D1239138

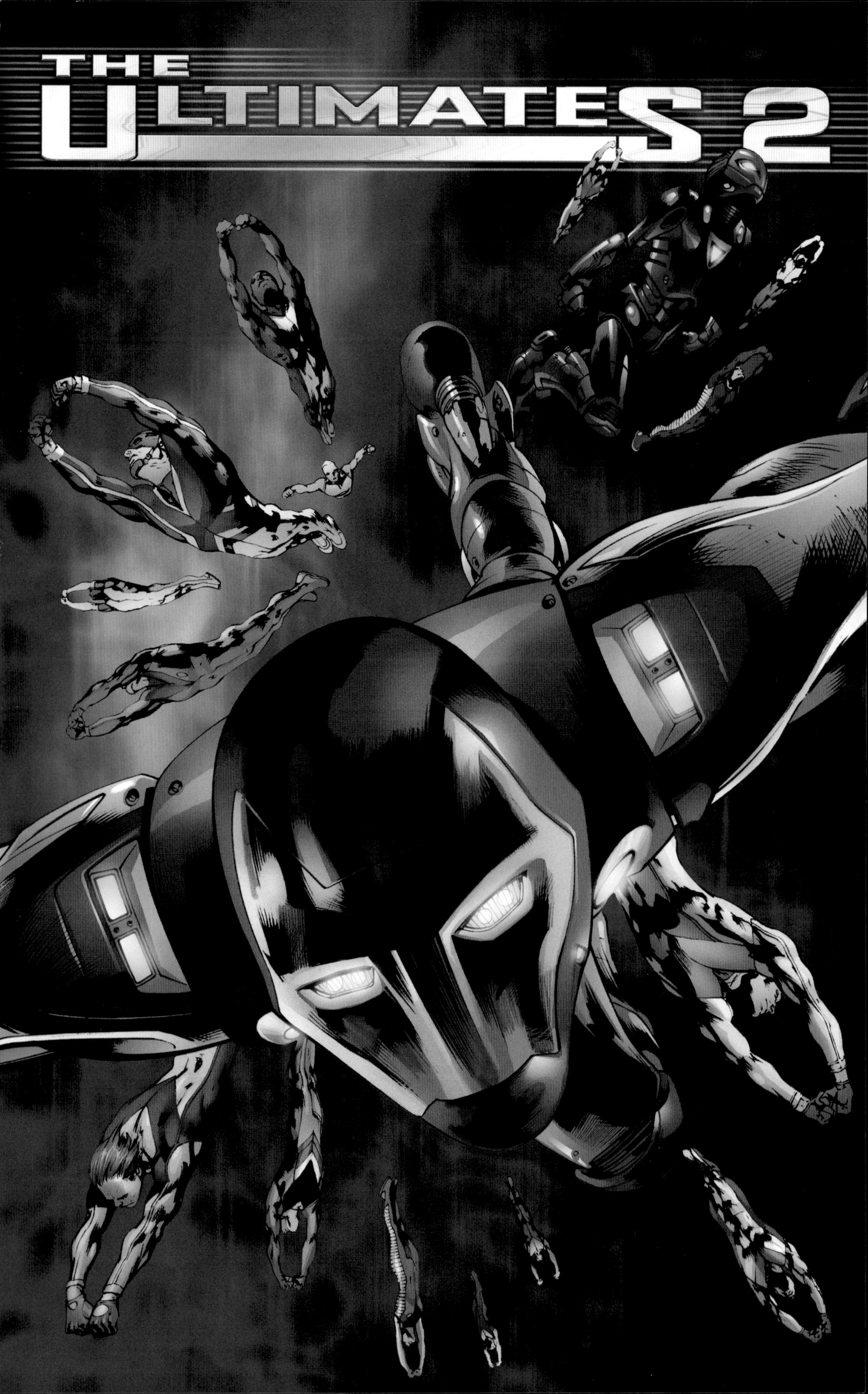
THE ULTIMATES 2

THE ULTIMATES 2

WRITER: MARK MILLAR

PENCILER: BRYAN HITCH

INKERS: PAUL NEARY & BRYAN HITCH

COLORISTS: LAURA MARTIN

WITH LARRY MOLINAR

LETTERERS: CHRIS ELIOPOULOS

WITH VC's CORY PETIT

ASSOCIATE EDITORS: JOHN BARBER, NICK LOWE
& NICOLE BOOSE
EDITOR: RALPH MACCHIO

CAPTAIN AMERICA CREATED BY JOE SIMON & JACK KIRBY

COLLECTION EDITOR: MARK D. BEAZLEY
ASSISTANT EDITORS: JOHN DENNING & CORY LEVINE
ASSOCIATE EDITOR: JENNIFER GRÜNWALD
SENIOR EDITOR, SPECIAL PROJECTS: JEFF YOUNGQUIST
SENIOR VICE PRESIDENT OF SALES: DAVID GABRIEL
PRODUCTION: JERRY KALINOWSKI

EDITOR IN CHIEF: JOE QUESADA
PUBLISHER: DAN BUCKLEY

ULTIMATES 2. Contains material originally published in magazine form as ULTIMATES 2 #1-13 and ULTIMATES 2 #1 (VARIANT SKETCH EDITION). First printing 2007. ISBN# 978-0-7851-2138-1. Published by MARVEL PUBLISHING, INC., a subsidiary of MARVEL ENTERTAINMENT, INC. OFFICE OF PUBLICATION: 417 5th Avenue, New York, NY 10016. Copyright © 2005, 2006 and 2007 Marvel Characters, Inc. All rights reserved. $34.99 per copy in the U.S. and $56.00 in Canada (GST #R127032852); Canadian Agreement #40668537. All characters featured in this issue and the distinctive names and likenesses thereof, and all related indicia are trademarks of Marvel Characters, Inc. No similarity between any of the names, characters, persons, and/or institutions in this magazine with those of any living or dead person or institution is intended, and any such similarity which may exist is purely coincidental. **Printed in the U.S.A.** ALAN FINE, CEO Marvel Toys & Publishing Divisions and CMO Marvel Entertainment, Inc.; DAVID GABRIEL, Senior VP of Publishing Sales & Circulation; DAVID BOGART, VP of Business Affairs & Editorial Operations; MICHAEL PASCIULLO, VP Merchandising & Communications; JIM BOYLE, VP of Publishing Operations; DAN CARR, Executive Director of Publishing Technology; JUSTIN F. GABRIE, Managing Editor; SUSAN CRESPI, Production Manager; STAN LEE, Chairman Emeritus. For information regarding advertising in Marvel Comics or on Marvel.com, please contact Mitch Dane, Advertising Director, at mdane@marvel.com.

10 9 8 7 6 5 4 3 2 1

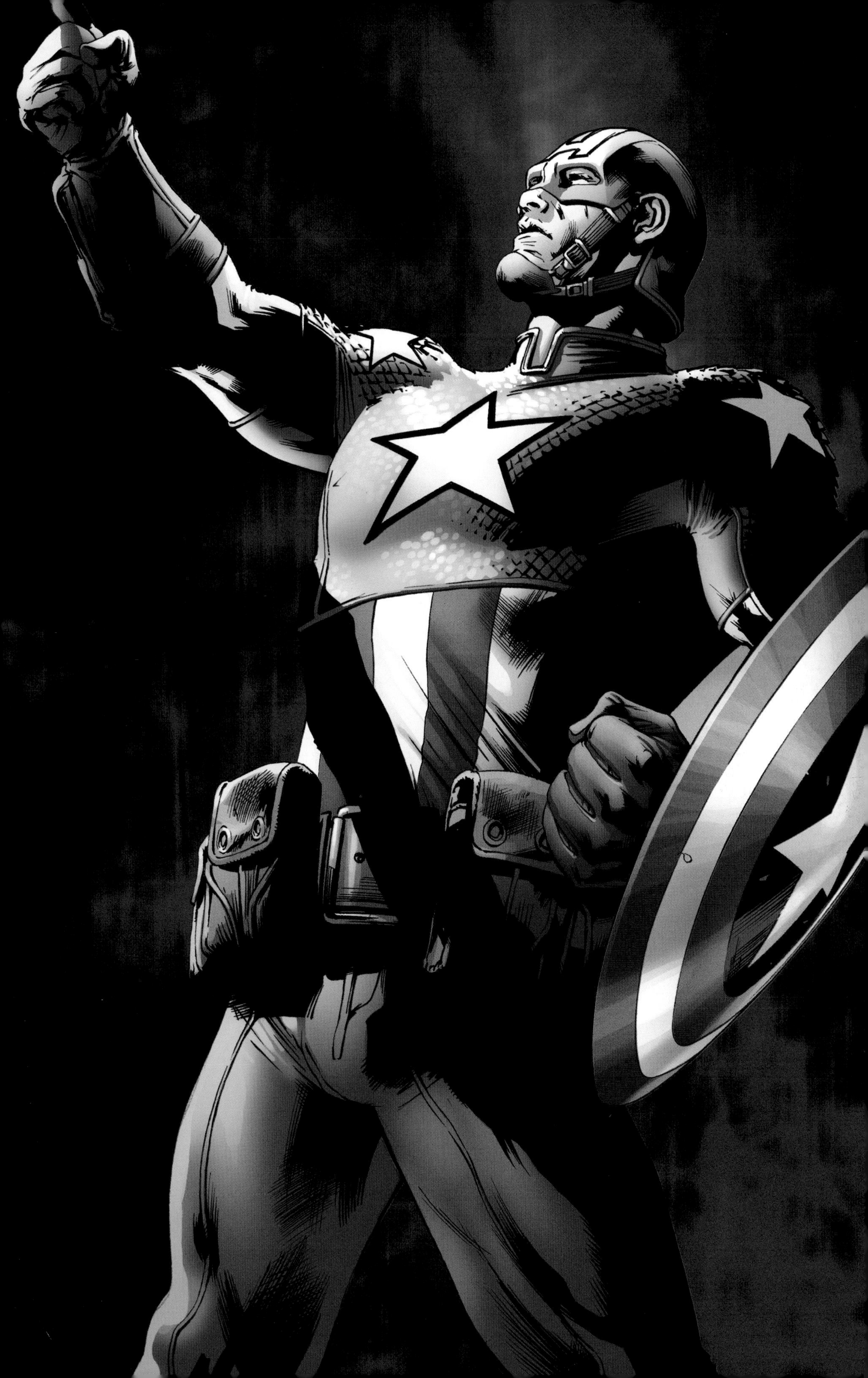

EARTH'S MIGHTIEST HEROES

If I ever bump into that Mark Millar guy, he better watch out, that's all I'm saying. I don't want to be too specific here and go into details and stuff but he is going to get a major beating from me. I am going to kick his skinny little Scottish rear all over the place, then take out some kung-fu vengeance on him. I haven't studied martial arts, that's true, but I've watched so many movies that I can perform the Snake Deadly Act and the wax-on wax-off without even breaking a sweat. He is not going to believe the moves I have been storing up for just such a righteous vengeance scenario as this. If there are any law-enforcement officers reading, then of course this is just a verbal warning, that's all. But the reality, should it ever occur, will be even scarier, I guarantee you. If I were that Mark Millar guy, I would be pretty scared right now. I would probably think about trying to get into the witness protection scheme, or maybe just going off and living somewhere remote. Well, more remote than where he lives now, which is pretty remote by the standards of most civilised people. Maybe he should live on a little haunted island somewhere that only gets supplies brought over once a month by a wizened old fisherman, and if he grows a beard and stops doing what he's been doing, I might just let it go. But if he doesn't heed this timely and generous warning, then he has only himself to blame. I mean it, Millar, your arse is mine.

Why? Why does he need to be taught a lesson from an older, wiser, fitter and better looking man? I'll tell you why, if you wait a second. Because of what he did, that's why. If you are at all smart you'll know what I mean by that, but if you are reading this, then you are probably a fan of his, and that means you are probably pretty stupid so I will elaborate for you. Slowly and loudly. And with hand gestures.

BECAUSE HE MADE ME START CARING ABOUT COMICS AGAIN, DAMN HIS BEADY LITTLE PINK EYES!

That's why. He got me hooked again. I had almost made it and he came along and did what he did and here I am, buying them and putting them in Mylar bags and getting excited about them all over again for at least the third time in my life. Damn him! I had just about gotten them out of my system when that irresponsible lowlife...well, maybe I should start at the beginning.

My tale is a common one for sure, but no less powerful or moving for that. First got addicted in my pre-teens. They used to push the stuff pretty hard to us little ones back then, in the Silver Age. You'd get your first few hits for free, from a brother maybe or an older guy at school or in some really sick, messed-up families, from your own dad. But the free supply soon dried up, and you'd get those withdrawal symptoms hard and need more. So you'd start searching for them, and buying them secondhand, and when you weren't reading them or trading them or trying to make your own, you were dreaming about them. Before long, comics are the only thing you want to get out of bed for. I can tell you know what I'm talking about—you've got the look of an addict about you. Pale skin, hollow eyes, not a lot of action on the girlfriend front. You were into super heroes too, weren't you? I feel your pain, brother.

While the supply is good and the quality held up, I didn't really have a problem. I can't say I was living, not in the traditional sense. But my life felt even more full and rich and colourful than those who somehow had the strength to look away from the four-colour monkey on my back. I started with only the best—Kirby, Lee, Ditko, and Co. Marvel was my flavor of choice, but when they weren't forthcoming I'd suck it in and settle for DC. Gotta admit they had a few cool characters, and in the early seventies when Kirby jumped ship I might even have preferred them for a while. They were golden days. I carried on buying and reading and storing and re-reading for far longer than was considered normal. I don't think I really looked out of my window from the age of 8 until I turned about 17. Those bastards took the best years of my youth from me! But in the late seventies the comics seemed to lose their way a bit. There were a were a few voices that called out to me still—Starlin, Wrightson, Chaykin, O'Neil to name a few. But the lure of punk rock and girls with badly applied make-up and—gasp—fresh air finally won out, and those kids comics that had once seemed so important to me were put away. I had the odd lapse, I'll admit—no one gets away clean the first time they try. That coldhearted genius, Alan Moore, almost broke me in the eighties, along with Gaiman and Frank Miller, Spiegelman and Charles Burns—but at least they were socially acceptable. Comics weren't just for kids anymore, we all crowed, knowing full well it was the strung out, messed up kid inside of us that was really getting off on the smarter, sexier, more violent books of that dark decade. But they all got tired or bored or something, and wandered off to make movies or write "graphic novels"—yeuchh.

I got married. Had kids. Bought a house, a car, four dogs. Got good at my job—all the things that my love of super-hero books had stopped me doing before. Then I made my mistake. I took a chance. I decided to peek at the covers, hoping—fully expecting—to see just how silly and laughable those men in their brightly colored spandex would look to a big grown-up dude like me. So I did. And I wasn't laughing. I think it was *Ultimates #2* that grabbed me—a cool-looking totally overhauled Iron Man on the cover. Then, inside, they'd cured Banner of being the Hulk and Stark was behaving just the way we all would in his position—he was having fun and sucking every last drop of juice from his playboy life—fighting crime, climbing Everest and knocking back martinis like Bond on holiday. I bought it! Why did I buy it? I could have made it out of the shop and got home and never been sucked back in. But I bought it and I loved it and damn it, if they didn't get better, issue after issue.

Series two is of course just about as good as a superhero book can get. I won't go into plot details because if you're buying then you're reading and if you're reading then you don't want me spoiling. But suffice to say that *Ultimates 2* is about as close to watching the perfect big budget *Avengers* movie of your dreams without actually having to risk the disappointment of ever going to see it, if you know what I mean. But I can't let the moment pass without at least acknowledging how out and out INSPIRED it is to have The Defenders crop up in a supporting role. They

always were a bit of a guilty pleasure of mine, a half-%#@ed assembly of the least interesting but somehow irresistible d-listers ever published by the House of Ideas. Just to see the Son of Satan and Nighthawk again would have been enough, but the storyline, as it plays out, is not just hilarious, but is also kind of poignant too. I'm secretly hoping that we can look forward to new storylines featuring Rom the Space Knight and the Human Fly in the next series. Maybe they could both ride in on Devil Dinosaur's back? Just a thought.

Of course it's not just Mr. Millar who's been cruising for a bruising. Bryan Hitch better watch his back as well. No one else makes the Hulk look as homicidally nutso and permanently pissed off as the Hitchattolah. No one can give Cap the gravitas and presence of a living legend but still make him look athletic and boyish enough to perform a triple flip off of the Triskelion and land on both feet, shield poised, ready for action. That's why I got hooked again, that's why I'm back to buying everything with the word Ultimates on the cover—that's why I'm mad. Great art, great stories, great dialogue and great characters, finally doing and saying the kind of things I wanted them to do and say without ever knowing it. No wonder I'm hooked. So watch it Millar, look out, Hitch. Because maybe you'll get a manly hug instead.

Jonathan Ross
May 2007

Jonathan Ross' prolific television career as a presenter has included: The Last Resort; The Incredibly Strange Film Show; One Hour with Jonathan Ross; Tonight With Jonathan Ross; The Late Jonathan Ross; In Search Of...; and Friday Night With Jonathan Ross garnering him numerous awards such as being made an Officer of the Order of the British Empire in Queen Elizabeth II's birthday honors for his services to broadcasting. Recent documentaries he's worked on have included Jonathan Ross' Asian Invasion and Japanorama dealing with his self-confessed love for anime and video games as well as Comics Britannia about the history of the British comic and Jonathan Ross in Search of Steve Ditko where he travels around the world to understand more about comics genius, Steve Ditko, and his incredible body of work. Jonathan lives in North London with his wife Jane Goldman, their three children and a menagerie of pets including a dog, cat, iguana, two salamanders, two chinchillas and a number of ferrets—he hopes to get a fruit bat soon.

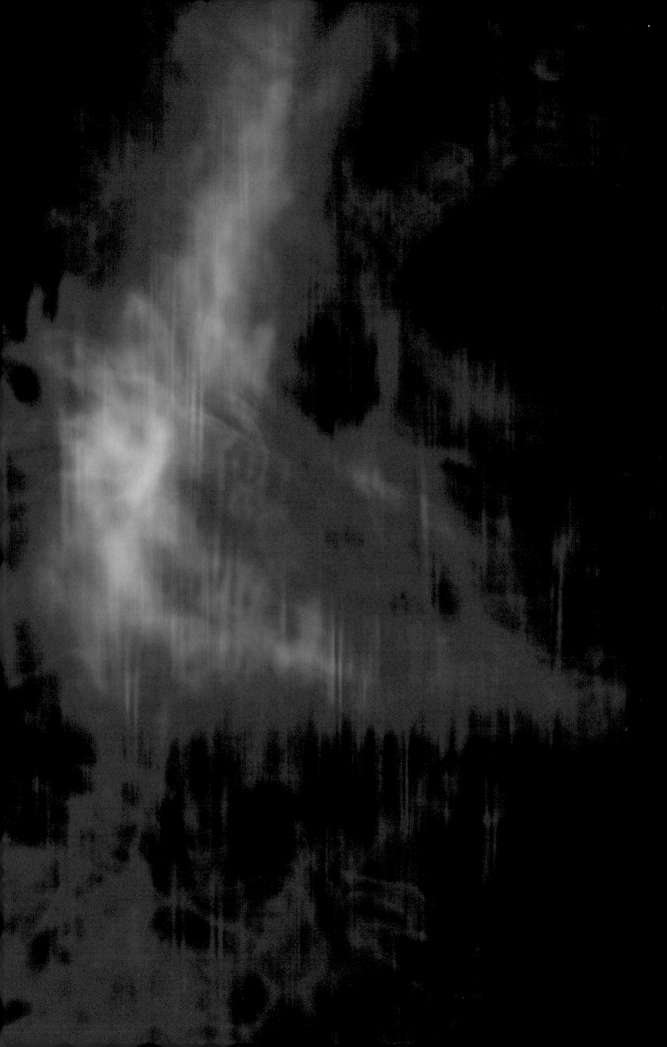

When faced with Nazi Germany's military advances, the U.S. government decided that the best weapon against them was a person, not a bomb. With this in mind, Steve Rogers volunteered for a covert military experiment that turned him into Captain America. After a few years of exemplary service, Captain America fell in battle-- his body wasn't recovered.

Years passed and Captain America was found frozen in suspended animation. When he awoke, he was convinced to join Iron Man, The Wasp, Giant Man, Black Widow, Hawkeye, and Thor in forming the superhuman defense initiative run by Nick Fury, called The Ultimates.

PREVIOUSLY IN THE ULTIMATES:

The Ultimates have had two decisive battles since Nick Fury brought them together. The first was when they saved New York City from the rampaging monster known as The Hulk. What the world at large doesn't know is that The Hulk is really Bruce Banner, a scientist who was working on the superhuman defense initiative.

The second battle The Ultimates won was against an army of shape-shifting aliens bent on destroying the world and killing all humankind. These two victories made The Ultimates the biggest celebrities the world has ever known.

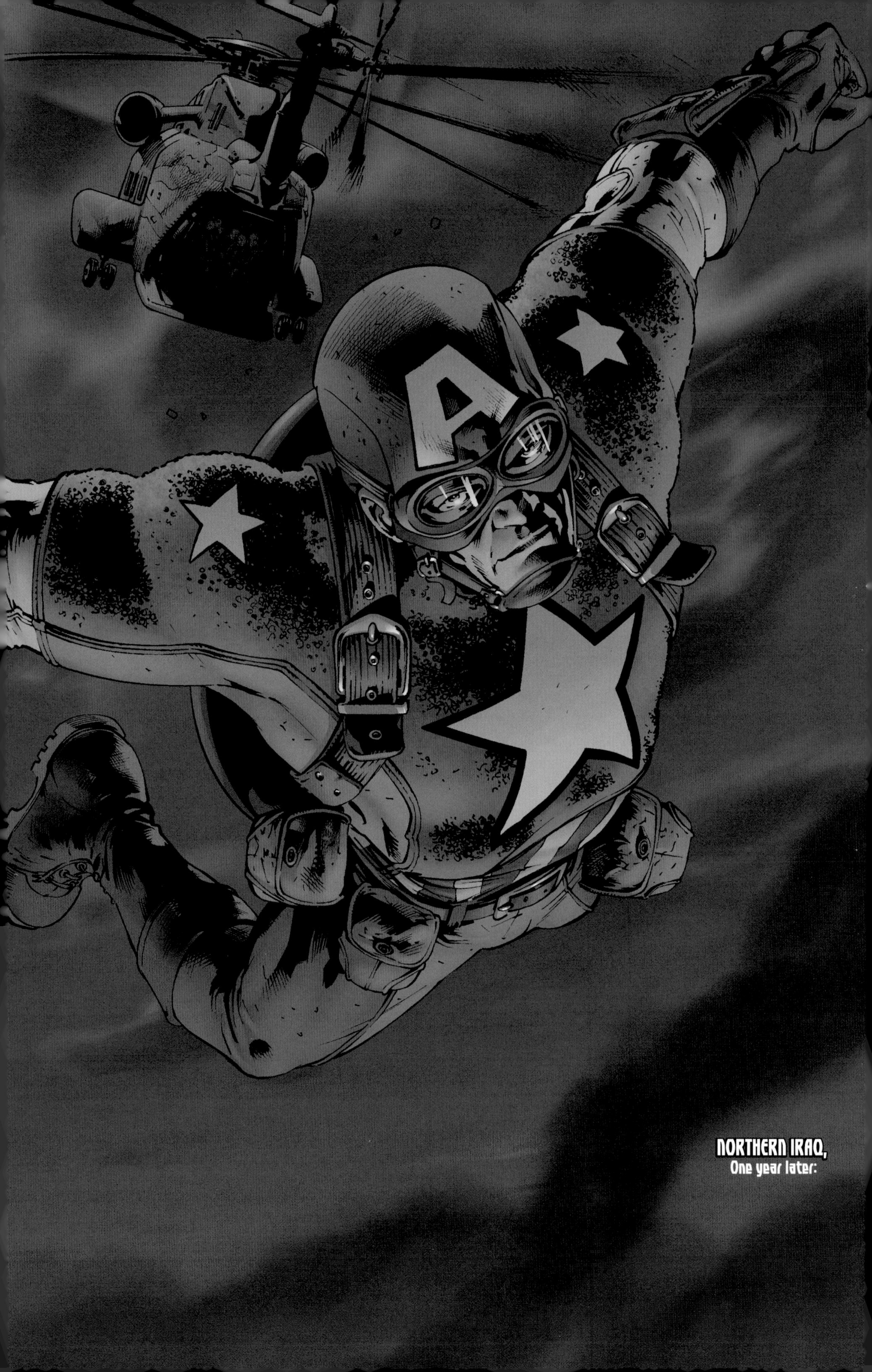
NORTHERN IRAQ,
One year later:

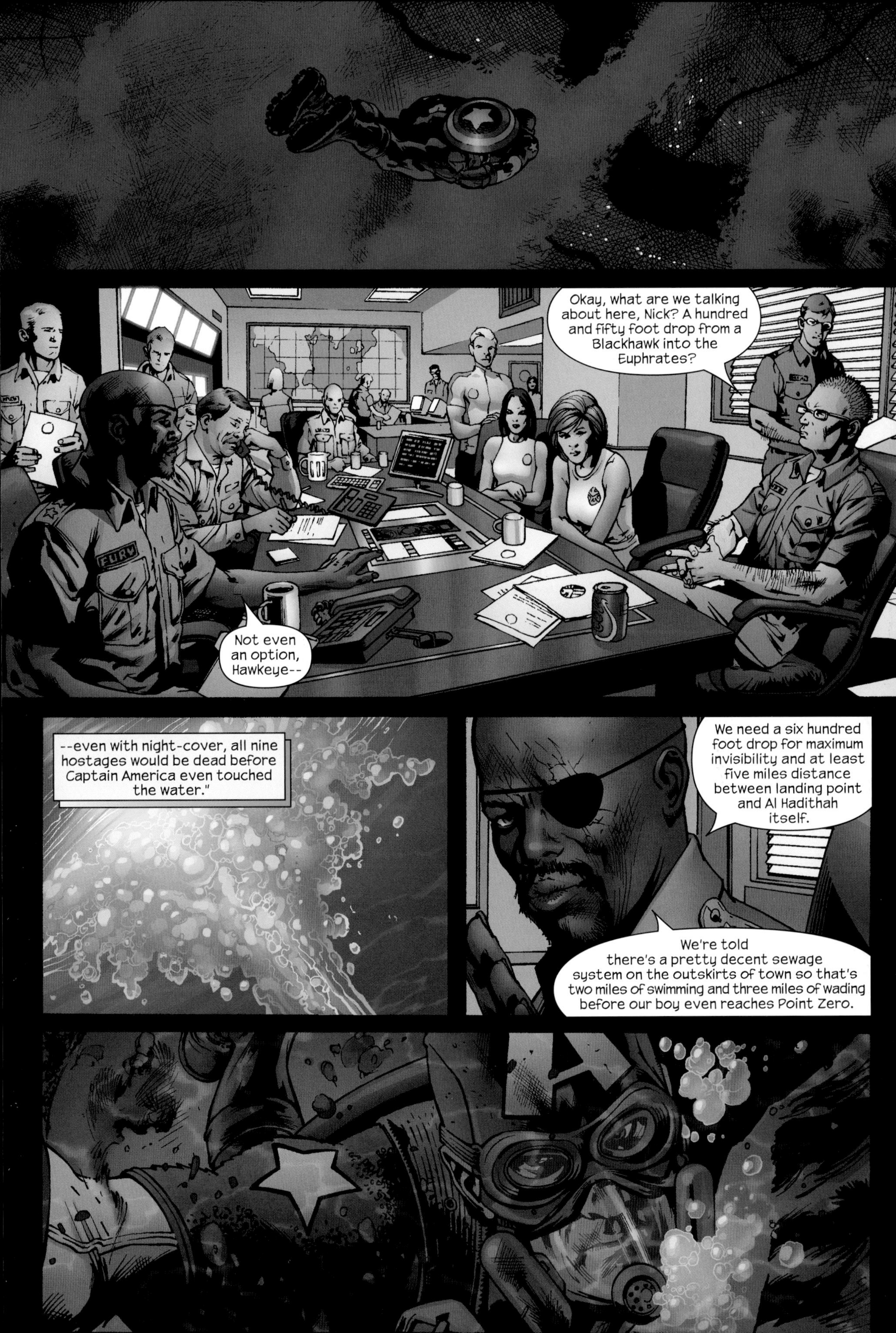

Okay, what are we talking about here, Nick? A hundred and fifty foot drop from a Blackhawk into the Euphrates?
Not even an option, Hawkeye--
--even with night-cover, all nine hostages would be dead before Captain America even touched the water."
We need a six hundred foot drop for maximum invisibility and at least five miles distance between landing point and Al Hadithah itself.
We're told there's a pretty decent sewage system on the outskirts of town so that's two miles of swimming and three miles of wading before our boy even reaches Point Zero.

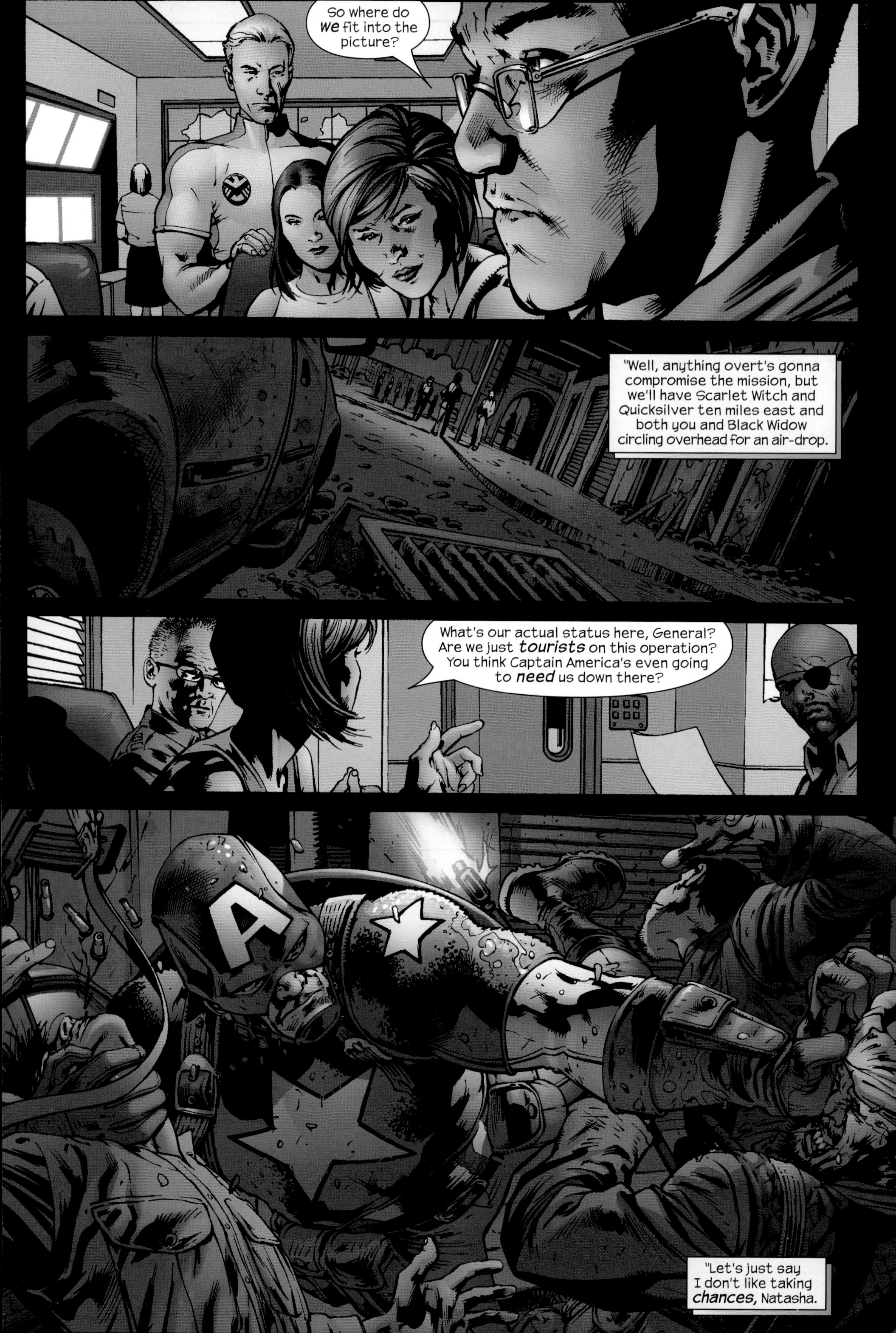
So where do *we* fit into the picture?
"Well, anything overt's gonna compromise the mission, but we'll have Scarlet Witch and Quicksilver ten miles east and both you and Black Widow circling overhead for an air-drop.
What's our actual status here, General? Are we just *tourists* on this operation? You think Captain America's even going to *need* us down there?
"Let's just say I don't like taking *chances,* Natasha.

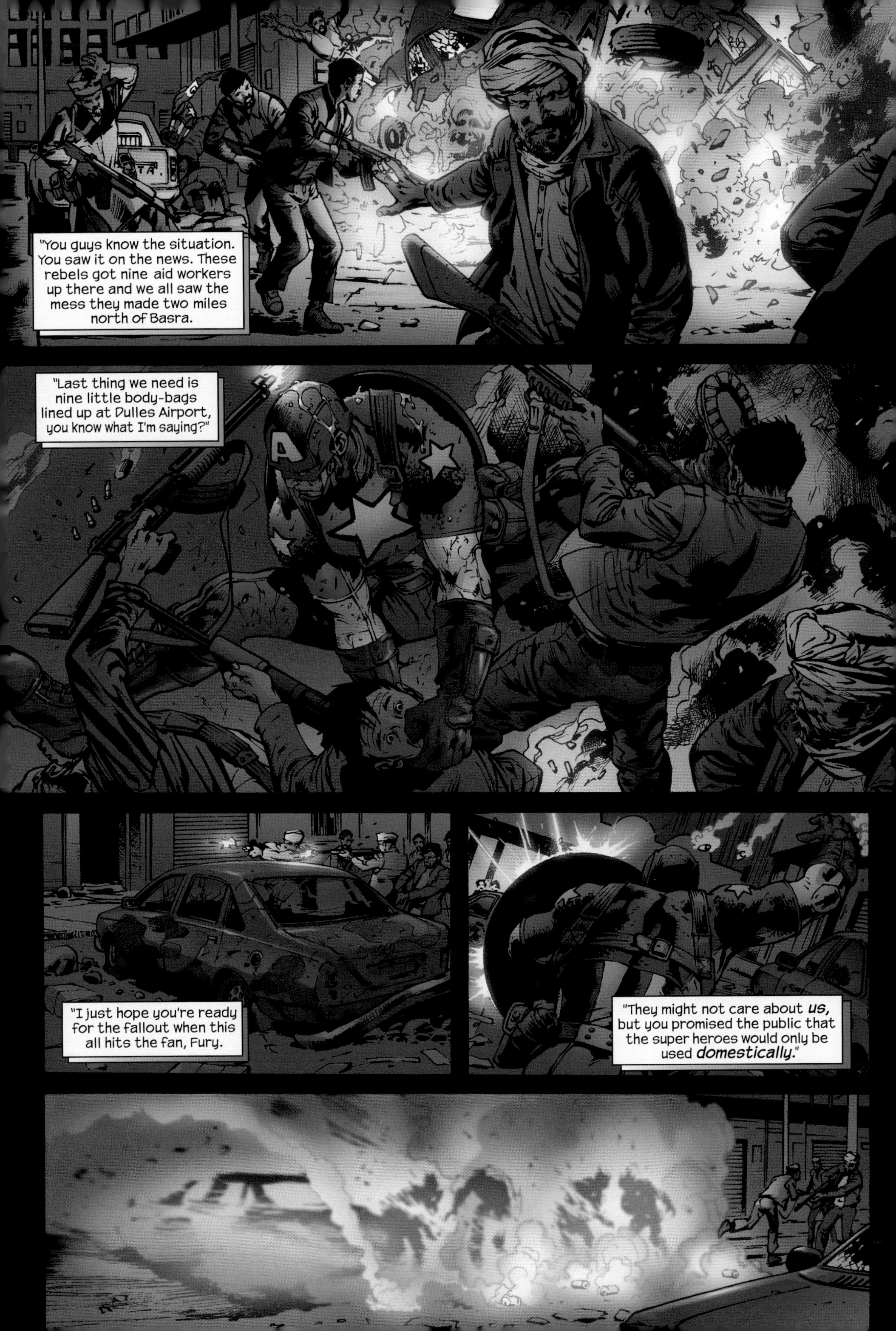
"You guys know the situation. You saw it on the news. These rebels got nine aid workers up there and we all saw the mess they made two miles north of Basra.
"Last thing we need is nine little body-bags lined up at Dulles Airport, you know what I'm saying?"
"I just hope you're ready for the fallout when this all hits the fan, Fury.
"They might not care about *us,* but you promised the public that the super heroes would only be used *domestically.*"

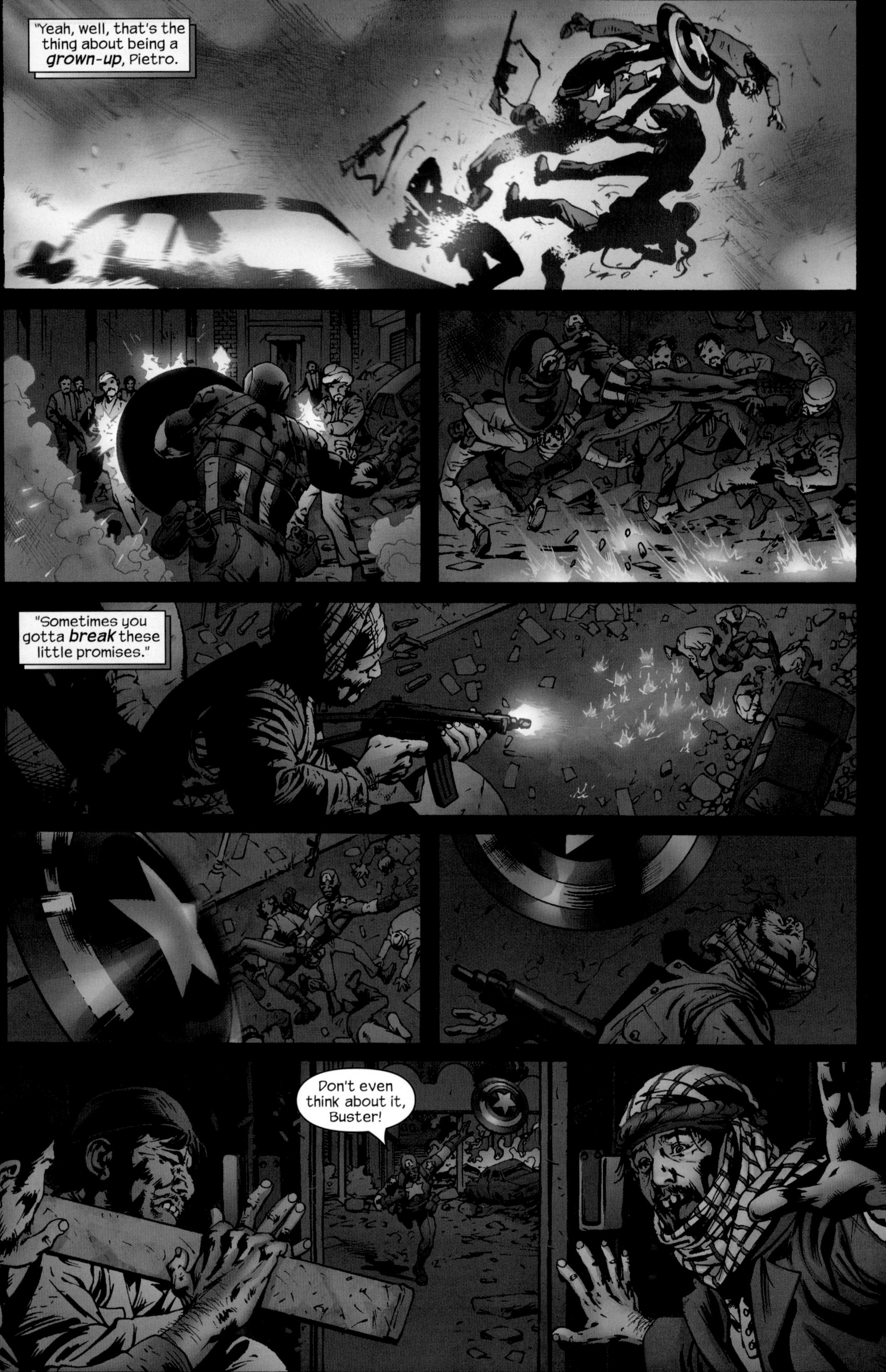
"Yeah, well, that's the thing about being a *grown-up*, Pietro.
"Sometimes you gotta *break* these little promises."
Don't even think about it, Buster!

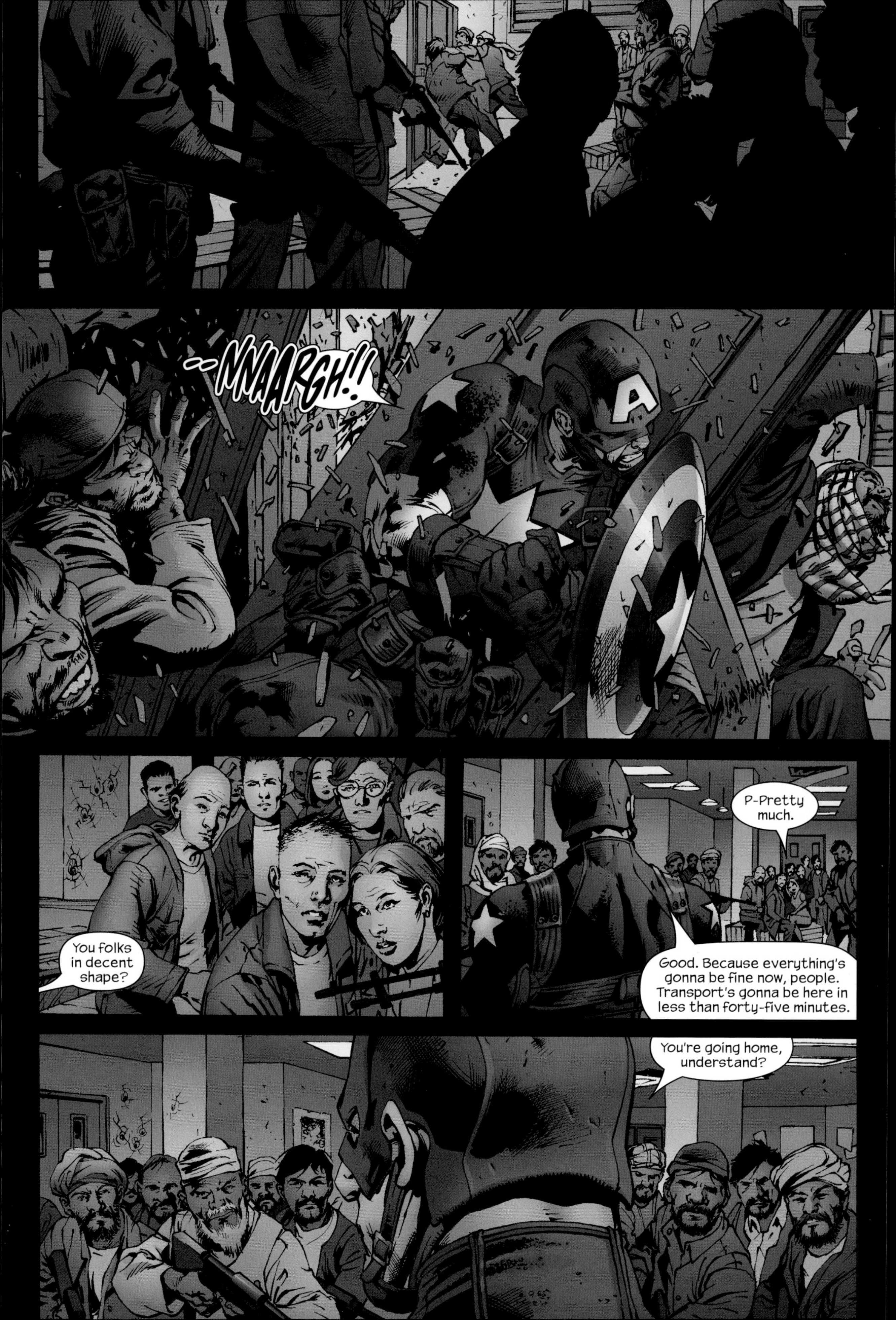
--NNAARGH!!
You folks in decent shape?
P-Pretty much.
Good. Because everything's gonna be fine now, people. Transport's gonna be here in less than forty-five minutes.
You're going home, understand?

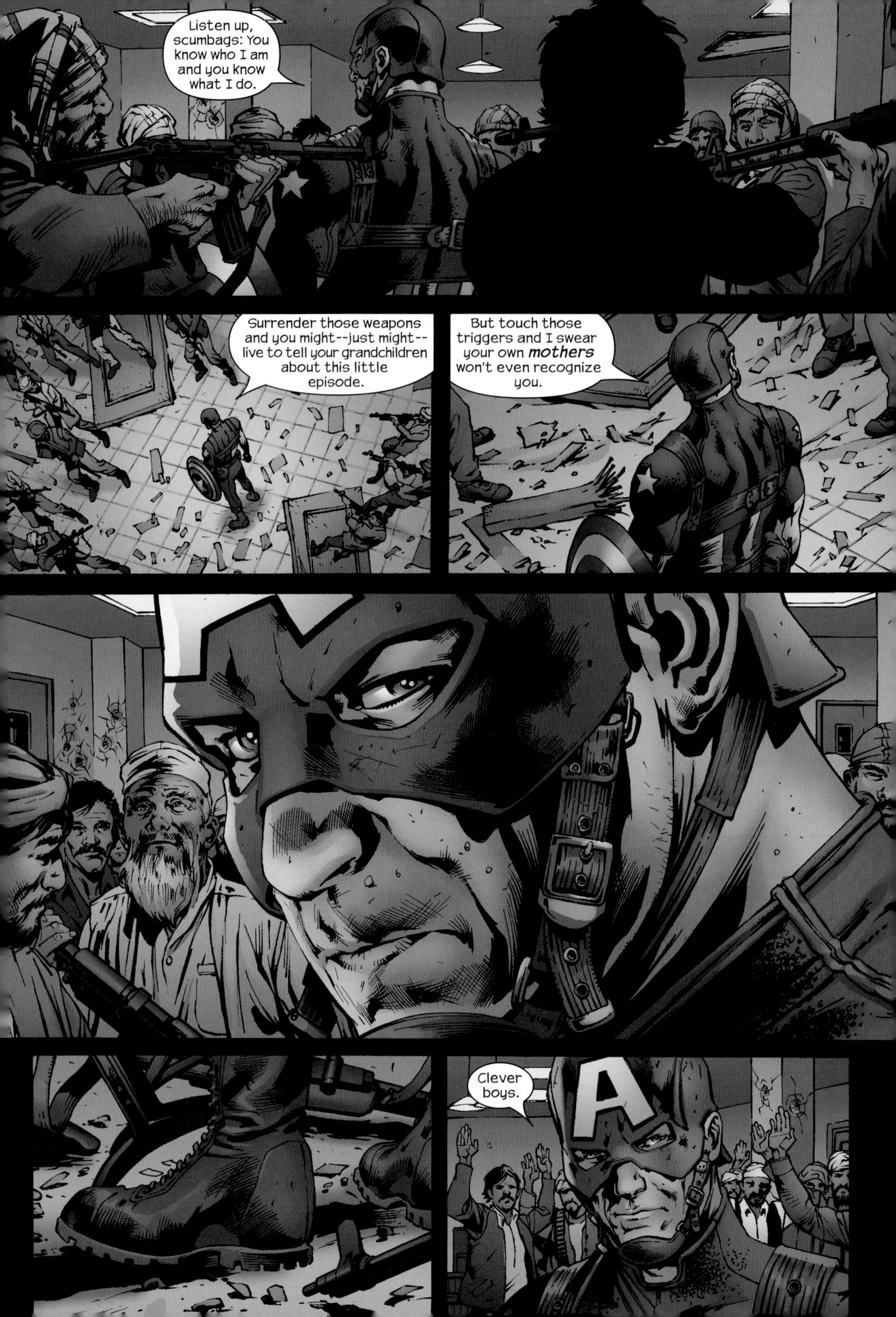
Listen up, scumbags: You know who I am and you know what I do.
Surrender those weapons and you might--just might--live to tell your grandchildren about this little episode.
But touch those triggers and I swear your own *mothers* won't even recognize you.
Clever boys.

--where the President was waiting with friends and family to greet these nine brave men and women after their terrifying fourteen-day ordeal.

What do I wanna say to Captain America? Man, you're the best, that's what. You're the reason we're still breathing, man. You're the reason we're back on American soil.

The reason they're still breathing? The reason they're back on American soil? That's not what *some* people are saying, Tony.

Some people are saying The Ultimates just overstepped their mandate and used a Person of Mass Destruction in a very delicate foreign policy situation.

Okay, first of all, I hardly think that Captain America qualifies as a Person of Mass Destruction, Larry.

Secondly, these aid-workers he rescued were all American citizens and this rescue operation had the backing of both the Red Cross and the U.N. Security Council.

LIVE

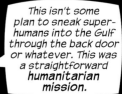

This isn't some plan to sneak super-humans into the Gulf through the back door or whatever. This was a straightforward **humanitarian mission.**

Not according to this guy, it wasn't. In fact, this morning Thor tendered his resignation from The Ultimates because he says that's *exactly* what Cap was doing in Iraq.

According to Thor, this whole Homeland Security thing was just one big scam to get public opinion on your side before launching preemptive strikes against anyone who ticks you off.

What do you say to that, Tony? You worried the government might be squandering all that public trust you guys built up after all those *big rescues* last year?

Listen, Thor's a good pal of mine. I was out for a drink with him just the other night, but we're talking about a former psychiatric patient who thinks he's a **Norse god**, Larry.

LIVE

CNC

DR. ANTHONY STARK
CEO, STARK INTERNATIONAL; IRON MAN

LIVE

The guy's great company, but this conspiracy theory he's putting around that The Ultimates are going to end up as some kind of storm-troopers for the oil industry...

Well, that's as outrageous as these **visions** he keeps having.

LIVE

Wait a second, wait a second.

Are you giving me a firm guarantee that you, Tony Stark, would never take part in a preemptive strike against any kind of rogue state acting contrary to American interests?

LIVE

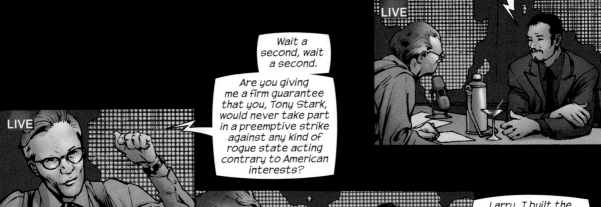

Larry, I built the **Iron Man** suit so that I could give something back and, hopefully, meet some cheeky, little honeys at the same time.

I'm honestly not interested in becoming some kind of Martini-swilling **smart-bomb.**

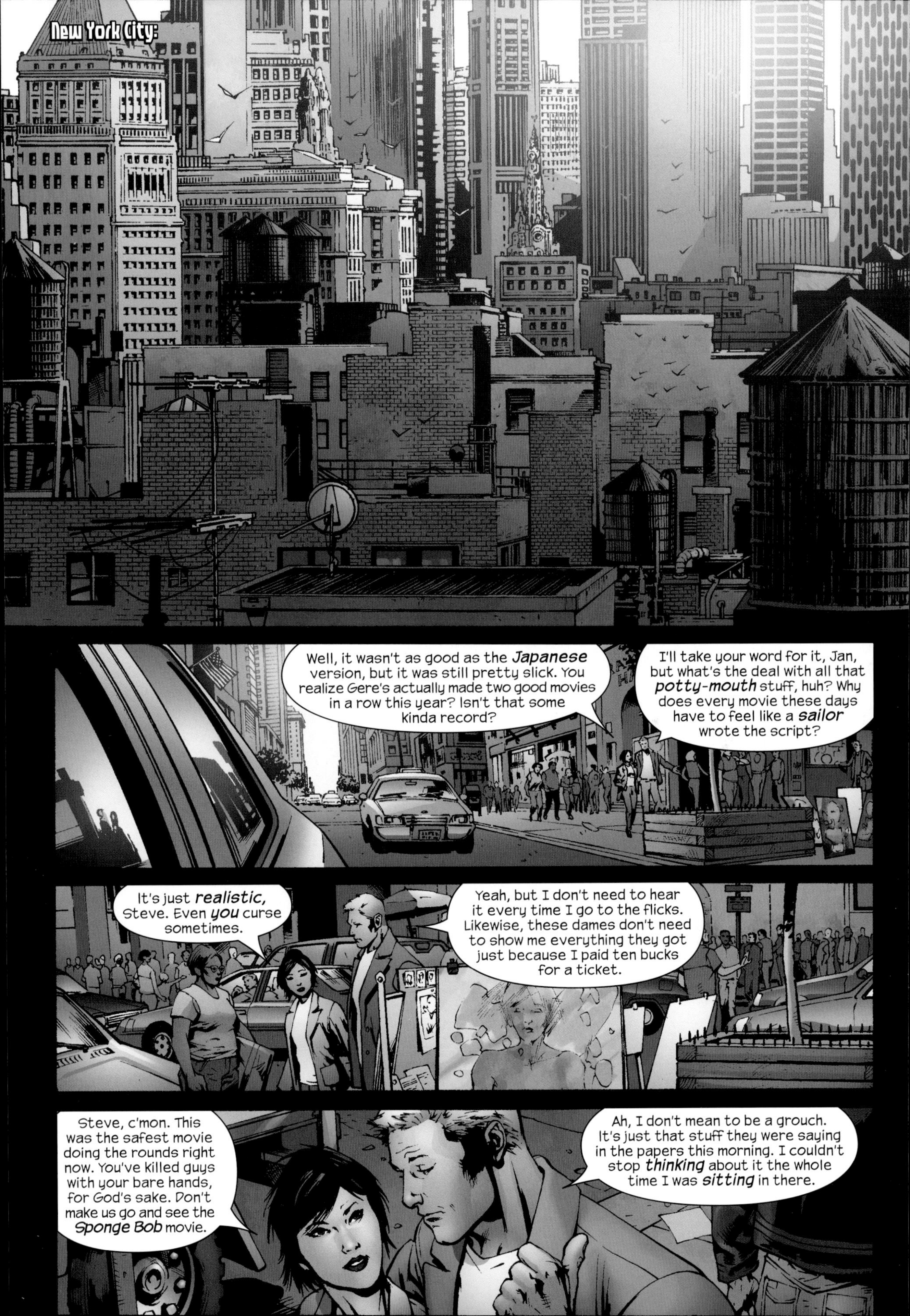
New York City:
Well, it wasn't as good as the Japanese version, but it was still pretty slick. You realize Gere's actually made two good movies in a row this year? Isn't that some kinda record?
I'll take your word for it, Jan, but what's the deal with all that potty-mouth stuff, huh? Why does every movie these days have to feel like a sailor wrote the script?
It's just realistic, Steve. Even you curse sometimes.
Yeah, but I don't need to hear it every time I go to the flicks. Likewise, these dames don't need to show me everything they got just because I paid ten bucks for a ticket.
Steve, c'mon. This was the safest movie doing the rounds right now. You've killed guys with your bare hands, for God's sake. Don't make us go and see the Sponge Bob movie.
Ah, I don't mean to be a grouch. It's just that stuff they were saying in the papers this morning. I couldn't stop thinking about it the whole time I was sitting in there.

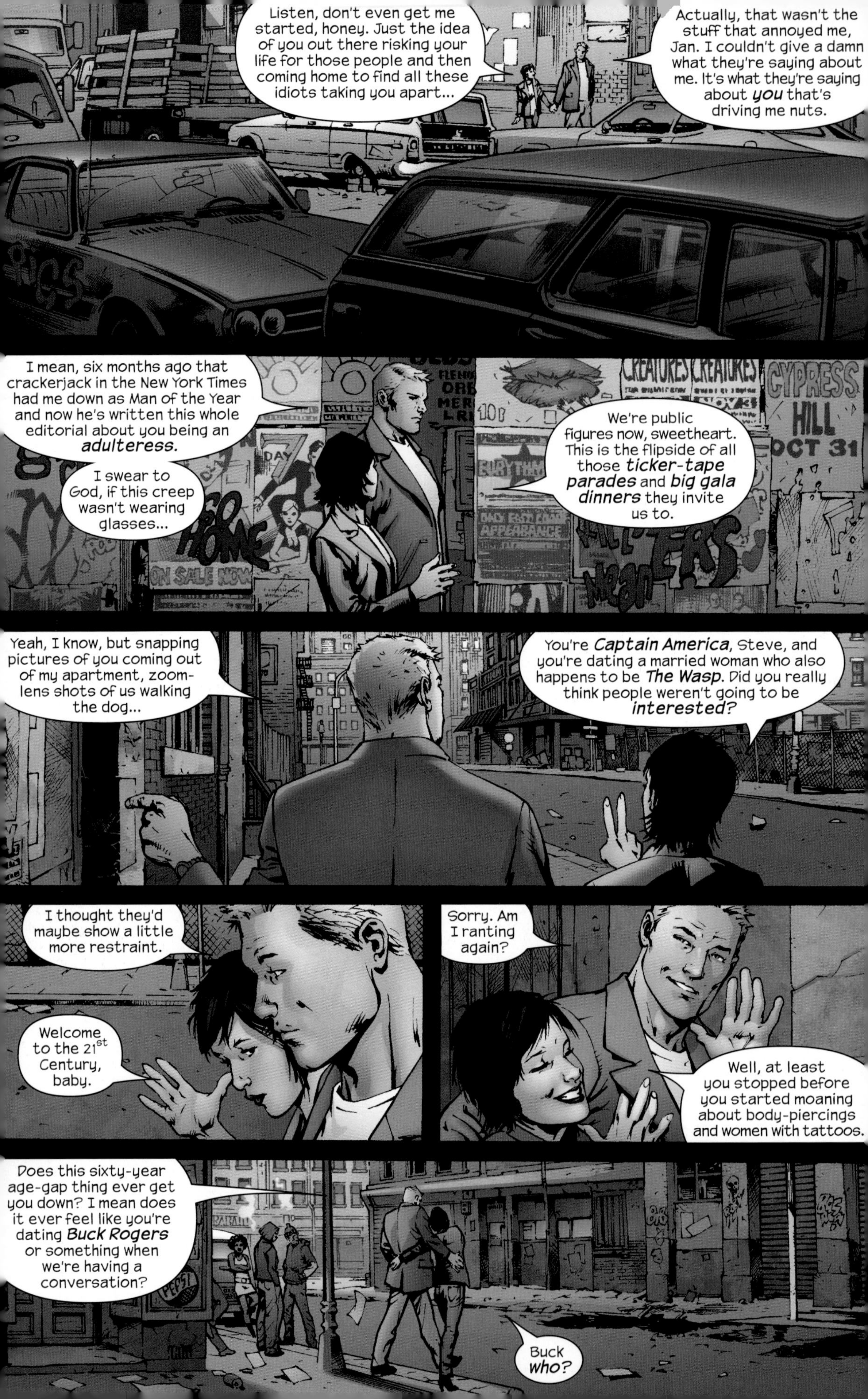
Listen, don't even get me started, honey. Just the idea of you out there risking your life for those people and then coming home to find all these idiots taking you apart...
Actually, that wasn't the stuff that annoyed me, Jan. I couldn't give a damn what they're saying about me. It's what they're saying about *you* that's driving me nuts.
I mean, six months ago that crackerjack in the New York Times had me down as Man of the Year and now he's written this whole editorial about you being an *adulteress.*
I swear to God, if this creep wasn't wearing glasses...
We're public figures now, sweetheart. This is the flipside of all those *ticker-tape parades* and *big gala dinners* they invite us to.
CREATURES
CREATURES
CYPRESS HILL OCT 31
ON SALE NOW
APPEARANCE
Yeah, I know, but snapping pictures of you coming out of my apartment, zoom-lens shots of us walking the dog...
You're *Captain America*, Steve, and you're dating a married woman who also happens to be *The Wasp*. Did you really think people weren't going to be *interested?*
I thought they'd maybe show a little more restraint.
Welcome to the 21st Century, baby.
Sorry. Am I ranting again?
Well, at least you stopped before you started moaning about body-piercings and women with tattoos.
Does this sixty-year age-gap thing ever get you down? I mean does it ever feel like you're dating *Buck Rogers* or something when we're having a conversation?
Buck *who?*

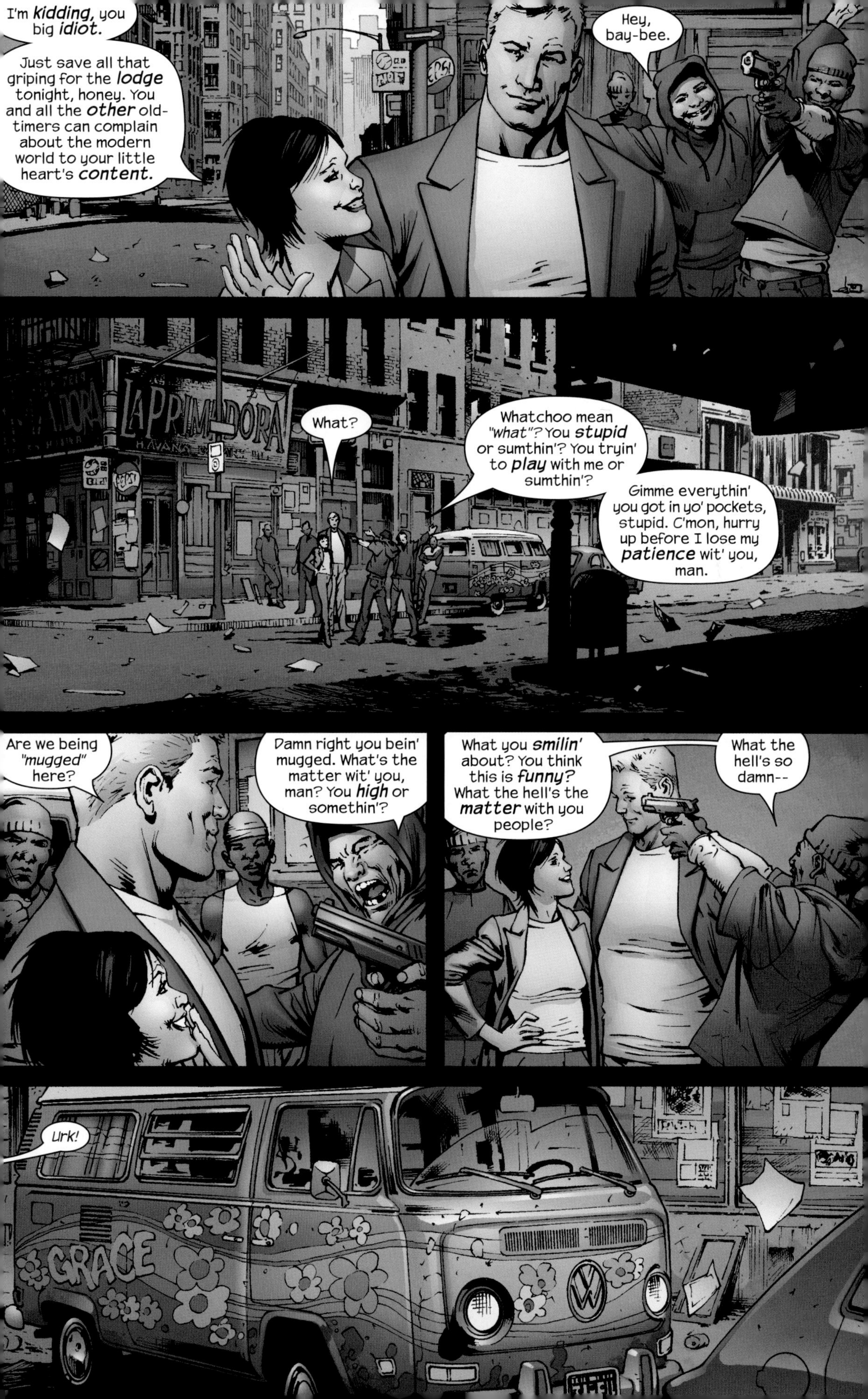
I'm kidding, you big idiot.
Just save all that griping for the lodge tonight, honey. You and all the other old-timers can complain about the modern world to your little heart's content.
Hey, bay-bee.
What?
Whatchoo mean "what"? You stupid or sumthin'? You tryin' to play with me or sumthin'?
Gimme everythin' you got in yo' pockets, stupid. C'mon, hurry up before I lose my patience wit' you, man.
Are we being "mugged" here?
Damn right you bein' mugged. What's the matter wit' you, man? You high or somethin'?
What you smilin' about? You think this is funny? What the hell's the matter with you people?
What the hell's so damn--
Urk!
GRACE

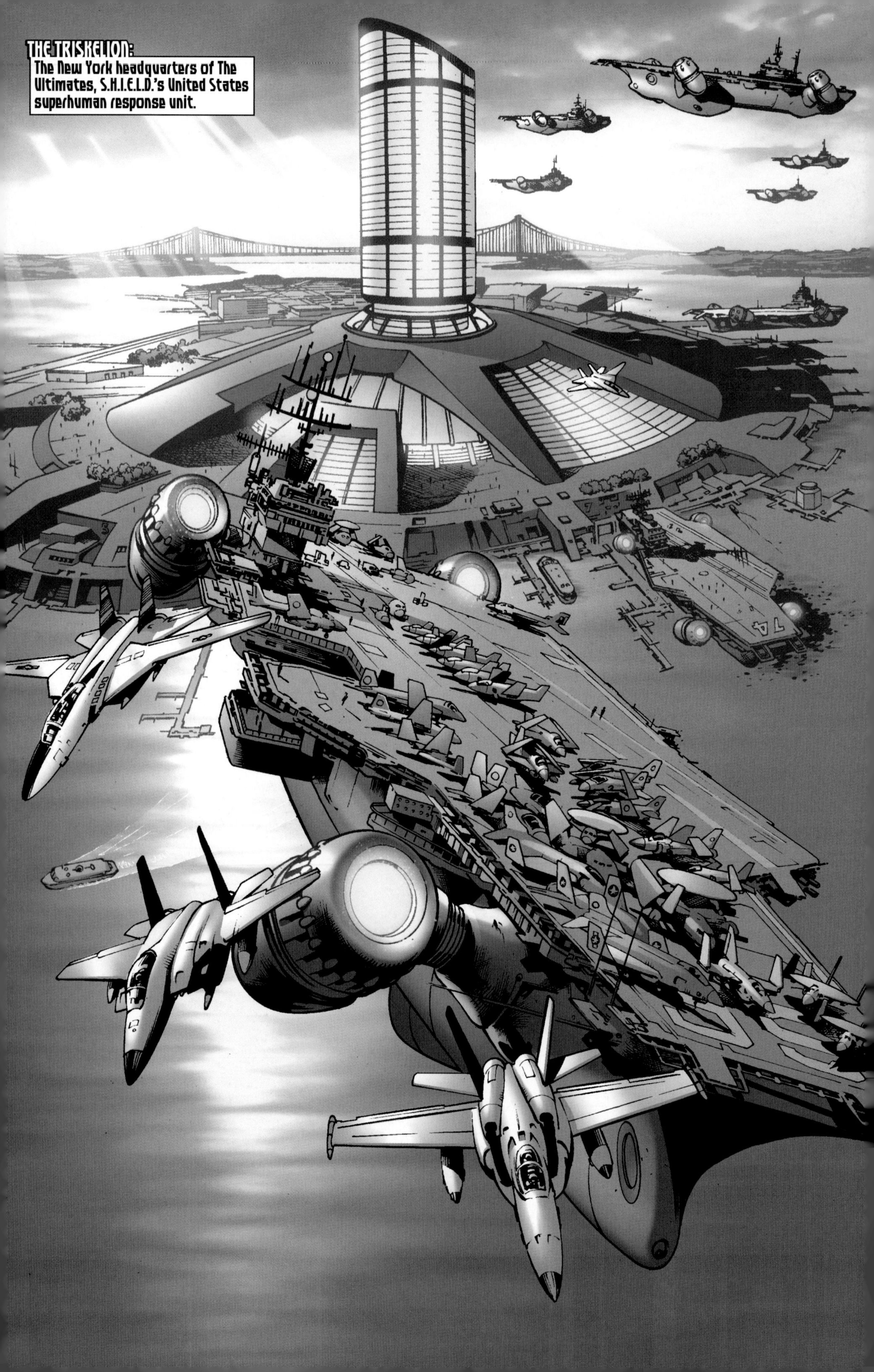
THE TRISKELION:
The New York headquarters of The Ultimates, S.H.I.E.L.D.'s United States superhuman response unit.

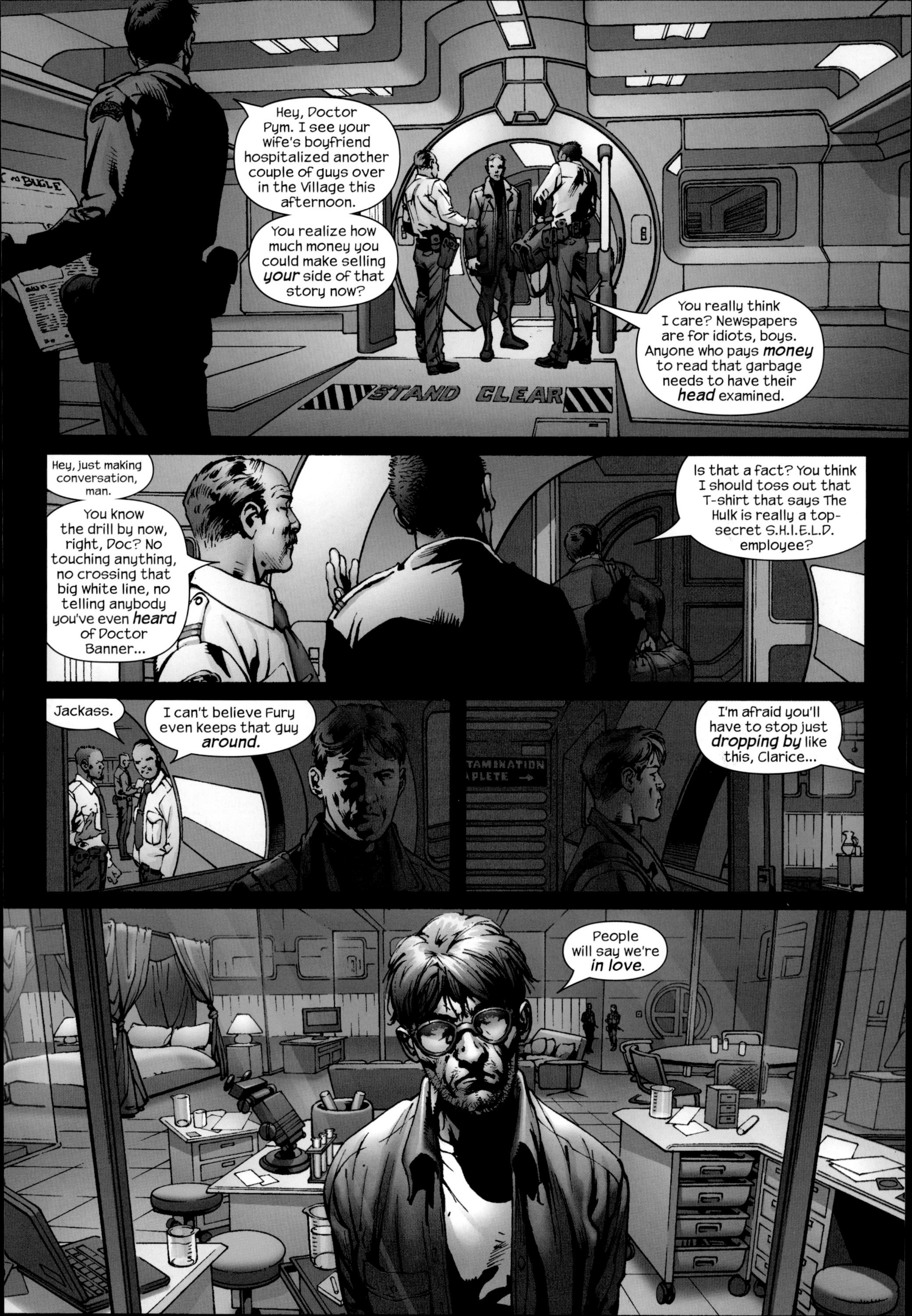

BUGLE
Hey, Doctor Pym. I see your wife's boyfriend hospitalized another couple of guys over in the Village this afternoon.
You realize how much money you could make selling *your* side of that story now?
You really think I care? Newspapers are for idiots, boys. Anyone who pays *money* to read that garbage needs to have their *head* examined.
STAND CLEAR
Hey, just making conversation, man.
You know the drill by now, right, Doc? No touching anything, no crossing that big white line, no telling anybody you've even *heard* of Doctor Banner...
Is that a fact? You think I should toss out that T-shirt that says The Hulk is really a top-secret S.H.I.E.L.D. employee?
Jackass.
I can't believe Fury even keeps that guy *around.*
TAMINATION
MPLETE →
I'm afraid you'll have to stop just *dropping by* like this, Clarice...
People will say we're *in love*.

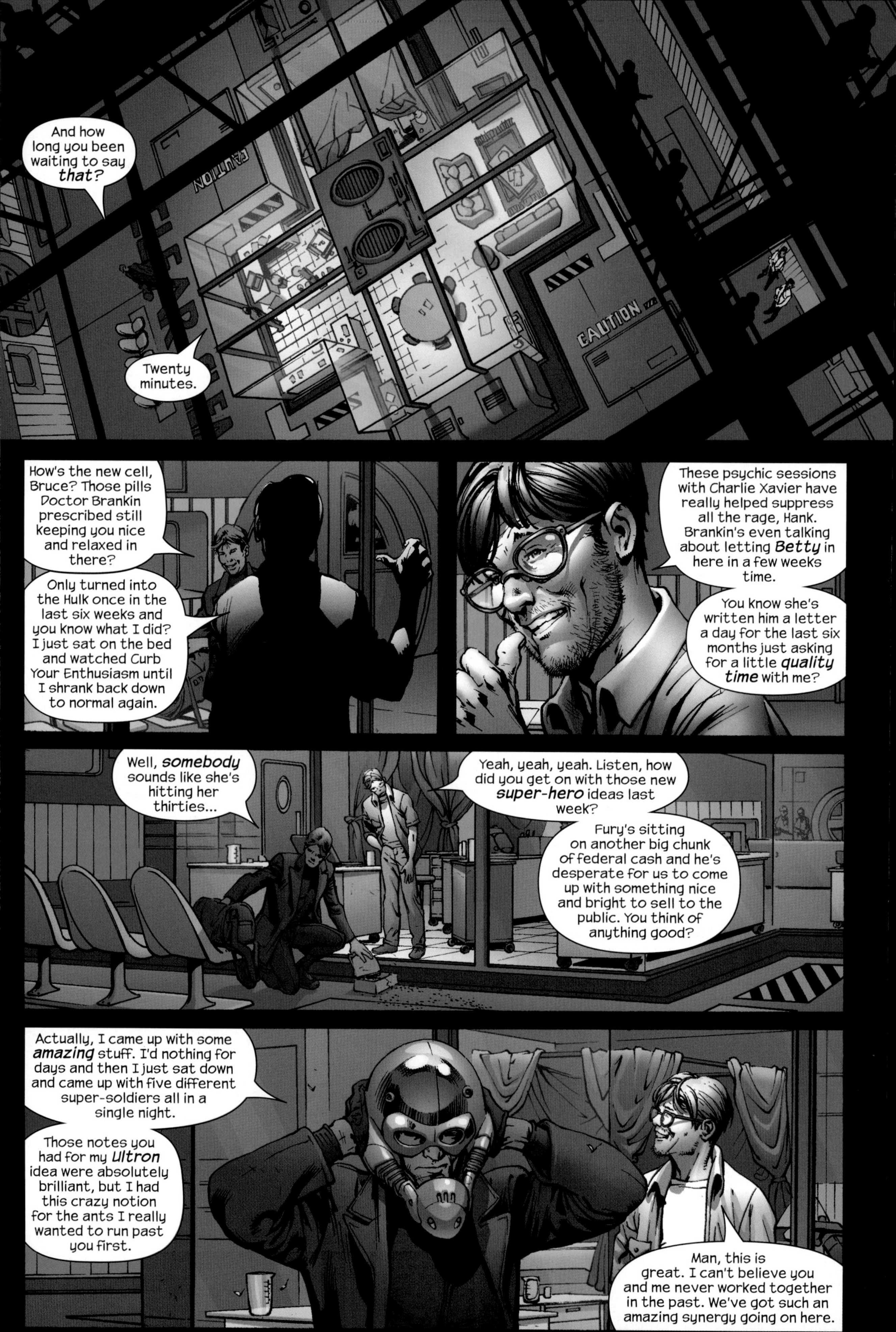
And how long you been waiting to say *that*?
Twenty minutes.
CAUTION
CAUTION
How's the new cell, Bruce? Those pills Doctor Brankin prescribed still keeping you nice and relaxed in there?
Only turned into the Hulk once in the last six weeks and you know what I did? I just sat on the bed and watched Curb Your Enthusiasm until I shrank back down to normal again.
These psychic sessions with Charlie Xavier have really helped suppress all the rage, Hank. Brankin's even talking about letting *Betty* in here in a few weeks time.
You know she's written him a letter a day for the last six months just asking for a little *quality time* with me?
Well, *somebody* sounds like she's hitting her thirties...
Yeah, yeah, yeah. Listen, how did you get on with those new *super-hero* ideas last week?
Fury's sitting on another big chunk of federal cash and he's desperate for us to come up with something nice and bright to sell to the public. You think of anything good?
Actually, I came up with some *amazing* stuff. I'd nothing for days and then I just sat down and came up with five different super-soldiers all in a single night.
Those notes you had for my *Ultron* idea were absolutely brilliant, but I had this crazy notion for the ants I really wanted to run past you first.
Man, this is great. I can't believe you and me never worked together in the past. We've got such an amazing synergy going on here.

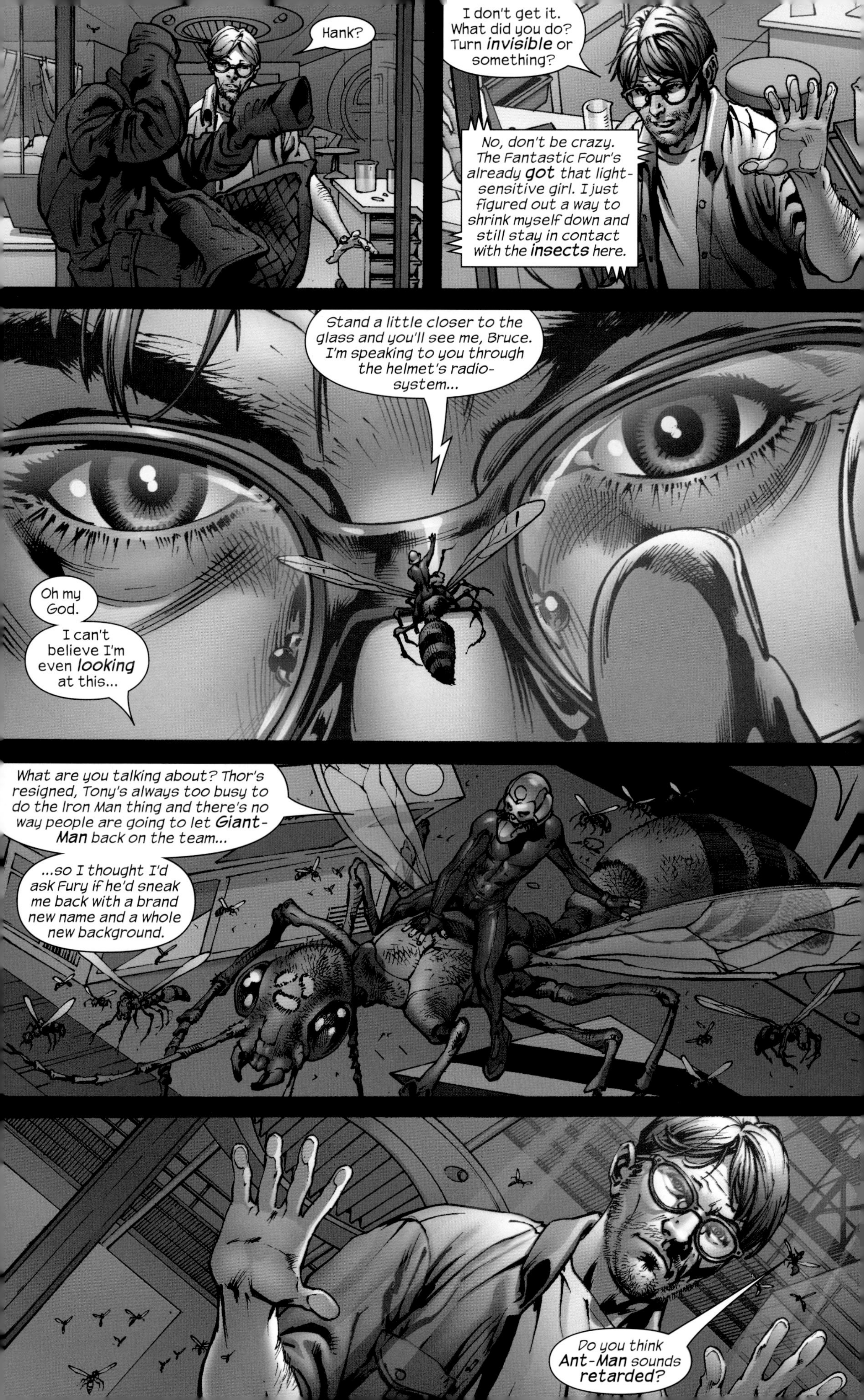
Hank?
I don't get it. What did you do? Turn invisible or something?
No, don't be crazy. The Fantastic Four's already got that light-sensitive girl. I just figured out a way to shrink myself down and still stay in contact with the insects here.
Stand a little closer to the glass and you'll see me, Bruce. I'm speaking to you through the helmet's radio-system...
Oh my God.
I can't believe I'm even looking at this...
What are you talking about? Thor's resigned, Tony's always too busy to do the Iron Man thing and there's no way people are going to let Giant-Man back on the team...
...so I thought I'd ask Fury if he'd sneak me back with a brand new name and a whole new background.
Do you think Ant-Man sounds retarded?

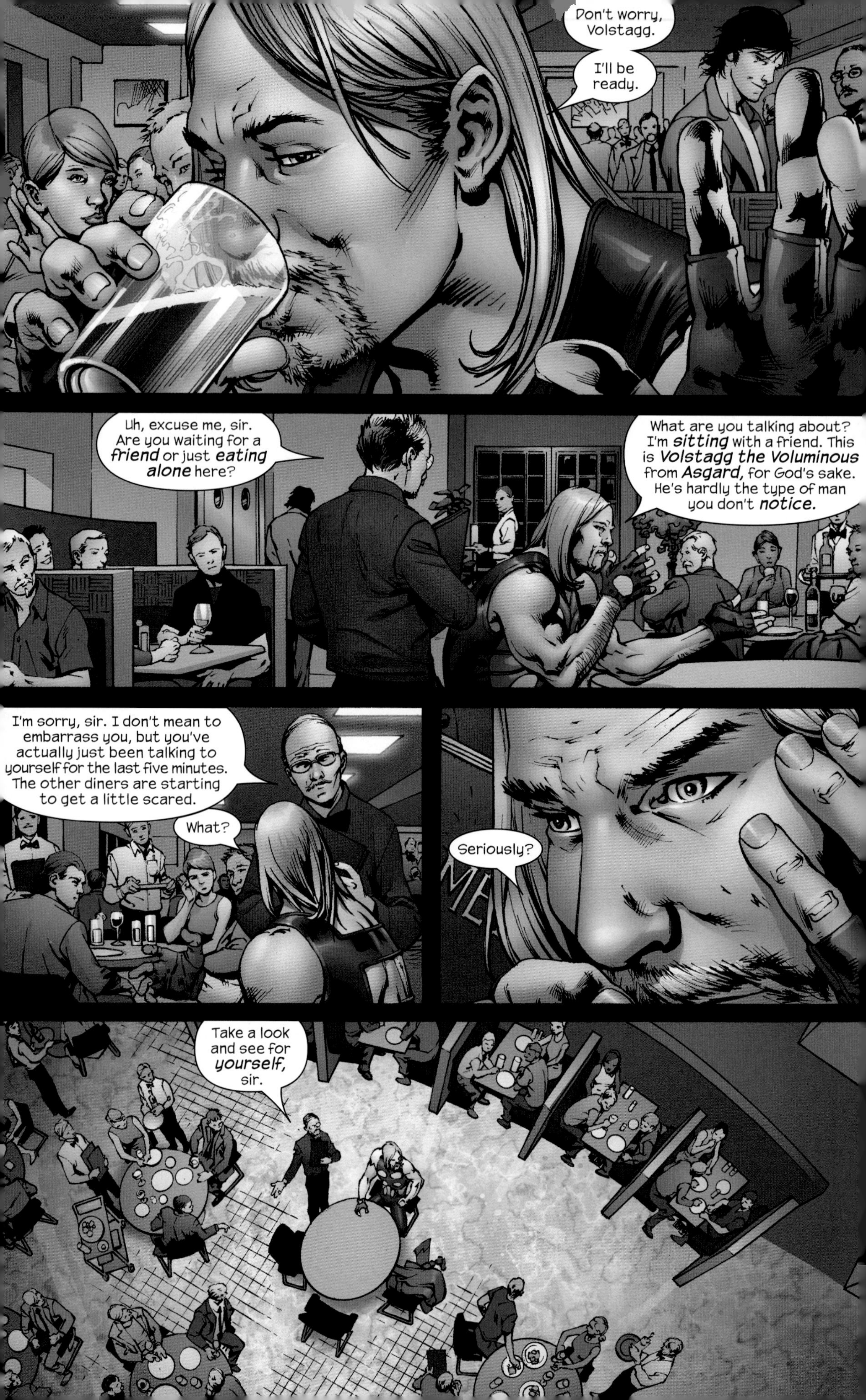

Don't worry, Volstagg.
I'll be ready.
Uh, excuse me, sir. Are you waiting for a *friend* or just *eating alone* here?
What are you talking about? I'm *sitting* with a friend. This is *Volstagg the Voluminous* from *Asgard,* for God's sake. He's hardly the type of man you don't *notice.*
I'm sorry, sir. I don't mean to embarrass you, but you've actually just been talking to yourself for the last five minutes. The other diners are starting to get a little scared.
What?
Seriously?
Take a look and see for *yourself,* sir.

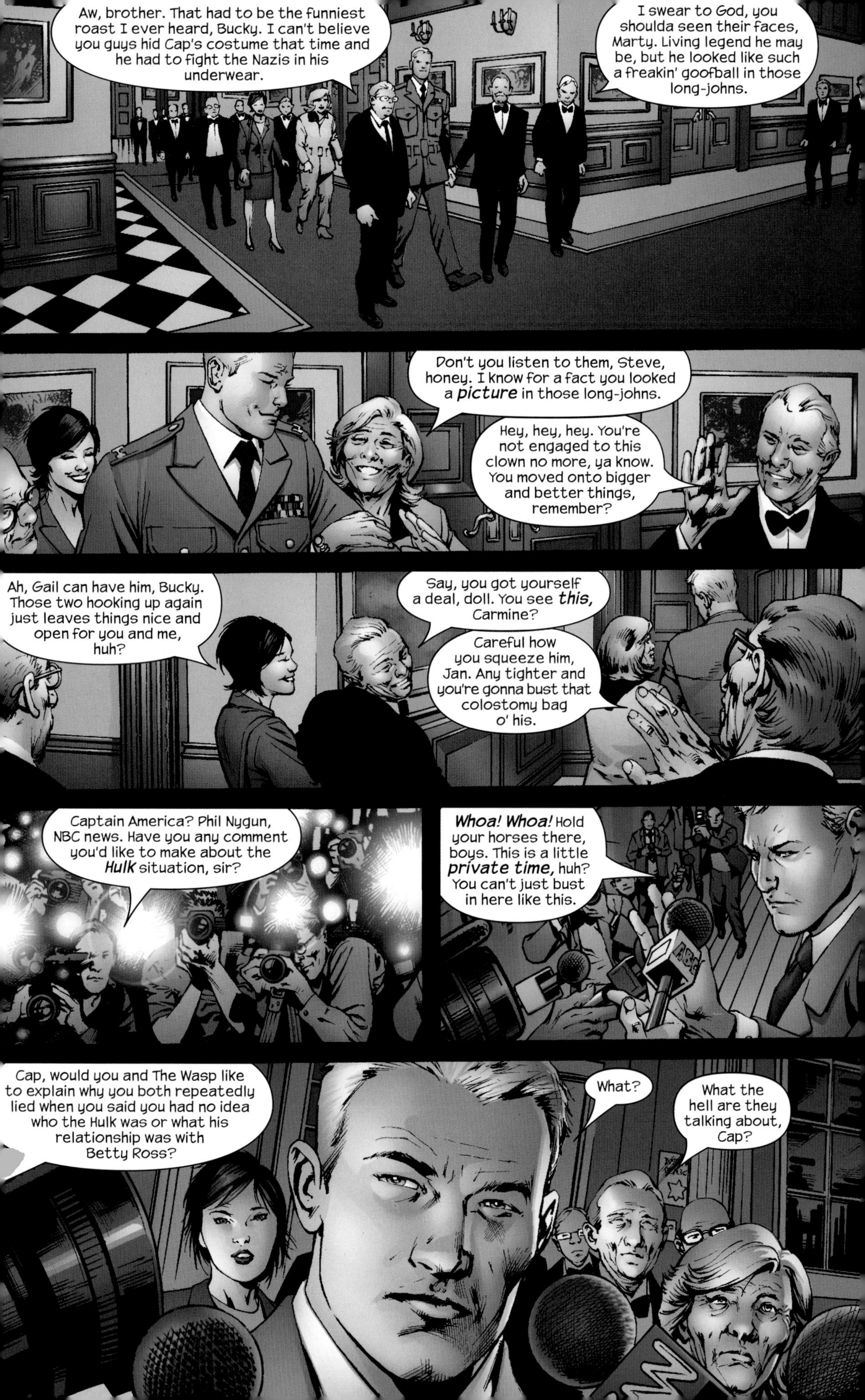
Aw, brother. That had to be the funniest roast I ever heard, Bucky. I can't believe you guys hid Cap's costume that time and he had to fight the Nazis in his underwear.
I swear to God, you shoulda seen their faces, Marty. Living legend he may be, but he looked like such a freakin' goofball in those long-johns.
Don't you listen to them, Steve, honey. I know for a fact you looked a *picture* in those long-johns.
Hey, hey, hey. You're not engaged to this clown no more, ya know. You moved onto bigger and better things, remember?
Ah, Gail can have him, Bucky. Those two hooking up again just leaves things nice and open for you and me, huh?
Say, you got yourself a deal, doll. You see *this,* Carmine?
Careful how you squeeze him, Jan. Any tighter and you're gonna bust that colostomy bag o' his.
Captain America? Phil Nygun, NBC news. Have you any comment you'd like to make about the *Hulk* situation, sir?
Whoa! Whoa! Hold your horses there, boys. This is a little *private time,* huh? You can't just bust in here like this.
Cap, would you and The Wasp like to explain why you both repeatedly lied when you said you had no idea who the Hulk was or what his relationship was with Betty Ross?
What?
What the hell are they talking about, Cap?

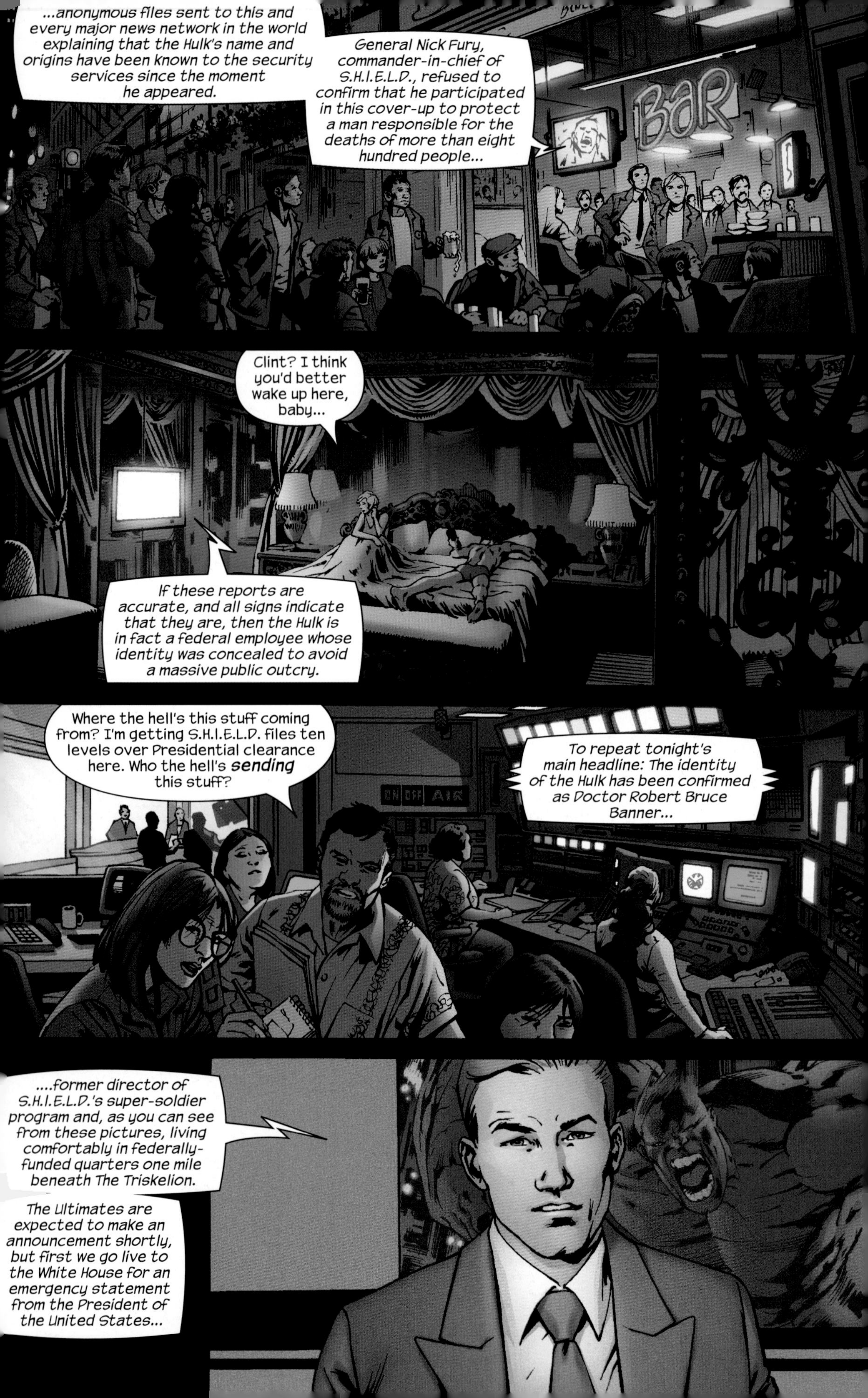
...anonymous files sent to this and every major news network in the world explaining that the Hulk's name and origins have been known to the security services since the moment he appeared.
General Nick Fury, commander-in-chief of S.H.I.E.L.D., refused to confirm that he participated in this cover-up to protect a man responsible for the deaths of more than eight hundred people...
BAR
Clint? I think you'd better wake up here, baby...
If these reports are accurate, and all signs indicate that they are, then the Hulk is in fact a federal employee whose identity was concealed to avoid a massive public outcry.
Where the hell's this stuff coming from? I'm getting S.H.I.E.L.D. files ten levels over Presidential clearance here. Who the hell's *sending* this stuff?
To repeat tonight's main headline: The identity of the Hulk has been confirmed as Doctor Robert Bruce Banner...
ON OFF AIR
....former director of S.H.I.E.L.D.'s super-soldier program and, as you can see from these pictures, living comfortably in federally-funded quarters one mile beneath The Triskelion.
The Ultimates are expected to make an announcement shortly, but first we go live to the White House for an emergency statement from the President of the United States...

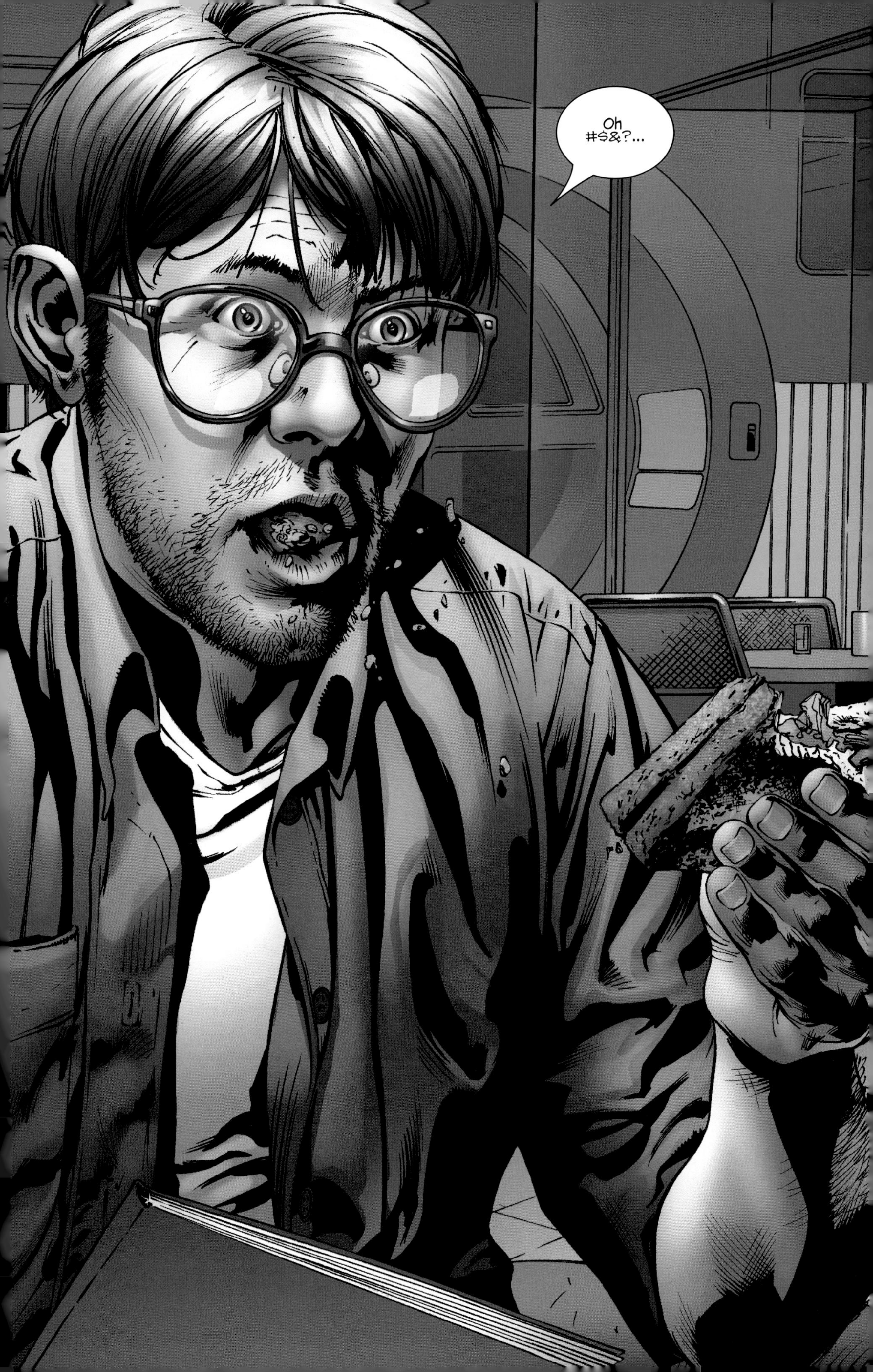
Oh #$&?...

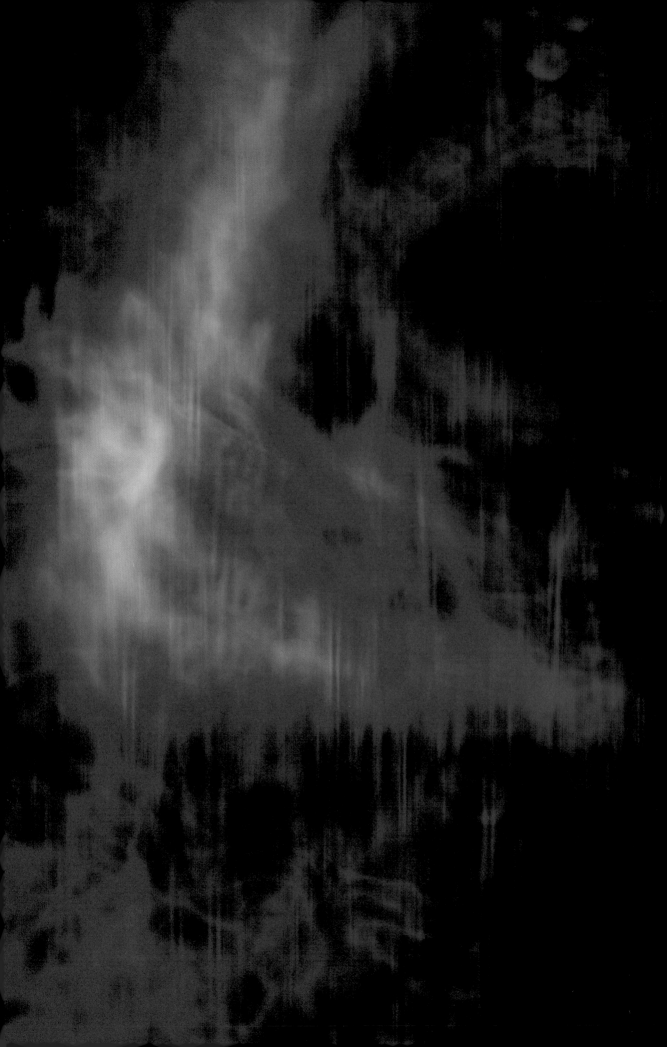

DEAD MAN WALKING

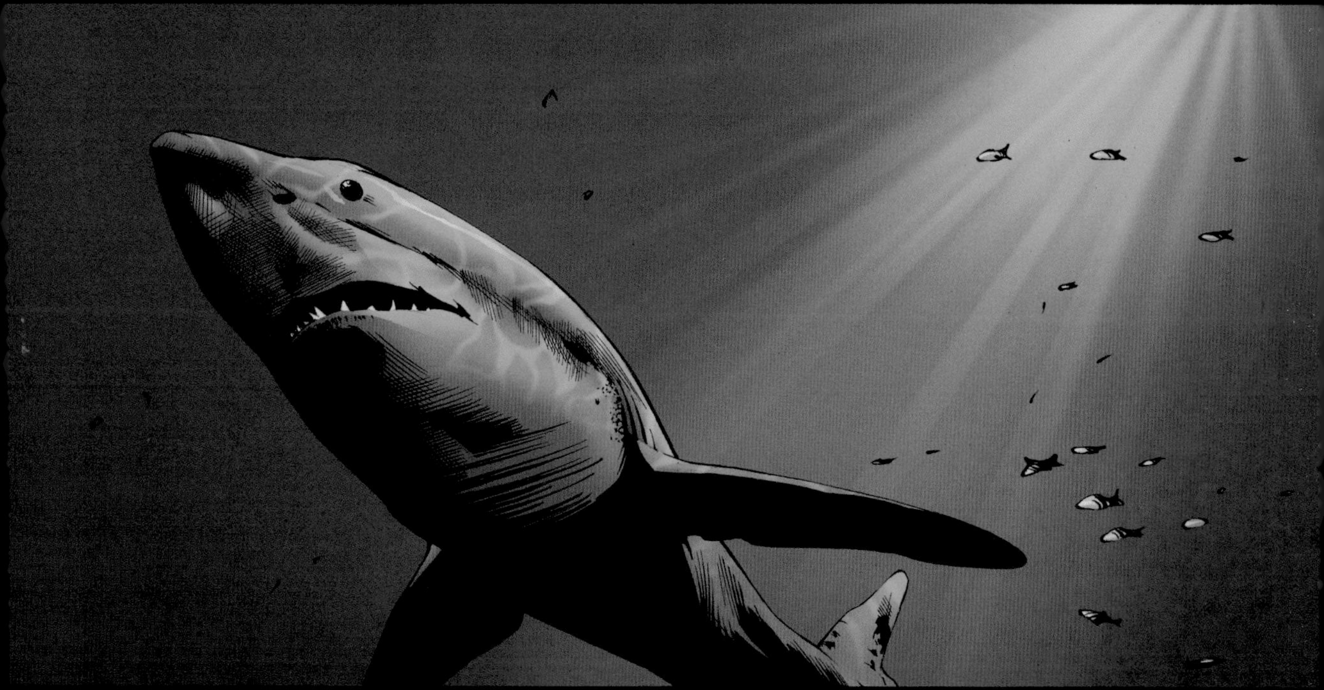

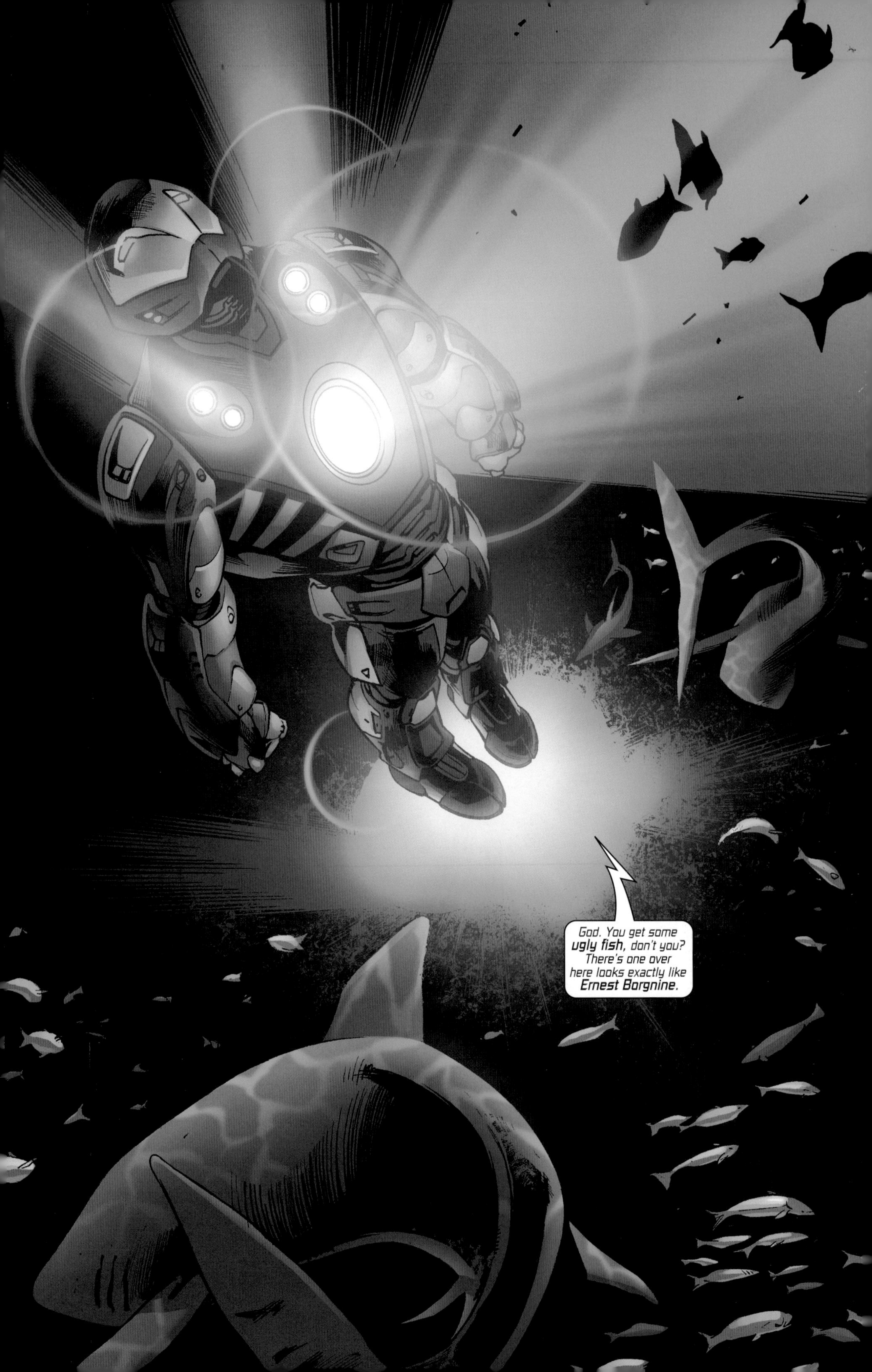
God. You get some ugly fish, don't you? There's one over here looks exactly like Ernest Borgnine.

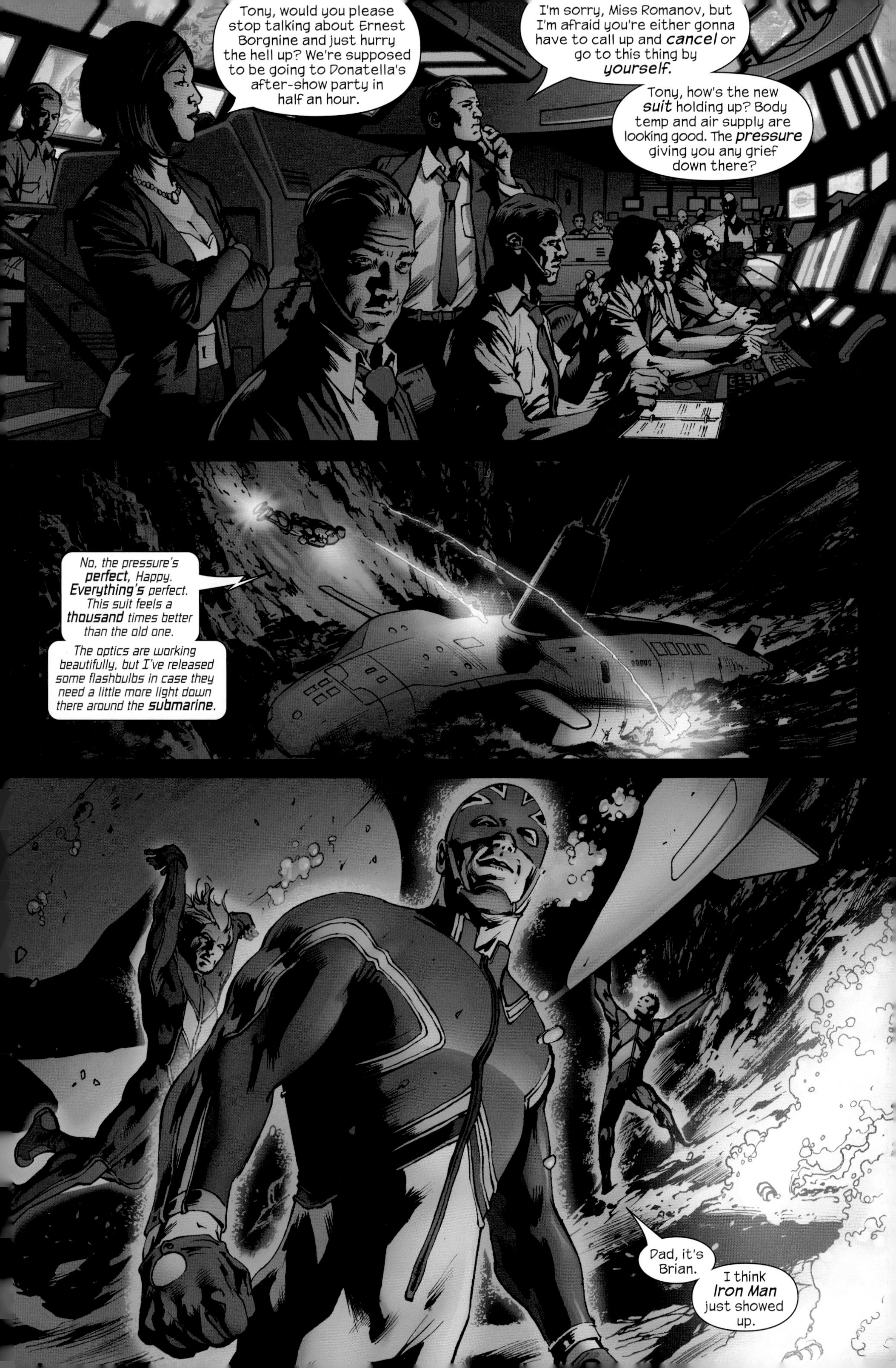
Tony, would you please stop talking about Ernest Borgnine and just hurry the hell up? We're supposed to be going to Donatella's after-show party in half an hour.
I'm sorry, Miss Romanov, but I'm afraid you're either gonna have to call up and cancel or go to this thing by yourself.
Tony, how's the new suit holding up? Body temp and air supply are looking good. The pressure giving you any grief down there?
No, the pressure's perfect, Happy. Everything's perfect. This suit feels a thousand times better than the old one.
The optics are working beautifully, but I've released some flashbulbs in case they need a little more light down there around the submarine.
Dad, it's Brian.
I think Iron Man just showed up.

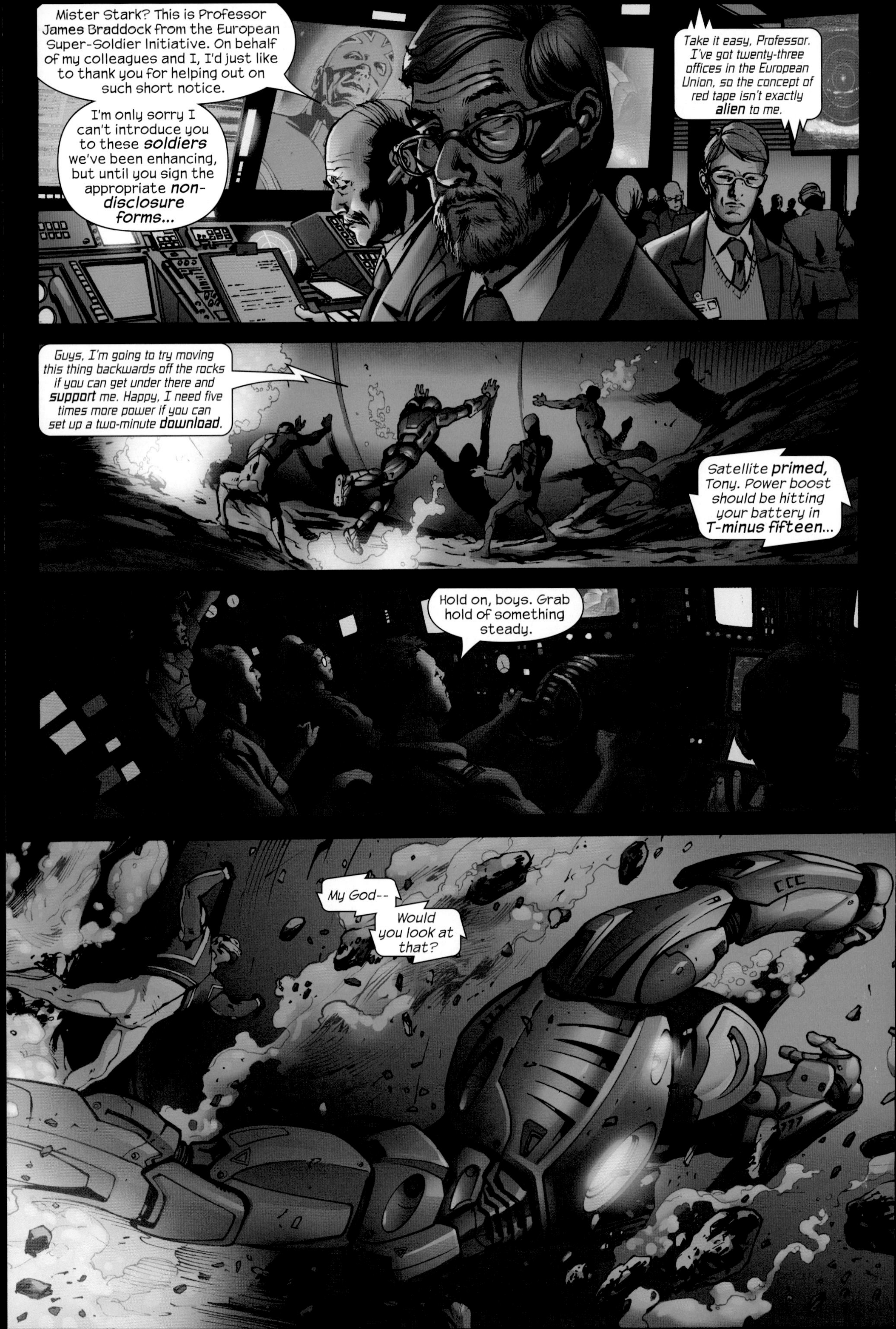

Mister Stark? This is Professor James Braddock from the European Super-Soldier Initiative. On behalf of my colleagues and I, I'd just like to thank you for helping out on such short notice.
I'm only sorry I can't introduce you to these **soldiers** we've been enhancing, but until you sign the appropriate **non-disclosure forms...**
Take it easy, Professor. I've got twenty-three offices in the European Union, so the concept of red tape isn't exactly **alien** to me.
Guys, I'm going to try moving this thing backwards off the rocks if you can get under there and **support** me. Happy, I need five times more power if you can set up a two-minute **download**.
Satellite **primed,** Tony. Power boost should be hitting your battery in **T-minus fifteen...**
Hold on, boys. Grab hold of something steady.
My God--
Would you look at that?

What did we **create** here, Tony?

A ten-billion-dollar means of rendering my weekends **miserable**, Mister Hogan. Now could somebody in this dump please fetch me a **drink?** Jarvis, what the hell are we **paying** you for?

Because I've still got the **negatives**, Miss Romanov. And you can fetch your **own** bloody drink. I've got my **hands** full at the moment playing **strip-monopoly.**

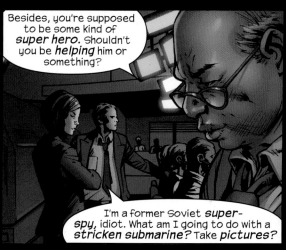

Besides, you're supposed to be some kind of **super hero.** Shouldn't you be **helping** him or something?

I'm a former Soviet **super-spy,** idiot. What am I going to do with a **stricken submarine?** Take **pictures?**

What Master Tony sees in you I'll **never** know, you slutty minx.

Well, I'm afraid you'll just have to get used to me, old man, because I'm not going **anywhere** as long as I'm giving him that one thing that even **you** can't deliver.

What's **that,** darling? Hungarian **goulash?**

Oh, hell.

What's wrong?

Just got a message from General Fury.

This is really **bad.**

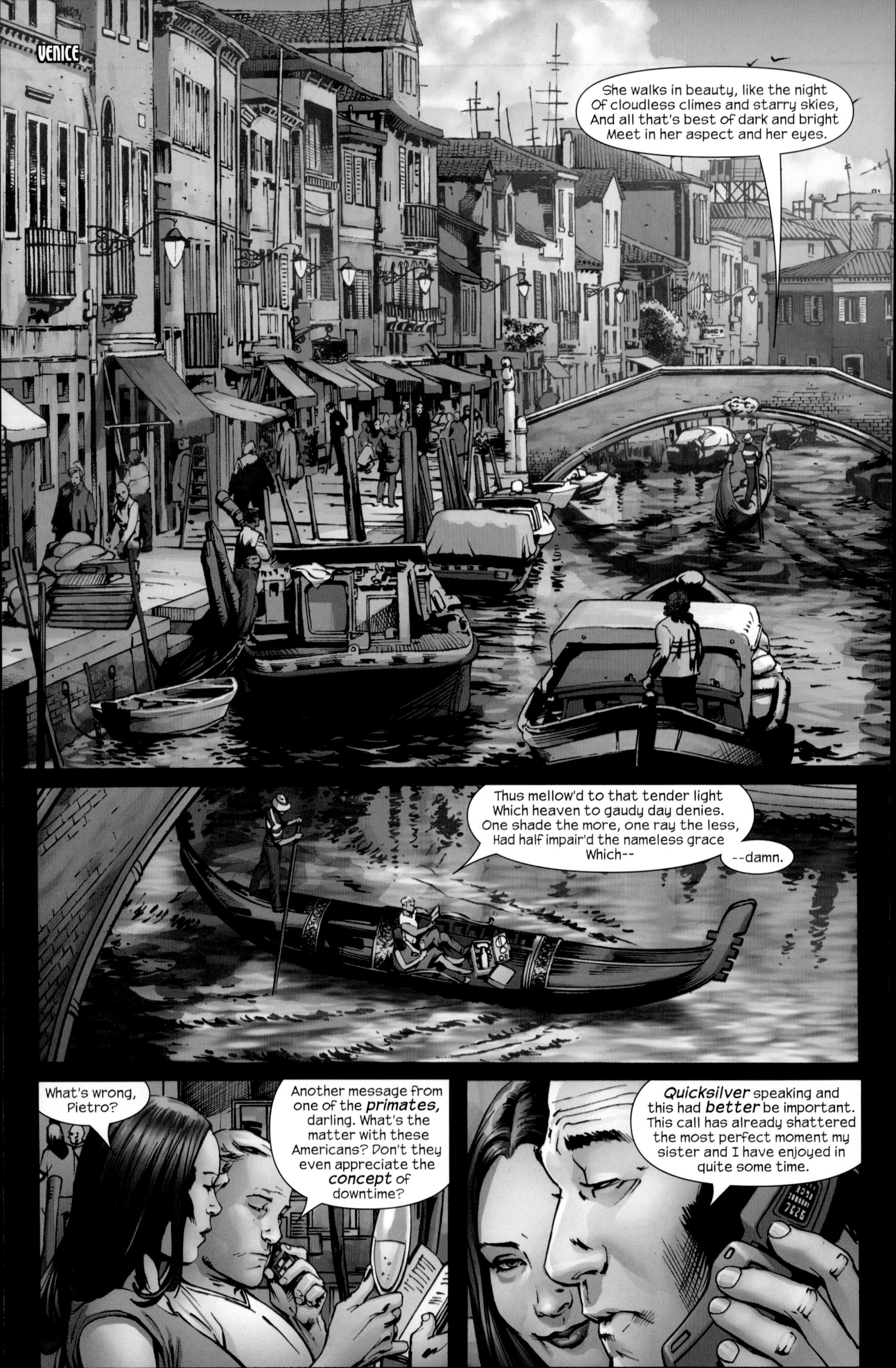
VENICE
She walks in beauty, like the night Of cloudless climes and starry skies, And all that's best of dark and bright Meet in her aspect and her eyes.
Thus mellow'd to that tender light Which heaven to gaudy day denies. One shade the more, one ray the less, Had half impair'd the nameless grace Which--
--damn.
What's wrong, Pietro?
Another message from one of the *primates,* darling. What's the matter with these Americans? Don't they even appreciate the *concept* of downtime?
Quicksilver speaking and this had *better* be important. This call has already shattered the most perfect moment my sister and I have enjoyed in quite some time.

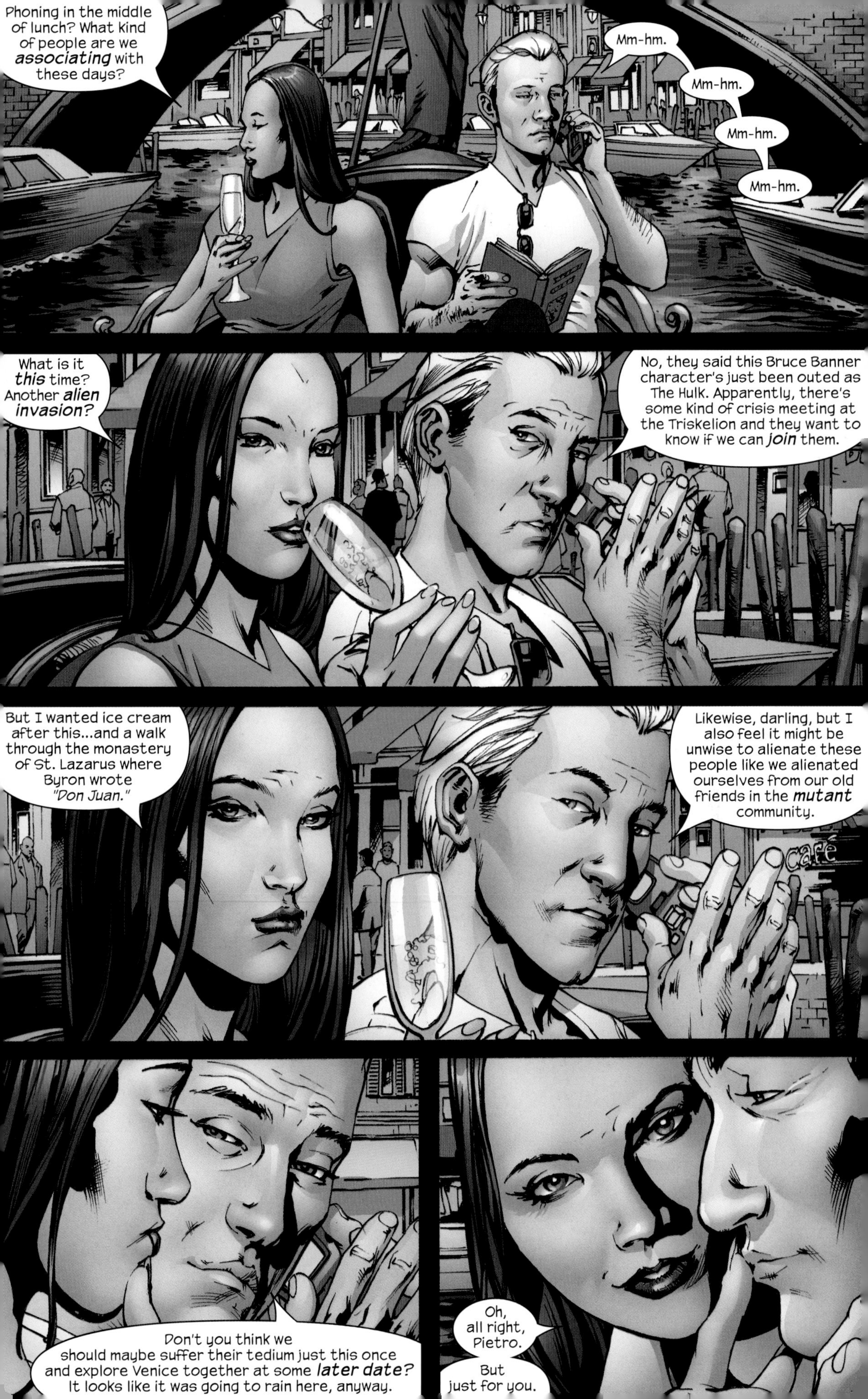
Phoning in the middle of lunch? What kind of people are we *associating* with these days?
Mm-hm.
Mm-hm.
Mm-hm.
Mm-hm.
What is it *this* time? Another *alien invasion?*
No, they said this Bruce Banner character's just been outed as The Hulk. Apparently, there's some kind of crisis meeting at the Triskelion and they want to know if we can *join* them.
But I wanted ice cream after this...and a walk through the monastery of St. Lazarus where Byron wrote *"Don Juan."*
Likewise, darling, but I also feel it might be unwise to alienate these people like we alienated ourselves from our old friends in the *mutant* community.
Café
Don't you think we should maybe suffer their tedium just this once and explore Venice together at some *later date?* It looks like it was going to rain here, anyway.
Oh, all right, Pietro.
But just for you.

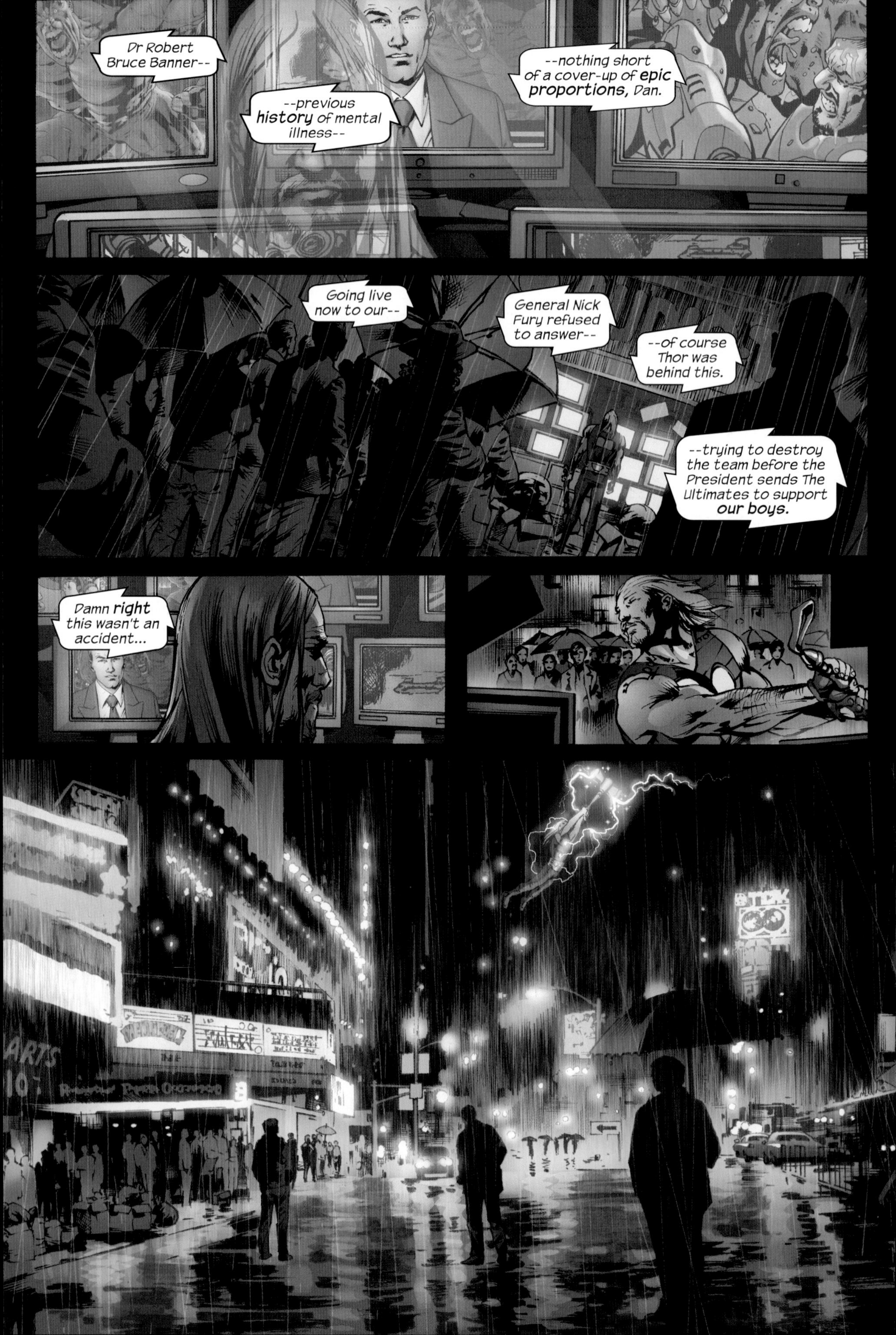
Dr Robert Bruce Banner--
--previous history of mental illness--
--nothing short of a cover-up of epic proportions, Dan.
Going live now to our--
General Nick Fury refused to answer--
--of course Thor was behind this.
--trying to destroy the team before the President sends The Ultimates to support our boys.
Damn right this wasn't an accident...

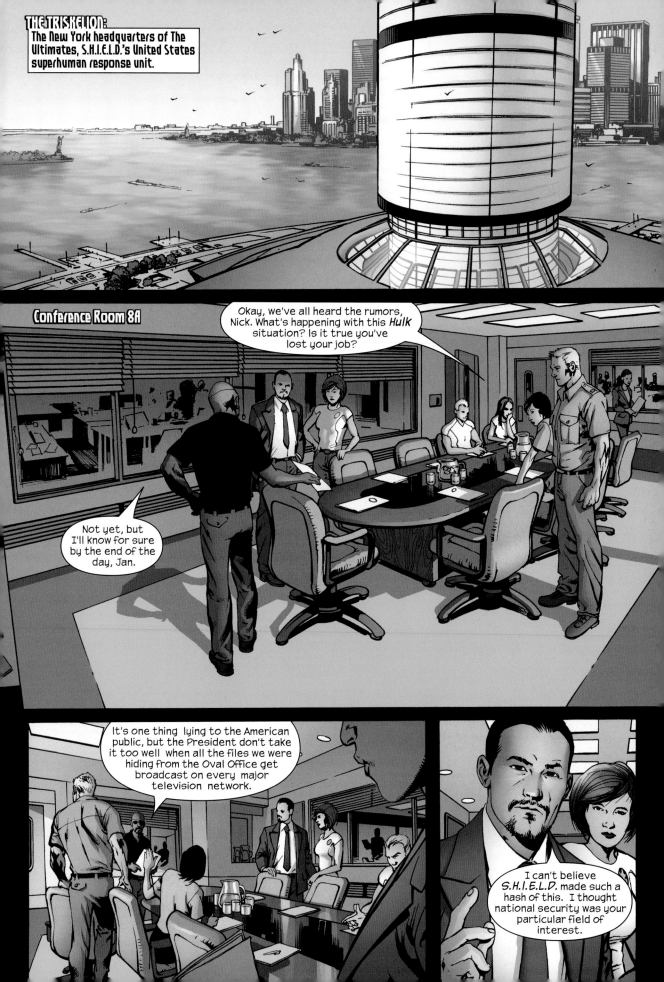

THE TRISKELION:
The New York headquarters of The Ultimates, S.H.I.E.L.D.'s United States superhuman response unit.

Conference Room 8A

Okay, we've all heard the rumors, Nick. What's happening with this *Hulk* situation? Is it true you've lost your job?

Not yet, but I'll know for sure by the end of the day, Jan.

It's one thing lying to the American public, but the President don't take it too well when all the files we were hiding from the Oval Office get broadcast on every major television network.

I can't believe *S.H.I.E.L.D.* made such a hash of this. I thought national security was your particular field of interest.

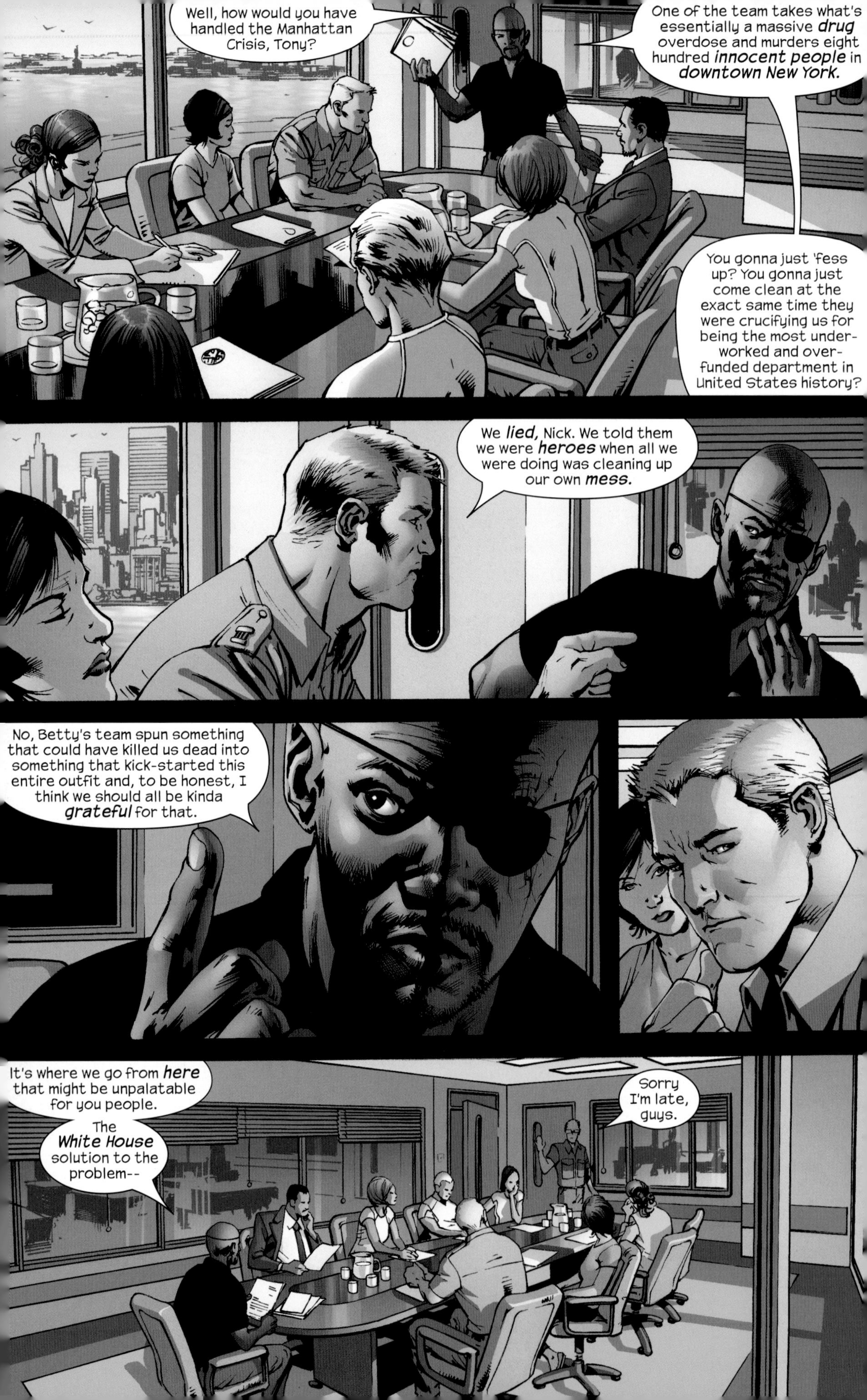

Well, how would you have handled the Manhattan Crisis, Tony?
One of the team takes what's essentially a massive *drug* overdose and murders eight hundred *innocent people* in *downtown New York.*
You gonna just 'fess up? You gonna just come clean at the exact same time they were crucifying us for being the most under-worked and over-funded department in United States history?
We *lied,* Nick. We told them we were *heroes* when all we were doing was cleaning up our own *mess.*
No, Betty's team spun something that could have killed us dead into something that kick-started this entire outfit and, to be honest, I think we should all be kinda *grateful* for that.
It's where we go from *here* that might be unpalatable for you people.
The *White House* solution to the problem--
Sorry I'm late, guys.

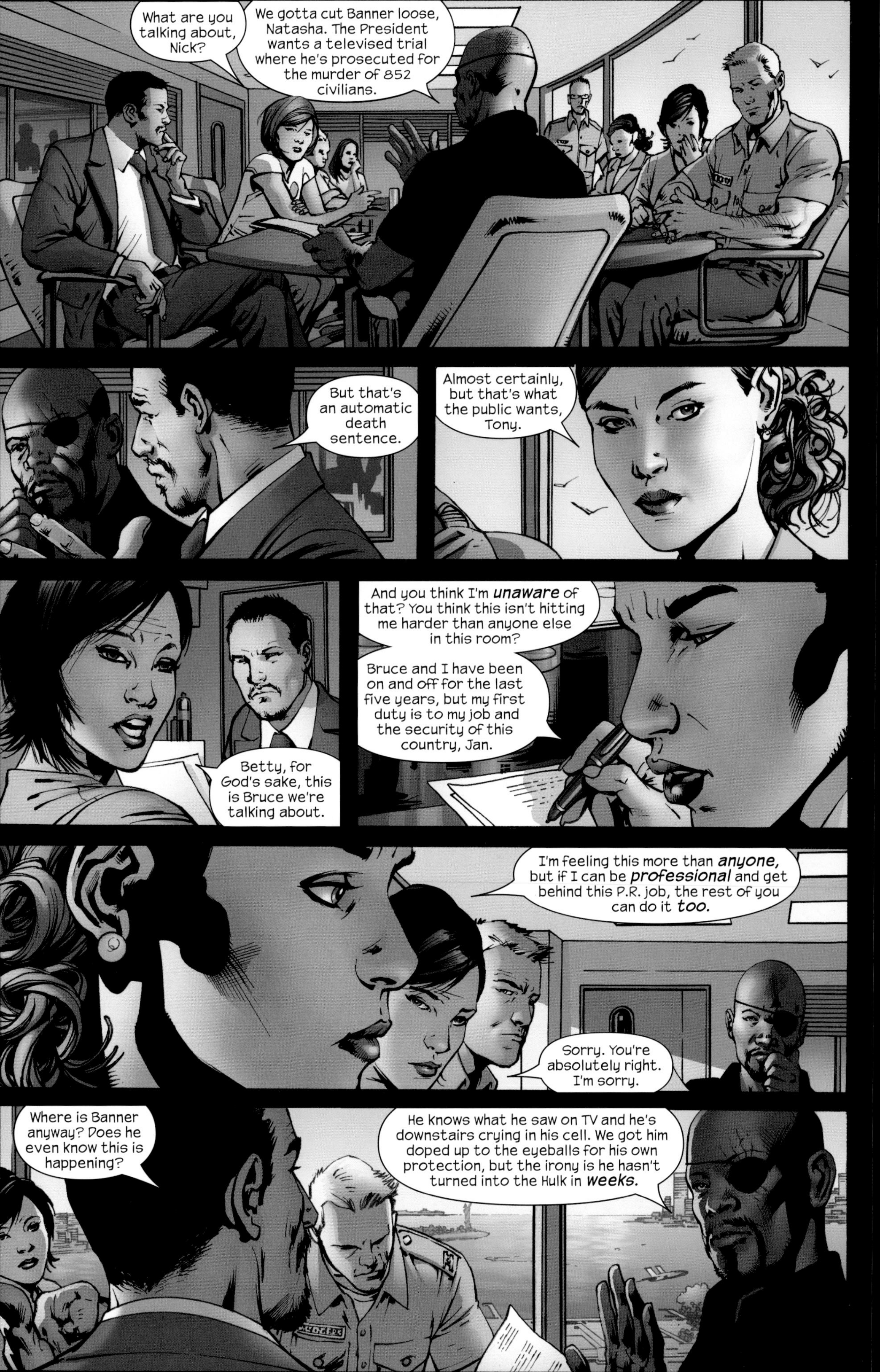
What are you talking about, Nick?
We gotta cut Banner loose, Natasha. The President wants a televised trial where he's prosecuted for the murder of 852 civilians.
But that's an automatic death sentence.
Almost certainly, but that's what the public wants, Tony.
Betty, for God's sake, this is Bruce we're talking about.
And you think I'm *unaware* of that? You think this isn't hitting me harder than anyone else in this room?
Bruce and I have been on and off for the last five years, but my first duty is to my job and the security of this country, Jan.
I'm feeling this more than *anyone,* but if I can be *professional* and get behind this P.R. job, the rest of you can do it *too.*
Sorry. You're absolutely right. I'm sorry.
Where is Banner anyway? Does he even know this is happening?
He knows what he saw on TV and he's downstairs crying in his cell. We got him doped up to the eyeballs for his own protection, but the irony is he hasn't turned into the Hulk in *weeks.*

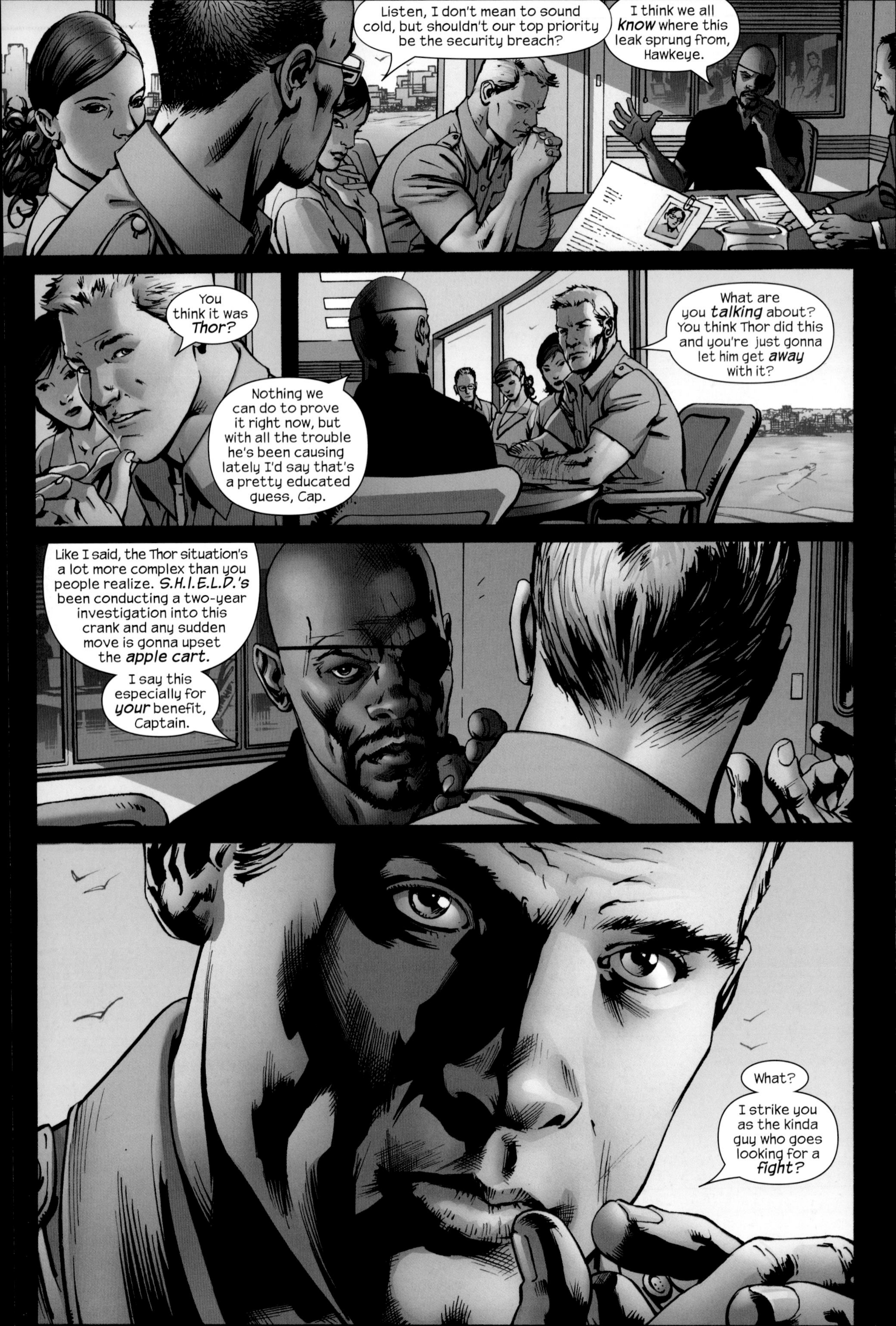
Listen, I don't mean to sound cold, but shouldn't our top priority be the security breach?
I think we all *know* where this leak sprung from, Hawkeye.
You think it was *Thor?*
What are you *talking* about? You think Thor did this and you're just gonna let him get *away* with it?
Nothing we can do to prove it right now, but with all the trouble he's been causing lately I'd say that's a pretty educated guess, Cap.
Like I said, the Thor situation's a lot more complex than you people realize. *S.H.I.E.L.D.'s* been conducting a two-year investigation into this crank and any sudden move is gonna upset the *apple cart.*
I say this especially for *your* benefit, Captain.
What?
I strike you as the kinda guy who goes looking for a *fight?*

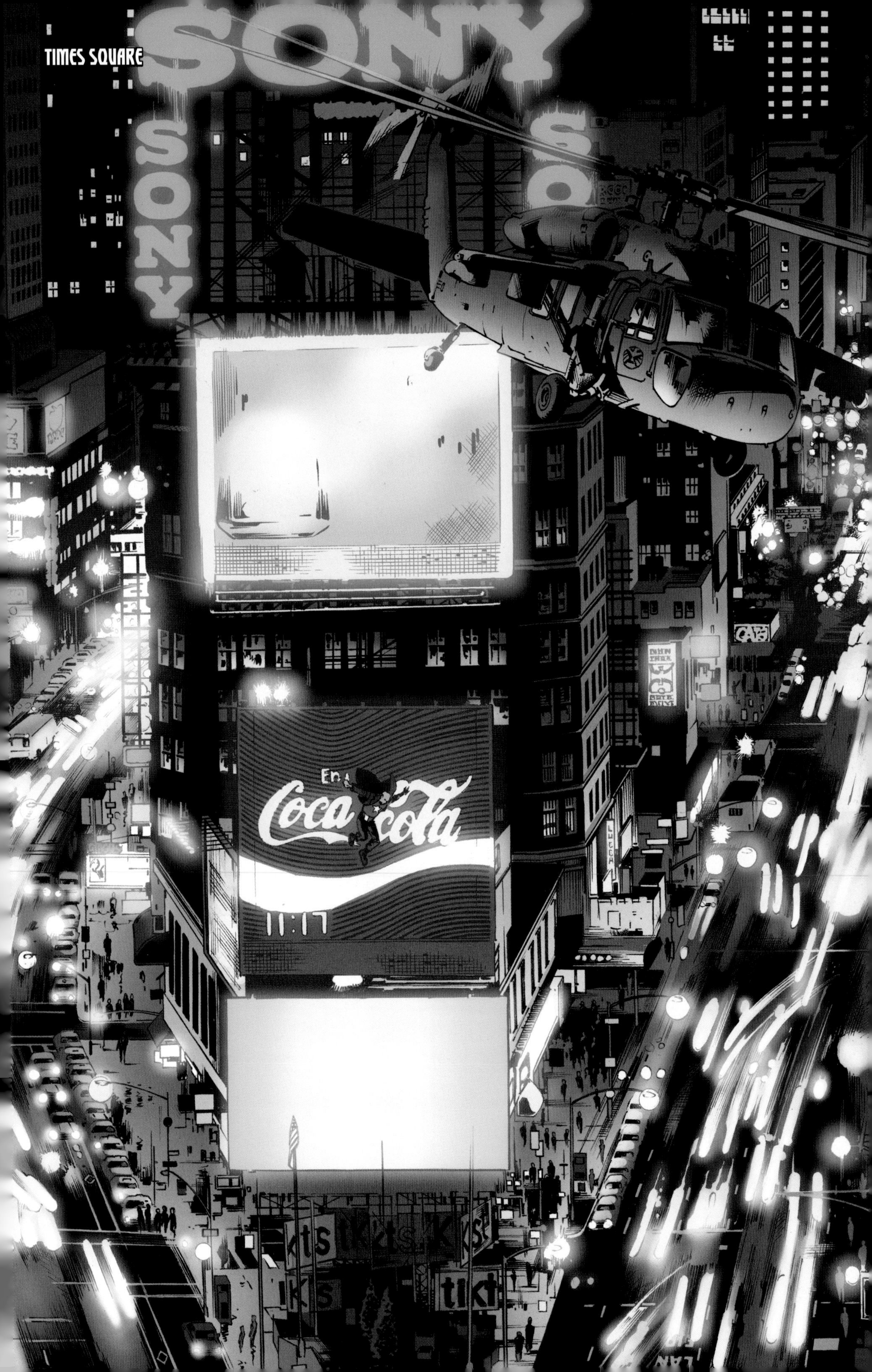

TIMES SQUARE
SONY
SONY
SO
Coca-Cola
11:17

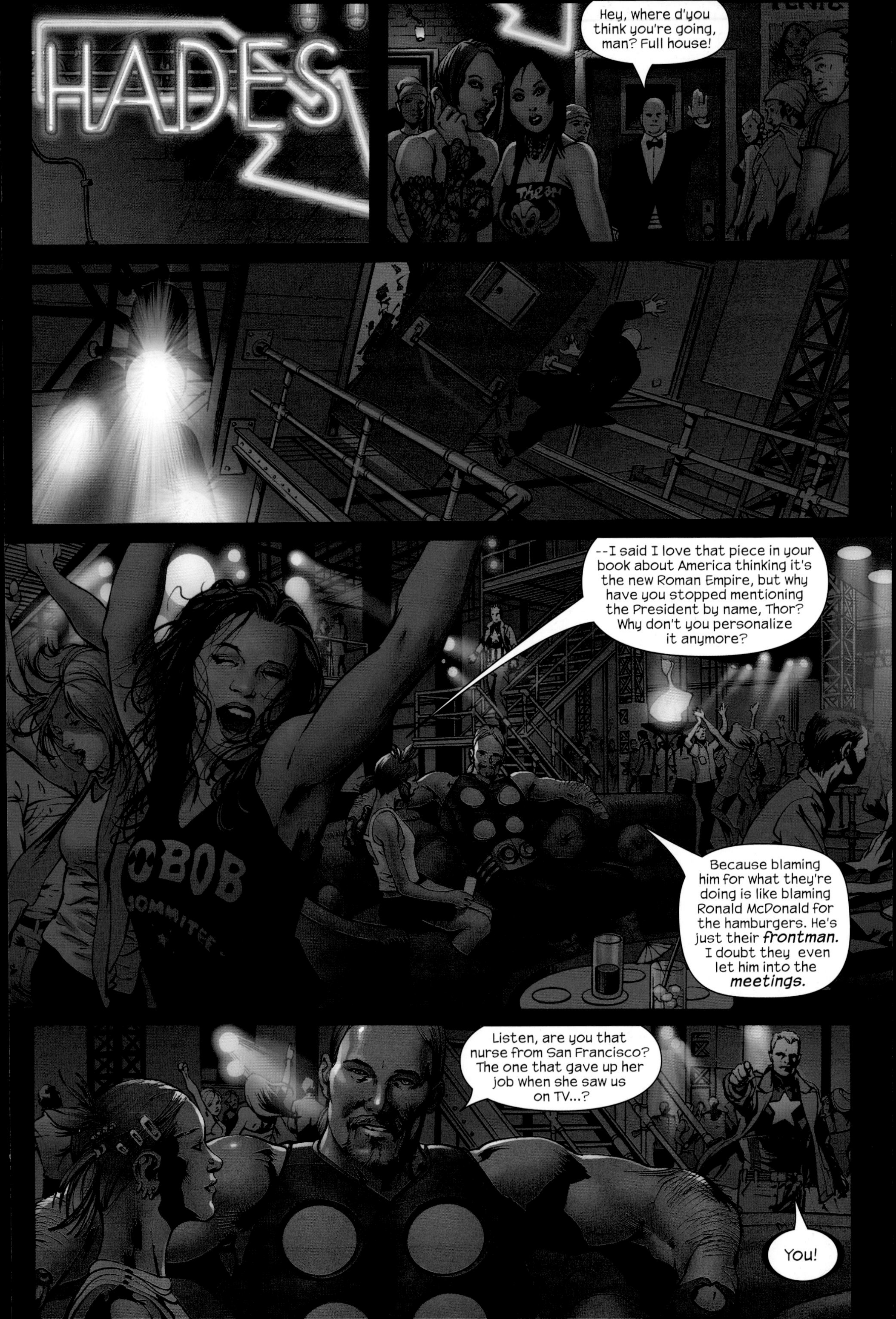
HADES
Hey, where d'you think you're going, man? Full house!
--I said I love that piece in your book about America thinking it's the new Roman Empire, but why have you stopped mentioning the President by name, Thor? Why don't you personalize it anymore?
Because blaming him for what they're doing is like blaming Ronald McDonald for the hamburgers. He's just their *frontman.* I doubt they even let him into the *meetings.*
Listen, are you that nurse from San Francisco? The one that gave up her job when she saw us on TV...?
You!

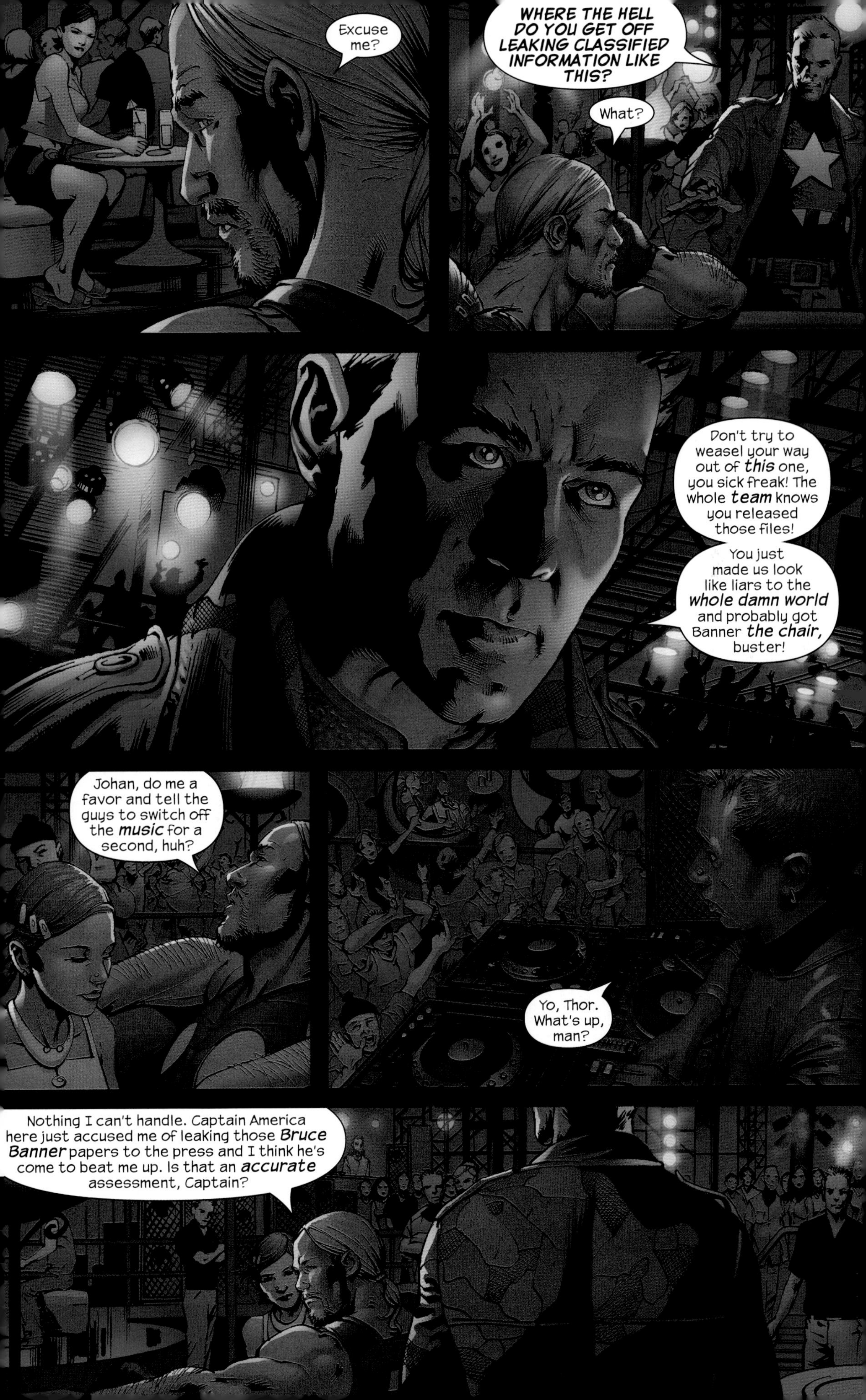
Excuse me?
WHERE THE HELL DO YOU GET OFF LEAKING CLASSIFIED INFORMATION LIKE THIS?
What?
Don't try to weasel your way out of *this* one, you sick freak! The whole *team* knows you released those files!
You just made us look like liars to the *whole damn world* and probably got Banner *the chair,* buster!
Johan, do me a favor and tell the guys to switch off the *music* for a second, huh?
Yo, Thor. What's up, man?
Nothing I can't handle. Captain America here just accused me of leaking those *Bruce Banner* papers to the press and I think he's come to beat me up. Is that an *accurate* assessment, Captain?

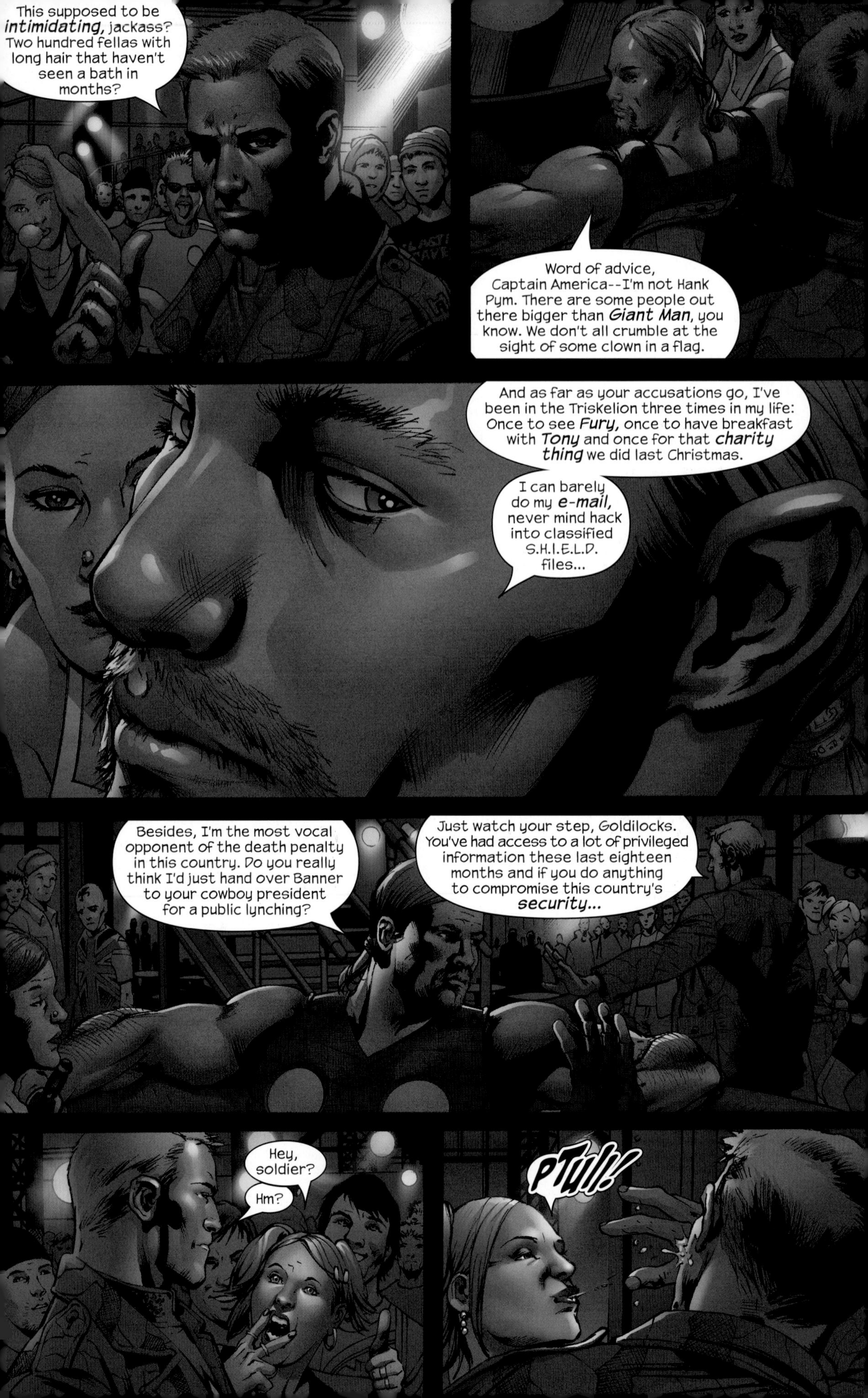
This supposed to be *intimidating,* jackass? Two hundred fellas with long hair that haven't seen a bath in months?
Word of advice, Captain America--I'm not Hank Pym. There are some people out there bigger than *Giant Man*, you know. We don't all crumble at the sight of some clown in a flag.
And as far as your accusations go, I've been in the Triskelion three times in my life: Once to see *Fury,* once to have breakfast with *Tony* and once for that *charity thing* we did last Christmas.
I can barely do my *e-mail,* never mind hack into classified S.H.I.E.L.D. files...
Besides, I'm the most vocal opponent of the death penalty in this country. Do you really think I'd just hand over Banner to your cowboy president for a public lynching?
Just watch your step, Goldilocks. You've had access to a lot of privileged information these last eighteen months and if you do anything to compromise this country's *security...*
Hey, soldier?
Hm?
PTUI!

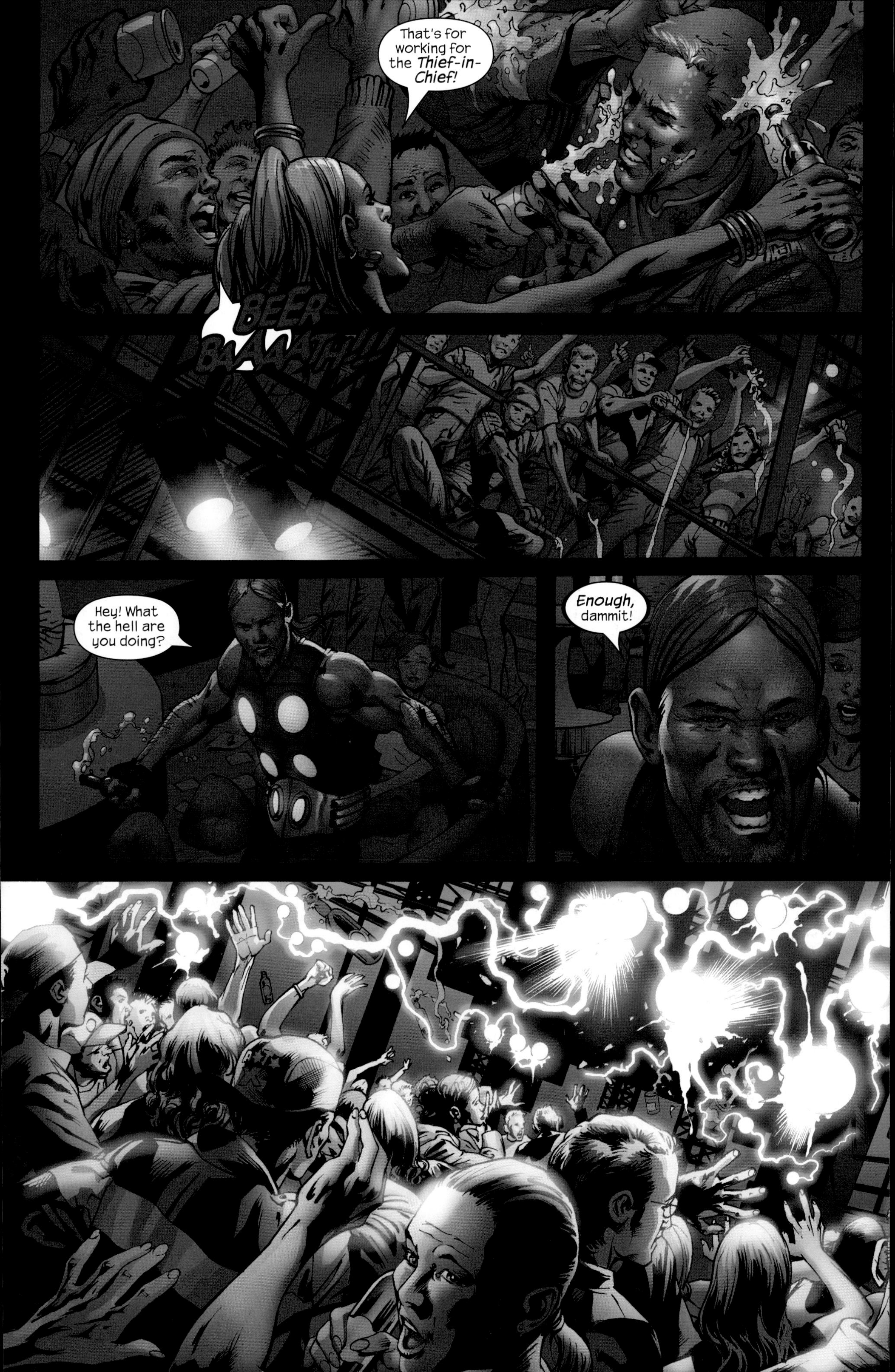

That's for working for the *Thief-in-Chief!*
BEER BAAATHH!!
Hey! What the hell are you doing?
Enough, dammit!

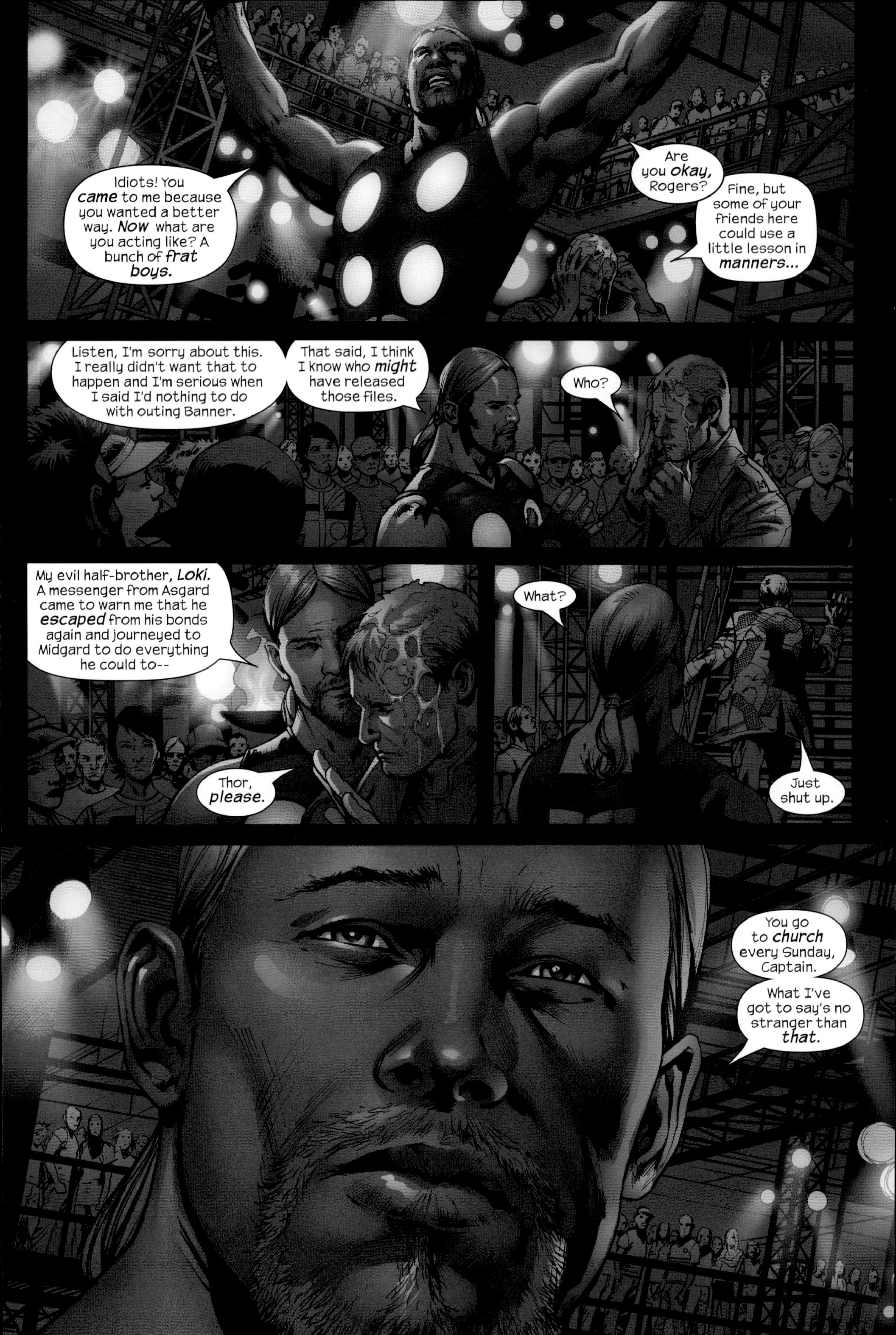
Idiots! You came to me because you wanted a better way. Now what are you acting like? A bunch of frat boys.
Are you okay, Rogers?
Fine, but some of your friends here could use a little lesson in manners...
Listen, I'm sorry about this. I really didn't want that to happen and I'm serious when I said I'd nothing to do with outing Banner.
That said, I think I know who might have released those files.
Who?
My evil half-brother, Loki. A messenger from Asgard came to warn me that he escaped from his bonds again and journeyed to Midgard to do everything he could to--
Thor, please.
What?
Just shut up.
You go to church every Sunday, Captain.
What I've got to say's no stranger than that.

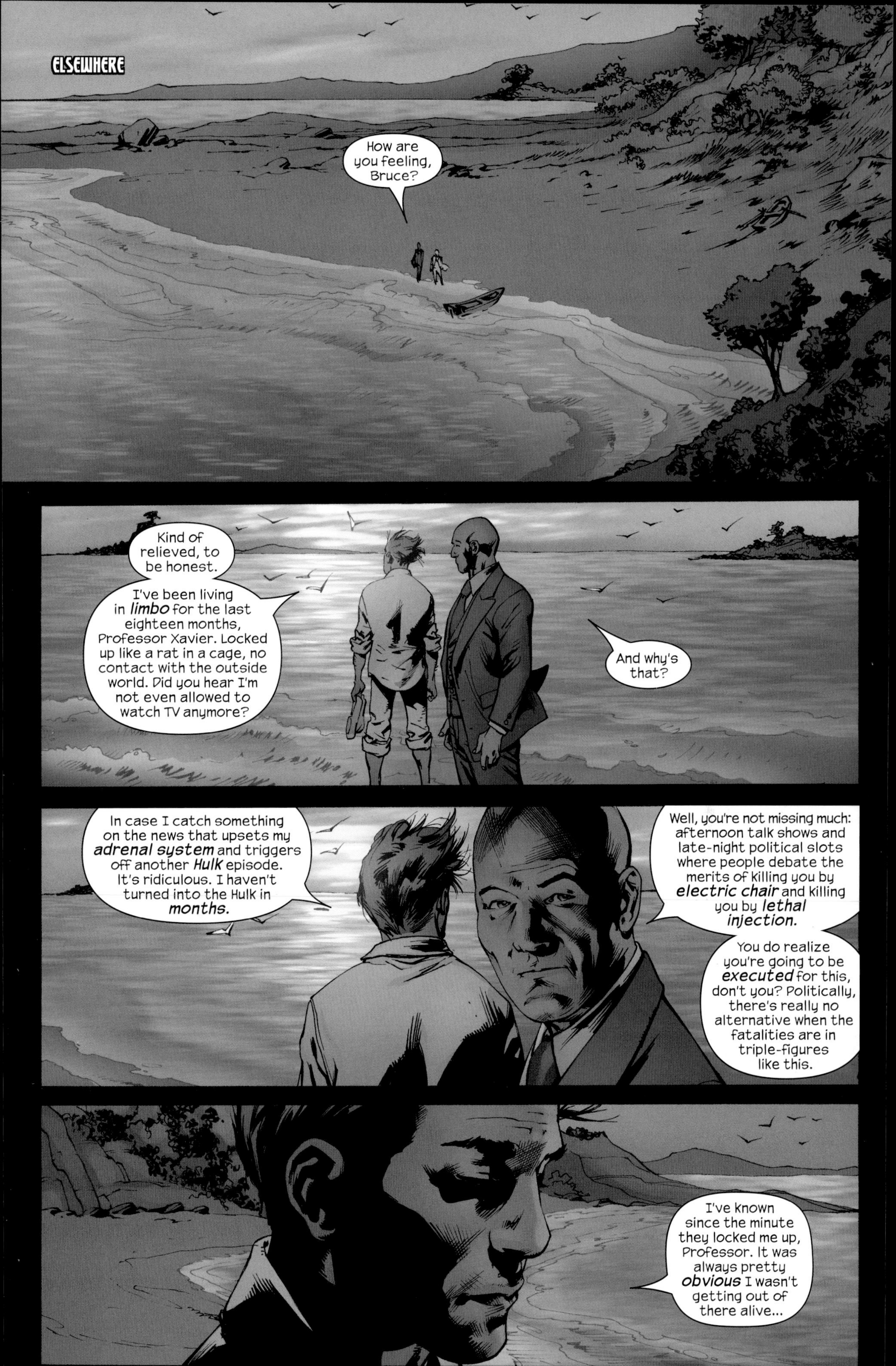
ELSEWHERE
How are you feeling, Bruce?
Kind of relieved, to be honest.
I've been living in *limbo* for the last eighteen months, Professor Xavier. Locked up like a rat in a cage, no contact with the outside world. Did you hear I'm not even allowed to watch TV anymore?
And why's that?
In case I catch something on the news that upsets my *adrenal system* and triggers off another *Hulk* episode. It's ridiculous. I haven't turned into the Hulk in *months.*
Well, you're not missing much: afternoon talk shows and late-night political slots where people debate the merits of killing you by *electric chair* and killing you by *lethal injection.*
You do realize you're going to be *executed* for this, don't you? Politically, there's really no alternative when the fatalities are in triple-figures like this.
I've known since the minute they locked me up, Professor. It was always pretty *obvious* I wasn't getting out of there alive...

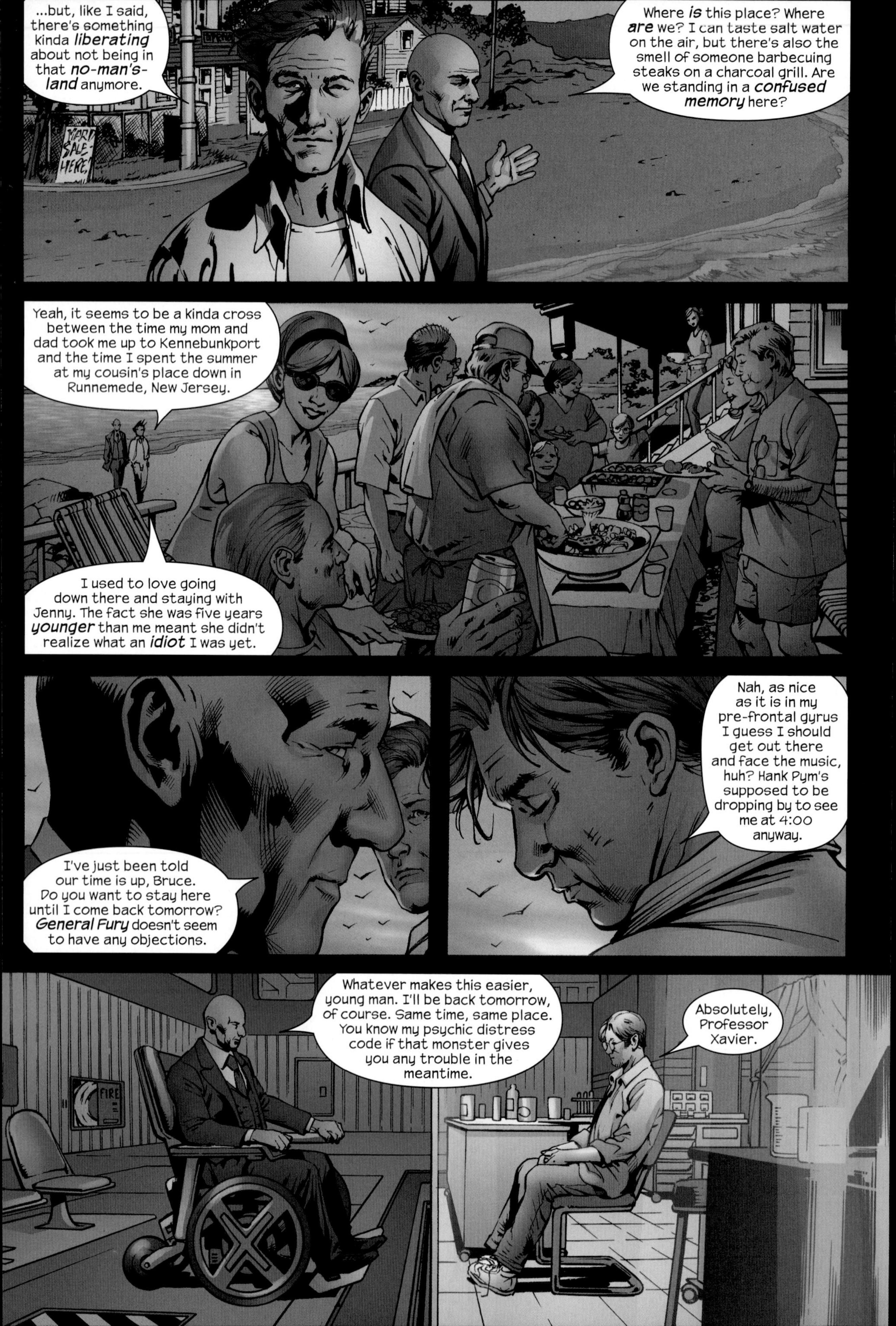

...but, like I said, there's something kinda *liberating* about not being in that *no-man's-land* anymore.
YARD SALE HERE!
Where *is* this place? Where *are* we? I can taste salt water on the air, but there's also the smell of someone barbecuing steaks on a charcoal grill. Are we standing in a *confused memory* here?
Yeah, it seems to be a kinda cross between the time my mom and dad took me up to Kennebunkport and the time I spent the summer at my cousin's place down in Runnemede, New Jersey.
I used to love going down there and staying with Jenny. The fact she was five years *younger* than me meant she didn't realize what an *idiot* I was yet.
I've just been told our time is up, Bruce. Do you want to stay here until I come back tomorrow? *General Fury* doesn't seem to have any objections.
Nah, as nice as it is in my pre-frontal gyrus I guess I should get out there and face the music, huh? Hank Pym's supposed to be dropping by to see me at 4:00 anyway.
Whatever makes this easier, young man. I'll be back tomorrow, of course. Same time, same place. You know my psychic distress code if that monster gives you any trouble in the meantime.
Absolutely, Professor Xavier.
FIRE

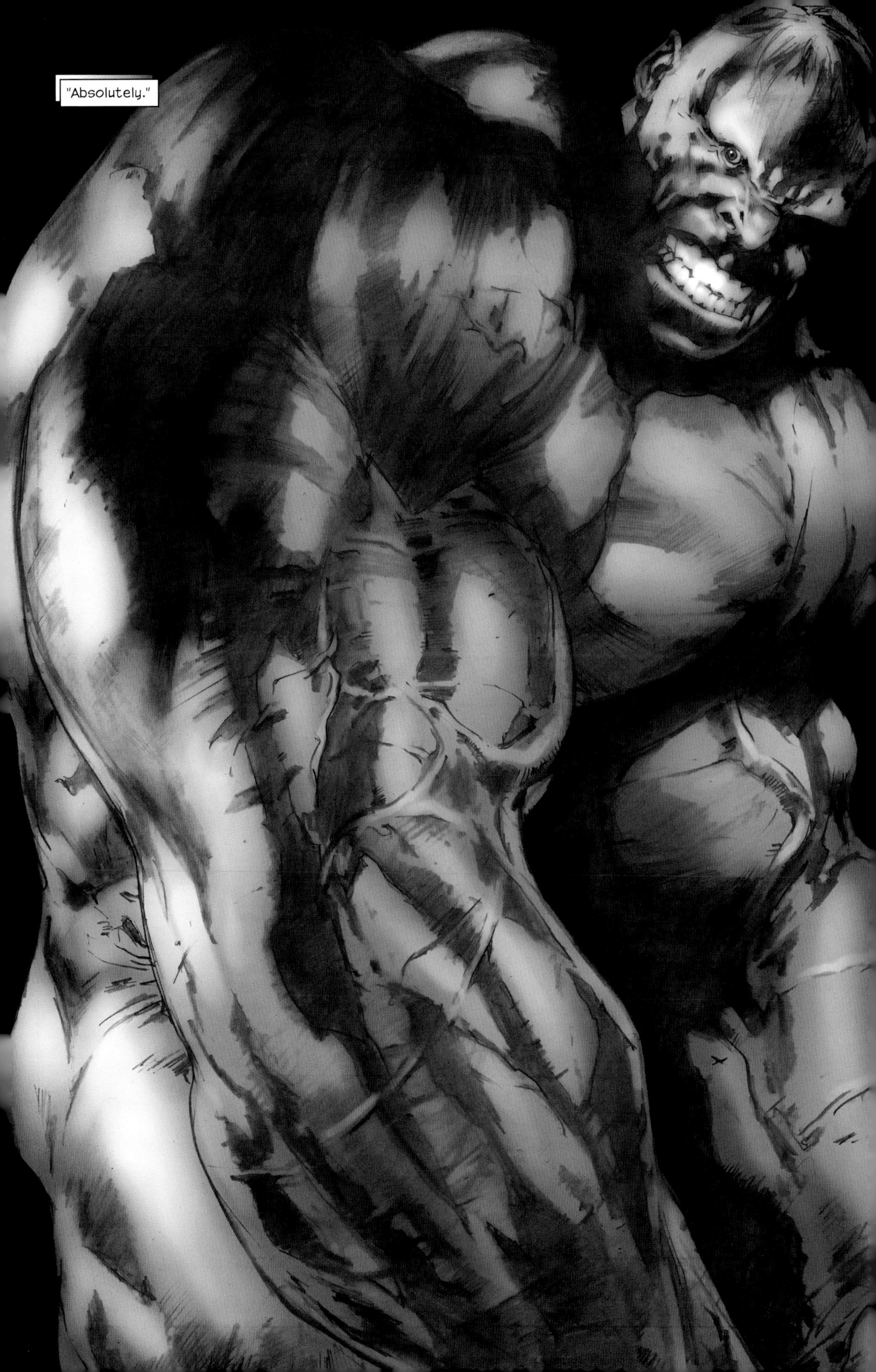
"Absolutely."

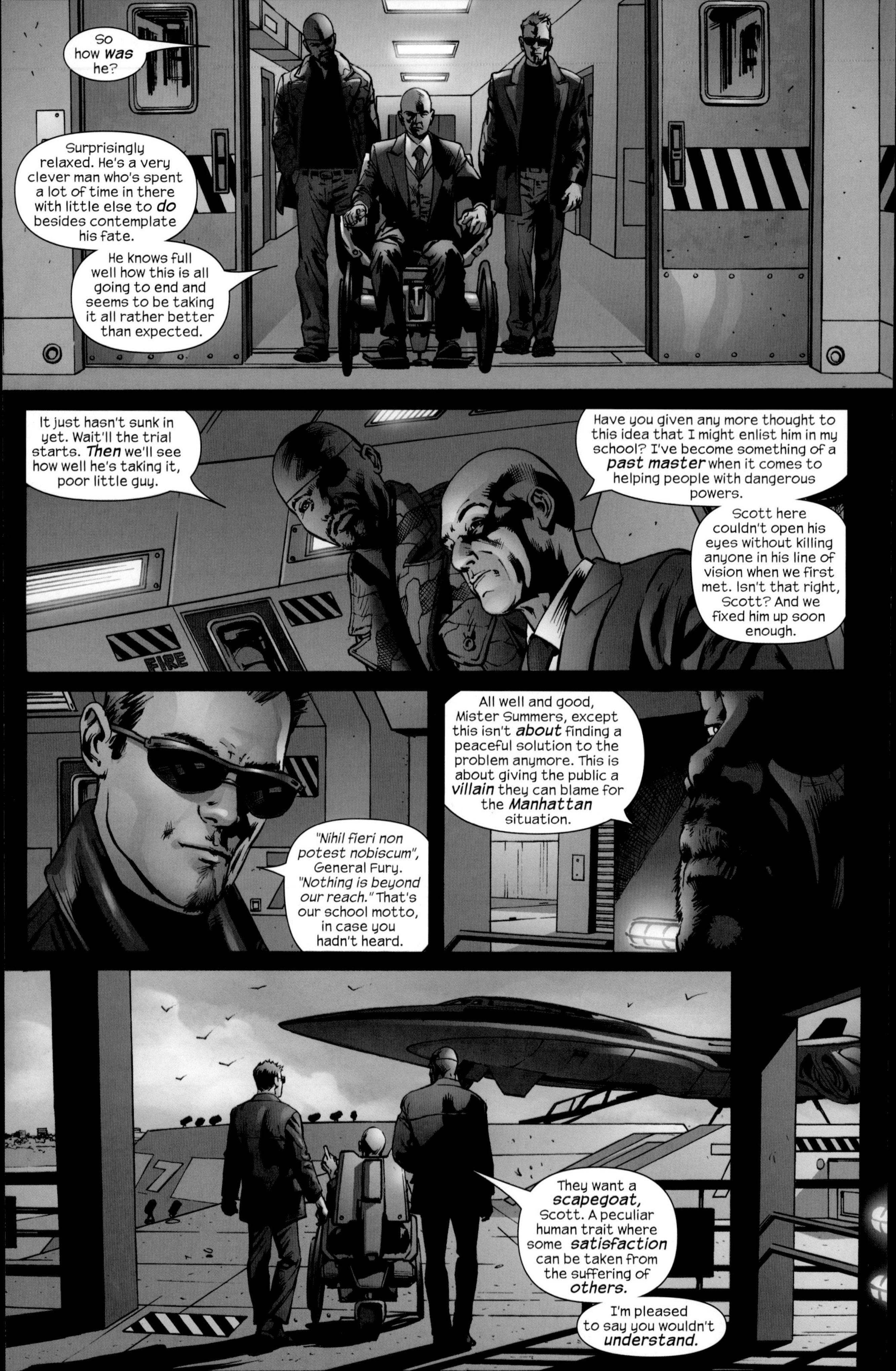

So how *was* he?
Surprisingly relaxed. He's a very clever man who's spent a lot of time in there with little else to *do* besides contemplate his fate.
He knows full well how this is all going to end and seems to be taking it all rather better than expected.
It just hasn't sunk in yet. Wait'll the trial starts. *Then* we'll see how well he's taking it, poor little guy.
Have you given any more thought to this idea that I might enlist him in my school? I've become something of a *past master* when it comes to helping people with dangerous powers.
Scott here couldn't open his eyes without killing anyone in his line of vision when we first met. Isn't that right, Scott? And we fixed him up soon enough.
FIRE
"Nihil fieri non potest nobiscum", General Fury. "Nothing is beyond our reach." That's our school motto, in case you hadn't heard.
All well and good, Mister Summers, except this isn't *about* finding a peaceful solution to the problem anymore. This is about giving the public a *villain* they can blame for the *Manhattan* situation.
They want a *scapegoat,* Scott. A peculiar human trait where some *satisfaction* can be taken from the suffering of *others.*
I'm pleased to say you wouldn't *understand.*

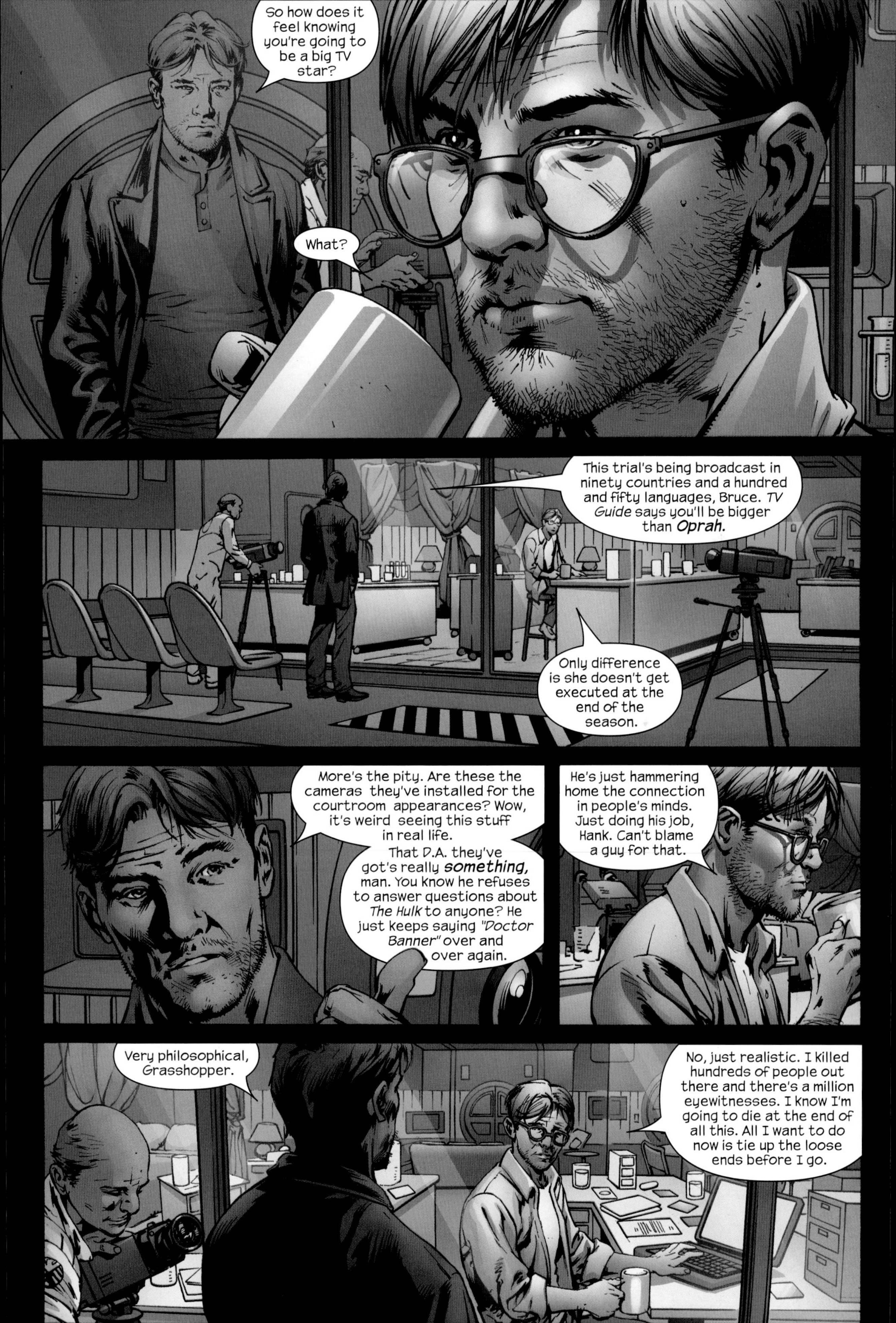
So how does it feel knowing you're going to be a big TV star?
What?
This trial's being broadcast in ninety countries and a hundred and fifty languages, Bruce. *TV Guide* says you'll be bigger than ***Oprah.***
Only difference is she doesn't get executed at the end of the season.
More's the pity. Are these the cameras they've installed for the courtroom appearances? Wow, it's weird seeing this stuff in real life.
That D.A. they've got's really ***something,*** man. You know he refuses to answer questions about *The Hulk* to anyone? He just keeps saying *"Doctor Banner"* over and over again.
He's just hammering home the connection in people's minds. Just doing his job, Hank. Can't blame a guy for that.
Very philosophical, Grasshopper.
No, just realistic. I killed hundreds of people out there and there's a million eyewitnesses. I know I'm going to die at the end of all this. All I want to do now is tie up the loose ends before I go.

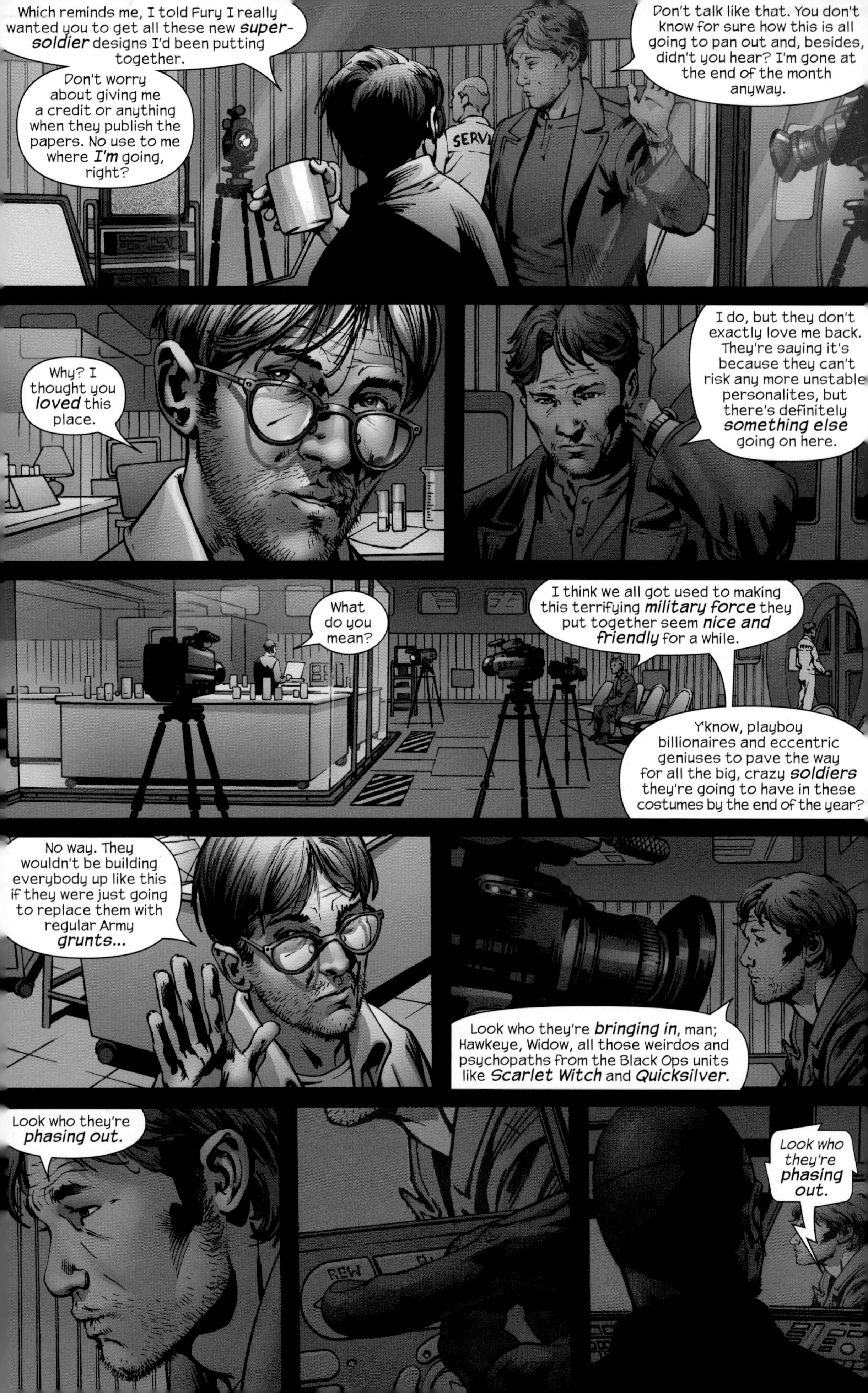

Which reminds me, I told Fury I really wanted you to get all these new super-soldier designs I'd been putting together.
Don't worry about giving me a credit or anything when they publish the papers. No use to me where I'm going, right?
Don't talk like that. You don't know for sure how this is all going to pan out and, besides, didn't you hear? I'm gone at the end of the month anyway.
SERVI
Why? I thought you loved this place.
I do, but they don't exactly love me back. They're saying it's because they can't risk any more unstable personalites, but there's definitely something else going on here.
What do you mean?
I think we all got used to making this terrifying military force they put together seem nice and friendly for a while.
Y'know, playboy billionaires and eccentric geniuses to pave the way for all the big, crazy soldiers they're going to have in these costumes by the end of the year?
No way. They wouldn't be building everybody up like this if they were just going to replace them with regular Army grunts...
Look who they're bringing in, man; Hawkeye, Widow, all those weirdos and psychopaths from the Black Ops units like Scarlet Witch and Quicksilver.
Look who they're phasing out.
REW
Look who they're phasing out.

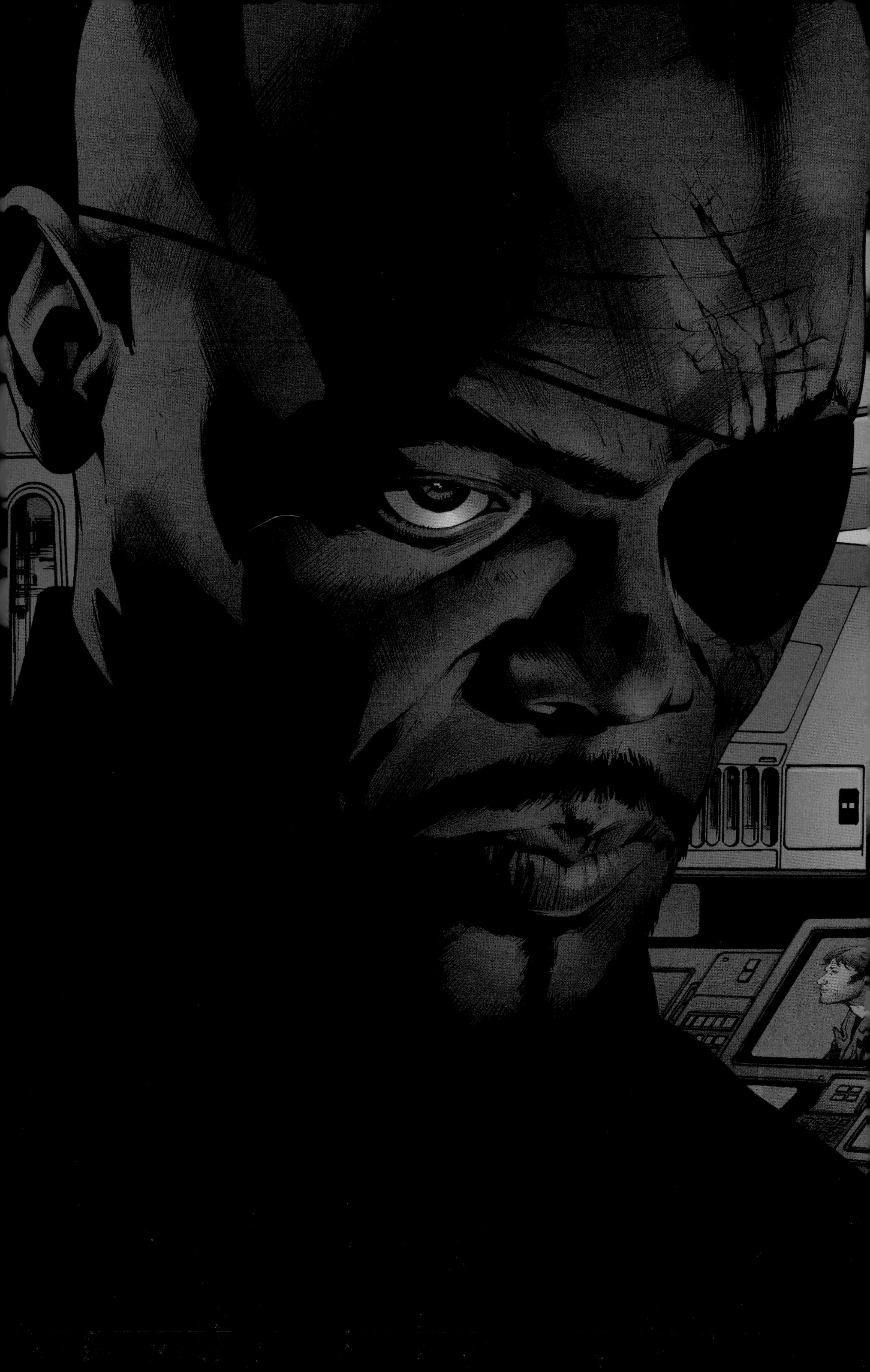

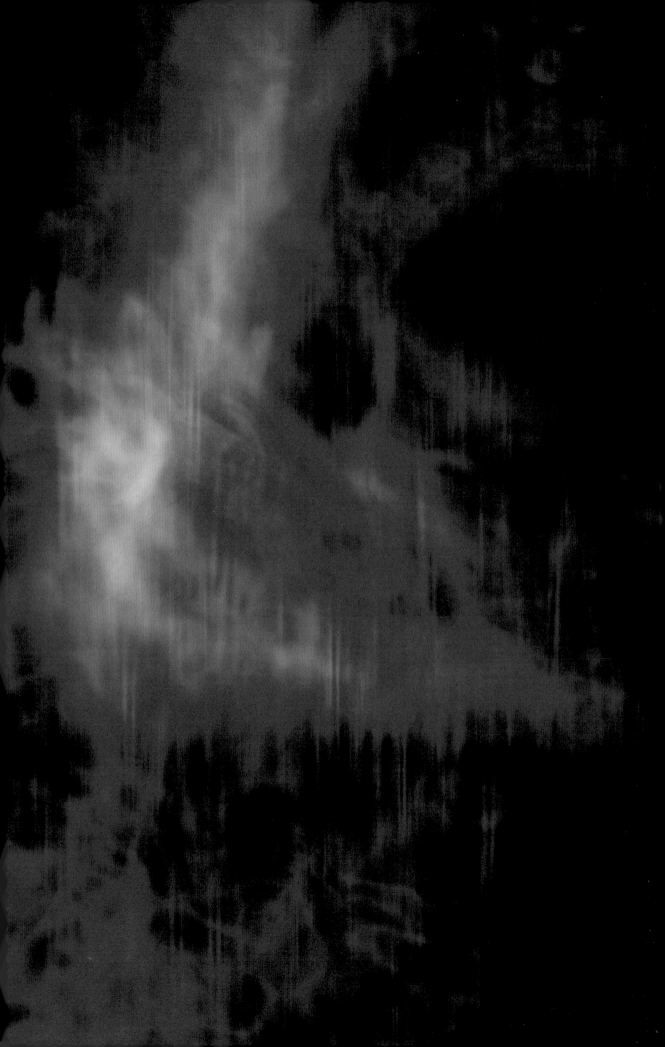

TRIAL OF THE INCREDIBLE HULK

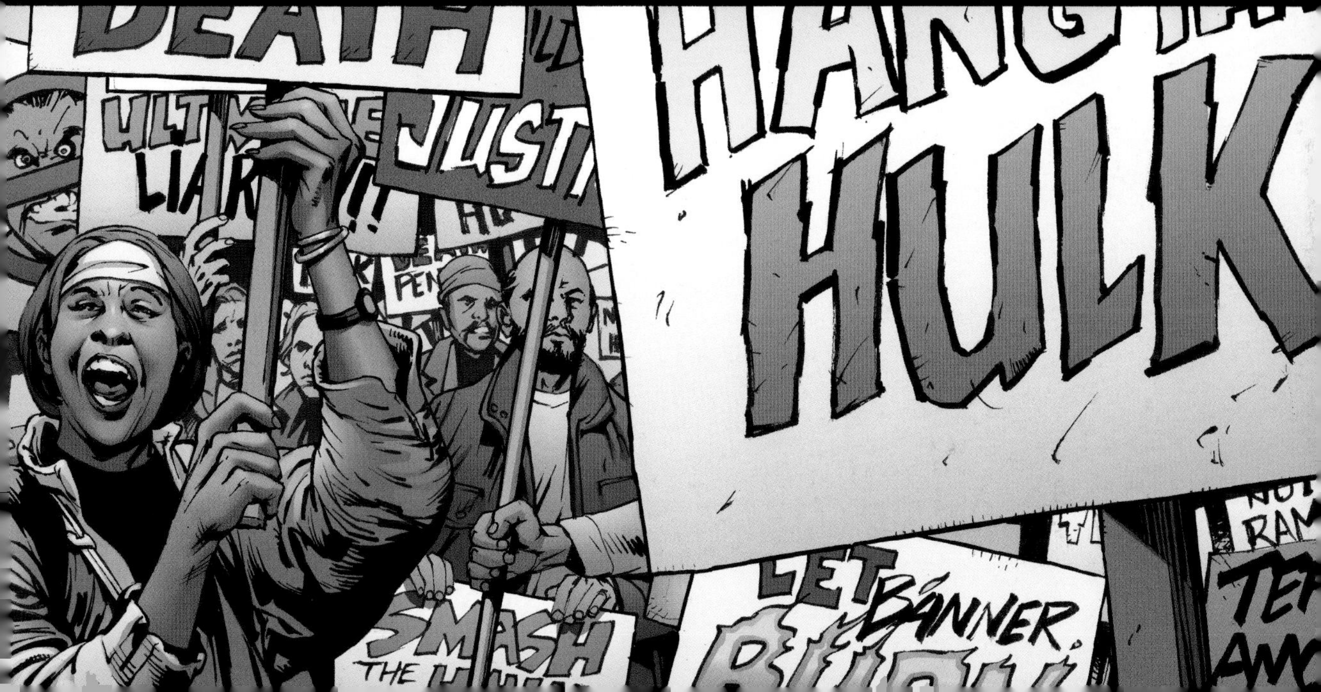
DEATH
HULK
LET BANNER
SMASH

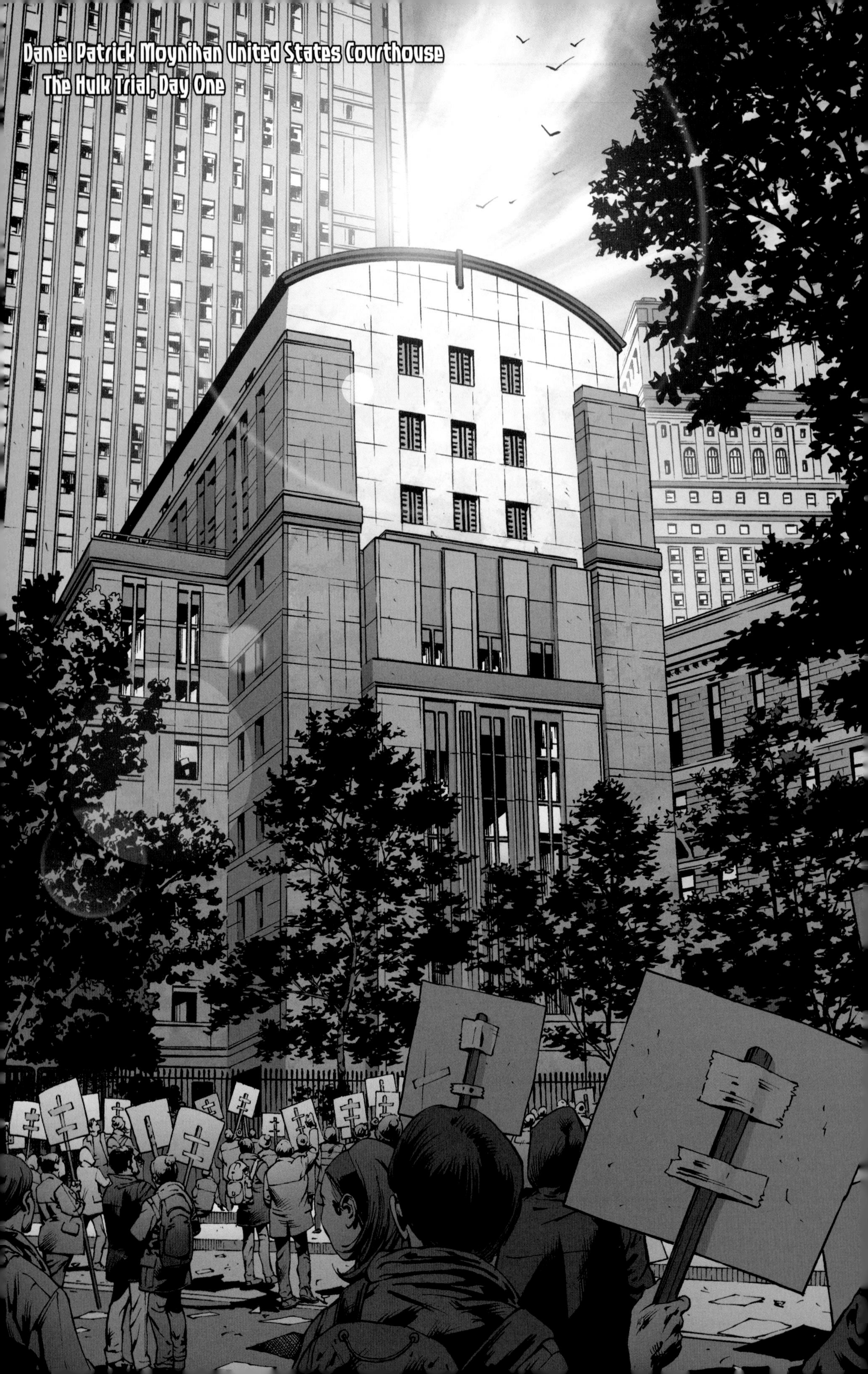
Daniel Patrick Moynihan United States Courthouse
The Hulk Trial, Day One

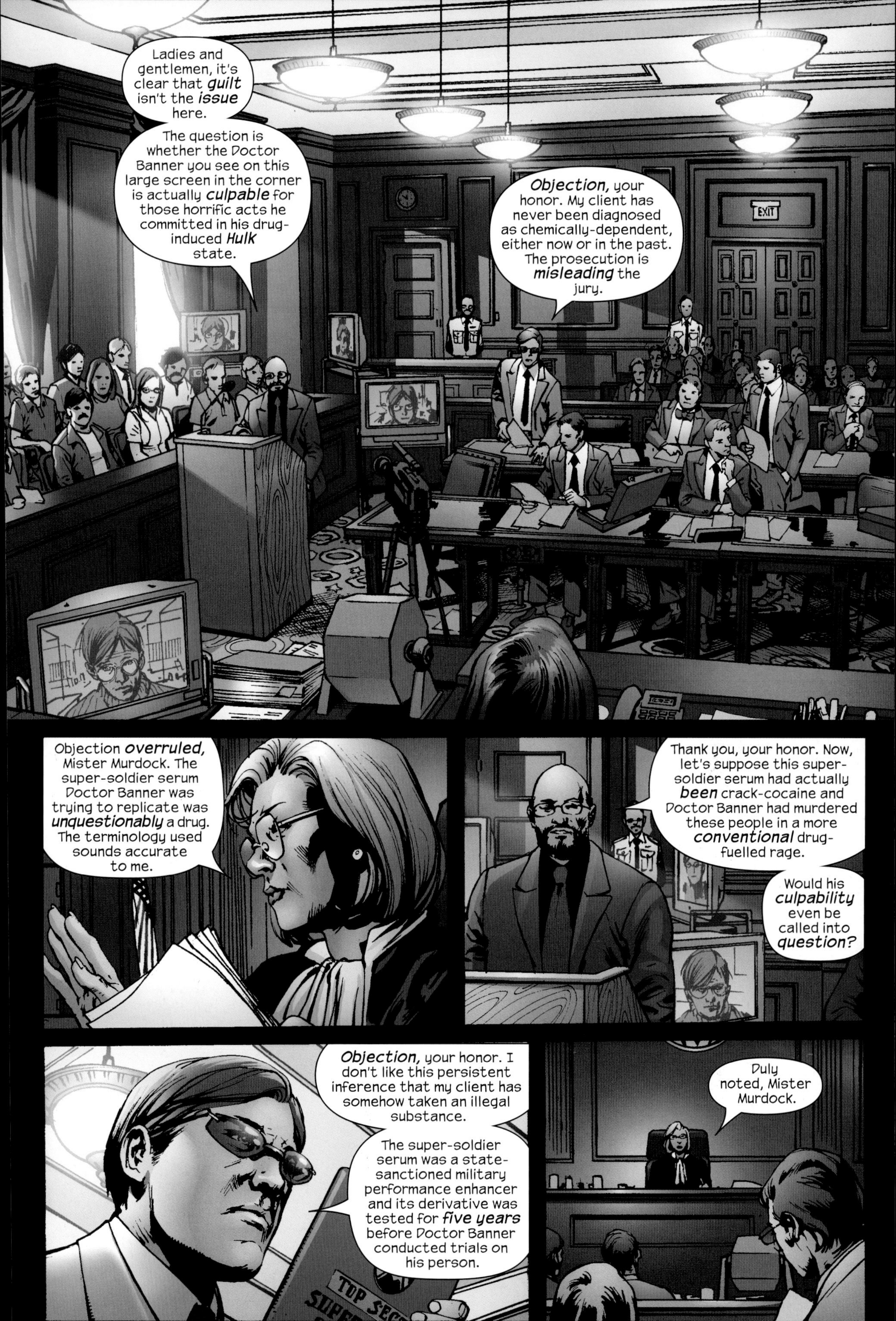
Ladies and gentlemen, it's clear that guilt isn't the issue here.
The question is whether the Doctor Banner you see on this large screen in the corner is actually culpable for those horrific acts he committed in his drug-induced Hulk state.
Objection, your honor. My client has never been diagnosed as chemically-dependent, either now or in the past. The prosecution is misleading the jury.
EXIT
Objection overruled, Mister Murdock. The super-soldier serum Doctor Banner was trying to replicate was unquestionably a drug. The terminology used sounds accurate to me.
Thank you, your honor. Now, let's suppose this super-soldier serum had actually been crack-cocaine and Doctor Banner had murdered these people in a more conventional drug-fuelled rage.
Would his culpability even be called into question?
Objection, your honor. I don't like this persistent inference that my client has somehow taken an illegal substance.
The super-soldier serum was a state-sanctioned military performance enhancer and its derivative was tested for five years before Doctor Banner conducted trials on his person.
Duly noted, Mister Murdock.

Well, let's use *alcohol* as an example. Doctor Banner is using the defense that he has no *memory* of what he does in his altered state, but is a homicide not a homicide if you're under the *influence*?

Is a pregnancy declared null and void if two teenagers have no *recollection* of falling into bed?

Ladies and gentlemen, pay no heed to the fact that the *Doctor Banner* you see on this screen looks different from the one you saw tearing a path through downtown Manhattan.

These were the acts of a *single individual* and that individual must now pay the *ultimate price.*

Turn it off, Steve. This guy's giving me a headache.

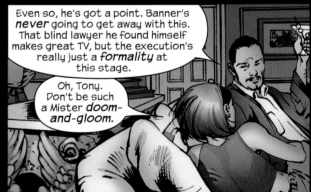

Even so, he's got a point. Banner's *never* going to get away with this. That blind lawyer he found himself makes great TV, but the execution's really just a *formality* at this stage.

Oh, Tony. Don't be such a Mister *doom-and-gloom.*

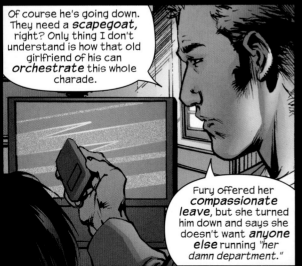

Of course he's going down. They need a *scapegoat*, right? Only thing I don't understand is how that old girlfriend of his can *orchestrate* this whole charade.

Fury offered her *compassionate leave*, but she turned him down and says she doesn't want *anyone else* running "her damn department."

She was exactly the same back in college. Betty Ross just likes to prove she's as tough as her old man. Did you know she hasn't even been down there to *see* him yet?

Cold-hearted witch. That's unbelievable.

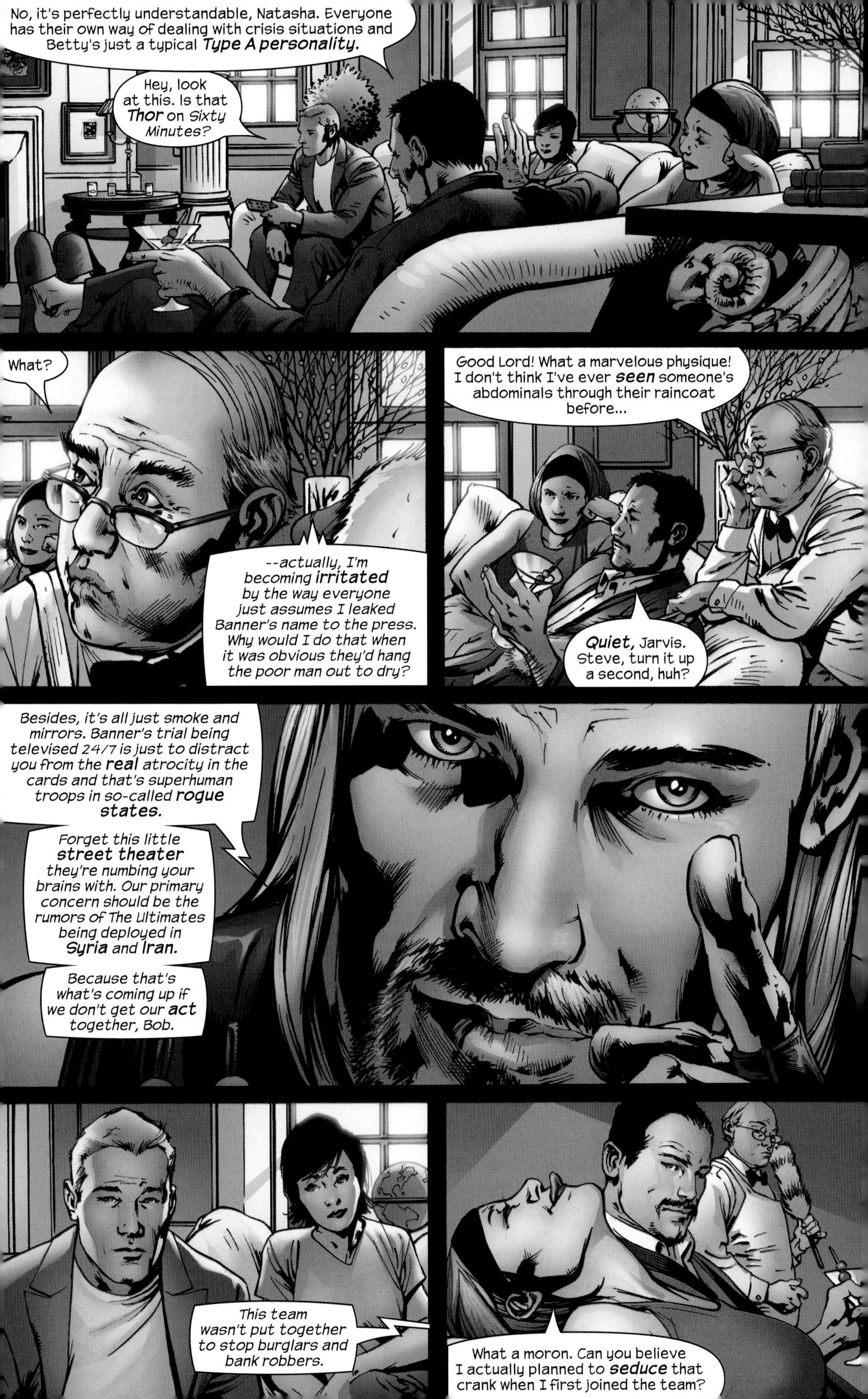
No, it's perfectly understandable, Natasha. Everyone has their own way of dealing with crisis situations and Betty's just a typical Type A personality.
Hey, look at this. Is that Thor on Sixty Minutes?
What?
--actually, I'm becoming irritated by the way everyone just assumes I leaked Banner's name to the press. Why would I do that when it was obvious they'd hang the poor man out to dry?
Good Lord! What a marvelous physique! I don't think I've ever seen someone's abdominals through their raincoat before...
Quiet, Jarvis. Steve, turn it up a second, huh?
Besides, it's all just smoke and mirrors. Banner's trial being televised 24/7 is just to distract you from the real atrocity in the cards and that's superhuman troops in so-called rogue states.
Forget this little street theater they're numbing your brains with. Our primary concern should be the rumors of The Ultimates being deployed in Syria and Iran.
Because that's what's coming up if we don't get our act together, Bob.
This team wasn't put together to stop burglars and bank robbers.
What a moron. Can you believe I actually planned to seduce that crank when I first joined the team?

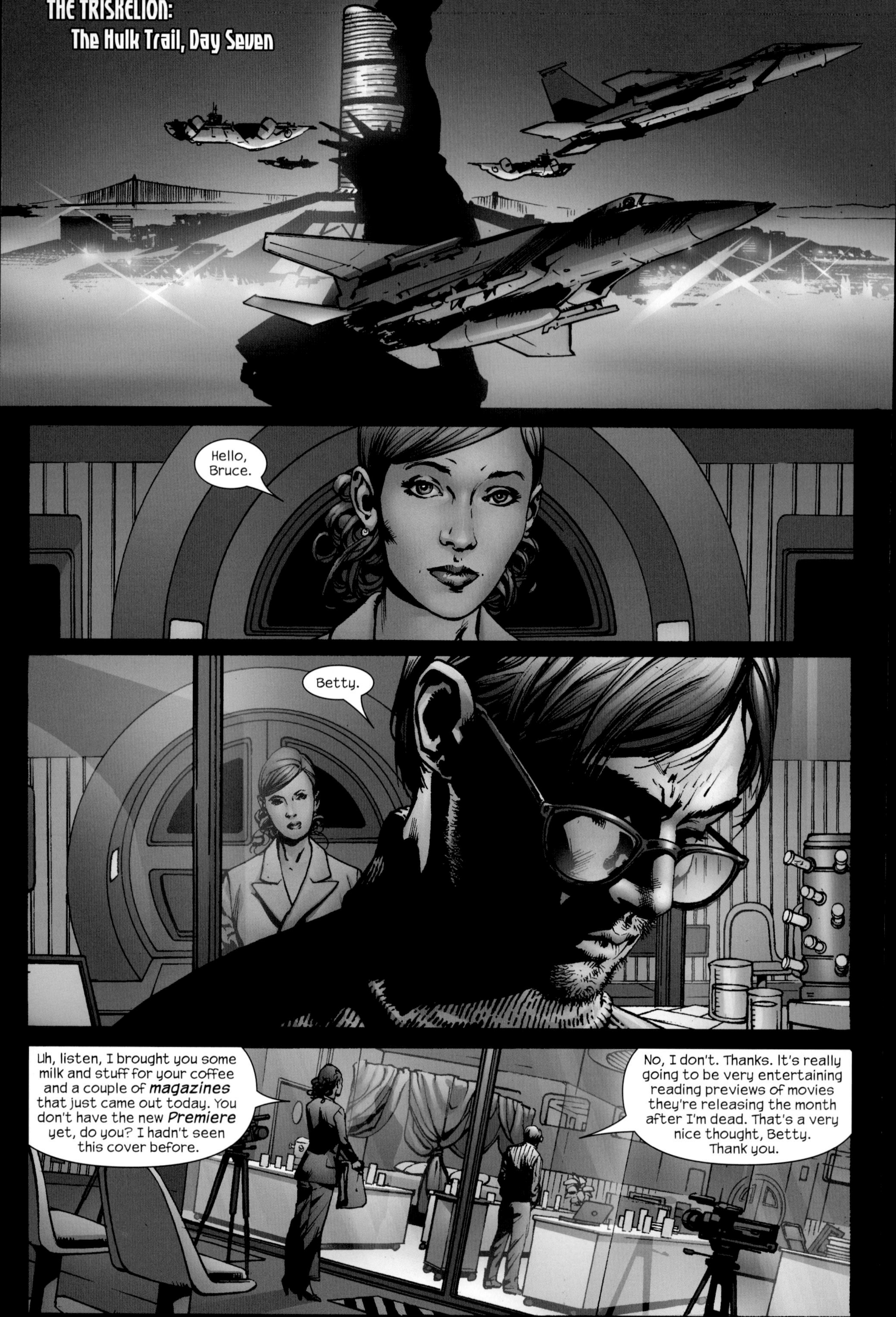
THE TRISKELION:
The Hulk Trail, Day Seven
Hello, Bruce.
Betty.
Uh, listen, I brought you some milk and stuff for your coffee and a couple of *magazines* that just came out today. You don't have the new *Premiere* yet, do you? I hadn't seen this cover before.
No, I don't. Thanks. It's really going to be very entertaining reading previews of movies they're releasing the month after I'm dead. That's a very nice thought, Betty. Thank you.

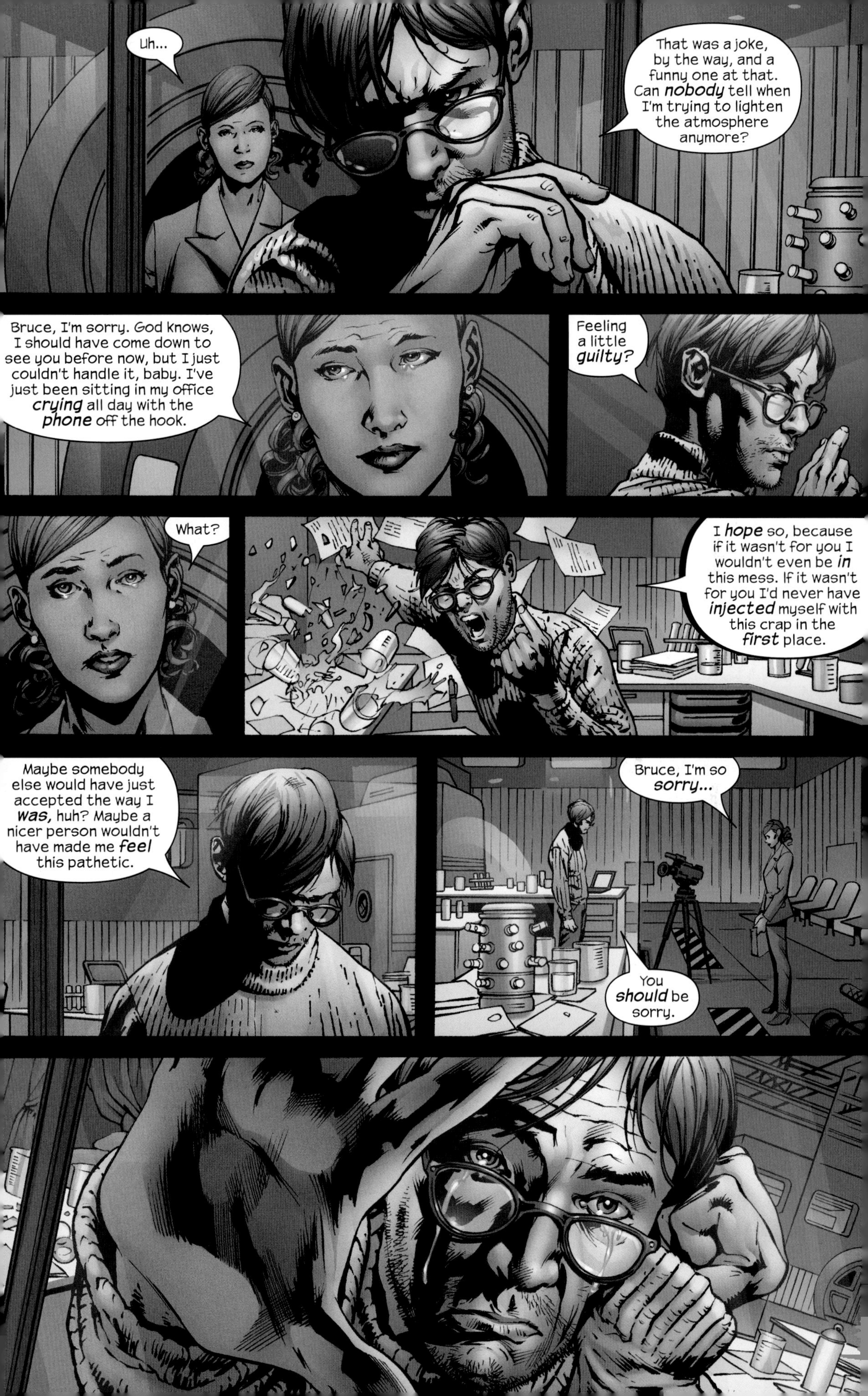

Uh...
That was a joke, by the way, and a funny one at that. Can *nobody* tell when I'm trying to lighten the atmosphere anymore?
Bruce, I'm sorry. God knows, I should have come down to see you before now, but I just couldn't handle it, baby. I've just been sitting in my office *crying* all day with the *phone* off the hook.
Feeling a little *guilty*?
What?
I *hope* so, because if it wasn't for you I wouldn't even be *in* this mess. If it wasn't for you I'd never have *injected* myself with this crap in the *first* place.
Maybe somebody else would have just accepted the way I *was,* huh? Maybe a nicer person wouldn't have made me *feel* this pathetic.
Bruce, I'm so *sorry...*
You *should* be sorry.

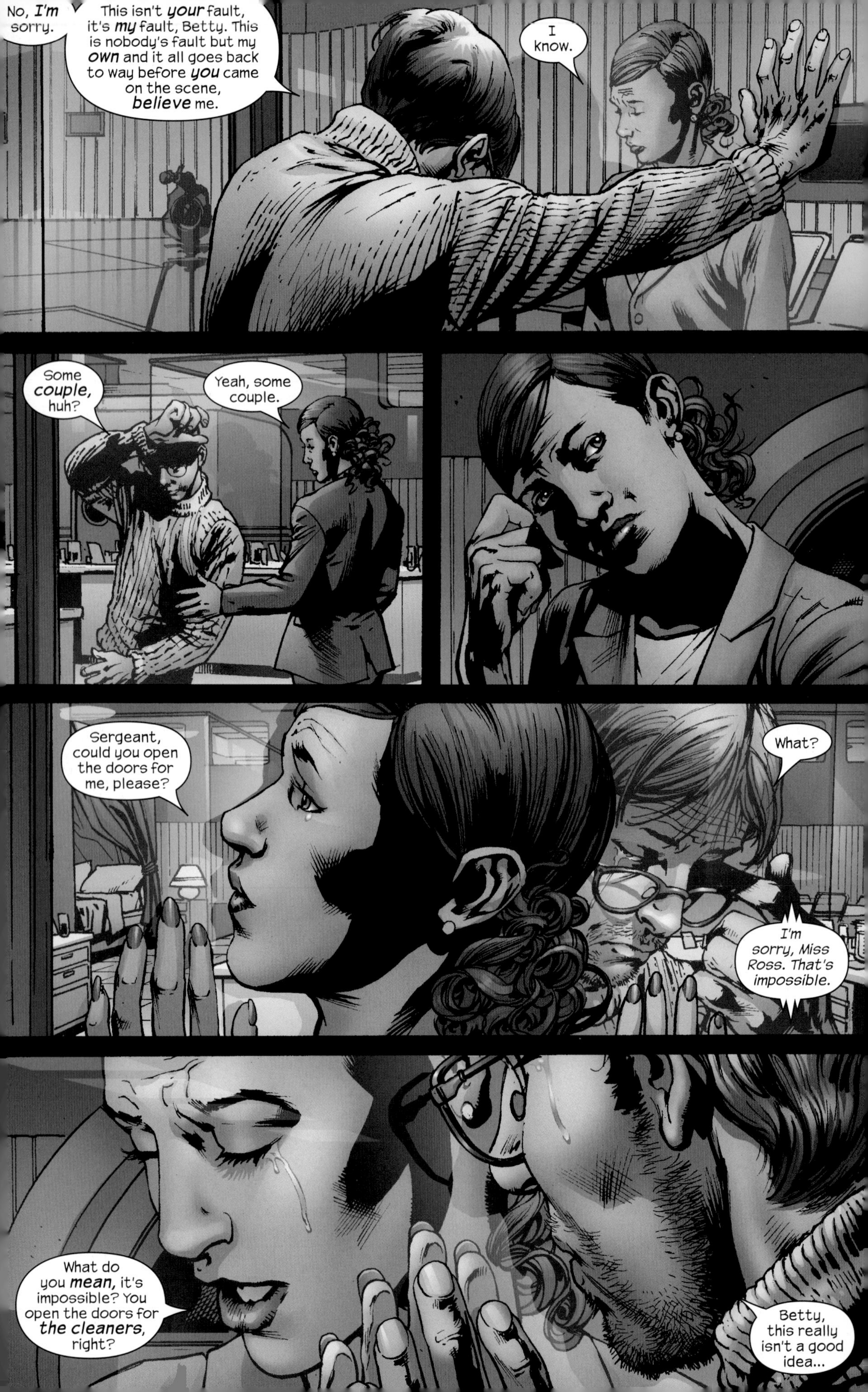
No, I'm sorry.
This isn't your fault, it's my fault, Betty. This is nobody's fault but my own and it all goes back to way before you came on the scene, believe me.
I know.
Some couple, huh?
Yeah, some couple.
Sergeant, could you open the doors for me, please?
What?
I'm sorry, Miss Ross. That's impossible.
What do you mean, it's impossible? You open the doors for the cleaners, right?
Betty, this really isn't a good idea...

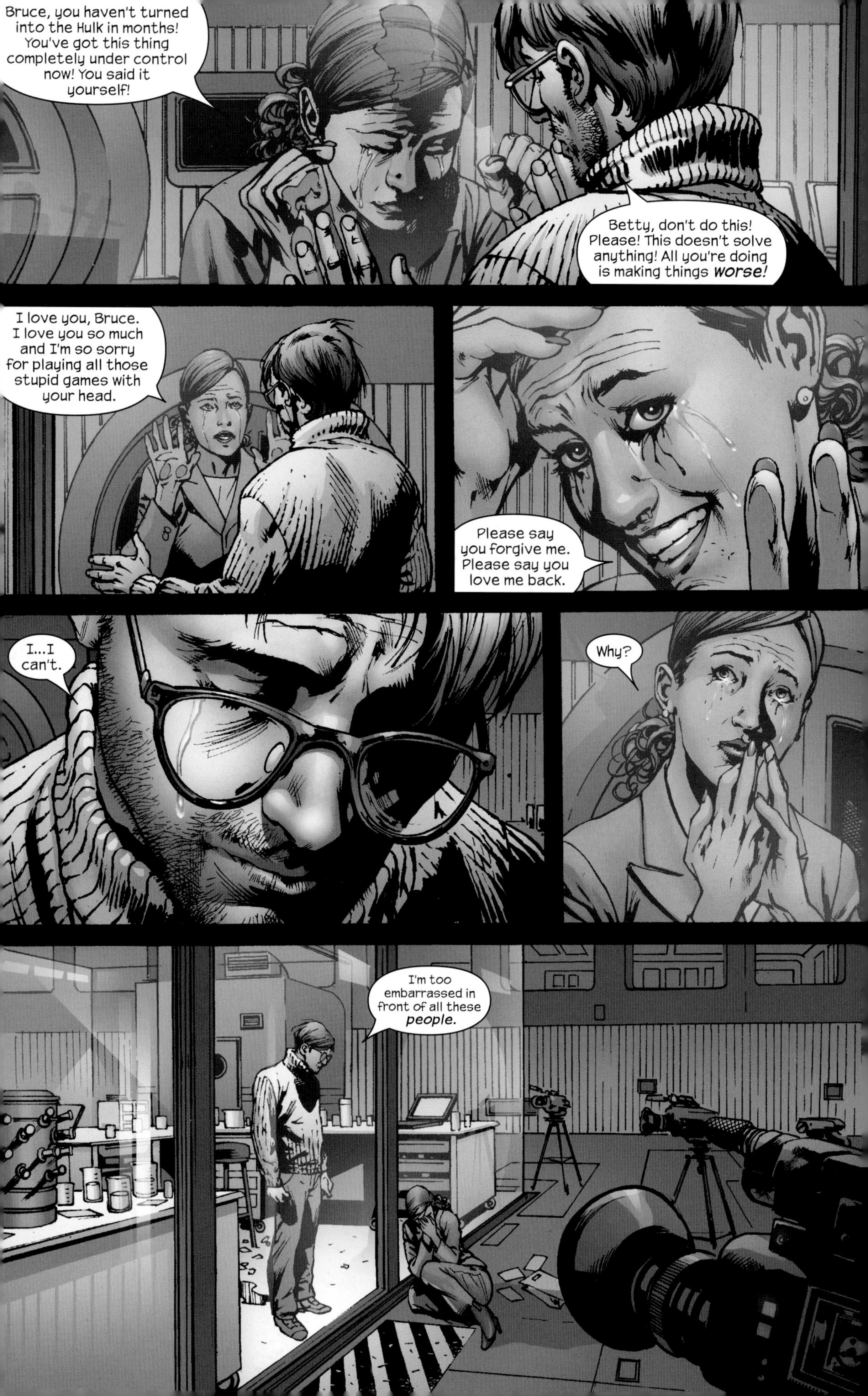
Bruce, you haven't turned into the Hulk in months! You've got this thing completely under control now! You said it yourself!
Betty, don't do this! Please! This doesn't solve anything! All you're doing is making things *worse!*
I love you, Bruce. I love you so much and I'm so sorry for playing all those stupid games with your head.
Please say you forgive me. Please say you love me back.
I...I can't.
Why?
I'm too embarrassed in front of all these *people.*

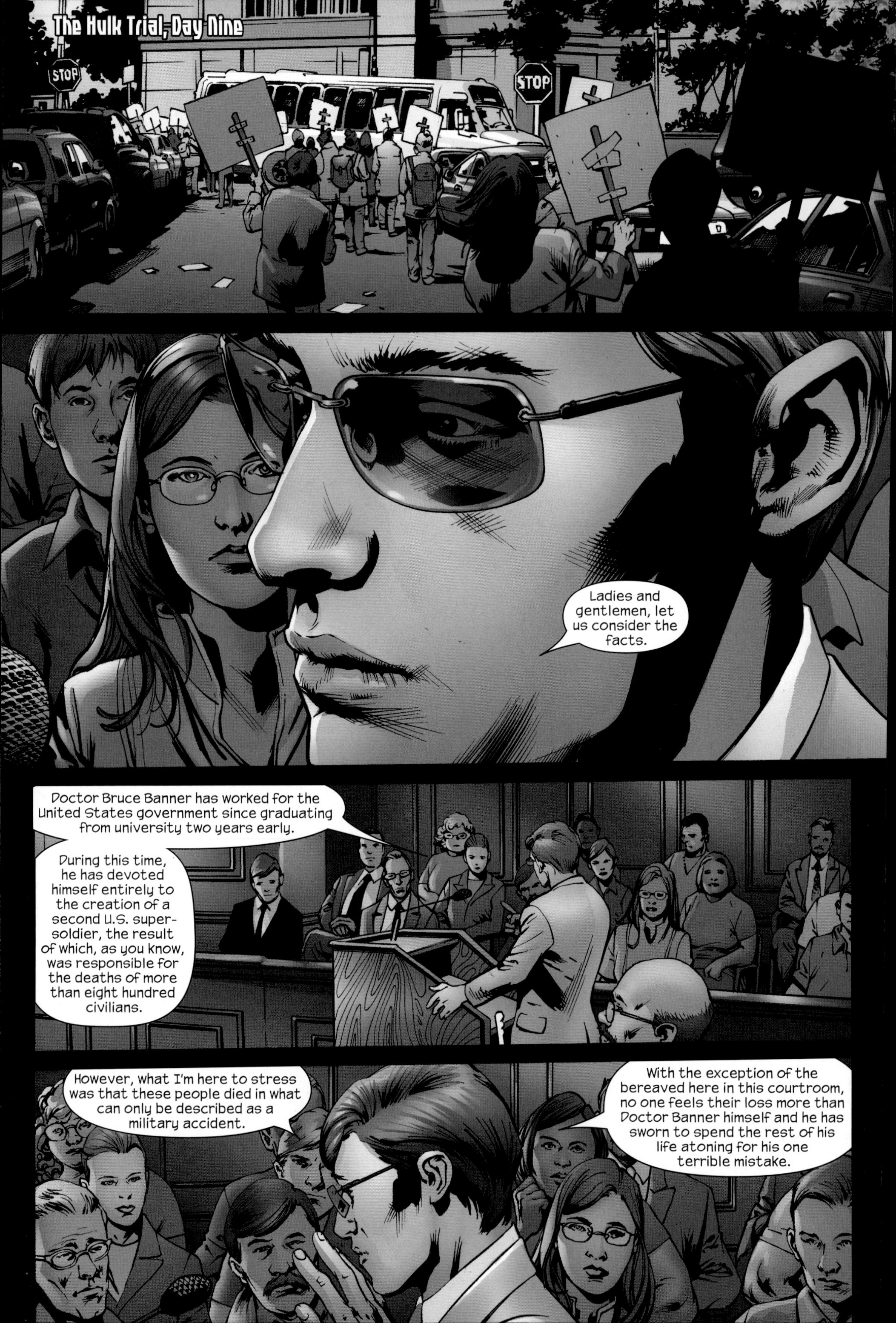
The Hulk Trial, Day Nine
STOP
STOP
Ladies and gentlemen, let us consider the facts.
Doctor Bruce Banner has worked for the United States government since graduating from university two years early.
During this time, he has devoted himself entirely to the creation of a second U.S. super-soldier, the result of which, as you know, was responsible for the deaths of more than eight hundred civilians.
However, what I'm here to stress was that these people died in what can only be described as a military accident.
With the exception of the bereaved here in this courtroom, no one feels their loss more than Doctor Banner himself and he has sworn to spend the rest of his life atoning for his one terrible mistake.

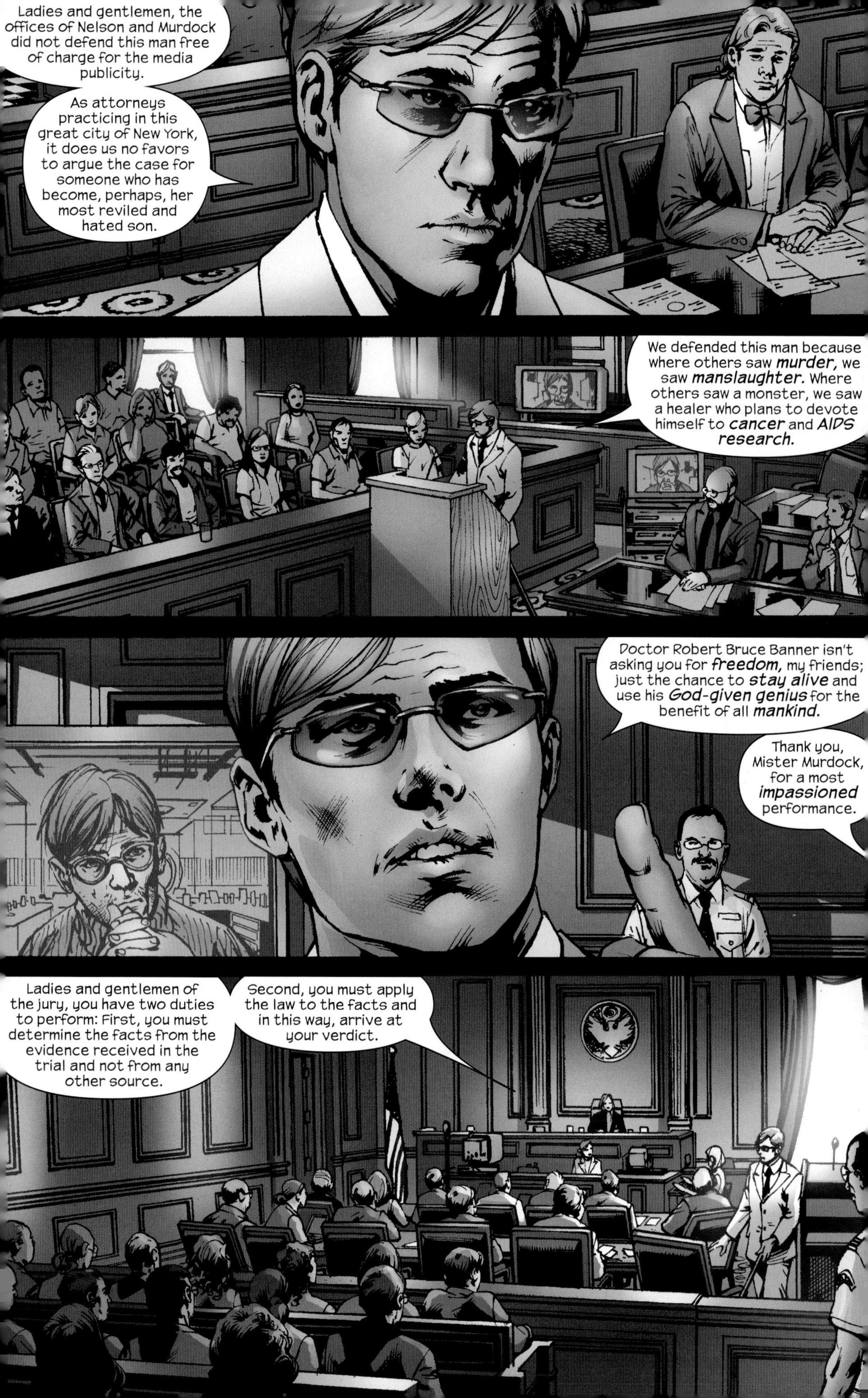
Ladies and gentlemen, the offices of Nelson and Murdock did not defend this man free of charge for the media publicity.
As attorneys practicing in this great city of New York, it does us no favors to argue the case for someone who has become, perhaps, her most reviled and hated son.
We defended this man because where others saw *murder*, we saw *manslaughter*. Where others saw a monster, we saw a healer who plans to devote himself to *cancer* and *AIDS research*.
Doctor Robert Bruce Banner isn't asking you for *freedom*, my friends; just the chance to *stay alive* and use his *God-given genius* for the benefit of all *mankind*.
Thank you, Mister Murdock, for a most *impassioned* performance.
Ladies and gentlemen of the jury, you have two duties to perform: First, you must determine the facts from the evidence received in the trial and not from any other source.
Second, you must apply the law to the facts and in this way, arrive at your verdict.

How am I feeling? Nervous as hell, I guess.

It's like you're back in high school waiting for your exam results, except much, much scarier because, well, I always used to score full marks in those things so that might not be the best analogy.

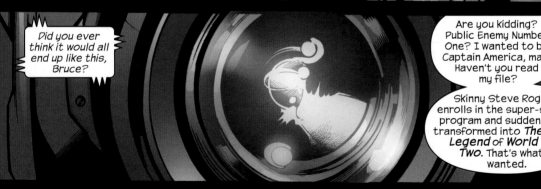

Did you ever think it would all end up like this, Bruce?

Are you kidding? Public Enemy Number One? I wanted to be Captain America, man. Haven't you read my file?

Skinny Steve Rogers enrolls in the super-soldier program and suddenly he's transformed into *The Living Legend* of *World War Two*. That's what *I* wanted.

I just wanted people to *like* me, y'know? That's why I spent all those hours working away in the lab.

Are you *prepared* for what's coming next?

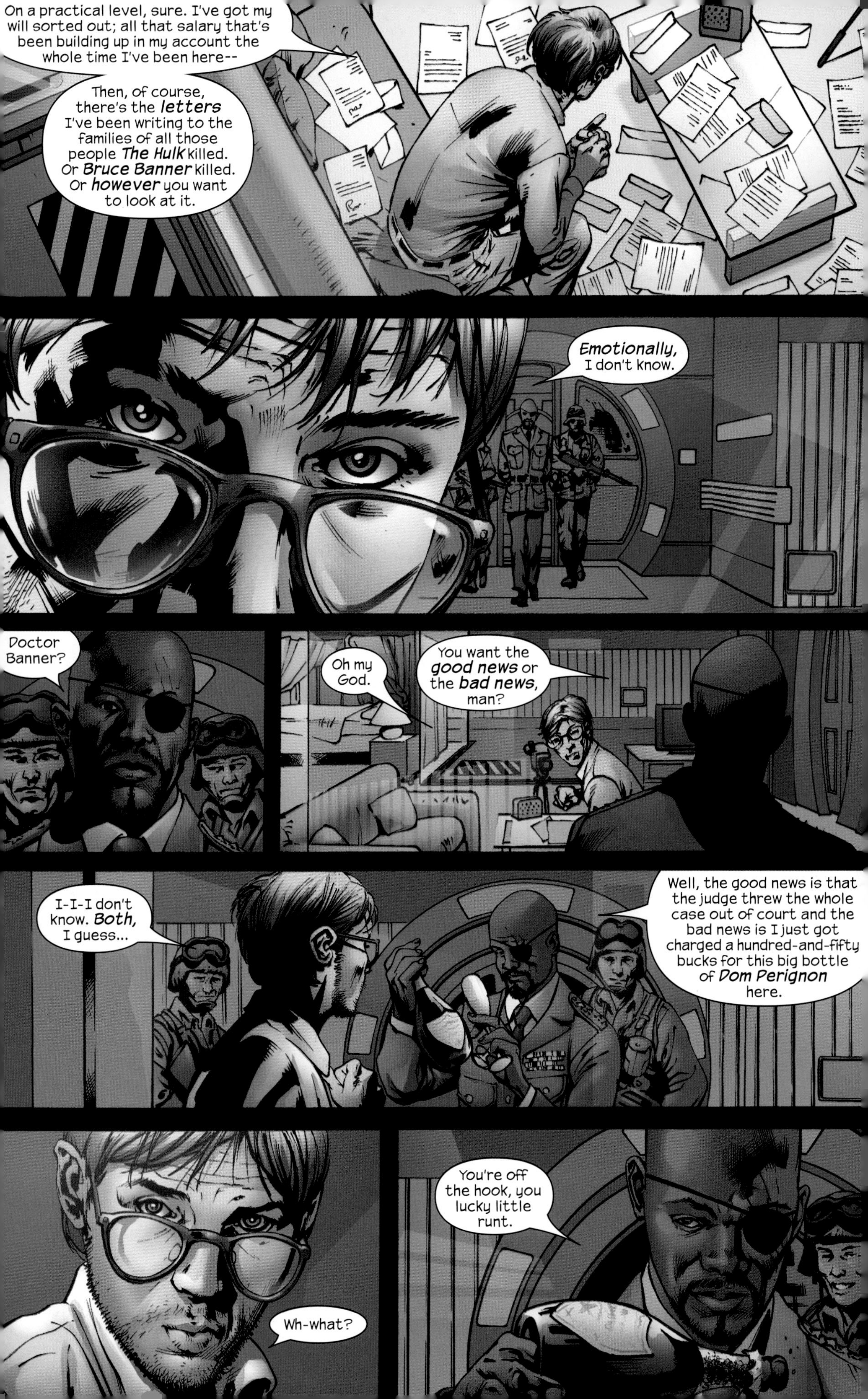
On a practical level, sure. I've got my will sorted out; all that salary that's been building up in my account the whole time I've been here--
Then, of course, there's the *letters* I've been writing to the families of all those people *The Hulk* killed. Or *Bruce Banner* killed. Or *however* you want to look at it.
Emotionally, I don't know.
Doctor Banner?
Oh my God.
You want the *good news* or the *bad news*, man?
I-I-I don't know. *Both,* I guess...
Well, the good news is that the judge threw the whole case out of court and the bad news is I just got charged a hundred-and-fifty bucks for this big bottle of *Dom Perignon* here.
You're off the hook, you lucky little runt.
Wh-what?

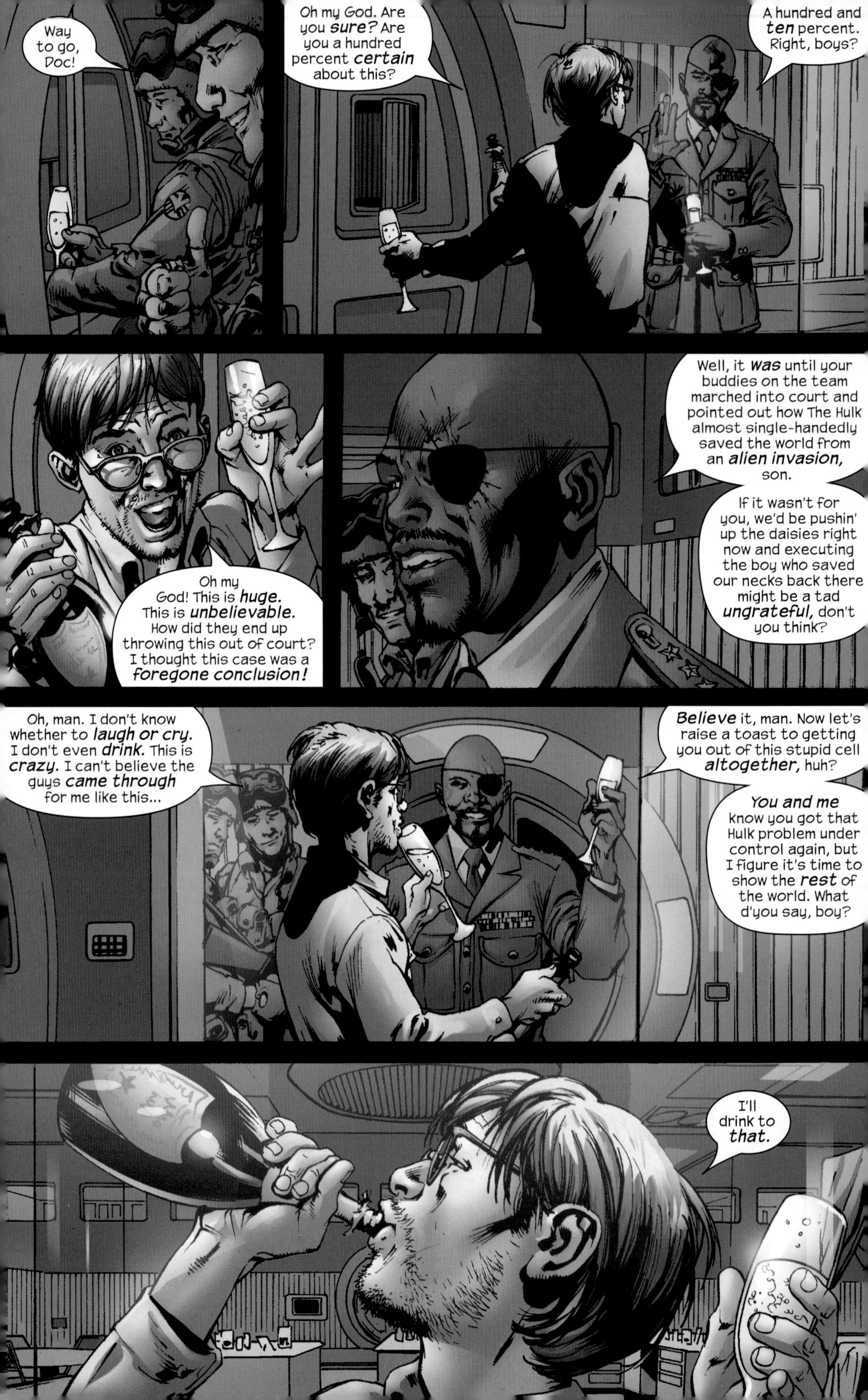
Way to go, Doc!
Oh my God. Are you sure? Are you a hundred percent certain about this?
A hundred and ten percent. Right, boys?
Oh my God! This is huge. This is unbelievable. How did they end up throwing this out of court? I thought this case was a foregone conclusion!
Well, it was until your buddies on the team marched into court and pointed out how The Hulk almost single-handedly saved the world from an alien invasion, son.
If it wasn't for you, we'd be pushin' up the daisies right now and executing the boy who saved our necks back there might be a tad ungrateful, don't you think?
Oh, man. I don't know whether to laugh or cry. I don't even drink. This is crazy. I can't believe the guys came through for me like this...
Believe it, man. Now let's raise a toast to getting you out of this stupid cell altogether, huh?
You and me know you got that Hulk problem under control again, but I figure it's time to show the rest of the world. What d'you say, boy?
I'll drink to that.

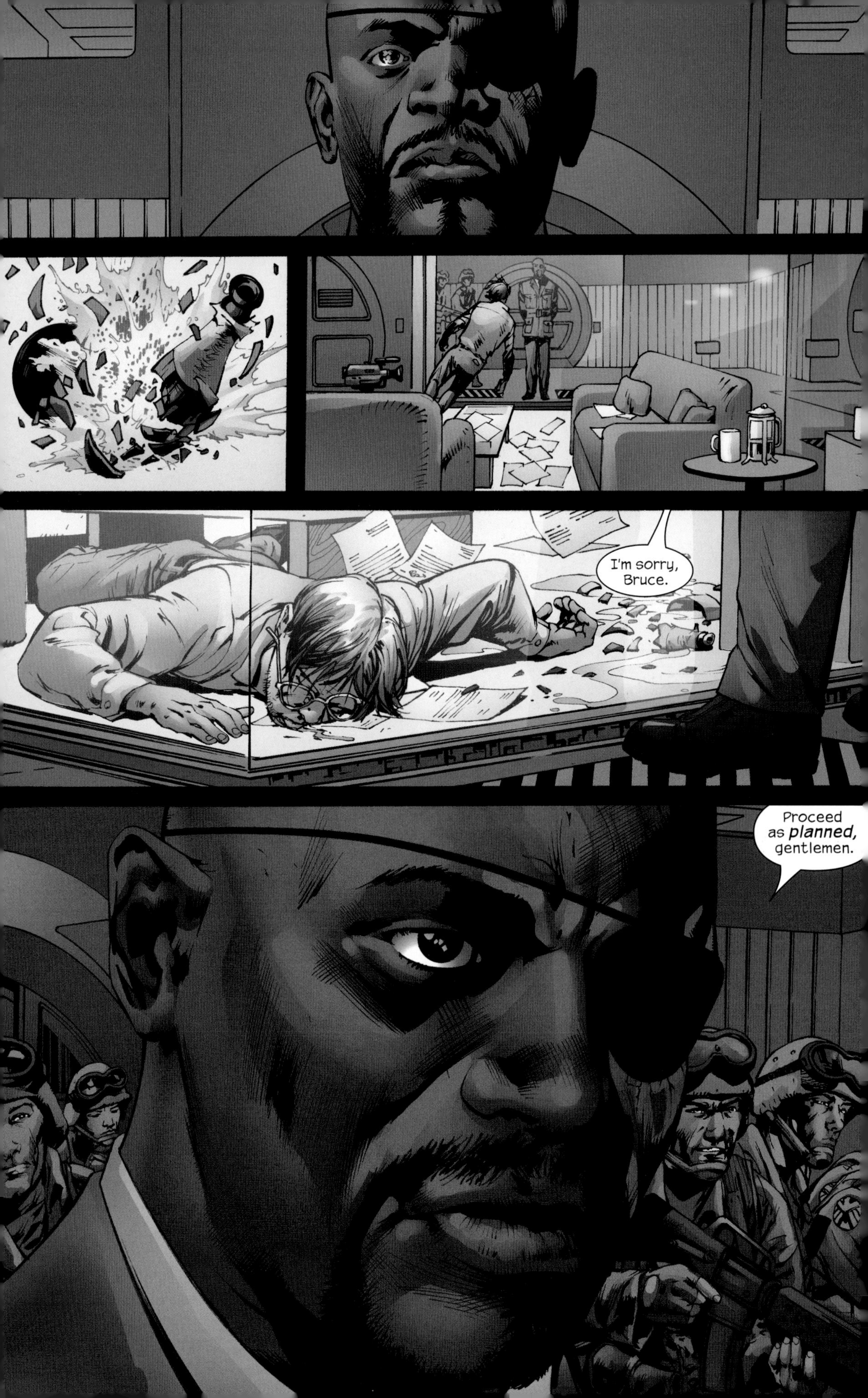
I'm sorry, Bruce.
Proceed as *planned,* gentlemen.

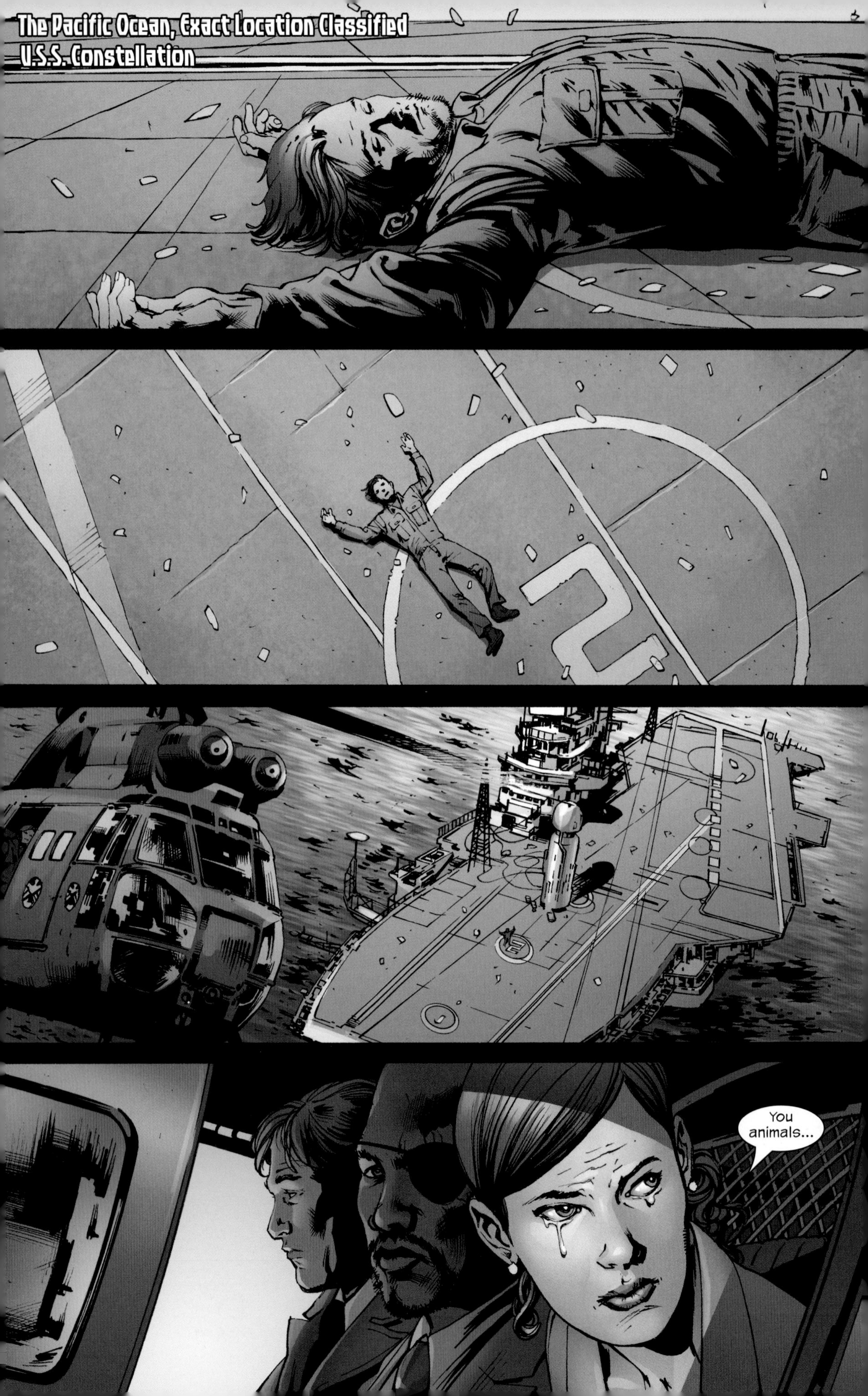

The Pacific Ocean, Exact Location Classified
U.S.S. Constellation
You animals...

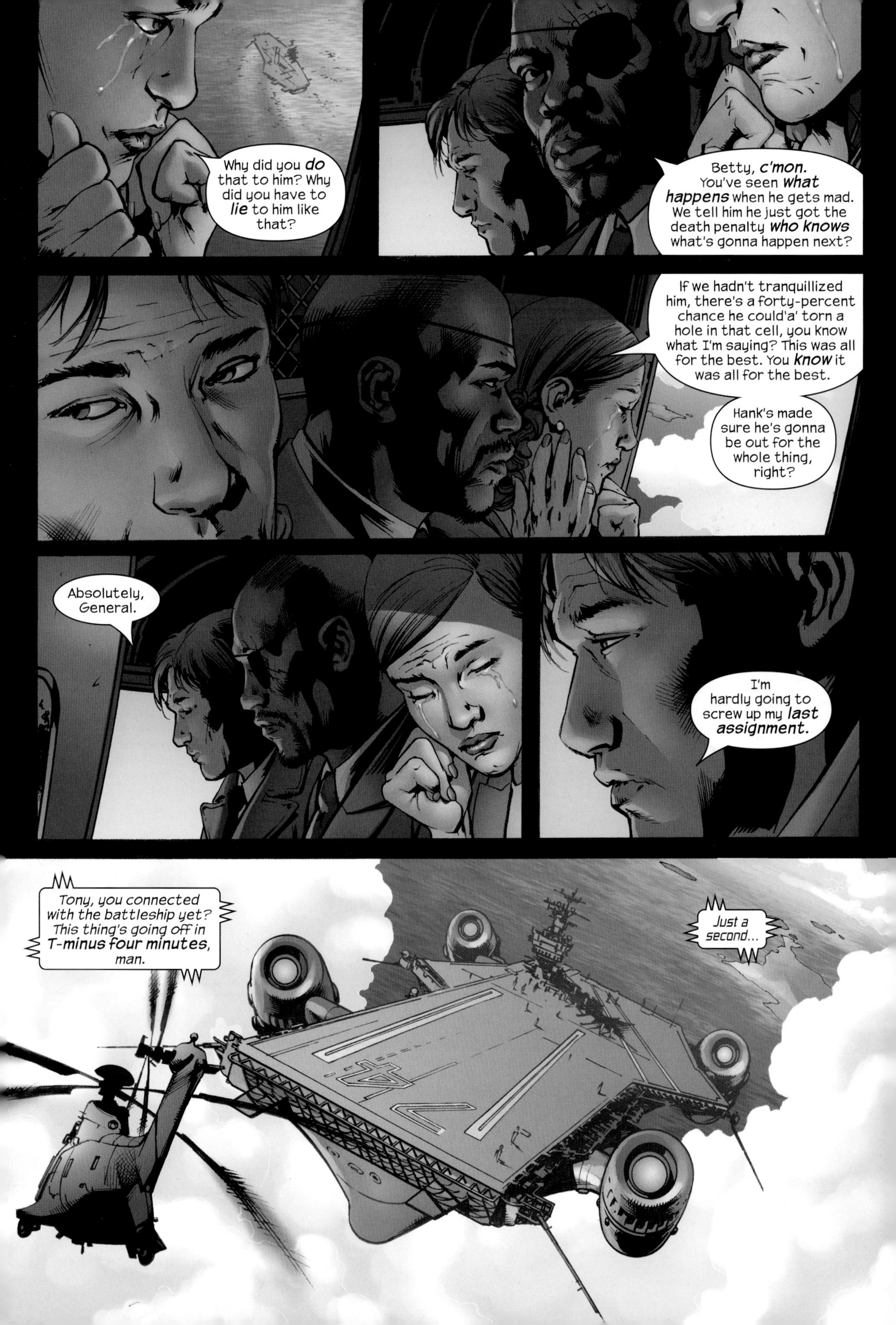

Why did you do that to him? Why did you have to lie to him like that?
Betty, c'mon. You've seen what happens when he gets mad. We tell him he just got the death penalty who knows what's gonna happen next?
If we hadn't tranquillized him, there's a forty-percent chance he could'a' torn a hole in that cell, you know what I'm saying? This was all for the best. You know it was all for the best.
Hank's made sure he's gonna be out for the whole thing, right?
Absolutely, General.
I'm hardly going to screw up my last assignment.
Tony, you connected with the battleship yet? This thing's going off in T-minus four minutes, man.
Just a second...

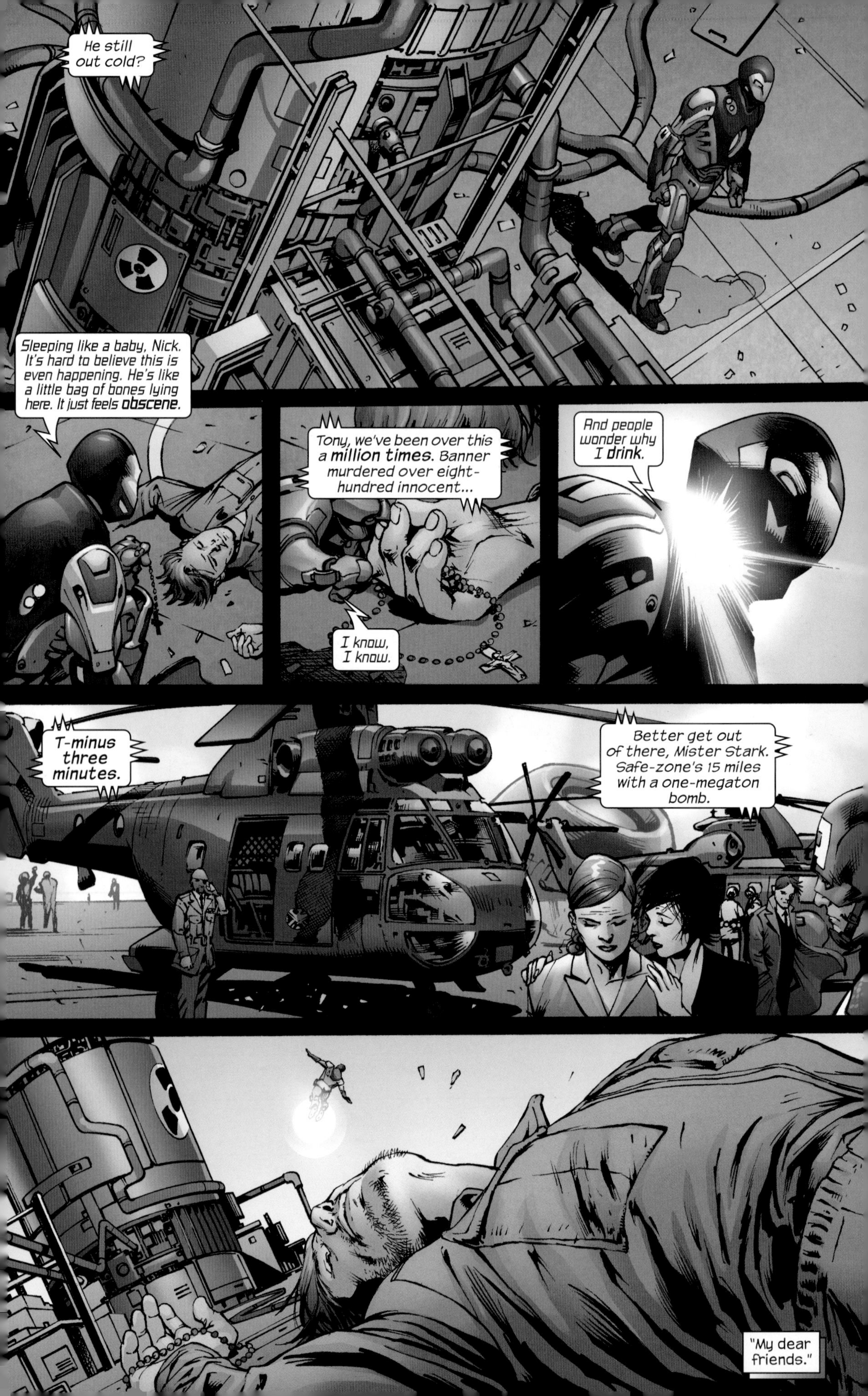
He still out cold?
Sleeping like a baby, Nick. It's hard to believe this is even happening. He's like a little bag of bones lying here. It just feels obscene.
Tony, we've been over this a million times. Banner murdered over eight-hundred innocent...
I know, I know.
And people wonder why I drink.
T-minus three minutes.
Better get out of there, Mister Stark. Safe-zone's 15 miles with a one-megaton bomb.
"My dear friends."

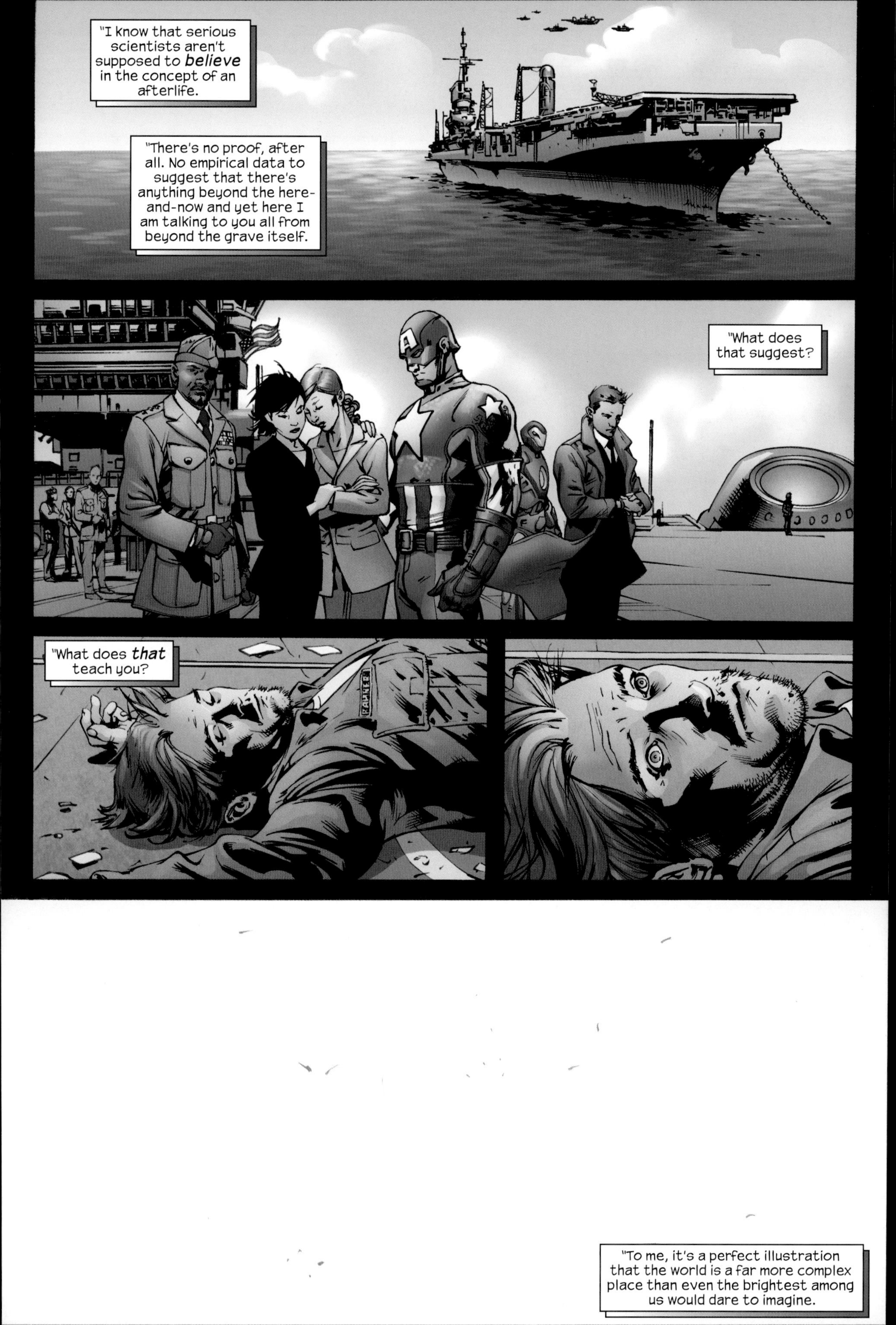
"I know that serious scientists aren't supposed to *believe* in the concept of an afterlife.
"There's no proof, after all. No empirical data to suggest that there's anything beyond the here-and-now and yet here I am talking to you all from beyond the grave itself.
"What does that suggest?
"What does *that* teach you?
"To me, it's a perfect illustration that the world is a far more complex place than even the brightest among us would dare to imagine.

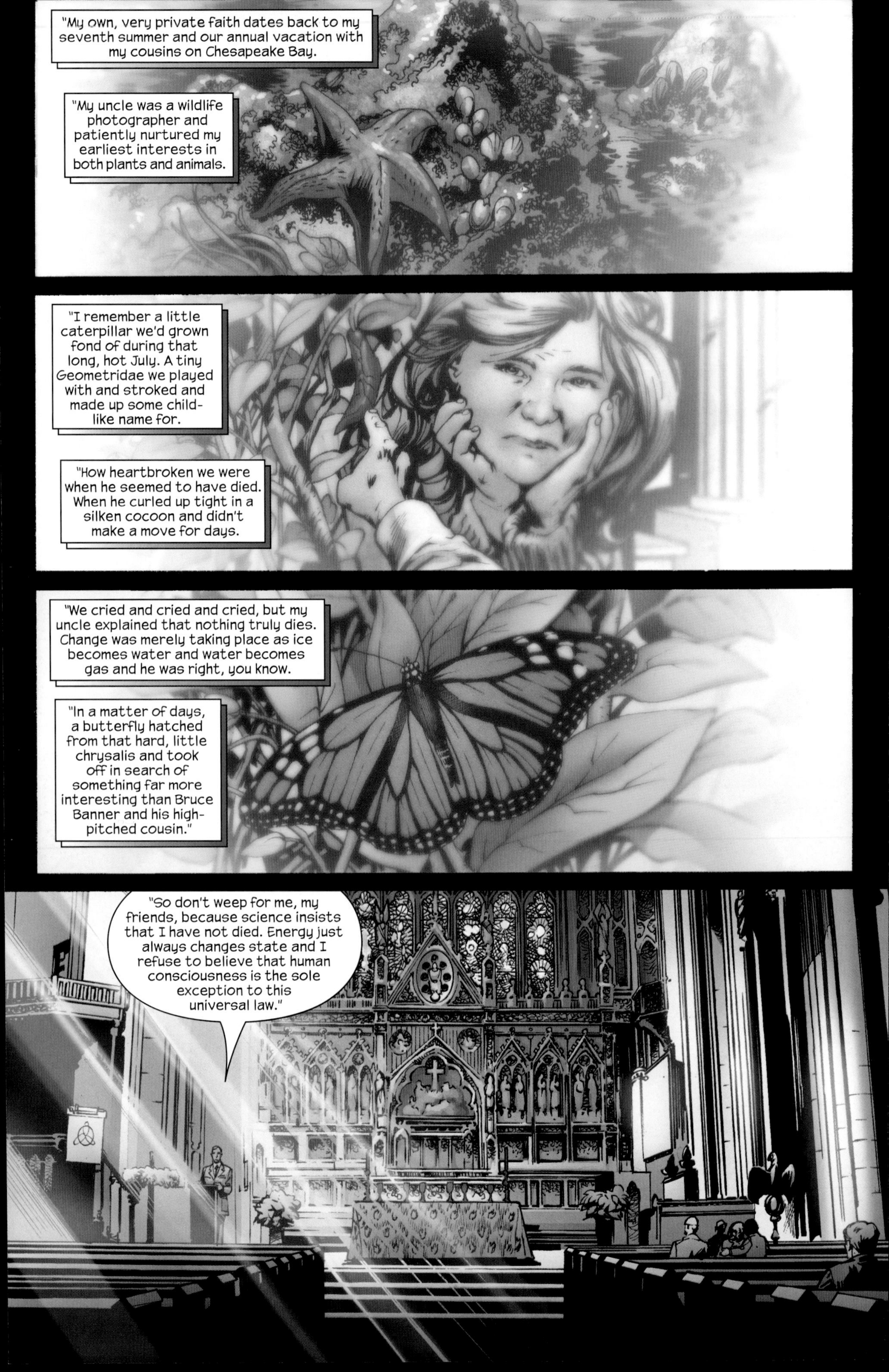
"My own, very private faith dates back to my seventh summer and our annual vacation with my cousins on Chesapeake Bay.
"My uncle was a wildlife photographer and patiently nurtured my earliest interests in both plants and animals.
"I remember a little caterpillar we'd grown fond of during that long, hot July. A tiny Geometridae we played with and stroked and made up some child-like name for.
"How heartbroken we were when he seemed to have died. When he curled up tight in a silken cocoon and didn't make a move for days.
"We cried and cried and cried, but my uncle explained that nothing truly dies. Change was merely taking place as ice becomes water and water becomes gas and he was right, you know.
"In a matter of days, a butterfly hatched from that hard, little chrysalis and took off in search of something far more interesting than Bruce Banner and his high-pitched cousin."
"So don't weep for me, my friends, because science insists that I have not died. Energy just always changes state and I refuse to believe that human consciousness is the sole exception to this universal law."

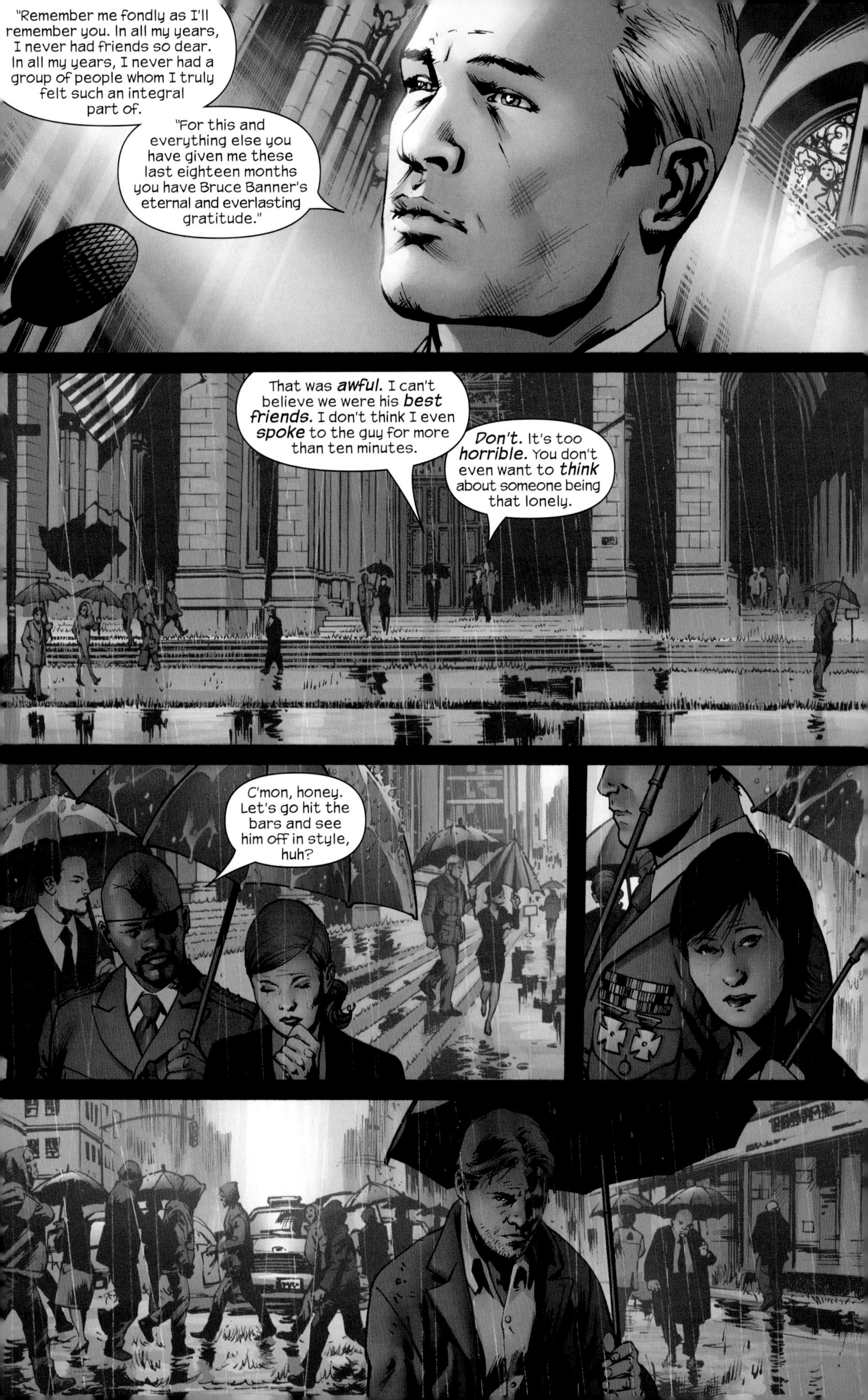
"Remember me fondly as I'll remember you. In all my years, I never had friends so dear. In all my years, I never had a group of people whom I truly felt such an integral part of.
"For this and everything else you have given me these last eighteen months you have Bruce Banner's eternal and everlasting gratitude."
That was *awful.* I can't believe we were his *best friends.* I don't think I even *spoke* to the guy for more than ten minutes.
Don't. It's too *horrible.* You don't even want to *think* about someone being that lonely.
C'mon, honey. Let's go hit the bars and see him off in style, huh?

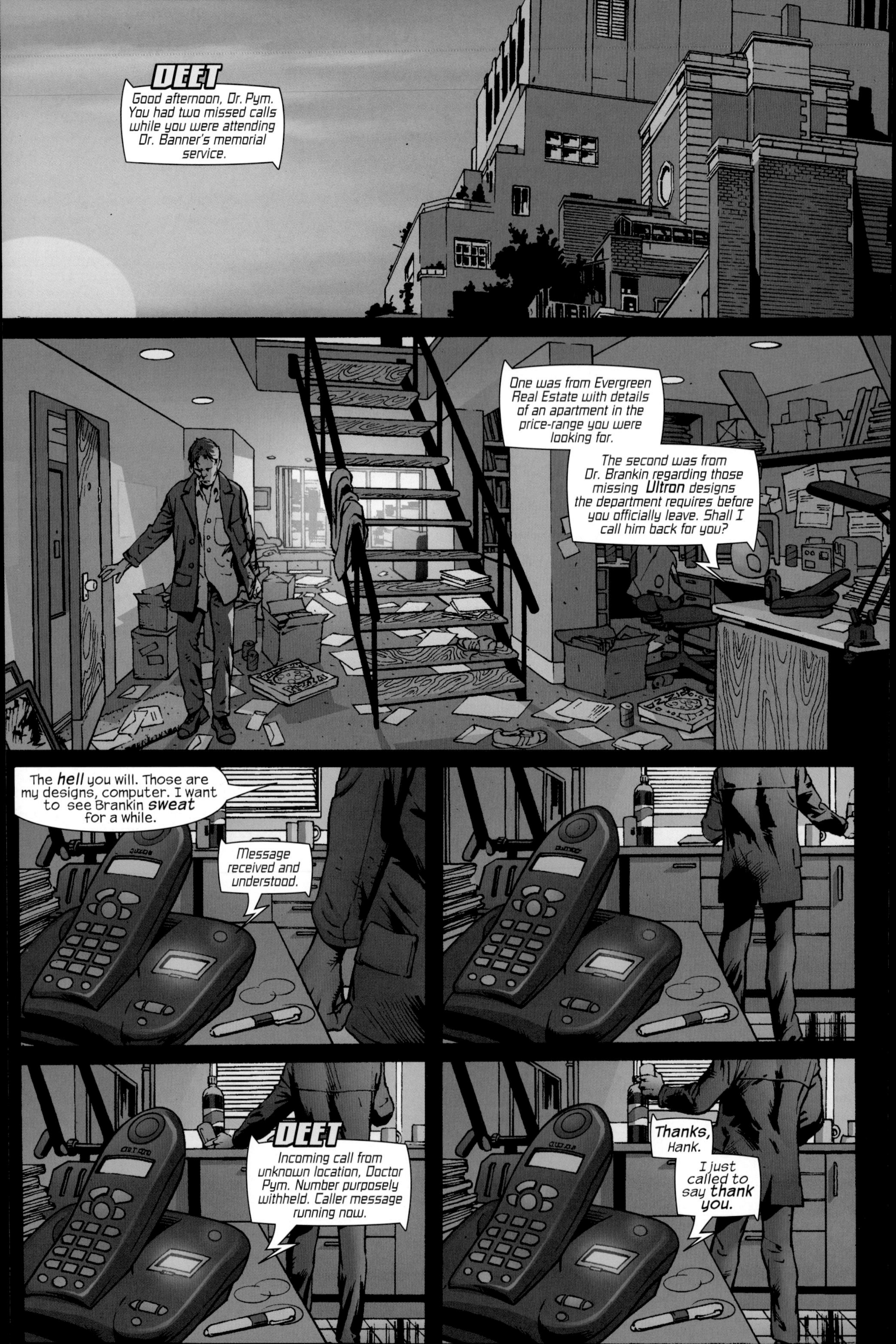
DEET
Good afternoon, Dr. Pym. You had two missed calls while you were attending Dr. Banner's memorial service.
One was from Evergreen Real Estate with details of an apartment in the price-range you were looking for.
The second was from Dr. Brankin regarding those missing Ultron designs the department requires before you officially leave. Shall I call him back for you?
The hell you will. Those are my designs, computer. I want to see Brankin sweat for a while.
Message received and understood.
DEET
Incoming call from unknown location, Doctor Pym. Number purposely withheld. Caller message running now.
Thanks, Hank.
I just called to say thank you.

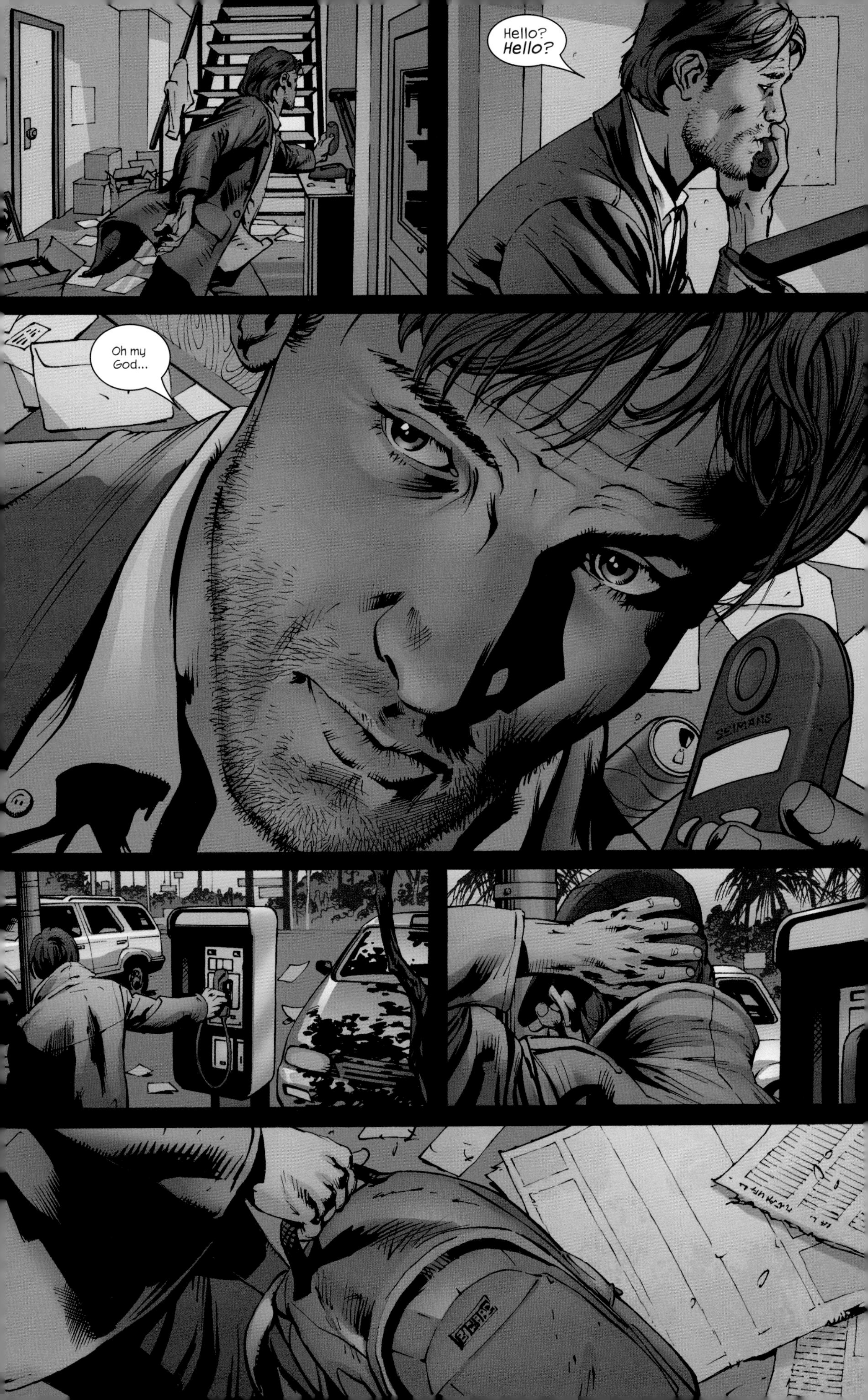
Hello? Hello?
Oh my God...

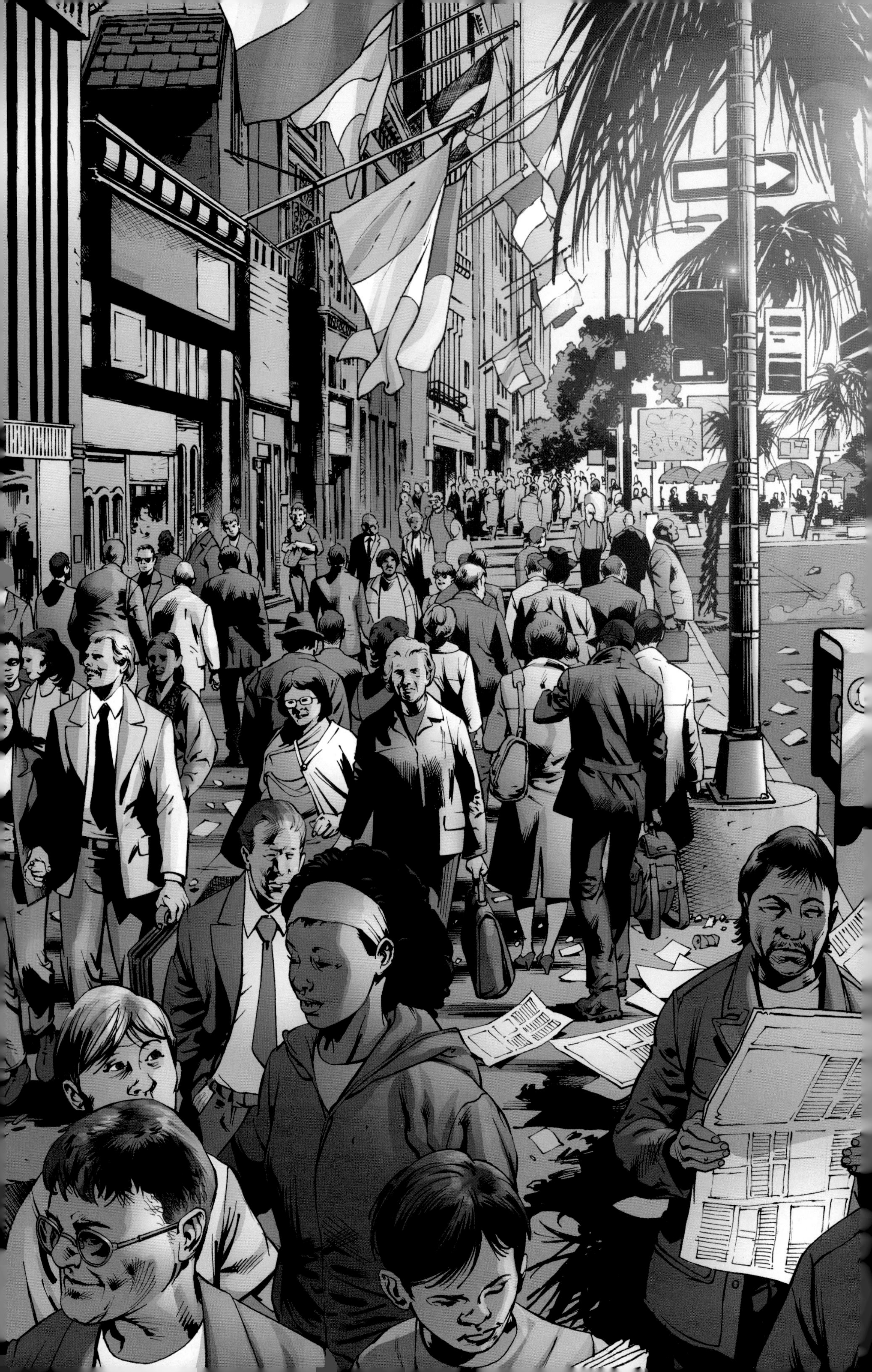

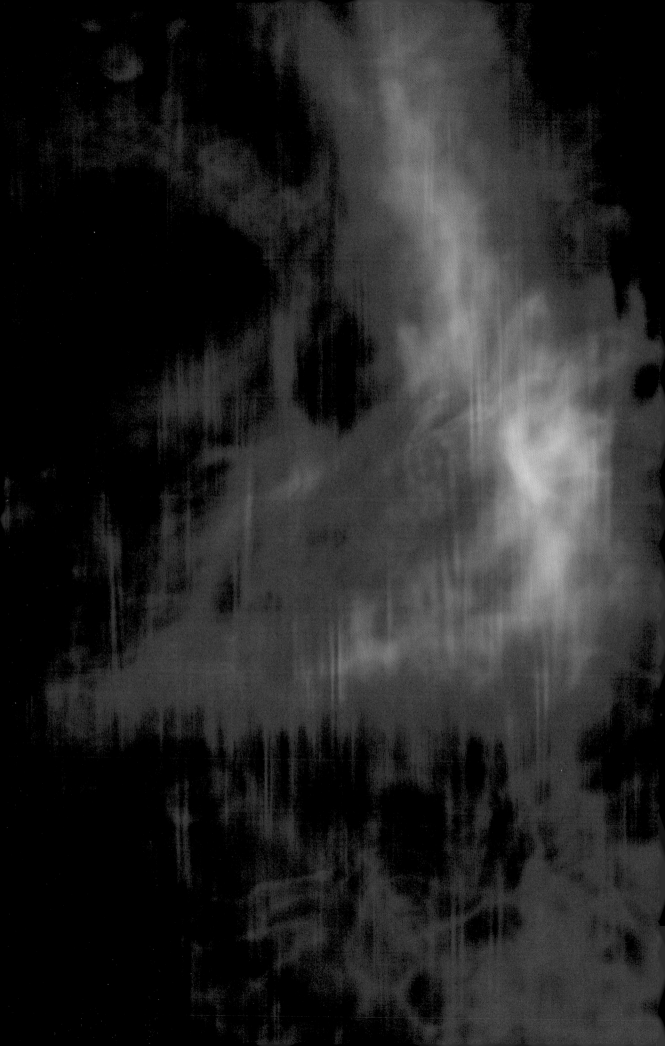

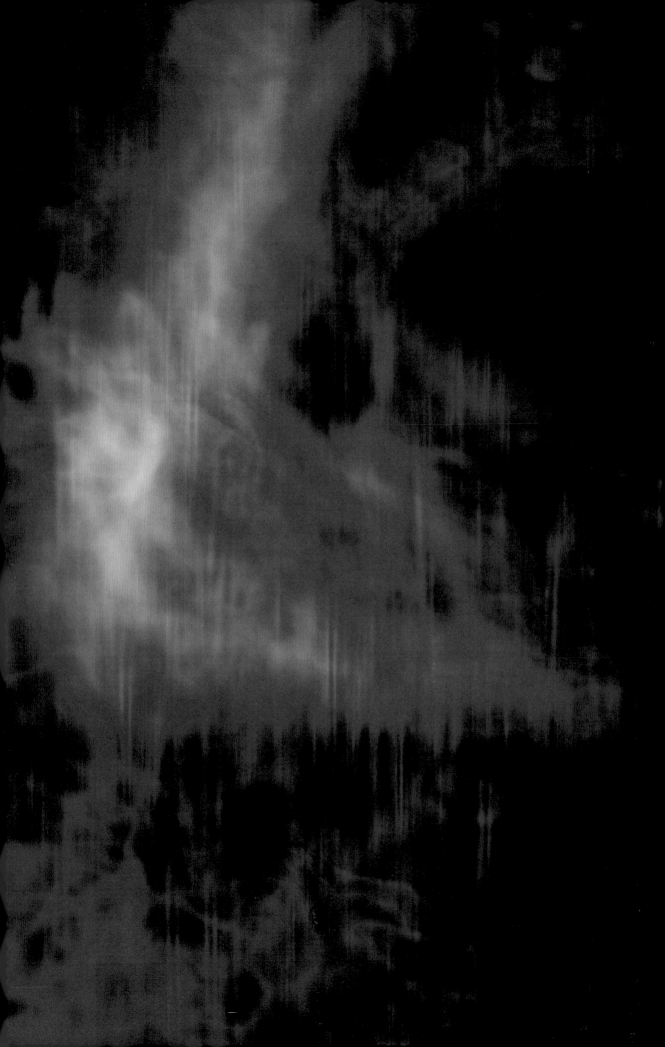

BROTHERS

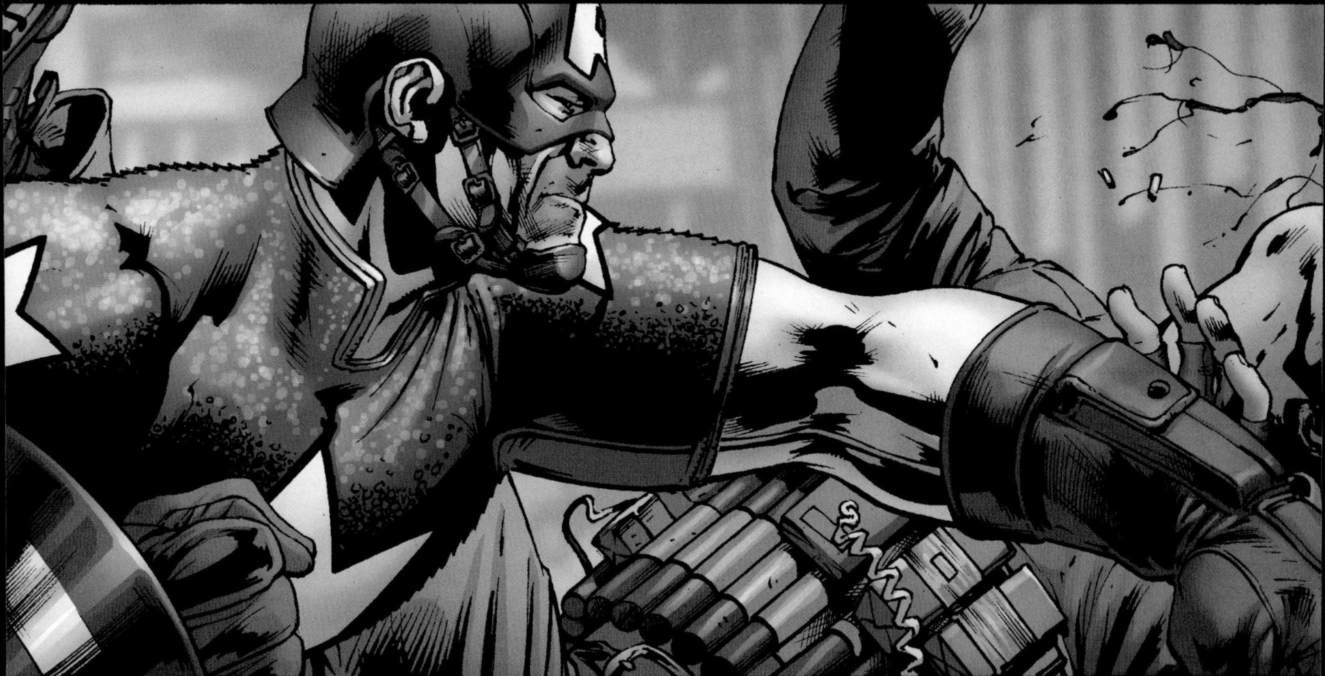

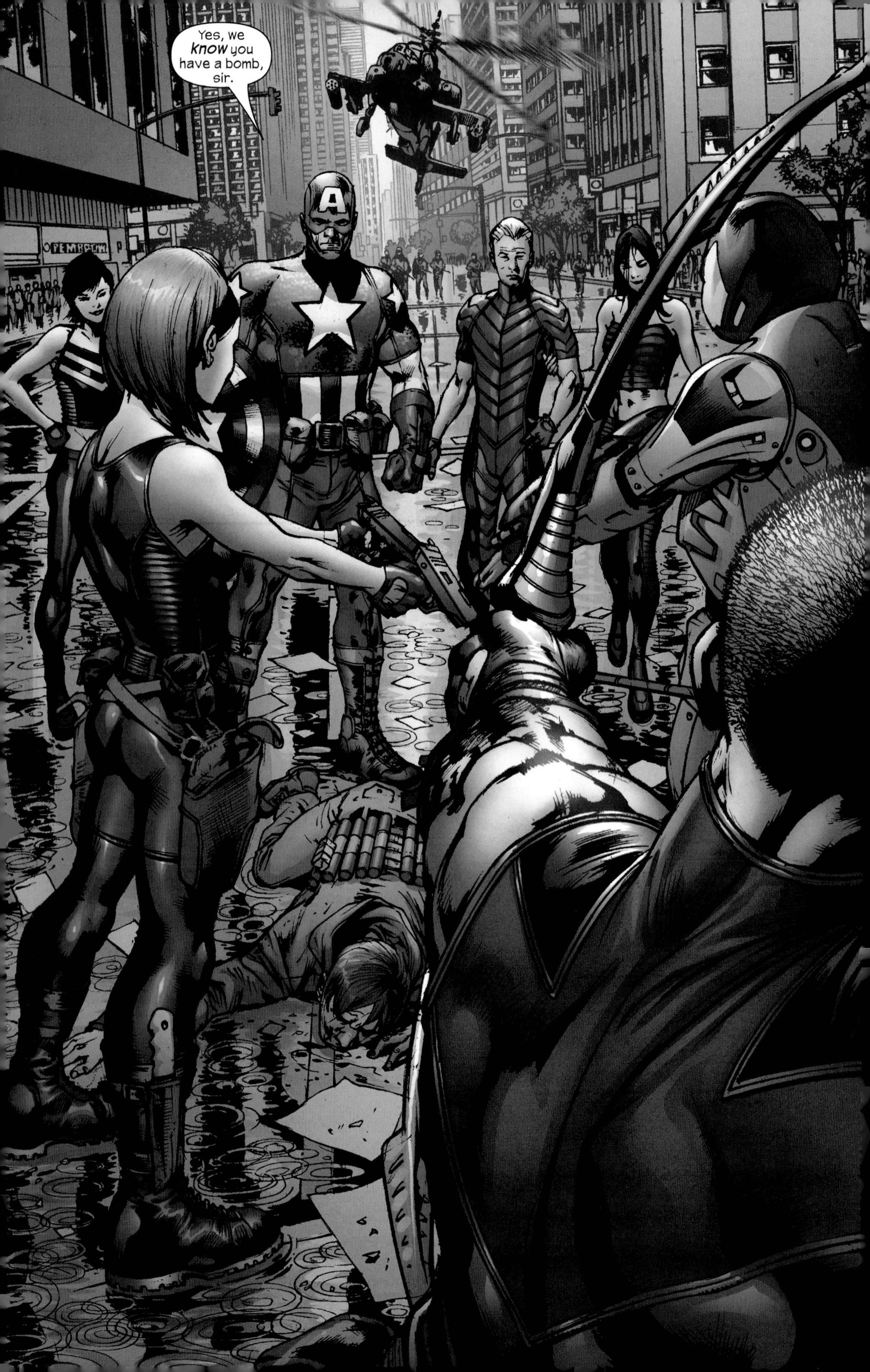
Yes, we KNOW you have a bomb, sir.

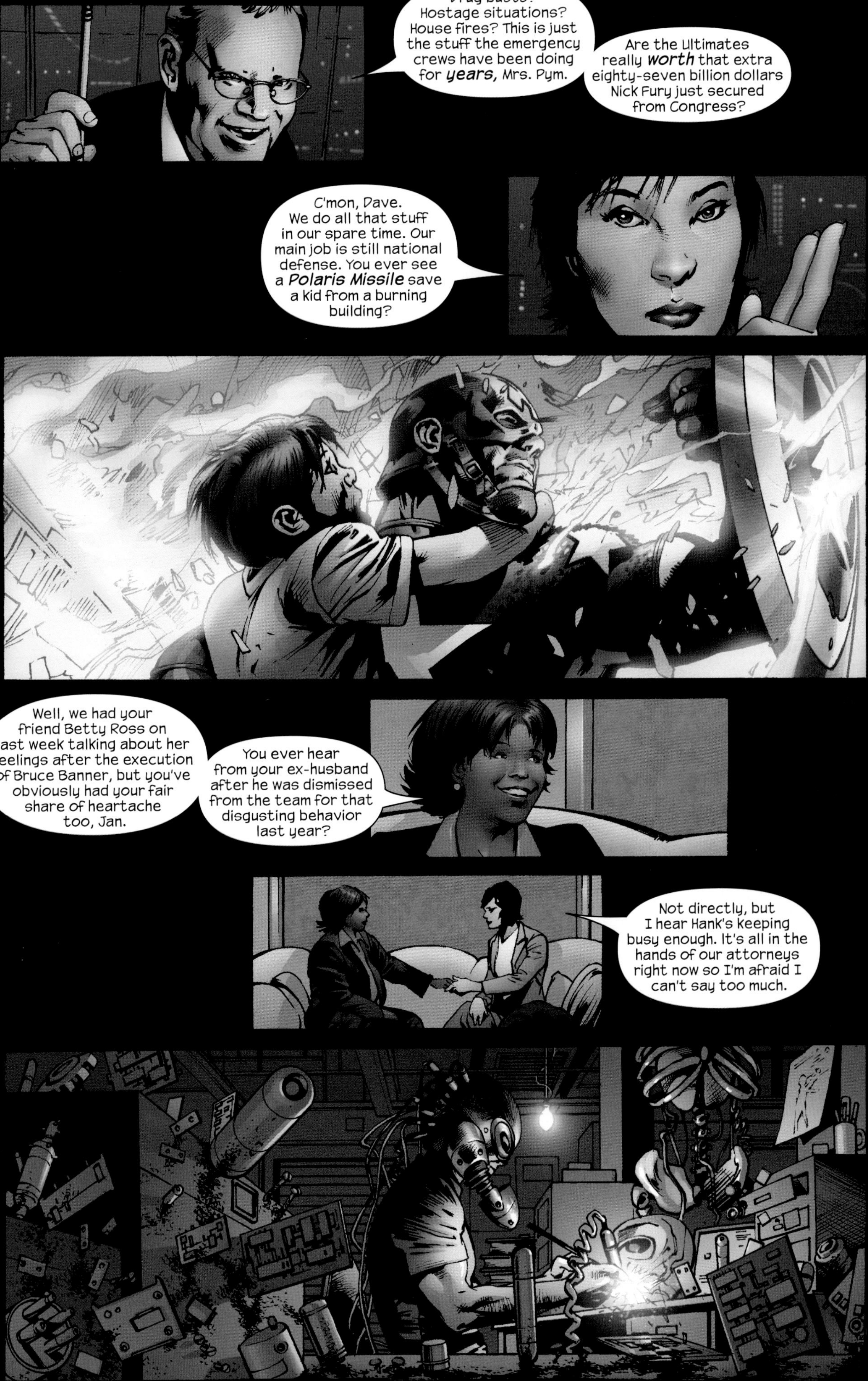
Drug busts? Hostage situations? House fires? This is just the stuff the emergency crews have been doing for *years,* Mrs. Pym.
Are the Ultimates really ***worth*** that extra eighty-seven billion dollars Nick Fury just secured from Congress?
C'mon, Dave. We do all that stuff in our spare time. Our main job is still national defense. You ever see a ***Polaris Missile*** save a kid from a burning building?
Well, we had your friend Betty Ross on last week talking about her feelings after the execution of Bruce Banner, but you've obviously had your fair share of heartache too, Jan.
You ever hear from your ex-husband after he was dismissed from the team for that disgusting behavior last year?
Not directly, but I hear Hank's keeping busy enough. It's all in the hands of our attorneys right now so I'm afraid I can't say too much.

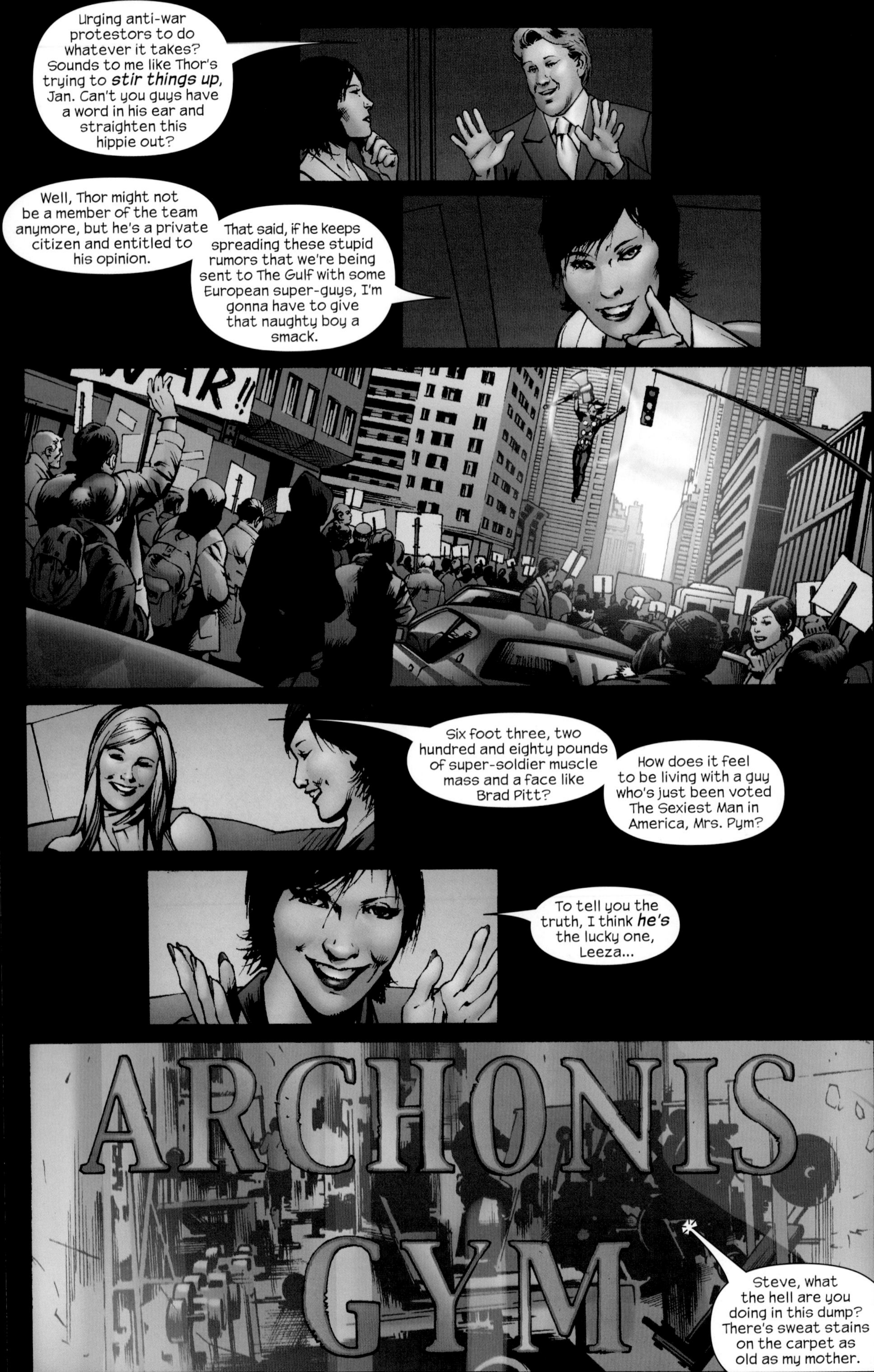
Urging anti-war protestors to do whatever it takes? Sounds to me like Thor's trying to *stir things up*, Jan. Can't you guys have a word in his ear and straighten this hippie out?
Well, Thor might not be a member of the team anymore, but he's a private citizen and entitled to his opinion.
That said, if he keeps spreading these stupid rumors that we're being sent to The Gulf with some European super-guys, I'm gonna have to give that naughty boy a smack.
Six foot three, two hundred and eighty pounds of super-soldier muscle mass and a face like Brad Pitt?
How does it feel to be living with a guy who's just been voted The Sexiest Man in America, Mrs. Pym?
To tell you the truth, I think *he's* the lucky one, Leeza...
ARCHONIS GYM
Steve, what the hell are you doing in this dump? There's sweat stains on the carpet as old as my mother.

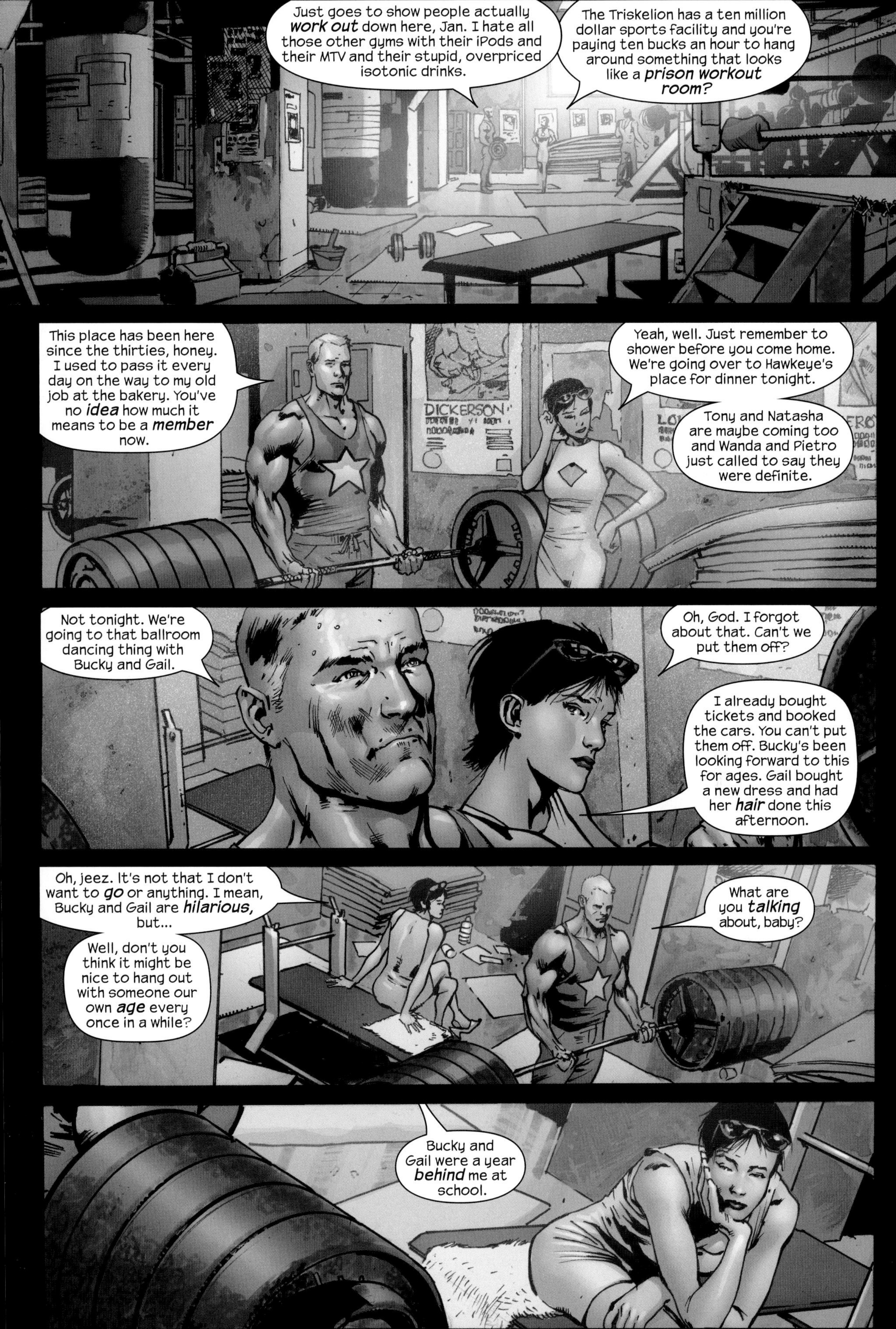
Just goes to show people actually work out down here, Jan. I hate all those other gyms with their iPods and their MTV and their stupid, overpriced isotonic drinks.
The Triskelion has a ten million dollar sports facility and you're paying ten bucks an hour to hang around something that looks like a prison workout room?
This place has been here since the thirties, honey. I used to pass it every day on the way to my old job at the bakery. You've no idea how much it means to be a member now.
Yeah, well. Just remember to shower before you come home. We're going over to Hawkeye's place for dinner tonight.
Tony and Natasha are maybe coming too and Wanda and Pietro just called to say they were definite.
DICKERSON
Not tonight. We're going to that ballroom dancing thing with Bucky and Gail.
Oh, God. I forgot about that. Can't we put them off?
I already bought tickets and booked the cars. You can't put them off. Bucky's been looking forward to this for ages. Gail bought a new dress and had her hair done this afternoon.
Oh, jeez. It's not that I don't want to go or anything. I mean, Bucky and Gail are hilarious, but...
Well, don't you think it might be nice to hang out with someone our own age every once in a while?
What are you talking about, baby?
Bucky and Gail were a year behind me at school.

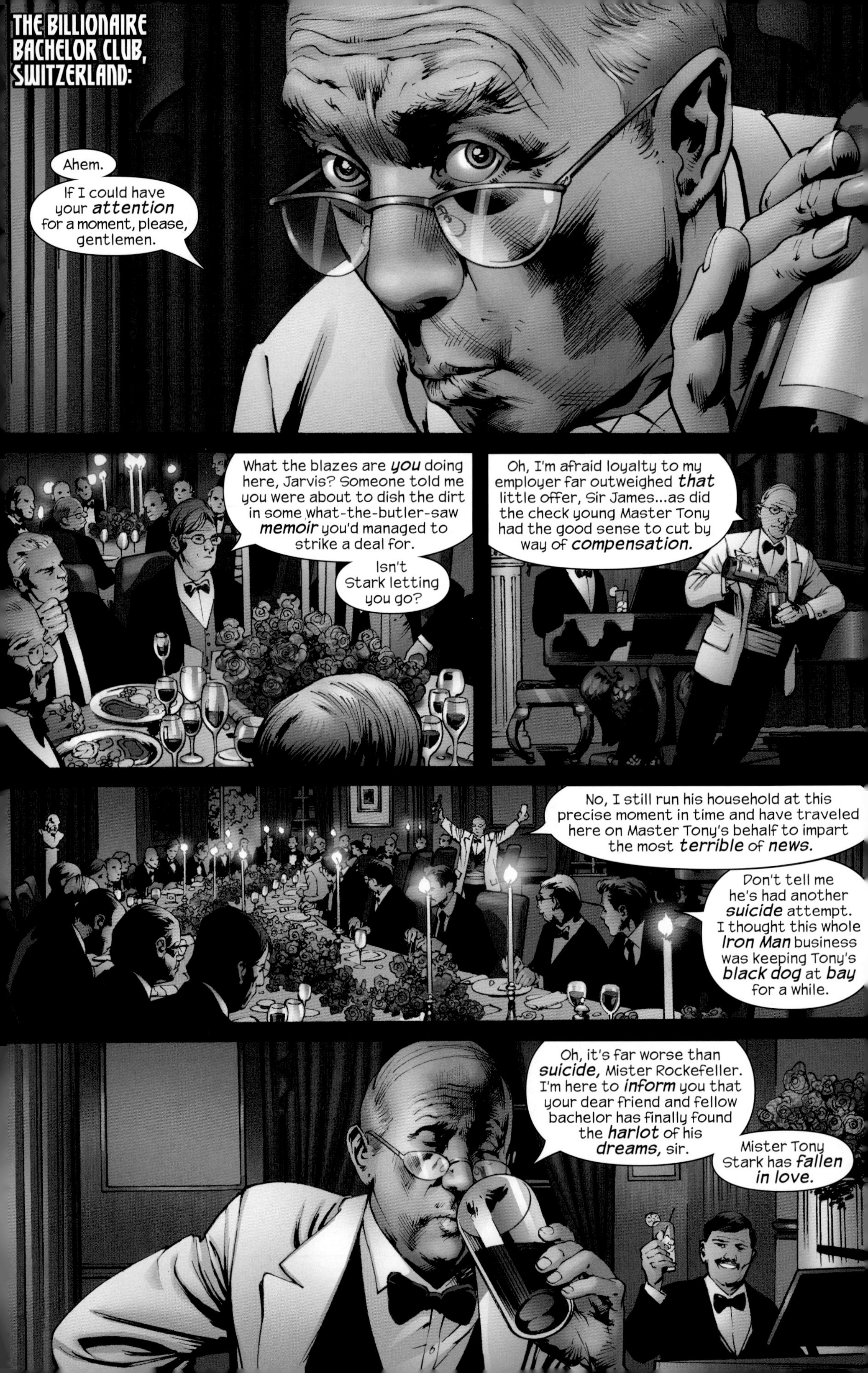
THE BILLIONAIRE BACHELOR CLUB, SWITZERLAND:
Ahem.
If I could have your attention for a moment, please, gentlemen.
What the blazes are you doing here, Jarvis? Someone told me you were about to dish the dirt in some what-the-butler-saw memoir you'd managed to strike a deal for.
Isn't Stark letting you go?
Oh, I'm afraid loyalty to my employer far outweighed that little offer, Sir James...as did the check young Master Tony had the good sense to cut by way of compensation.
No, I still run his household at this precise moment in time and have traveled here on Master Tony's behalf to impart the most terrible of news.
Don't tell me he's had another suicide attempt. I thought this whole Iron Man business was keeping Tony's black dog at bay for a while.
Oh, it's far worse than suicide, Mister Rockefeller. I'm here to inform you that your dear friend and fellow bachelor has finally found the harlot of his dreams, sir.
Mister Tony Stark has fallen in love.

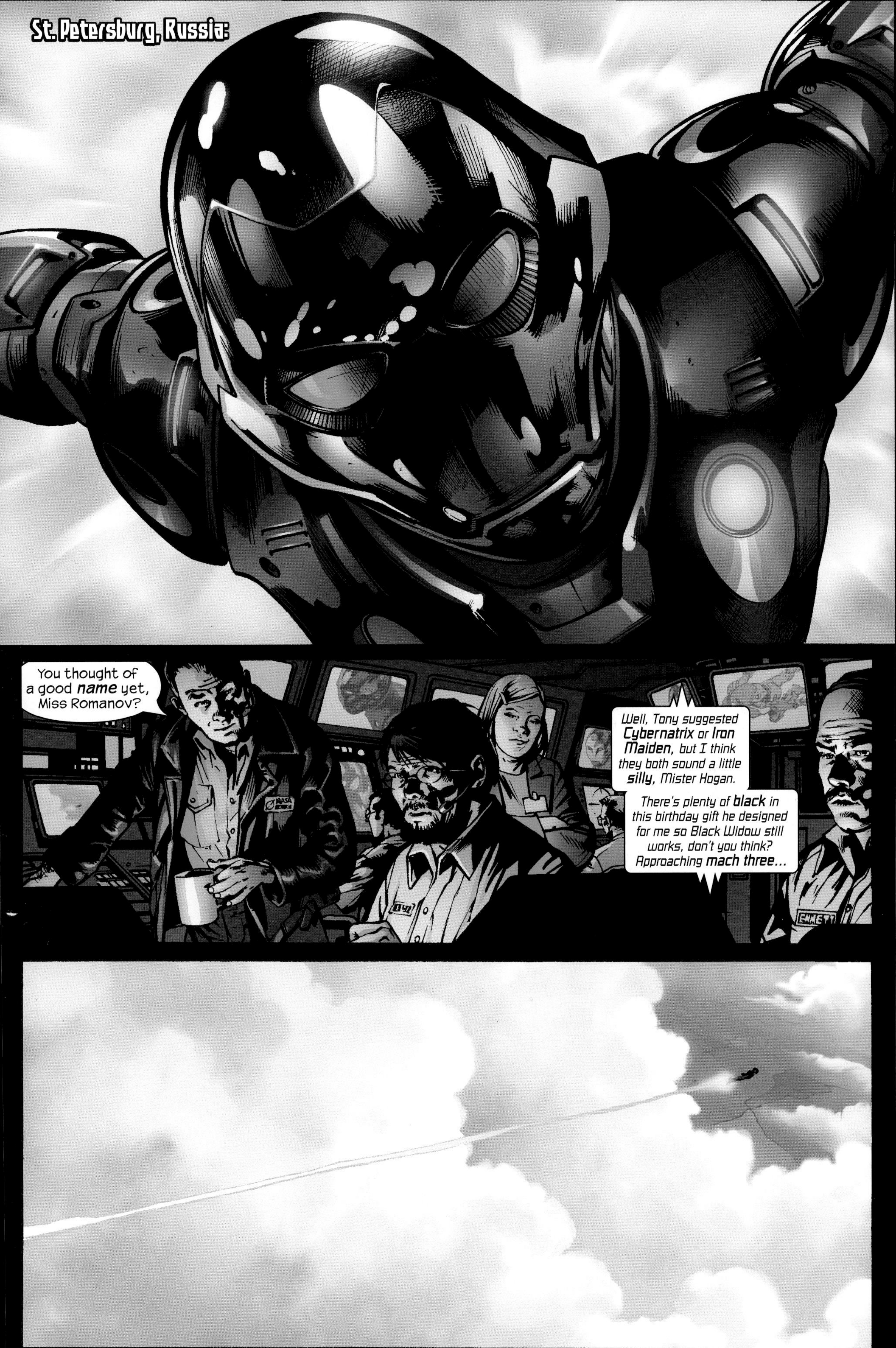
St. Petersburg, Russia:
You thought of a good name yet, Miss Romanov?
Well, Tony suggested Cybernatrix or Iron Maiden, but I think they both sound a little silly, Mister Hogan.
There's plenty of black in this birthday gift he designed for me so Black Widow still works, don't you think? Approaching mach three...

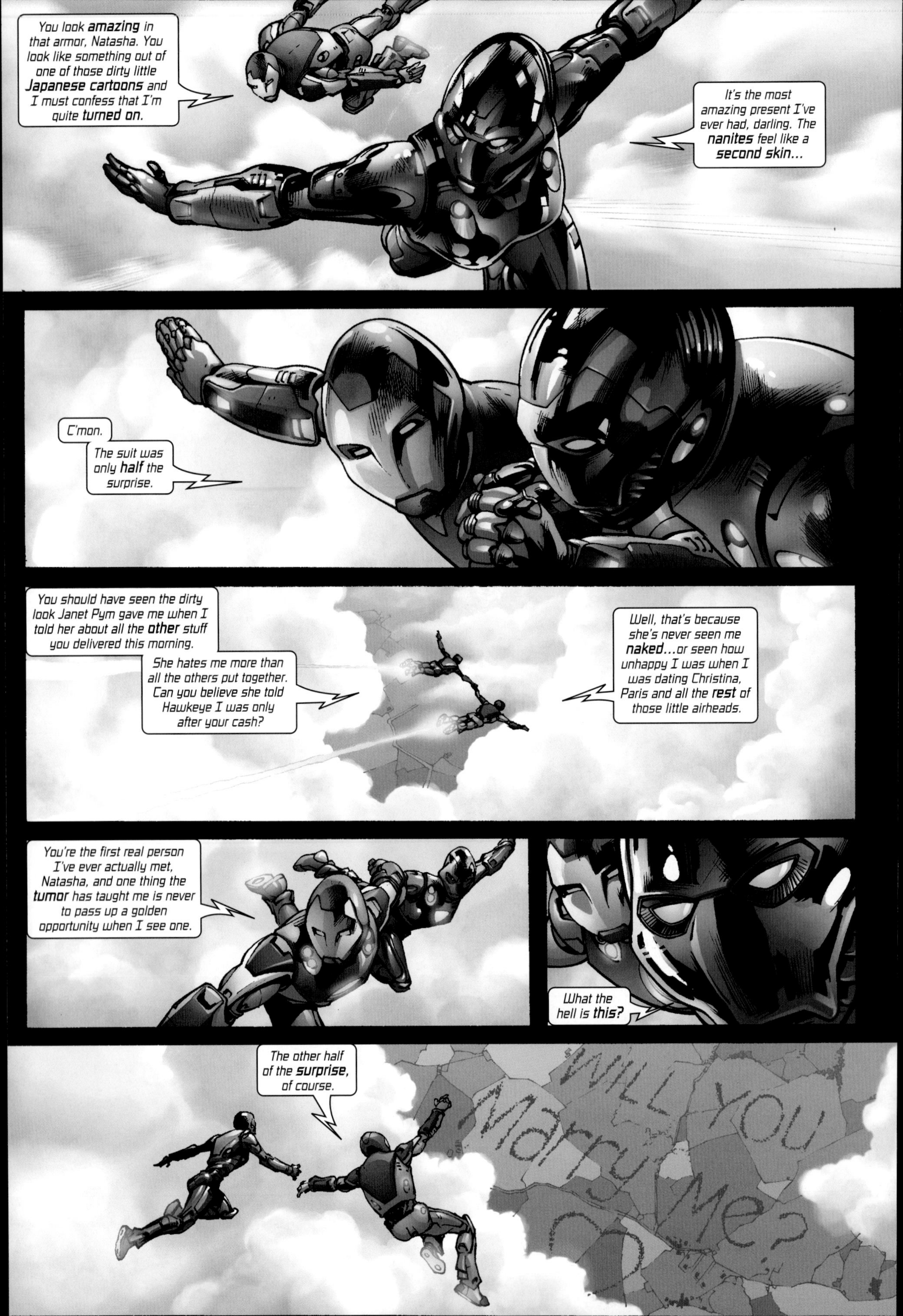
You look amazing in that armor, Natasha. You look like something out of one of those dirty little Japanese cartoons and I must confess that I'm quite turned on.
It's the most amazing present I've ever had, darling. The nanites feel like a second skin...
C'mon.
The suit was only half the surprise.
You should have seen the dirty look Janet Pym gave me when I told her about all the other stuff you delivered this morning.
She hates me more than all the others put together. Can you believe she told Hawkeye I was only after your cash?
Well, that's because she's never seen me naked...or seen how unhappy I was when I was dating Christina, Paris and all the rest of those little airheads.
You're the first real person I've ever actually met, Natasha, and one thing the tumor has taught me is never to pass up a golden opportunity when I see one.
What the hell is this?
The other half of the surprise, of course.
WILL YOU MARRY ME?

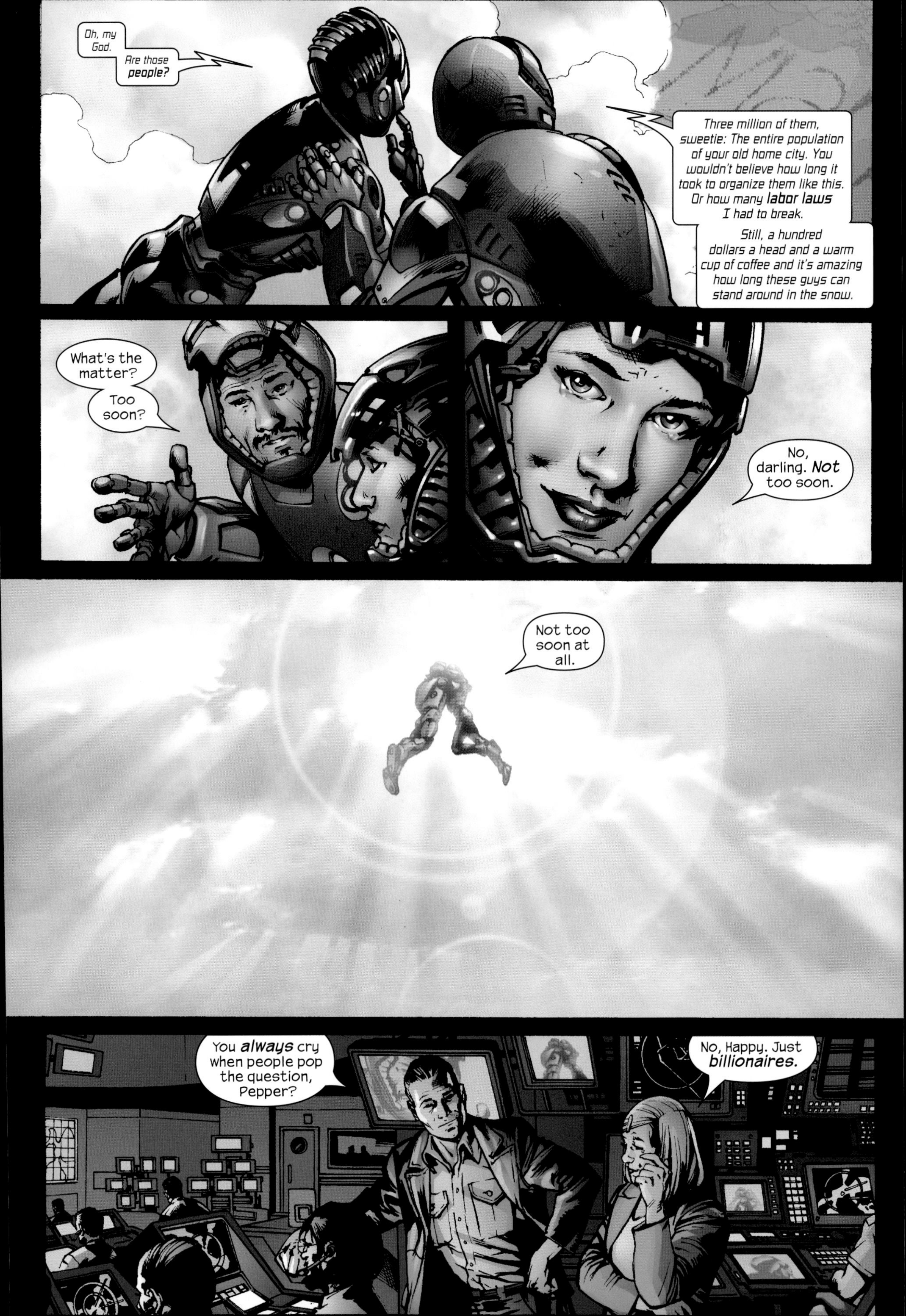

Oh, my God.
Are those *people?*
Three million of them, sweetie: The entire population of your old home city. You wouldn't believe how long it took to organize them like this. Or how many **labor laws** I had to break.
Still, a hundred dollars a head and a warm cup of coffee and it's amazing how long these guys can stand around in the snow.
What's the matter?
Too soon?
No, darling. ***Not*** too soon.
Not too soon at all.
You ***always*** cry when people pop the question, Pepper?
No, Happy. Just ***billionaires.***

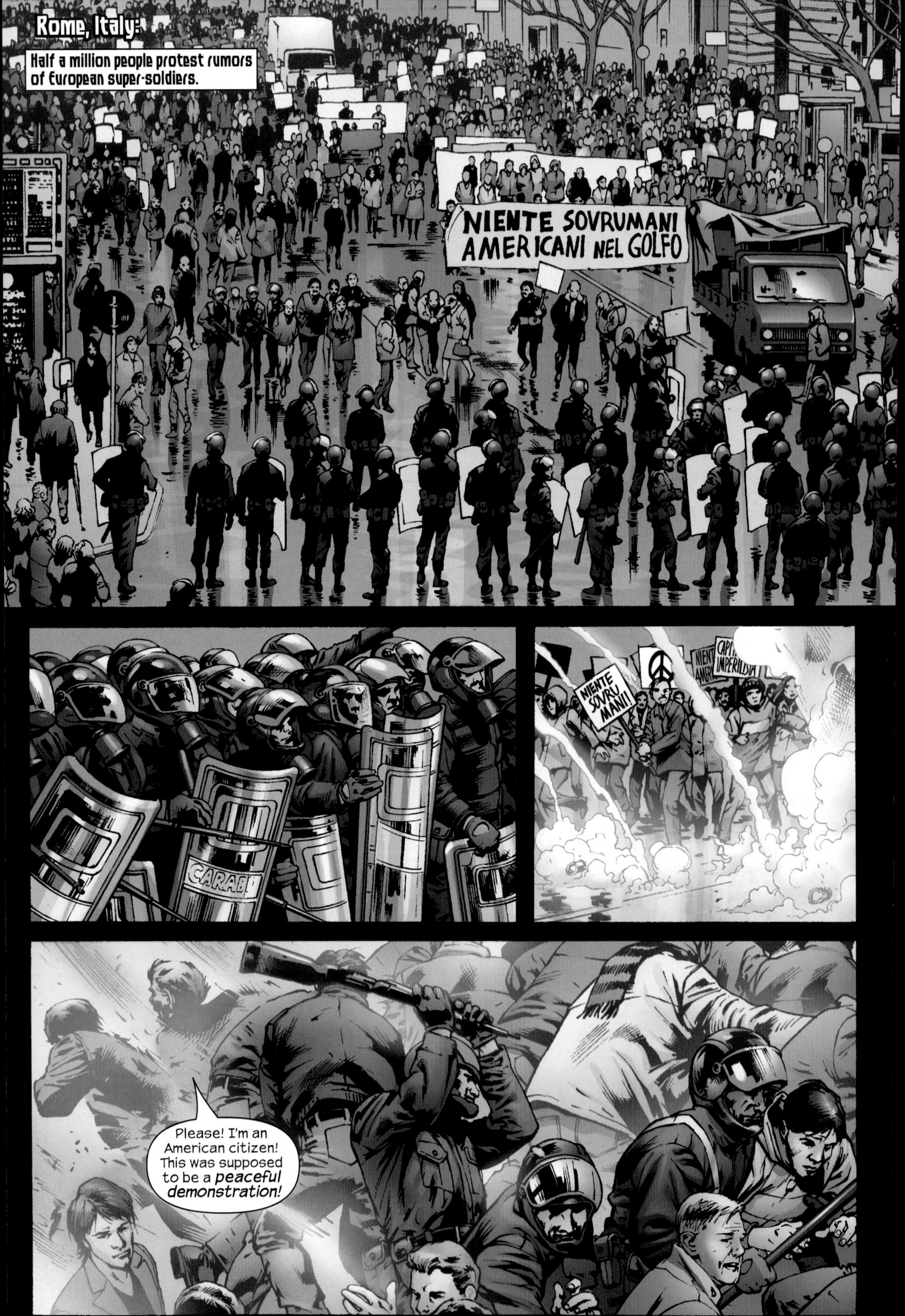
Rome, Italy:
Half a million people protest rumors of European super-soldiers.
NIENTE SOVRUMANI AMERICANI NEL GOLFO
CARAB
NIENTE SOVRU MANI!
IMPERILISTA
Please! I'm an American citizen! This was supposed to be a *peaceful demonstration!*

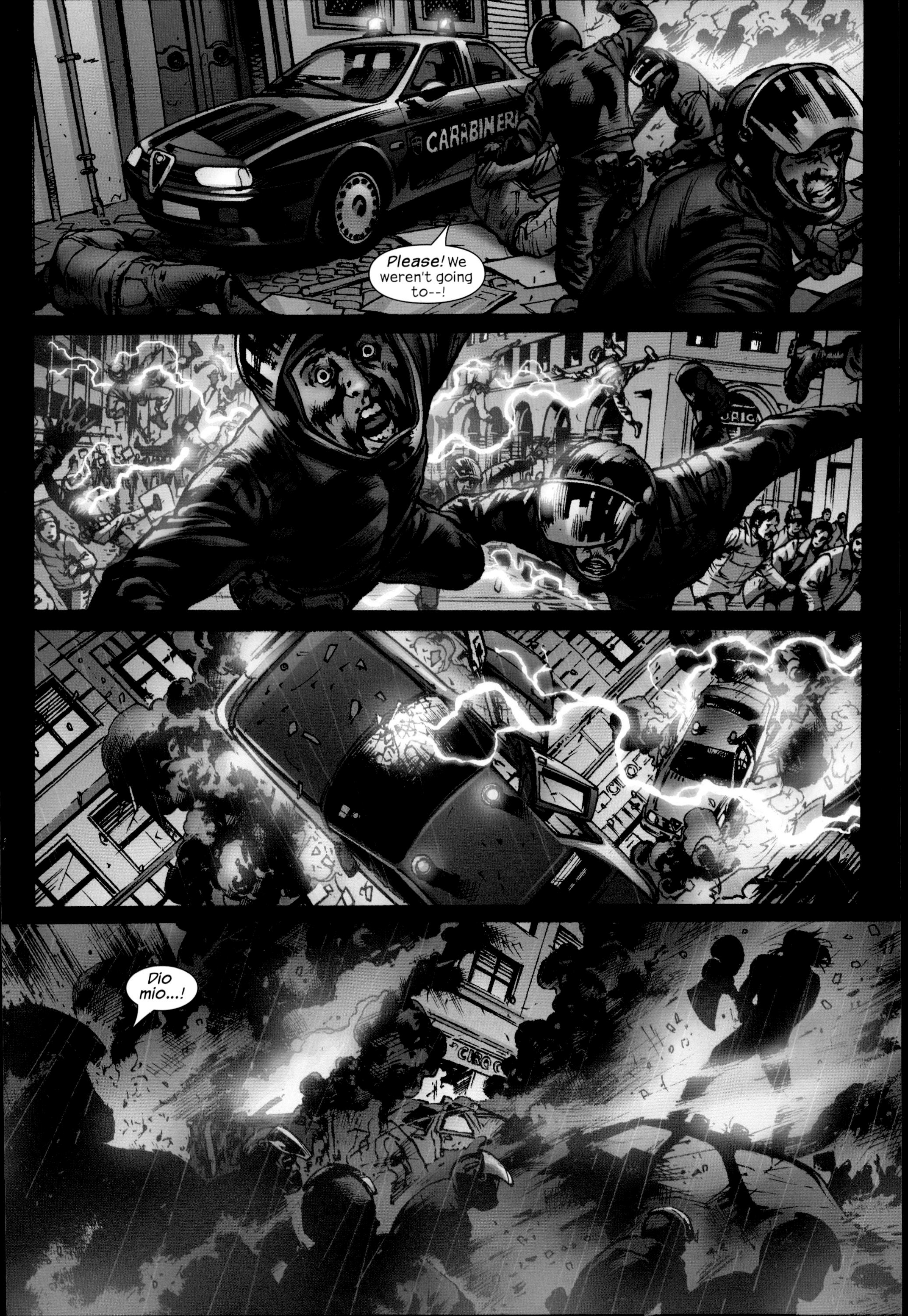
CARABINIERI
Please! We weren't going to--!
Dio mio...!

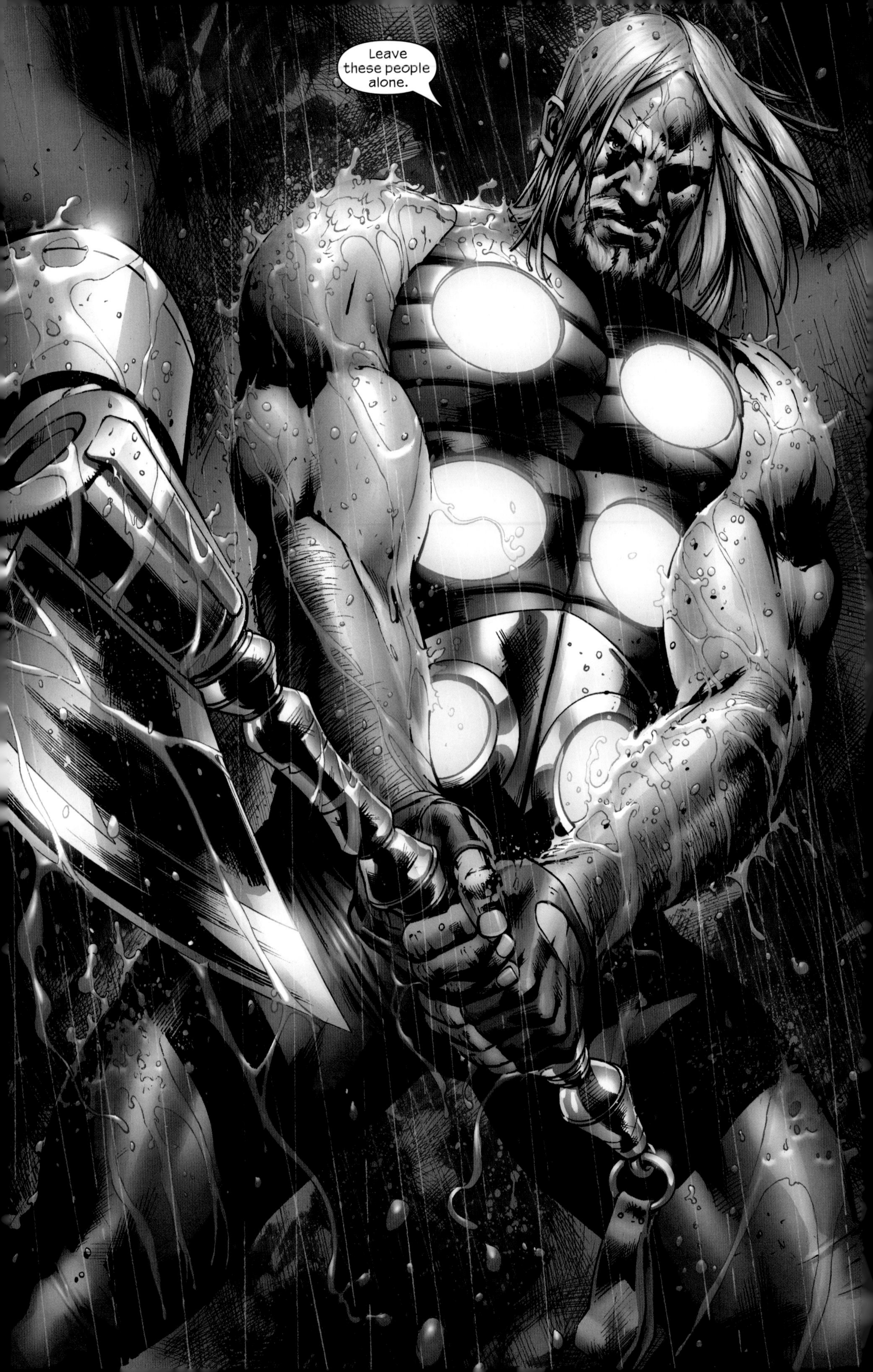
Leave these people alone.

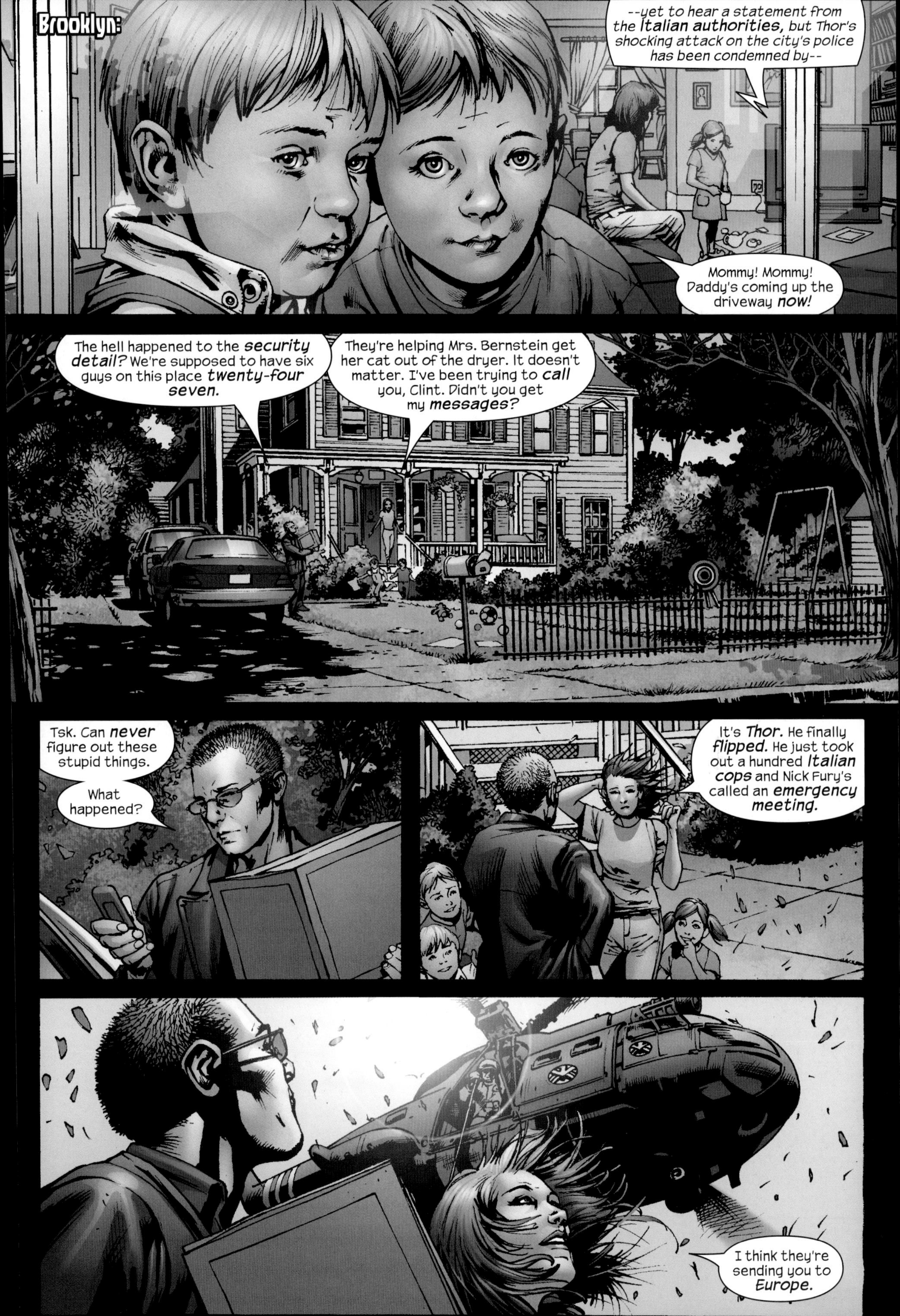

Brooklyn:
--yet to hear a statement from the Italian authorities, but Thor's shocking attack on the city's police has been condemned by--
Mommy! Mommy! Daddy's coming up the driveway now!
The hell happened to the security detail? We're supposed to have six guys on this place twenty-four seven.
They're helping Mrs. Bernstein get her cat out of the dryer. It doesn't matter. I've been trying to call you, Clint. Didn't you get my messages?
Tsk. Can never figure out these stupid things.
What happened?
It's Thor. He finally flipped. He just took out a hundred Italian cops and Nick Fury's called an emergency meeting.
I think they're sending you to Europe.

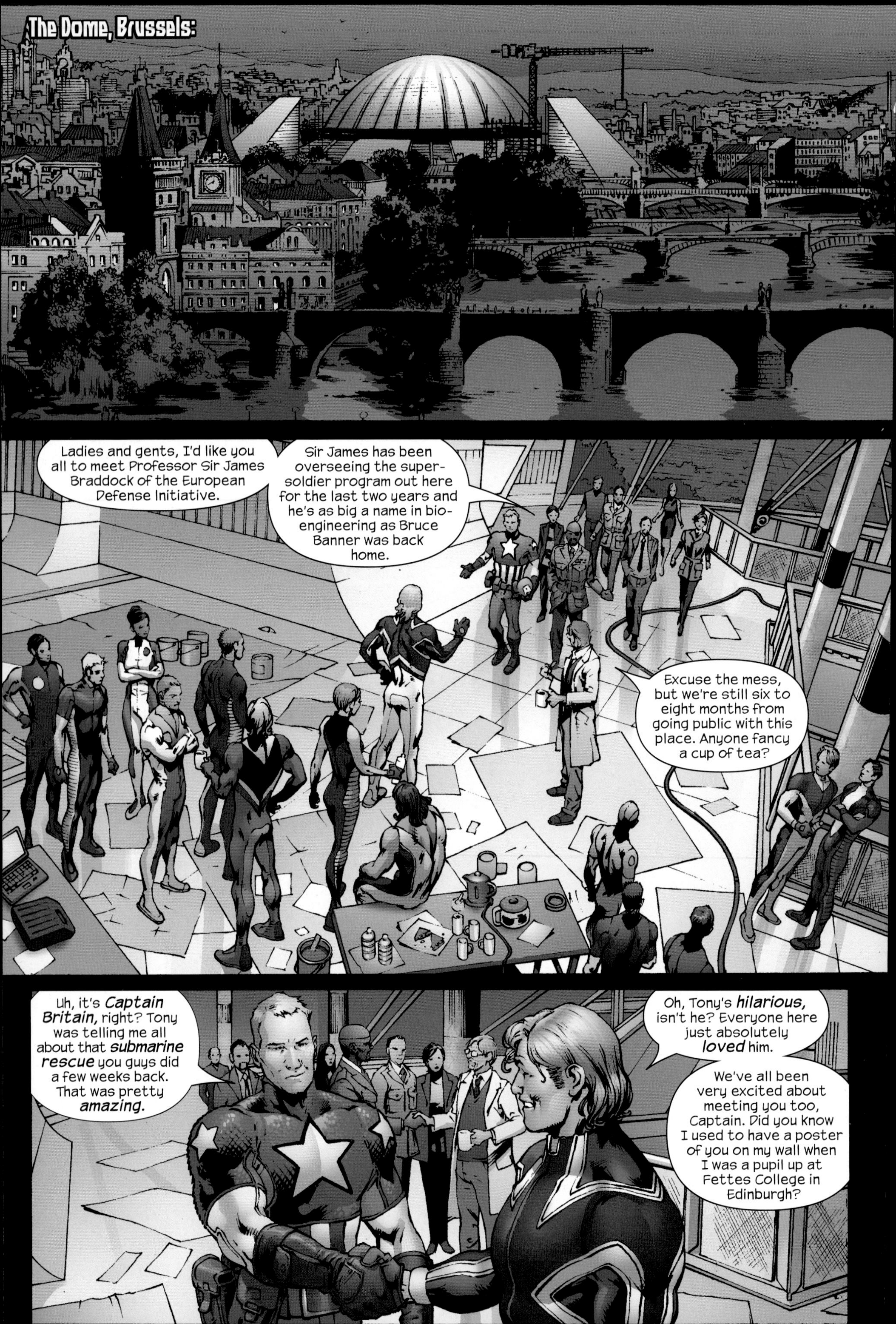
The Dome, Brussels:
Ladies and gents, I'd like you all to meet Professor Sir James Braddock of the European Defense Initiative.
Sir James has been overseeing the super-soldier program out here for the last two years and he's as big a name in bio-engineering as Bruce Banner was back home.
Excuse the mess, but we're still six to eight months from going public with this place. Anyone fancy a cup of tea?
Uh, it's *Captain Britain,* right? Tony was telling me all about that ***submarine rescue*** you guys did a few weeks back. That was pretty ***amazing.***
Oh, Tony's ***hilarious,*** isn't he? Everyone here just absolutely ***loved*** him.
We've all been very excited about meeting you too, Captain. Did you know I used to have a poster of you on my wall when I was a pupil up at Fettes College in Edinburgh?

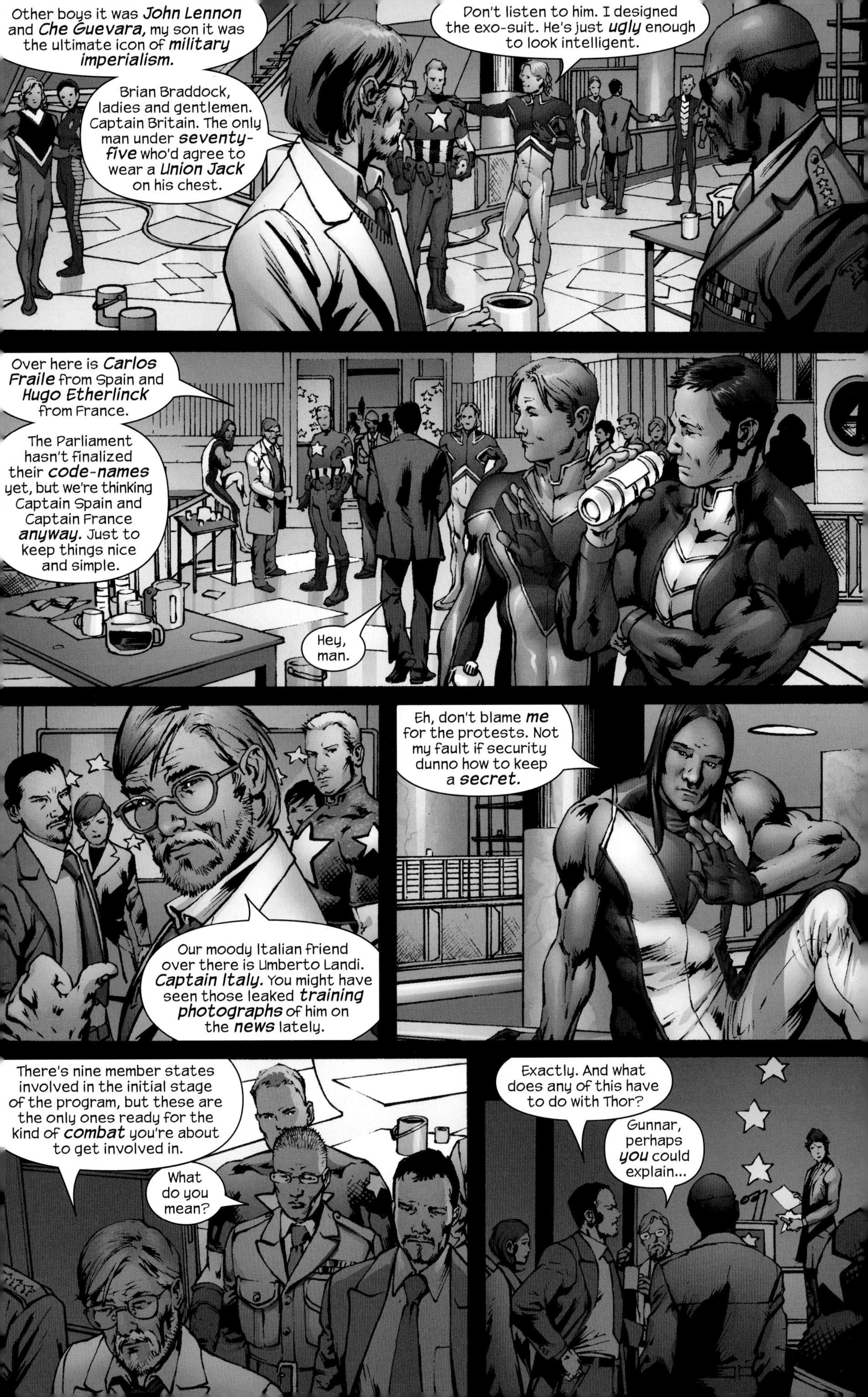
Other boys it was John Lennon and Che Guevara, my son it was the ultimate icon of military imperialism.
Brian Braddock, ladies and gentlemen. Captain Britain. The only man under seventy-five who'd agree to wear a Union Jack on his chest.
Don't listen to him. I designed the exo-suit. He's just ugly enough to look intelligent.
Over here is Carlos Fraile from Spain and Hugo Etherlinck from France.
The Parliament hasn't finalized their code-names yet, but we're thinking Captain Spain and Captain France anyway. Just to keep things nice and simple.
Hey, man.
Our moody Italian friend over there is Umberto Landi. Captain Italy. You might have seen those leaked training photographs of him on the news lately.
Eh, don't blame me for the protests. Not my fault if security dunno how to keep a secret.
There's nine member states involved in the initial stage of the program, but these are the only ones ready for the kind of combat you're about to get involved in.
What do you mean?
Exactly. And what does any of this have to do with Thor?
Gunnar, perhaps you could explain...

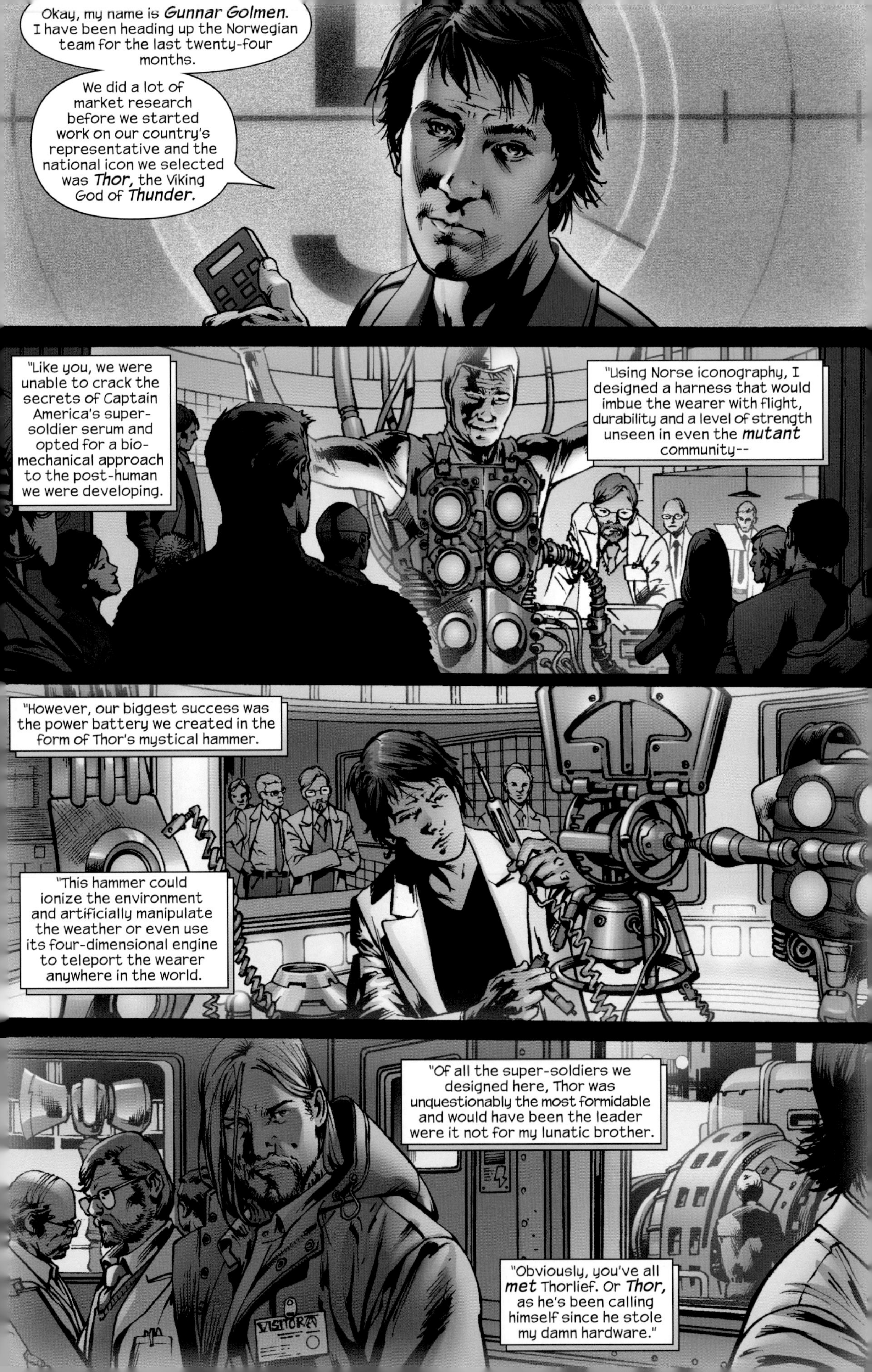
Okay, my name is *Gunnar Golmen.* I have been heading up the Norwegian team for the last twenty-four months.
We did a lot of market research before we started work on our country's representative and the national icon we selected was *Thor,* the Viking God of *Thunder.*
"Like you, we were unable to crack the secrets of Captain America's super-soldier serum and opted for a bio-mechanical approach to the post-human we were developing.
"Using Norse iconography, I designed a harness that would imbue the wearer with flight, durability and a level of strength unseen in even the *mutant* community--
"However, our biggest success was the power battery we created in the form of Thor's mystical hammer.
"This hammer could ionize the environment and artificially manipulate the weather or even use its four-dimensional engine to teleport the wearer anywhere in the world.
"Of all the super-soldiers we designed here, Thor was unquestionably the most formidable and would have been the leader were it not for my lunatic brother.
"Obviously, you've all *met* Thorlief. Or *Thor,* as he's been calling himself since he stole my damn hardware."
VISITOR

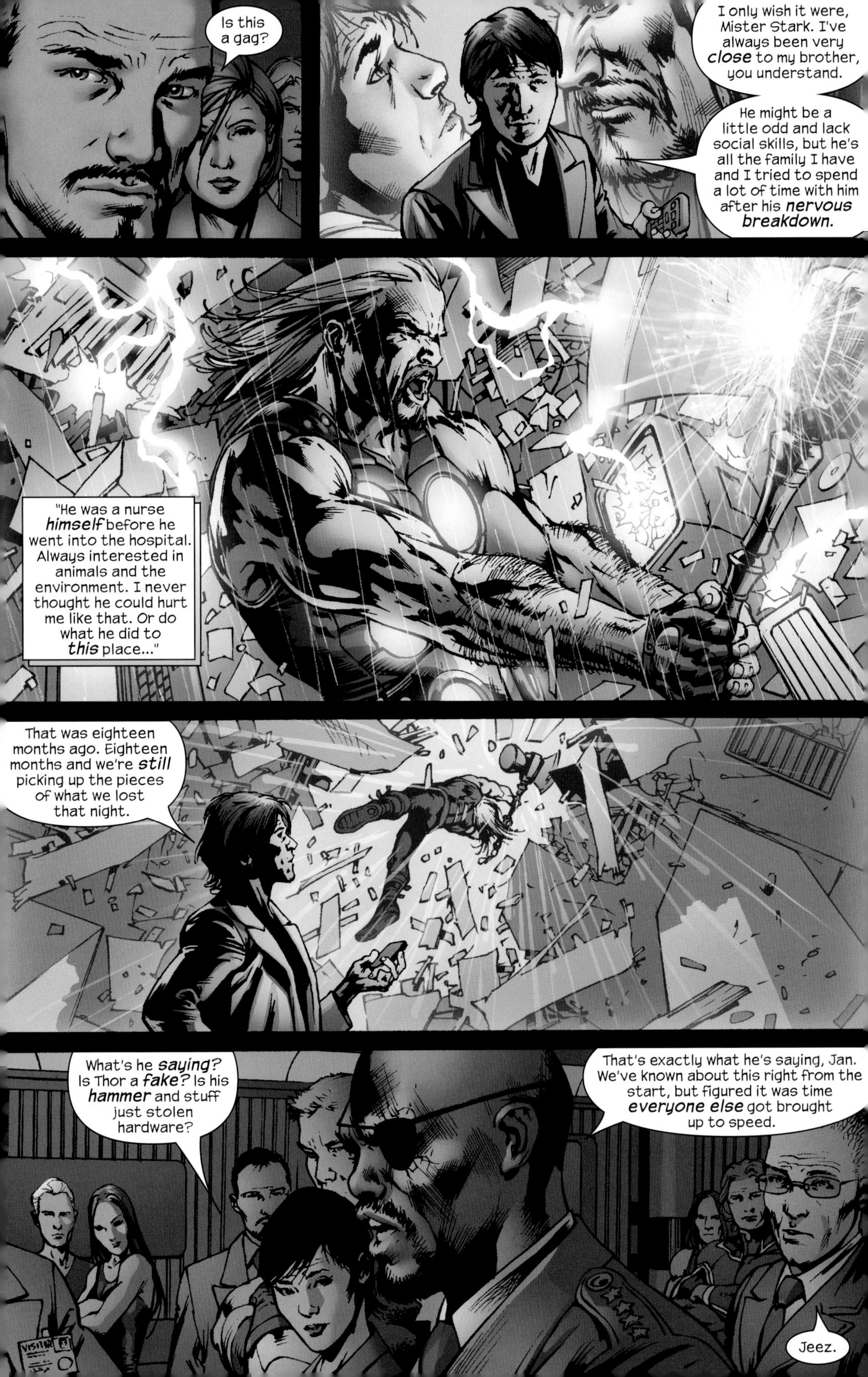
Is this a gag?
I only wish it were, Mister Stark. I've always been very close to my brother, you understand.
He might be a little odd and lack social skills, but he's all the family I have and I tried to spend a lot of time with him after his nervous breakdown.
"He was a nurse himself before he went into the hospital. Always interested in animals and the environment. I never thought he could hurt me like that. Or do what he did to this place..."
That was eighteen months ago. Eighteen months and we're still picking up the pieces of what we lost that night.
What's he saying? Is Thor a fake? Is his hammer and stuff just stolen hardware?
That's exactly what he's saying, Jan. We've known about this right from the start, but figured it was time everyone else got brought up to speed.
Jeez.

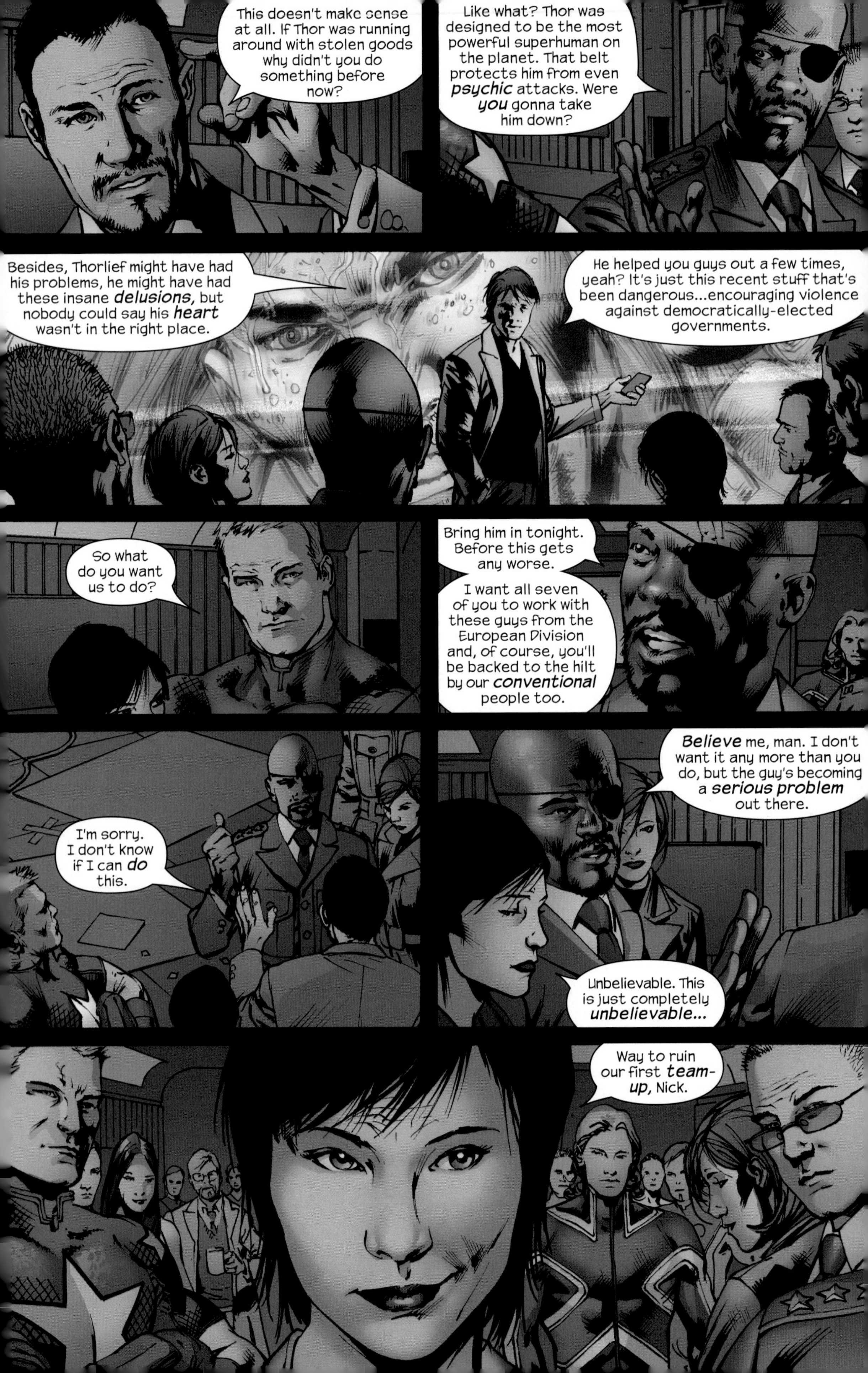
This doesn't make sense at all. If Thor was running around with stolen goods why didn't you do something before now?
Like what? Thor was designed to be the most powerful superhuman on the planet. That belt protects him from even psychic attacks. Were you gonna take him down?
Besides, Thorlief might have had his problems, he might have had these insane delusions, but nobody could say his heart wasn't in the right place.
He helped you guys out a few times, yeah? It's just this recent stuff that's been dangerous...encouraging violence against democratically-elected governments.
So what do you want us to do?
Bring him in tonight. Before this gets any worse.
I want all seven of you to work with these guys from the European Division and, of course, you'll be backed to the hilt by our conventional people too.
I'm sorry. I don't know if I can do this.
Believe me, man. I don't want it any more than you do, but the guy's becoming a serious problem out there.
Unbelievable. This is just completely unbelievable...
Way to ruin our first team-up, Nick.

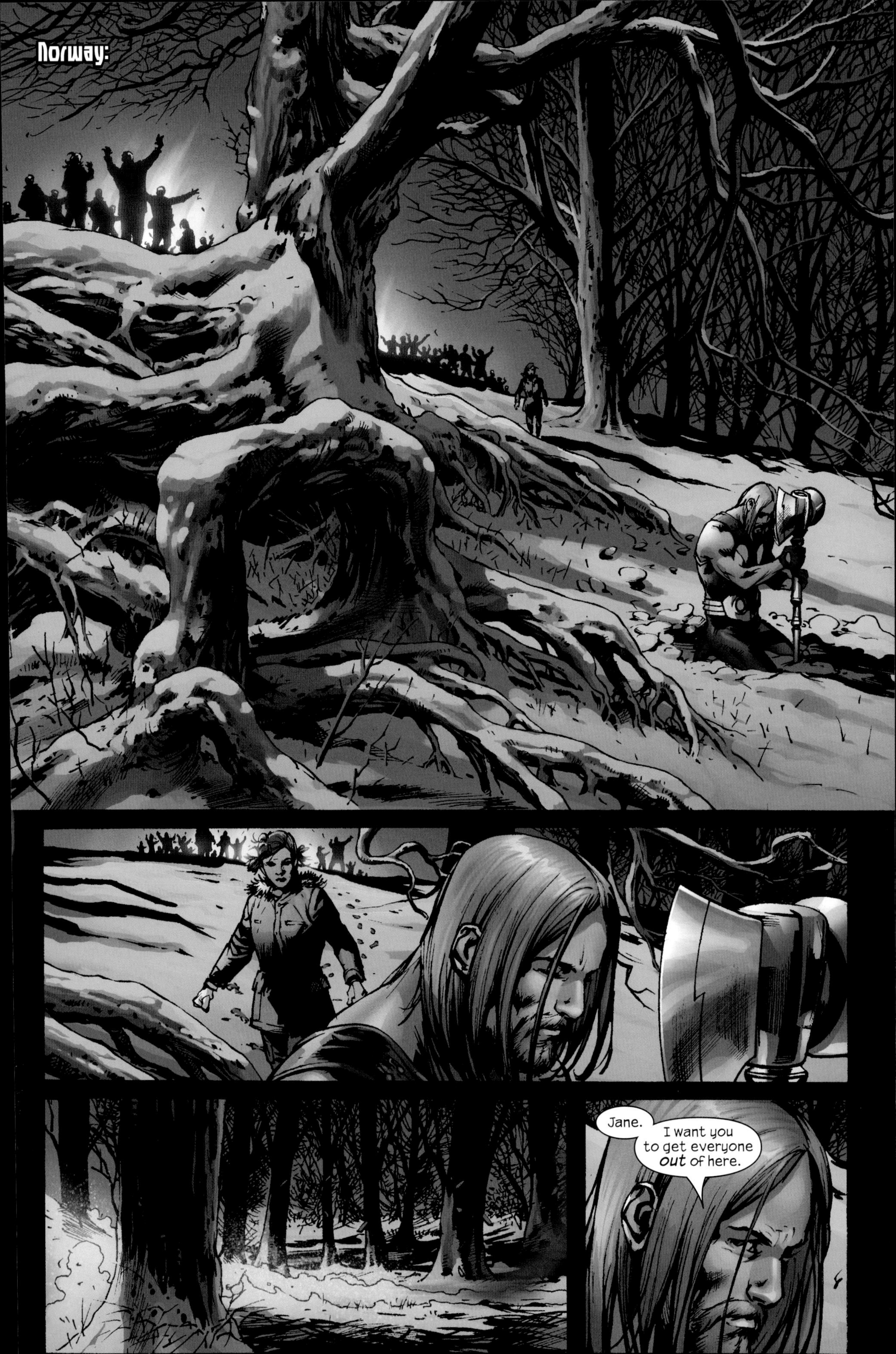
Norway:
Jane.
I want you to get everyone *out* of here.

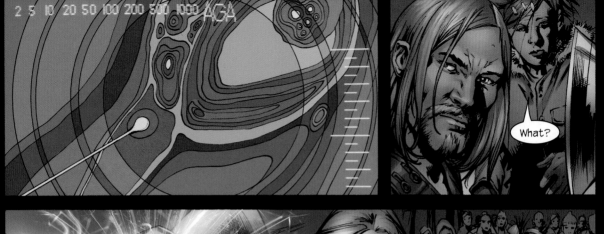

2 5 10 20 50 100 200 300 1000 AGA

What?

Get them *out* of here *now!*

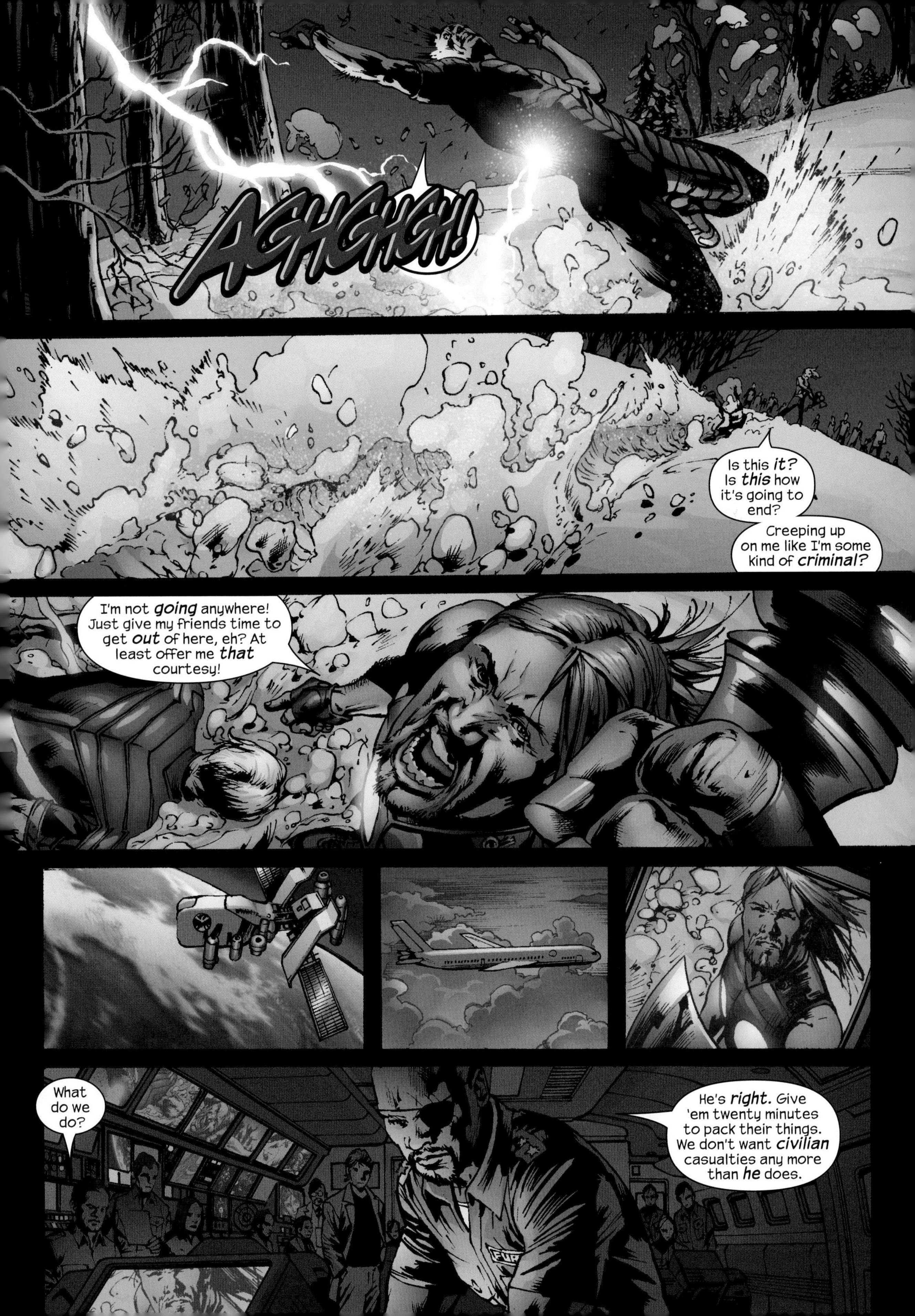
AGHGHGH!
Is this it? Is this how it's going to end?
Creeping up on me like I'm some kind of criminal?
I'm not going anywhere! Just give my friends time to get out of here, eh? At least offer me that courtesy!
What do we do?
He's right. Give 'em twenty minutes to pack their things. We don't want civilian casualties any more than he does.

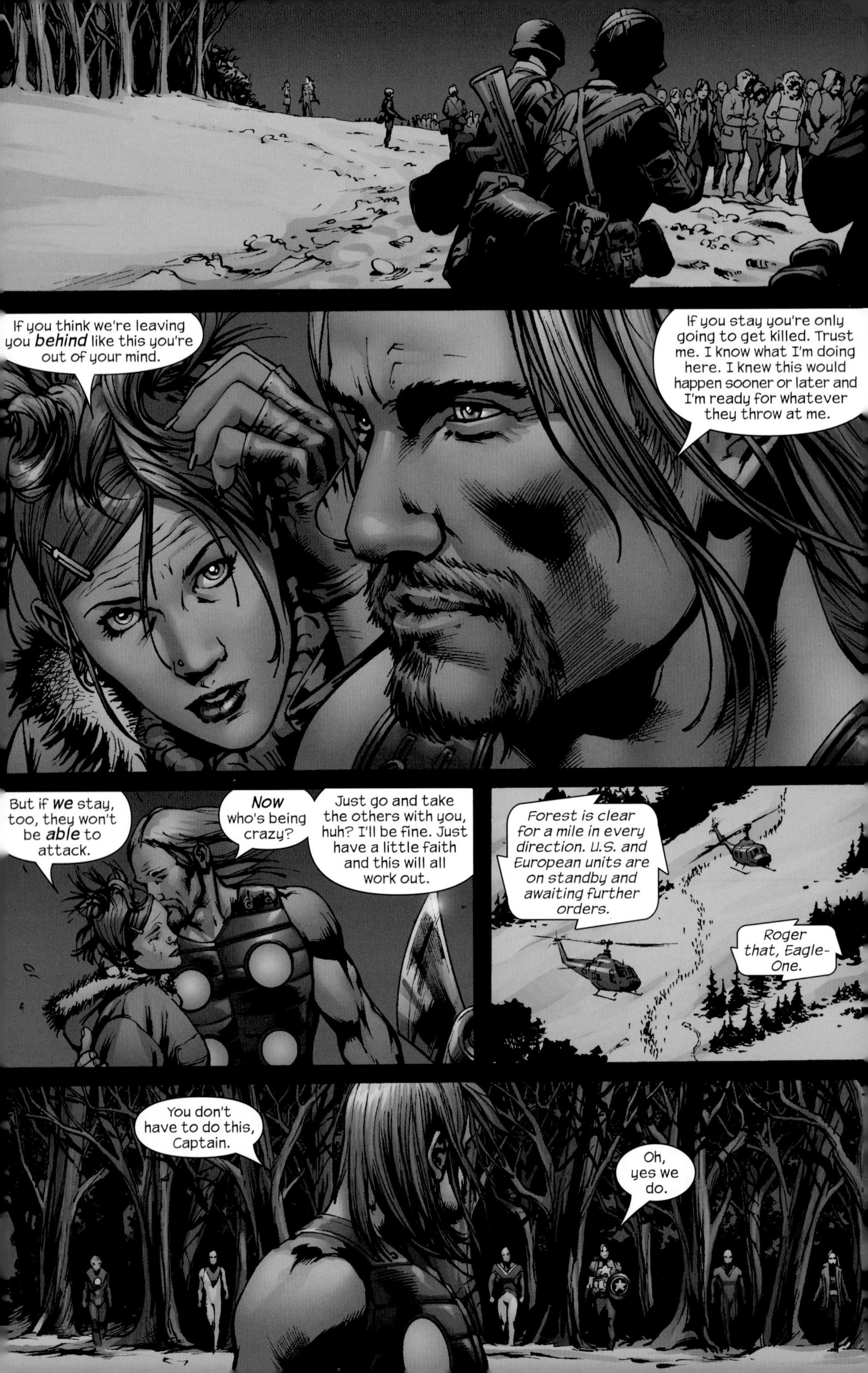
If you think we're leaving you *behind* like this you're out of your mind.
If you stay you're only going to get killed. Trust me. I know what I'm doing here. I knew this would happen sooner or later and I'm ready for whatever they throw at me.
But if *we* stay, too, they won't be *able* to attack.
Now who's being crazy?
Just go and take the others with you, huh? I'll be fine. Just have a little faith and this will all work out.
Forest is clear for a mile in every direction. U.S. and European units are on standby and awaiting further orders.
Roger that, Eagle-One.
You don't have to do this, Captain.
Oh, yes we do.

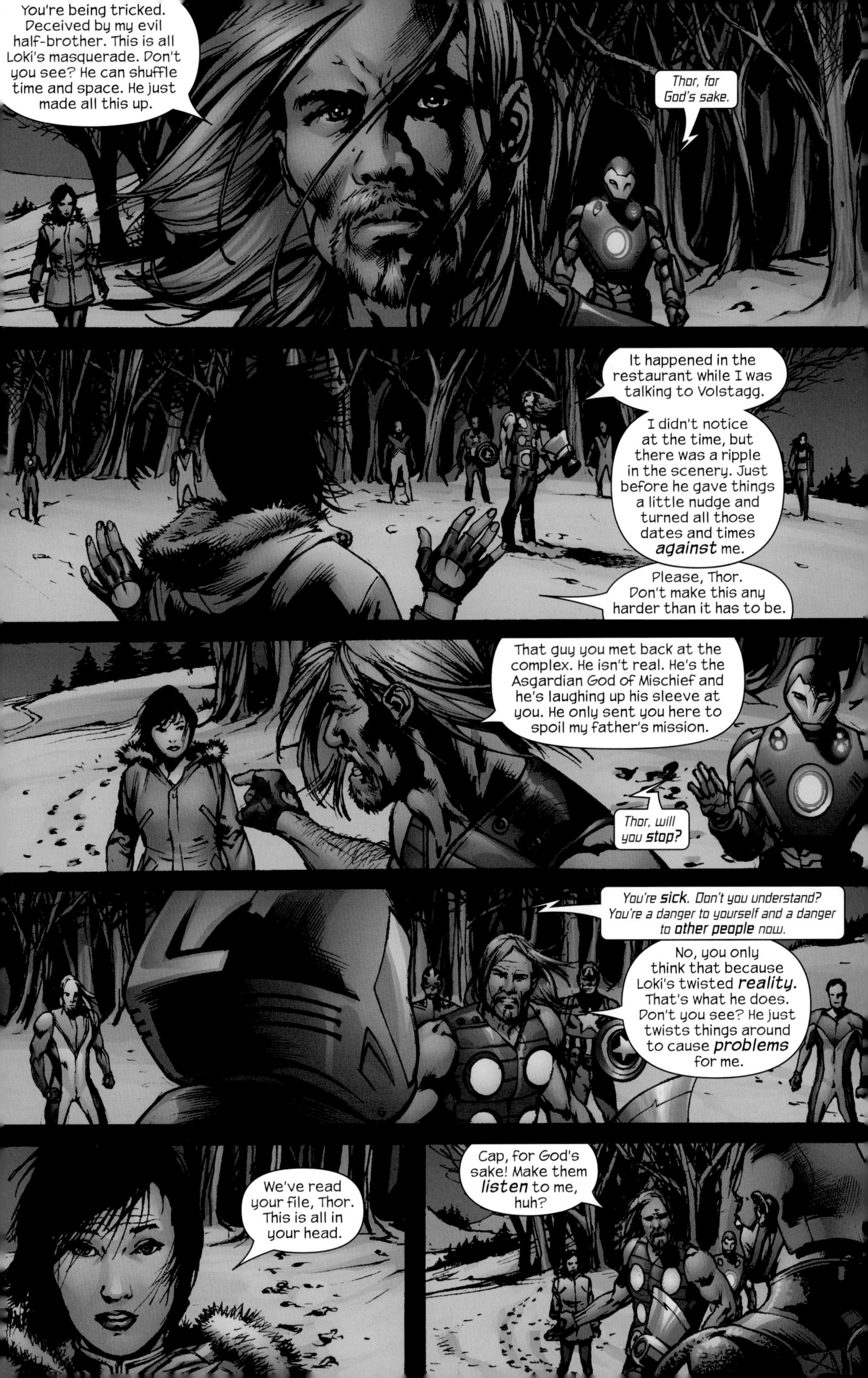
You're being tricked. Deceived by my evil half-brother. This is all Loki's masquerade. Don't you see? He can shuffle time and space. He just made all this up.
Thor, for God's sake.
It happened in the restaurant while I was talking to Volstagg.
I didn't notice at the time, but there was a ripple in the scenery. Just before he gave things a little nudge and turned all those dates and times against me.
Please, Thor. Don't make this any harder than it has to be.
That guy you met back at the complex. He isn't real. He's the Asgardian God of Mischief and he's laughing up his sleeve at you. He only sent you here to spoil my father's mission.
Thor, will you stop?
You're sick. Don't you understand? You're a danger to yourself and a danger to other people now.
No, you only think that because Loki's twisted reality. That's what he does. Don't you see? He just twists things around to cause problems for me.
We've read your file, Thor. This is all in your head.
Cap, for God's sake! Make them listen to me, huh?

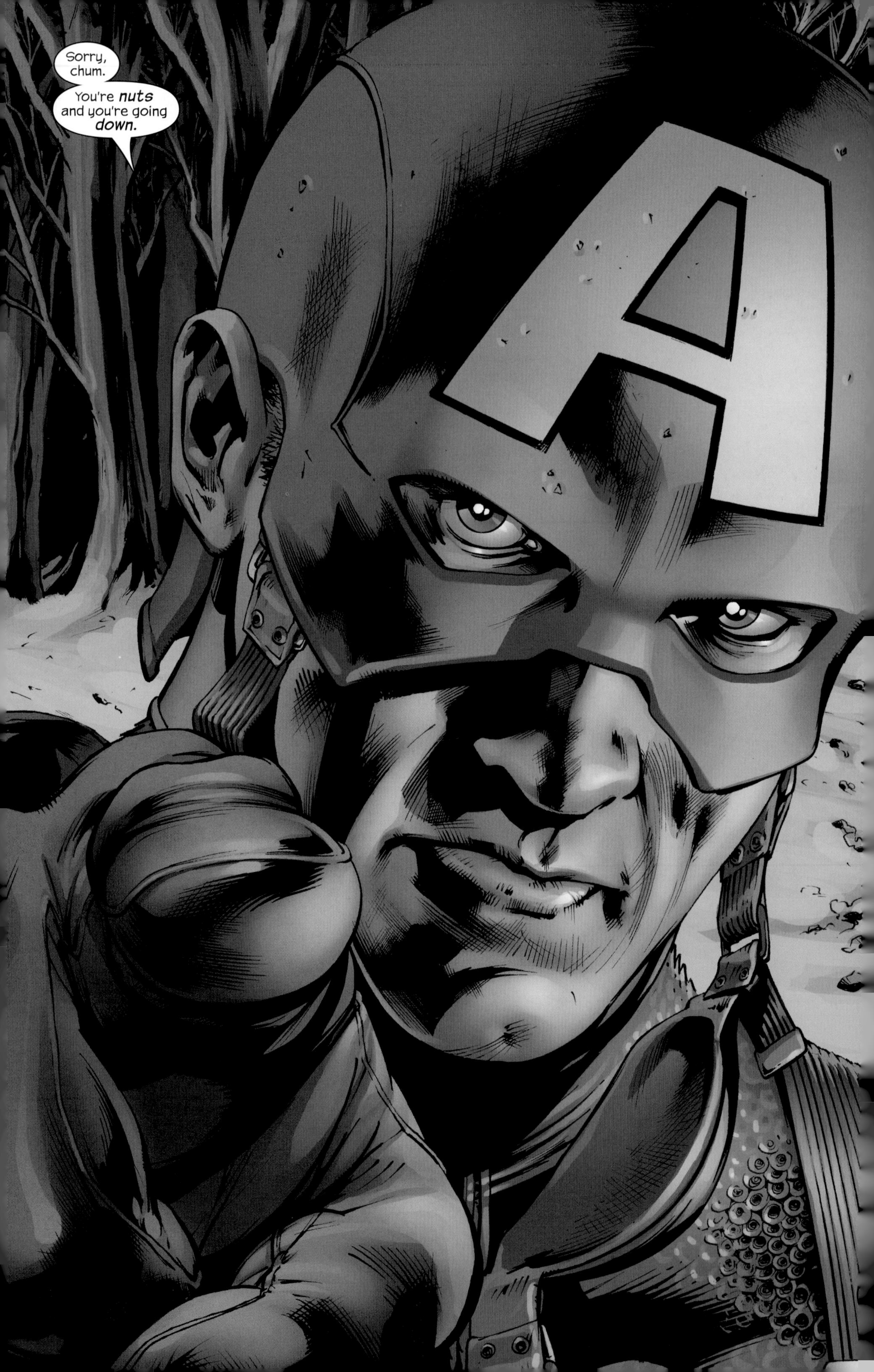
Sorry, chum.
You're **nuts** and you're going ***down.***

THE PASSION

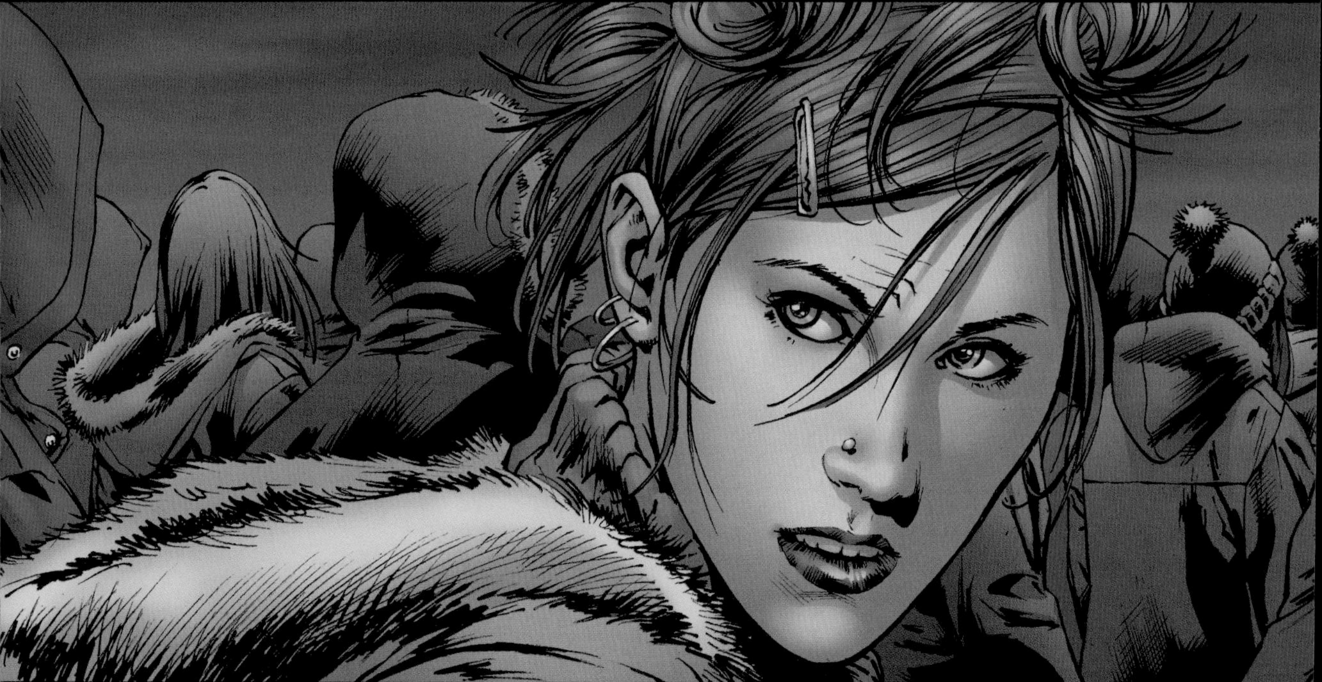

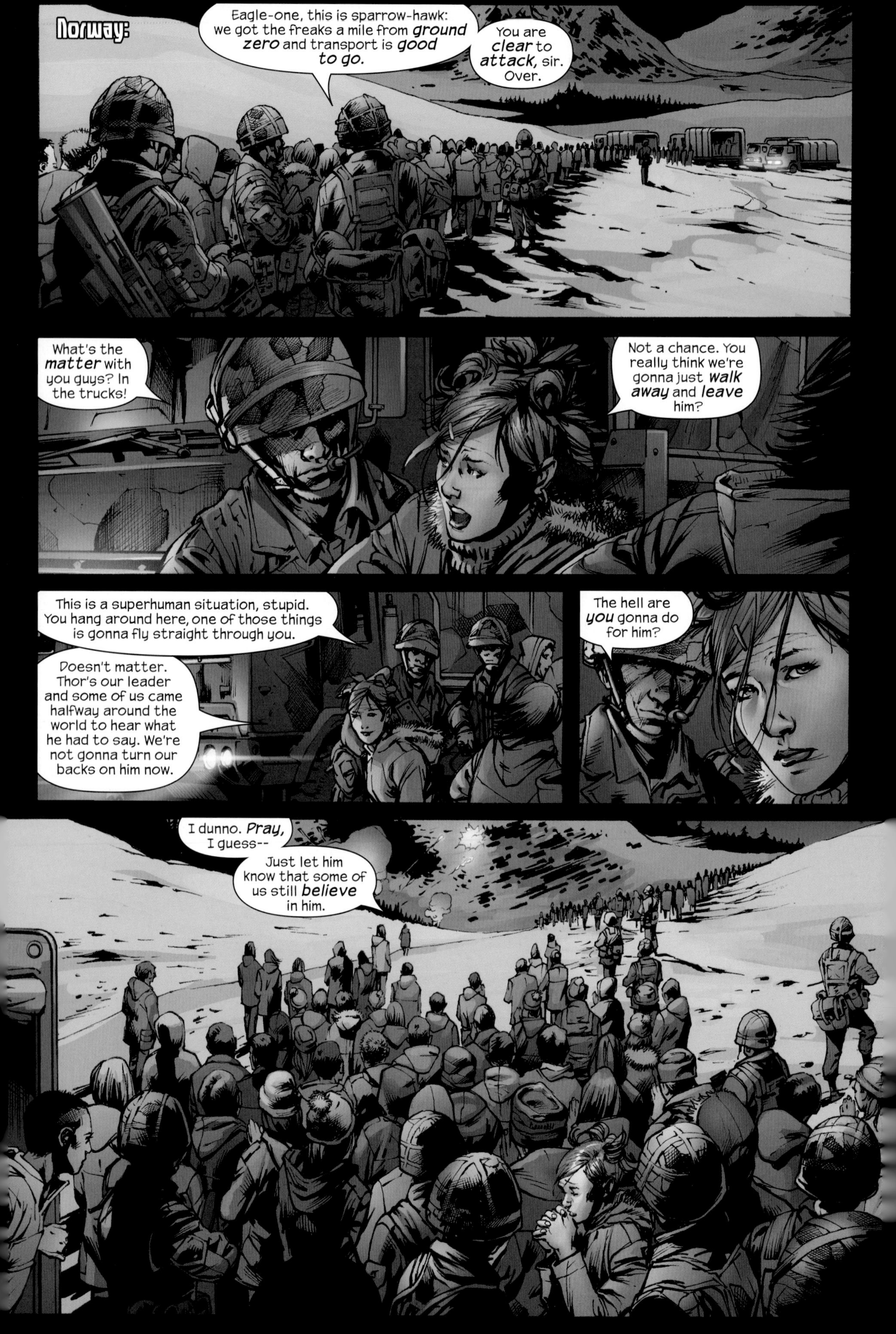

Norway:
Eagle-one, this is sparrow-hawk: we got the freaks a mile from ground zero and transport is good to go.
You are clear to attack, sir. Over.
What's the matter with you guys? In the trucks!
Not a chance. You really think we're gonna just walk away and leave him?
This is a superhuman situation, stupid. You hang around here, one of those things is gonna fly straight through you.
Doesn't matter. Thor's our leader and some of us came halfway around the world to hear what he had to say. We're not gonna turn our backs on him now.
The hell are you gonna do for him?
I dunno. Pray, I guess--
Just let him know that some of us still believe in him.

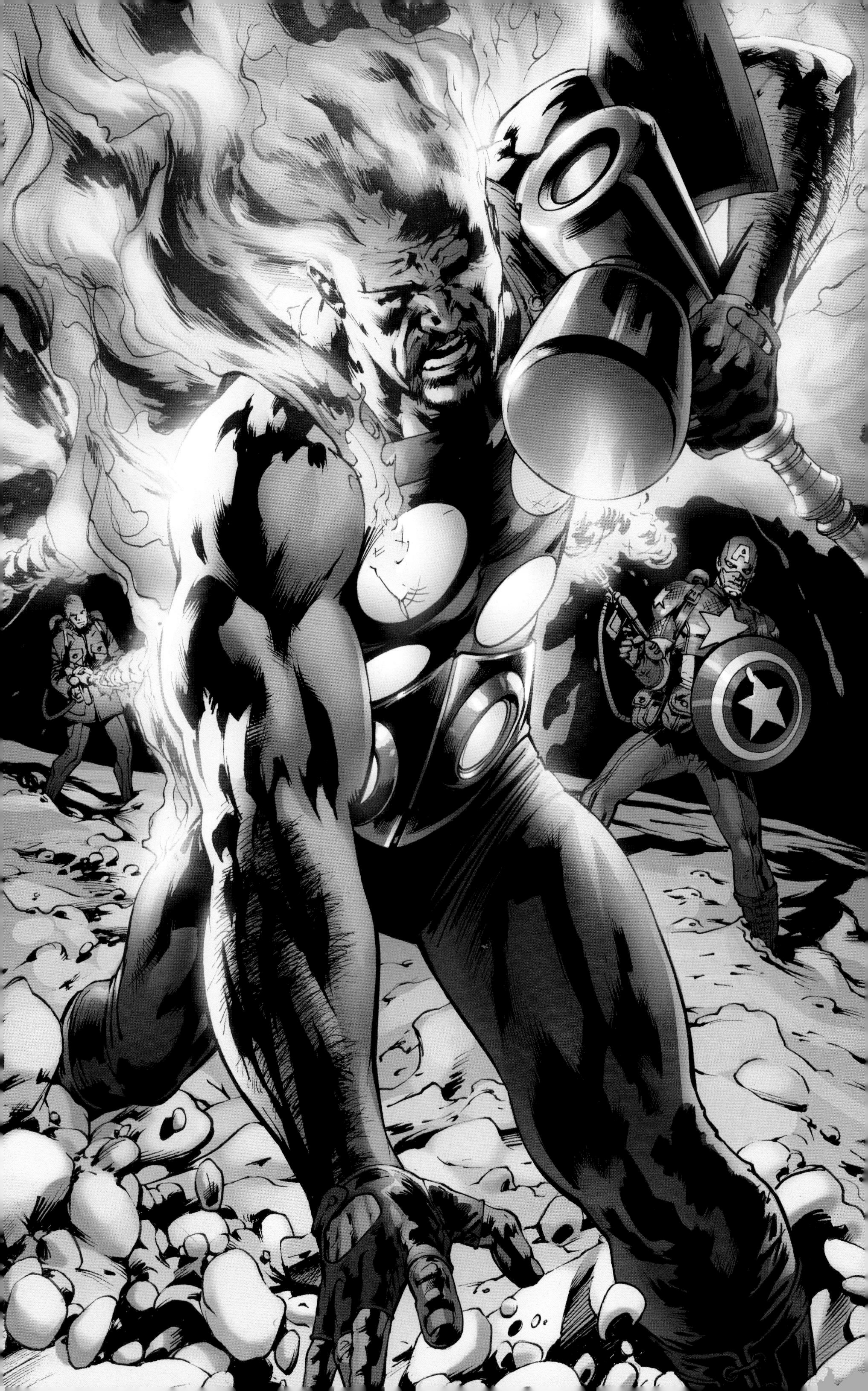

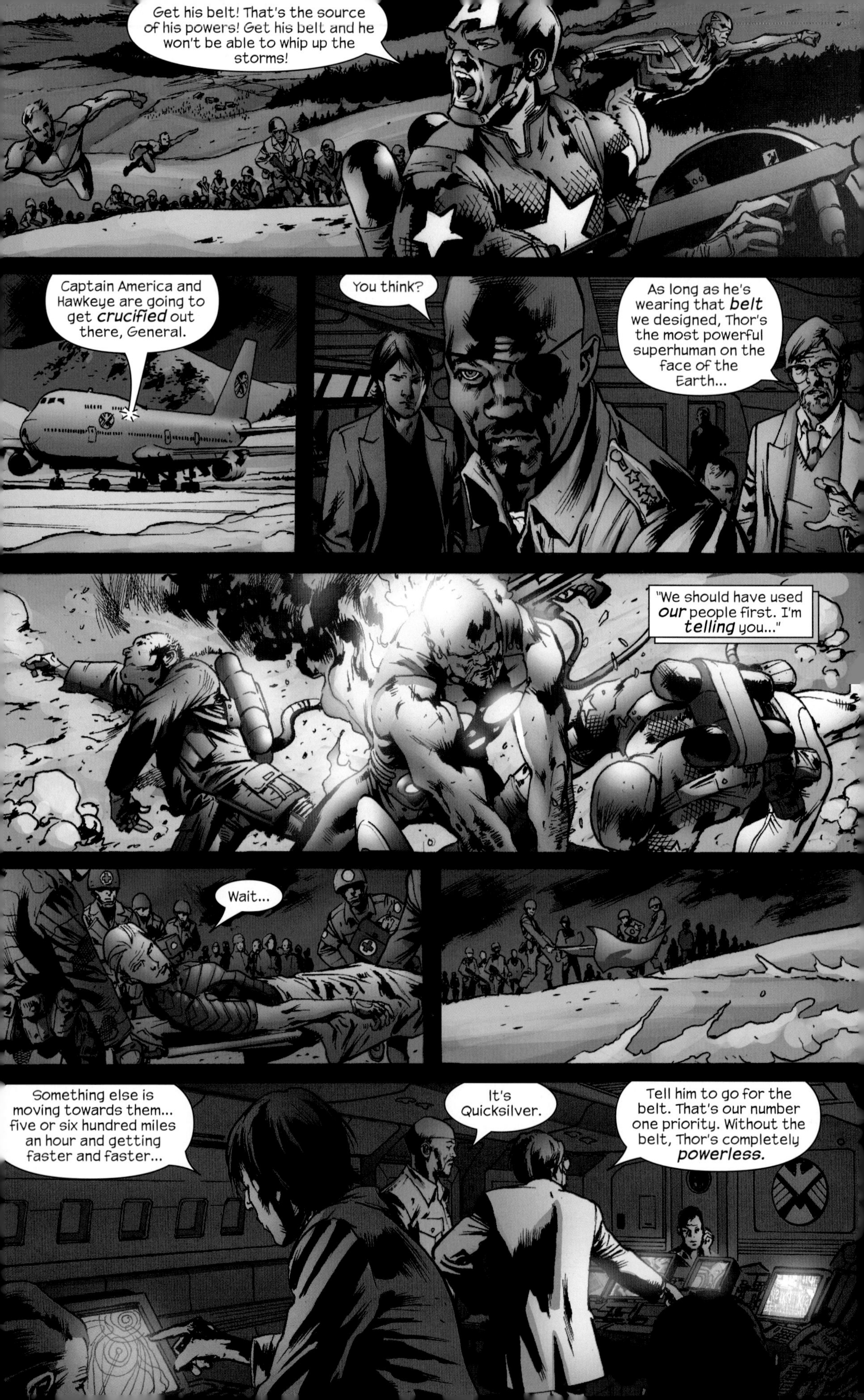
Get his belt! That's the source of his powers! Get his belt and he won't be able to whip up the storms!
Captain America and Hawkeye are going to get *crucified* out there, General.
You think?
As long as he's wearing that *belt* we designed, Thor's the most powerful superhuman on the face of the Earth...
"We should have used *our* people first. I'm *telling* you..."
Wait...
Something else is moving towards them... five or six hundred miles an hour and getting faster and faster...
It's Quicksilver.
Tell him to go for the belt. That's our number one priority. Without the belt, Thor's completely *powerless.*

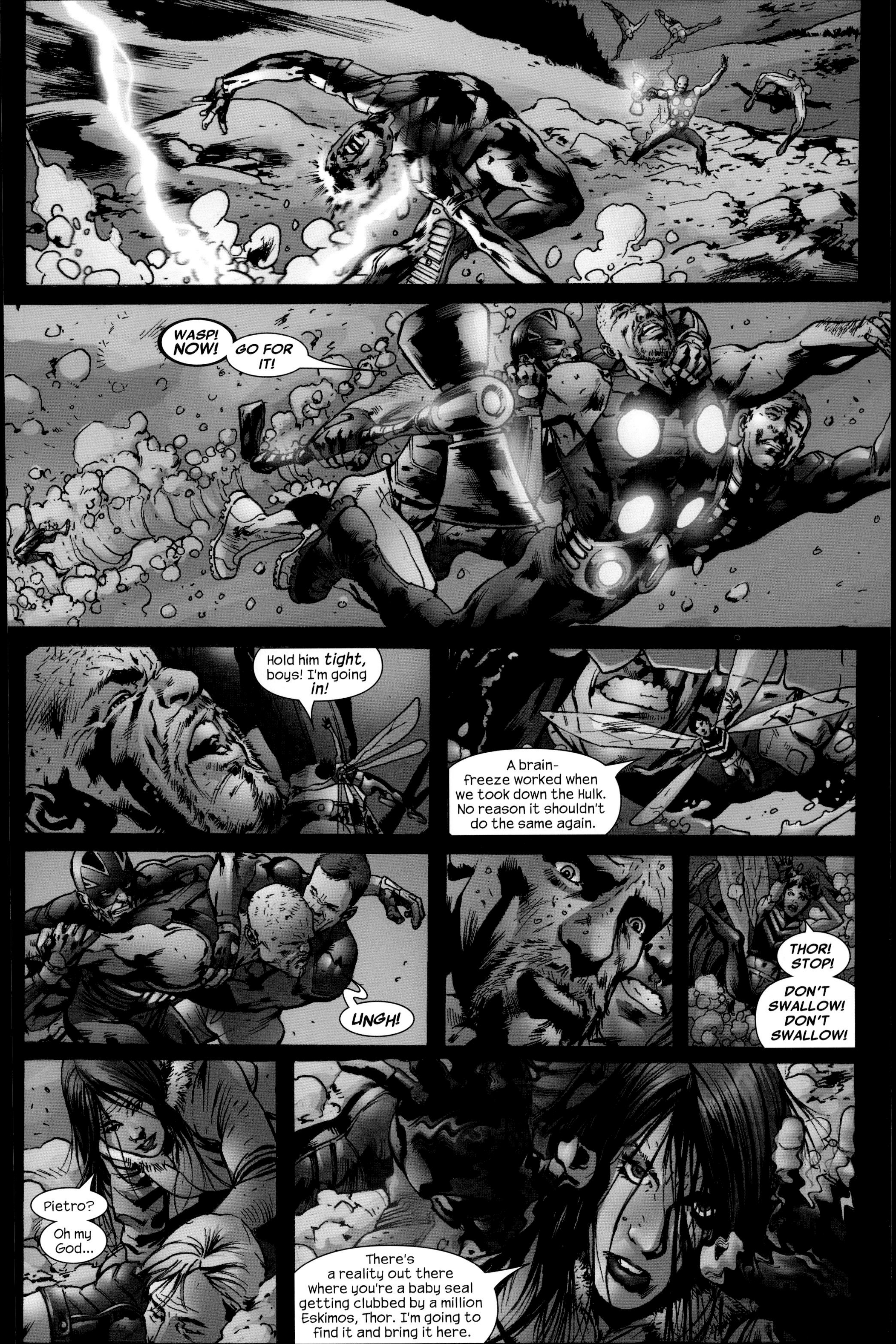
WASP! NOW!
GO FOR IT!
Hold him tight, boys! I'm going in!
A brain-freeze worked when we took down the Hulk. No reason it shouldn't do the same again.
UNGH!
THOR! STOP!
DON'T SWALLOW! DON'T SWALLOW!
Pietro?
Oh my God...
There's a reality out there where you're a baby seal getting clubbed by a million Eskimos, Thor. I'm going to find it and bring it here.

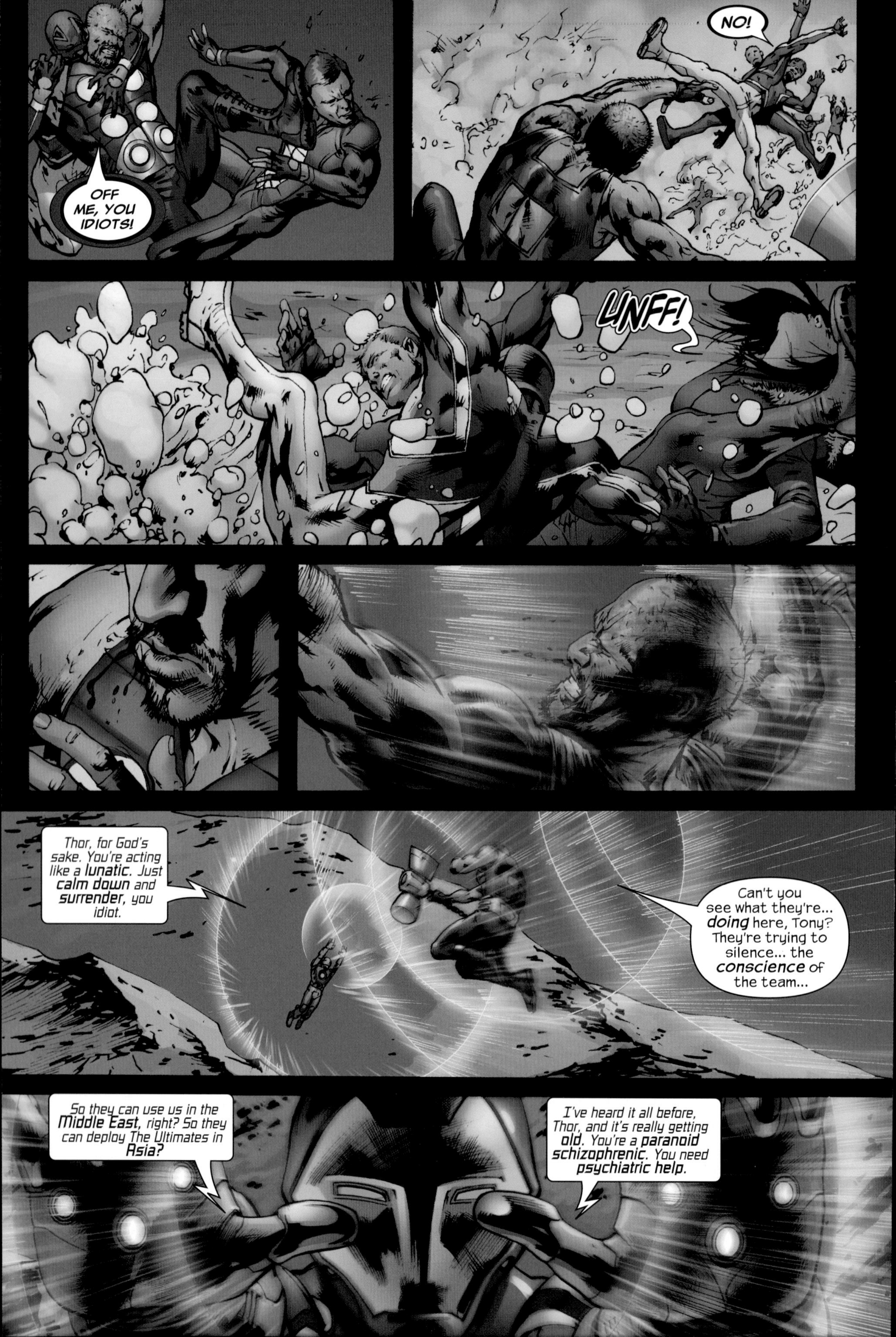
OFF ME, YOU IDIOTS!
NO!
UNFF!
Thor, for God's sake. You're acting like a lunatic. Just calm down and surrender, you idiot.
Can't you see what they're... doing here, Tony? They're trying to silence... the conscience of the team...
So they can use us in the Middle East, right? So they can deploy The Ultimates in Asia?
I've heard it all before, Thor, and it's really getting old. You're a paranoid schizophrenic. You need psychiatric help.

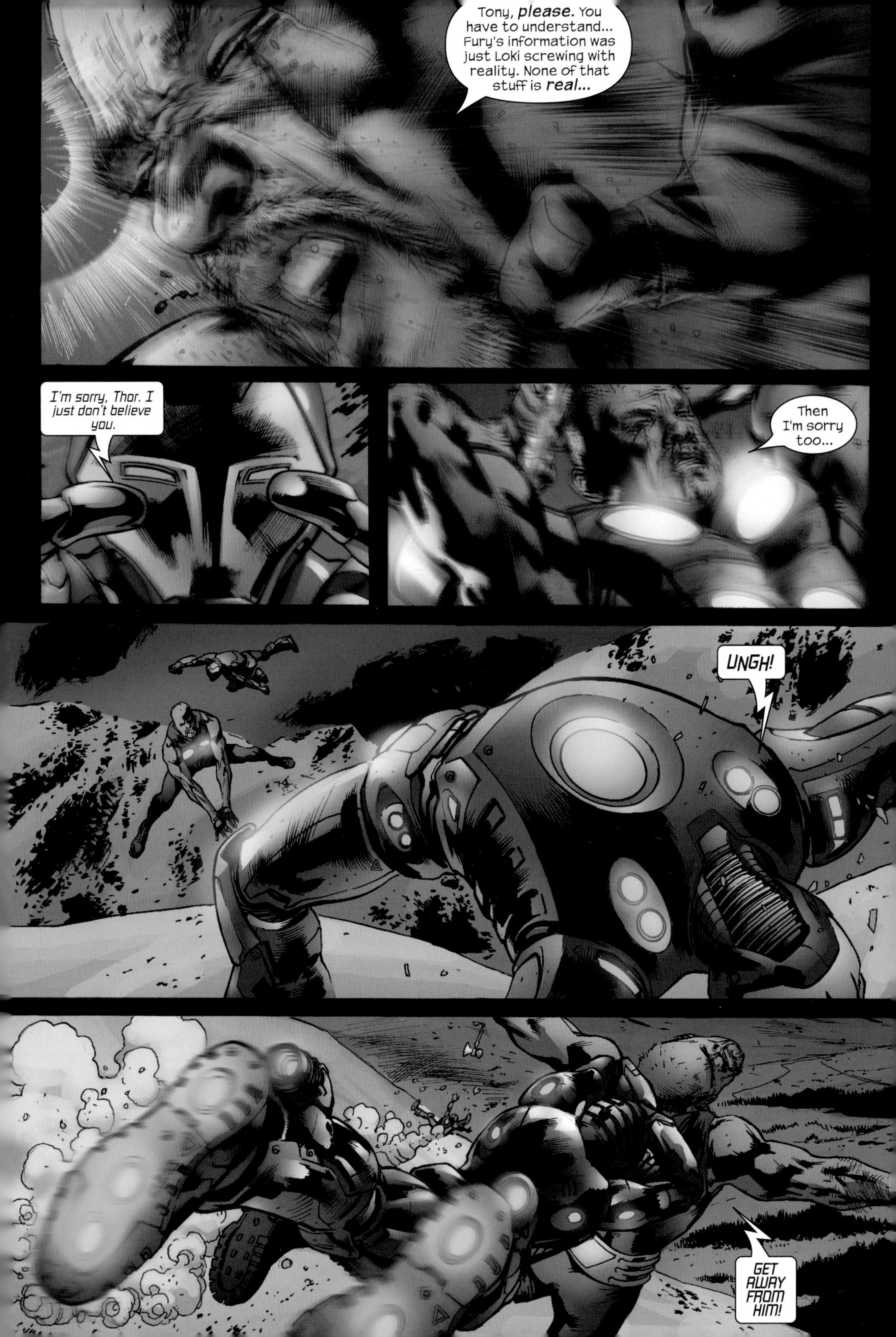

Tony, *please.* You have to understand... Fury's information was just Loki screwing with reality. None of that stuff is *real...*
I'm sorry, Thor. I just don't believe you.
Then I'm sorry too...
UNGH!
GET AWAY FROM HIM!

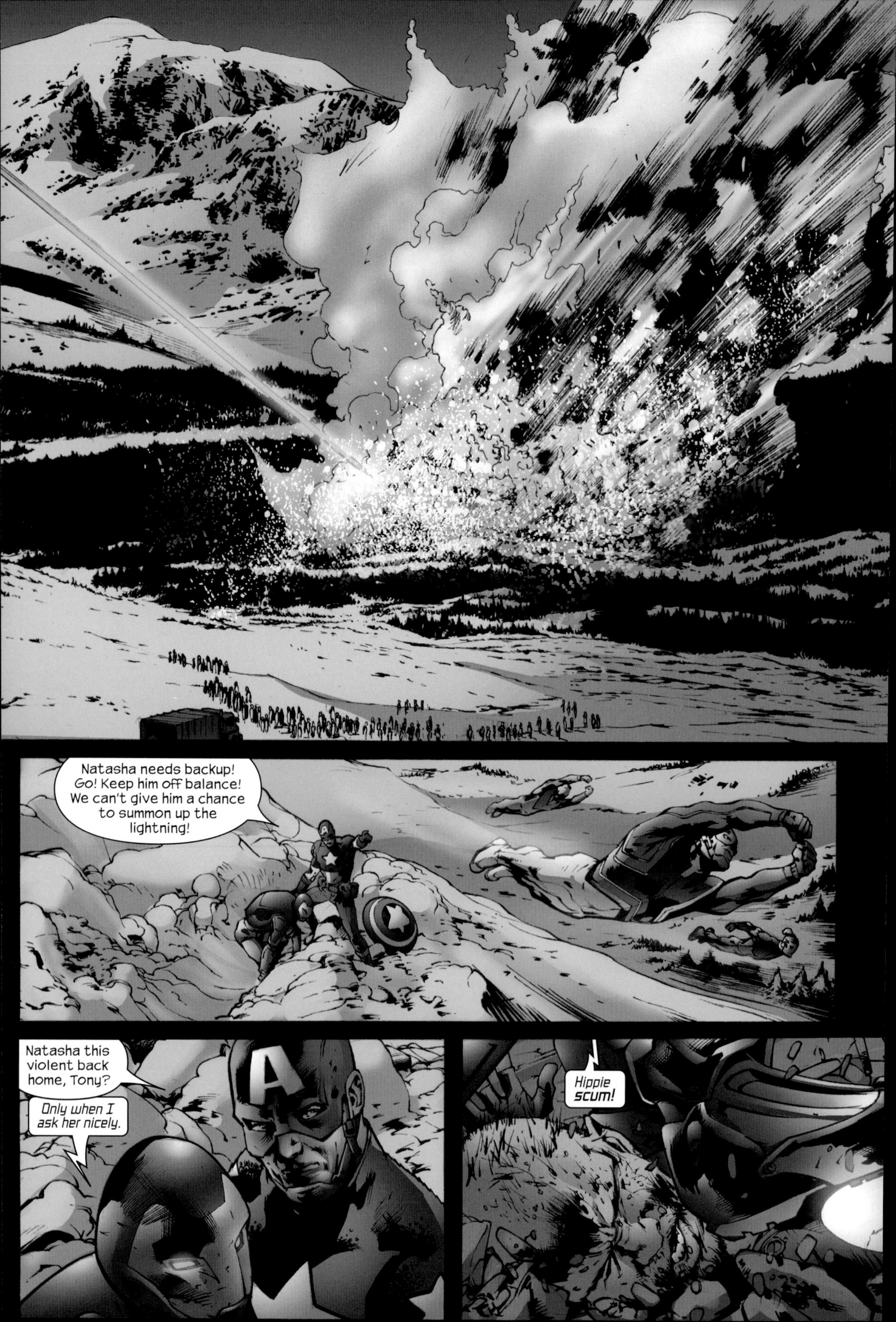

Natasha needs backup! Go! Keep him off balance! We can't give him a chance to summon up the lightning!
Natasha this violent back home, Tony?
Only when I ask her nicely.
Hippie scum!

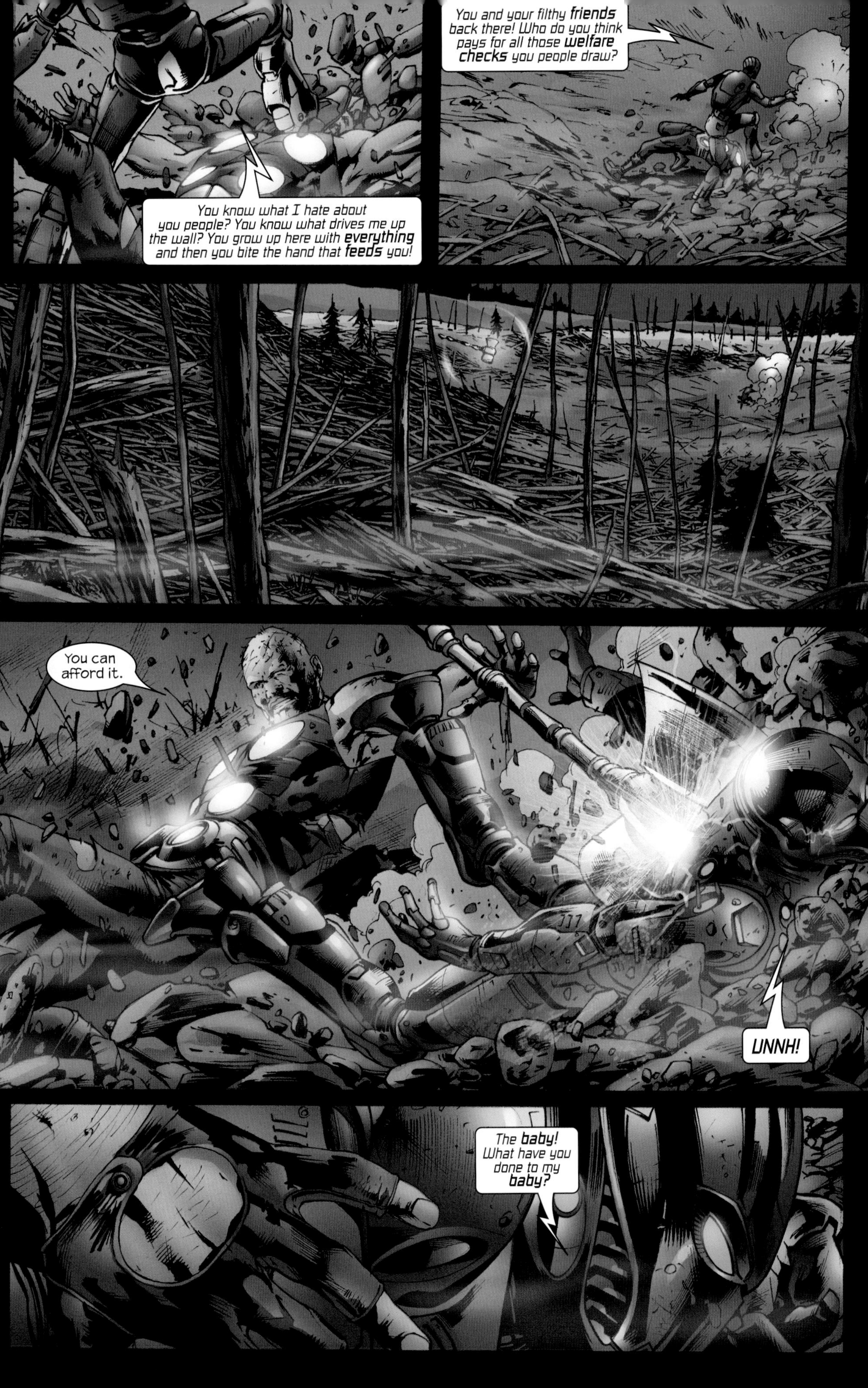
You know what I hate about you people? You know what drives me up the wall? You grow up here with everything and then you bite the hand that feeds you!
You and your filthy friends back there! Who do you think pays for all those welfare checks you people draw?
You can afford it.
UNNH!
The baby! What have you done to my baby?

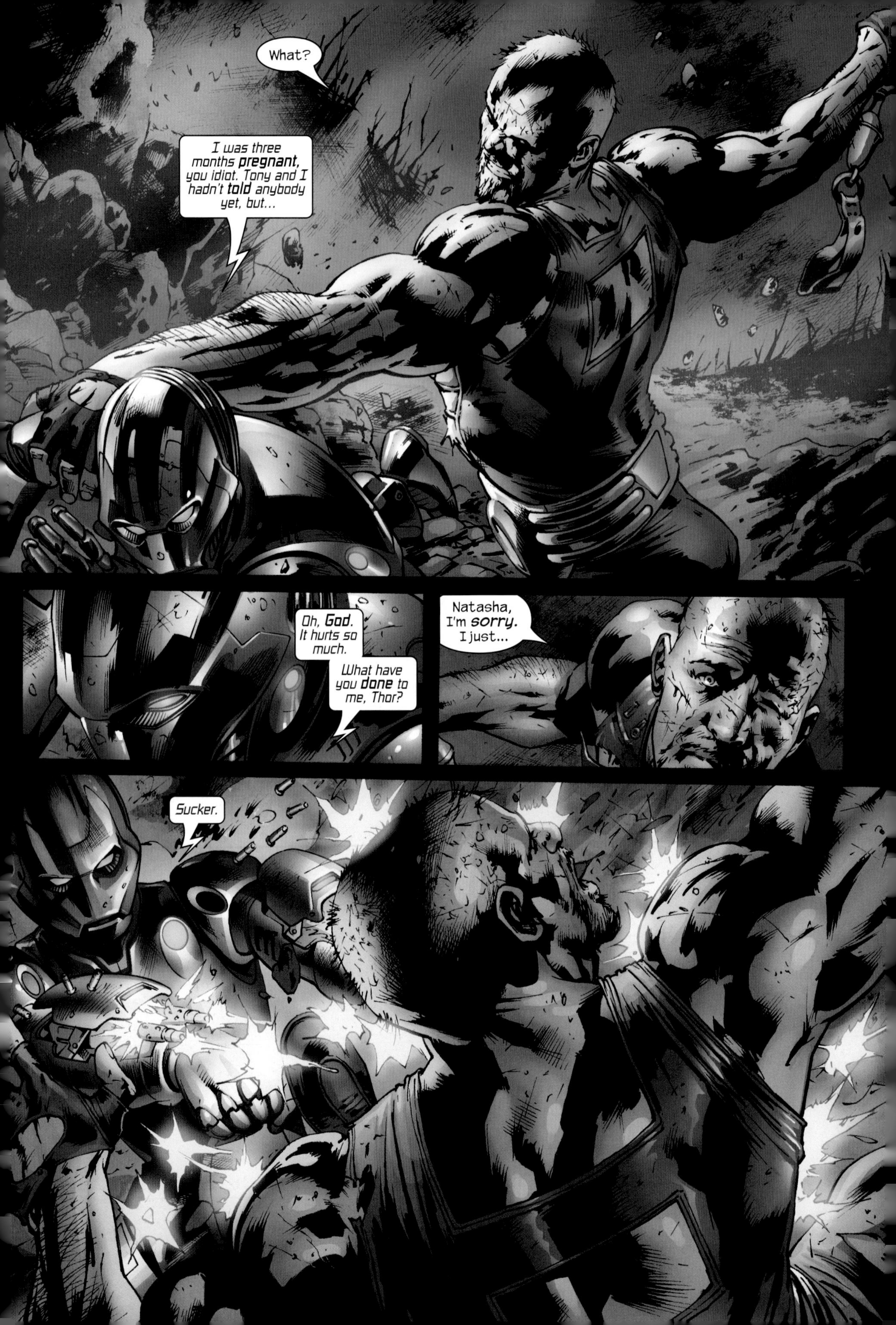
What?
I was three months **pregnant**, you idiot. Tony and I hadn't **told** anybody yet, but...
Oh, **God**. It hurts so much.
What have you **done** to me, Thor?
Natasha, I'm **sorry.** I just...
Sucker.

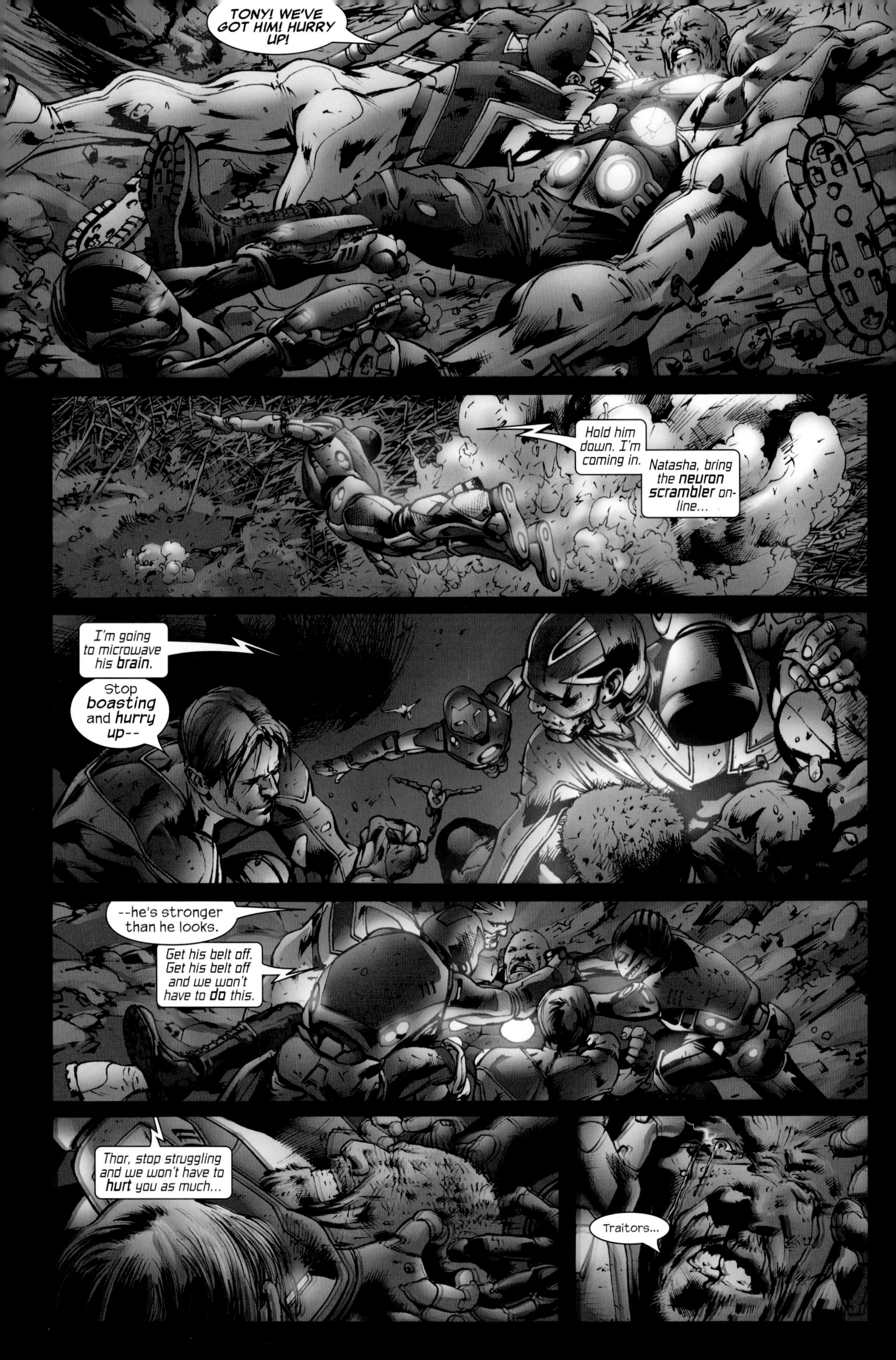
TONY! WE'VE GOT HIM! HURRY UP!
Hold him down. I'm coming in.
Natasha, bring the neuron scrambler on-line...
I'm going to microwave his brain.
Stop boasting and hurry up--
--he's stronger than he looks.
Get his belt off. Get his belt off and we won't have to do this.
Thor, stop struggling and we won't have to hurt you as much...
Traitors...

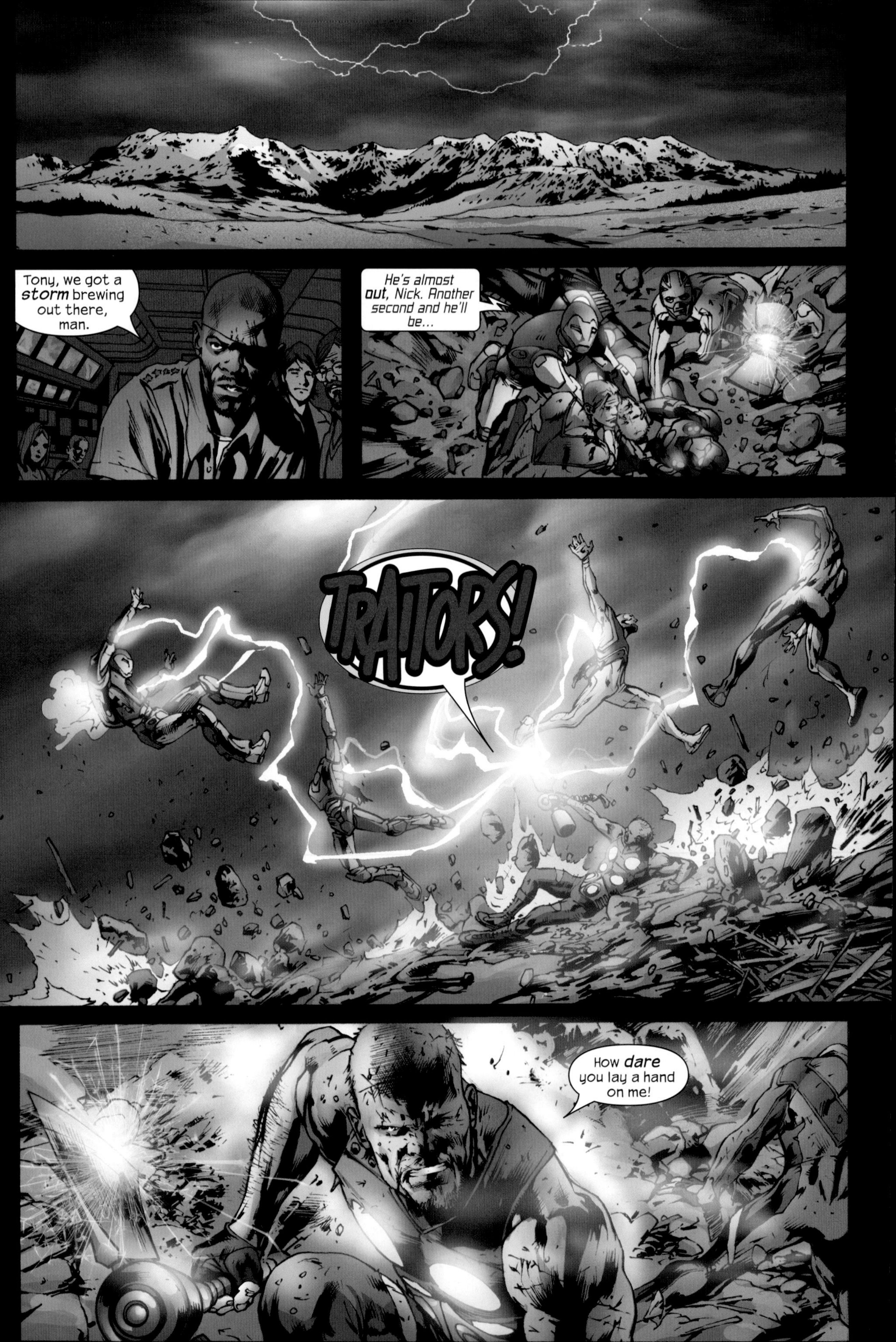

Tony, we got a storm brewing out there, man.
He's almost out, Nick. Another second and he'll be...
TRAITORS!
How dare you lay a hand on me!

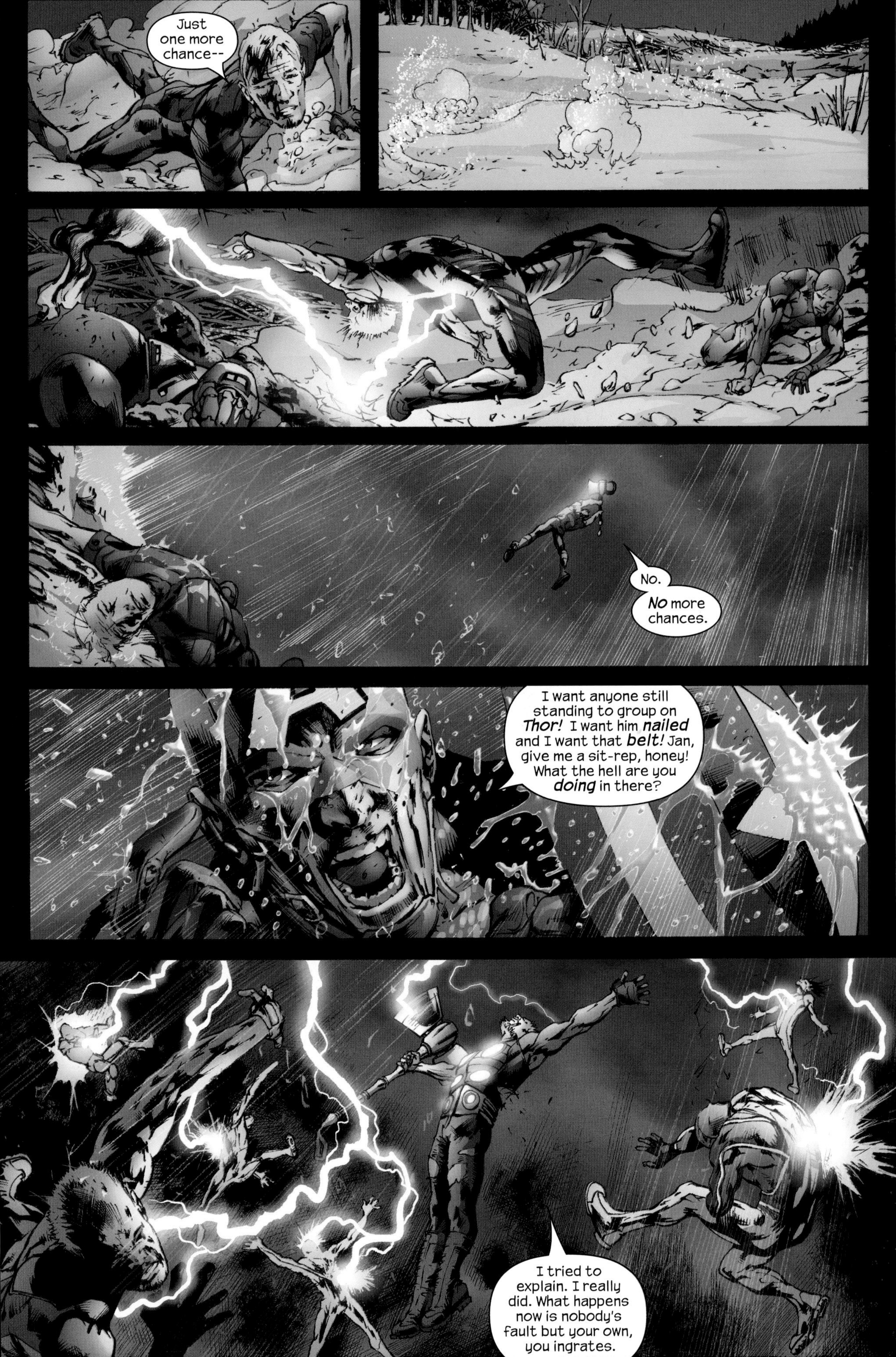
Just one more chance--
No. *No* more chances.
I want anyone still standing to group on *Thor!* I want him *nailed* and I want that *belt!* Jan, give me a sit-rep, honey! What the hell are you *doing* in there?
I tried to explain. I really did. What happens now is nobody's fault but your own, you ingrates.

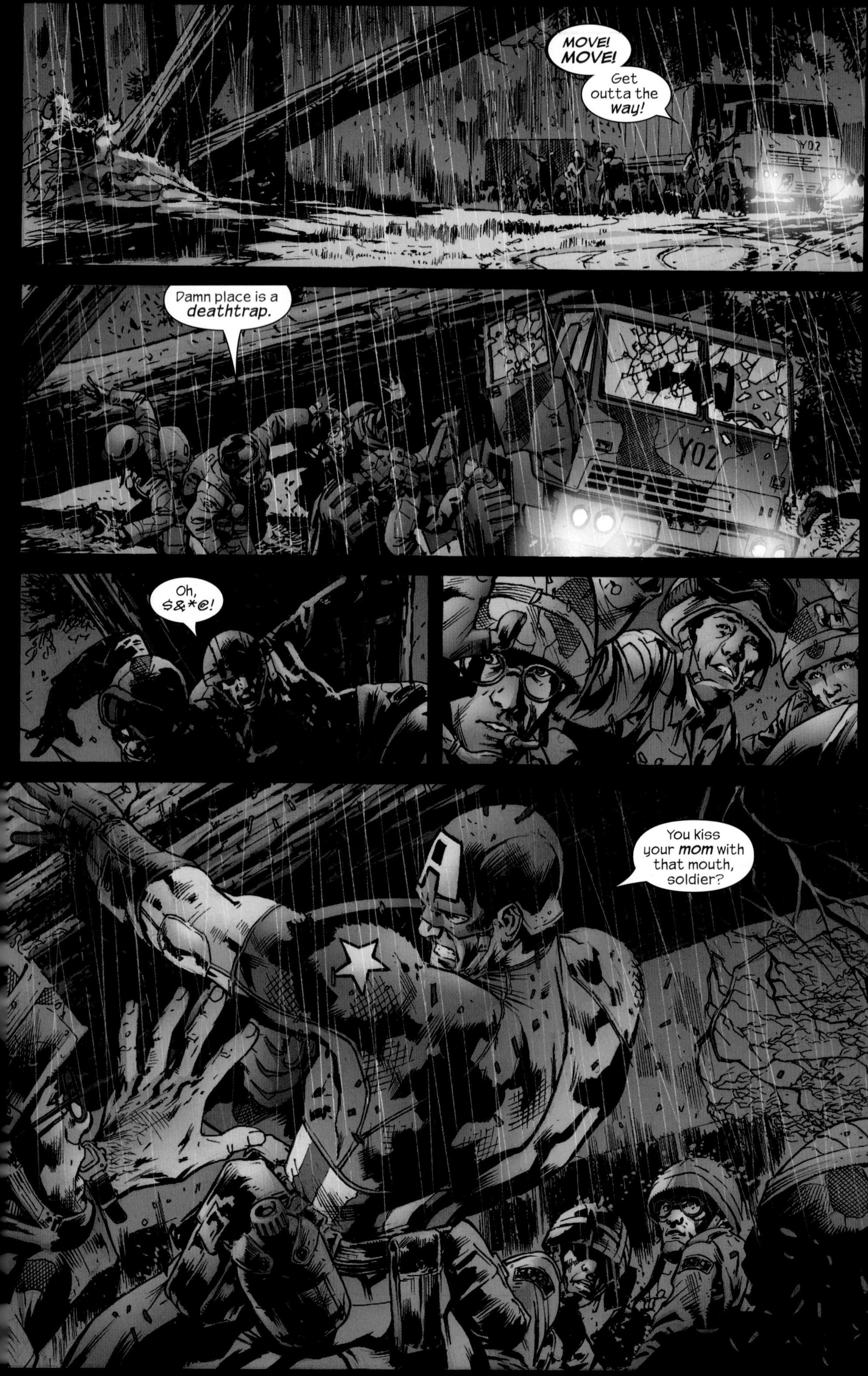
MOVE! MOVE!
Get outta the way!
Damn place is a deathtrap.
Oh, $&*@!
You kiss your mom with that mouth, soldier?

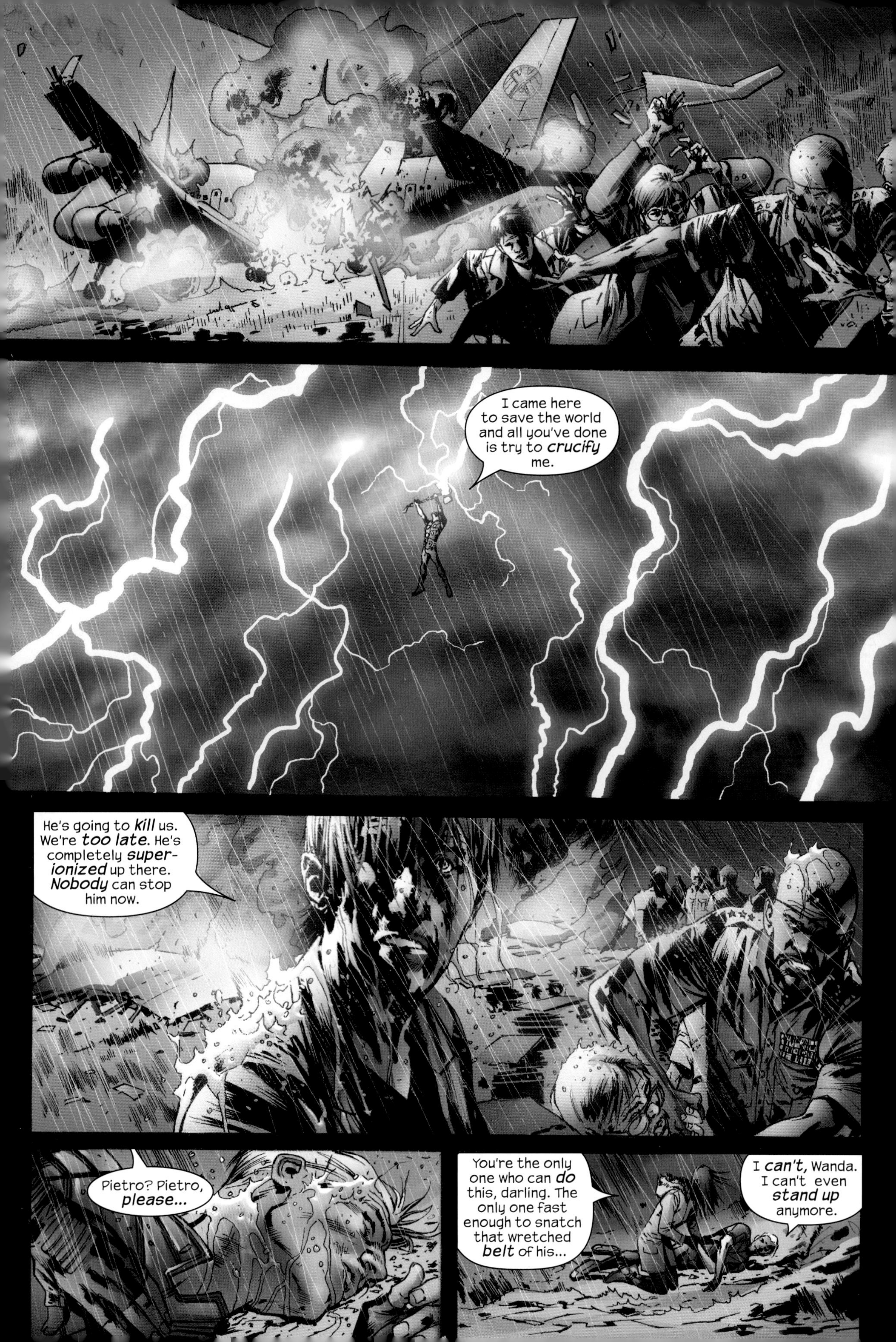
I came here to save the world and all you've done is try to *crucify* me.
He's going to *kill* us. We're *too late*. He's completely *super-ionized* up there. *Nobody* can stop him now.
Pietro? Pietro, *please...*
You're the only one who can *do* this, darling. The only one fast enough to snatch that wretched *belt* of his...
I *can't,* Wanda. I can't even *stand up* anymore.

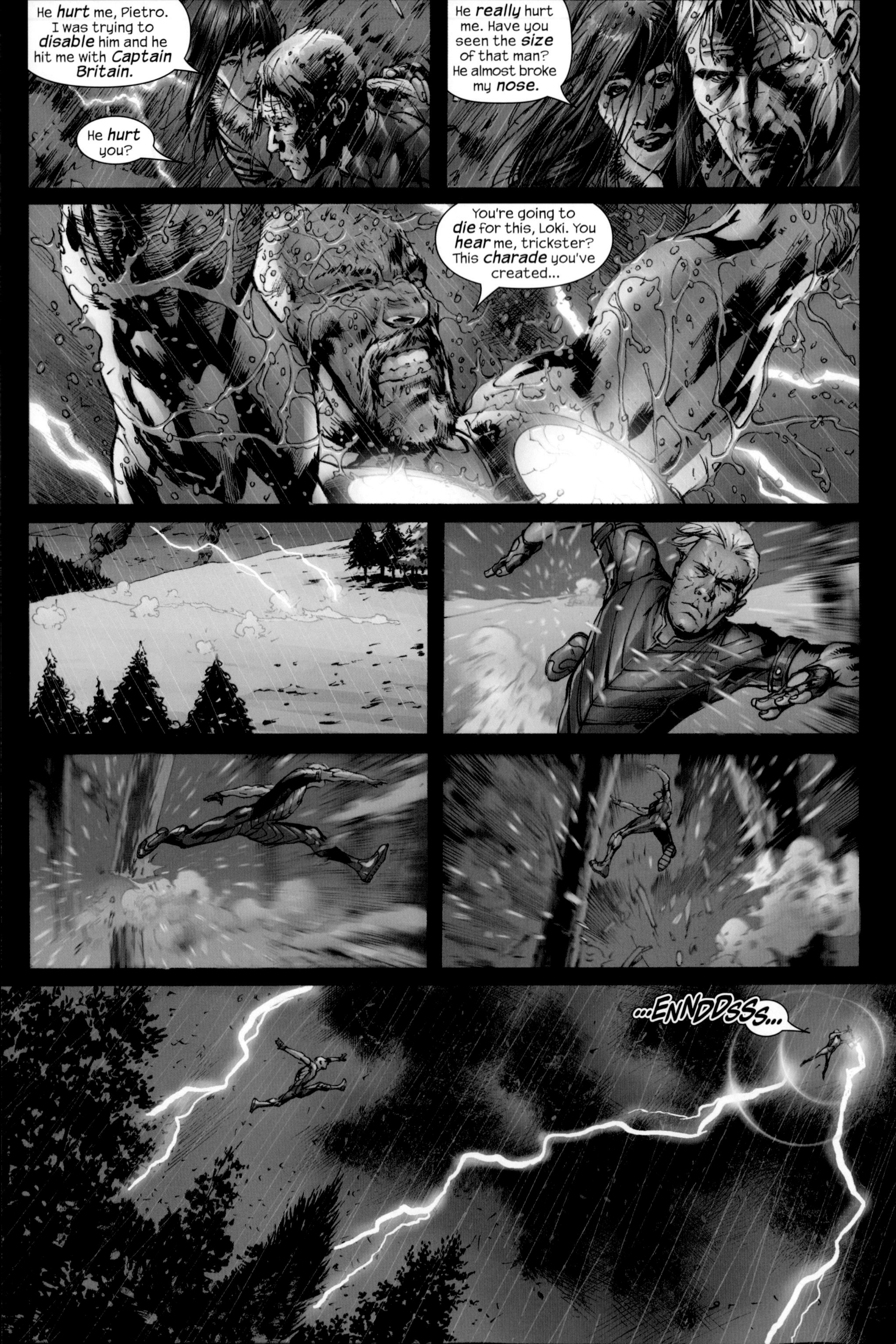

He hurt me, Pietro. I was trying to disable him and he hit me with Captain Britain.
He hurt you?
He really hurt me. Have you seen the size of that man? He almost broke my nose.
You're going to die for this, Loki. You hear me, trickster? This charade you've created...
...ENNDDSSS...

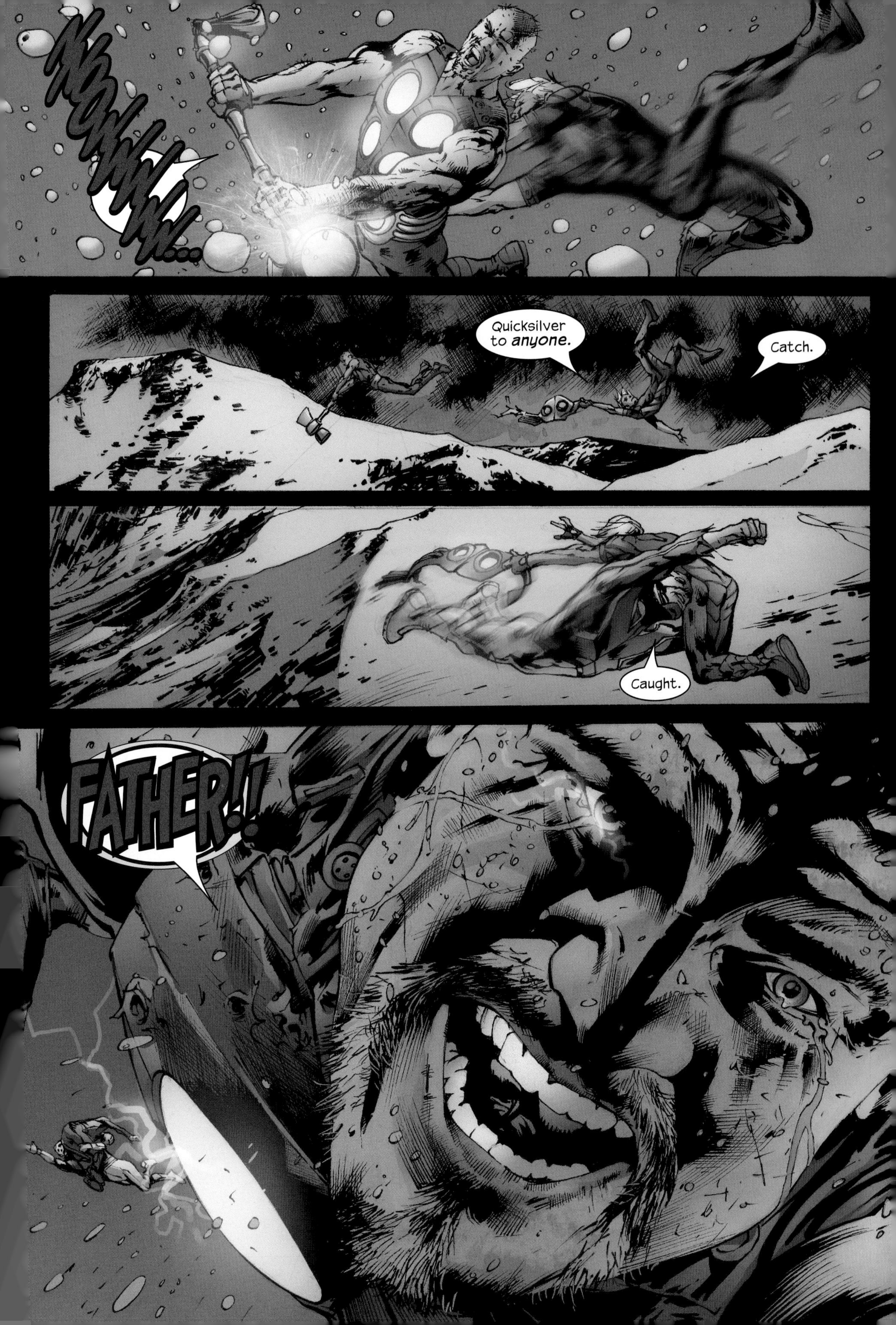
NNNNOOWWWW...
Quicksilver to *anyone.*
Catch.
Caught.
FATHER!!

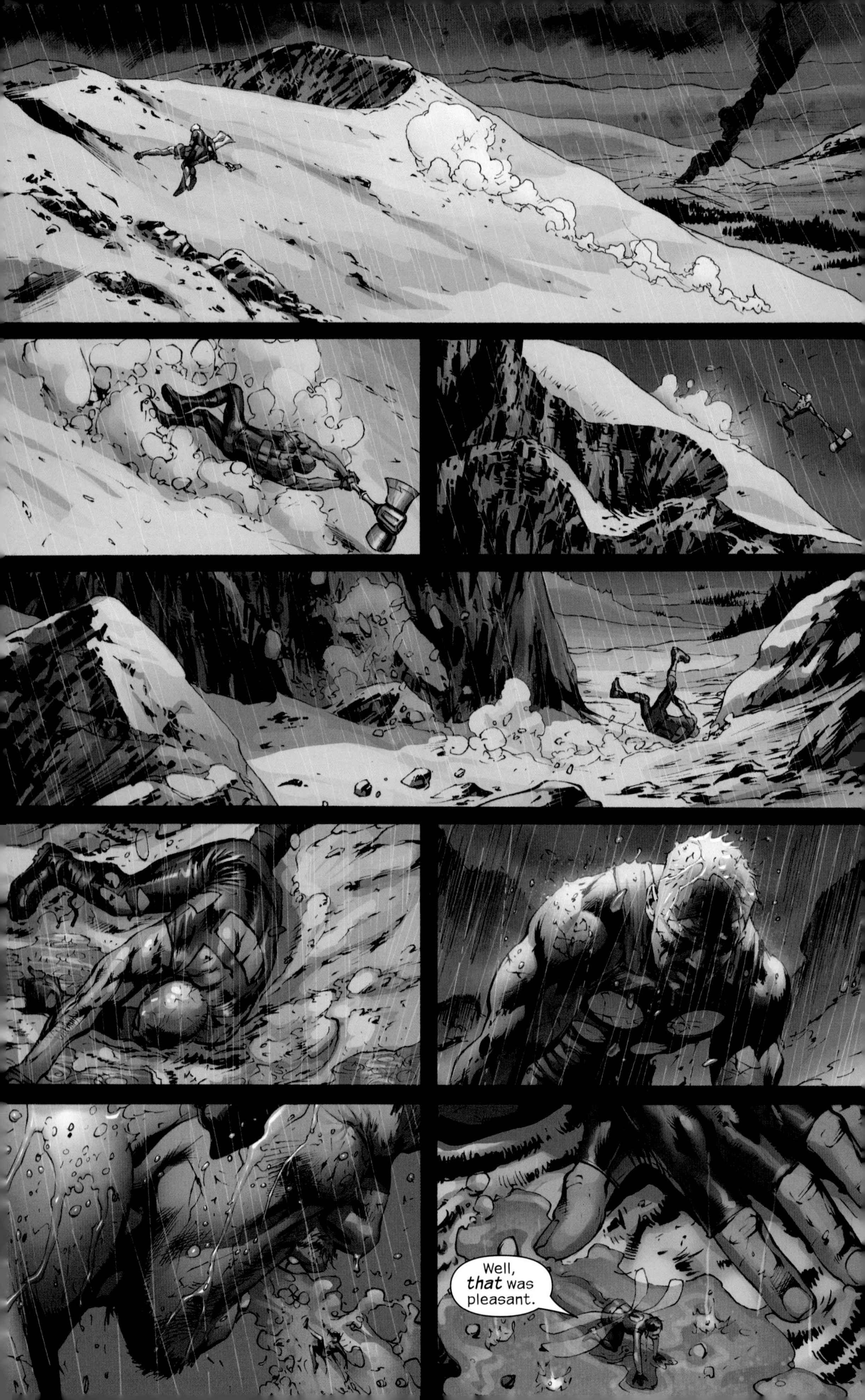
Well, *that* was pleasant.

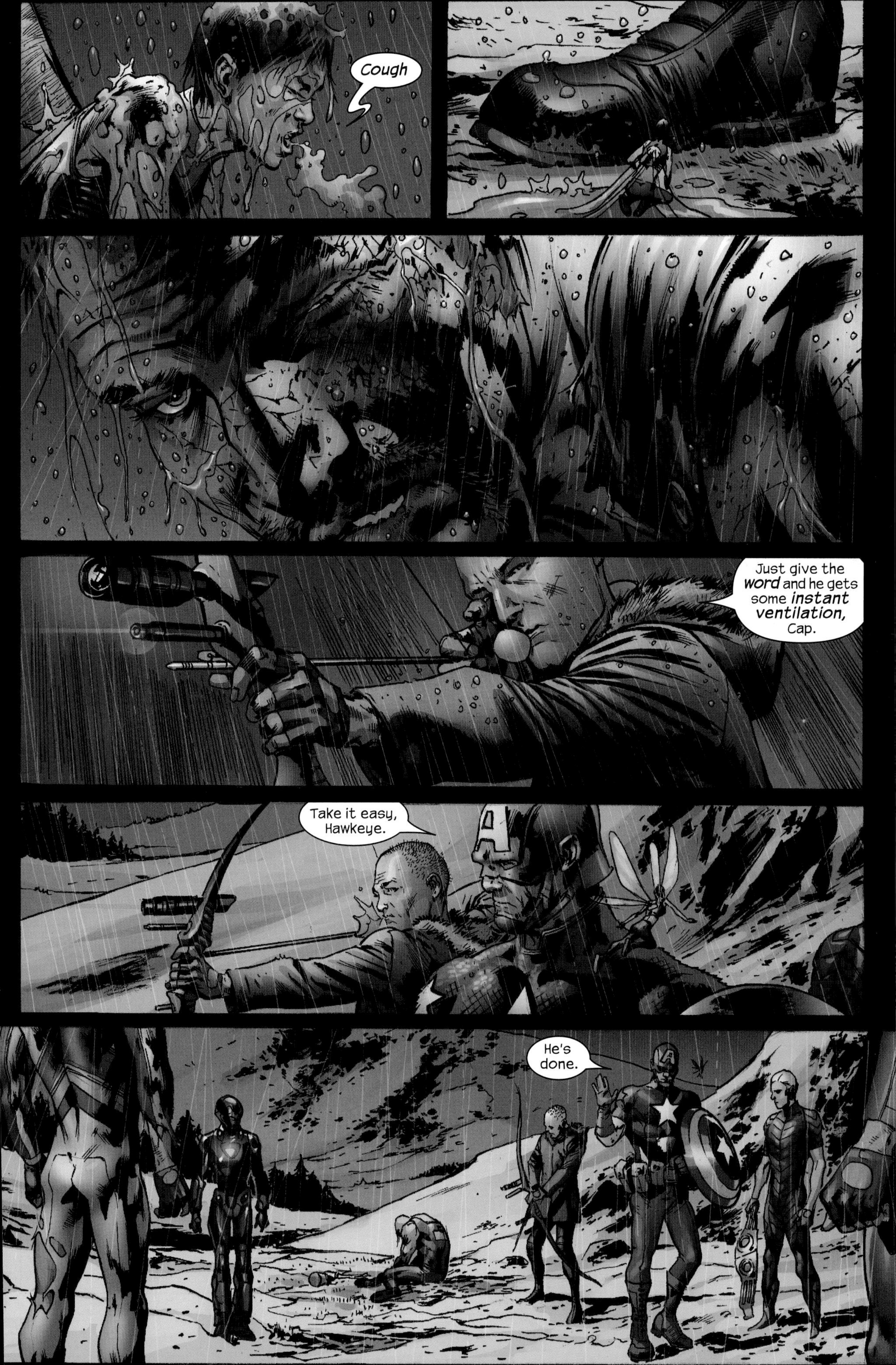
Cough
Just give the *word* and he gets some *instant ventilation,* Cap.
Take it easy, Hawkeye.
He's done.

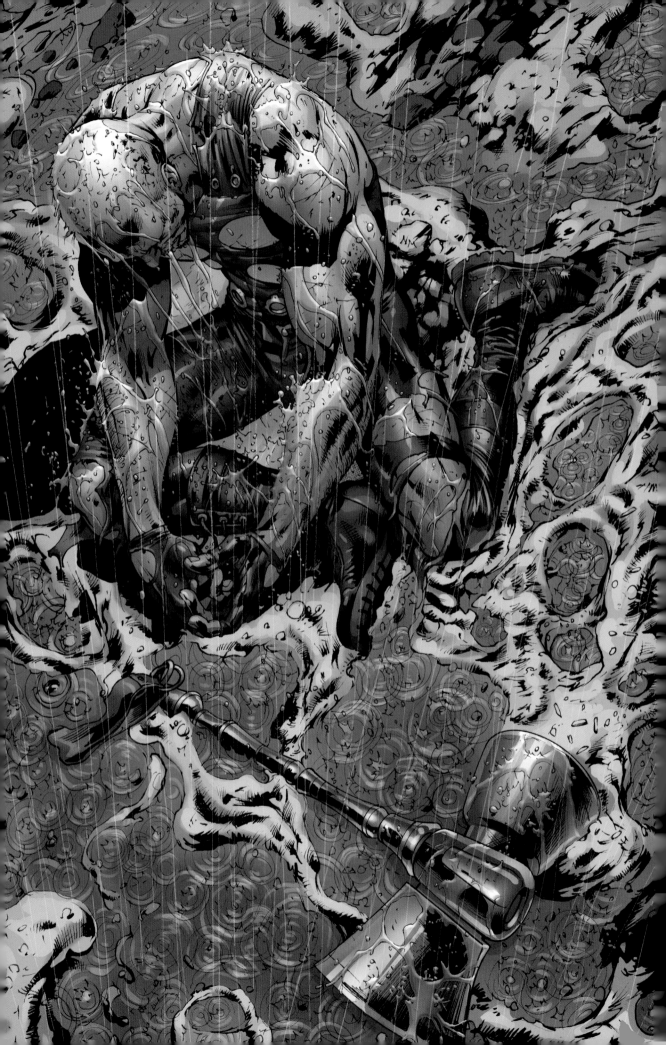

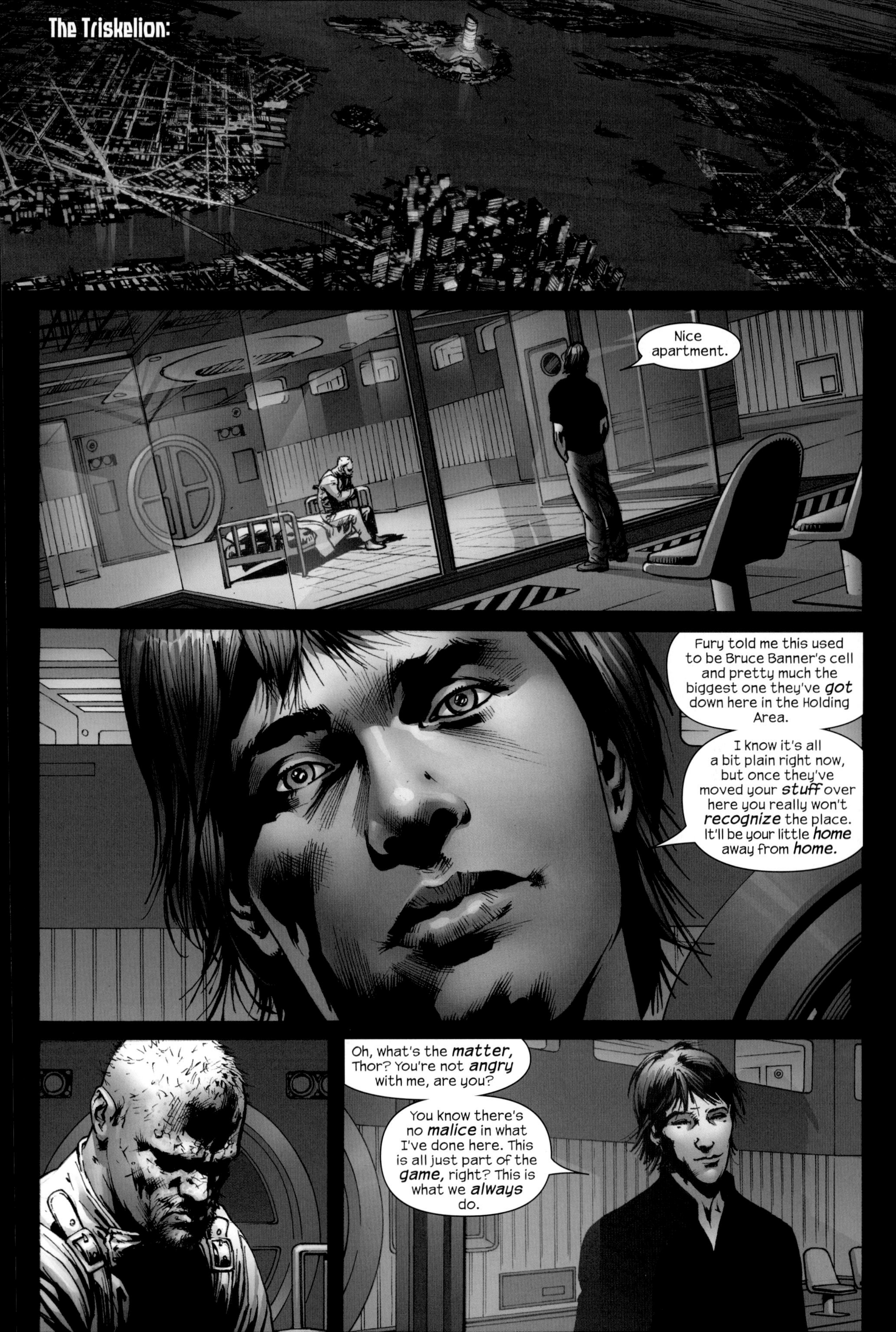

The Triskelion:
Nice apartment.
Fury told me this used to be Bruce Banner's cell and pretty much the biggest one they've got down here in the Holding Area.
I know it's all a bit plain right now, but once they've moved your stuff over here you really won't recognize the place. It'll be your little home away from home.
Oh, what's the matter, Thor? You're not angry with me, are you?
You know there's no malice in what I've done here. This is all just part of the game, right? This is what we always do.

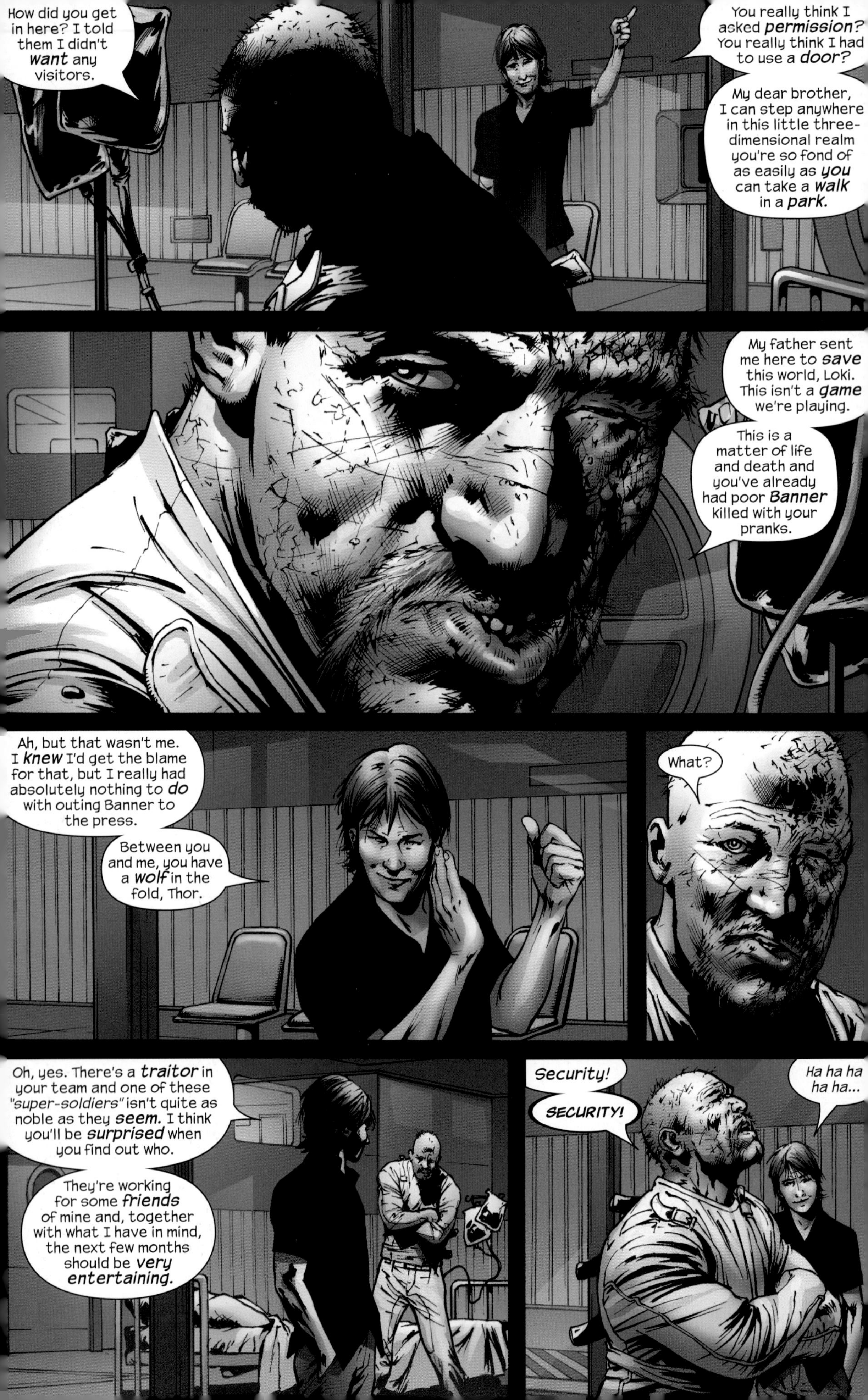
How did you get in here? I told them I didn't want any visitors.
You really think I asked permission? You really think I had to use a door?
My dear brother, I can step anywhere in this little three-dimensional realm you're so fond of as easily as you can take a walk in a park.
My father sent me here to save this world, Loki. This isn't a game we're playing.
This is a matter of life and death and you've already had poor Banner killed with your pranks.
Ah, but that wasn't me. I knew I'd get the blame for that, but I really had absolutely nothing to do with outing Banner to the press.
Between you and me, you have a wolf in the fold, Thor.
What?
Oh, yes. There's a traitor in your team and one of these "super-soldiers" isn't quite as noble as they seem. I think you'll be surprised when you find out who.
They're working for some friends of mine and, together with what I have in mind, the next few months should be very entertaining.
Security!
SECURITY!
Ha ha ha ha ha...

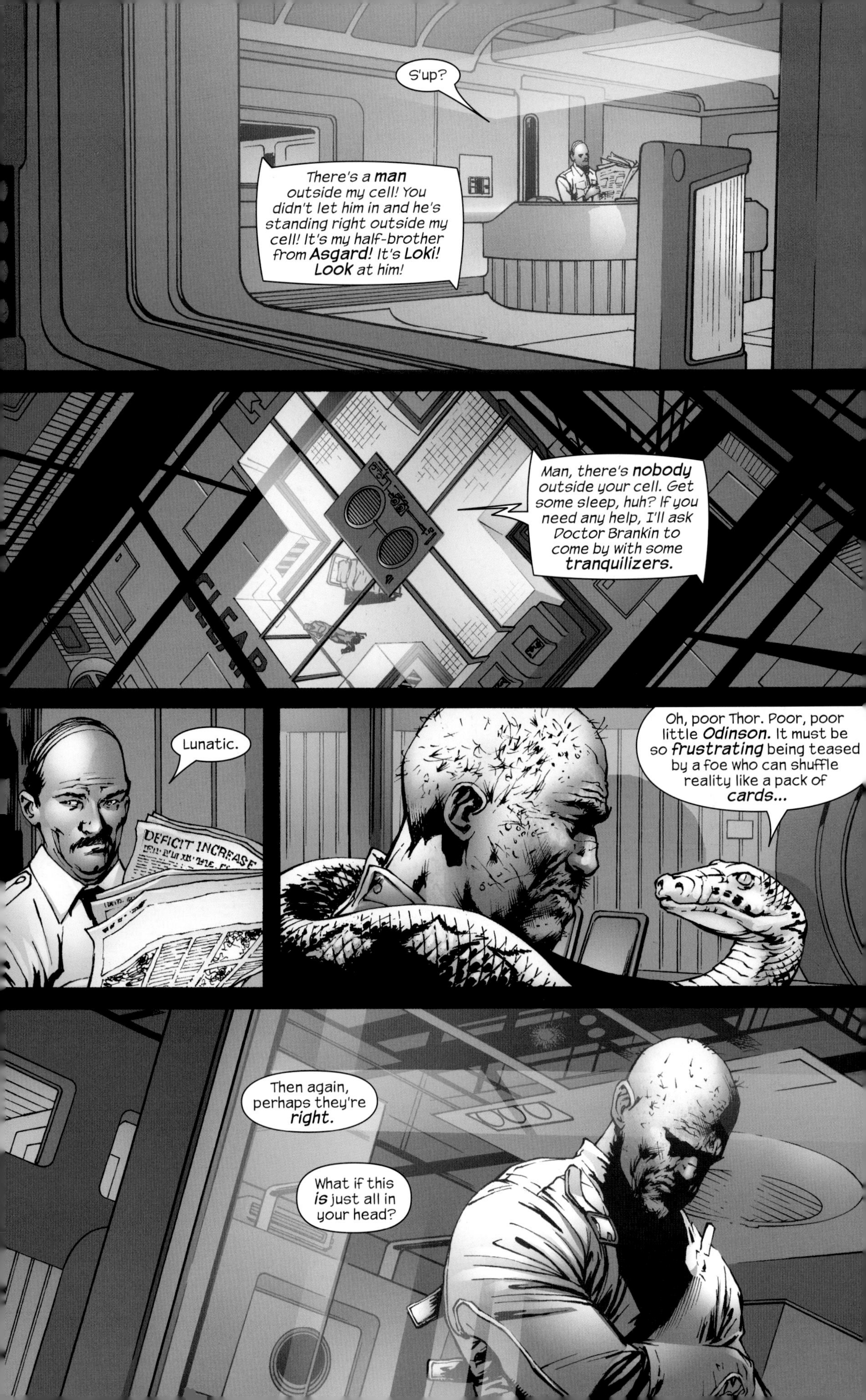
S'up?
There's a man outside my cell! You didn't let him in and he's standing right outside my cell! It's my half-brother from Asgard! It's Loki! Look at him!
Man, there's nobody outside your cell. Get some sleep, huh? If you need any help, I'll ask Doctor Brankin to come by with some tranquilizers.
CLEAR
Lunatic.
DEFICIT INCREASE
Oh, poor Thor. Poor, poor little Odinson. It must be so frustrating being teased by a foe who can shuffle reality like a pack of cards...
Then again, perhaps they're right.
What if this is just all in your head?

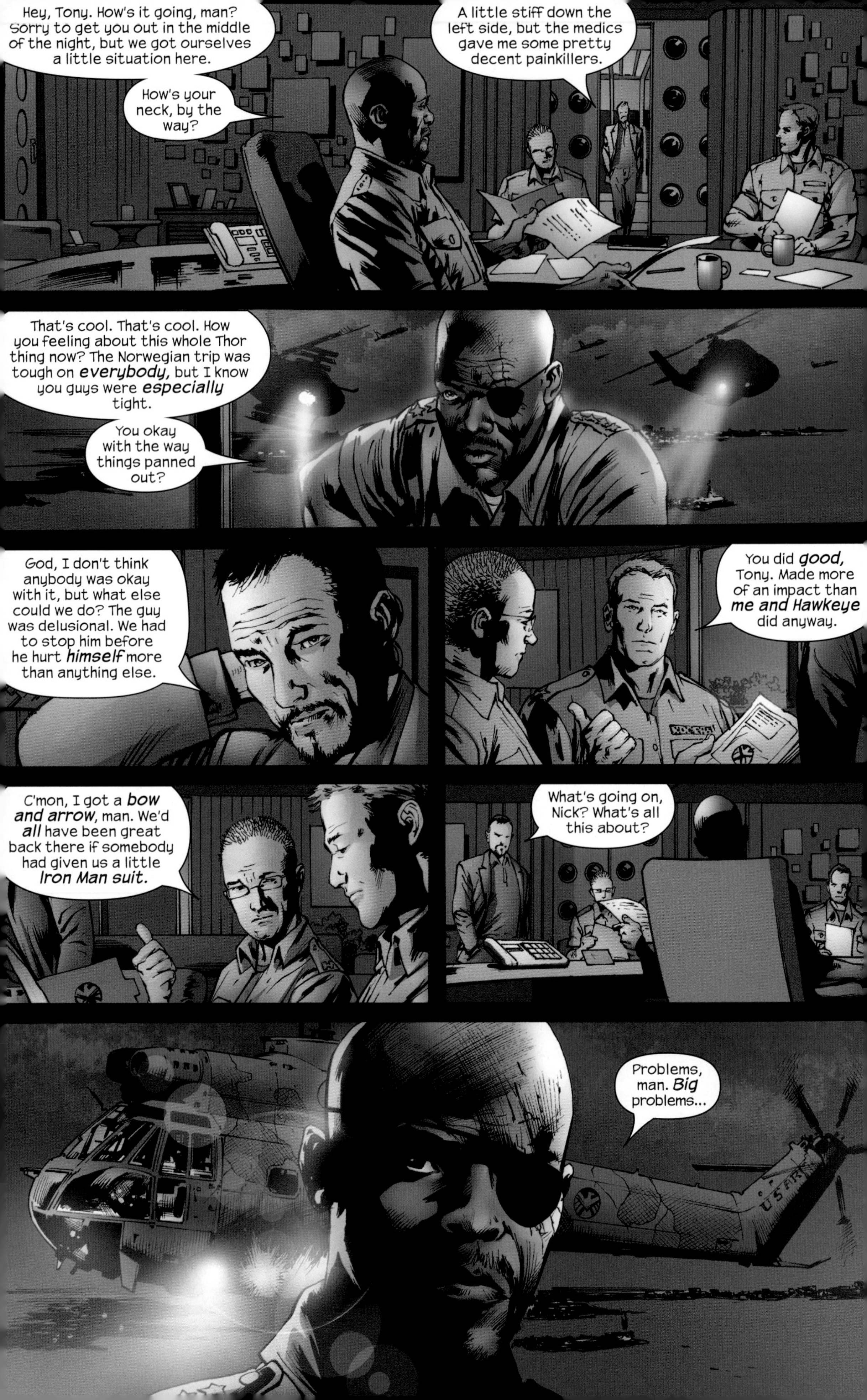
Hey, Tony. How's it going, man? Sorry to get you out in the middle of the night, but we got ourselves a little situation here.
How's your neck, by the way?
A little stiff down the left side, but the medics gave me some pretty decent painkillers.
That's cool. That's cool. How you feeling about this whole Thor thing now? The Norwegian trip was tough on everybody, but I know you guys were especially tight.
You okay with the way things panned out?
God, I don't think anybody was okay with it, but what else could we do? The guy was delusional. We had to stop him before he hurt himself more than anything else.
You did good, Tony. Made more of an impact than me and Hawkeye did anyway.
C'mon, I got a bow and arrow, man. We'd all have been great back there if somebody had given us a little Iron Man suit.
What's going on, Nick? What's all this about?
Problems, man. Big problems...

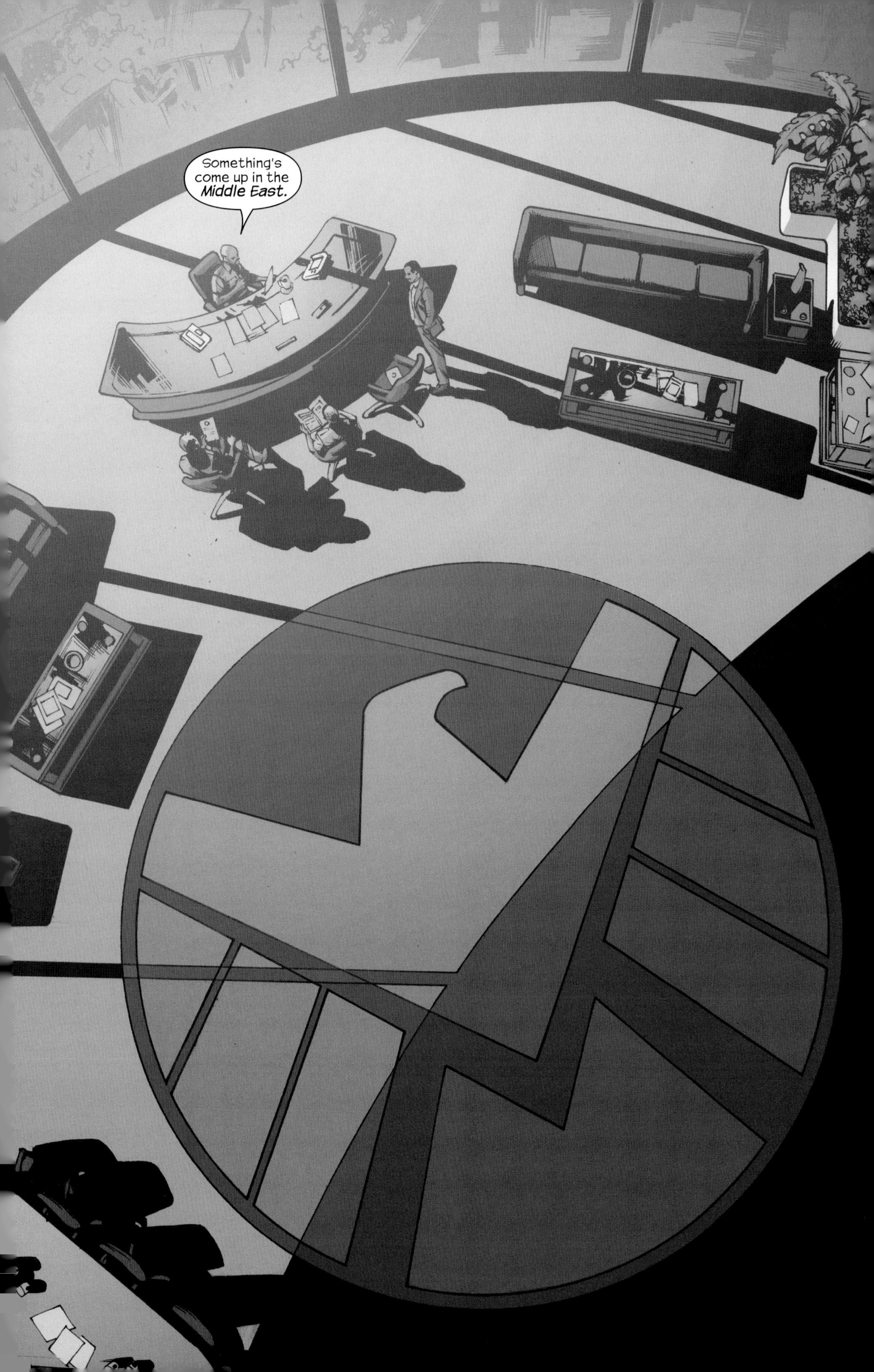
Something's come up in the *Middle East.*

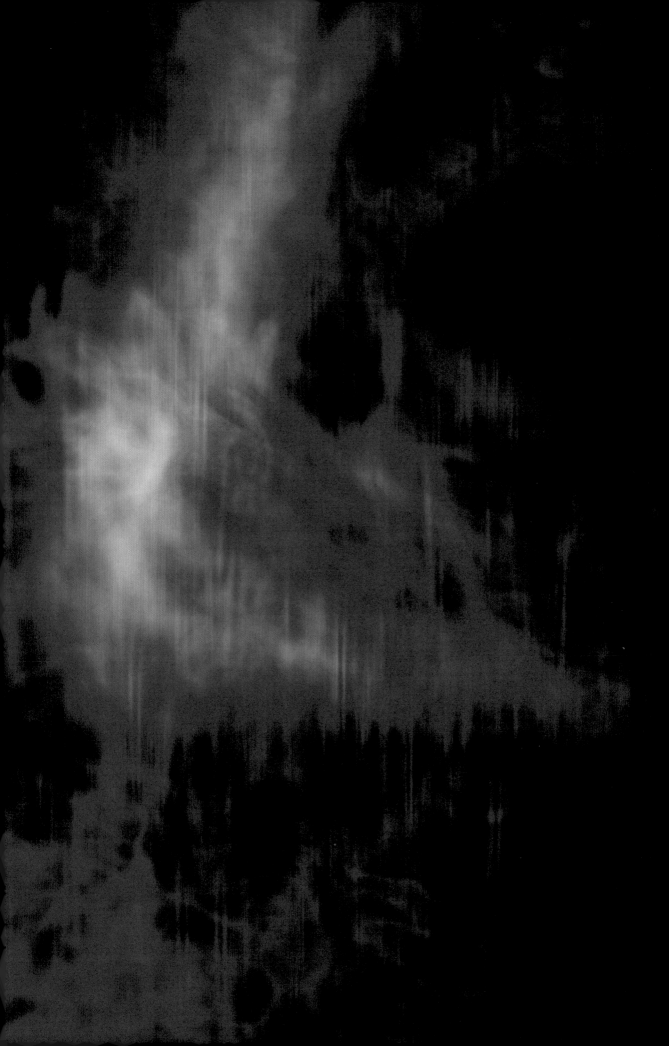

THE DEFENDERS

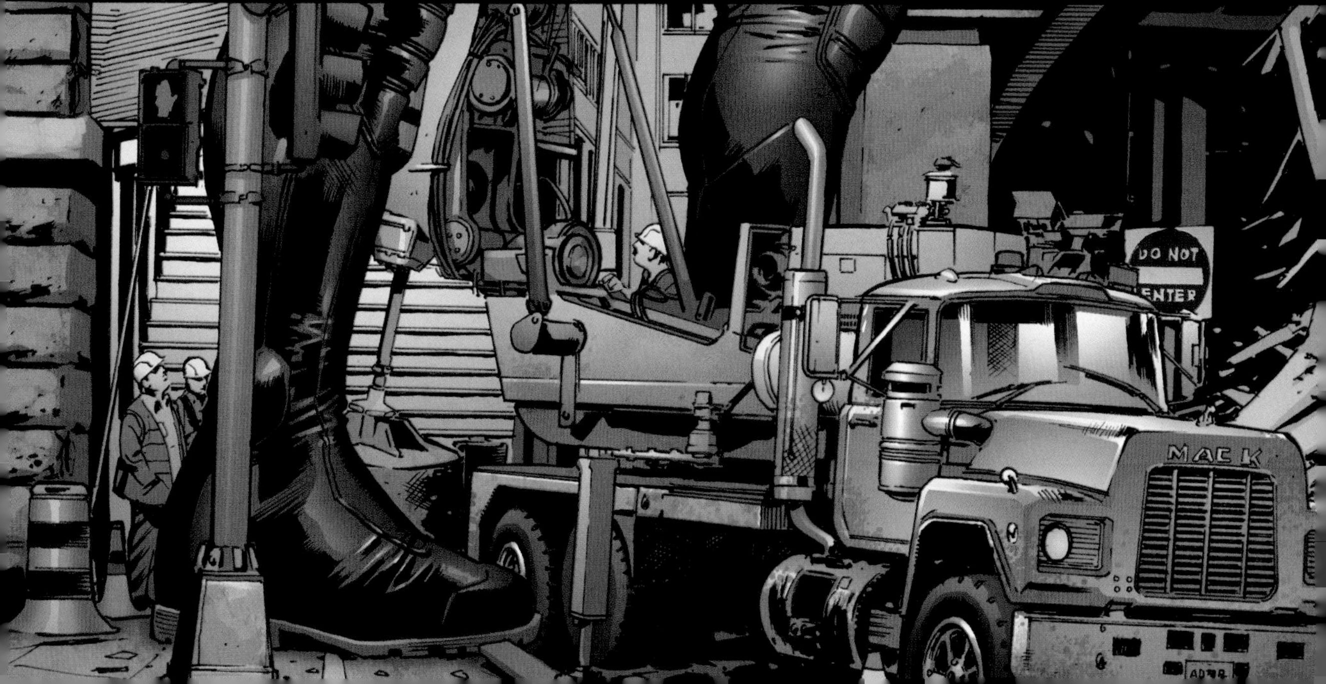
DO NOT
ENTER
MACK

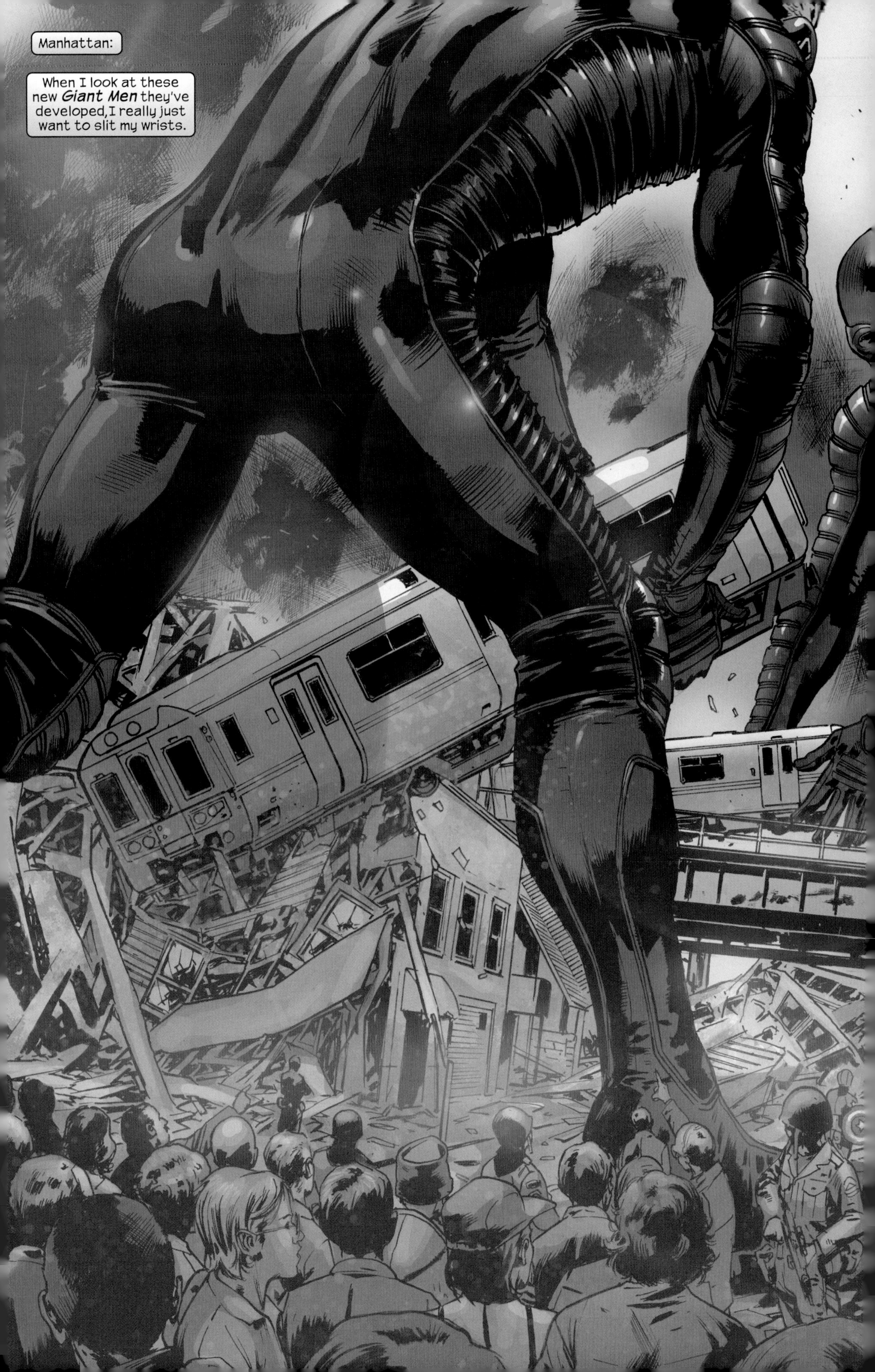
Manhattan:
When I look at these new *Giant Men* they've developed, I really just want to slit my wrists.

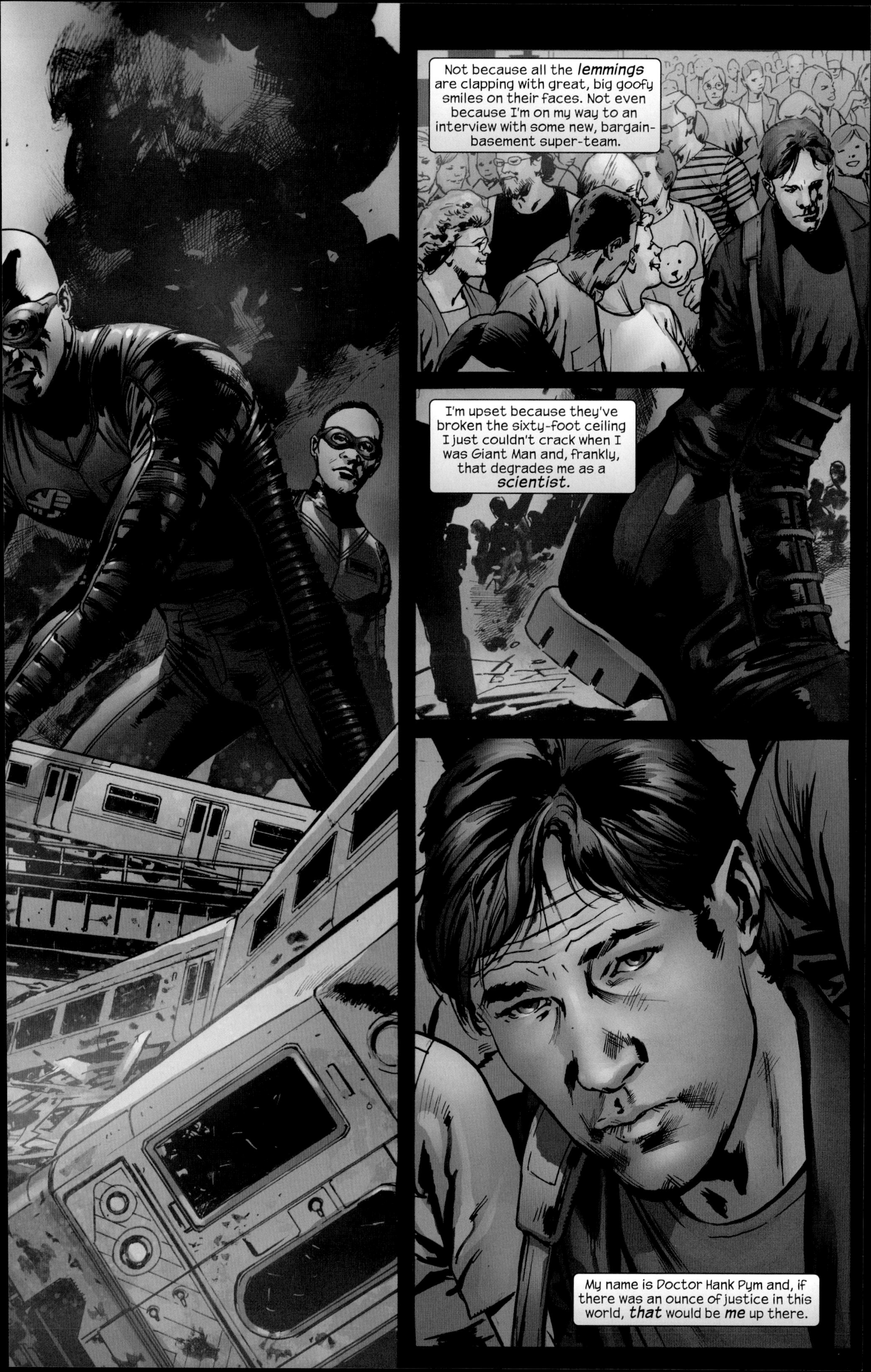
Not because all the lemmings are clapping with great, big goofy smiles on their faces. Not even because I'm on my way to an interview with some new, bargain-basement super-team.
I'm upset because they've broken the sixty-foot ceiling I just couldn't crack when I was Giant Man and, frankly, that degrades me as a scientist.
My name is Doctor Hank Pym and, if there was an ounce of justice in this world, that would be me up there.

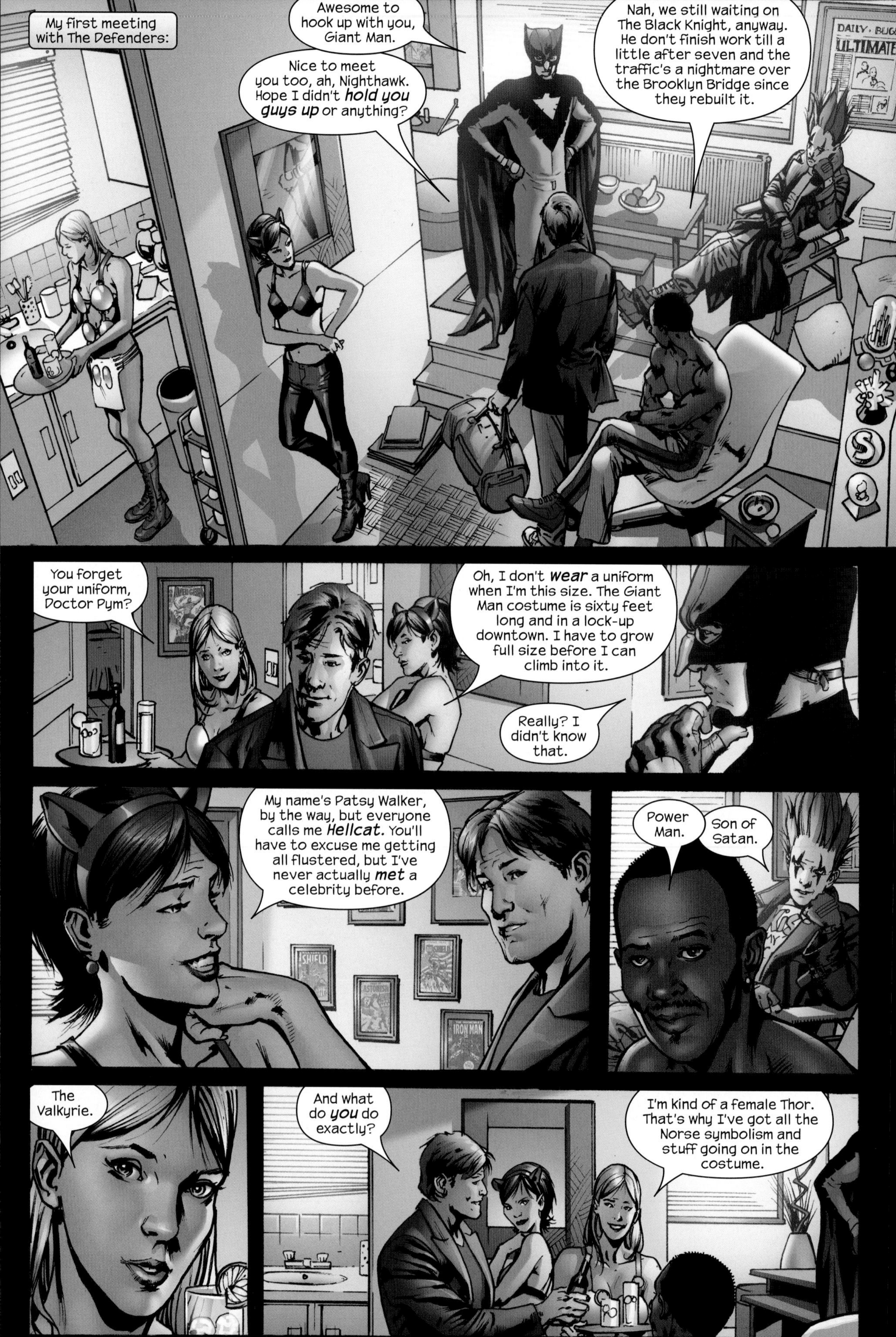
My first meeting with The Defenders:
Awesome to hook up with you, Giant Man.
Nice to meet you too, ah, Nighthawk. Hope I didn't hold you guys up or anything?
Nah, we still waiting on The Black Knight, anyway. He don't finish work till a little after seven and the traffic's a nightmare over the Brooklyn Bridge since they rebuilt it.
DAILY BUG
ULTIMATE
You forget your uniform, Doctor Pym?
Oh, I don't wear a uniform when I'm this size. The Giant Man costume is sixty feet long and in a lock-up downtown. I have to grow full size before I can climb into it.
Really? I didn't know that.
My name's Patsy Walker, by the way, but everyone calls me Hellcat. You'll have to excuse me getting all flustered, but I've never actually met a celebrity before.
SHIELD
ASTONISH
IRON MAN
Power Man.
Son of Satan.
The Valkyrie.
And what do you do exactly?
I'm kind of a female Thor. That's why I've got all the Norse symbolism and stuff going on in the costume.

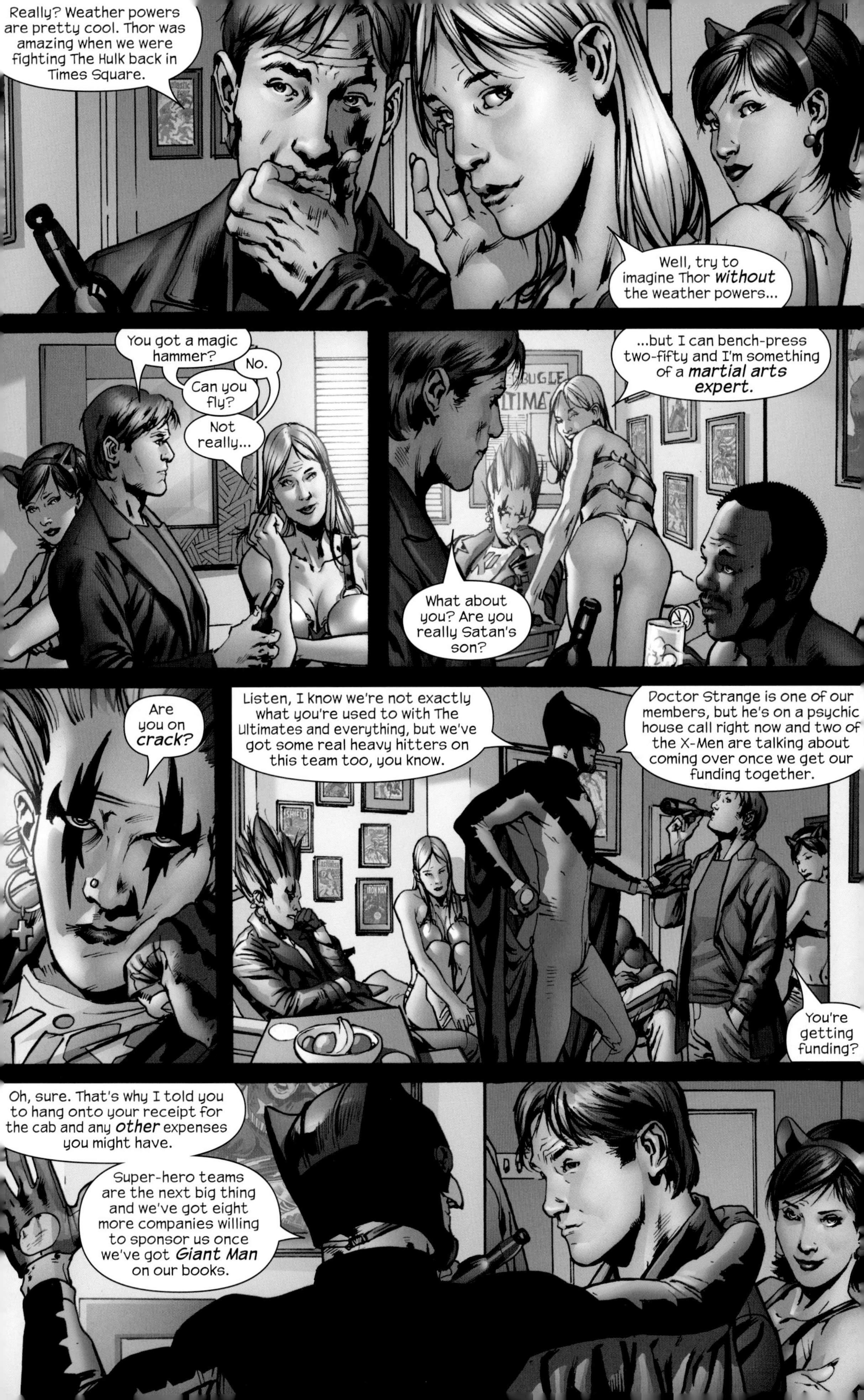
Really? Weather powers are pretty cool. Thor was amazing when we were fighting The Hulk back in Times Square.
Well, try to imagine Thor *without* the weather powers...
You got a magic hammer?
No.
Can you fly?
Not really...
...but I can bench-press two-fifty and I'm something of a *martial arts expert.*
What about you? Are you really Satan's son?
Are you on *crack?*
Listen, I know we're not exactly what you're used to with The Ultimates and everything, but we've got some real heavy hitters on this team too, you know.
Doctor Strange is one of our members, but he's on a psychic house call right now and two of the X-Men are talking about coming over once we get our funding together.
You're getting funding?
Oh, sure. That's why I told you to hang onto your receipt for the cab and any *other* expenses you might have.
Super-hero teams are the next big thing and we've got eight more companies willing to sponsor us once we've got *Giant Man* on our books.

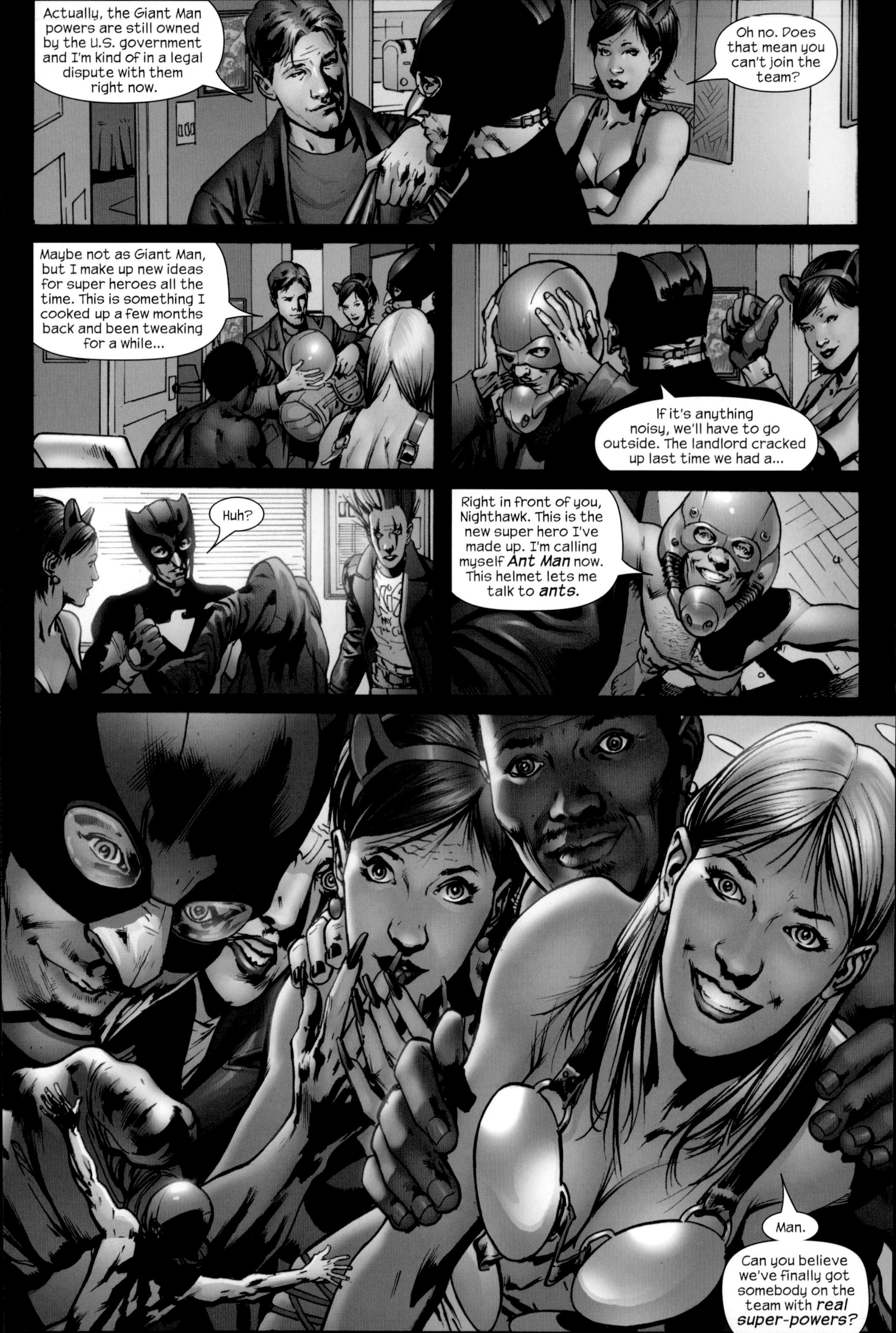
Actually, the Giant Man powers are still owned by the U.S. government and I'm kind of in a legal dispute with them right now.
Oh no. Does that mean you can't join the team?
Maybe not as Giant Man, but I make up new ideas for super heroes all the time. This is something I cooked up a few months back and been tweaking for a while...
If it's anything noisy, we'll have to go outside. The landlord cracked up last time we had a...
Huh?
Right in front of you, Nighthawk. This is the new super hero I've made up. I'm calling myself *Ant Man* now. This helmet lets me talk to ***ants.***
Man.
Can you believe we've finally got somebody on the team with ***real super-powers?***

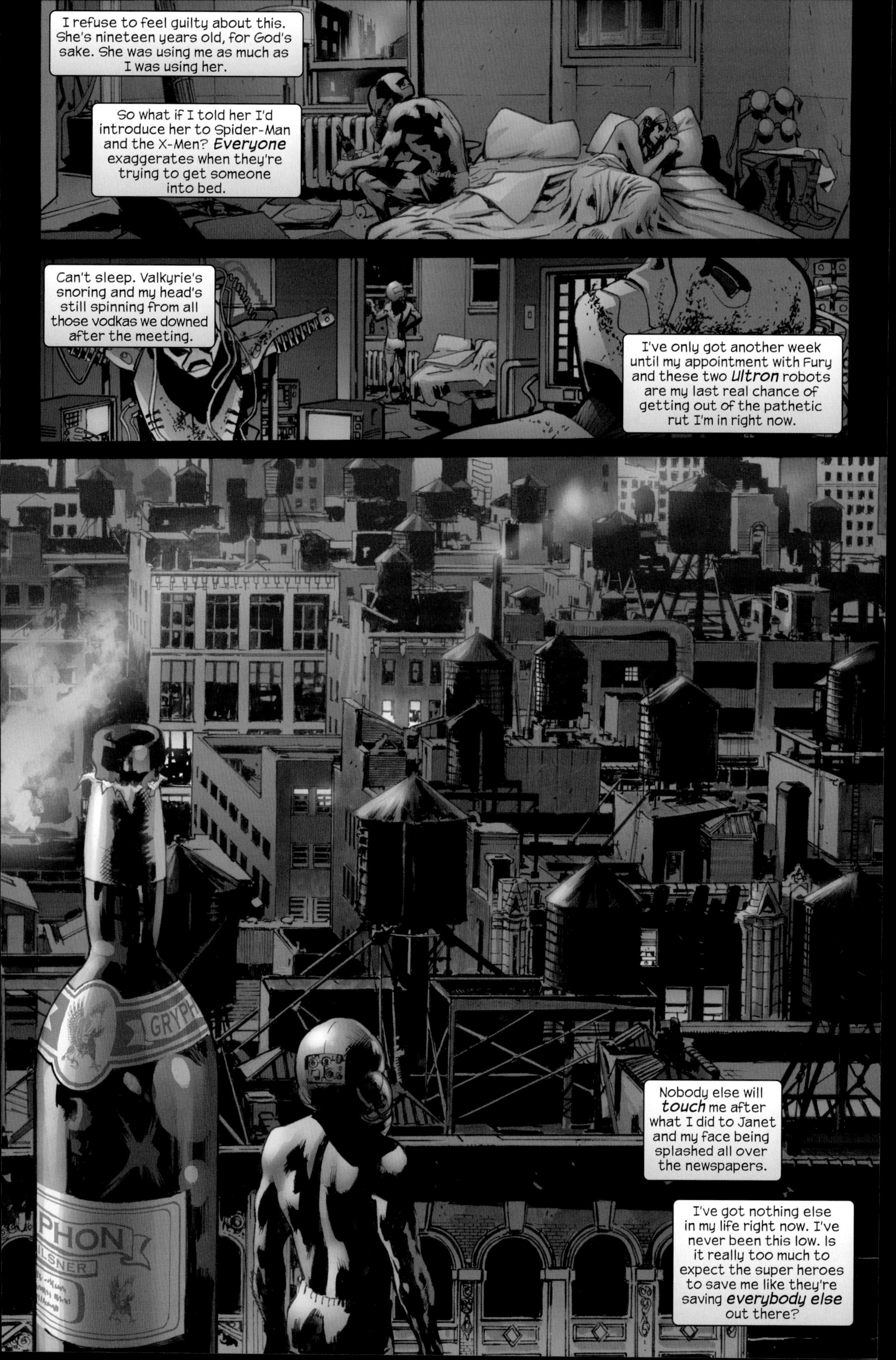
I refuse to feel guilty about this. She's nineteen years old, for God's sake. She was using me as much as I was using her.
So what if I told her I'd introduce her to Spider-Man and the X-Men? *Everyone* exaggerates when they're trying to get someone into bed.
Can't sleep. Valkyrie's snoring and my head's still spinning from all those vodkas we downed after the meeting.
I've only got another week until my appointment with Fury and these two *Ultron* robots are my last real chance of getting out of the pathetic rut I'm in right now.
GRYPH
PHON
ILSNER
Nobody else will *touch* me after what I did to Janet and my face being splashed all over the newspapers.
I've got nothing else in my life right now. I've never been this low. Is it really too much to expect the super heroes to save me like they're saving *everybody else* out there?

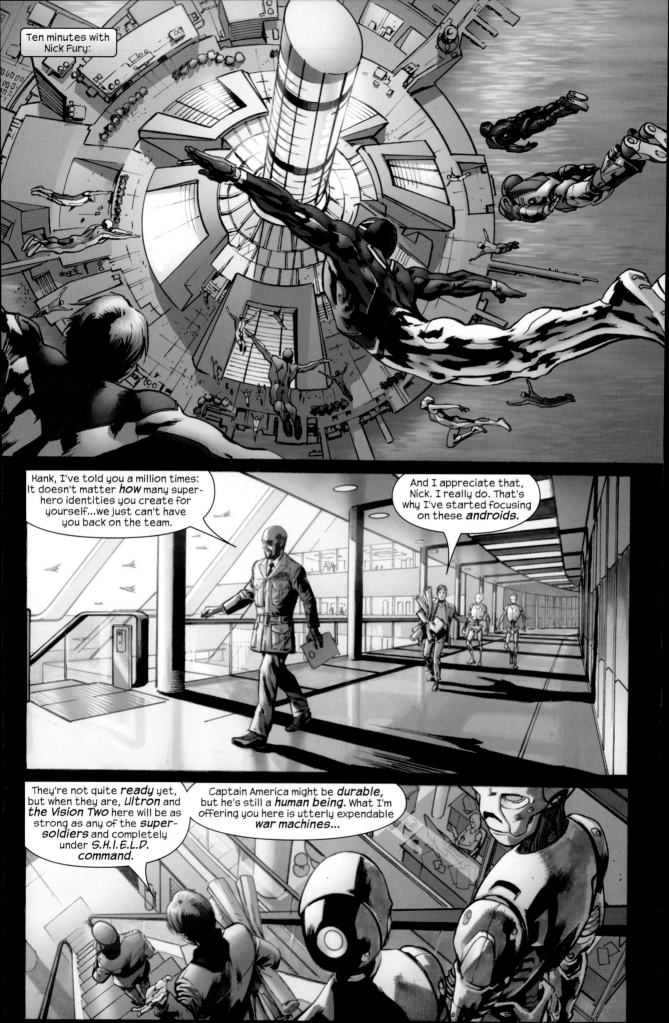

Ten minutes with Nick Fury:

Hank, I've told you a million times: It doesn't matter *how* many super-hero identities you create for yourself...we just can't have you back on the team.

And I appreciate that, Nick. I really do. That's why I've started focusing on these *androids*.

They're not quite *ready* yet, but when they are, *Ultron* and *the Vision Two* here will be as strong as any of the *super-soldiers* and completely under S.H.I.E.L.D. command.

Captain America might be *durable*, but he's still a *human being*. What I'm offering you here is utterly expendable *war machines*...

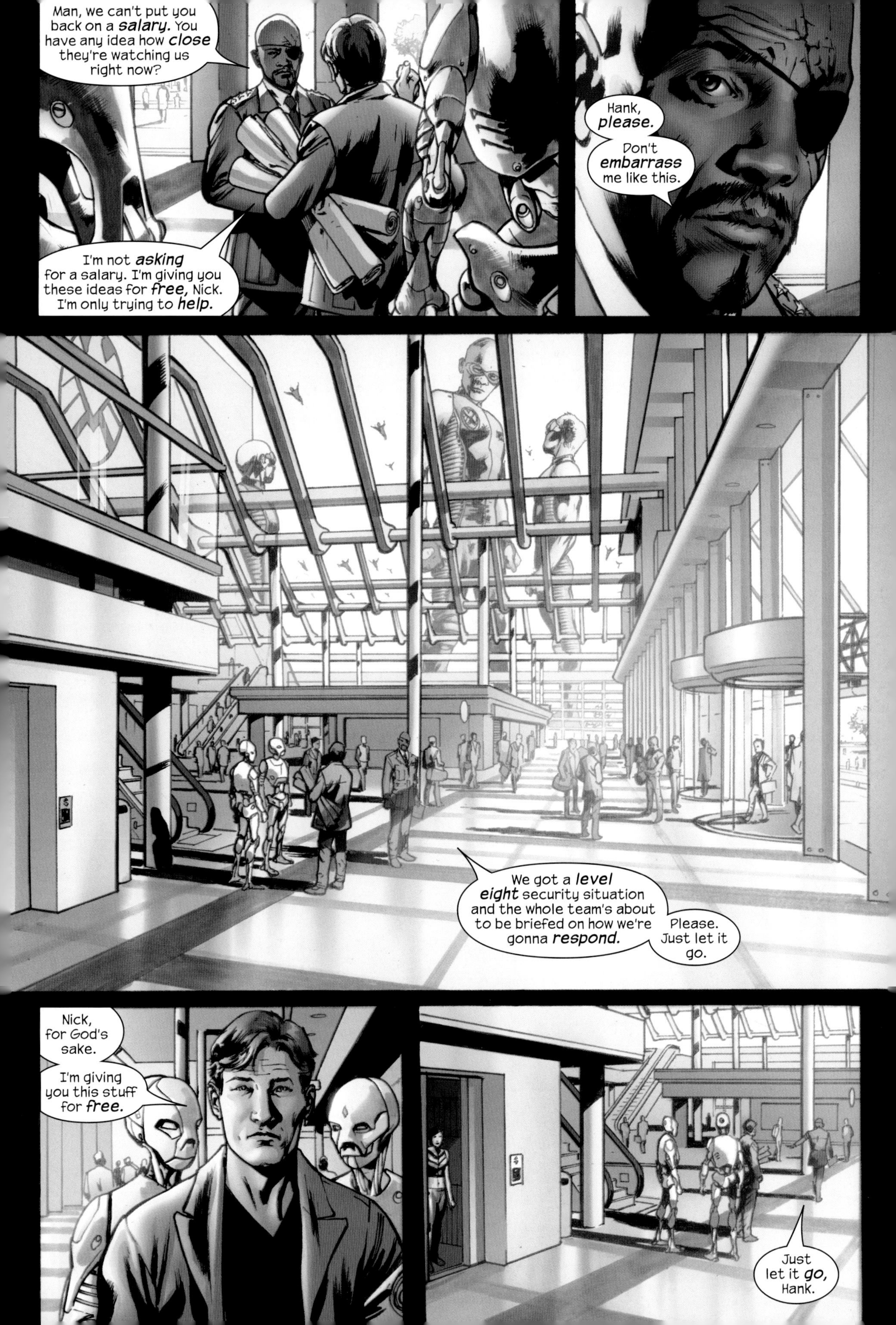

Man, we can't put you back on a salary. You have any idea how close they're watching us right now?
I'm not asking for a salary. I'm giving you these ideas for free, Nick. I'm only trying to help.
Hank, please.
Don't embarrass me like this.
We got a level eight security situation and the whole team's about to be briefed on how we're gonna respond.
Please. Just let it go.
Nick, for God's sake.
I'm giving you this stuff for free.
Just let it go, Hank.

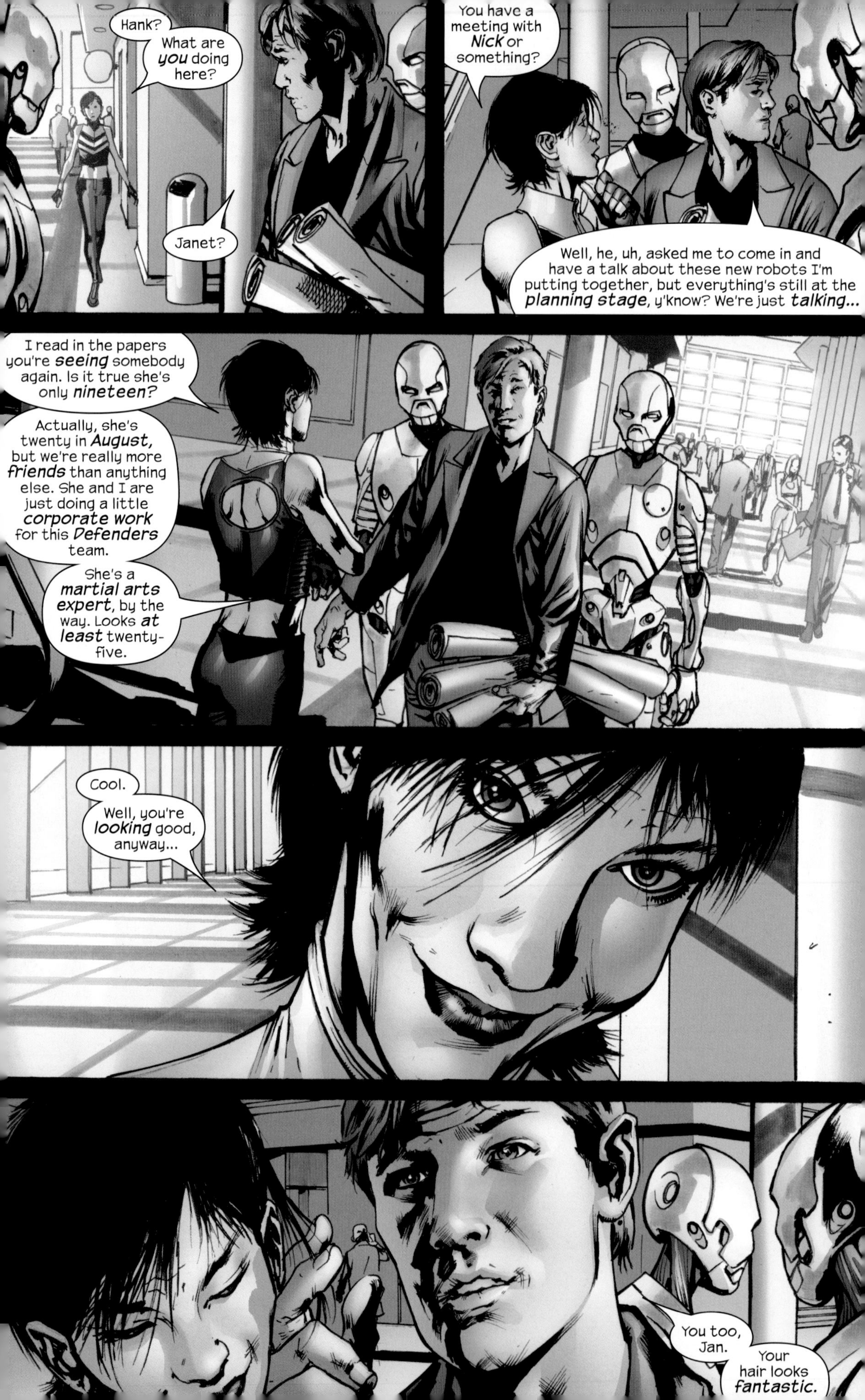

Hank? What are *you* doing here?
Janet?
You have a meeting with *Nick* or something?
Well, he, uh, asked me to come in and have a talk about these new robots I'm putting together, but everything's still at the *planning stage*, y'know? We're just *talking...*
I read in the papers you're *seeing* somebody again. Is it true she's only *nineteen?*
Actually, she's twenty in *August,* but we're really more *friends* than anything else. She and I are just doing a little *corporate work* for this *Defenders* team.
She's a *martial arts expert*, by the way. Looks *at least* twenty-five.
Cool.
Well, you're *looking* good, anyway...
You too, Jan.
Your hair looks *fantastic.*

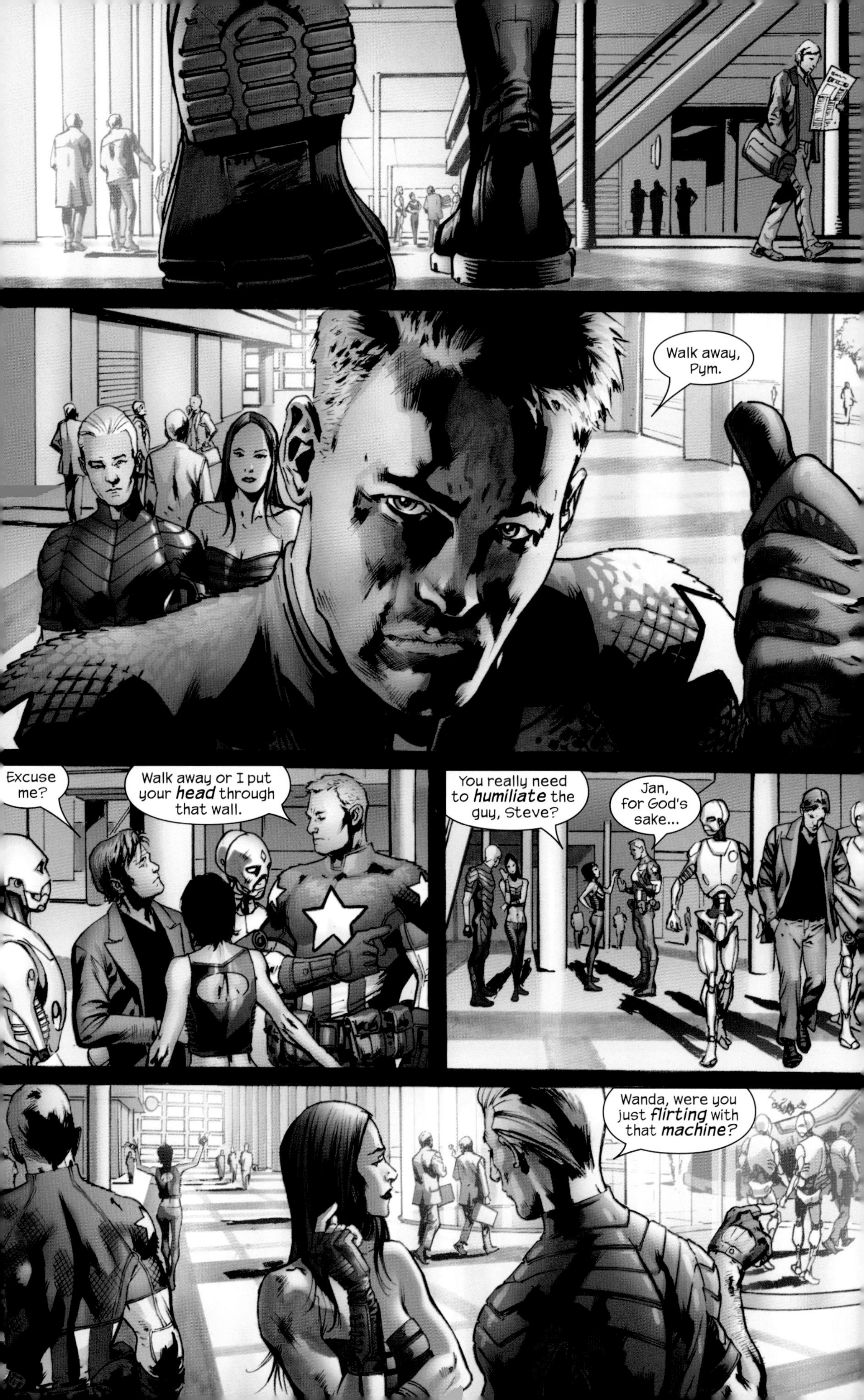
Walk away, Pym.
Excuse me?
Walk away or I put your *head* through that wall.
You really need to *humiliate* the guy, Steve?
Jan, for God's sake...
Wanda, were you just *flirting* with that *machine*?

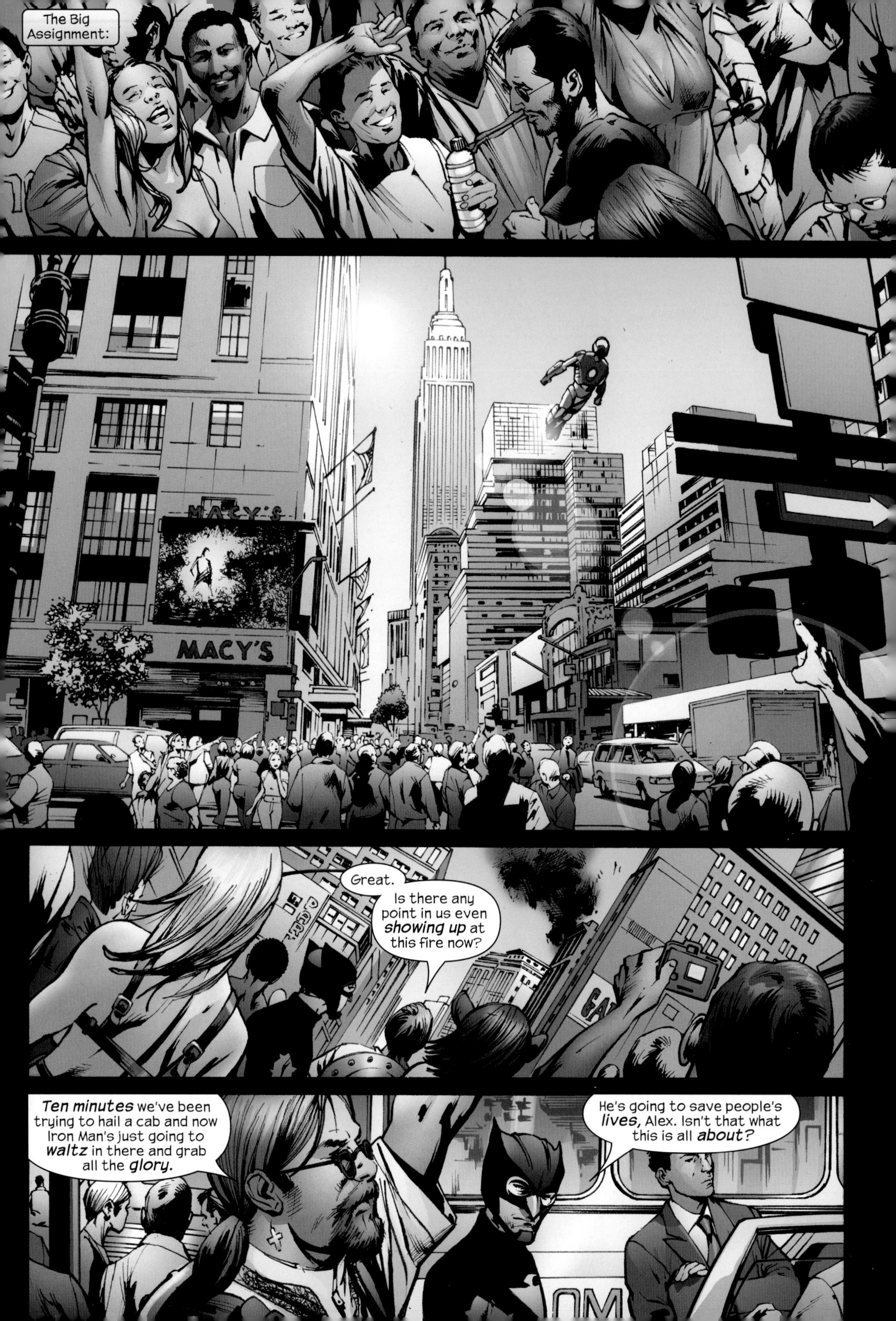
The Big Assignment:
MACY'S
MACY'S
Great.
Is there any point in us even *showing up* at this fire now?
Ten minutes we've been trying to hail a cab and now Iron Man's just going to *waltz* in there and grab all the *glory.*
He's going to save people's *lives,* Alex. Isn't that what this is all *about?*

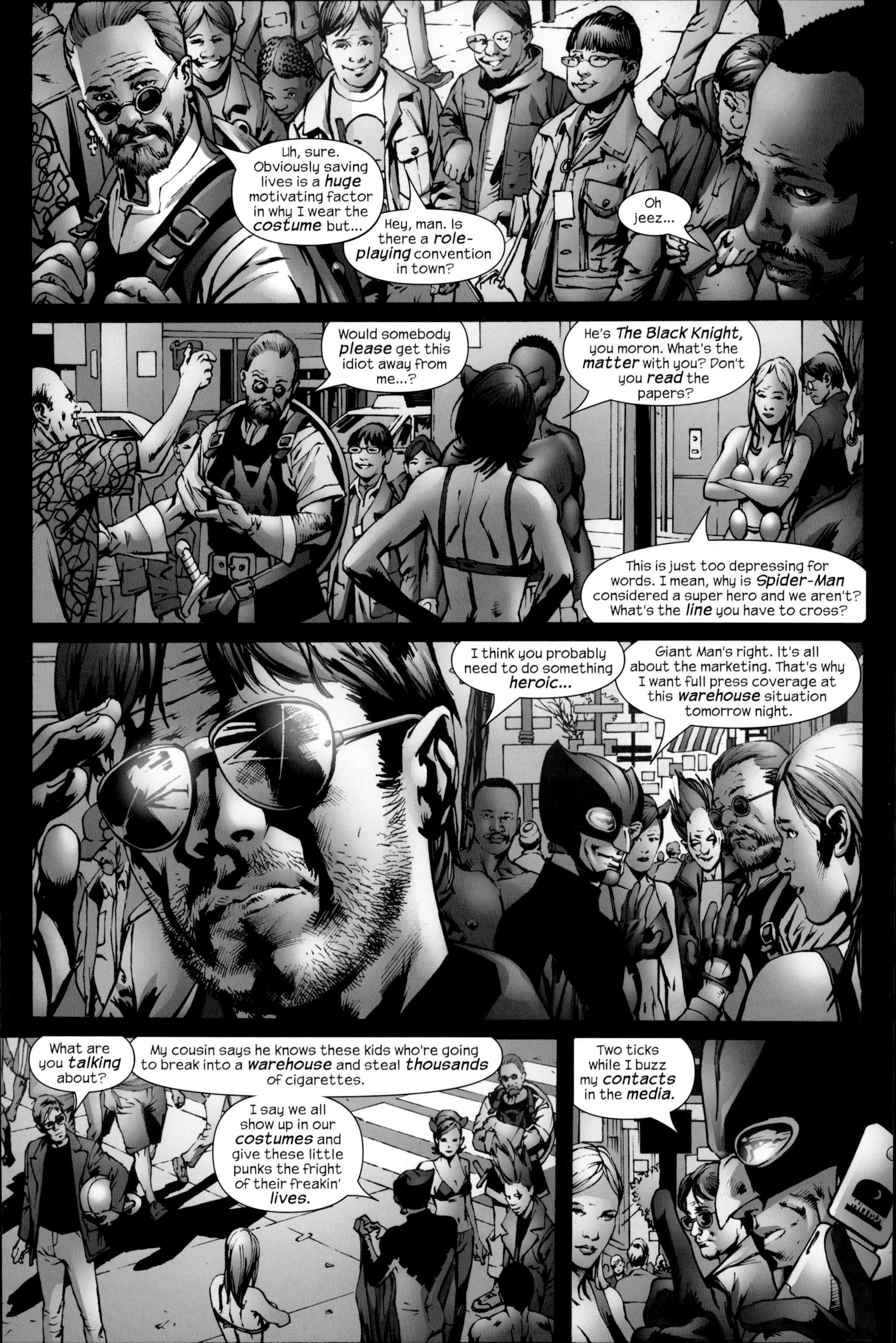
Uh, sure. Obviously saving lives is a huge motivating factor in why I wear the costume but...
Hey, man. Is there a role-playing convention in town?
Oh jeez...
Would somebody please get this idiot away from me...?
He's The Black Knight, you moron. What's the matter with you? Don't you read the papers?
This is just too depressing for words. I mean, why is Spider-Man considered a super hero and we aren't? What's the line you have to cross?
I think you probably need to do something heroic...
Giant Man's right. It's all about the marketing. That's why I want full press coverage at this warehouse situation tomorrow night.
What are you talking about?
My cousin says he knows these kids who're going to break into a warehouse and steal thousands of cigarettes.
I say we all show up in our costumes and give these little punks the fright of their freakin' lives.
Two ticks while I buzz my contacts in the media.

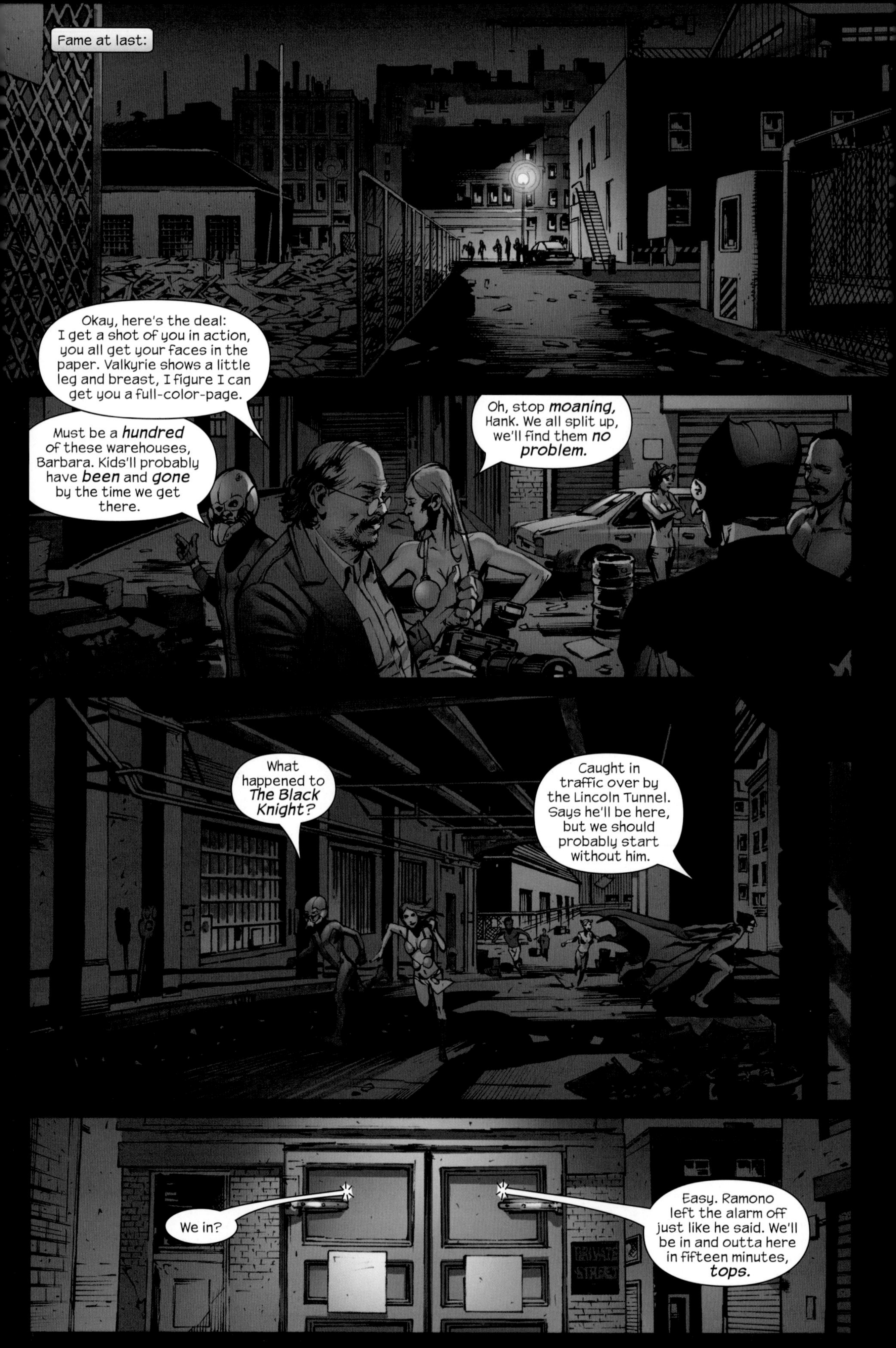
Fame at last:
Okay, here's the deal: I get a shot of you in action, you all get your faces in the paper. Valkyrie shows a little leg and breast, I figure I can get you a full-color-page.
Must be a *hundred* of these warehouses, Barbara. Kids'll probably have *been* and *gone* by the time we get there.
Oh, stop *moaning,* Hank. We all split up, we'll find them *no problem.*
What happened to *The Black Knight?*
Caught in traffic over by the Lincoln Tunnel. Says he'll be here, but we should probably start without him.
We in?
Easy. Ramono left the alarm off just like he said. We'll be in and outta here in fifteen minutes, *tops.*

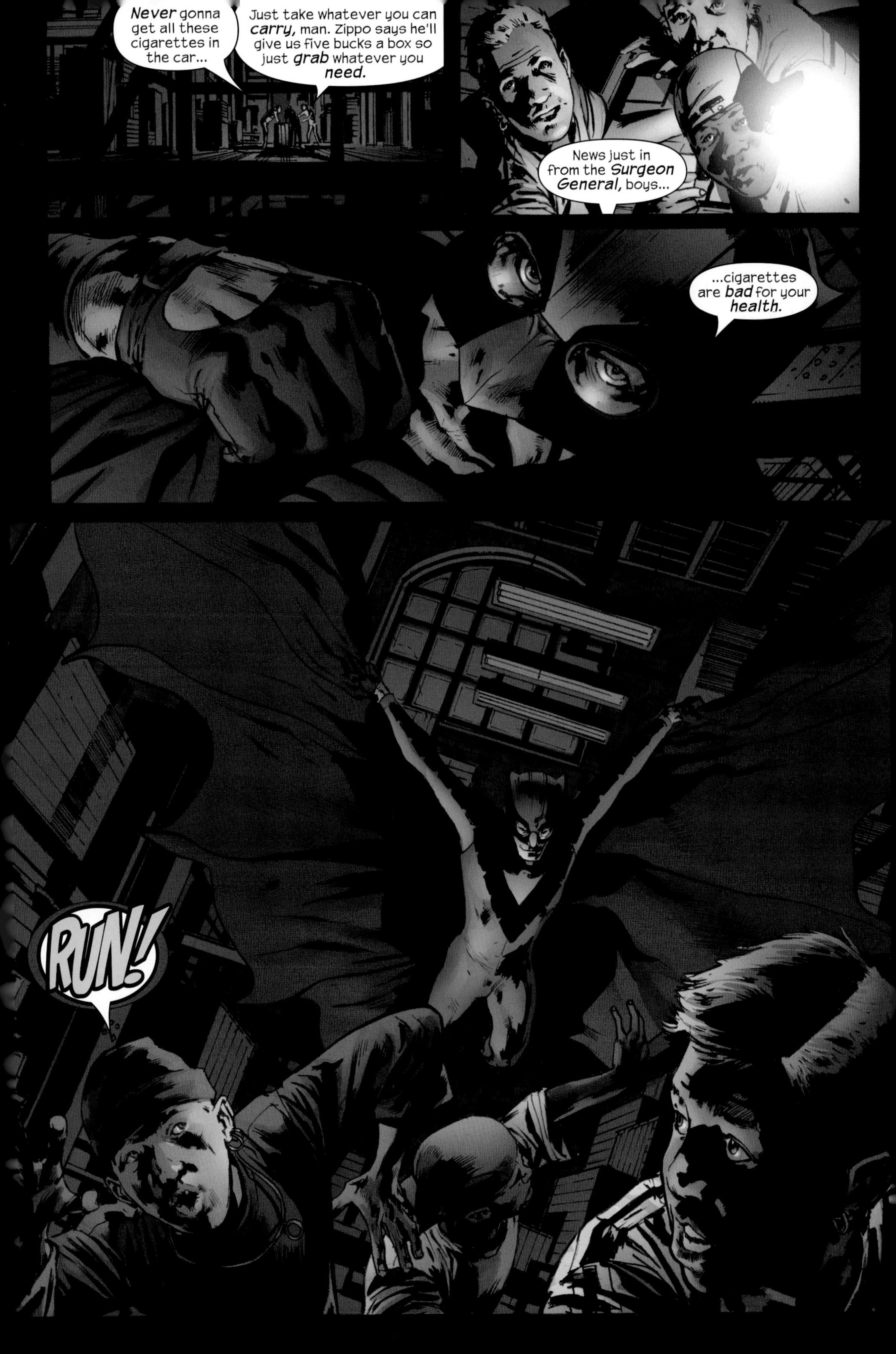

Never gonna get all these cigarettes in the car...
Just take whatever you can carry, man. Zippo says he'll give us five bucks a box so just grab whatever you need.
News just in from the Surgeon General, boys...
...cigarettes are bad for your health.
RUN!

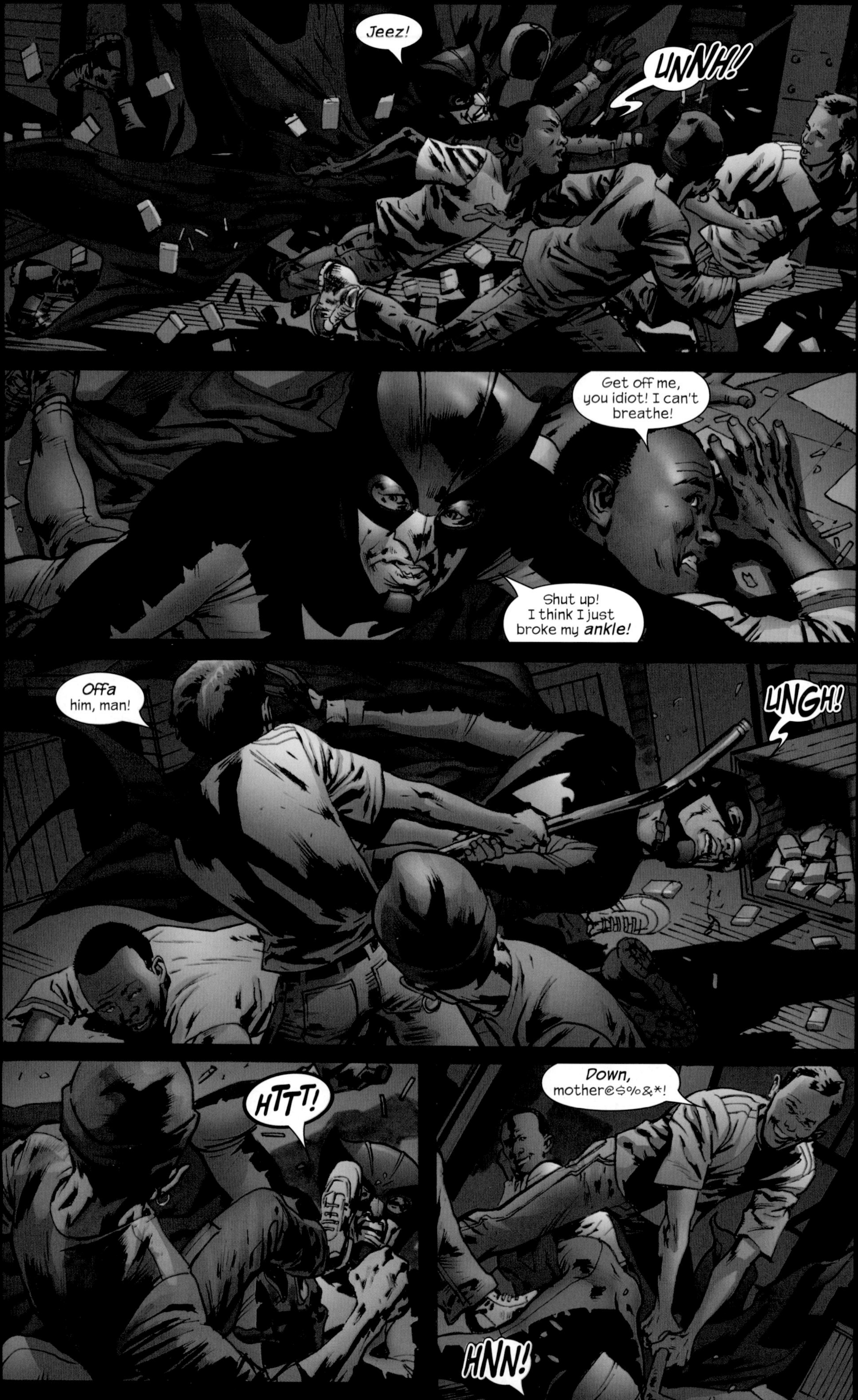
Jeez!
UNNH!
Get off me, you idiot! I can't breathe!
Shut up! I think I just broke my *ankle!*
Offa him, man!
UNGH!
HTTT!
Down, mother@$%&*!
HNN!

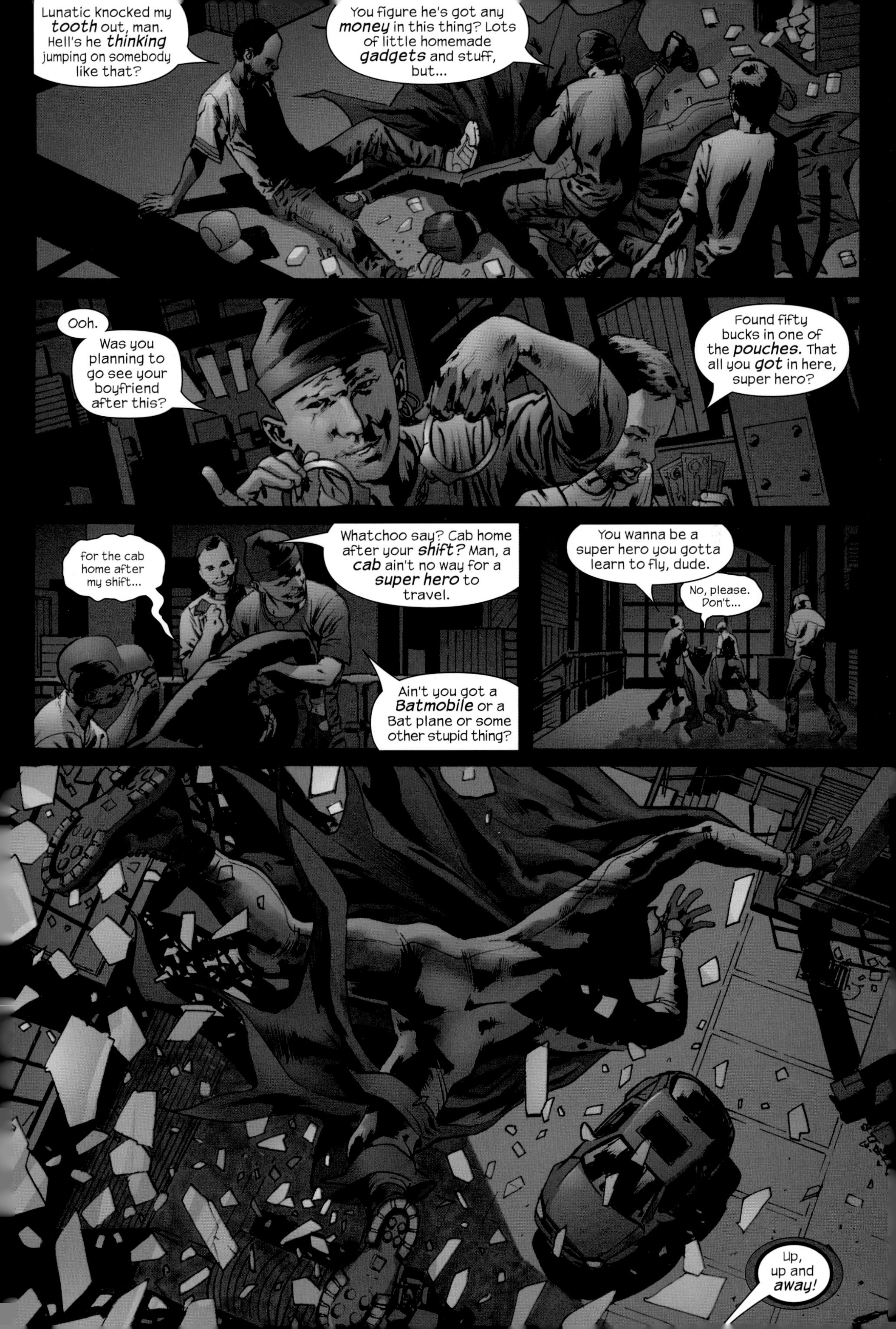
Lunatic knocked my tooth out, man. Hell's he thinking jumping on somebody like that?
You figure he's got any money in this thing? Lots of little homemade gadgets and stuff, but...
Ooh.
Was you planning to go see your boyfriend after this?
Found fifty bucks in one of the pouches. That all you got in here, super hero?
for the cab home after my shift...
Whatchoo say? Cab home after your shift? Man, a cab ain't no way for a super hero to travel.
Ain't you got a Batmobile or a Bat plane or some other stupid thing?
You wanna be a super hero you gotta learn to fly, dude.
No, please. Don't...
Up, up and away!

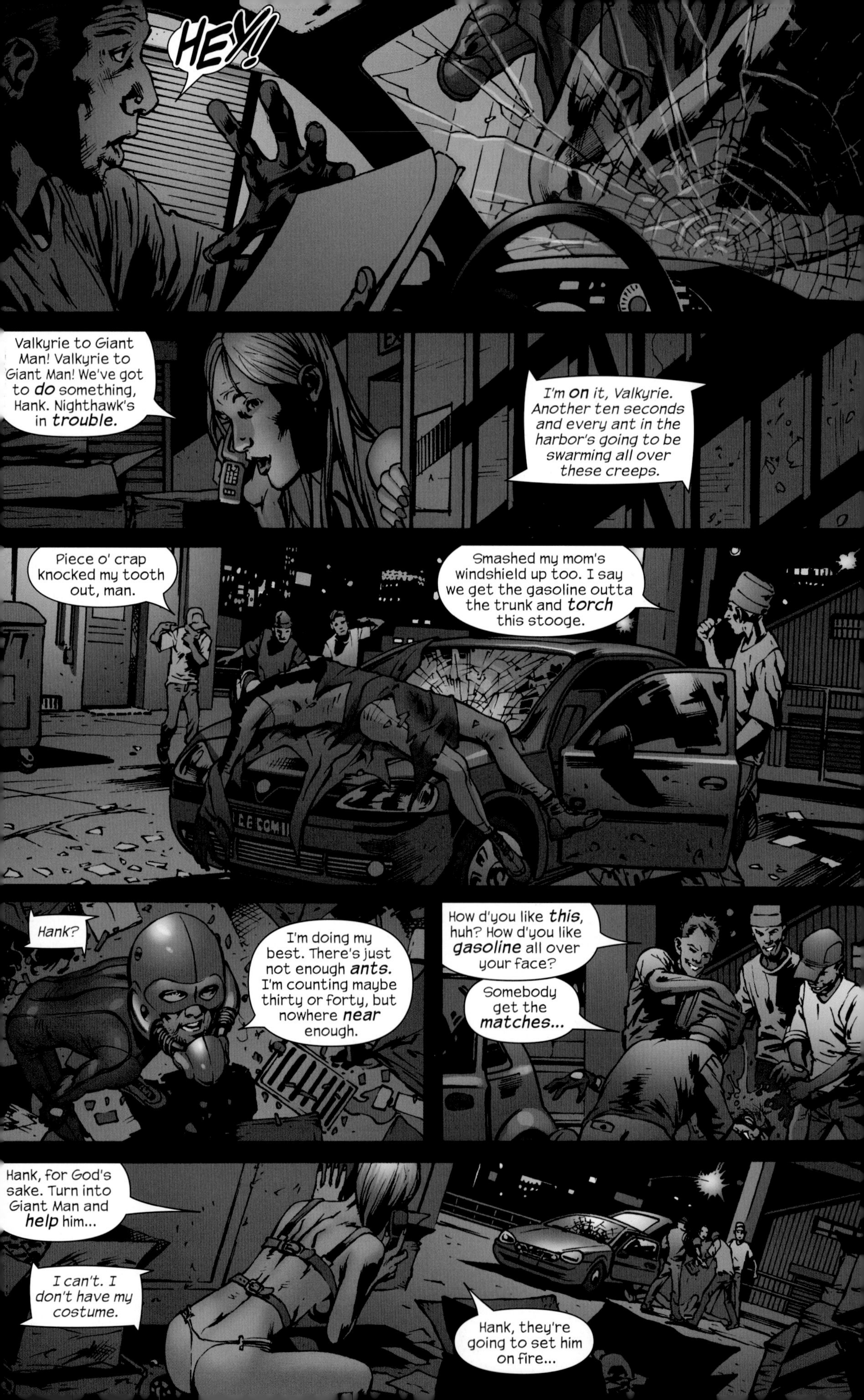
HEY!
Valkyrie to Giant Man! Valkyrie to Giant Man! We've got to *do* something, Hank. Nighthawk's in *trouble.*
*I'm **on** it, Valkyrie. Another ten seconds and every ant in the harbor's going to be swarming all over these creeps.*
Piece o' crap knocked my tooth out, man.
Smashed my mom's windshield up too. I say we get the gasoline outta the trunk and *torch* this stooge.
Hank?
I'm doing my best. There's just not enough *ants.* I'm counting maybe thirty or forty, but nowhere *near* enough.
How d'you like *this*, huh? How d'you like *gasoline* all over your face?
Somebody get the *matches...*
Hank, for God's sake. Turn into Giant Man and *help* him...
I can't. I don't have my costume.
Hank, they're going to set him on fire...

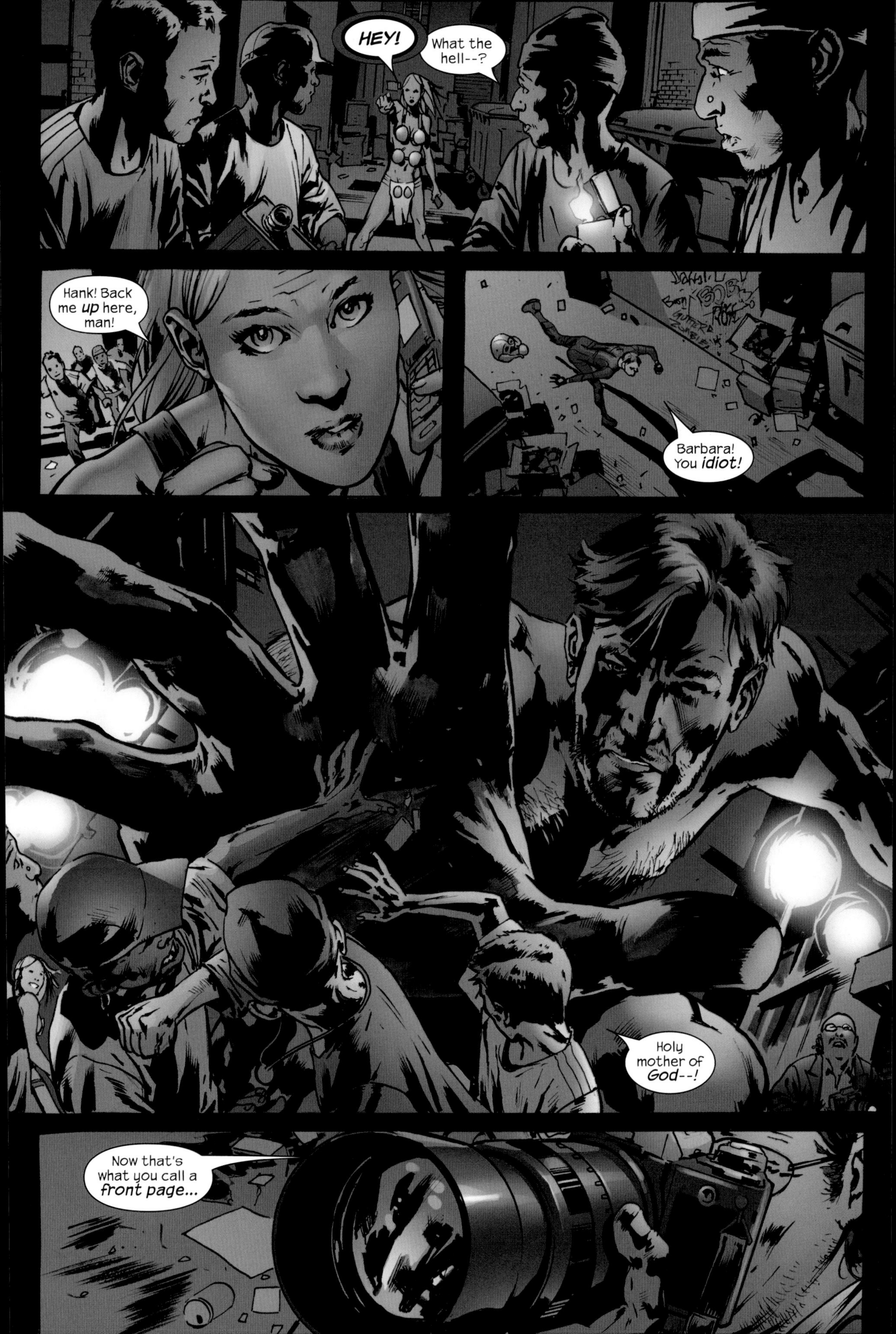
HEY!
What the hell--?
Hank! Back me up here, man!
Barbara! You idiot!
Holy mother of God--!
Now that's what you call a front page...

DAILY BUGLE

NEW YORK'S FINEST DAILY PAPER

BUTT-ER LUCK NEXT TIME

uper-Hero Debut Descends Into Farce

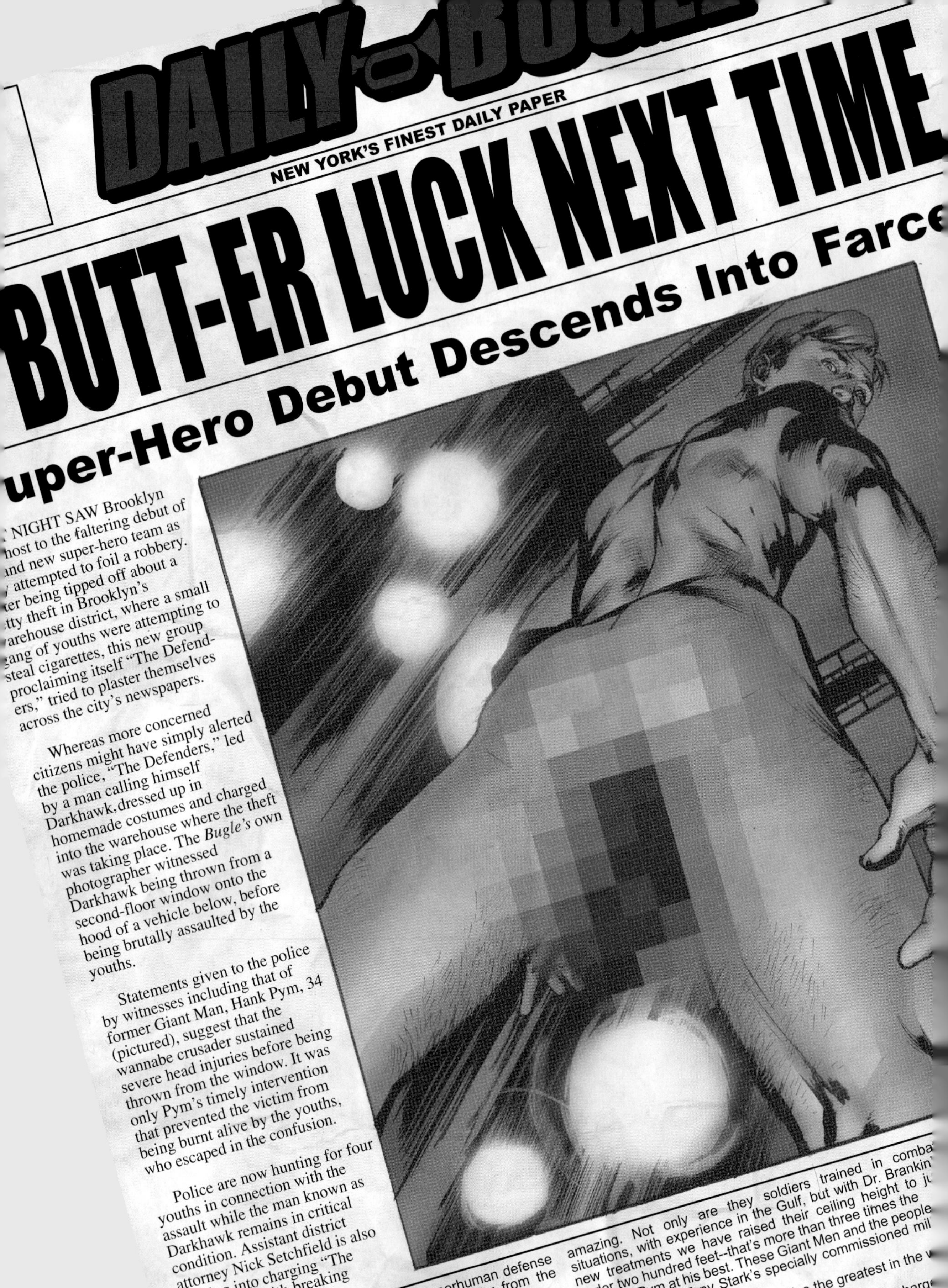

T NIGHT SAW Brooklyn host to the faltering debut of and new super-hero team as y attempted to foil a robbery. ter being tipped off about a tty theft in Brooklyn's arehouse district, where a small gang of youths were attempting to steal cigarettes, this new group proclaiming itself "The Defenders," tried to plaster themselves across the city's newspapers.

Whereas more concerned citizens might have simply alerted the police, "The Defenders," led by a man calling himself Darkhawk, dressed up in homemade costumes and charged into the warehouse where the theft was taking place. The *Bugle's* own photographer witnessed Darkhawk being thrown from a second-floor window onto the hood of a vehicle below, before being brutally assaulted by the youths.

Statements given to the police by witnesses including that of former Giant Man, Hank Pym, 34 (pictured), suggest that the wannabe crusader sustained severe head injuries before being thrown from the window. It was only Pym's timely intervention that prevented the victim from being burnt alive by the youths, who escaped in the confusion.

Police are now hunting for four youths in connection with the assault while the man known as Darkhawk remains in critical condition. Assistant district attorney Nick Setchfield is also looking into charging "The Defenders" with breaking anti-vigilante laws.

Once a member of the world's leading superhuman defense group, The Ultimates, Dr. Hank Pym's life is far from the glamor of Hollywood celebrity.
Aside from his much-publicized divorce from fellow teammate Janet van Dyne (also known as The Wasp), he was fired from his position as head of the ultra-secret Super Soldier program at S.H.I.E.L.D. following allegations of physical abuse and a public brawl with Captain America in the streets of Chicago.
's position, medical breakthroughs saw a introduced to the Ultimates' line- guys are

amazing. Not only are they soldiers trained in comba situations, with experience in the Gulf, but with Dr. Brankin's new treatments we have raised their ceiling height to ju under two hundred feet--that's more than three times the height of Pym at his best. These Giant Men and the people have training in Tony Stark's specially commissioned mil exo-suits will make our Super Human Defense Initiative the greatest in the w

Triskelion insiders also suggest that Pym may be charge illegal use of a controlled substance following his u tioned height multiplication in Brooklyn last night.

Dr. Pym was not available for comment.

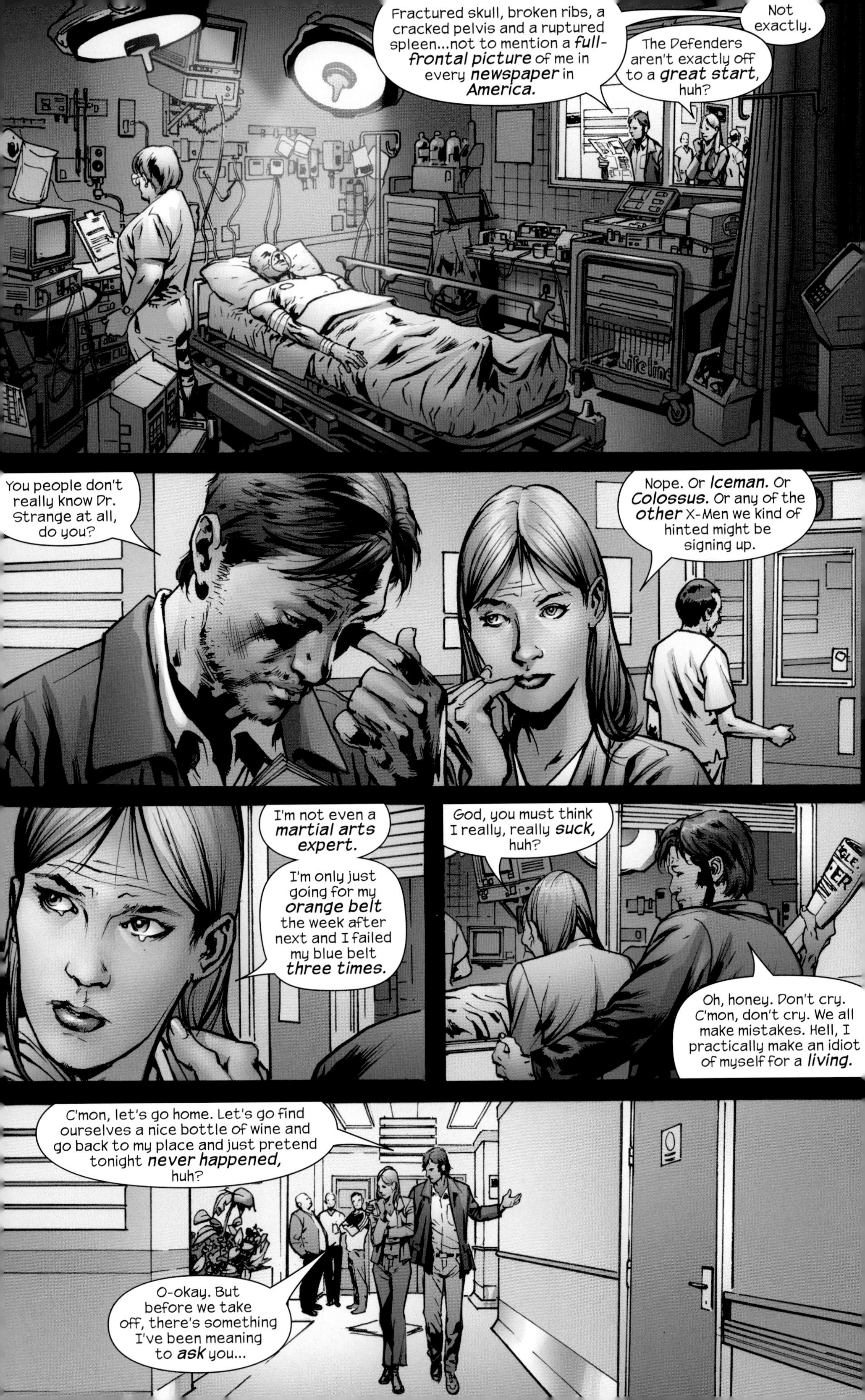
Fractured skull, broken ribs, a cracked pelvis and a ruptured spleen...not to mention a *full-frontal picture* of me in every *newspaper* in *America.*
Not exactly.
The Defenders aren't exactly off to a *great start*, huh?
You people don't really know Dr. Strange at all, do you?
Nope. Or *Iceman.* Or *Colossus.* Or any of the *other* X-Men we kind of hinted might be signing up.
I'm not even a *martial arts expert.*
I'm only just going for my *orange belt* the week after next and I failed my blue belt *three times.*
God, you must think I really, really *suck,* huh?
Oh, honey. Don't cry. C'mon, don't cry. We all make mistakes. Hell, I practically make an idiot of myself for a *living.*
C'mon, let's go home. Let's go find ourselves a nice bottle of wine and go back to my place and just pretend tonight *never happened,* huh?
O-okay. But before we take off, there's something I've been meaning to *ask* you...

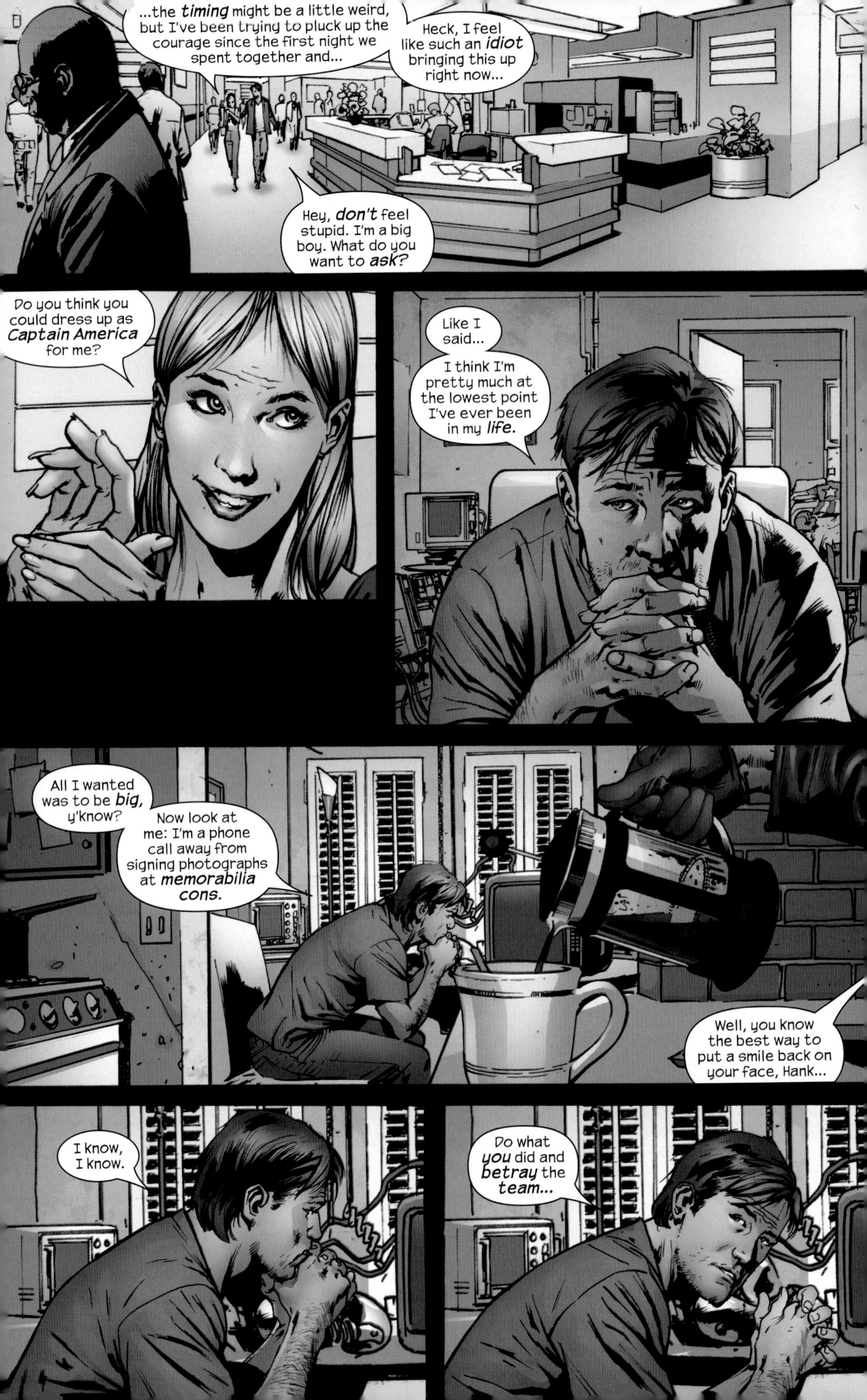
...the timing might be a little weird, but I've been trying to pluck up the courage since the first night we spent together and...
Heck, I feel like such an idiot bringing this up right now...
Hey, don't feel stupid. I'm a big boy. What do you want to ask?
Do you think you could dress up as Captain America for me?
Like I said...
I think I'm pretty much at the lowest point I've ever been in my life.
All I wanted was to be big, y'know?
Now look at me: I'm a phone call away from signing photographs at memorabilia cons.
Well, you know the best way to put a smile back on your face, Hank...
I know, I know.
Do what you did and betray the team...

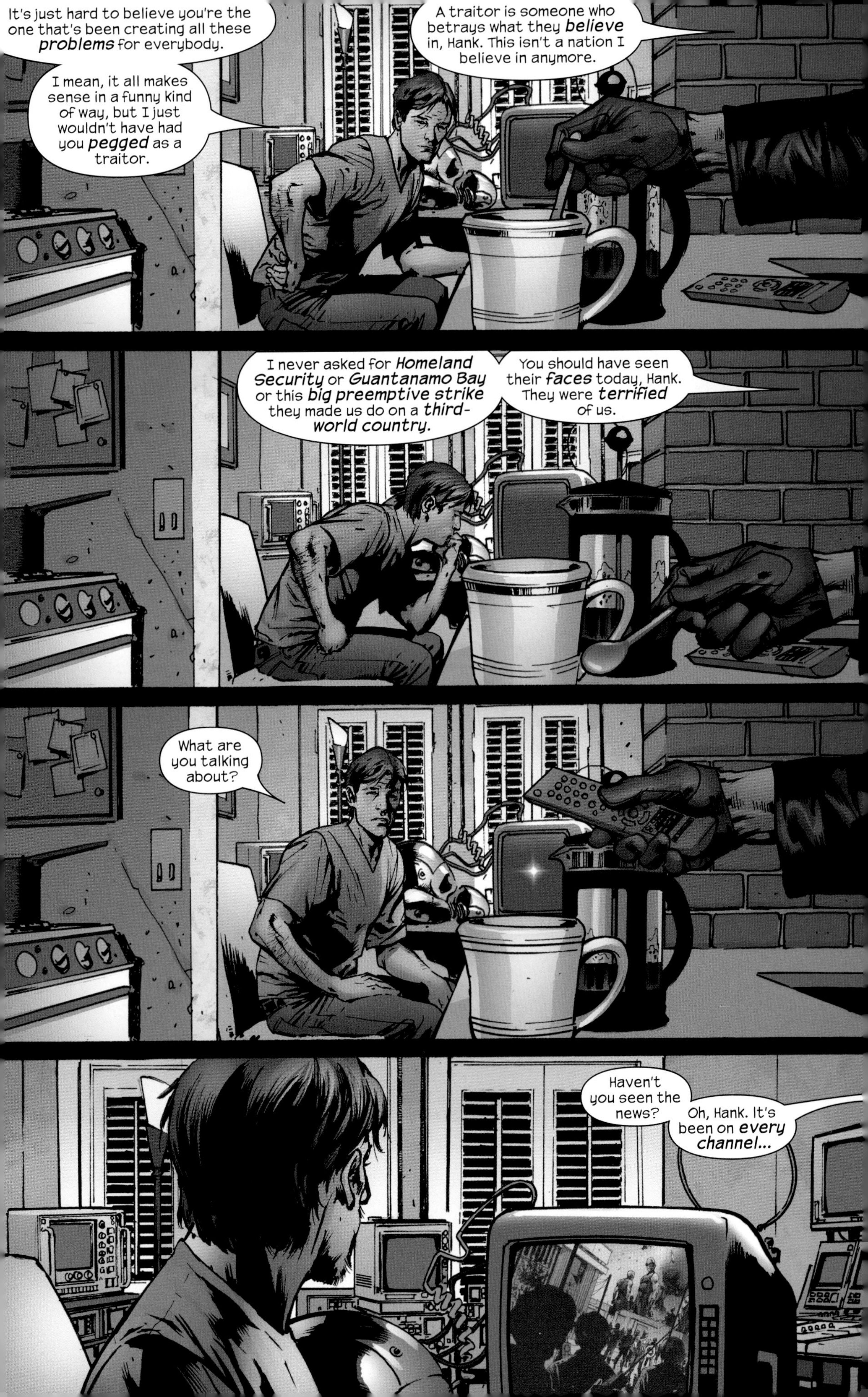
It's just hard to believe you're the one that's been creating all these *problems* for everybody.
I mean, it all makes sense in a funny kind of way, but I just wouldn't have had you *pegged* as a traitor.
A traitor is someone who betrays what they *believe* in, Hank. This isn't a nation I believe in anymore.
I never asked for *Homeland Security* or *Guantanamo Bay* or this *big preemptive strike* they made us do on a *third-world country.*
You should have seen their *faces* today, Hank. They were *terrified* of us.
What are you talking about?
Haven't you seen the news?
Oh, Hank. It's been on *every channel...*

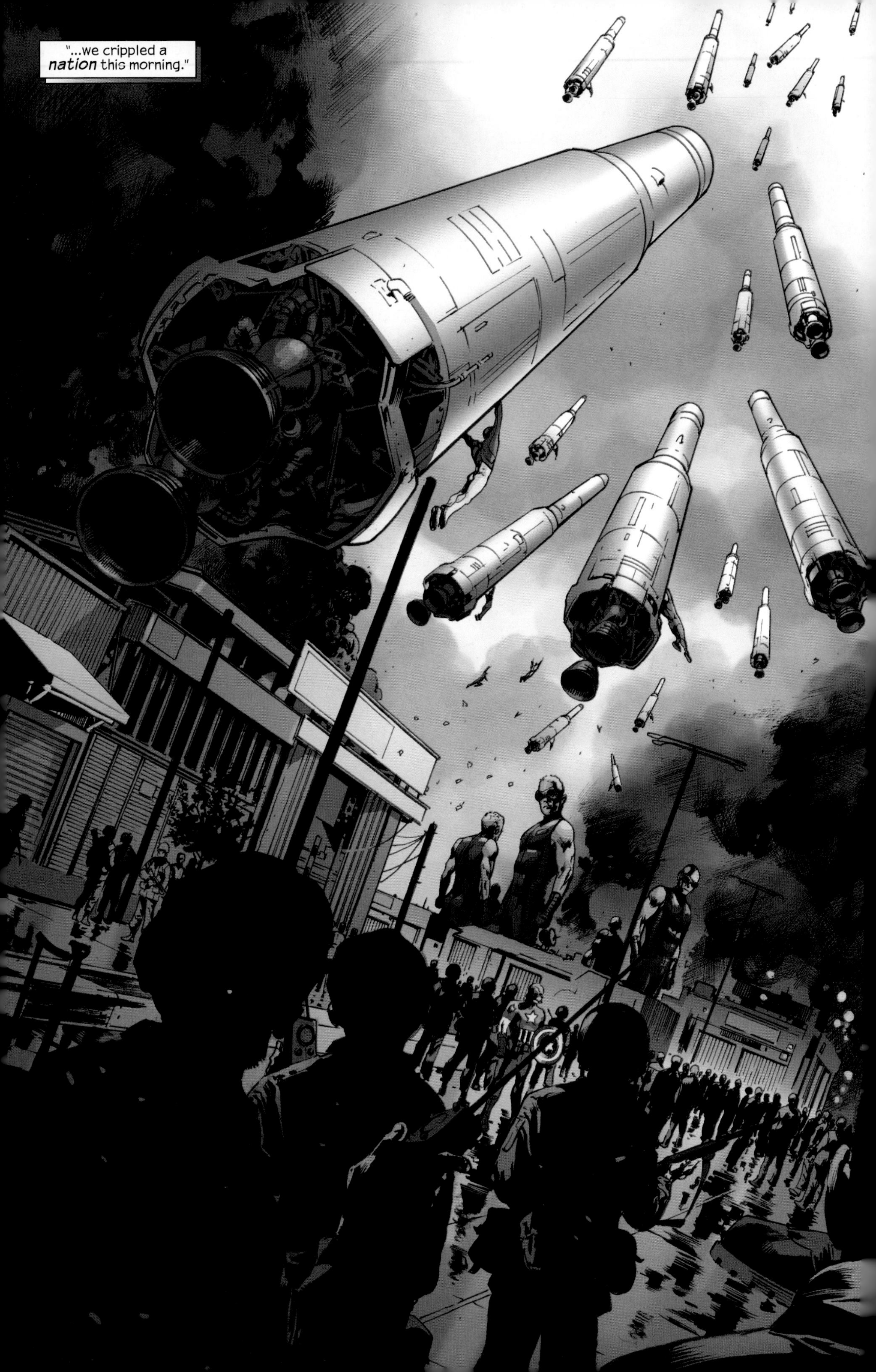
"...we crippled a *nation* this morning."

WOLF IN THE FOLD

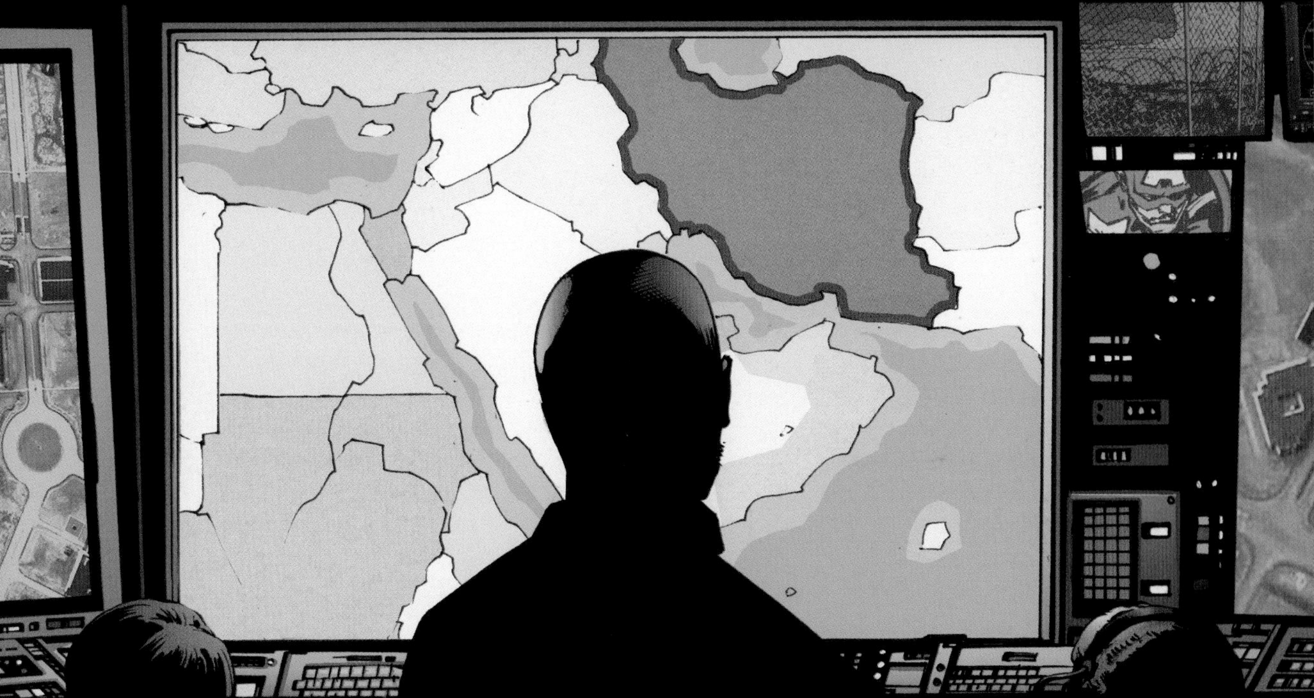

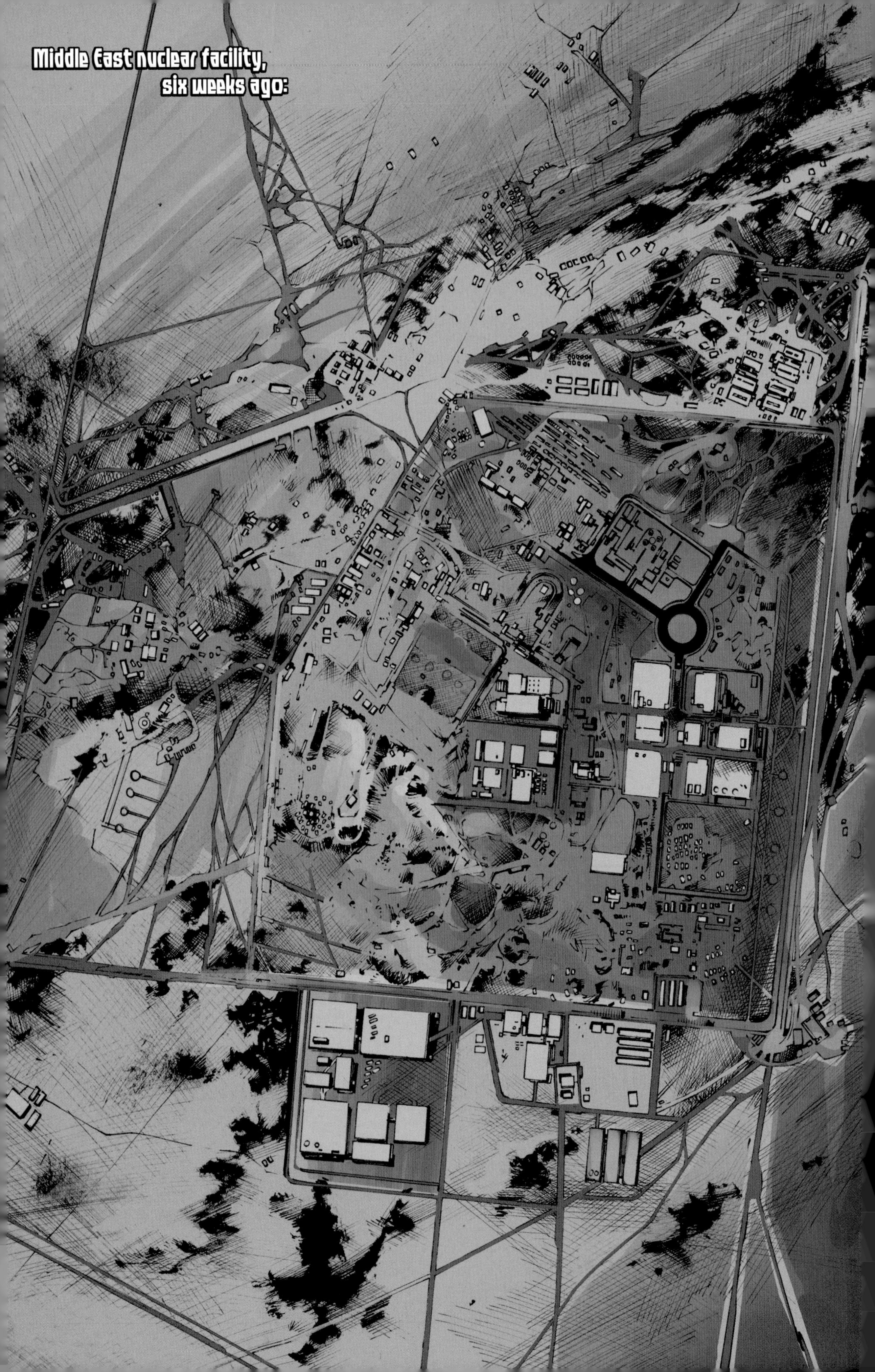
Middle East nuclear facility,
six weeks ago:

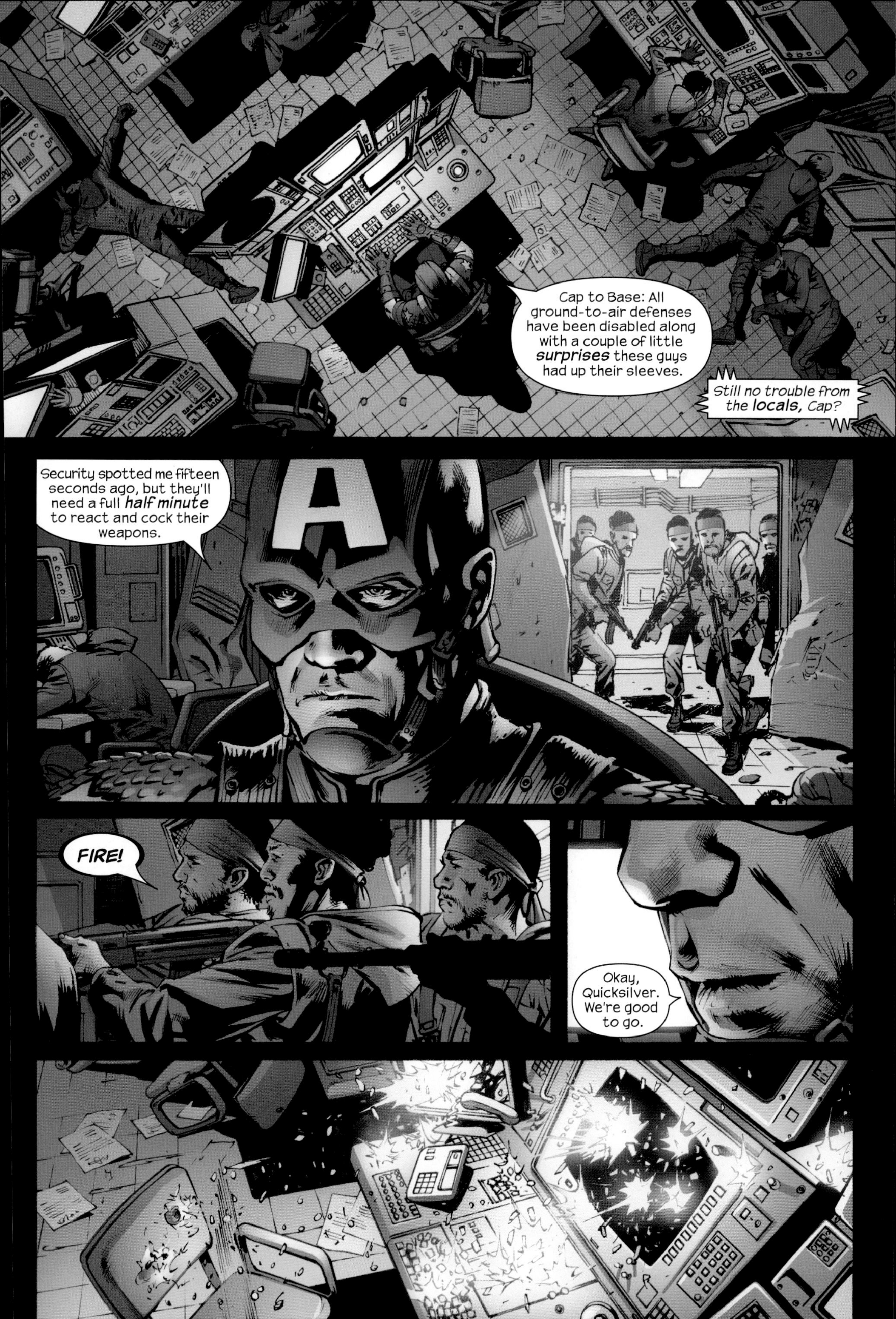
Cap to Base: All ground-to-air defenses have been disabled along with a couple of little *surprises* these guys had up their sleeves.
Still no trouble from the ***locals,*** *Cap?*
Security spotted me fifteen seconds ago, but they'll need a full ***half minute*** to react and cock their weapons.
FIRE!
Okay, Quicksilver. We're good to go.

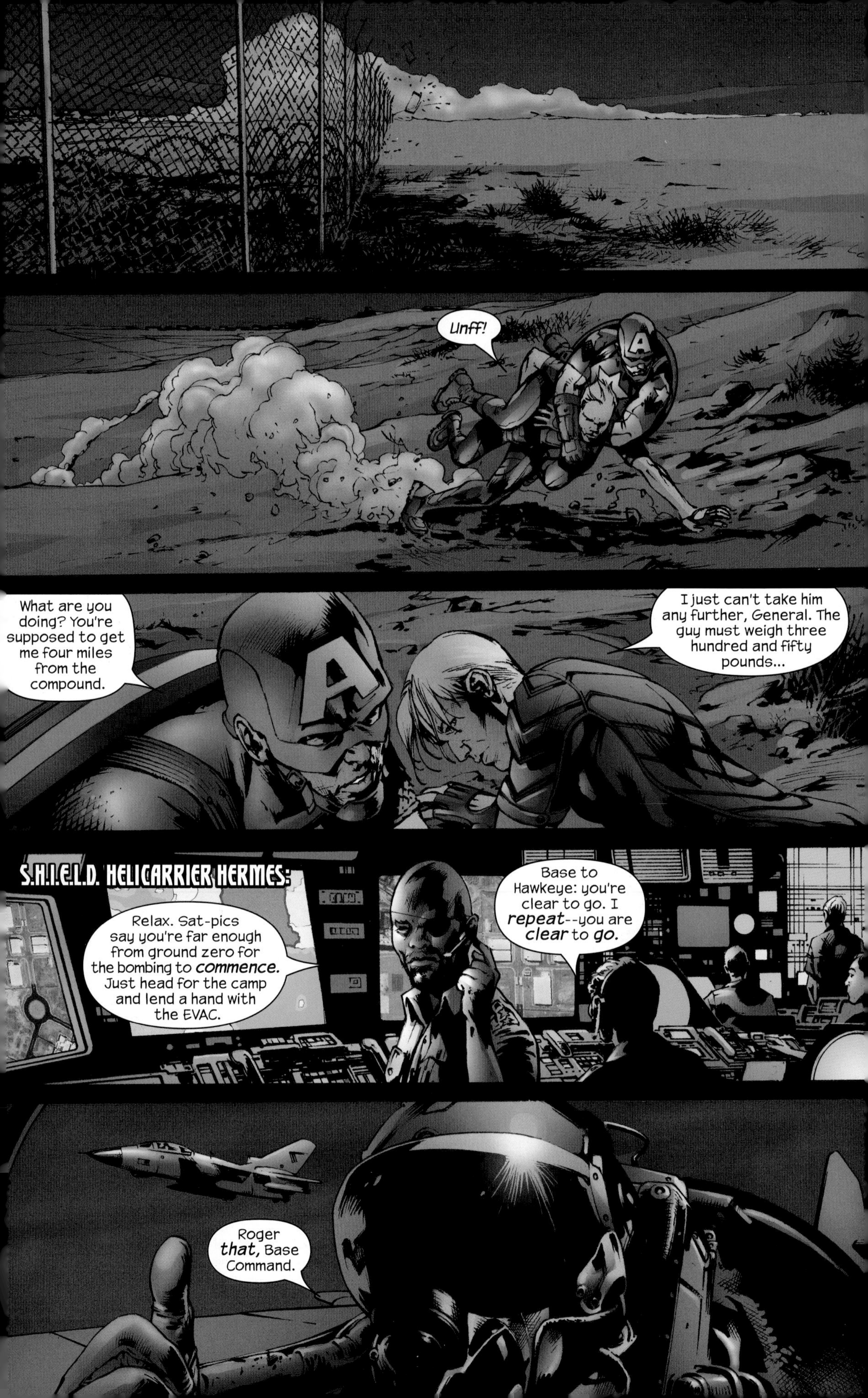
Unff!
What are you doing? You're supposed to get me four miles from the compound.
I just can't take him any further, General. The guy must weigh three hundred and fifty pounds...
S.H.I.E.L.D. HELICARRIER HERMES:
Relax. Sat-pics say you're far enough from ground zero for the bombing to commence. Just head for the camp and lend a hand with the EVAC.
Base to Hawkeye: you're clear to go. I repeat--you are clear to go.
Roger that, Base Command.

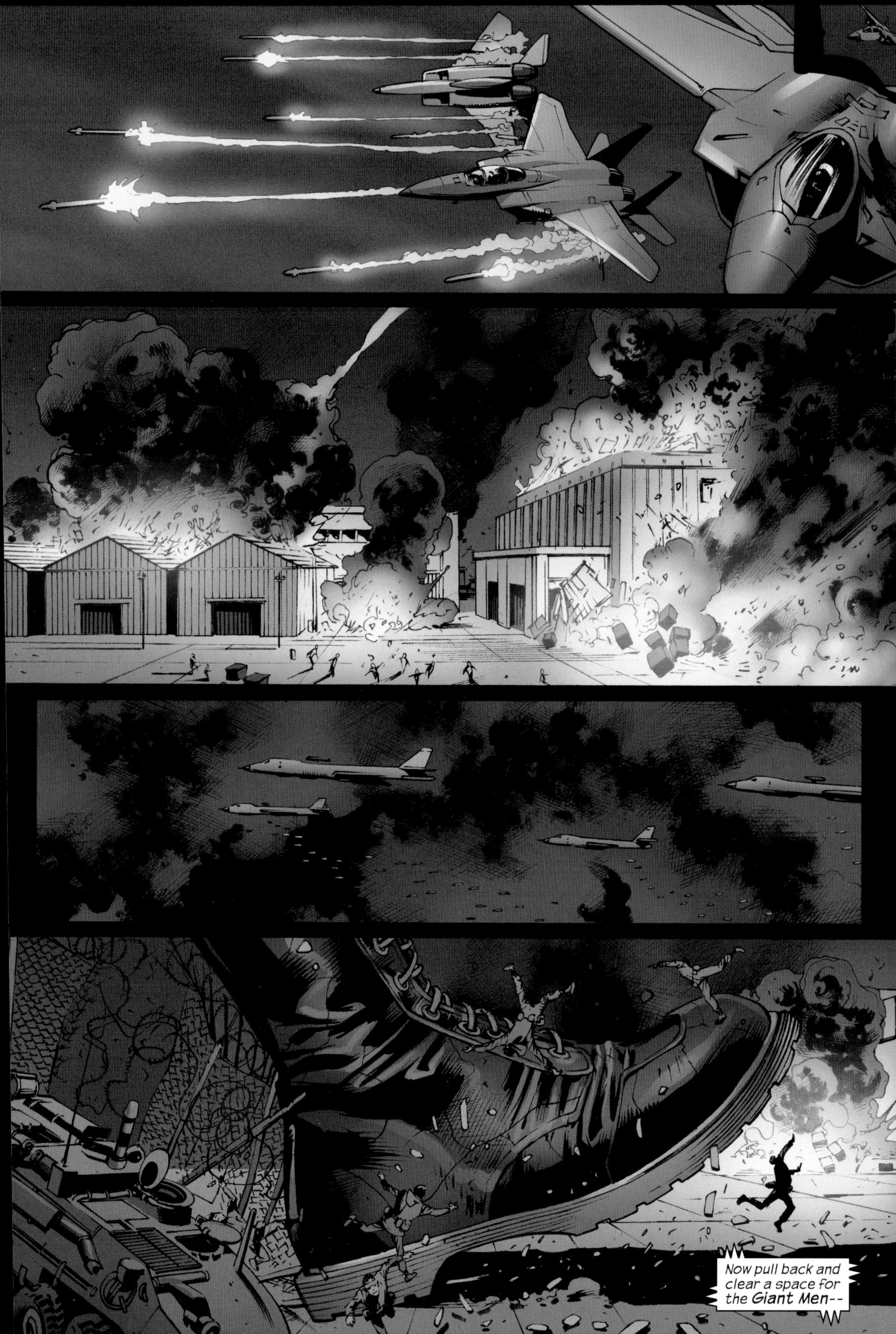
Now pull back and clear a space for the Giant Men--

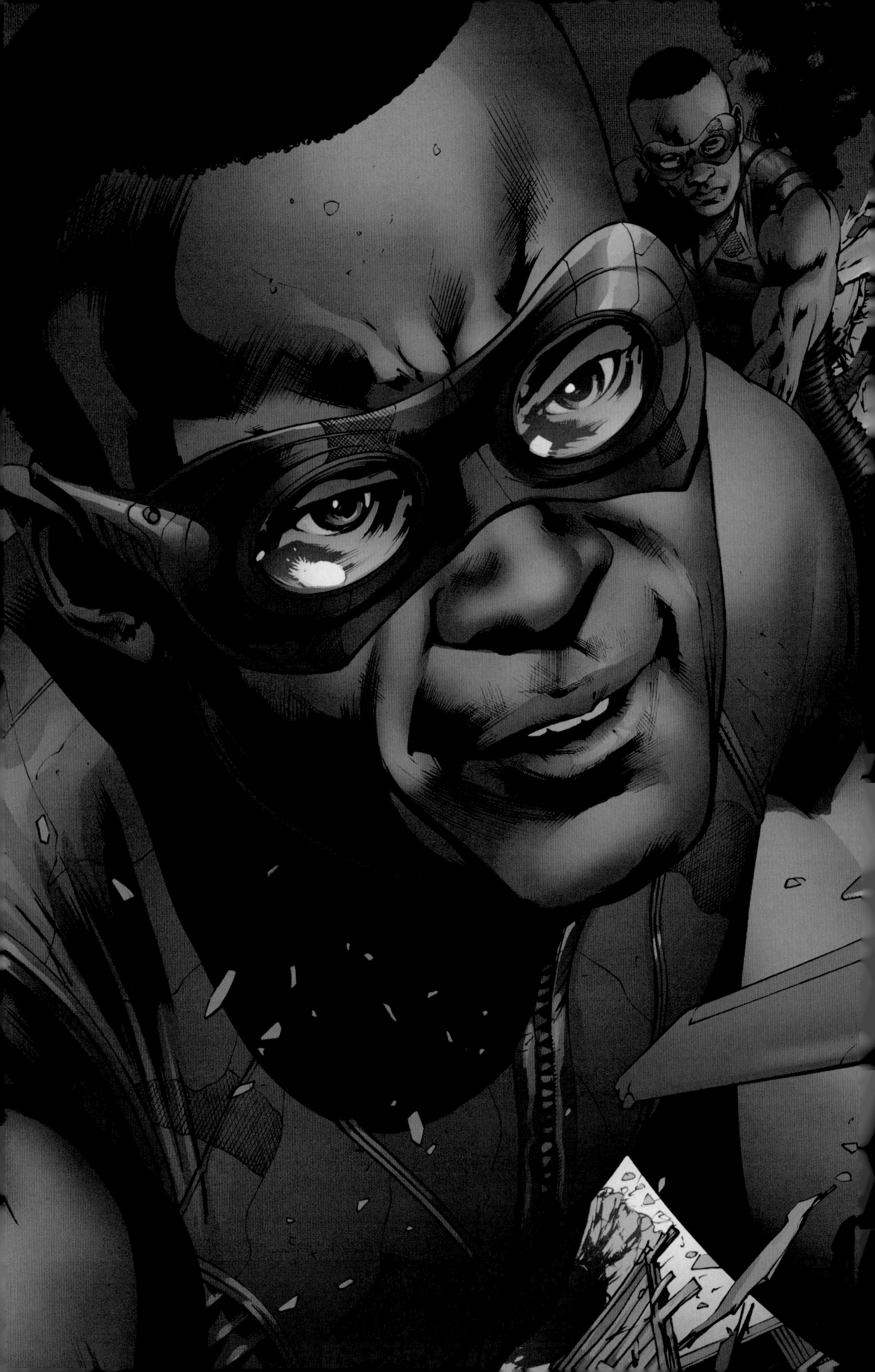

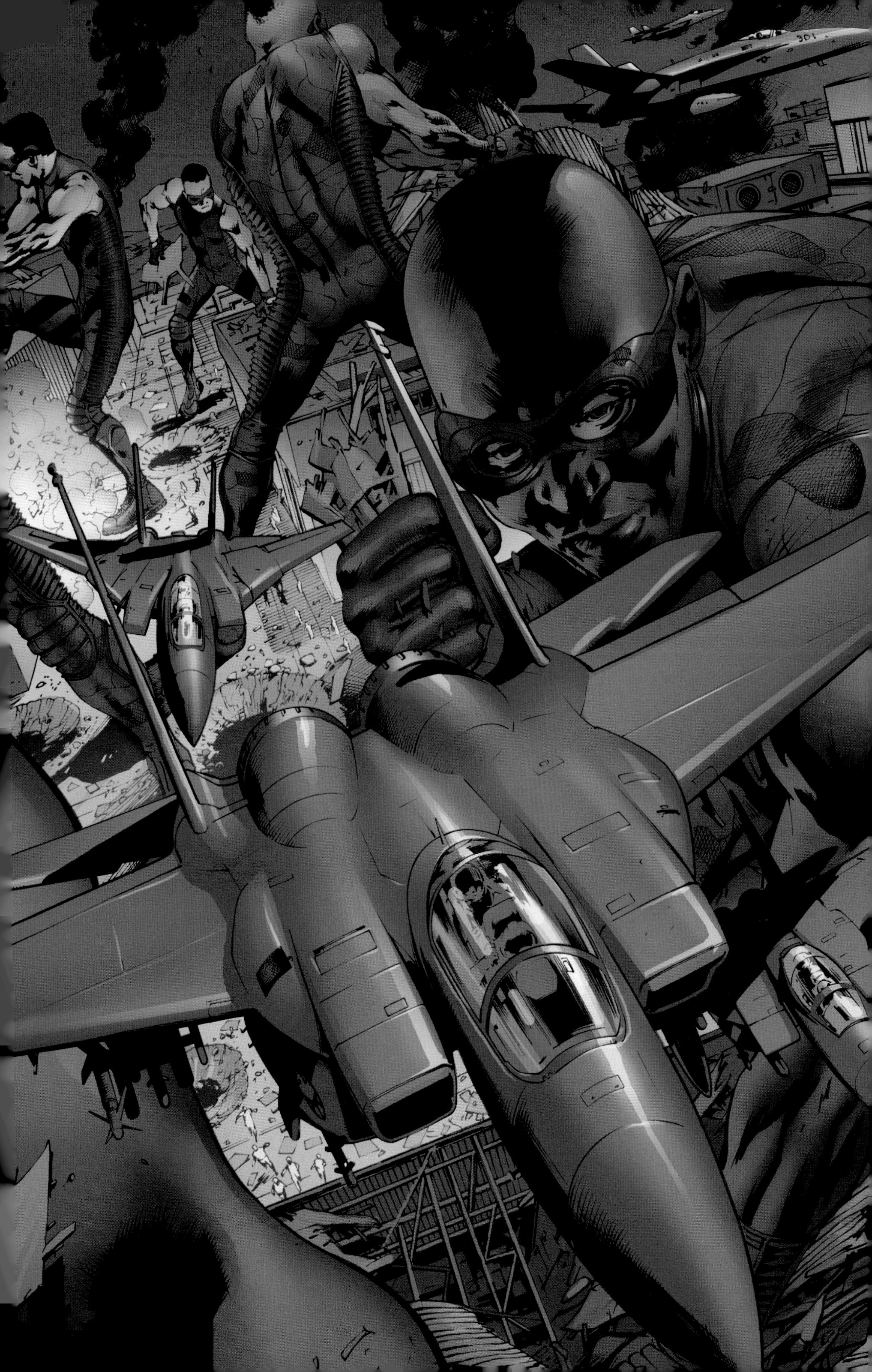

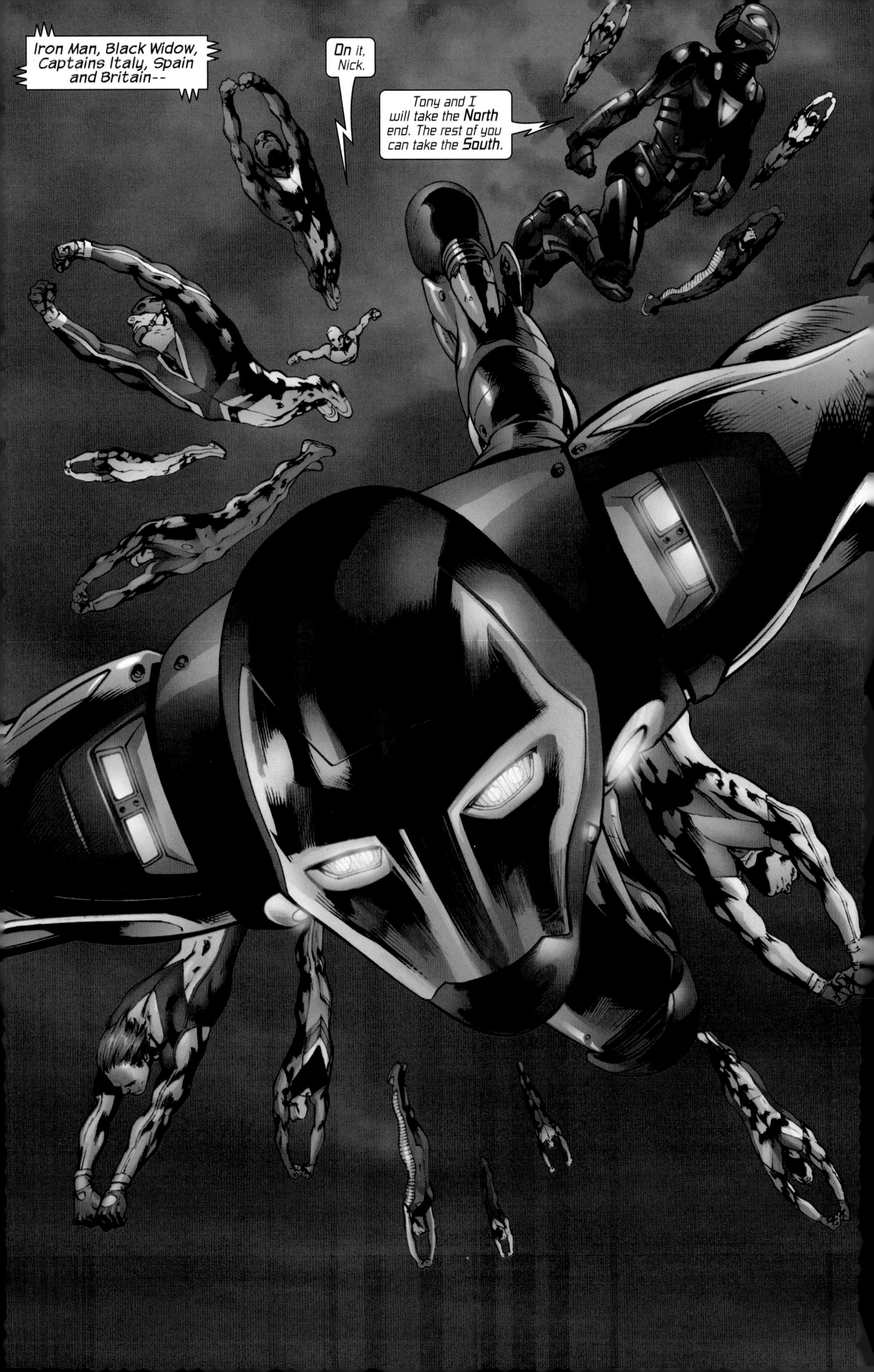

Iron Man, Black Widow, Captains Italy, Spain and Britain--
On it, Nick.
Tony and I will take the North end. The rest of you can take the South.

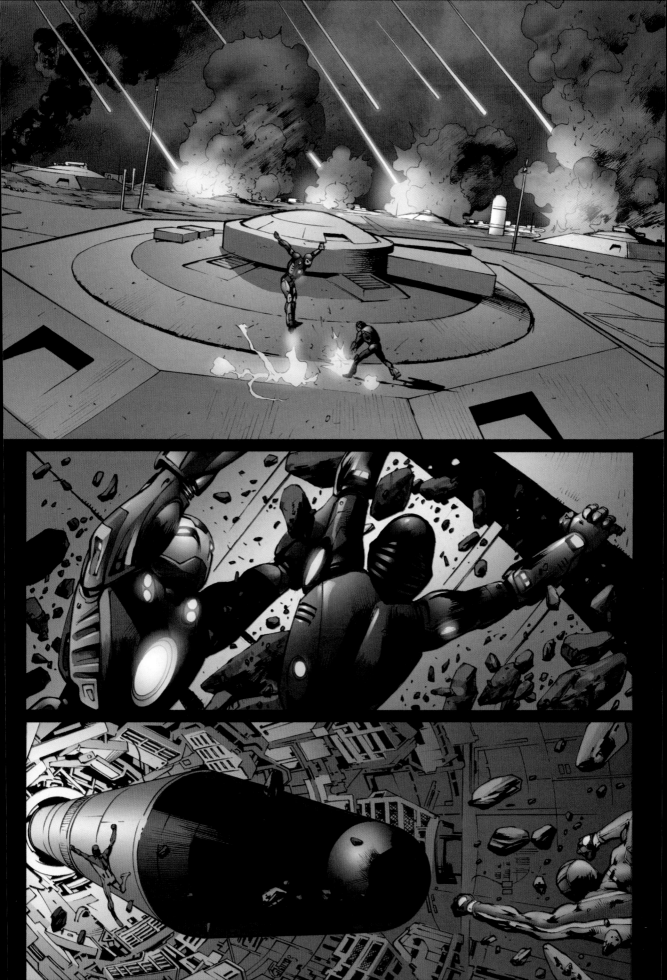

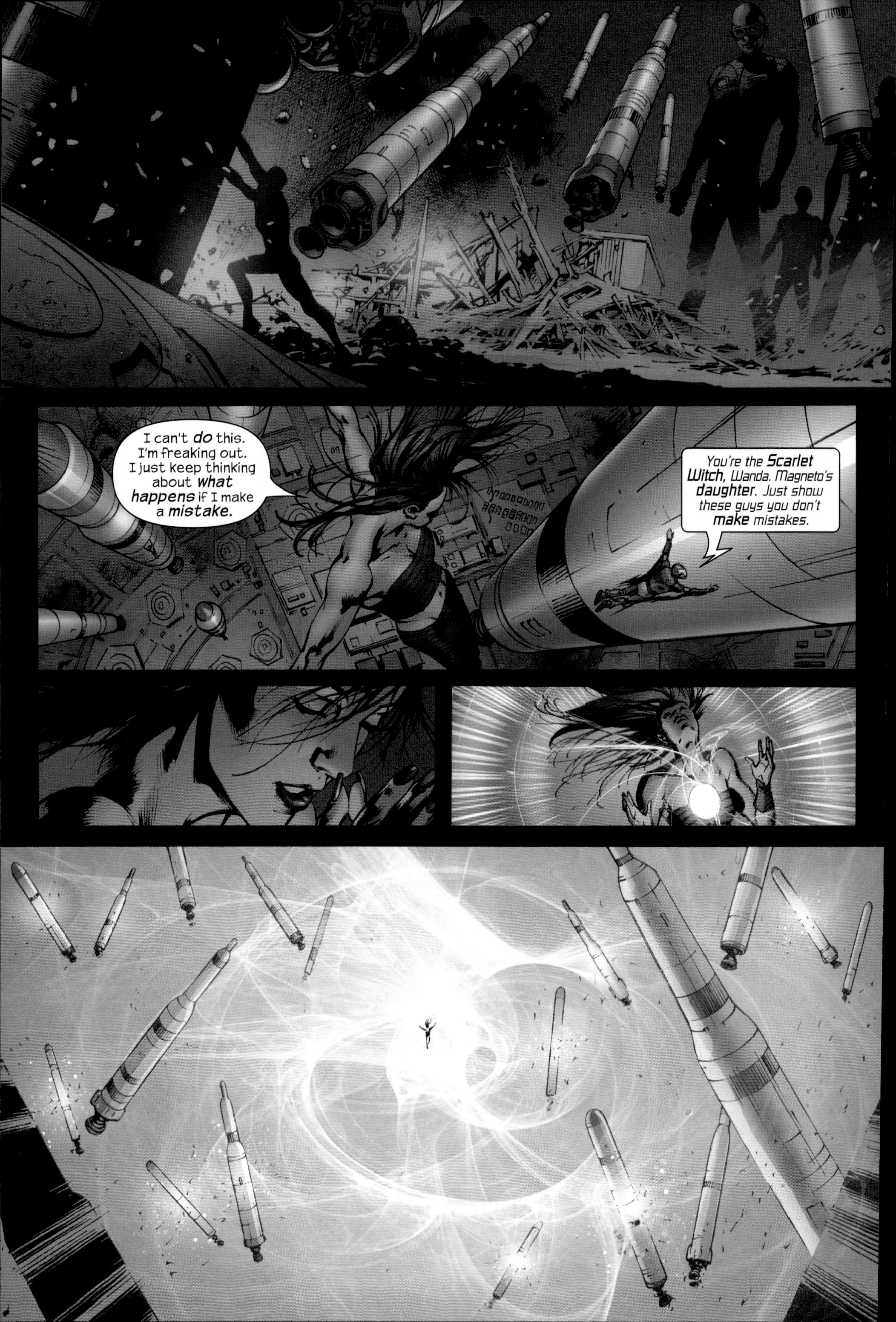
I can't **do** this. I'm freaking out. I just keep thinking about **what happens** if I make a **mistake.**
*You're the **Scarlet Witch**, Wanda. Magneto's **daughter**. Just show these guys you don't **make** mistakes.*

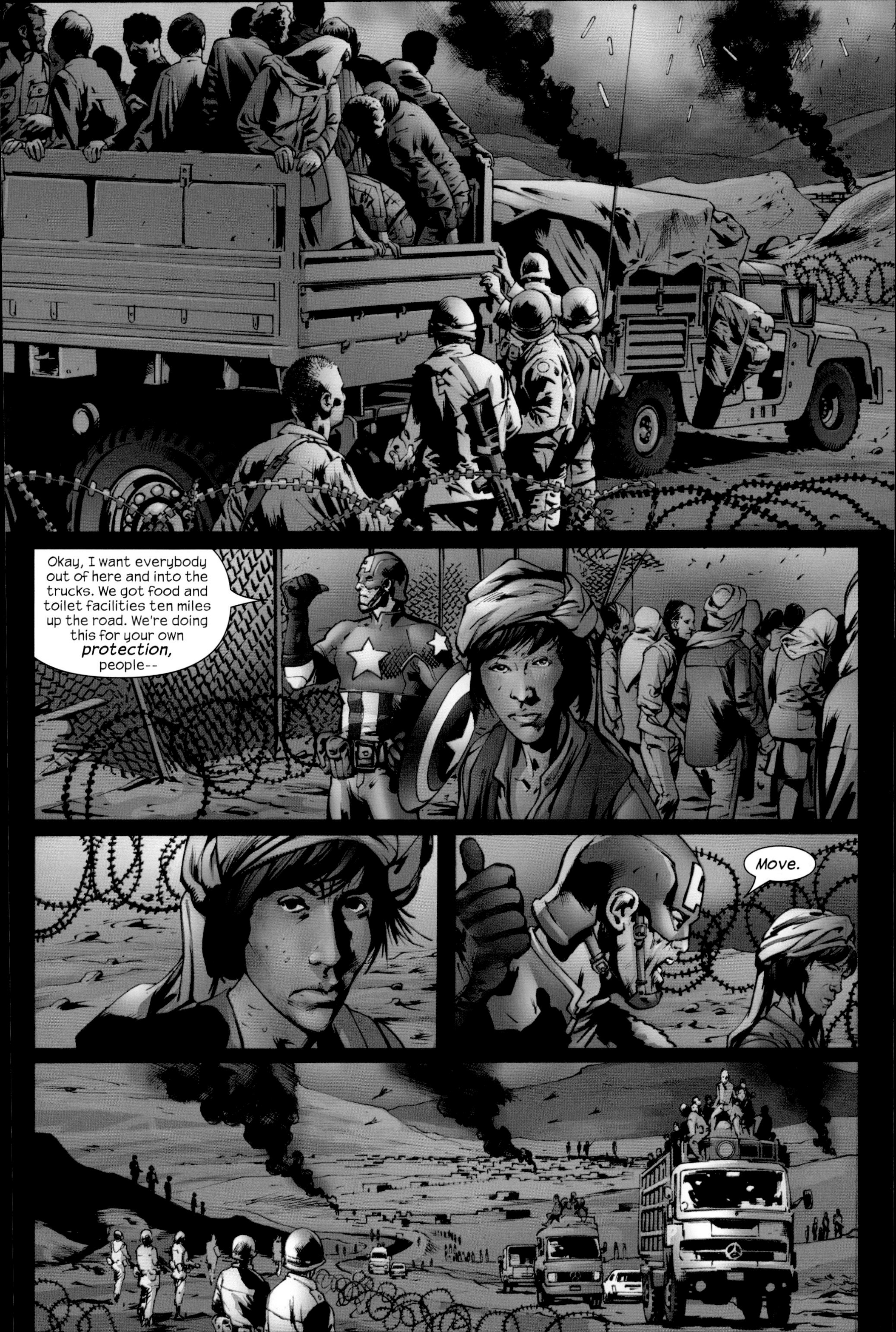
Okay, I want everybody out of here and into the trucks. We got food and toilet facilities ten miles up the road. We're doing this for your own *protection,* people--
Move.

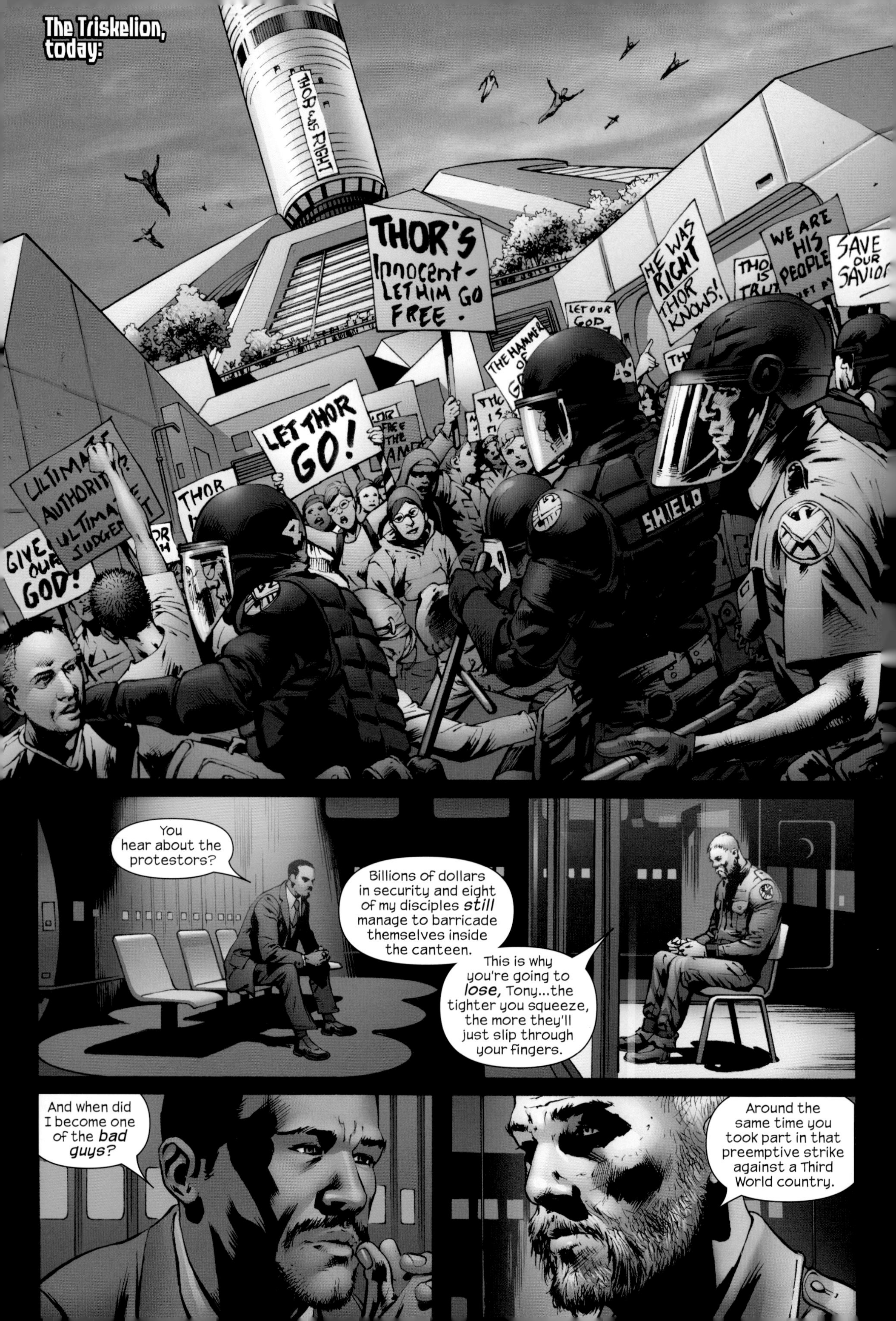
The Triskelion, today:
THOR WAS RIGHT
THOR'S Innocent- LET HIM GO FREE.
WE ARE HIS PEOPLE
HE WAS RIGHT THOR KNOWS!
LET THOR GO!
S.H.I.E.L.D
You hear about the protestors?
Billions of dollars in security and eight of my disciples *still* manage to barricade themselves inside the canteen.
This is why you're going to *lose,* Tony...the tighter you squeeze, the more they'll just slip through your fingers.
And when did I become one of the *bad guys?*
Around the same time you took part in that preemptive strike against a Third World country.

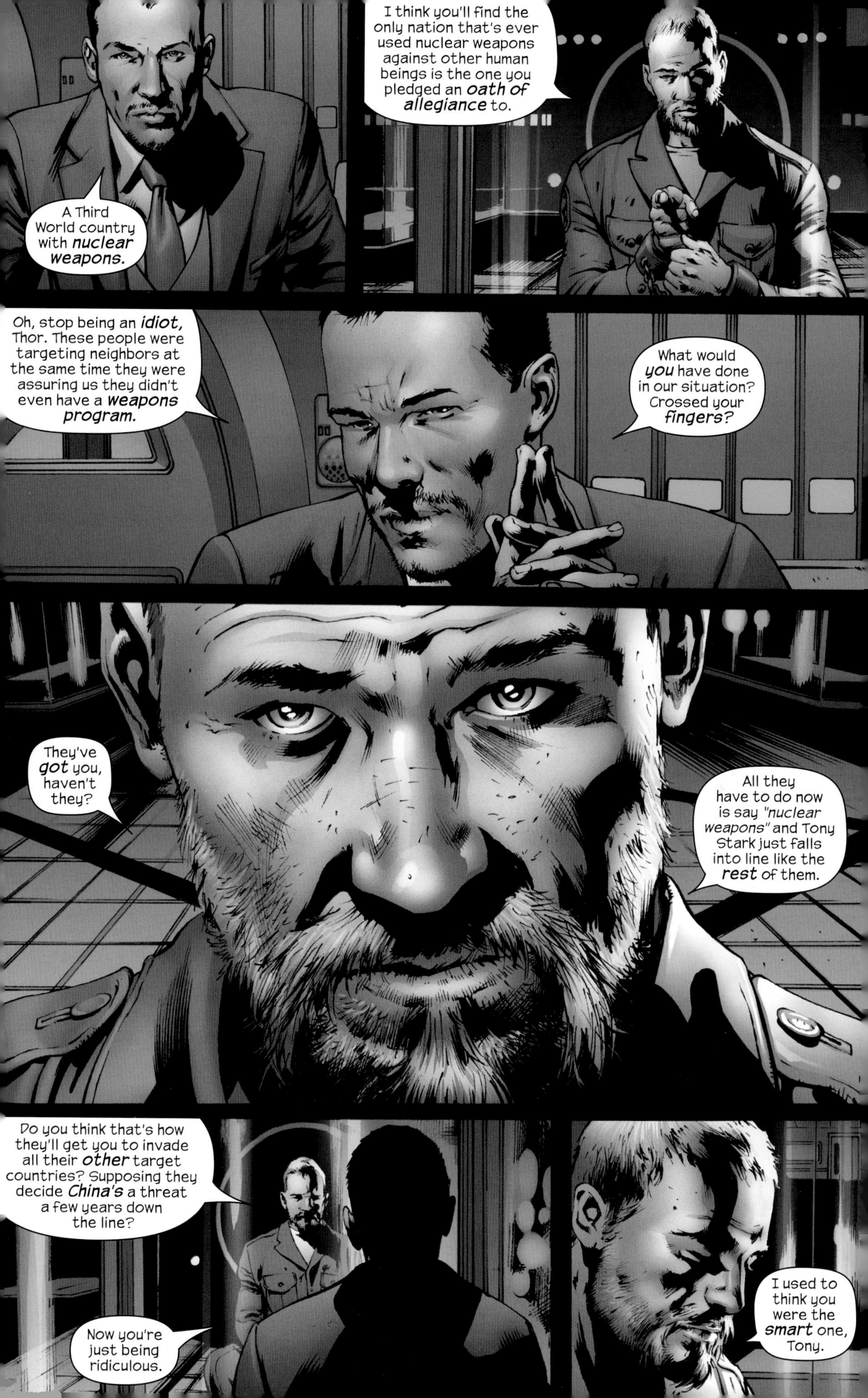
I think you'll find the only nation that's ever used nuclear weapons against other human beings is the one you pledged an *oath of allegiance* to.
A Third World country with *nuclear weapons.*
Oh, stop being an *idiot,* Thor. These people were targeting neighbors at the same time they were assuring us they didn't even have a *weapons program.*
What would *you* have done in our situation? Crossed your *fingers?*
They've *got* you, haven't they?
All they have to do now is say *"nuclear weapons"* and Tony Stark just falls into line like the *rest* of them.
Do you think that's how they'll get you to invade all their *other* target countries? Supposing they decide *China's* a threat a few years down the line?
Now you're just being ridiculous.
I used to think you were the *smart* one, Tony.

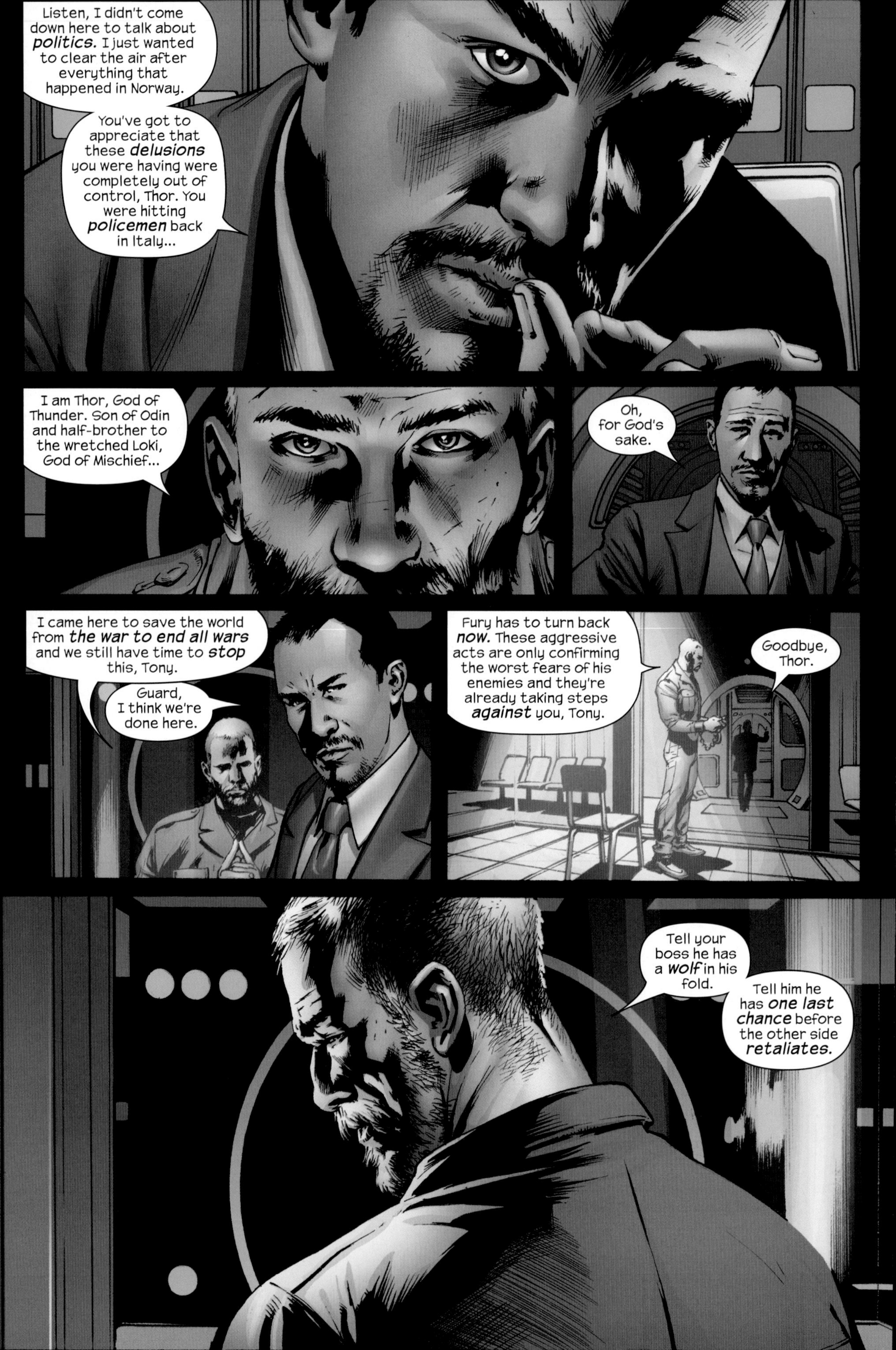
Listen, I didn't come down here to talk about politics. I just wanted to clear the air after everything that happened in Norway.
You've got to appreciate that these delusions you were having were completely out of control, Thor. You were hitting policemen back in Italy...
I am Thor, God of Thunder. Son of Odin and half-brother to the wretched Loki, God of Mischief...
Oh, for God's sake.
I came here to save the world from the war to end all wars and we still have time to stop this, Tony.
Guard, I think we're done here.
Fury has to turn back now. These aggressive acts are only confirming the worst fears of his enemies and they're already taking steps against you, Tony.
Goodbye, Thor.
Tell your boss he has a wolf in his fold.
Tell him he has one last chance before the other side retaliates.

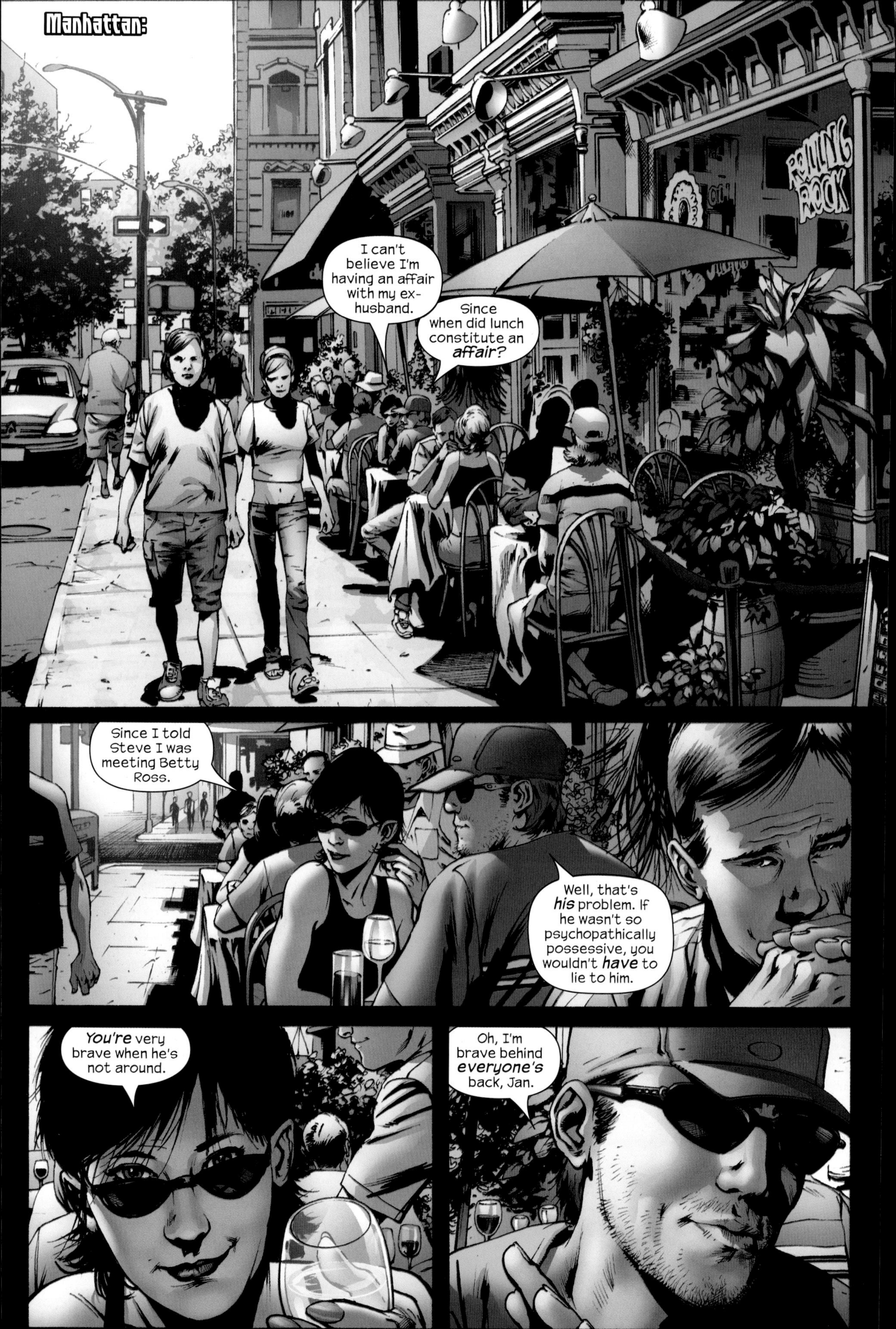
Manhattan:
I can't believe I'm having an affair with my ex-husband.
Since when did lunch constitute an *affair?*
Since I told Steve I was meeting Betty Ross.
Well, that's *his* problem. If he wasn't so psychopathically possessive, you wouldn't *have* to lie to him.
You're very brave when he's not around.
Oh, I'm brave behind *everyone's* back, Jan.

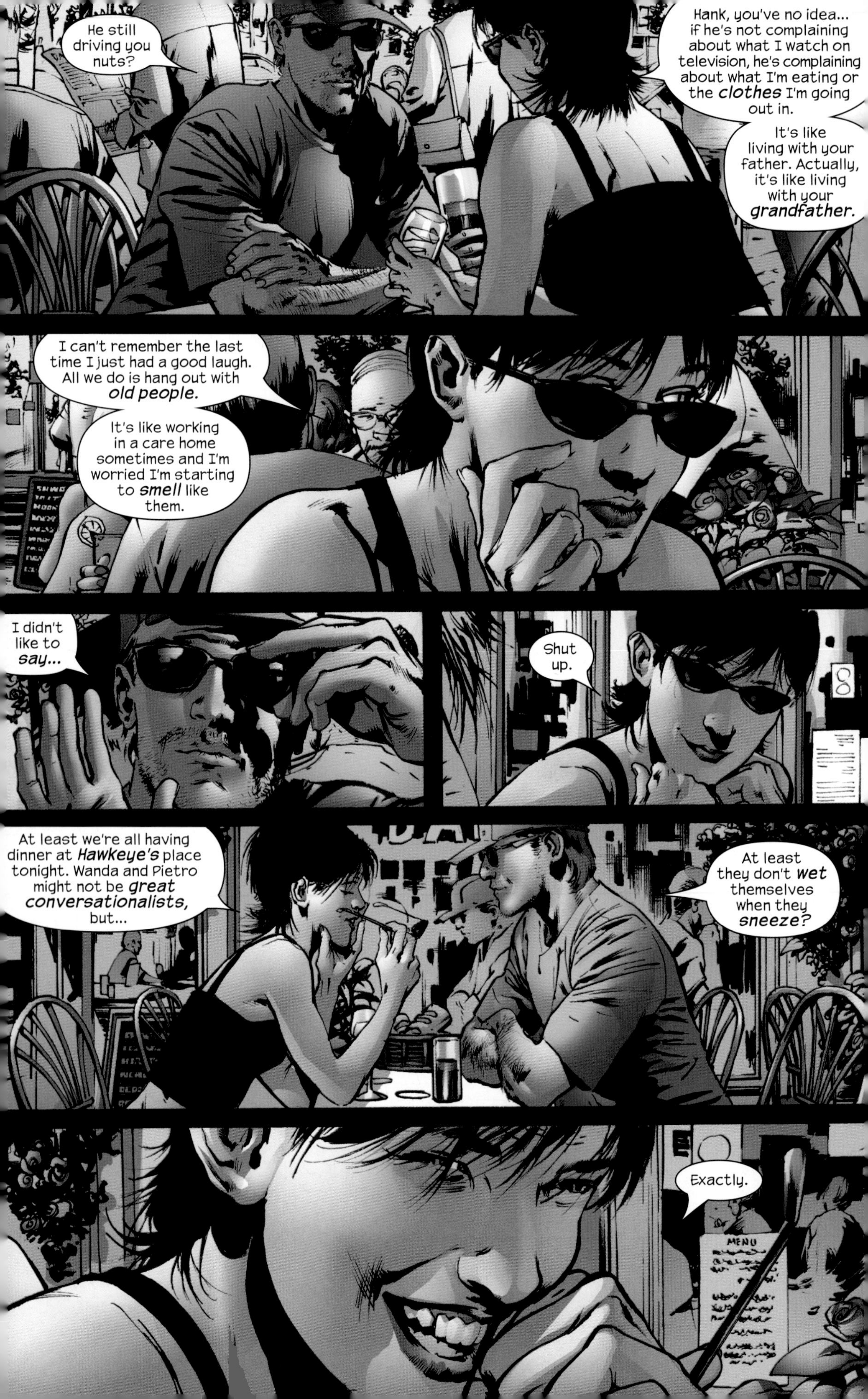
He still driving you nuts?
Hank, you've no idea... if he's not complaining about what I watch on television, he's complaining about what I'm eating or the clothes I'm going out in.
It's like living with your father. Actually, it's like living with your grandfather.
I can't remember the last time I just had a good laugh. All we do is hang out with old people.
It's like working in a care home sometimes and I'm worried I'm starting to smell like them.
I didn't like to say...
Shut up.
At least we're all having dinner at Hawkeye's place tonight. Wanda and Pietro might not be great conversationalists, but...
At least they don't wet themselves when they sneeze?
Exactly.
MENU

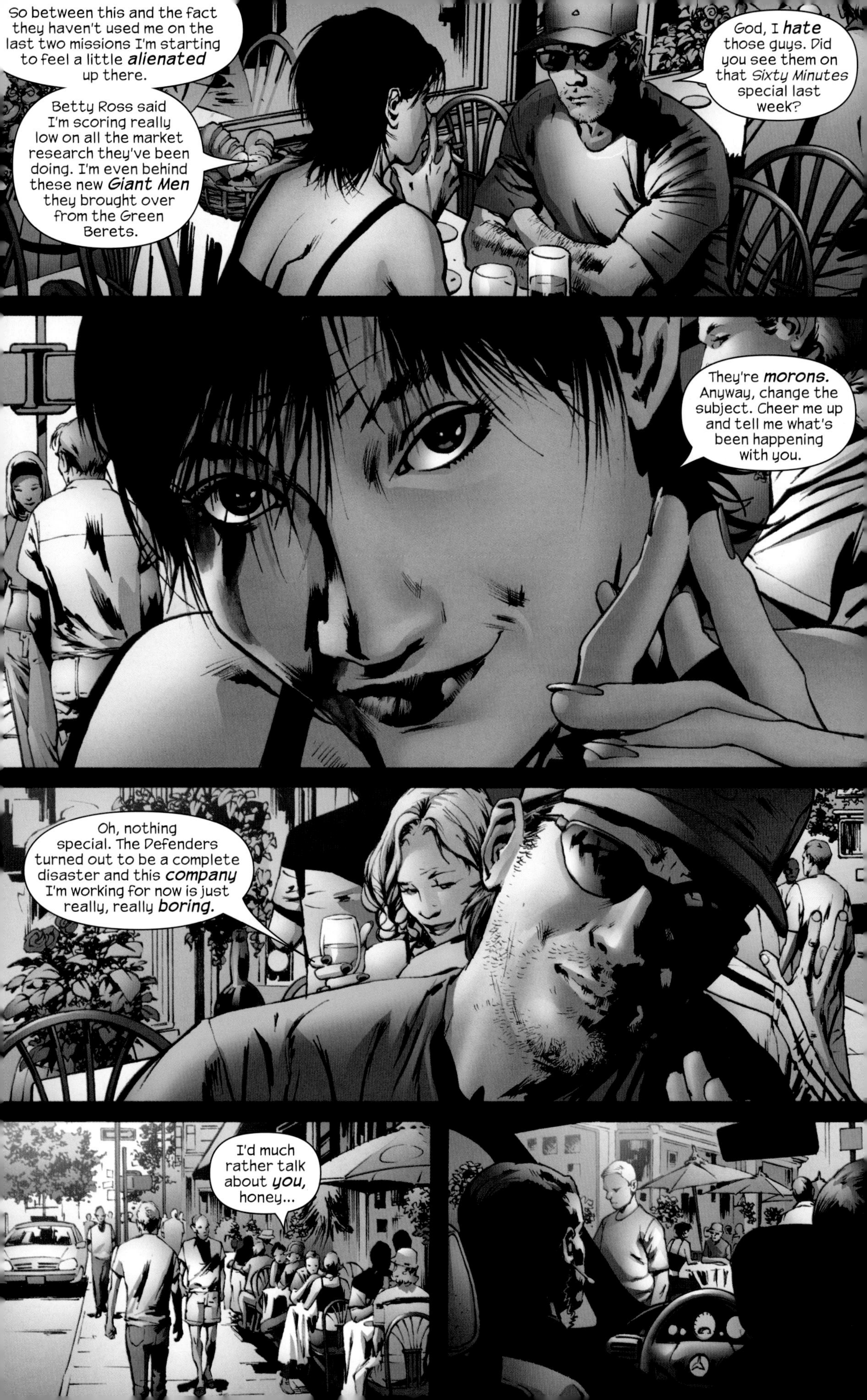
So between this and the fact they haven't used me on the last two missions I'm starting to feel a little *alienated* up there.
Betty Ross said I'm scoring really low on all the market research they've been doing. I'm even behind these new *Giant Men* they brought over from the Green Berets.
God, I *hate* those guys. Did you see them on that *Sixty Minutes* special last week?
They're *morons.* Anyway, change the subject. Cheer me up and tell me what's been happening with you.
Oh, nothing special. The Defenders turned out to be a complete disaster and this *company* I'm working for now is just really, really *boring.*
I'd much rather talk about *you,* honey...

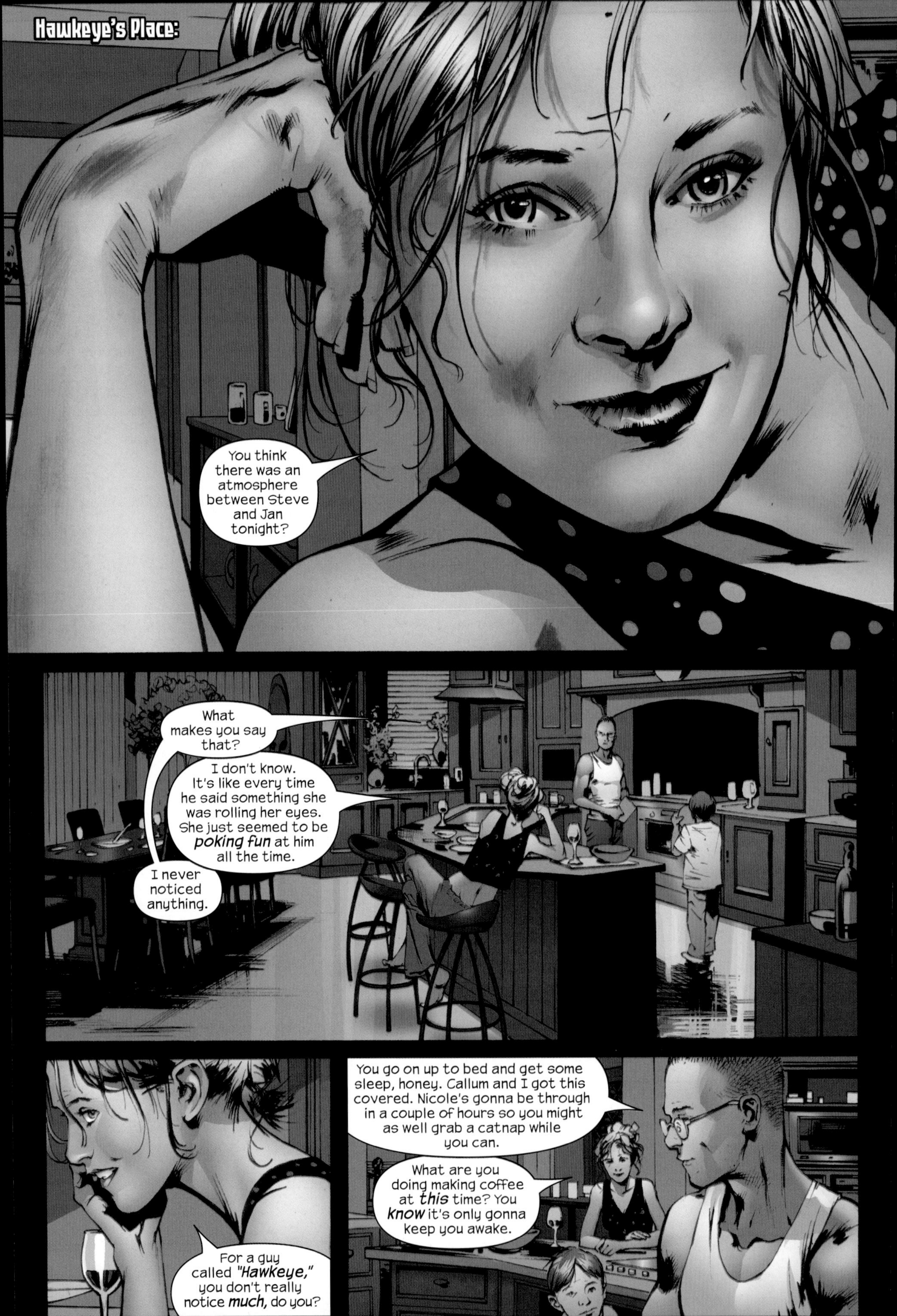
Hawkeye's Place:
You think there was an atmosphere between Steve and Jan tonight?
What makes you say that?
I don't know. It's like every time he said something she was rolling her eyes. She just seemed to be *poking fun* at him all the time.
I never noticed anything.
For a guy called *"Hawkeye,"* you don't really notice *much,* do you?
You go on up to bed and get some sleep, honey. Callum and I got this covered. Nicole's gonna be through in a couple of hours so you might as well grab a catnap while you can.
What are you doing making coffee at *this* time? You *know* it's only gonna keep you awake.

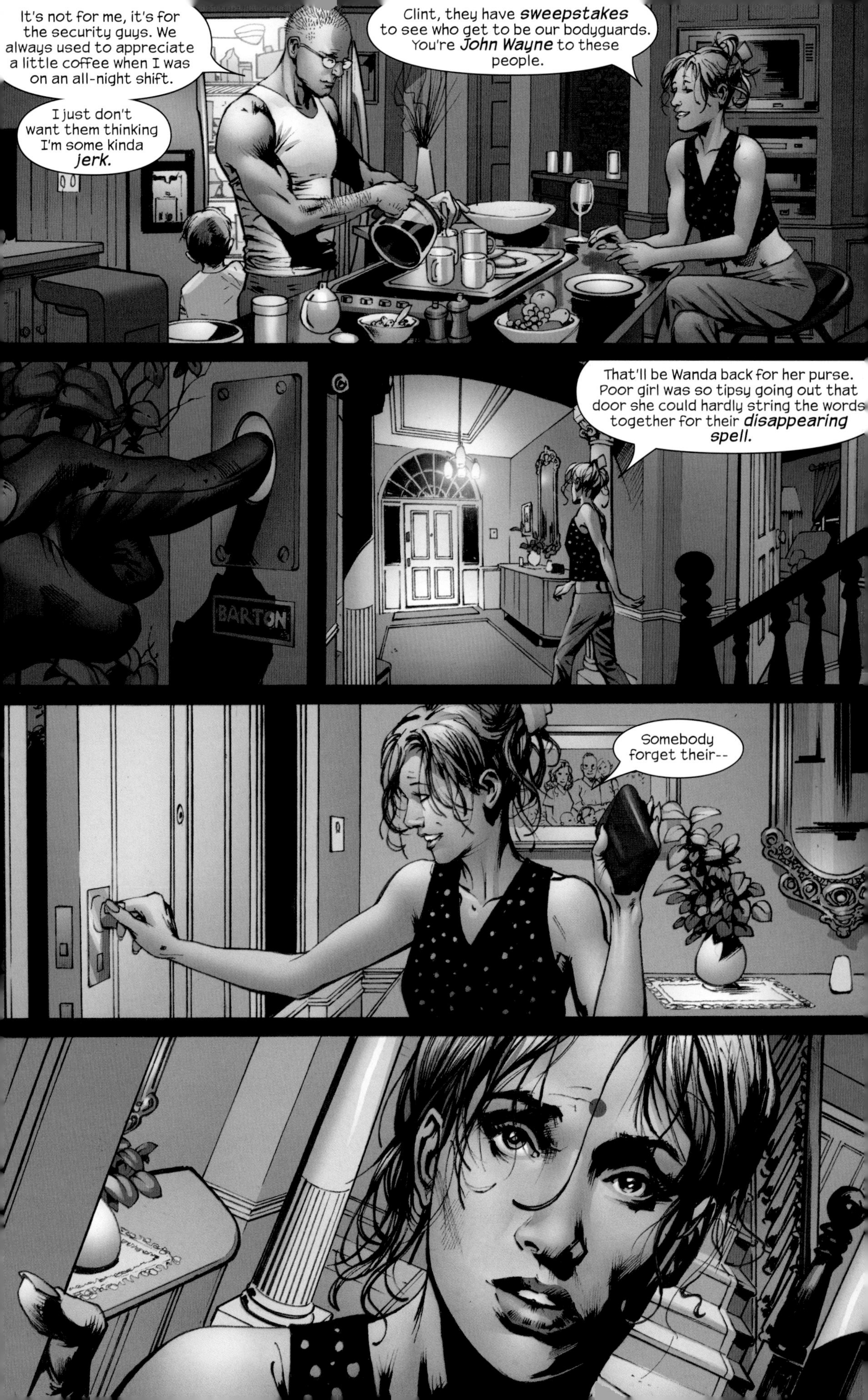
It's not for me, it's for the security guys. We always used to appreciate a little coffee when I was on an all-night shift.
I just don't want them thinking I'm some kinda jerk.
Clint, they have sweepstakes to see who get to be our bodyguards. You're John Wayne to these people.
BARTON
That'll be Wanda back for her purse. Poor girl was so tipsy going out that door she could hardly string the words together for their disappearing spell.
Somebody forget their--

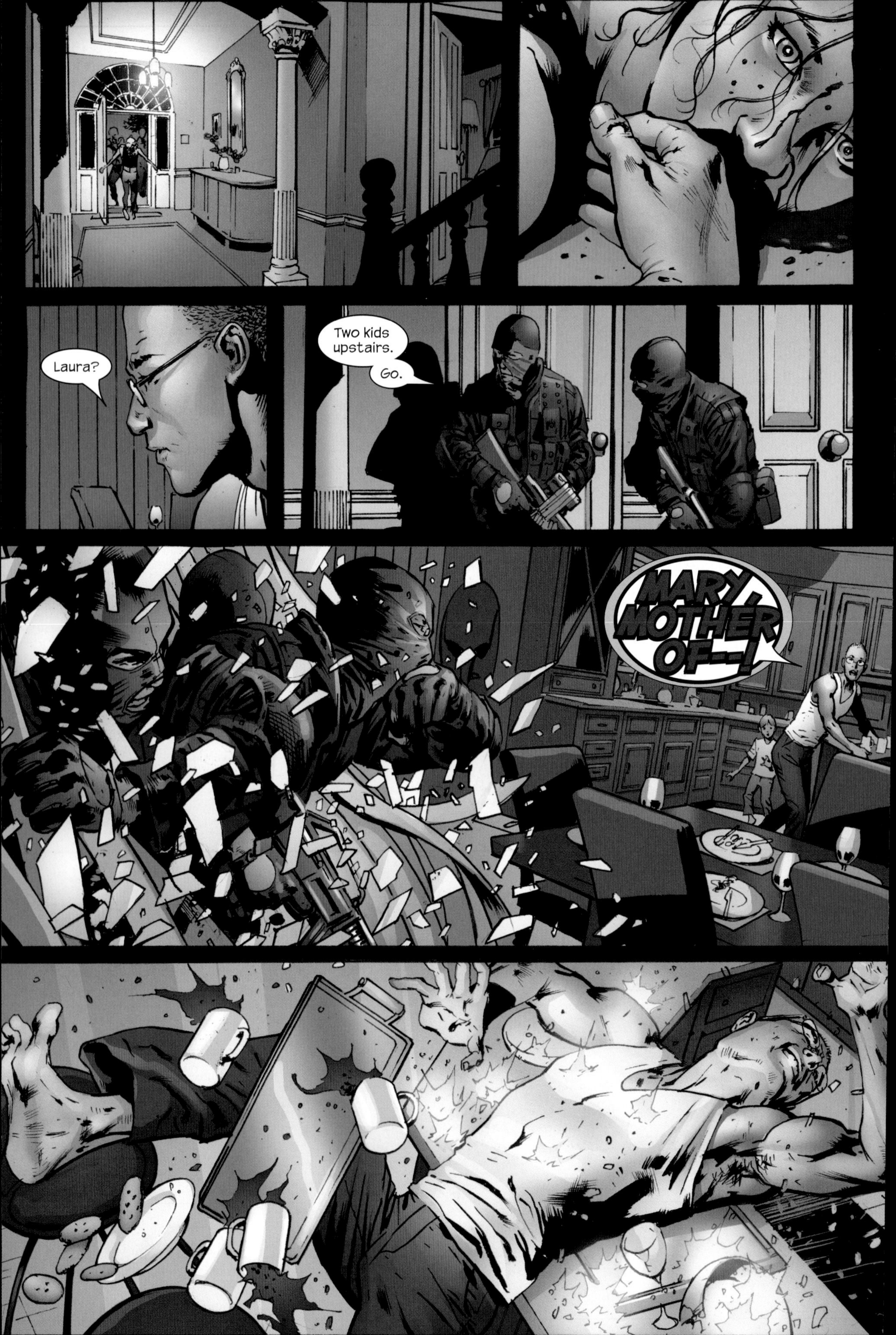
Laura?
Two kids upstairs.
Go.
MARY, MOTHER OF--!

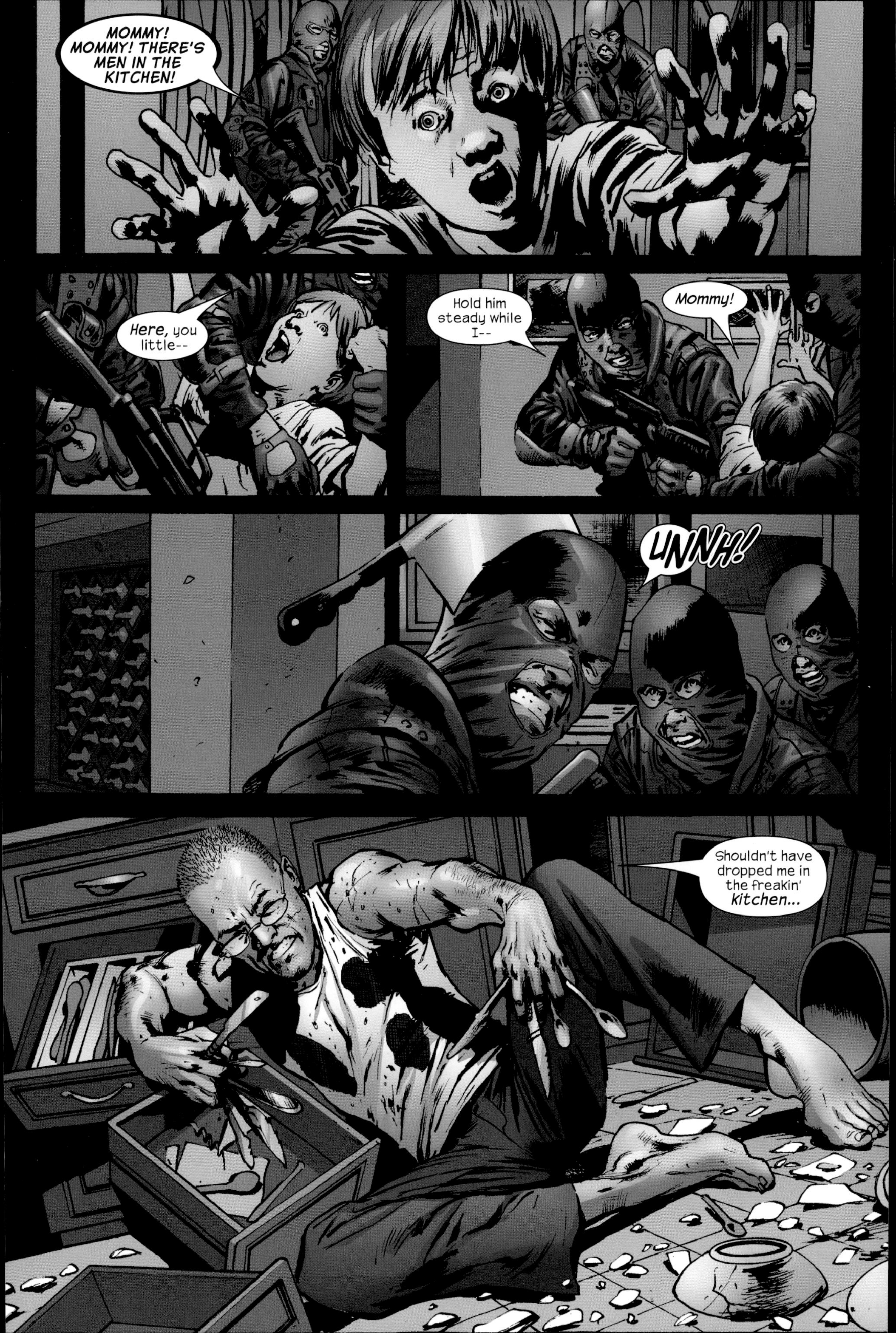

MOMMY! MOMMY! THERE'S MEN IN THE KITCHEN!
Here, you little--
Hold him steady while I--
Mommy!
UNNH!
Shouldn't have dropped me in the freakin' kitchen...

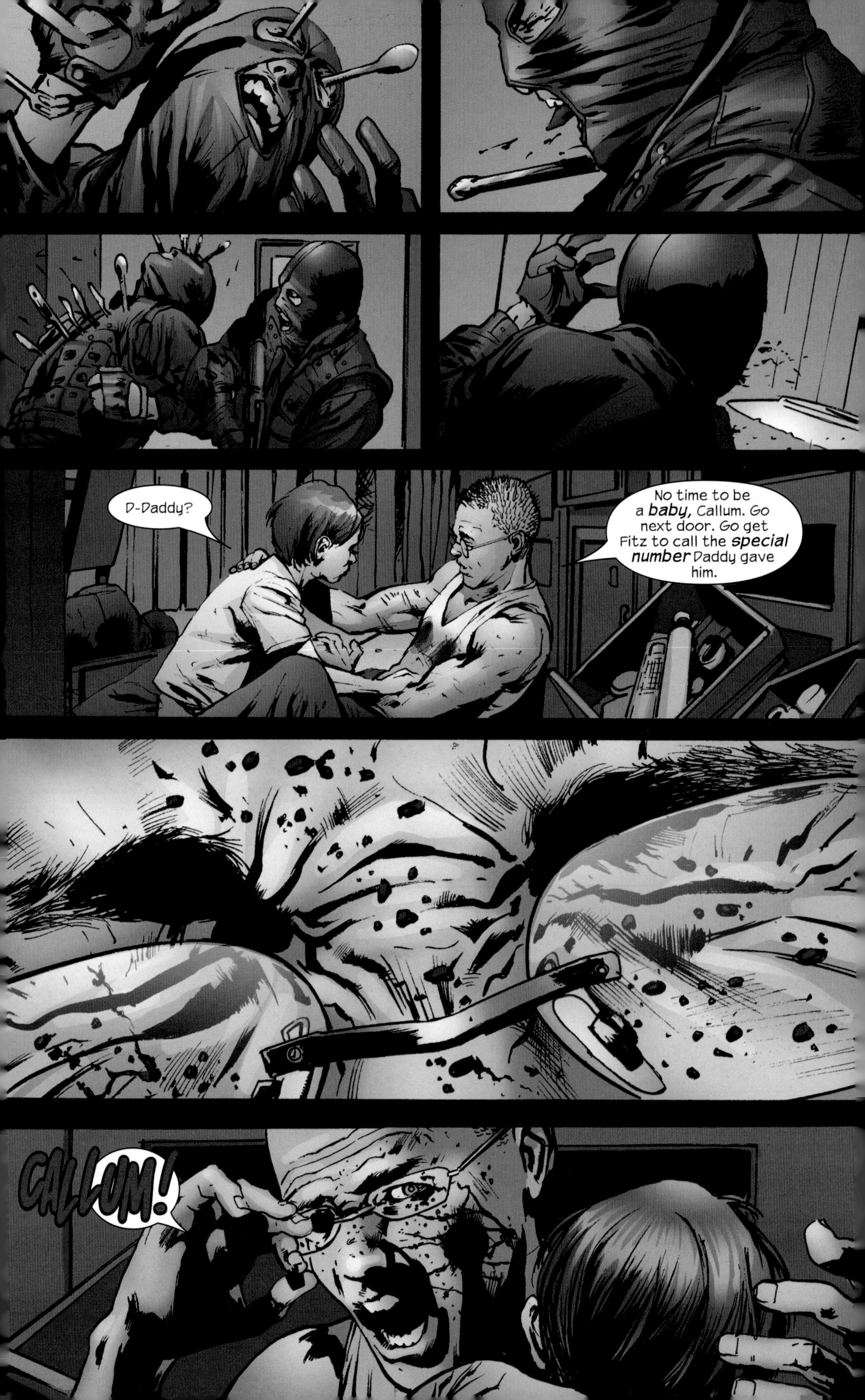
D-Daddy?
No time to be a *baby,* Callum. Go next door. Go get Fitz to call the *special number* Daddy gave him.
CALLUM!

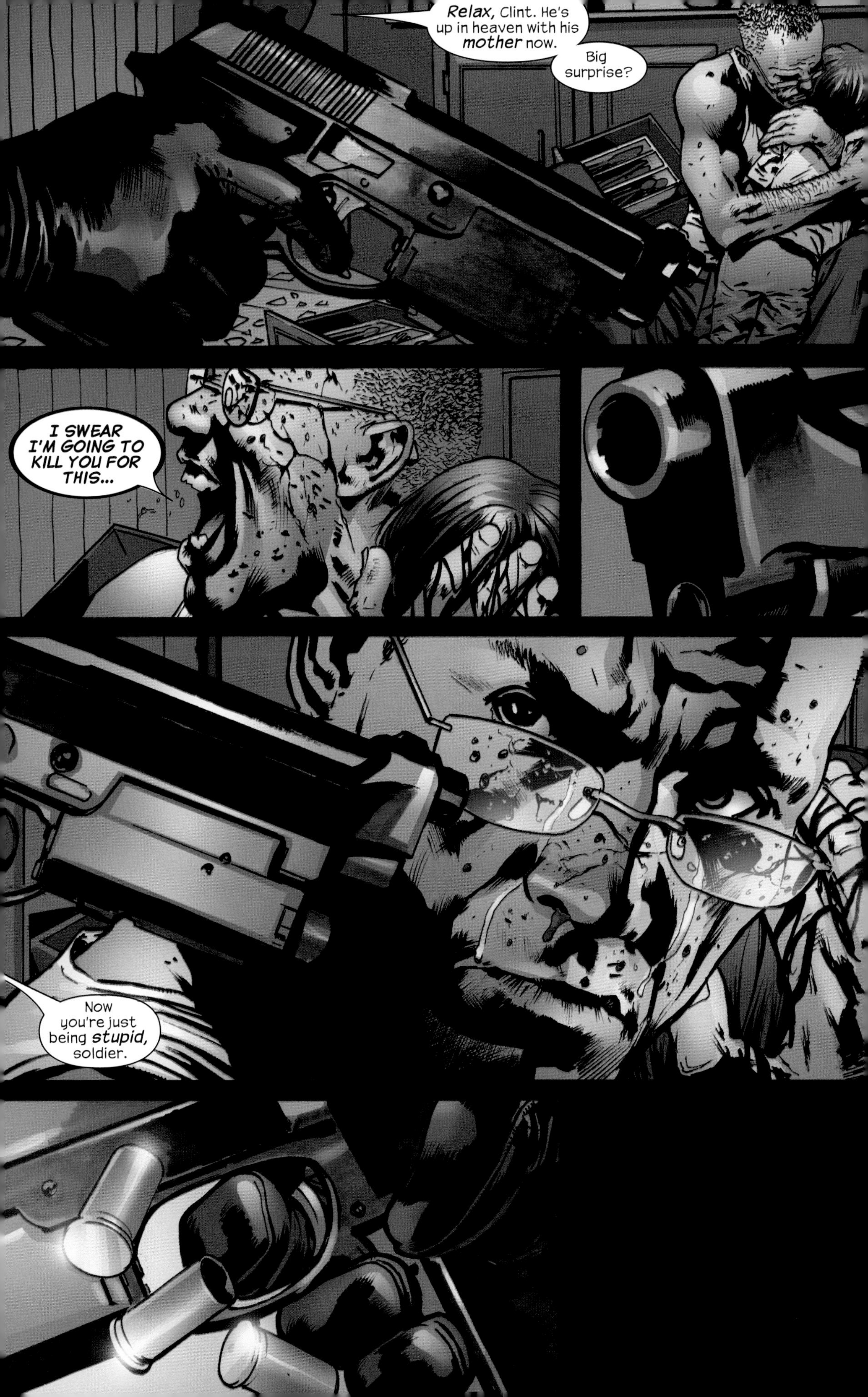
Relax, Clint. He's up in heaven with his ***mother*** now.
Big surprise?
I SWEAR I'M GOING TO KILL YOU FOR THIS...
Now you're just being ***stupid,*** soldier.

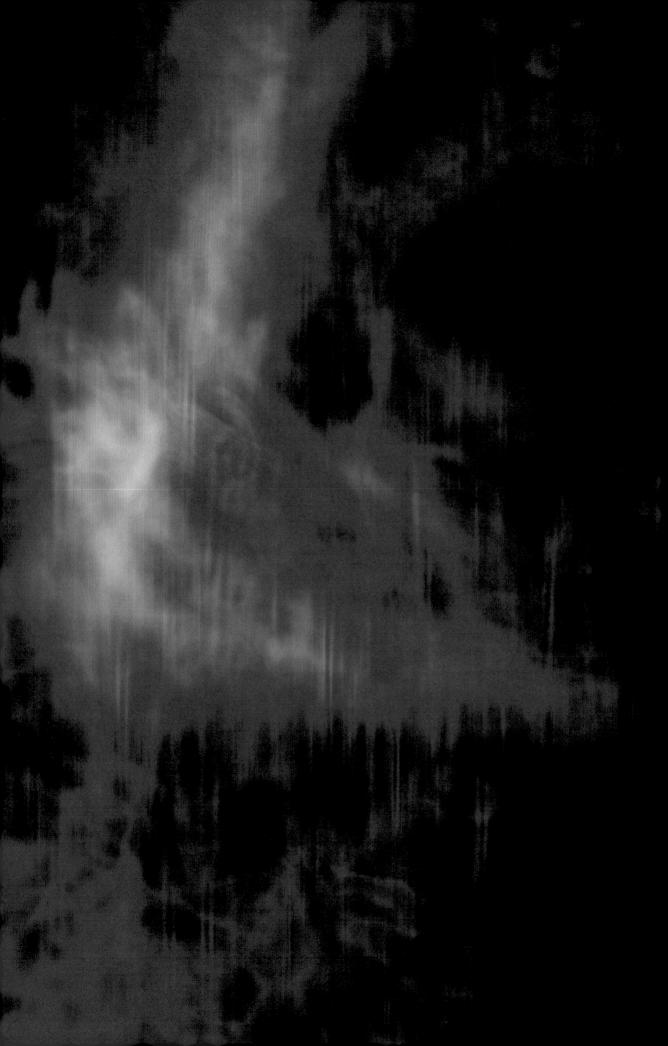

BORN ON THE FOURTH OF JULY

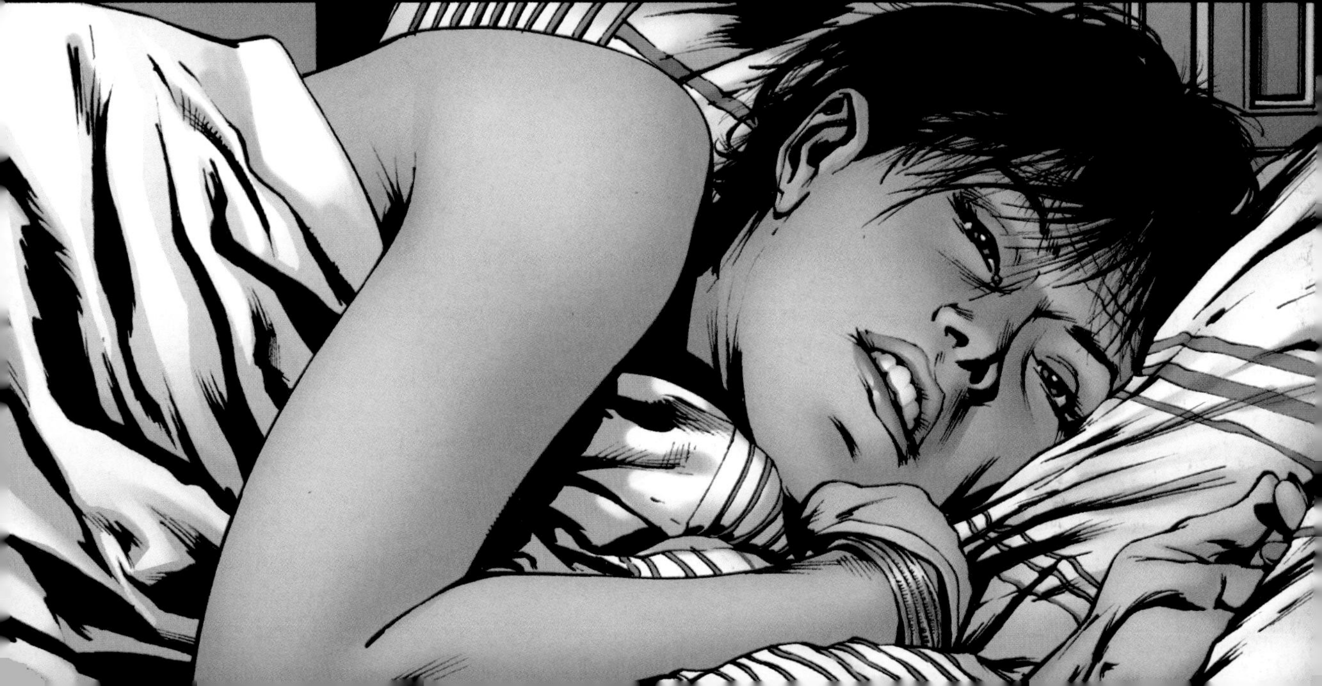

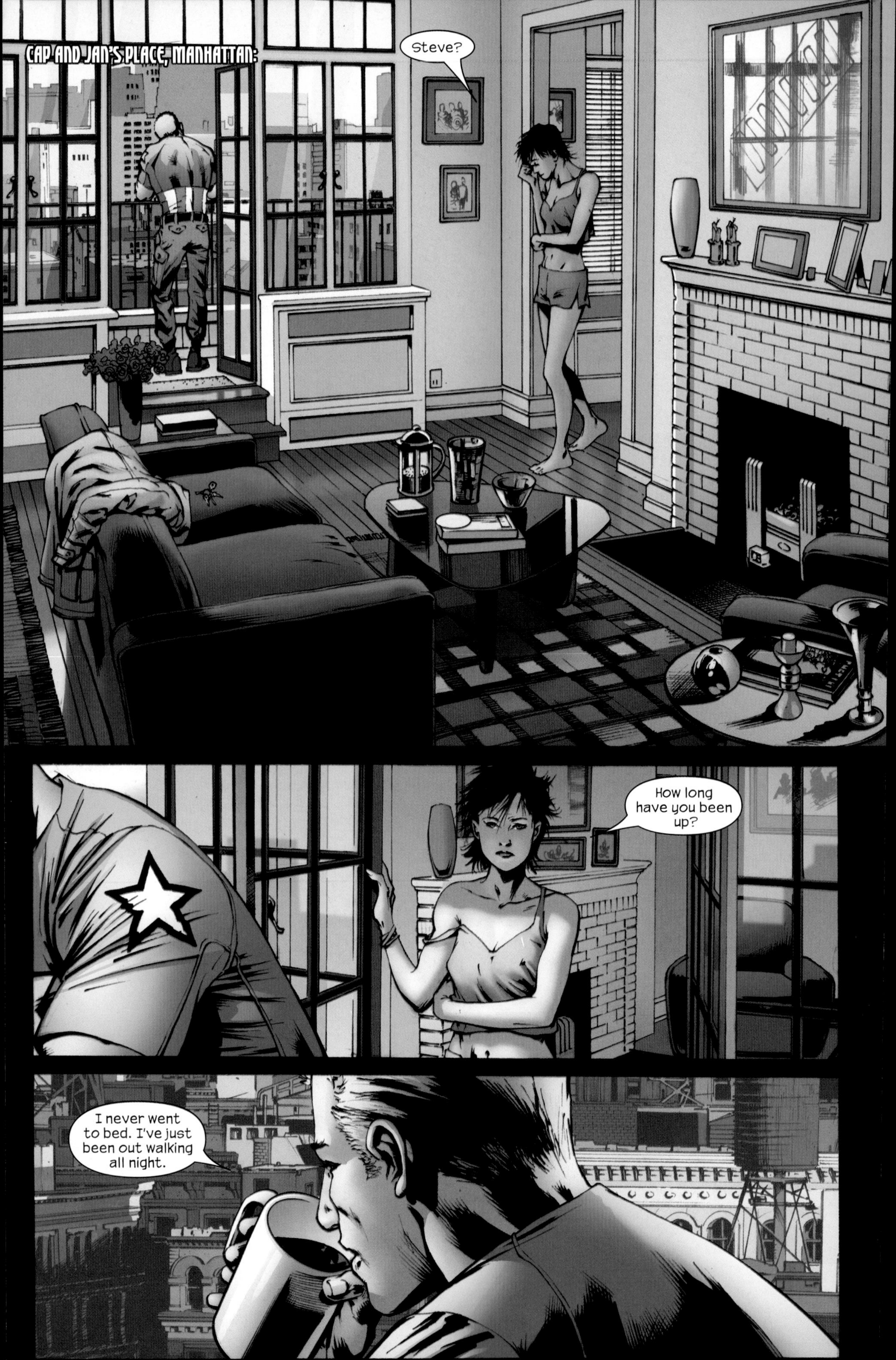
CAP AND JAN'S PLACE, MANHATTAN:
Steve?
How long have you been up?
I never went to bed. I've just been out walking all night.

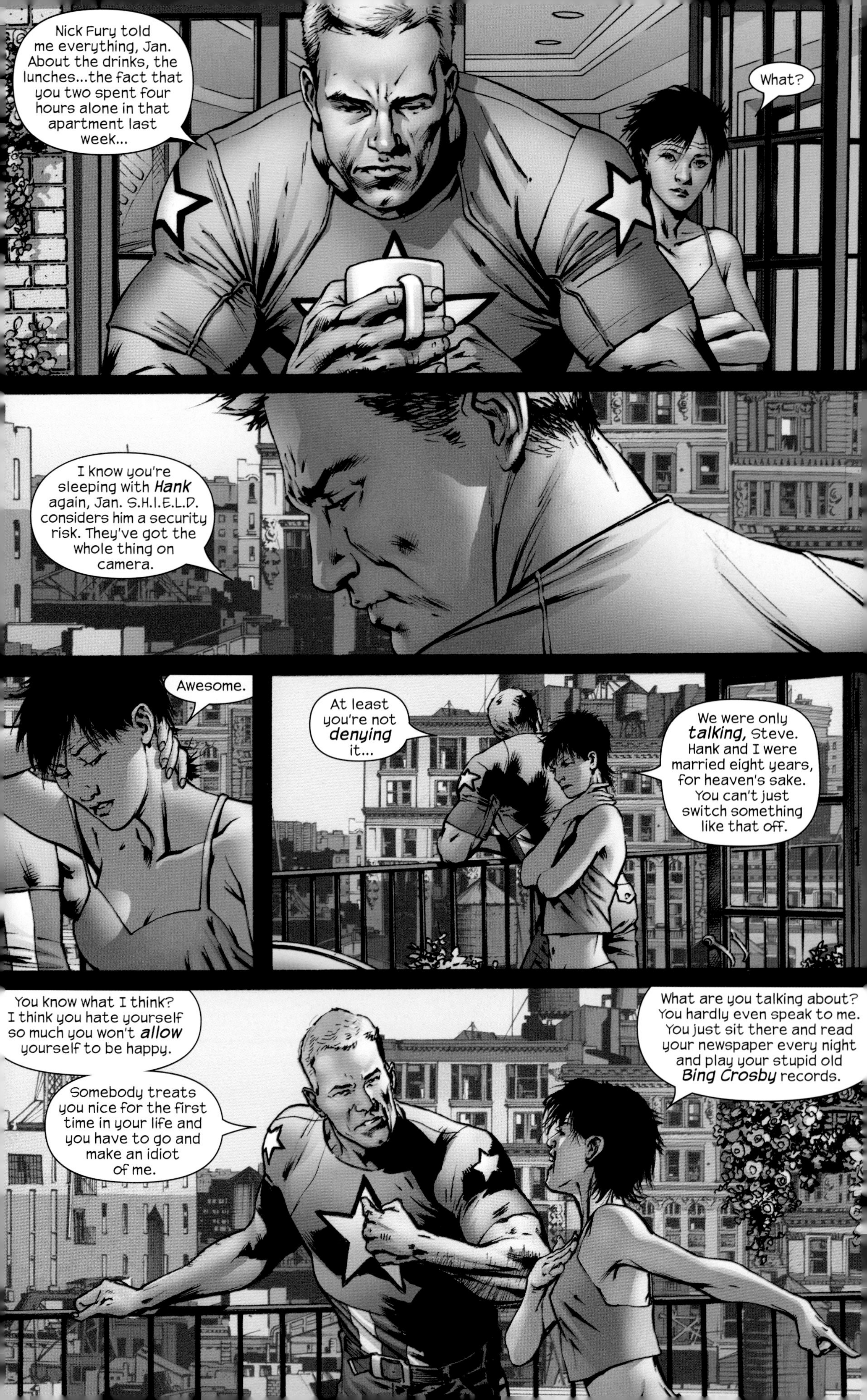
Nick Fury told me everything, Jan. About the drinks, the lunches...the fact that you two spent four hours alone in that apartment last week...
What?
I know you're sleeping with *Hank* again, Jan. S.H.I.E.L.D. considers him a security risk. They've got the whole thing on camera.
Awesome.
At least you're not *denying* it...
We were only *talking,* Steve. Hank and I were married eight years, for heaven's sake. You can't just switch something like that off.
You know what I think? I think you hate yourself so much you won't *allow* yourself to be happy.
Somebody treats you nice for the first time in your life and you have to go and make an idiot of me.
What are you talking about? You hardly even speak to me. You just sit there and read your newspaper every night and play your stupid old *Bing Crosby* records.

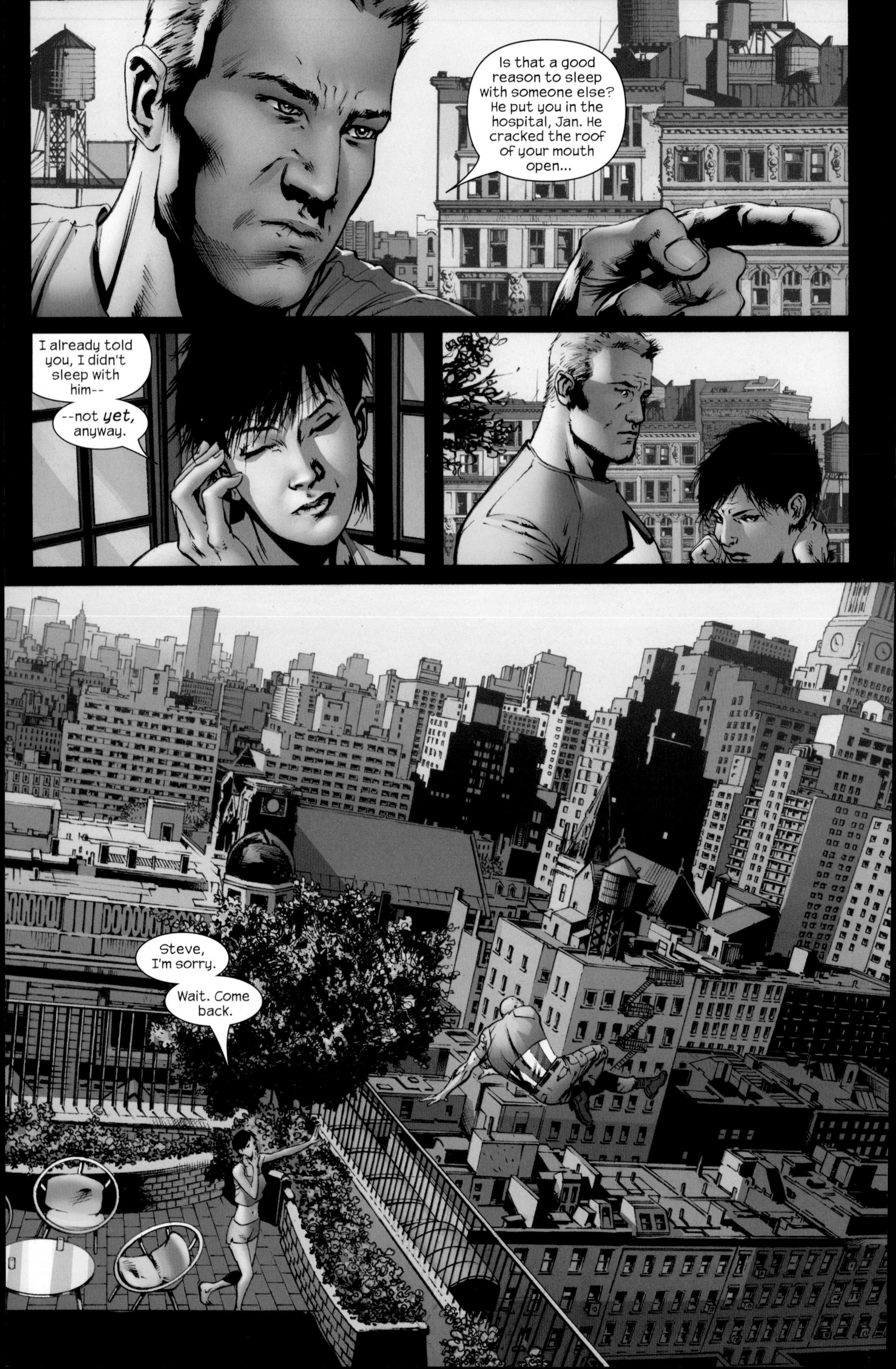

Is that a good reason to sleep with someone else? He put you in the hospital, Jan. He cracked the roof of your mouth open...
I already told you, I didn't sleep with him--
--not *yet,* anyway.
Steve, I'm sorry.
Wait. Come back.

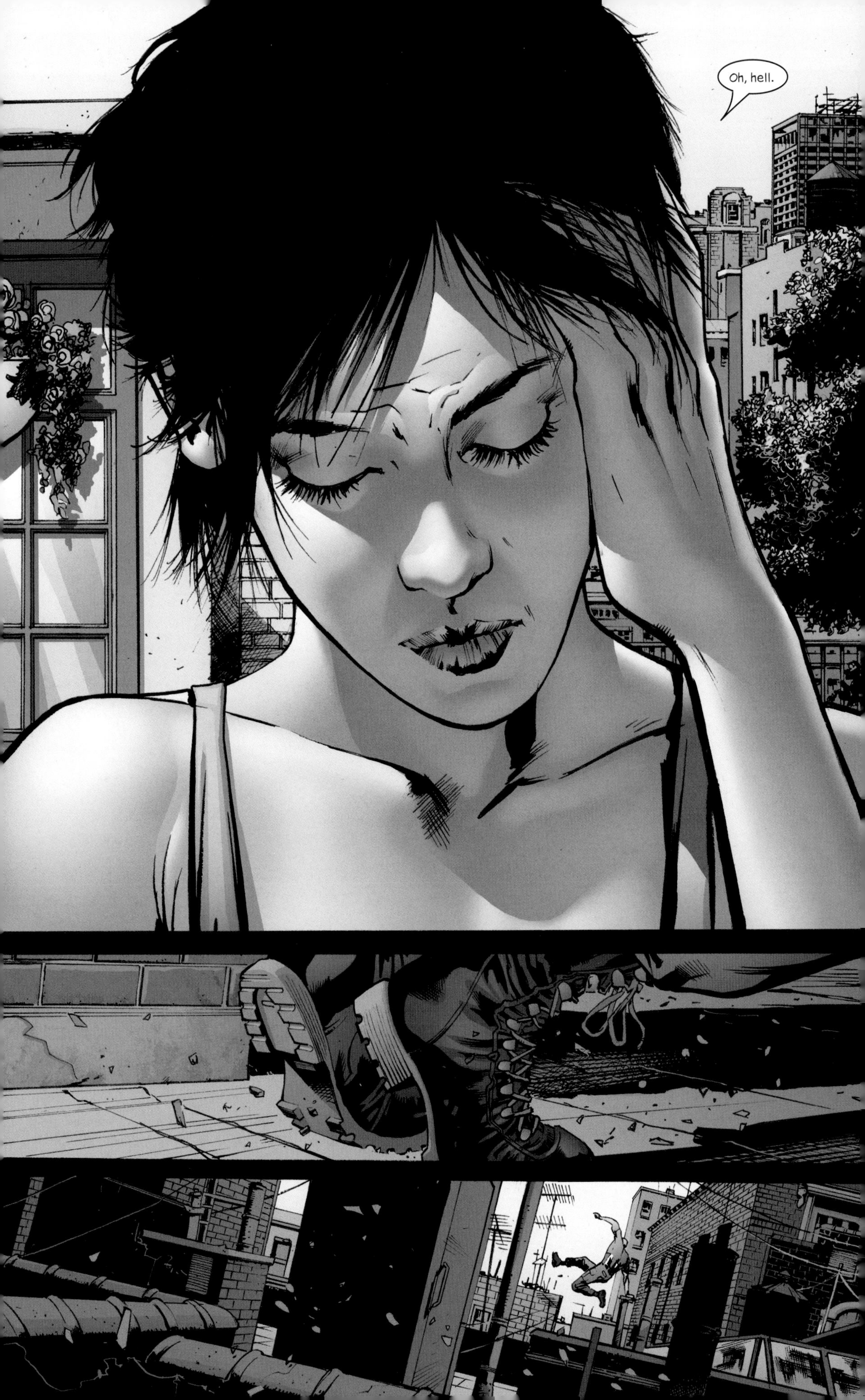
Oh, hell.

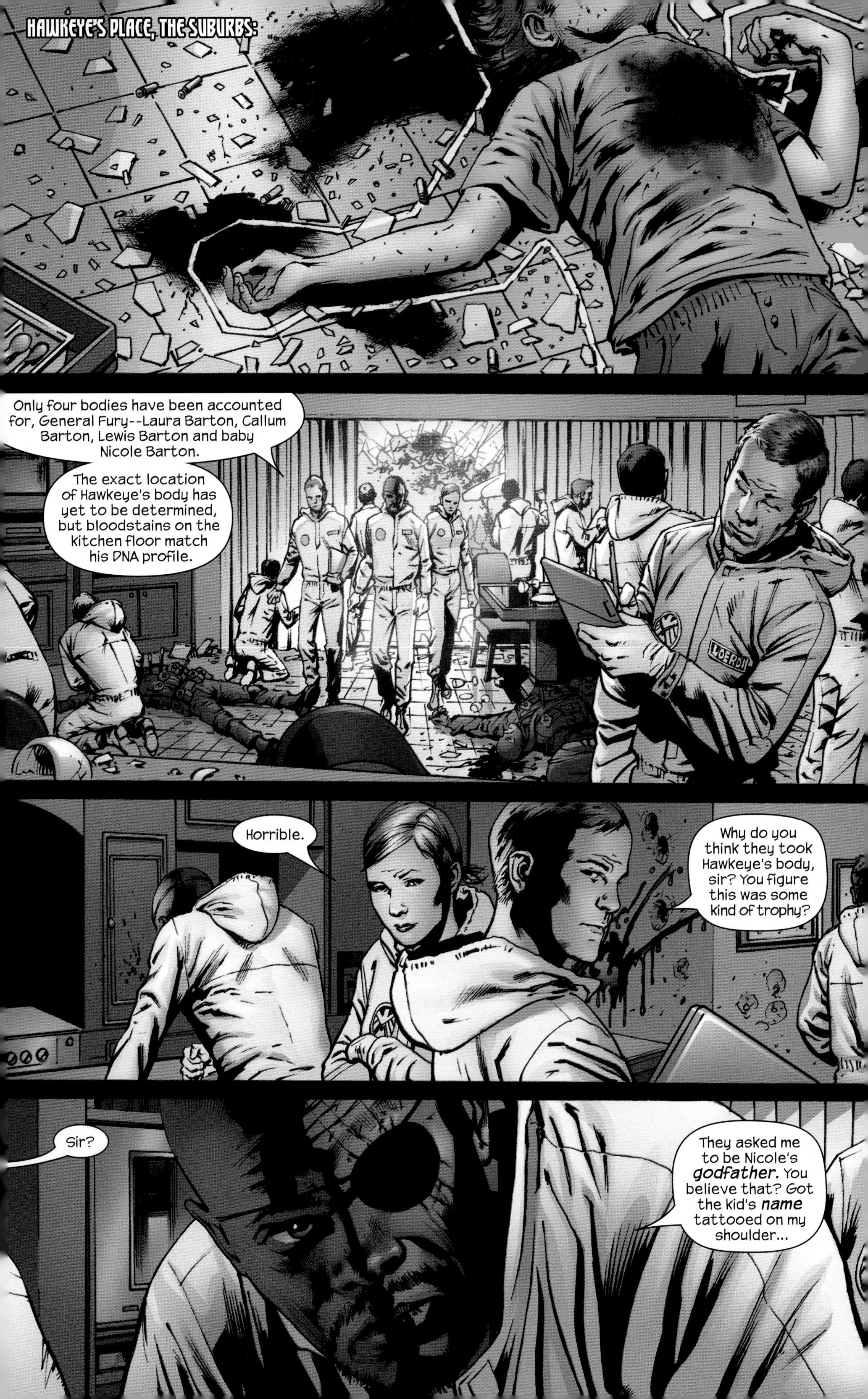
HAWKEYE'S PLACE, THE SUBURBS:
Only four bodies have been accounted for, General Fury--Laura Barton, Callum Barton, Lewis Barton and baby Nicole Barton.
The exact location of Hawkeye's body has yet to be determined, but bloodstains on the kitchen floor match his DNA profile.
Horrible.
Why do you think they took Hawkeye's body, sir? You figure this was some kind of trophy?
Sir?
They asked me to be Nicole's *godfather*. You believe that? Got the kid's *name* tattooed on my shoulder...

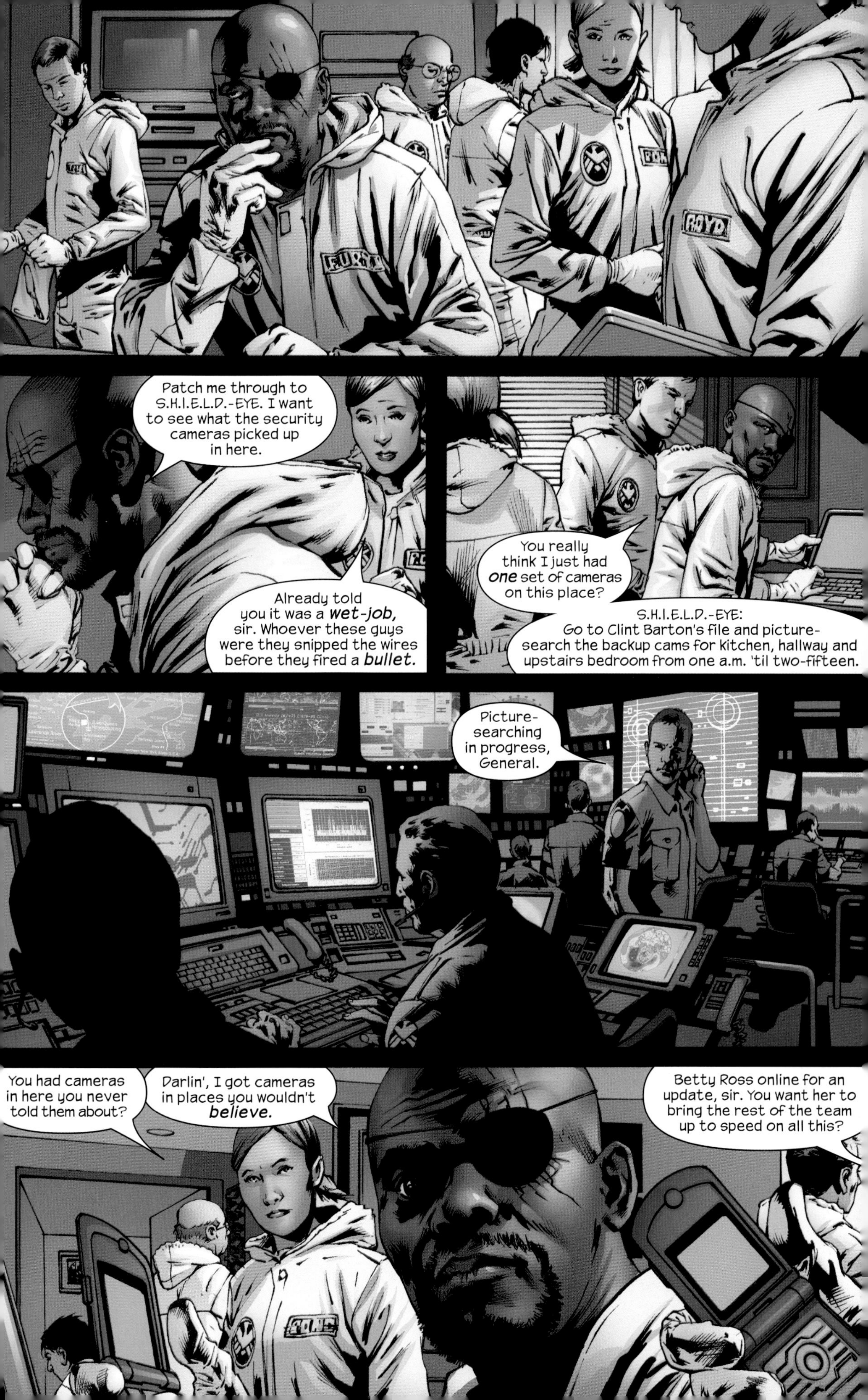
FURY
ROYD
Patch me through to S.H.I.E.L.D.-EYE. I want to see what the security cameras picked up in here.
Already told you it was a wet-job, sir. Whoever these guys were they snipped the wires before they fired a bullet.
You really think I just had one set of cameras on this place?
S.H.I.E.L.D.-EYE: Go to Clint Barton's file and picture-search the backup cams for kitchen, hallway and upstairs bedroom from one a.m. 'til two-fifteen.
Picture-searching in progress, General.
You had cameras in here you never told them about?
Darlin', I got cameras in places you wouldn't believe.
Betty Ross online for an update, sir. You want her to bring the rest of the team up to speed on all this?

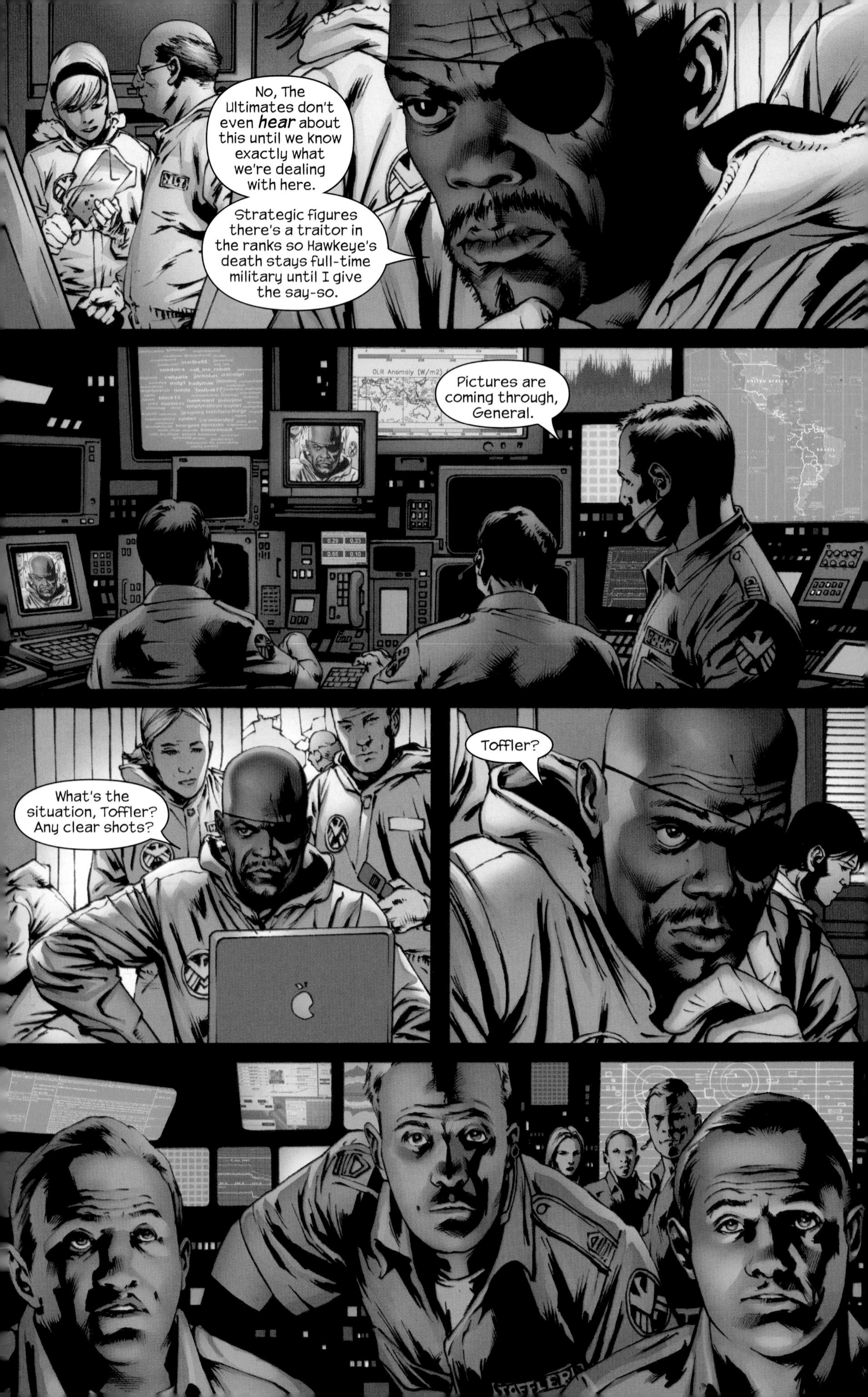
No, The Ultimates don't even *hear* about this until we know exactly what we're dealing with here.
Strategic figures there's a traitor in the ranks so Hawkeye's death stays full-time military until I give the say-so.
Pictures are coming through, General.
What's the situation, Toffler? Any clear shots?
Toffler?

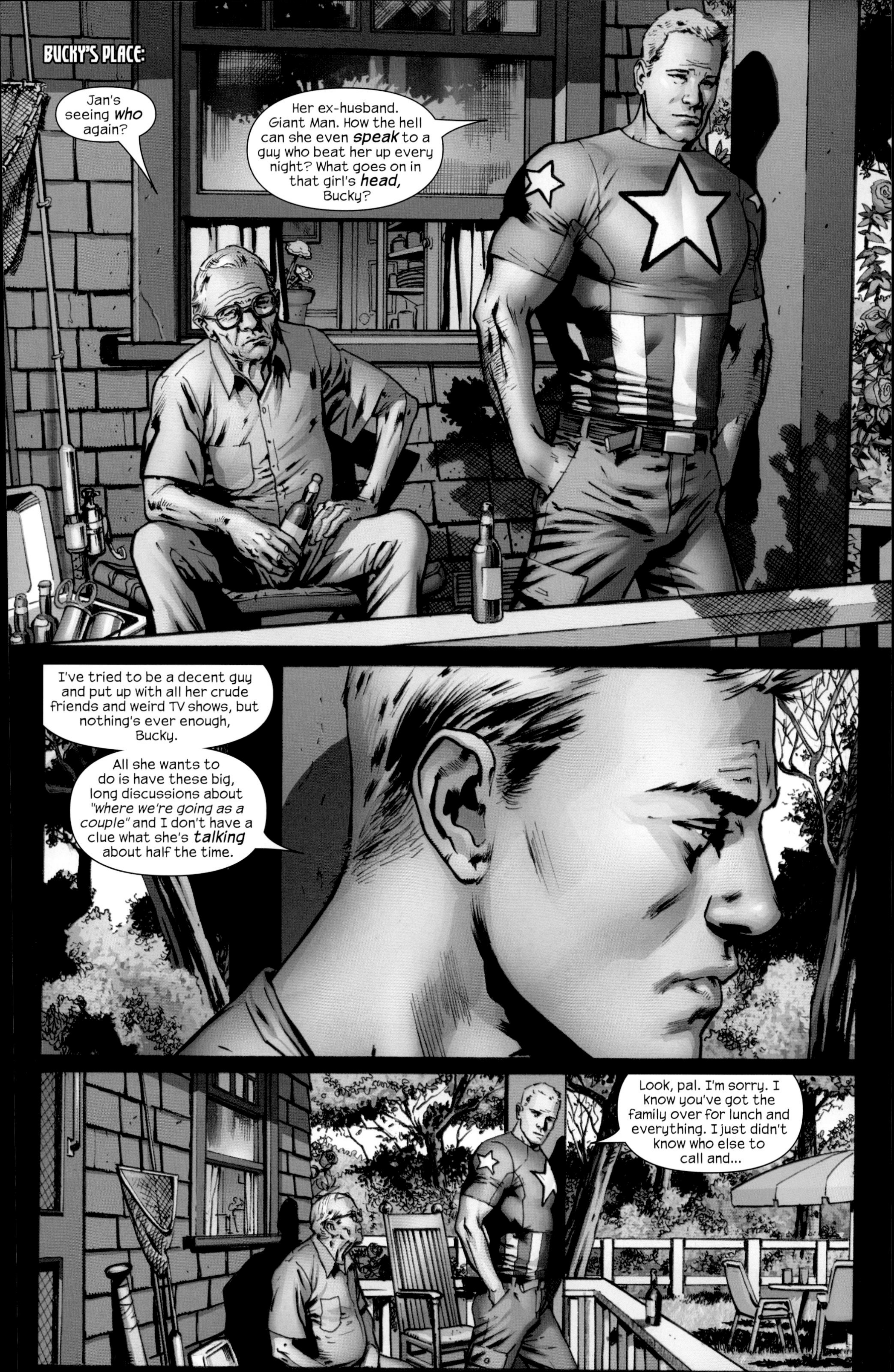
BUCKY'S PLACE:
Jan's seeing *who* again?
Her ex-husband. Giant Man. How the hell can she even **speak** to a guy who beat her up every night? What goes on in that girl's **head,** Bucky?
I've tried to be a decent guy and put up with all her crude friends and weird TV shows, but nothing's ever enough, Bucky.
All she wants to do is have these big, long discussions about *"where we're going as a couple"* and I don't have a clue what she's ***talking*** about half the time.
Look, pal. I'm sorry. I know you've got the family over for lunch and everything. I just didn't know who else to call and...

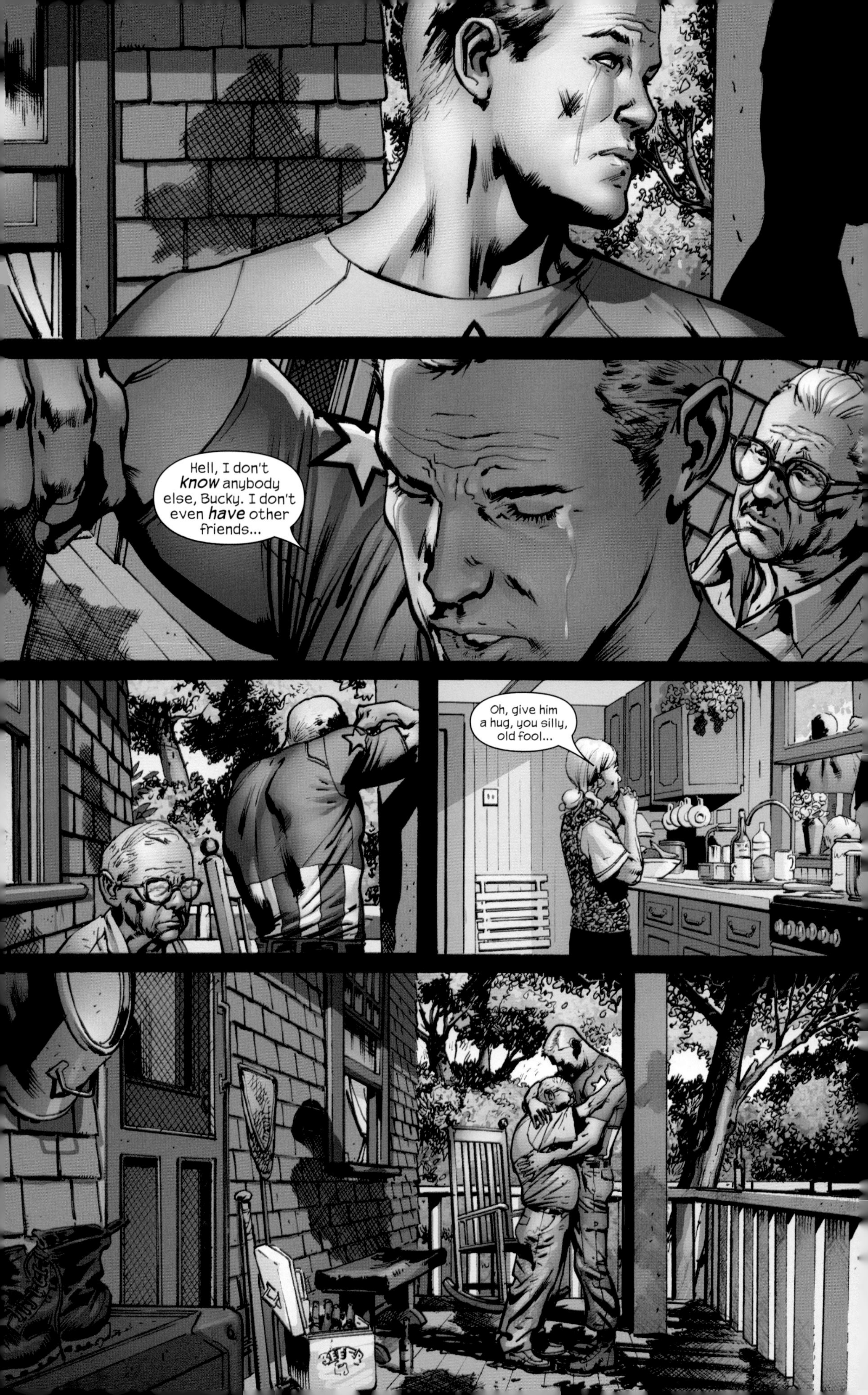
Hell, I don't *know* anybody else, Bucky. I don't even *have* other friends...
Oh, give him a hug, you silly, old fool...

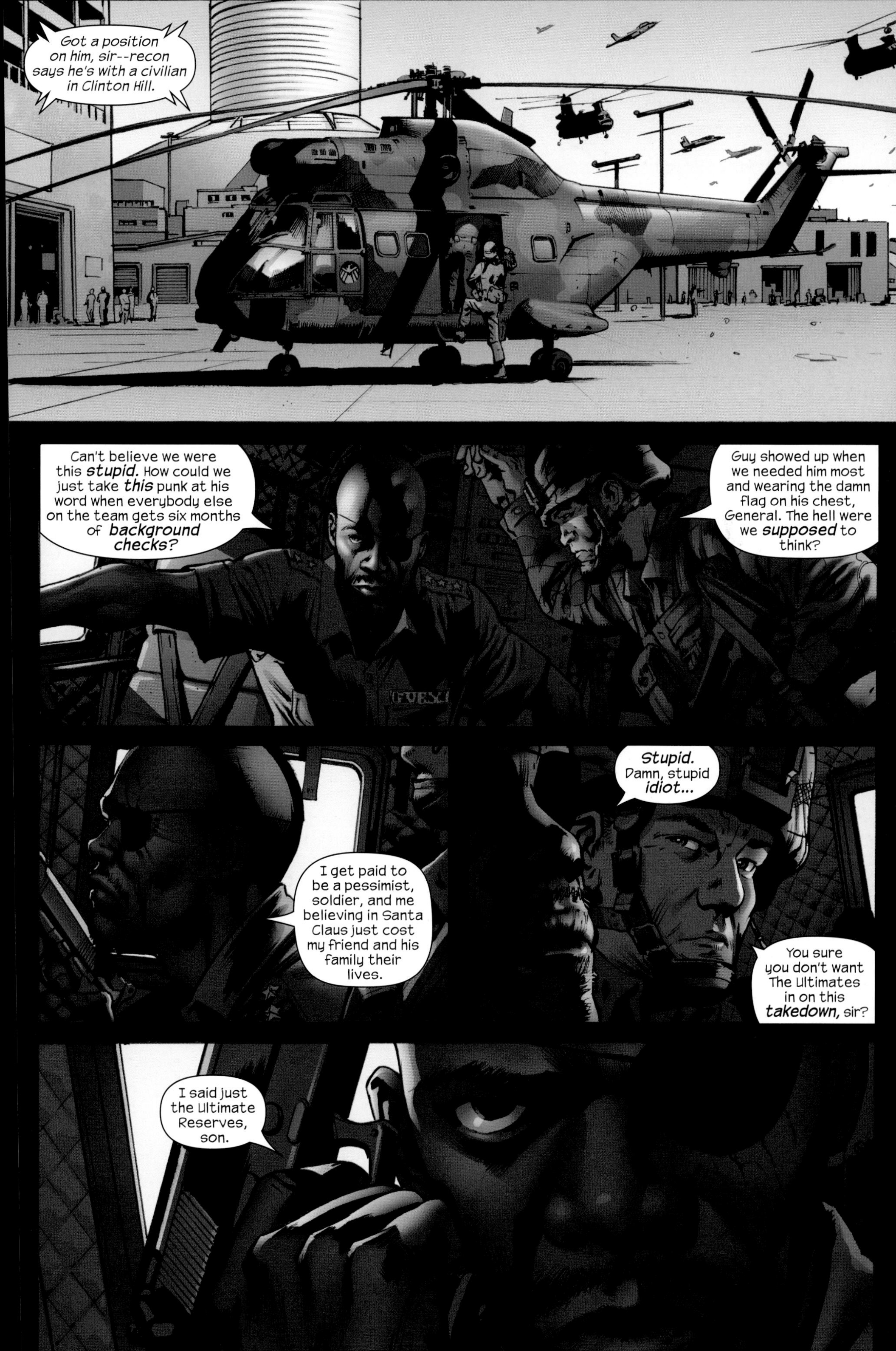
Got a position on him, sir--recon says he's with a civilian in Clinton Hill.
Can't believe we were this stupid. How could we just take this punk at his word when everybody else on the team gets six months of background checks?
Guy showed up when we needed him most and wearing the damn flag on his chest, General. The hell were we supposed to think?
FURY
I get paid to be a pessimist, soldier, and me believing in Santa Claus just cost my friend and his family their lives.
Stupid. Damn, stupid idiot...
You sure you don't want The Ultimates in on this takedown, sir?
I said just the Ultimate Reserves, son.

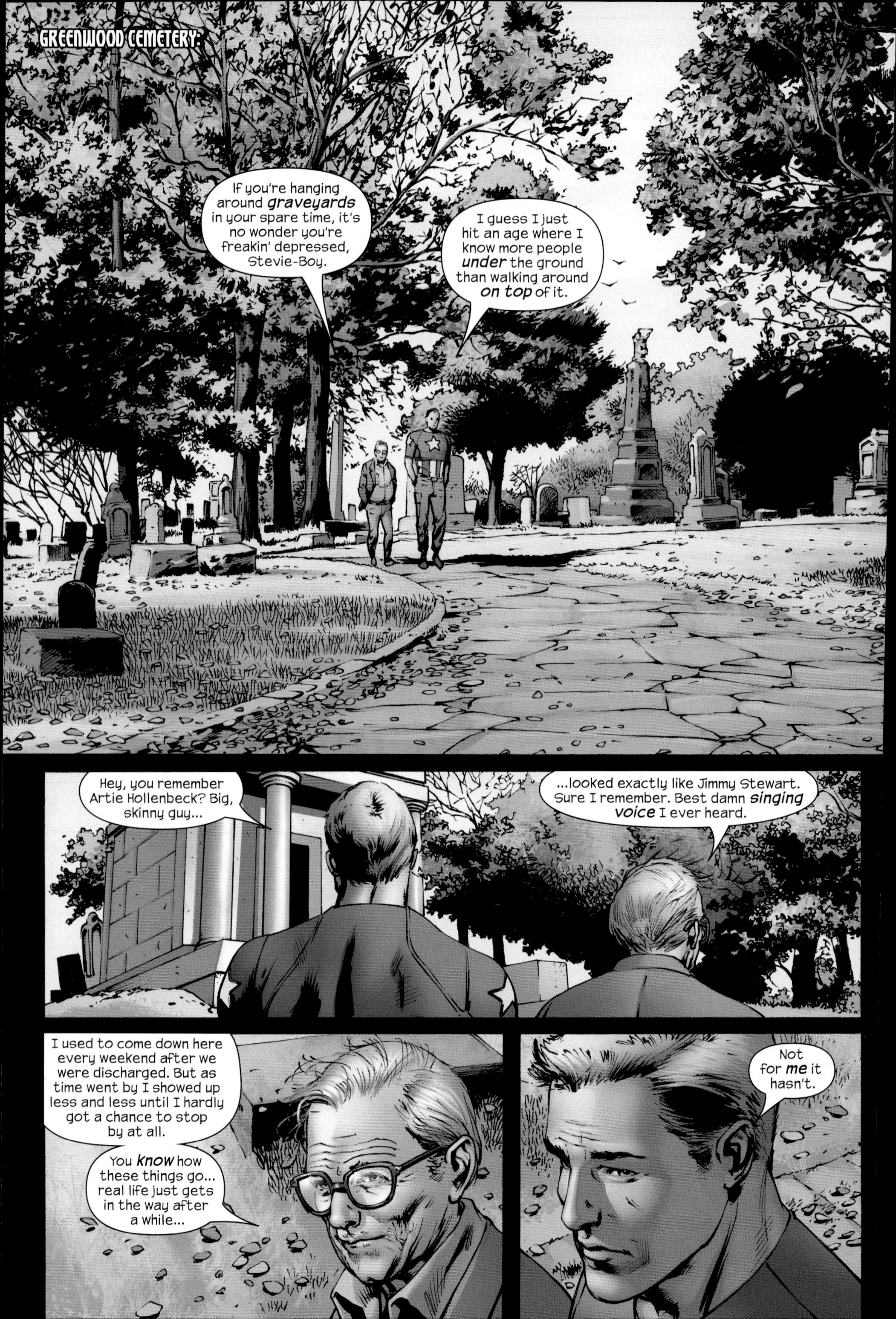

GREENWOOD CEMETERY:
If you're hanging around graveyards in your spare time, it's no wonder you're freakin' depressed, Stevie-Boy.
I guess I just hit an age where I know more people under the ground than walking around on top of it.
Hey, you remember Artie Hollenbeck? Big, skinny guy...
...looked exactly like Jimmy Stewart. Sure I remember. Best damn singing voice I ever heard.
I used to come down here every weekend after we were discharged. But as time went by I showed up less and less until I hardly got a chance to stop by at all.
You know how these things go... real life just gets in the way after a while...
Not for me it hasn't.

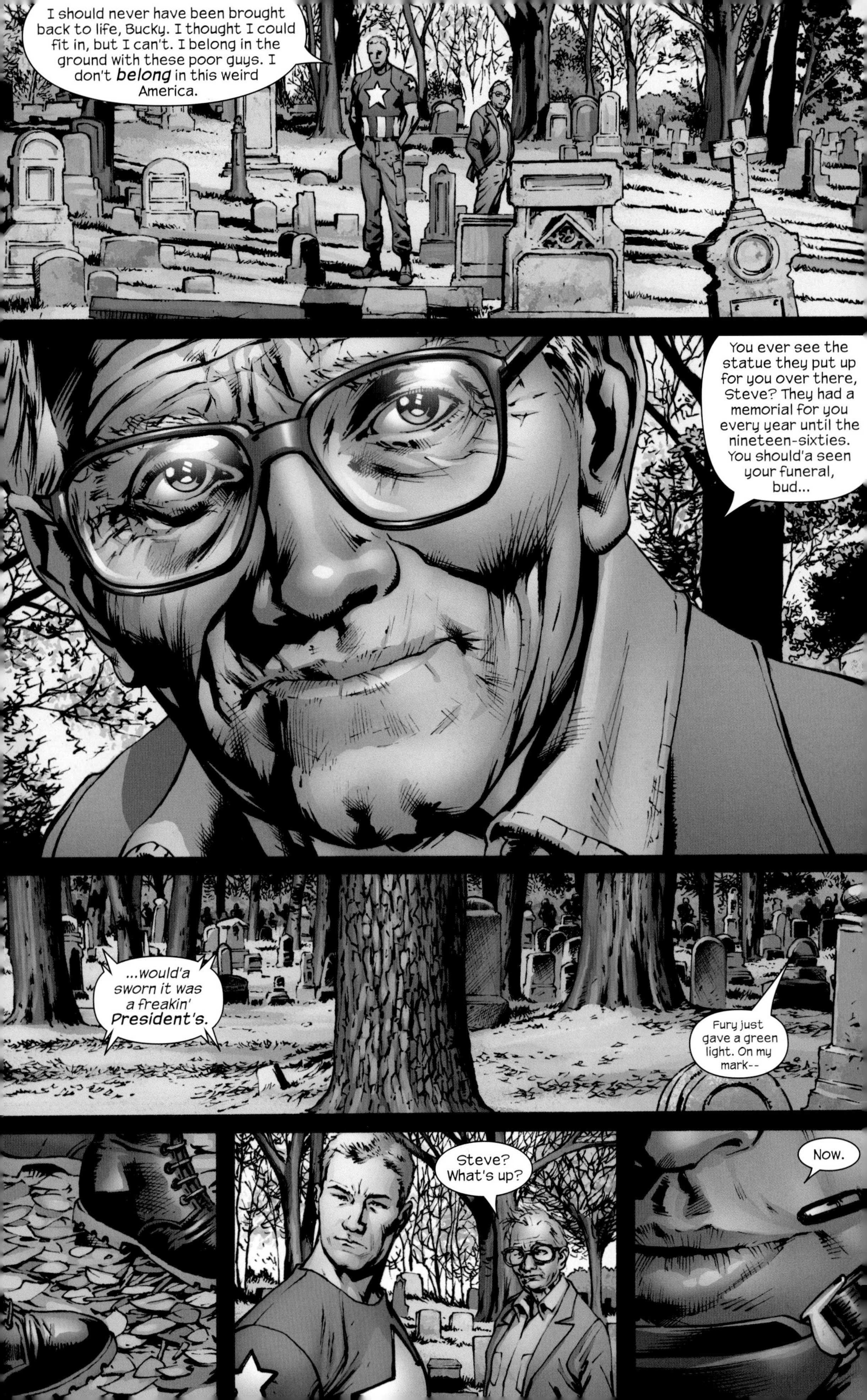
I should never have been brought back to life, Bucky. I thought I could fit in, but I can't. I belong in the ground with these poor guys. I don't *belong* in this weird America.
You ever see the statue they put up for you over there, Steve? They had a memorial for you every year until the nineteen-sixties. You should'a seen your funeral, bud...
...would'a sworn it was a freakin' President's.
Fury just gave a green light. On my mark--
Steve? What's up?
Now.

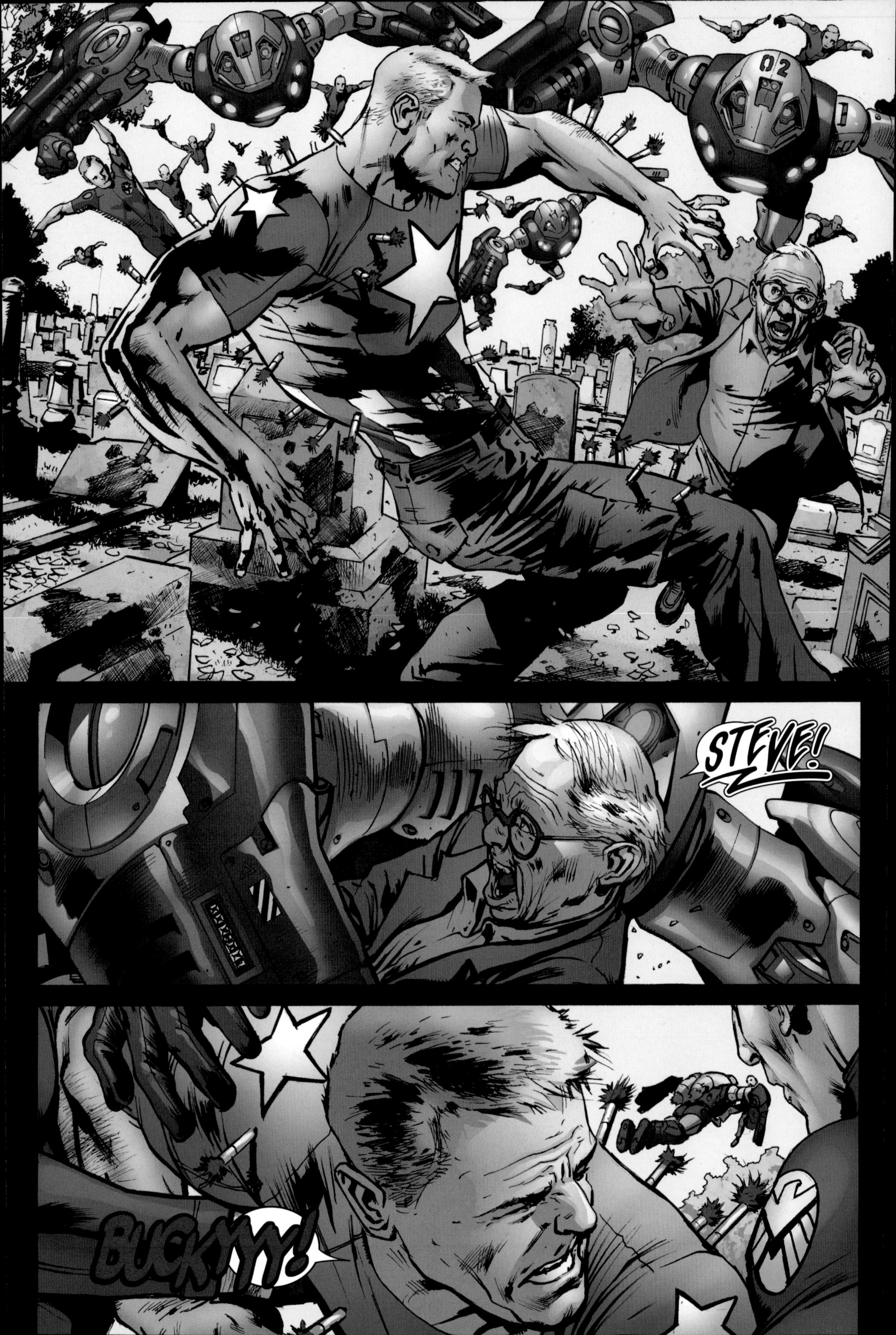
STEVE!
BUCKYYY!

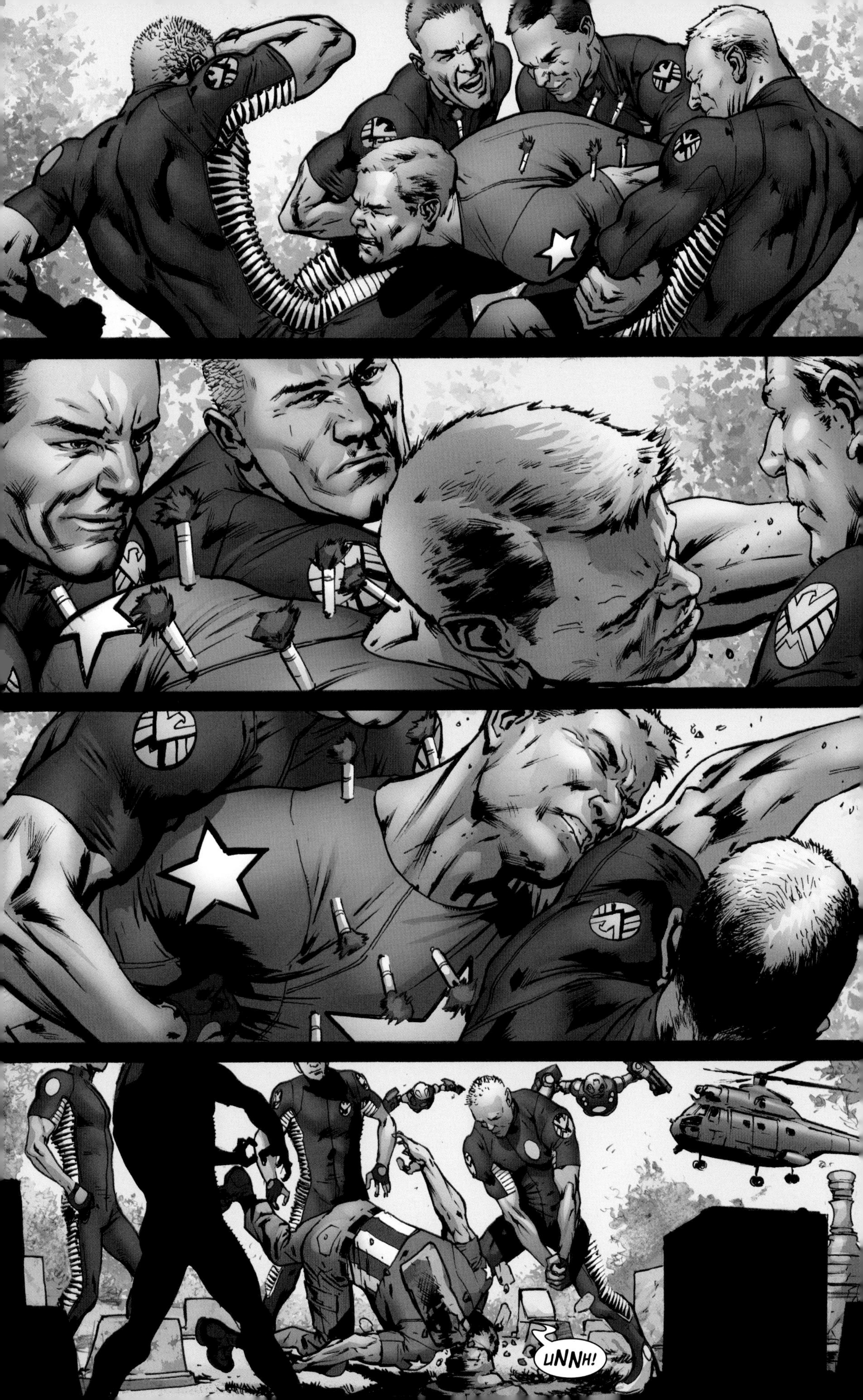
UNNH!

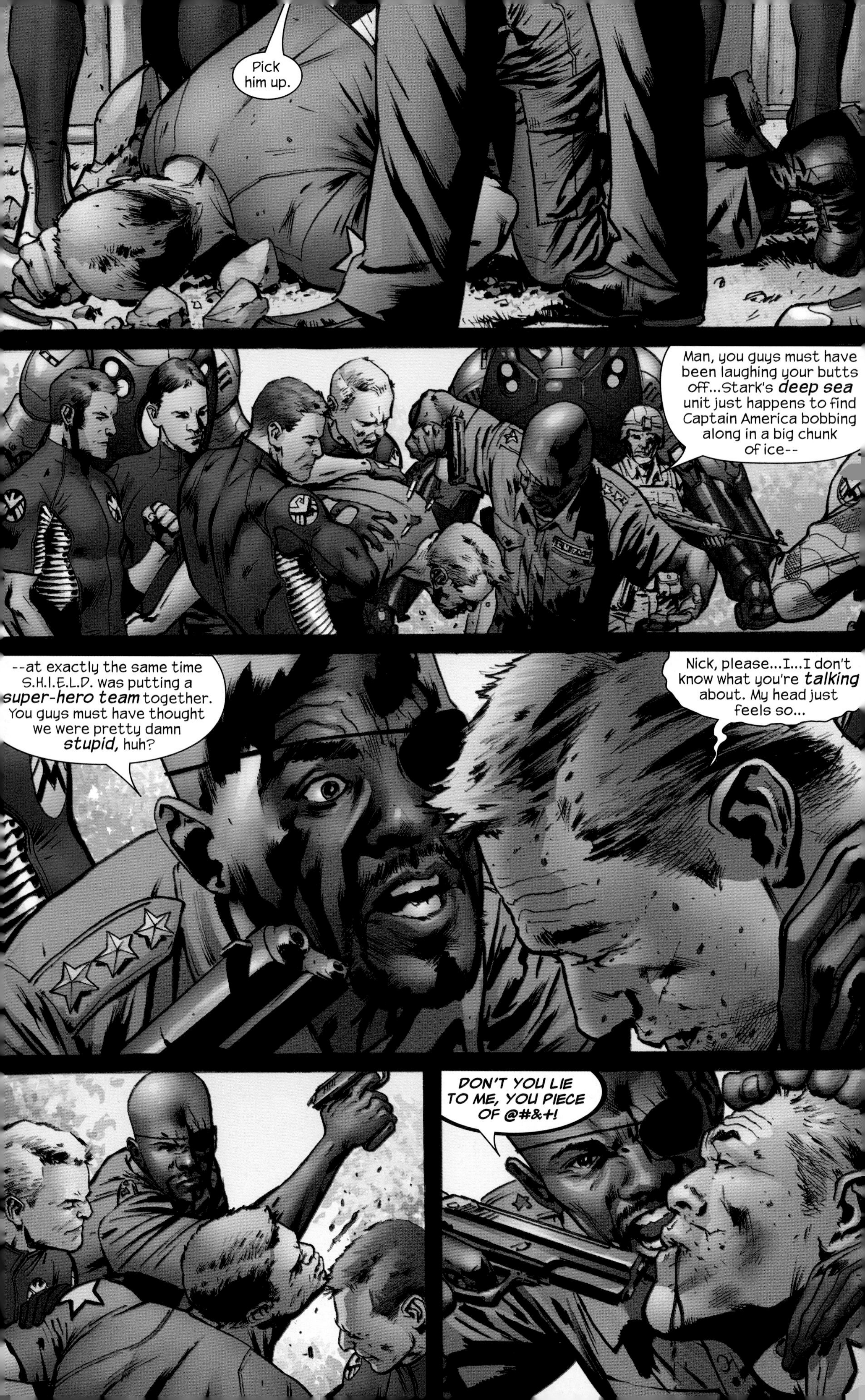
Pick him up.
Man, you guys must have been laughing your butts off...Stark's **deep sea** unit just happens to find Captain America bobbing along in a big chunk of ice--
--at exactly the same time S.H.I.E.L.D. was putting a **super-hero team** together. You guys must have thought we were pretty damn **stupid,** huh?
Nick, please...I...I don't know what you're **talking** about. My head just feels so...
DON'T YOU LIE TO ME, YOU PIECE OF @#&+!

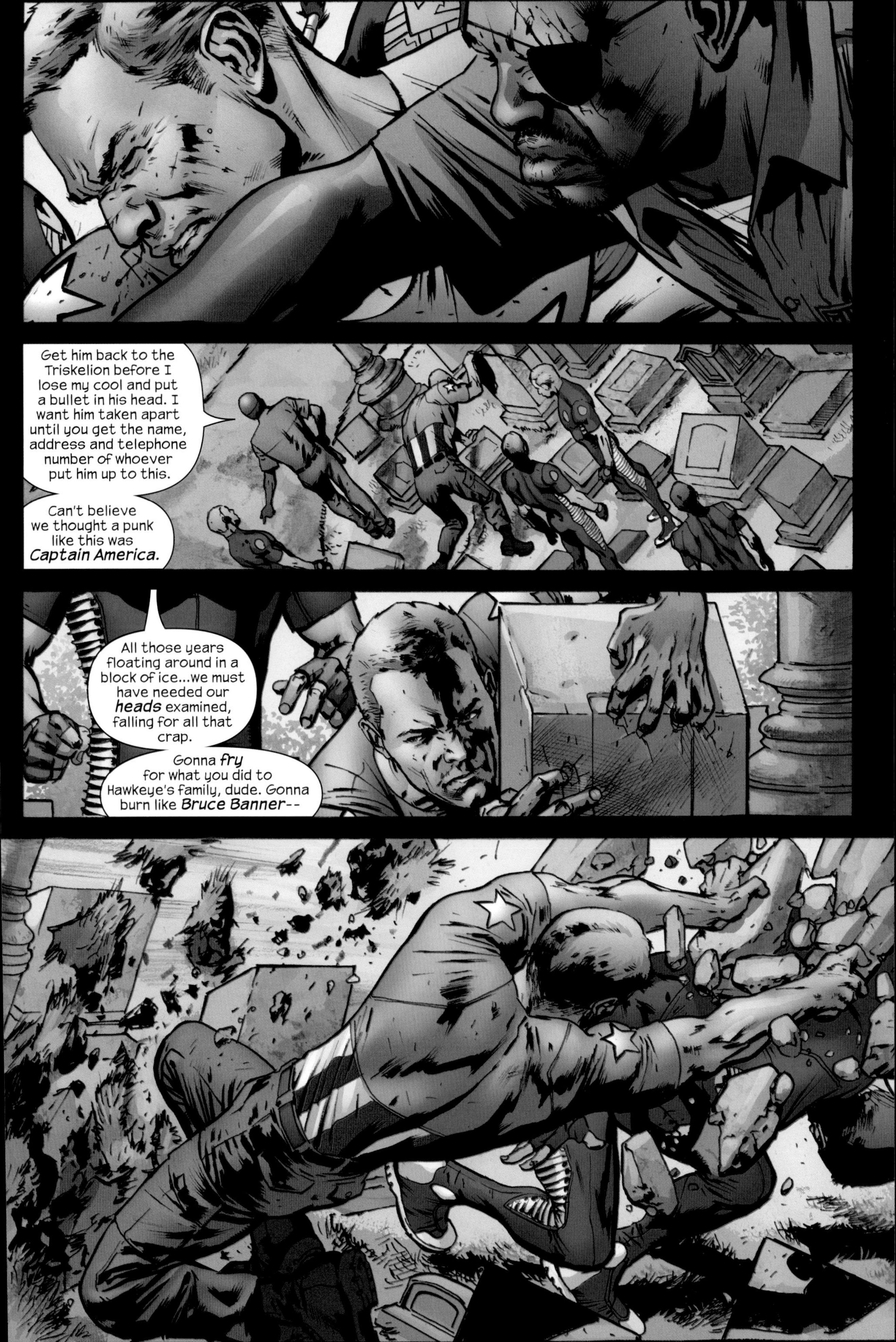
Get him back to the Triskelion before I lose my cool and put a bullet in his head. I want him taken apart until you get the name, address and telephone number of whoever put him up to this.
Can't believe we thought a punk like this was *Captain America.*
All those years floating around in a block of ice...we must have needed our **heads** examined, falling for all that crap.
Gonna *fry* for what you did to Hawkeye's family, dude. Gonna burn like *Bruce Banner*--

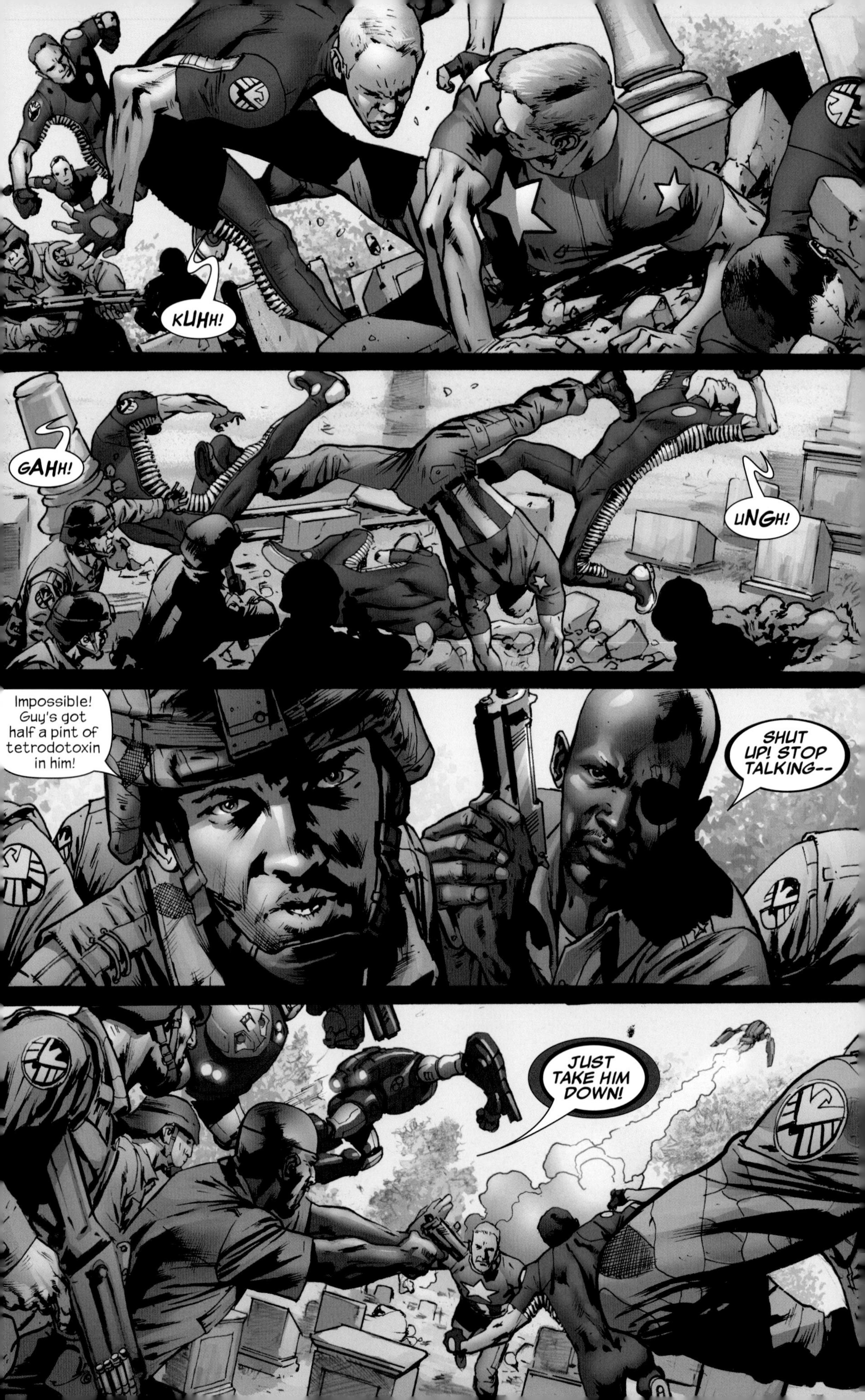
KUHH!
GAHH!
UNGH!
Impossible! Guy's got half a pint of tetrodotoxin in him!
SHUT UP! STOP TALKING--
JUST TAKE HIM DOWN!

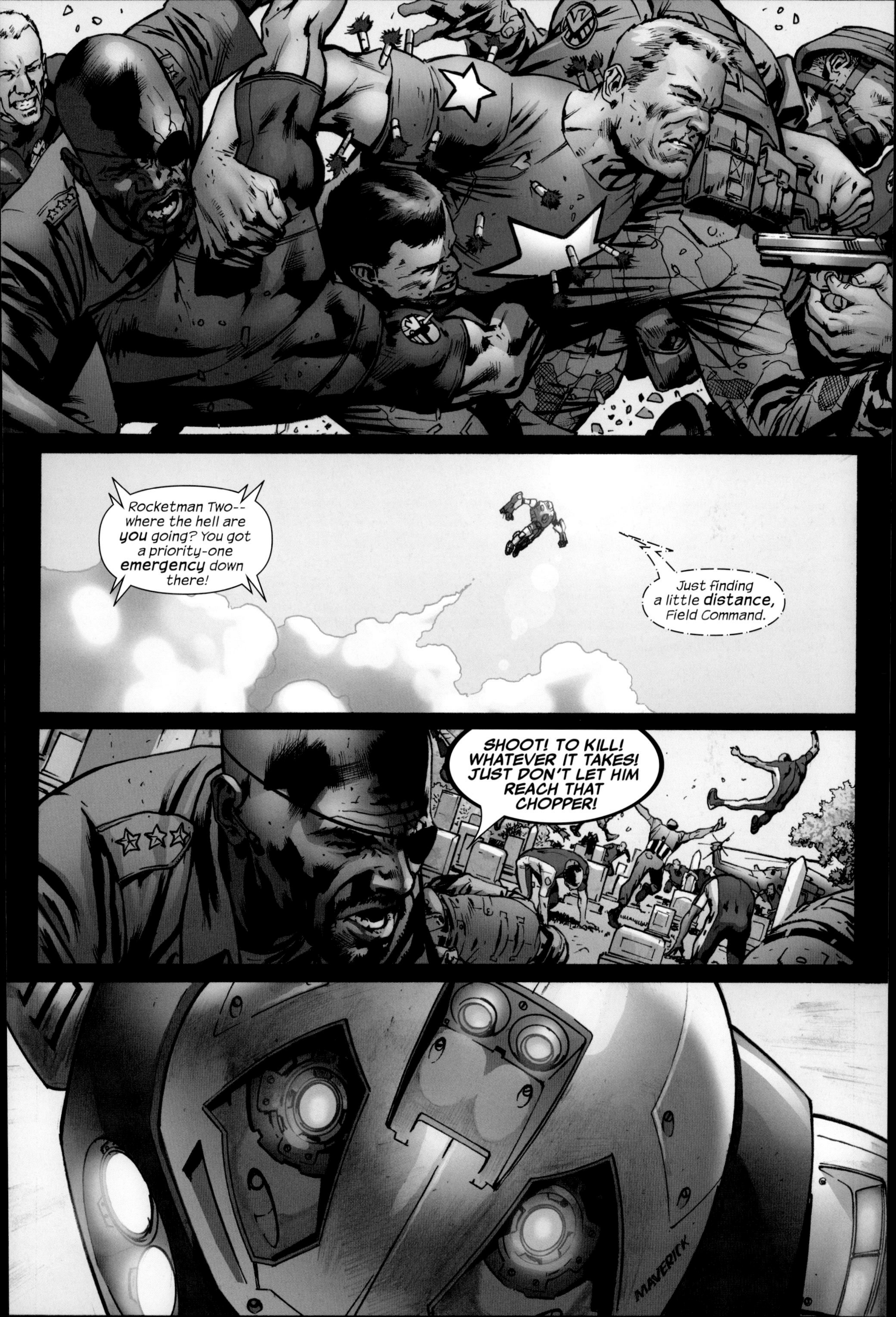

Rocketman Two-- where the hell are **you** going? You got a priority-one **emergency** down there!
Just finding a little **distance,** Field Command.
SHOOT! TO KILL! WHATEVER IT TAKES! JUST DON'T LET HIM REACH THAT CHOPPER!
MAVERICK

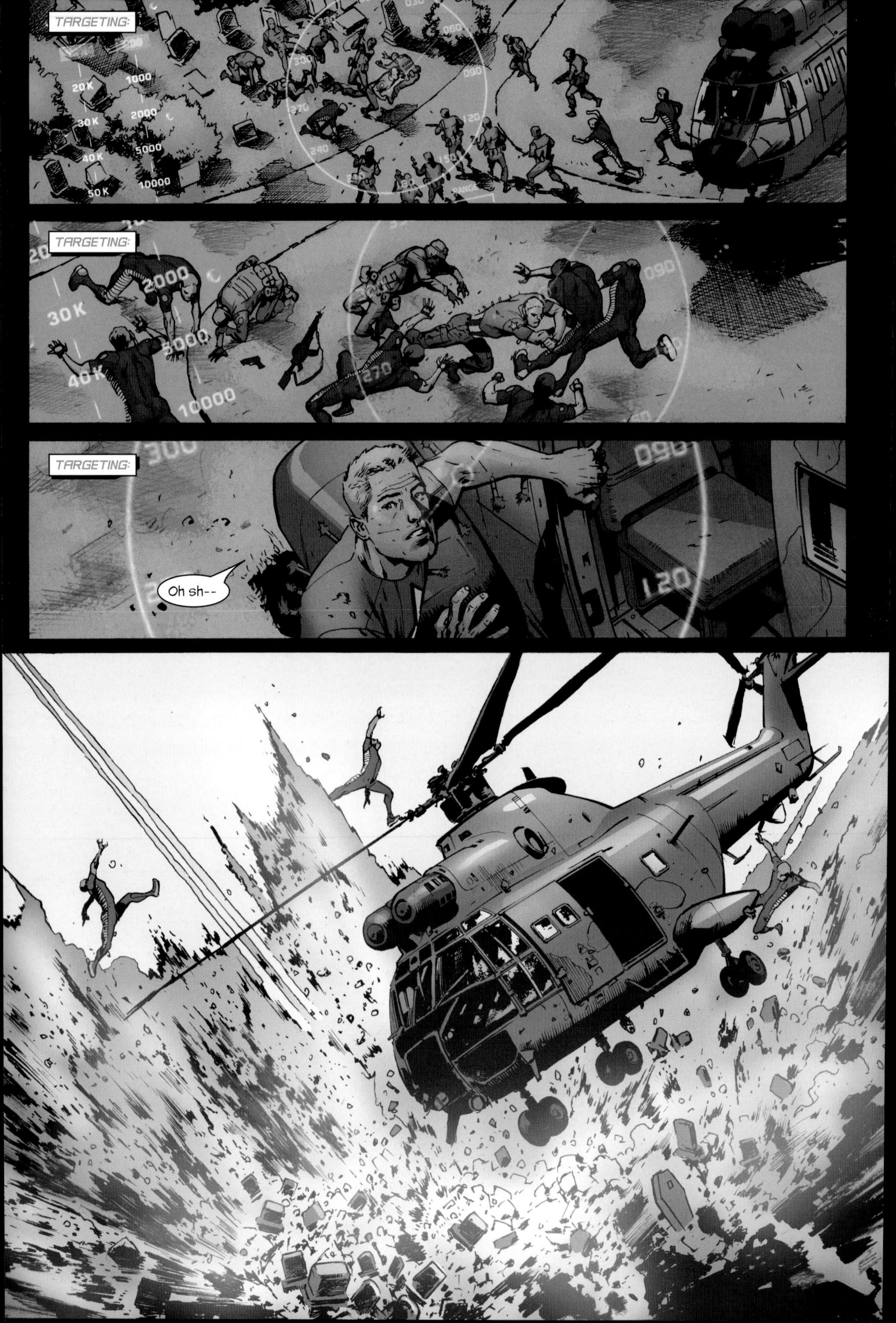

TARGETING:
TARGETING:
TARGETING:
Oh sh--

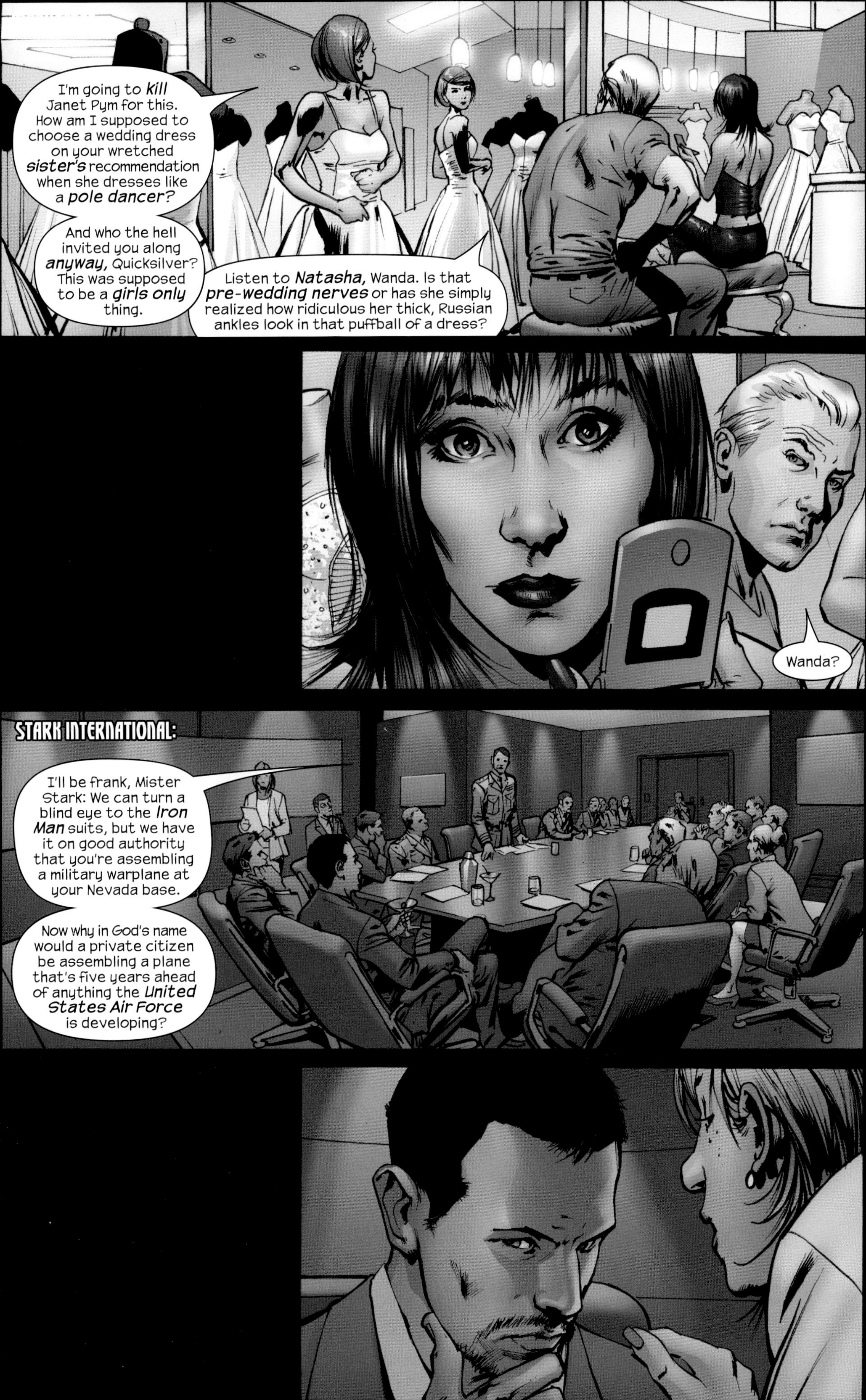
I'm going to kill Janet Pym for this. How am I supposed to choose a wedding dress on your wretched sister's recommendation when she dresses like a pole dancer?
And who the hell invited you along anyway, Quicksilver? This was supposed to be a girls only thing.
Listen to Natasha, Wanda. Is that pre-wedding nerves or has she simply realized how ridiculous her thick, Russian ankles look in that puffball of a dress?
Wanda?
STARK INTERNATIONAL:
I'll be frank, Mister Stark: We can turn a blind eye to the Iron Man suits, but we have it on good authority that you're assembling a military warplane at your Nevada base.
Now why in God's name would a private citizen be assembling a plane that's five years ahead of anything the United States Air Force is developing?

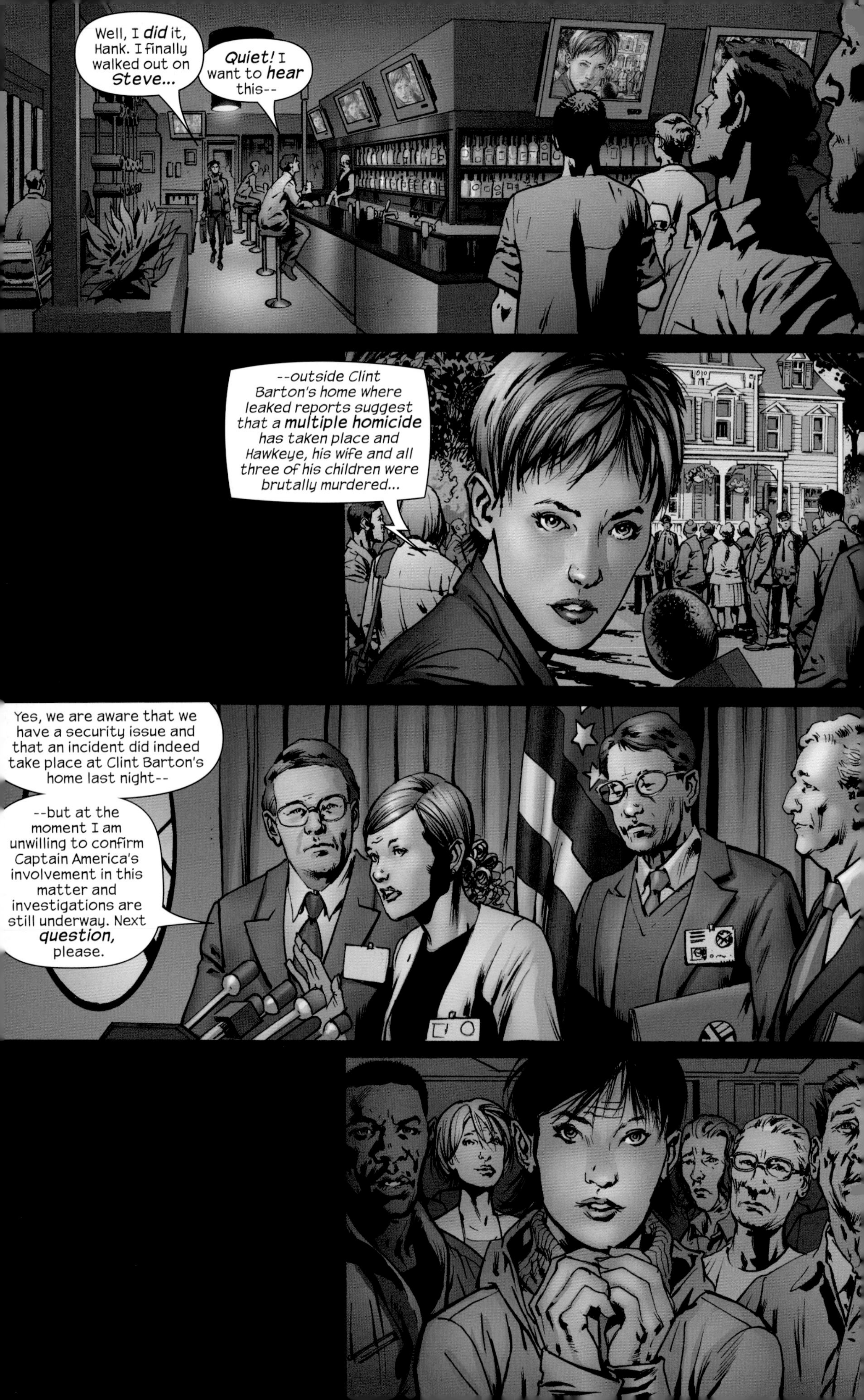
Well, I did it, Hank. I finally walked out on Steve...
Quiet! I want to hear this--
--outside Clint Barton's home where leaked reports suggest that a multiple homicide has taken place and Hawkeye, his wife and all three of his children were brutally murdered...
Yes, we are aware that we have a security issue and that an incident did indeed take place at Clint Barton's home last night--
--but at the moment I am unwilling to confirm Captain America's involvement in this matter and investigations are still underway. Next question, please.

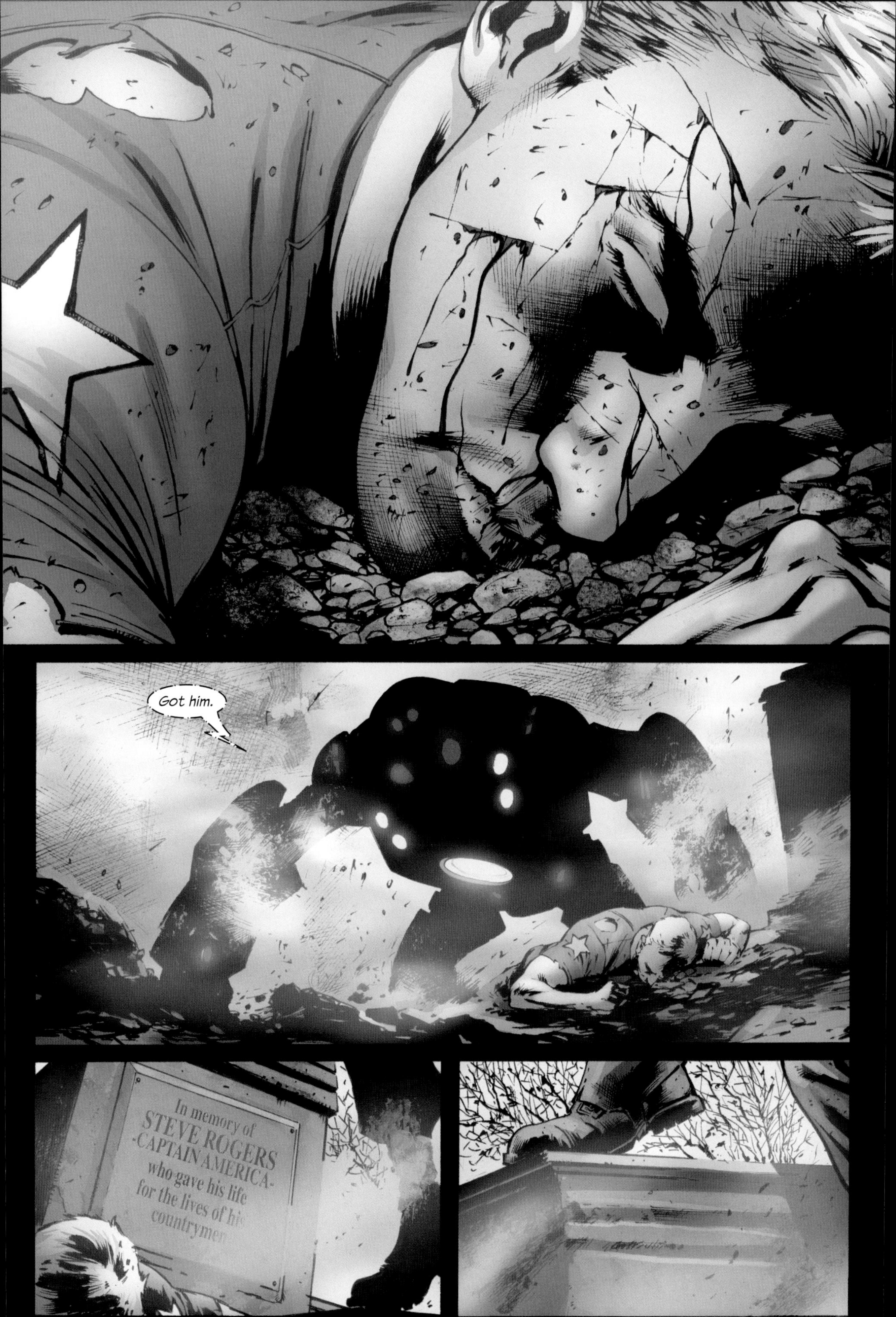
Got him.
In memory of
STEVE ROGERS
-CAPTAIN AMERICA-
who gave his life
for the lives of his
countrymen

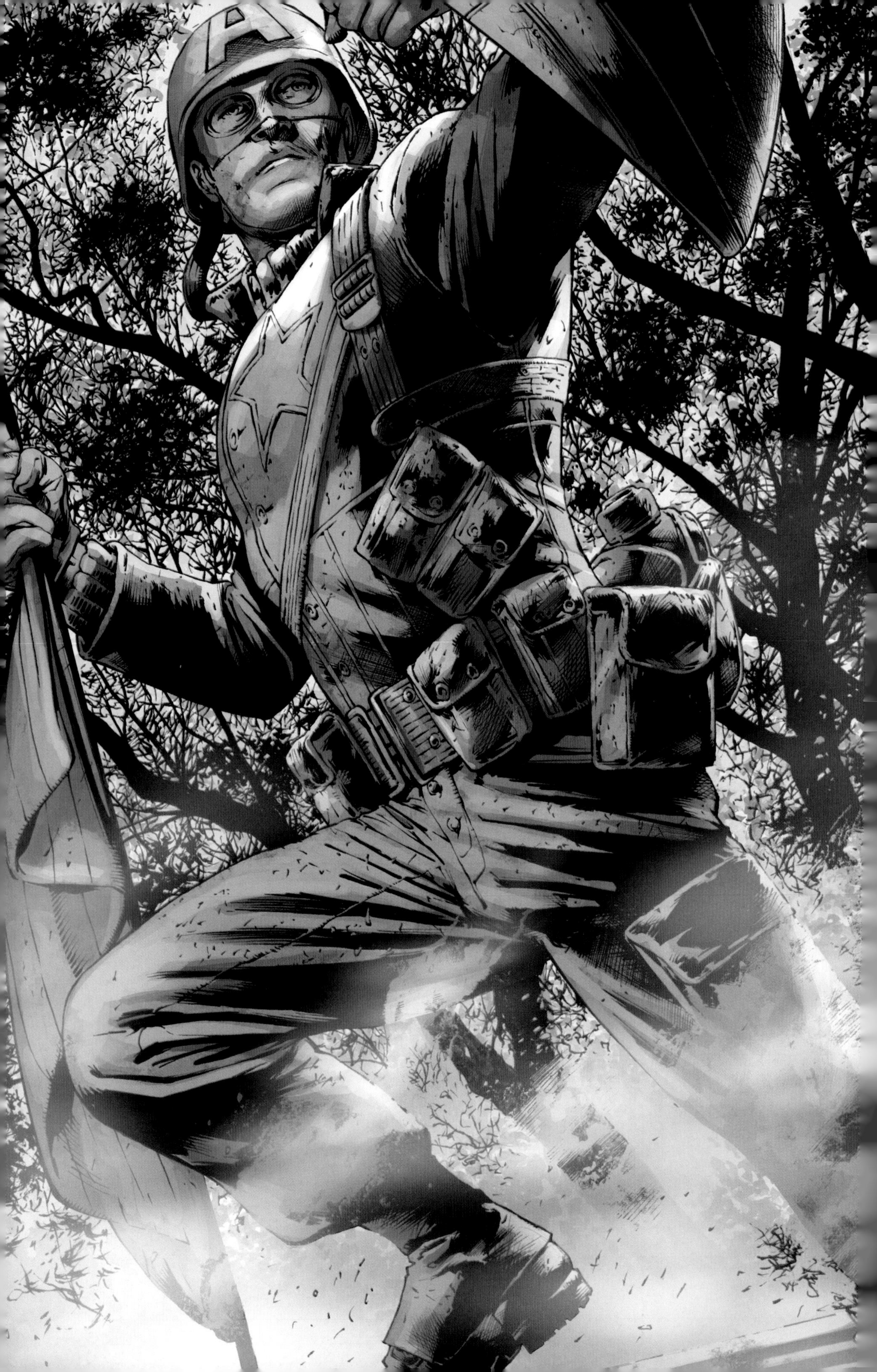

GRAND THEFT AMERICA

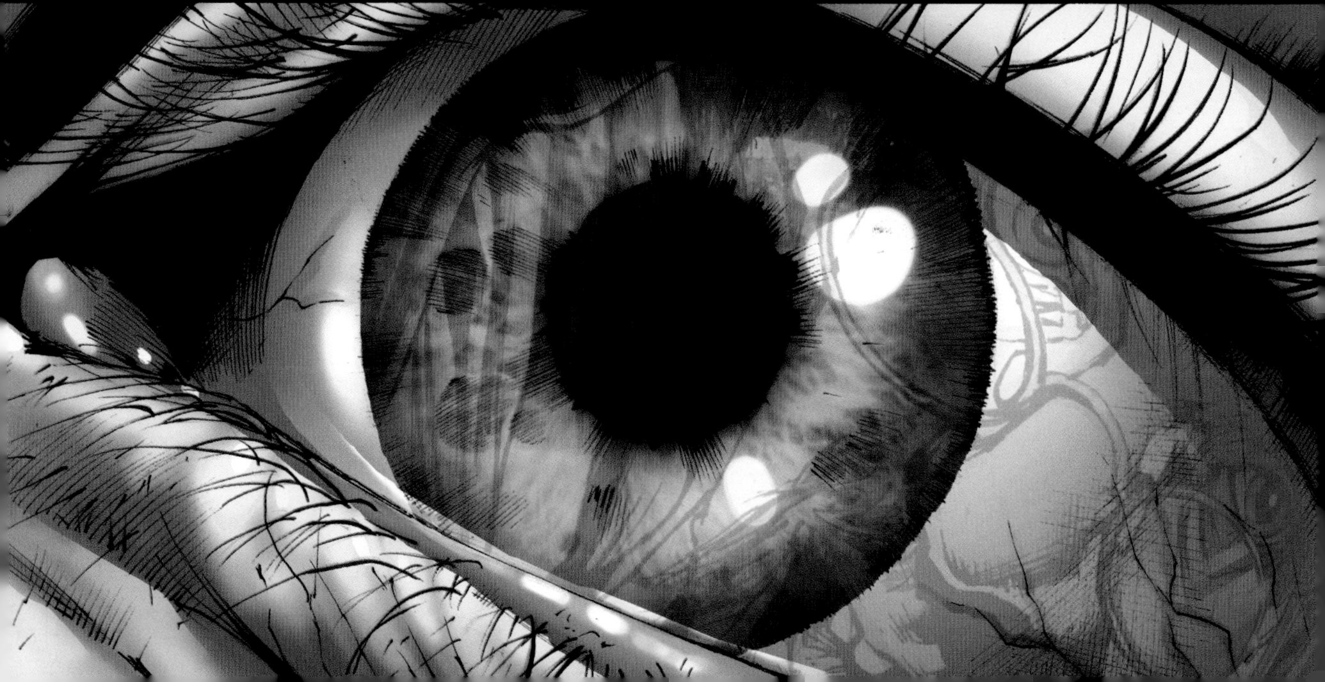

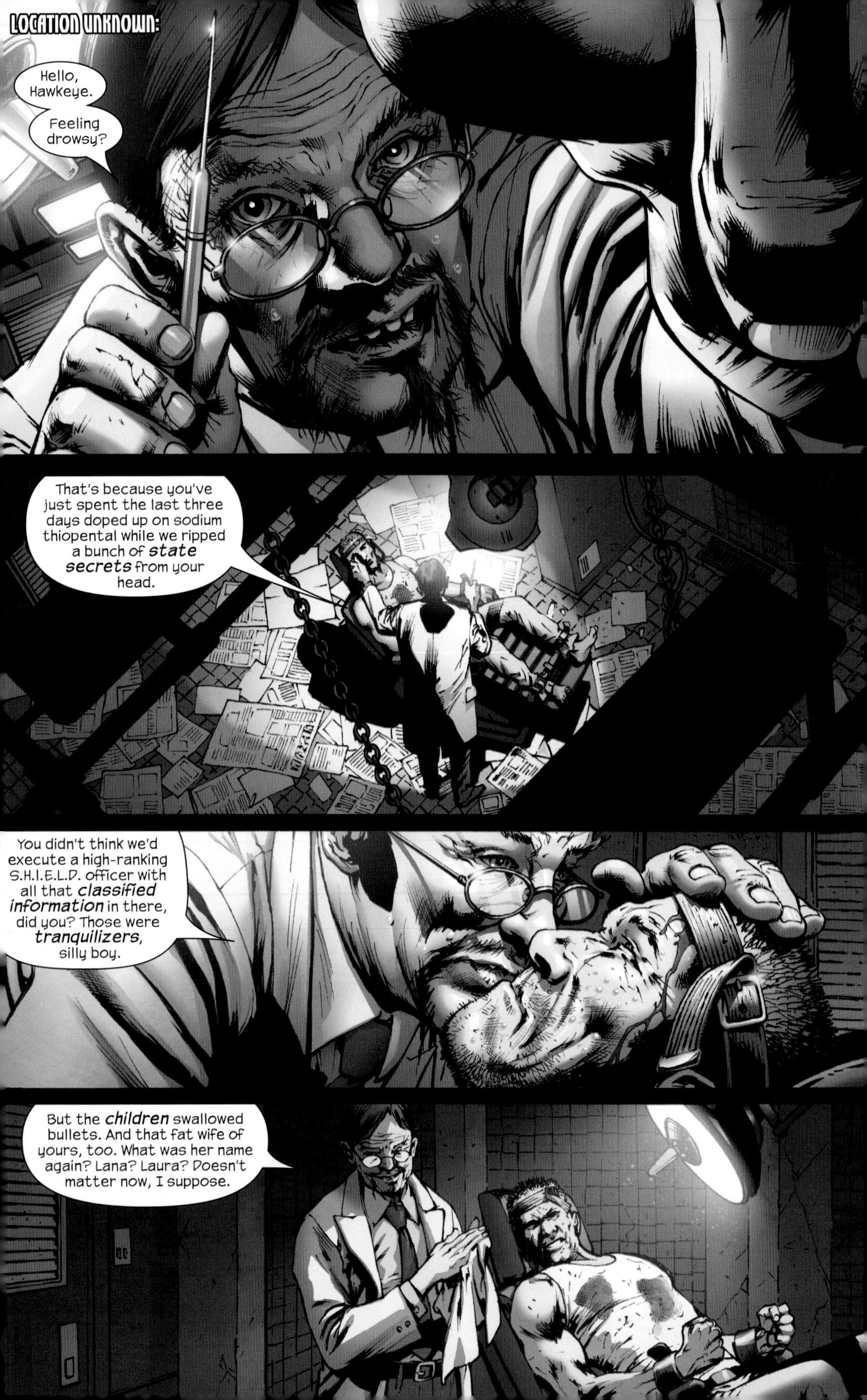
LOCATION UNKNOWN:
Hello, Hawkeye.
Feeling drowsy?
That's because you've just spent the last three days doped up on sodium thiopental while we ripped a bunch of state secrets from your head.
You didn't think we'd execute a high-ranking S.H.I.E.L.D. officer with all that classified information in there, did you? Those were tranquilizers, silly boy.
But the children swallowed bullets. And that fat wife of yours, too. What was her name again? Lana? Laura? Doesn't matter now, I suppose.

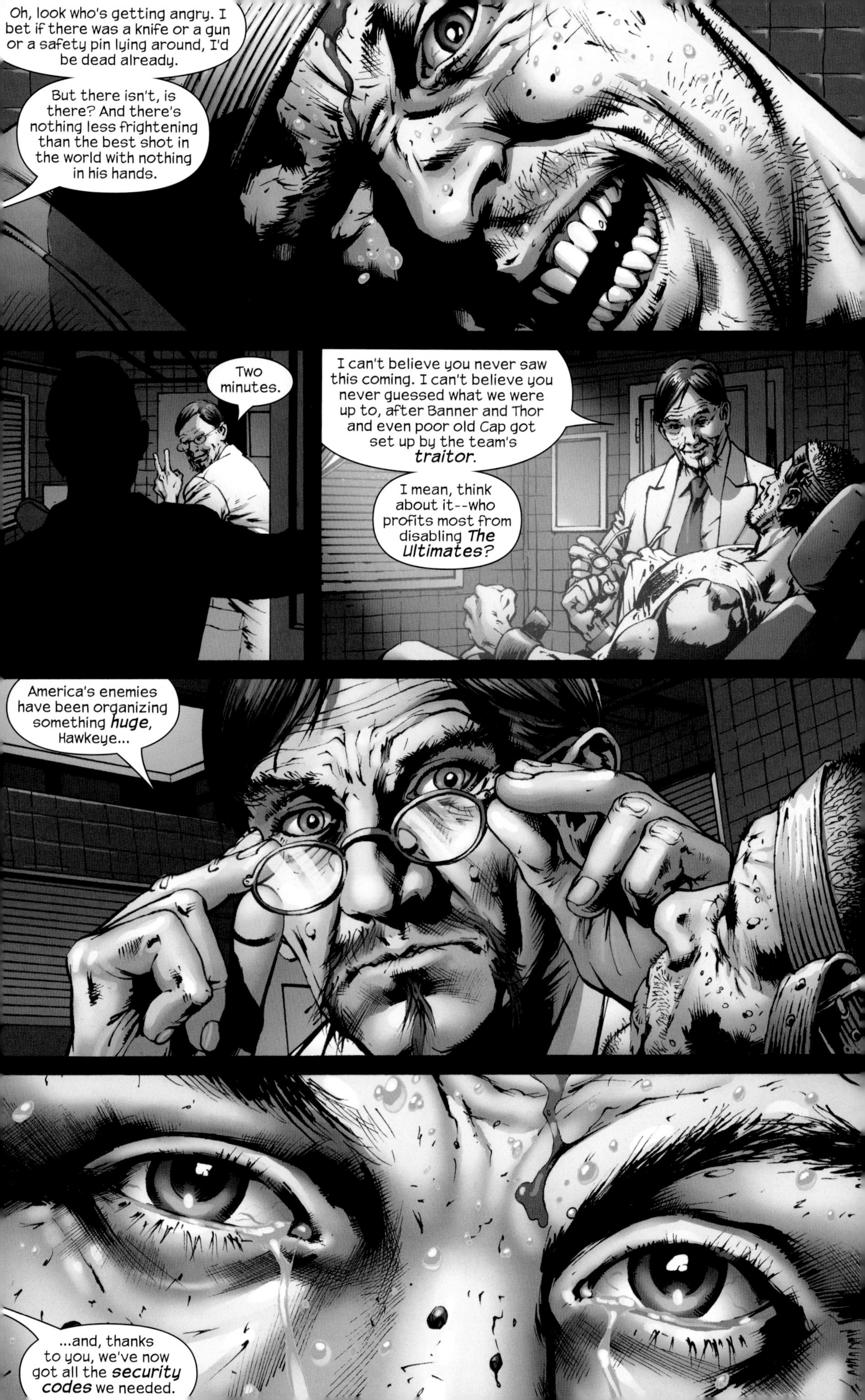
Oh, look who's getting angry. I bet if there was a knife or a gun or a safety pin lying around, I'd be dead already.
But there isn't, is there? And there's nothing less frightening than the best shot in the world with nothing in his hands.
Two minutes.
I can't believe you never saw this coming. I can't believe you never guessed what we were up to, after Banner and Thor and even poor old Cap got set up by the team's *traitor*.
I mean, think about it--who profits most from disabling *The Ultimates*?
America's enemies have been organizing something *huge*, Hawkeye...
...and, thanks to you, we've now got all the *security codes* we needed.

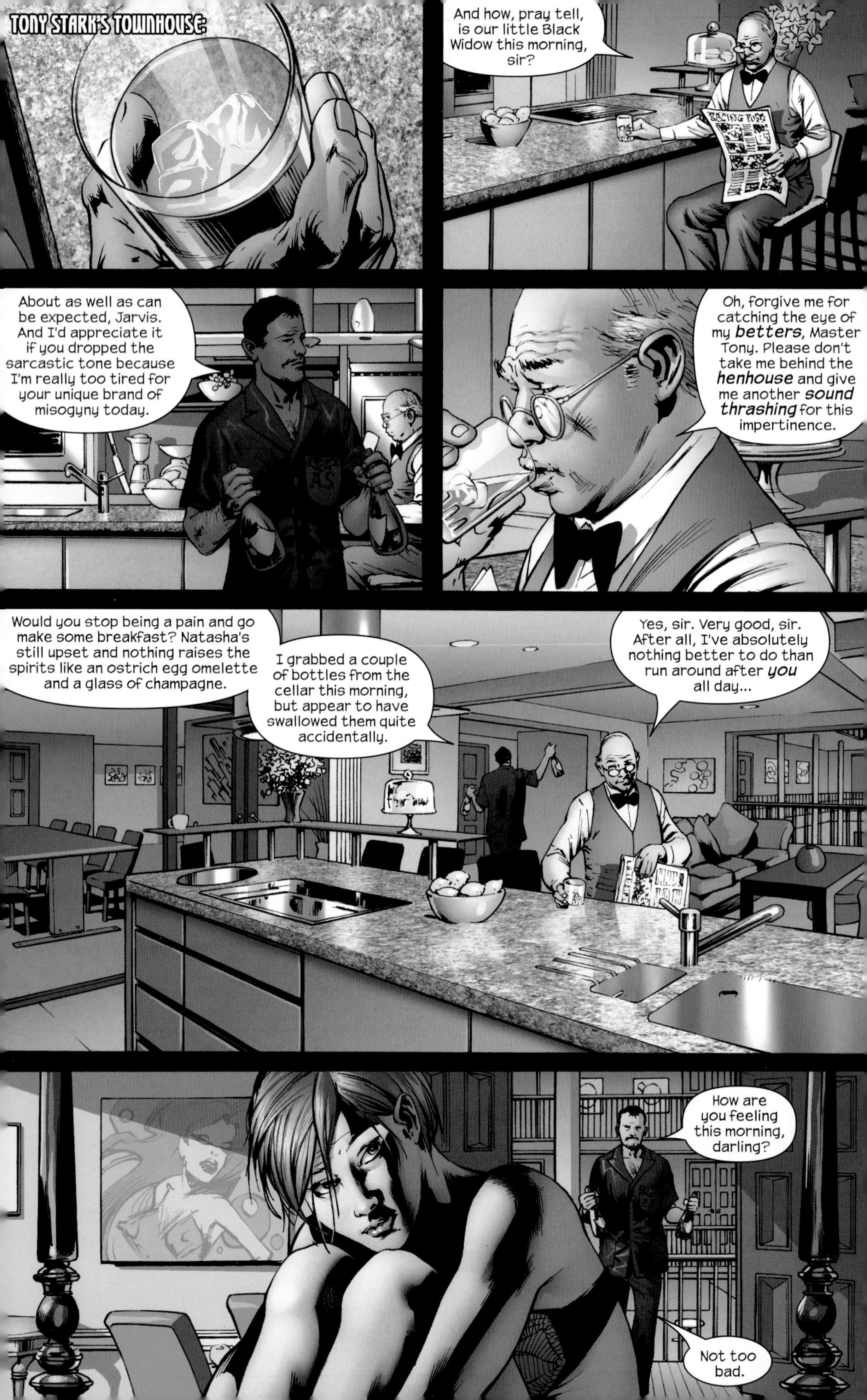
TONY STARK'S TOWNHOUSE:
And how, pray tell, is our little Black Widow this morning, sir?
About as well as can be expected, Jarvis. And I'd appreciate it if you dropped the sarcastic tone because I'm really too tired for your unique brand of misogyny today.
Oh, forgive me for catching the eye of my **betters**, Master Tony. Please don't take me behind the **henhouse** and give me another **sound thrashing** for this impertinence.
Would you stop being a pain and go make some breakfast? Natasha's still upset and nothing raises the spirits like an ostrich egg omelette and a glass of champagne.
I grabbed a couple of bottles from the cellar this morning, but appear to have swallowed them quite accidentally.
Yes, sir. Very good, sir. After all, I've absolutely nothing better to do than run around after ***you*** all day...
How are you feeling this morning, darling?
Not too bad.

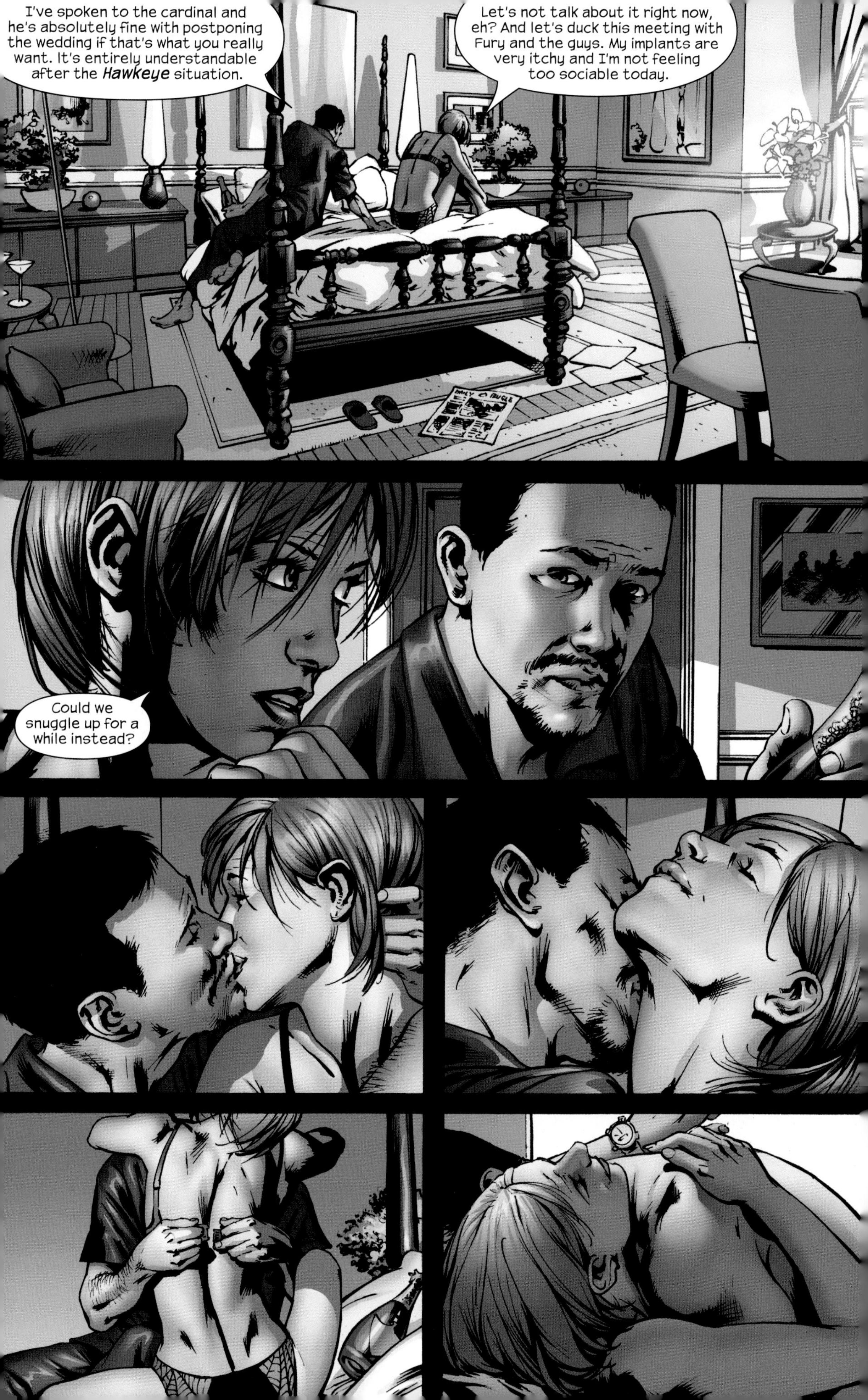

I've spoken to the cardinal and he's absolutely fine with postponing the wedding if that's what you really want. It's entirely understandable after the *Hawkeye* situation.
Let's not talk about it right now, eh? And let's duck this meeting with Fury and the guys. My implants are very itchy and I'm not feeling too sociable today.
Could we snuggle up for a while instead?

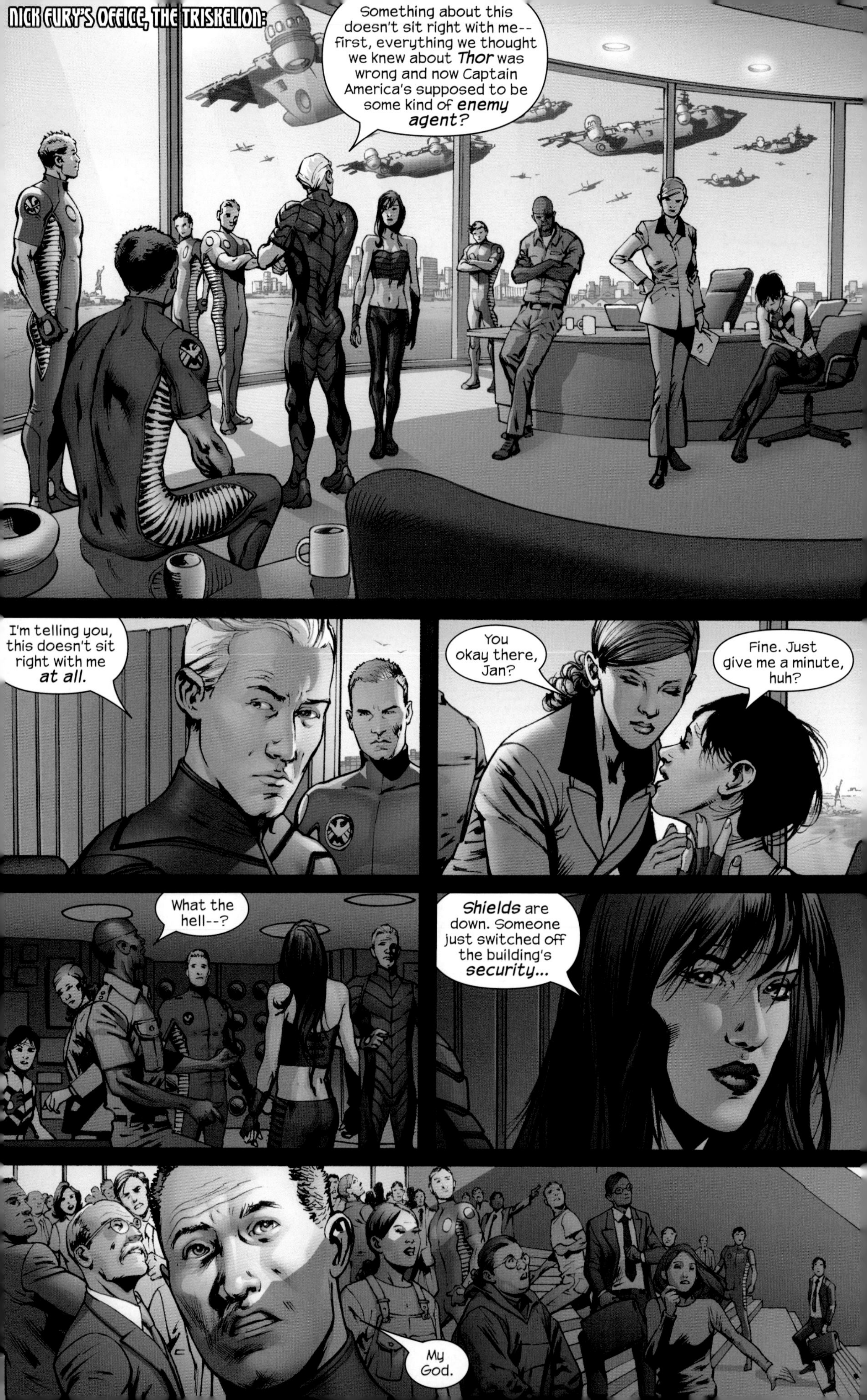

NICK FURY'S OFFICE, THE TRISKELION:
Something about this doesn't sit right with me-- first, everything we thought we knew about Thor was wrong and now Captain America's supposed to be some kind of enemy agent?
I'm telling you, this doesn't sit right with me at all.
You okay there, Jan?
Fine. Just give me a minute, huh?
What the hell--?
Shields are down. Someone just switched off the building's security...
My God.

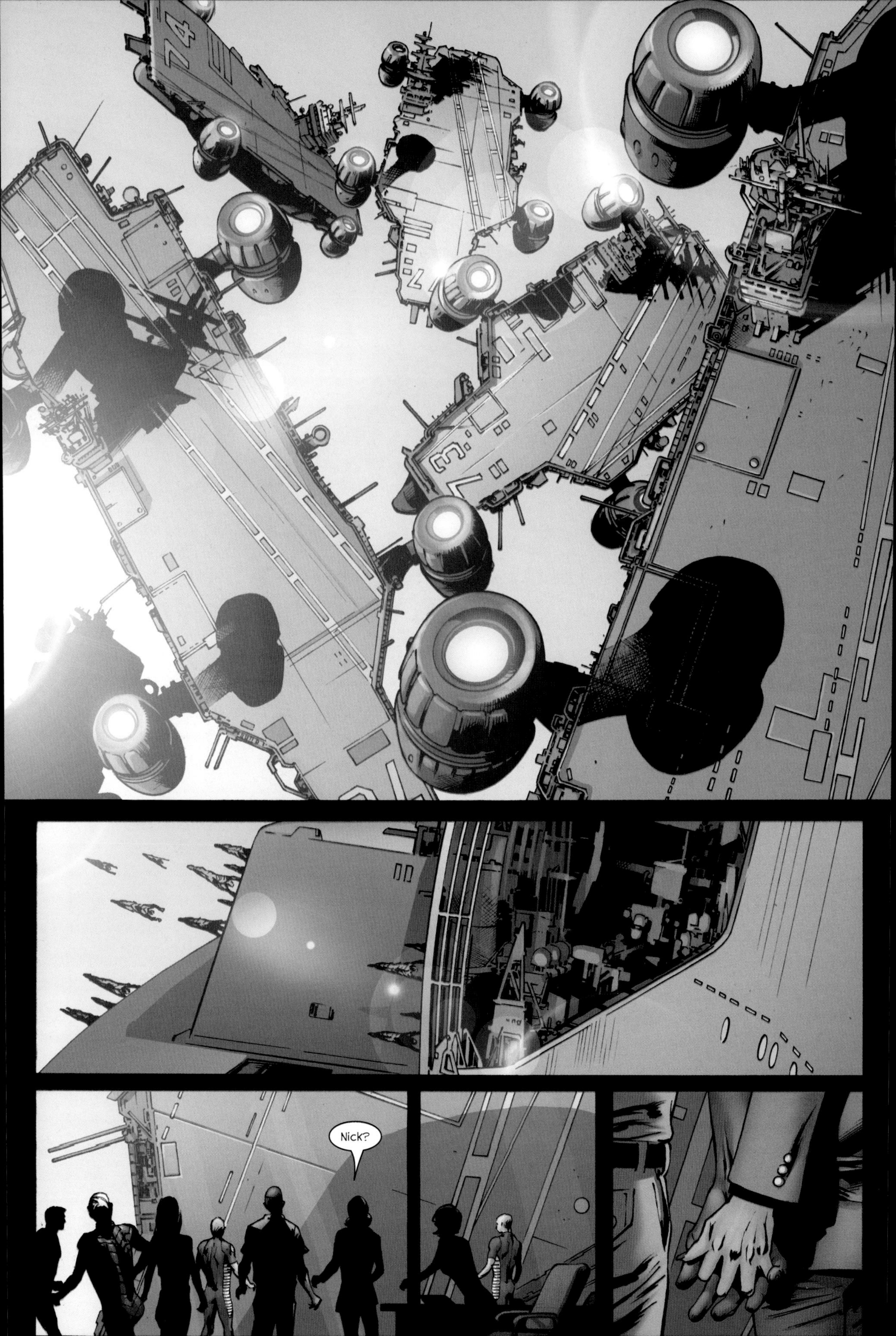
Nick?

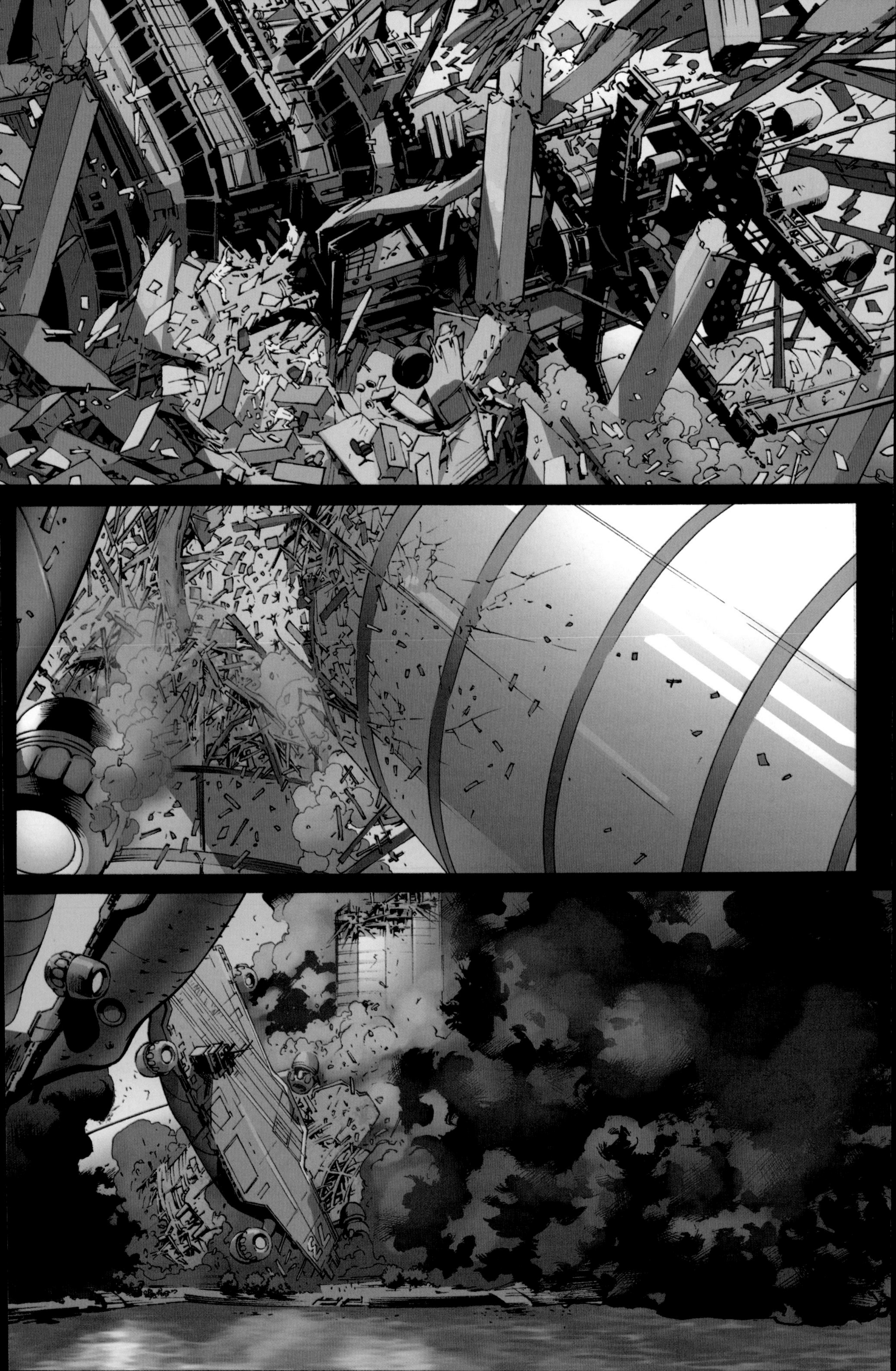

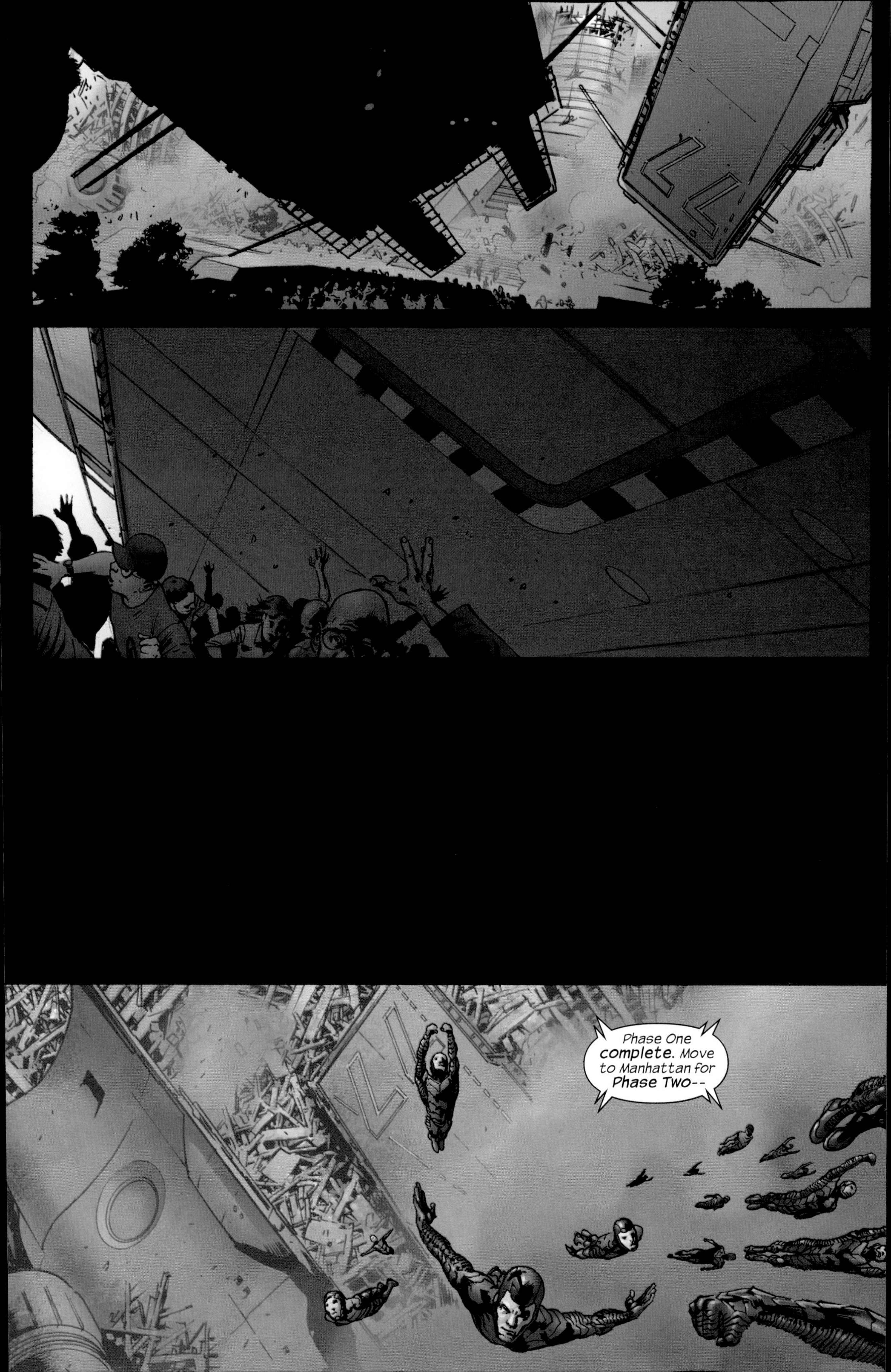
Phase One complete. Move to Manhattan for Phase Two--

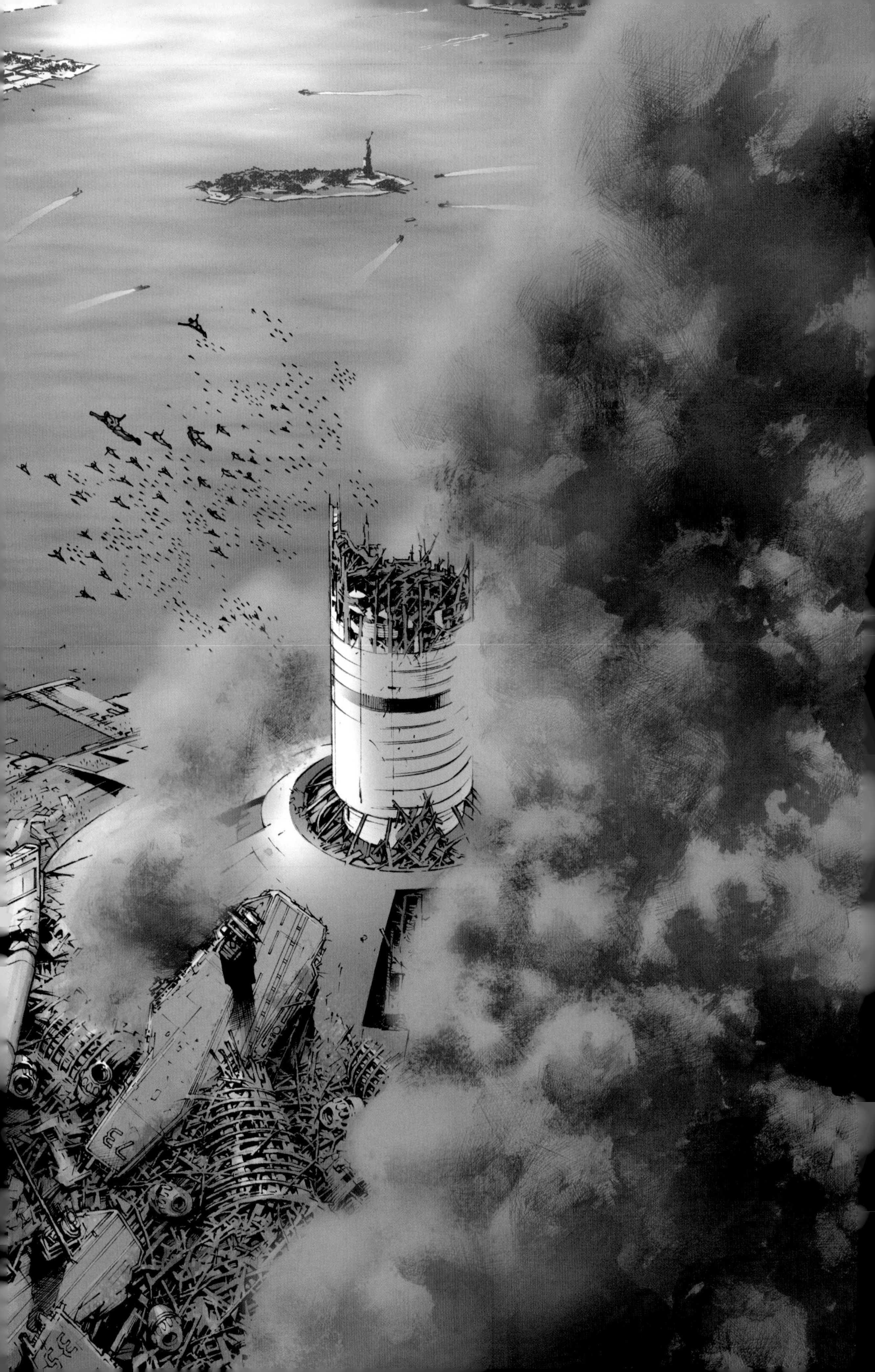

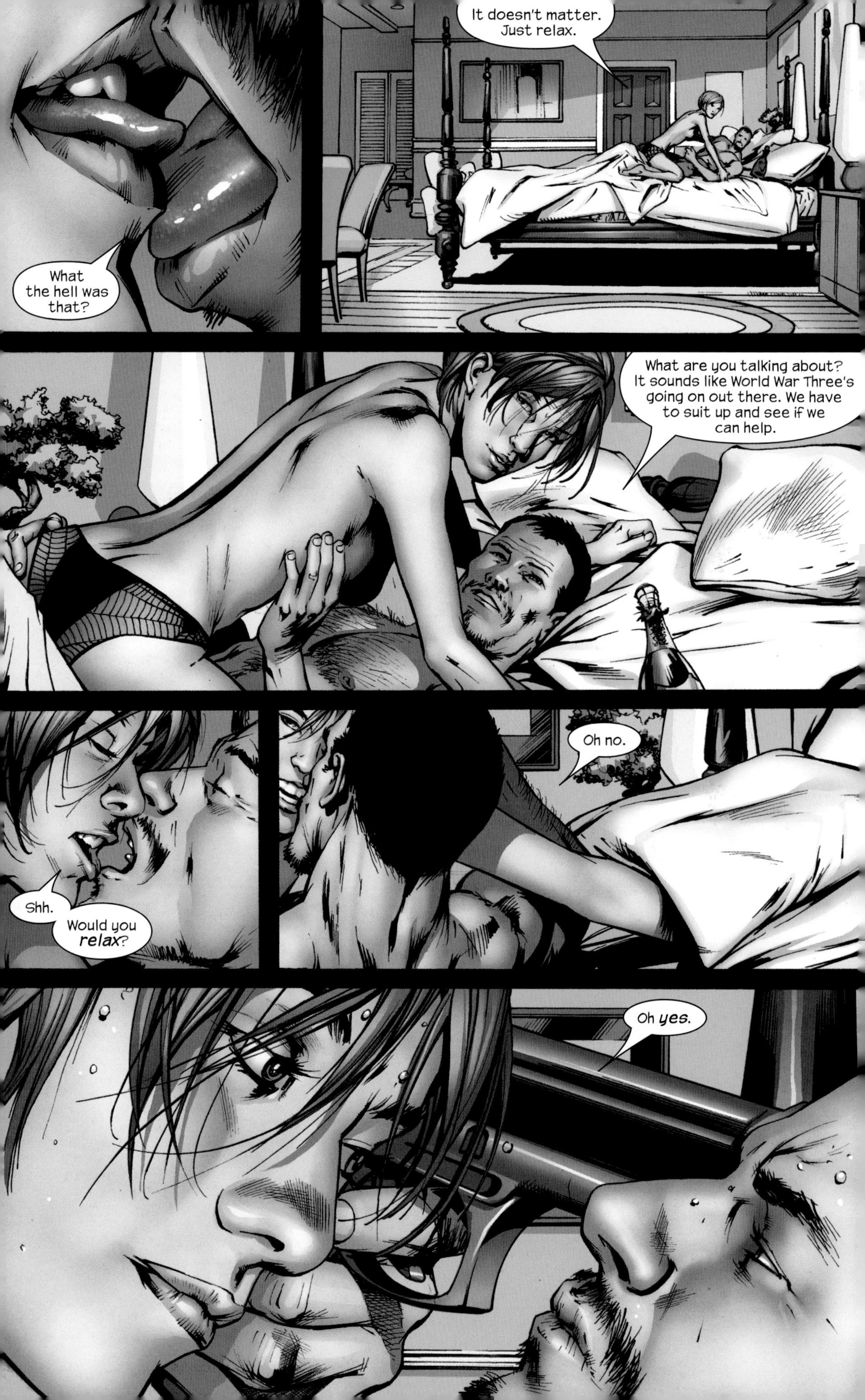
What the hell was that?
It doesn't matter. Just relax.
What are you talking about? It sounds like World War Three's going on out there. We have to suit up and see if we can help.
Shh.
Would you *relax*?
Oh no.
Oh *yes*.

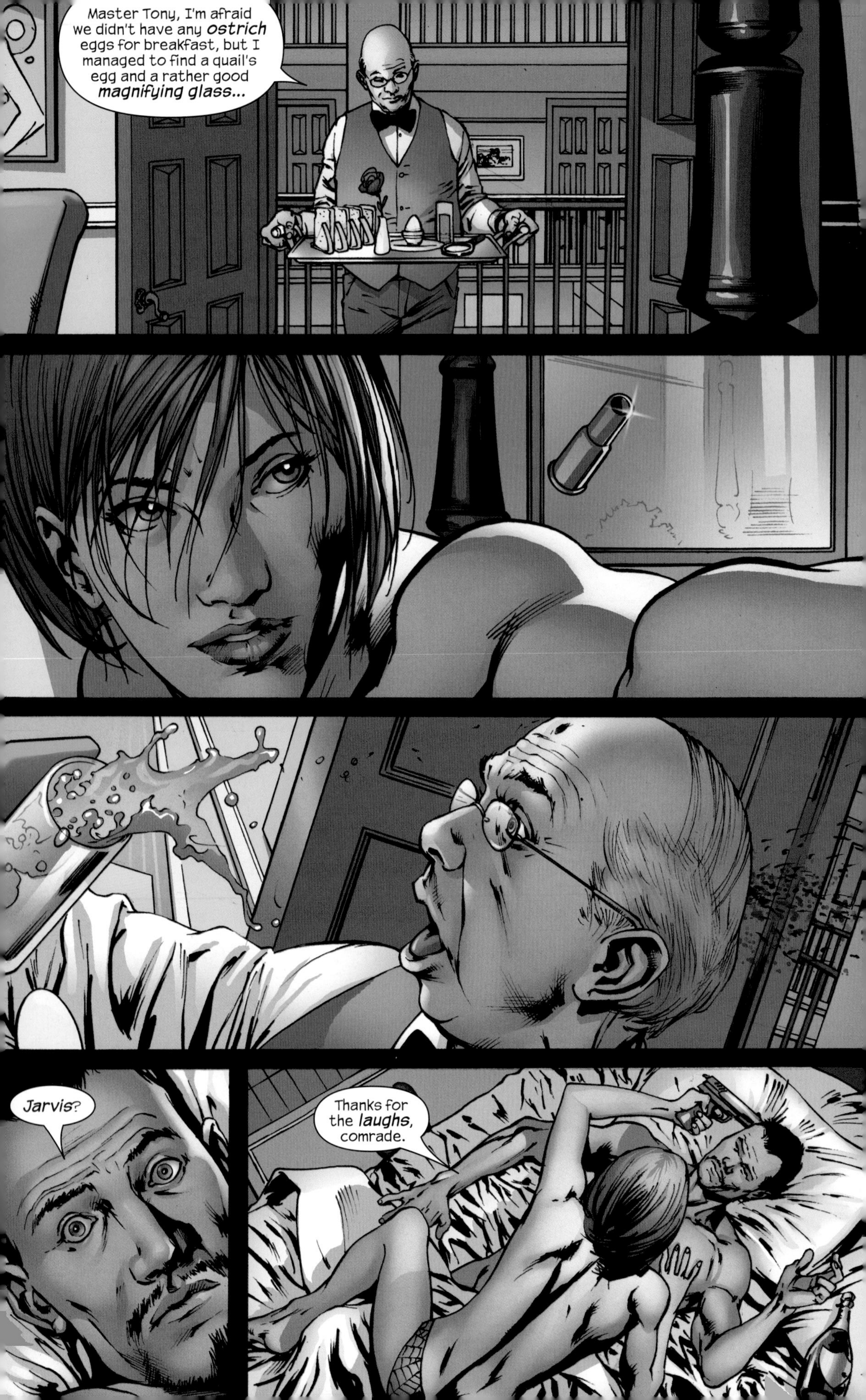
Master Tony, I'm afraid we didn't have any ostrich eggs for breakfast, but I managed to find a quail's egg and a rather good magnifying glass...
Jarvis?
Thanks for the laughs, comrade.

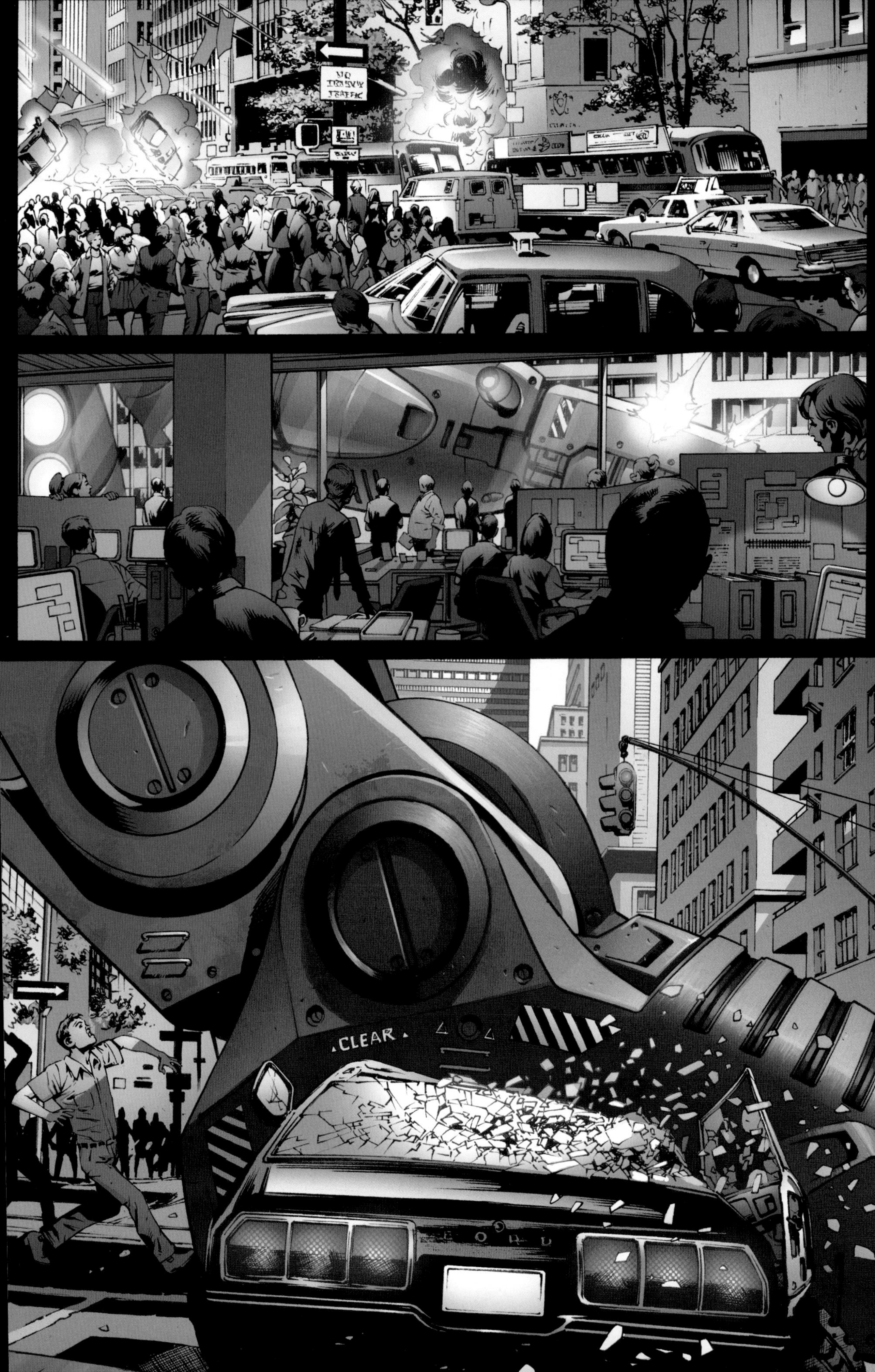
CLEAR

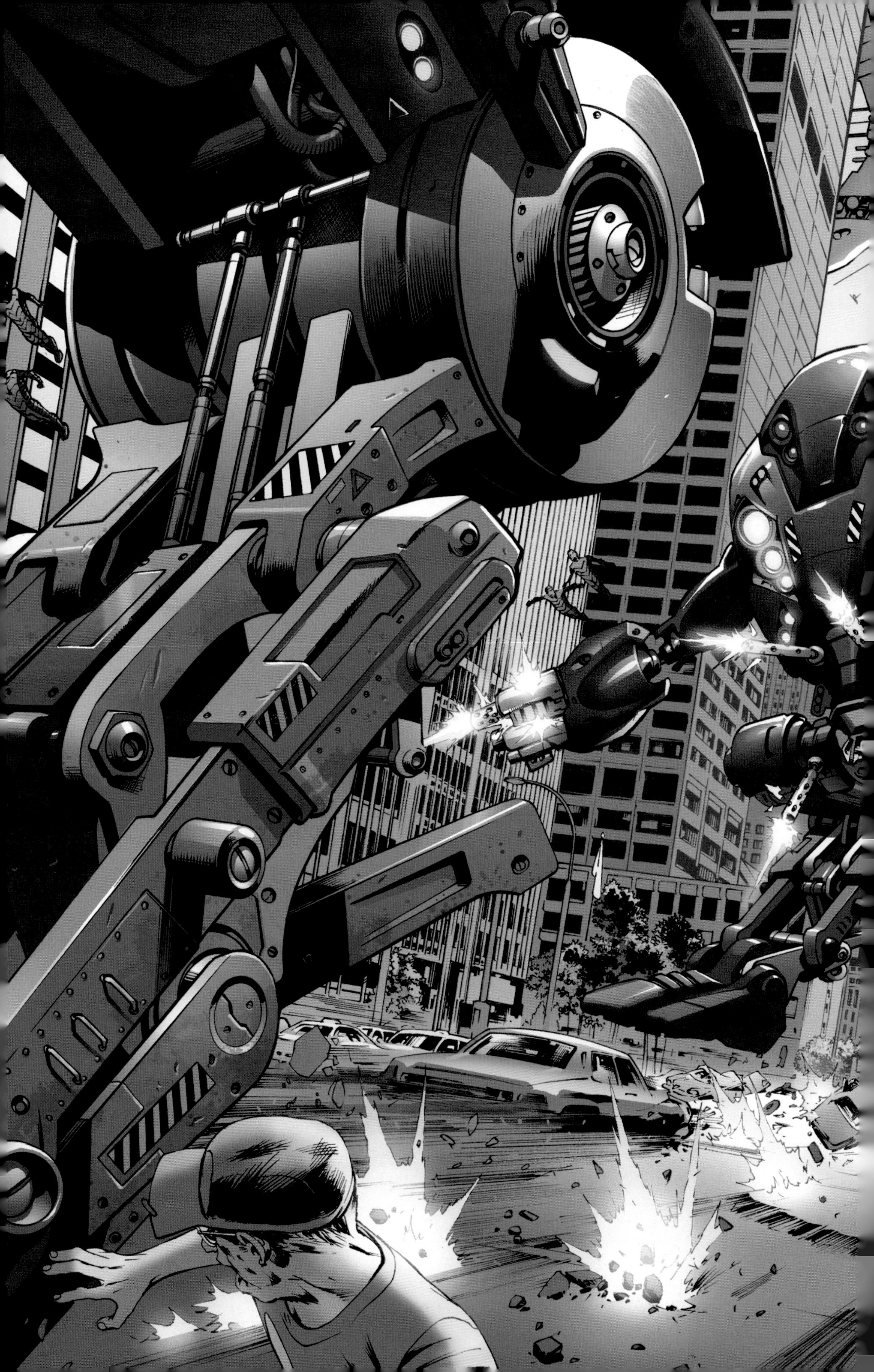

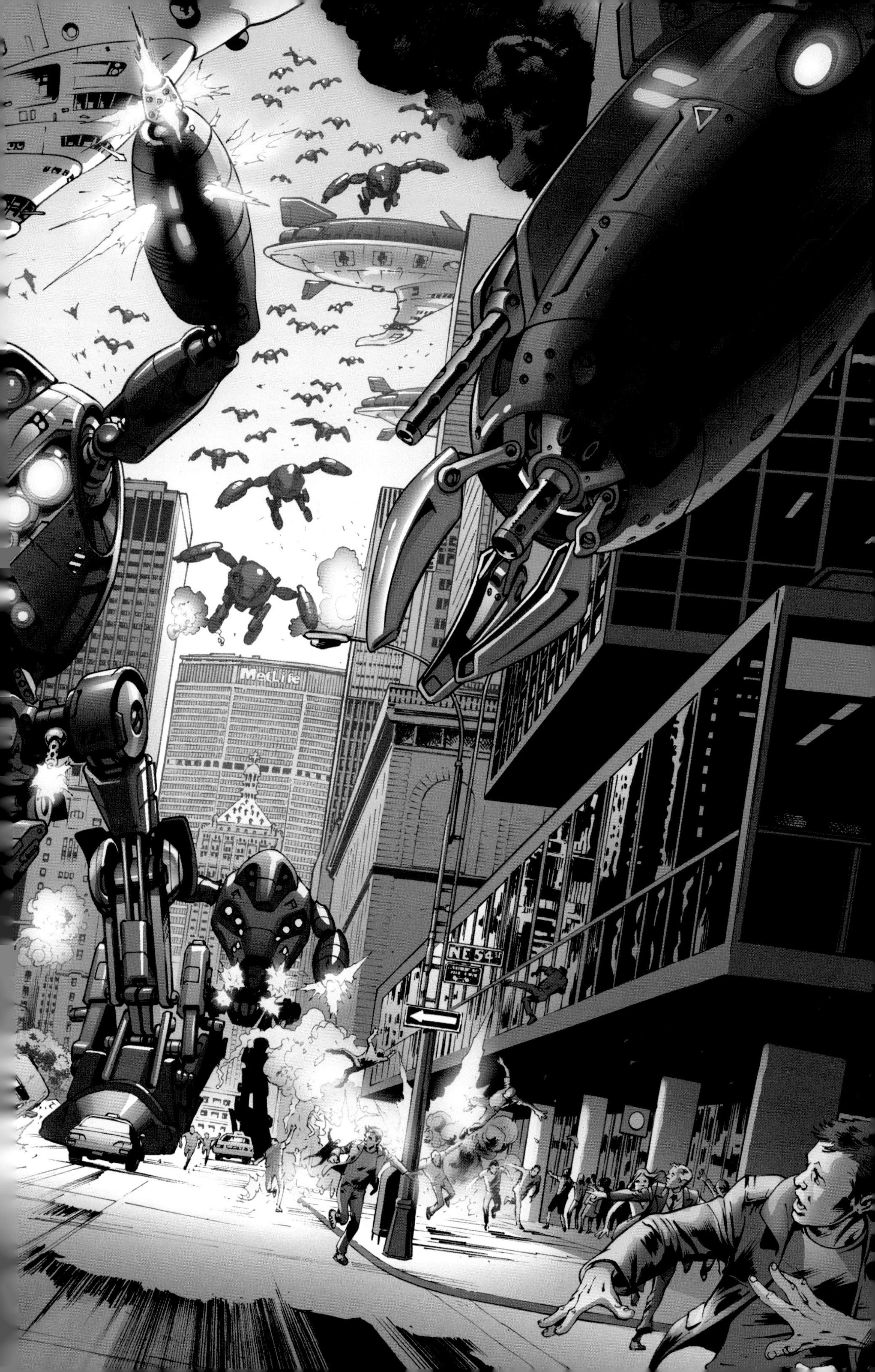
MetLife
NE 54 St

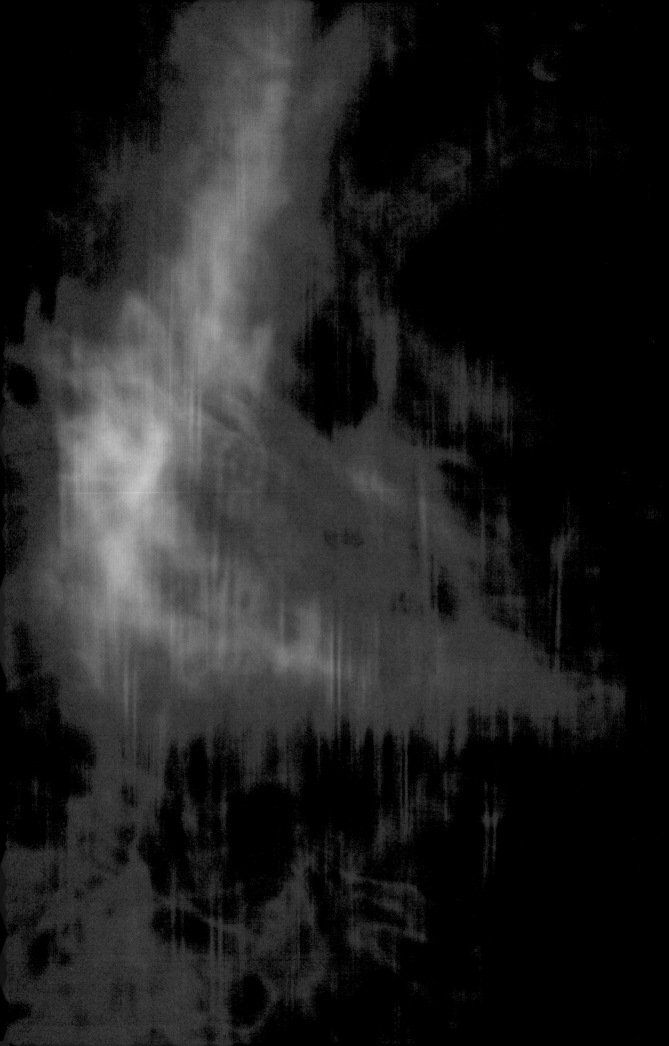

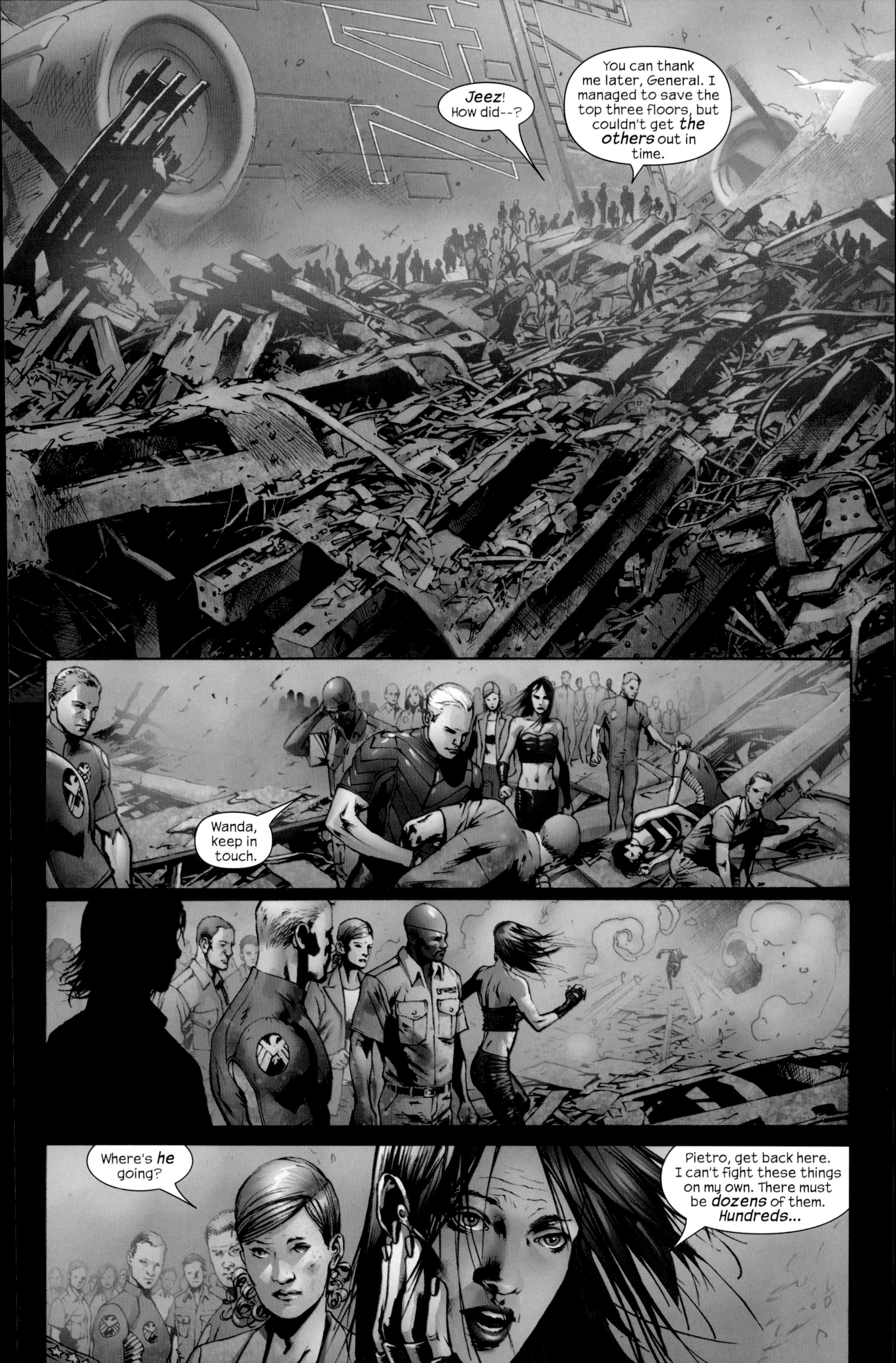
Jeez! How did--?
You can thank me later, General. I managed to save the top three floors, but couldn't get the others out in time.
Wanda, keep in touch.
Where's he going?
Pietro, get back here. I can't fight these things on my own. There must be dozens of them. Hundreds...

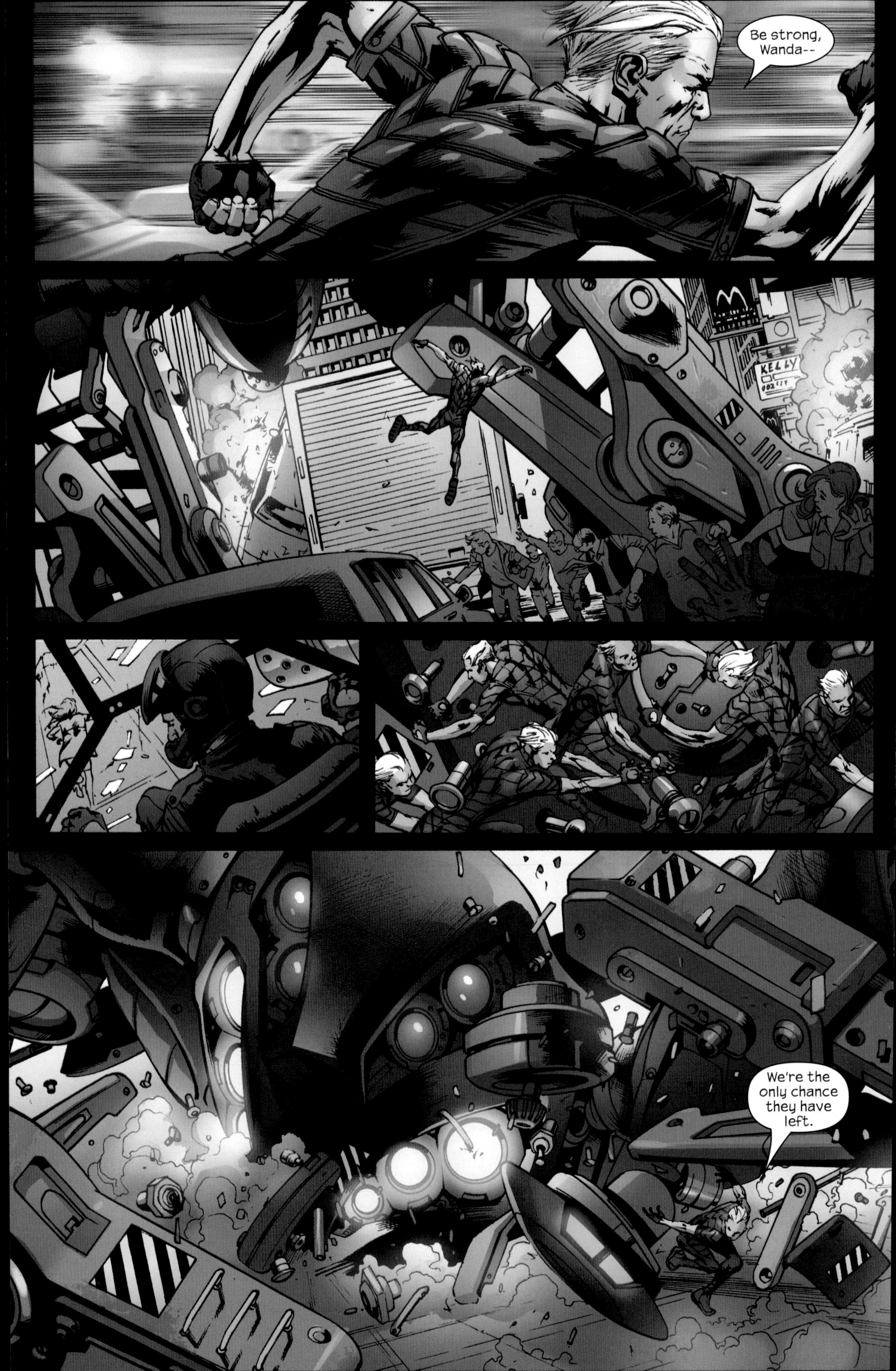
Be strong, Wanda--
We're the only chance they have left.

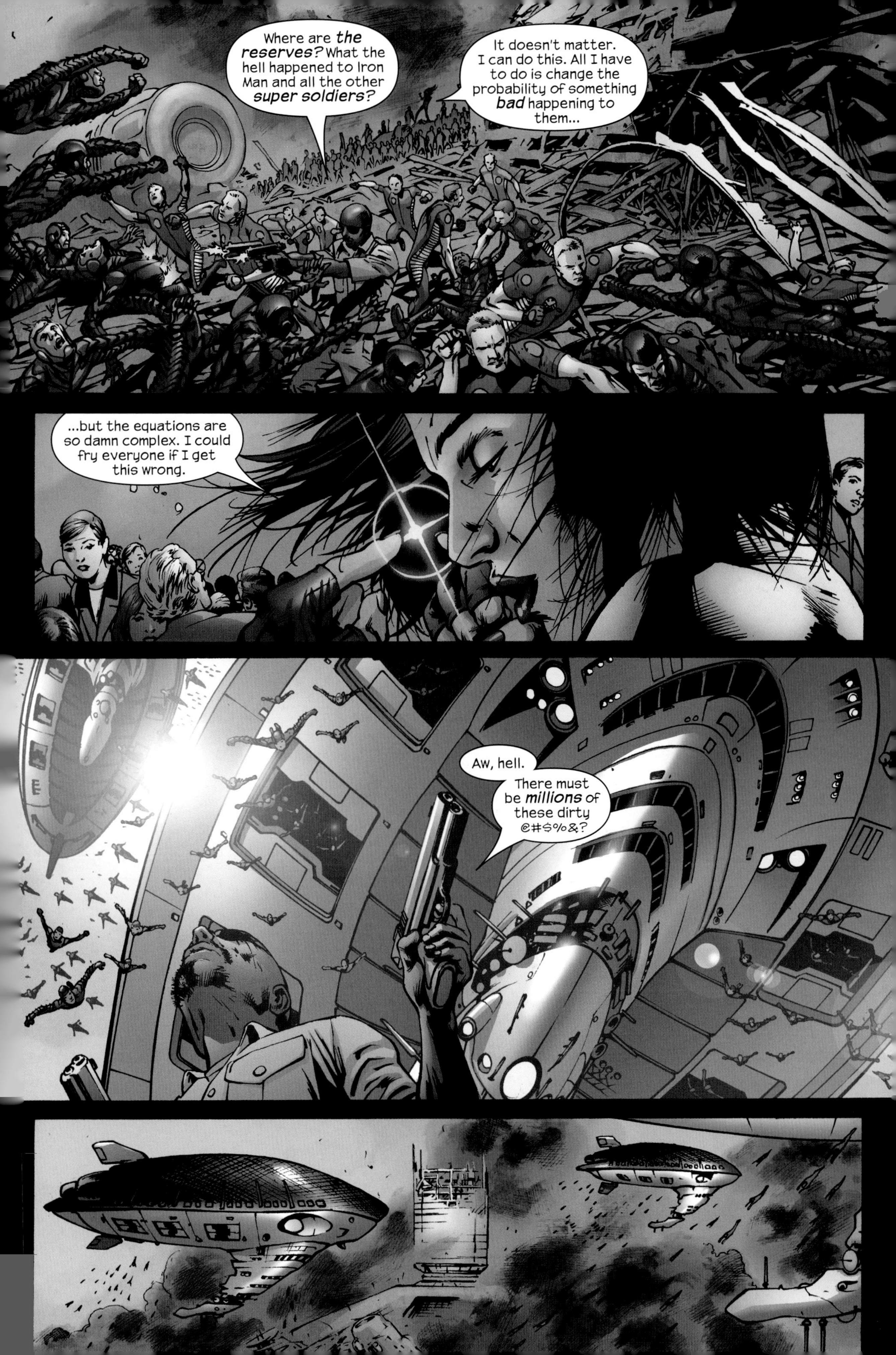
Where are the reserves? What the hell happened to Iron Man and all the other super soldiers?
It doesn't matter. I can do this. All I have to do is change the probability of something bad happening to them...
...but the equations are so damn complex. I could fry everyone if I get this wrong.
Aw, hell.
There must be millions of these dirty @#$%&?

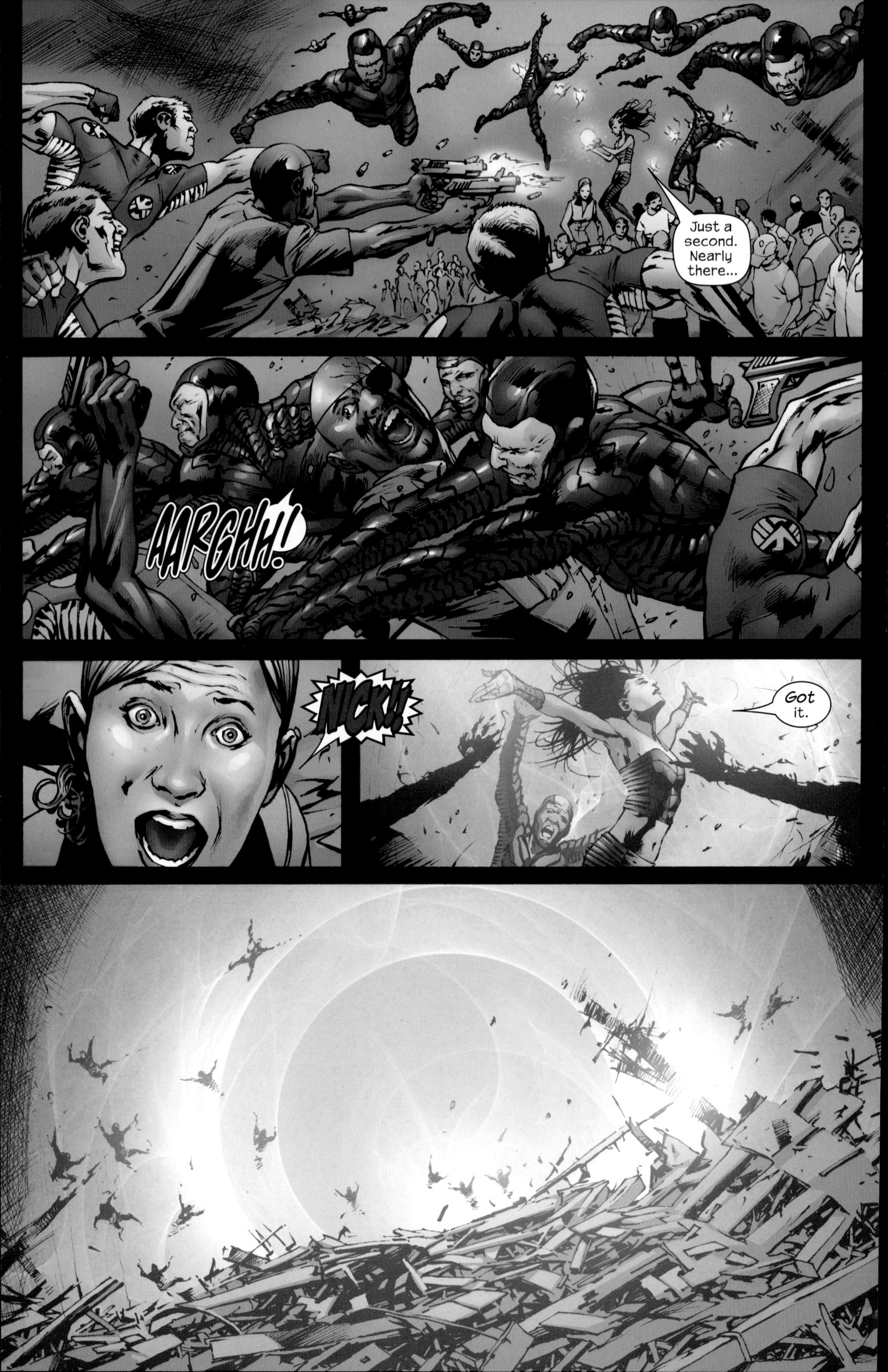
Just a second. Nearly there...
AARGHH!
NICK!!
Got it.

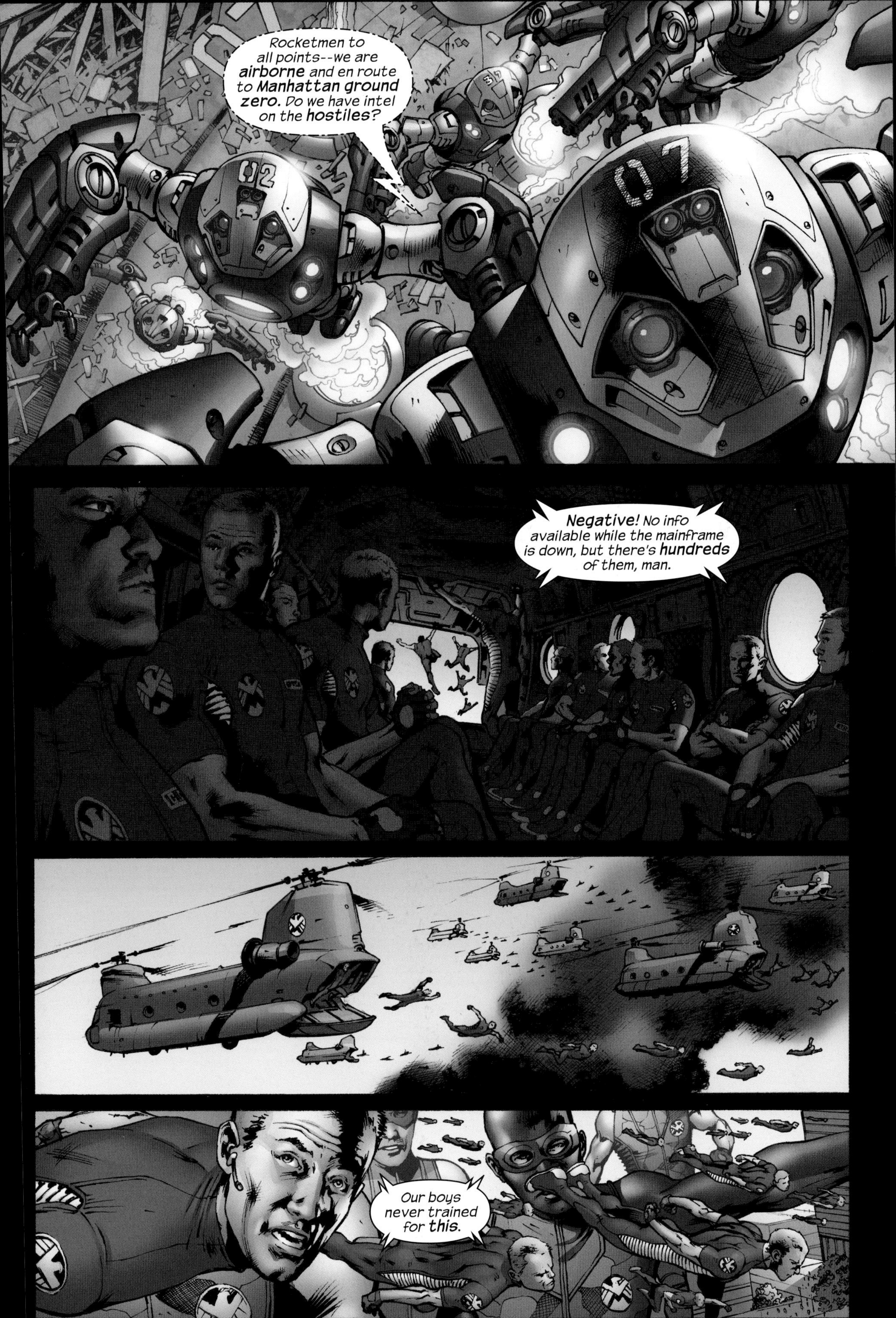
Rocketmen to all points--we are airborne and en route to Manhattan ground zero. Do we have intel on the hostiles?
Negative! No info available while the mainframe is down, but there's hundreds of them, man.
Our boys never trained for this.

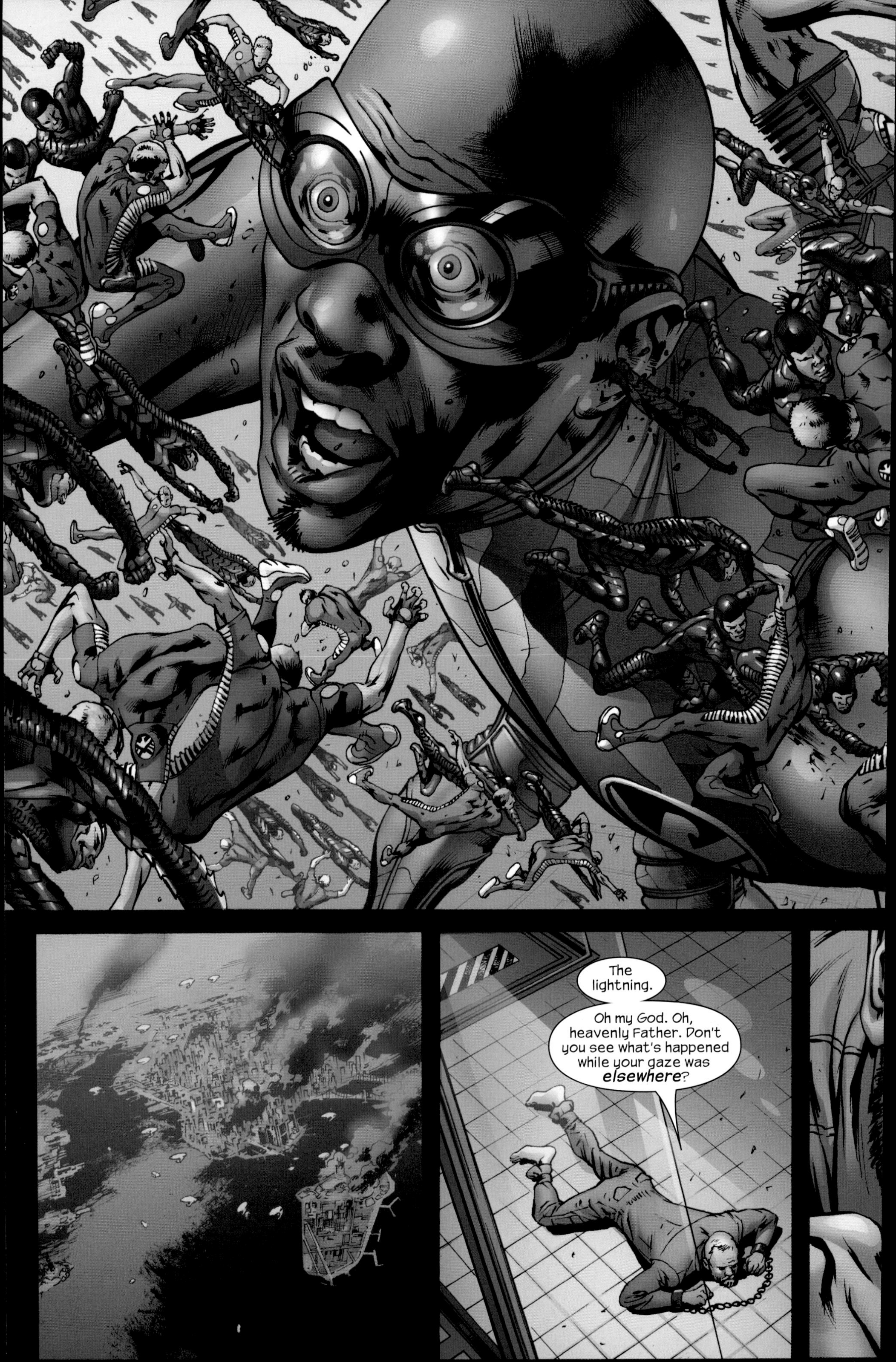
The lightning.
Oh my God. Oh, heavenly Father. Don't you see what's happened while your gaze was *elsewhere*?

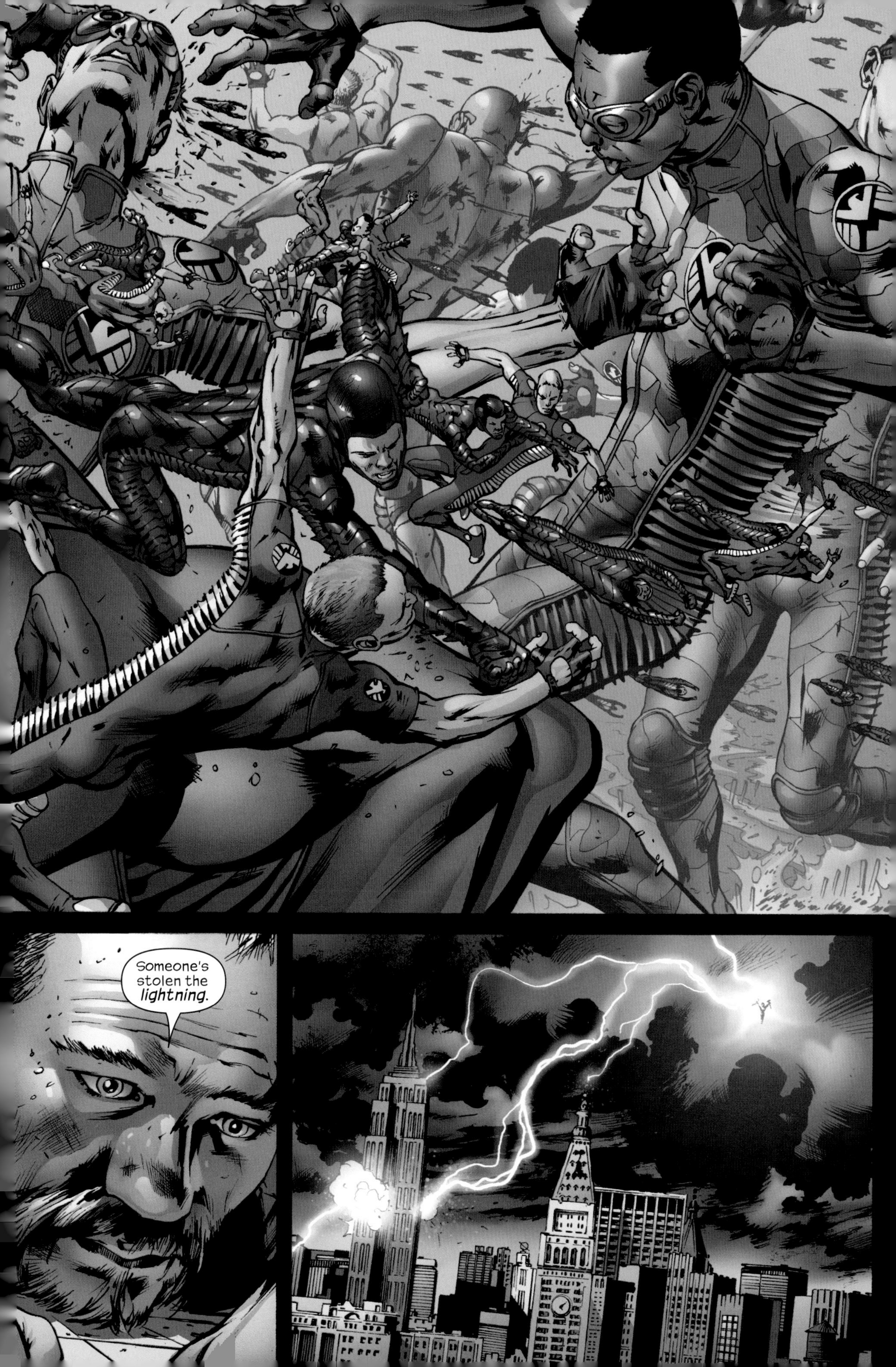
Someone's stolen the *lightning*.

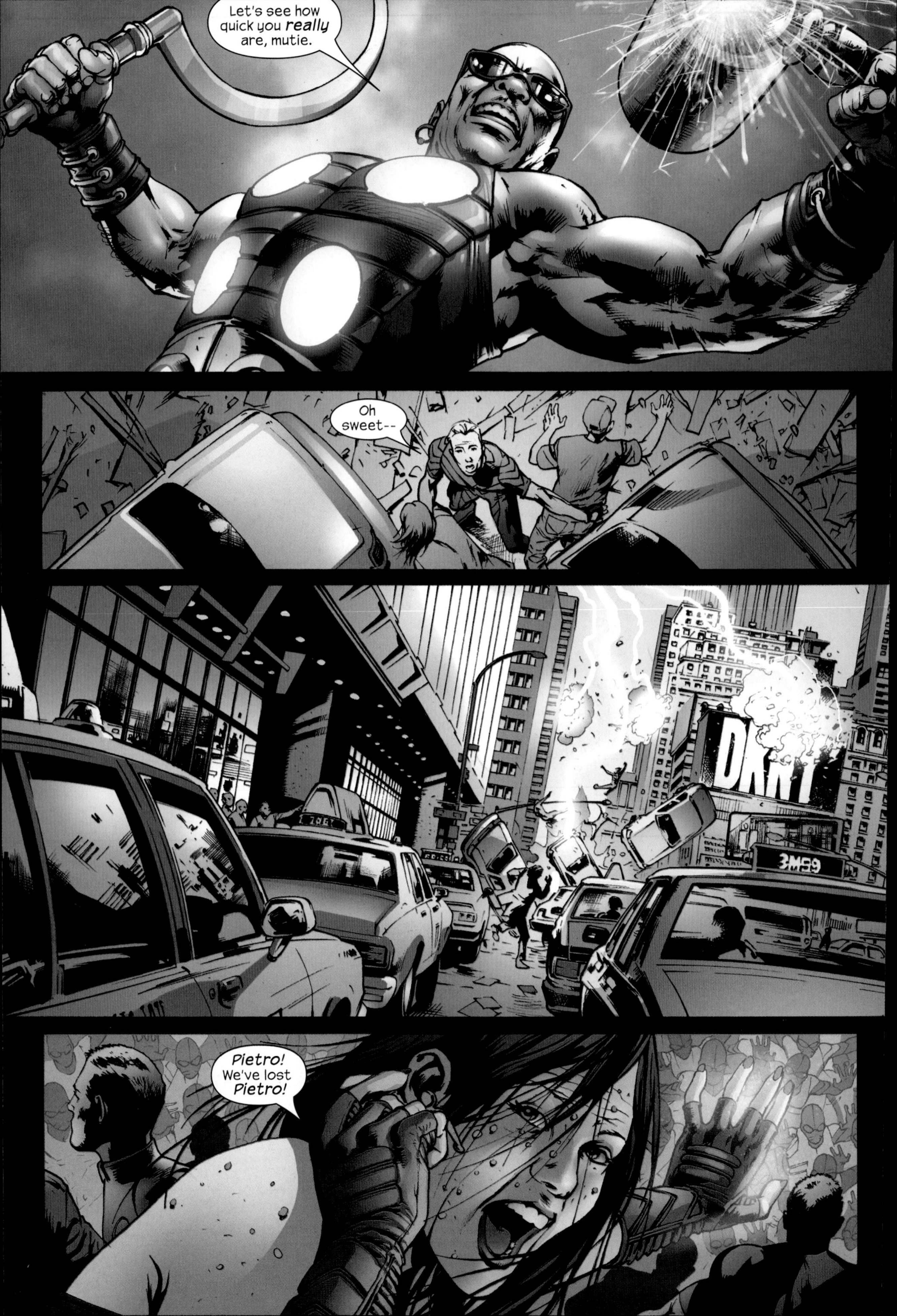
Let's see how quick you *really* are, mutie.
Oh sweet--
Pietro! We've lost Pietro!

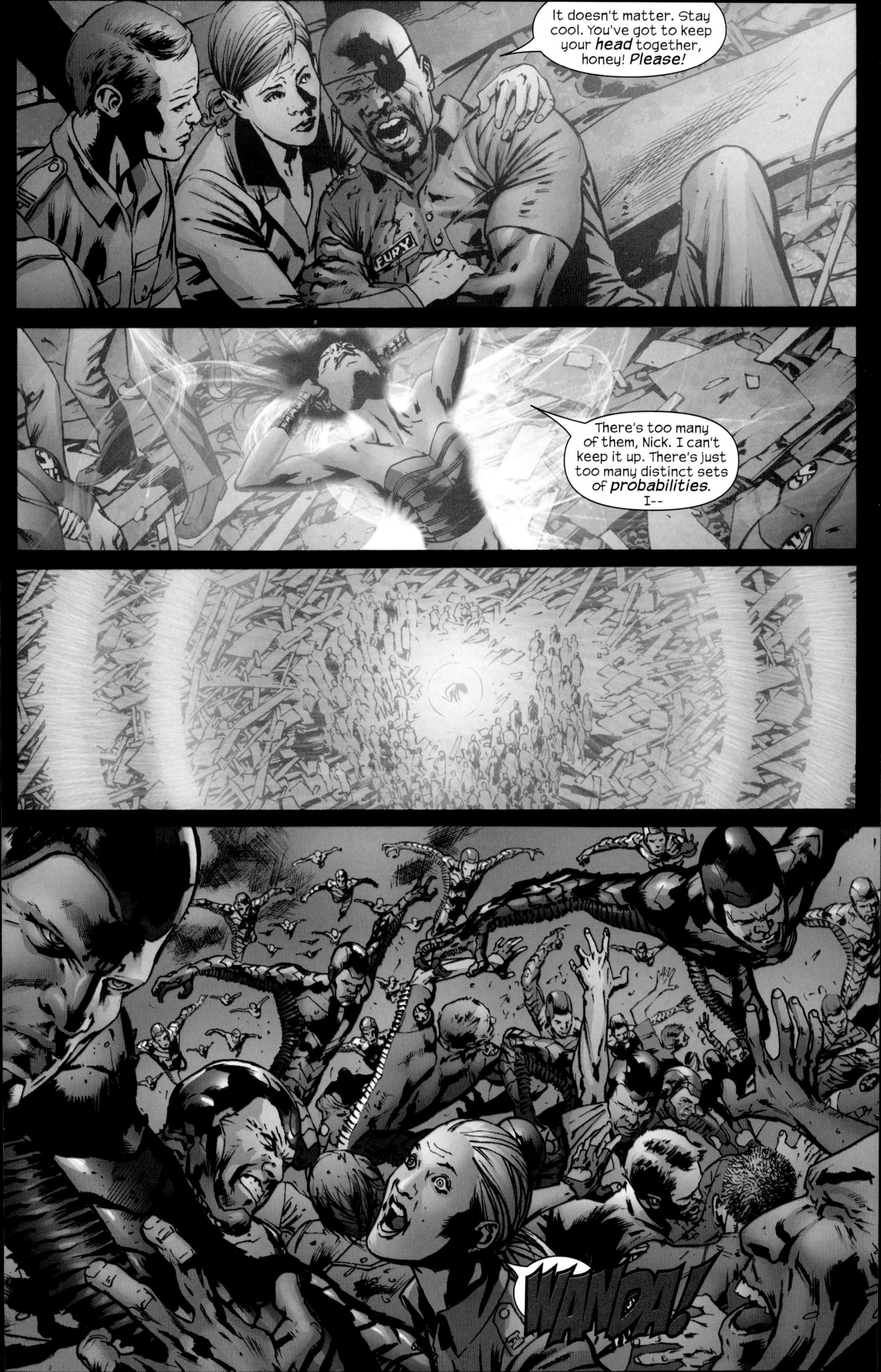
It doesn't matter. Stay cool. You've got to keep your **head** together, honey! ***Please!***
There's too many of them, Nick. I can't keep it up. There's just too many distinct sets of ***probabilities***. I--
WANDA!

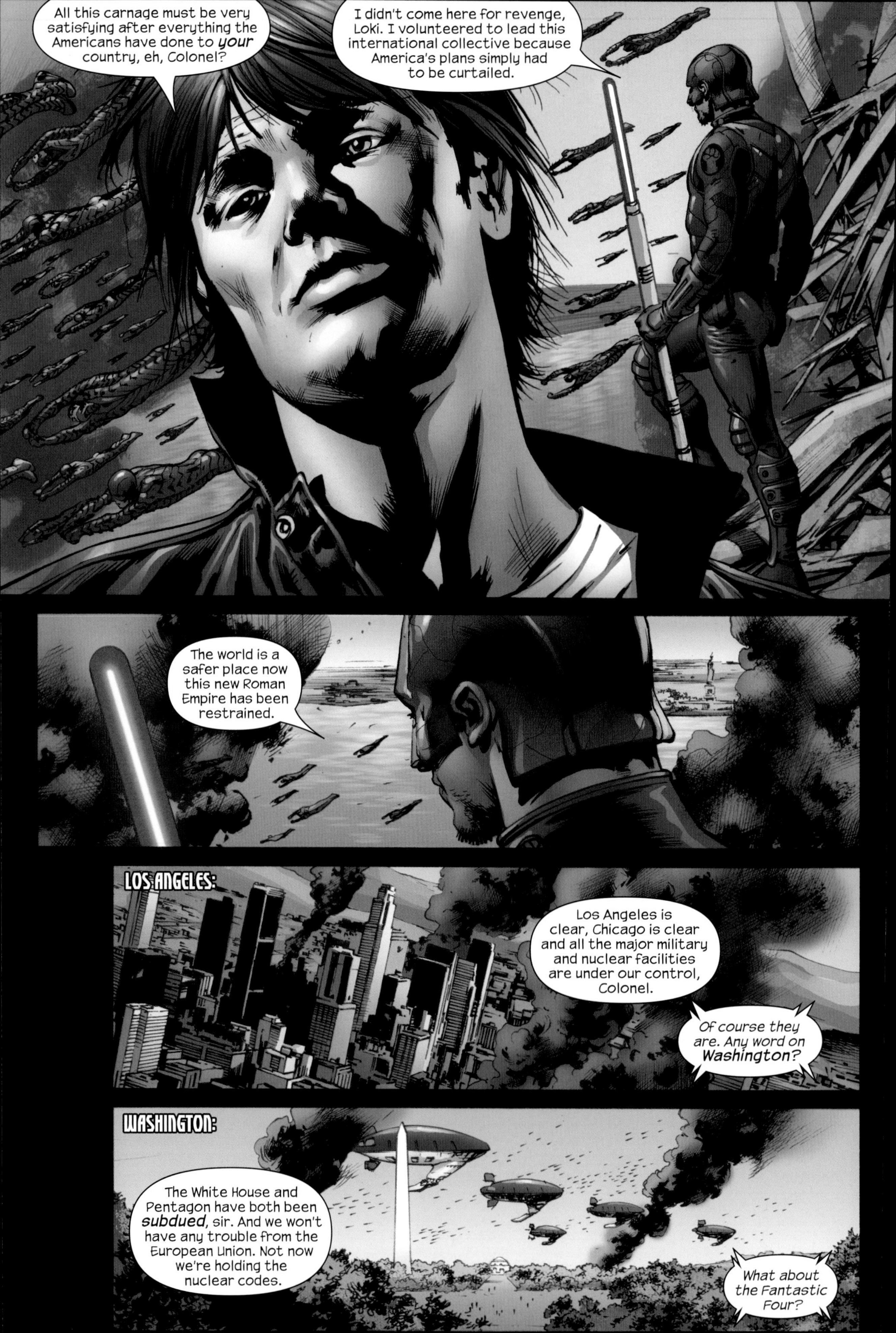
All this carnage must be very satisfying after everything the Americans have done to *your* country, eh, Colonel?
I didn't come here for revenge, Loki. I volunteered to lead this international collective because America's plans simply had to be curtailed.
The world is a safer place now this new Roman Empire has been restrained.
LOS ANGELES:
Los Angeles is clear, Chicago is clear and all the major military and nuclear facilities are under our control, Colonel.
Of course they are. Any word on ***Washington****?*
WASHINGTON:
The White House and Pentagon have both been ***subdued***, sir. And we won't have any trouble from the European Union. Not now we're holding the nuclear codes.
What about the Fantastic Four?

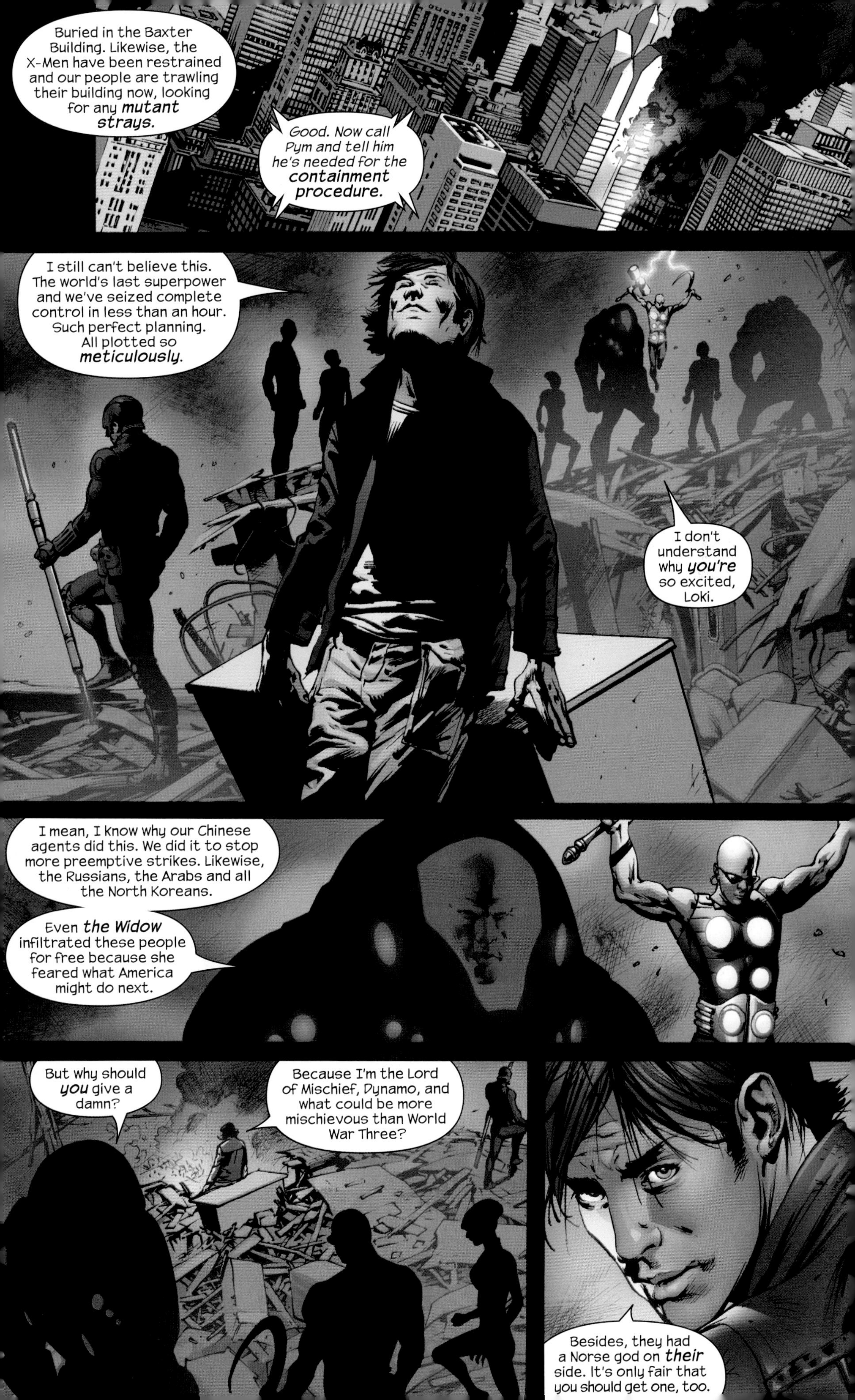

Buried in the Baxter Building. Likewise, the X-Men have been restrained and our people are trawling their building now, looking for any *mutant strays.*
Good. Now call Pym and tell him he's needed for the ***containment procedure.***
I still can't believe this. The world's last superpower and we've seized complete control in less than an hour. Such perfect planning. All plotted so ***meticulously***.
I don't understand why ***you're*** so excited, Loki.
I mean, I know why our Chinese agents did this. We did it to stop more preemptive strikes. Likewise, the Russians, the Arabs and all the North Koreans.
Even ***the Widow*** infiltrated these people for free because she feared what America might do next.
But why should ***you*** give a damn?
Because I'm the Lord of Mischief, Dynamo, and what could be more mischievous than World War Three?
Besides, they had a Norse god on ***their*** side. It's only fair that you should get one, too.

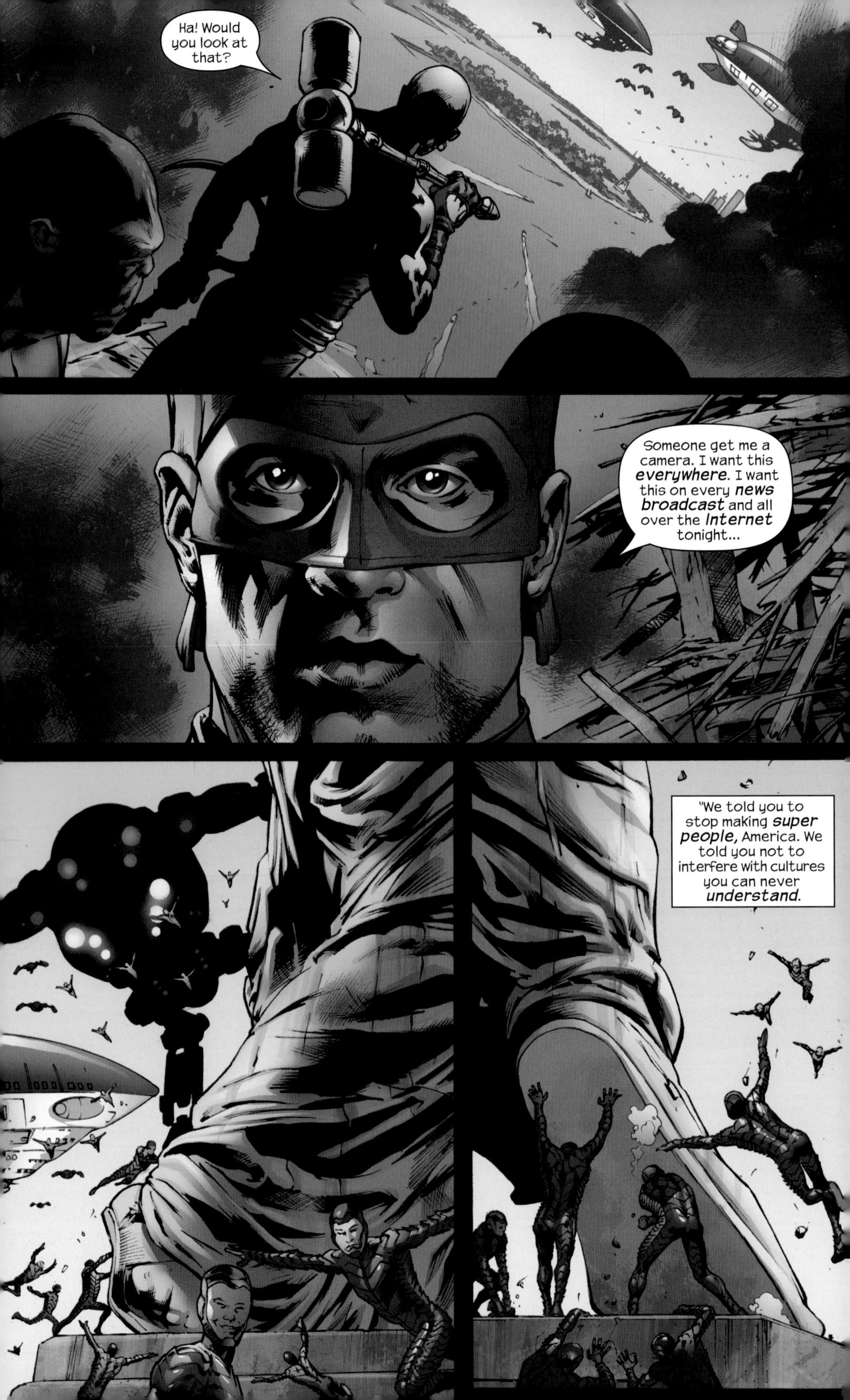
Ha! Would you look at that?
Someone get me a camera. I want this everywhere. I want this on every news broadcast and all over the Internet tonight...
"We told you to stop making super people, America. We told you not to interfere with cultures you can never understand.

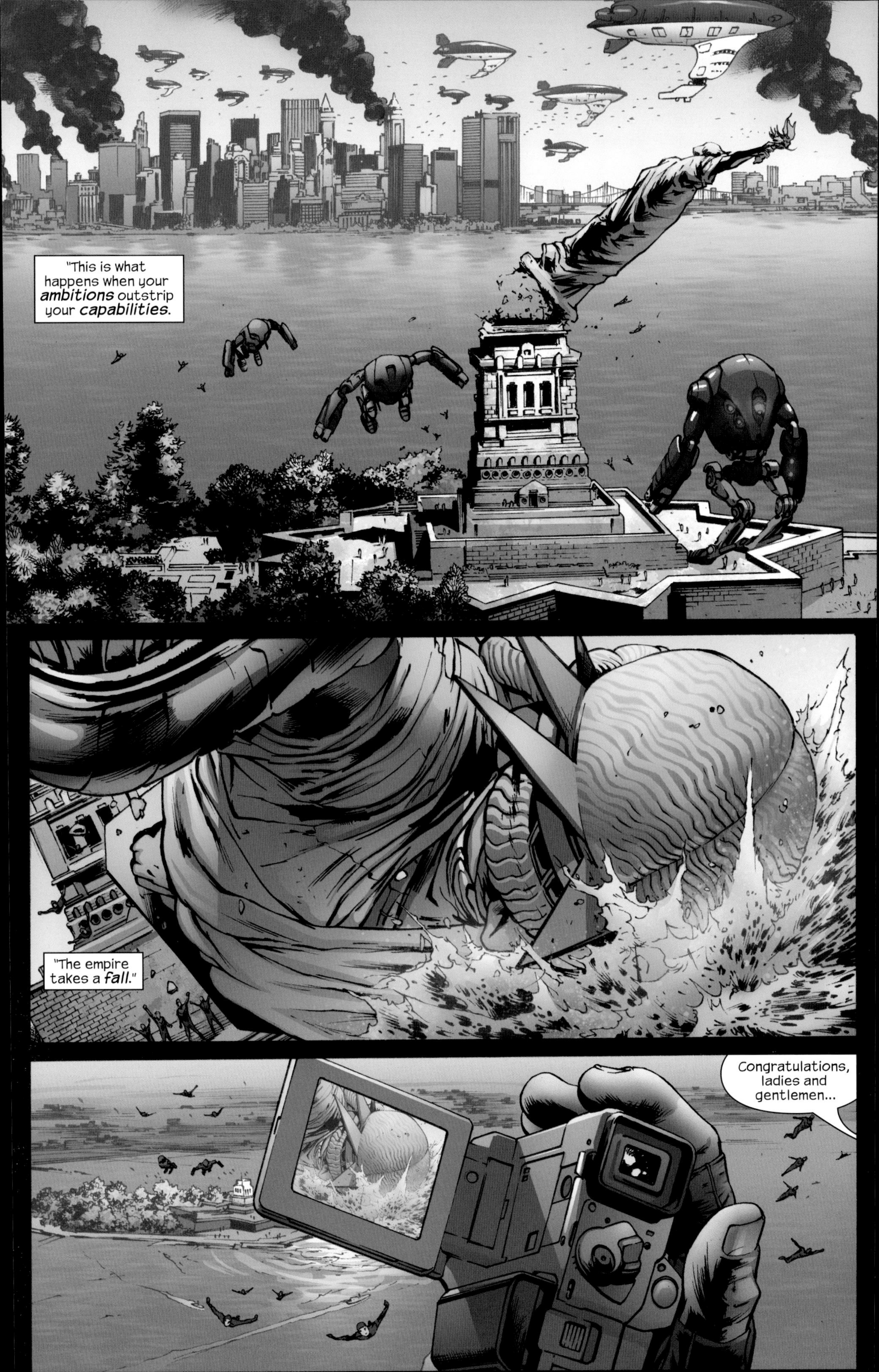
"This is what happens when your ambitions outstrip your capabilities.
"The empire takes a fall."
Congratulations, ladies and gentlemen...

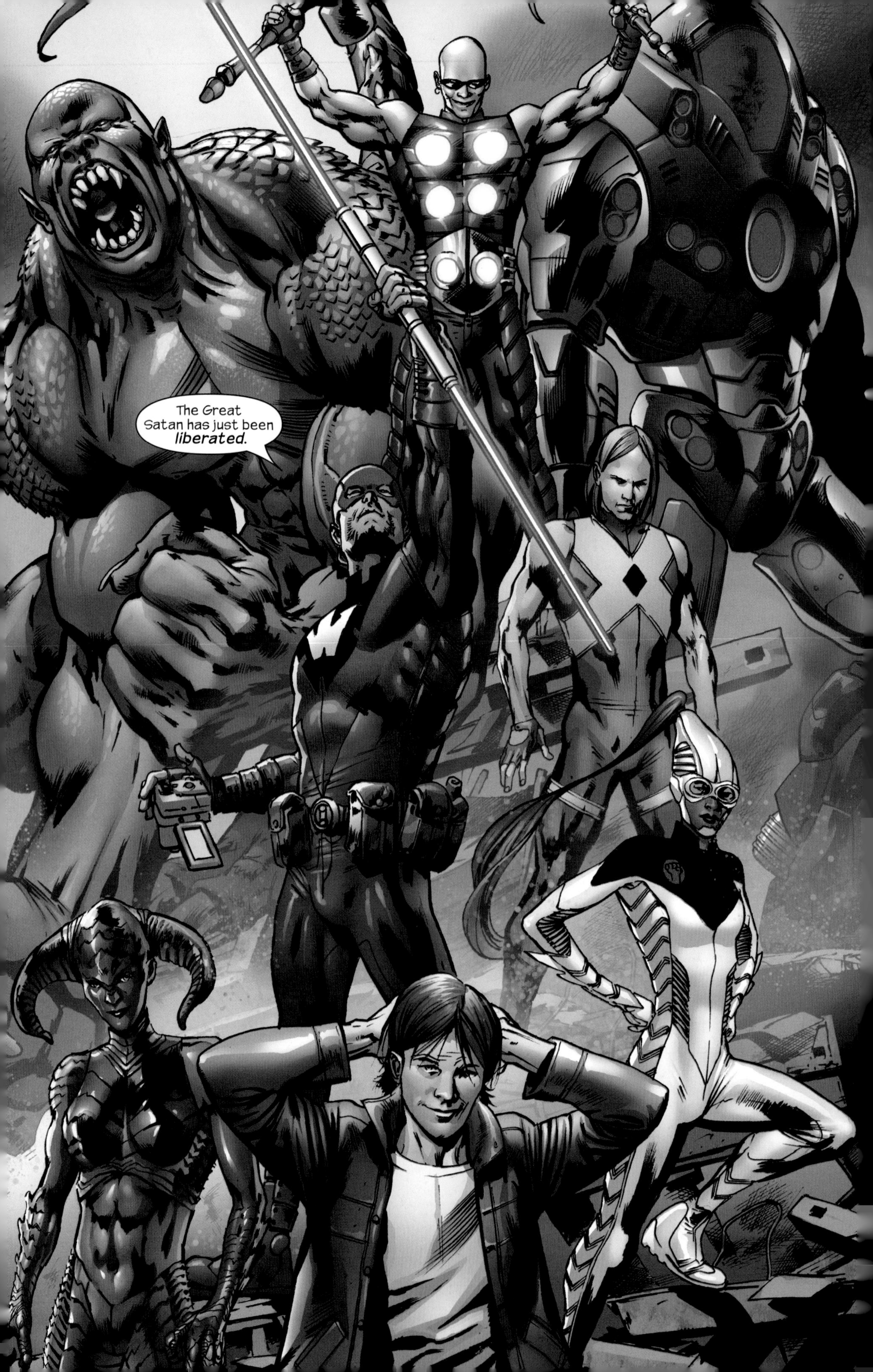
The Great Satan has just been *liberated*.

THE AXIS OF EVIL

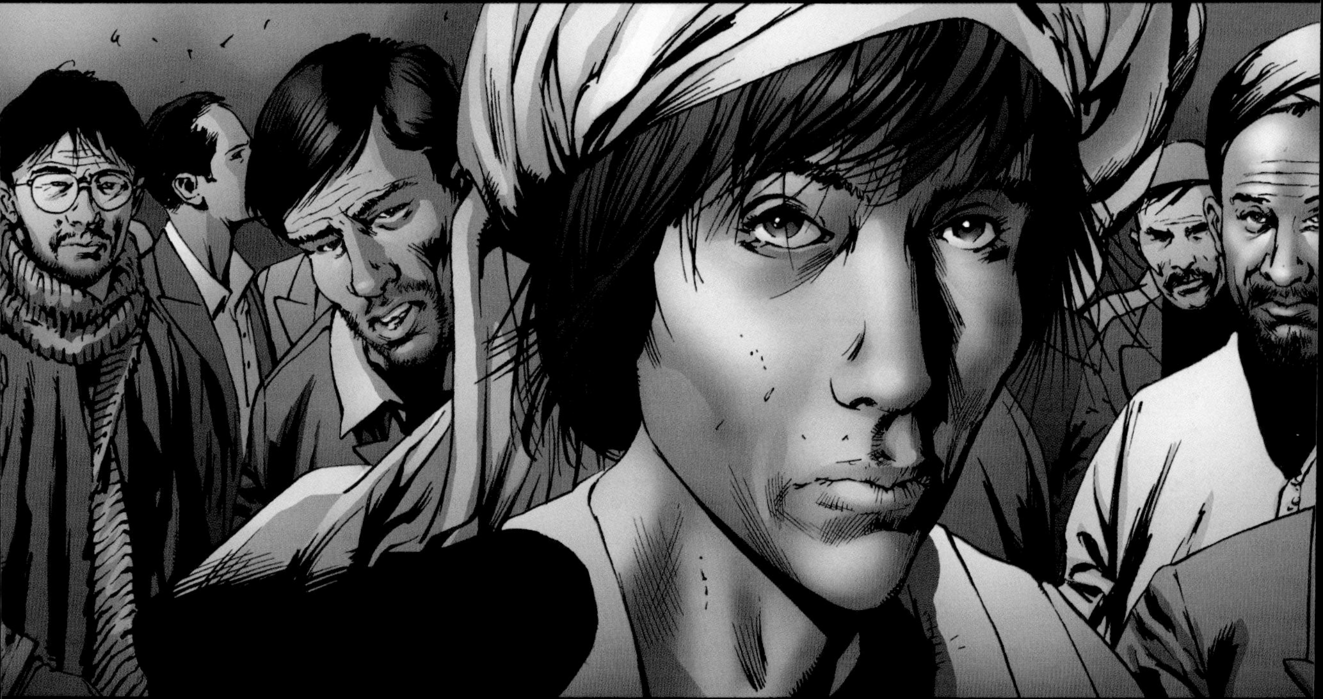

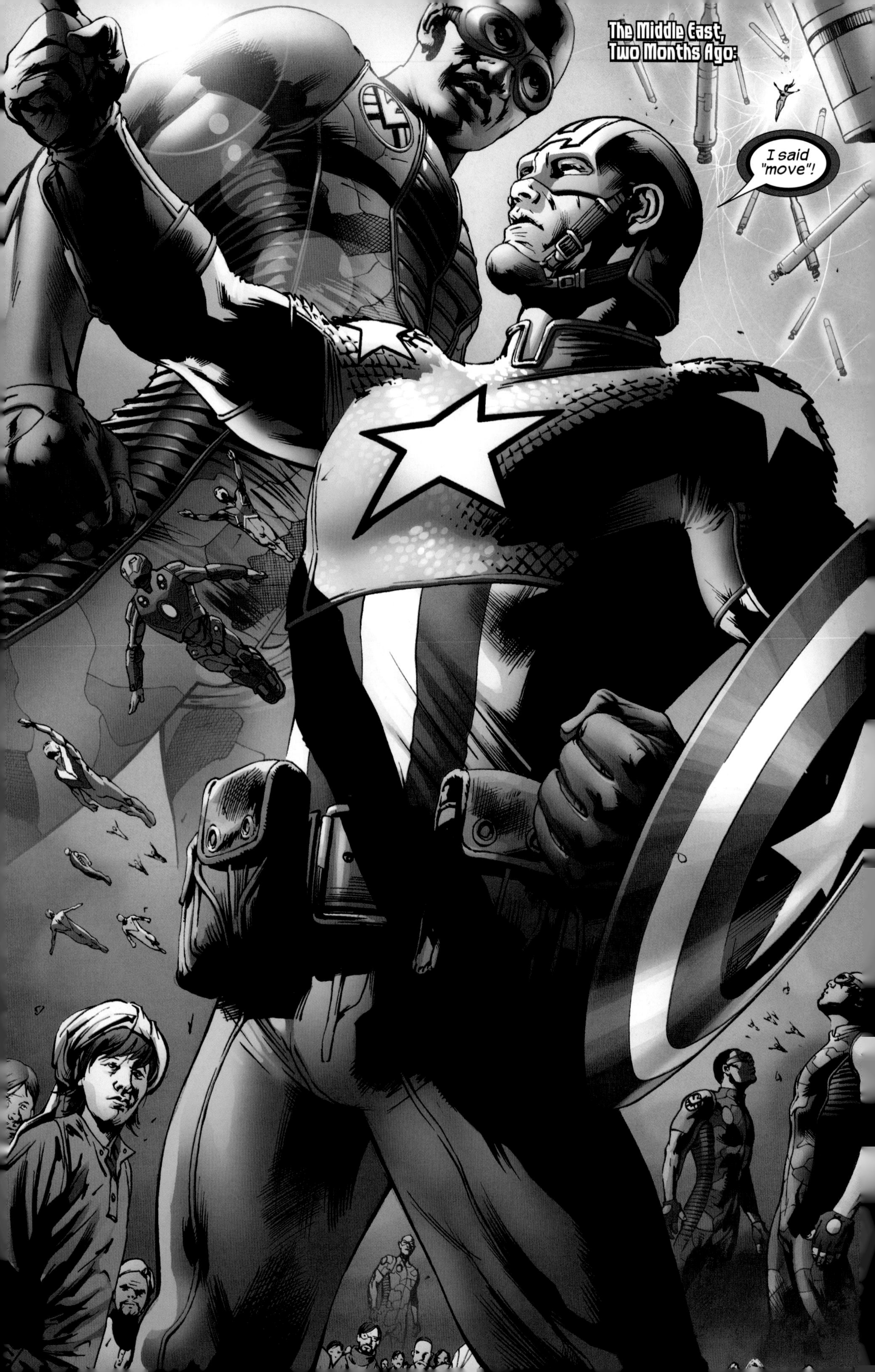
The Middle East, Two Months Ago:
I said "move"!

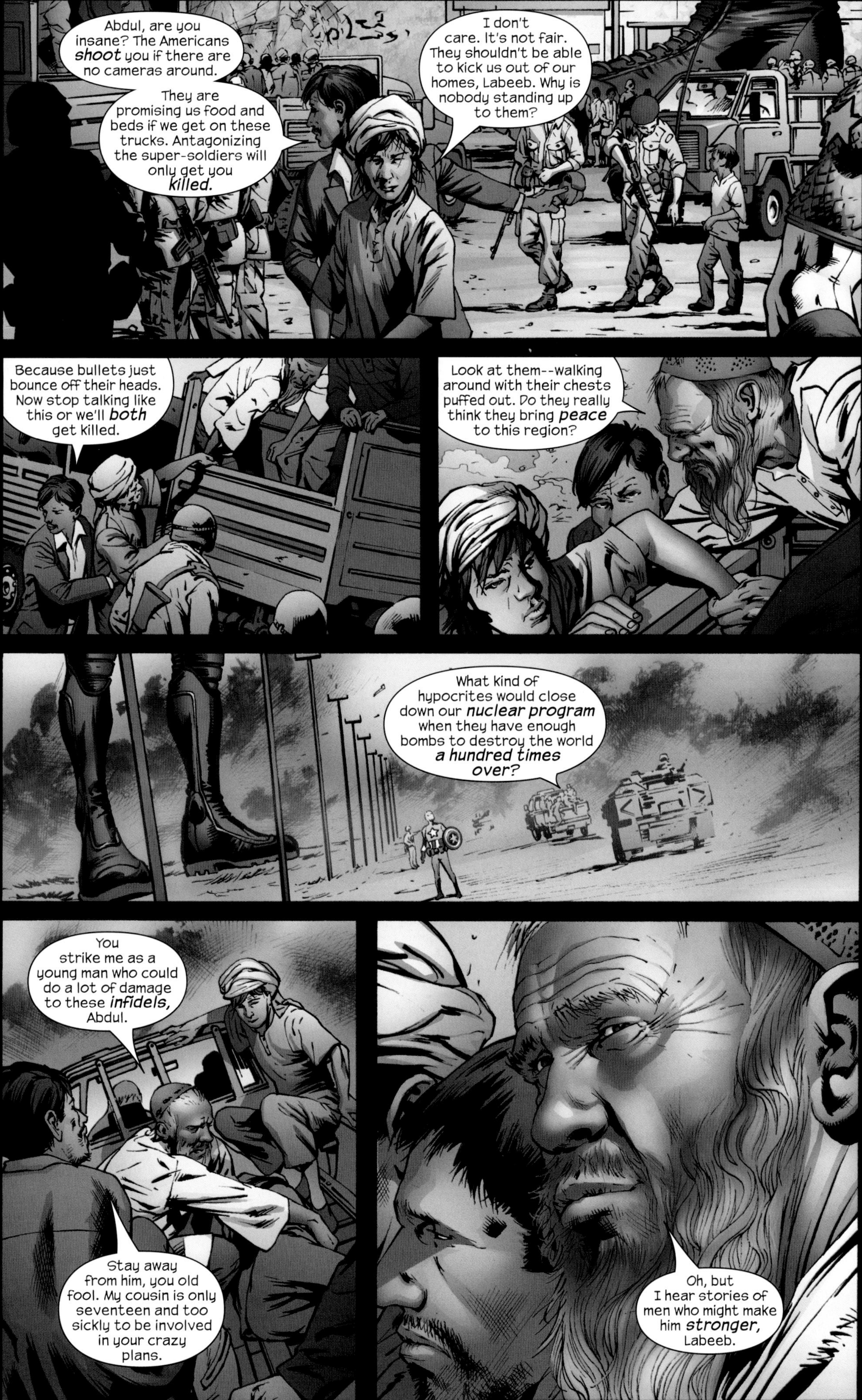
Abdul, are you insane? The Americans *shoot* you if there are no cameras around.
They are promising us food and beds if we get on these trucks. Antagonizing the super-soldiers will only get you *killed.*
I don't care. It's not fair. They shouldn't be able to kick us out of our homes, Labeeb. Why is nobody standing up to them?
Because bullets just bounce off their heads. Now stop talking like this or we'll *both* get killed.
Look at them--walking around with their chests puffed out. Do they really think they bring *peace* to this region?
What kind of hypocrites would close down our *nuclear program* when they have enough bombs to destroy the world *a hundred times over?*
You strike me as a young man who could do a lot of damage to these *infidels,* Abdul.
Stay away from him, you old fool. My cousin is only seventeen and too sickly to be involved in your crazy plans.
Oh, but I hear stories of men who might make him *stronger,* Labeeb.

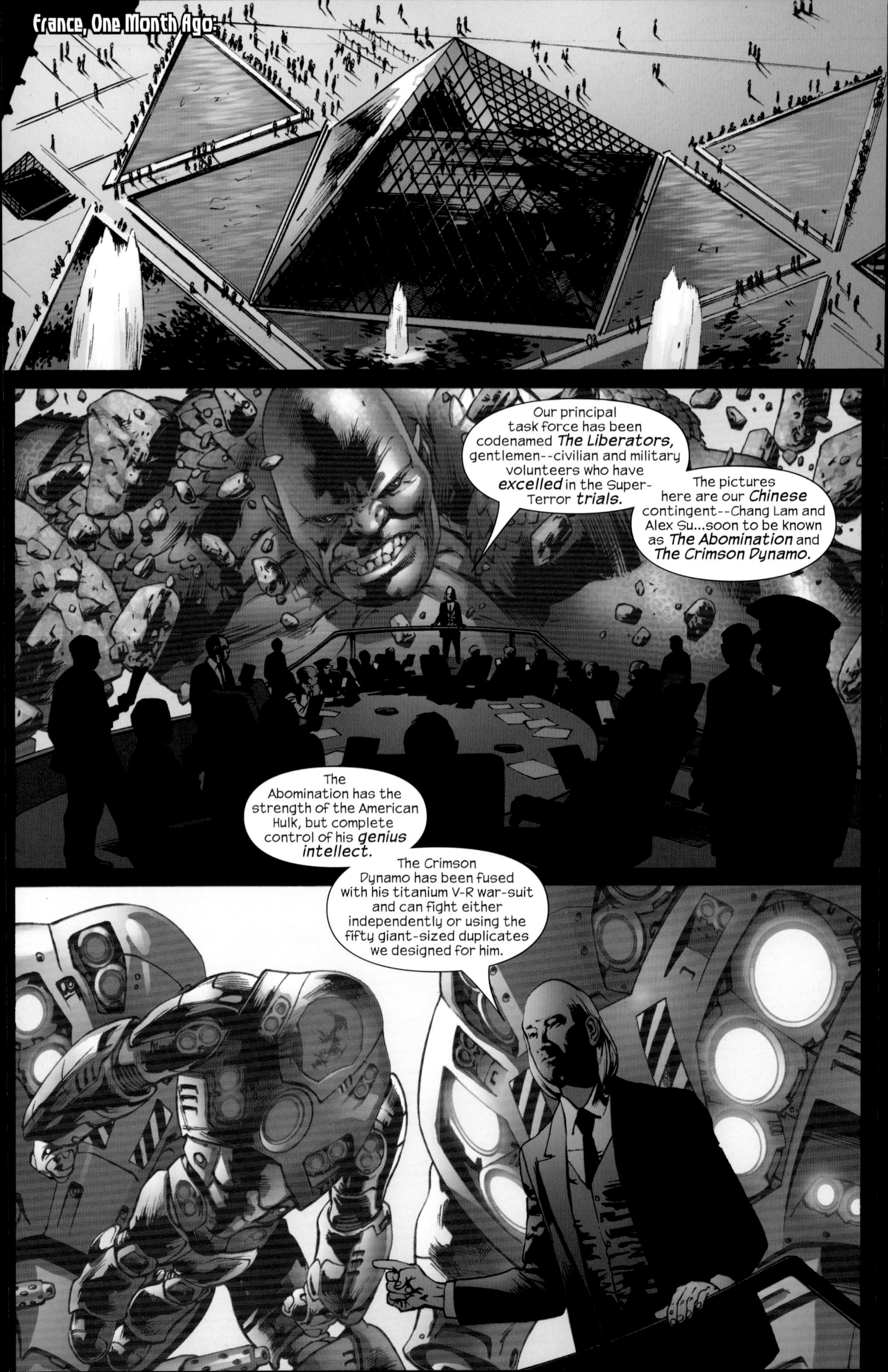
France, One Month Ago:
Our principal task force has been codenamed The Liberators, gentlemen--civilian and military volunteers who have excelled in the Super-Terror trials.
The pictures here are our Chinese contingent--Chang Lam and Alex Su...soon to be known as The Abomination and The Crimson Dynamo.
The Abomination has the strength of the American Hulk, but complete control of his genius intellect.
The Crimson Dynamo has been fused with his titanium V-R war-suit and can fight either independently or using the fifty giant-sized duplicates we designed for him.

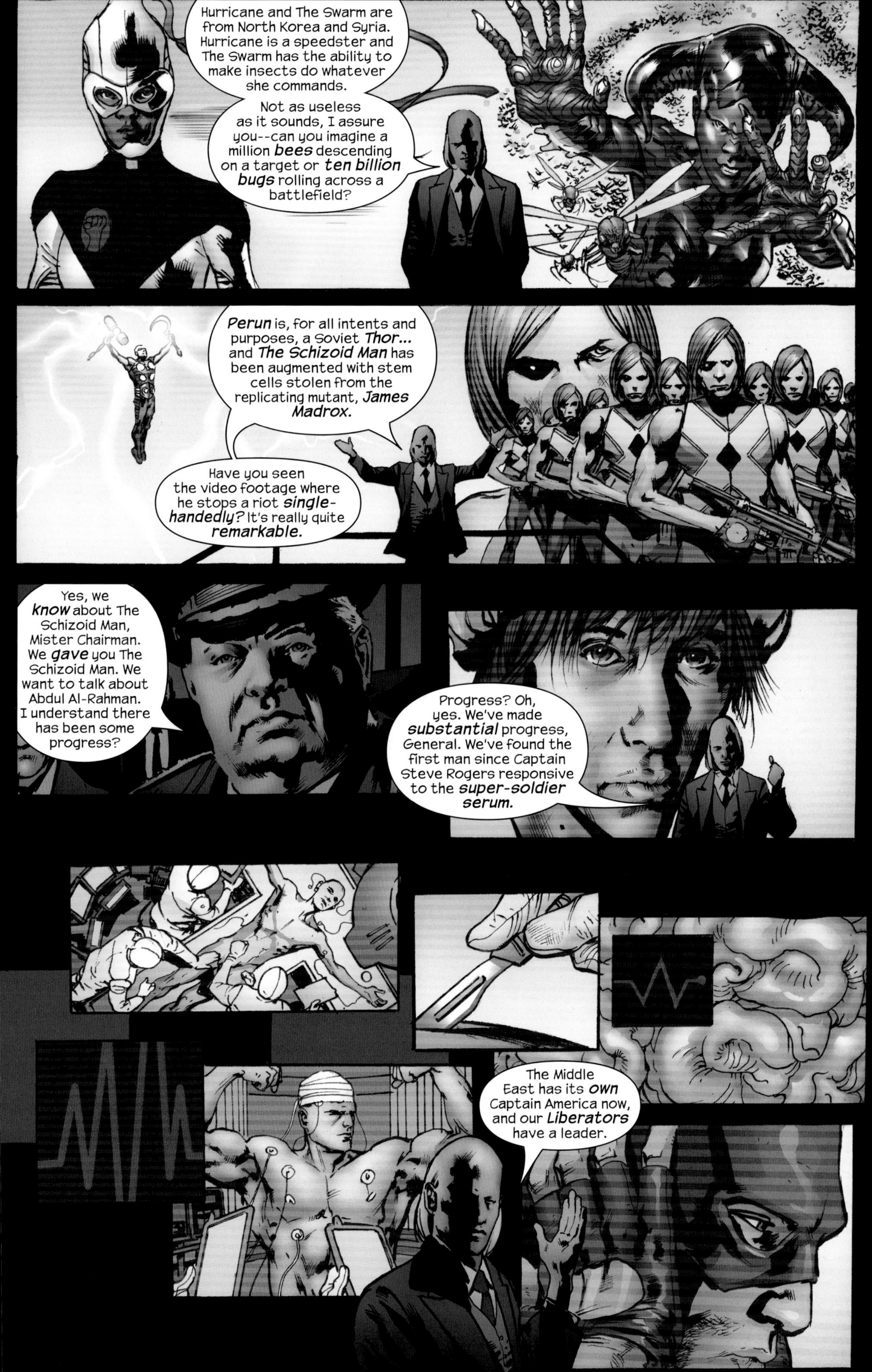
Hurricane and The Swarm are from North Korea and Syria. Hurricane is a speedster and The Swarm has the ability to make insects do whatever she commands.
Not as useless as it sounds, I assure you--can you imagine a million bees descending on a target or ten billion bugs rolling across a battlefield?
Perun is, for all intents and purposes, a Soviet Thor... and The Schizoid Man has been augmented with stem cells stolen from the replicating mutant, James Madrox.
Have you seen the video footage where he stops a riot single-handedly? It's really quite remarkable.
Yes, we know about The Schizoid Man, Mister Chairman. We gave you The Schizoid Man. We want to talk about Abdul Al-Rahman. I understand there has been some progress?
Progress? Oh, yes. We've made substantial progress, General. We've found the first man since Captain Steve Rogers responsive to the super-soldier serum.
The Middle East has its own Captain America now, and our Liberators have a leader.

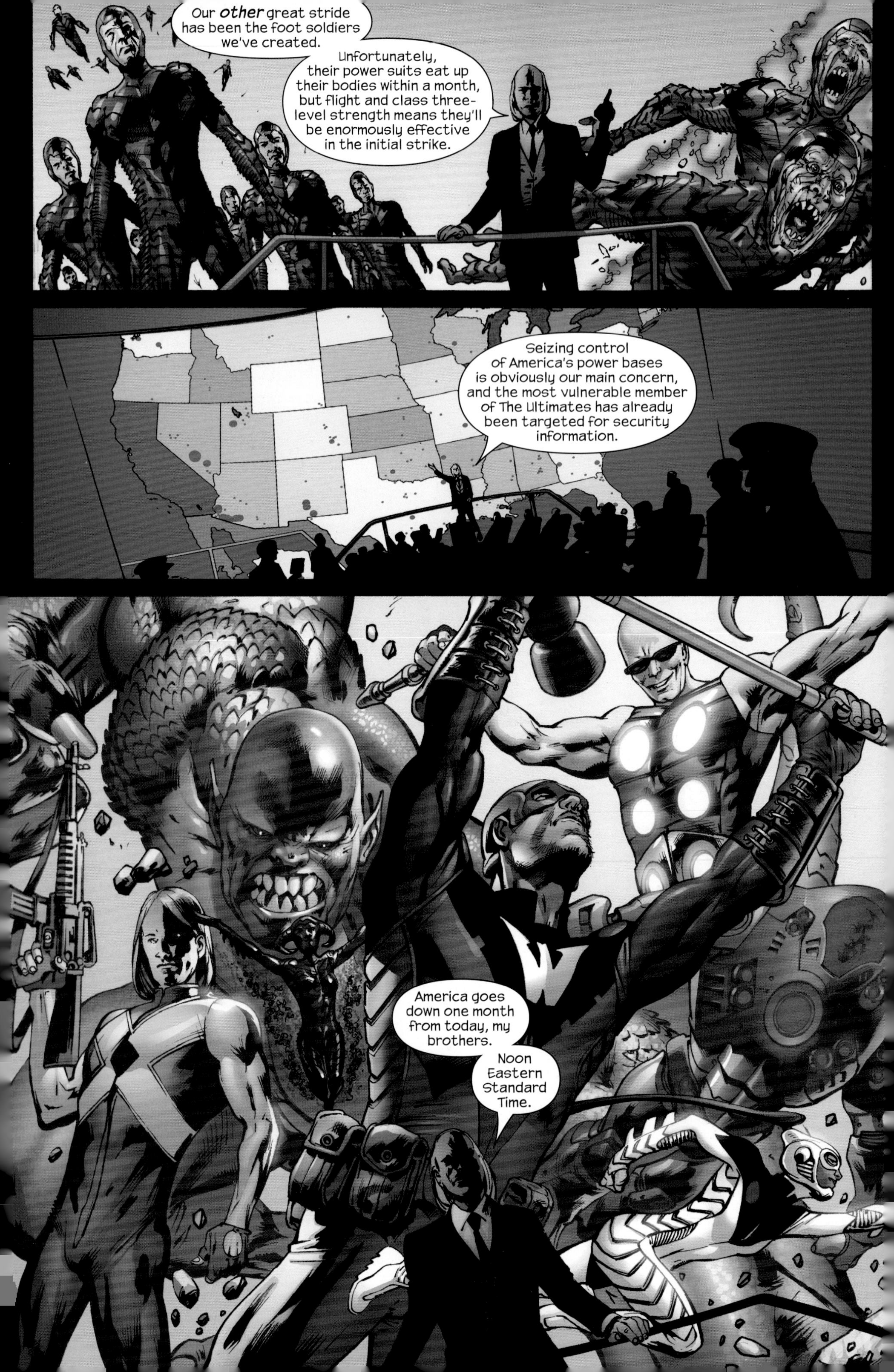
Our *other* great stride has been the foot soldiers we've created.
Unfortunately, their power suits eat up their bodies within a month, but flight and class three-level strength means they'll be enormously effective in the initial strike.
Seizing control of America's power bases is obviously our main concern, and the most vulnerable member of The Ultimates has already been targeted for security information.
America goes down one month from today, my brothers.
Noon Eastern Standard Time.

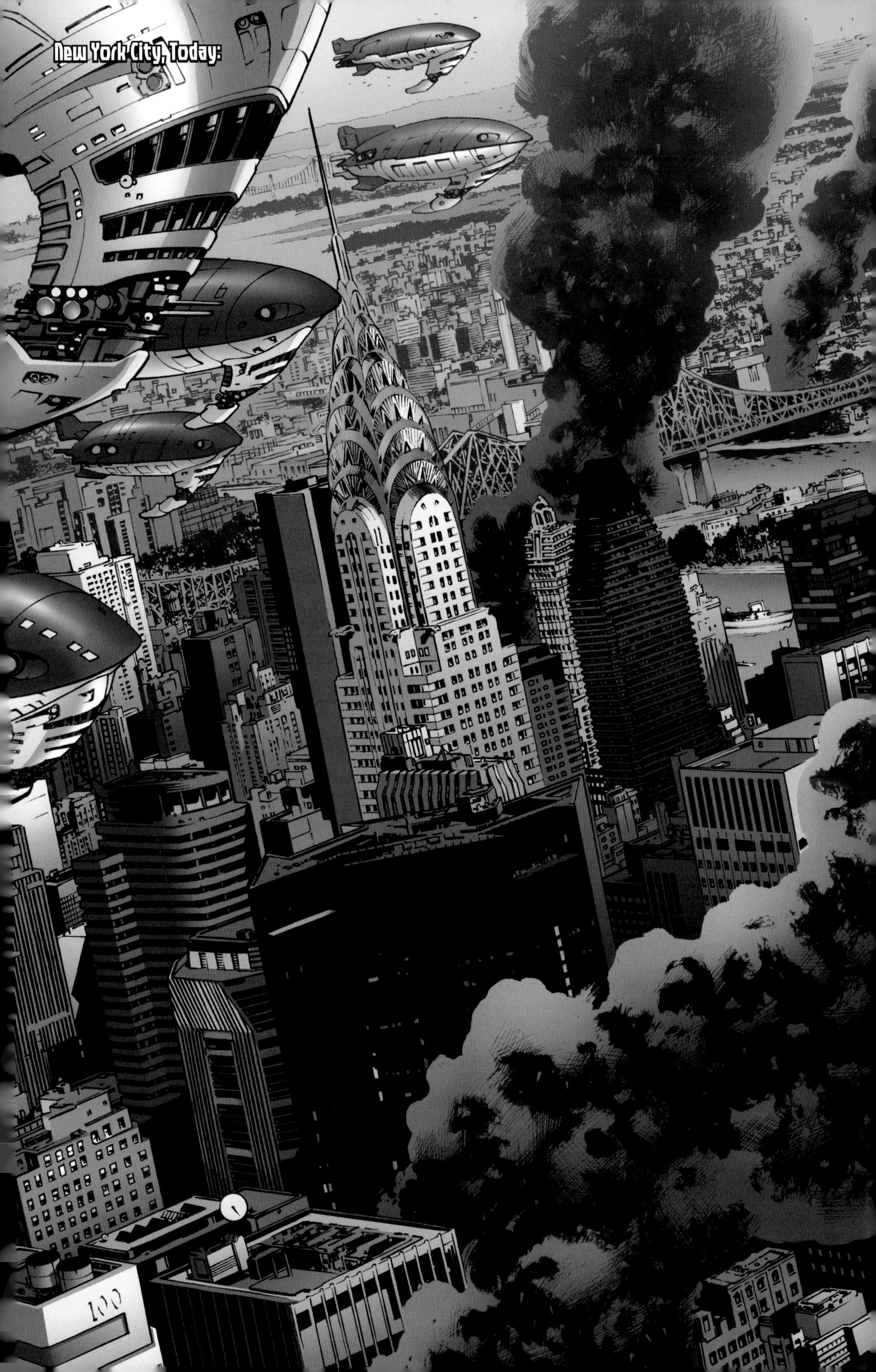
New York City, Today:
100

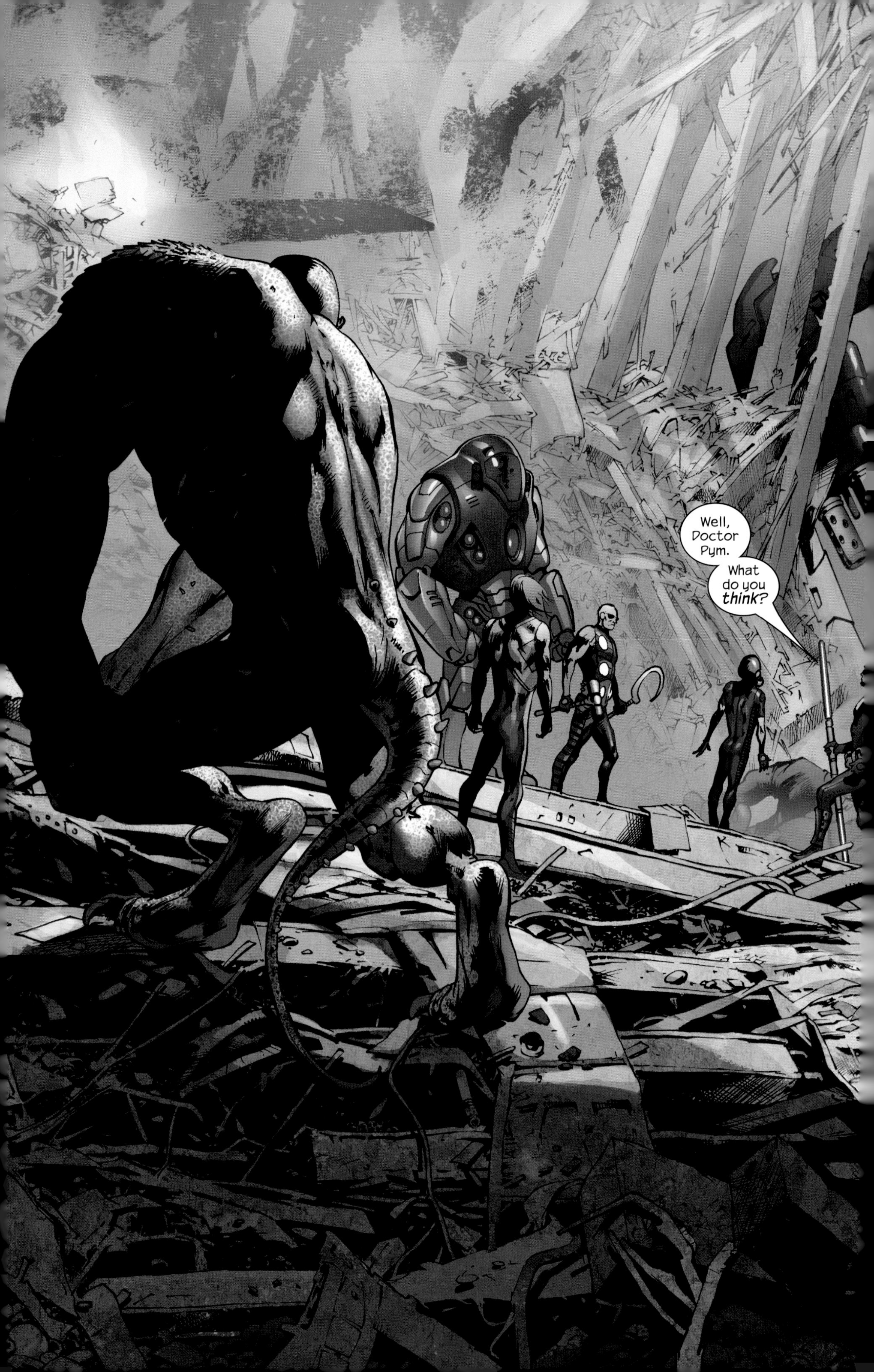
Well, Doctor Pym.
What do you *think*?

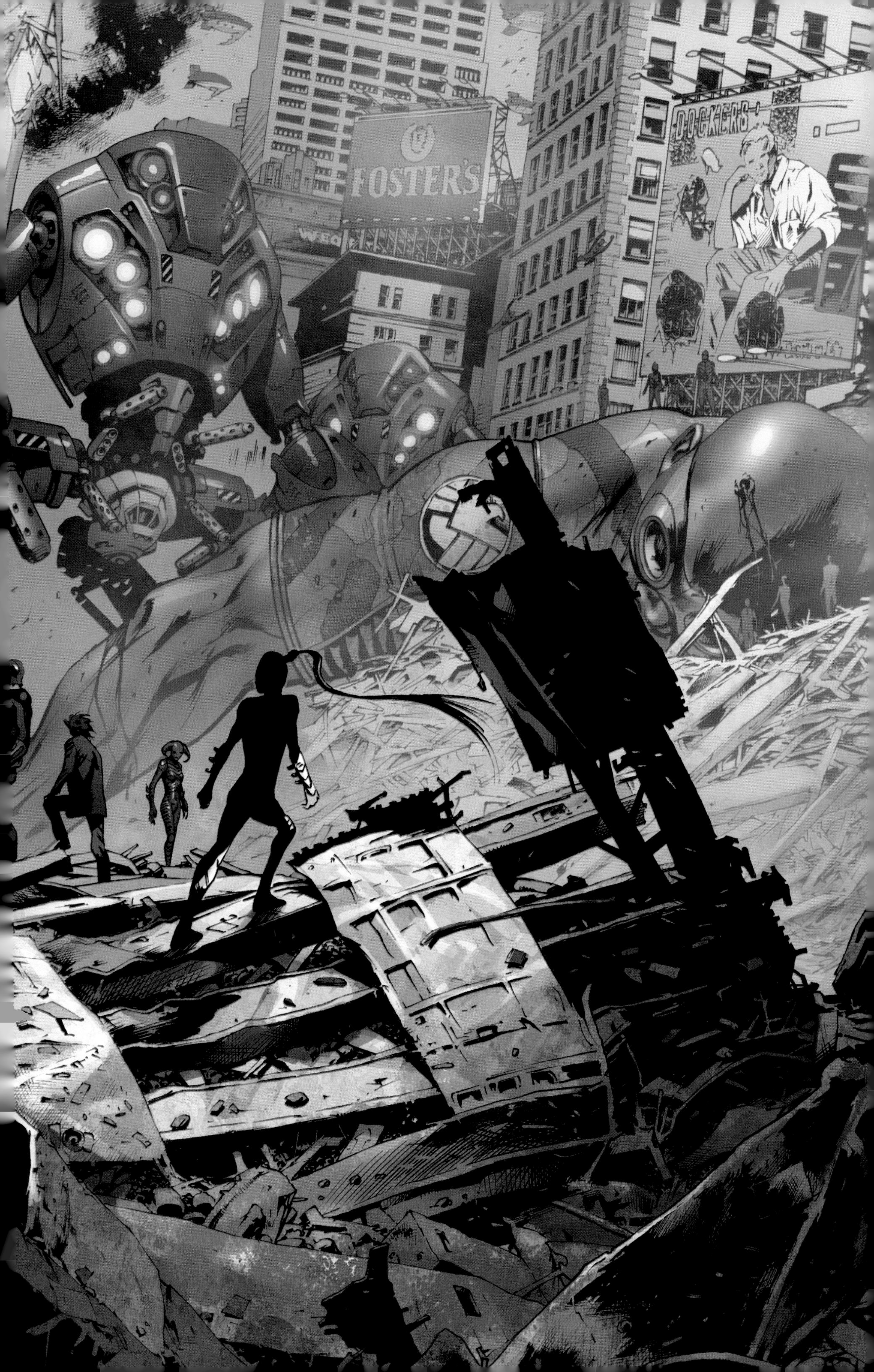
FOSTER'S
DOCKERS

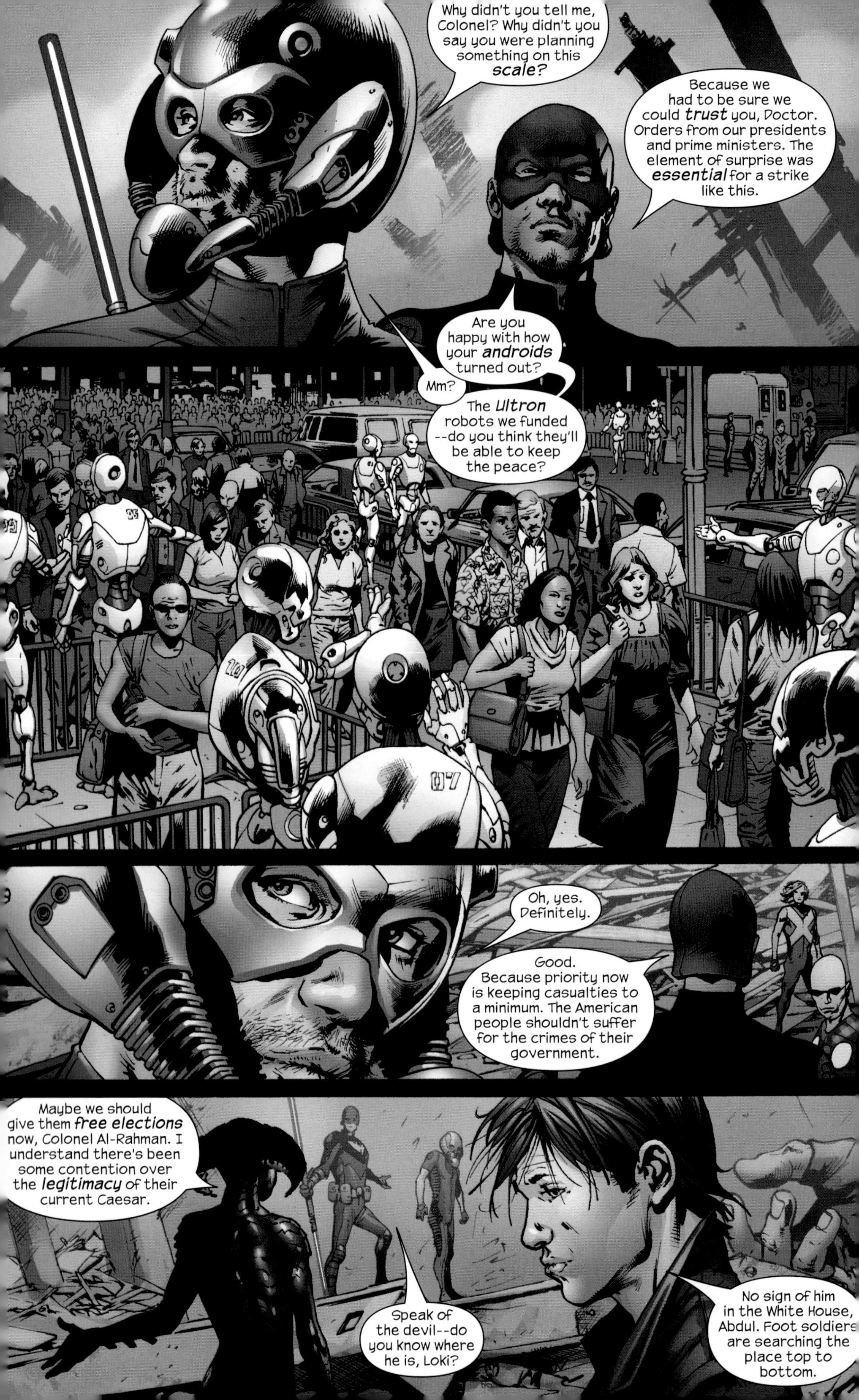

Why didn't you tell me, Colonel? Why didn't you say you were planning something on this *scale*?
Because we had to be sure we could *trust* you, Doctor. Orders from our presidents and prime ministers. The element of surprise was *essential* for a strike like this.
Are you happy with how your *androids* turned out?
Mm?
The *Ultron* robots we funded --do you think they'll be able to keep the peace?
Oh, yes. Definitely.
Good. Because priority now is keeping casualties to a minimum. The American people shouldn't suffer for the crimes of their government.
Maybe we should give them *free elections* now, Colonel Al-Rahman. I understand there's been some contention over the *legitimacy* of their current Caesar.
Speak of the devil--do you know where he is, Loki?
No sign of him in the White House, Abdul. Foot soldiers are searching the place top to bottom.

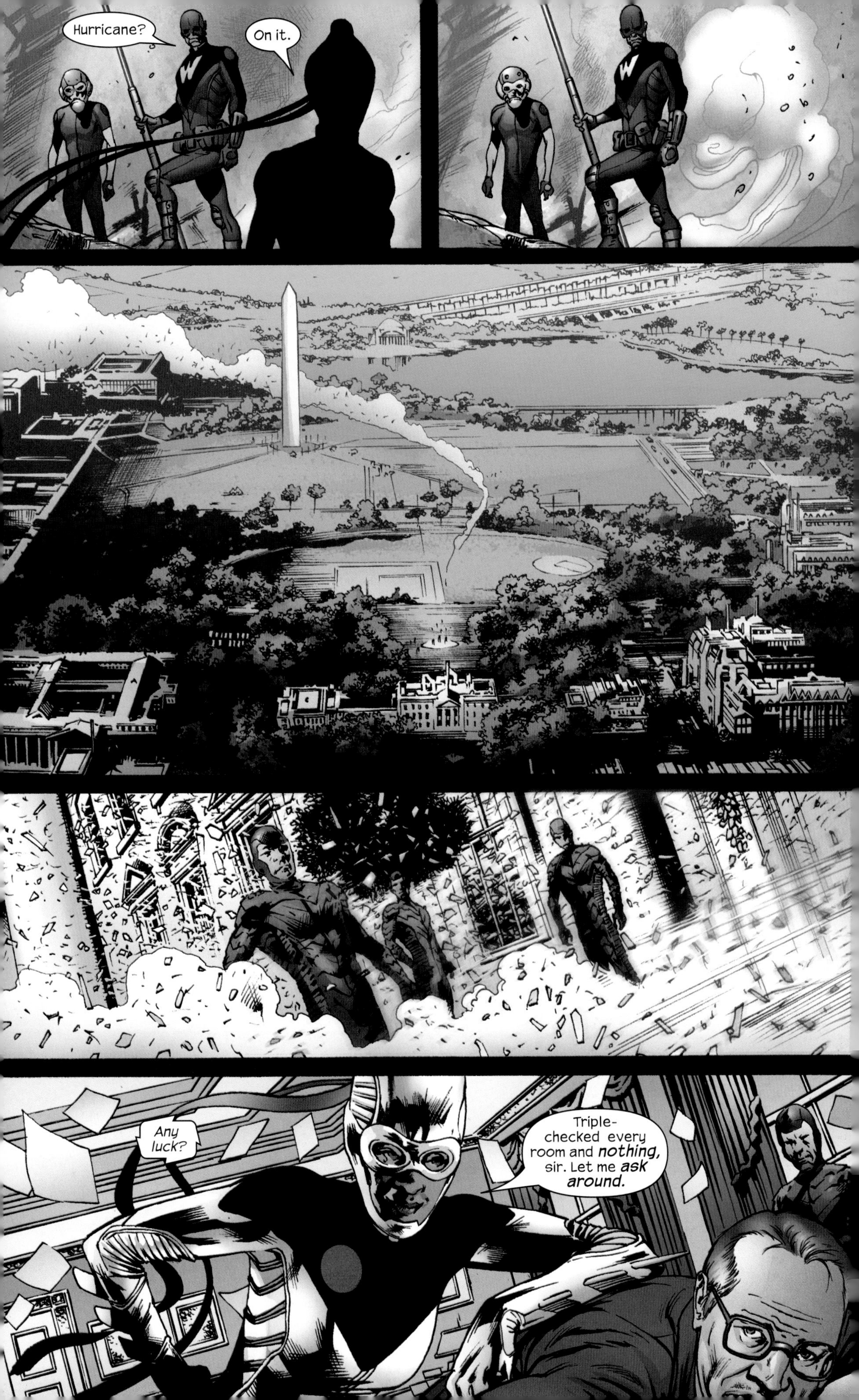
Hurricane?
On it.
Any luck?
Triple-checked every room and *nothing,* sir. Let me *ask around.*

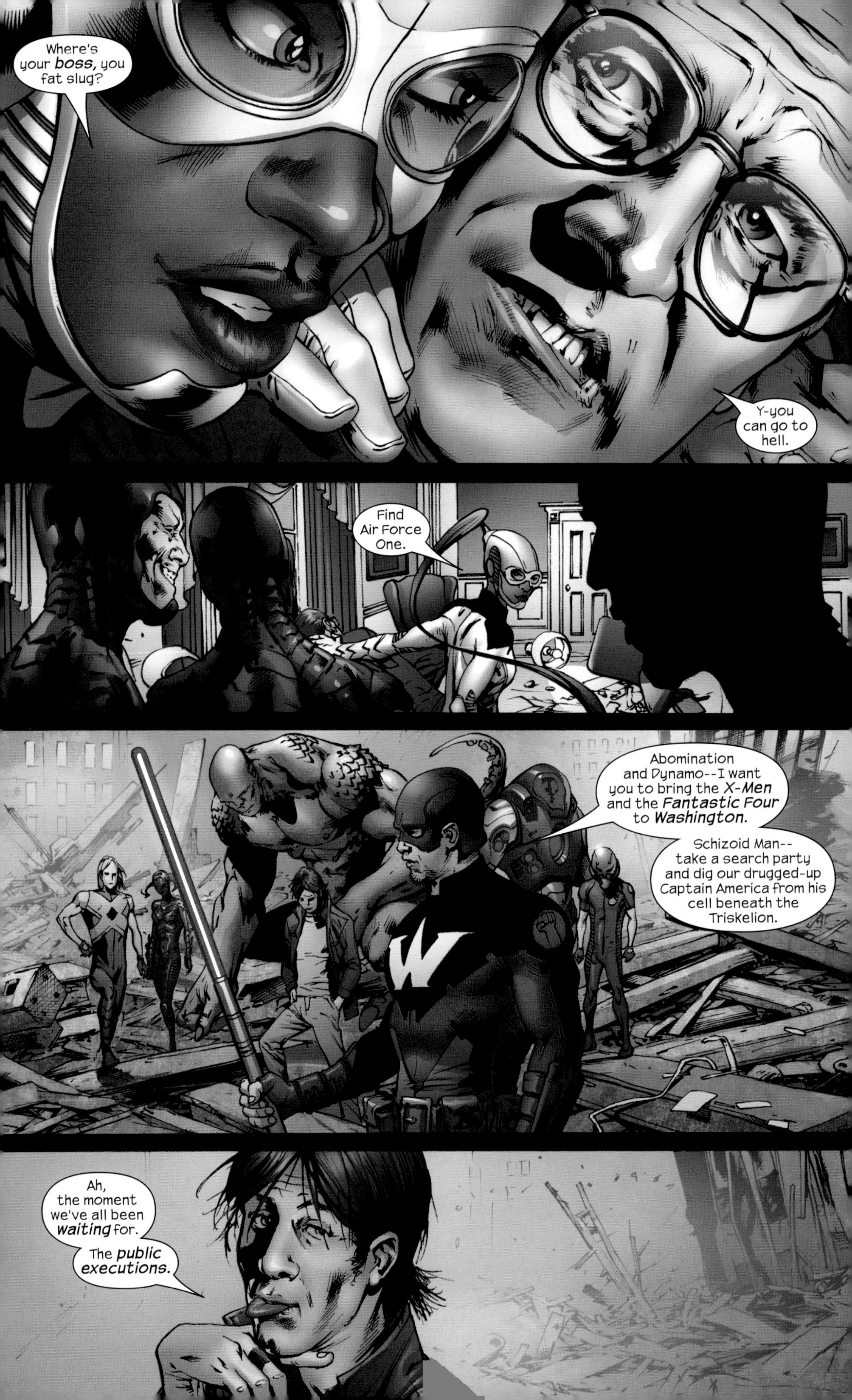
Where's your *boss,* you fat slug?
Y-you can go to hell.
Find Air Force One.
Abomination and Dynamo--I want you to bring the *X-Men* and the *Fantastic Four* to *Washington.*
Schizoid Man--take a search party and dig our drugged-up Captain America from his cell beneath the Triskelion.
Ah, the moment we've all been *waiting* for.
The *public executions.*

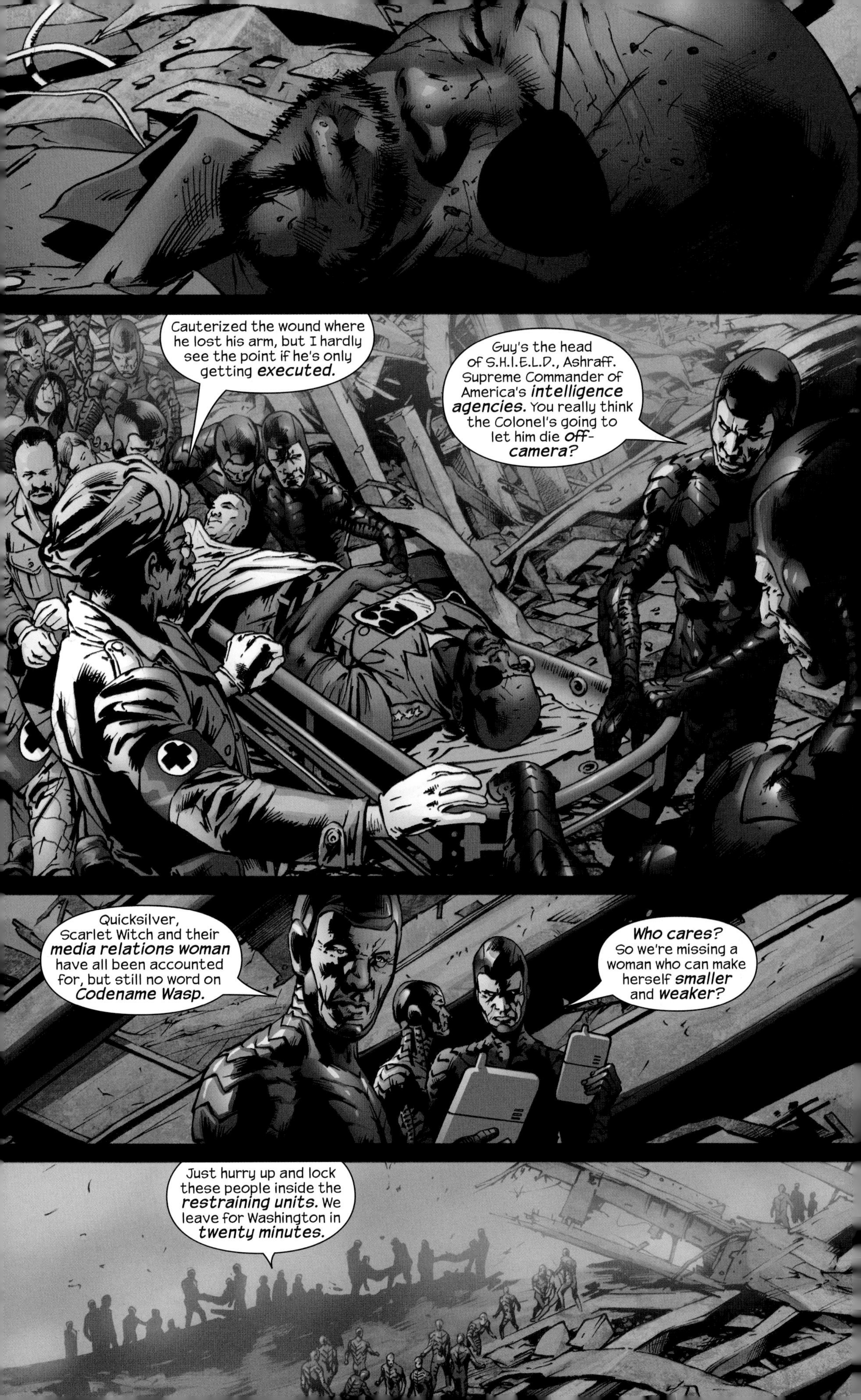
Cauterized the wound where he lost his arm, but I hardly see the point if he's only getting executed.
Guy's the head of S.H.I.E.L.D., Ashraff. Supreme Commander of America's intelligence agencies. You really think the Colonel's going to let him die off-camera?
Quicksilver, Scarlet Witch and their media relations woman have all been accounted for, but still no word on Codename Wasp.
Who cares? So we're missing a woman who can make herself smaller and weaker?
Just hurry up and lock these people inside the restraining units. We leave for Washington in twenty minutes.

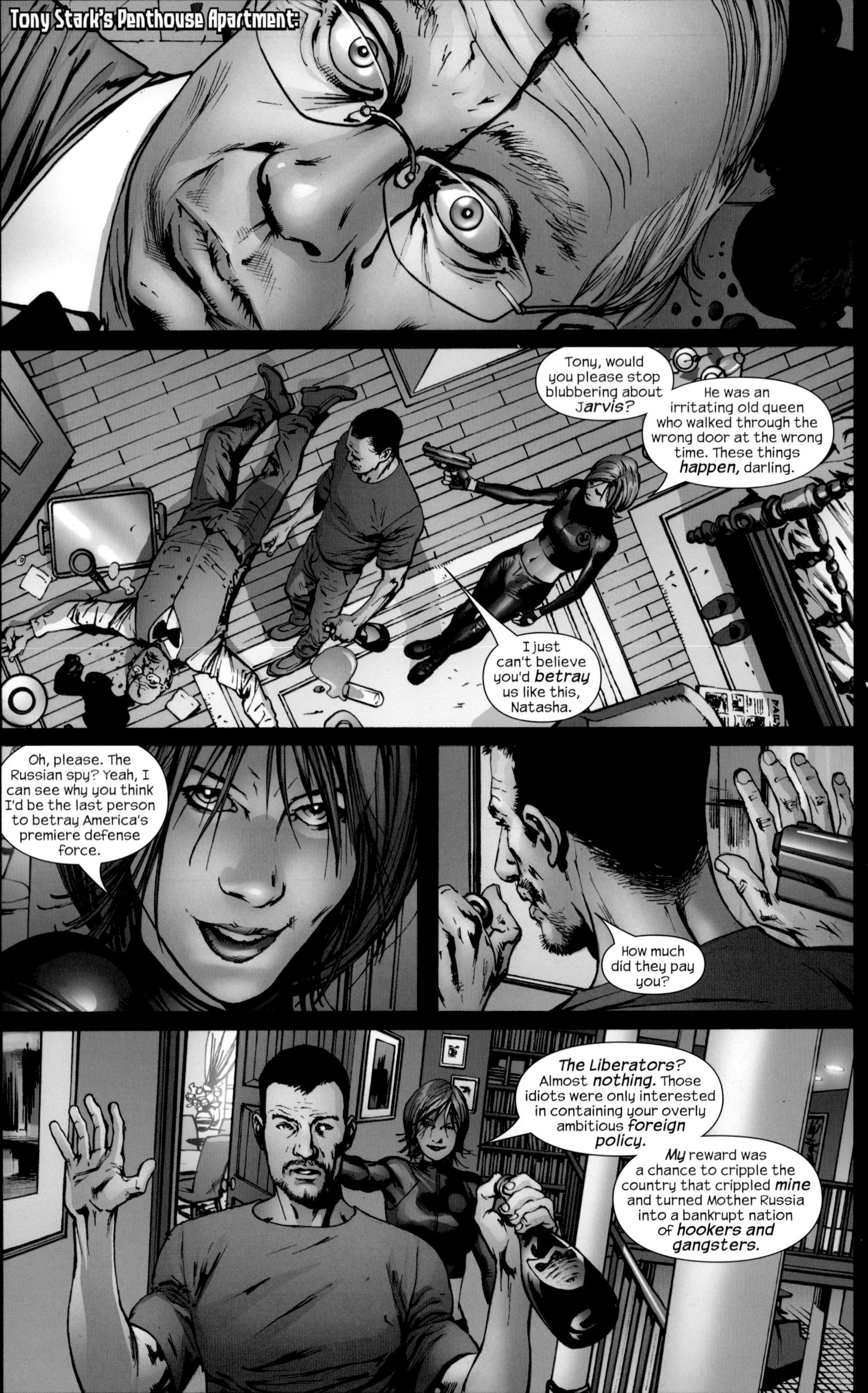

Tony Stark's Penthouse Apartment:
Tony, would you please stop blubbering about Jarvis?
He was an irritating old queen who walked through the wrong door at the wrong time. These things happen, darling.
I just can't believe you'd betray us like this, Natasha.
Oh, please. The Russian spy? Yeah, I can see why you think I'd be the last person to betray America's premiere defense force.
How much did they pay you?
The Liberators? Almost nothing. Those idiots were only interested in containing your overly ambitious foreign policy.
My reward was a chance to cripple the country that crippled mine and turned Mother Russia into a bankrupt nation of hookers and gangsters.

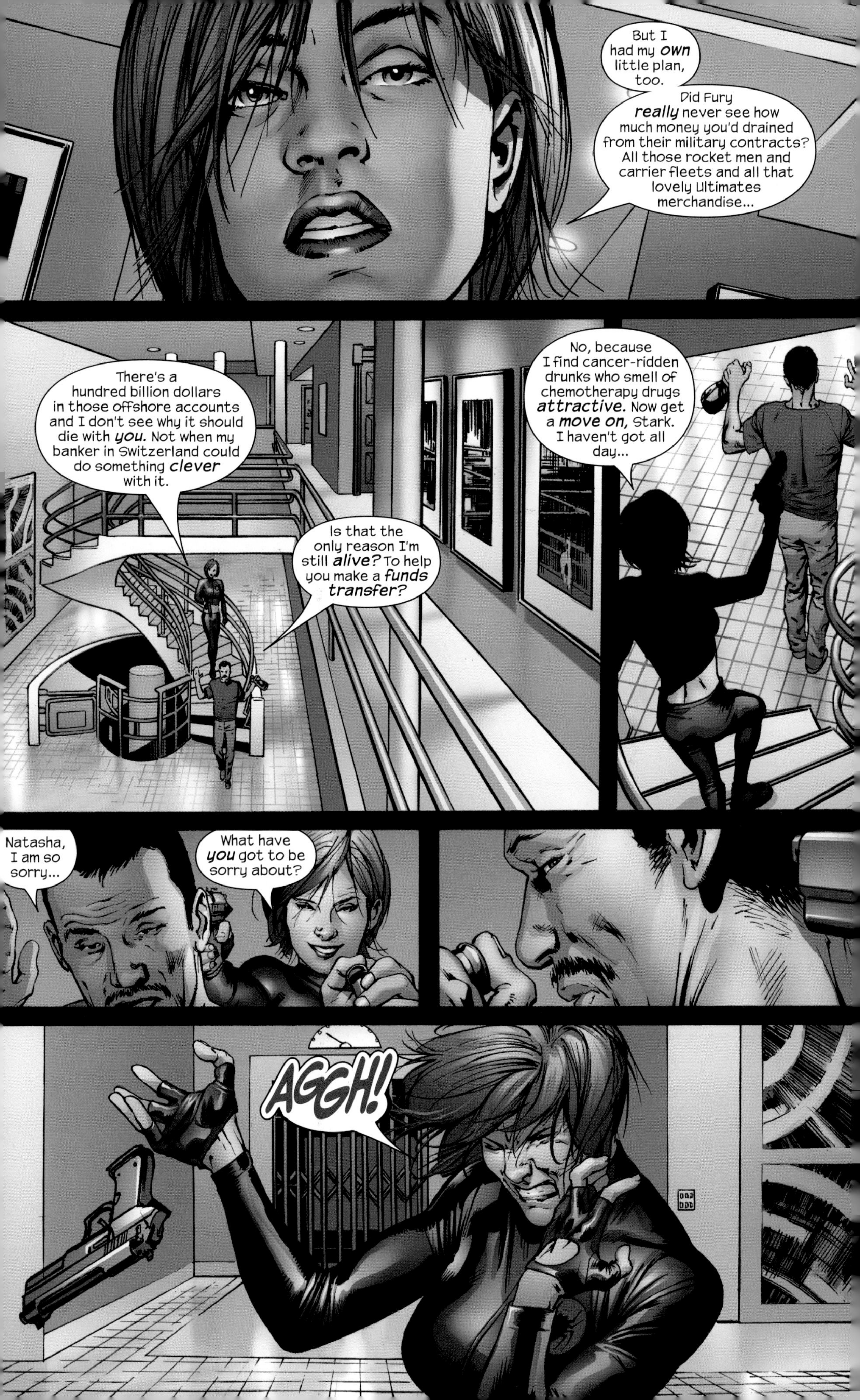

But I had my own little plan, too.
Did Fury really never see how much money you'd drained from their military contracts? All those rocket men and carrier fleets and all that lovely Ultimates merchandise...
There's a hundred billion dollars in those offshore accounts and I don't see why it should die with you. Not when my banker in Switzerland could do something clever with it.
Is that the only reason I'm still alive? To help you make a funds transfer?
No, because I find cancer-ridden drunks who smell of chemotherapy drugs attractive. Now get a move on, Stark. I haven't got all day...
Natasha, I am so sorry...
What have you got to be sorry about?
AGGH!

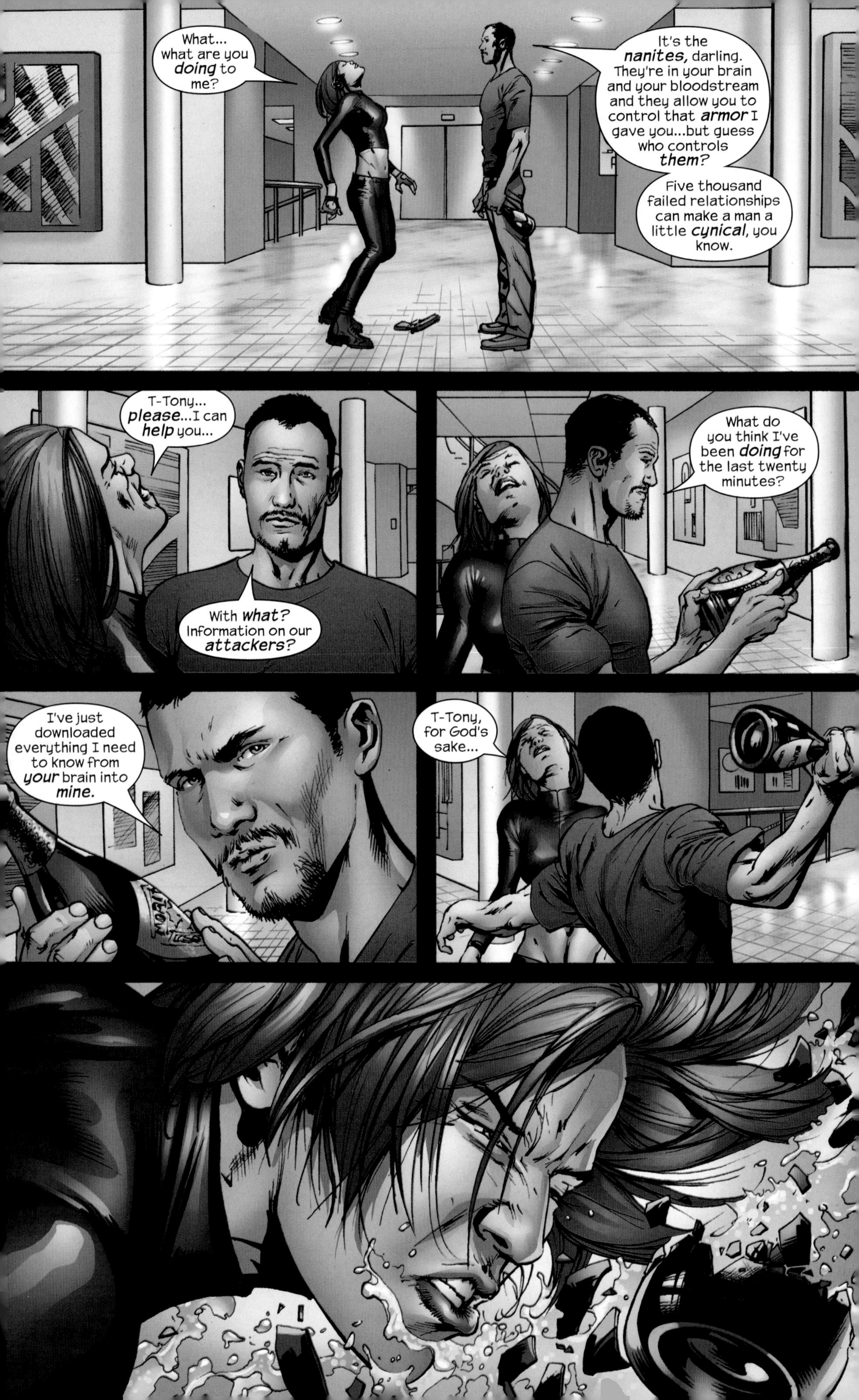

What... what are you doing to me?
It's the nanites, darling. They're in your brain and your bloodstream and they allow you to control that armor I gave you...but guess who controls them?
Five thousand failed relationships can make a man a little cynical, you know.
T-Tony... please...I can help you...
With what? Information on our attackers?
What do you think I've been doing for the last twenty minutes?
I've just downloaded everything I need to know from your brain into mine.
T-Tony, for God's sake...

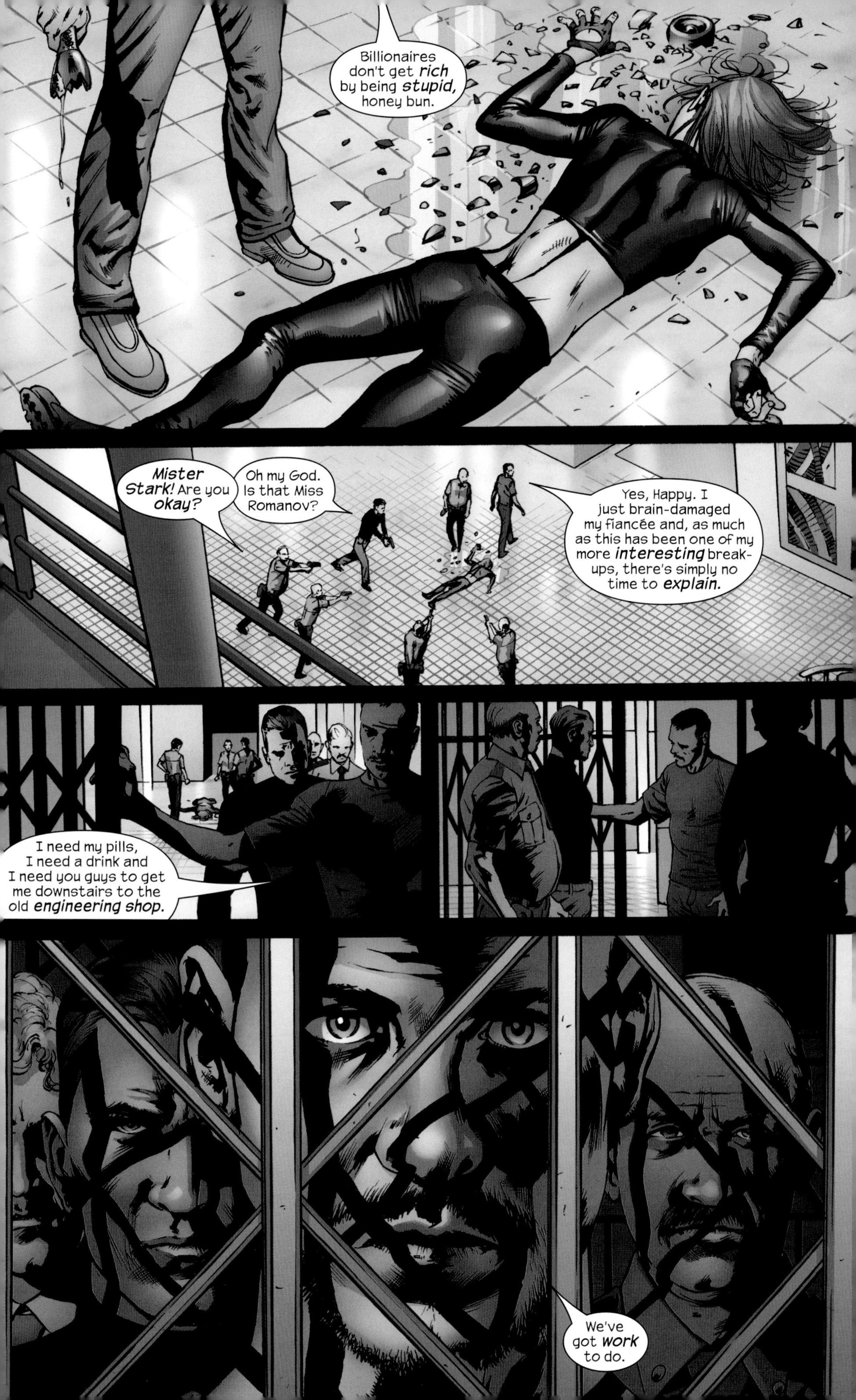
Billionaires don't get rich by being stupid, honey bun.
Mister Stark! Are you okay?
Oh my God. Is that Miss Romanov?
Yes, Happy. I just brain-damaged my fiancée and, as much as this has been one of my more interesting break-ups, there's simply no time to explain.
I need my pills, I need a drink and I need you guys to get me downstairs to the old engineering shop.
We've got work to do.

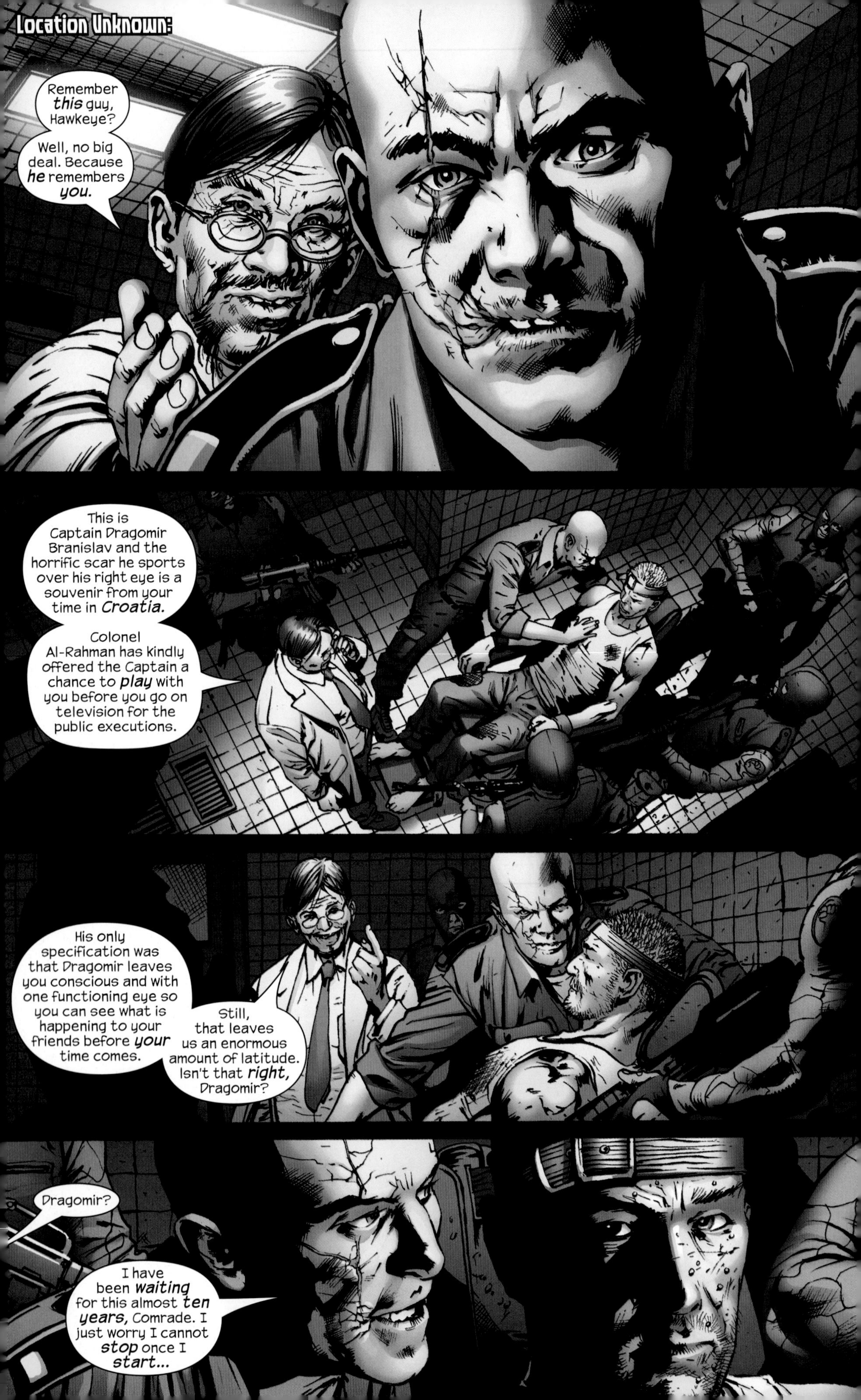
Location Unknown:
Remember this guy, Hawkeye?
Well, no big deal. Because he remembers you.
This is Captain Dragomir Branislav and the horrific scar he sports over his right eye is a souvenir from your time in Croatia.
Colonel Al-Rahman has kindly offered the Captain a chance to play with you before you go on television for the public executions.
His only specification was that Dragomir leaves you conscious and with one functioning eye so you can see what is happening to your friends before your time comes.
Still, that leaves us an enormous amount of latitude. Isn't that right, Dragomir?
Dragomir?
I have been waiting for this almost ten years, Comrade. I just worry I cannot stop once I start...

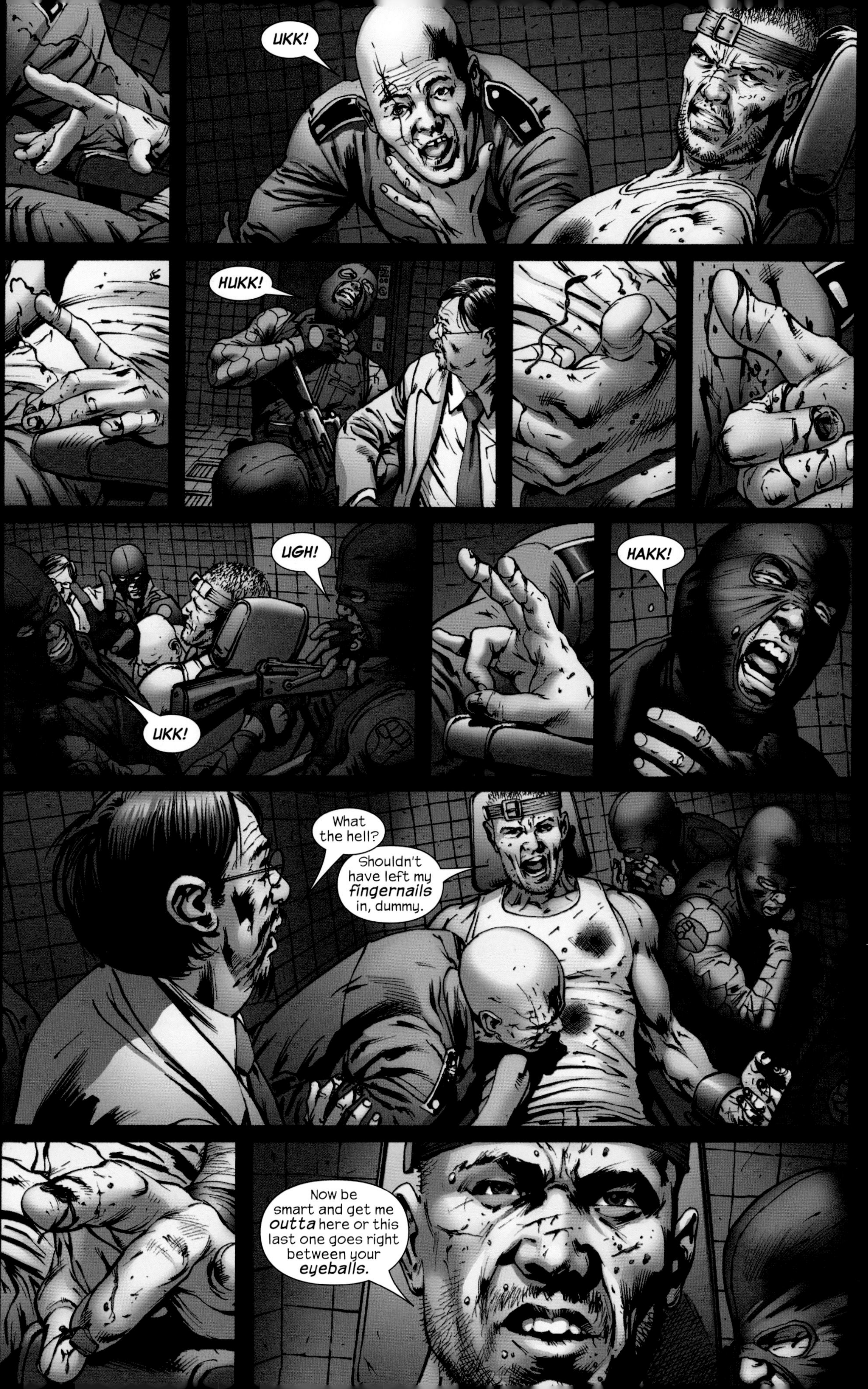
UKK!
HUKK!
UGH!
UKK!
HAKK!
What the hell?
Shouldn't have left my *fingernails* in, dummy.
Now be smart and get me *outta* here or this last one goes right between your *eyeballs.*

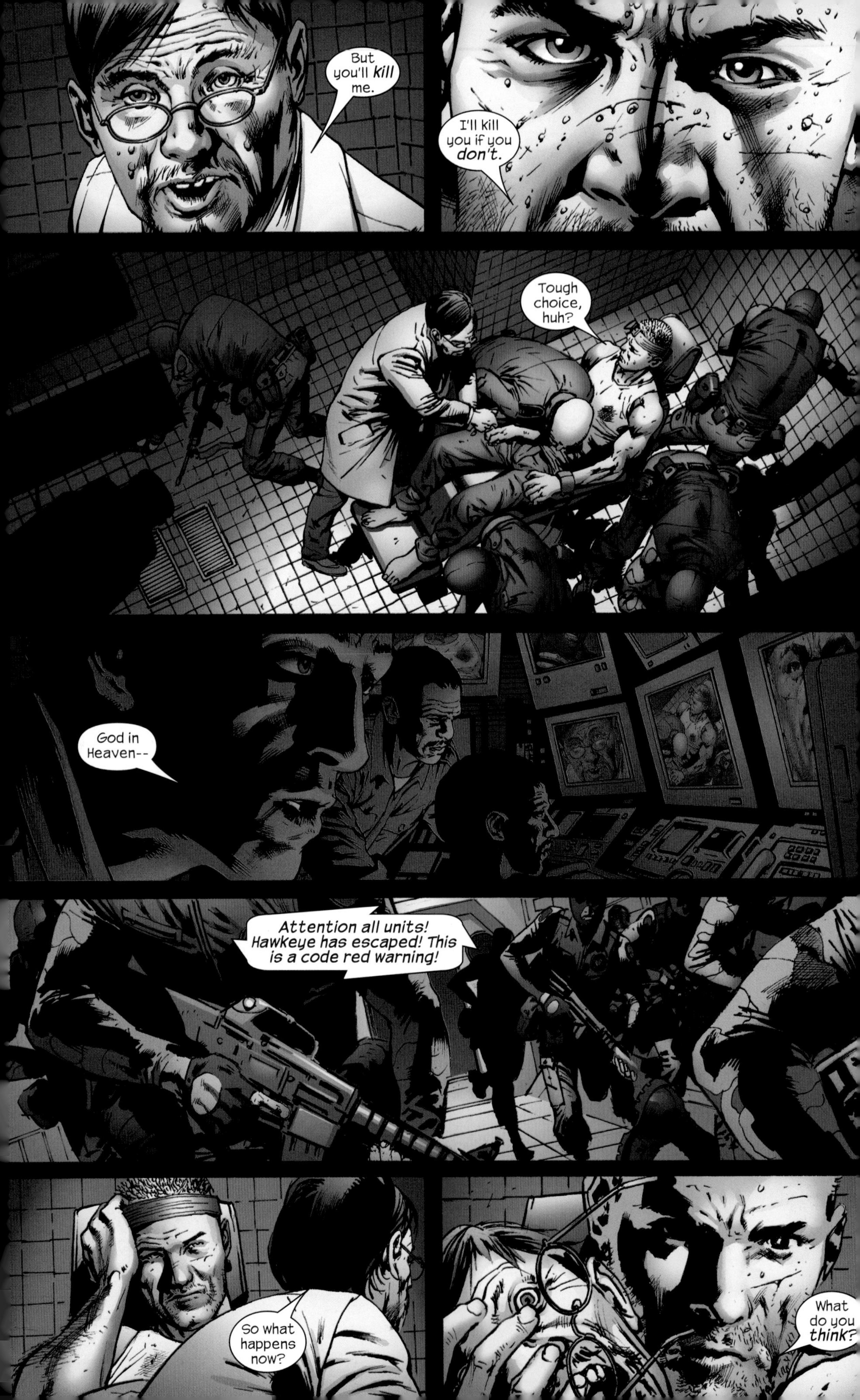
But you'll *kill* me.
I'll kill you if you *don't*.
Tough choice, huh?
God in Heaven--
Attention all units! Hawkeye has escaped! This is a code red warning!
So what happens now?
What do you *think*?

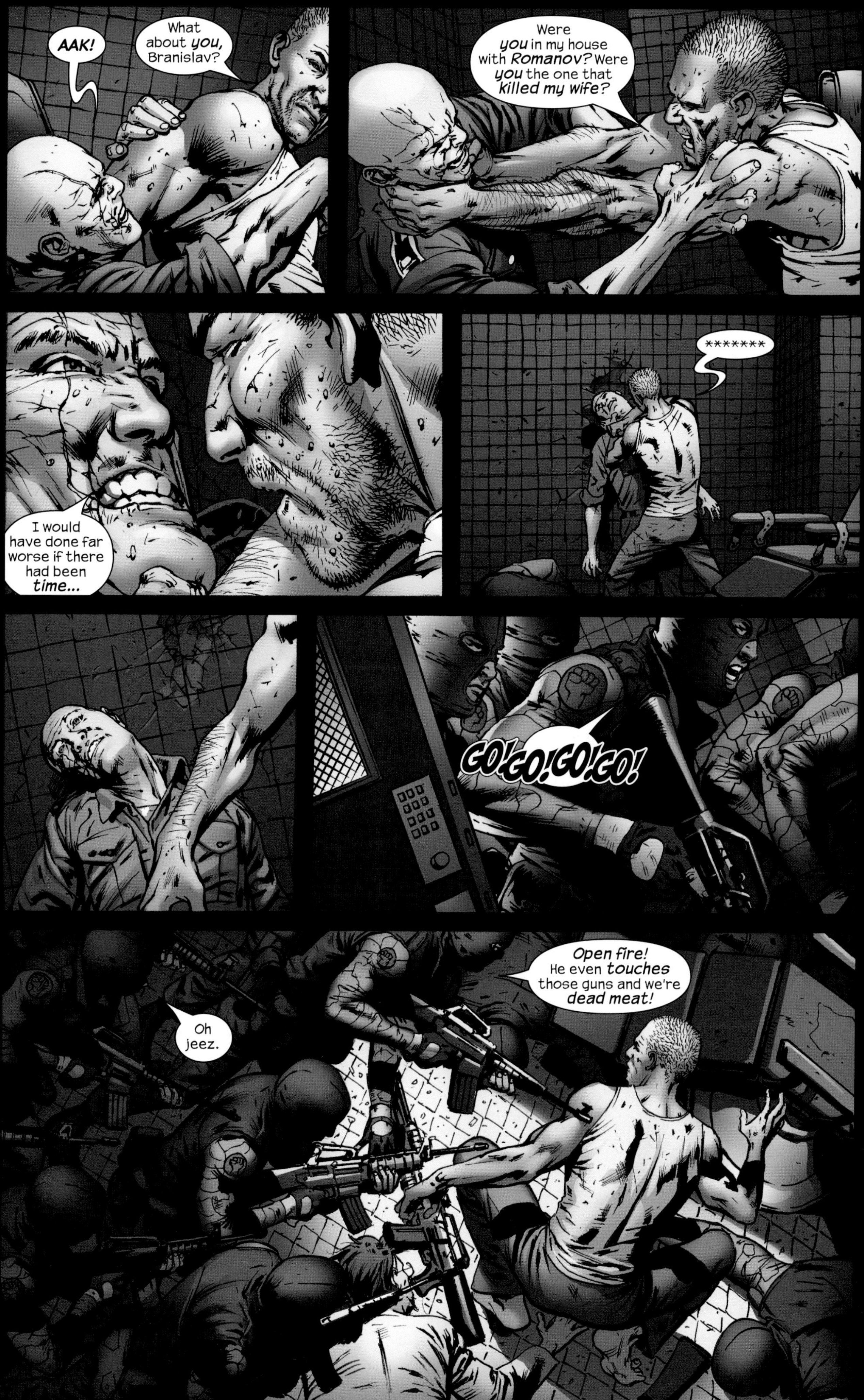
AAK!
What about you, Branislav?
Were you in my house with Romanov? Were you the one that killed my wife?
I would have done far worse if there had been time...
****
GO! GO! GO! GO!
Open fire! He even touches those guns and we're dead meat!
Oh jeez.

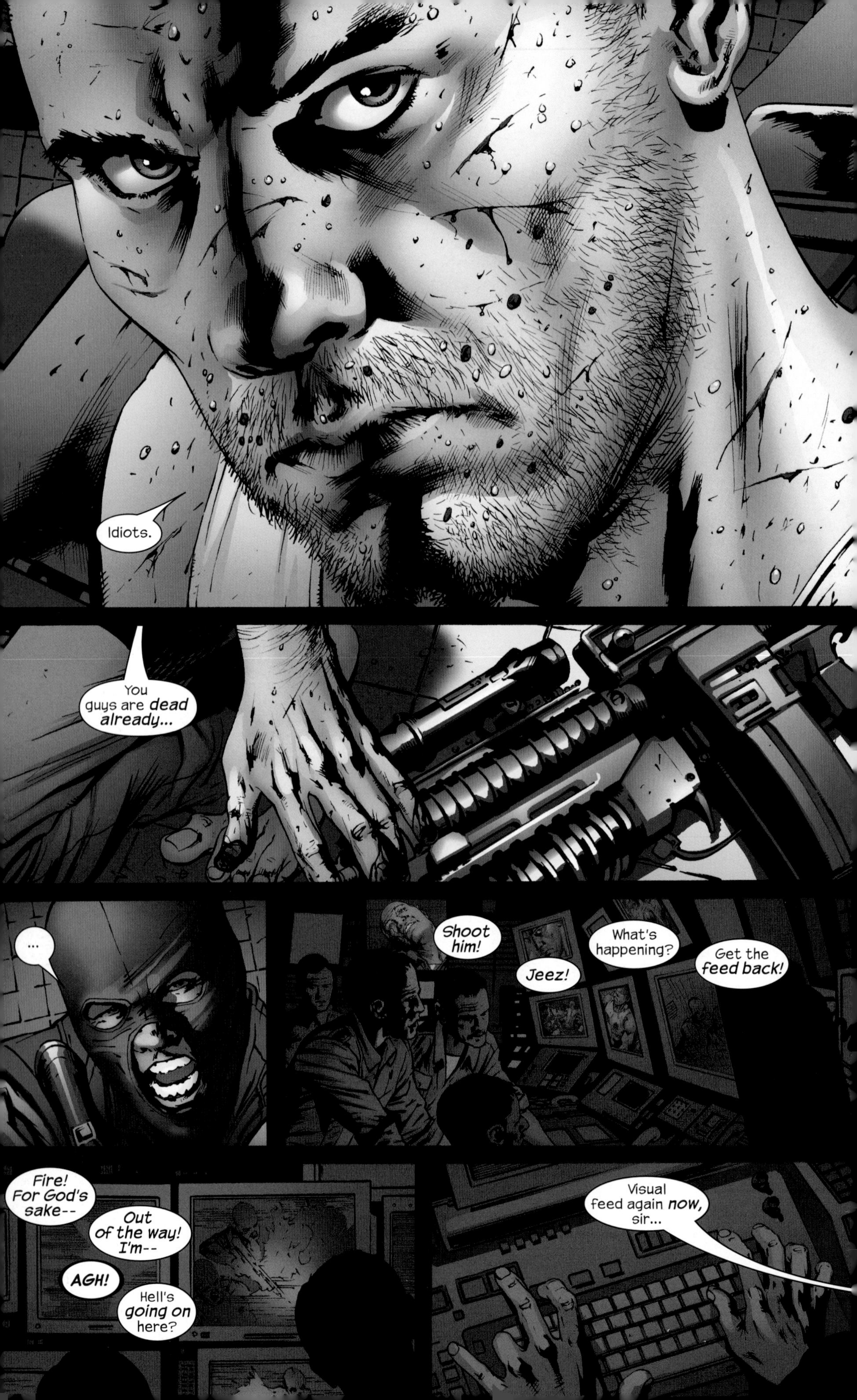
Idiots.
You guys are *dead already...*
...
Shoot him!
Jeez!
What's happening?
Get the *feed back!*
Fire! For God's sake--
Out of the way! I'm--
AGH!
Hell's *going on* here?
Visual feed again *now,* sir...

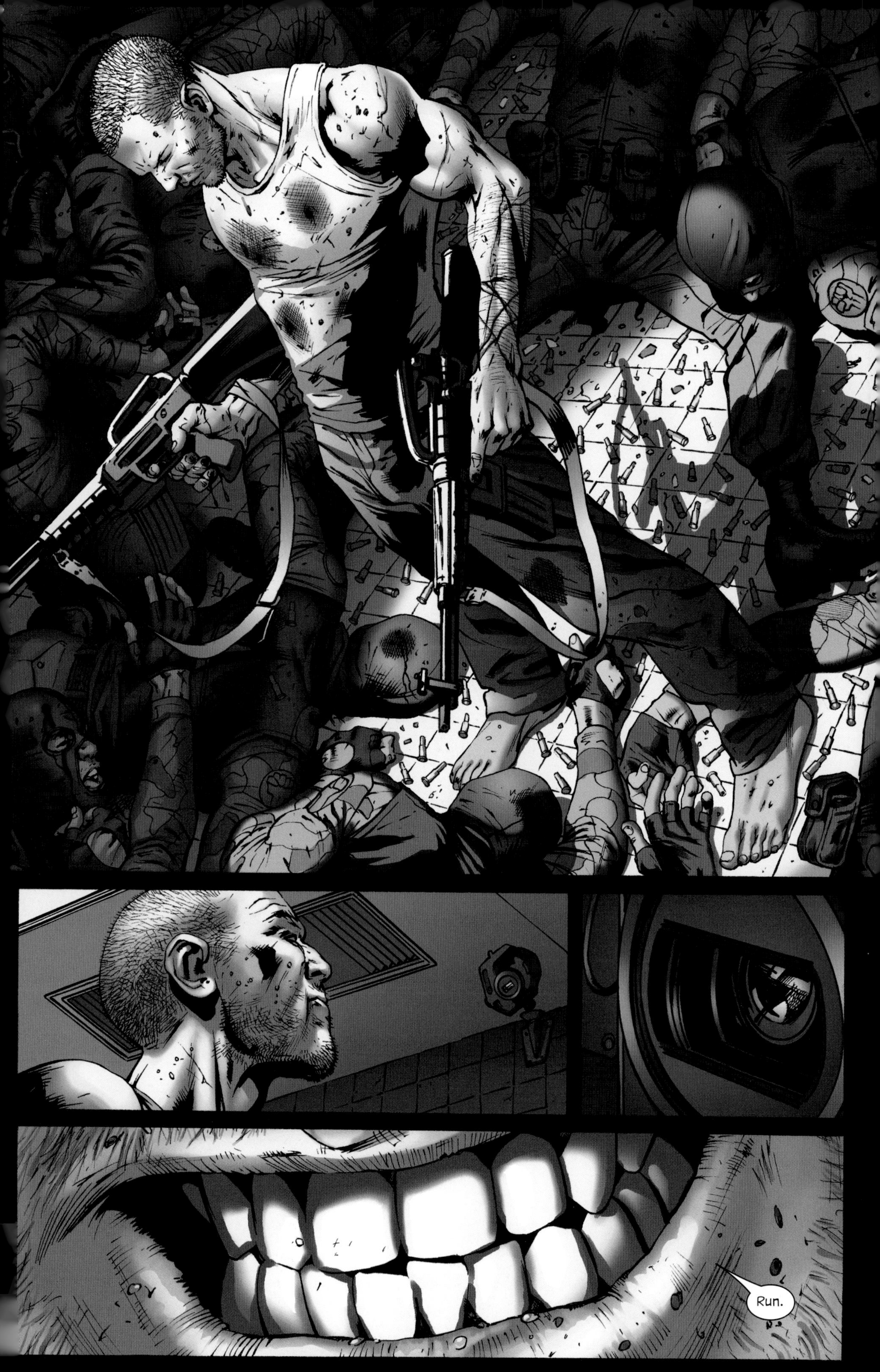
Run.

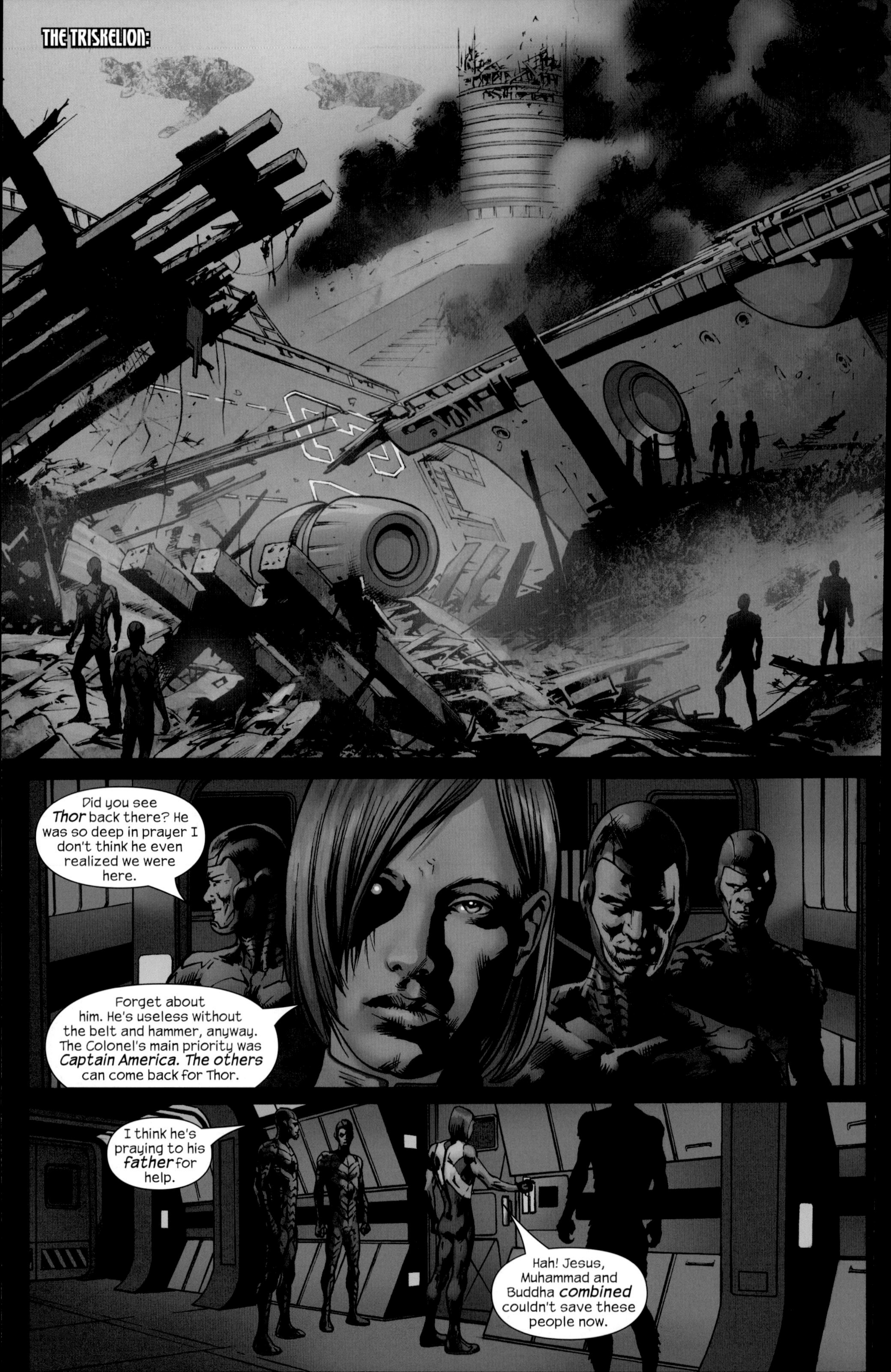
THE TRISKELION:
Did you see Thor back there? He was so deep in prayer I don't think he even realized we were here.
Forget about him. He's useless without the belt and hammer, anyway. The Colonel's main priority was Captain America. The others can come back for Thor.
I think he's praying to his father for help.
Hah! Jesus, Muhammad and Buddha combined couldn't save these people now.

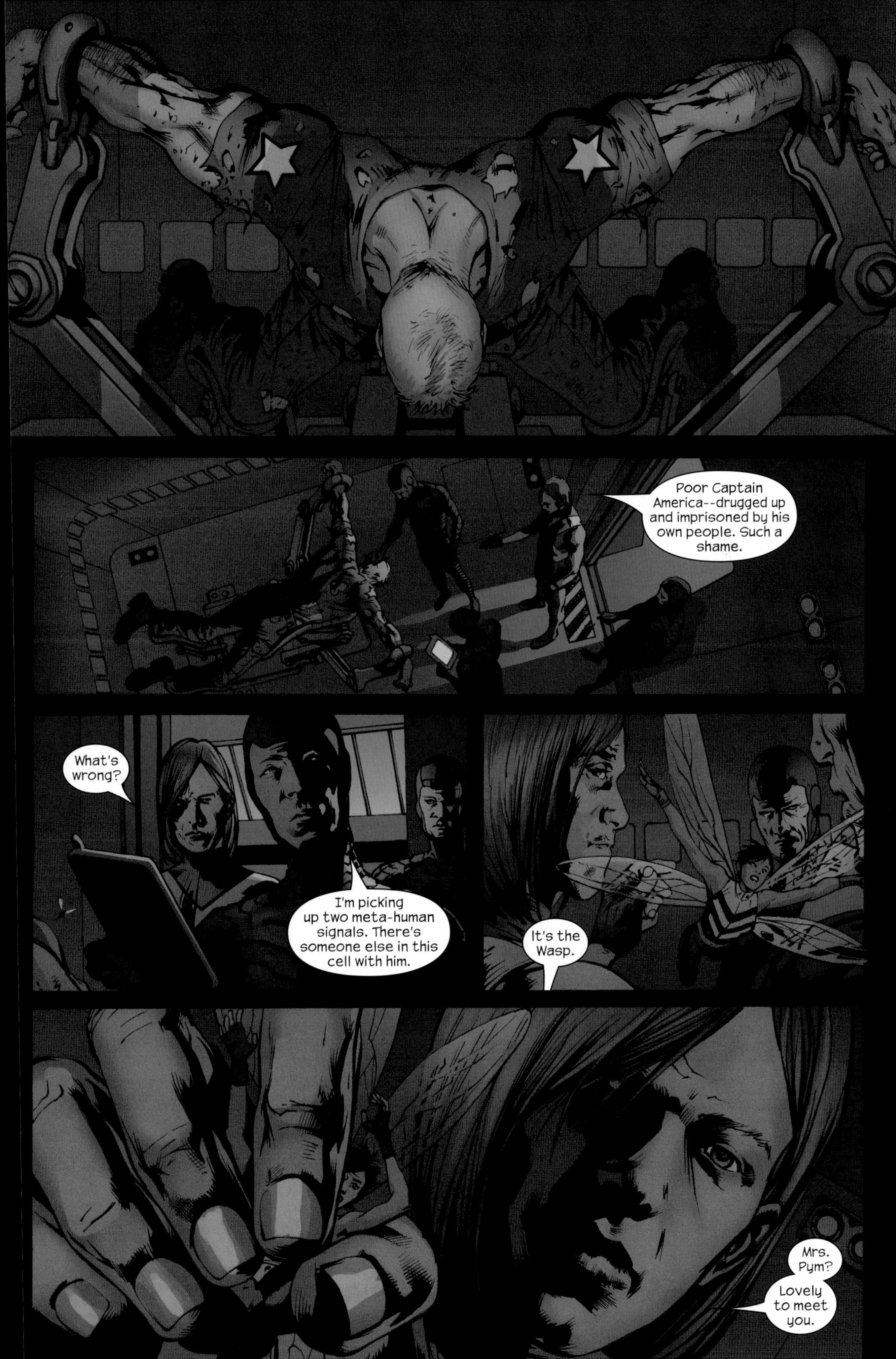

Poor Captain America--drugged up and imprisoned by his own people. Such a shame.
What's wrong?
I'm picking up two meta-human signals. There's someone else in this cell with him.
It's the Wasp.
Mrs. Pym?
Lovely to meet you.

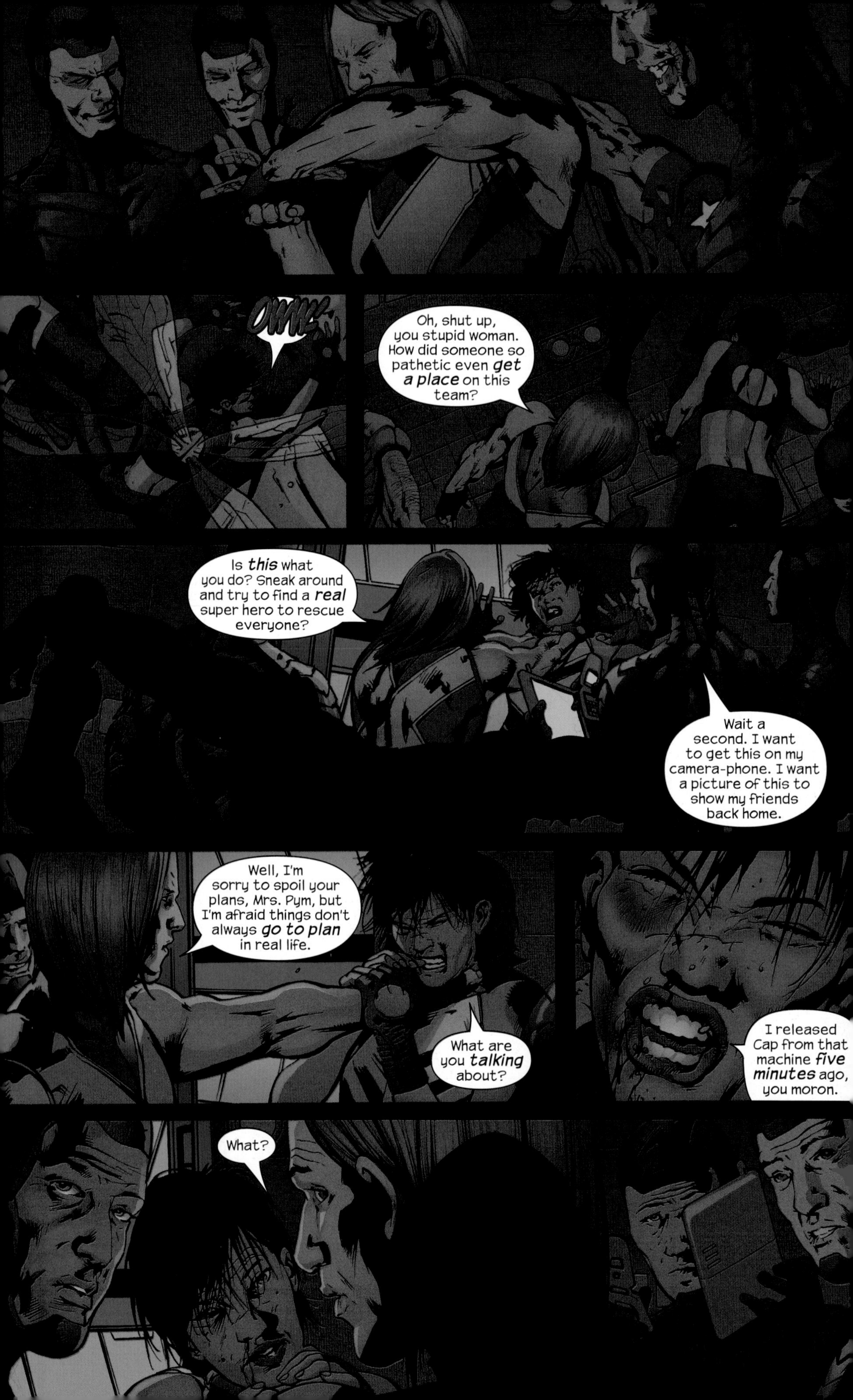
OWW!
Oh, shut up, you stupid woman. How did someone so pathetic even get a place on this team?
Is this what you do? Sneak around and try to find a real super hero to rescue everyone?
Wait a second. I want to get this on my camera-phone. I want a picture of this to show my friends back home.
Well, I'm sorry to spoil your plans, Mrs. Pym, but I'm afraid things don't always go to plan in real life.
What are you talking about?
I released Cap from that machine five minutes ago, you moron.
What?

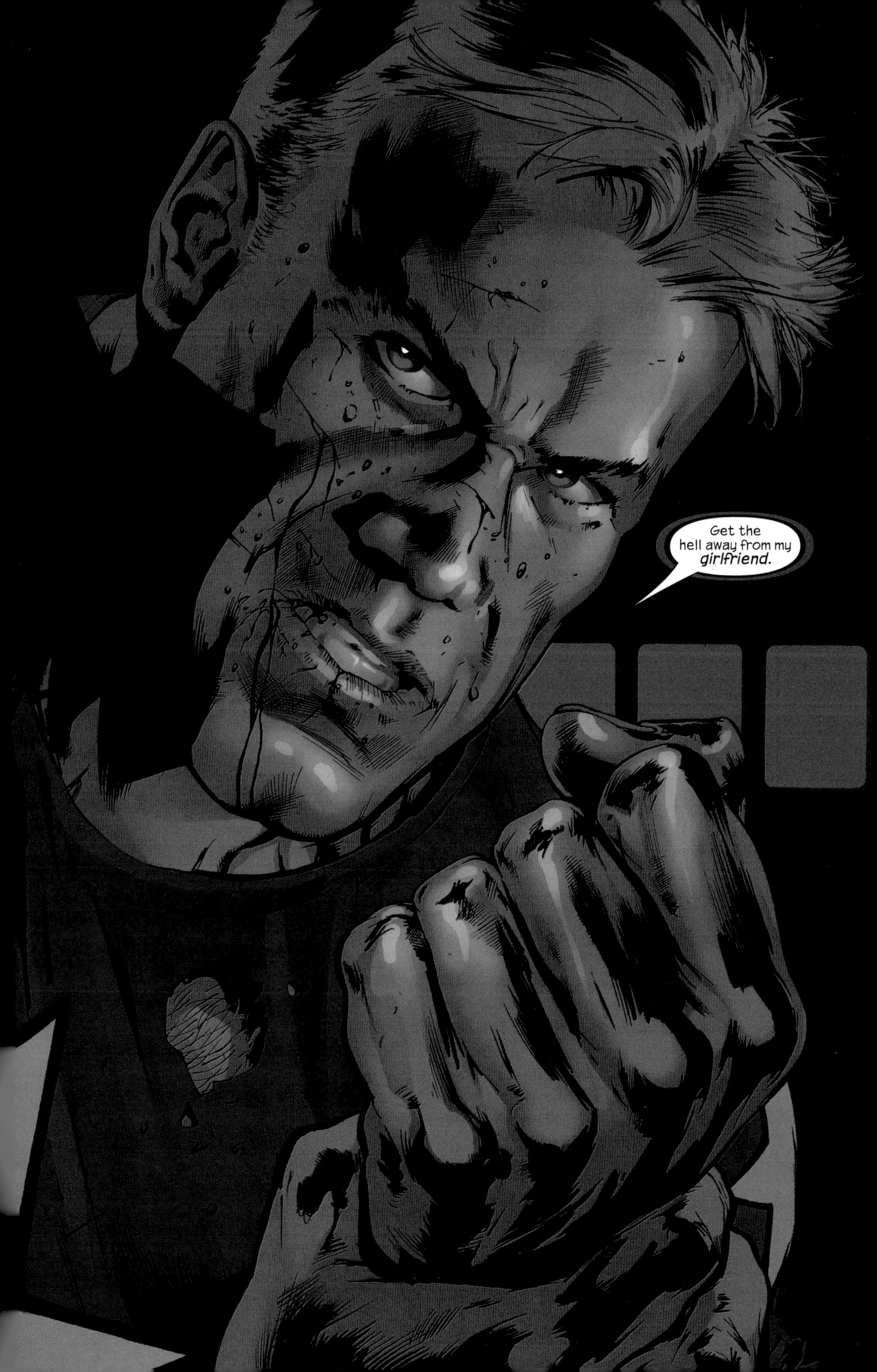
Get the hell away from my *girlfriend.*

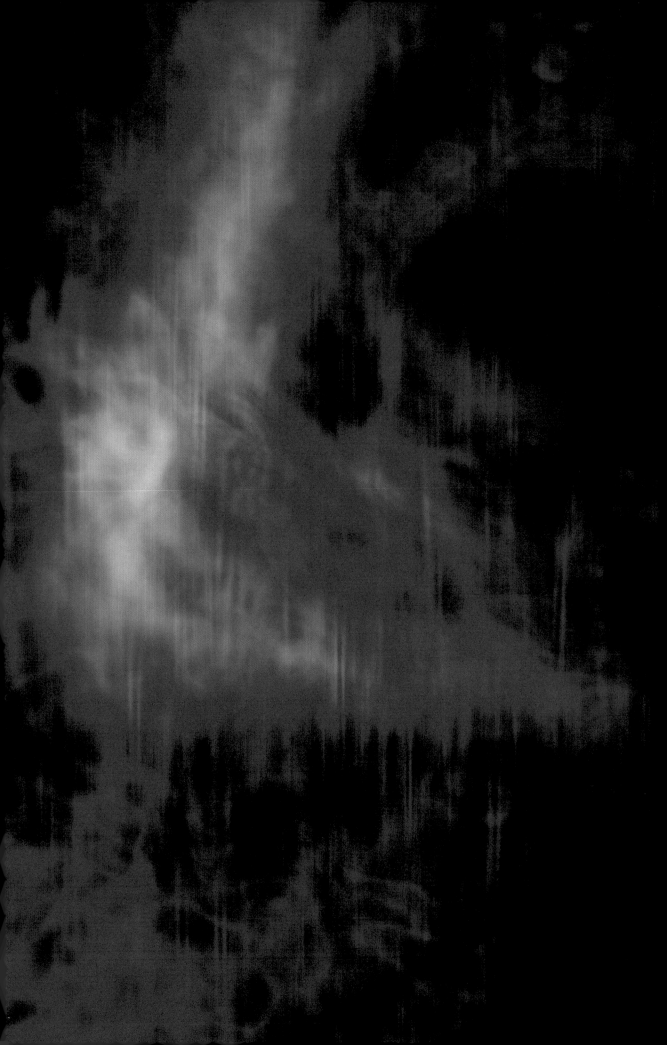

AMERICA STRIKES BACK

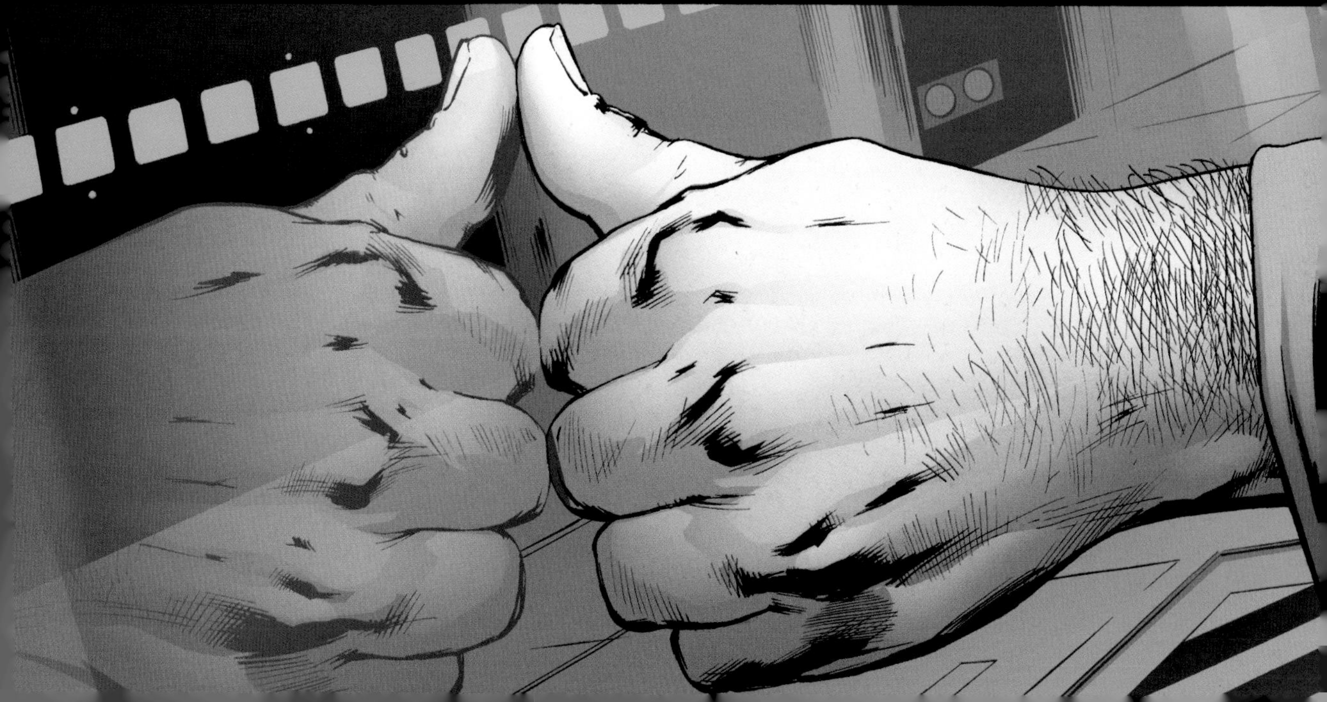

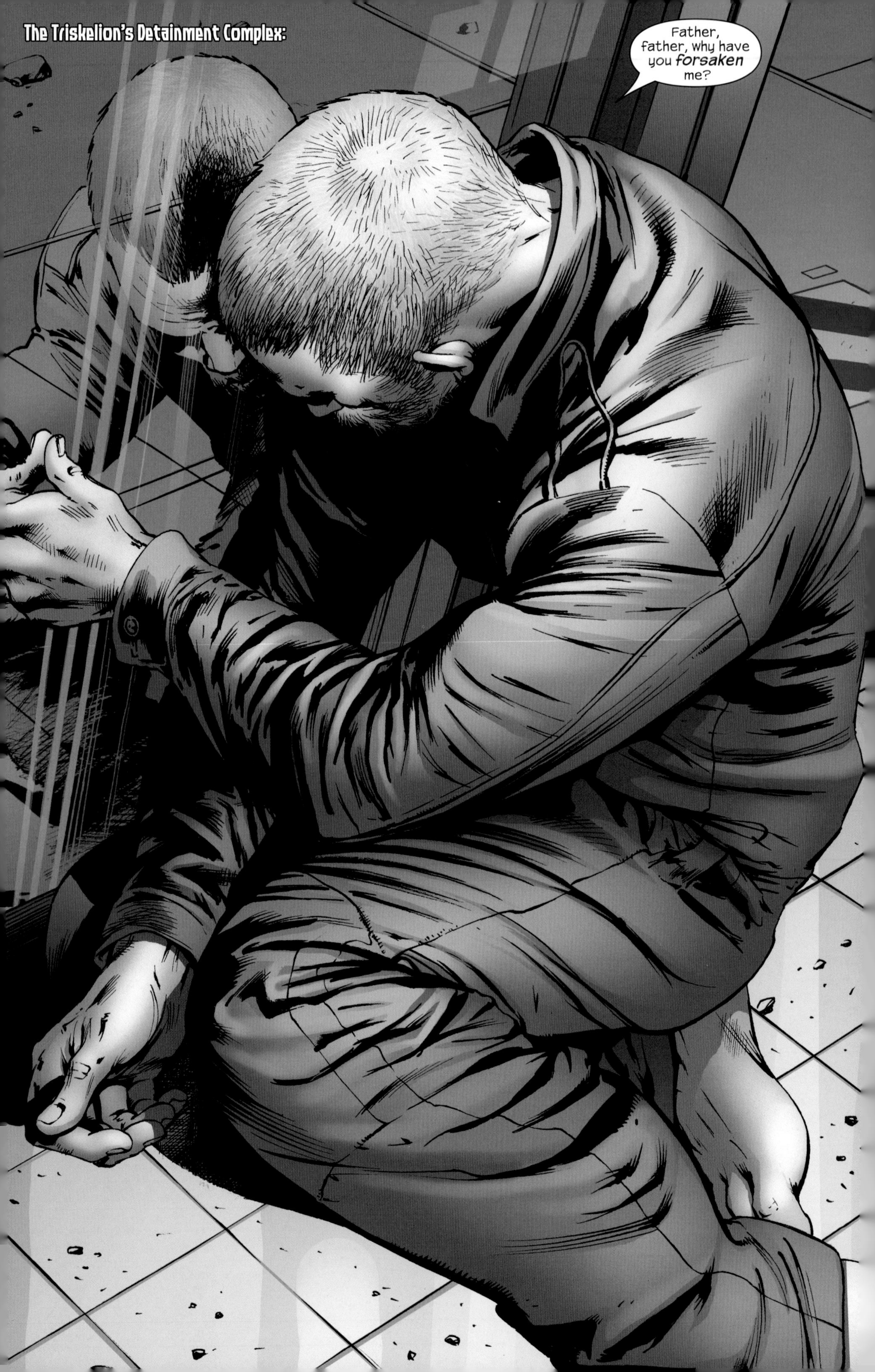
The Triskelion's Detainment Complex:
Father, father, why have you *forsaken* me?

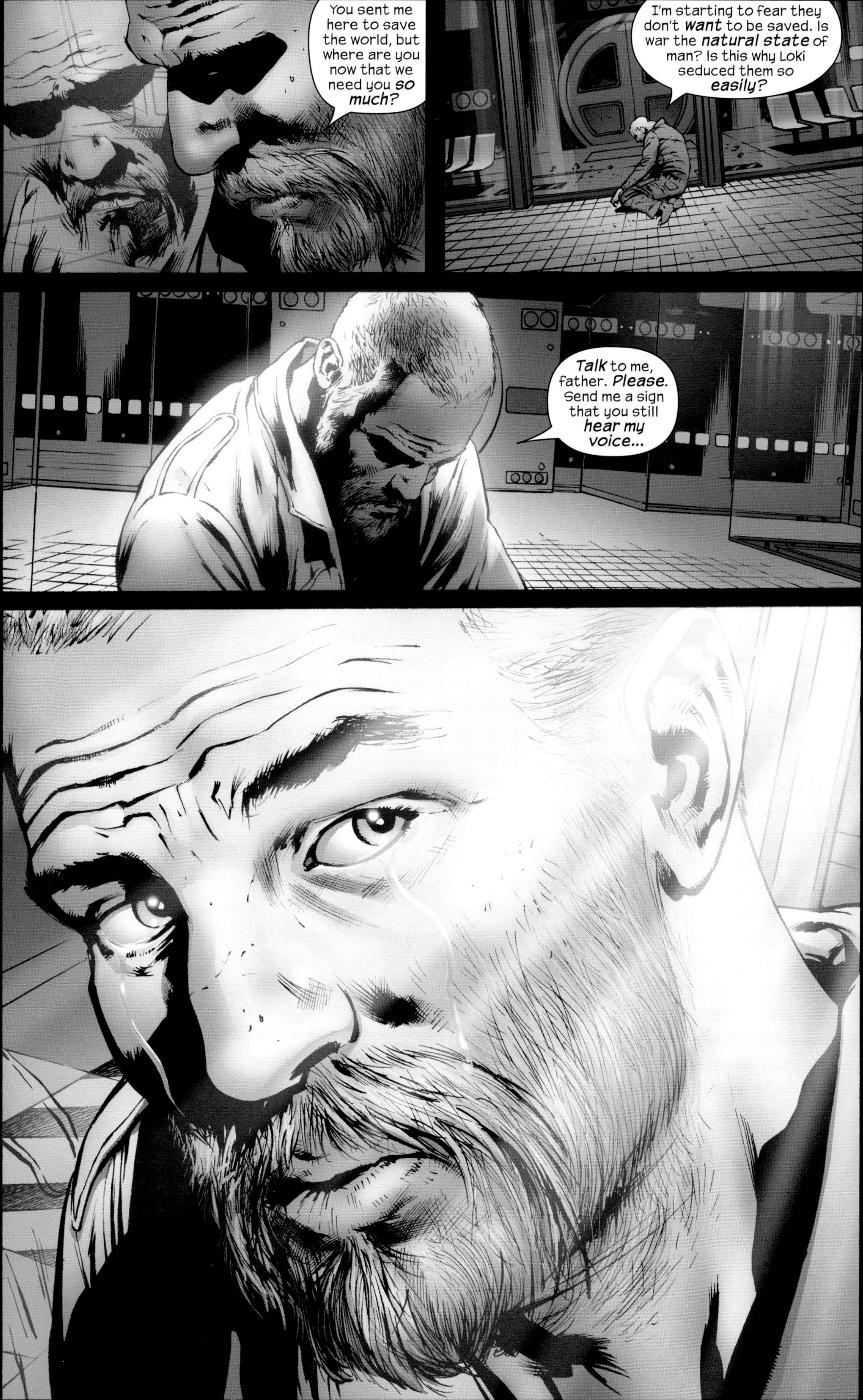
You sent me here to save the world, but where are you now that we need you **so much**?
I'm starting to fear they don't **want** to be saved. Is war the **natural state** of man? Is this why Loki seduced them so **easily**?
Talk to me, father. **Please.** Send me a sign that you still **hear my voice...**

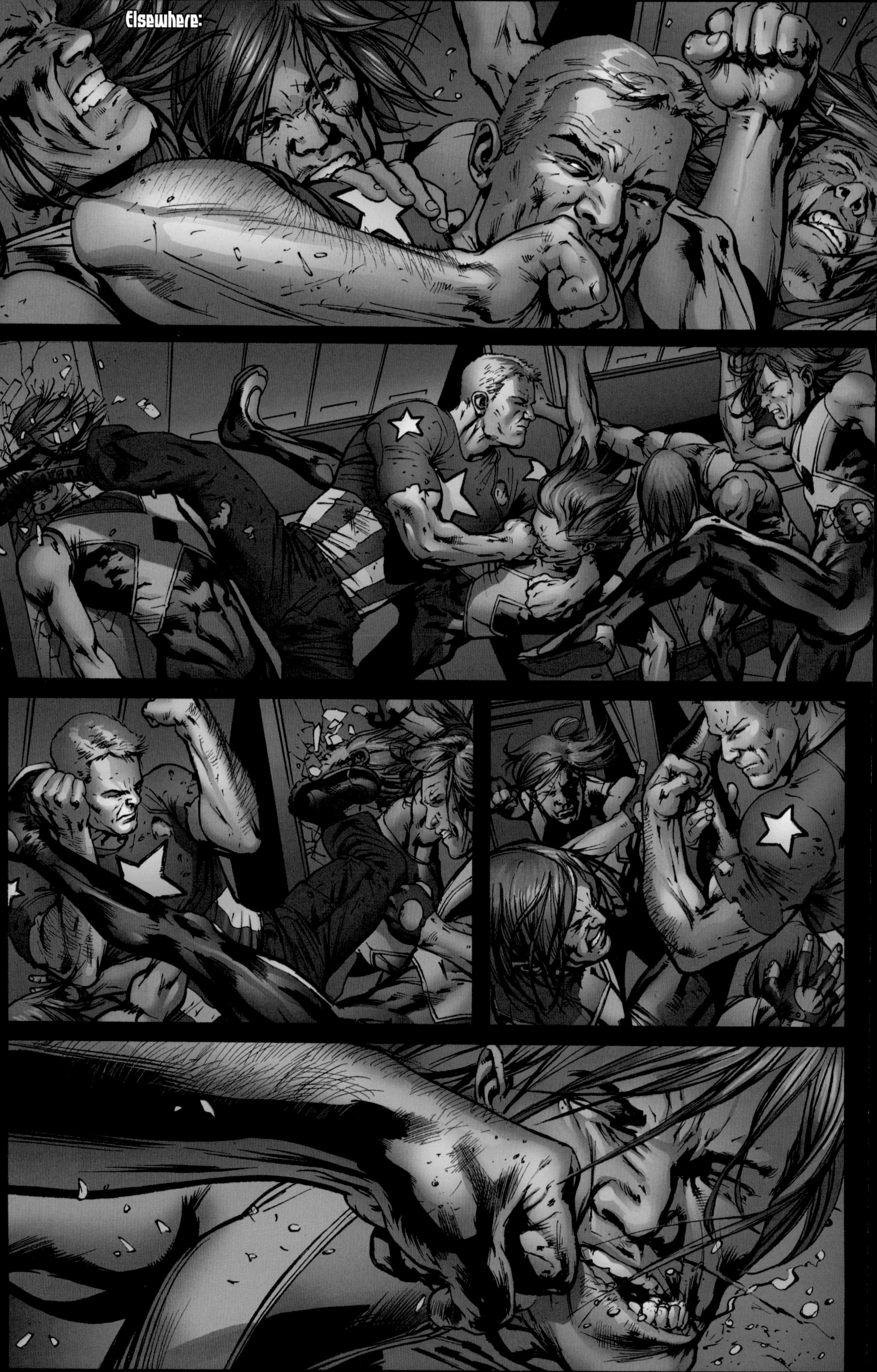
Elsewhere:

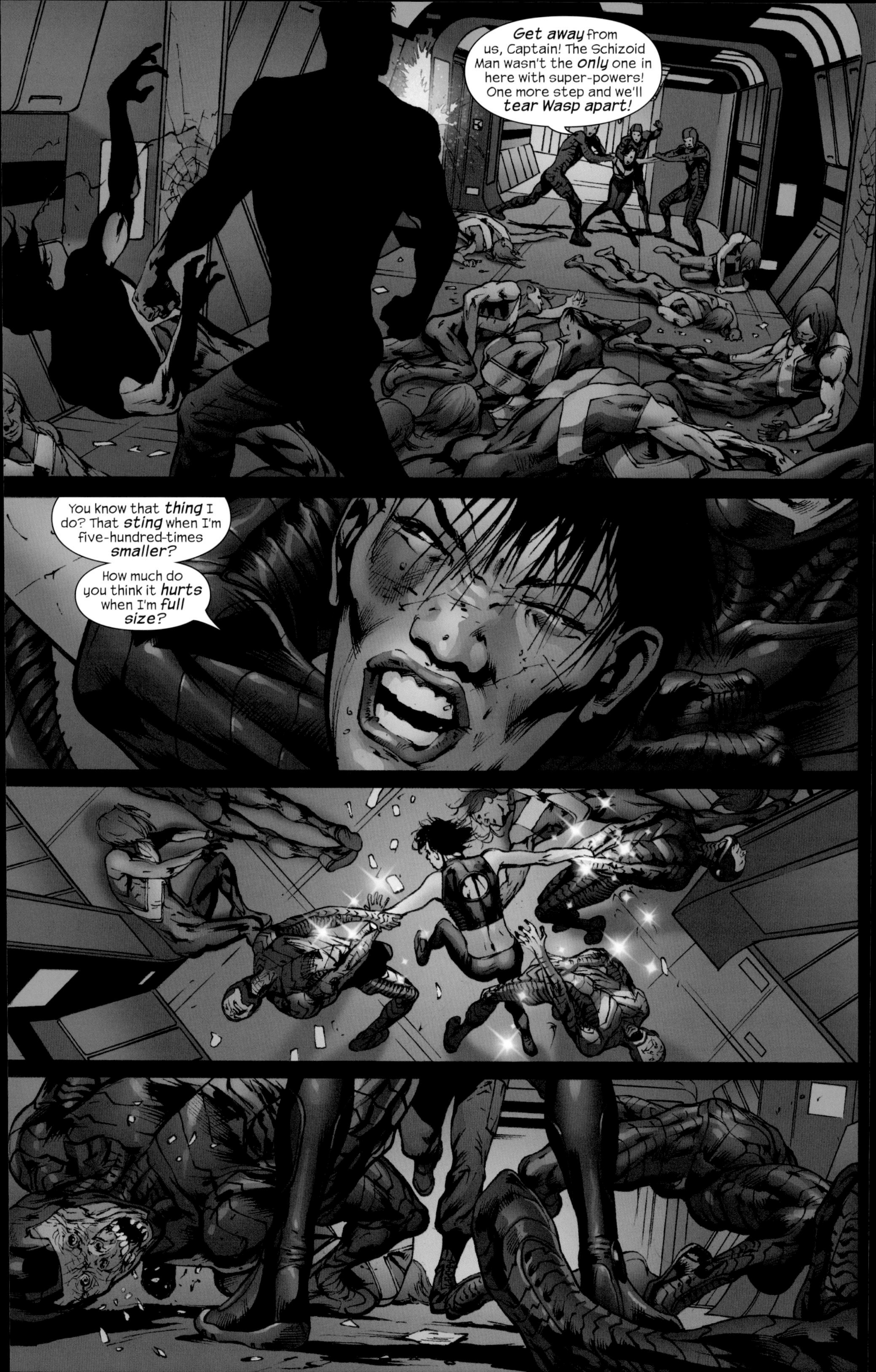
Get away from us, Captain! The Schizoid Man wasn't the only one in here with super-powers! One more step and we'll tear Wasp apart!
You know that thing I do? That sting when I'm five-hundred-times smaller?
How much do you think it hurts when I'm full size?

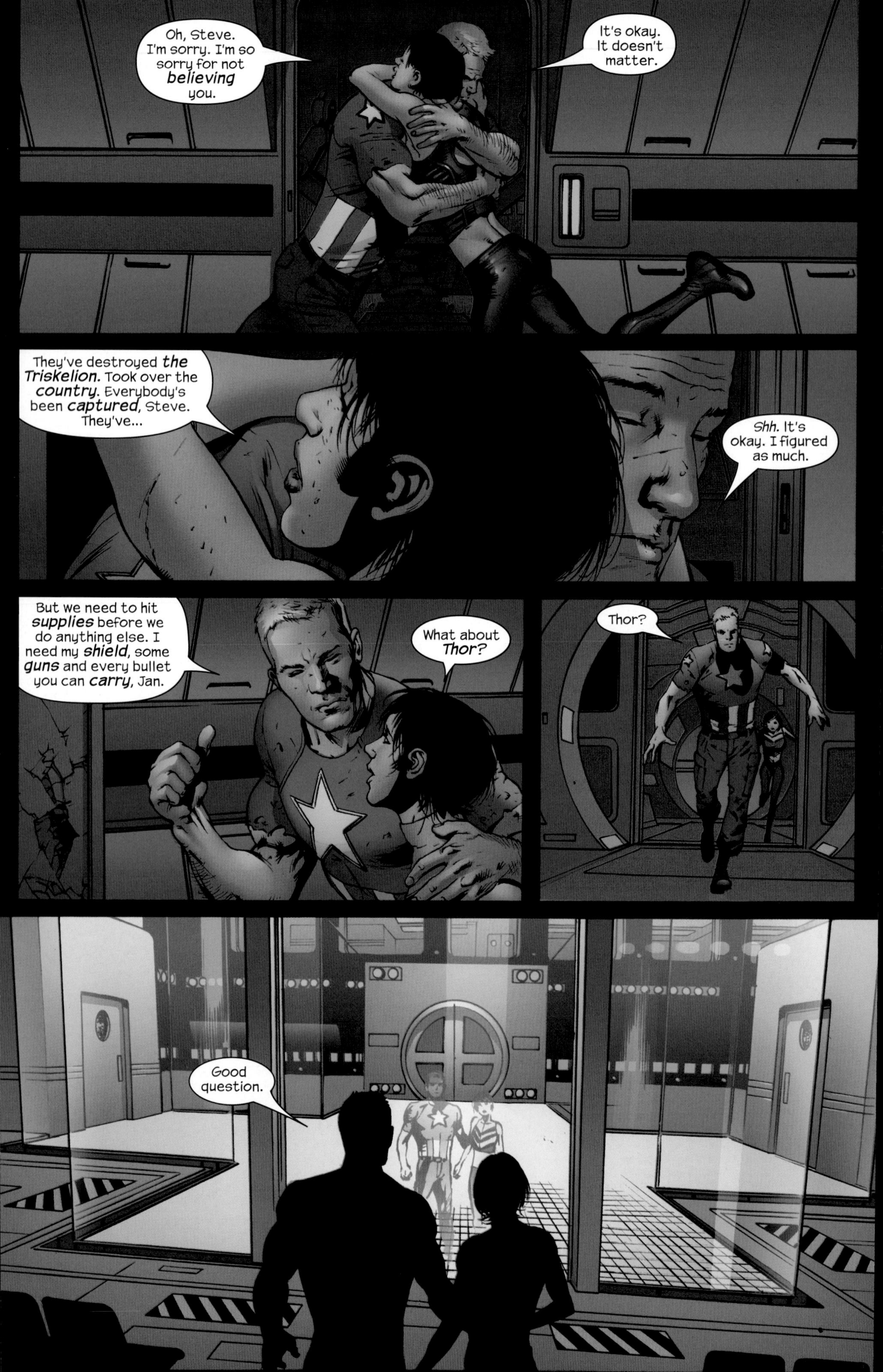
Oh, Steve. I'm sorry. I'm so sorry for not *believing* you.
It's okay. It doesn't matter.
They've destroyed *the Triskelion.* Took over the *country.* Everybody's been *captured*, Steve. They've...
Shh. It's okay. I figured as much.
But we need to hit *supplies* before we do anything else. I need my *shield*, some *guns* and every bullet you can *carry*, Jan.
What about *Thor?*
Thor?
Good question.

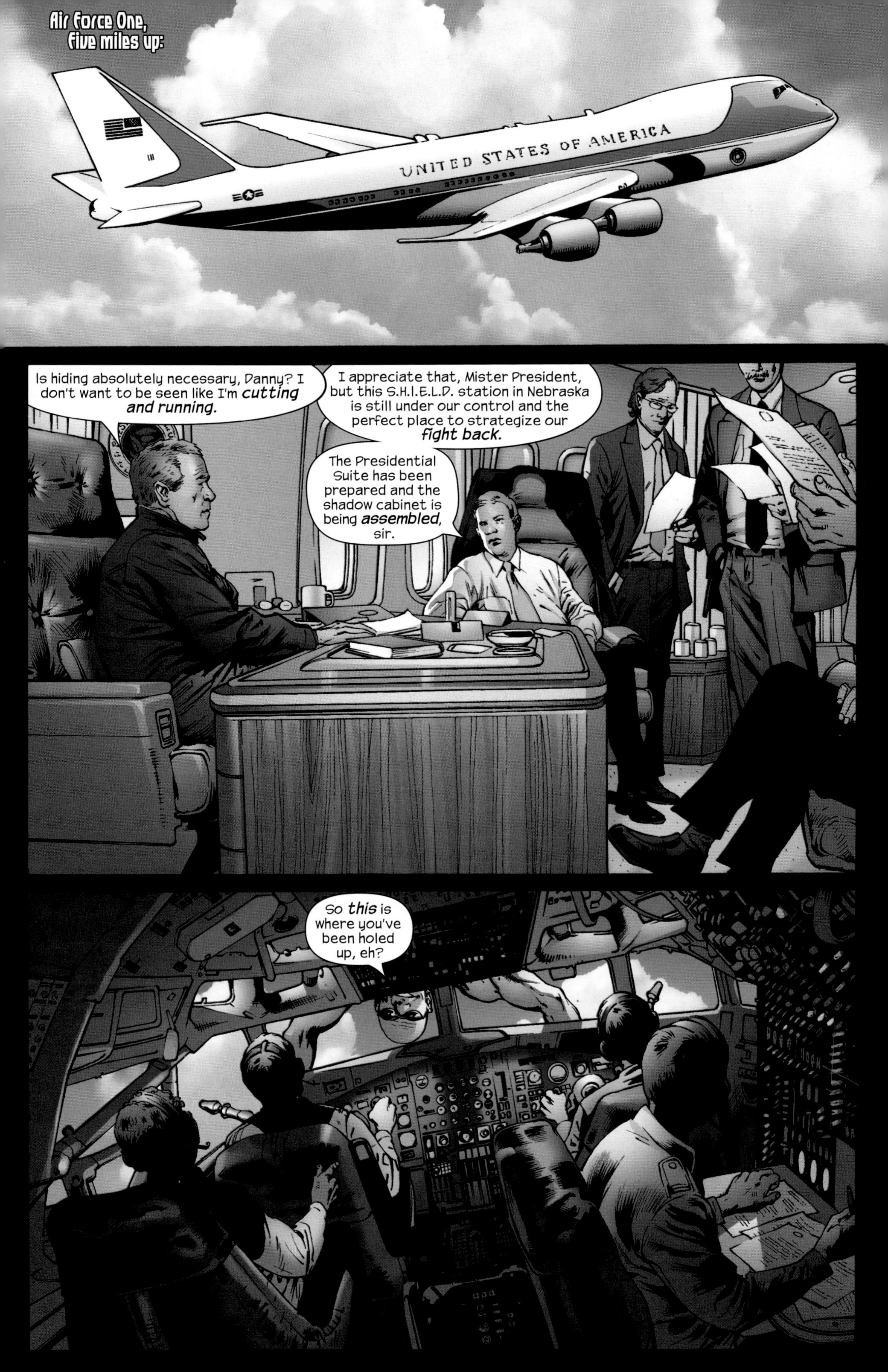

Air Force One, five miles up:
UNITED STATES OF AMERICA
Is hiding absolutely necessary, Danny? I don't want to be seen like I'm *cutting and running.*
I appreciate that, Mister President, but this S.H.I.E.L.D. station in Nebraska is still under our control and the perfect place to strategize our ***fight back.***
The Presidential Suite has been prepared and the shadow cabinet is being ***assembled***, sir.
So ***this*** is where you've been holed up, eh?

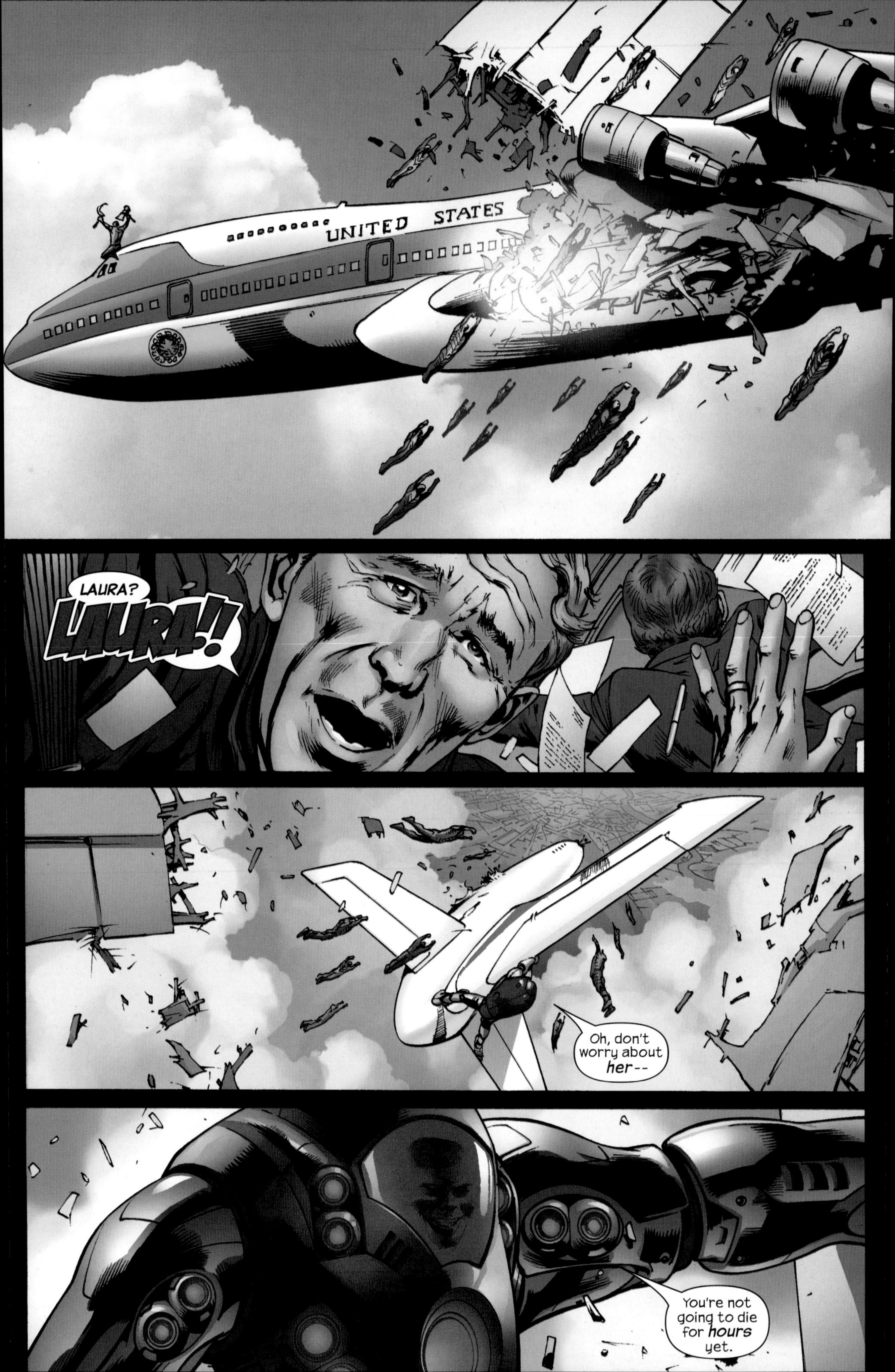
UNITED STATES
LAURA?
LAURA!!
Oh, don't worry about her--
You're not going to die for hours yet.

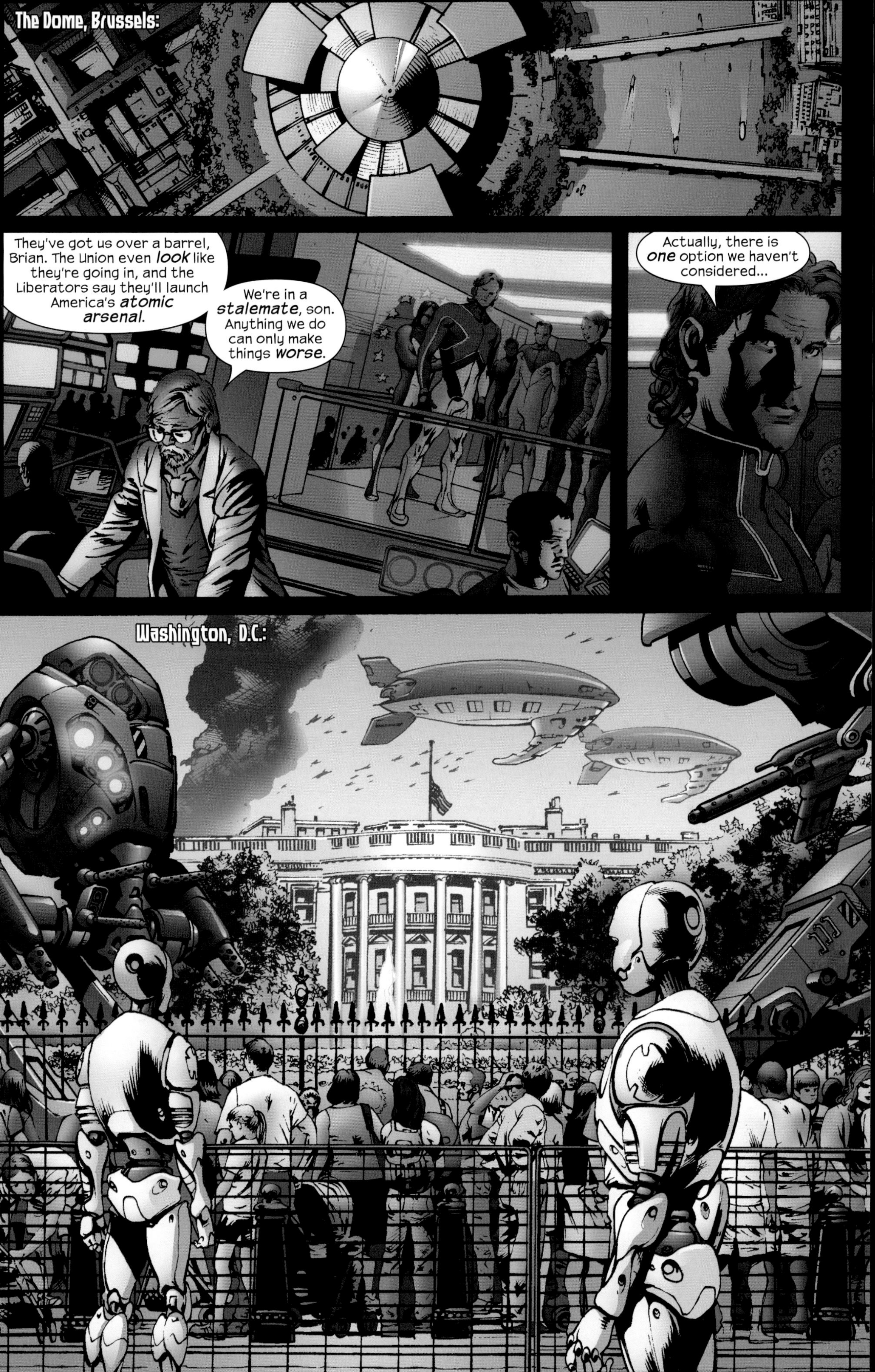

The Dome, Brussels:
They've got us over a barrel, Brian. The Union even *look* like they're going in, and the Liberators say they'll launch America's *atomic arsenal*.
We're in a *stalemate*, son. Anything we do can only make things *worse*.
Actually, there is *one* option we haven't considered...
Washington, D.C.:

He's *escaped*?

New York:

We *presume* he's escaped, Colonel Al-Rahman. He wasn't in his cell and the Schizoid Man's bodies were scattered all over *the Triskelion*.

What should we do with the *others* we've captured? Does this *change* things in any way?

No, it changes nothing. Everyone convenes in Washington precisely as planned. Loki wants the executions to go ahead at *midnight*.

I think you're underestimating Rogers, Colonel. Seriously, you need to focus your attention on *finding* him or you're putting this *entire mission* in danger.

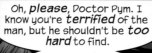

Oh, *please*, Doctor Pym. I know you're *terrified* of the man, but he shouldn't be *too hard* to find.

We've *crippled* his country, *captured* his President and plan to behead his *friends* very shortly.

Do you honestly think this isn't going to *smoke him out*?

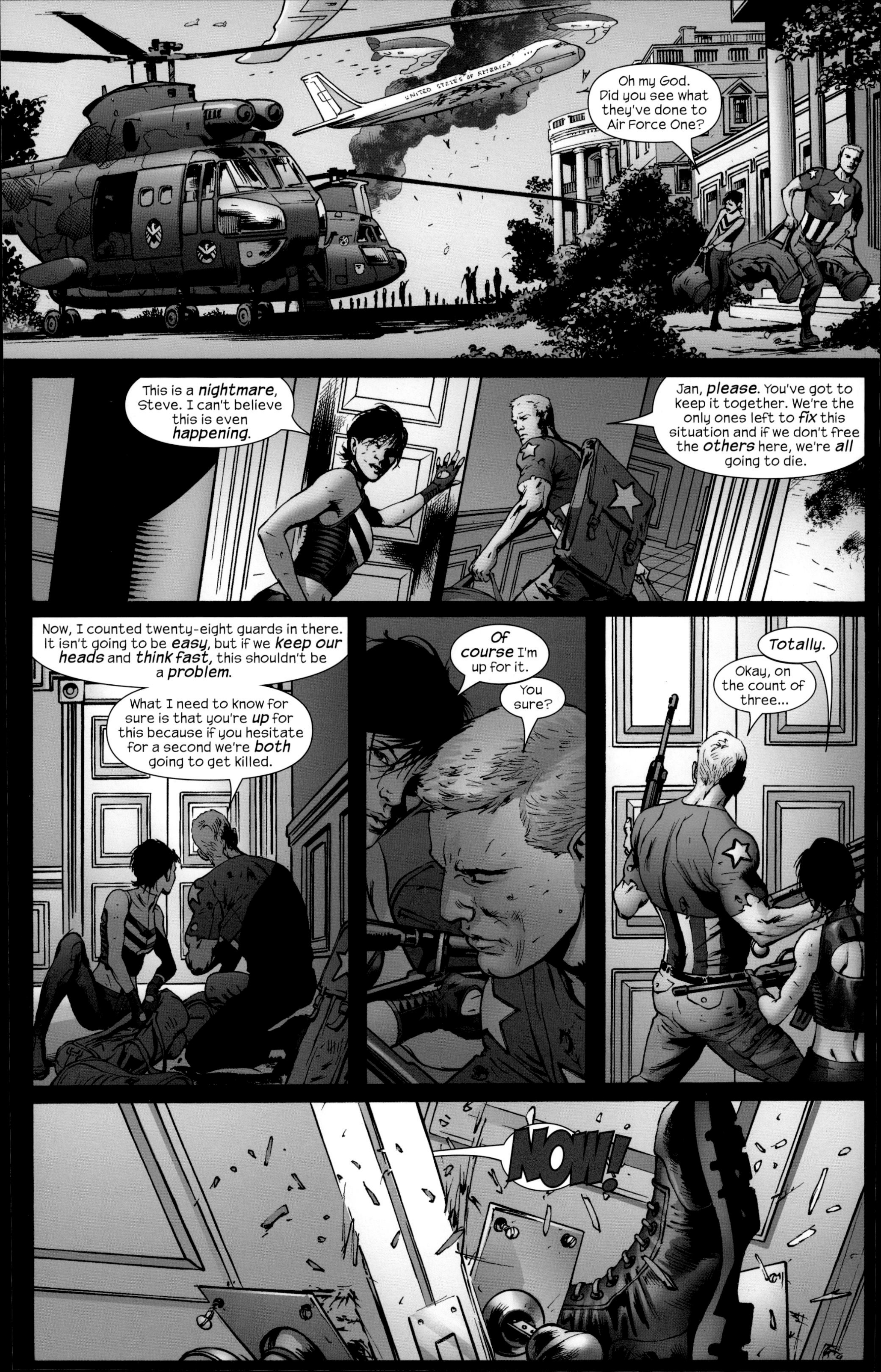
UNITED STATES OF AMERICA
Oh my God. Did you see what they've done to Air Force One?
This is a *nightmare*, Steve. I can't believe this is even *happening*.
Jan, *please*. You've got to keep it together. We're the only ones left to *fix* this situation and if we don't free the *others* here, we're *all* going to die.
Now, I counted twenty-eight guards in there. It isn't going to be *easy*, but if we *keep our heads* and *think fast*, this shouldn't be a *problem*.
What I need to know for sure is that you're *up* for this because if you hesitate for a second we're *both* going to get killed.
Of course I'm up for it.
You sure?
Totally.
Okay, on the count of three...
NOW!

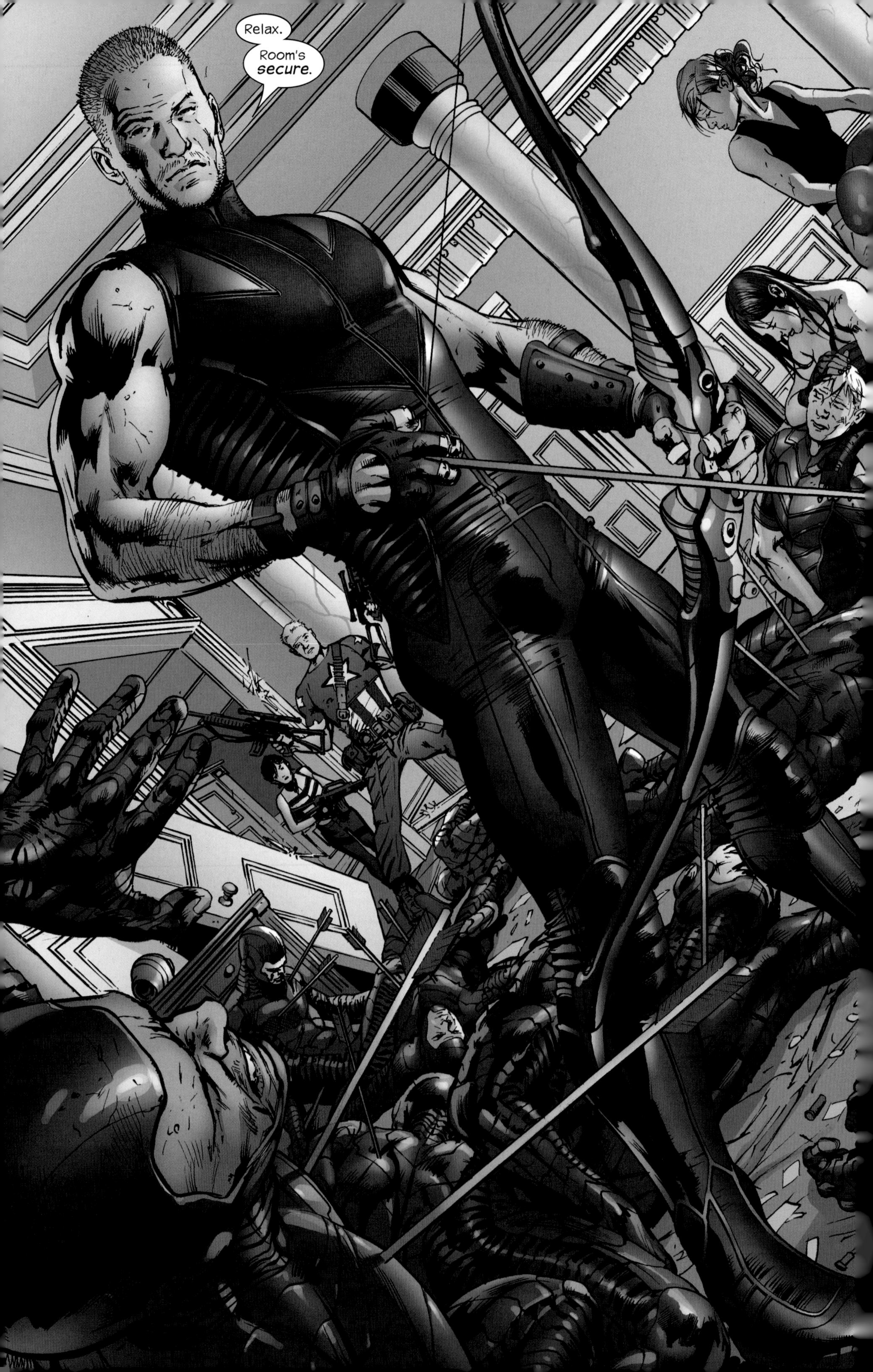
Relax.
Room's secure.

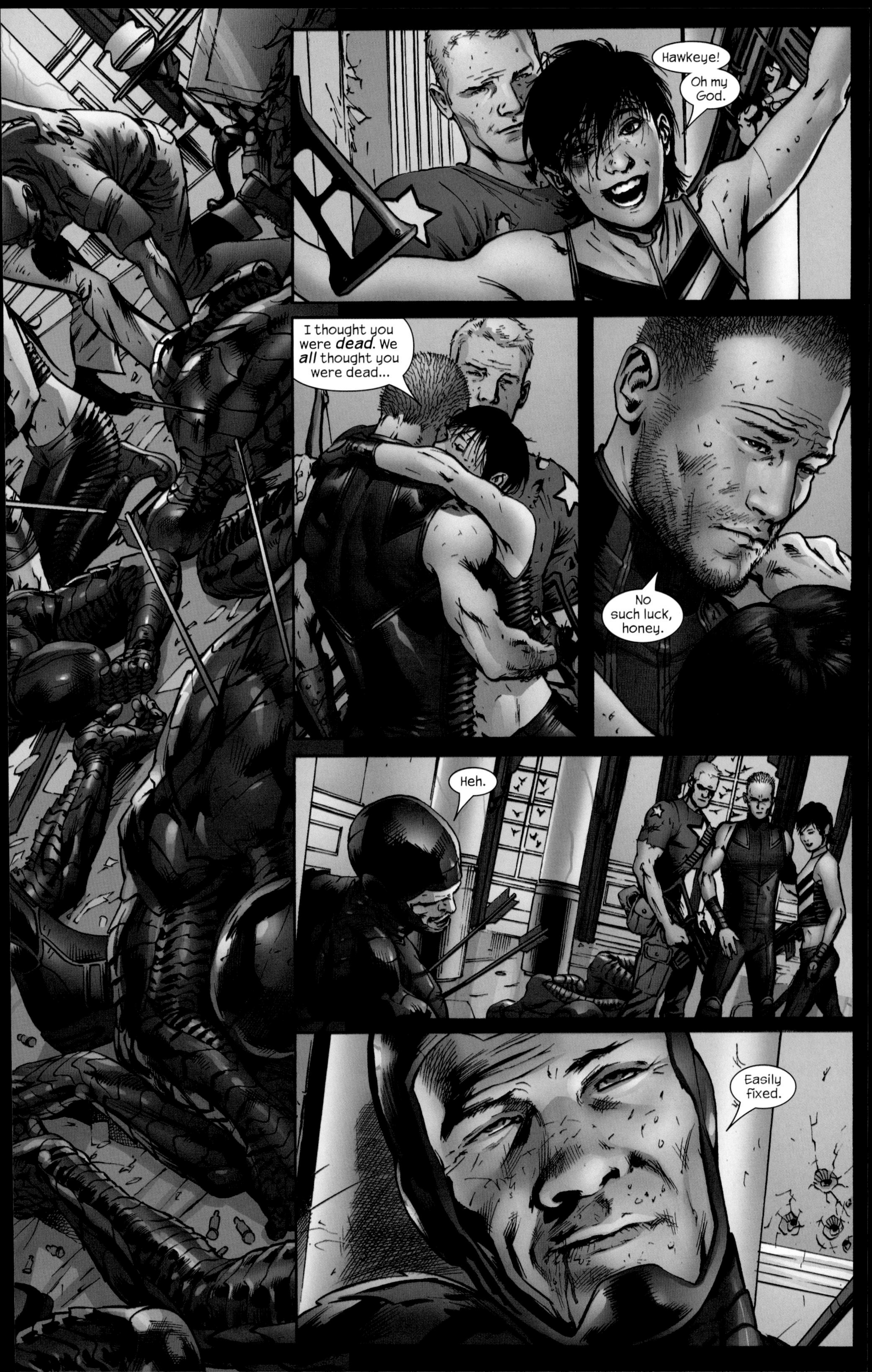
Hawkeye!
Oh my God.
I thought you were *dead*. We *all* thought you were dead...
No such luck, honey.
Heh.
Easily fixed.

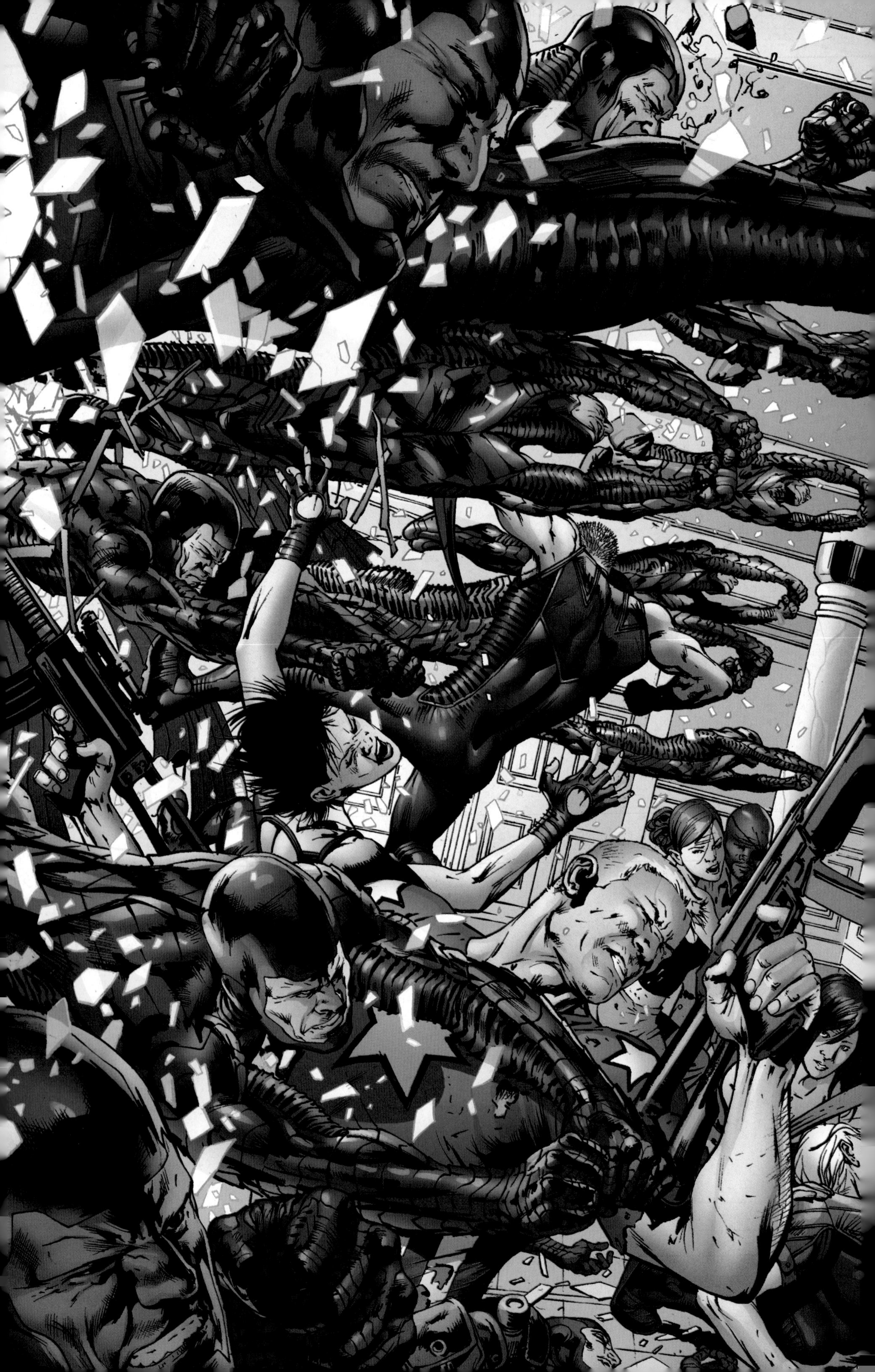

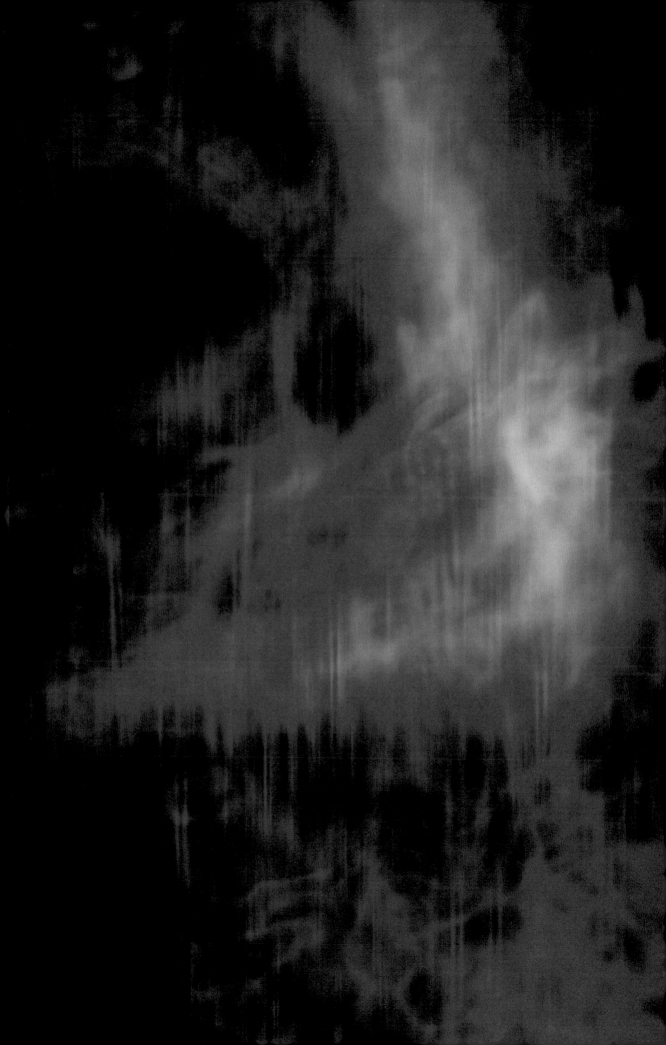

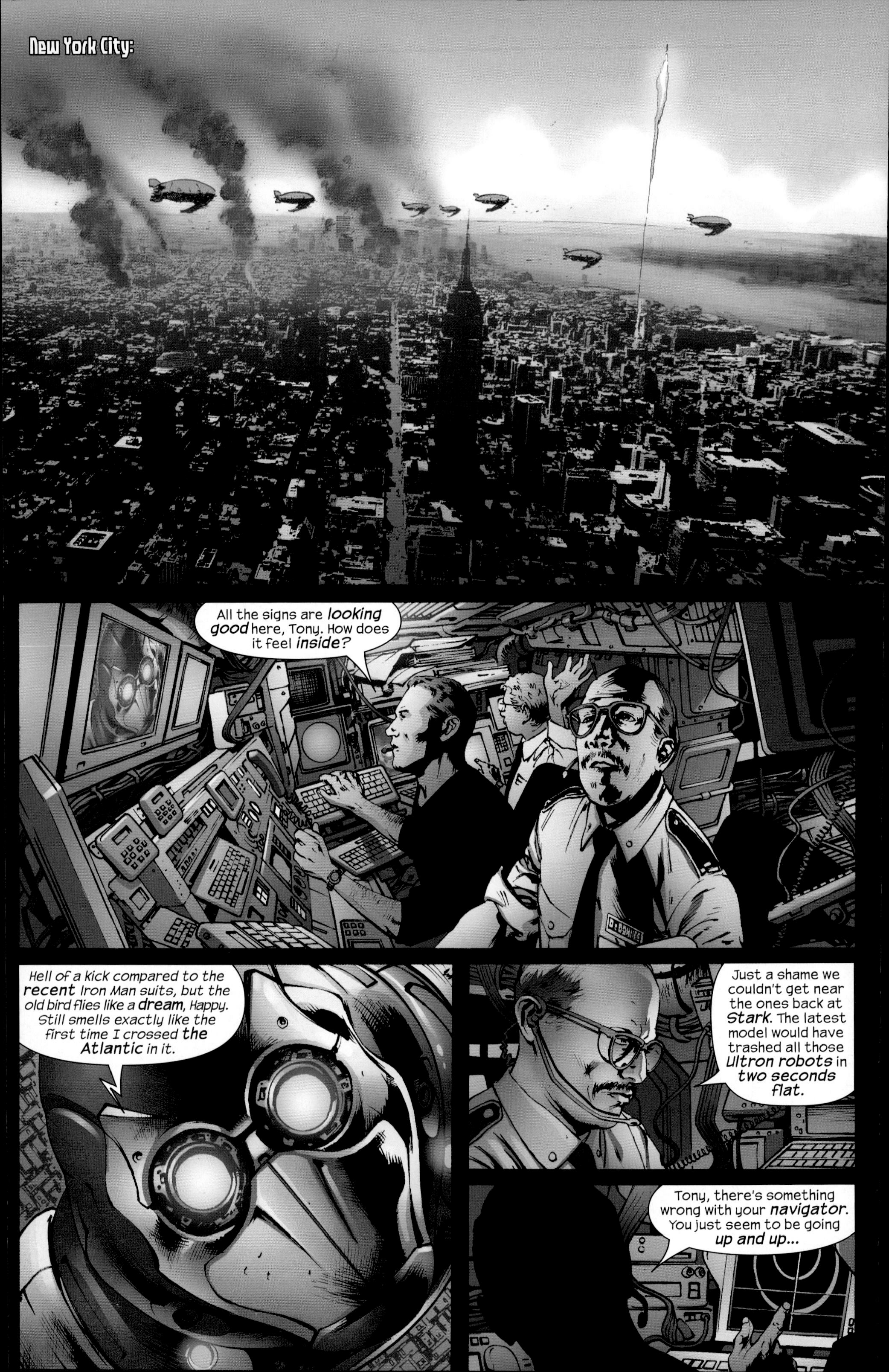
New York City:
All the signs are *looking good* here, Tony. How does it feel *inside*?
Hell of a kick compared to the **recent** Iron Man suits, but the old bird flies like a **dream**, Happy. Still smells exactly like the first time I crossed **the Atlantic** in it.
Just a shame we couldn't get near the ones back at *Stark*. The latest model would have trashed all those *Ultron robots* in *two seconds flat*.
Tony, there's something wrong with your *navigator*. You just seem to be going *up and up*...

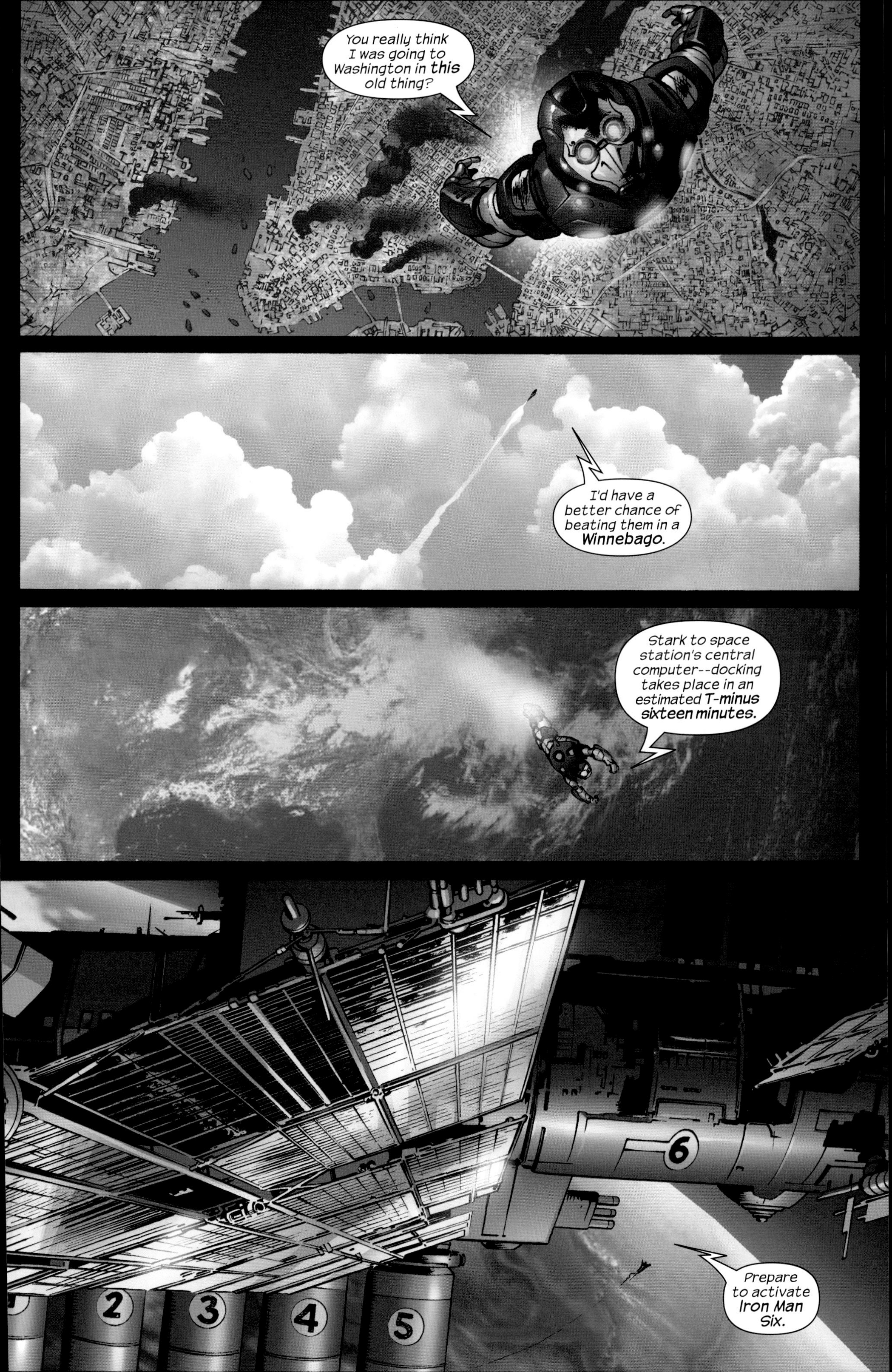
You really think I was going to Washington in this old thing?
I'd have a better chance of beating them in a Winnebago.
Stark to space station's central computer--docking takes place in an estimated T-minus sixteen minutes.
Prepare to activate Iron Man Six.
2
3
4
5
6

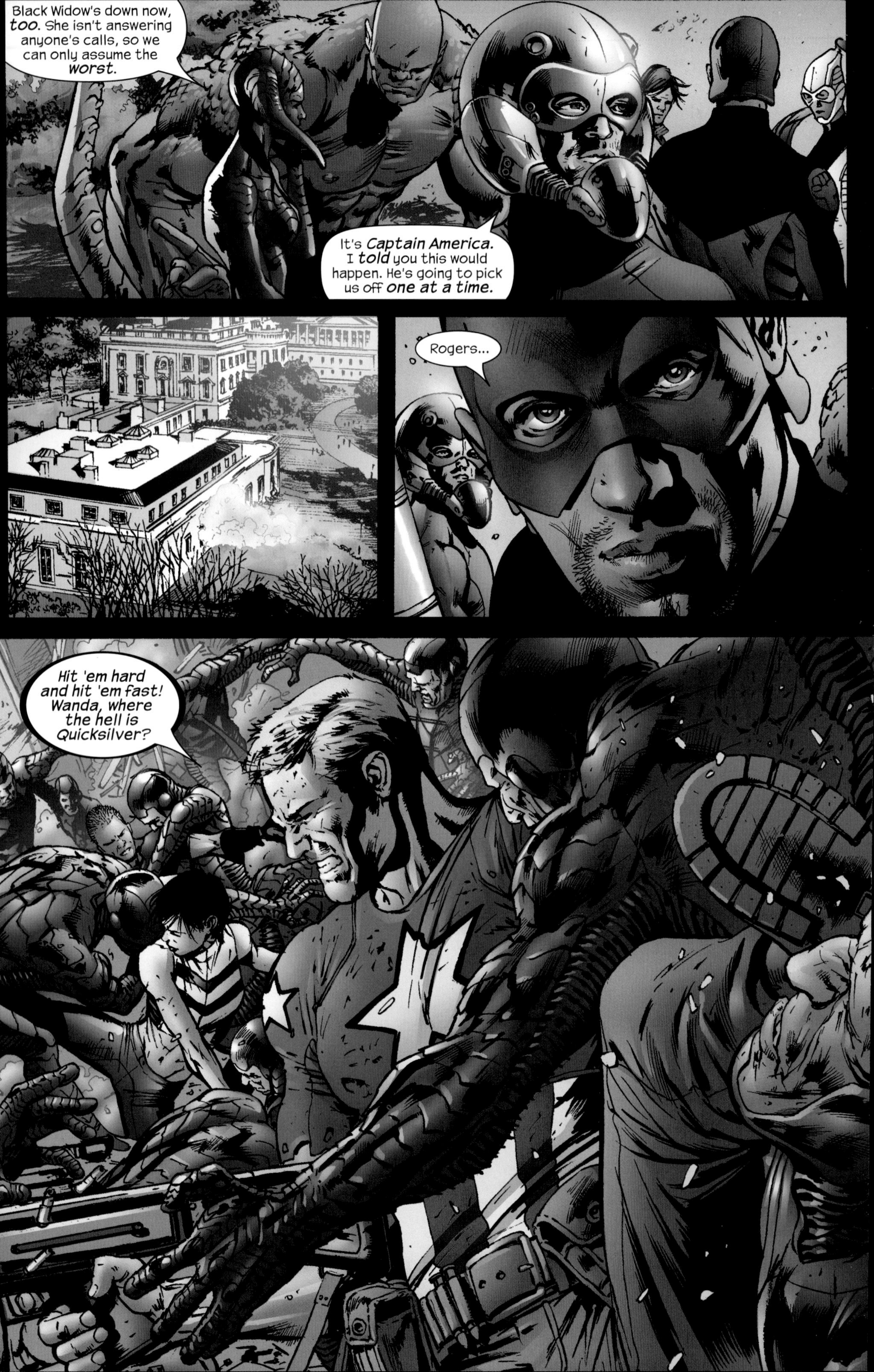

Black Widow's down now, too. She isn't answering anyone's calls, so we can only assume the worst.
It's Captain America. I told you this would happen. He's going to pick us off one at a time.
Rogers...
Hit 'em hard and hit 'em fast! Wanda, where the hell is Quicksilver?

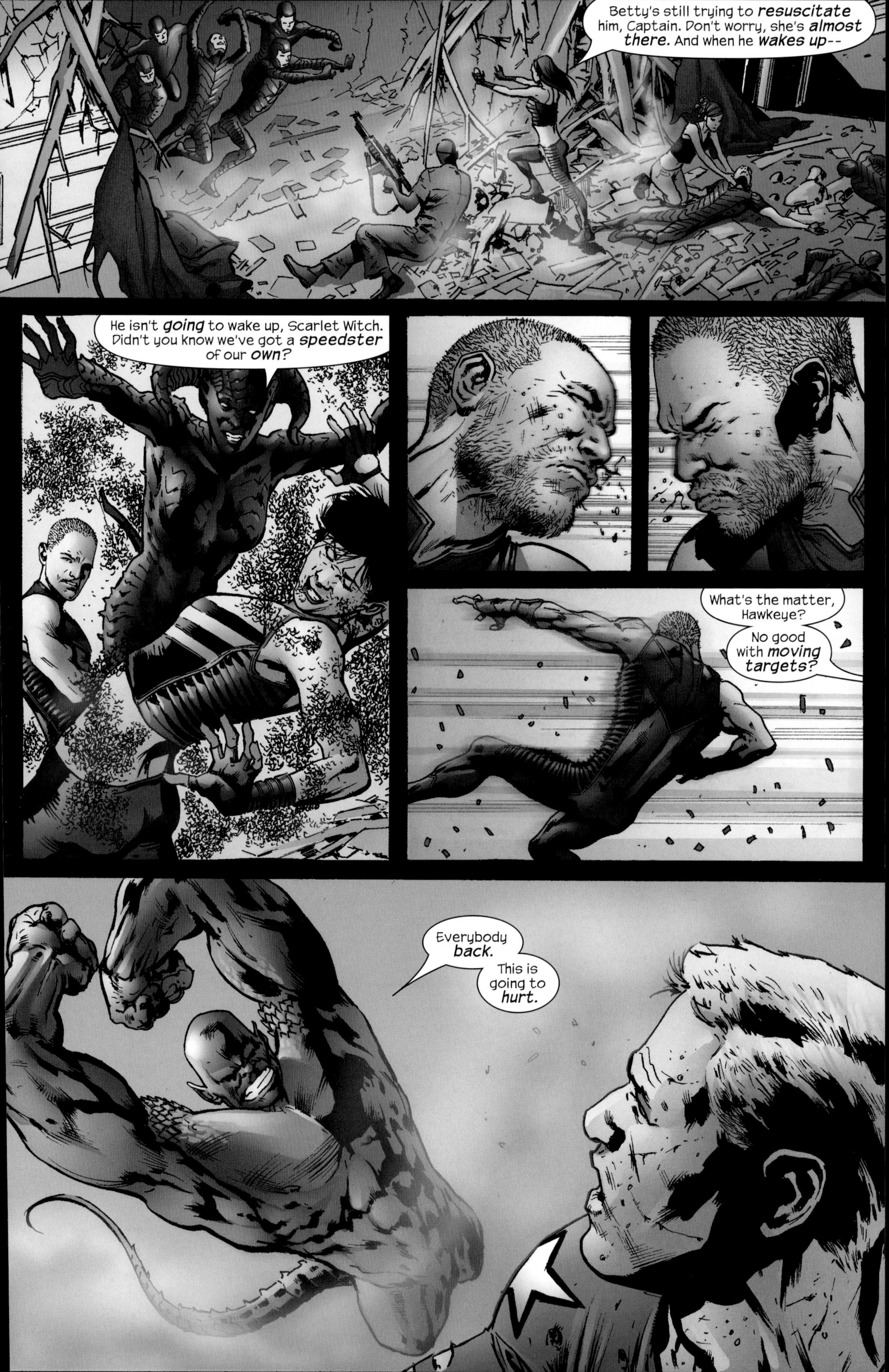
Betty's still trying to resuscitate him, Captain. Don't worry, she's almost there. And when he wakes up--
He isn't going to wake up, Scarlet Witch. Didn't you know we've got a speedster of our own?
What's the matter, Hawkeye?
No good with moving targets?
Everybody back.
This is going to hurt.

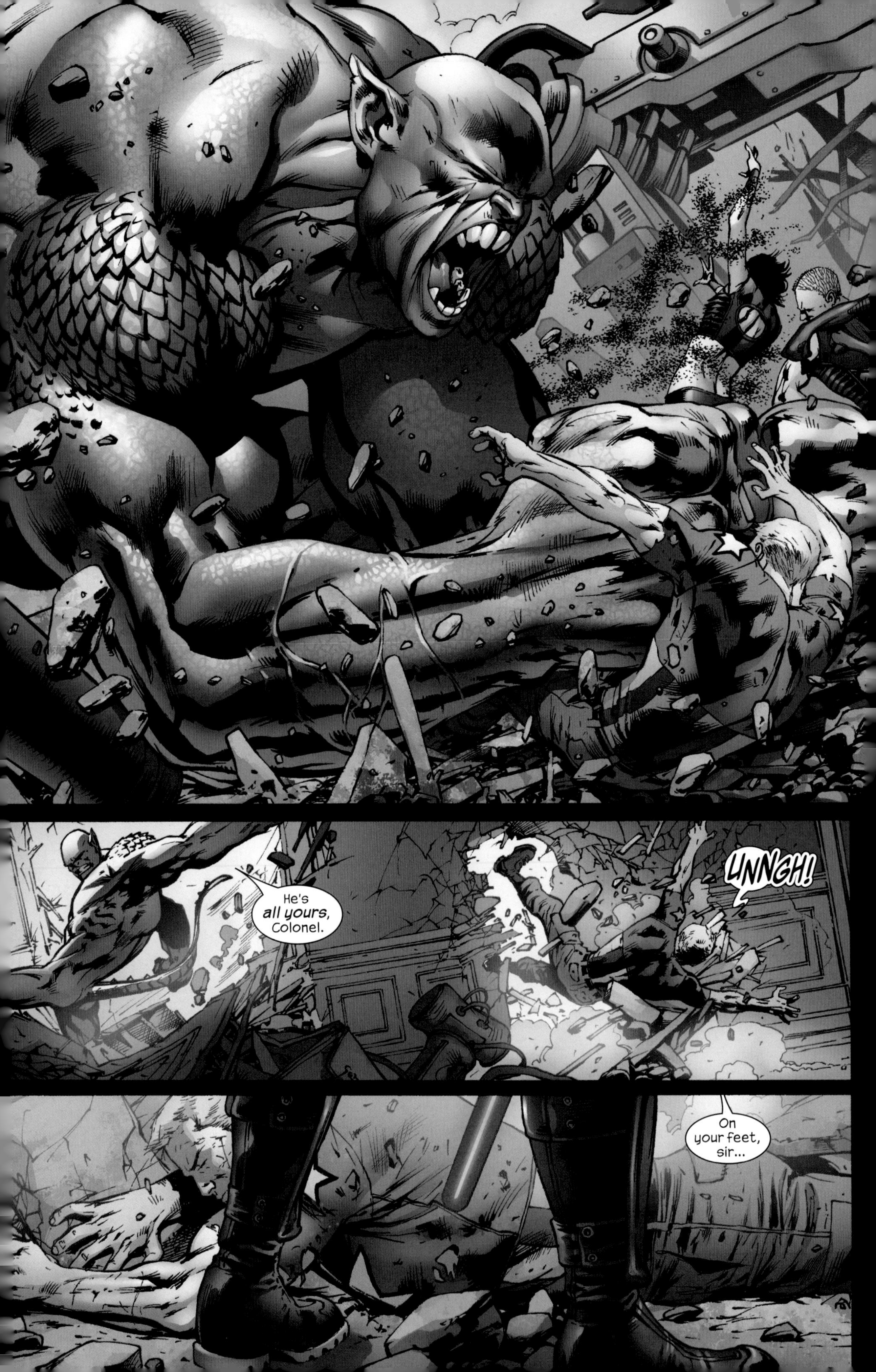
He's all yours, Colonel.
UNNGH!
On your feet, sir...

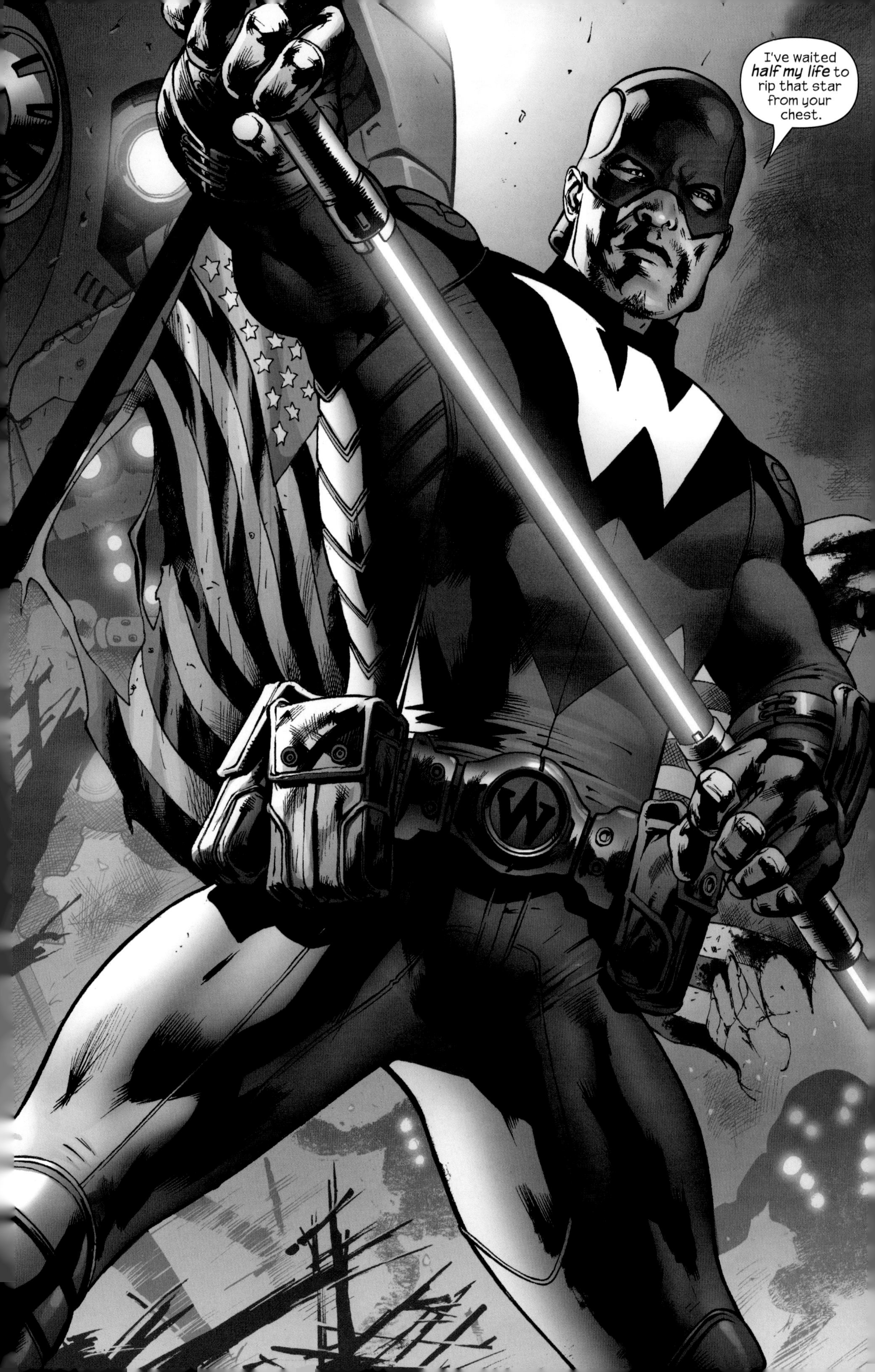
I've waited half my life to rip that star from your chest.

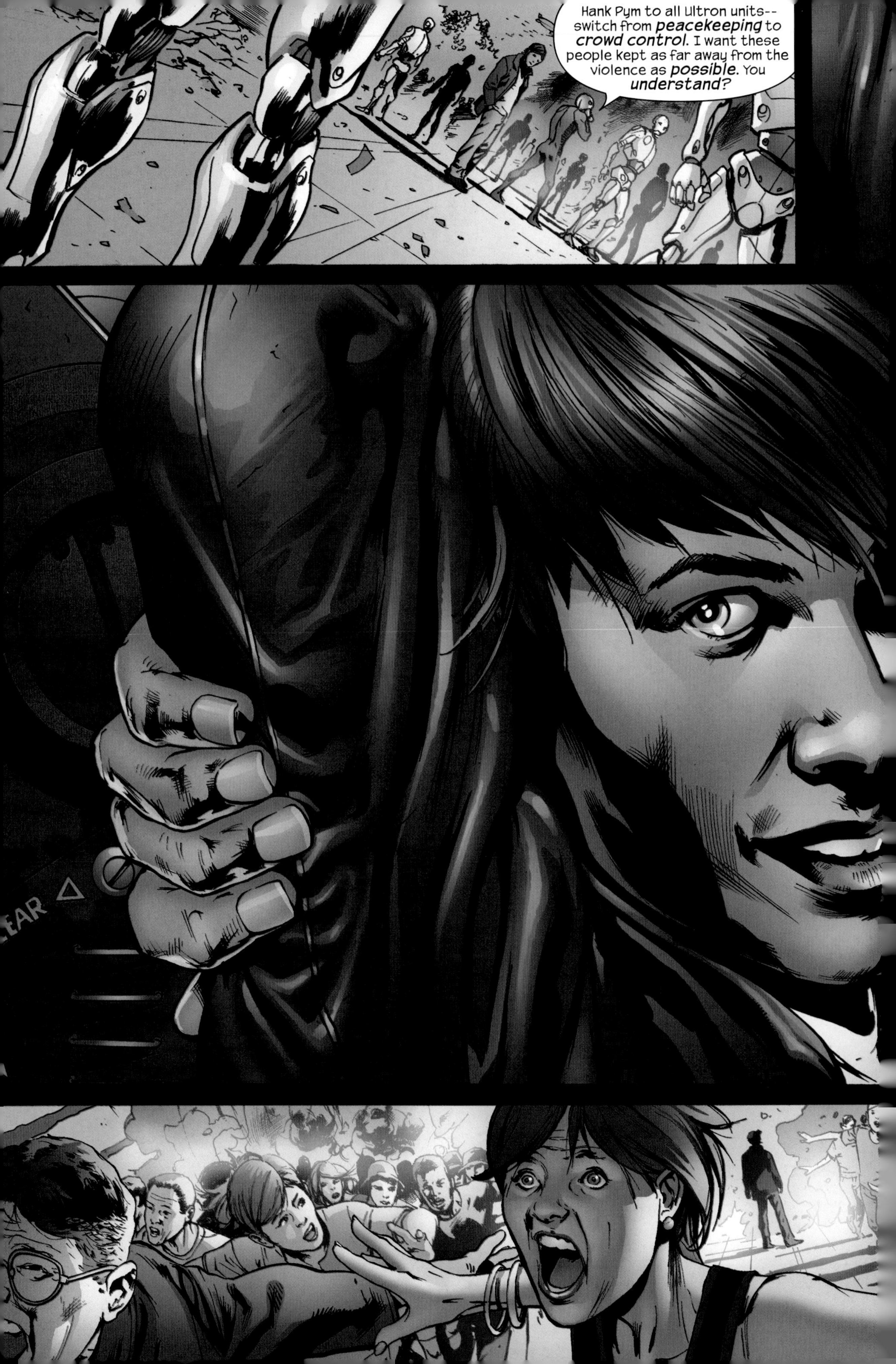
Hank Pym to all Ultron units--switch from *peacekeeping* to *crowd control*. I want these people kept as far away from the violence as *possible*. You *understand*?

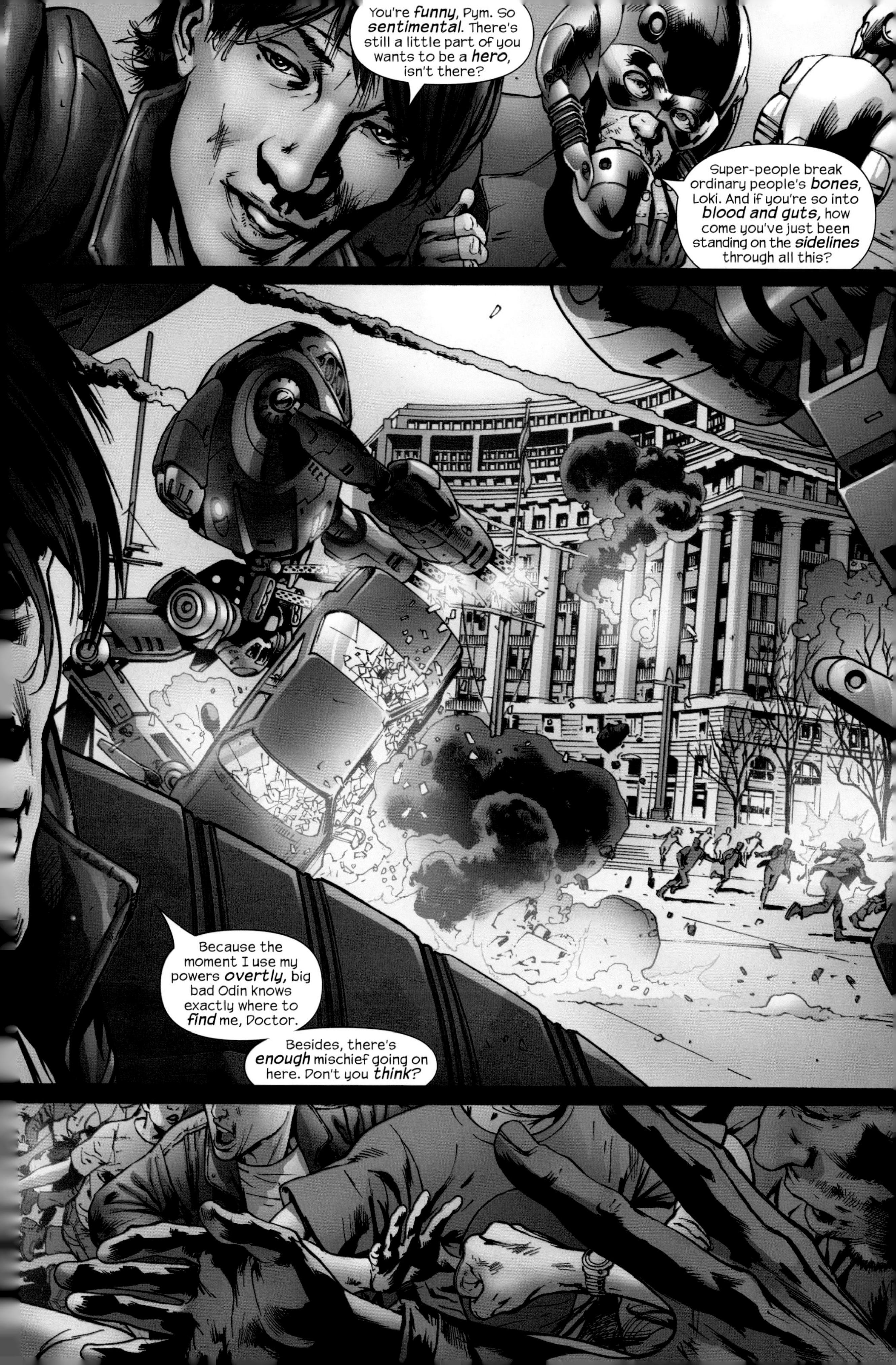
You're funny, Pym. So sentimental. There's still a little part of you wants to be a hero, isn't there?
Super-people break ordinary people's bones, Loki. And if you're so into blood and guts, how come you've just been standing on the sidelines through all this?
Because the moment I use my powers overtly, big bad Odin knows exactly where to find me, Doctor.
Besides, there's enough mischief going on here. Don't you think?

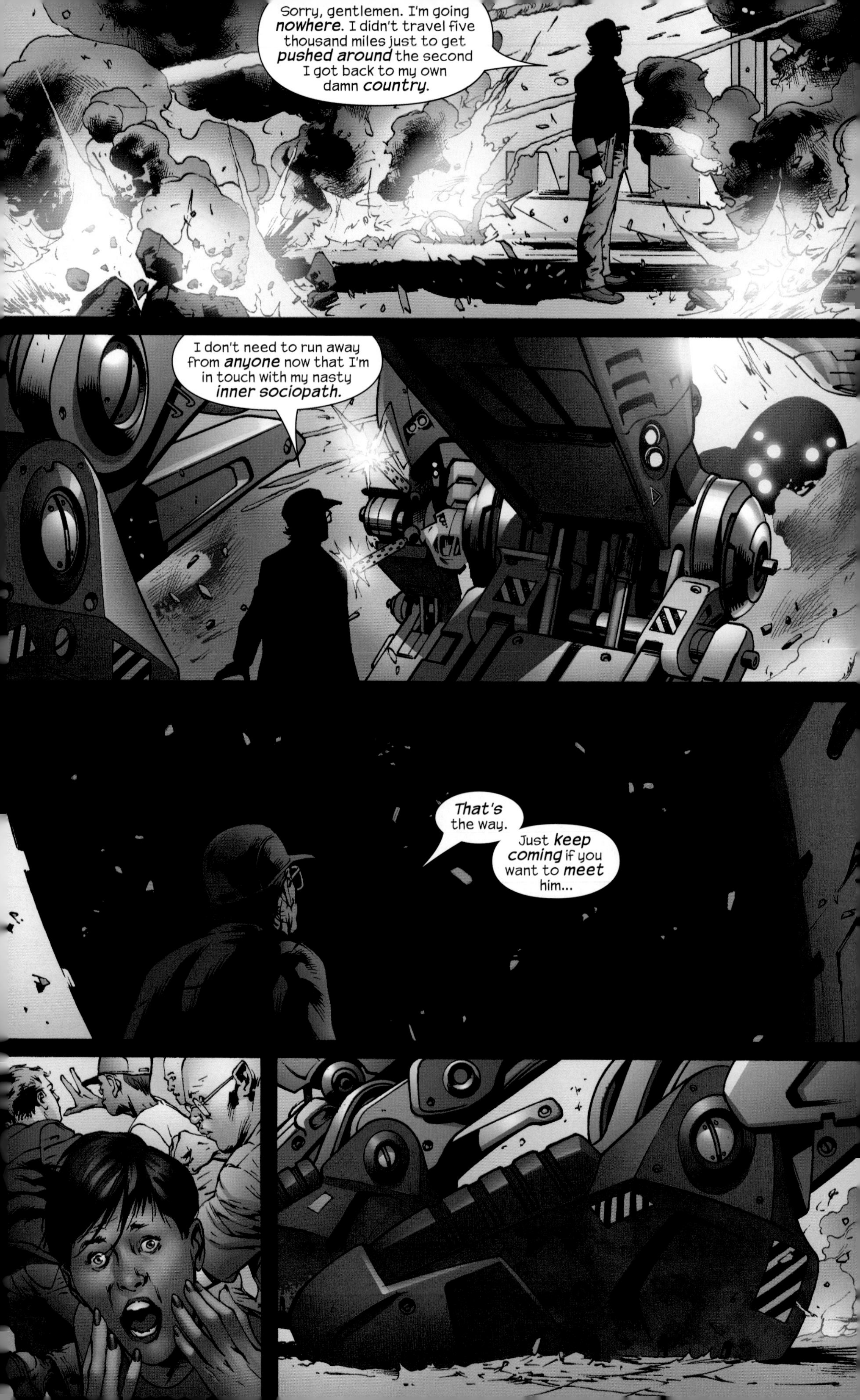
Sorry, gentlemen. I'm going nowhere. I didn't travel five thousand miles just to get pushed around the second I got back to my own damn country.
I don't need to run away from anyone now that I'm in touch with my nasty inner sociopath.
That's the way.
Just keep coming if you want to meet him...

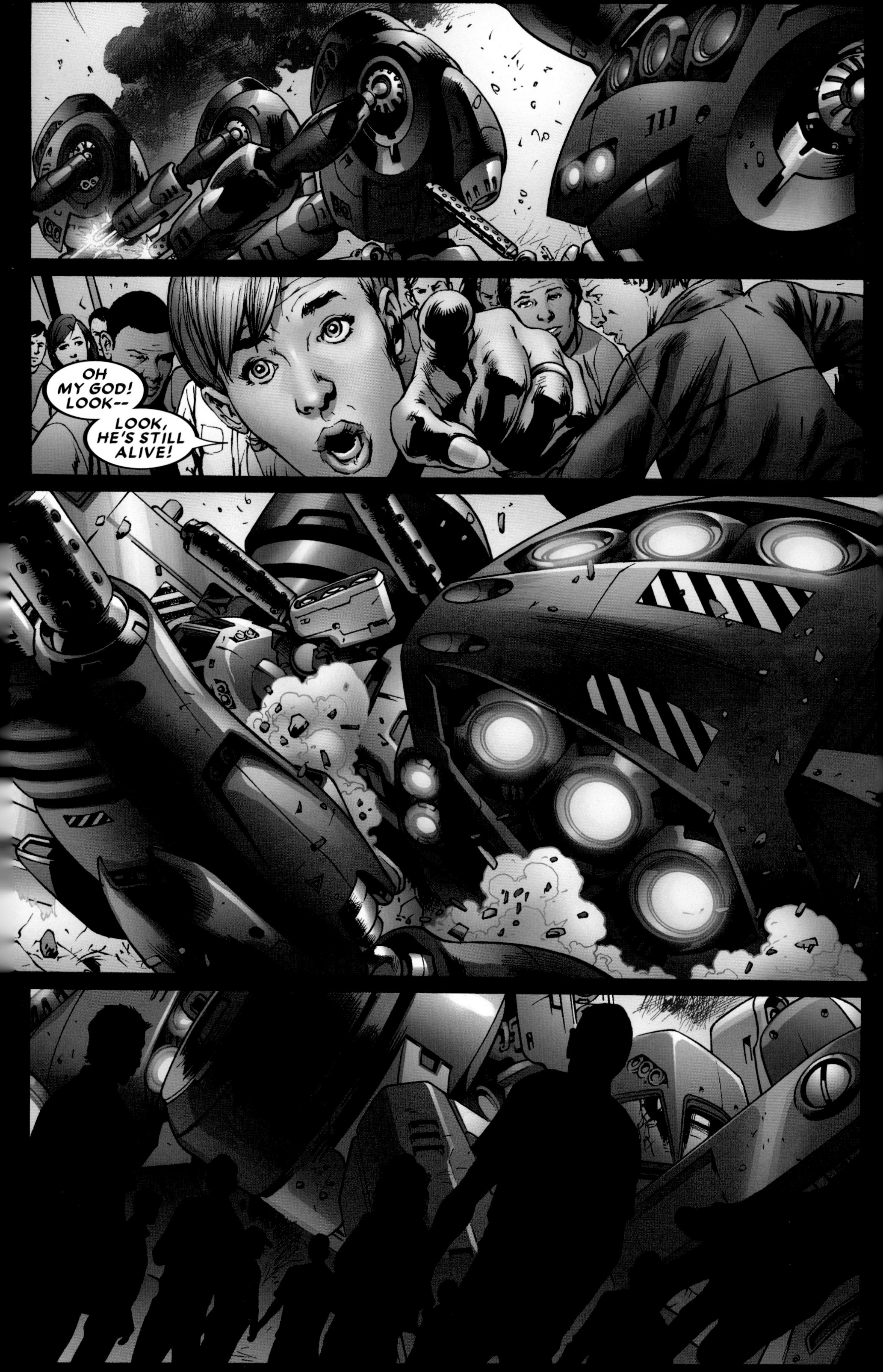
OH MY GOD! LOOK--
LOOK, HE'S STILL ALIVE!

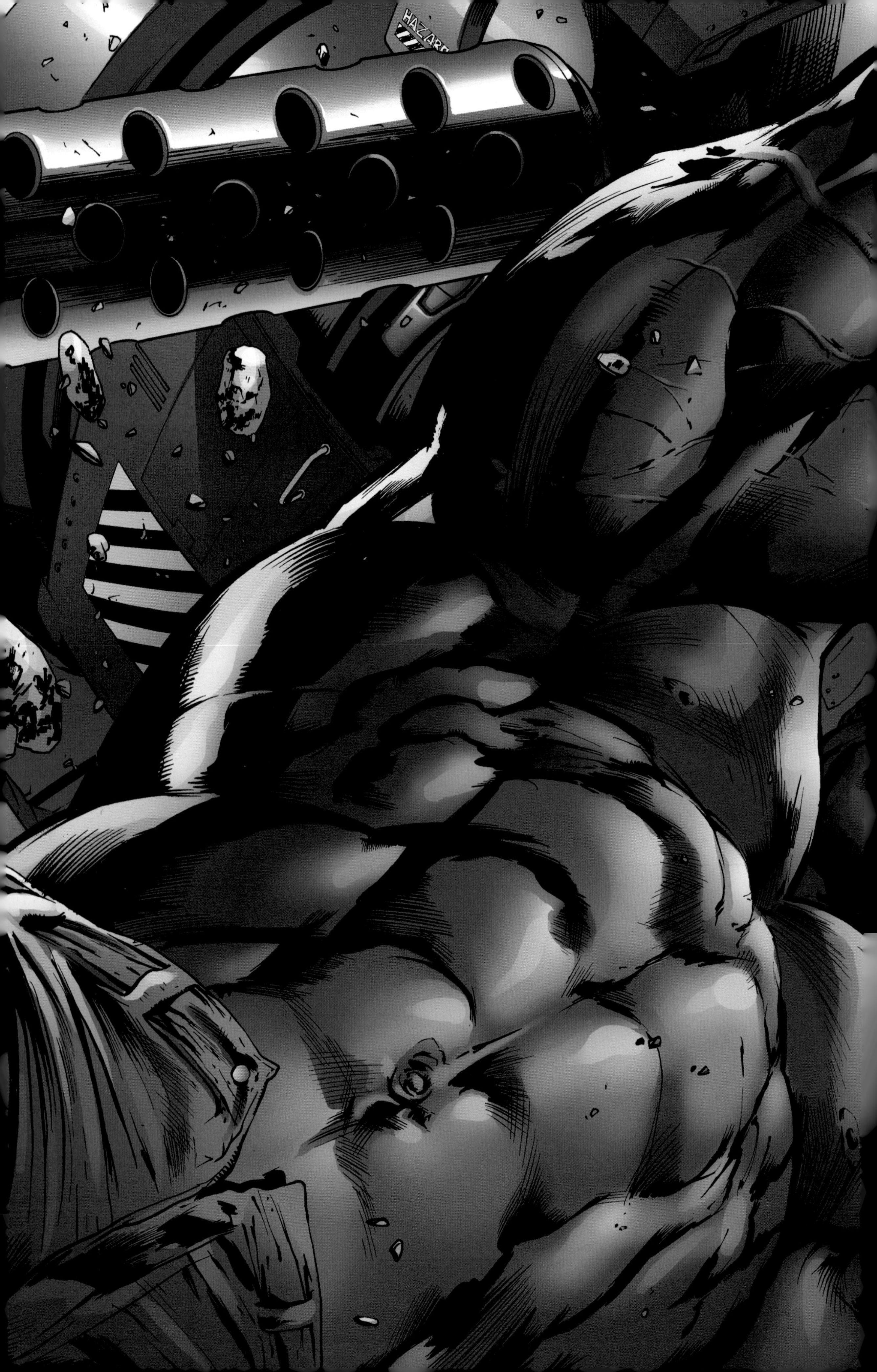

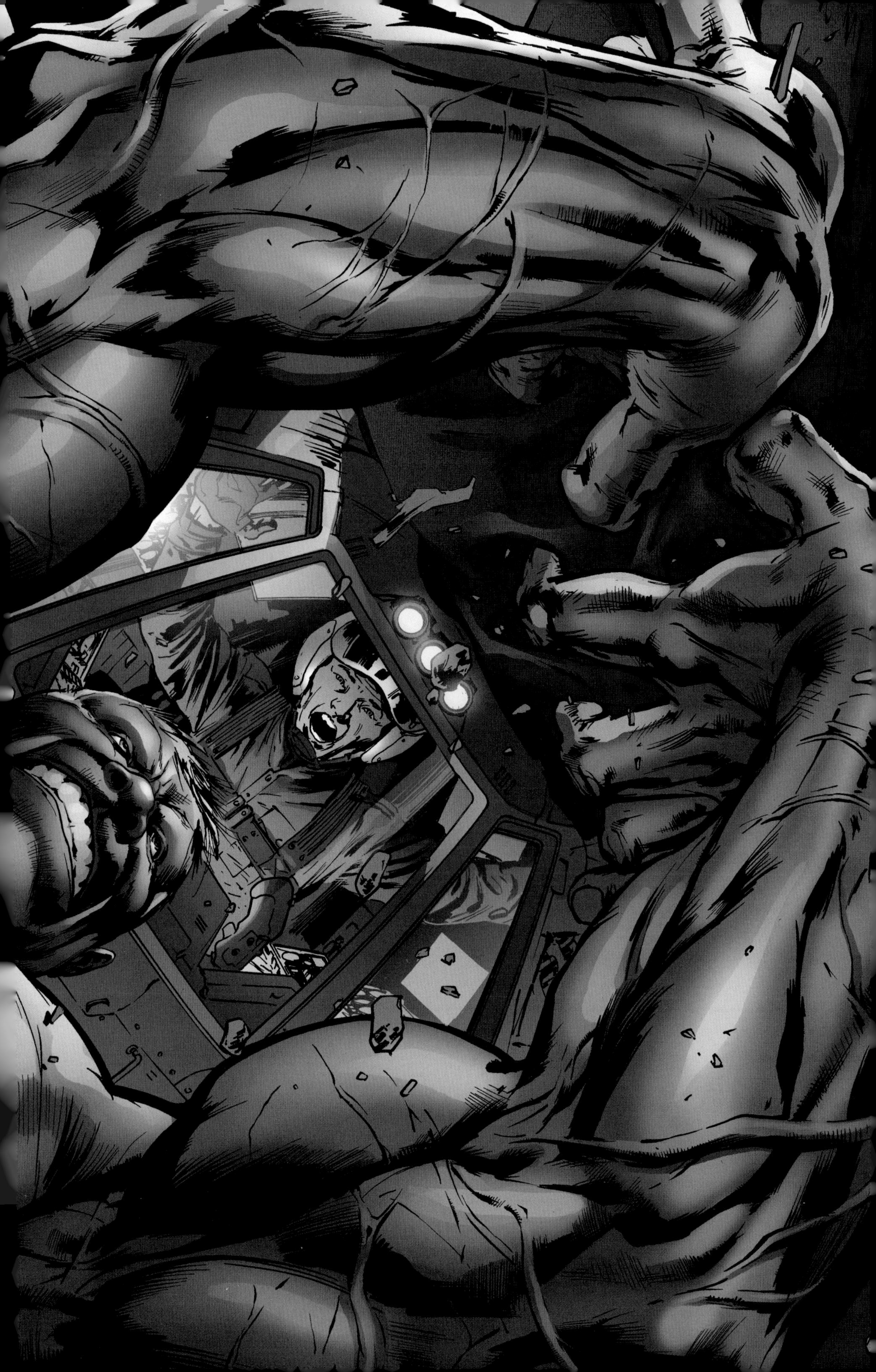

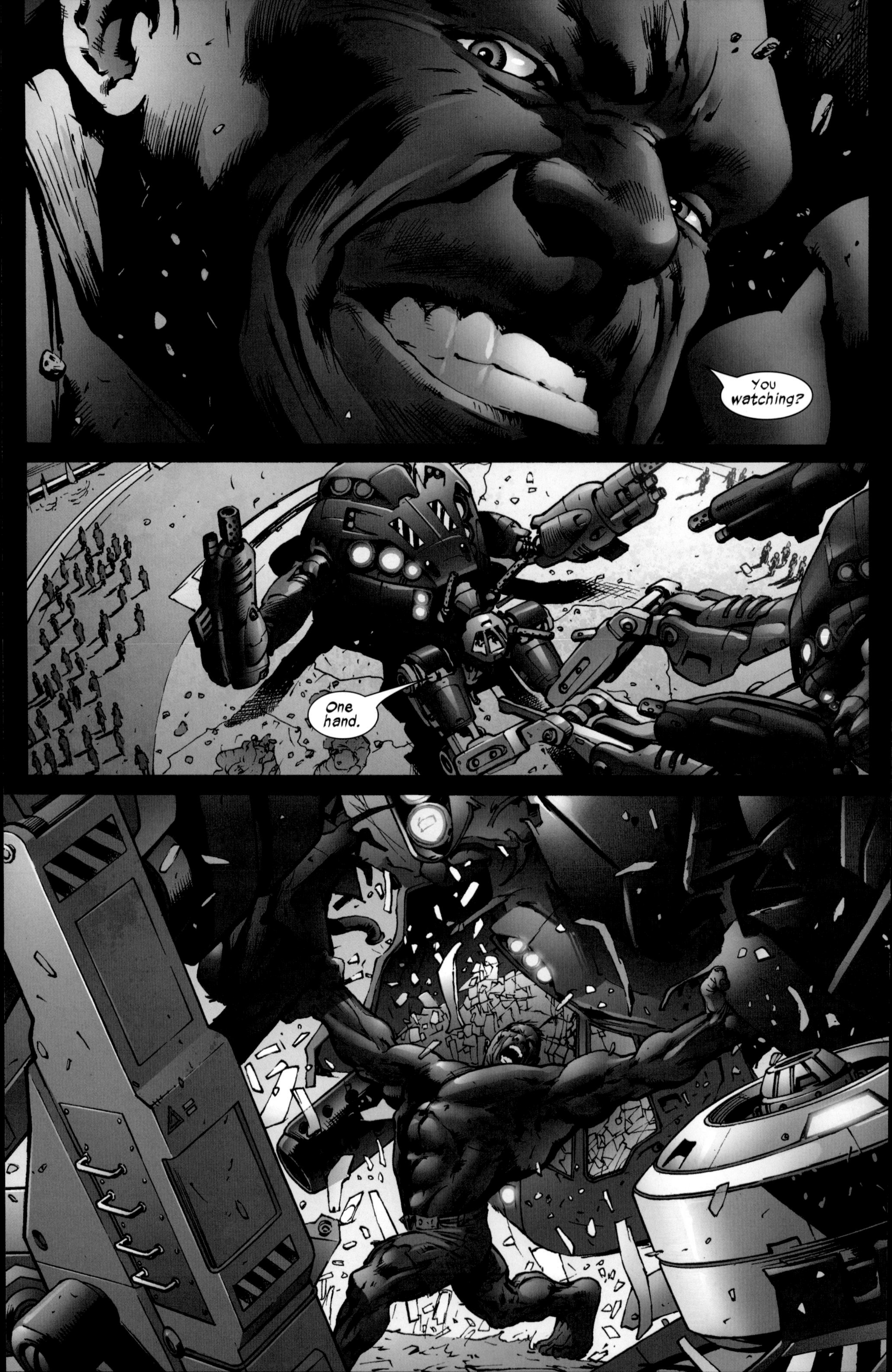
You watching?
One hand.

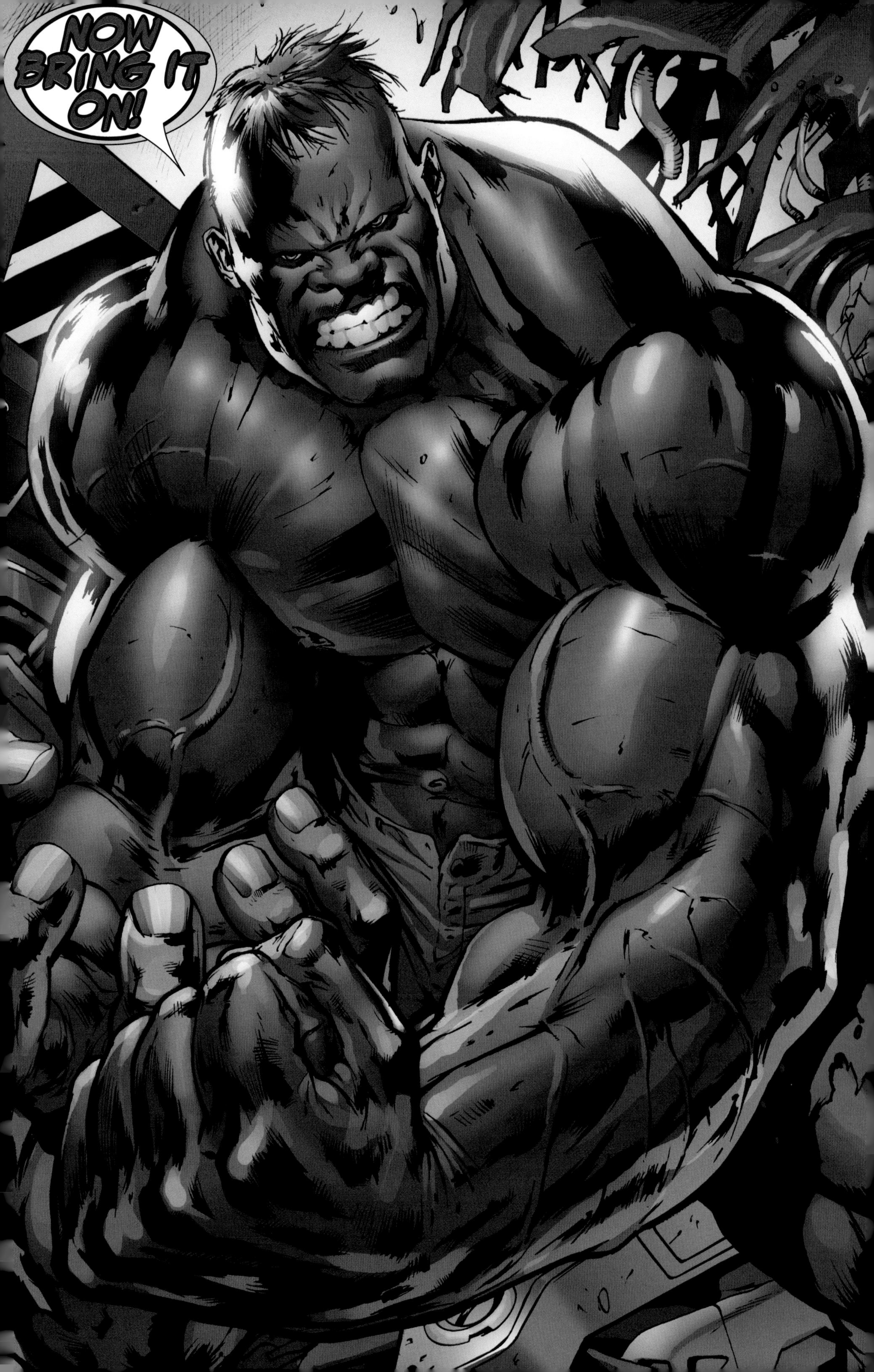
NOW BRING IT ON!

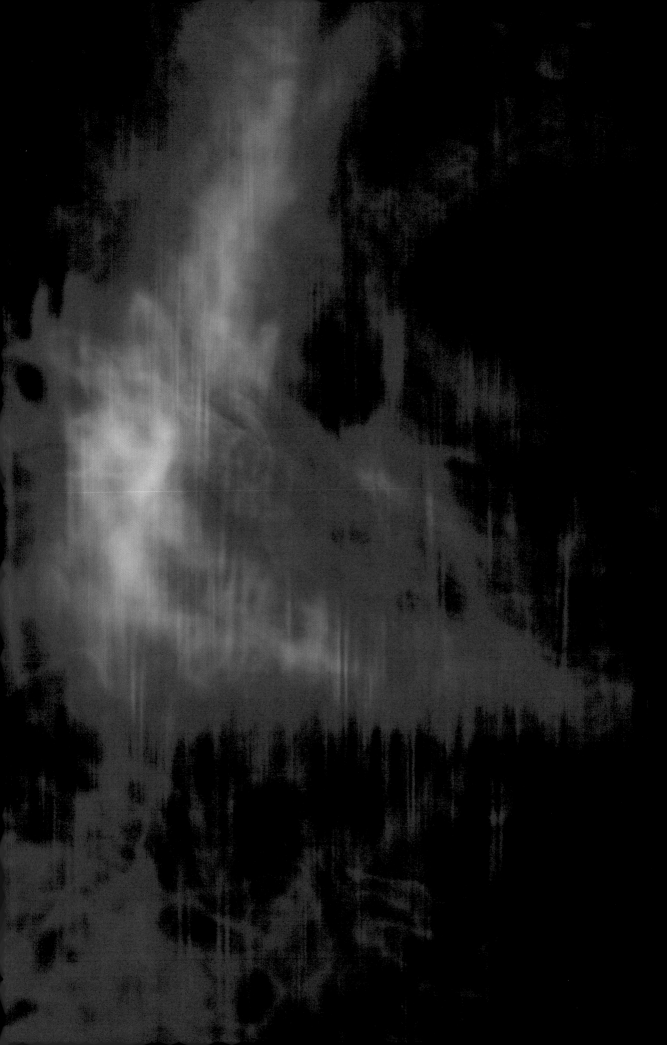

THE AVENGERS

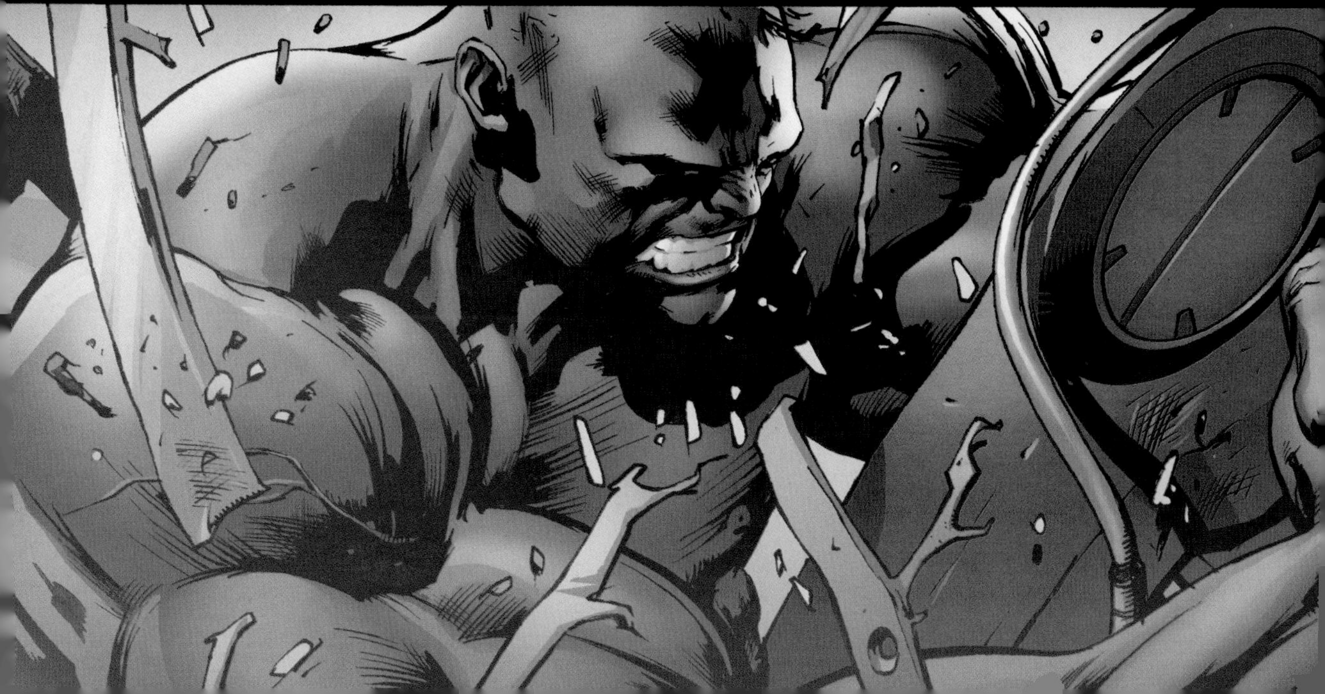

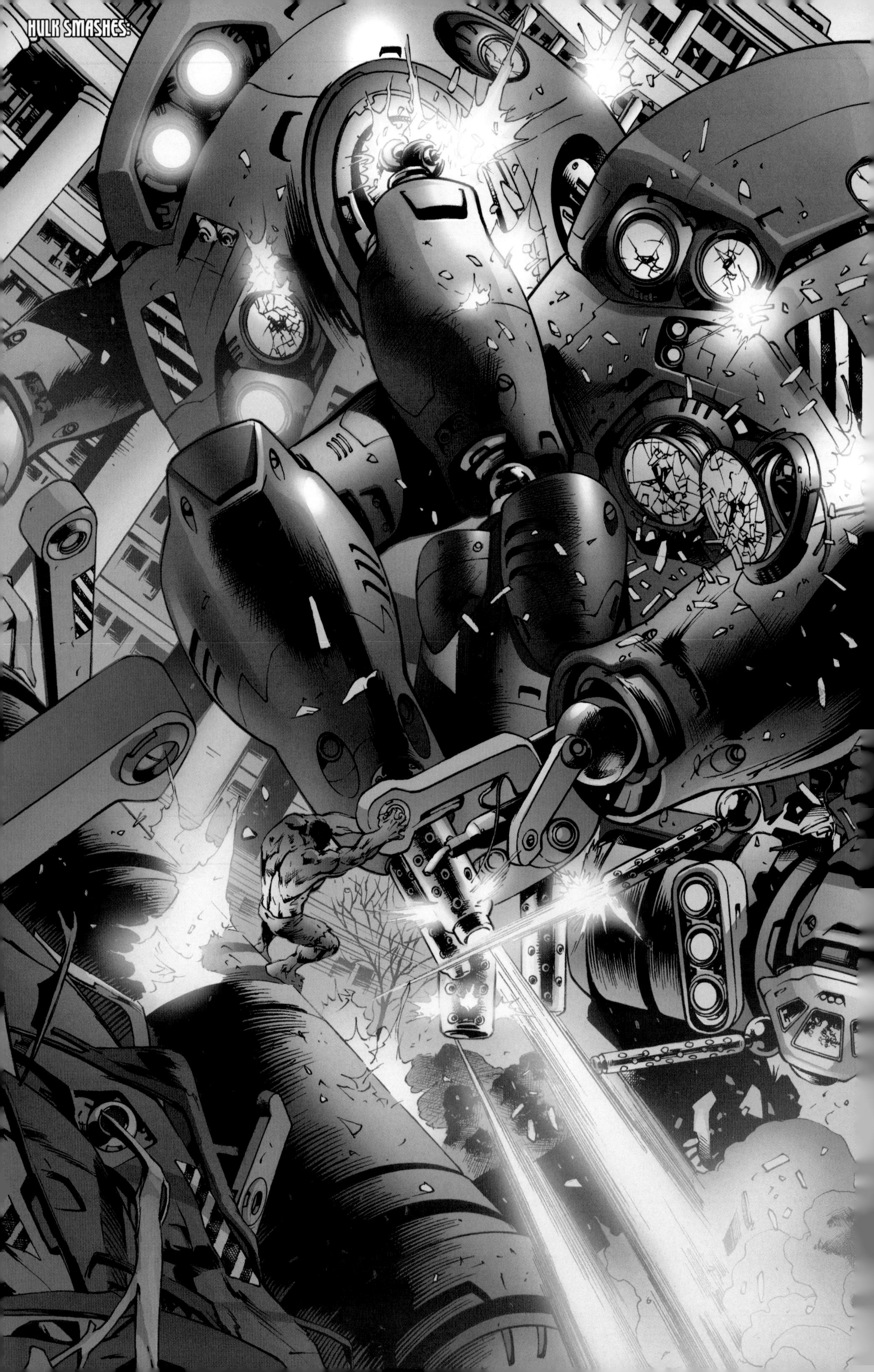
HULK SMASHES:

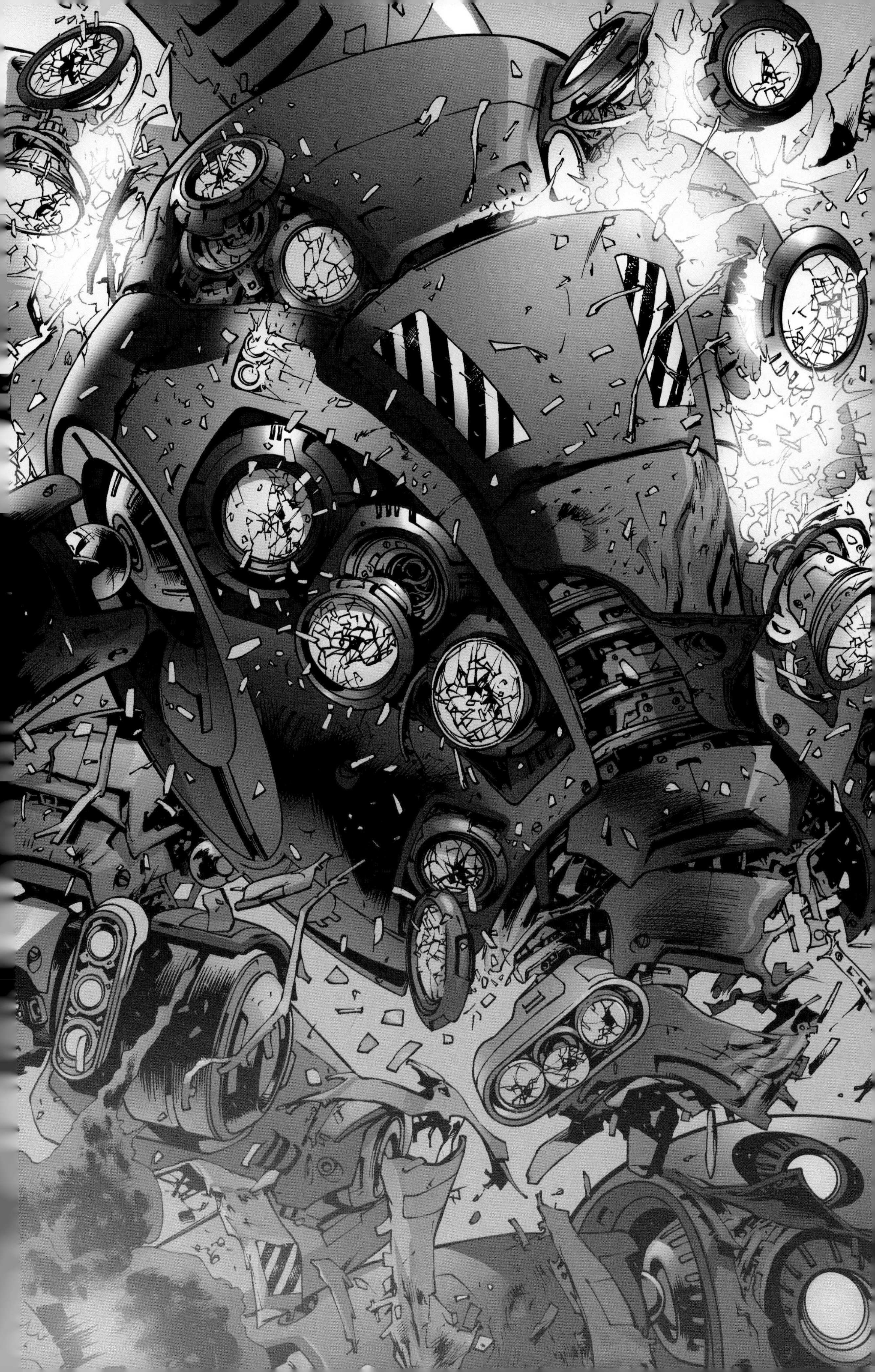

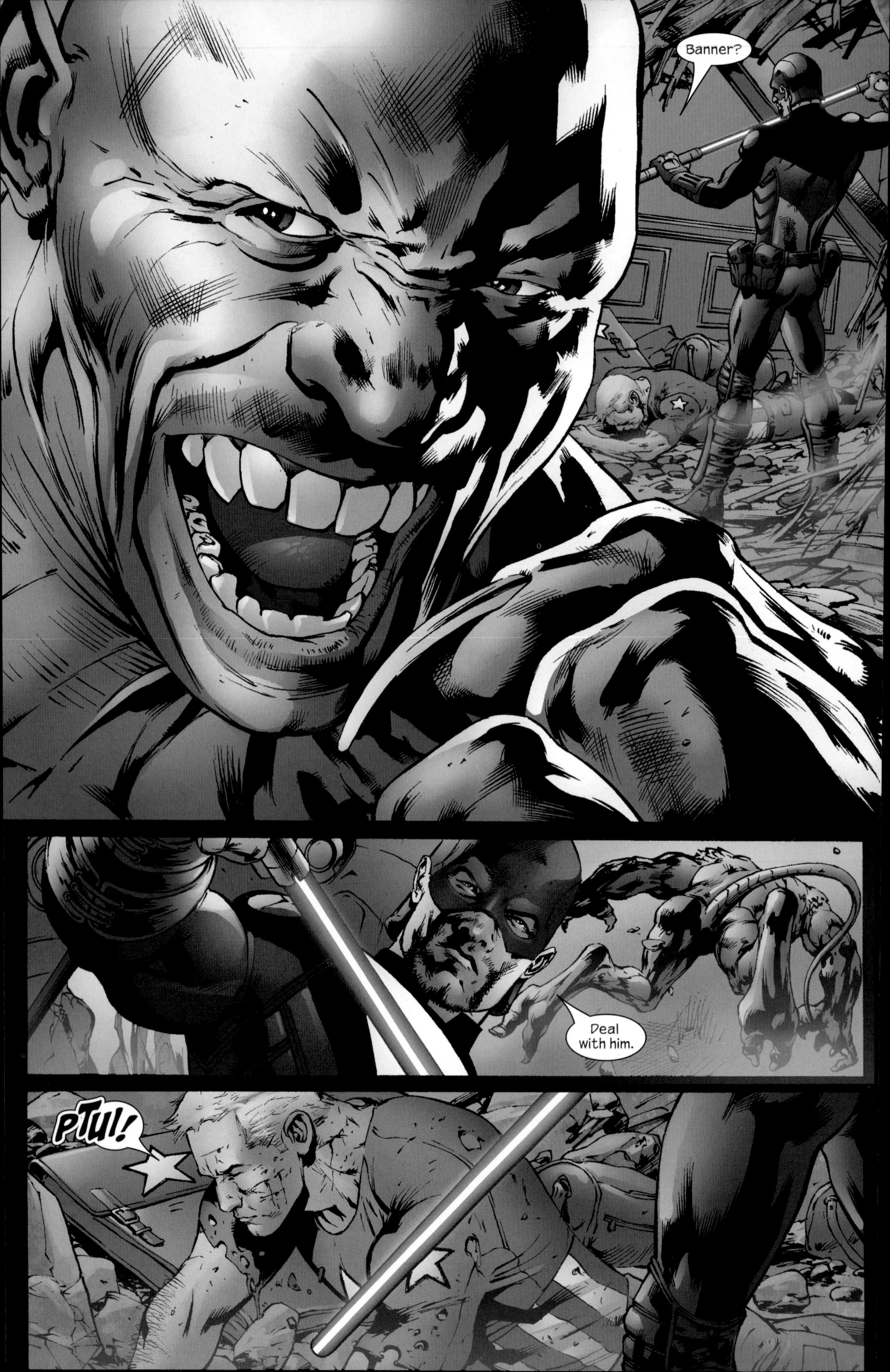
Banner?
Deal with him.
PTUI!

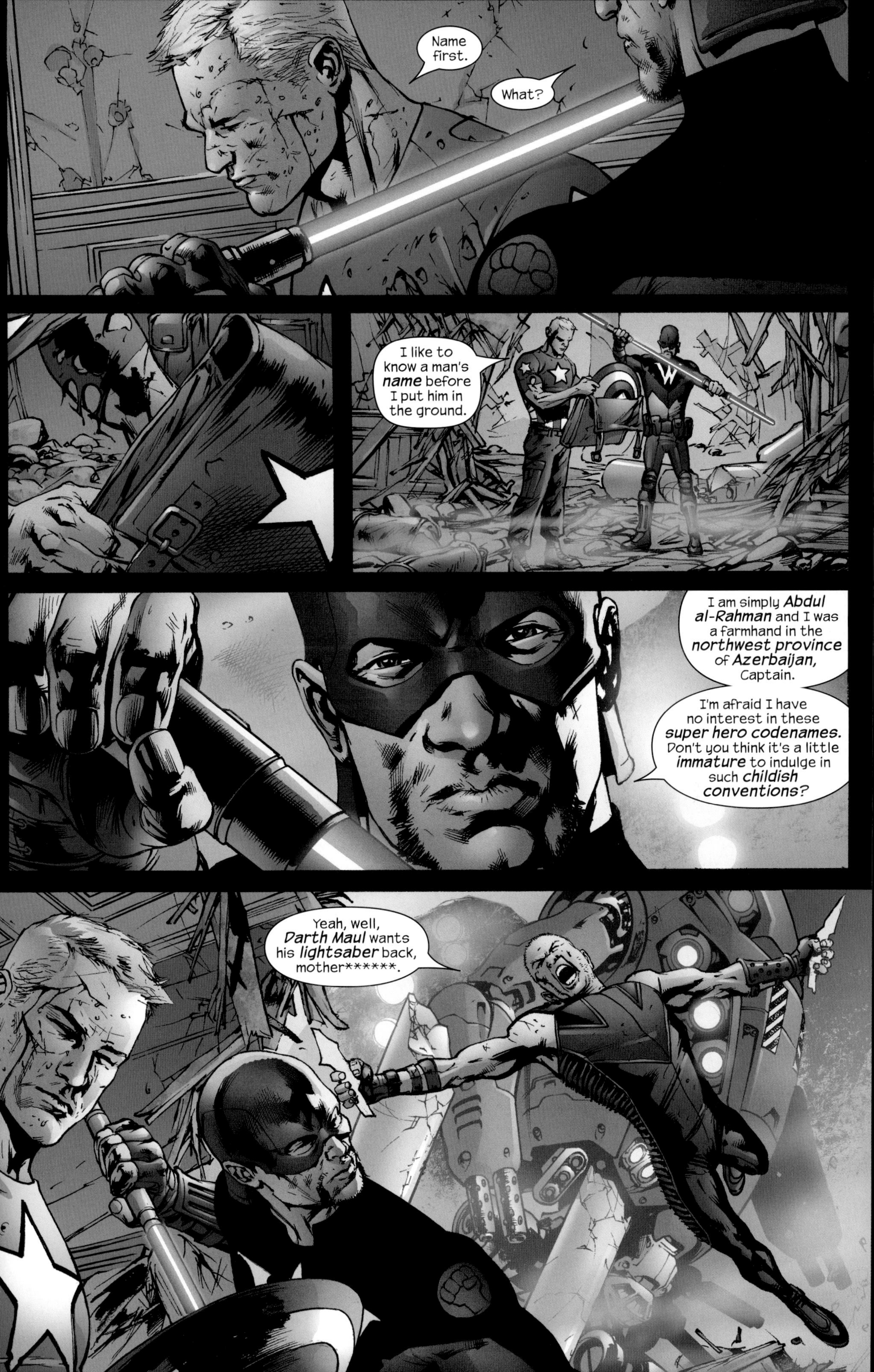
Name first.
What?
I like to know a man's *name* before I put him in the ground.
I am simply *Abdul al-Rahman* and I was a farmhand in the *northwest province* of *Azerbaijan,* Captain.
I'm afraid I have no interest in these *super hero codenames.* Don't you think it's a little *immature* to indulge in such *childish conventions?*
Yeah, well, *Darth Maul* wants his *lightsaber* back, mother******.

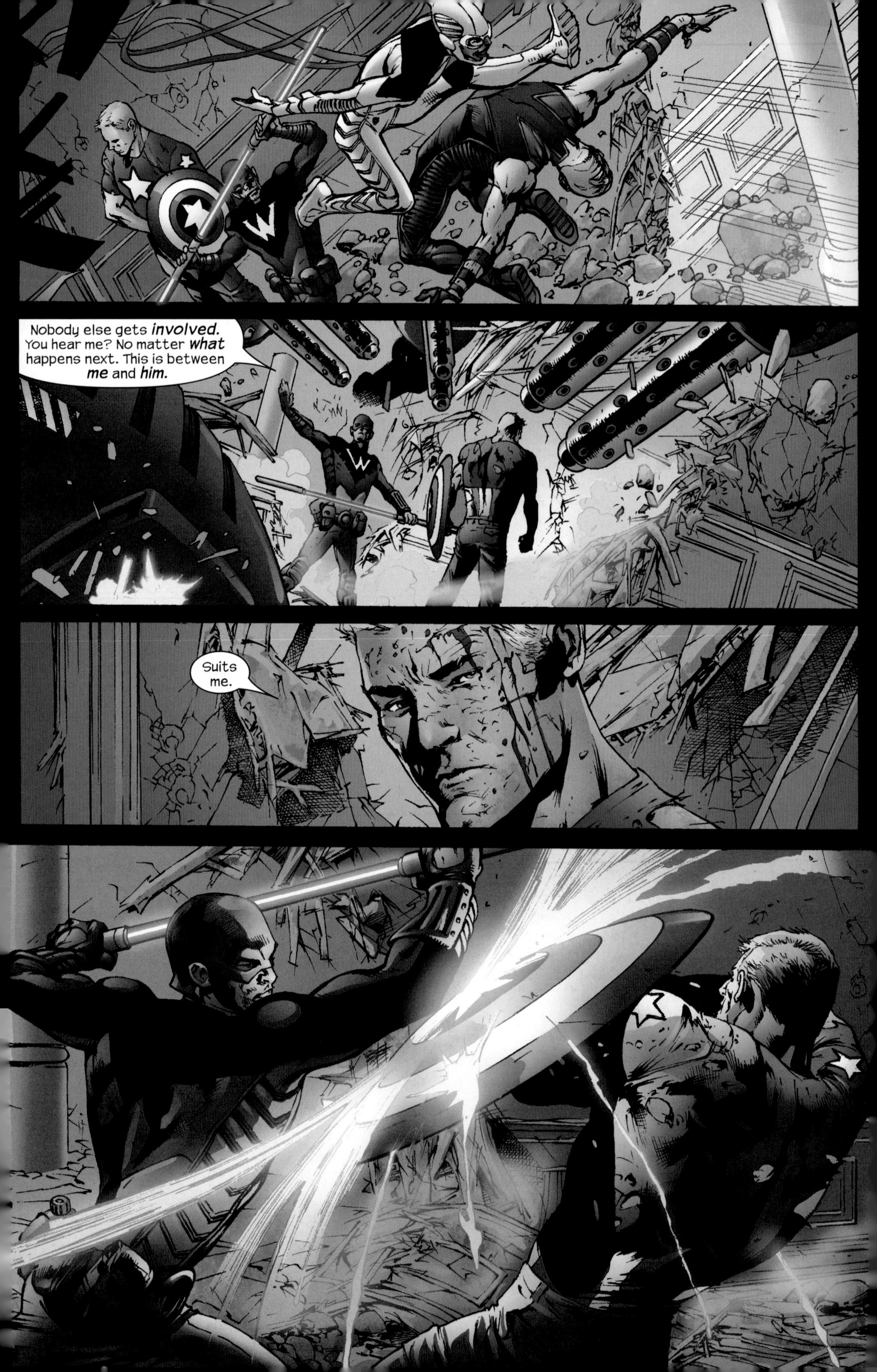

Nobody else gets *involved.* You hear me? No matter *what* happens next. This is between *me* and *him.*
Suits me.

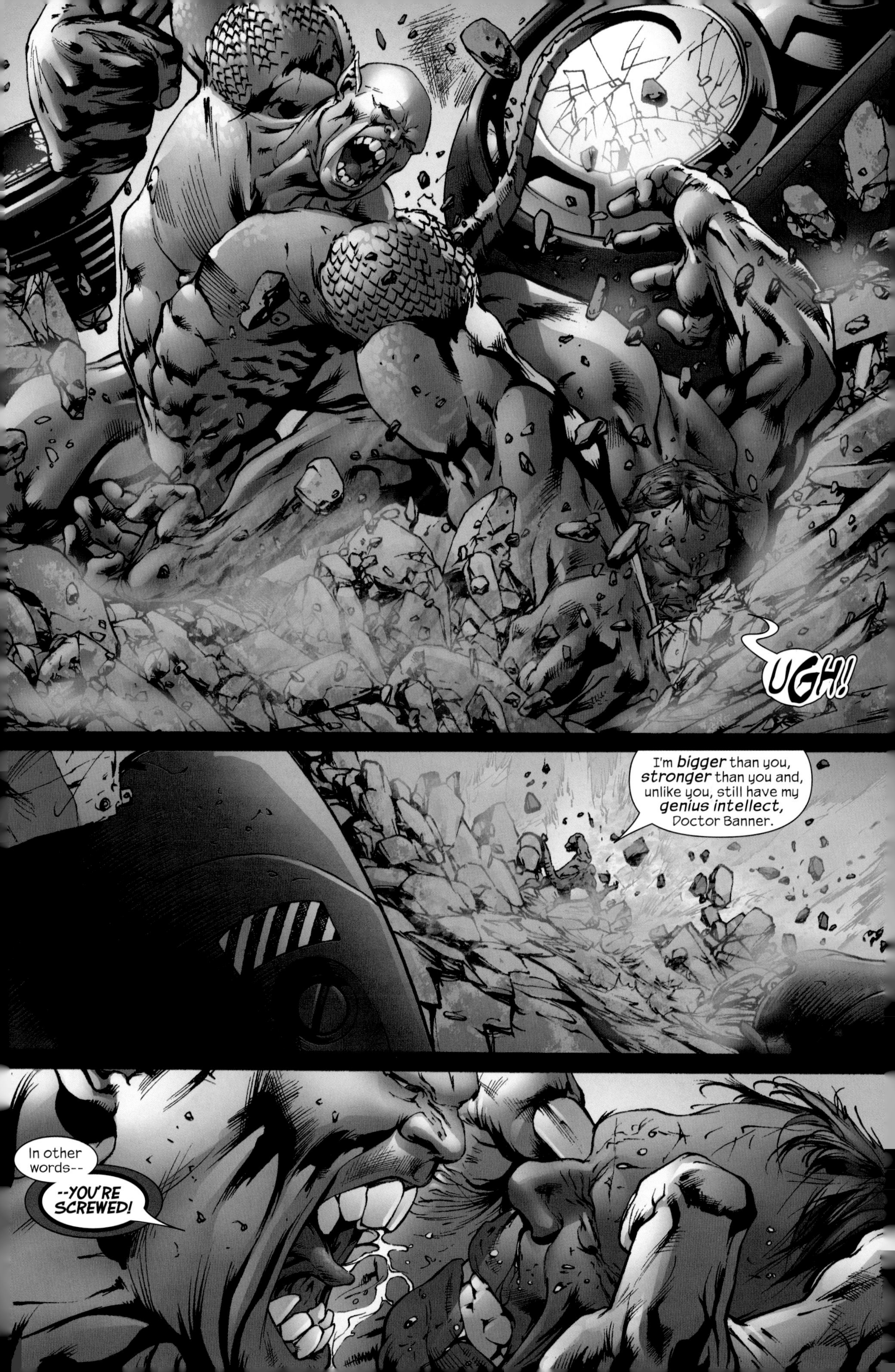
UGH!
I'm bigger than you, stronger than you and, unlike you, still have my genius intellect, Doctor Banner.
In other words--
--YOU'RE SCREWED!

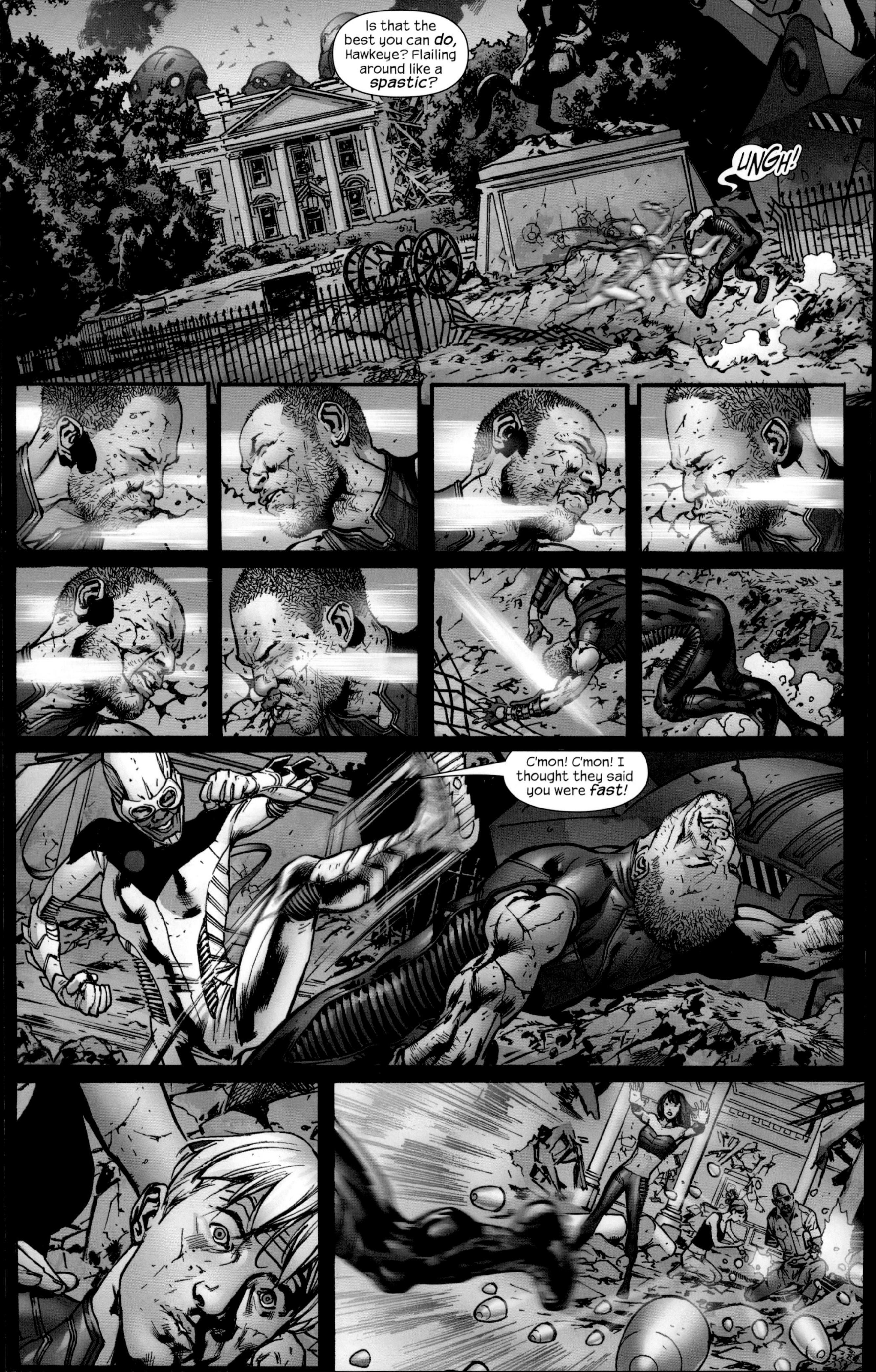

Is that the best you can *do,* Hawkeye? Flailing around like a *spastic?*
UNGH!
C'mon! C'mon! I thought they said you were *fast!*

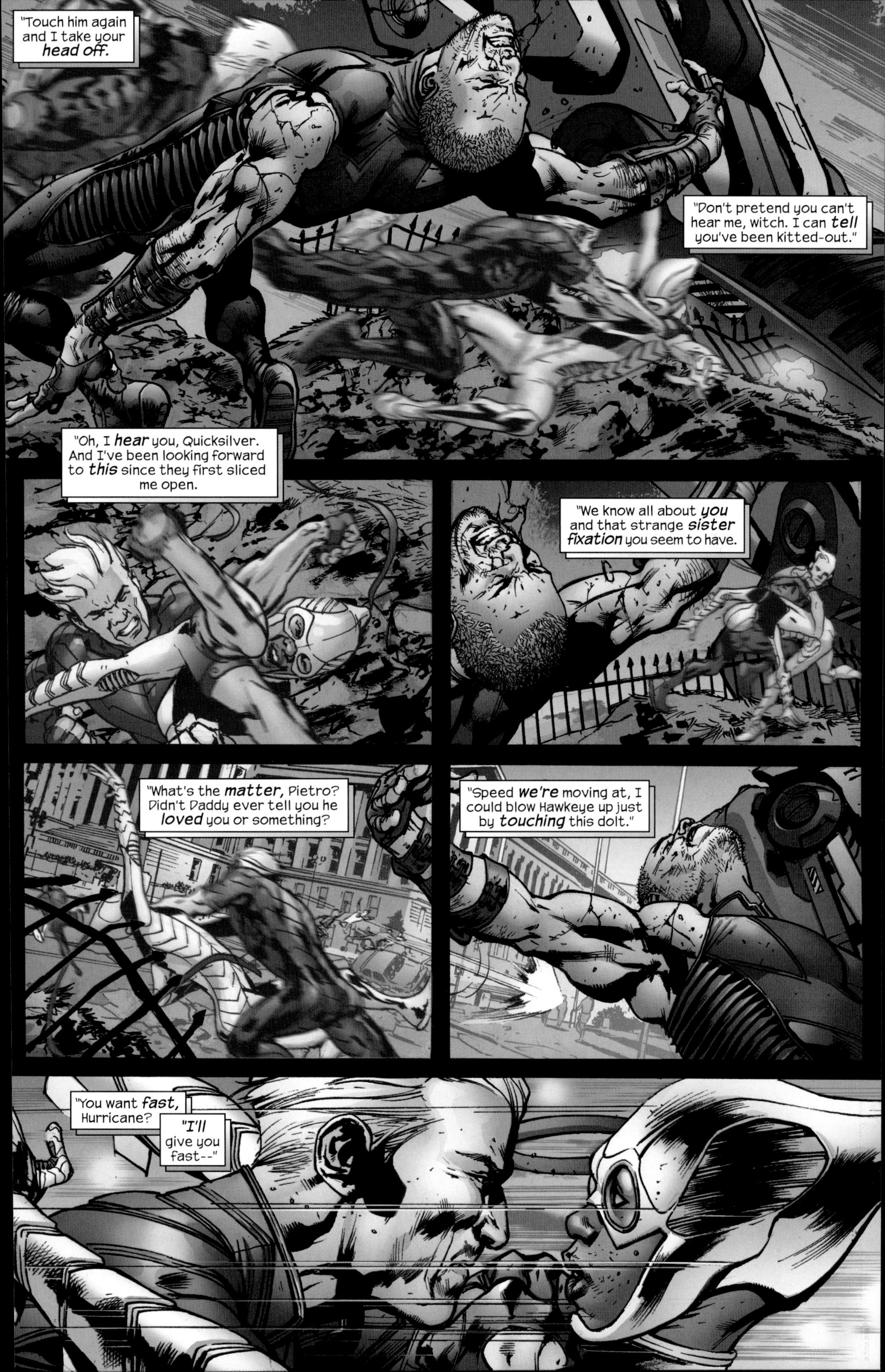
"Touch him again and I take your head off.
"Don't pretend you can't hear me, witch. I can tell you've been kitted-out."
"Oh, I hear you, Quicksilver. And I've been looking forward to this since they first sliced me open.
"We know all about you and that strange sister fixation you seem to have.
"What's the matter, Pietro? Didn't Daddy ever tell you he loved you or something?
"Speed we're moving at, I could blow Hawkeye up just by touching this dolt."
"You want fast, Hurricane?
"I'll give you fast--"

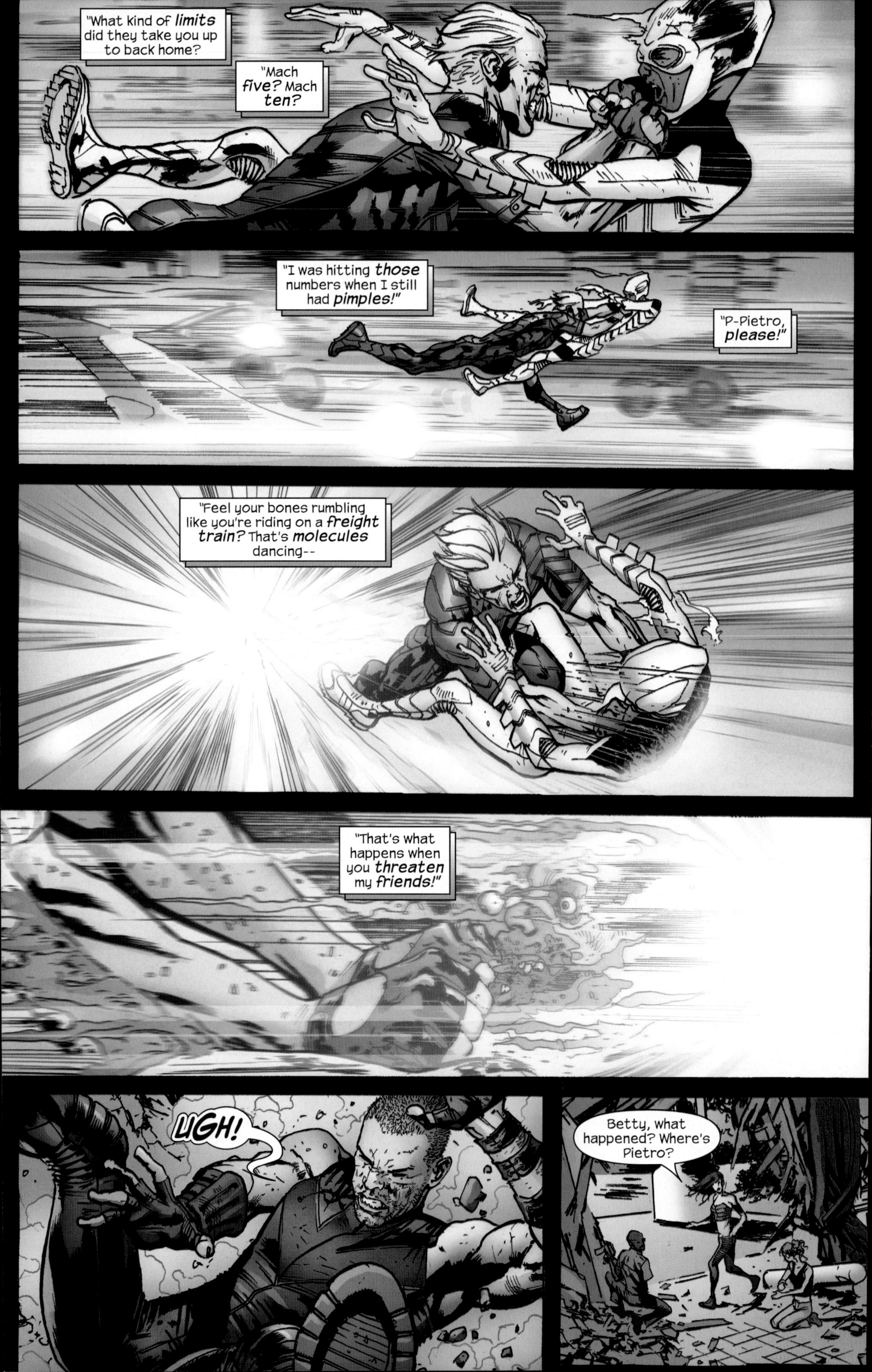
"What kind of limits did they take you up to back home?
"Mach five? Mach ten?
"I was hitting those numbers when I still had pimples!"
"P-Pietro, please!"
"Feel your bones rumbling like you're riding on a freight train? That's molecules dancing--
"That's what happens when you threaten my friends!"
UGH!
Betty, what happened? Where's Pietro?

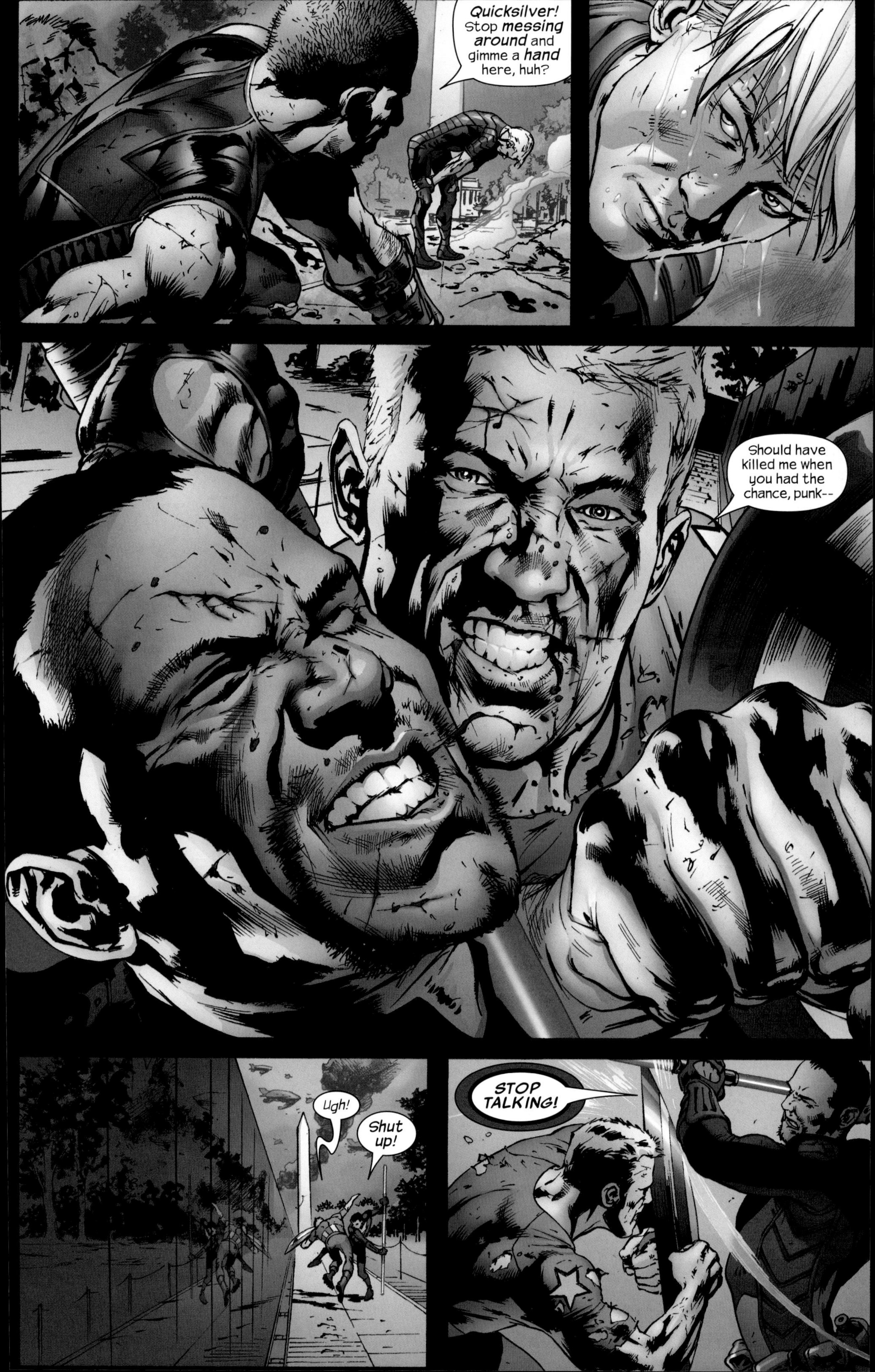
Quicksilver! Stop messing around and gimme a hand here, huh?
Should have killed me when you had the chance, punk--
Ugh!
Shut up!
STOP TALKING!

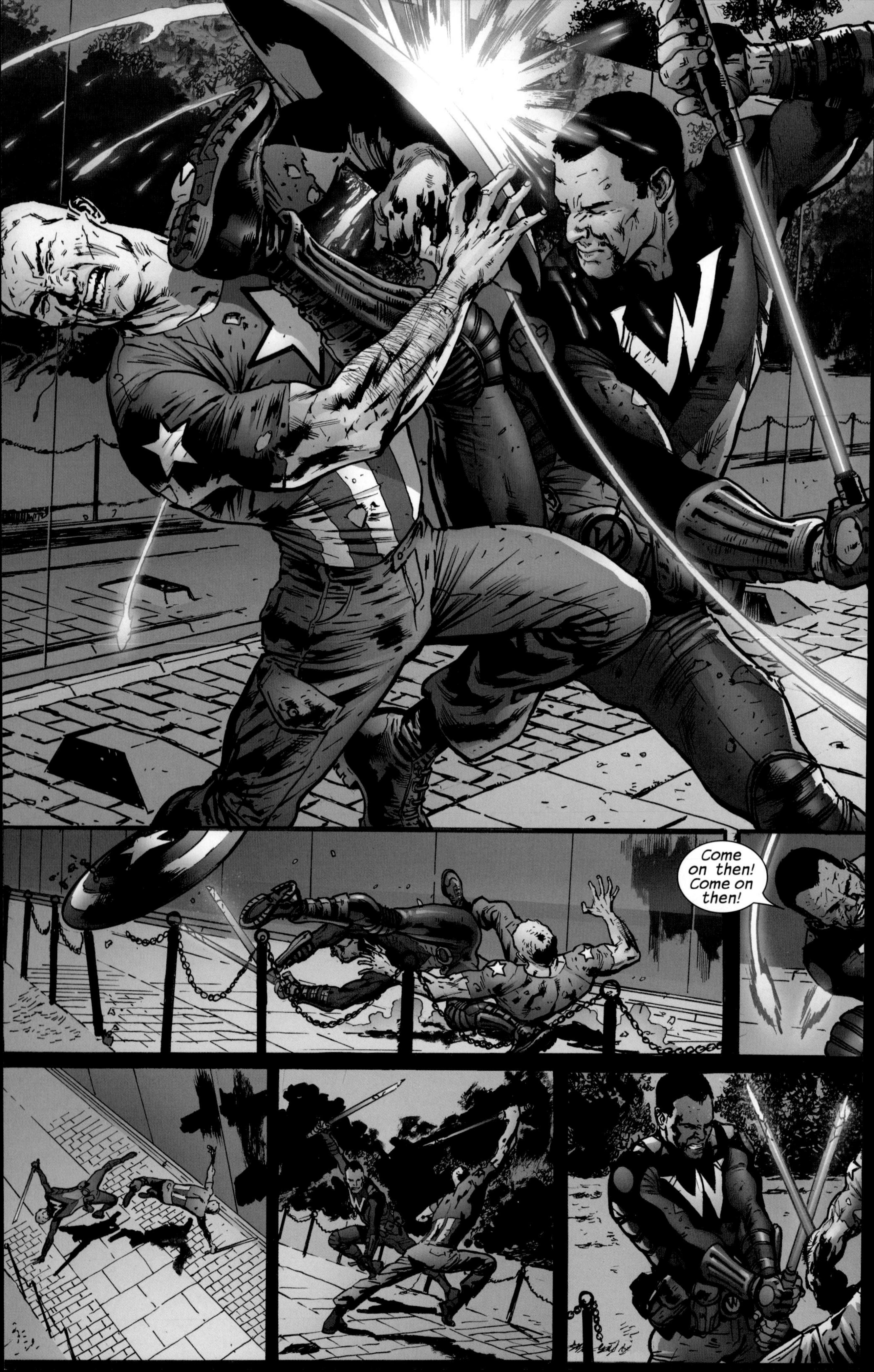
Come on then! Come on then!

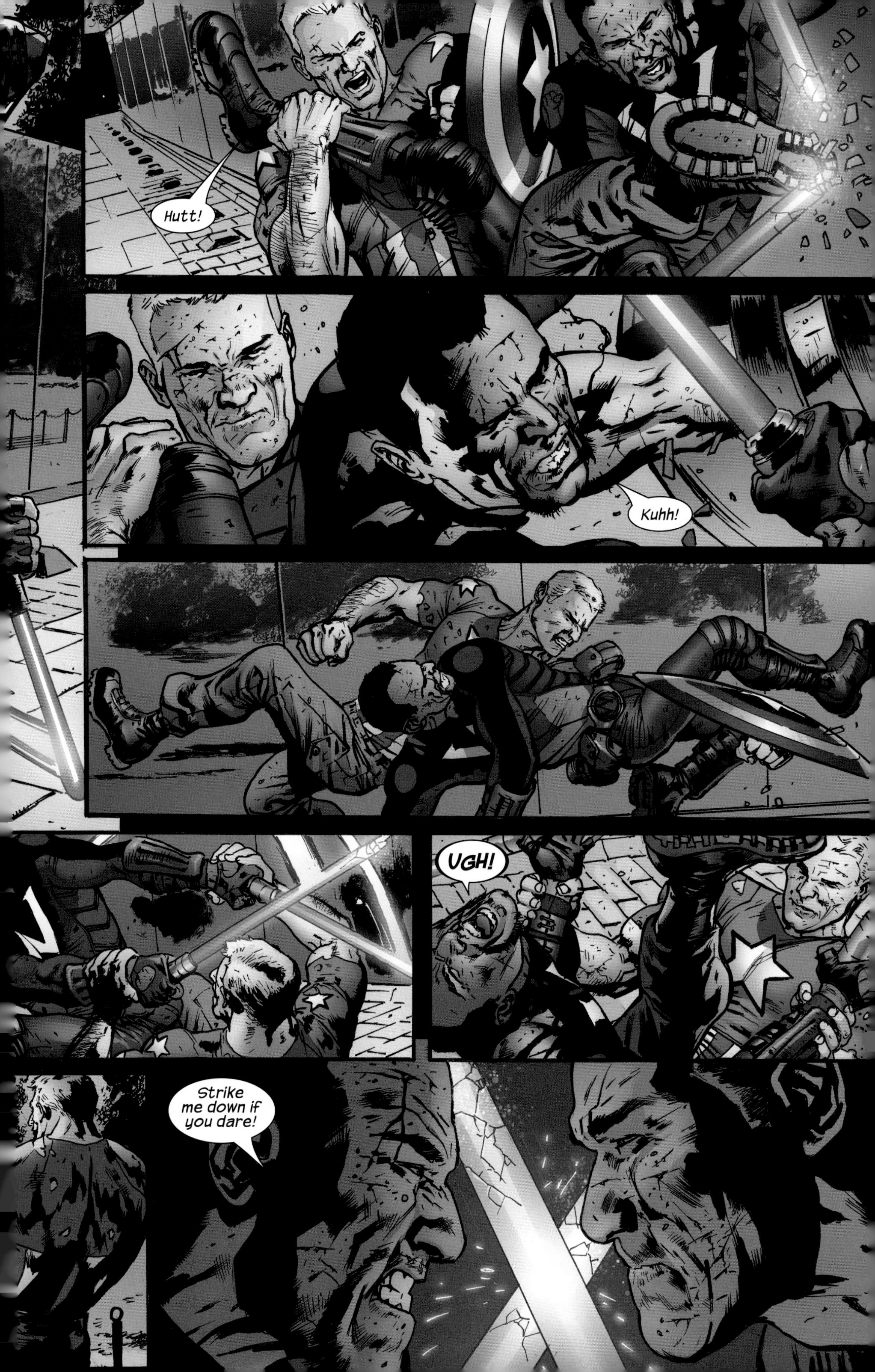
Hutt!
Kuhh!
UGH!
Strike me down if you dare!

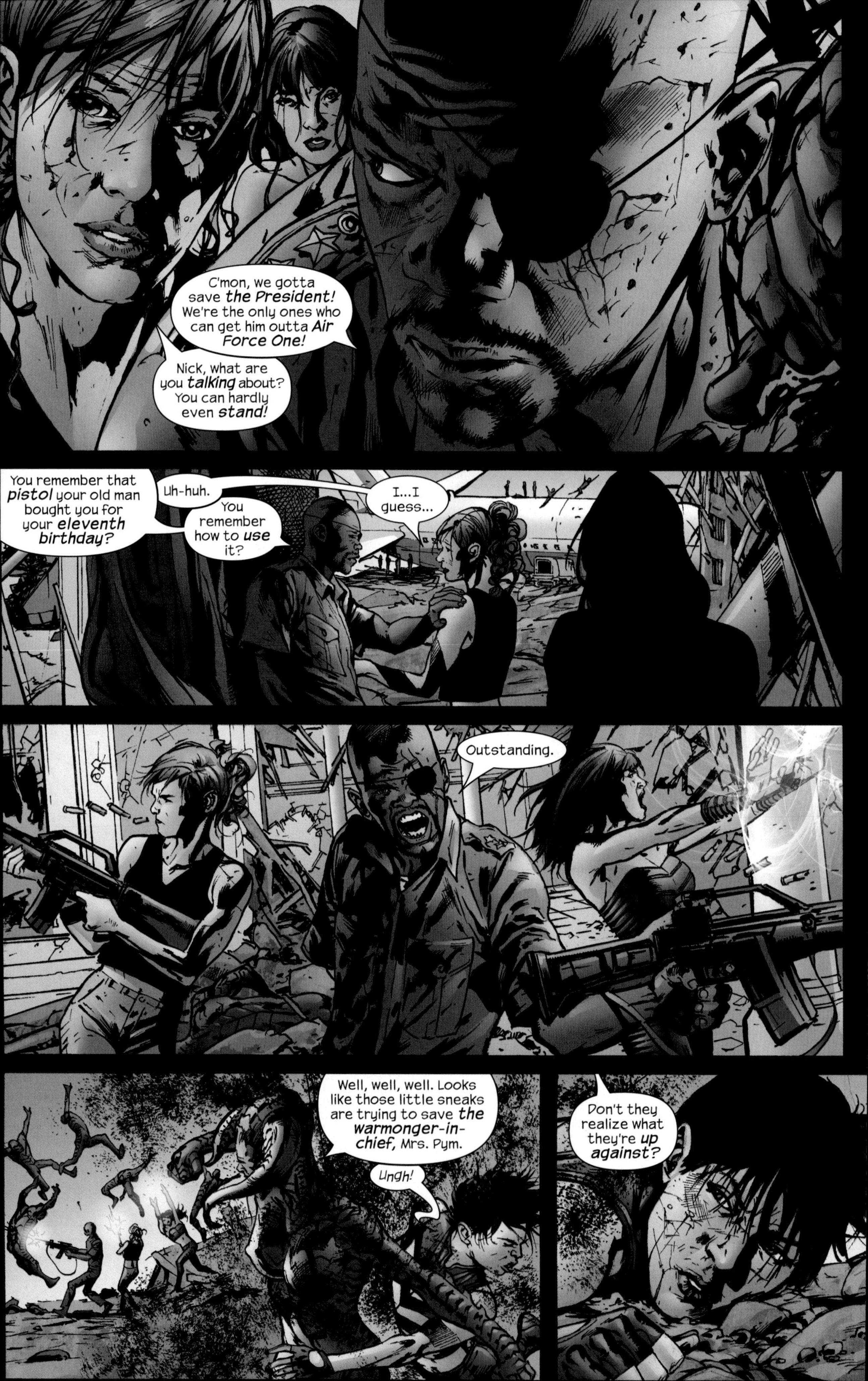
C'mon, we gotta save the President! We're the only ones who can get him outta Air Force One!
Nick, what are you talking about? You can hardly even stand!
You remember that pistol your old man bought you for your eleventh birthday?
Uh-huh.
You remember how to use it?
I...I guess...
Outstanding.
Well, well, well. Looks like those little sneaks are trying to save the warmonger-in-chief, Mrs. Pym.
Ungh!
Don't they realize what they're up against?

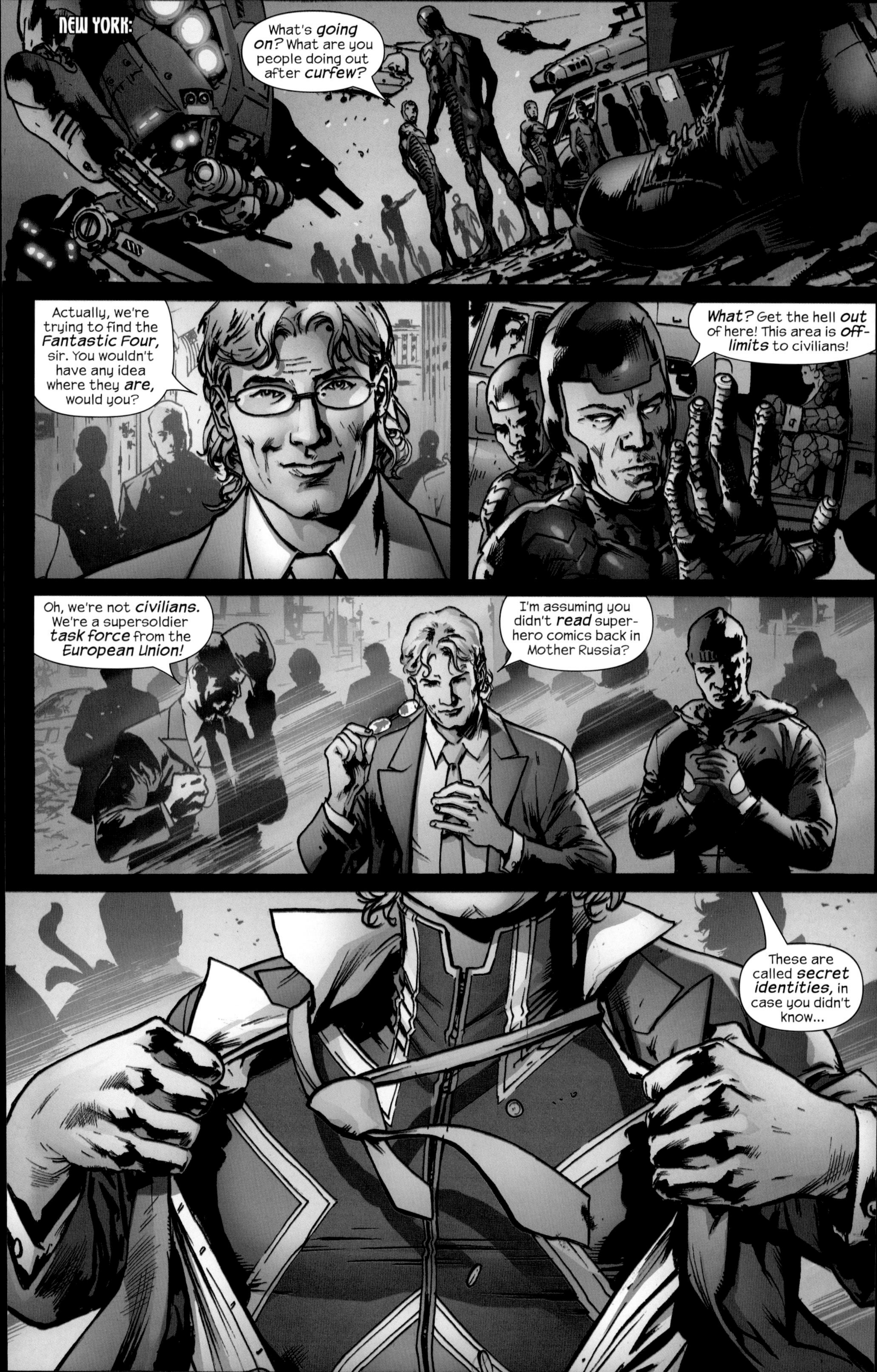
NEW YORK:
What's going on? What are you people doing out after curfew?
Actually, we're trying to find the Fantastic Four, sir. You wouldn't have any idea where they are, would you?
What? Get the hell out of here! This area is off-limits to civilians!
Oh, we're not civilians. We're a supersoldier task force from the European Union!
I'm assuming you didn't read super-hero comics back in Mother Russia?
These are called secret identities, in case you didn't know...

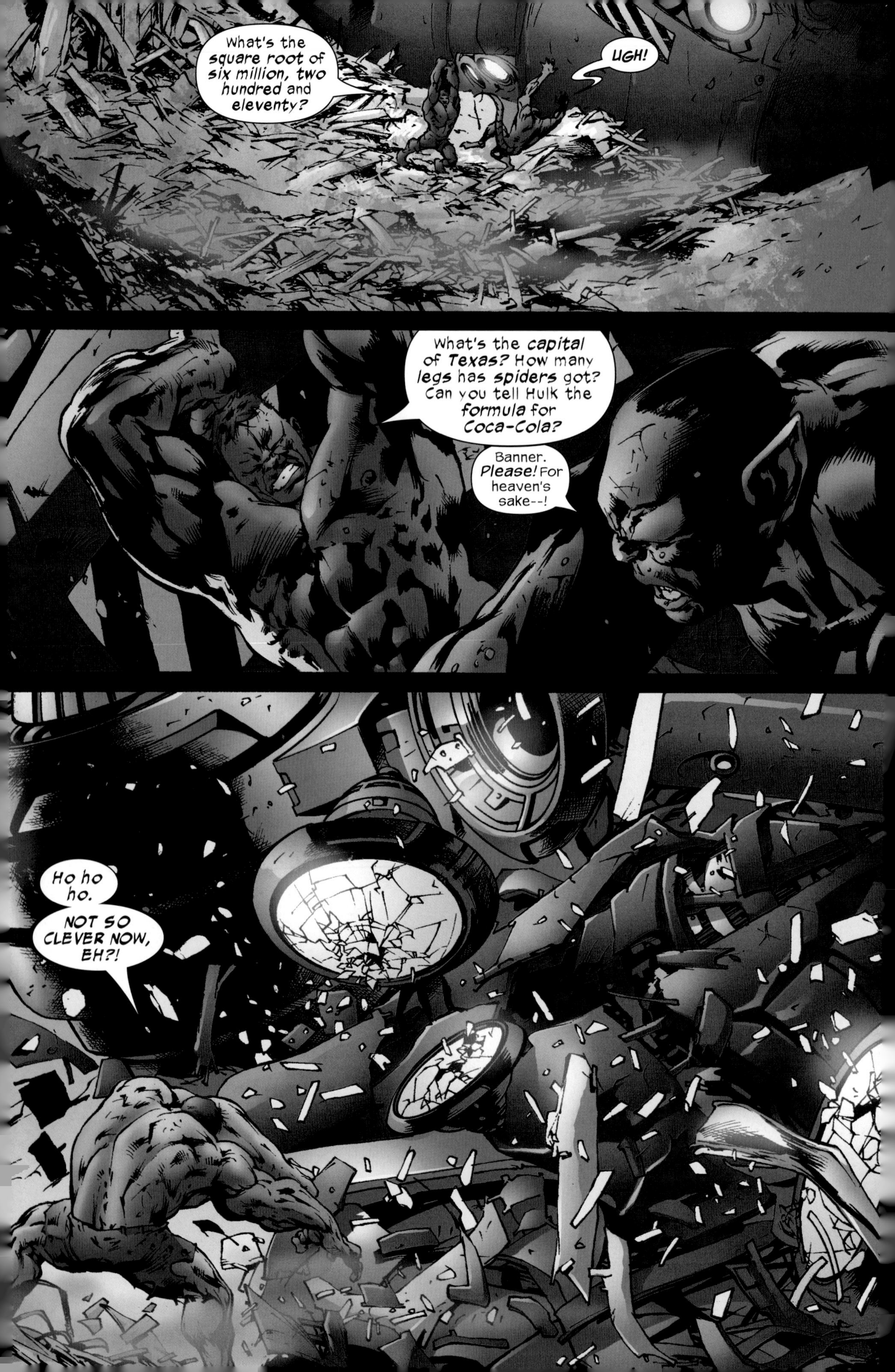
What's the square root of six million, two hundred and eleventy?
UGH!
What's the capital of Texas? How many legs has spiders got? Can you tell Hulk the formula for Coca-Cola?
Banner. Please! For heaven's sake--!
Ho ho ho.
NOT SO CLEVER NOW, EH?!

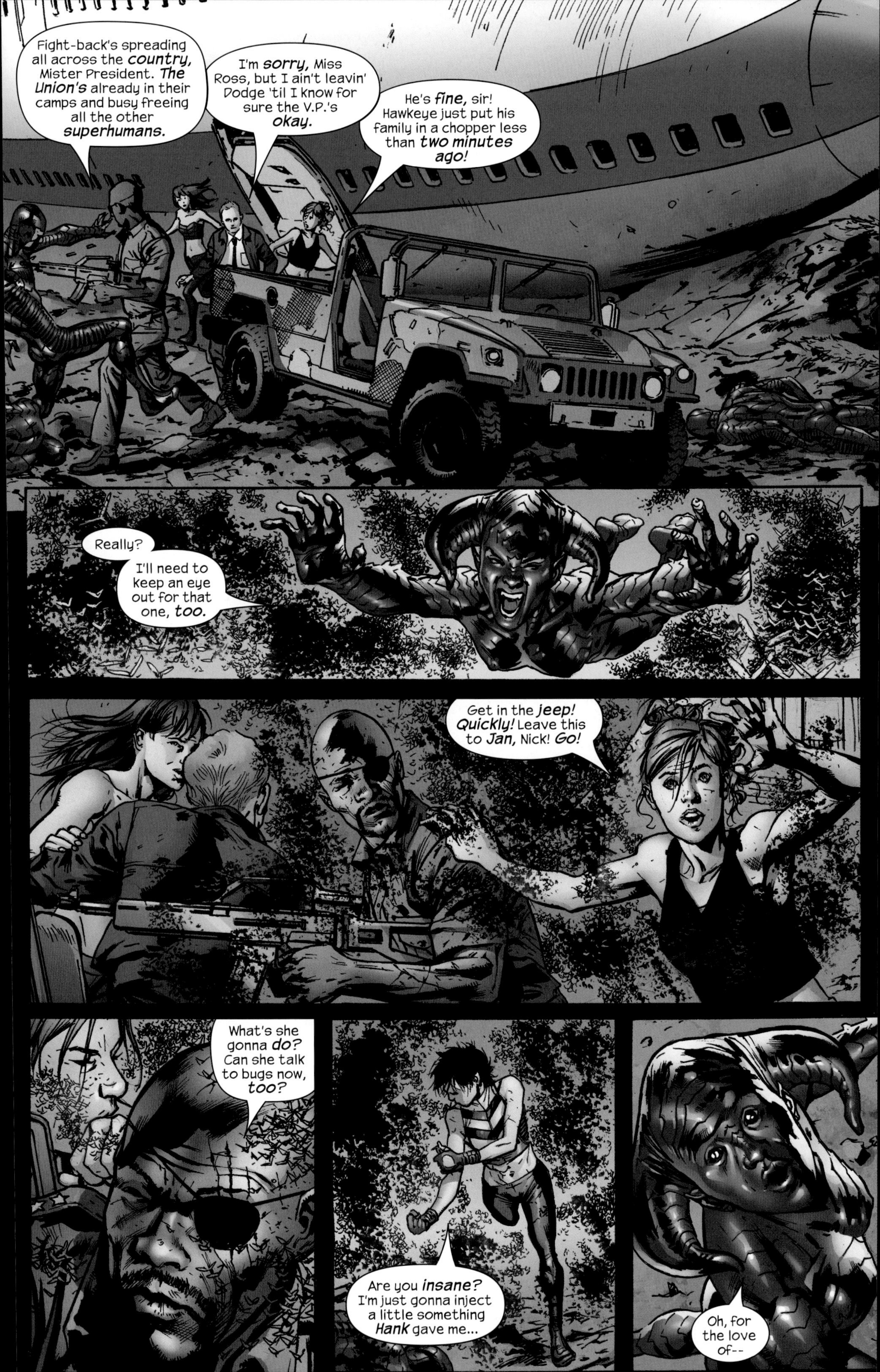

Fight-back's spreading all across the *country,* Mister President. *The Union's* already in their camps and busy freeing all the other *superhumans.*
I'm *sorry,* Miss Ross, but I ain't leavin' Dodge 'til I know for sure the V.P.'s *okay.*
He's *fine,* sir! Hawkeye just put his family in a chopper less than *two minutes ago!*
Really?
I'll need to keep an eye out for that one, *too.*
Get in the *jeep! Quickly!* Leave this to *Jan,* Nick! *Go!*
What's she gonna *do?* Can she talk to bugs now, *too?*
Are you *insane?* I'm just gonna inject a little something *Hank* gave me...
Oh, for the love of--

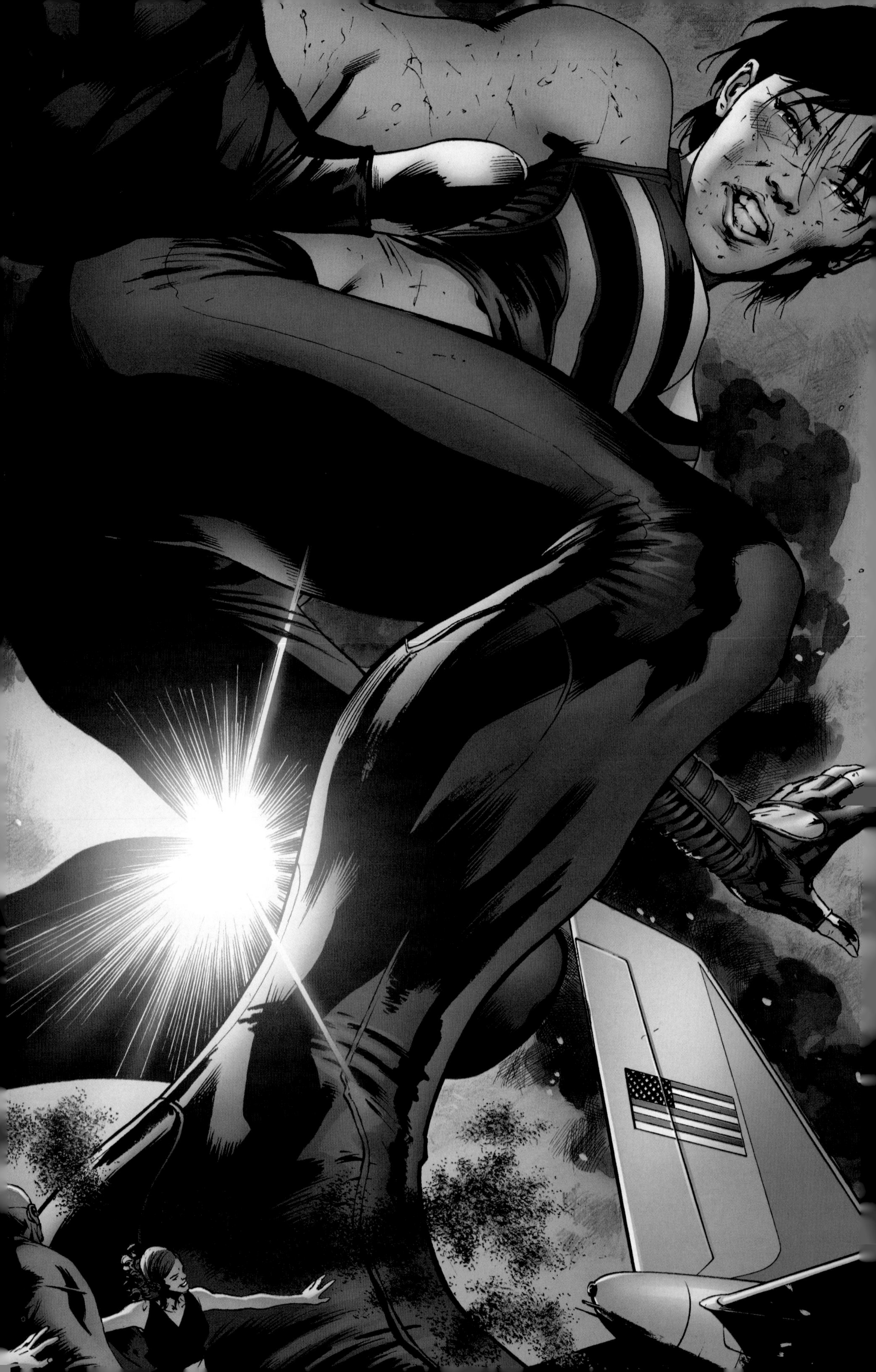

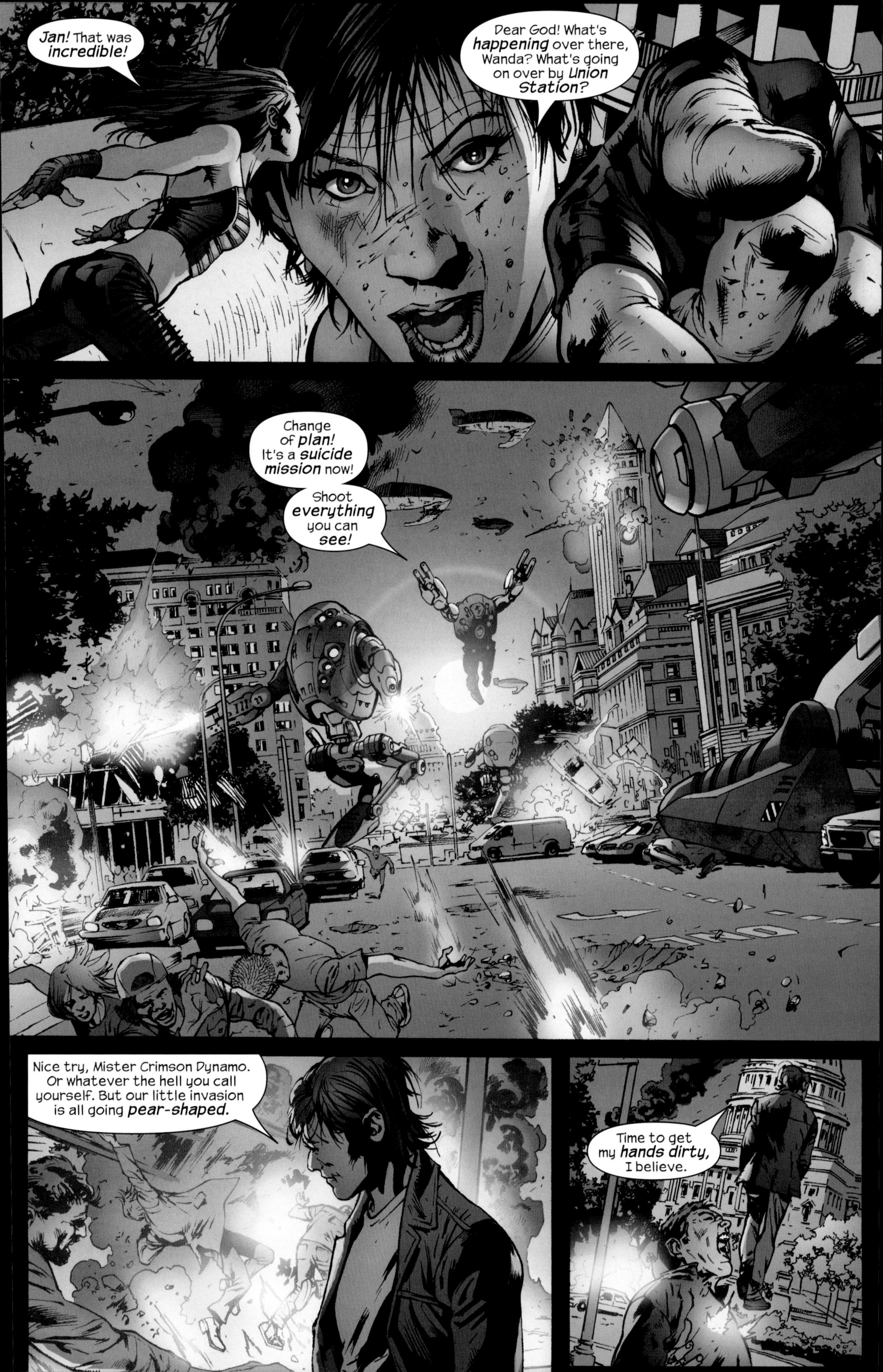
Jan! That was incredible!
Dear God! What's happening over there, Wanda? What's going on over by Union Station?
Change of plan! It's a suicide mission now!
Shoot everything you can see!
Nice try, Mister Crimson Dynamo. Or whatever the hell you call yourself. But our little invasion is all going pear-shaped.
Time to get my hands dirty, I believe.

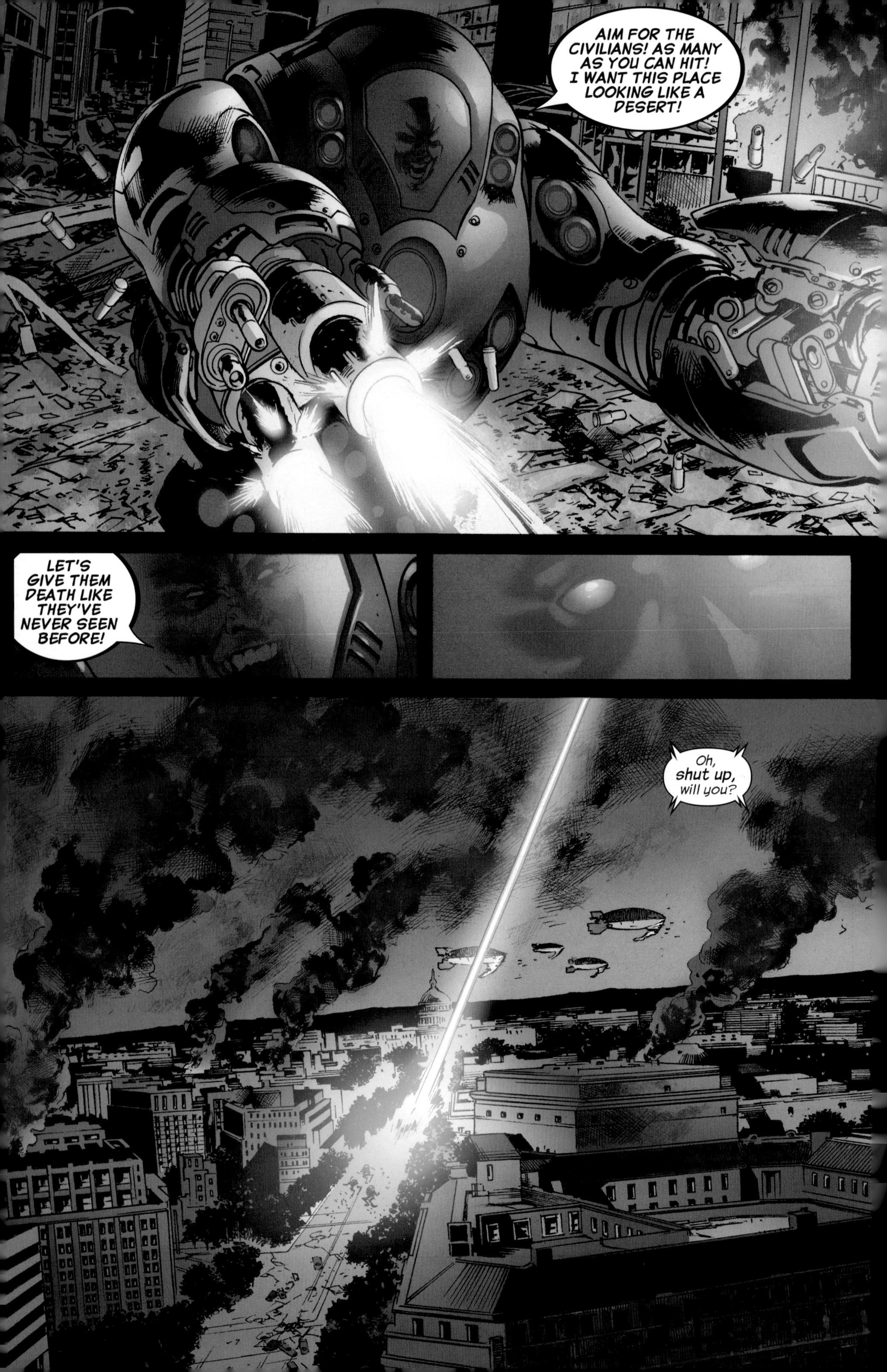
AIM FOR THE CIVILIANS! AS MANY AS YOU CAN HIT! I WANT THIS PLACE LOOKING LIKE A DESERT!
LET'S GIVE THEM DEATH LIKE THEY'VE NEVER SEEN BEFORE!
Oh, shut up, will you?

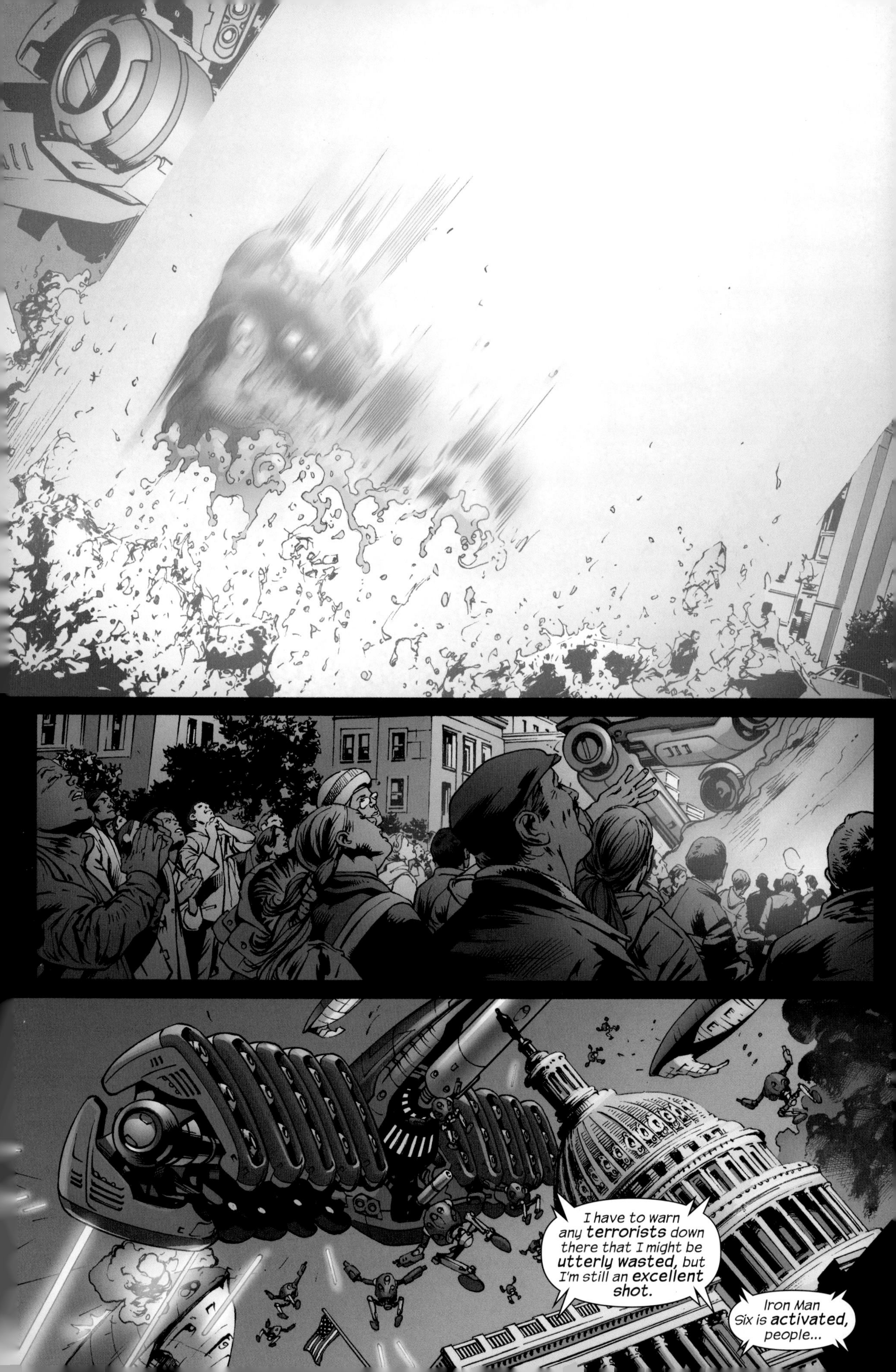
I have to warn any terrorists down there that I might be utterly wasted, but I'm still an excellent shot.
Iron Man Six is activated, people...

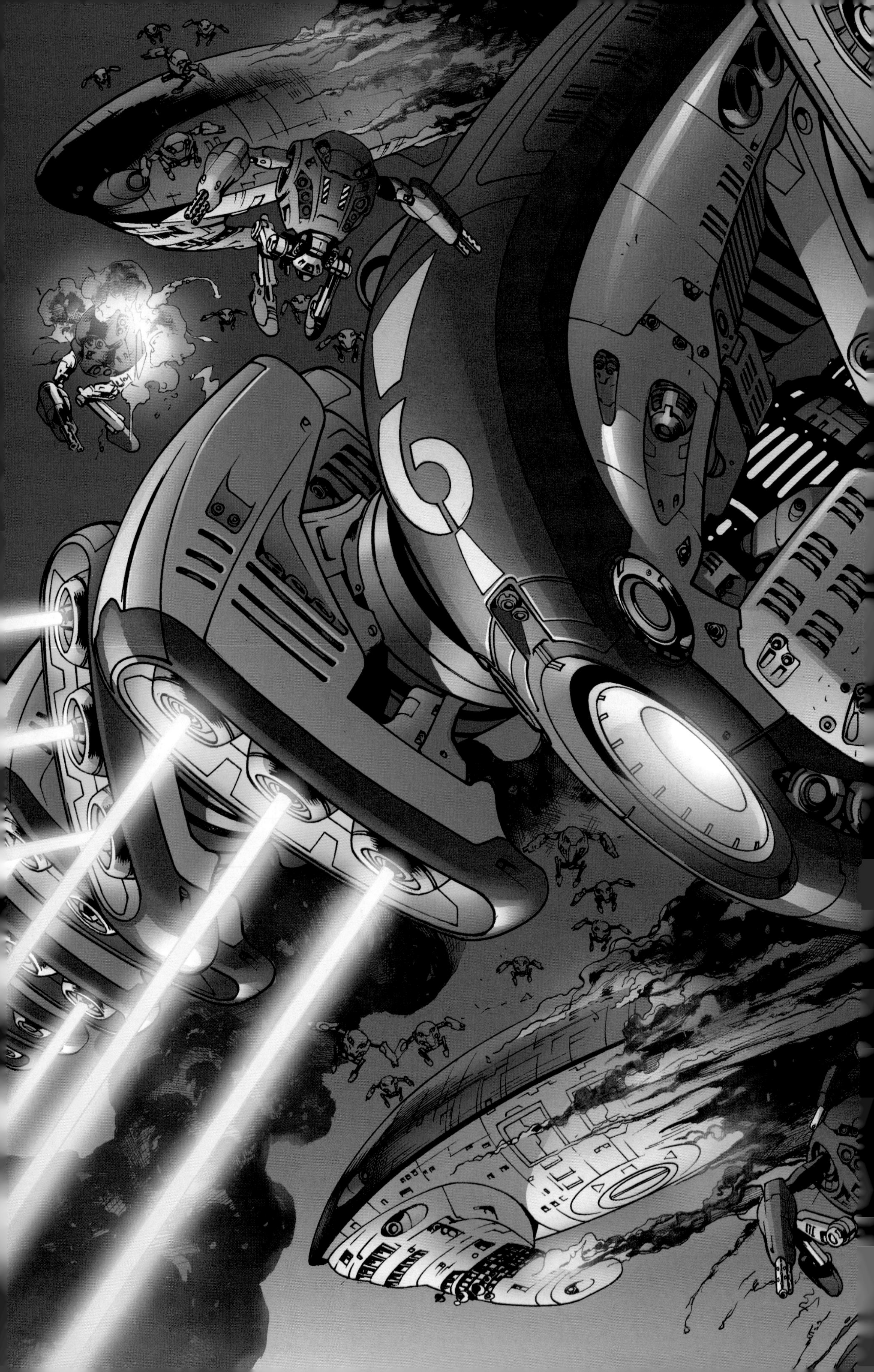

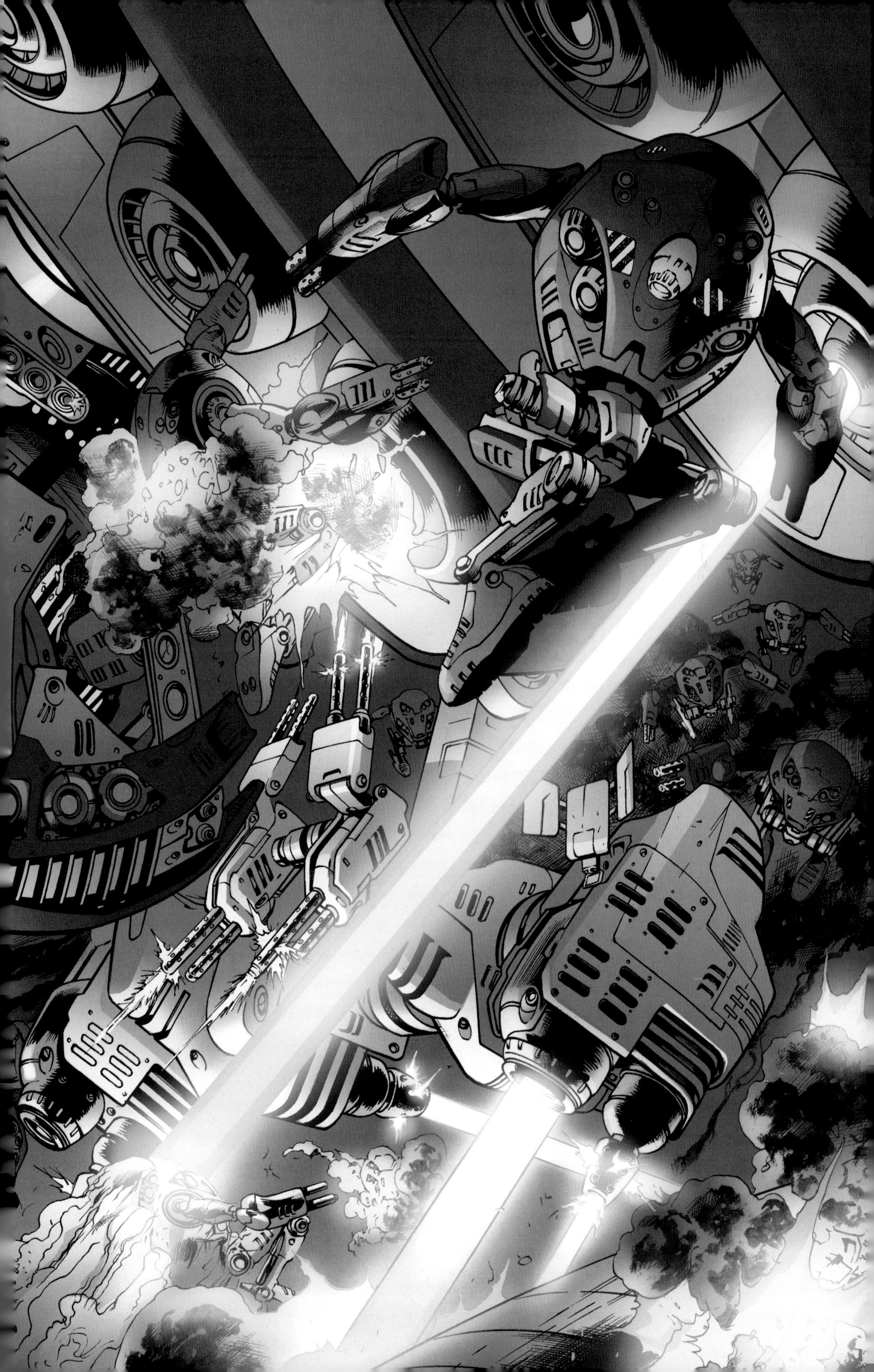

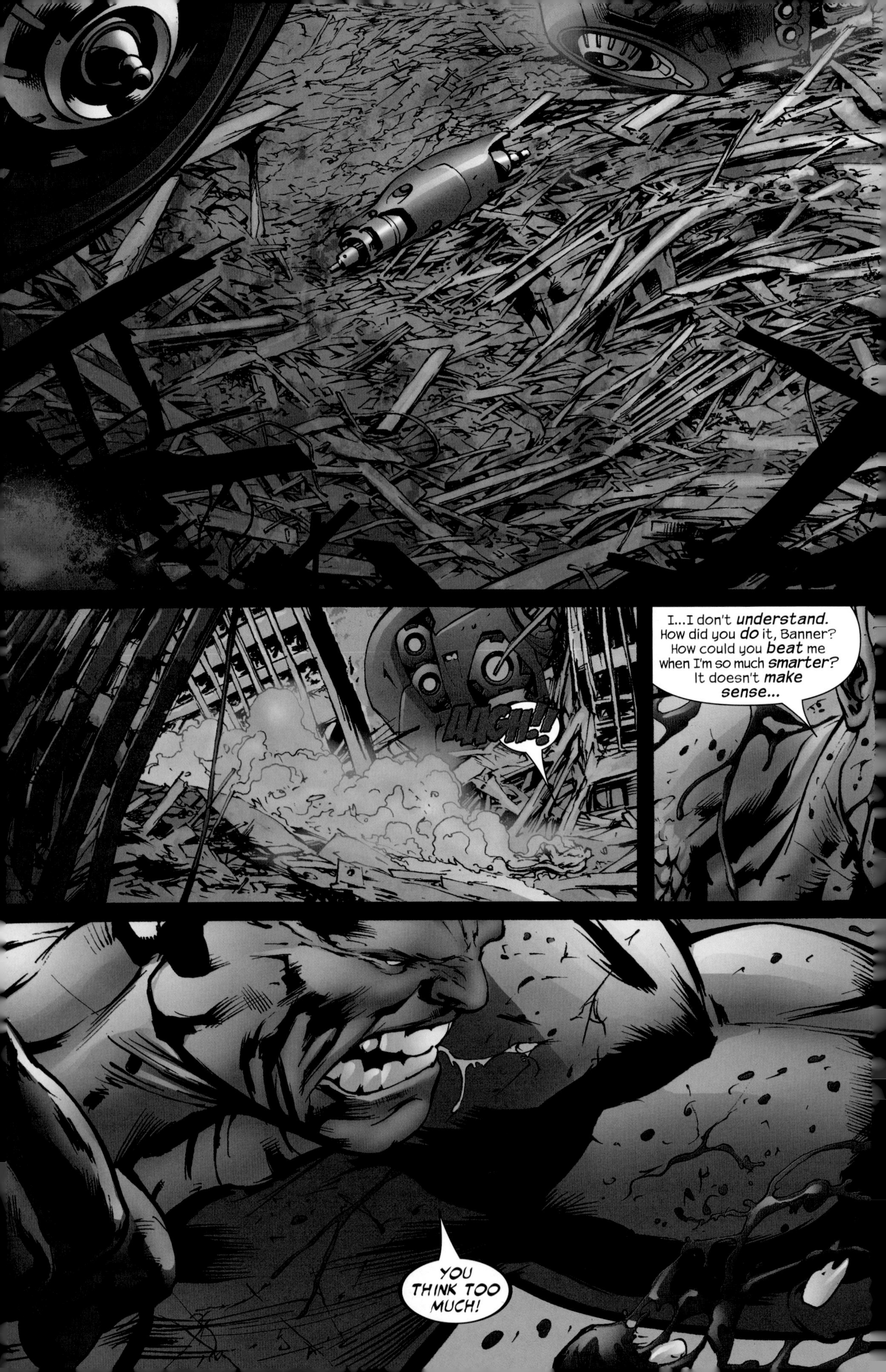
AAAGH!!
I...I don't understand. How did you do it, Banner? How could you beat me when I'm so much smarter? It doesn't make sense...
YOU THINK TOO MUCH!

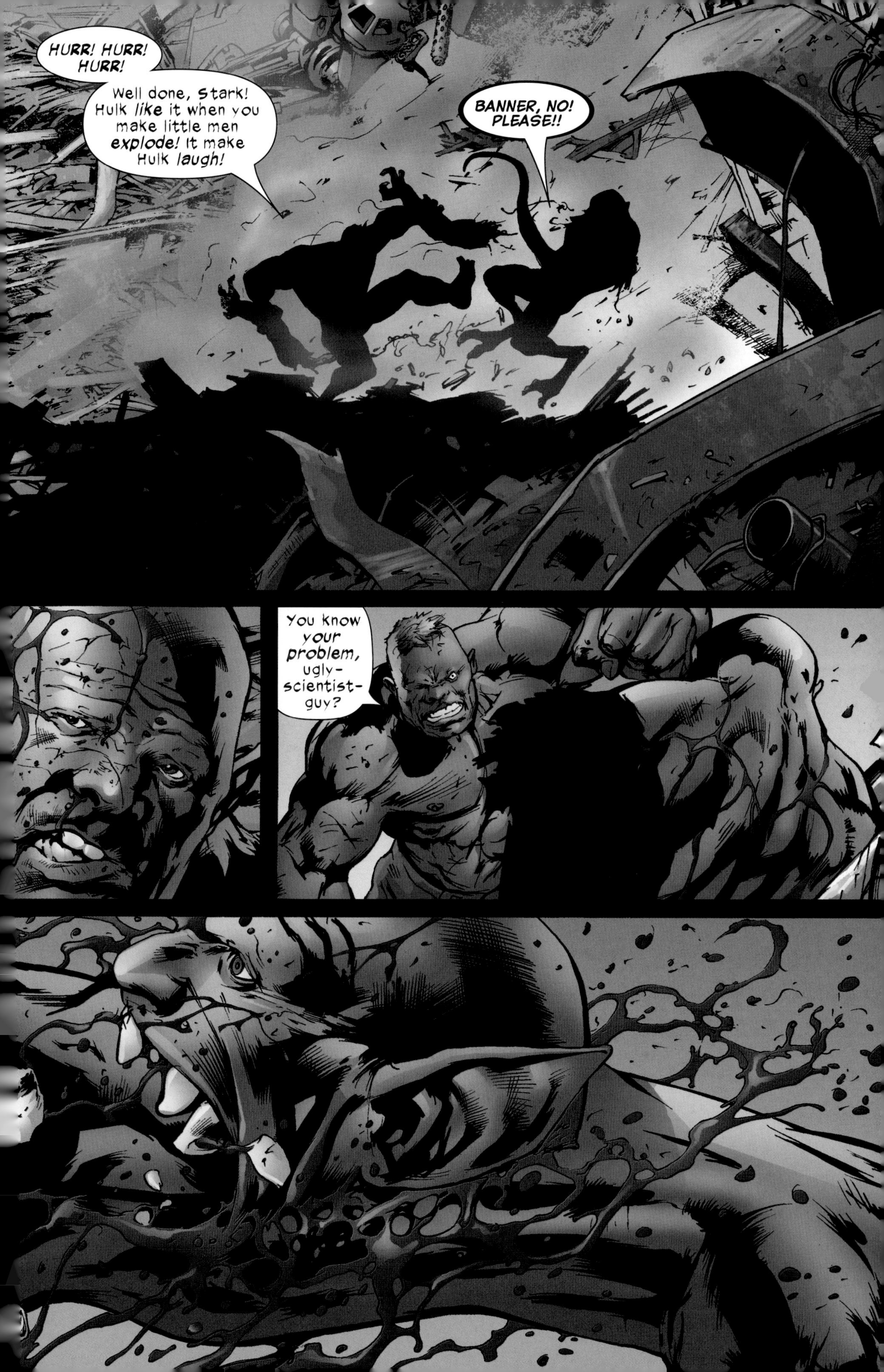
HURR! HURR! HURR!
Well done, Stark! Hulk like it when you make little men explode! It make Hulk laugh!
BANNER, NO! PLEASE!!
You know your problem, ugly-scientist-guy?

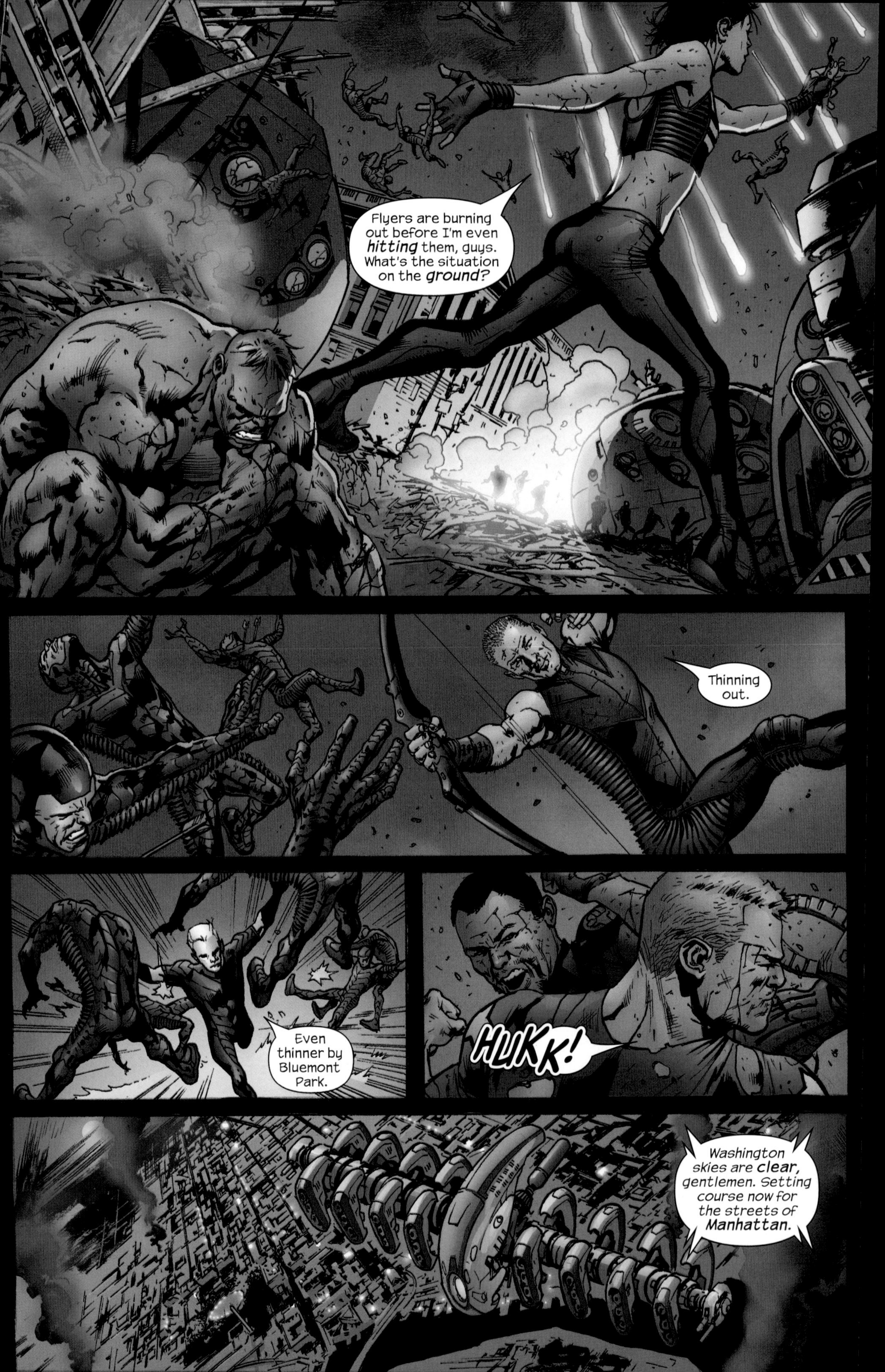
Flyers are burning out before I'm even *hitting* them, guys. What's the situation on the *ground*?
Thinning out.
Even thinner by Bluemont Park.
HUKK!
*Washington skies are **clear**, gentlemen. Setting course now for the streets of **Manhattan**.*

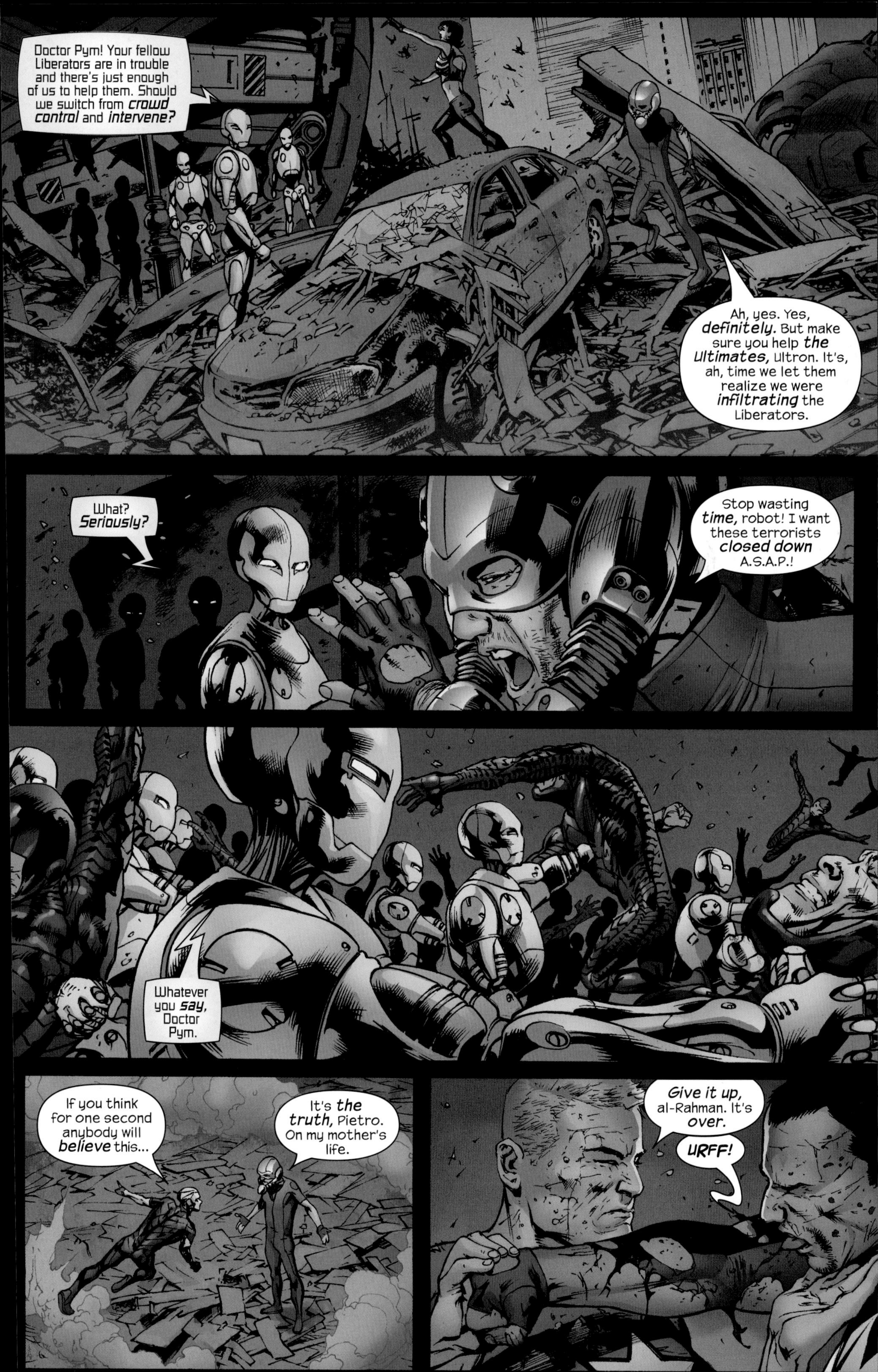
Doctor Pym! Your fellow Liberators are in trouble and there's just enough of us to help them. Should we switch from *crowd control* and *intervene?*
Ah, yes. Yes, *definitely.* But make sure you help *the Ultimates,* Ultron. It's, ah, time we let them realize we were *infiltrating* the Liberators.
What? *Seriously?*
Stop wasting *time,* robot! I want these terrorists *closed down* A.S.A.P.!
Whatever you *say,* Doctor Pym.
If you think for one second anybody will *believe* this...
It's *the truth,* Pietro. On my mother's life.
Give it up, al-Rahman. It's *over.*
URFF!

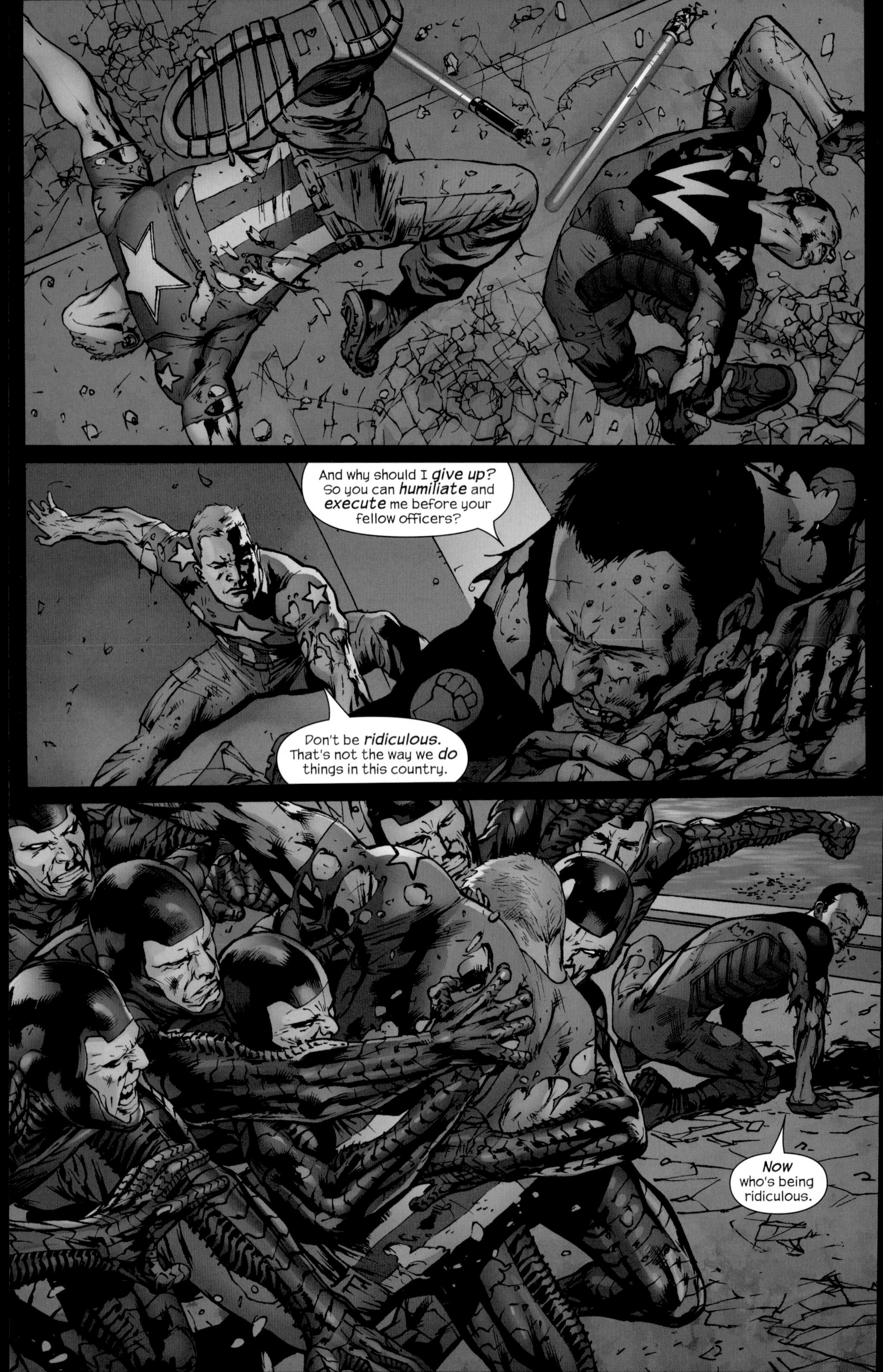
And why should I *give up*? So you can *humiliate* and *execute* me before your fellow officers?
Don't be *ridiculous*. That's not the way we *do* things in this country.
NOW who's being ridiculous.

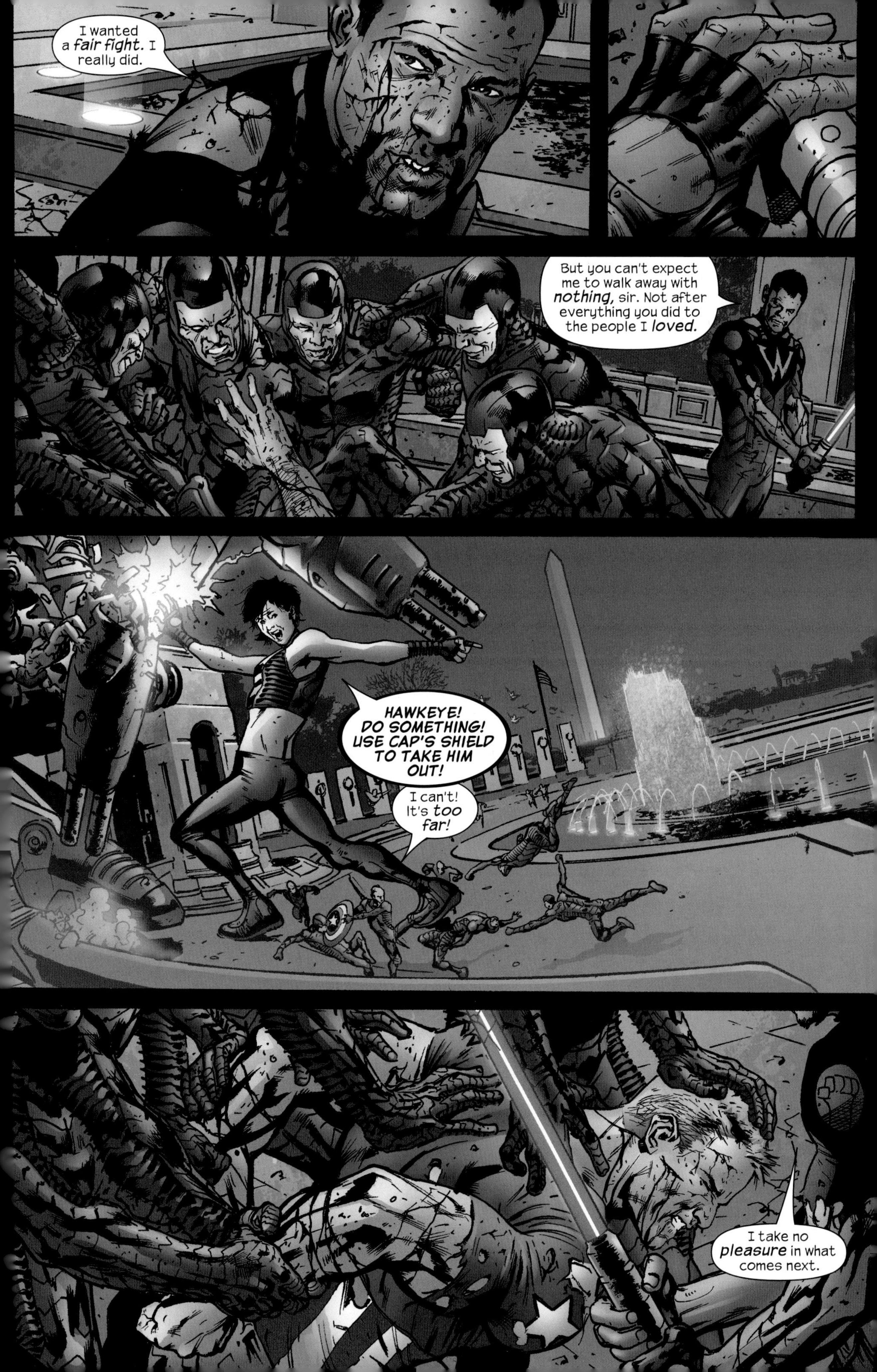
I wanted a *fair fight.* I really did.
But you can't expect me to walk away with *nothing,* sir. Not after everything you did to the people I *loved.*
HAWKEYE! DO SOMETHING! USE CAP'S SHIELD TO TAKE HIM OUT!
I can't! It's *too far!*
I take no *pleasure* in what comes next.

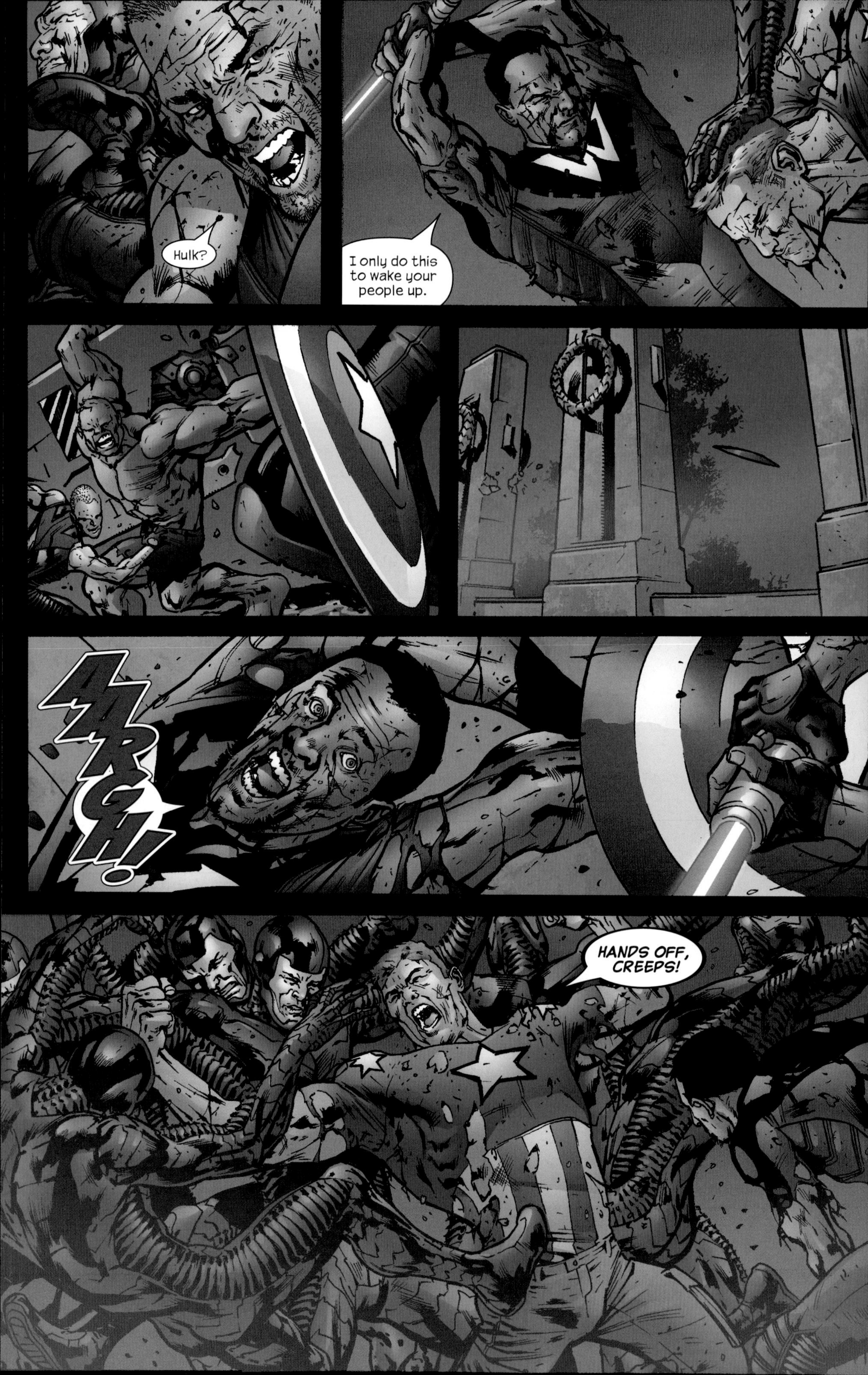
Hulk?
I only do this to wake your people up.
AARGH!
HANDS OFF, CREEPS!

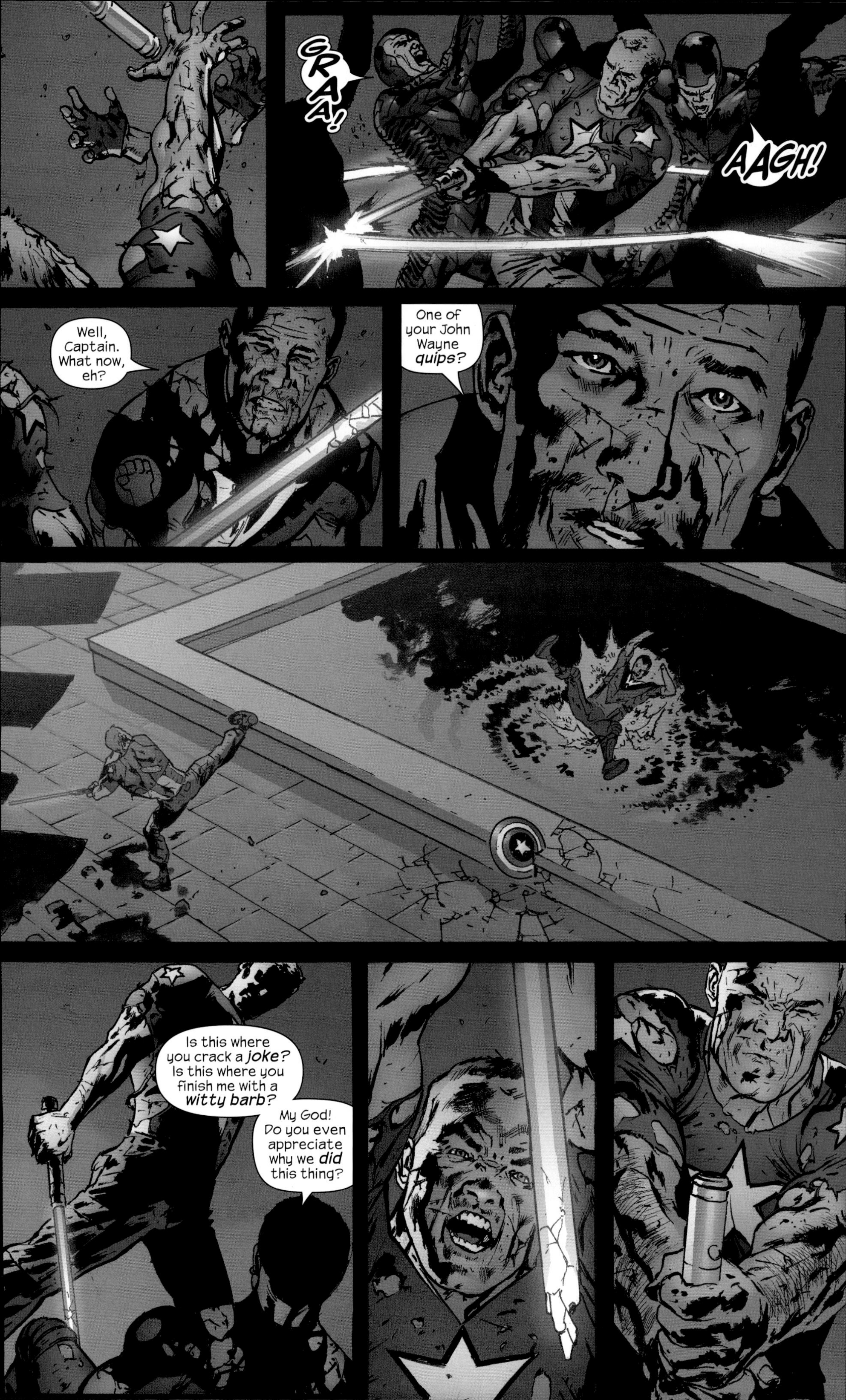
GRAA!
AAGH!
Well, Captain. What now, eh?
One of your John Wayne *quips?*
Is this where you crack a *joke?* Is this where you finish me with a *witty barb?*
My God! Do you even appreciate why we *did* this thing?

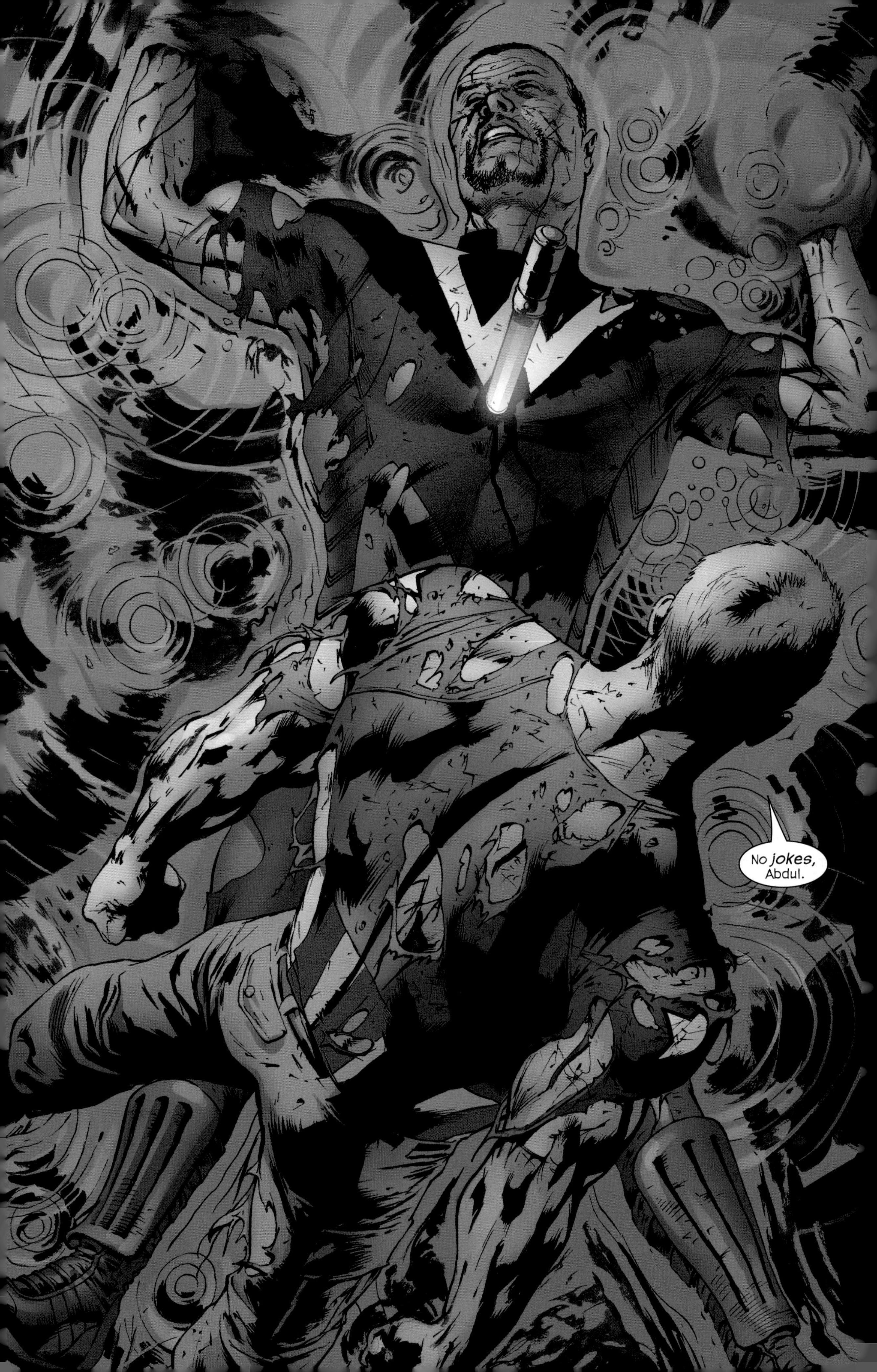
No jokes, Abdul.

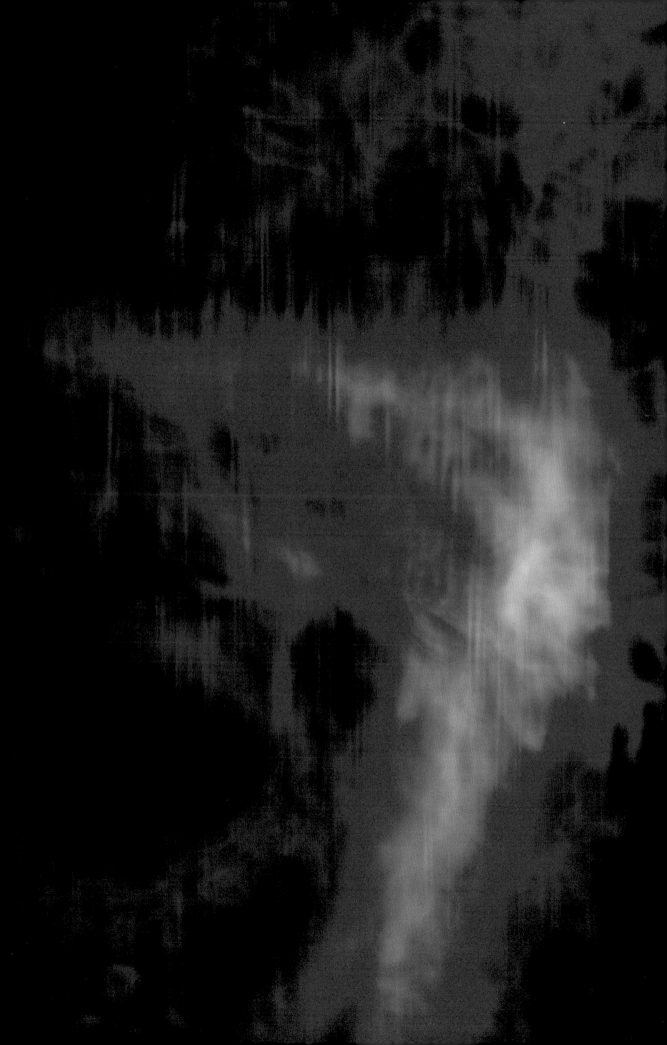

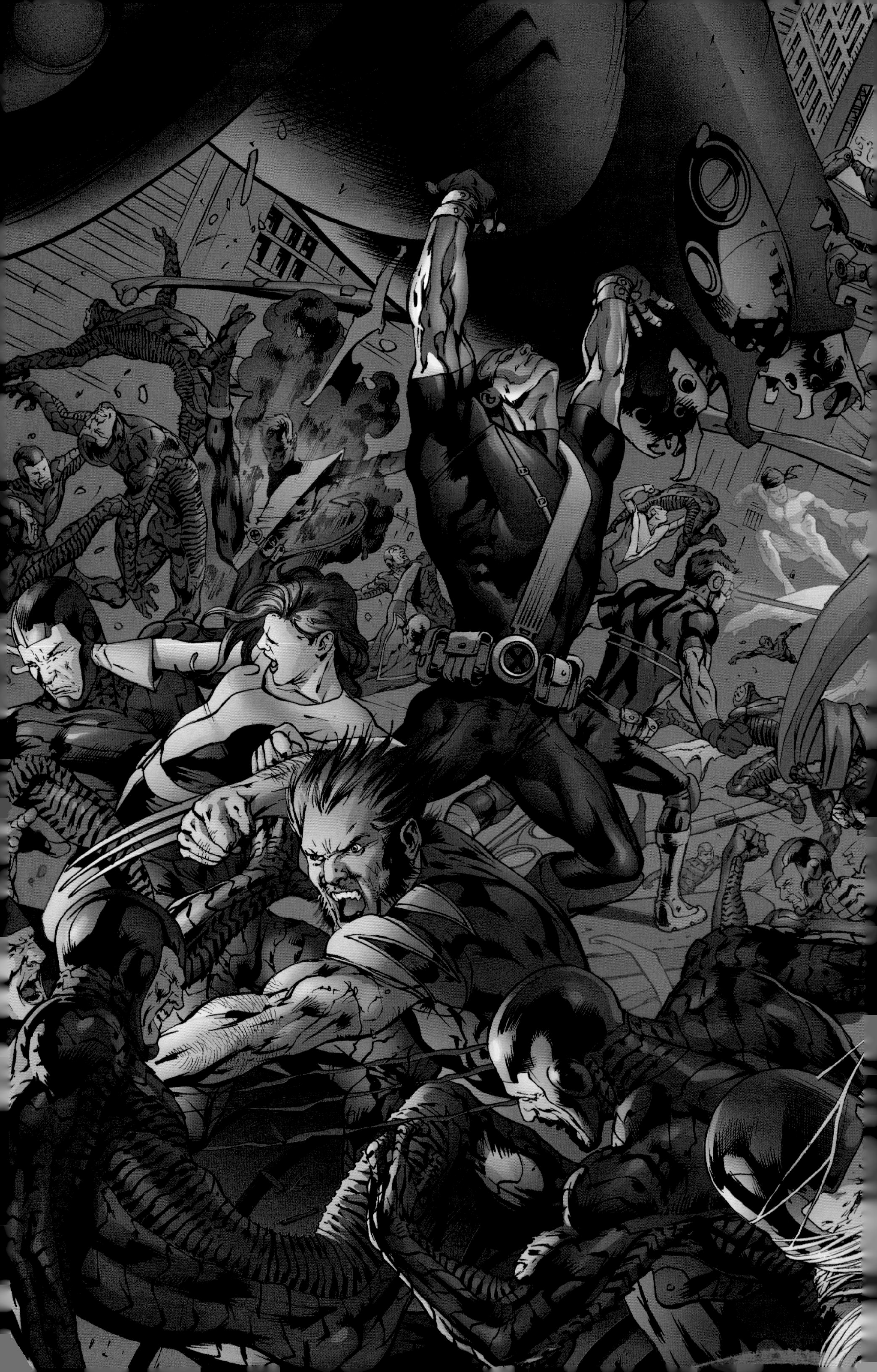

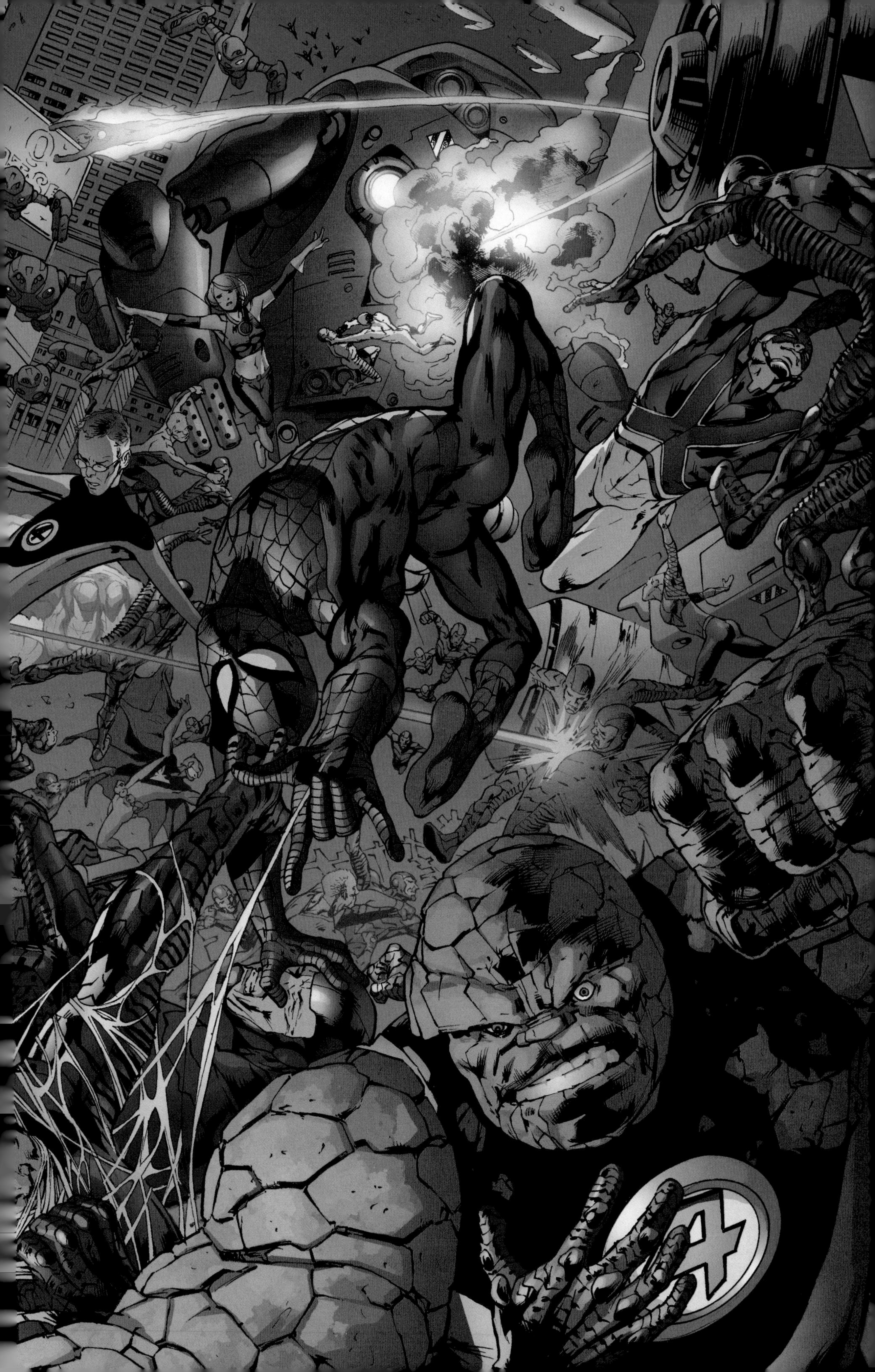

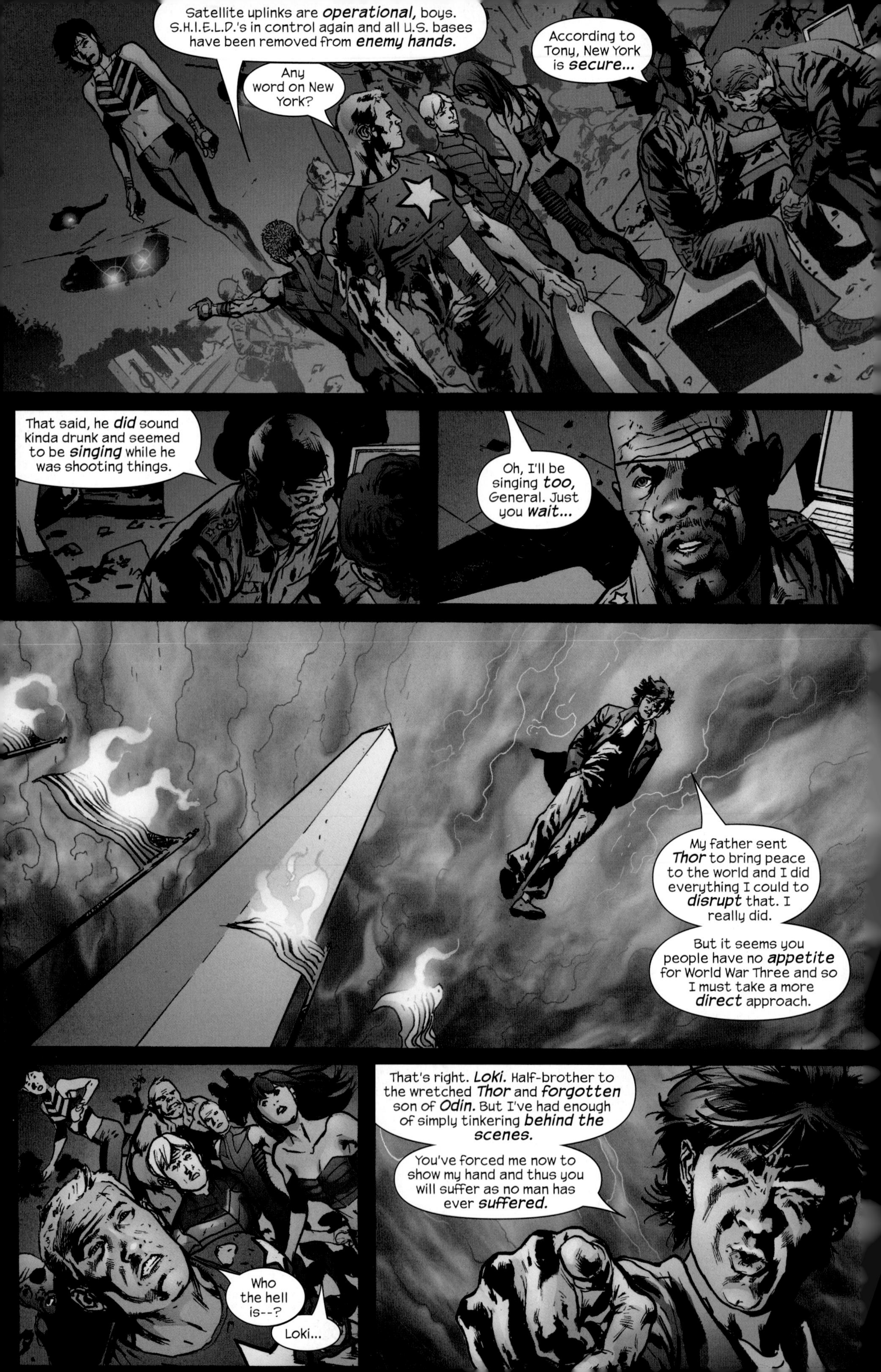
Satellite uplinks are operational, boys. S.H.I.E.L.D.'s in control again and all U.S. bases have been removed from enemy hands.
Any word on New York?
According to Tony, New York is secure...
That said, he did sound kinda drunk and seemed to be singing while he was shooting things.
Oh, I'll be singing too, General. Just you wait...
My father sent Thor to bring peace to the world and I did everything I could to disrupt that. I really did.
But it seems you people have no appetite for World War Three and so I must take a more direct approach.
Who the hell is--?
Loki...
That's right. Loki. Half-brother to the wretched Thor and forgotten son of Odin. But I've had enough of simply tinkering behind the scenes.
You've forced me now to show my hand and thus you will suffer as no man has ever suffered.

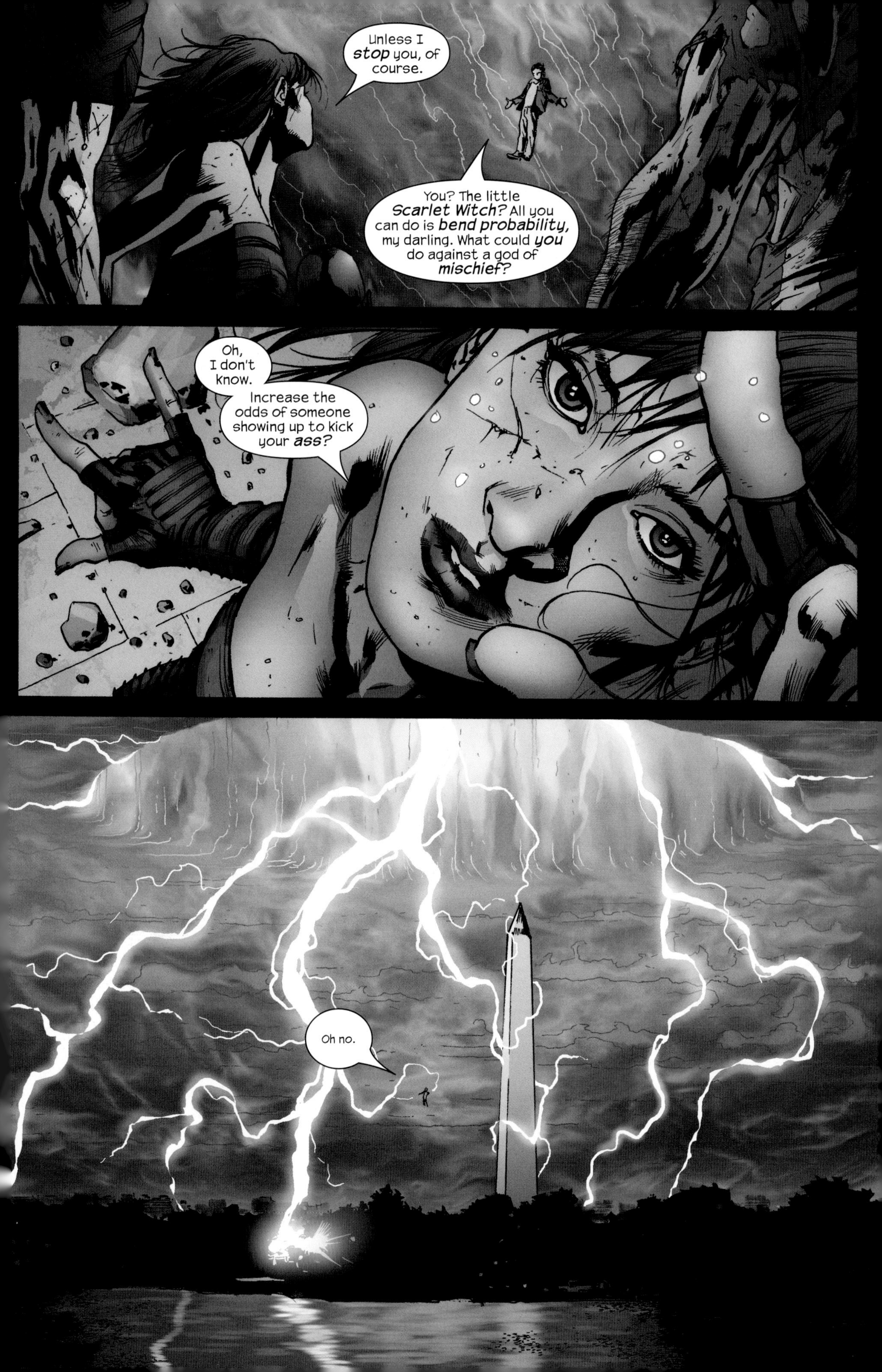
Unless I stop you, of course.
You? The little Scarlet Witch? All you can do is bend probability, my darling. What could you do against a god of mischief?
Oh, I don't know.
Increase the odds of someone showing up to kick your ass?
Oh no.

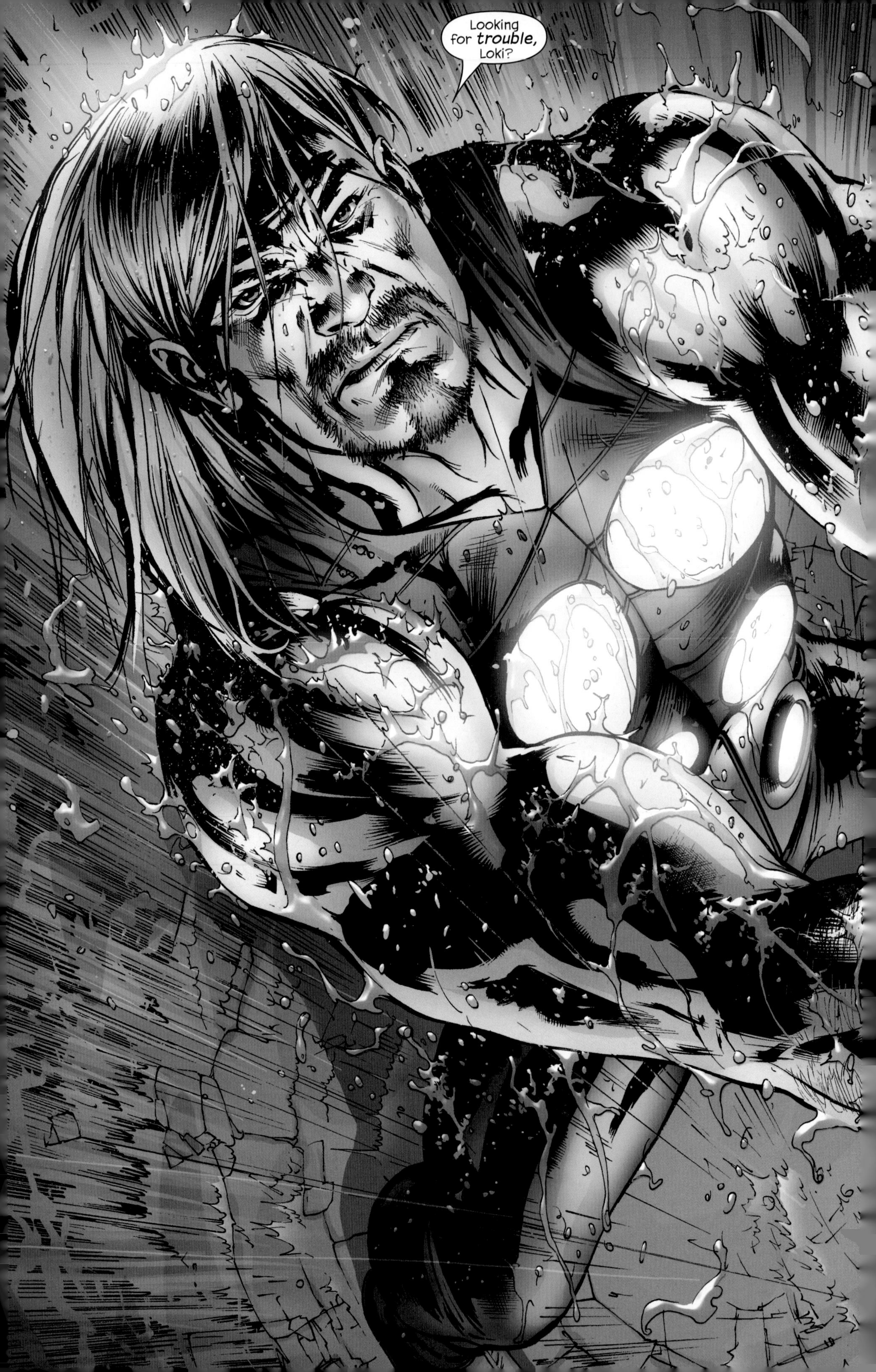
Looking for trouble, Loki?

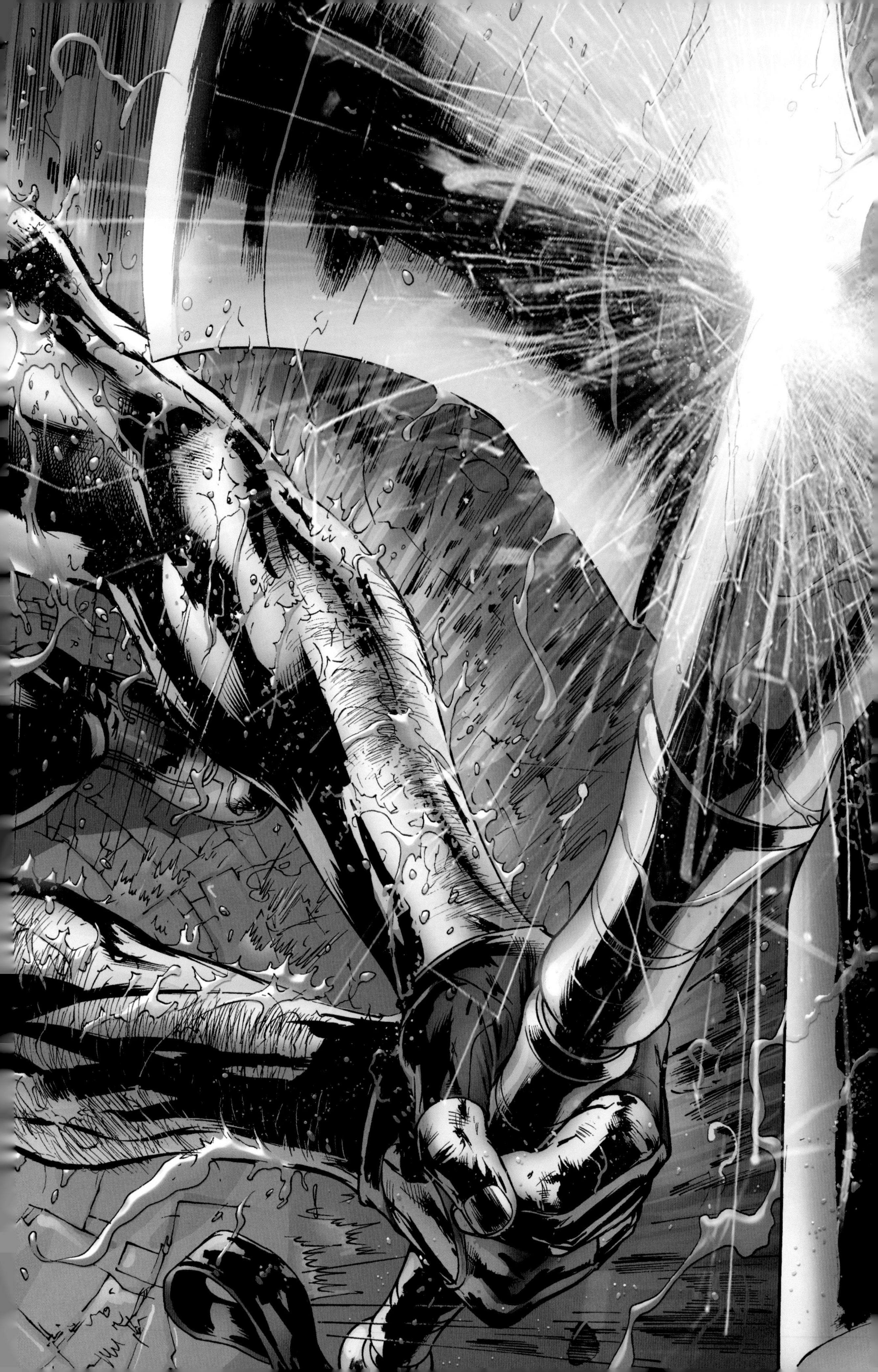

INDEPENDENCE DAY

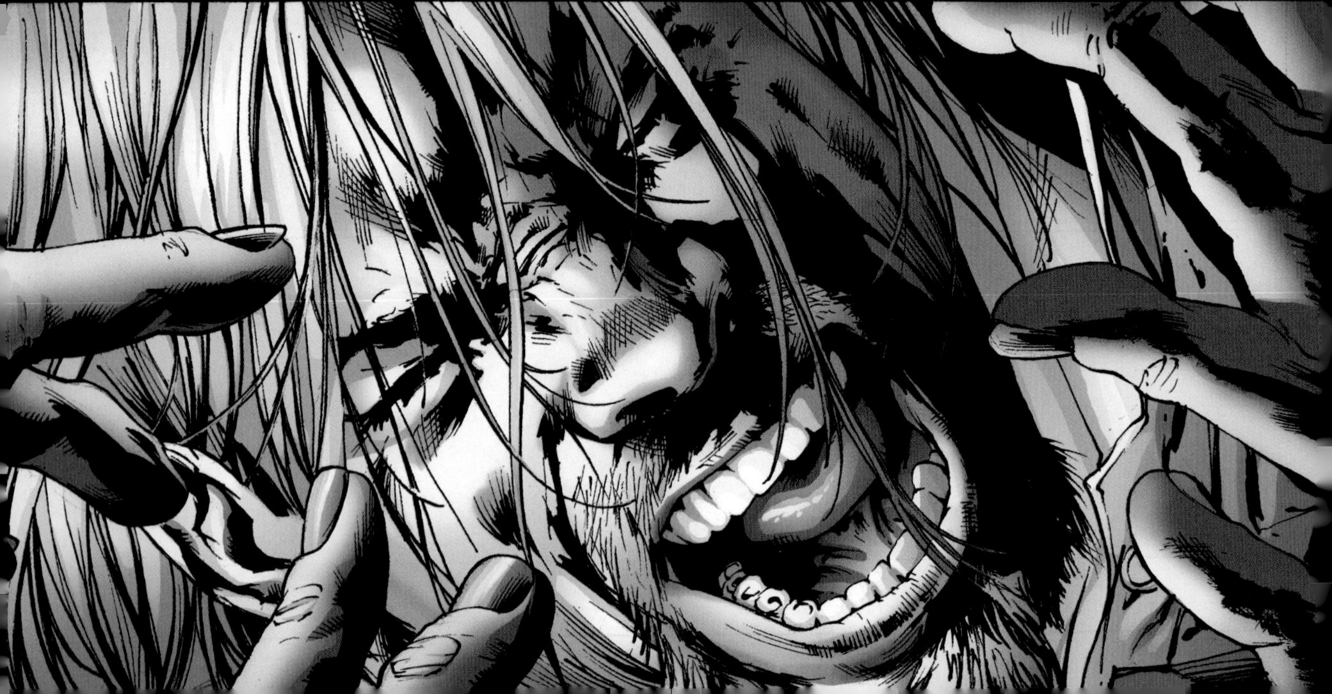

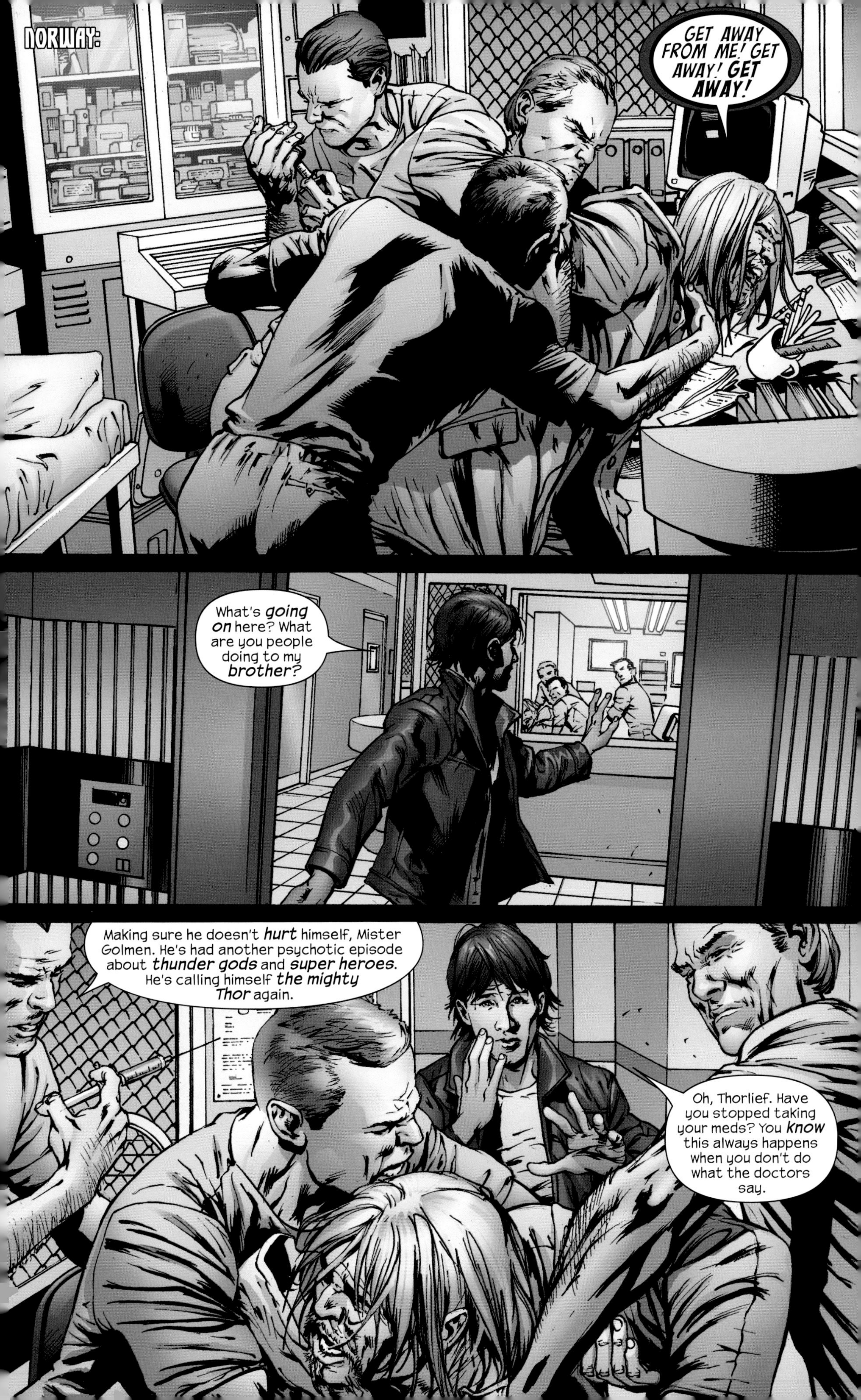
NORWAY:
GET AWAY FROM ME! GET AWAY! GET AWAY!
What's going on here? What are you people doing to my brother?
Making sure he doesn't hurt himself, Mister Golmen. He's had another psychotic episode about thunder gods and super heroes. He's calling himself the mighty Thor again.
Oh, Thorlief. Have you stopped taking your meds? You know this always happens when you don't do what the doctors say.

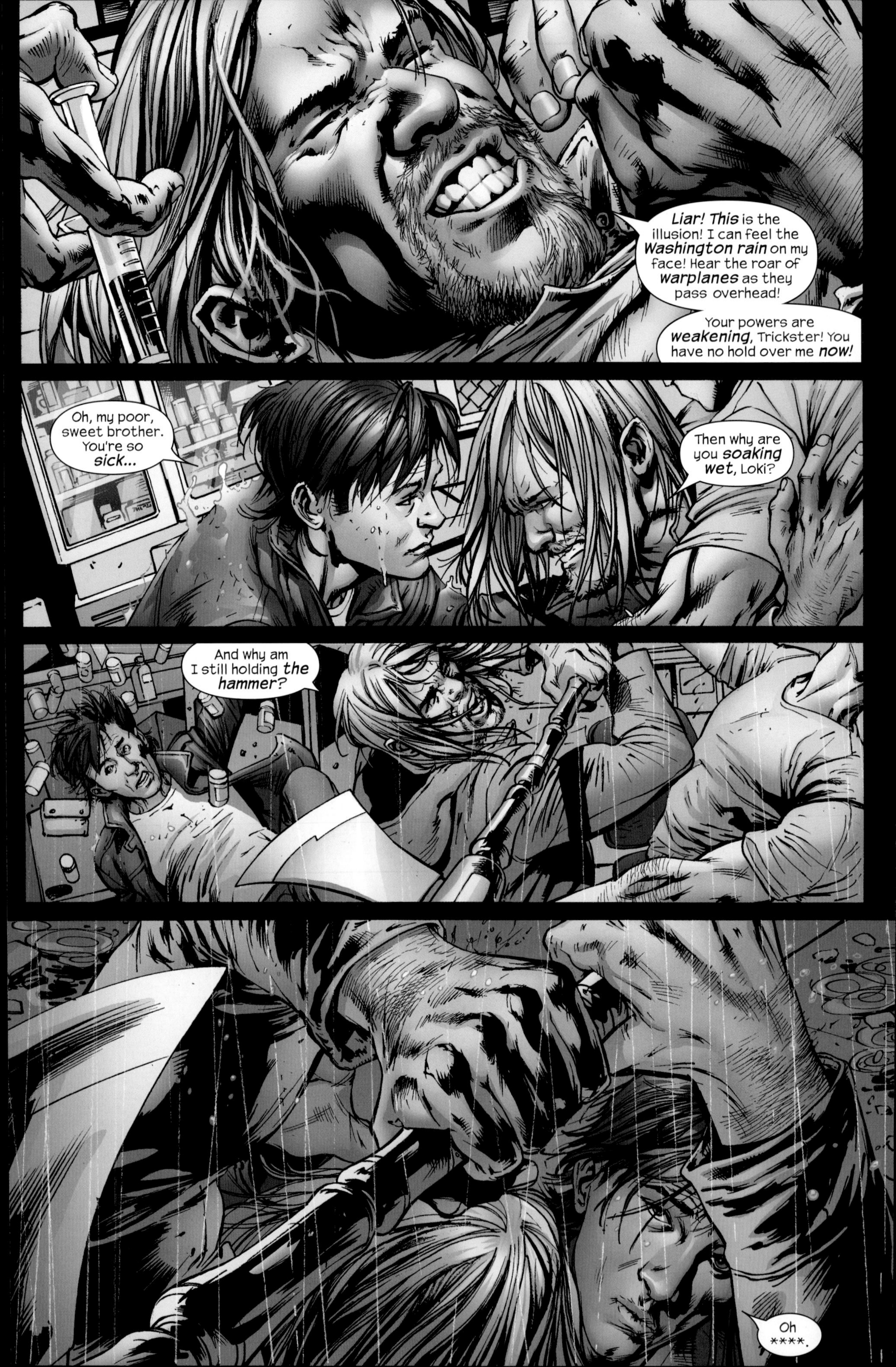
Liar! This is the illusion! I can feel the Washington rain on my face! Hear the roar of warplanes as they pass overhead!
Your powers are weakening, Trickster! You have no hold over me now!
Oh, my poor, sweet brother. You're so sick...
Then why are you soaking wet, Loki?
And why am I still holding the hammer?
Oh ****.

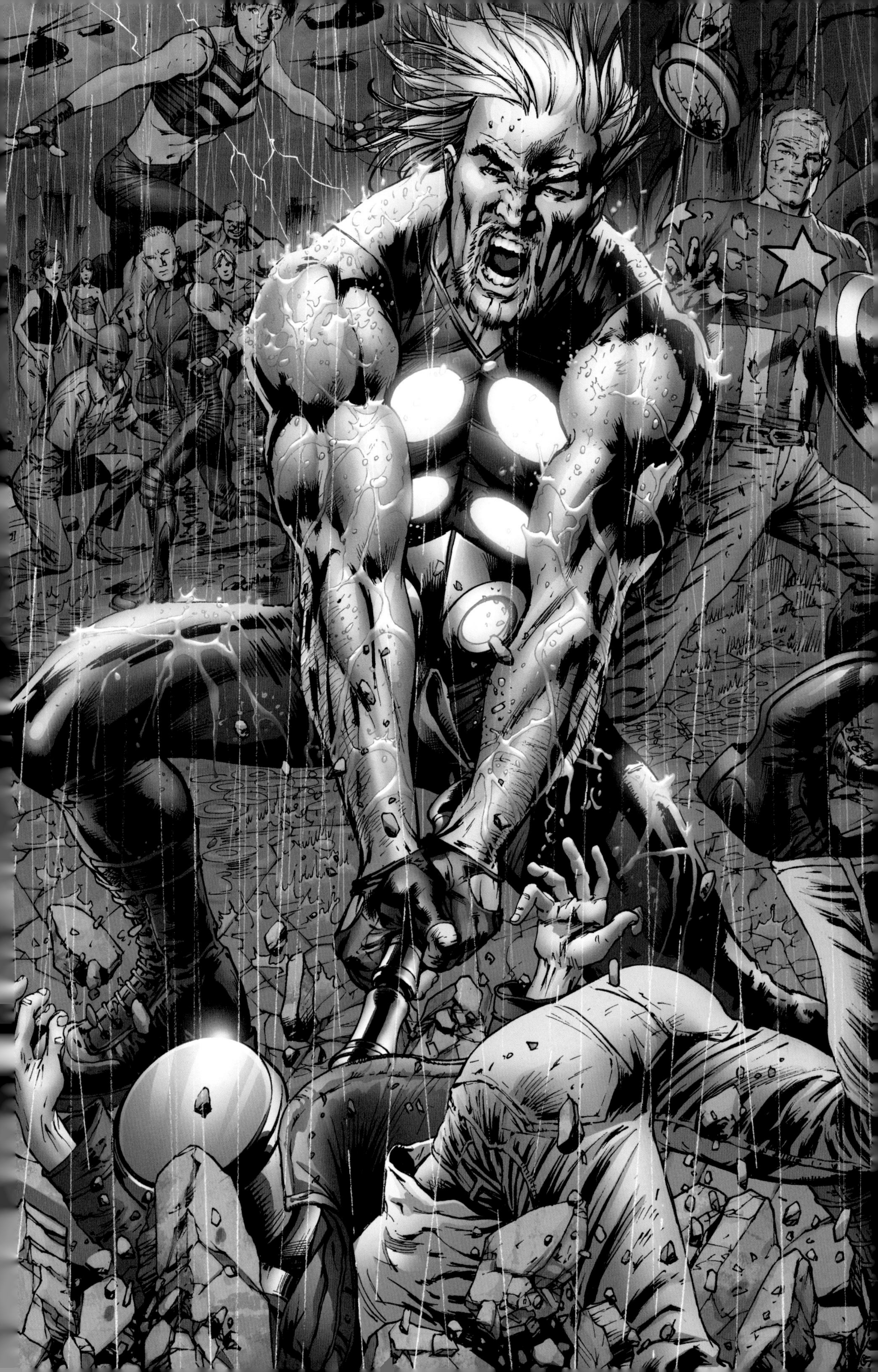

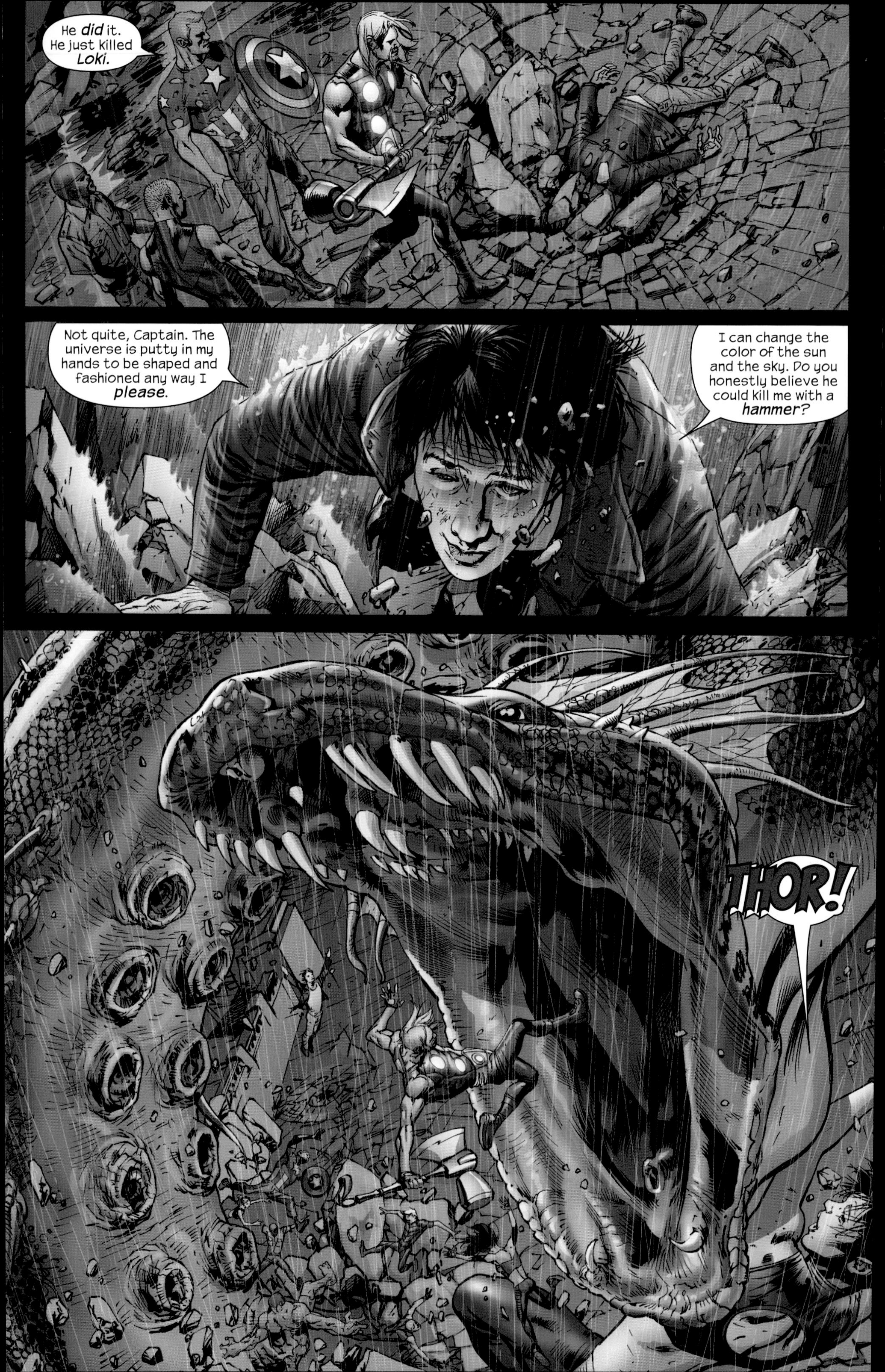
He did it. He just killed Loki.
Not quite, Captain. The universe is putty in my hands to be shaped and fashioned any way I please.
I can change the color of the sun and the sky. Do you honestly believe he could kill me with a hammer?
THOR!

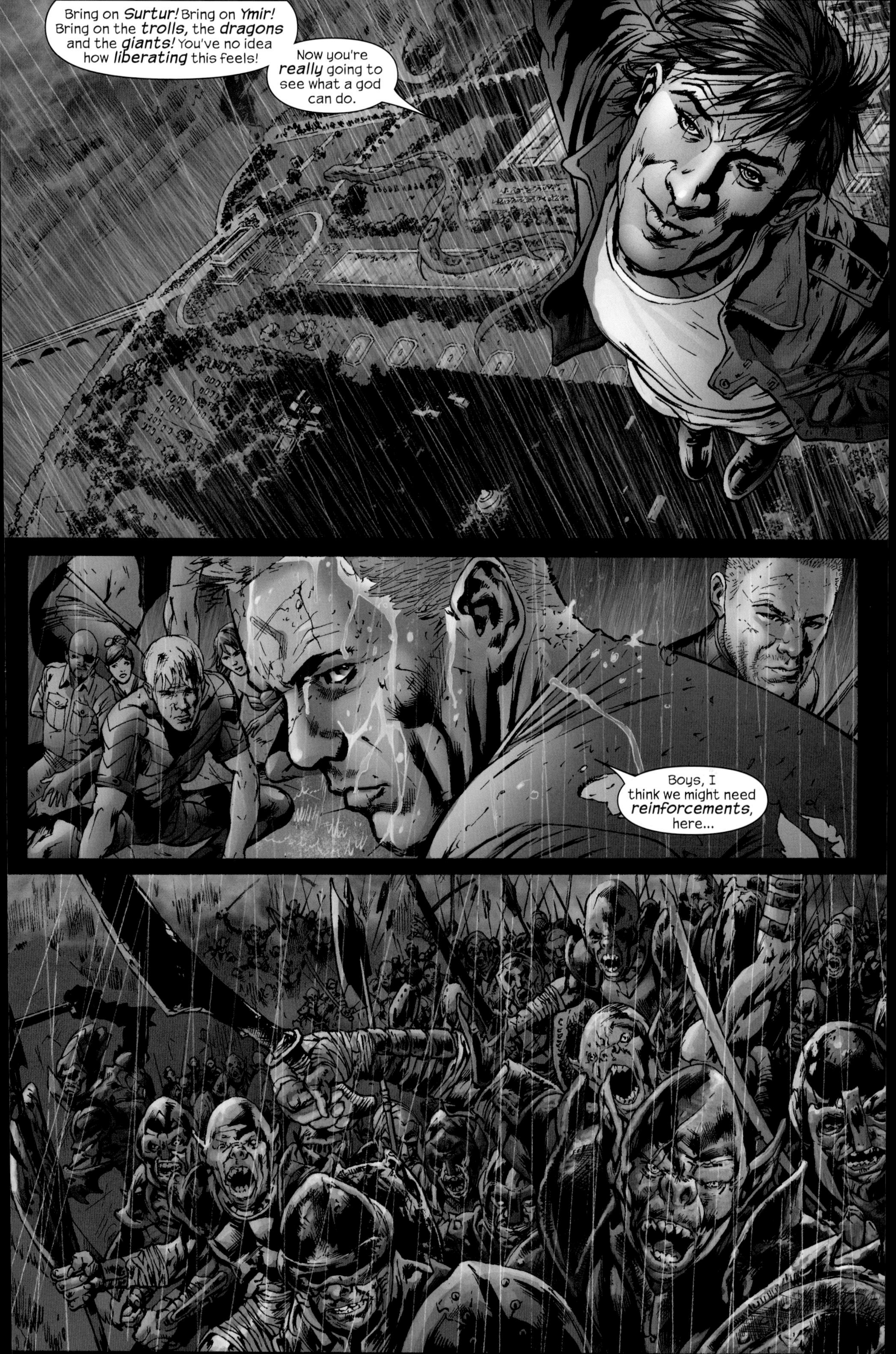
Bring on Surtur! Bring on Ymir! Bring on the trolls, the dragons and the giants! You've no idea how liberating this feels!
Now you're really going to see what a god can do.
Boys, I think we might need reinforcements, here...

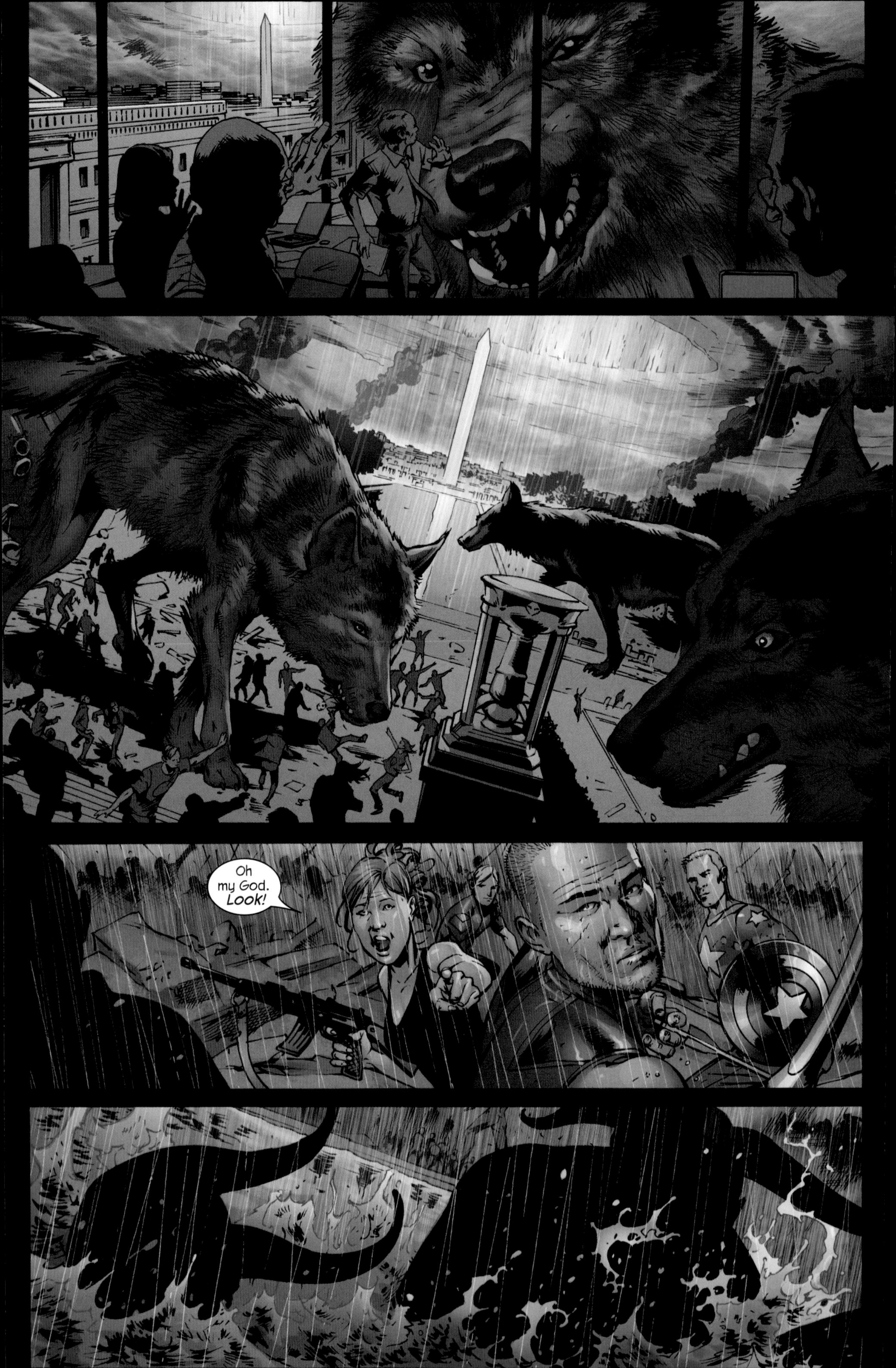
Oh my God. Look!

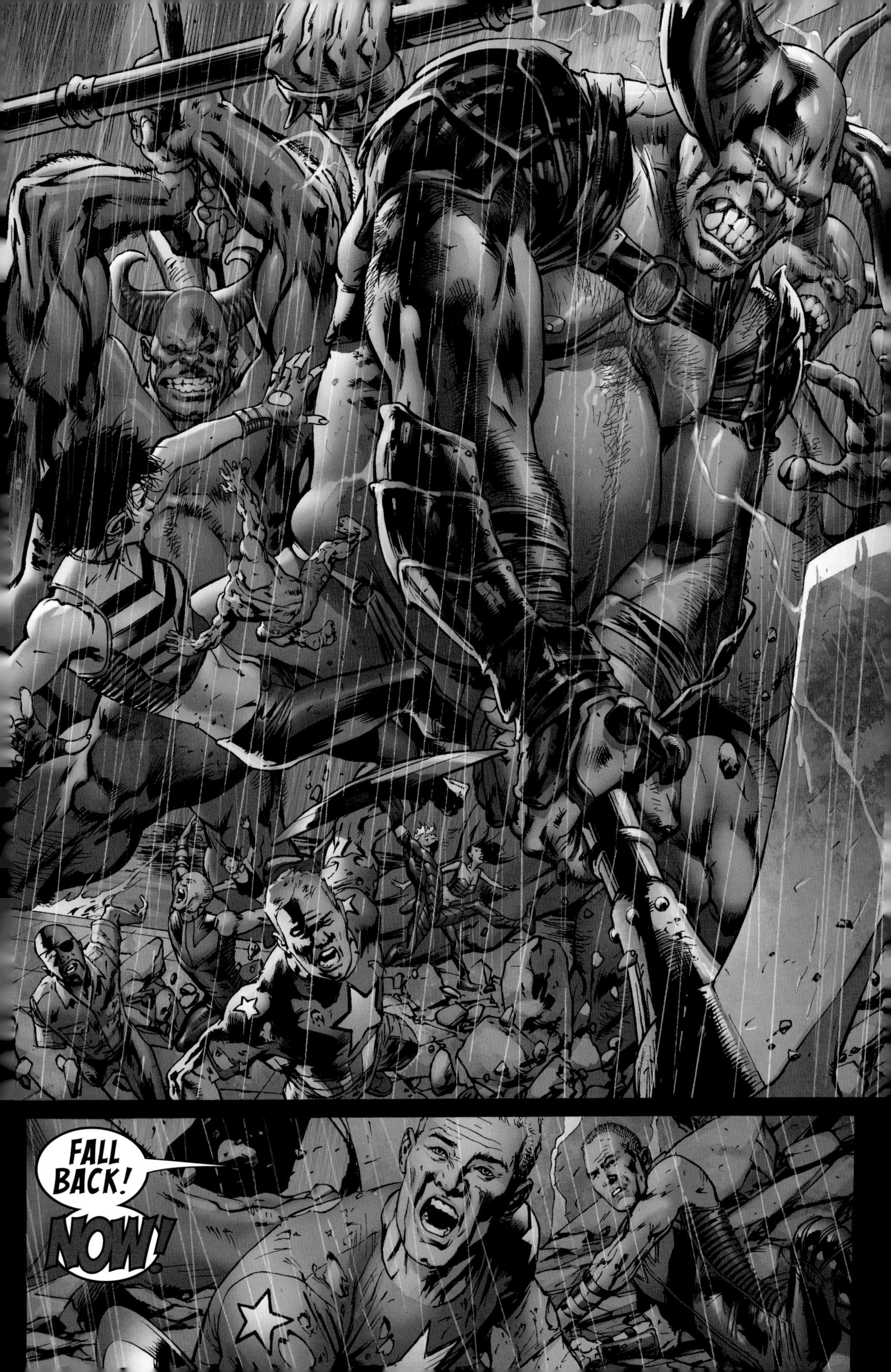
FALL BACK!
NOW!

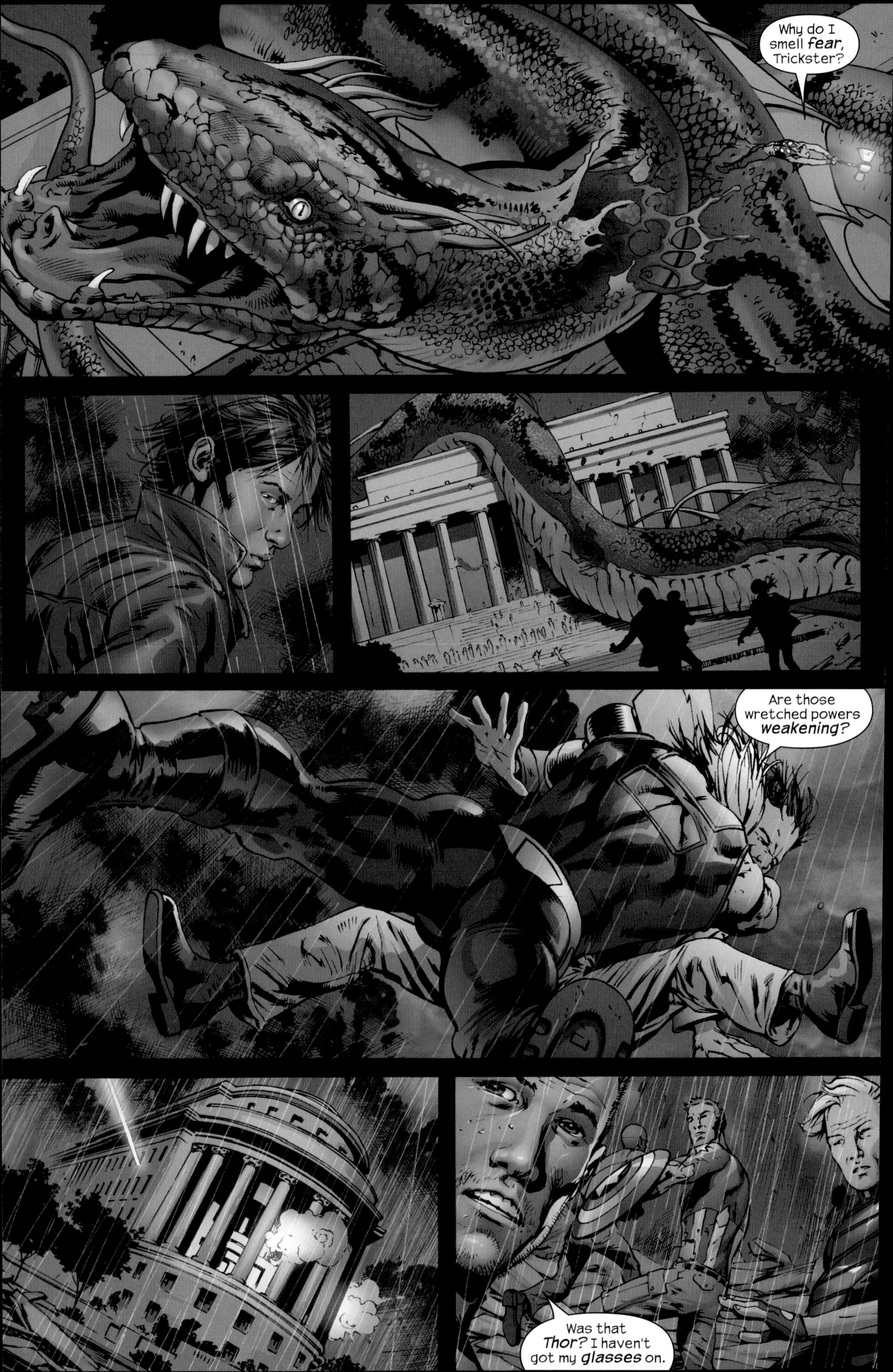
Why do I smell fear, Trickster?
Are those wretched powers weakening?
Was that Thor? I haven't got my glasses on.

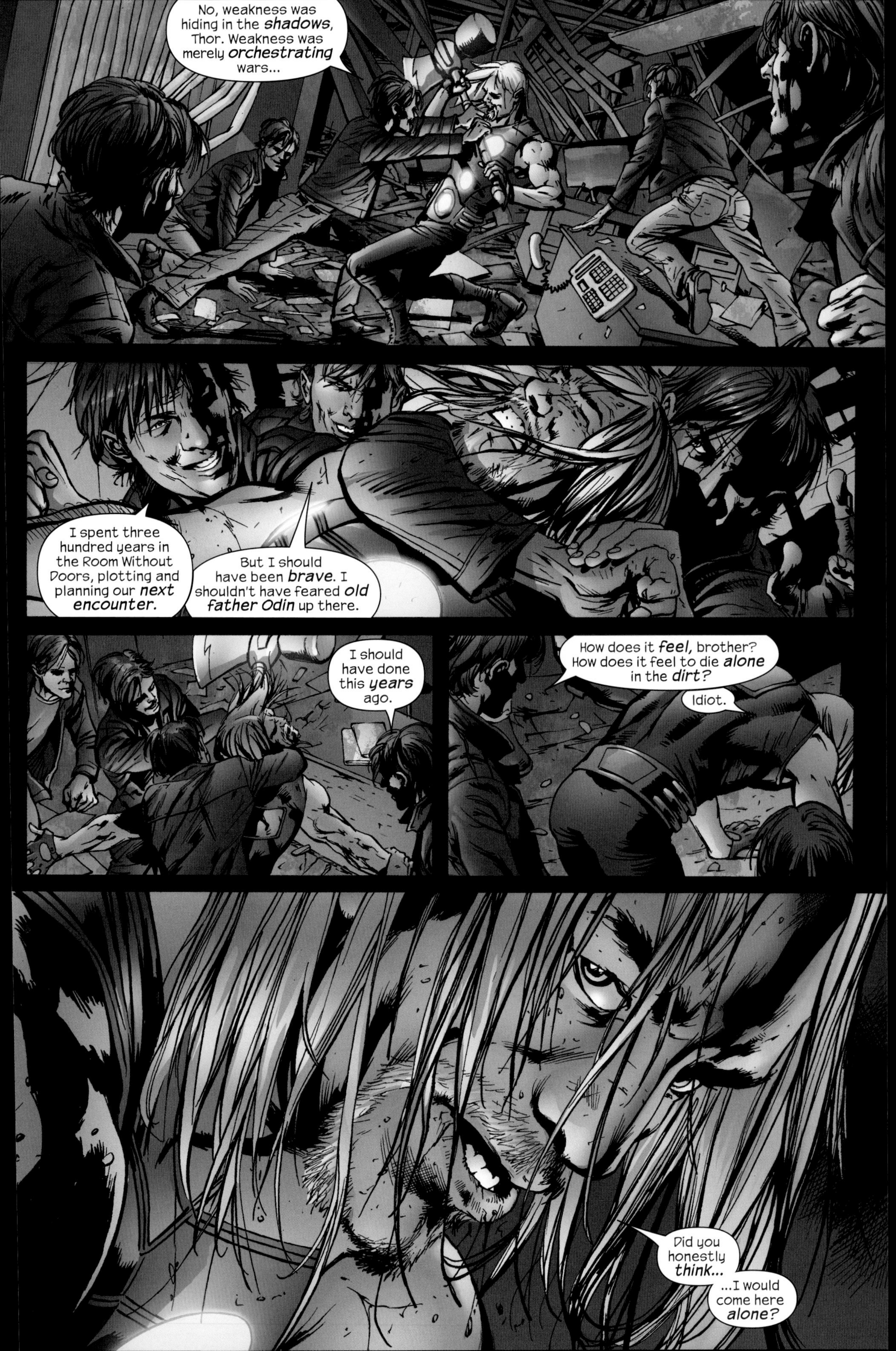
No, weakness was hiding in the shadows, Thor. Weakness was merely orchestrating wars...
I spent three hundred years in the Room Without Doors, plotting and planning our next encounter.
But I should have been brave. I shouldn't have feared old father Odin up there.
I should have done this years ago.
How does it feel, brother? How does it feel to die alone in the dirt?
Idiot.
Did you honestly think...
...I would come here alone?

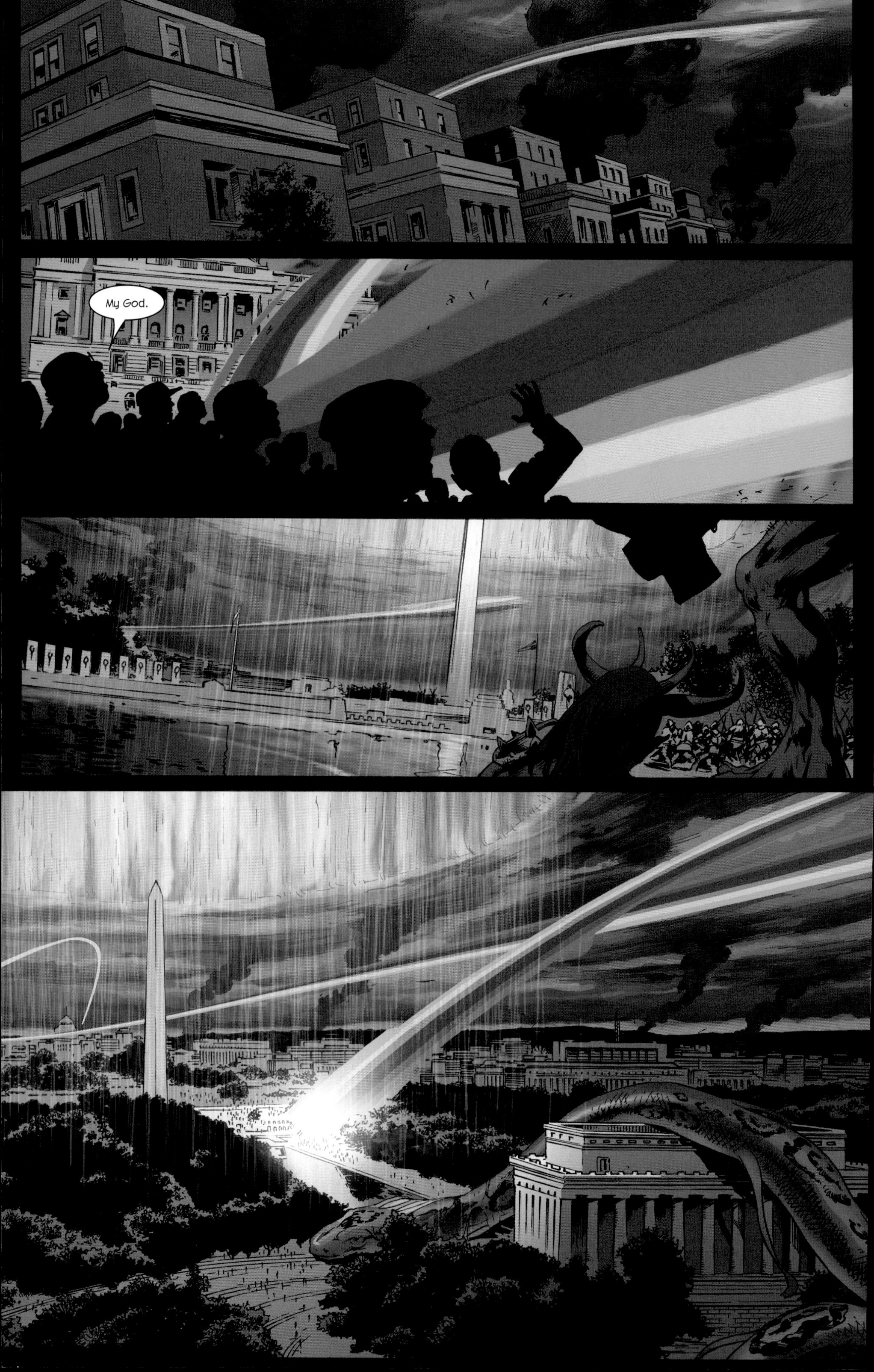
My God.

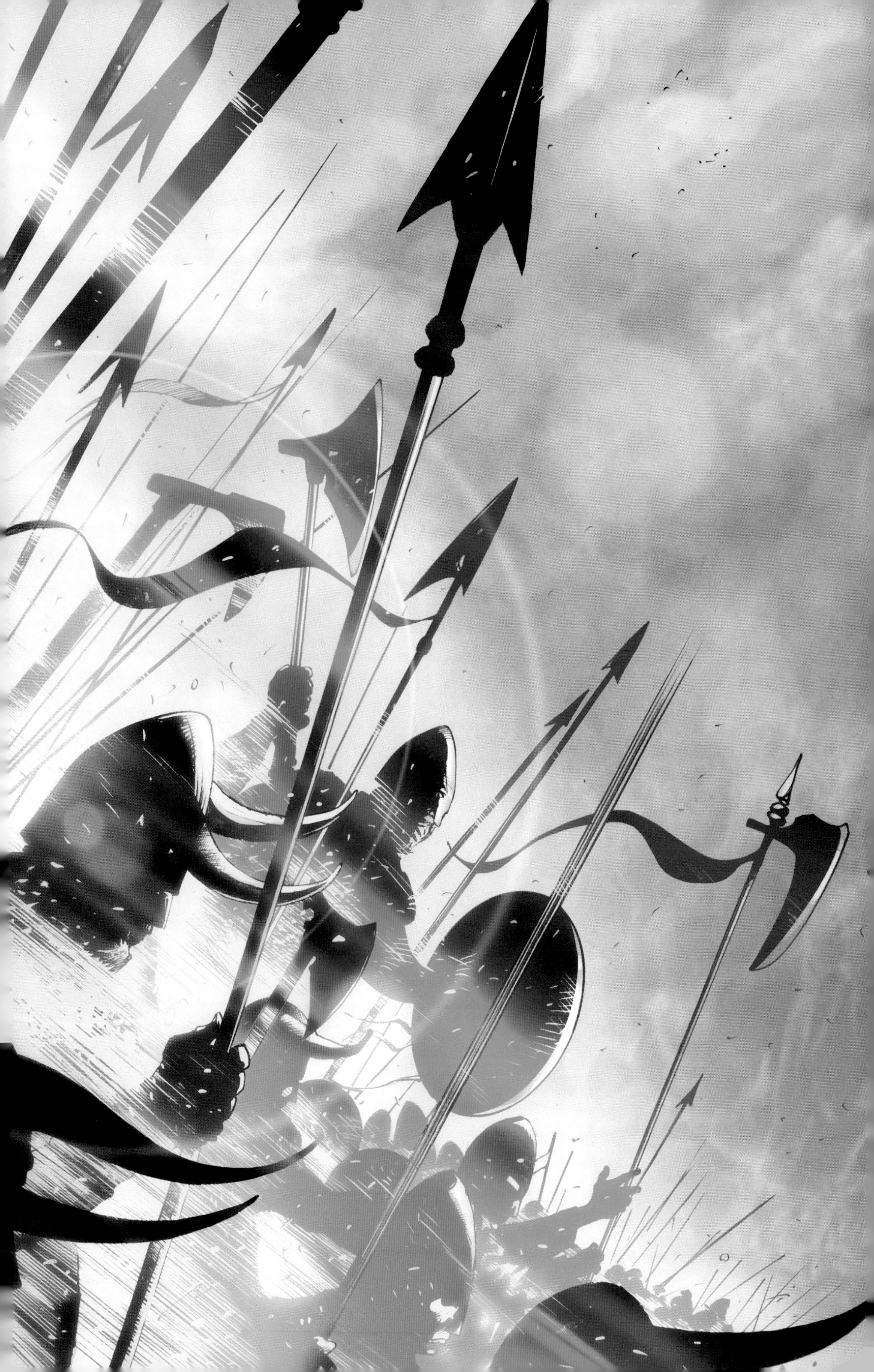

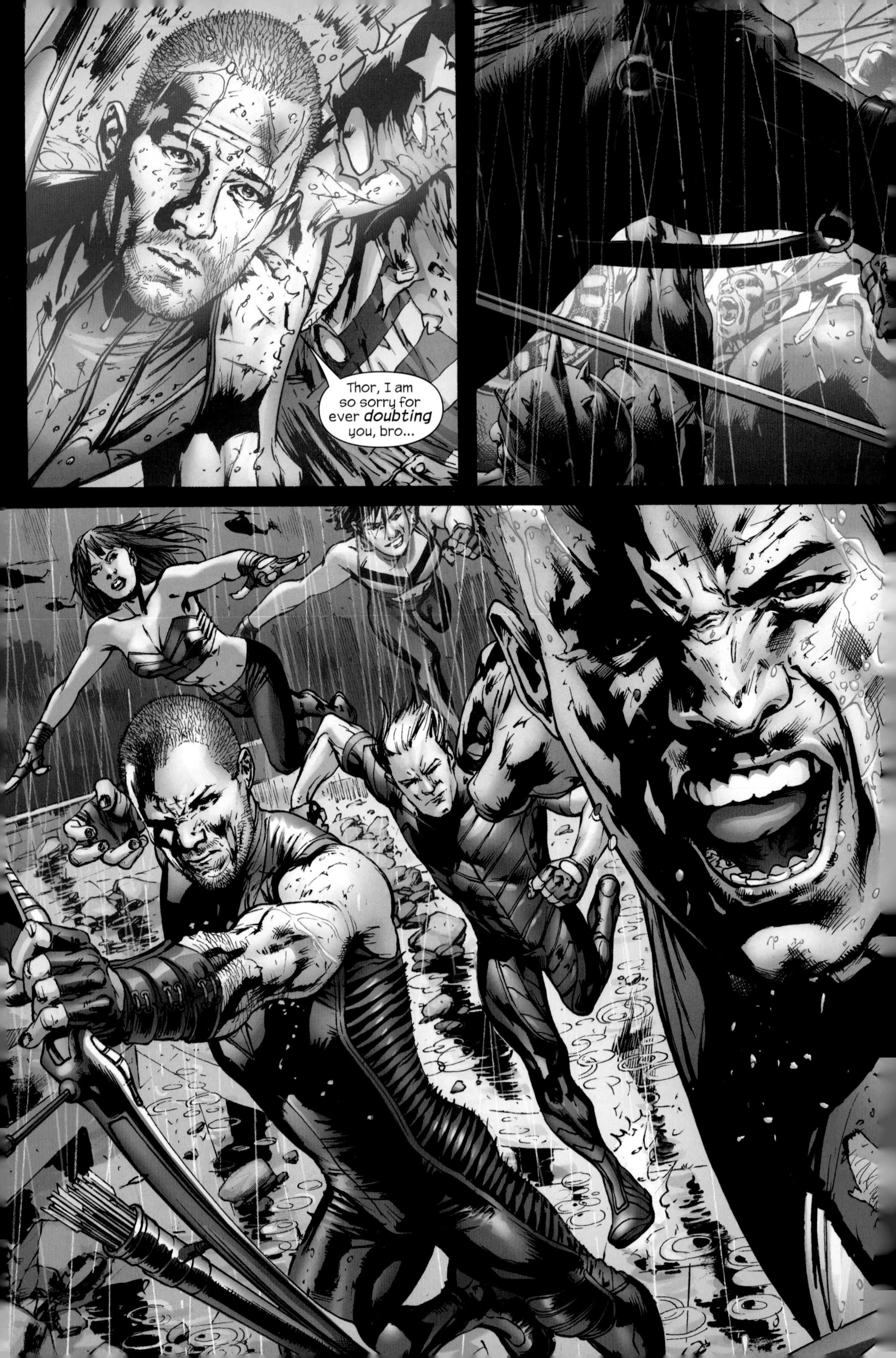
Thor, I am so sorry for ever *doubting* you, bro...

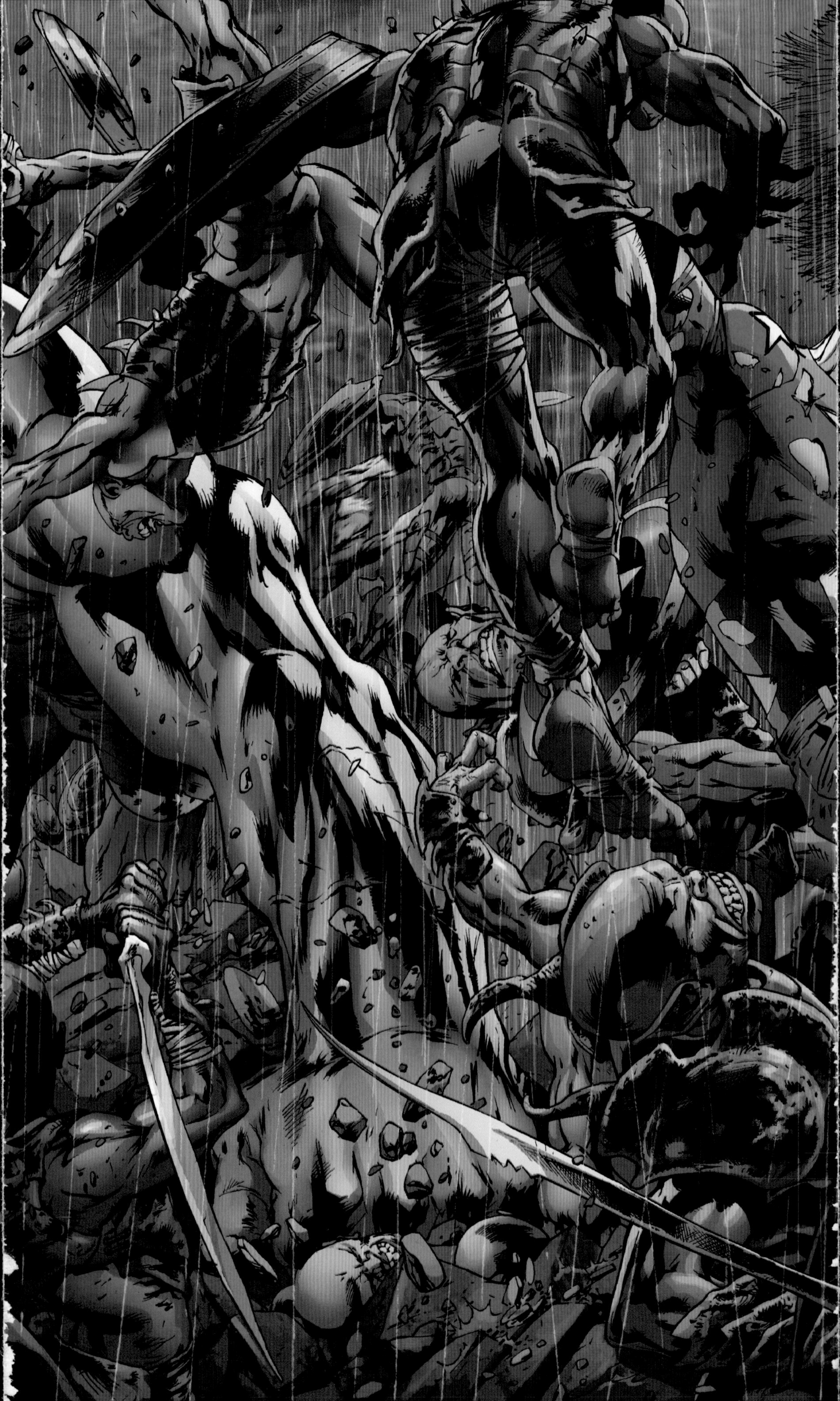

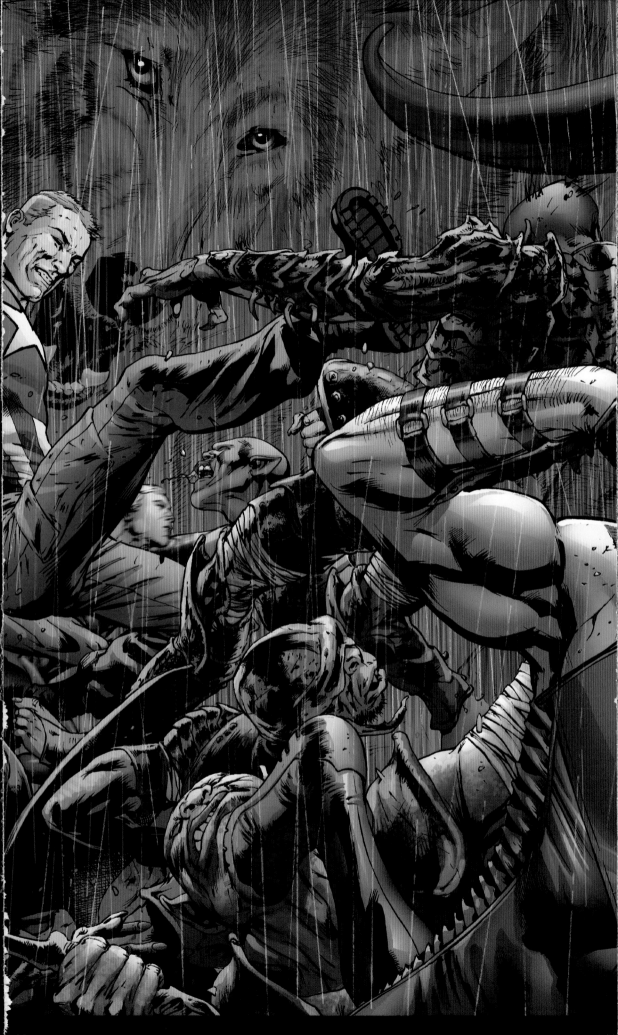

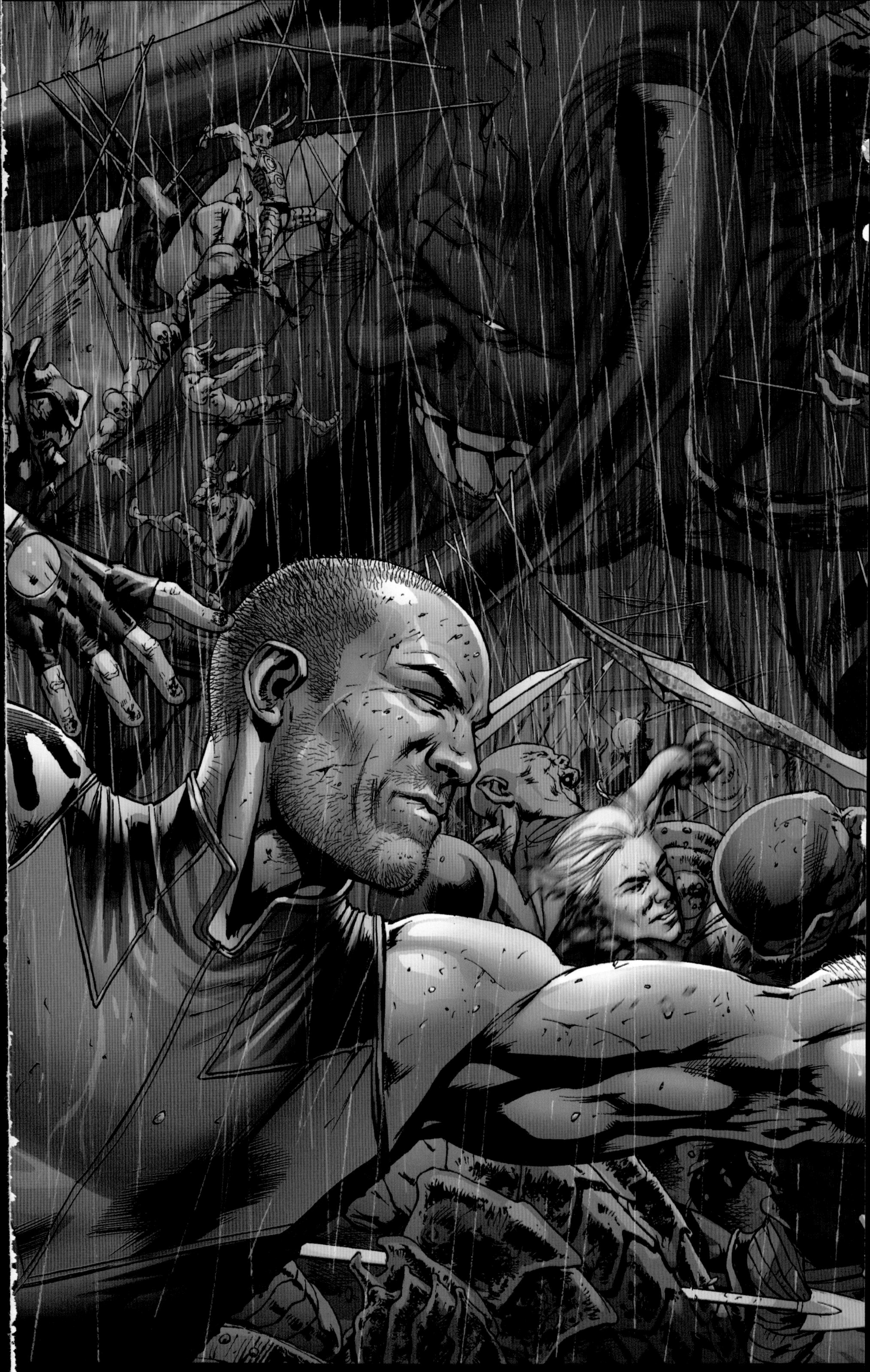

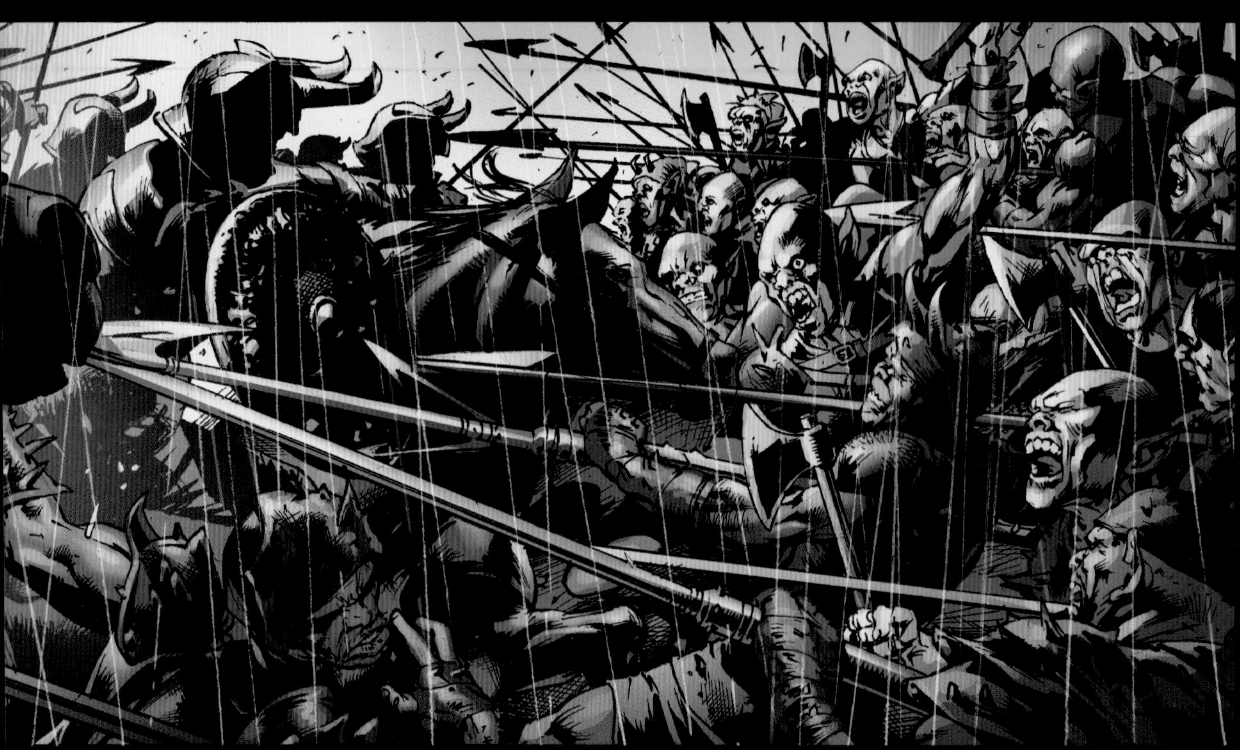
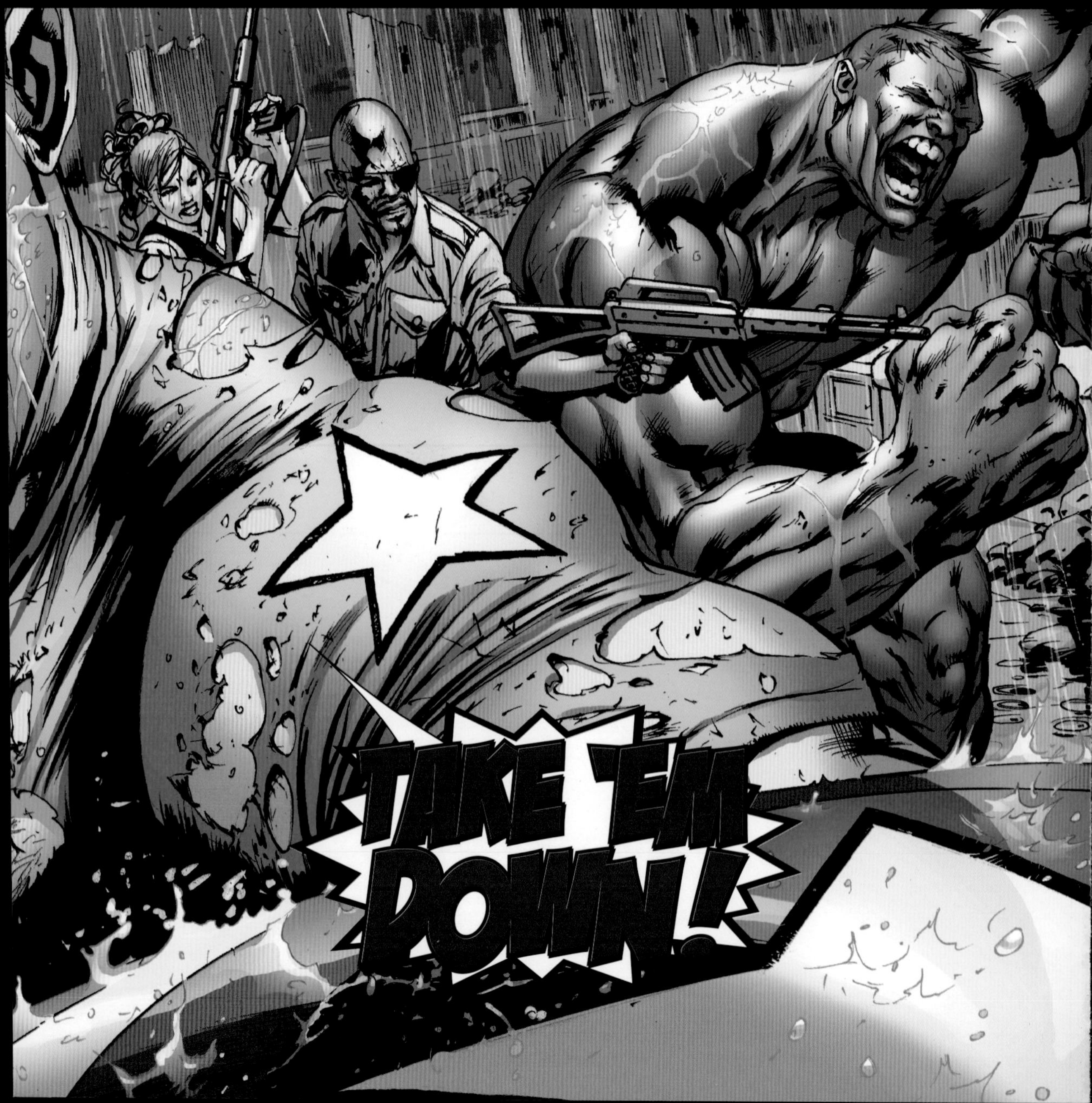
TAKE 'EM DOWN!

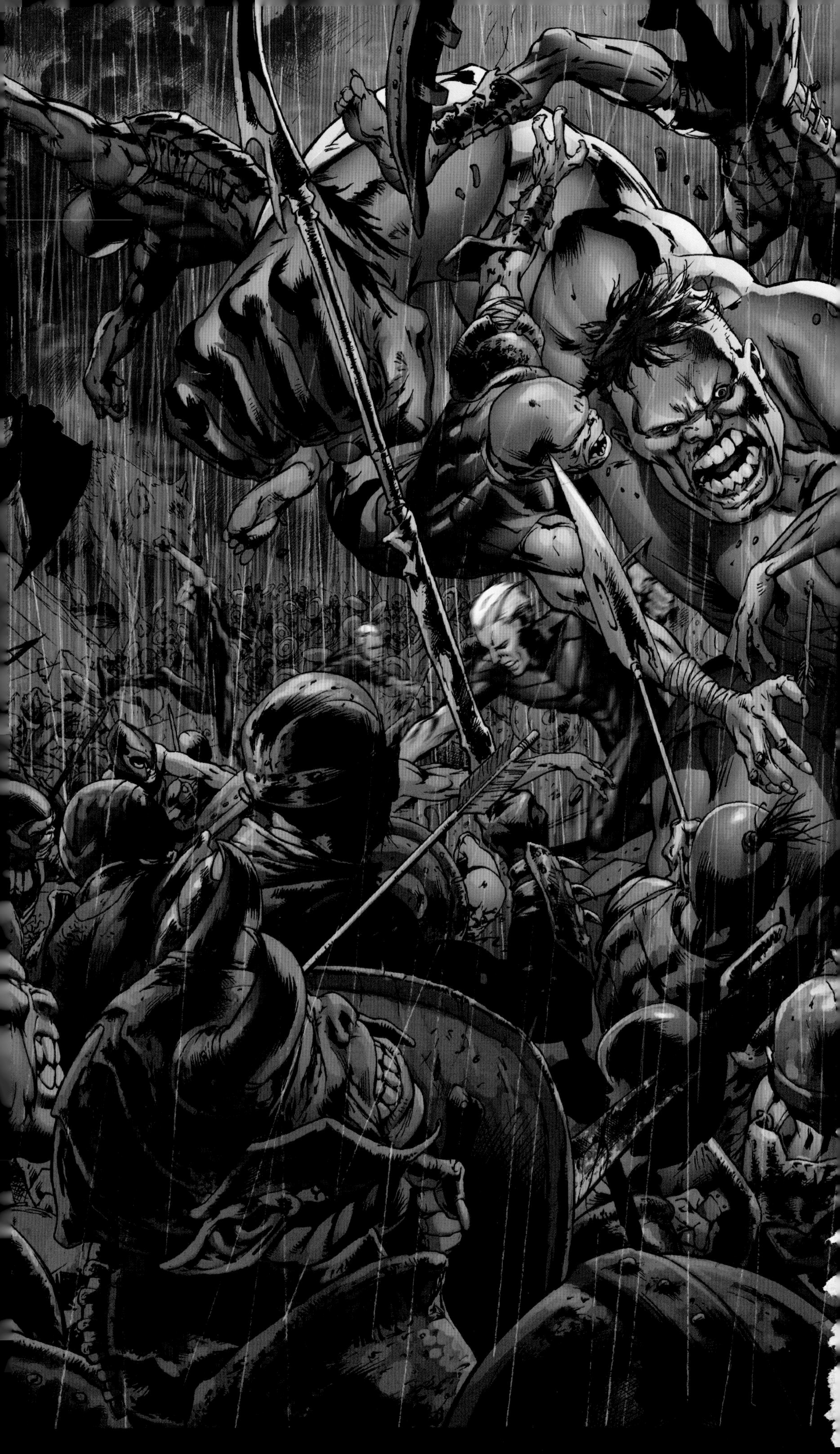

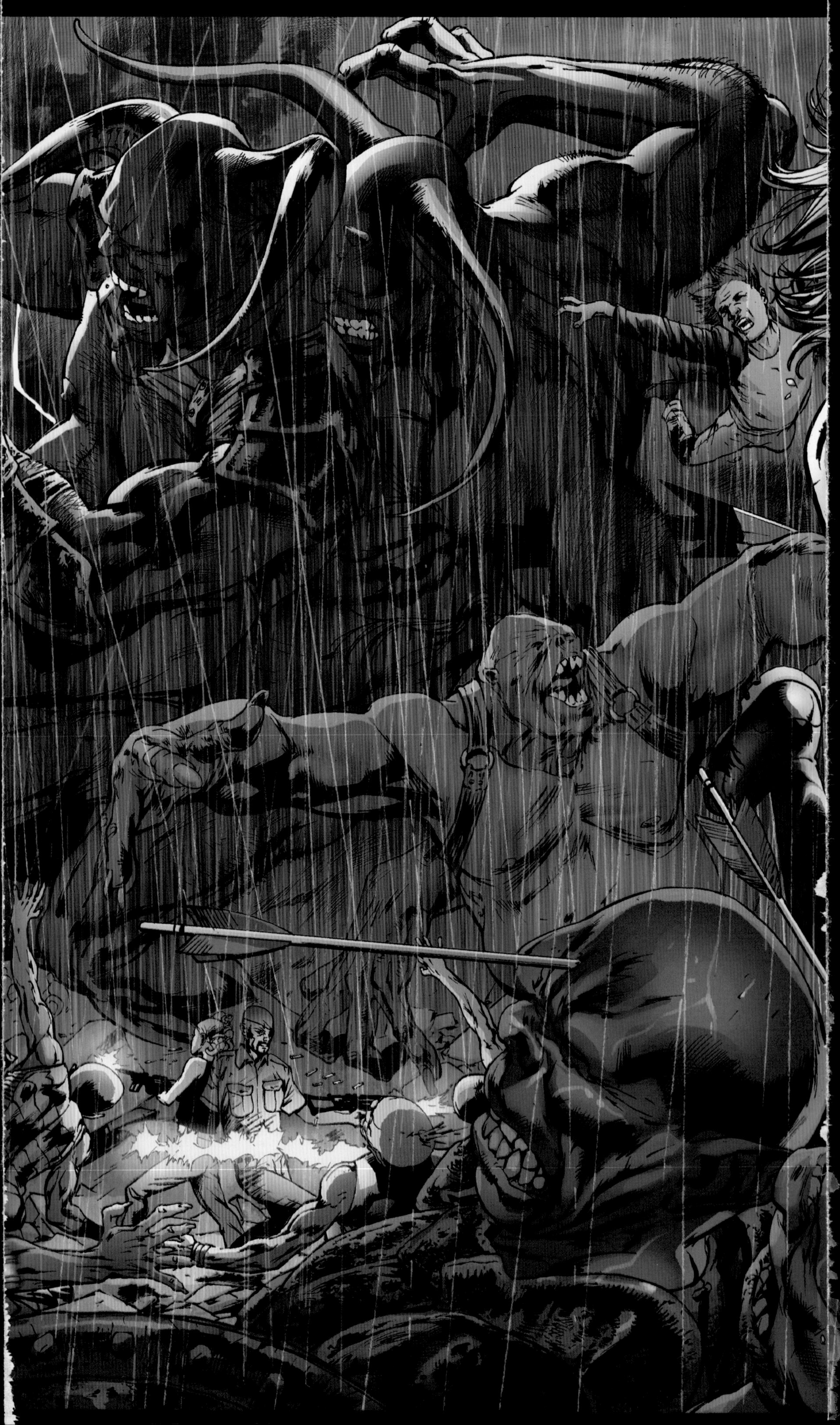

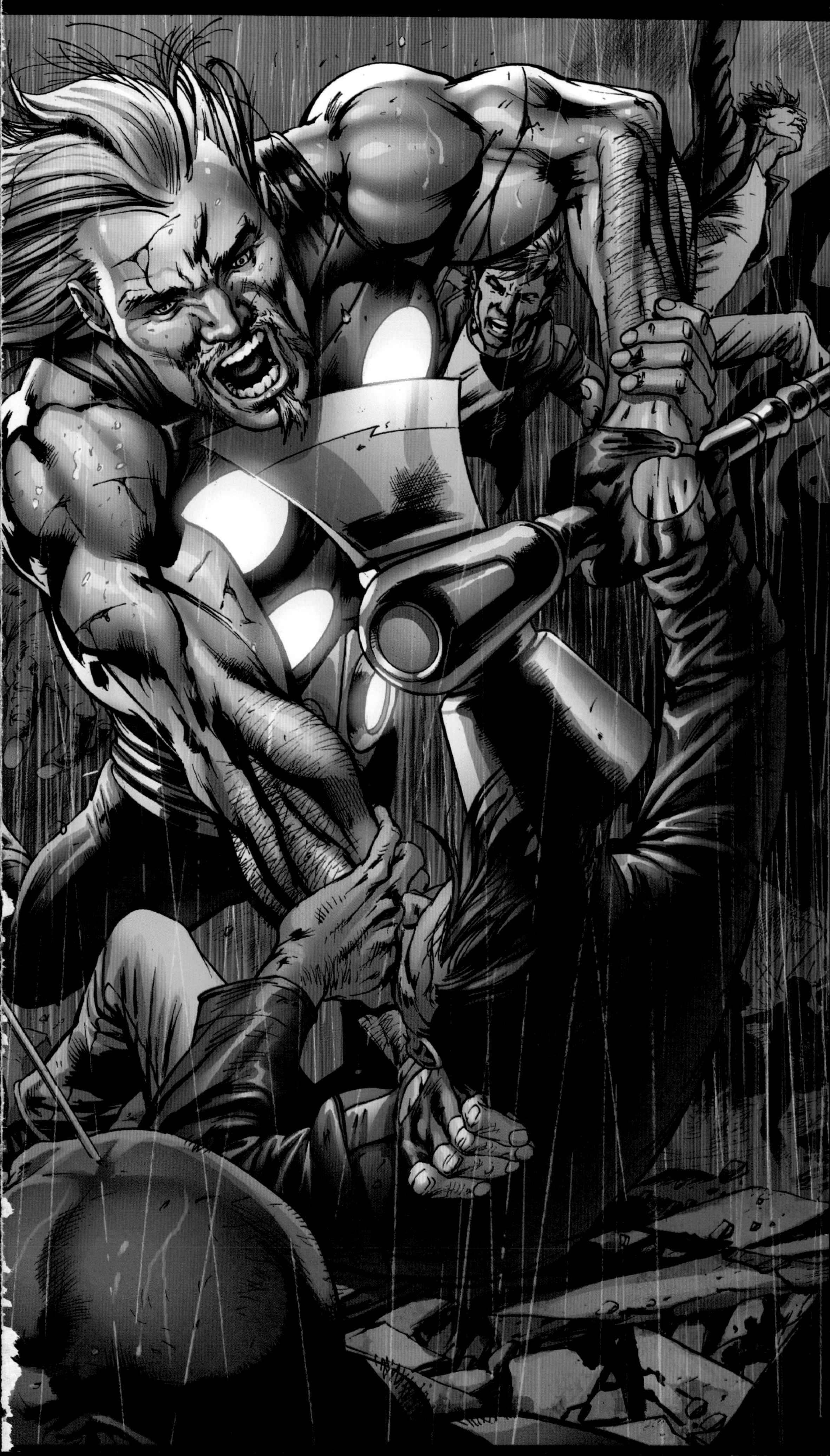

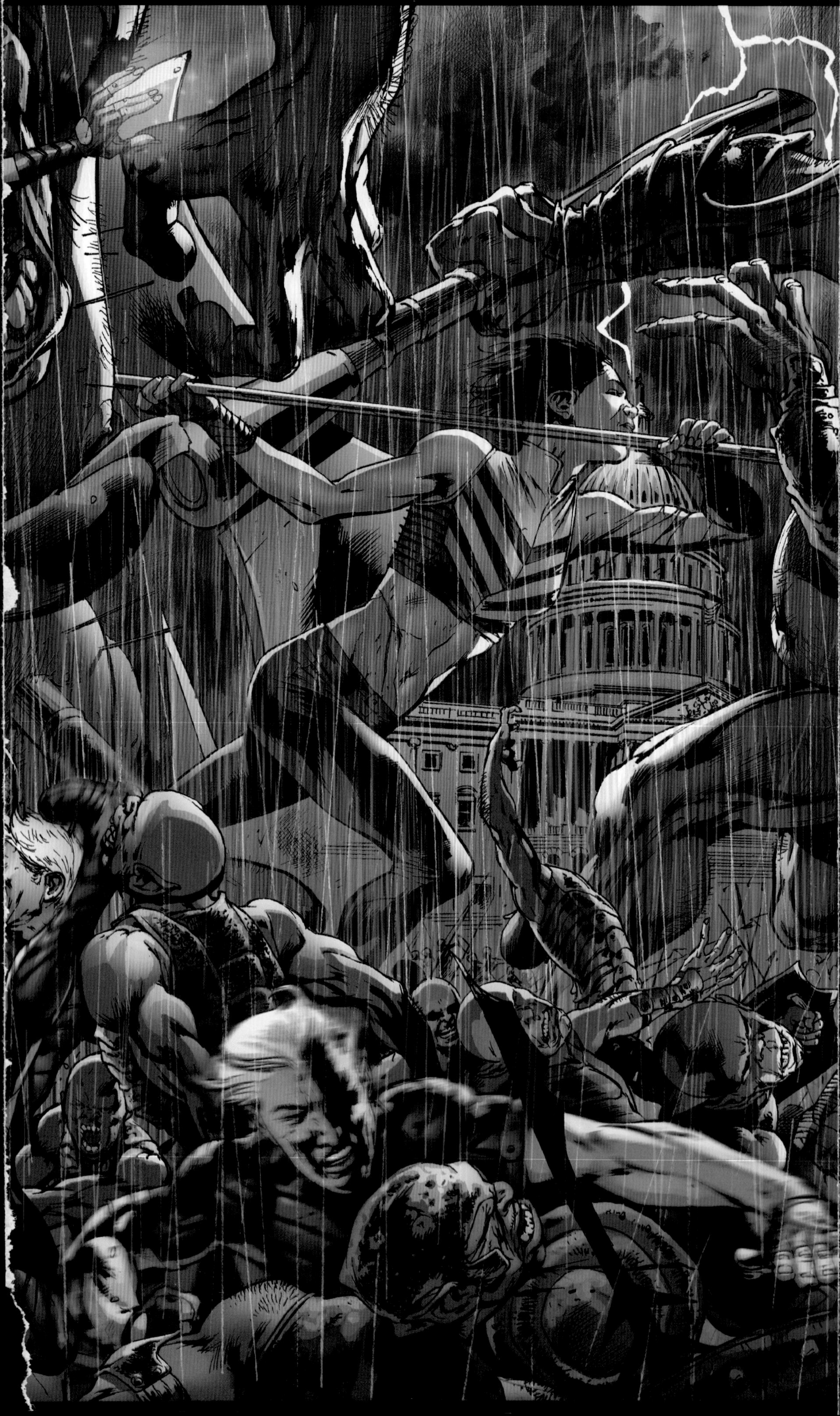

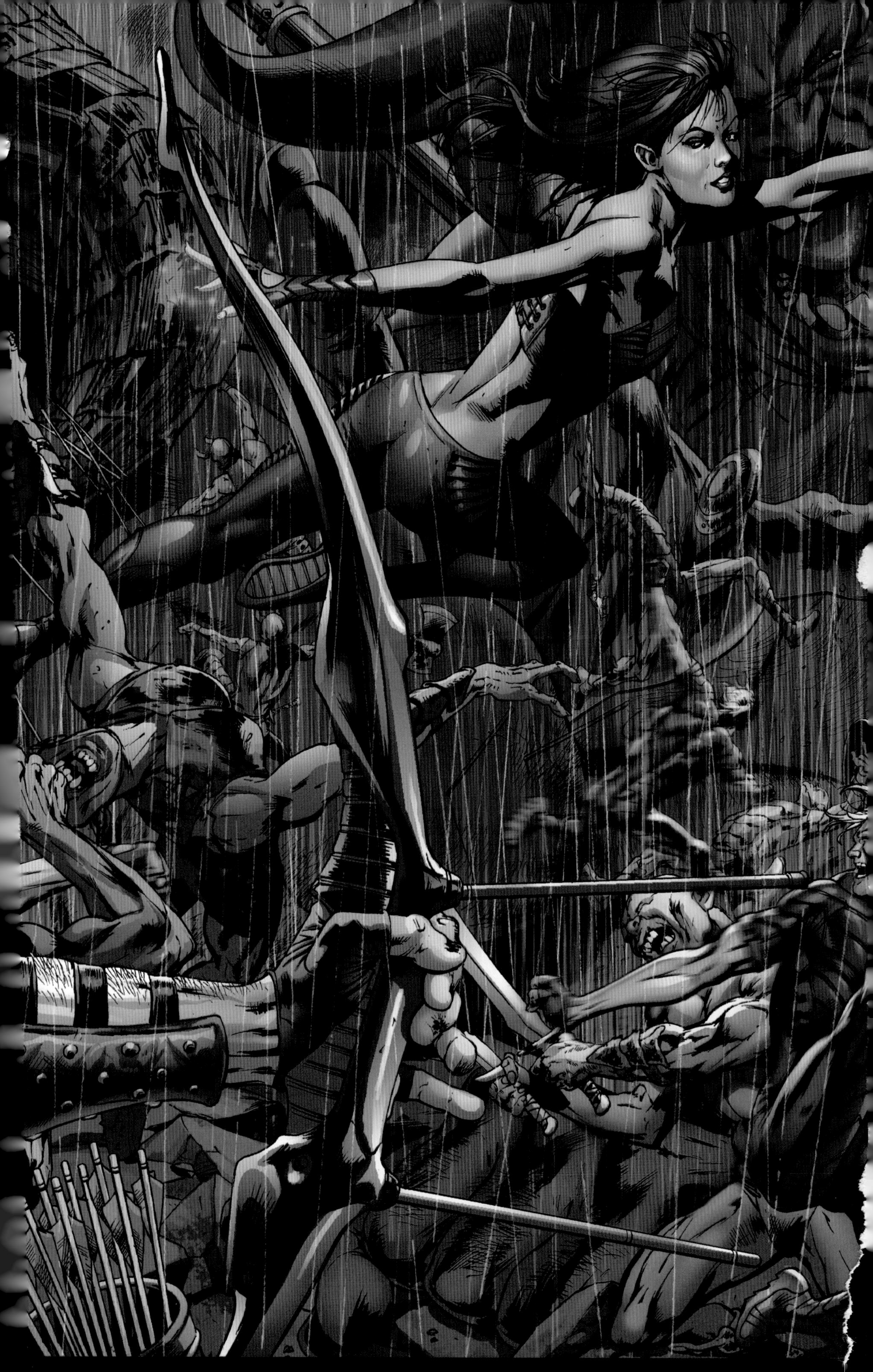

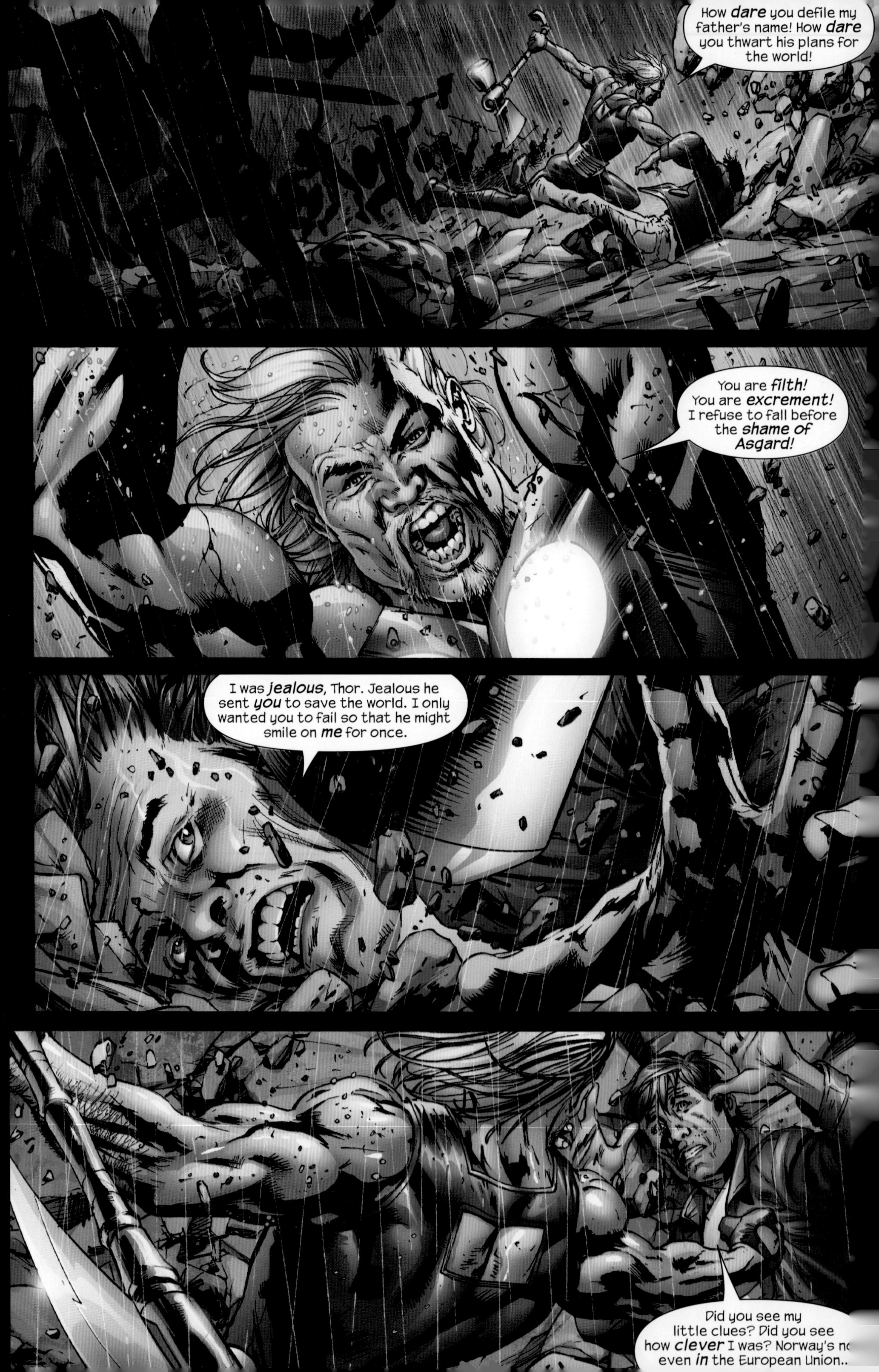
How dare you defile my father's name! How dare you thwart his plans for the world!
You are filth! You are excrement! I refuse to fall before the shame of Asgard!
I was jealous, Thor. Jealous he sent you to save the world. I only wanted you to fail so that he might smile on me for once.
Did you see my little clues? Did you see how clever I was? Norway's not even in the European Union..

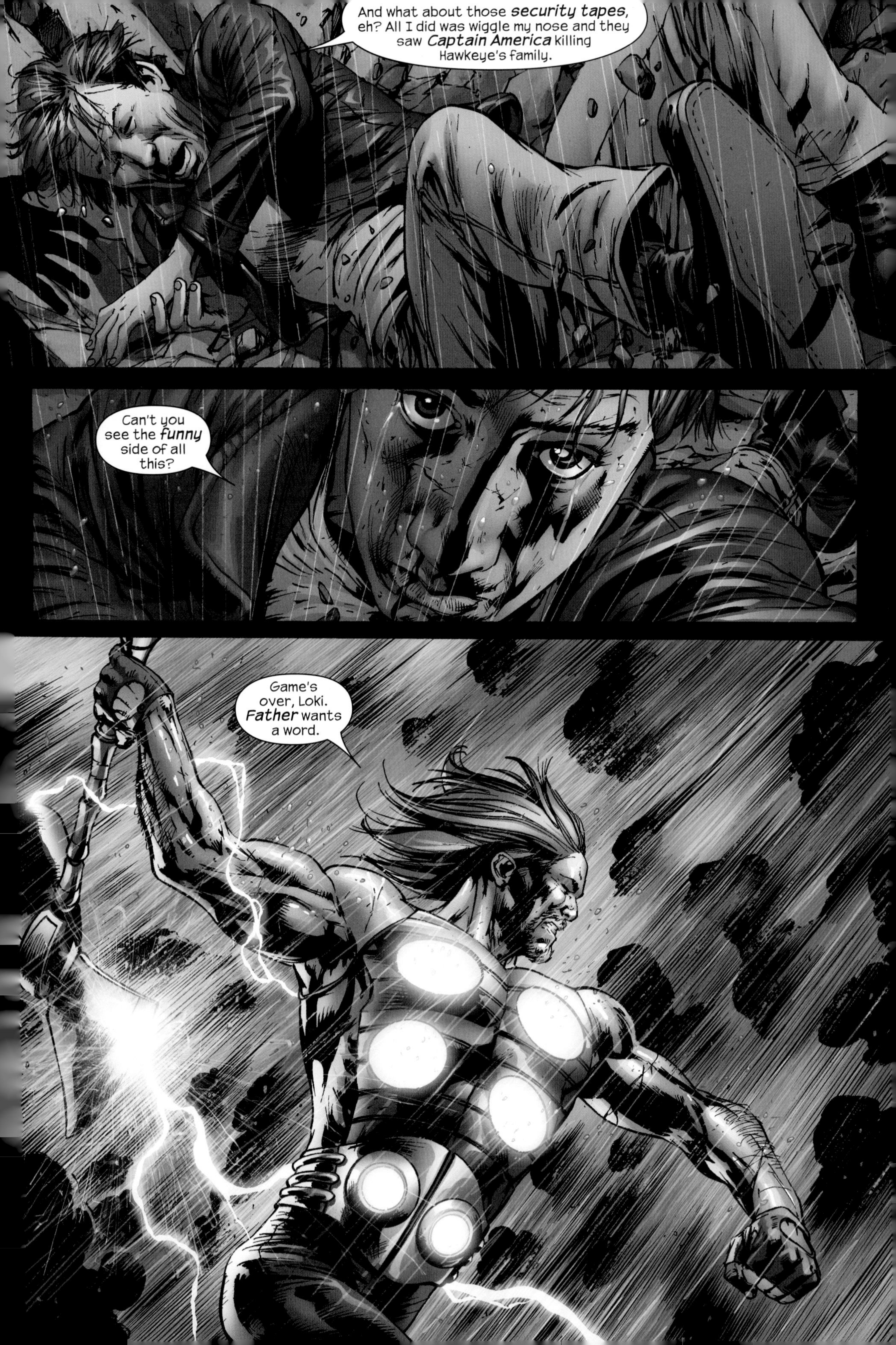
And what about those *security tapes*, eh? All I did was wiggle my nose and they saw *Captain America* killing Hawkeye's family.
Can't you see the *funny* side of all this?
Game's over, Loki. *Father* wants a word.

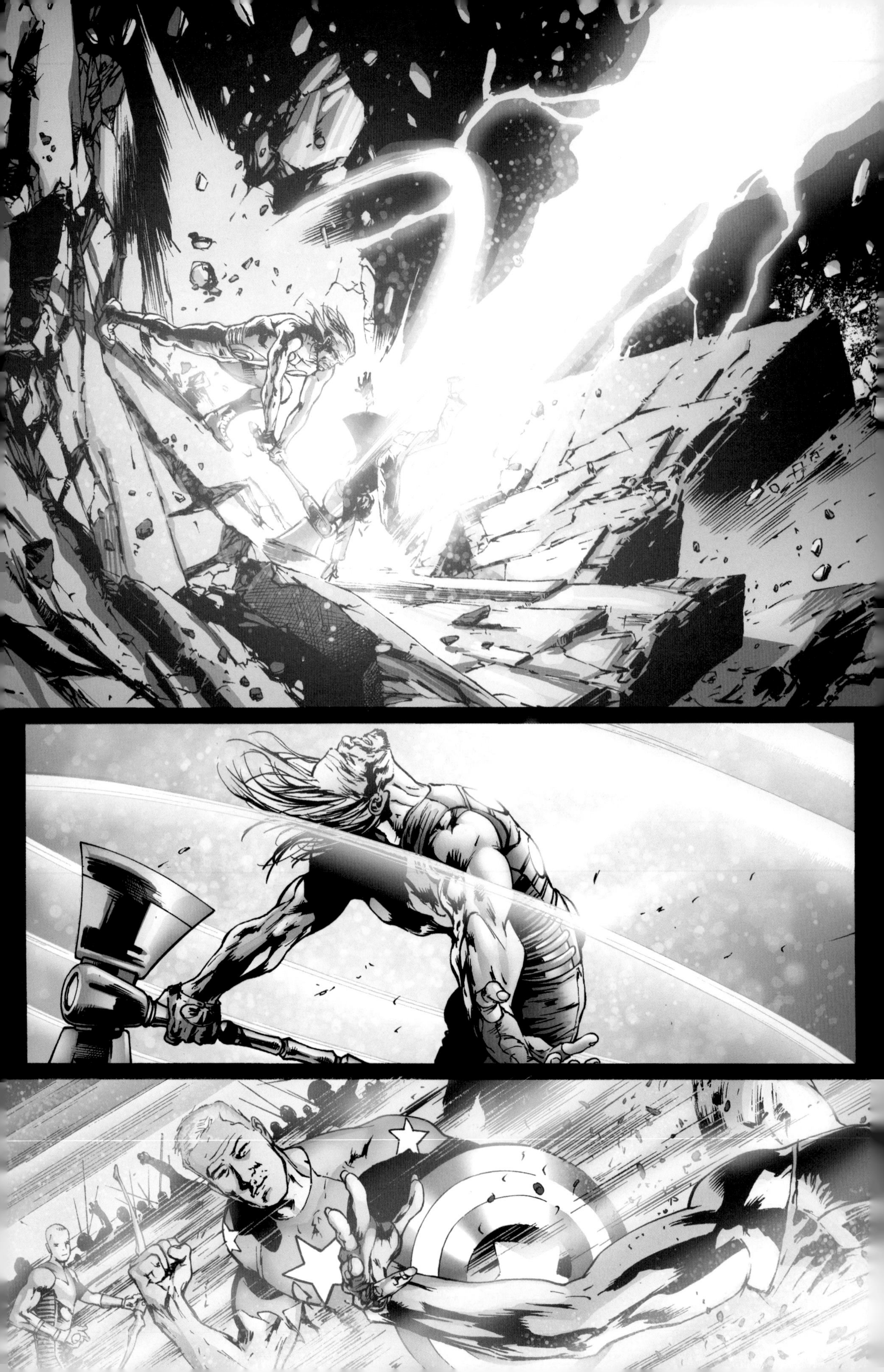

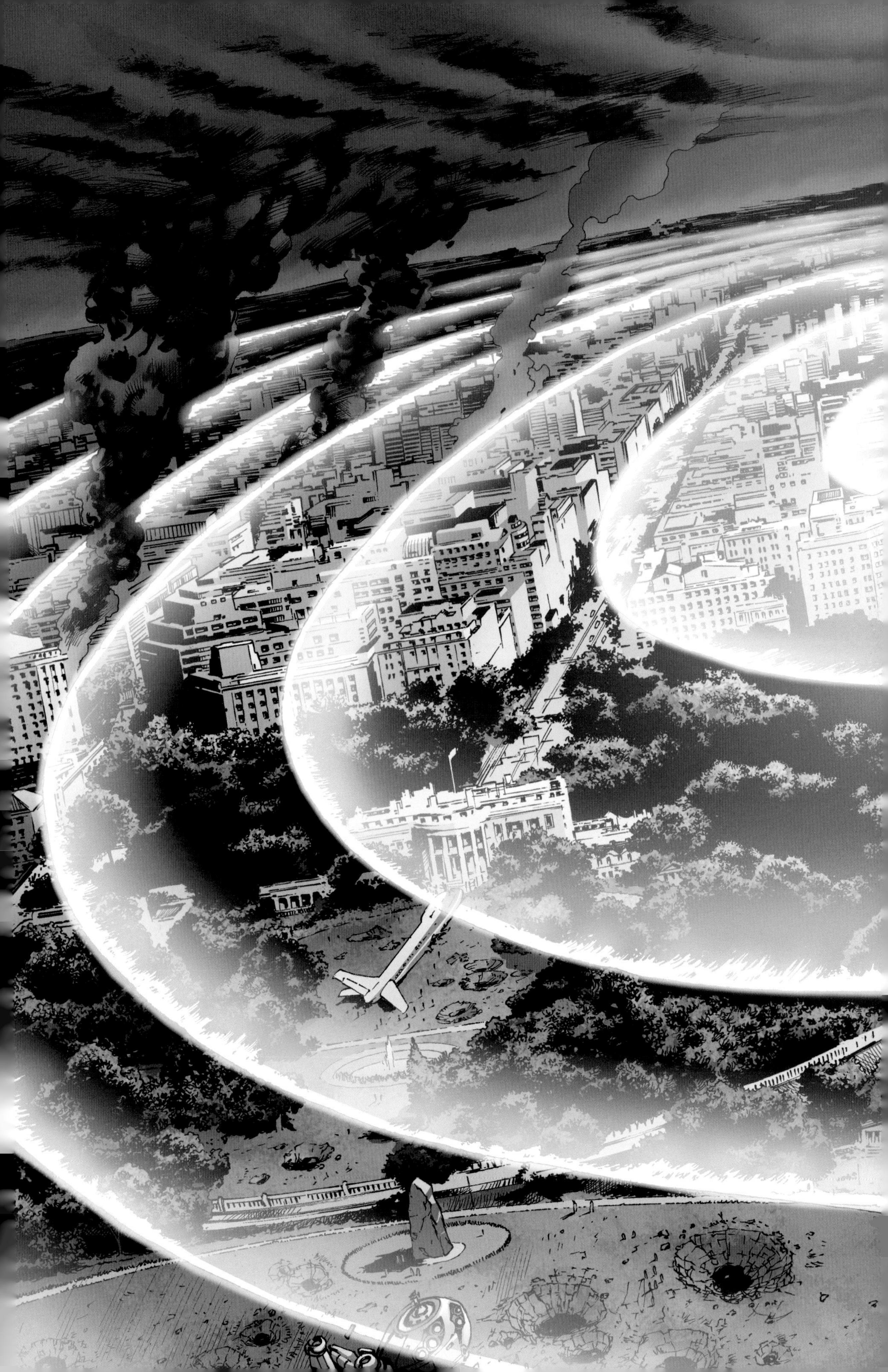

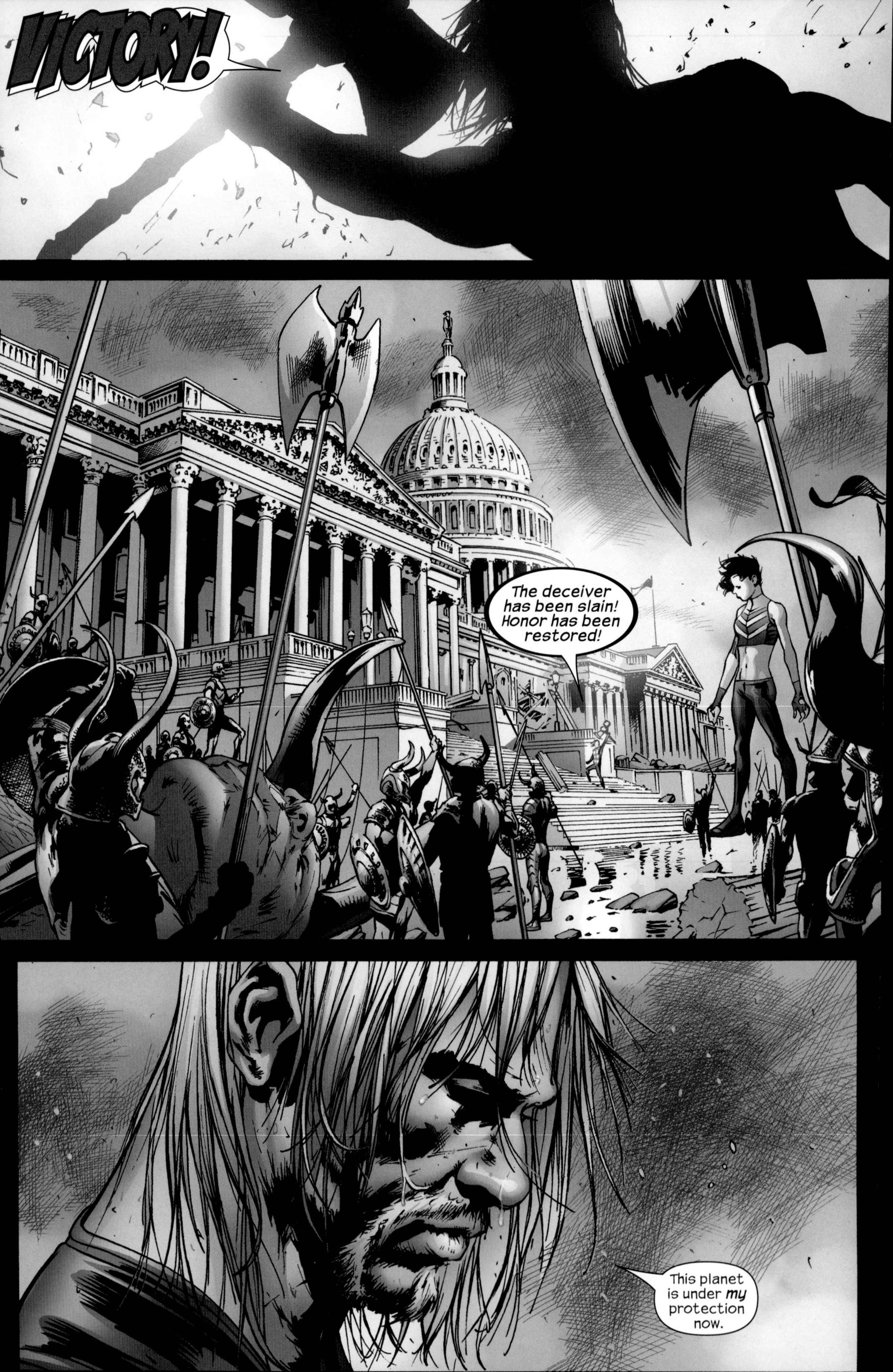
VICTORY!
The deceiver has been slain! Honor has been restored!
This planet is under *my* protection now.

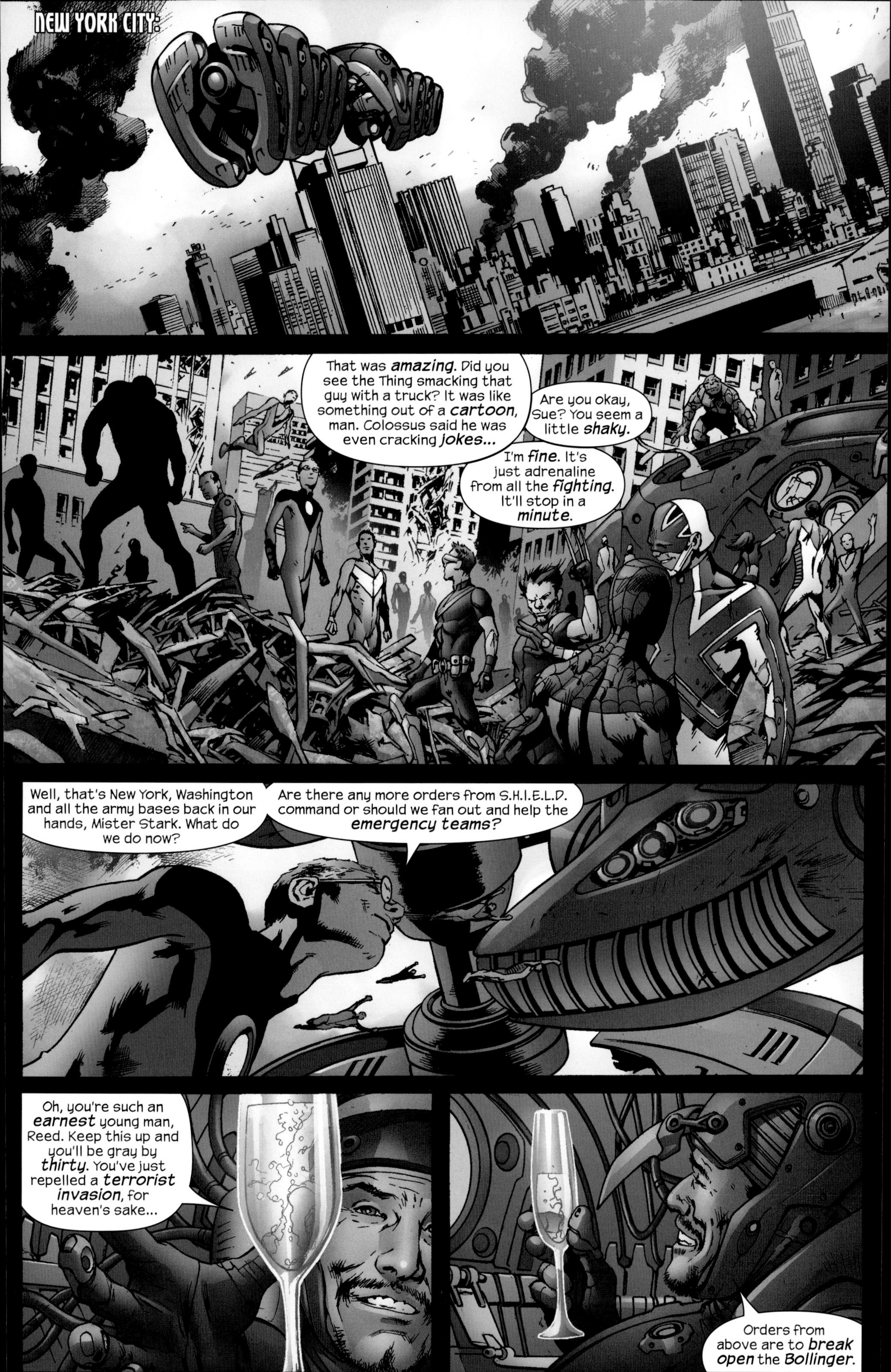

NEW YORK CITY:
That was amazing. Did you see the Thing smacking that guy with a truck? It was like something out of a cartoon, man. Colossus said he was even cracking jokes...
Are you okay, Sue? You seem a little shaky.
I'm fine. It's just adrenaline from all the fighting. It'll stop in a minute.
Well, that's New York, Washington and all the army bases back in our hands, Mister Stark. What do we do now?
Are there any more orders from S.H.I.E.L.D. command or should we fan out and help the emergency teams?
Oh, you're such an earnest young man, Reed. Keep this up and you'll be gray by thirty. You've just repelled a terrorist invasion, for heaven's sake...
Orders from above are to break open the Bollinger.

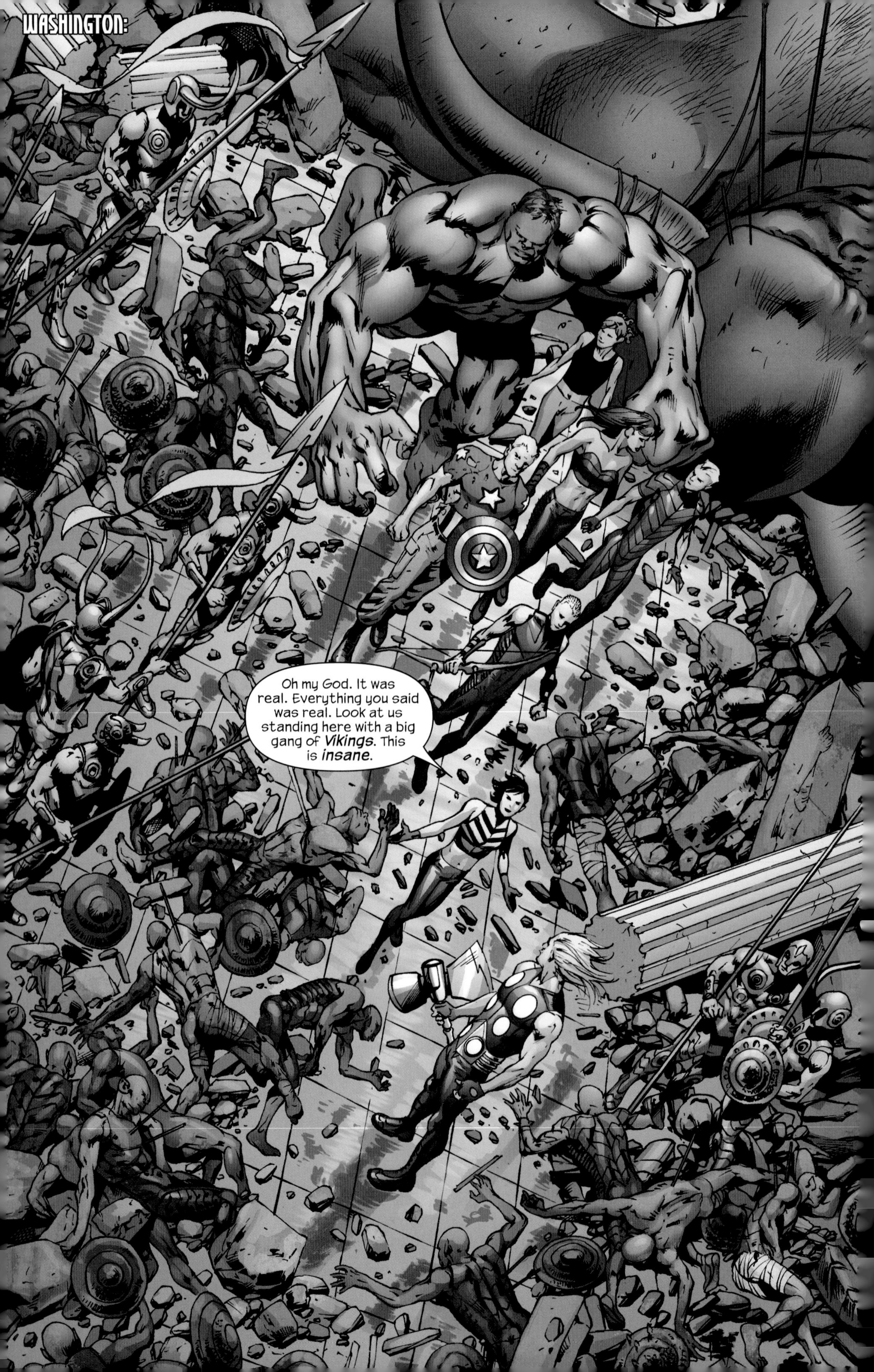
WASHINGTON:
Oh my God. It was real. Everything you said was real. Look at us standing here with a big gang of *Vikings*. This is *insane*.

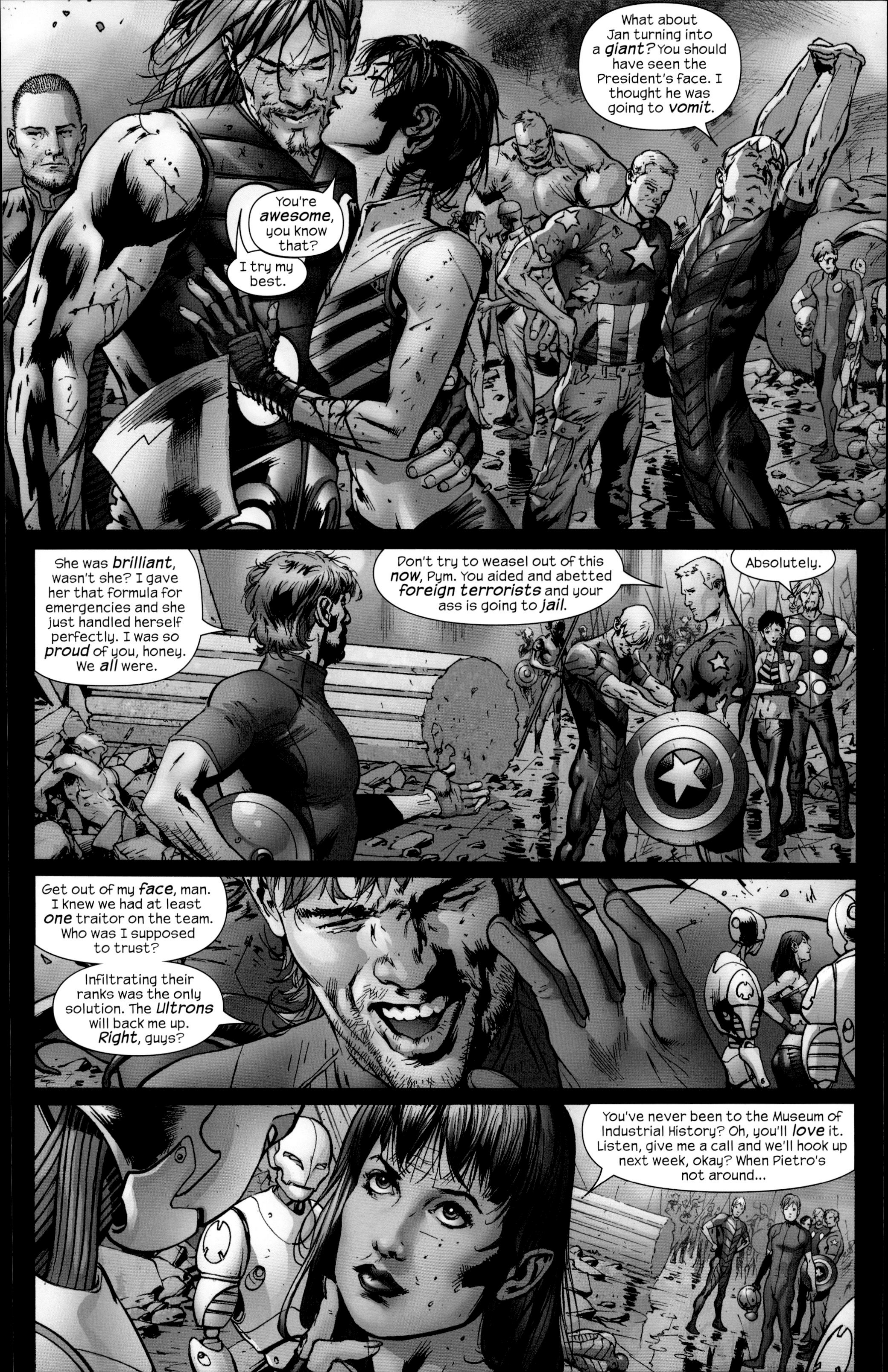
What about Jan turning into a *giant?* You should have seen the President's face. I thought he was going to *vomit*.
You're *awesome*, you know that?
I try my best.
She was *brilliant*, wasn't she? I gave her that formula for emergencies and she just handled herself perfectly. I was so *proud* of you, honey. We *all* were.
Don't try to weasel out of this *now*, Pym. You aided and abetted *foreign terrorists* and your ass is going to *jail*.
Absolutely.
Get out of my *face*, man. I knew we had at least *one* traitor on the team. Who was I supposed to trust?
Infiltrating their ranks was the only solution. The *Ultrons* will back me up. *Right*, guys?
You've never been to the Museum of Industrial History? Oh, you'll *love* it. Listen, give me a call and we'll hook up next week, okay? When Pietro's not around...

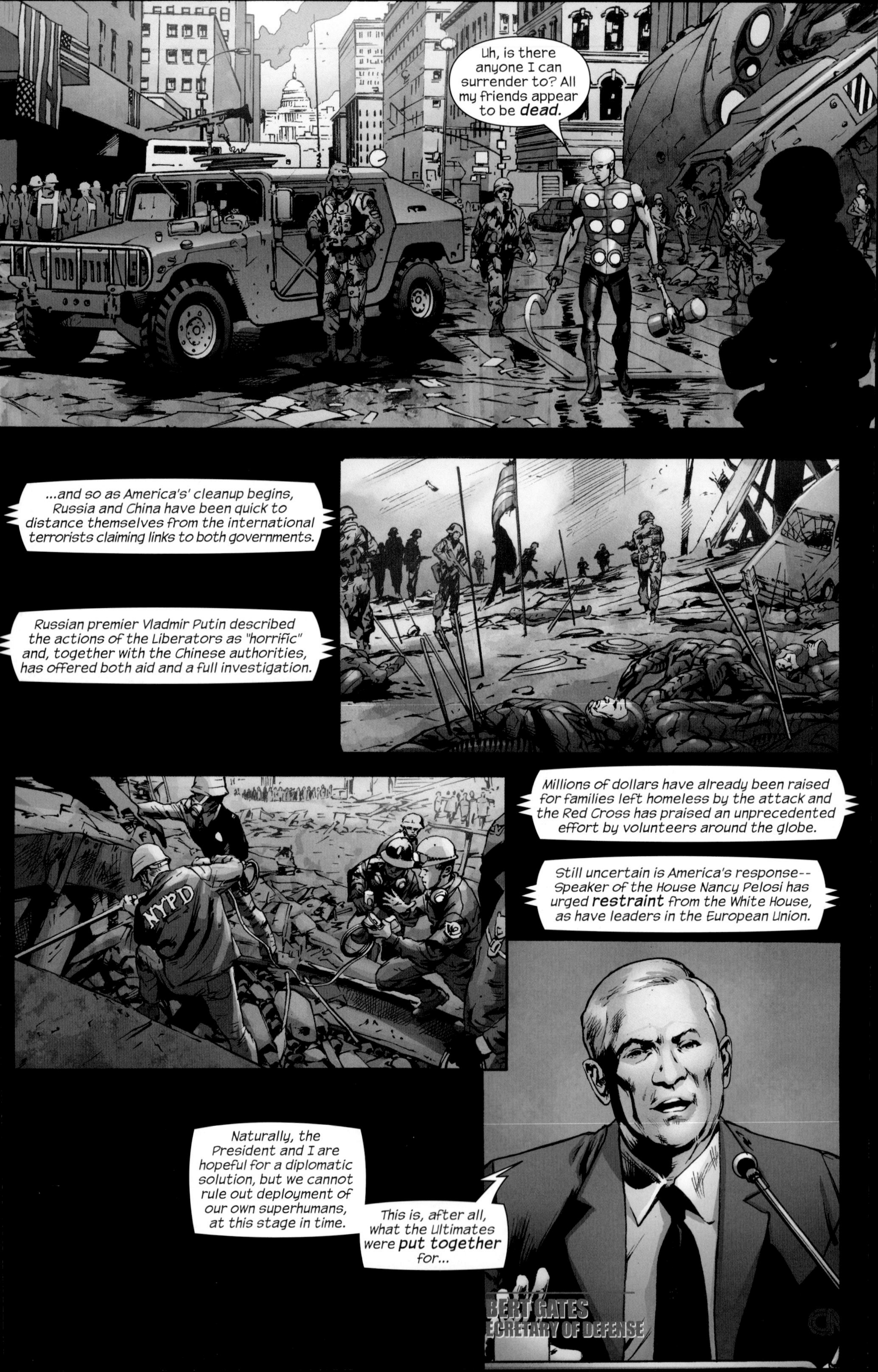
Uh, is there anyone I can surrender to? All my friends appear to be **dead.**
...and so as America's' cleanup begins, Russia and China have been quick to distance themselves from the international terrorists claiming links to both governments.
Russian premier Vladmir Putin described the actions of the Liberators as "horrific" and, together with the Chinese authorities, has offered both aid and a full investigation.
NYPD
Millions of dollars have already been raised for families left homeless by the attack and the Red Cross has praised an unprecedented effort by volunteers around the globe.
Still uncertain is America's response-- Speaker of the House Nancy Pelosi has urged **restraint** from the White House, as have leaders in the European Union.
Naturally, the President and I are hopeful for a diplomatic solution, but we cannot rule out deployment of our own superhumans, at this stage in time.
This is, after all, what the Ultimates were **put together** for...
BERT GATES
ECRETARY OF DEFENSE

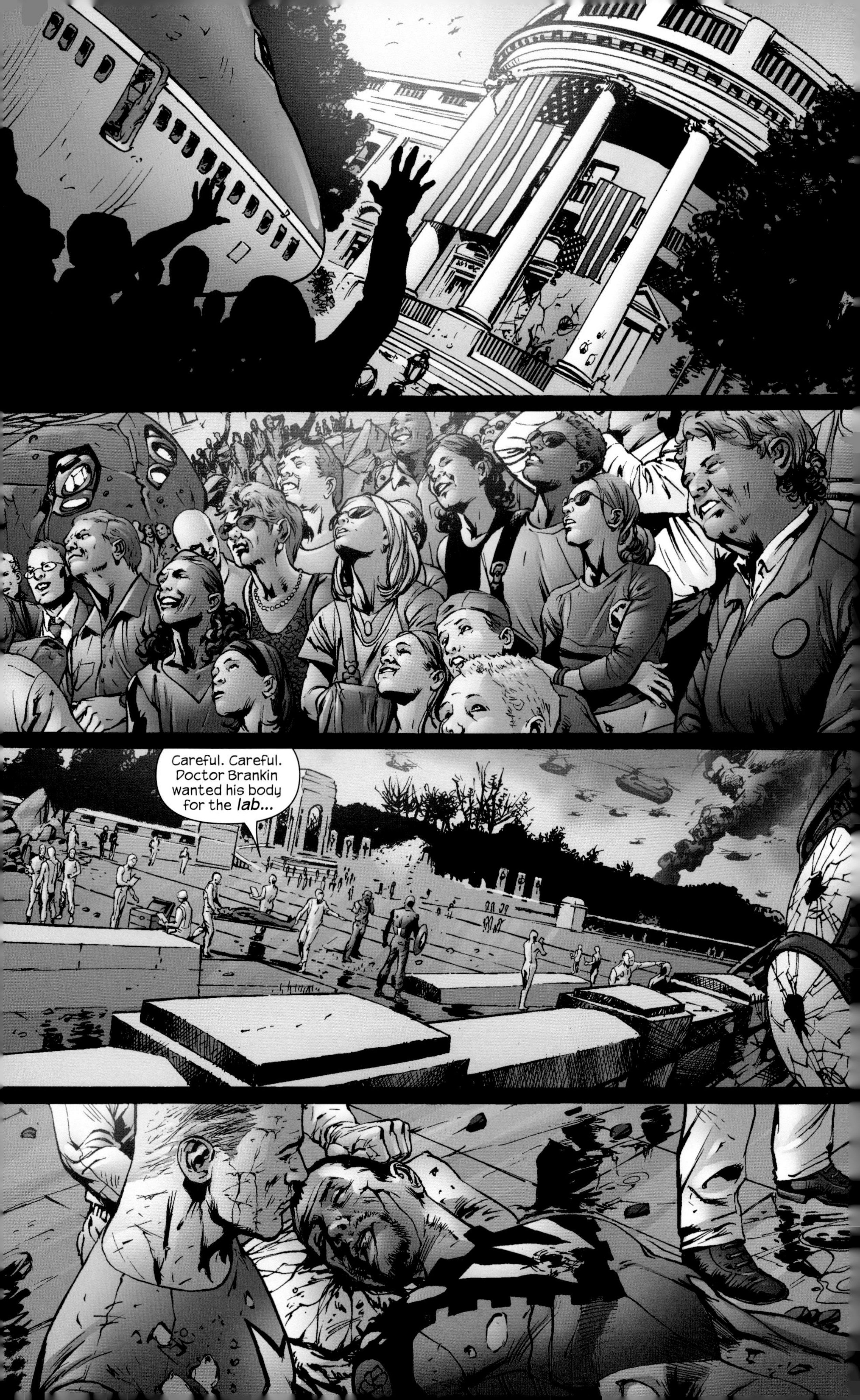
Careful. Careful. Doctor Brankin wanted his body for the *lab*...

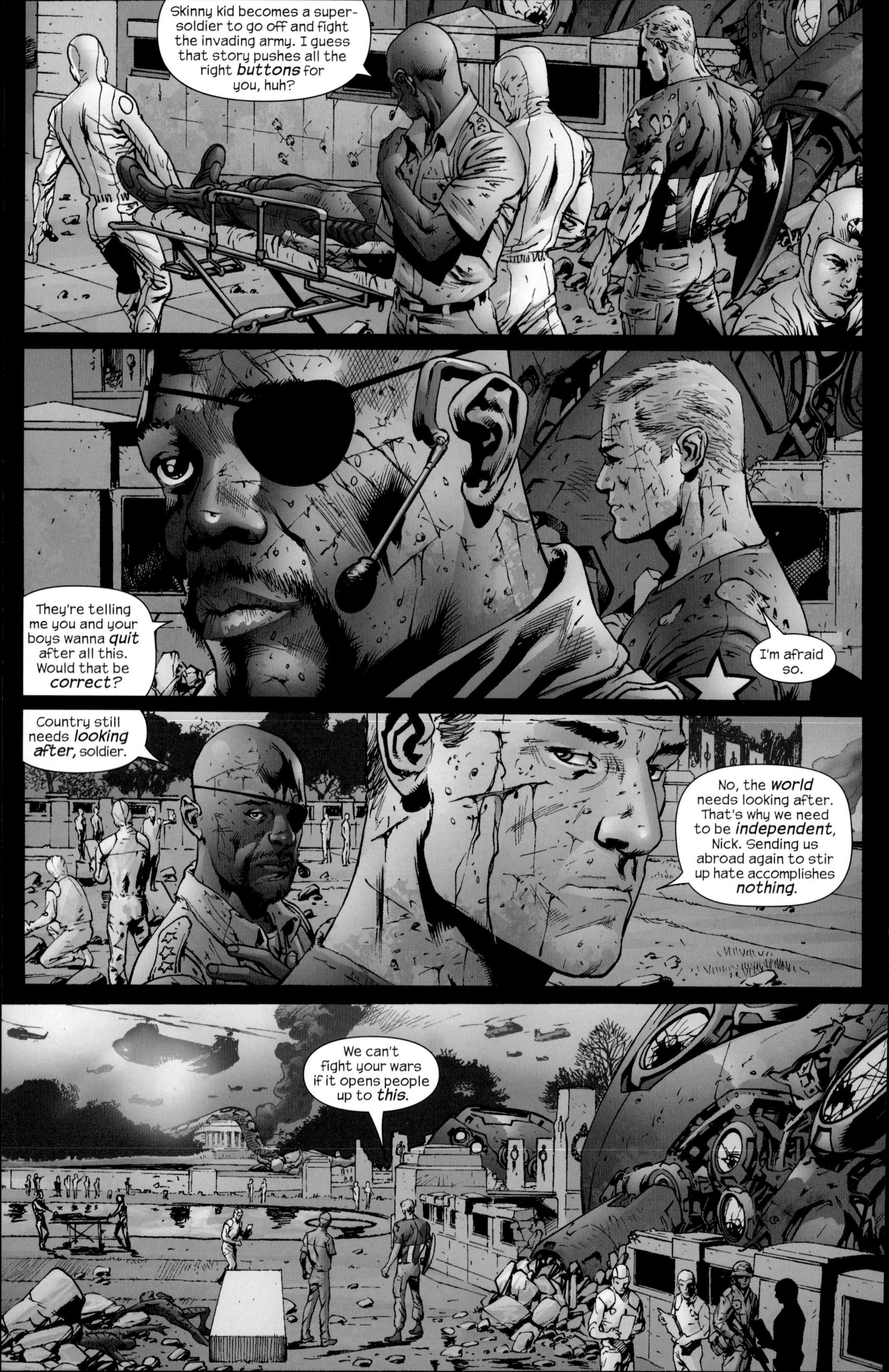
Skinny kid becomes a super-soldier to go off and fight the invading army. I guess that story pushes all the right *buttons* for you, huh?
They're telling me you and your boys wanna *quit* after all this. Would that be *correct?*
I'm afraid so.
Country still needs *looking after,* soldier.
No, the *world* needs looking after. That's why we need to be *independent*, Nick. Sending us abroad again to stir up hate accomplishes *nothing*.
We can't fight your wars if it opens people up to *this*.

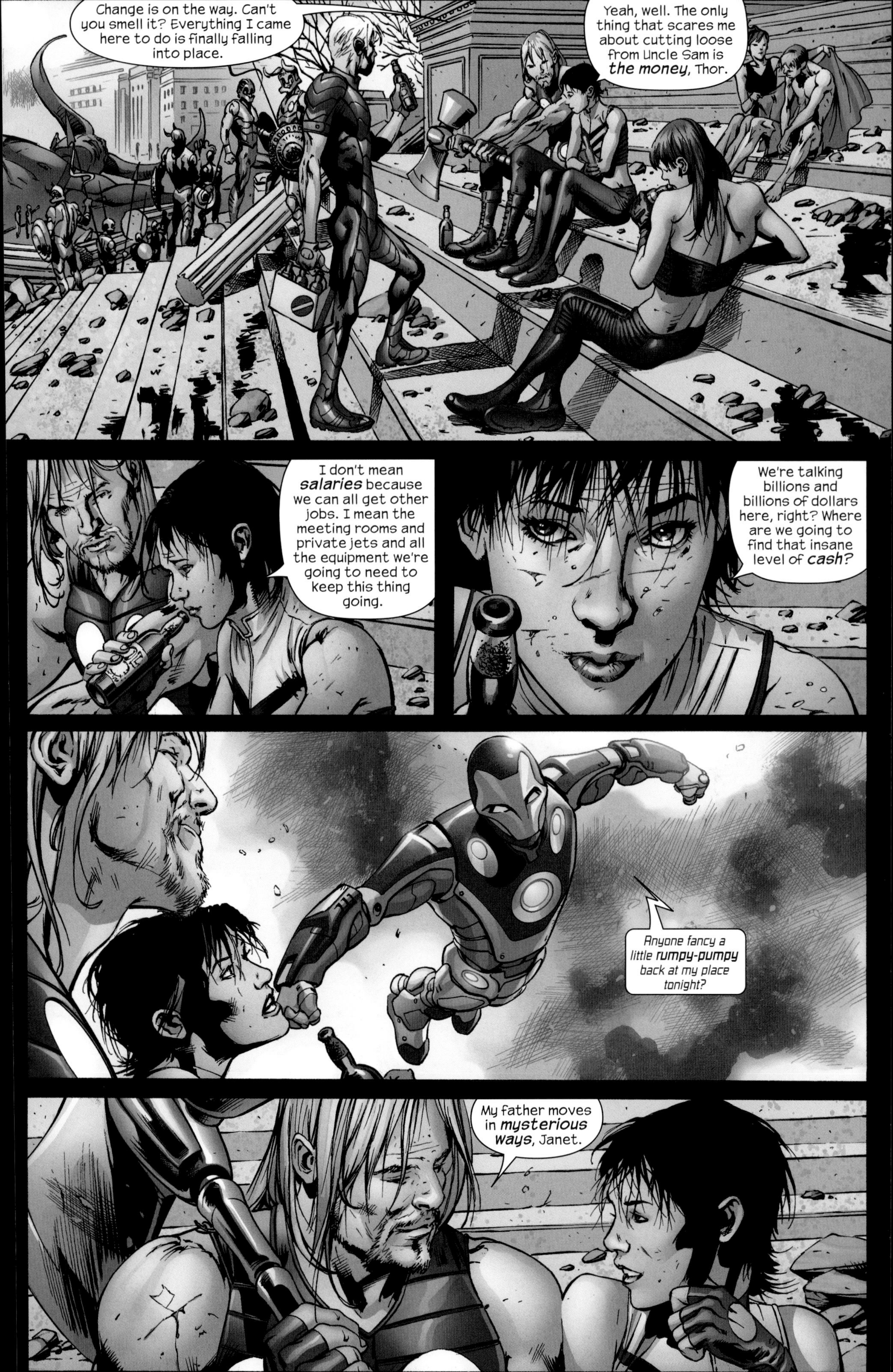

Change is on the way. Can't you smell it? Everything I came here to do is finally falling into place.
Yeah, well. The only thing that scares me about cutting loose from Uncle Sam is the money, Thor.
I don't mean salaries because we can all get other jobs. I mean the meeting rooms and private jets and all the equipment we're going to need to keep this thing going.
We're talking billions and billions of dollars here, right? Where are we going to find that insane level of cash?
Anyone fancy a little rumpy-pumpy back at my place tonight?
My father moves in mysterious ways, Janet.

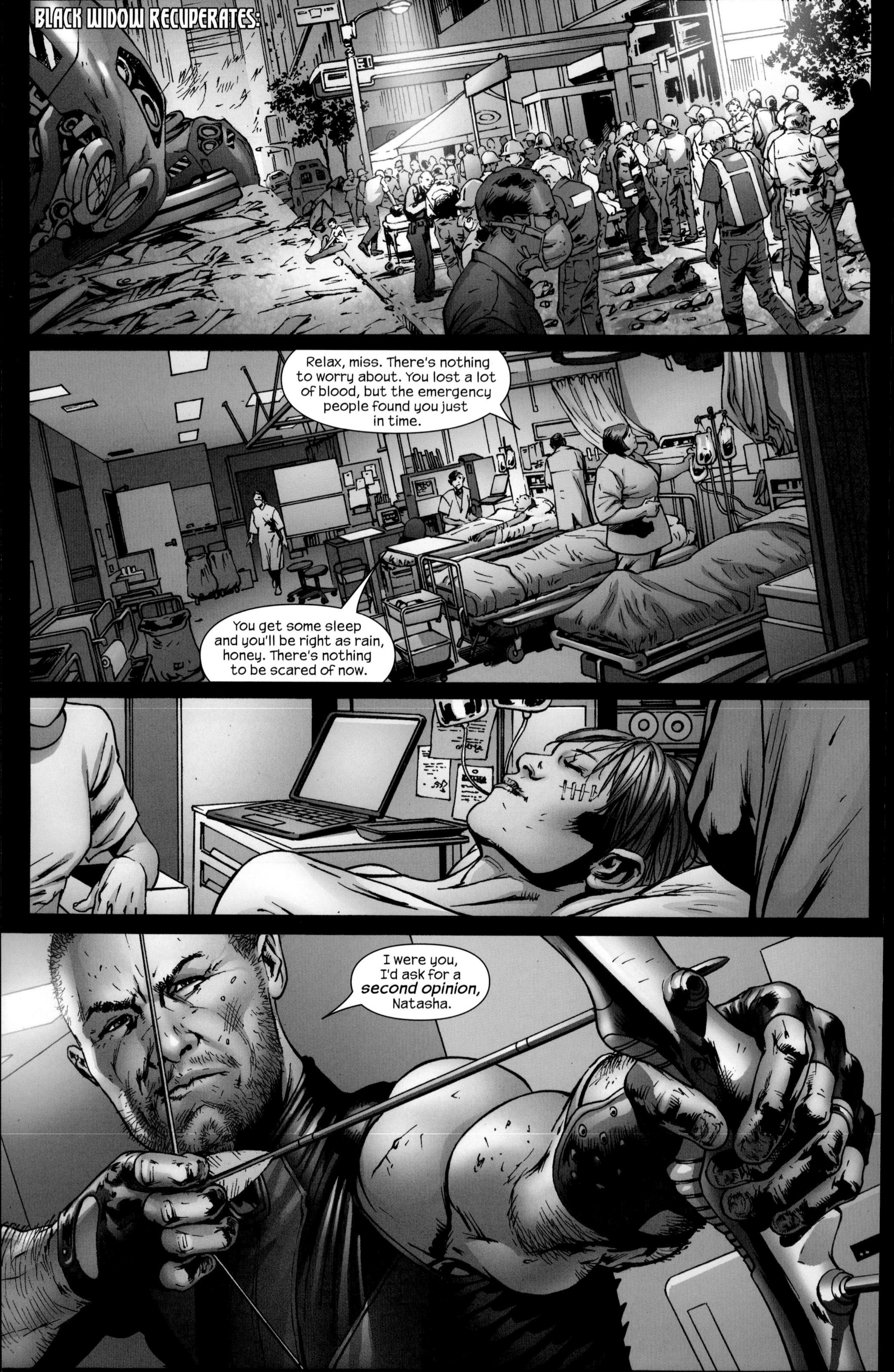
BLACK WIDOW RECUPERATES:
Relax, miss. There's nothing to worry about. You lost a lot of blood, but the emergency people found you just in time.
You get some sleep and you'll be right as rain, honey. There's nothing to be scared of now.
I were you, I'd ask for a *second opinion,* Natasha.

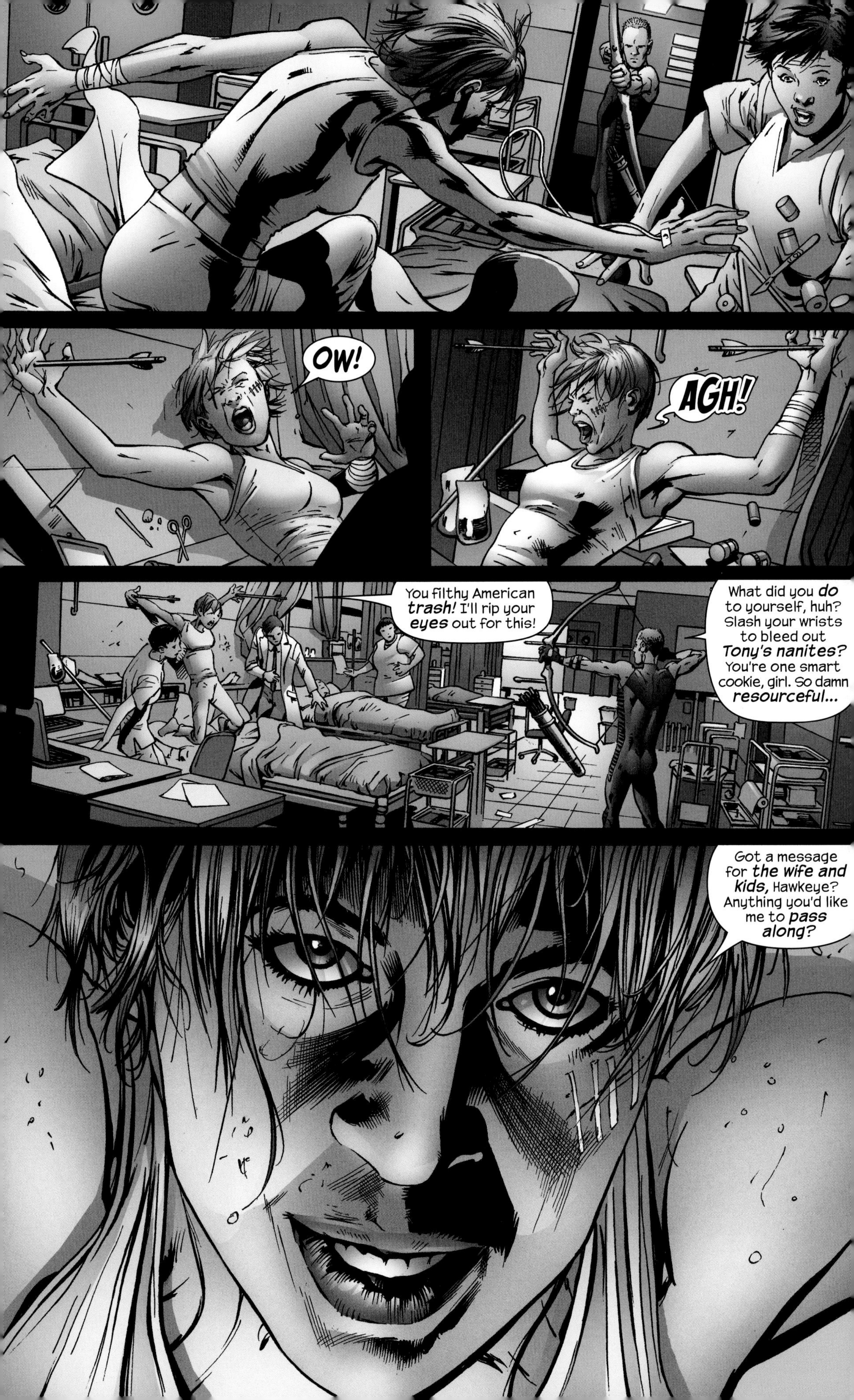
OW!
AGH!
You filthy American trash! I'll rip your eyes out for this!
What did you do to yourself, huh? Slash your wrists to bleed out Tony's nanites? You're one smart cookie, girl. So damn resourceful...
Got a message for the wife and kids, Hawkeye? Anything you'd like me to pass along?

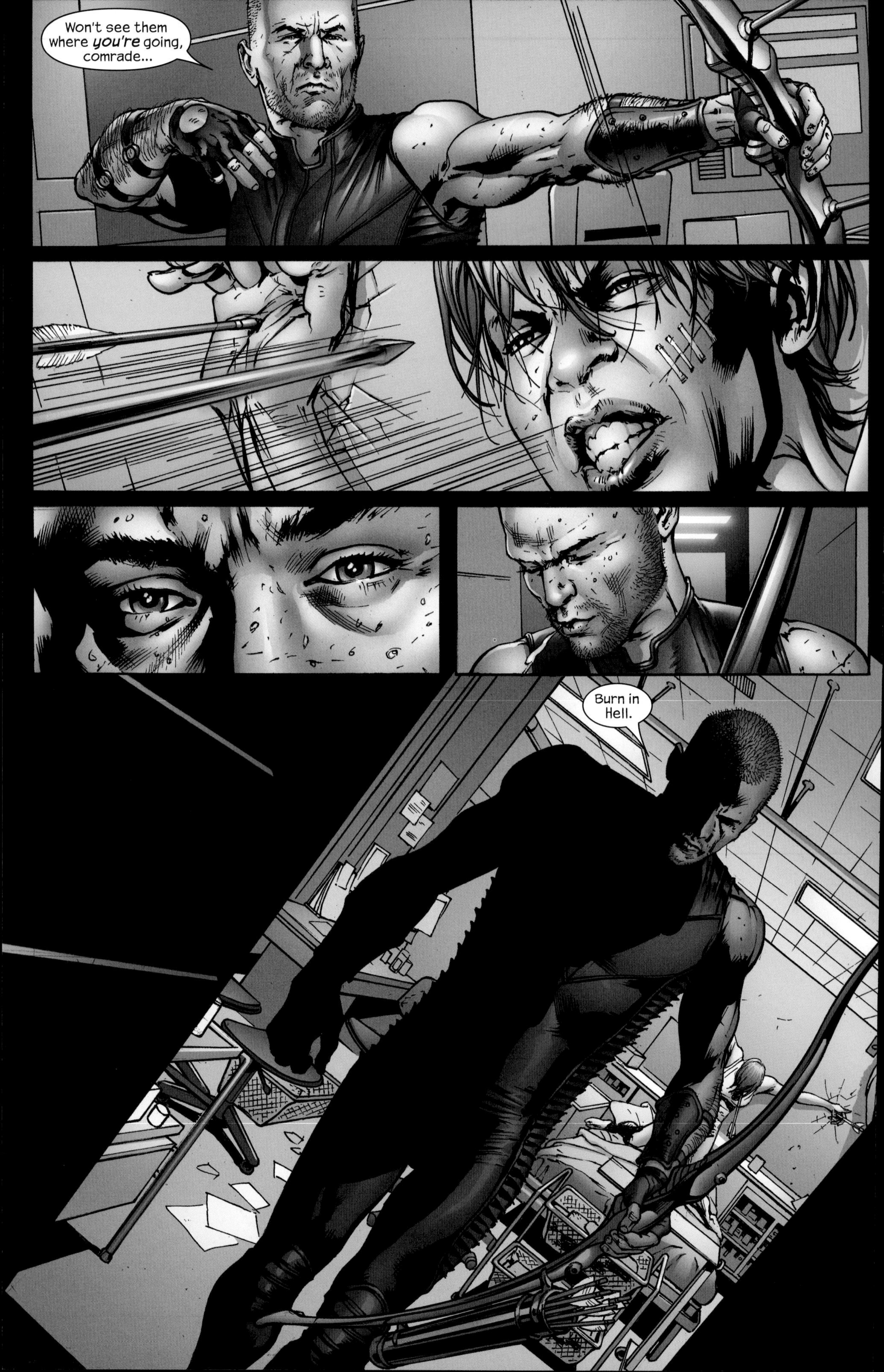
Won't see them where *you're* going, comrade...
Burn in Hell.

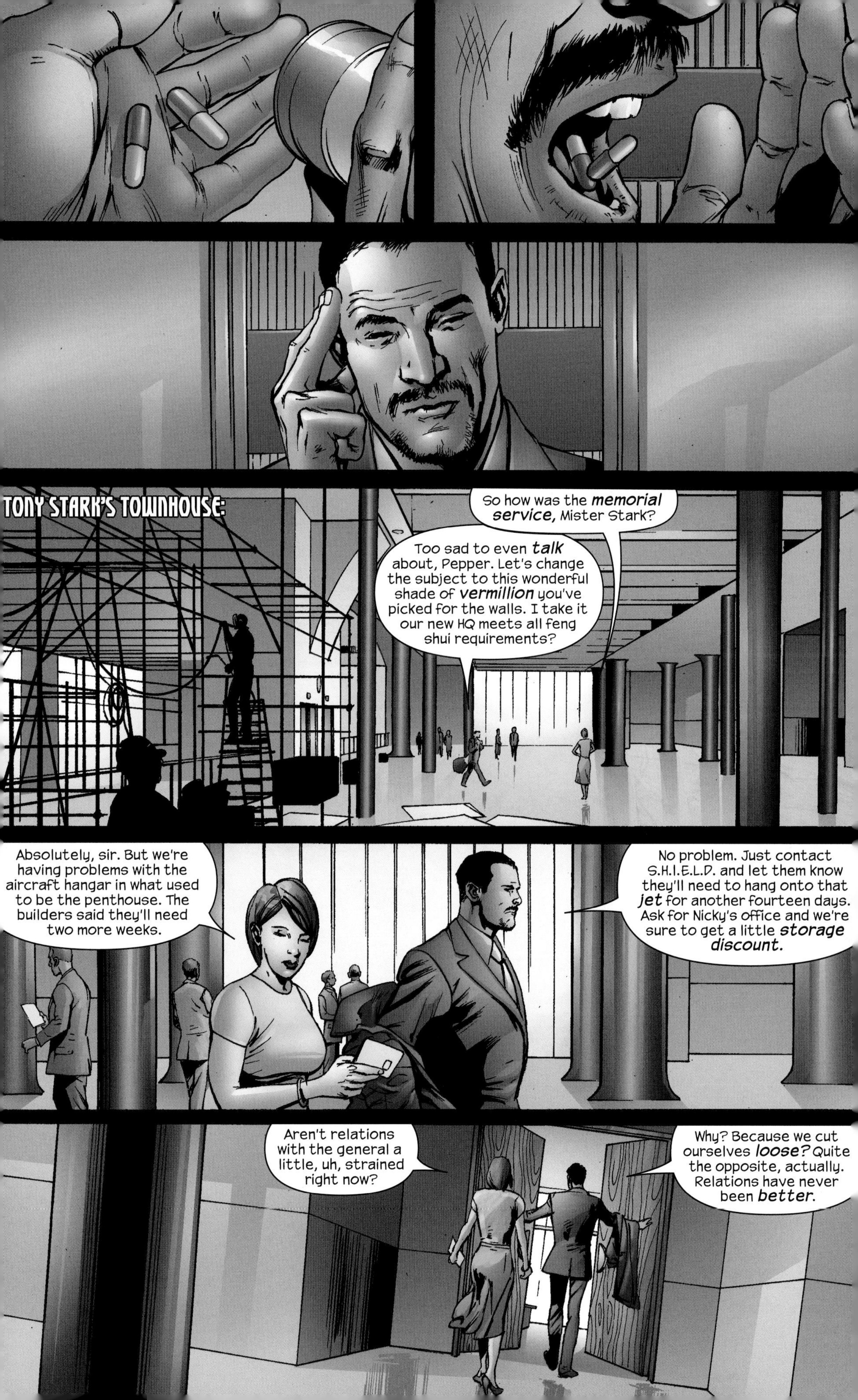
TONY STARK'S TOWNHOUSE:
So how was the memorial service, Mister Stark?
Too sad to even talk about, Pepper. Let's change the subject to this wonderful shade of vermillion you've picked for the walls. I take it our new HQ meets all feng shui requirements?
Absolutely, sir. But we're having problems with the aircraft hangar in what used to be the penthouse. The builders said they'll need two more weeks.
No problem. Just contact S.H.I.E.L.D. and let them know they'll need to hang onto that jet for another fourteen days. Ask for Nicky's office and we're sure to get a little storage discount.
Aren't relations with the general a little, uh, strained right now?
Why? Because we cut ourselves loose? Quite the opposite, actually. Relations have never been better.

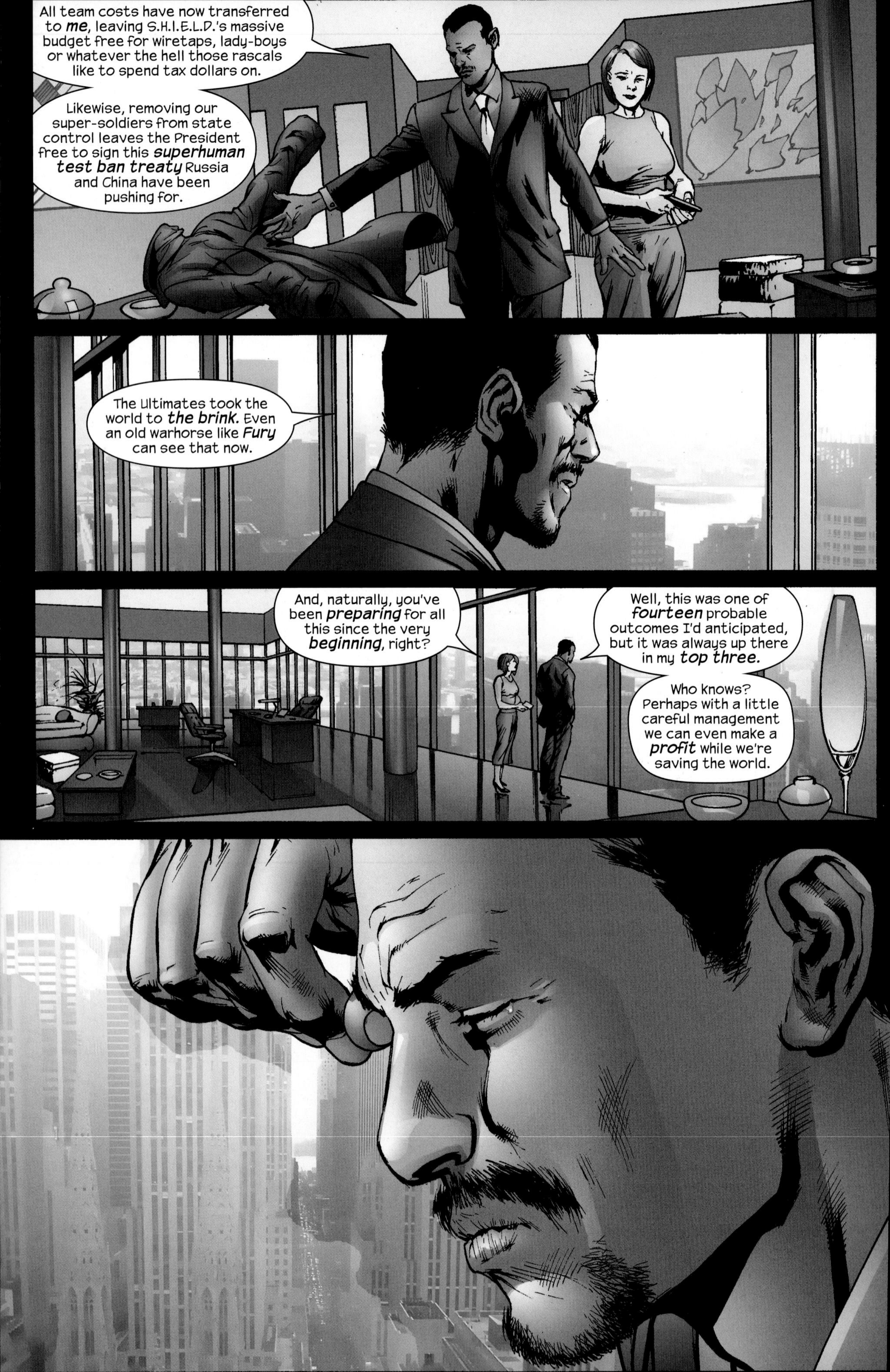

All team costs have now transferred to **me**, leaving S.H.I.E.L.D.'s massive budget free for wiretaps, lady-boys or whatever the hell those rascals like to spend tax dollars on.
Likewise, removing our super-soldiers from state control leaves the President free to sign this ***superhuman test ban treaty*** Russia and China have been pushing for.
The Ultimates took the world to ***the brink.*** Even an old warhorse like ***Fury*** can see that now.
And, naturally, you've been ***preparing*** for all this since the very ***beginning***, right?
Well, this was one of ***fourteen*** probable outcomes I'd anticipated, but it was always up there in my ***top three.***
Who knows? Perhaps with a little careful management we can even make a ***profit*** while we're saving the world.

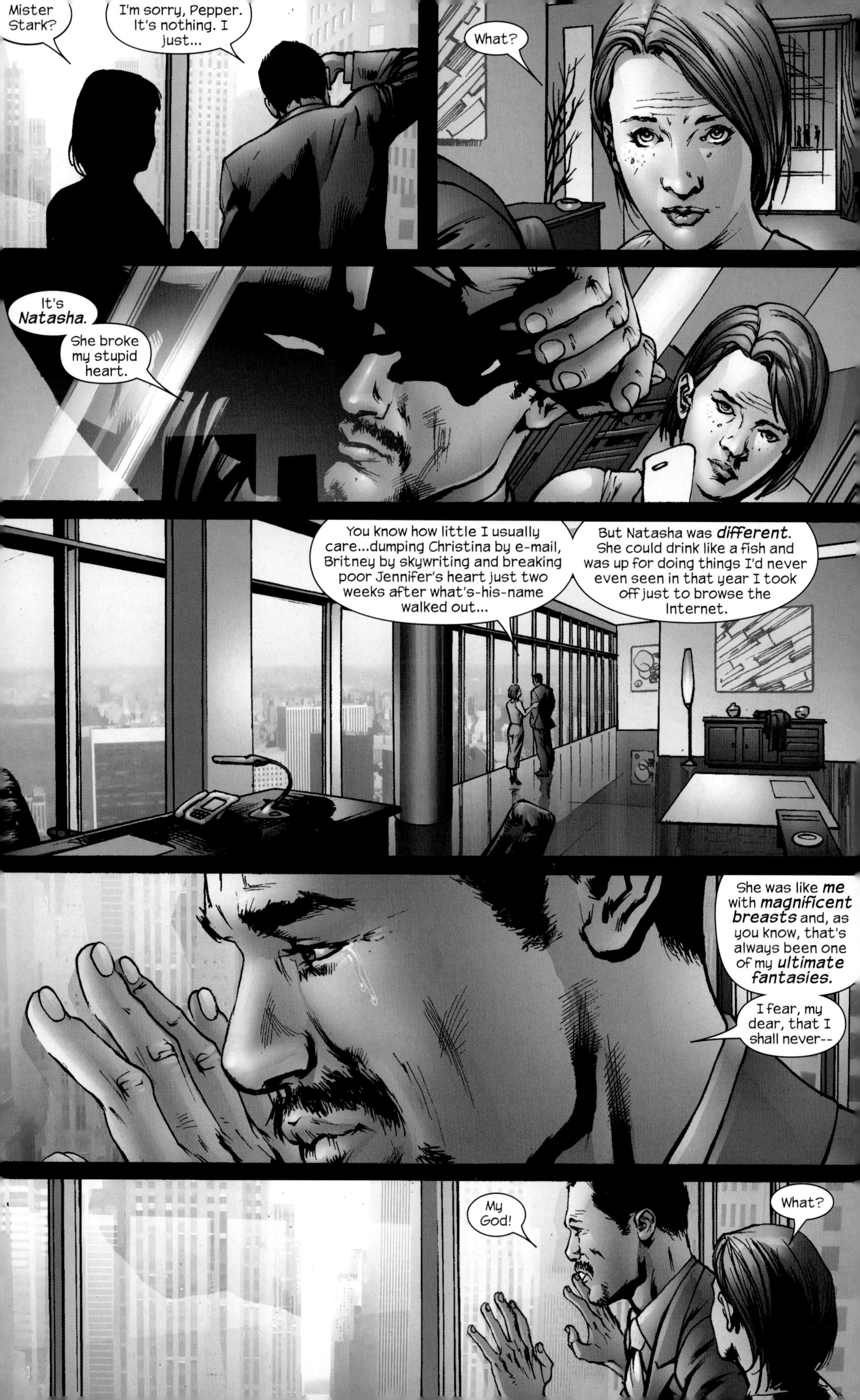
Mister Stark?
I'm sorry, Pepper. It's nothing. I just...
What?
It's *Natasha*.
She broke my stupid heart.
You know how little I usually care...dumping Christina by e-mail, Britney by skywriting and breaking poor Jennifer's heart just two weeks after what's-his-name walked out...
But Natasha was ***different***. She could drink like a fish and was up for doing things I'd never even seen in that year I took off just to browse the Internet.
She was like ***me*** with ***magnificent breasts*** and, as you know, that's always been one of my ***ultimate fantasies.***
I fear, my dear, that I shall never--
My God!
What?

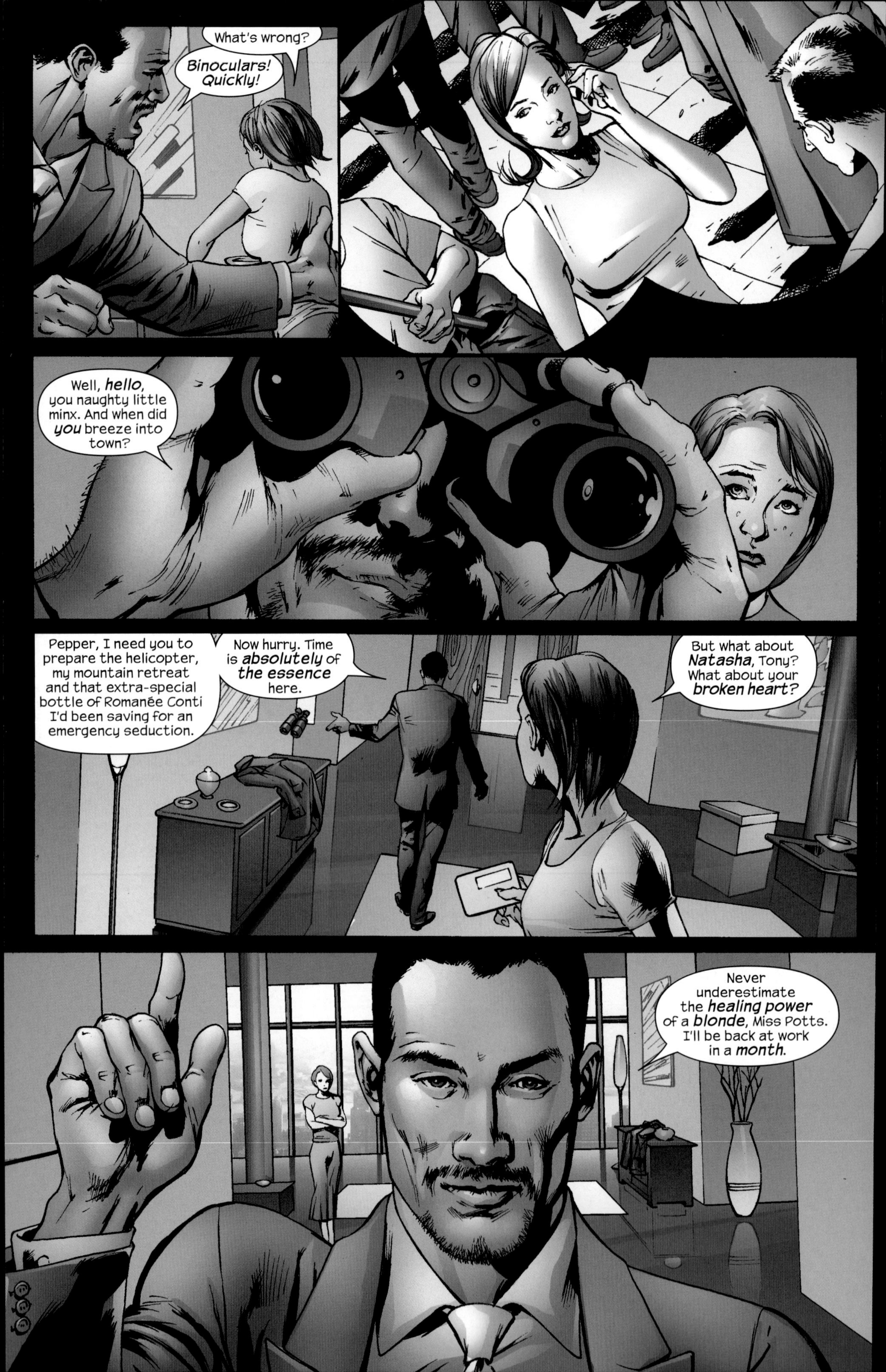
What's wrong?
Binoculars! Quickly!
Well, hello, you naughty little minx. And when did you breeze into town?
Pepper, I need you to prepare the helicopter, my mountain retreat and that extra-special bottle of Romanée Conti I'd been saving for an emergency seduction.
Now hurry. Time is absolutely of the essence here.
But what about Natasha, Tony? What about your broken heart?
Never underestimate the healing power of a blonde, Miss Potts. I'll be back at work in a month.

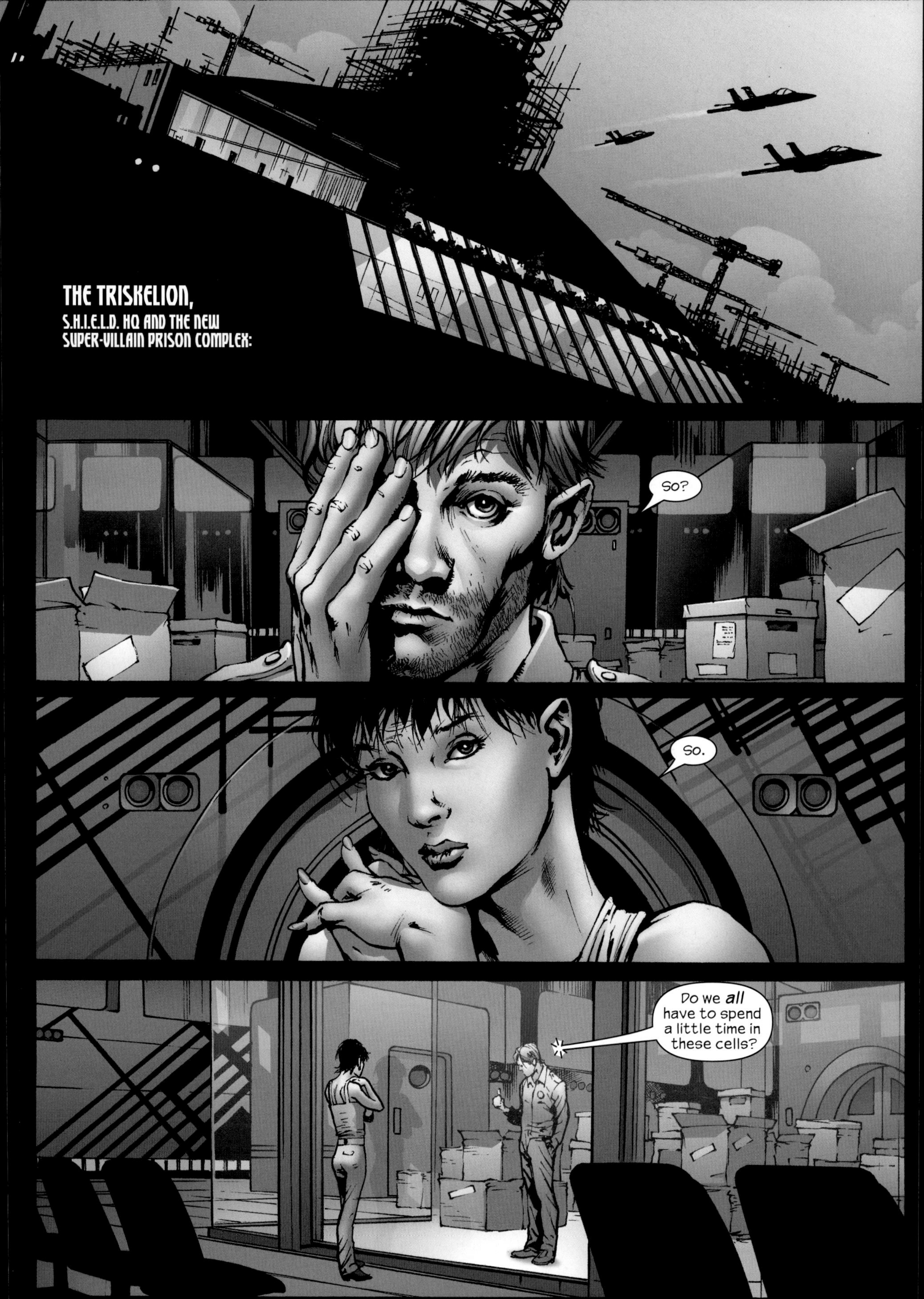
THE TRISKELION,
S.H.I.E.L.D. HQ AND THE NEW SUPER-VILLAIN PRISON COMPLEX:
So?
So.
Do we *all* have to spend a little time in these cells?

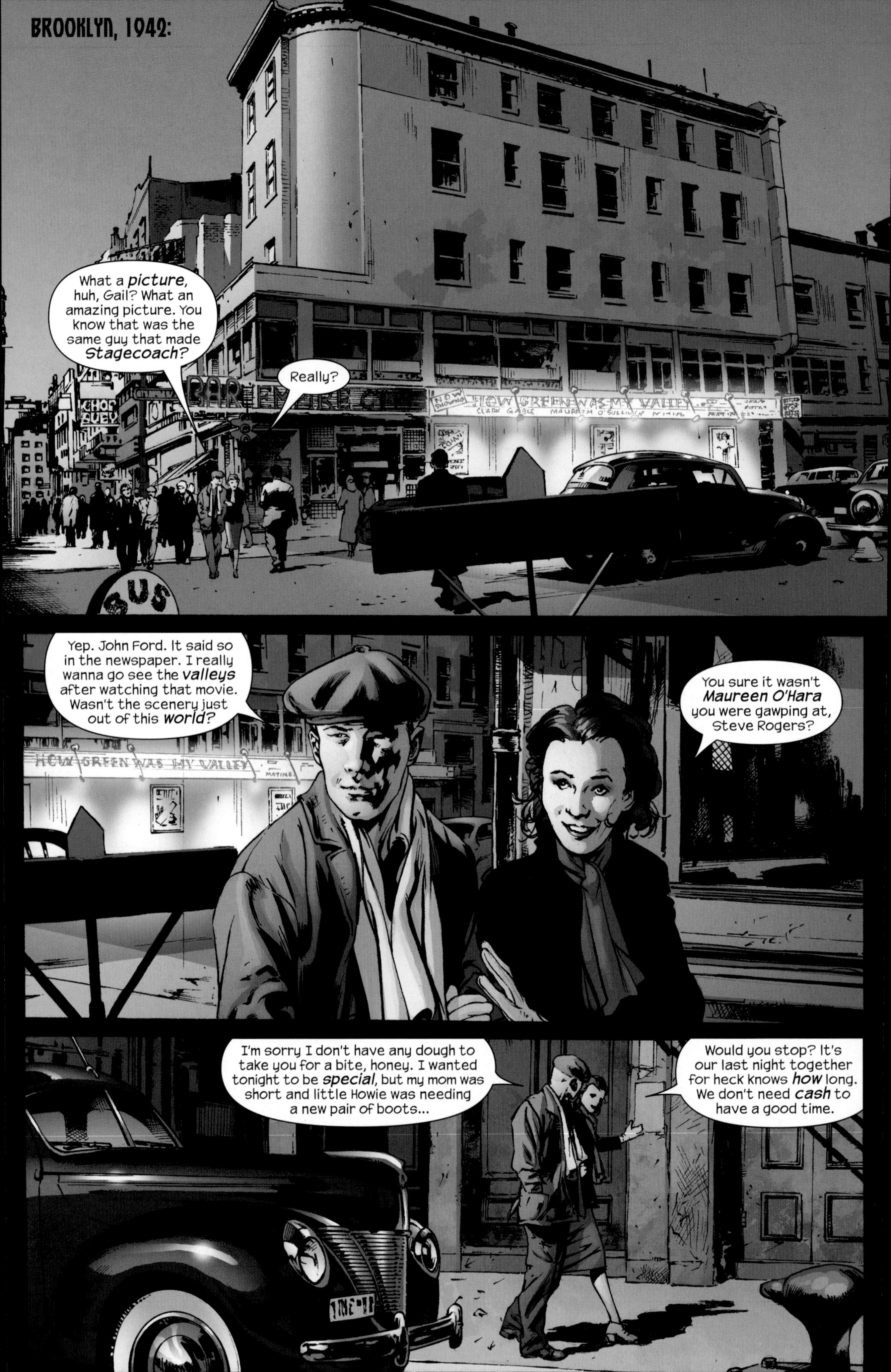

BROOKLYN, 1942:
What a *picture*, huh, Gail? What an amazing picture. You know that was the same guy that made *Stagecoach*?
Really?
BAR
CHOP SUEY
NOW SHOWING
HOW GREEN WAS MY VALLEY
BUS
Yep. John Ford. It said so in the newspaper. I really wanna go see the *valleys* after watching that movie. Wasn't the scenery just out of this *world*?
HOW GREEN WAS MY VALLEY
You sure it wasn't *Maureen O'Hara* you were gawping at, Steve Rogers?
I'm sorry I don't have any dough to take you for a bite, honey. I wanted tonight to be *special*, but my mom was short and little Howie was needing a new pair of boots...
Would you stop? It's our last night together for heck knows *how* long. We don't need *cash* to have a good time.

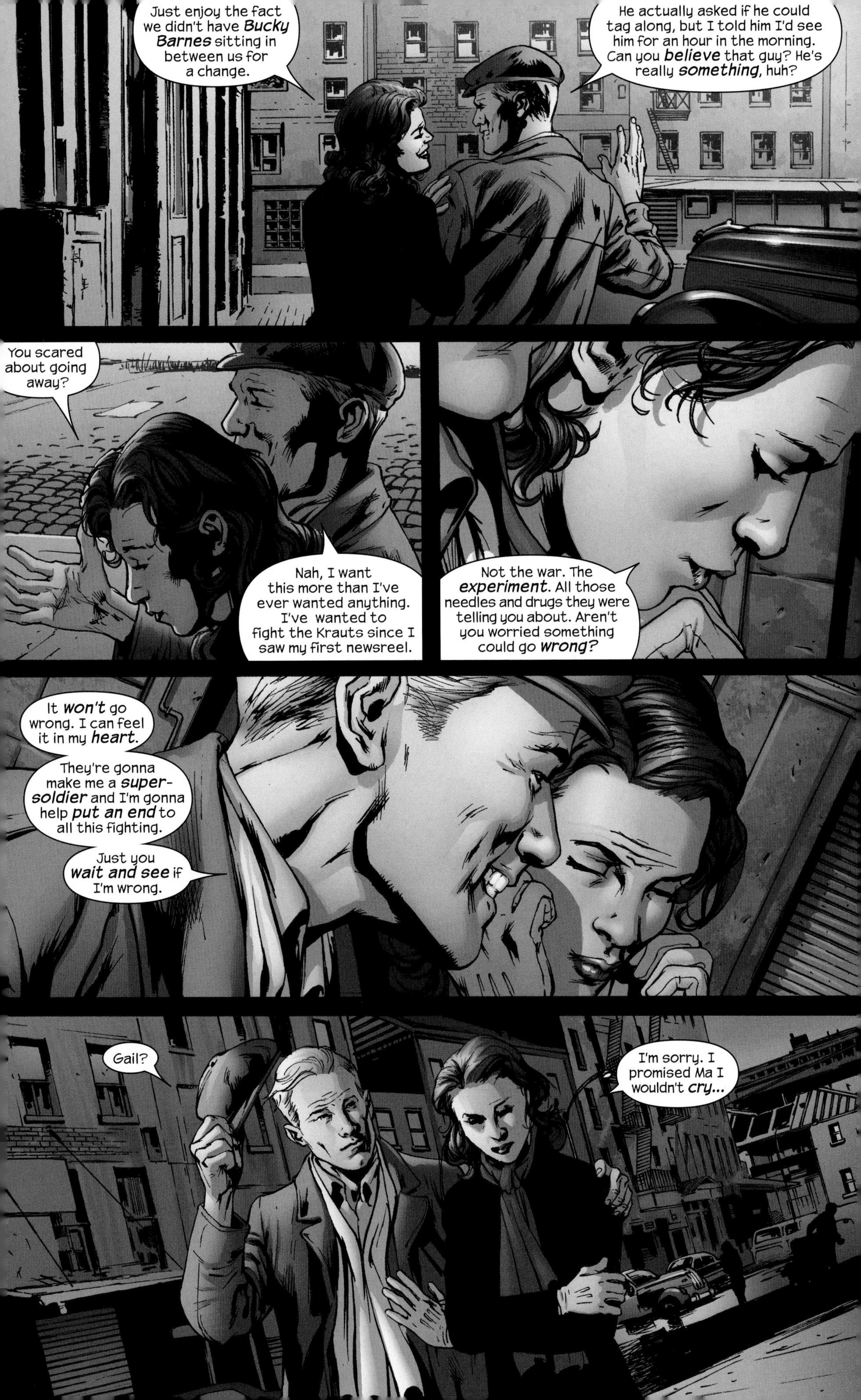
Just enjoy the fact we didn't have Bucky Barnes sitting in between us for a change.
He actually asked if he could tag along, but I told him I'd see him for an hour in the morning. Can you believe that guy? He's really something, huh?
You scared about going away?
Nah, I want this more than I've ever wanted anything. I've wanted to fight the Krauts since I saw my first newsreel.
Not the war. The experiment. All those needles and drugs they were telling you about. Aren't you worried something could go wrong?
It won't go wrong. I can feel it in my heart.
They're gonna make me a super-soldier and I'm gonna help put an end to all this fighting.
Just you wait and see if I'm wrong.
Gail?
I'm sorry. I promised Ma I wouldn't cry...

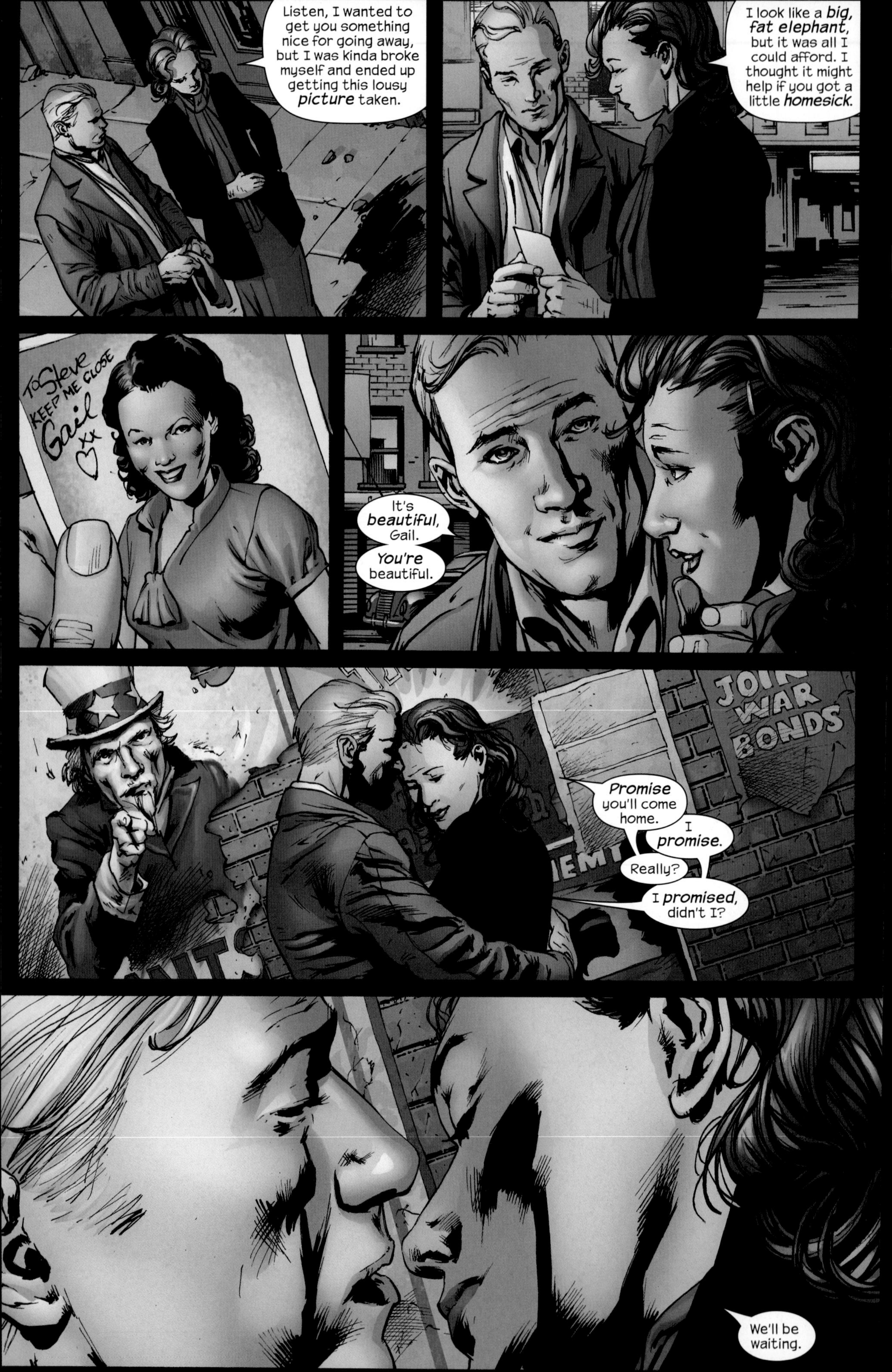

Listen, I wanted to get you something nice for going away, but I was kinda broke myself and ended up getting this lousy picture taken.
I look like a big, fat elephant, but it was all I could afford. I thought it might help if you got a little homesick.
To Steve KEEP ME CLOSE Gail XX
It's beautiful, Gail.
You're beautiful.
JOIN WAR BONDS
Promise you'll come home.
I promise.
Really?
I promised, didn't I?
We'll be waiting.

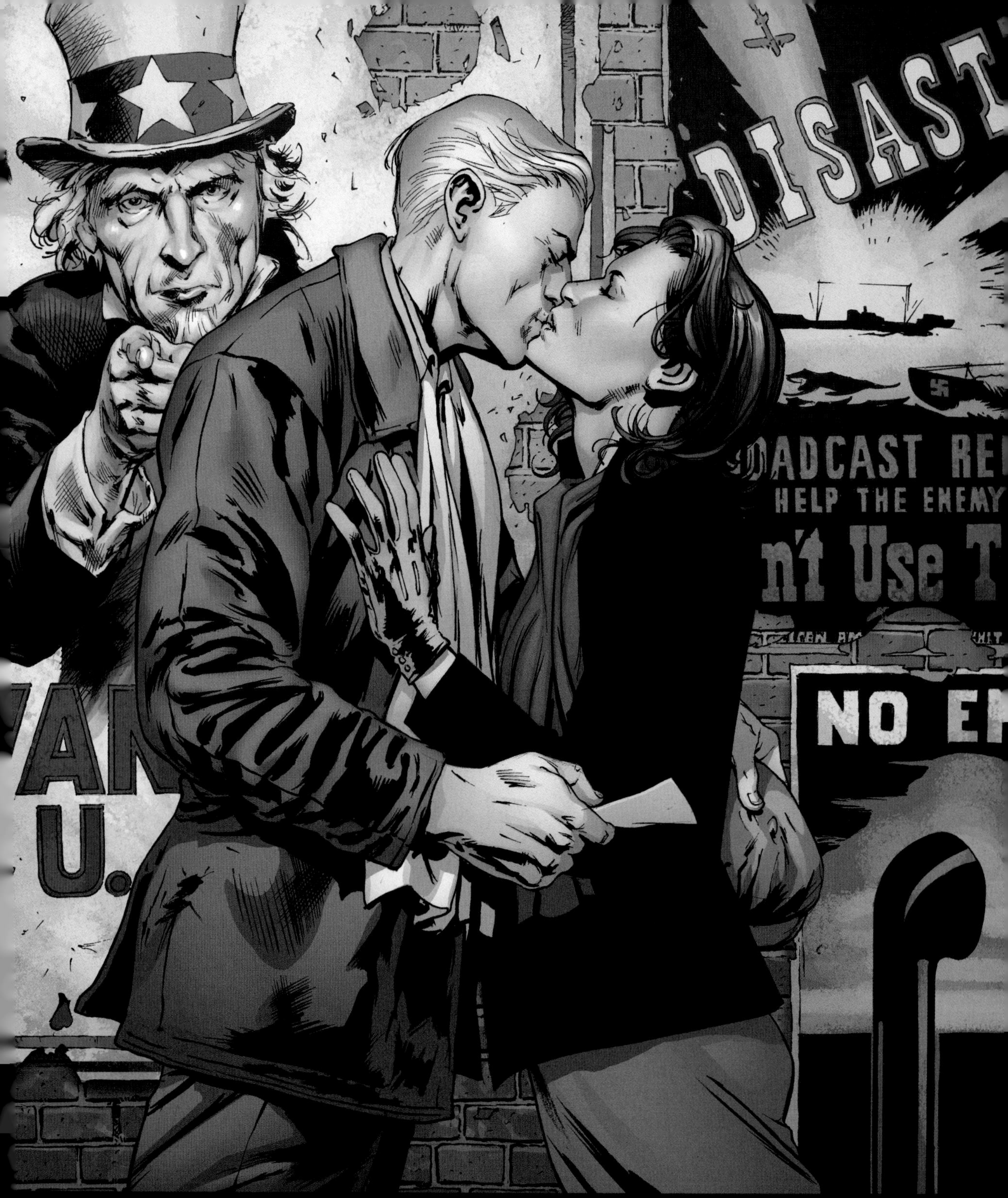
DISAST
ADCAST RE
HELP THE ENEMY
n't Use T
NO E
U.

THE ULTIMATES VOLUMES ONE AND TWO
DEDICATED WITH LOVE TO STAN AND JACK

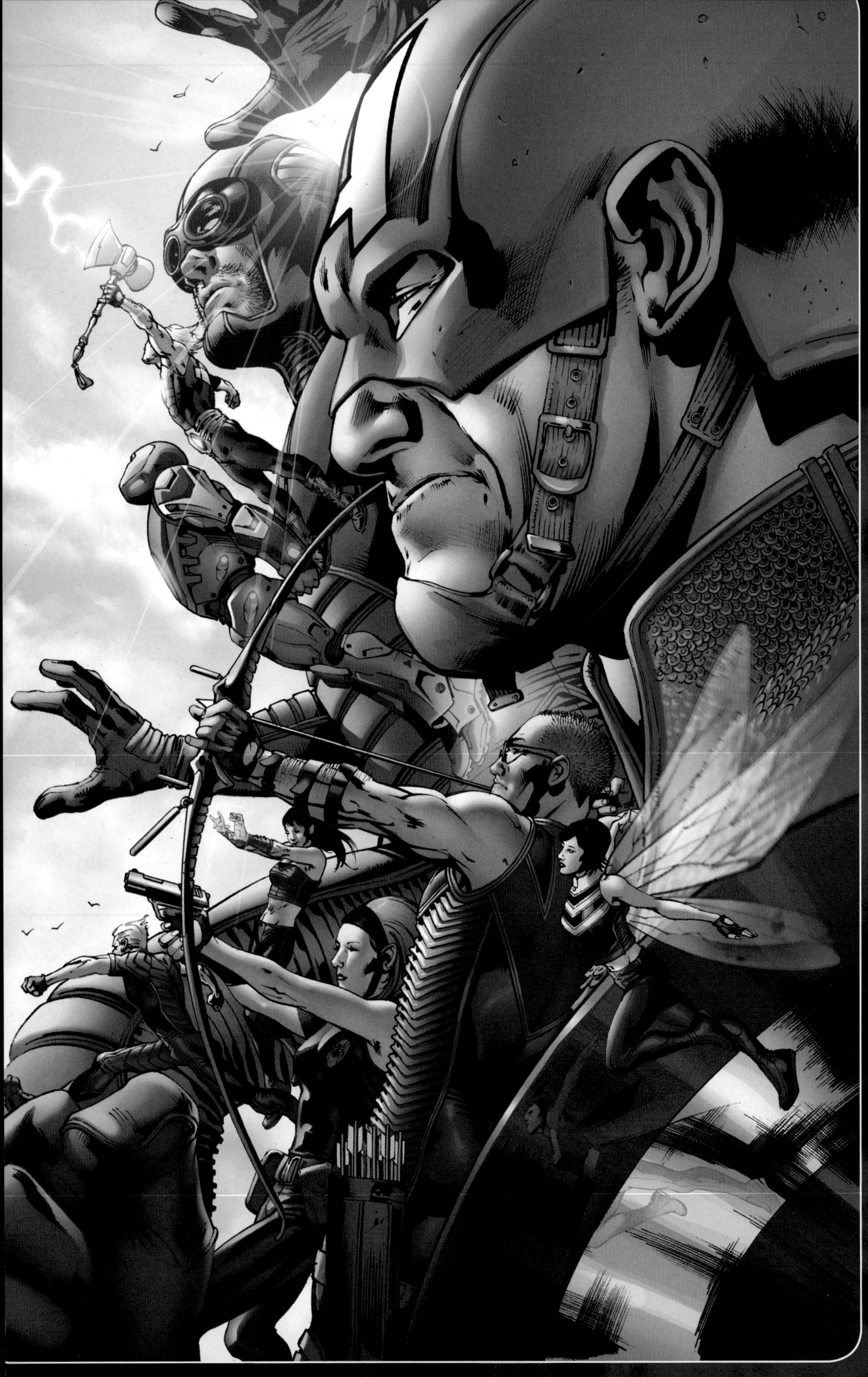

ONE

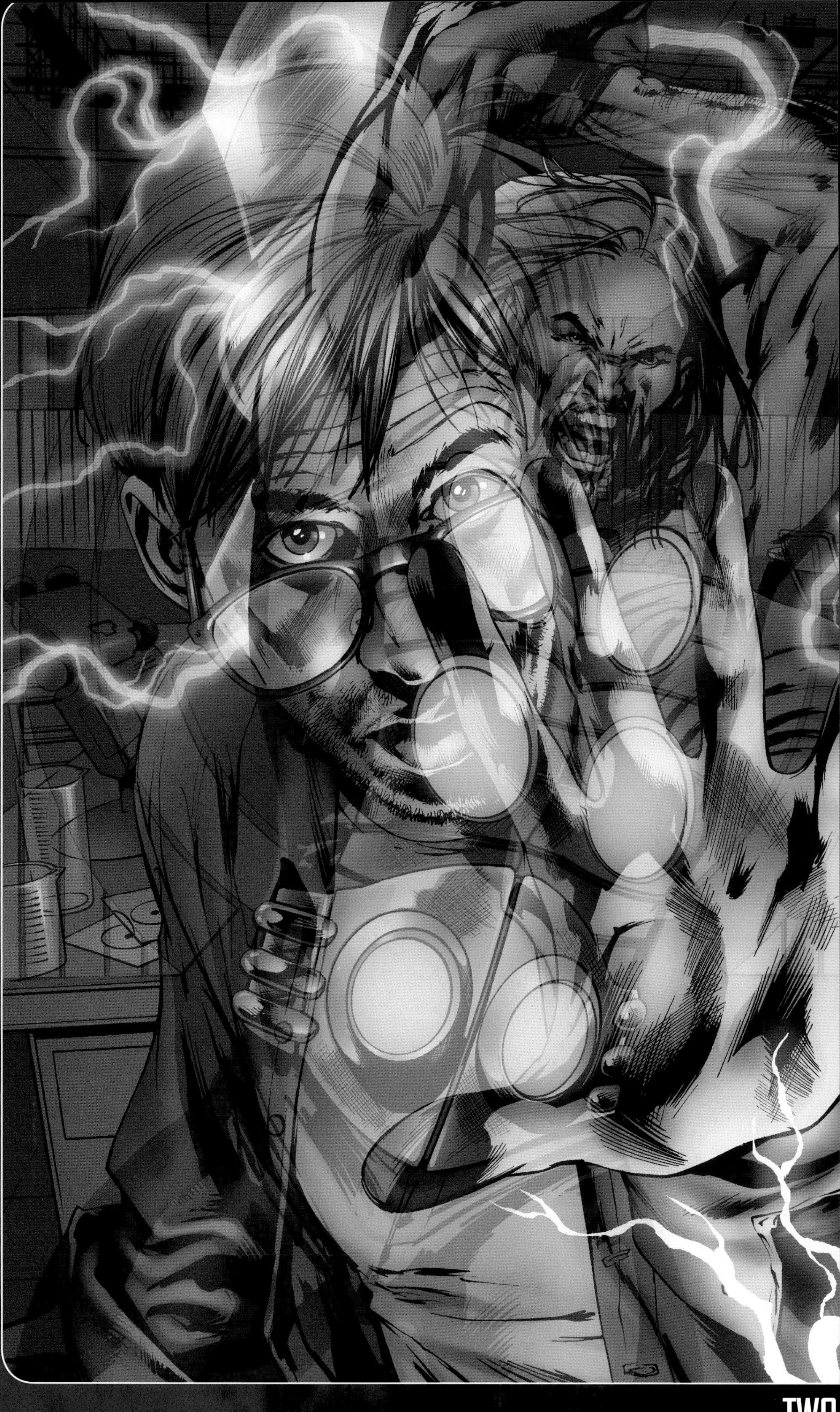

TWO

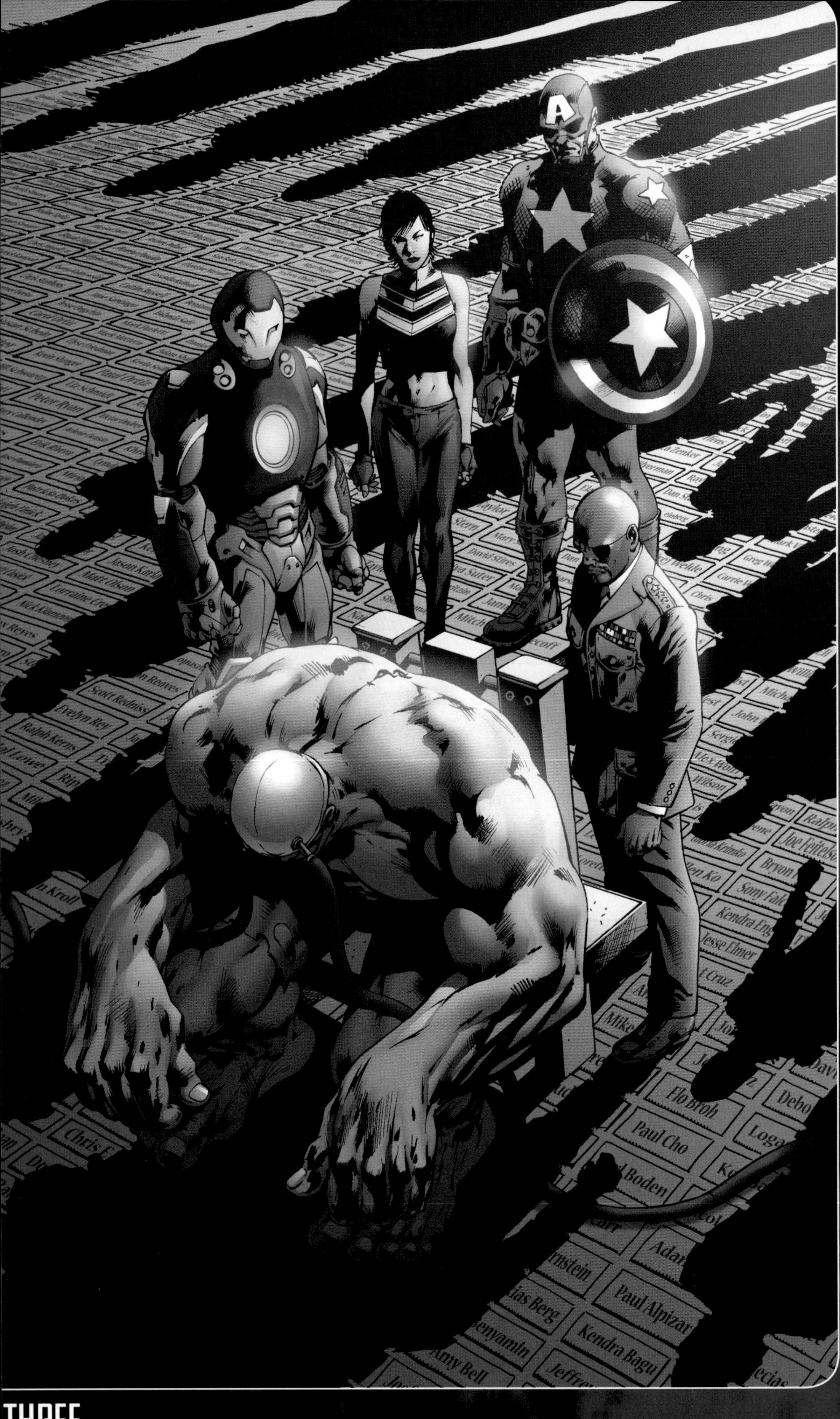
Paul Cho
Flo Broh
Paul Alpizar
Amy Bell
Evelyn Rey
Ralph Kerns
Jesse Elmer
Matt Olsen
David Stires

THREE

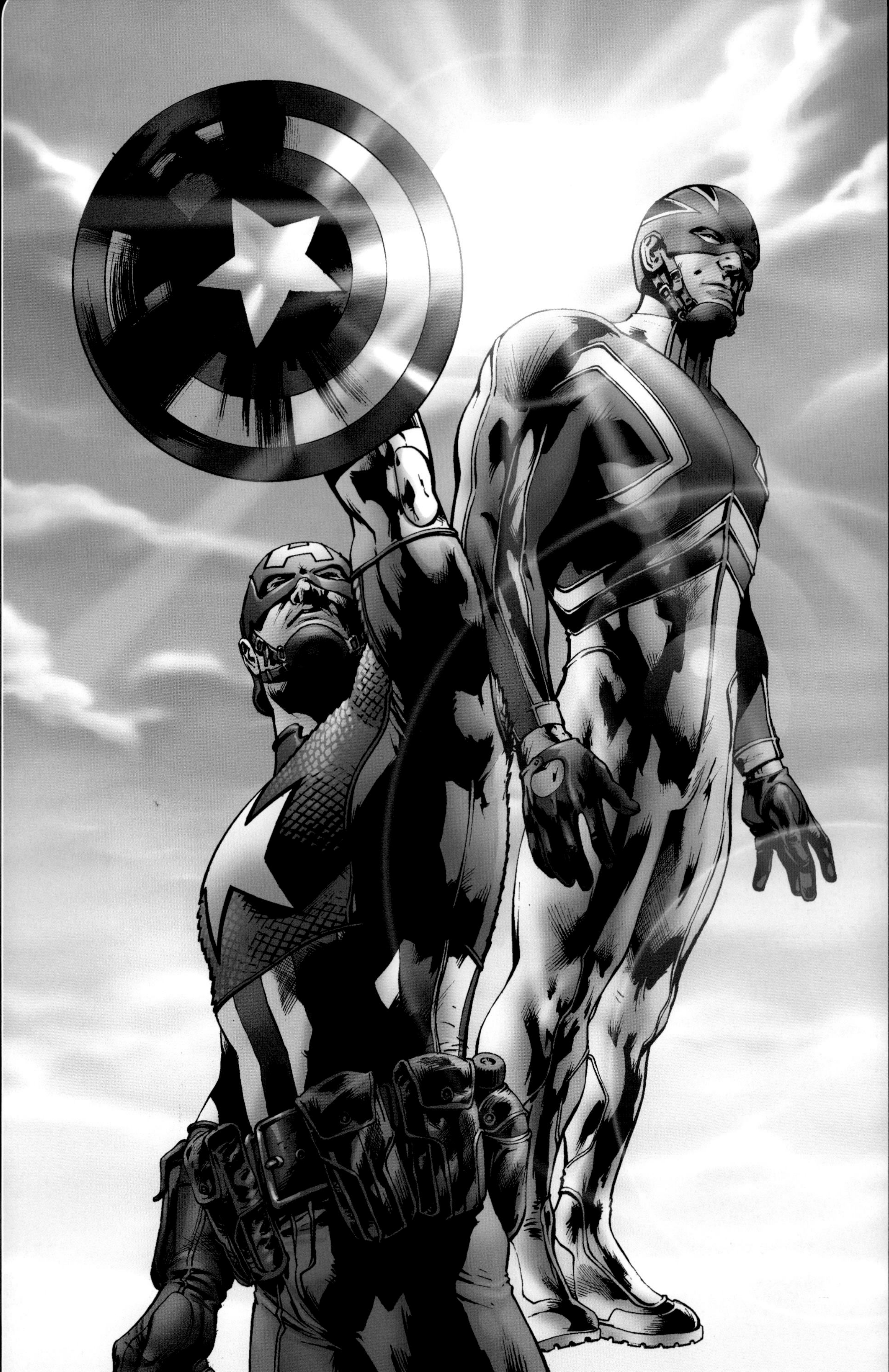

FOUR

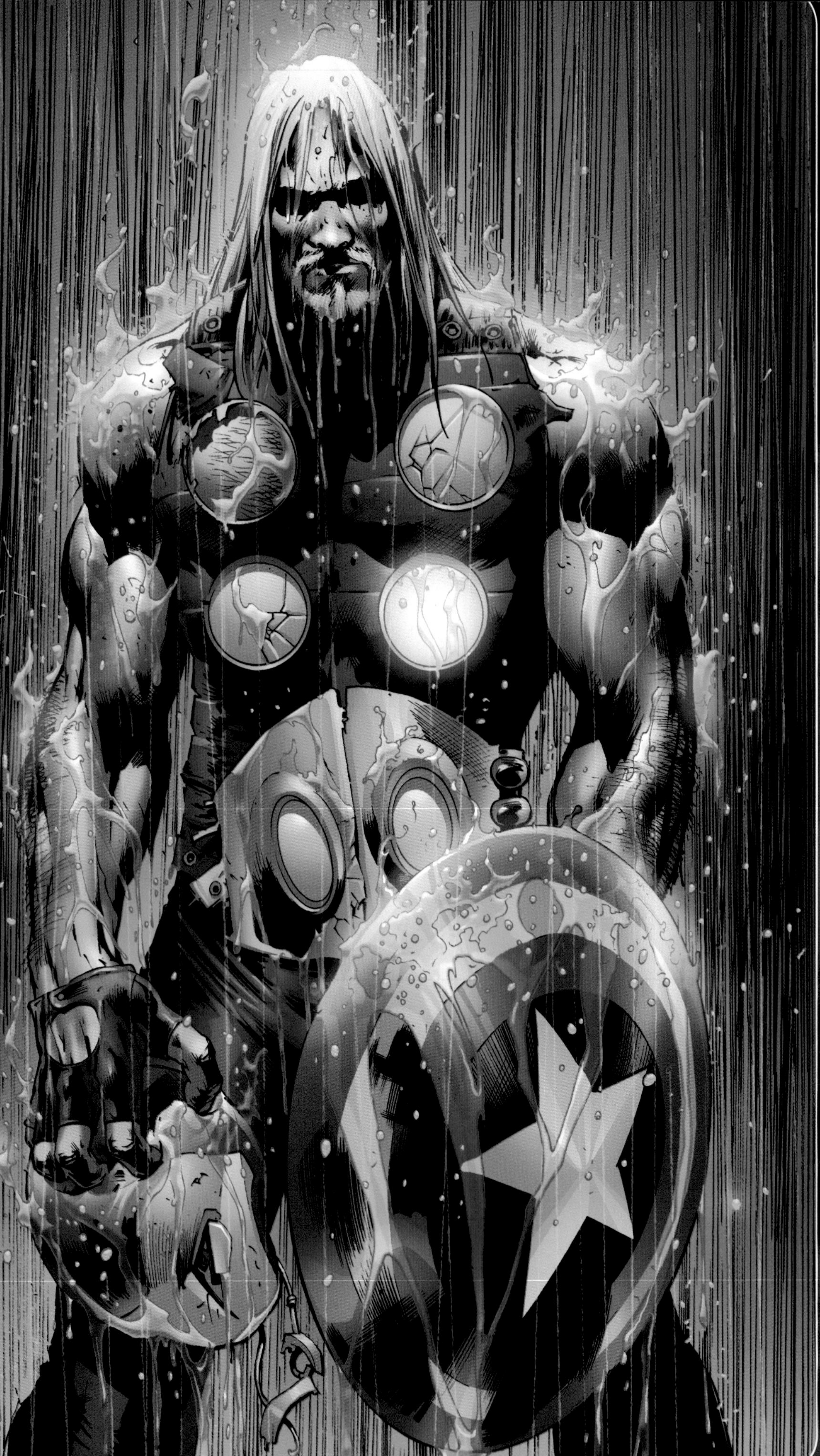

FIVE

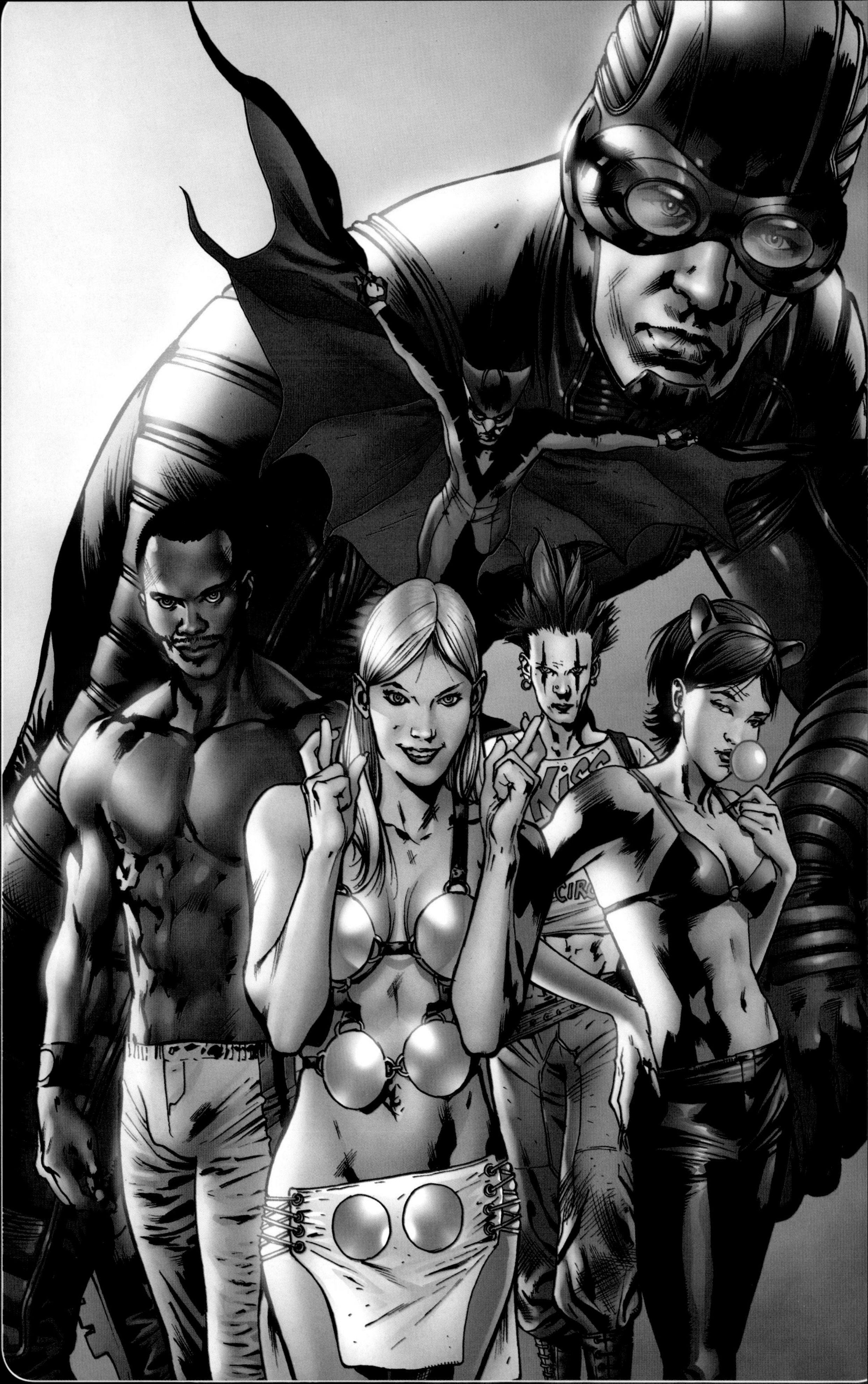

SIX

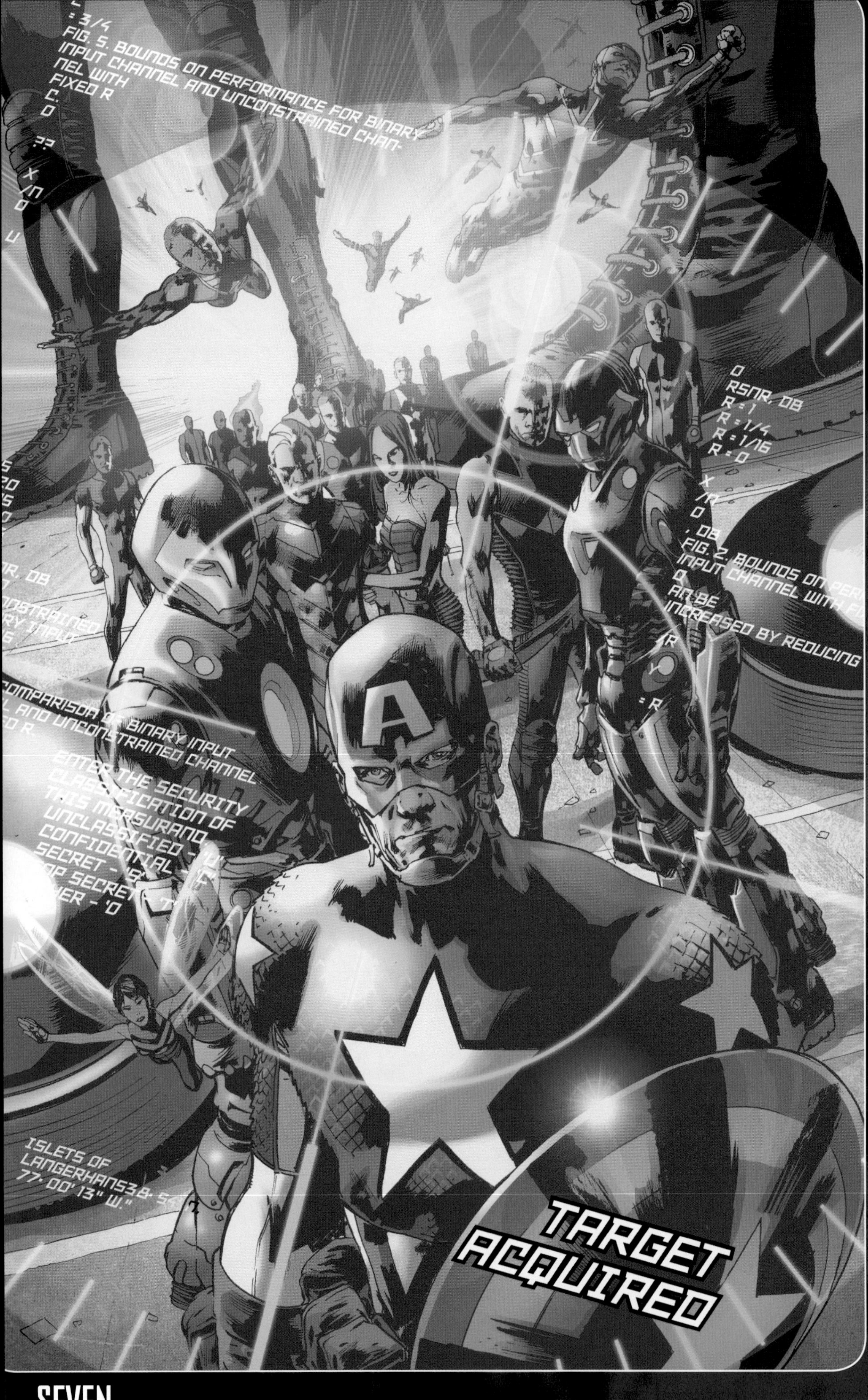
FIG. 5. BOUNDS ON PERFORMANCE FOR BINARY INPUT CHANNEL AND UNCONSTRAINED CHANNEL WITH FIXED R
RSNR, DB
R = 1
R = 1/4
R = 1/16
R = 0
FIG. 2. BOUNDS ON PERF
INPUT CHANNEL WITH FI
INCREASED BY REDUCING
COMPARISON OF BINARY INPUT
L AND UNCONSTRAINED CHANNEL
ENTER THE SECURITY
CLASSIFICATION OF
THIS MEASURAND
UNCLASSIFIED
CONFIDENTIAL
SECRET
TOP SECRET
ISLETS OF
LANGERHANS
TARGET ACQUIRED

SEVEN

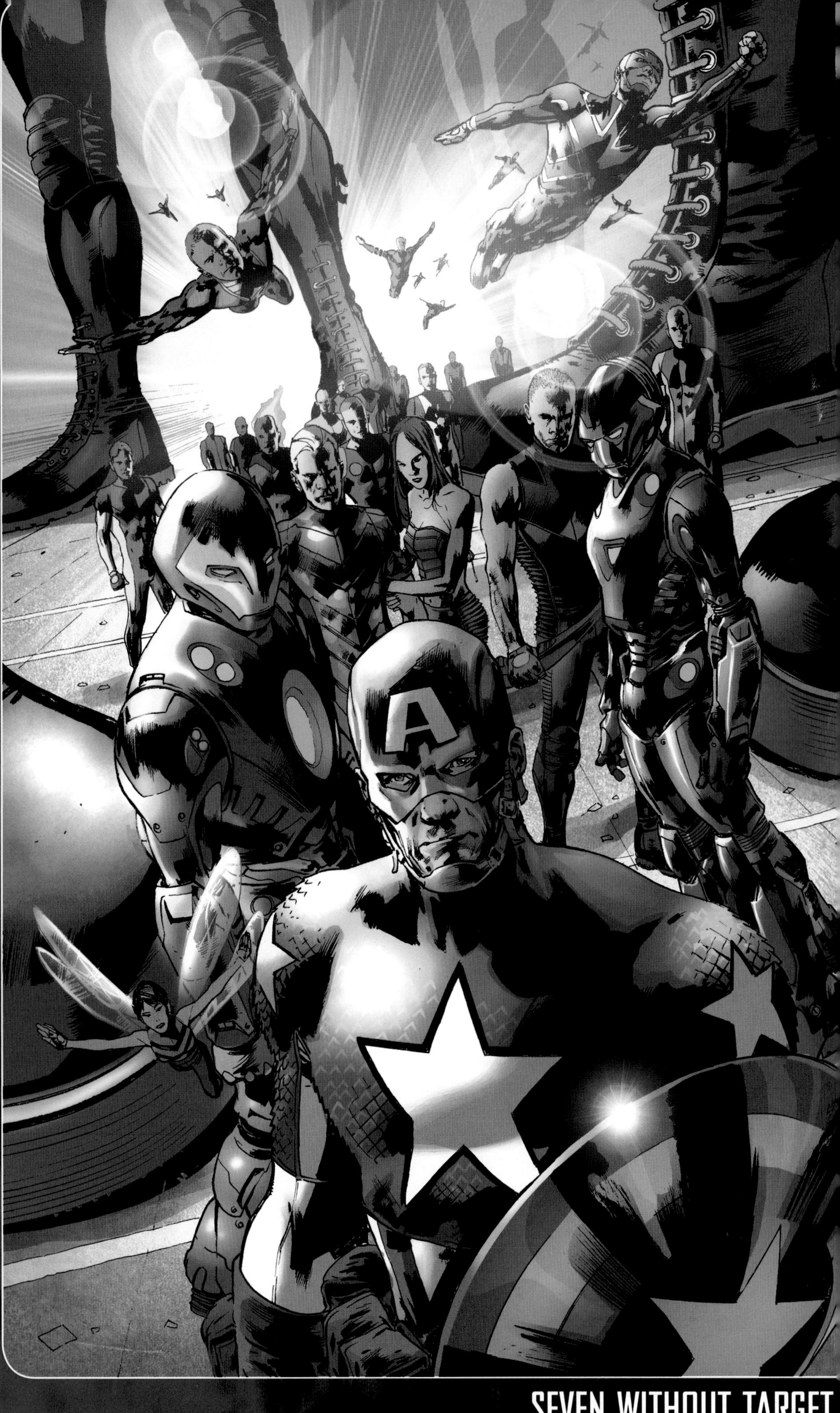

SEVEN WITHOUT TARGET

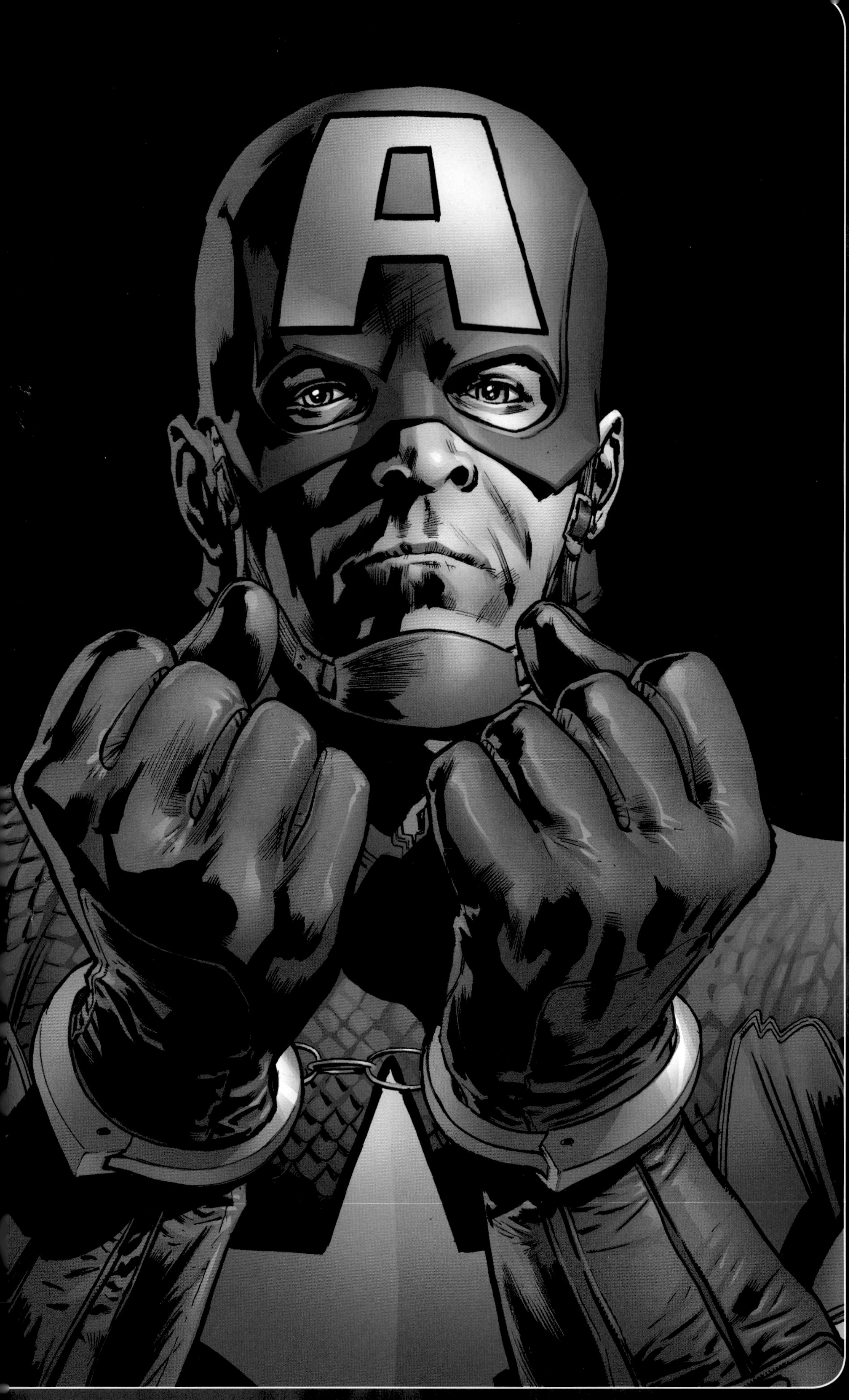

EIGHT

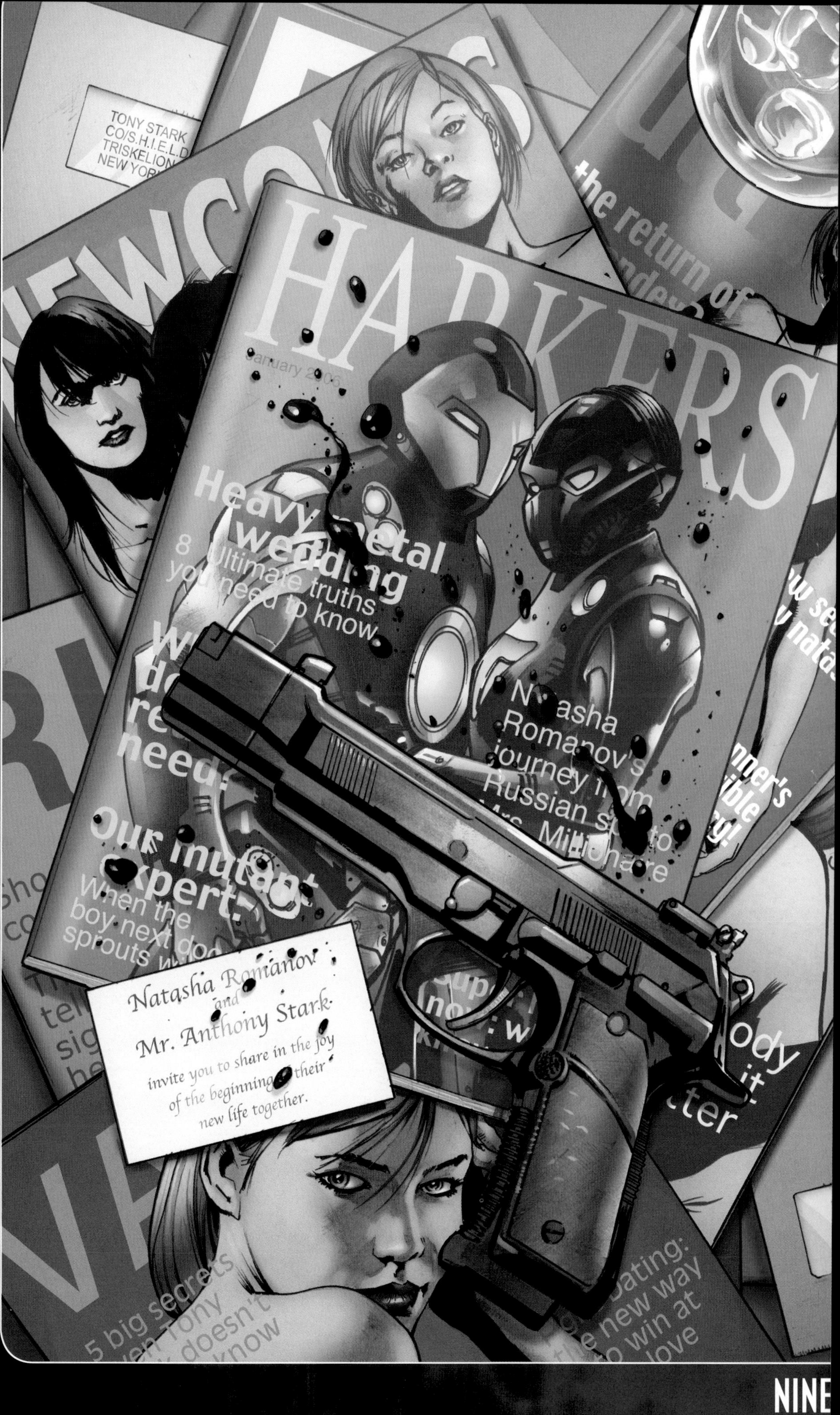
TONY STARK
CO/S.H.I.E.L.D.
TRISKELION
NEW YORK
HARKERS
Heavy metal wedding
8 Ultimate truths you need to know
Our mutant expert:
When the boy next door sprouts
Natasha Romanov's journey from Russian spy to Mrs. Millionaire
the return of
Natasha Romanov
and
Mr. Anthony Stark
invite you to share in the joy
of the beginning of their
new life together.
5 big secrets
even Tony doesn't know
Dating:
the new way to win at love

NINE

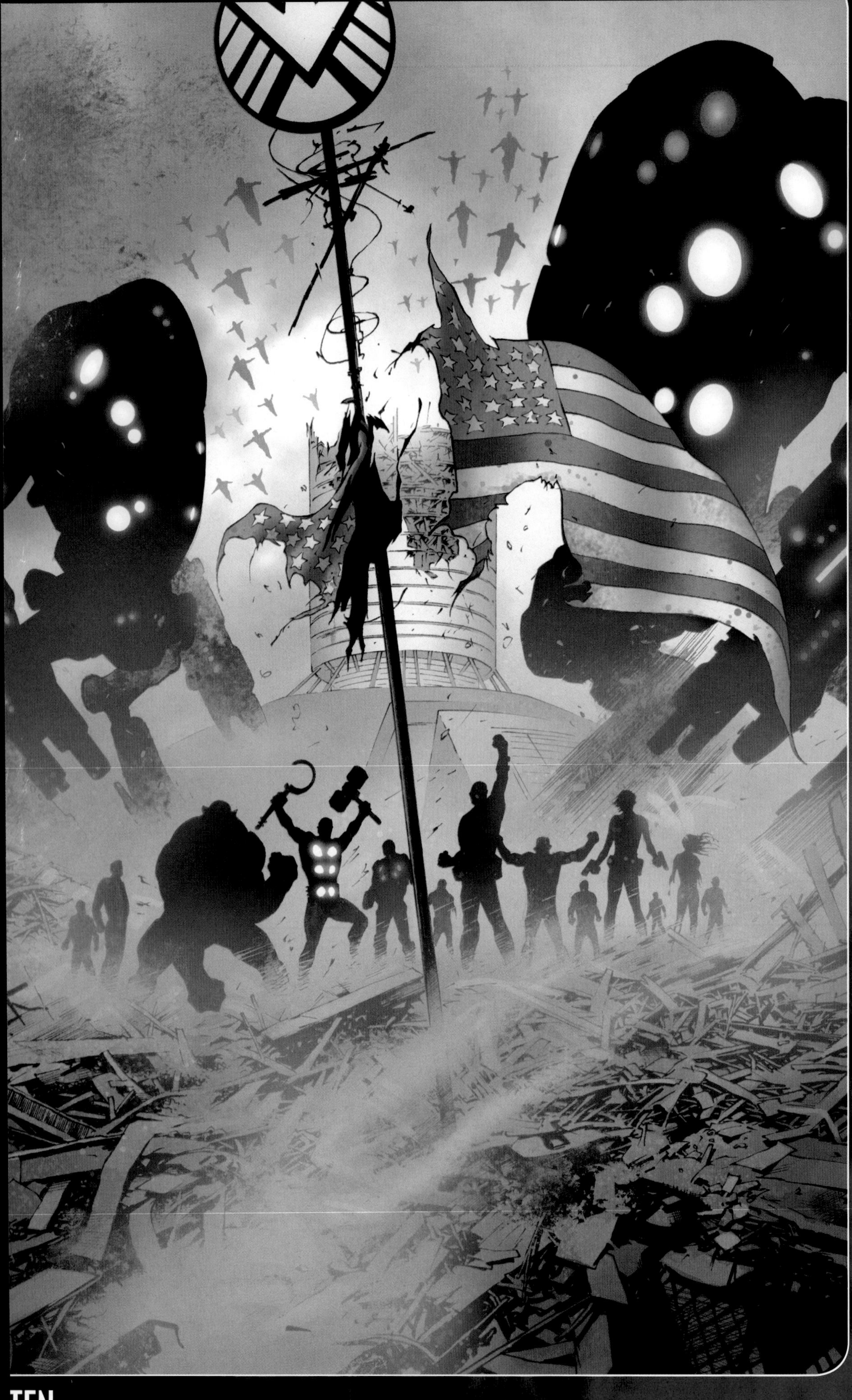

TEN

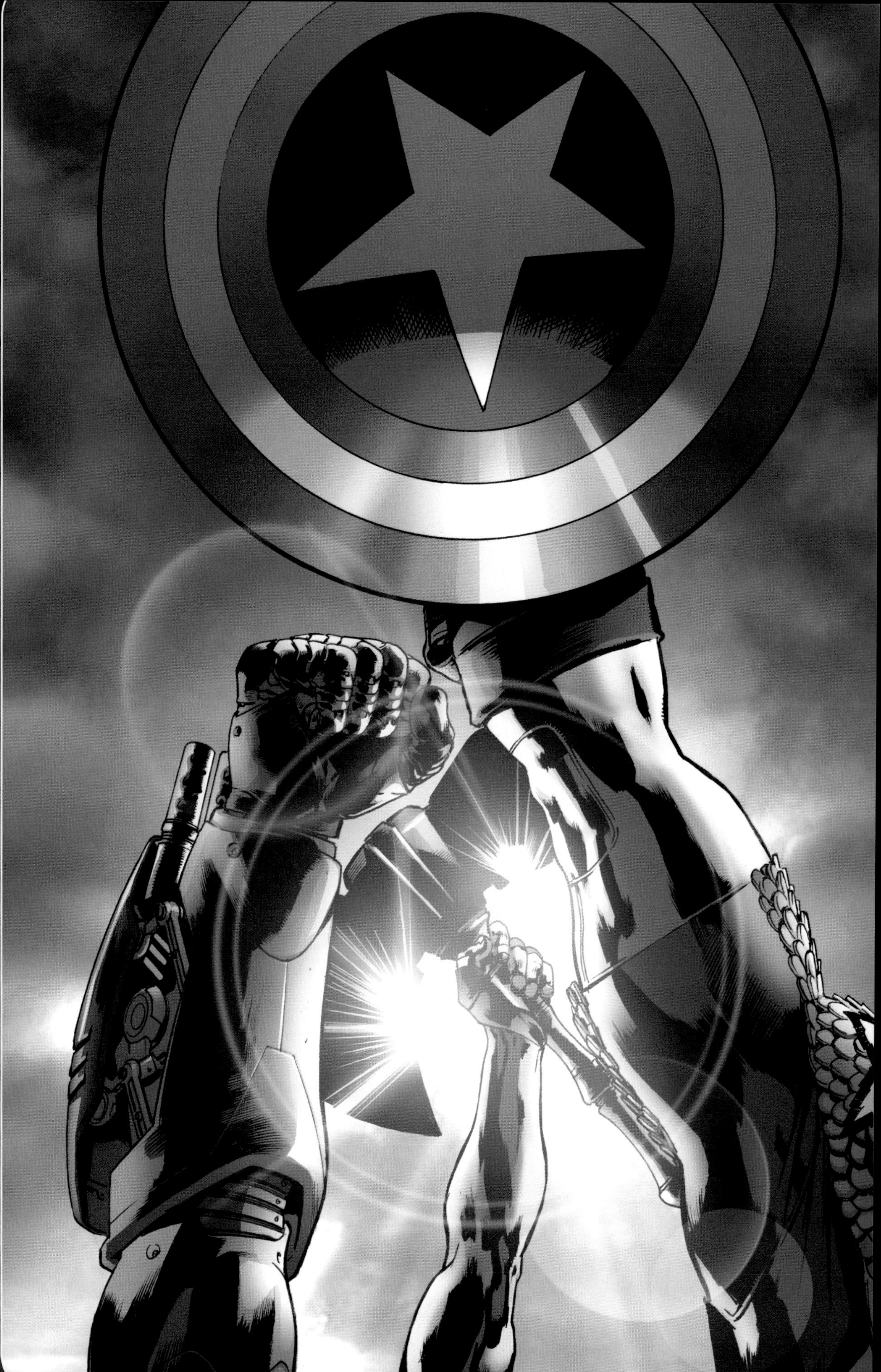

ELEVEN

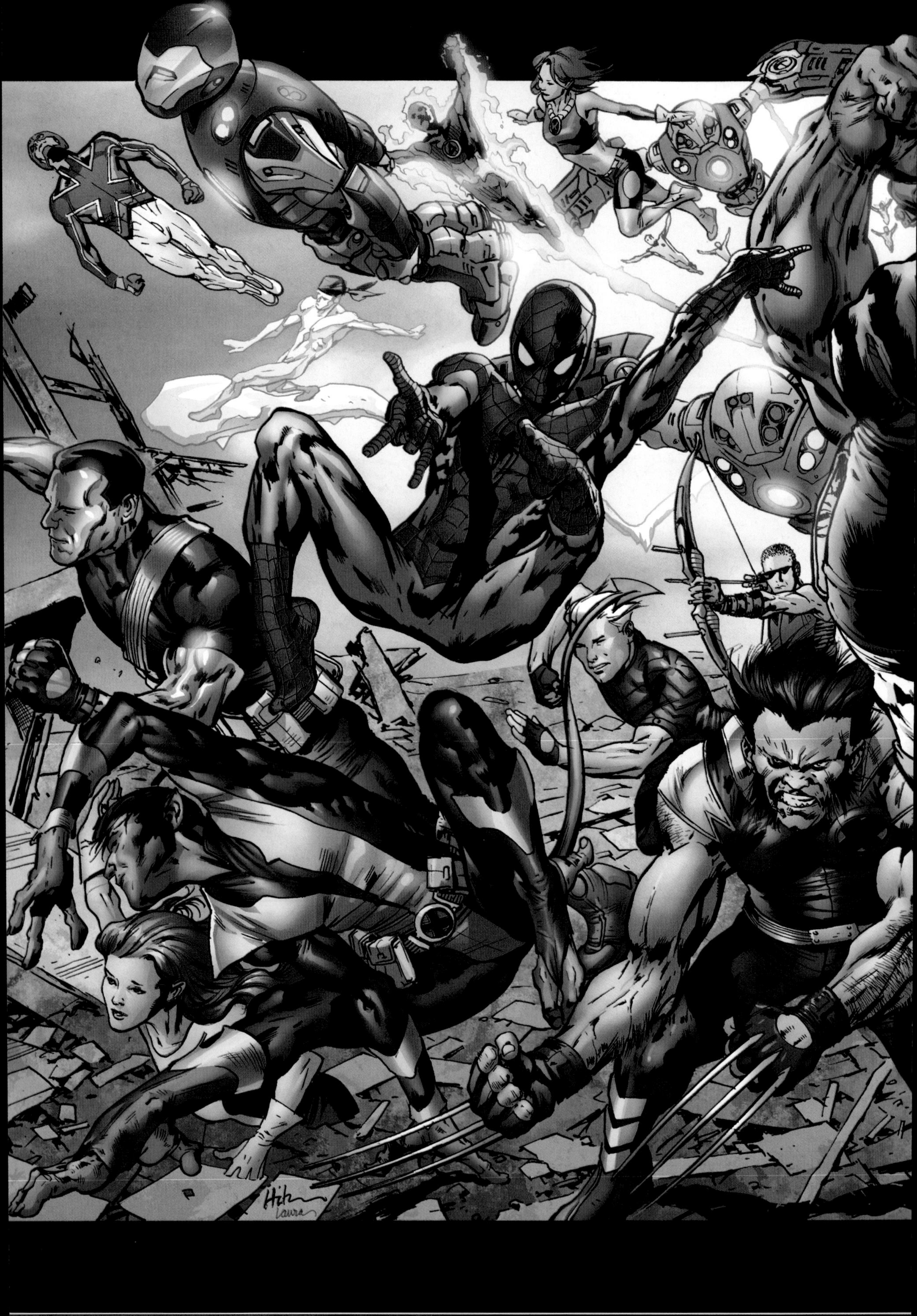

TWELVE

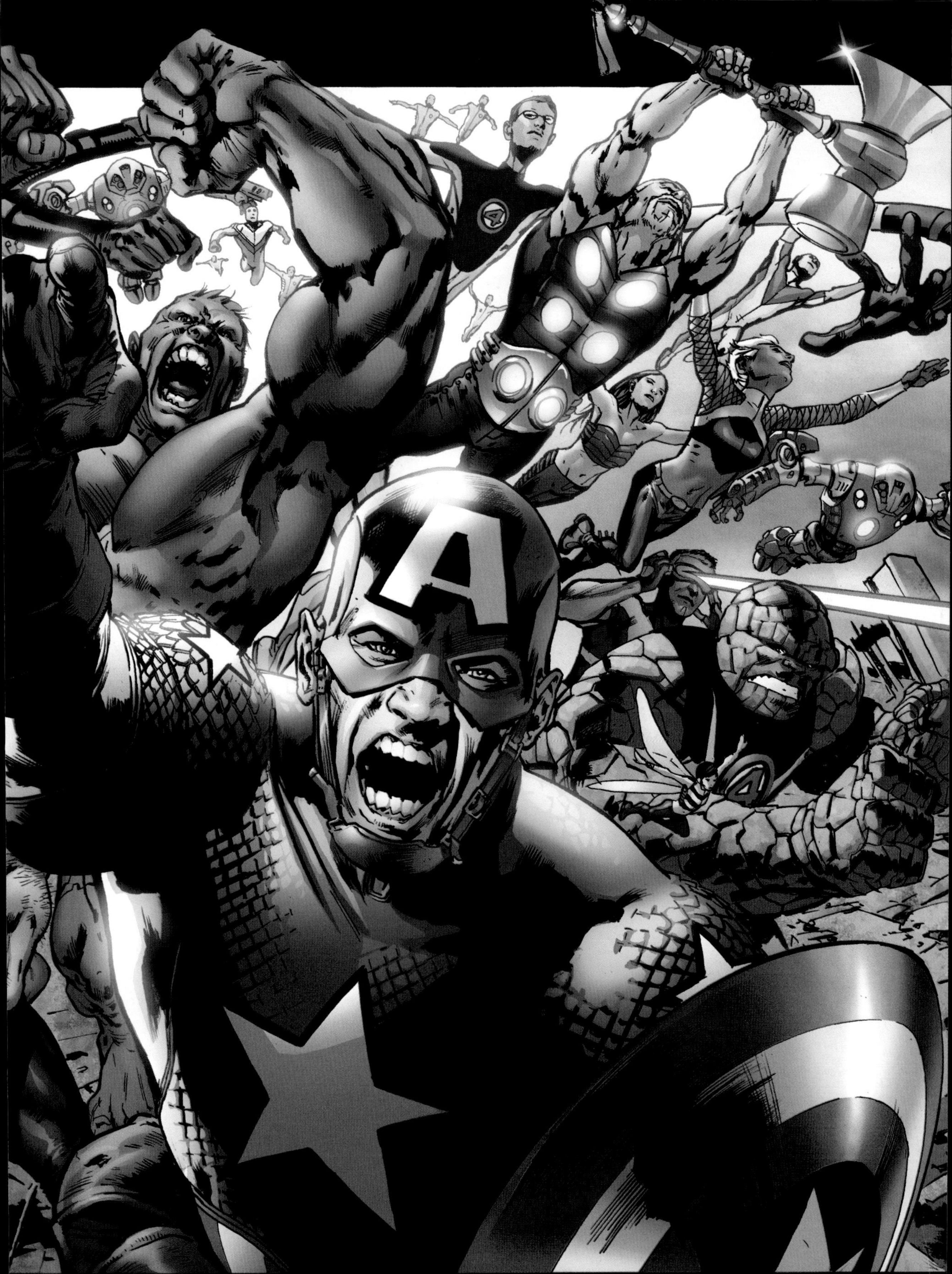

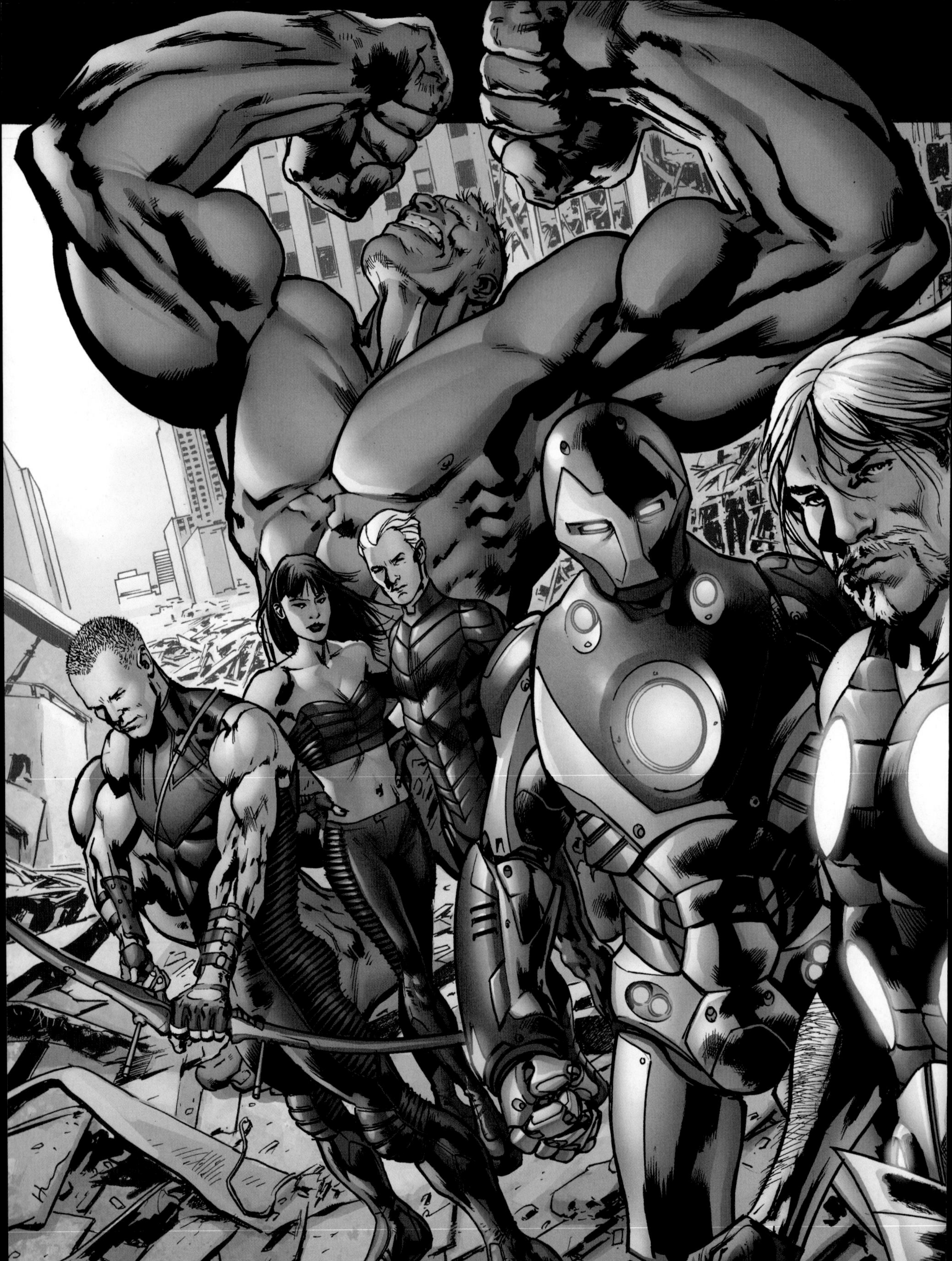

THIRTEEN

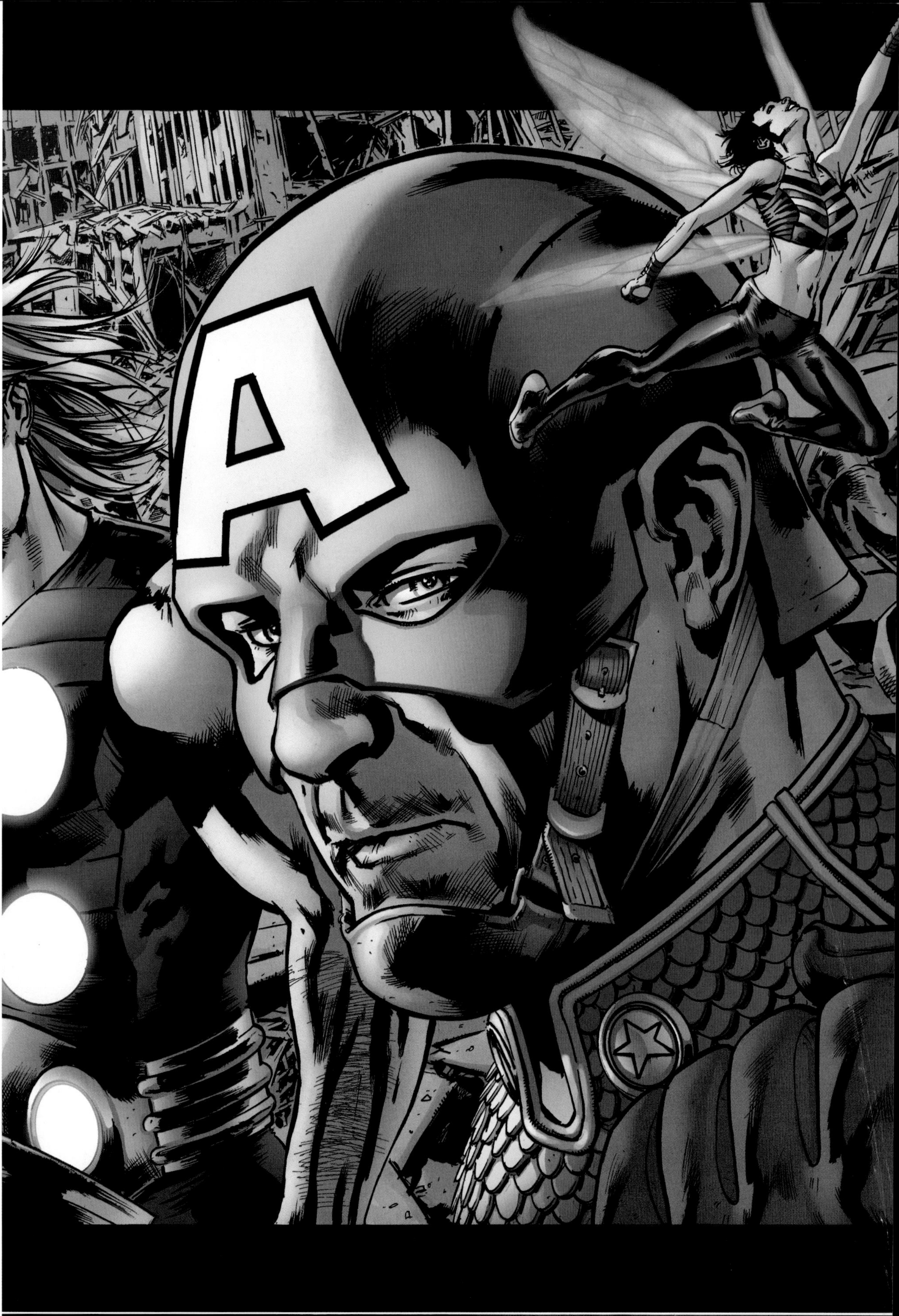

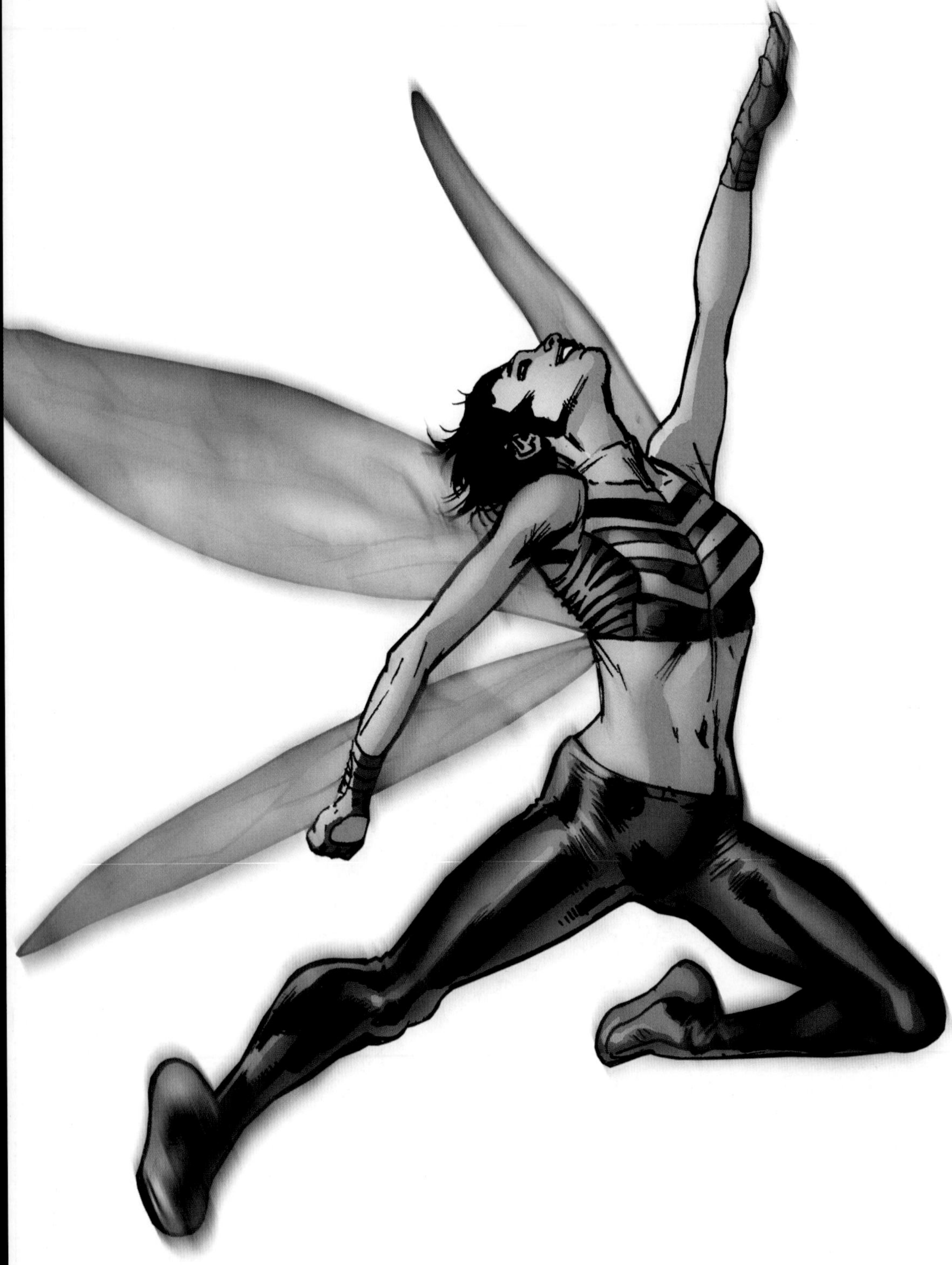

THIRTEEN VARIANT

COMMENTARY
featuring Mark Millar
and Bryan Hitch

ISSUE ONE

MARK MILLAR: I love the opening to issue one. I know it's bad form to say things like that when it's a book you've actually written, but those opening eight pages are just glorious to look at. I might be the most dripping-wet liberal in comics, but I never tire of seeing Cap kick the ass of America's international enemies. I wish he was real.

BRYAN HITCH: He's always fun to draw and I could have carried on drawing him forever. Actually I feel that way about the whole core team whenever I'm doing any particular character as they always seemed so real and fully believable. It's true to say that once you have the characters so well nailed they begin to write and draw themselves, you just need an idea to drop them into. That opening sequence I remember being like having my teeth pulled because I was so tired and burned out after the first volume and being so behind there was no time for a break, as we had to get going. I did, anyway. Still, Cap leaping out of an aircraft without a parachute was also a nice way of touching the first issue of the previous volume.

MM: Yeah, parachutes are for girls.

BH: I think, though, that my favourite scenes with the Ultimates were always the quiet ones with characters just talking, such as the fun one you wrote with Jan and Steve walking his neighbourhood. Those streets don't exist anymore by the way, or at least not like that. As they leave the cinema in modern New York and they are talking about Steve's early life on their way back to his old neighbourhood, I started using stuff from the real 1940's for the backgrounds that had long since been redeveloped. It lent a certain authenticity to keeping his personality rooted in the past and that's a theme which later came to cause problems in his relationship with Jan.

MM: You're insane. I didn't even know that and we talk every day. Still, it's not every artist who will actually go to the bother of inventing time-travel for a three-page conversation. No wonder the book was often late. If only these buggers knew what you went through as you cracked the fourth dimension.

BH: Don't you think that if I HAD invented time travel the book actually wouldn't have been late? It would have been both early and with all 26 mostly extra-sized issues out at once before you had written them and I had even drawn them. We could have swiped from ourselves...

MM: Good point. But man, look at this stuff. Alex Ross is the only other artist I can think of who puts so much thought into every panel. These books are just laden with Easter eggs and as much as I'd like to claim the credit, so much of this stuff and so many little subtle moments really come from the art. I will ritually slit the throat of anyone who moans about this book ever being late. Hold up a page from Bryan and hold up a typical comic page, and if you can't see the difference, you're either blind or stupid. Harsh, I know, but it has to be said.

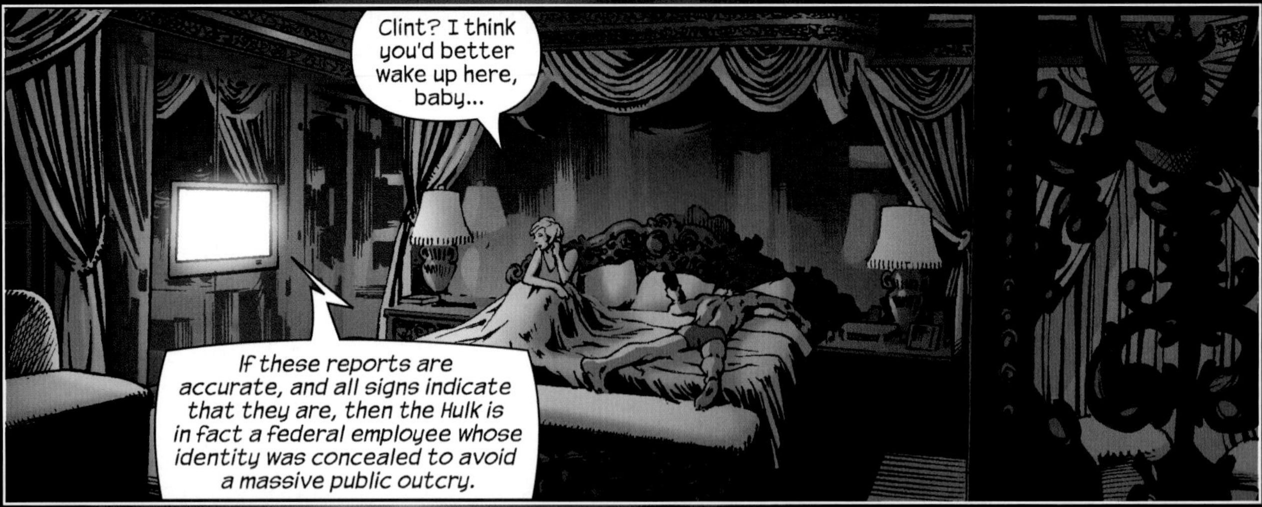
Clint? I think you'd better wake up here, baby...
If these reports are accurate, and all signs indicate that they are, then the Hulk is in fact a federal employee whose identity was concealed to avoid a massive public outcry.

BH: Did anybody notice on the penultimate page that panel two shows Tony and Black Widow in bed watching the news, but we changed the dialogue to Clint and his wife when we realised after drawing issue number two that Tony was simultaneously under the sea with Captain Britain whilst that scene took place?

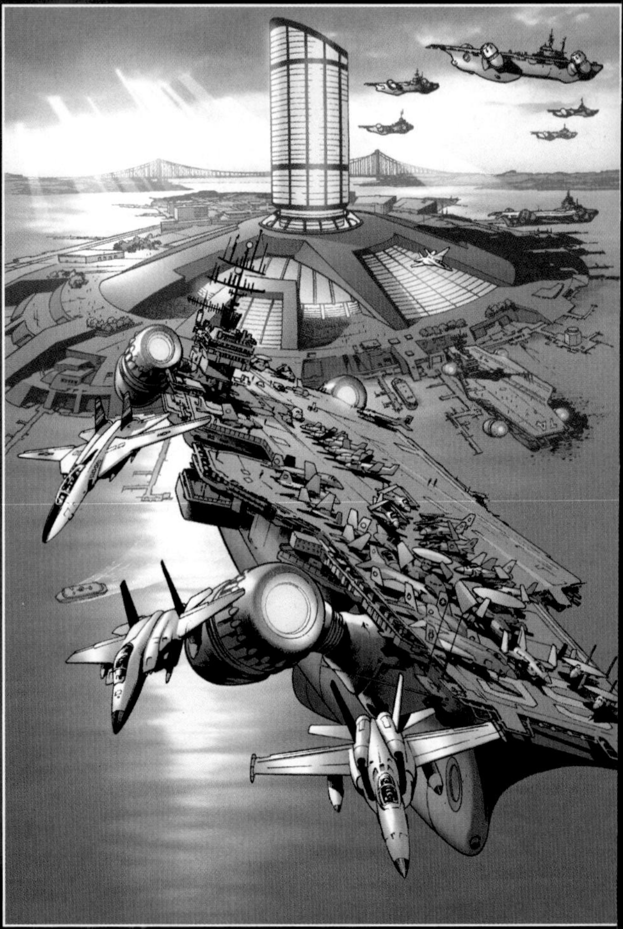

MM: Yeah, that was my fault, but we managed to fudge it cleverly so it isn't actually a mistake. As you know, I wrote and rewrote every issue constantly and the original opening to issue two didn't feature an underwater Iron Man. But once it did, I had to go back at the last minute and clean up that panel so he wasn't in two different places at the same time. The original opening to issue two was a chat with Banner again and just not visual enough. Plus, this allowed us to bring in the European team early, which is obviously something I'd wanted to do for plot reasons. Also, can I just say that the splash page of the Triskelion with the helicarriers floating around it gave me my first full-blown multiple nerdgasm this morning. I'd forgotten just how beautiful this book looked. Were I another artist poring over Hitchy's pages I think I'd have to write a suicide note to Wizard magazine and just open a vein. How can people compete with drawings like that?

BH: Er, well. Thanks. A little embarrassing shuffle of my feet. I drew that page only a few days before going to press as I thought it needed that big musical chord before the cut to inside. Eagle-eyed folk might notice that the security area Hank goes through on his way to Bruce's cell is the same as Magneto's from X2. Our thought was to suggest Mags was being held in the Triskelion as a little bit of fun. I would have preferred to keep the big tough-looking cylindrical cell Bruce had from volume one but it made interaction difficult and knowing what was

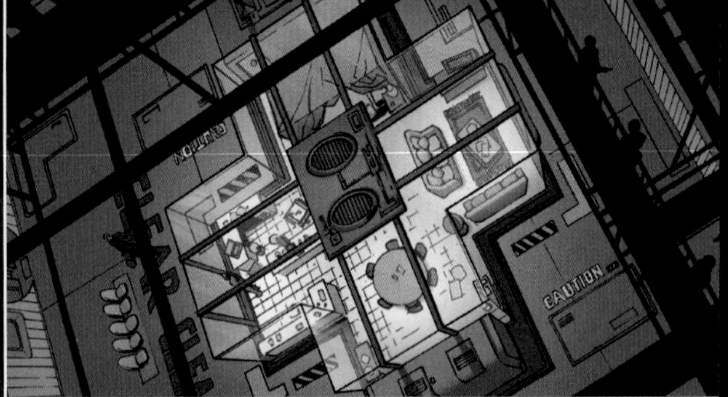
CAUTION

happening over the first three issues meant I needed a way to have more close contact

MM: Yeah, I loved that little touch with Magneto in The Triskelion. The upcoming Marvel movies from Iron Man to The Avengers are all clearly set in the Ultimate universe too, so I think this makes sense.

BH: Do you remember when you sent the script over it originally had Thor talking to Balder the Brave in a forest? We both felt, on reflection, that it didn't quite work, so you went away and came back with Vostagg in a restaurant, which seemed so much more like an Ultimates scene.

MM: Yeah, I had us jumping right into the mythological stuff and Bryan's instincts were right. It was just too soon. We really had to build up to that and people would only accept it if we worked it all in very gradually. So I went away and rewrote this as a scene in a restaurant as opposed to a magical forest on the edges of Asgard. God, we really worked hard on this. There's so many versions of each script on my hard drive, I'm quite embarrassed.

BH: You should be.

MM: Look closely and you'll see that Bryan has added another one of his little Easter eggs here. Can you see Loki wandering around in the background just as they're talking about reality shifting? That wasn't in the script, but this, along with all the other Loki cameos throughout the book, enhanced the thing enormously. It became a great "Where's Wally?" kind of thing for me as much as the readers.

BH: Oddly though, readers kept seeing him even in volume one issues, so the real Loki was obviously playing tricks.

MM: Get real, loser. He's a mythological character.

ISSUE TWO

MM: Captain Britain's appearance in issue two really happened for two reasons. The first is that if America has The Ultimates,

then Europe would need to have their own superhuman response team (as China and others would, too). But on a more fanboy level, I just wanted to write Captain Britain. The original run was published here in the U.K. back in 1977 and advertised on television as Britain's first ever superhero, so every boy in my class was into it and we all had the little mask you got free with the first issue. Years later, I got into the Alan Moore/Alan Davis run too so it was a double-whammy of nostalgia for me to write the good Captain. Moore's Cap run, I think, is one of the three best works of his career. It had an enormous impact on me as both a fan and a writer, so it felt all nice and tingly to write him here.

BH: I came to that Captain Britain stuff a little later than you, as I was getting it on with bikes and loose girls as a seven-year-old, but I thought that the CB stuff was amongst his most visually dynamic work. I still do. I can see he's improved and learned far more about how to draw since then (25 years ago), but that and his Marvelman stuff (his proper name, True Believers) were his most energetically experimental work; he tried everything visually to see what worked and it had a unique freshness to it, however comparatively crude it may be.

MM: I love Alan Davis. He and Moore are possibly my favourite creative team in the history of the medium. They were the U.K.'s Stan and Jack. Everything they did was just gold when I was a kid. Obviously, their work was a little rough around the edges compared to later technical genius, but there was such an amazing energy to their collaborations.

BH: I think that's often true when you are just trying anything and everything. The process of refinement might make something more technically assured, but it can sometimes be at the cost of a little something extra, an essential energy, maybe. My Ultimates work is far more involved, assured and in all ways technically superior to my Authority work, but the earlier Authority is still often cited by readers as a preferred favourite. A lesson there possibly, considering the time, effort, energy and struggle involved in putting this baby together.

BH: So what about the traitor story line? One of the biggest deliberate misdirections we ever did.

MM: I'd forgotten just how early we were flagging the traitor plot in the books. Nothing gets the readers going mad quite like the old wolf-in-the-fold story line and this had the internet message boards buzzing for a long time. We were hinting heavily towards Thor and Fury in the opening chapters and obviously shifted this around to pretty much every character at some point. My favourite post on the boards was a kid who thought it had to be Tony because the beard and moustache made him look kind of evil. In hindsight, I wish we'd made it Jarvis, just so we could have had a book where the butler did it.

BH: Well, the butler GOT it later from the traitor, so it was almost there. Funny, too, looking back to these early issues and noting the scene of Jarvis playing strip poker whilst Natasha watches Tony's undersea rescue with CB in issue two. She later shot him in the head, of course, so perhaps she didn't like his under-hosiery.

MM: I think Ultimate Jarvis is perhaps the seediest character in the history of the medium. We didn't even see what he was getting up to, but we knew it was bad and it somehow combined humans, animals AND the insect kingdom. He was a deeply, deeply disturbed man and so the perfect friend for Tony. Didn't you base his visual on one of your friends?

BH: Yes, one of my deeply disturbed friends; the kind with which I always try to surround myself, especially at parties.

ISSUE THREE

MM: Oh, big thanks to a mate of mine called Jim for all his help on issue three. He helped with a lot of the legal jargon and, I think, took lots of photographs of the courthouse for Bryan to use as ref. I haven't heard from him in a little while, which makes me think he might have been arrested for all those pics under new Homeland Security laws. I hope the guards of Guantanamo Bay are treating you well, Jimbo. See you in twenty years.

BH: Actually, the photos came from editorial. I don't remember which of Karate Kid and Editor Ralph Macchio's assistants took them for me; it may actually have been Nick Lowe, but I do remember John Barber was skulking around in them to show me the human scale for the jury box. He HAS since been arrested but the reasons for which are a closely guarded secret known only by myself and three million loyal Americans.

MM: I loved writing the Bruce and Betty scenes. Their relationship was so poisonous and built entirely on one having power over the other. And yet at the same time you could tell that they both cared for one another. Likeable, but they were hopefully always real. God, I miss these guys. I loved them. Why did we leave this book?

BH: Because we'd had enough and you should never stay at the party until somebody suggests you help tidy up. However many issues we'd done, I'd lived with it for so long I needed to move on. I wasn't entirely convinced I wanted to do this second volume and Nick Lowe had to patiently listen to me quitting every Friday and talk me back on the book. I am glad we got there in the end, as I am very proud of the work we did on it overall, no matter how many nervous breakdowns I had to endure. It's been the most enduring and successful working relationship I've ever had.

MM: You're absolutely right. We really are brilliant. I sit this next to the Bible on my bookshelves at home, you know.

BH: Unlike the Bible though, our work is not a complete fiction.

MM: You'll regret saying that when you die in an Omen-style accident, smart-ass.

BH: I'll take my chances. But, it's having great material like that to work with that makes the drawing so much easier. As much as the old Marvel Method of plot, art and script produced some real winners over the years, I can't imagine not having the dialogue to work from. How can you have characters emote and act without knowing what they are saying?

of the leading lights on my www.millarworld.tv message board and the biggest Captain America fan in the world outside of John Cassaday. He's a bodyguard and personal trainer too, so the idea of Cap working out in his gym gave him a warm glow and a big surprise when he picked up the issue.

BH: I think he has the original page, probably now sweat-stained, hanging on his real gym wall, too.

MM: Hey, here's that little cameo from Matt Murdock. I love the fact we were so cocky about the book that we felt we could do Murdock without needing to have a big Daredevil appearance. It reminds me of something Sam Loeb said to me shortly after this issue was published. Sam, for those who didn't know him, was the brilliantly smart and funny son of our friend Jeph Loeb who sadly passed away a couple of years ago. But he was a hilarious kid and the first time I met him, he shook my hand and said he was digging Ultimates, but wouldn't it be great if something actually **HAPPENED** in the book. He said it with a smirk and I remember liking him immediately. How cheeky is THAT?

ISSUE FOUR

MM: The first thing to jump out at me in issue four is the Archonis Gym. Archonis is one

Steve and Jan's relationship disintegrating was great fun to write and I loved all the scenes like this. Captain America just seemed like the perfect catch at first, but as reality seeps in Jan comes to realize he might look like Brad Pitt, but his sense of humour is probably stuck in 1941 Marx Brothers movies and they have very little in common. That and he loves hanging out with the elderly. Imagine a double date with two octogenarians when you're as hot as Jan. As ever, she's attracted to absolutely the wrong man.

BH: Originally I'd thought of Hank as a Sam Neil kind of look, an older, irascible type. My thought was that Hank was a little guy trying to make himself bigger and Jan was tiny but had a huge heart and intellect in need of a father figure. That need for an older guy came through in Cap, but she ended up with a great-grandfather figure instead!.

MM: Oh God. Hawkeye's kids. Turning the page and seeing their little faces made me uneasy for a moment because I know what happens to them three issues down the line. But this is made so much worse by Bryan basing these tots on his own little

sons. Tragically, he had no idea what I had planned for these little darlings further down the line and was no doubt traumatized when the script for issue seven arrived. Either that or it was wildly cathartic for him as the boys had been especially badly behaved that particular week. I think he should have a copy of their execution hanging in the kitchen as a warning of what they can expect if they give him any crap.

BH: This wee story is becoming an urban legend of its own. They aren't my kids, but since I hadn't really drawn children much I grabbed some snaps from our family photo box to help with Hawk's brood. They are sort of an amalgam of my nephews (on my wife's side) and some friends, but nobody specific and I DID know what was going to happen to them, you daft whiskey-swiller, as we thought this stuff up together years ago! Still, why let truth get in the way of a great anecdote! It was a great piece of action to draw though. I remember the script started with an exterior shot of the house but since I wanted to keep it intimate rather than spacious, I opened with a close-up of Mrs. Hawkeye. We hadn't really seen her before so I thought it was important to immediately identify with her, especially as we had that lovely personal family dialogue. If you can get the readers to care about her in the short space you have, it gives her killing that bit more emotional impact. The writing of the character was note-perfect, so the images and the shot choices needed to match that. Also starting inside the house, rather than outside the house, gives us the family point of view rather than the attackers' and that was important too.

I had fun creating those European super-soldiers and based a few on friends and family. My sister is engaged to an Italian guy called Umberto Landi, so he was quite chuffed about becoming Captain Italy. My friend Carlos Fraile was a shoo-in for Captain Spain and I bought him this page as a birthday present. God, I am so, so generous and nice. Like Jesus, really, but with Sean Connery's accent.

BH: Jesus could probably shrug better than you though and he was a better bring-your-own-bottle party guest.

MM: Can I just say that my favourite panel in the entire series is featured here? The image of Captain America and the rest of the team walking through this snowy forest is just haunting. We've seen them step from the shadows countless times, but taking superheroes away from the big city and into this almost Brothers Grimm-like setting was very eerie. I know it's just a little panel on the bottom of a page, but I thought the image was absolutely amazing. Again, well done, Hitchy.

BH: Well, as ever, you exaggerate charmingly, as this was another of those instances where you called the shot perfectly, so I can't take credit for it. Drawn exactly as scripted. We dipped into each other's work areas so much on this series and I think it made for stronger storytelling all-round. Take your own bow, Mighty Mark.

ISSUE FIVE:

MM: I will go down on record as saying that this fight scene is the best-drawn of the whole series. I remember coming to the studio with a guy from Wizard and we were just gawping at these pages. It was perfect, just beautiful storytelling. The scene where Thor gets football tackled by two of the heroes was just amazing. That shot was just perfect.

BH: Thanks, too kind. I bask indulgently in your warm glow of praise. Really, I do...

MM: I don't know if you remember, but you had to nip back to the house for ten

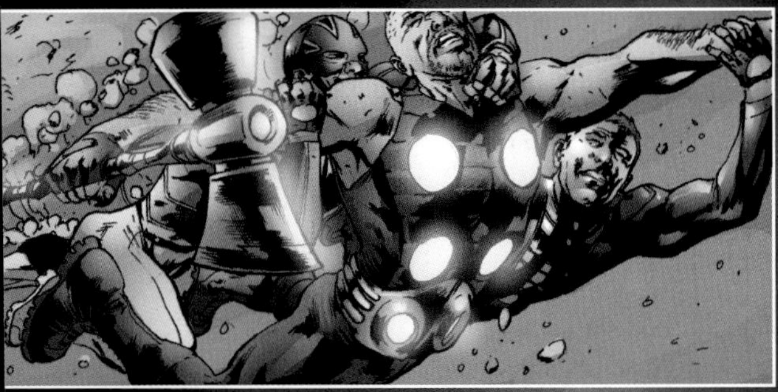

minutes and you left us in your studio alone. Being swines, we immediately checked your computer for porn and you know what? We found almost nothing. Either you're a monk or you have hidden files even a Wizard writer couldn't find. But one disturbing thing I'll never forget was finding just two nude shots. They looked like something from the '40s. They were literally just bland nude shots of a girl smiling and looking over her shoulder. Is that what you get off on? Is that the limit of your tastes?

BH: Naturally I have no idea what you are talking about and my legal team will be in touch.

MM: That scene at the end with Thor talking to Loki is just horrible. I had something a little more special effects going on, but you were absolutely right to just have him as a simple snake. I think I suggested Loki's head on the body, but as ever you kept it real and that always worked best for this book.

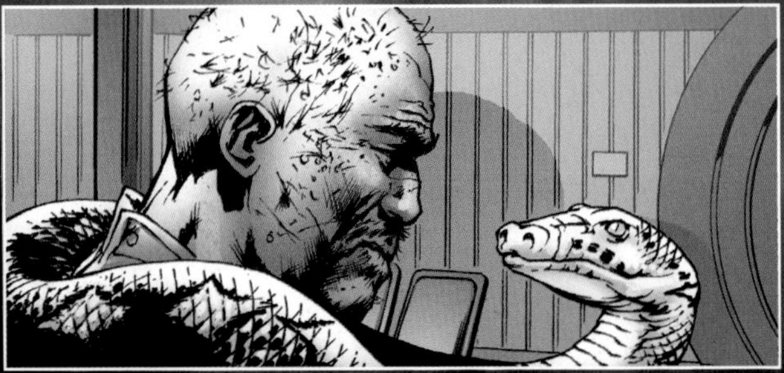

BH: I never really knew how anything would actually play when I worked on it; there was always just this nebulous FEEL to what it was supposed to be in my head and the shots had to match that feel. It's often why stuff got redrawn so much. I could have drawn all of this stuff more quickly and more easily but finding that elusive flavour often proved hard. It's certainly a contributing factor to why it seemed to take so long and to be a massive indulgence. I don't know whether it made the work any better or just different, but there you go. I'd probably redraw and edit so much of it now, as my approach is from a different place for Fantastic Four. I look at those pages now and think "I wouldn't do THAT now." My special edition would be shorter than the original. Pay more, readers and get less; a great new deal!

ISSUE SIX:

MM: This was my favourite issue of the whole run. In terms of actual writing, this was the issue I was most pleased with and was so excited about, I wrote it about six months earlier than the preceding issues. There's nothing more interesting than a superhero failing. I don't know why. But it just seemed very Marvel to me. It was just a flawed guy trying to do the right thing and everything just going wrong.

BH: I suppose it plays to much of the tragedy of the original Marvel stuff. Spidey and Hulk were sympathetic because they were heroic despite their ordinary lives and failings, rather than godlike heroes such as the never-failing DC icons.

MM: Is it true you based the nude shot of Giant Man on a polaroid of yourself?

BH: Unfortunately for my public modesty, yes. I was wearing trunks, but it was a difficult shot to get right at that angle, so I stood over a camera and set the timer. I drew the piece without any blur and, shall we say, fully rendered; it was also the first

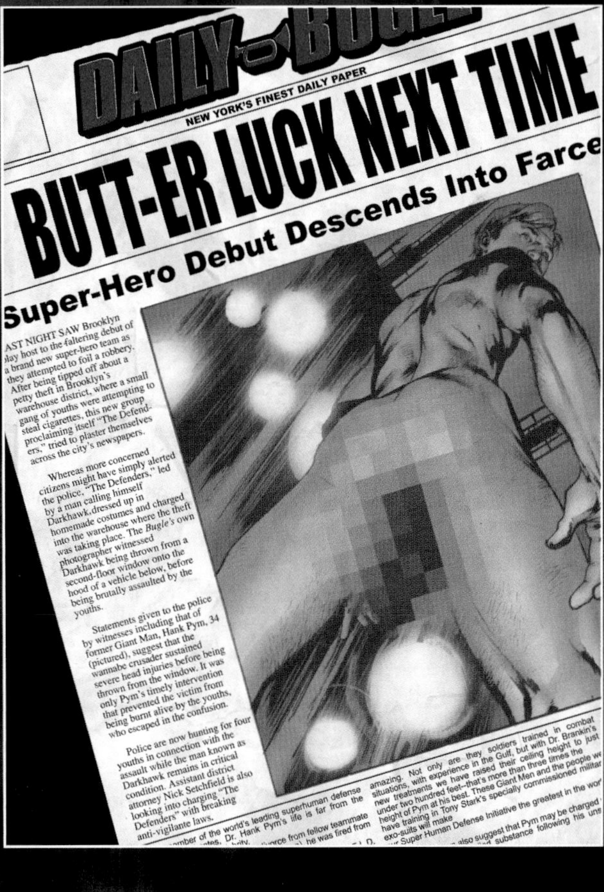

DAILY BUGLE
NEW YORK'S FINEST DAILY PAPER
BUTT-ER LUCK NEXT TIME
Super-Hero Debut Descends Into Farce
AST NIGHT SAW Brooklyn play host to the faltering debut of a brand new super-hero team as they attempted to foil a robbery. After being tipped off about a petty theft in Brooklyn's warehouse district, where a small gang of youths were attempting to steal cigarettes, this new group proclaiming itself "The Defenders," tried to plaster themselves across the city's newspapers.
Whereas more concerned citizens might have simply alerted the police, "The Defenders," led by a man calling himself Darkhawk, dressed up in homemade costumes and charged into the warehouse where the theft was taking place. The Bugle's own photographer witnessed Darkhawk being thrown from a second-floor window onto the hood of a vehicle below, before being brutally assaulted by the youths.
Statements given to the police by witnesses including that of former Giant Man, Hank Pym, 34 (pictured), suggest that the wannabe crusader sustained severe head injuries before being thrown from the window. It was only Pym's timely intervention that prevented the victim from being burnt alive by the youths, who escaped in the confusion.
Police are now hunting for four youths in connection with the assault while the man known as Darkhawk remains in critical condition. Assistant district attorney Nick Setchfield is also looking into charging "The Defenders" with breaking anti-vigilante laws.

piece of original art to sell. It may not have sold as quickly had it been known that was my own gentlemen's area staring back, but it does say a lot about what sells.

MM: The best little touch in the issue was something Bryan added in the art. We had that soul-destroying moment where this girl (who's clearly using Hank as much as he's using her) asks him if he'll dress up as Cap in bed. It was just so, so awful, but Bryan made it ten times worse by having the Cap costume in the background panel of the next scene. It made me feel like crying, as he felt so low, he did it. He actually just dressed up as this guy he couldn't stand just to sleep with a nineteen-year-old girl.

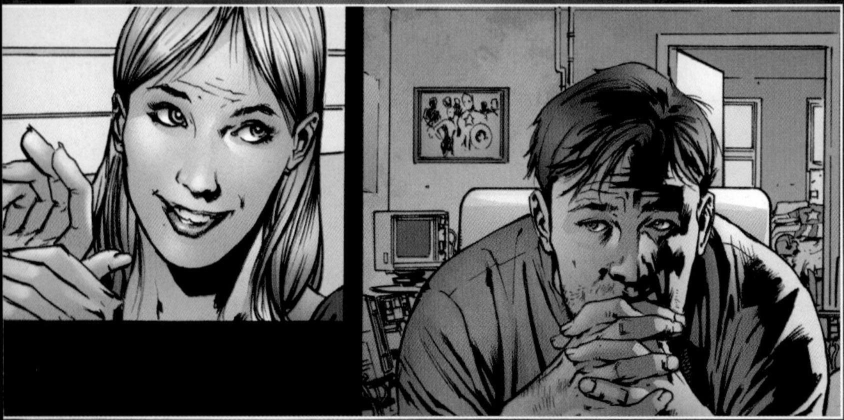

BH: I ALWAYS go further than Mark with this stuff. Besides, it's fun to put this stuff in for readers to dig out; not everything has to be telegraphed with caption boxes and dialogue.

MM: The traitor thing was good, though, wasn't it? I loved the speculation on the boards and it was always fun feeding that.

BH: Yeah, it played out very well and yet it was always so obvious who it was. It was a nice little thread, along with the "Who is Thor?" stuff; gives it a bit more depth. Well done, you.

ISSUE SEVEN:

MM: I'm amazed how political we were allowed to go. Gulf War 2 had just started and Bush had 80% approval and people had flags all over their cars and we were criticizing them instantly. We were saying America was stealing Iraq's oil and had designs on Iran, Syria, North Korea and eventually China. That chat between Thor and Tony just said it all and nobody made us change a line.

BH: Is that because nobody was really reading it?

MM: Hollywood is just touching on stuff like this now, three years later, and that makes me very proud of comics– how immediate we can be. It's like being newspaper cartoonists. We don't have a legal department watching over us.

BH: I was saying this to a large table of Hollywood types only the other day. Comics are so wonderfully immediate (even the late ones that don't arrive immediately) in a way that movies can't be. We could get a book out in two months, start to finish (really we COULD, we didn't, but we could) whereas a movie is anything from two to three years. Advantage us. I think.

MM: Oh God. There's the kids dying. People never saw that one coming, did they? I remember that's when the book just kicked into high gear and the readers were going nuts. The momentum was going really well here too, as we'd had about seven issues out in nine months at that point, so a lot of people were talking between issues. The traitor thing worked well, as it got very nasty very quickly. I loved Hawkeye. He could have had a whole book to himself if done right. Why are the conservative characters the most fun to do?

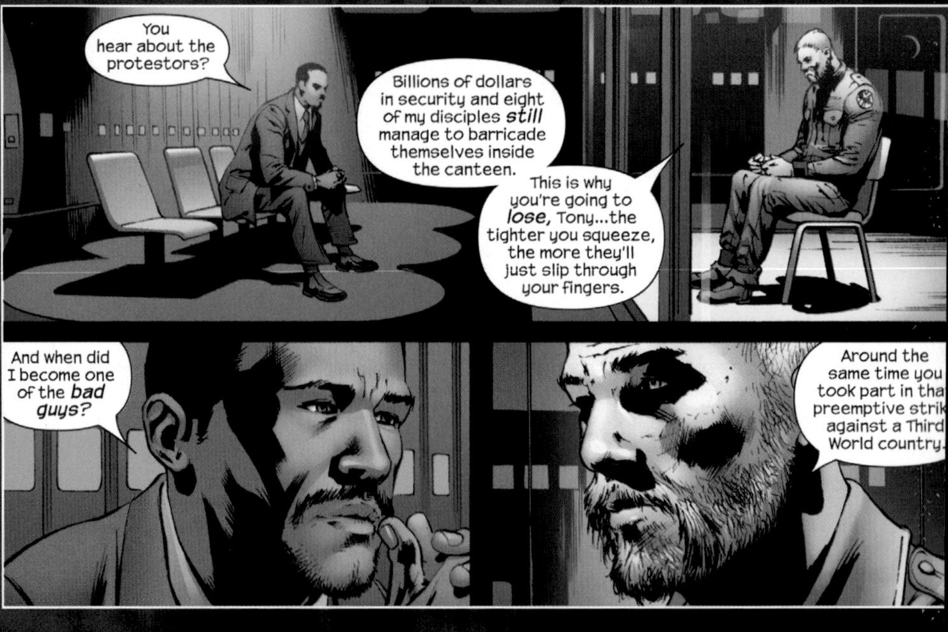
You hear about the protestors?
Billions of dollars in security and eight of my disciples *still* manage to barricade themselves inside the canteen.
This is why you're going to *lose,* Tony...the tighter you squeeze, the more they'll just slip through your fingers.
And when did I become one of the *bad guys?*
Around the same time you took part in tha preemptive strik against a Third World country.

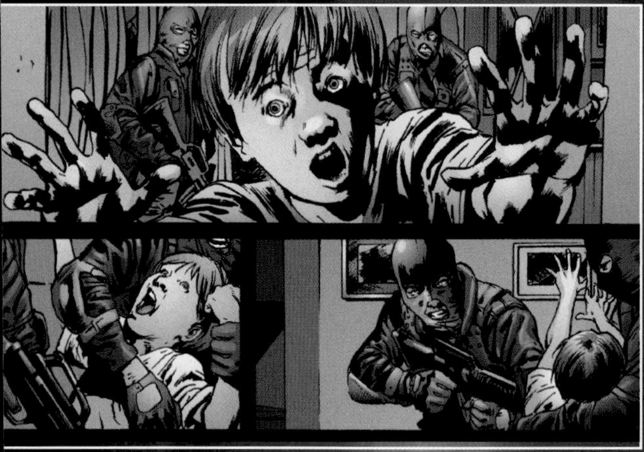

BH: Dunno, cos politically they are dull as dirty ditch water. I'd always love to do more Hawkeye; I think he could have beaten the Punisher for popularity, too, and I'd always be up for more Hawkeye.

MM: Hawkeye is da bomb, bitches.

BH: Did you really just say that out loud?

MM: Yes. And I apologize.

ISSUE EIGHT:

MM: Genuinely the hardest thing about this book was finding the space for everything you wanted to say. Cap and Bucky had such an interesting relationship, but we didn't have time to do much with it and so I treasured chances to get these little chats about the old days. Seeing Fury and his guys taking Cap down when he was at his lowest ebb here was really affecting. You really got a lot of emotion into these scenes, Bry.

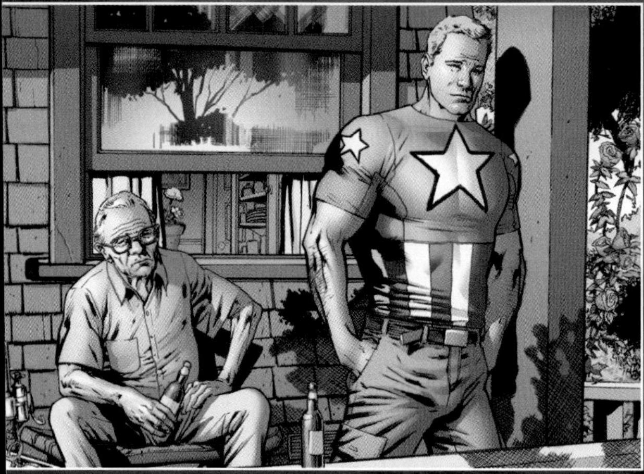

I tried but in reading them I can see where I didn't manage it. Some of it fits okay, but much of it doesn't. It's where movies and TV have the advantage in that they have actors and a chance to edit afterwards. I'm glad you think it hit where you want, but if I had to redraw anything it would be these scenes. It's that they were so well written that holds it together, not the art. Still, thanks, Old Hobbit.

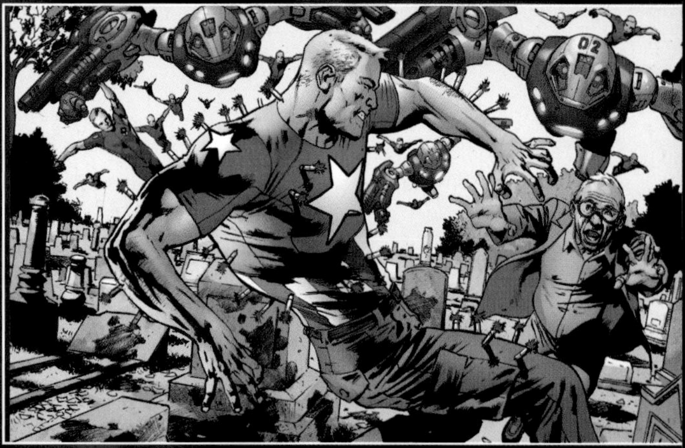

MM: That last page is just brilliant. As a kid, I always wondered why we never saw Cap's grave, as everybody thought he'd died at the end of World War II, and so we shoved a scene about that into volume one. But seeing him go down here just felt awful. It makes me laugh, though, when I think about the guy online who thought the statue on the last page was the real Cap showing up. What made it worse is that he loved it and said he couldn't wait to see what happened next issue. He had no idea it was a statue.

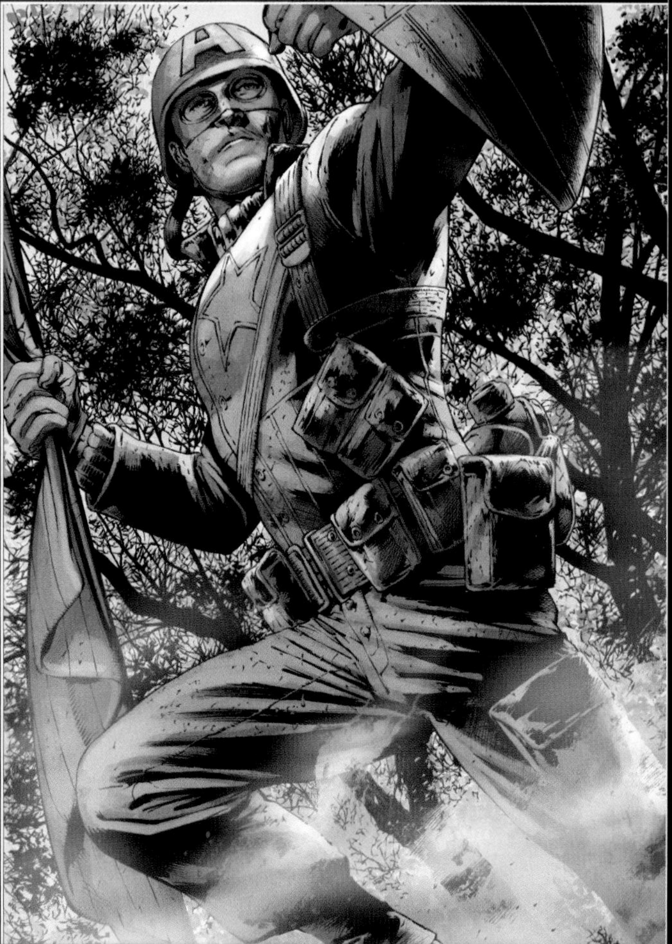

ISSUE NINE:

MM: Oh, Tony and Natasha's sex scene. I think the script just had them kissing for a panel and Natasha looking at her watch, but Bryan added in all the little naughty bits I never thought we'd get away with. One of the nice things about the book starting to get late by this stage is that there was never time to redraw anything. It always just went to the printers without a single comment. But this is pretty racy for an all-ages book.

had in our heads but never really made a big deal of. Offices always have secret relationships and this was the secret in the S.H.I.E.L.D. office. It also makes the Banner scenes in previous issues a little more complex. Read them again with this in mind.

BH: It's what I said earlier; you and I stuffed this book with more information than was immediately explicit and it makes for a more intelligent and involving read, if I do say so myself. Which I did. It also makes it much more fun to work on, too.

MM: Poor Jarvis. Shot through the head. In my original script it was a bullet in the chest and he was saved by his hip flask. But Bry wanted to draw his head exploding and again it was the right call.

BH: This was **NEVER** an all-ages book. I know that was the original intent for the Ultimates line in general, but ours never fitted that. We always wanted to keep punching; I would have happily made it far more adult, pushing the super-powered violence and having more sex depicted too.

MM: Did you see that little panel where Nick Fury and Betty hold hands?

BH: I should do; drew it. Are you paying attention to who you work with here?

MM: From issue three we'd planted the seeds that she was secretly sleeping with Nick. He's an old friend of her father's and it was a little background thing we

BH: I needed a casualty. I wanted those reading to feel like anything could happen and anyone could die. I was planning on killing Fury during the attack on the Triskelion, but when that was nixed by the higher powers, I had the Jarvis head shot (Nat would **NEVER** miss) and Fury losing an arm. That fit with Fury's warhorse persona, but also suggested that a normal guy in a super battle wouldn't do too well.

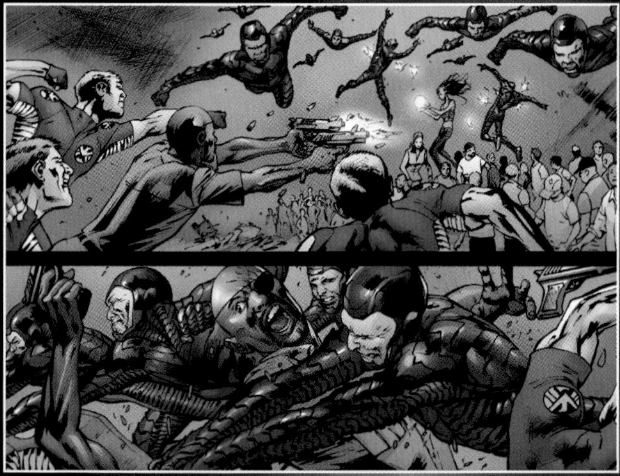

MM: This issue reads like something an Islamic fundamentalist would write. I'm amazed we got away with it. It seemed very anti-American on one level, but nobody said a word. The fans loved it too. I think it was maybe our best-received of the whole run, as people were so busy talking about the traitor we'd misdirected them from the real issue.

ISSUE TEN:

MM: Ah, that little opener was obviously an Islamic version of Captain America's origin. The parallels between the war on terror and the Nazi's preemptive strikes were very interesting.

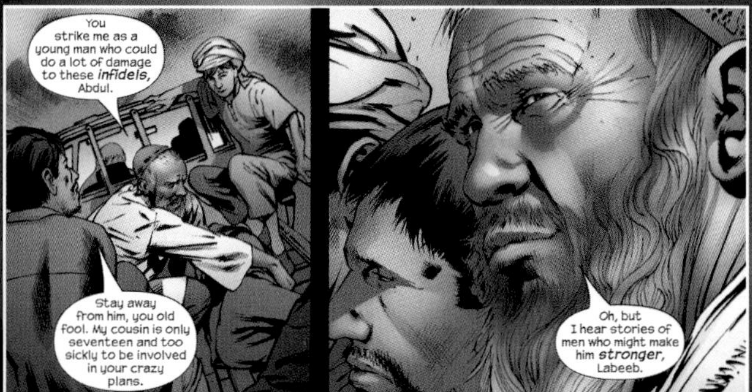
You strike me as a young man who could do a lot of damage to these *infidels*, Abdul.
Stay away from him, you old fool. My cousin is only seventeen and too sickly to be involved in your crazy plans.
Oh, but I hear stories of men who might make him *stronger*, Labeeb.

BH: Of course how he AGED so much in just a few months is washed over slightly...

MM: I love the scene where Hawkeye escapes. I stroked my chin over that fingernail sequence for a couple of days, but it worked so well. Only Bryan could have pulled this off. It could have looked incredibly stupid, but he makes all my worst excesses look believable.

BH: First rule with this stuff: verisimilitude. If you wink at the camera, it's all gone; you have to play the sillier stuff absolutely straight. I don't think this would have worked on film, but it's an excellent example of the

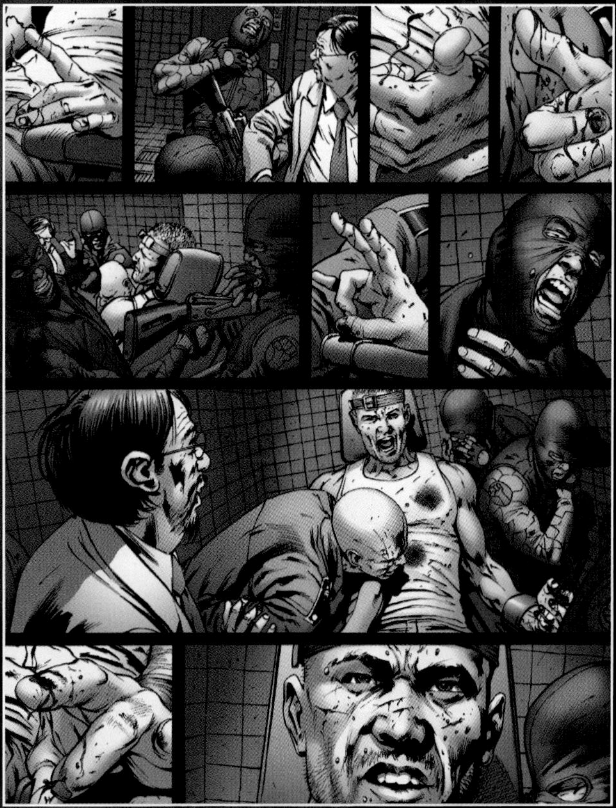

glorious excesses of comics! Speaking of excesses, I quite like the scene in Cap's cell and the shot where the bad guy catches Jan and punches her full-strength when she's Wasp-sized; it's almost missed but awfully brutal.

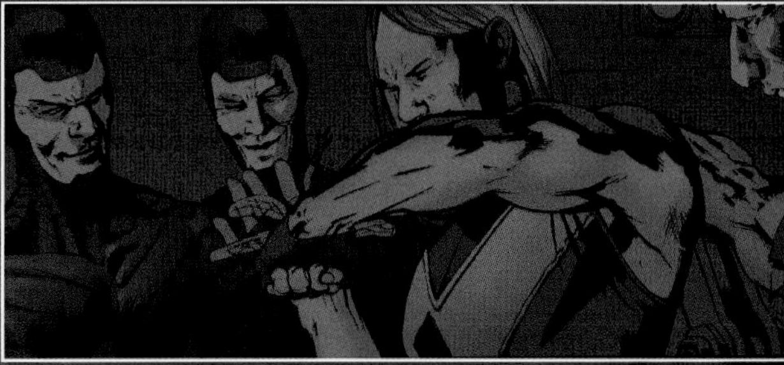

Great finish with Cap released, as you know, no matter what follows, it's the fight back.

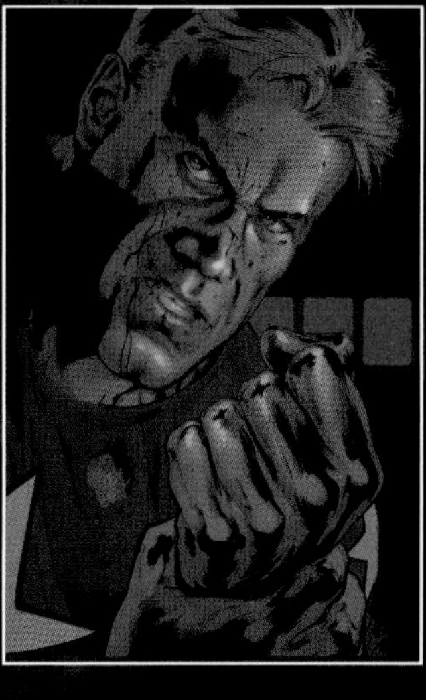

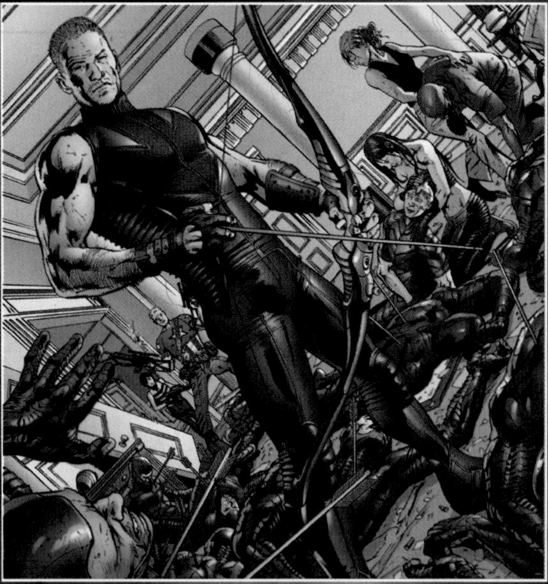

ISSUE ELEVEN:

MM: I love that shot of Hawkeye coming back. I remember you played around with the storytelling there and made it fifty times better than the script.

BH: Did I? Thanks, chum. I loved the simple emotion of Hawk's response when Jan says, " I thought you were dead" and he replies, "No such luck." After a few issues it reminds us of what he's been through in what would have been just a few days. It's beautiful in its simplicity. Too many other writers would have been tempted to have recaps, thought balloons and captions to go over it all, but there you are. Joss Whedon said it was one of his favourite scenes. I drew Jan hugging Hawk there too, because it's a nice human moment amidst all of that destruction and chaos.

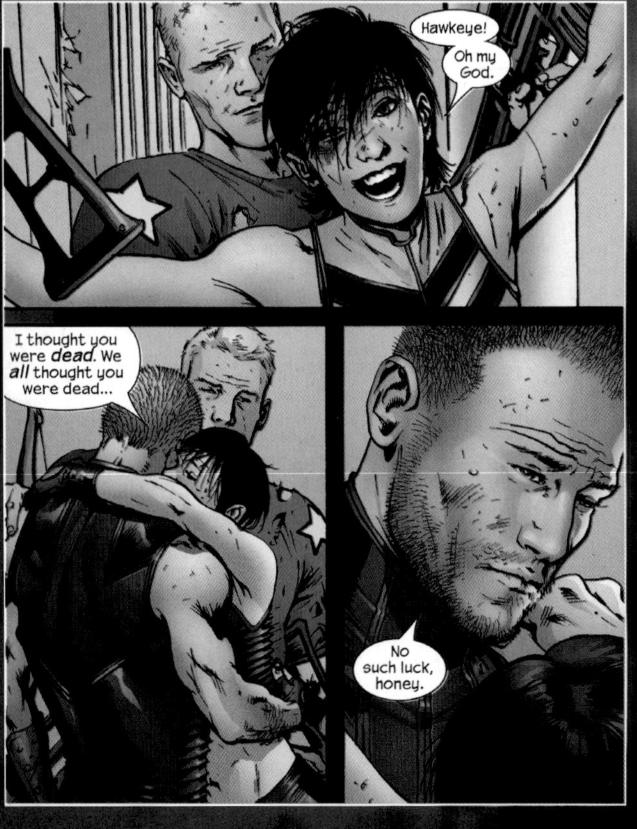
Hawkeye!
Oh my God.
I thought you were *dead*. We *all* thought you were dead...
No such luck, honey.

MM: The return of Bruce Banner. Who'da thunk? Even if you saw it coming a million miles off, it was still cool. That spread is amazing. Were you a truly great friend, you'd have sent me that for my wall. McNiven, Quitely, Adam Kubert and all my most treasured pals always send me pages.

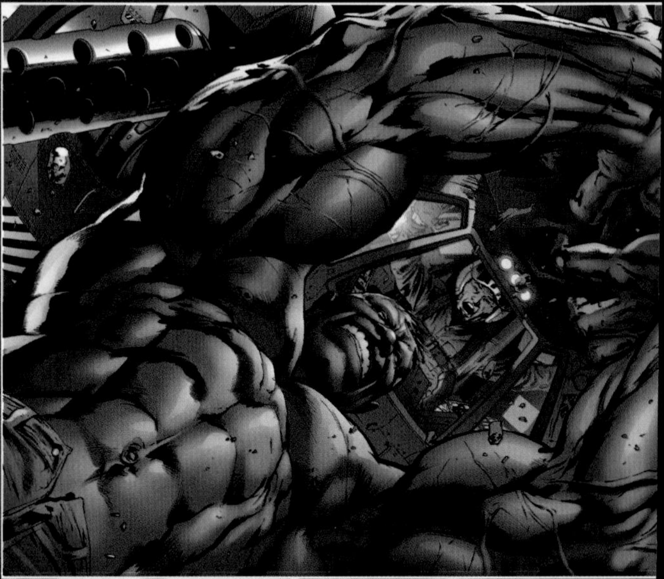

BH: Upon your furnishing me with a vast cheque, duly signed and correctly dated, any page can be yours absolutely free of charge, my friend. Least I can do.

ISSUE TWELVE:

MM: God, this fight just goes on forever, doesn't it?

BH: I think it lasted about a year for me...

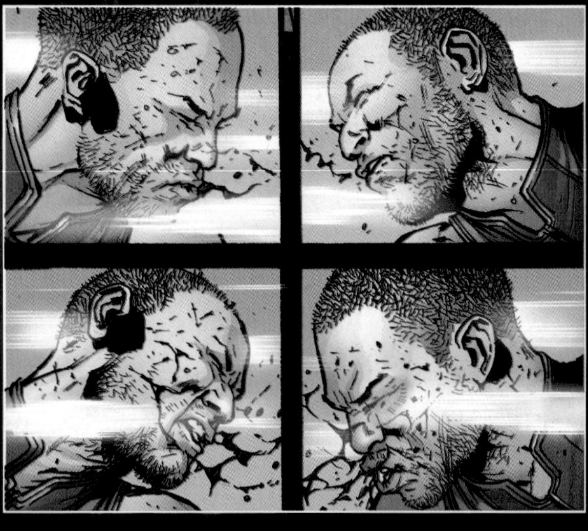

MM: I remember Marvel saying we couldn't have an extra-sized issue 12 for some reason. I think they wanted the issue out in a particular quarter to clobber DC's market share or whatever and so we were told to turn issue 12 into two issues. But they BOTH ended up extra-sized [laughs].

BH: Yeah; Dan Buckley thought it would give us more pages to have two 22-pagers instead of one. That learned him! Issue 12 was 41 pages, issue 13 was about 48 pages. Insane.

MM: That was brilliant. The fight just kept getting bigger and bigger. Bryan was adding extra spreads and cityscapes every day. We had to taser him to stop eventually. I'll never forget his little eyes and that scream... "Don't TASER me, bro!"

BH: That's patently ridiculous. I NEVER say "Bro."

MM: That fight between Cap and Al-Rahman is amazing. It's so beautifully choreographed. But I remember Bryan got so carried away he had Cap grab the guy's weapon and carve an "A" onto his chest once he was dead. It was the only time I think I ever asked him to redraw something as it seemed a bit mean. It took away from the poignancy I was going for, but Bry was already covered in sweat and pro-American pheromones by that point. He just couldn't help himself. It was hilarious.

BH: Possibly a bit much; true. I was aiming for a Zorro and pro-American moment from Cap and didn't think he'd have the time to carve the Stars-and-Stripes on his chest.

We went back and forth on whether Al-Rahman would be dead or not, too, as you had him unconscious. I think the script called for the water to boil with the light-sabre and turn him into the Red Skull, too. We both had our moments of insanity with that one. In the end I just moved the light-sabre into his chest and called quits.

MM: That spread with every hero fighting is just insane. At a stroke, he just kicks the ass of every other artist holding a pencil.

BH: Not so, and only because they would be so busy drawing, I'd have the chance to sneak up behind them. Truth to tell, I think that's one of the weaker images in the book.

MM: Stop lying. You're just trying to get me to say you're great again.

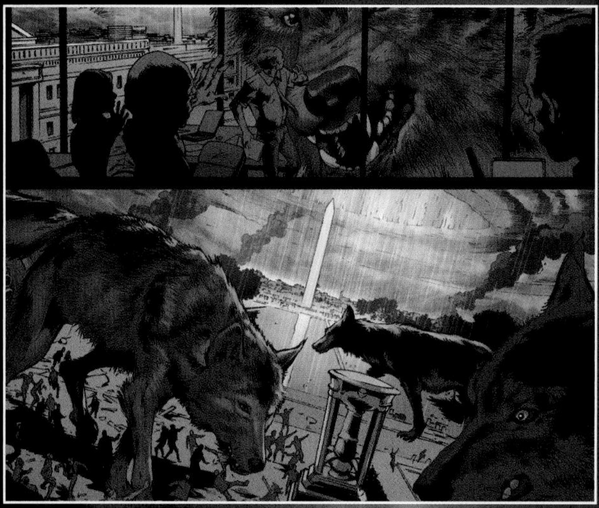

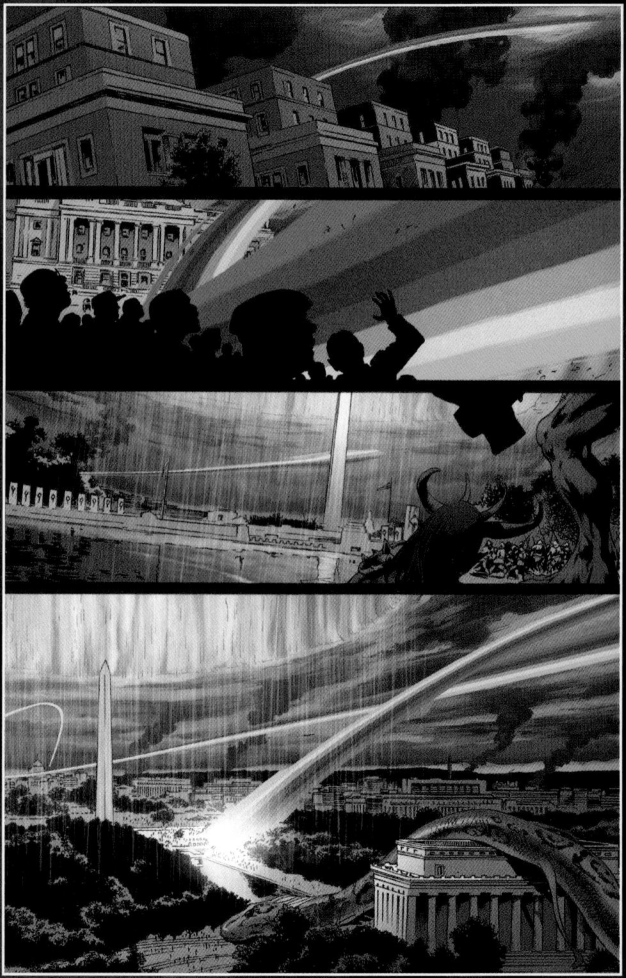

ISSUE THIRTEEN:

MM: Just when you thought it was all over, here comes Loki. So much of the visuals I find inspiring come from TV ads, believe it or not, and the big wolves looking in the windows of city blocks was straight from an insurance commercial over here. But the weirdest reference I shoved in a script had to be the visual I had in mind for the Rainbow Bridge opening up. There's a courier company here called DHL and this was from an ad they had on TV about fifteen years ago. Bryan is very possibly the only other person alive who even remembered it, so that worked out great.

BH: Er, well, I didn't remember it at all, but I got your gist well enough and it was an idea that worked out well. I don't think it was clear enough on page 12 when the Asgardians arrive, but my thought was that they burst out of the bridge as though through a waterfall with light cascading everywhere. It seemed more elegant than running over it.

MM: God, would you look at that eight-page spread. I was really, really against this at first. Yes, it's going in the Guinness Book of Records as the longest published comic panel ever, but I was worried it would hurt the beats of the story. I was even moaning about it as it was being drawn, as it seemed more like a stunt than a part of the book, but when the pages came through I just exhaled and relaxed. It's probably the greatest single piece Bryan has ever drawn. The little spread I had in mind is

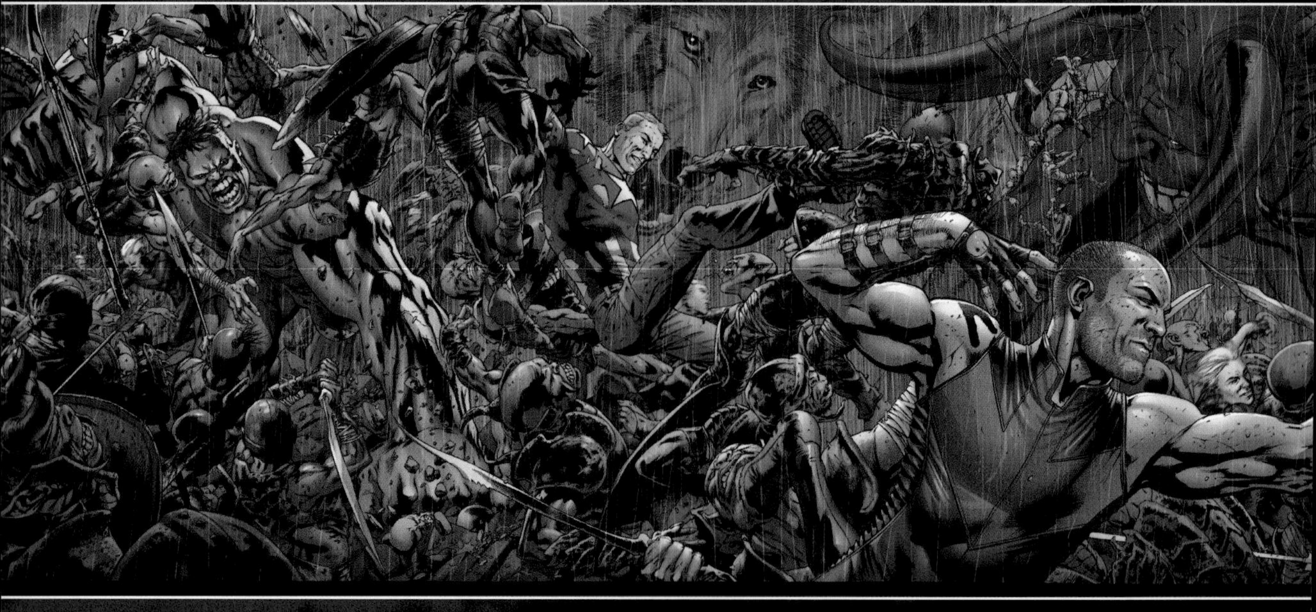

nothing compared to this. It tells a story in itself and in a way that only comics can do. It's just unique. Well done, Englishman.

BH: Well, thanks. I too was unsure about it all the way. I'd asked for a three-page spread so it was bigger than the preceding two-pager, making the image just a bit bigger. Marvel, insanely (insanity was catching on this gig) asked me to make it eight. It was actually very easy to work out, too. The image being so very wide and no taller than a normal panel meant it was more like a Roman wall frieze or the Bayeux Tapestry and since you had to move your head left to right and not just your eyes, the only places you could put any real depth was on both the left and the right edges; where you start and where you stop. Everything else had to be designed to keep your eyes moving that way, so the composition was straightforward. I drew it on three large art boards in a week and Paul took three weeks to ink it. By that point I was flying, as the end was nigh!

MM: The epilogues all worked well. I was almost in tears when I wrote them because it really was goodbye to these characters (for a long time, anyway). The only one that really made me smile was the Tony one. The Hawkeye piece was very satisfying because we really, really wanted to see the Widow get it in the neck, but the

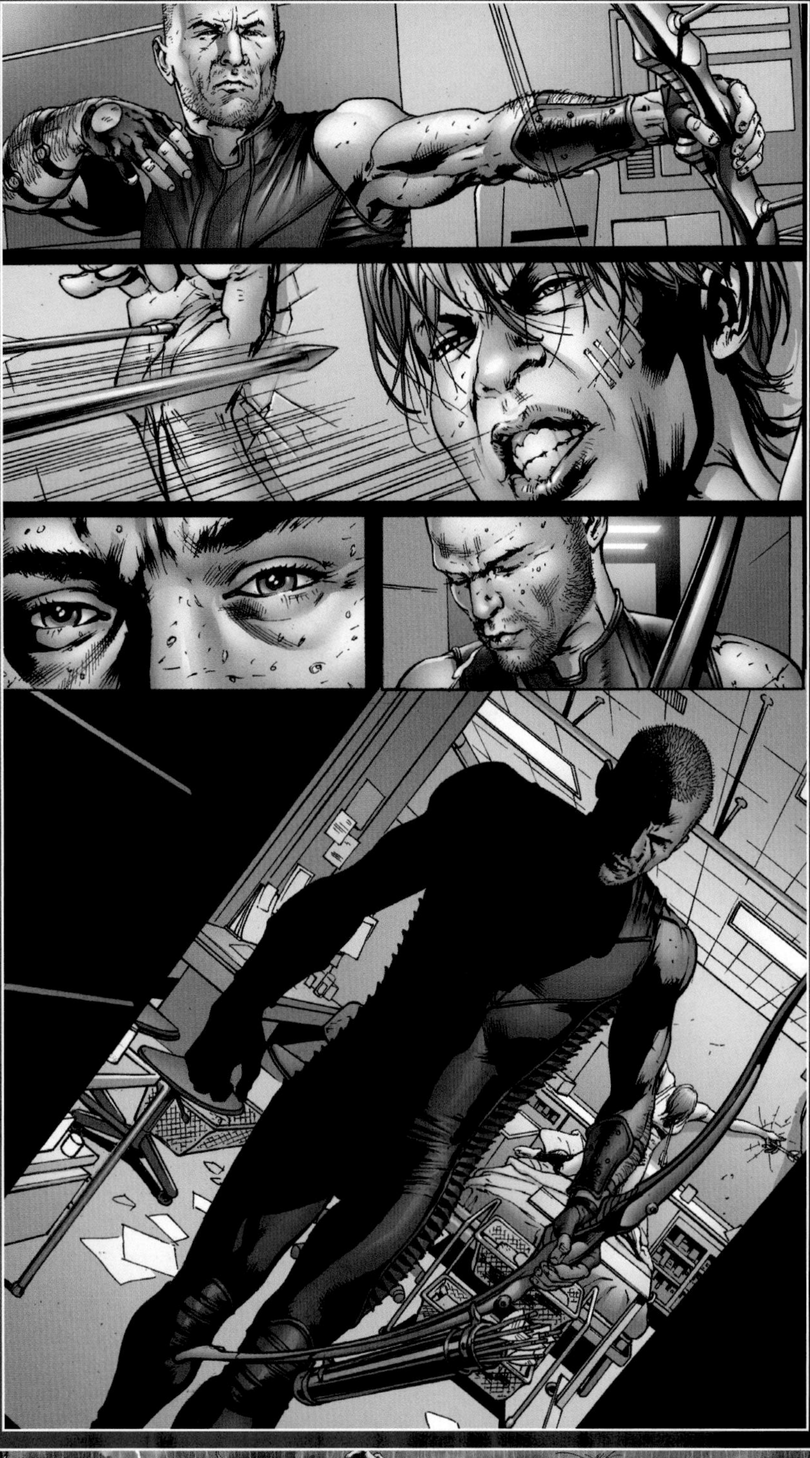

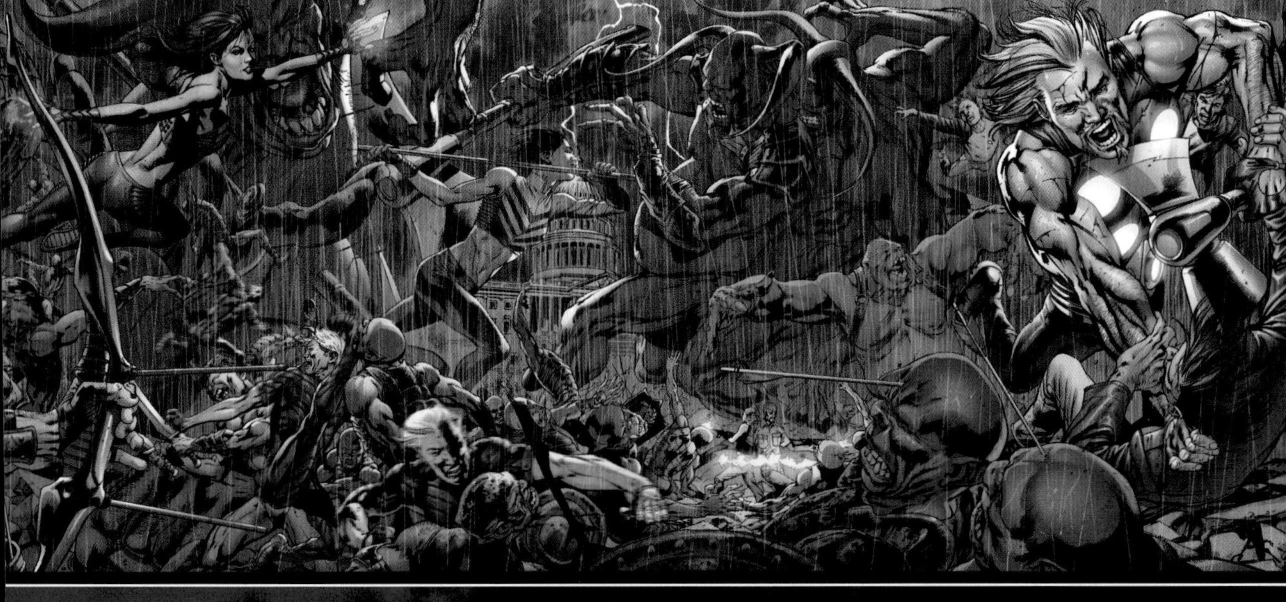

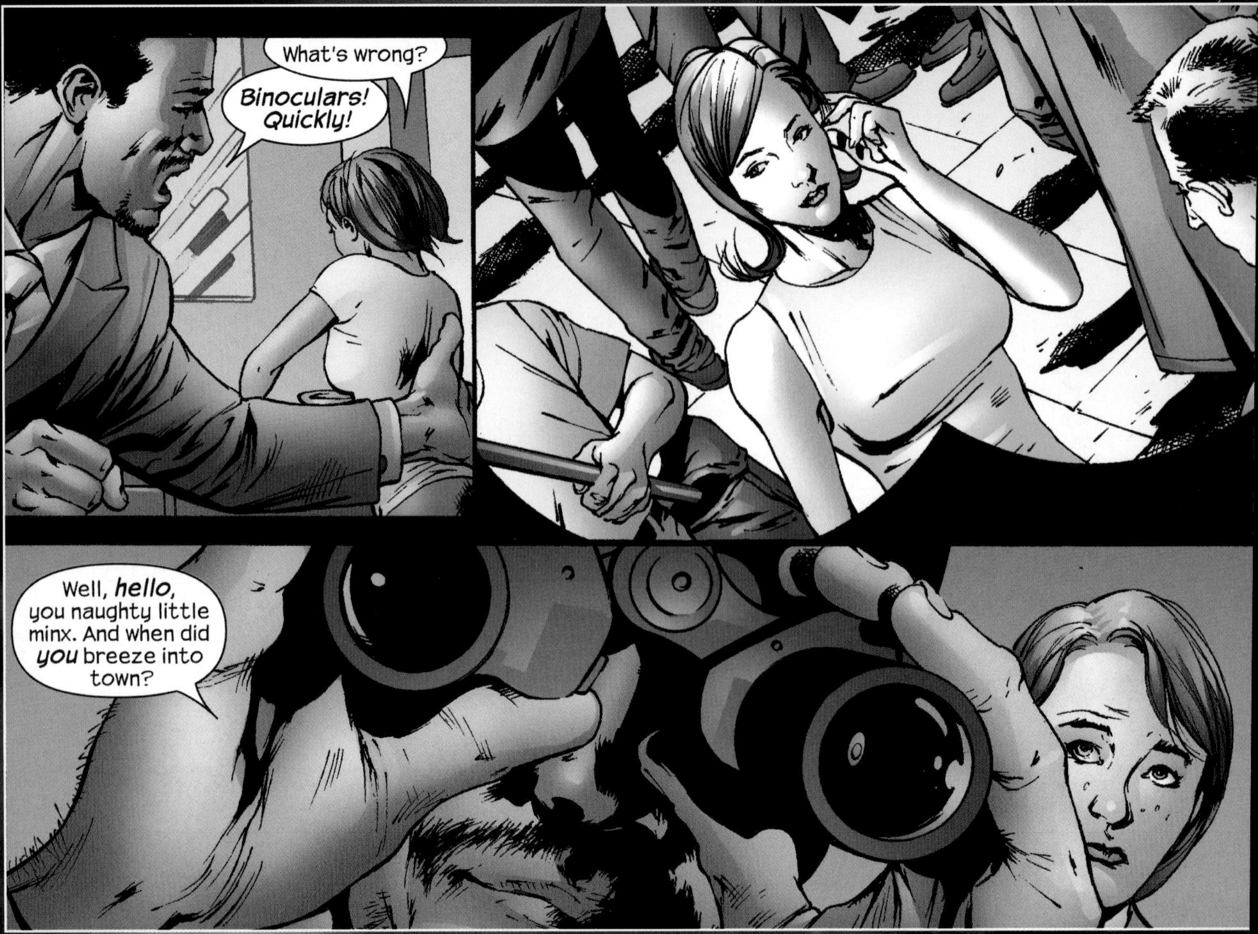
What's wrong?
Binoculars! Quickly!
Well, *hello*, you naughty little minx. And when did *you* breeze into town?

Tony piece looked so sad for a moment and then just snapped Tony straight back into character when he saw that new blonde. I probably relate to Tony more than any of the other characters. I love the fact that they're playing him like this in the movie. I hate seeing Tony tortured. He should embrace his shallowness and revel in his booze.

BH: Yeah, as fun as all that action was I'd been drawing fight scenes for six months by then and craved the smaller stuff. The Hawkeye scene was my favourite in the whole book and absolutely satisfying.

MM: We had the epilogue worked out five years ago, didn't we? So much changed as we were doing the book. We made up new stuff every day and scrapped so much as the times around us changed, too. Bu a couple of little things remained and thi ending, set prior to the opening scene fron the first volume, was something we wante to do right from the start. I don't know i I told you this, but I nicked the idea fron the first two Godfather movies. Copoll didn't know how to end the second on without everyone being on a downer an so he set it before the first scene in th first movie when everyone was very hopefu and innocent. It thus makes you feel happ because it ends on a high with everyone o a high, but it's sad, too, because you kno absolutely everything that awaits them. An all good stories should end with a kiss, right

BH: My lips are yours, chum.

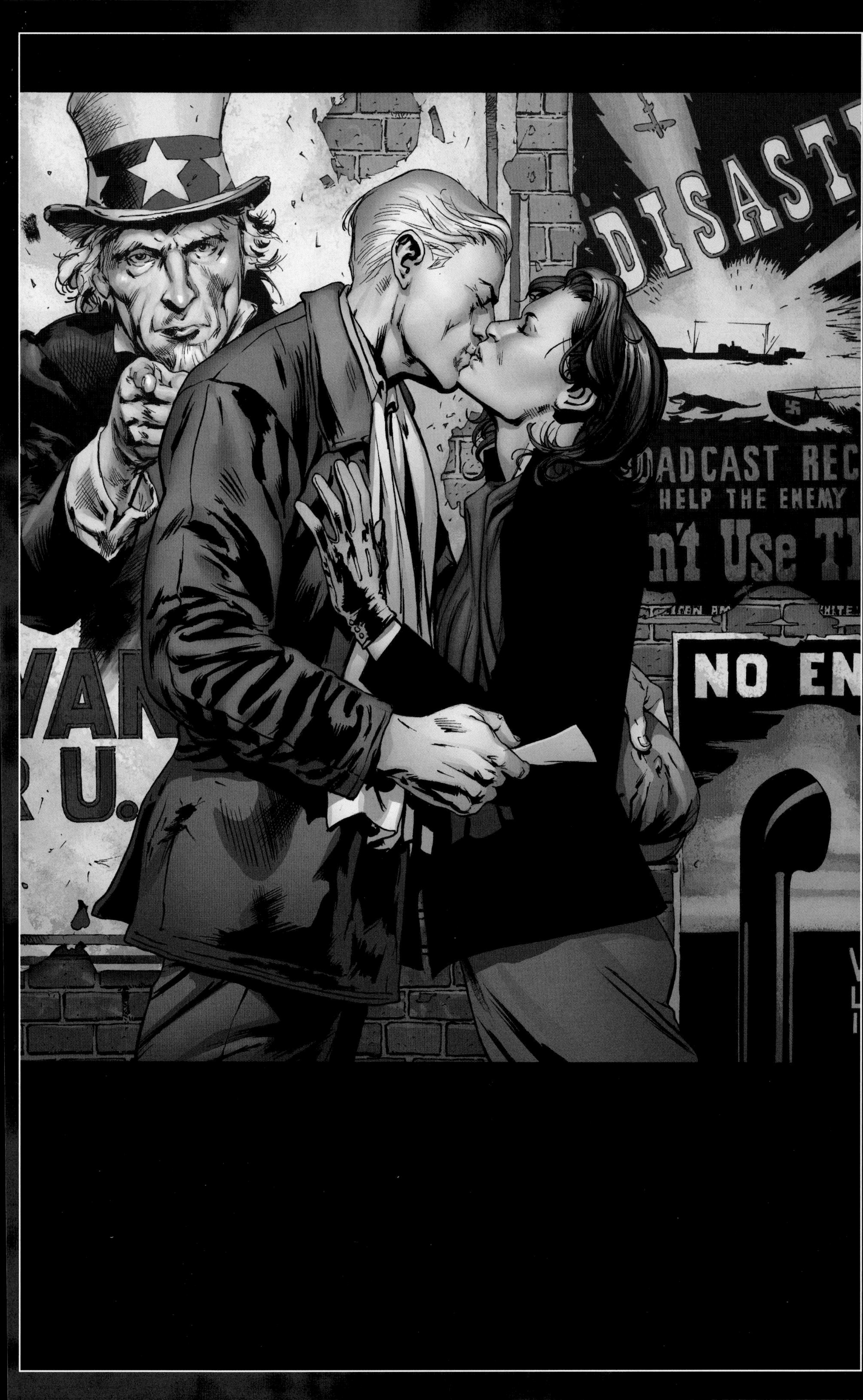
DISAST
ADCAST REC
HELP THE ENEMY
n't Use TH
NO EN
WAN
R U.

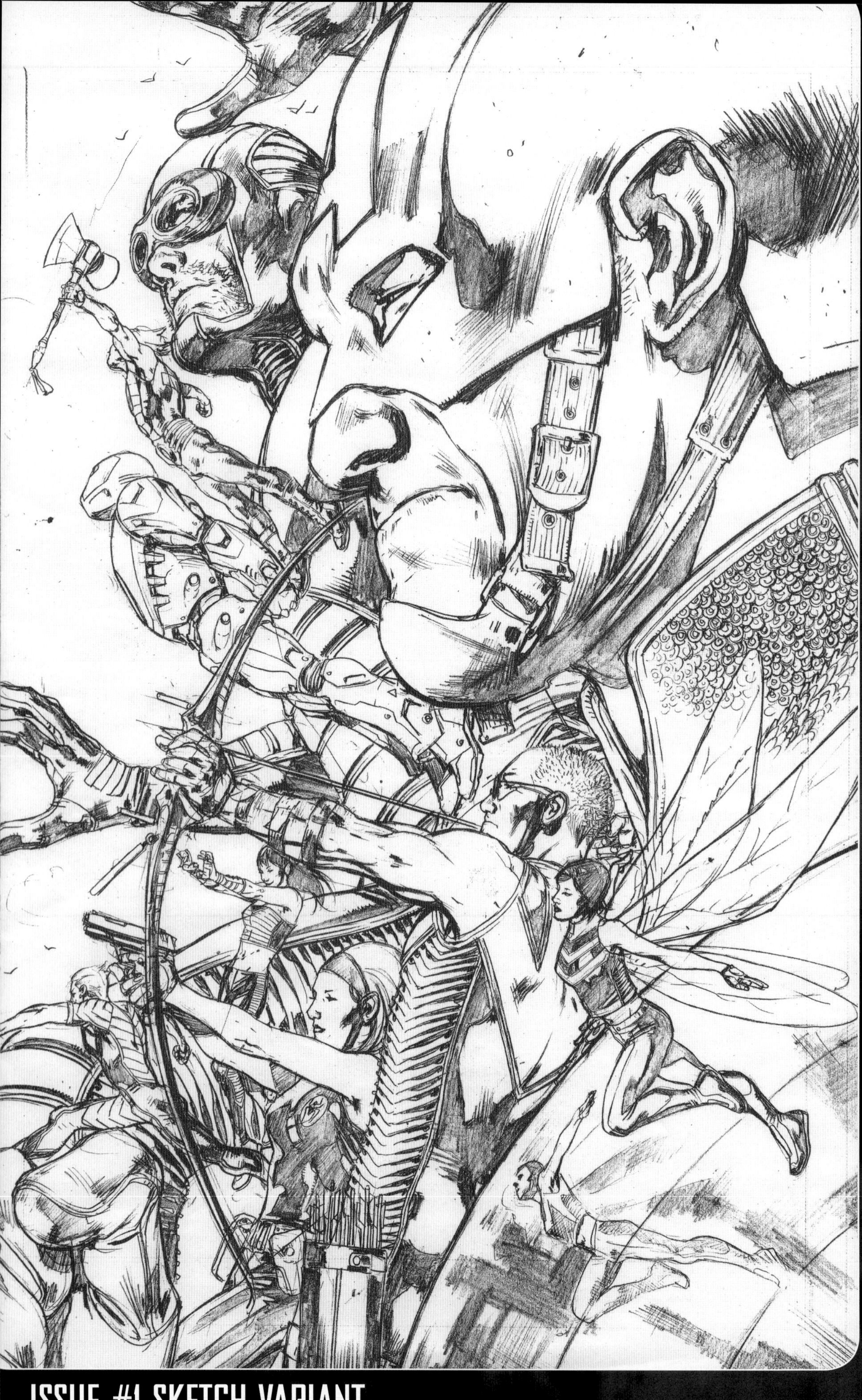

ISSUE #1 SKETCH VARIANT

RECAP —

X

X X Y

RED UGHILG / MOONLIGHT EXTERIOR

X

X

x2 458207

TITLE, CREDITS & INDICIA —

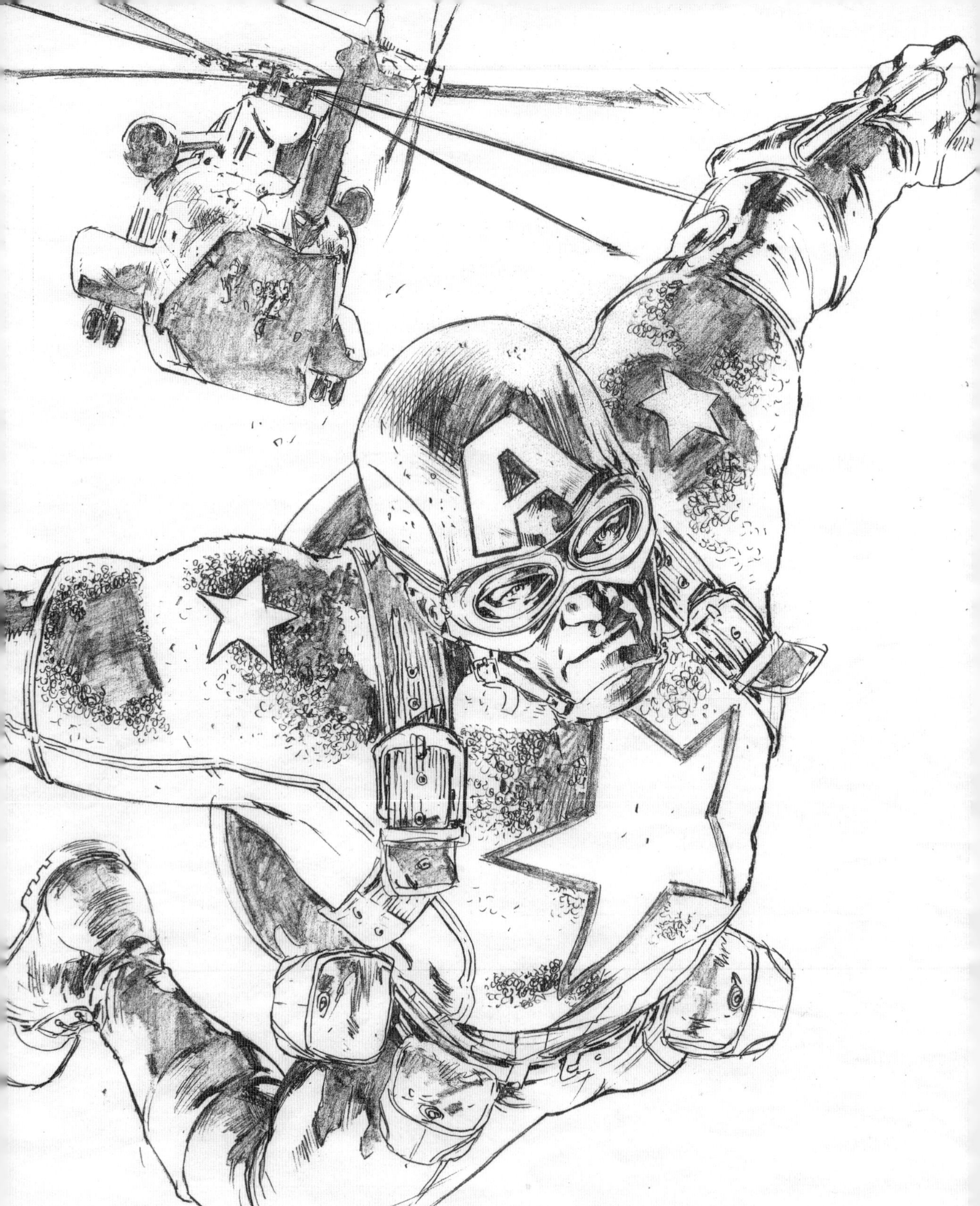

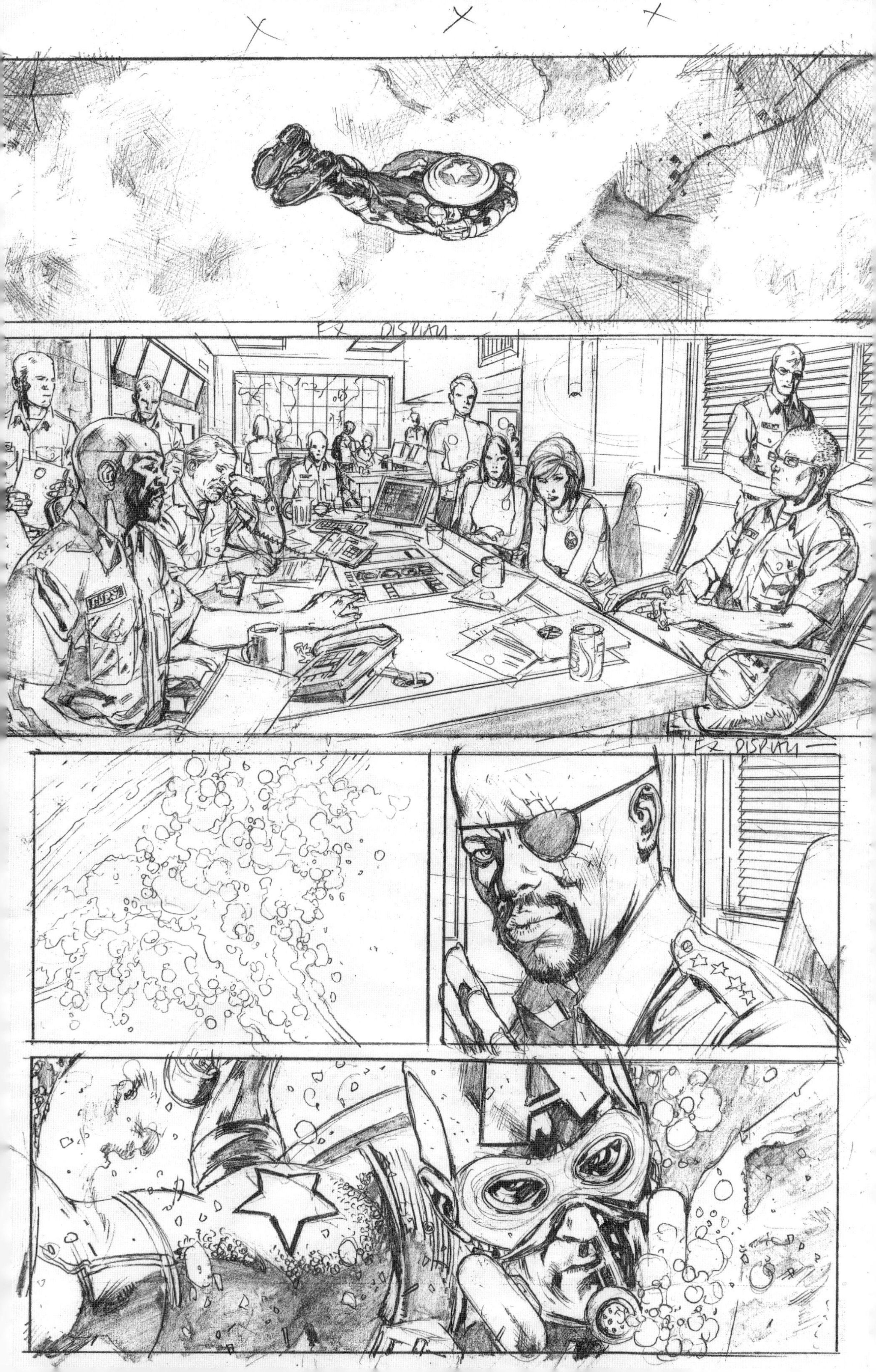
FX DISPLAY
FX DISPLAY

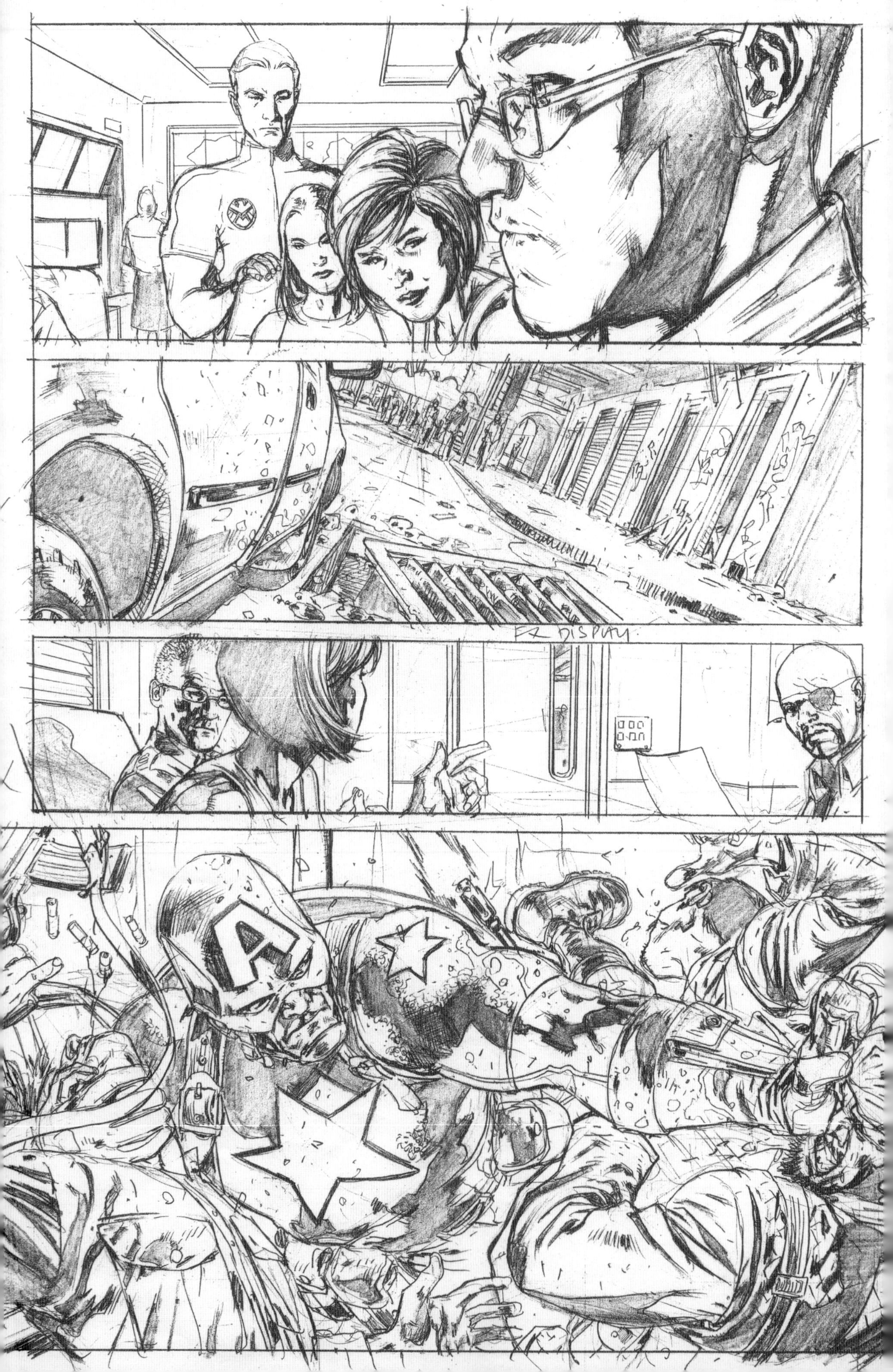
FX DISPLAY

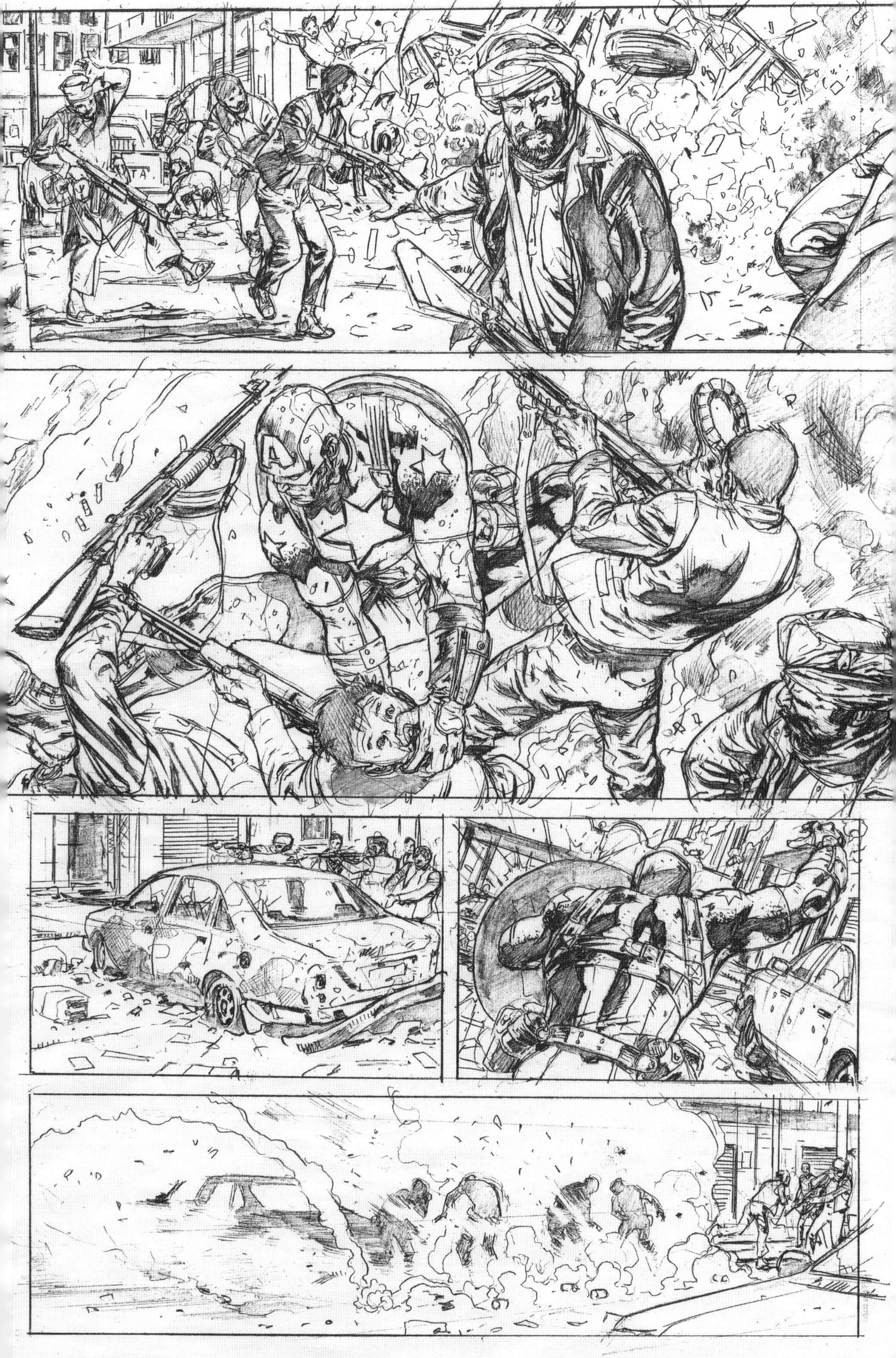

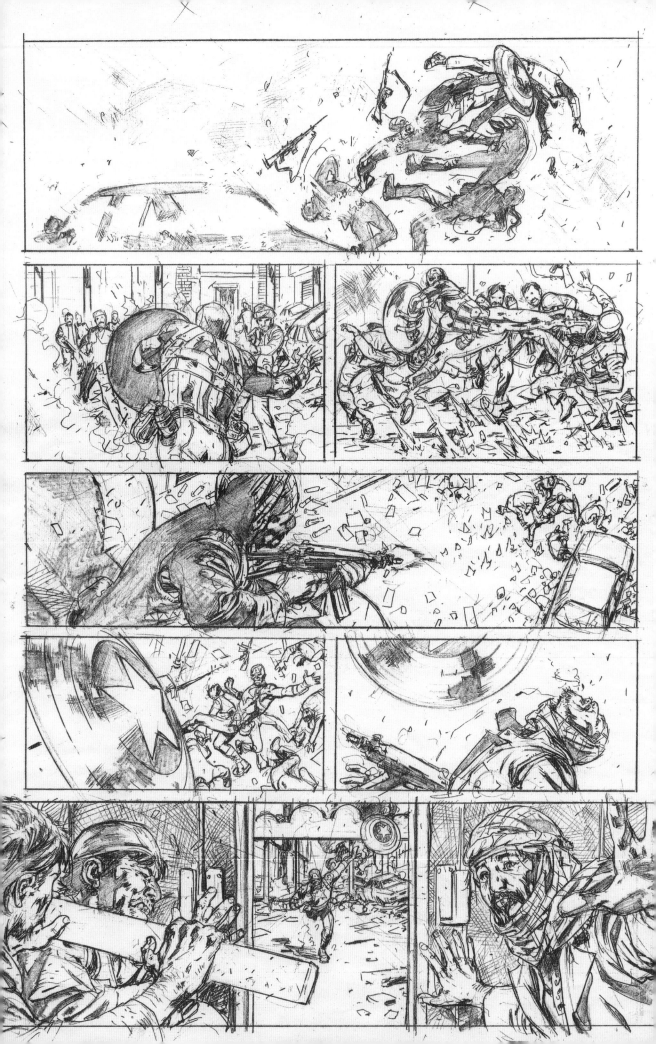

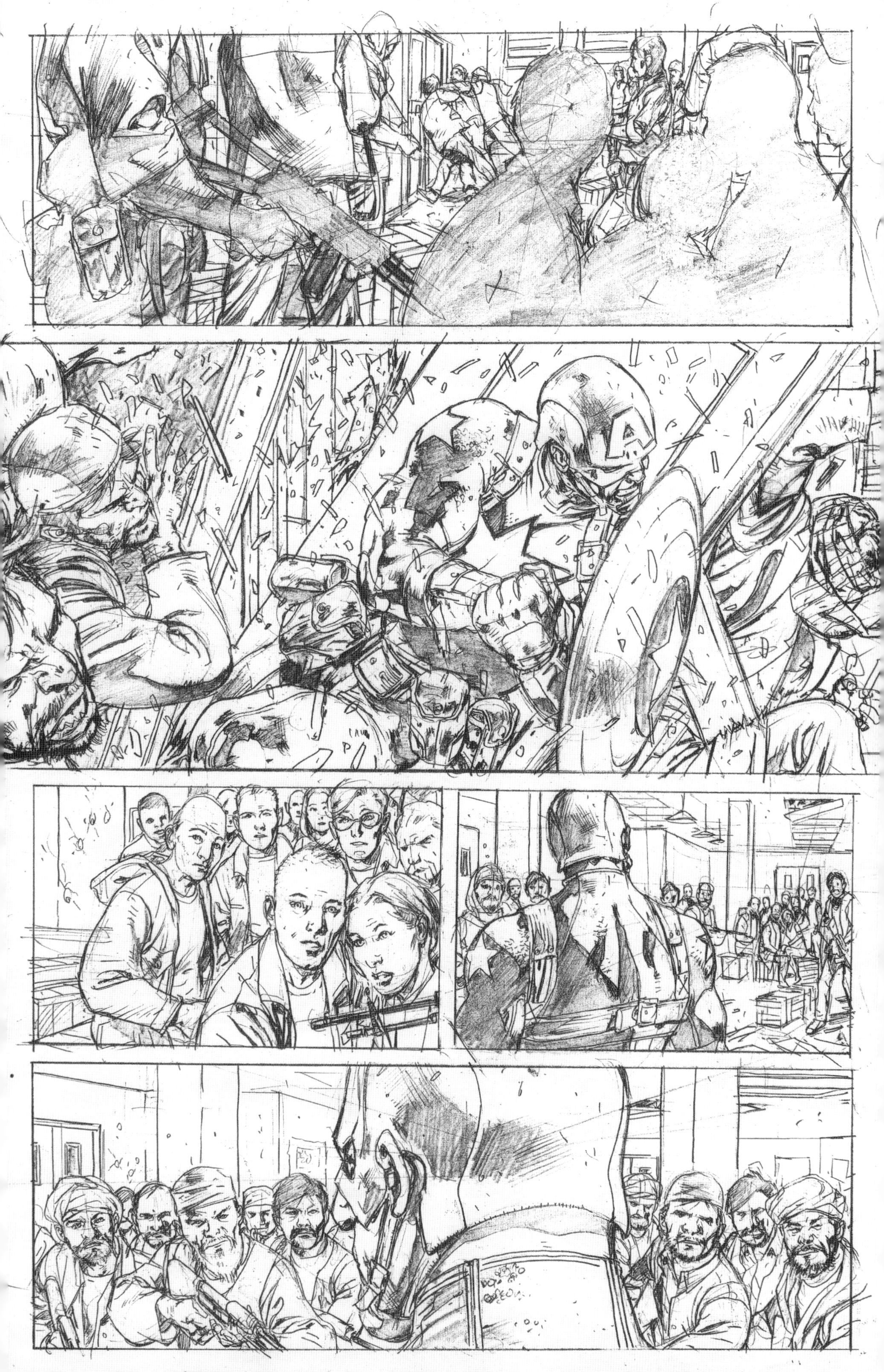

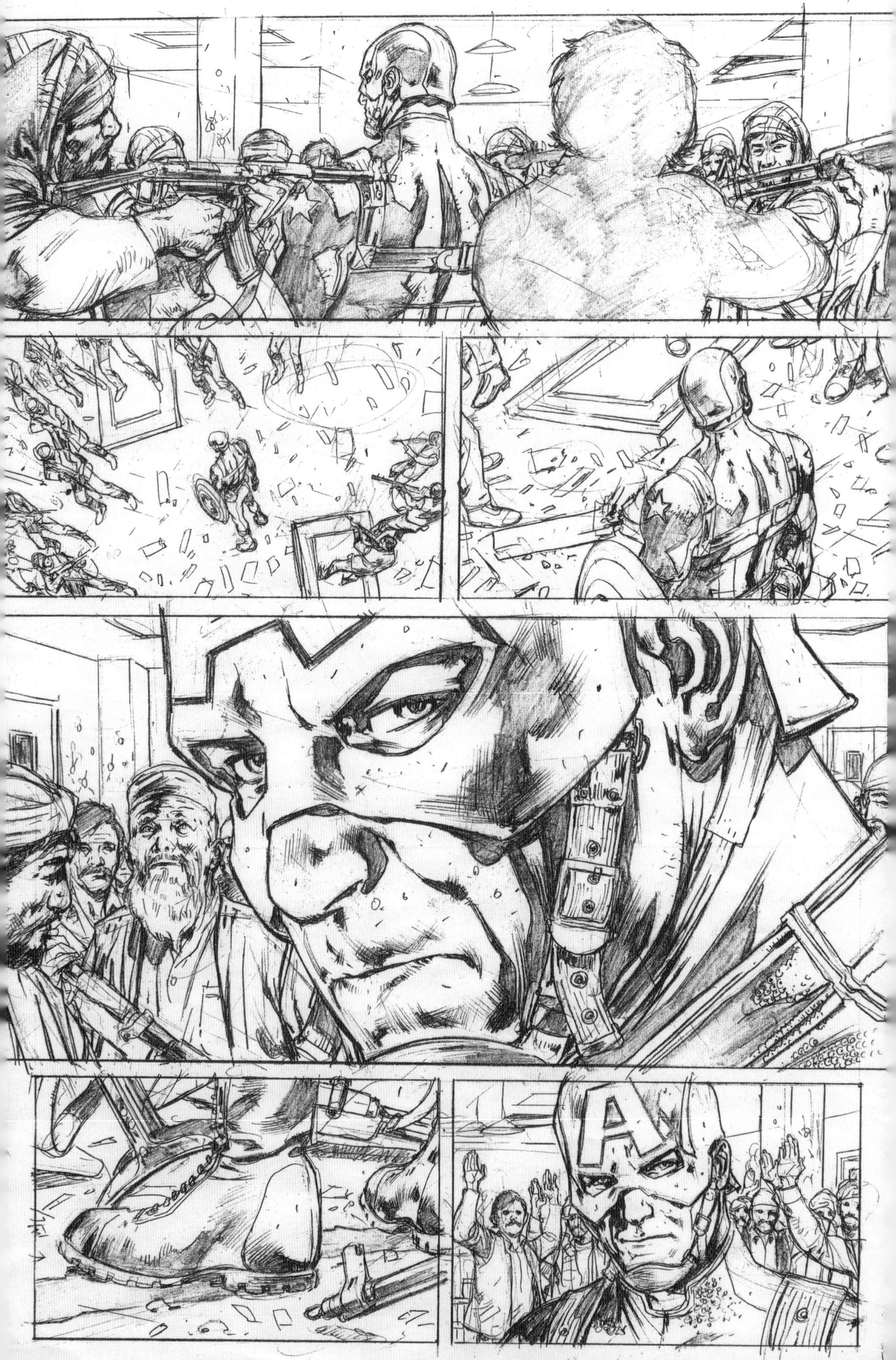

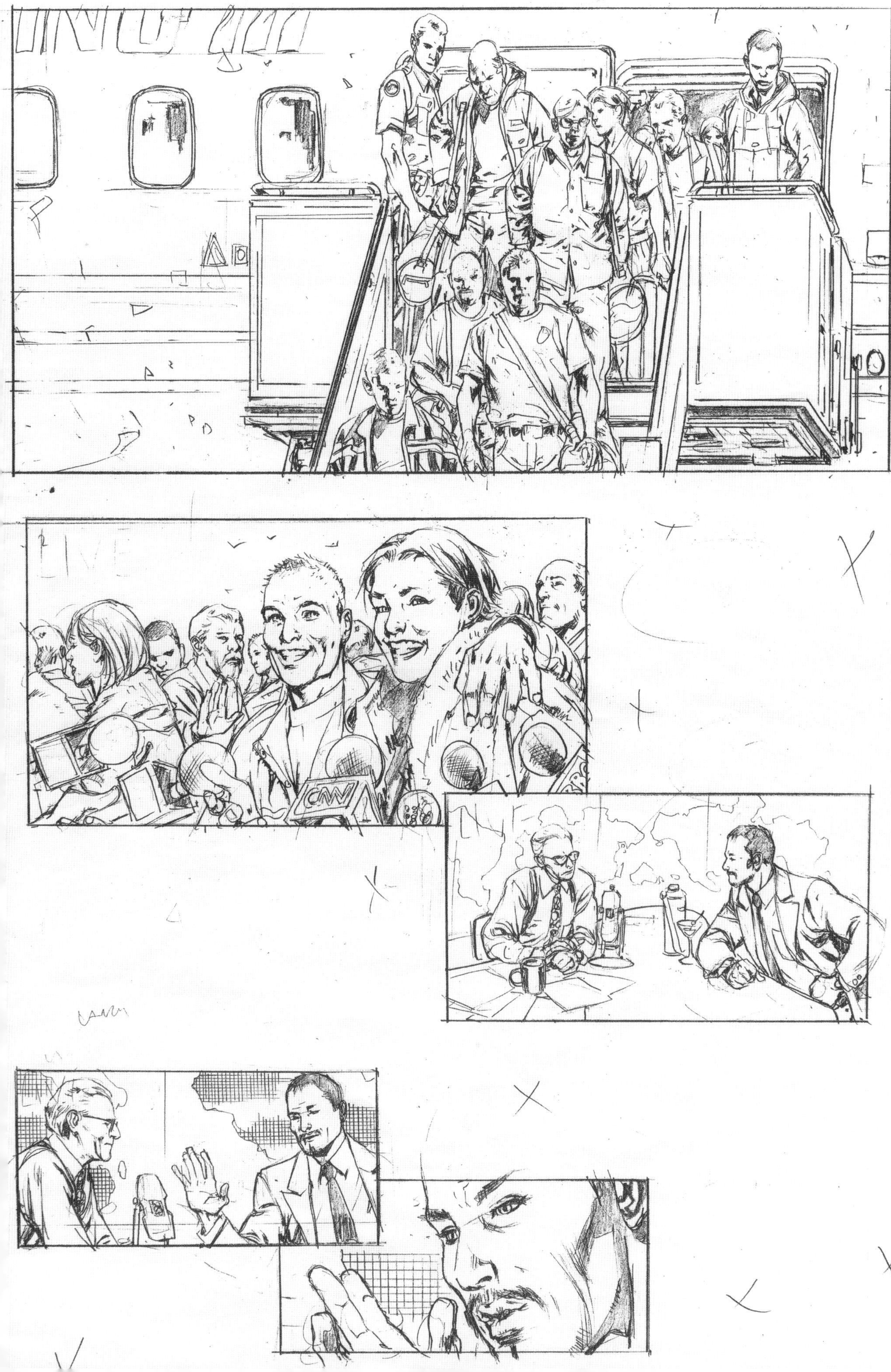
CNN

ISSUE 5 HULK ATTACK GROUND ZER

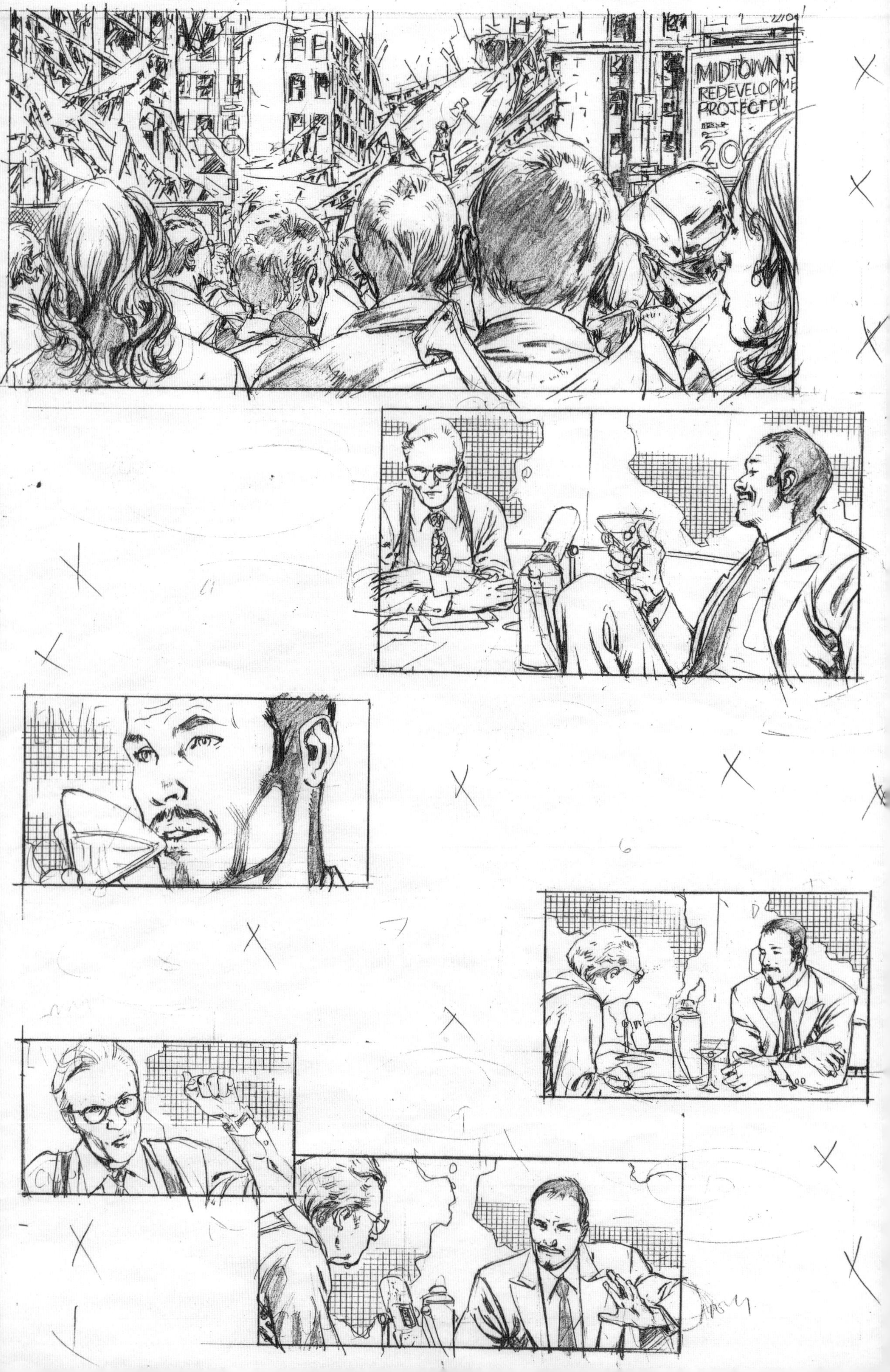
MIDTOWN
REDEVELOPME
PROJECT

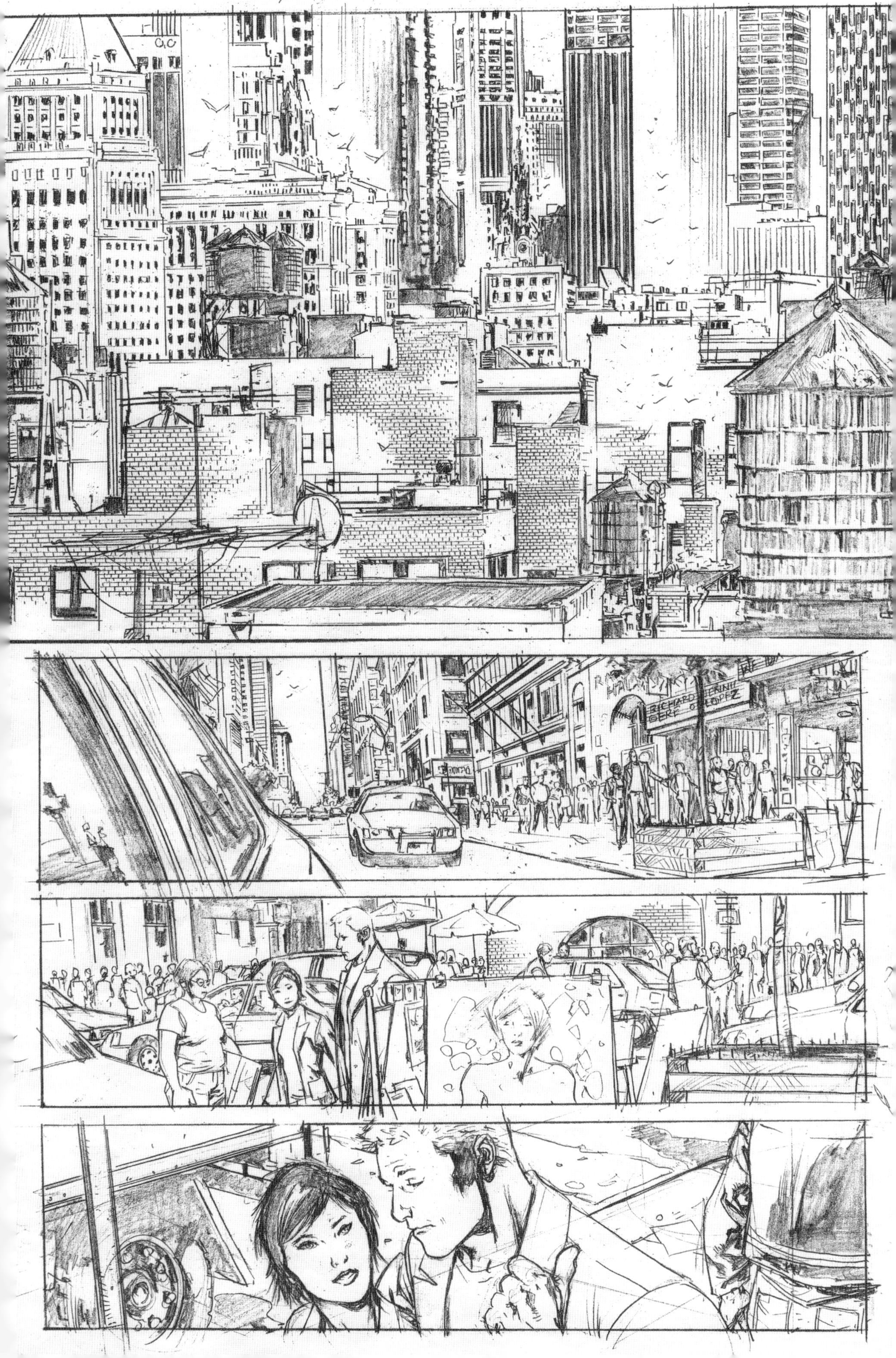
RICHARD
GERE
LOPEZ

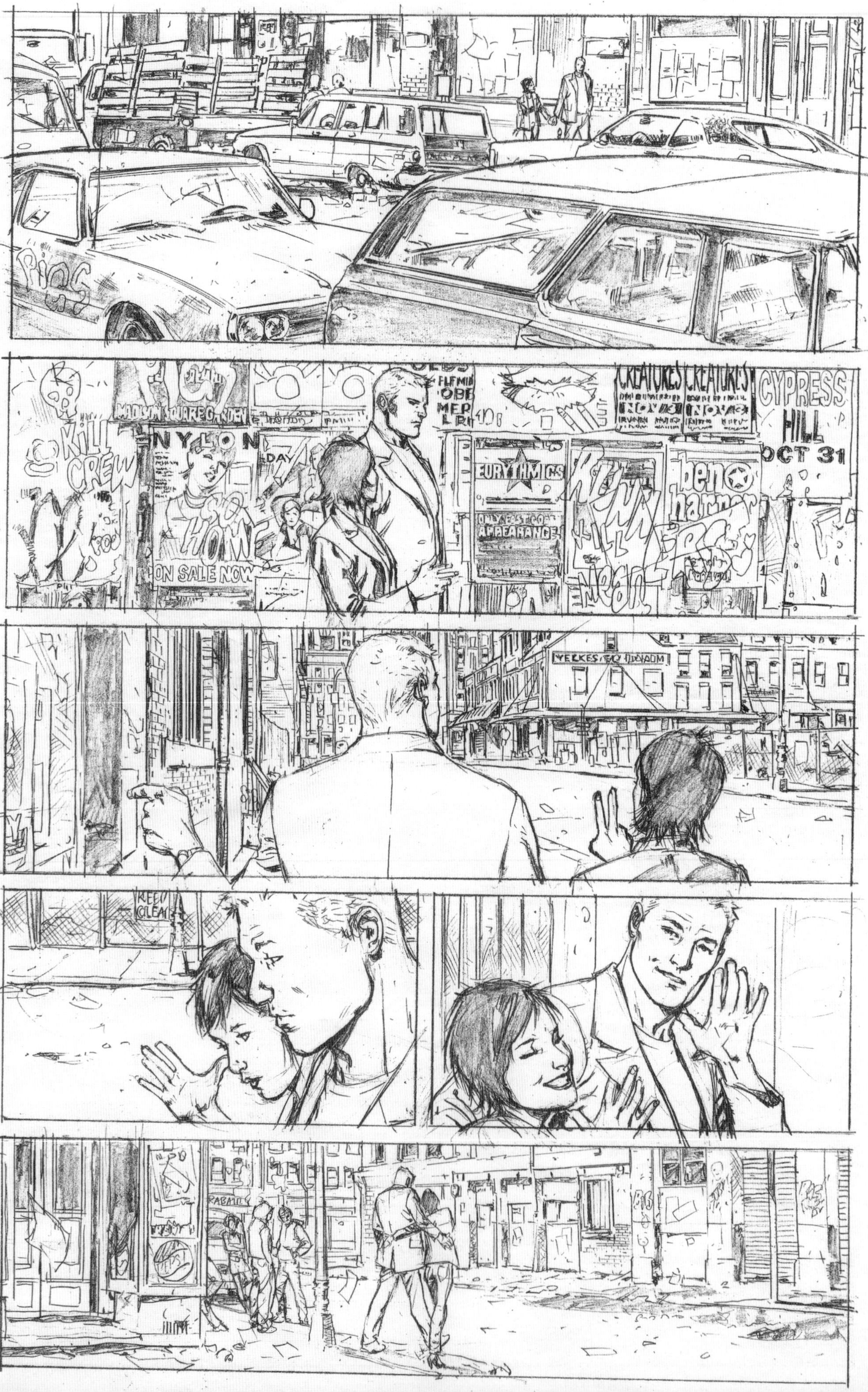

PIGS
MADISON SQUARE GARDEN
NYLON
KILL CREW
ON SALE NOW
EURYTHMICS
CREATURES
CREATURES
CYPRESS HILL
OCT 31
ben harper

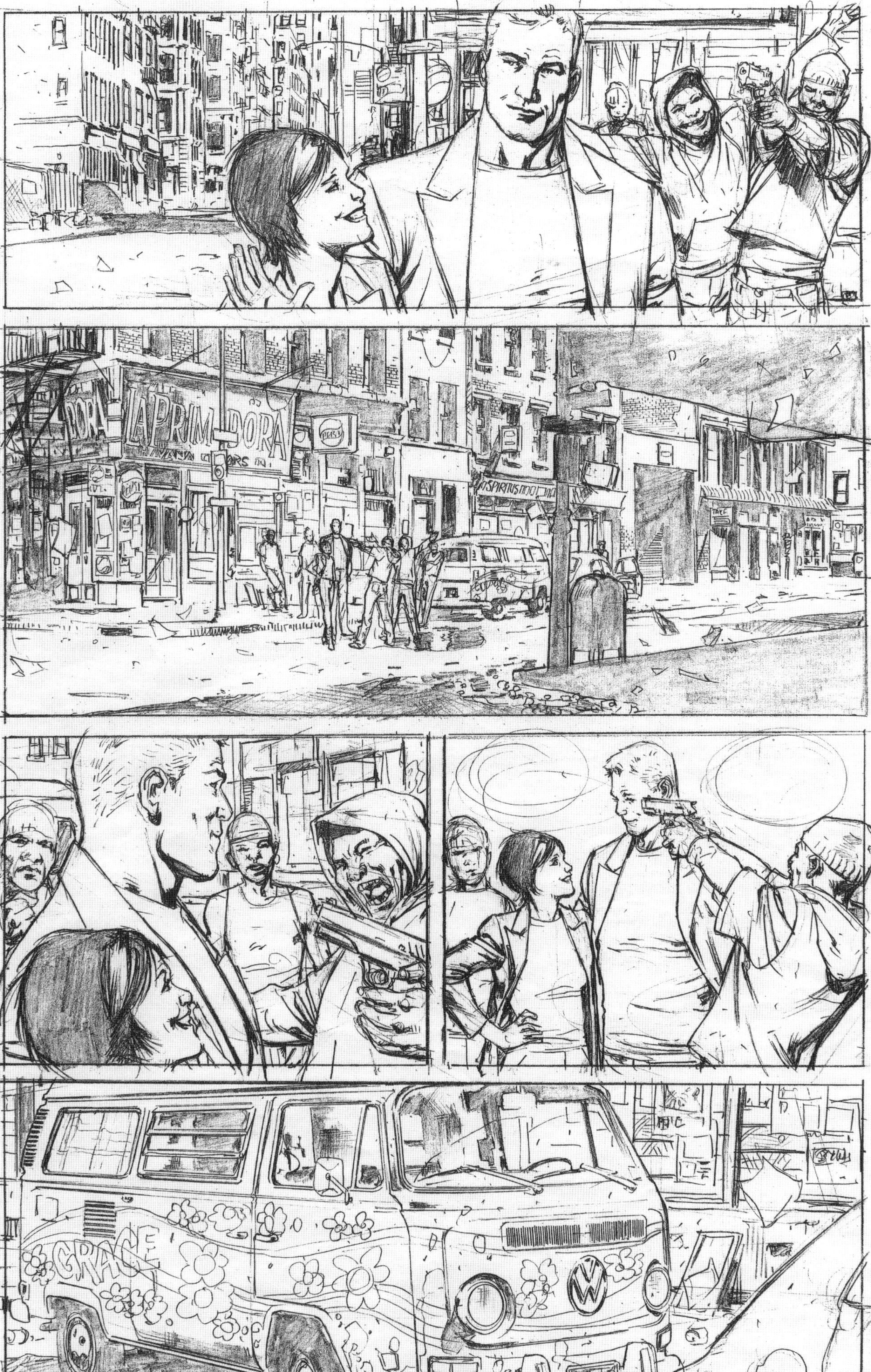
DORA
LAPRIM DORA
GRACE

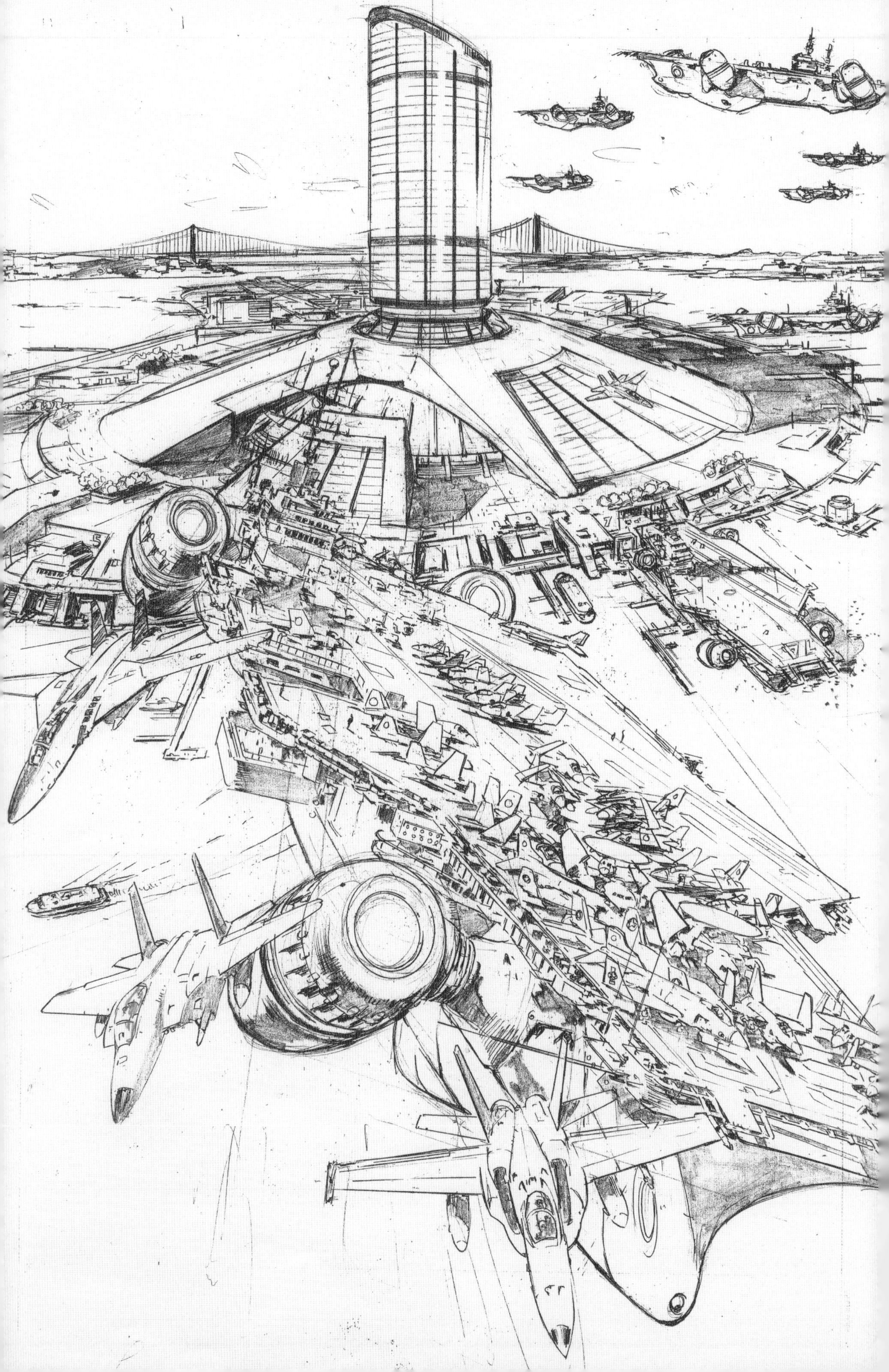

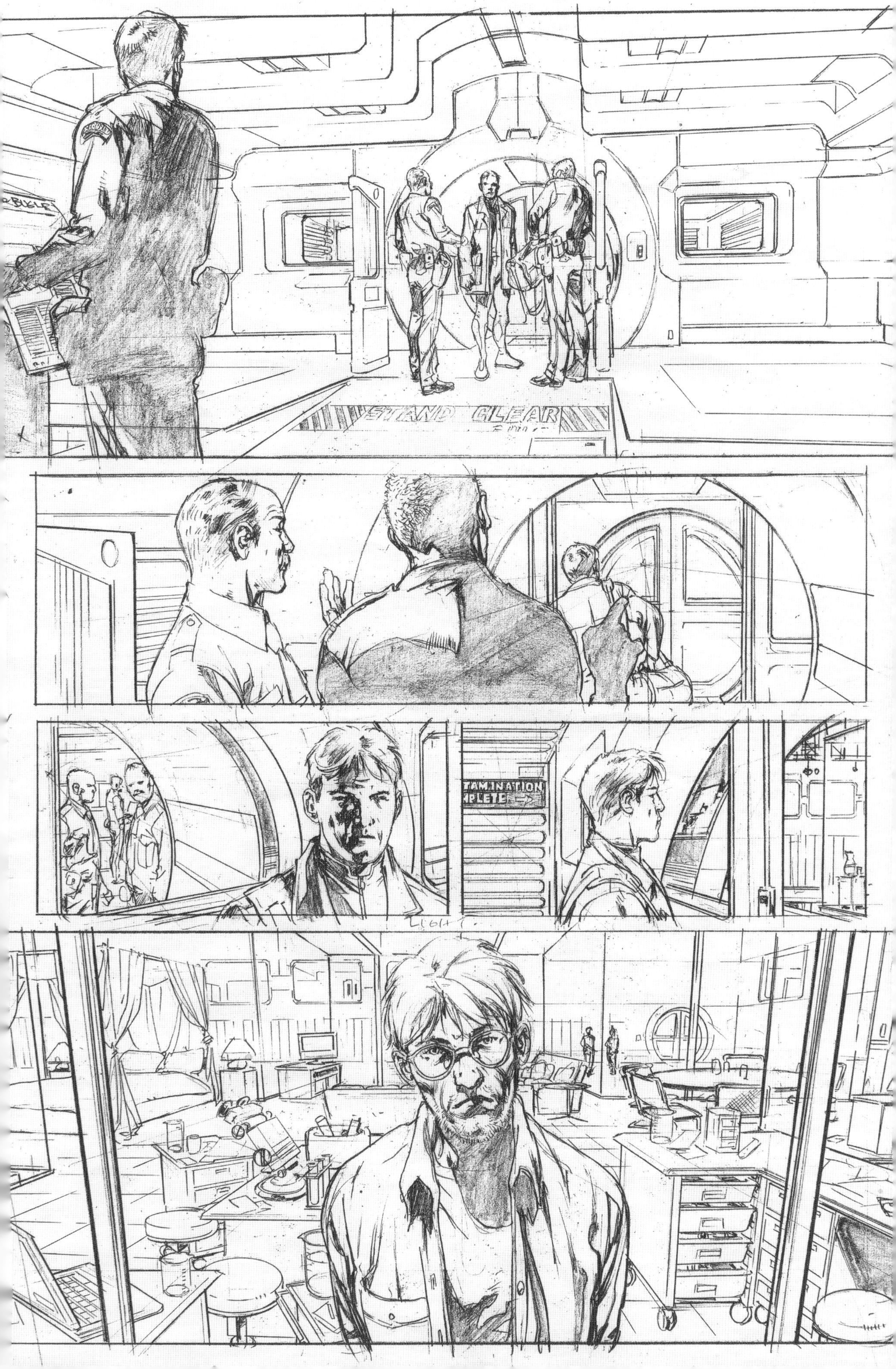
STAND CLEAR
TAMINATION
MPLETE

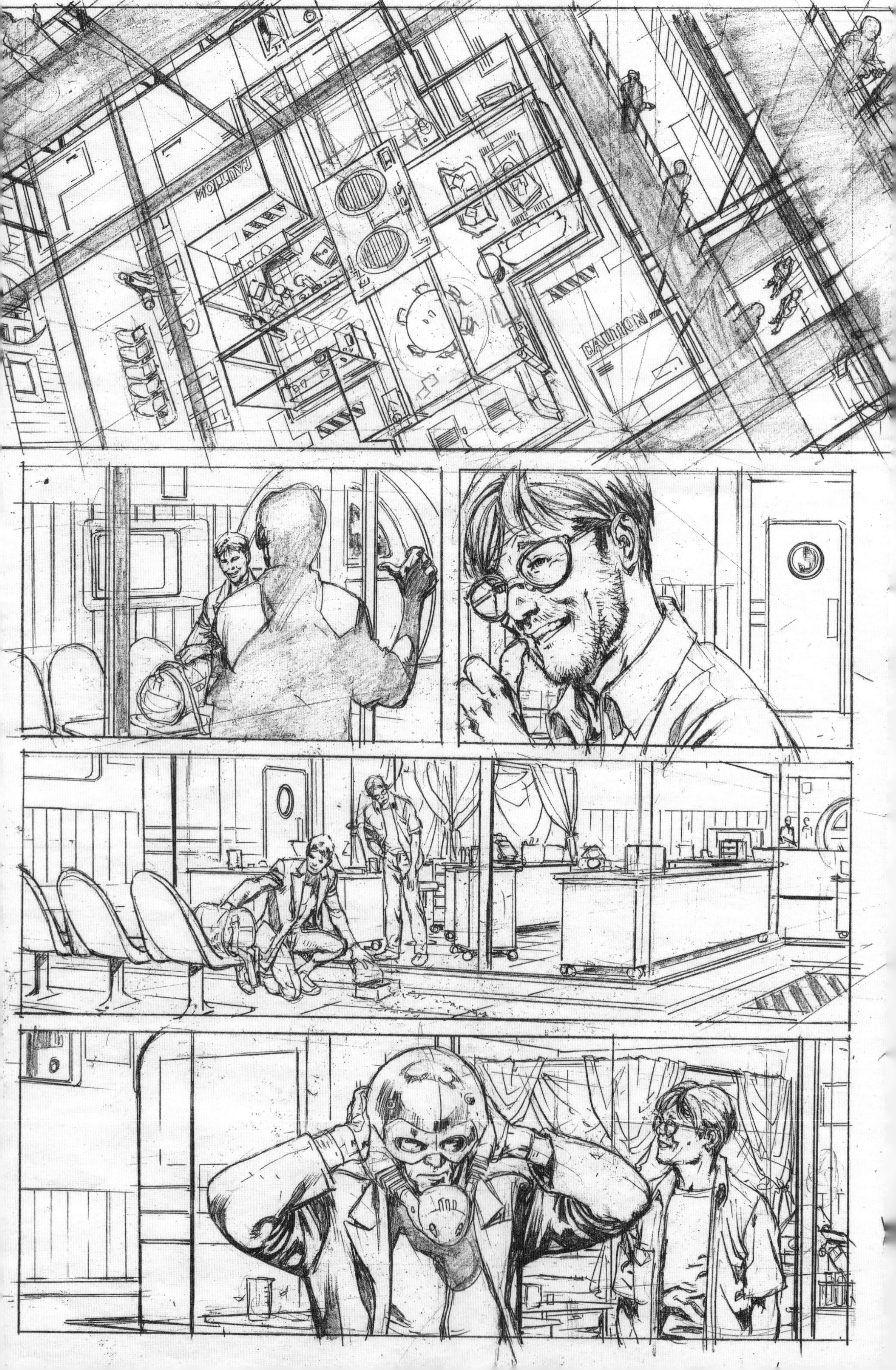
CAUTION
CAUTION

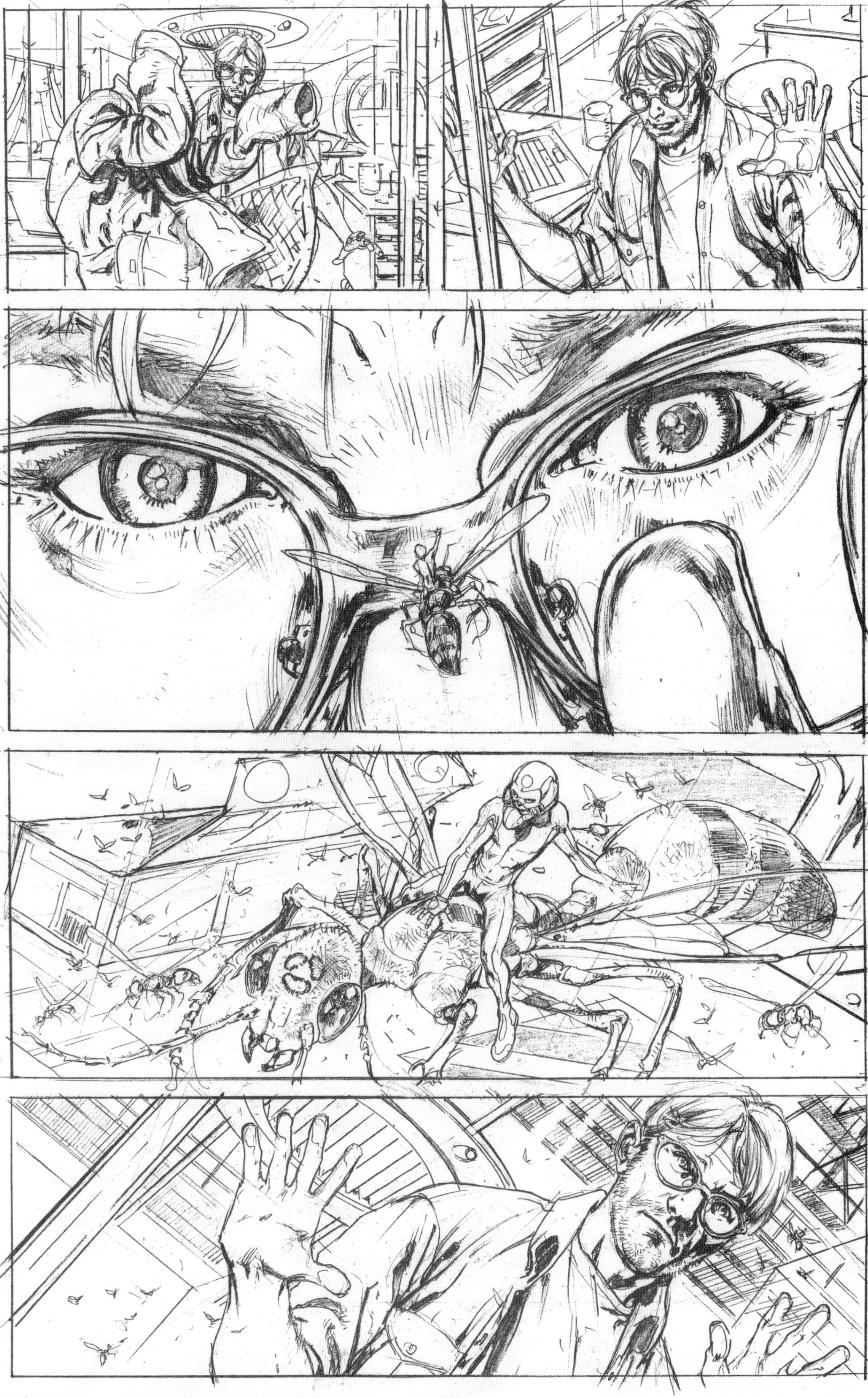

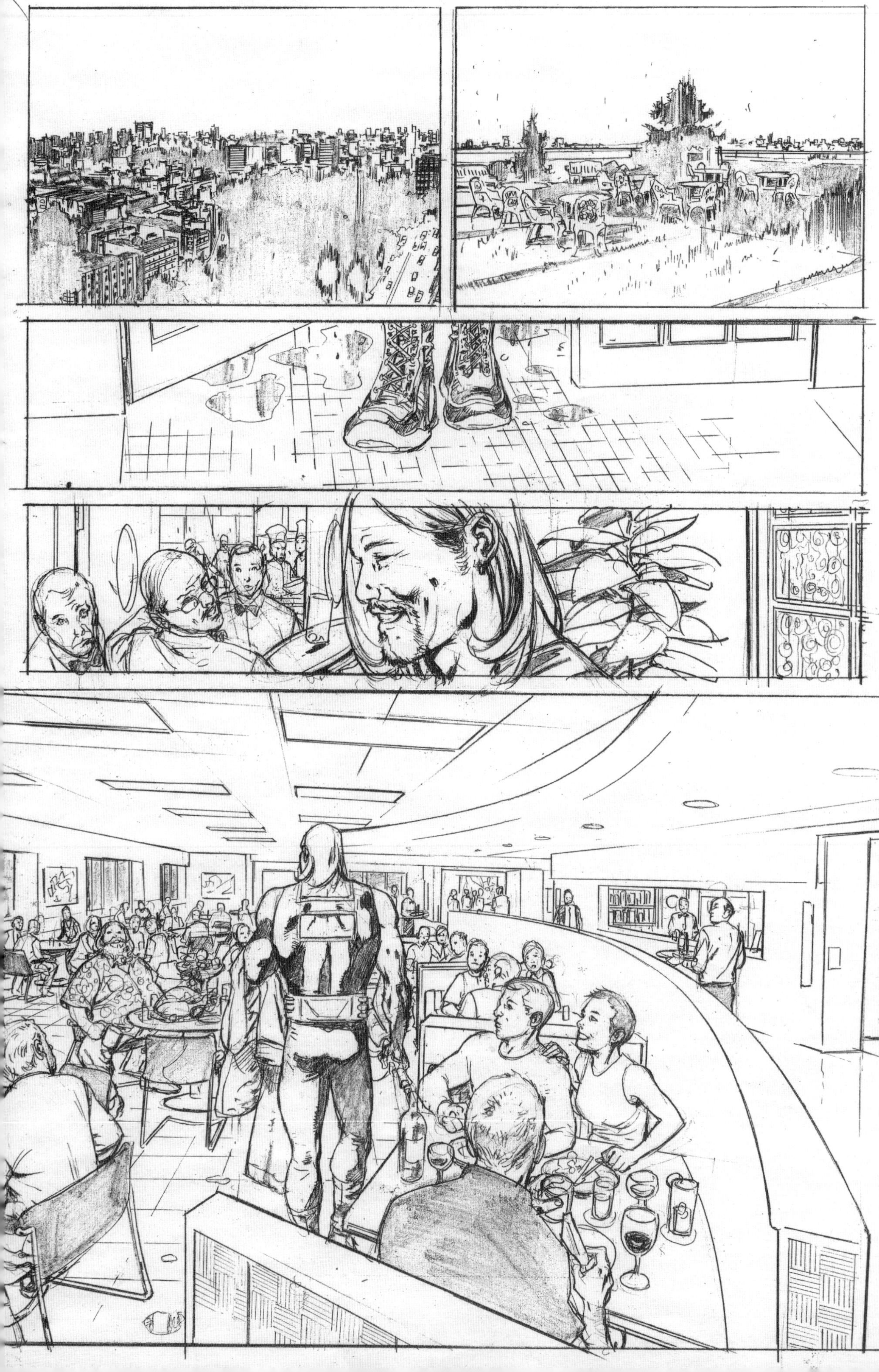

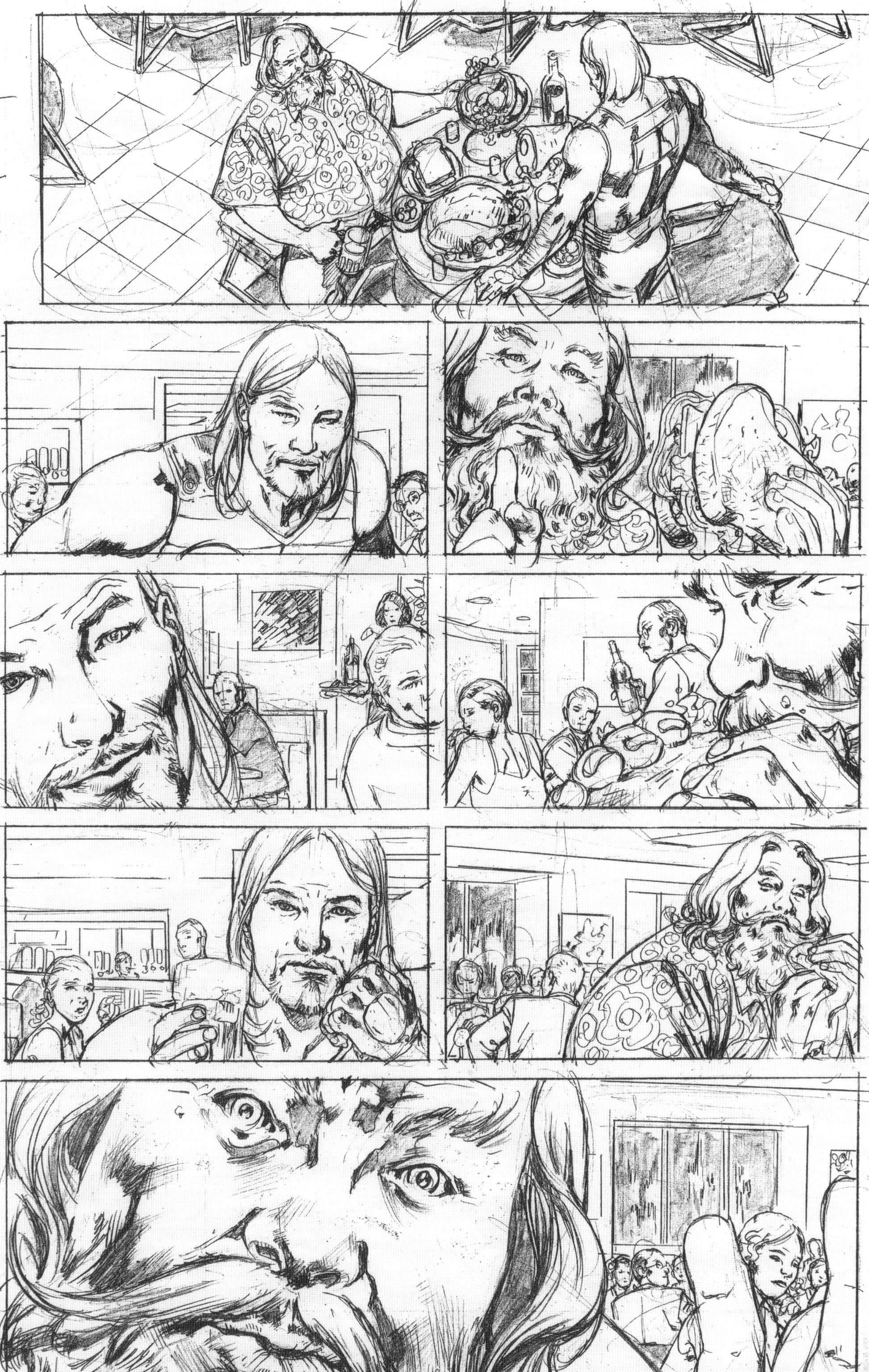

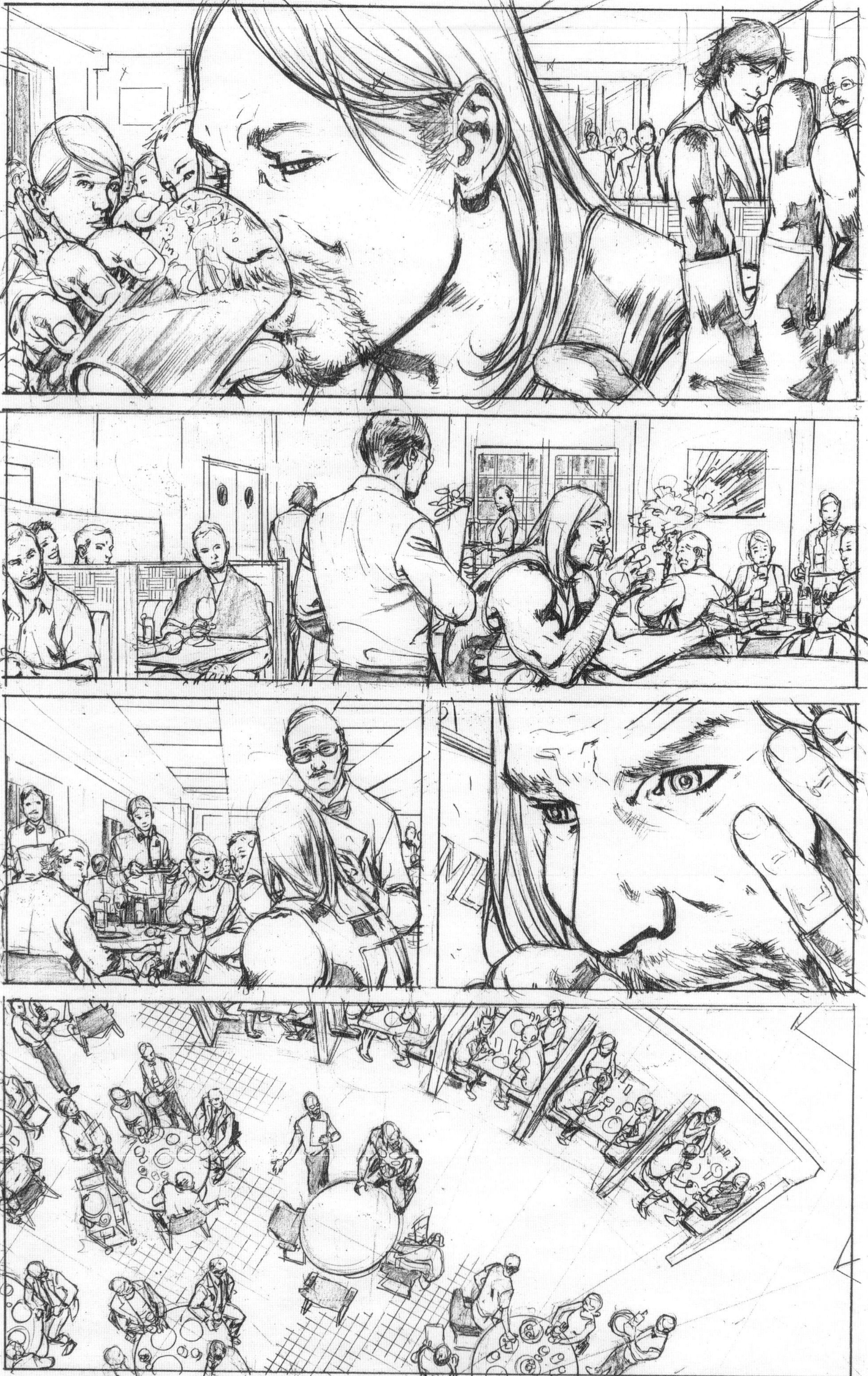

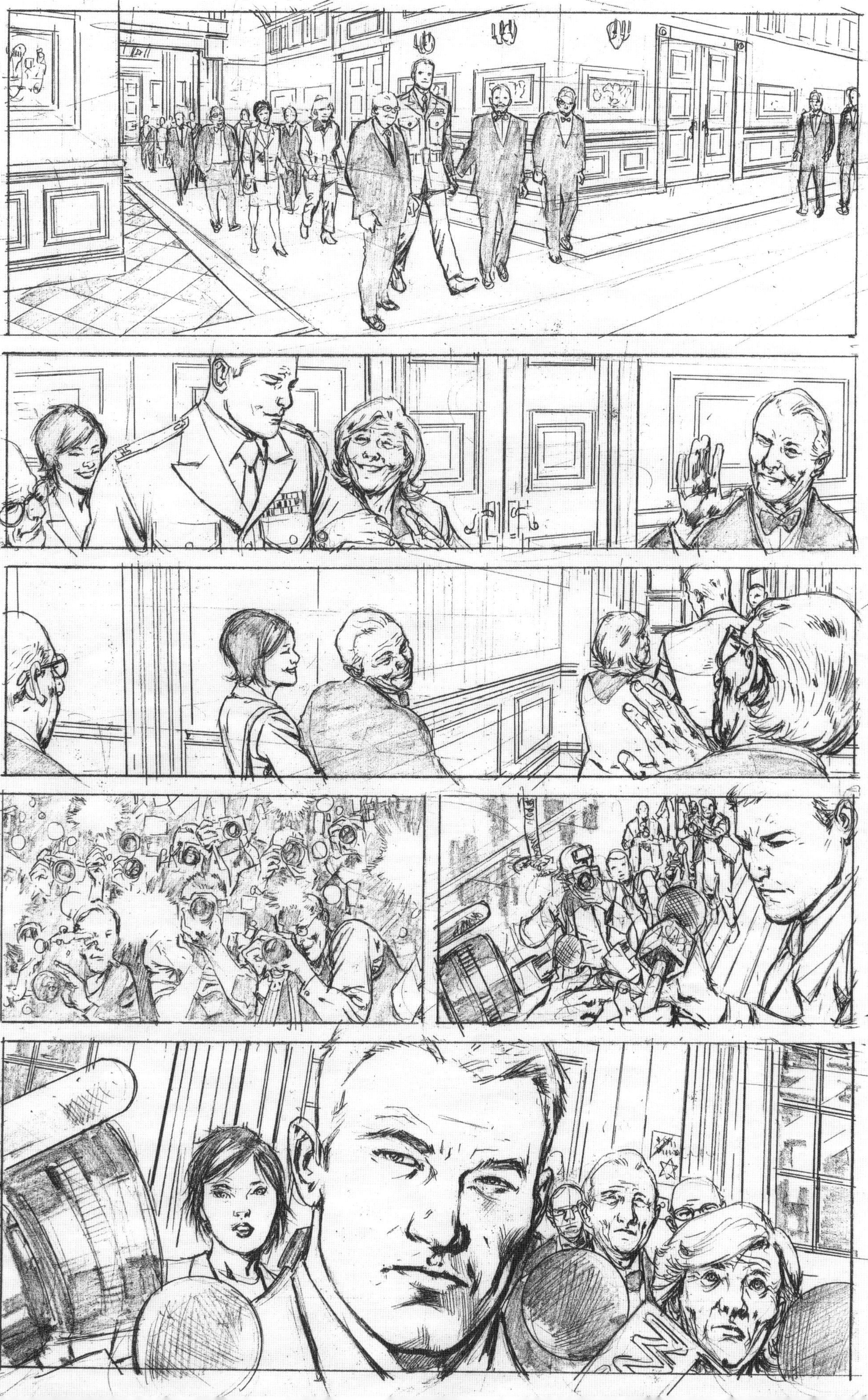

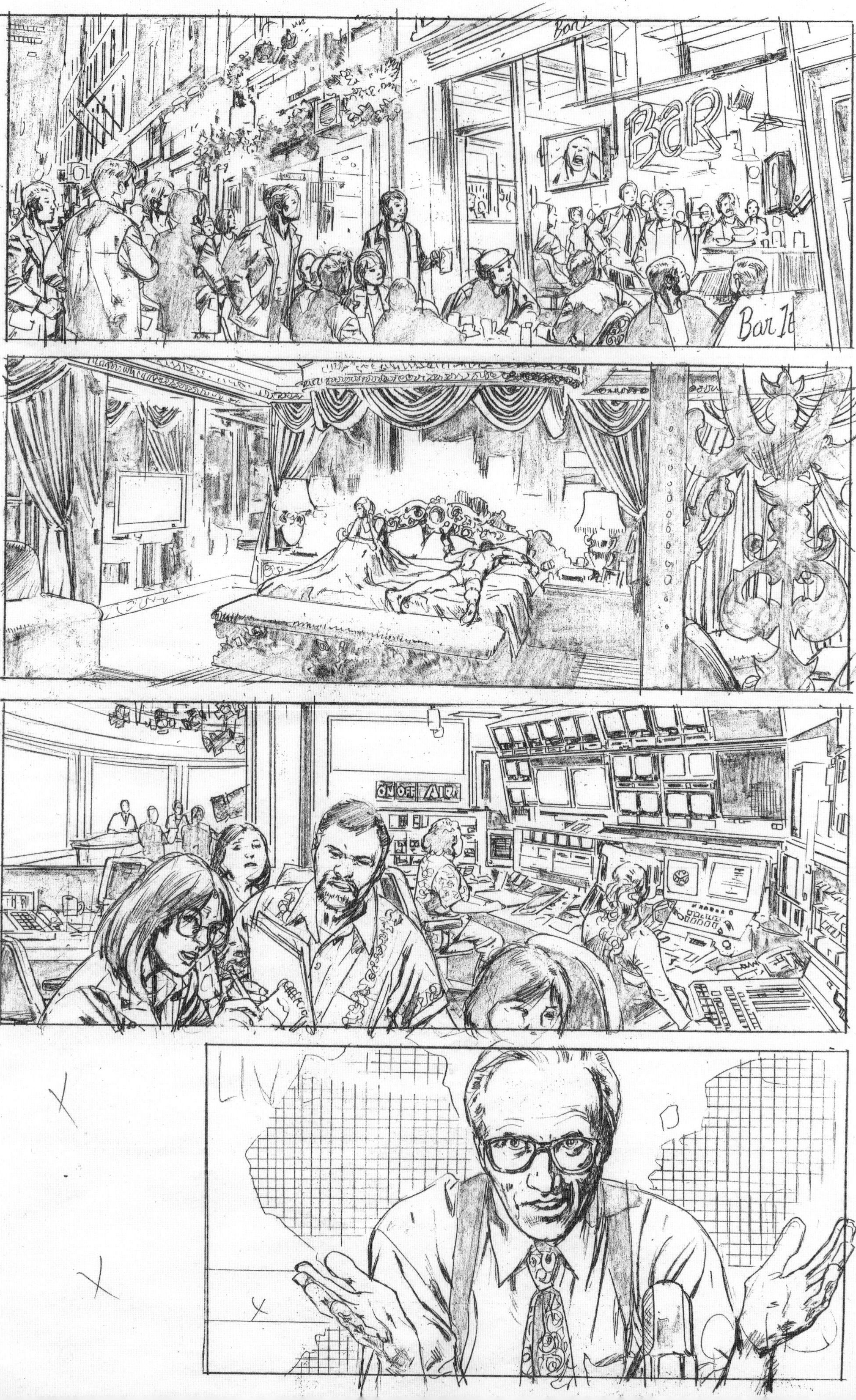
BAR
ON OFF AIR

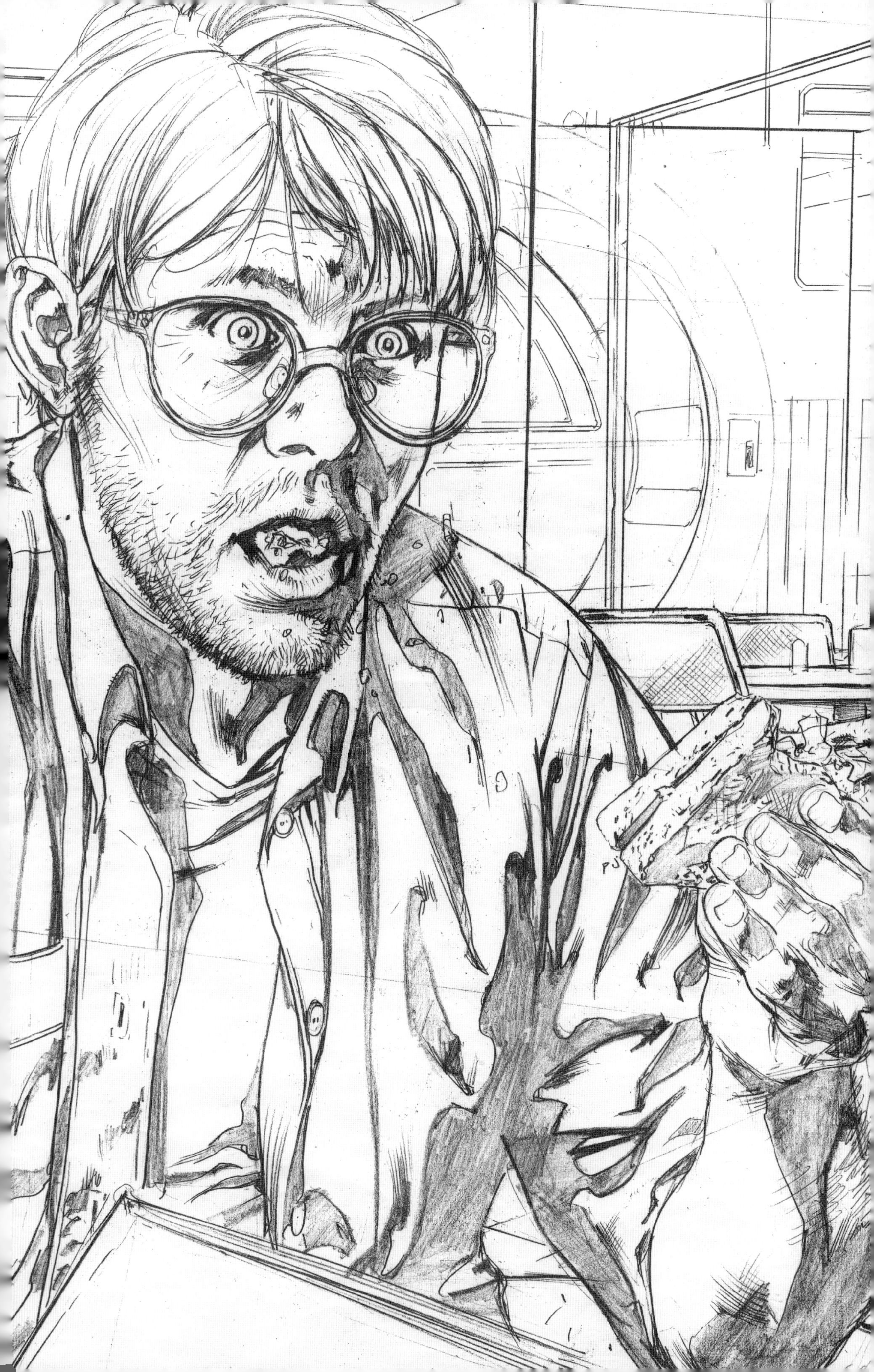

THE ULTIMATES #1
GODS AND MONSTERS

Script By Mark Millar
Pencils by Bryan Hitch

22 Script Pages
FINAL DRAFT: 11th February 2004

Page One

1/ Opening image of Hitchy's choosing with the recap and titles for anyone crazy enough to miss volume one and the greatest comics they've ever shelled out $2.25 on. Bryan will handle the recap here so don't pay me for this page, Ralph and Smitty.

NO DIALOGUE

Page Two

1/ Turn over for a full-page, Superman-style image of a soldier dropping down from the sky towards the Euphrates. He's got no parachute, but is wearing desert combat-gear, big boots, a helmet and is suitably tooled-up. This is Captain America and he's just been dropped at night by plane and he tumbles towards us in all his glory, heading for the off-camera river and neighboring Iraqi town (see Royd's map, Bryan). This is the last time we see Cap's face clearly until a few pages down the line so place this for mystery with lots of unusual angles and tight close-ups in this sequence.

3/ Cut back to this meeting around the map-table as they plan what's coming next and we see Nick Fury a little more clearly.

NICK FURY: We need a six-hundred-foot drop for maximum invisibility and at least five miles distance between landing point and Al Hadithah itself.

4/ Cut back to the Gulf and an underwater shot of the semi-shadowed Captain America swimming inside a big, open sewage pipe. He's on a covert mission here and everything about his movements just scream deadly to us.

CAPTION: "We're told there's a pretty decent sewage system on the outskirts of town so that's two miles of swimming and three miles of wading before our boy even reaches Point Zero."

Page Four

1/ Cut back to the meeting room and we rotate the camera a little to see what's going on here. Hawkeye's standing with his arms folded and we see Widow, Quicksilver and Scarlet Witch a little more clearly. Keep it shadowed and conspiratorial, though.

HAWKEYE: So where do WE fit into the picture?

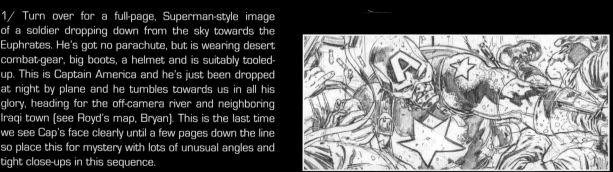

CAPTION: "Let's just say I don't like taking CHANCES, Natasha."

Page Five

1/ Cut to a small explosion in another part of the town where we see some guards and their vehicle all blasted into the air. Other guards react with surprise.

CAPTION: "You guys know the situation. You saw it on the news. These rebels got nine female aid workers up there and we all saw the mess they made two miles north of Basra."

2/ Cap steps out of the shadows and breaks someone's neck, James Bond-style. These guys are all bloodthirsty terrorists, but make it vague enough if this seems a little harsh.

CAPTION: "Last thing we need in an ELECTION YEAR is nine little body bags lined up at Dulles Airport, you know what I'm saying?"

3/ Cut to another part of the area as we see some smoke bombs going off among another gang of rebels guarding the first floor of a building.

CAPTION: "I just hope you're ready for the fall-out when this all hits the fan, Fury. They might not care about US, but you promised the public that the super heroes would only be used DOMESTICALLY."

4/ Switch angles and another extreme close-up shot as we see one of the guards getting a rifle-butt in the face, cracking his head back against a wall here as Cap continues his assault on the area.

CAPTION: "Yeah, well, that's the thing about being a GROWN-UP, Pietro; sometimes you gotta BREAK these little promises."

Page Six

1/ Cut to a quite spectacular shot of Cap maintaining this forward momentum, leaping into the air between two roofs and curling into a ball as further guards start to fire upon him. In the background, we can see the remains of the smoke bomb dispersing and all the other unconscious or dead Iraqi guards.

NO DIALOGUE

2/ Switch angles and close in on another brutal shot of his big boots crushing at least one of these Iraqi troops to the floor as he continues his forward momentum, swinging his shield back and preparing to take out several of the many troops guarding this area.

NO DIALOGUE

3/ Cut to a beautiful impact shot as the shield just takes out a whole bunch of these guys in a single swoop.

NO DIALOGUE

4/ Cut back to Cap as he continues this forward momentum and just charges towards the hospital where the hostages are holed up. Cap's grabbing the shield

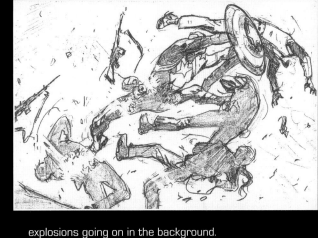

explosions going on in the background.

NO DIALOGUE

Page Seven

1/ Cut to inside the hospital itself and we see Captain America looking cool as Hell looking right at us as he pushes open the twin doors at the entrance, all the Iraqis sweating and trying their best to hold these doors closed. Think about Aragorn's big entrance in *Lord of the Rings*.

CAPT AMERICA: HNNnnnn—
IRAQI GUARD: [translation to come].

2/ Pull back and we see Cap just pushing these doors off their hinges and knocking all these Iraqis back like they're little cartoon characters. Other guards are staring straight ahead and looking shocked.

CAPT AMERICA (big): —NNAARGH!!

3/ Switch angles and the other guards all fall into line there, raising their rifles and aiming at Cap as he just stands there and ignores them, looking around at the badly-shaken Red Cross girls tied to the radiators as hostages always seem to be. Cap just raises a hand, as though he's telling these guys to shut up for a second.

CAPT AMERICA: You girls in decent shape?

RED CROSS CHICK: P-Pretty much.

4/ Switch angles again and we see a whole horde of these guys assembled here and Cap's still ignoring them. One of the Iraqi commanders is here and yelling at the others to take down Cap, but he isn't even looking around, preferring to reassure the girls.

CAPT AMERICA: Good. Because everything's gonna be fine now, ladies.Transport's gonna be here in less than forty-five minutes.

CAPT AMERICA: You're going home, understand?

IRAQI GUARD: [translation to come].

Page Eight

1/ Cap finally gives his attention to the aiming Iraqis.
CAPT AMERICA: [translation to come].

CAPTION: Listen up, scumbags: You know who I am and you know what I do.

2/ Switch angles and we see this collection of worried-looking Iraqi guards assembled here as they point their guns at Cap and he just faces them all down. Think Uma Thurman facing all those Green Hornet guys in *Kill Bill*. The odds just look preposterous here.

CAPT AMERICA: (translation to come).

CAPTION: Surrender those weapons and you might—just might—live to tell your grand-children about this little episode.

3/ Cut to a reaction shot of these terrified Iraqis sweating.

NO DIALOGUE

4/ Head-and-shoulders shot of Cap for the first time and we clearly see the blue of his mask as he looks out from under the shadow of his helmet. Think about the cover of the *Fight Club* DVD for the kind of moody perspective we want here, Cap looking up and catching the reader's eye for the first time this issue and a dangerous glint as he just cracks his knuckles. Really give him a snarl here.

CAPT AMERICA: (translation to come).

CAPTION: But touch those triggers and I swear your own MOTHERS won't even recognize you.

5/ Reaction shot as we see all the Iraqis just dropping their rifles. Reaction shot from Cap, quietly pleased as everyone surrenders.

CAPT AMERICA: (translation to come).

CAPTION: Clever boys.

Page Nine

1/ Cut to news footage of these hostages being brought home in a military plane and hundreds of friends and well-wishers meeting them at the airport. There's TV crews everywhere and a nice wide shot of the proceedings as the whole thing gets broadcast on *Larry King Live*.

TV BALLOON: —where both the President and all remaining Democratic contenders were waiting with friends and family to greet these nine brave women after their terrifying fourteen-day ordeal.

2/ Head-and-shoulders shot of one of the female hostages being interviewed, a microphone stuck in her face as she smiles and gushes about the rescue operation, how cool

Captain America is and so on. There's a real feel-good Homeland Security kind of thing going on here and we get the usual little CNN banner across the bottom of the panel explaining who this person is and what they do.

HOSTAGE: What do I wanna say to Captain America? Man, you're the best, that's what. You're the reason we're still breathing, man. You're the reason we're back on American soil.

3/ Cut back to the studio and a shot of Larry King sitting across his desk from a very dapper-looking Tony Stark.

LARRY KING: The reason they're still breathing? The reason they're back on American soil? That's not what SOME people are saying, Tony.

LARRY KING: Some people are saying The Ultimates just overstepped their mandate and used a Person of Mass Destruction in a very delicate foreign policy situation.

TONY STARK: Okay, first of all, I hardly think that Captain America qualifies as a Person of Mass Destruction, Larry.

4/ Closer on the super-smooth Stark as he sits here and we get a head-and-shoulders shot of him explaining the situation. Again, we should have a little CNN Banner explaining that this is Professor Tony Stark, that he's the CEO of Stark International and also just happens to be Iron Man.

TONY STARK: Secondly, these aid-workers he rescued were all American citizens and this rescue operation had the backing of both the Red Cross and the U.N. security council.

TONY STARK: This isn't some plan to sneak super-humans into The Gulf through the back door or whatever. This was a straightforward HUMANITARIAN MISSION.

Page Ten

1/ Cut to a nice, big image of Thor standing here and giving a speech to thousands of protestors. Thor's really got some authority here as he shouts about Cap's mission.

TV BALLOON: Not according to this guy, it wasn't. In fact, this morning Thor tendered his resignation from The Ultimates because he says that's EXACTLY what Cap was doing in Iraq.

TV BALLOON: According to Thor, this whole Homeland Security thing was just one big scam to get public opinion on your side before launching preemptive strikes against anyone who ticks you off.

2/ Cut back to the studio and we see a relaxed-looking Tony sitting here with a Martini as he rebuffs Larry King's questions, Thor's image on a big screen in the background. Don't do little TV panels here for every pic, it'll be more interesting to see the cameras and a little of the studio sometimes.

LARRY KING: What do you say to that, Tony? You worried the government might be squandering all that public trust you guys built up after all those BIG RESCUES last year?

TONY STARK: Listen, Thor's a good pal of mine. I was out for a drink with him just the other night, but we're talking about a former psychiatric patient who thinks he's a NORSE GOD, Larry.

3/ Closer on Stark as he scoffs.

TONY STARK: The guy's great company, but this conspiracy theory he's putting around that The Ultimates are going to end up as some kind of storm troopers for the oil industry...

TONY STARK: Well, that's as outrageous as these VISIONS he keeps having.

4/ Reaction from Larry as he raises his hands, trying to make him clarify a point.

LARRY KING: Wait a second, wait a second.

LARRY KING: Are you giving me a firm guarantee that you, Tony Stark, would never take part in a pre-emptive strike against any kind of rogue state acting contrary to American interests?

5/ Cut back to Tony here on TV as he takes another sip of his Martini and looks sufficiently cool as a cucumber.

TONY STARK: Larry, I built the IRON MAN suit so that I could give something back and, hopefully, meet some cheeky little honeys at the same time.

TONY STARK: I'm honestly not interested in becoming some kind of Martini-swilling SMART-BOMB.

Page Eleven

1/ Cut to an establishing shot of New York in daytime. After the initial draft, Bryan requested an extra page here to turn this panel into a full-page picture to get a little wide-screen scope into the first issue and that's fine with me.

CAPTION: New York City:

Page Twelve

1/ Cut to a cinema in Cap's neighborhood and an exterior shot of a crowd coming out of a performance of "SHALL WE DANCE?" and we see Steve Rogers and Janet Pym among them. This movie is an upcoming Jennifer Lopez/ Richard Gere picture that will be out by the time we launch in the autumn.

JANET PYM: Well, it wasn't as good as the JAPANESE version, but it was still pretty slick. You realize Gere's actually made two good movies in a row this year? Isn't that some kinda record?

STEVE ROGERS: I'll take your word for it, Jan, but what's the deal with all that POTTY-MOUTH stuff, huh? Why does every movie these days have to feel like a SAILOR wrote the script?

2/ Closer and we see them a little more clearly here. As they come back into the afternoon light, we can see them sticking on the kind of sunglasses and baseball caps Hollywood celebrities stick on to avoid being noticed.

JANET PYM: It's just REALISTIC, Steve. Even YOU curse sometimes.

STEVE ROGERS: Yeah, but I don't need to hear it every time I go to the flicks. Likewise, these dames don't need to show me everything they got just because I paid ten bucks for a ticket.

3/ Steve slings an arm around Jan and apologizes for moaning.

JANET PYM: Steve, c'mon. This was the safest movie doing the rounds right now. You've killed guys with your bare hands, for God's sake. Don't make us go and see the PIGLET movie.

STEVE ROGERS: Ah, I don't mean to be a grouch. It's just that stuff they were saying in the papers this morning. I couldn't stop THINKING about it the whole time I was SITTING in there.

4/ Pull back and see them taking off down the street. This isn't the best of areas.

JANET PYM: Listen, don't even get me started, honey. Just the idea of you out there risking your life for those people and then coming home to find all these idiots taking you apart...

STEVE ROGERS: Actually, that wasn't the stuff that annoyed me, Jan. I couldn't give a damn what they're saying about me. It's what they're saying about YOU that's driving me nuts.

Page Thirteen

1/ The talk continues as they walk down the street, snuggling into each other. It's actually pretty desolate as they head for Steve's apartment.

STEVE ROGERS: I mean, six months ago that crackerjack in the *New York Times* had me down as Man of the Year and now he's written this whole editorial about you being an ADULTRESS.

STEVE ROGERS: I swear to God, if this creep wasn't wearing glasses...

JANET PYM: We're public figures now, sweetheart. This is the flipside of all those TICKER-TAPE PARADES and BIG GALA DINNERS they invite us to.

2/ Closer on them.

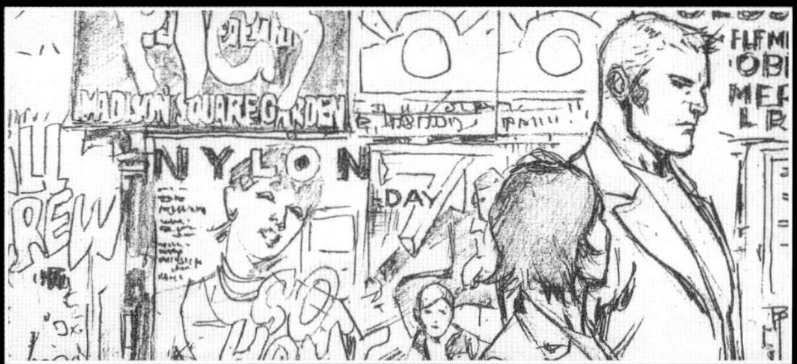
MADISON SQUARE GARDEN
NYLON
DAY

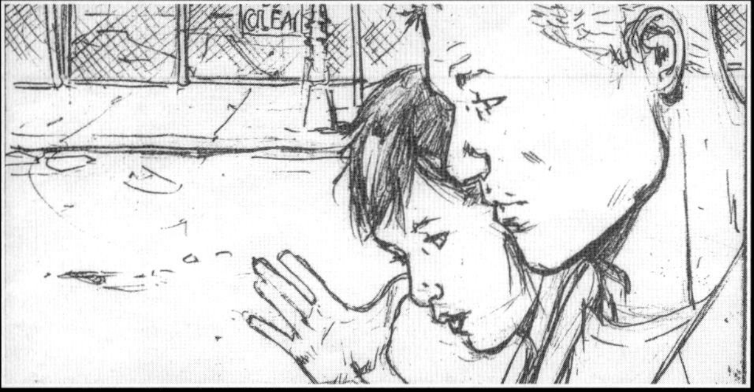
CLEAN

STEVE ROGERS: Yeah, I know, but snapping pictures of you coming out of my apartment, zoom-lens shots of us walking the dog...

JANET PYM: You're CAPTAIN AMERICA, Steve, and you're dating a married woman who also happens to be THE WASP. Did you really think people weren't going to be INTERESTED?

3/ Steve looks a little disappointed, but Jan was expecting exactly this kind of outcry. We should start to get the impression that a gang of kids have singled them out as they walk down the street here, so pepper this scene with nods in the background and a sense of fifteen, sixteen-year-olds tailing them.

STEVE ROGERS: I thought they'd maybe show a little more restraint.

JANET PYM: Welcome to the 21st Century, baby.

4/ Steve catches himself and Jan gives a little smile.

STEVE ROGERS: Sorry. Am I ranting again?

JANET PYM: Well, at least you stopped before you started moaning about body-piercings and women with tattoos.

5/ The sense that these kids have completely cut them off becomes a little more apparent as the figures behind and in front of them seem a little more predatory. Steve and Jan don't even seem to notice, Jan faking ignorance of what Steve's talking about.

STEVE ROGERS: Does this sixty-year age-gap thing ever get you down? I mean does it ever feel like you're dating BUCK ROGERS or something when we're having a conversation?

JANET PYM: Buck WHO?

Page Fourteen

1/ Steve groans and Jan cuddles him, laughing a little as she teases him. One of the kids points a gun at them from behind or the side or whatever looks best.

JANET PYM: I'm KIDDING, you big IDIOT.

JANET PYM: Just save all that griping for the LODGE tonight, honey. You and all the OTHER old-timers can complain about the modern world until your little heart's CONTENT.

MUGGER ONE: Hey, bay-bee.

2/ Steve and Jan, still keeping their arms around each other, look a little surprised as these kids move in, some looking threatening and the others watching out from the side of the truck they're using to shield what's happening here.

STEVE ROGERS: What?

MUGGER ONE: Whatchoo mean "what"? You STUPID or sumthin', bitch? You tryin' to PLAY with me or sumthin'?

MUGGER TWO: Gimme everythin' you got in yo' pockets, stupid. C'mon, hurry up before I lose my PATIENCE wit' you, man.

3/ Steve and Jan look a little amused by all this, but the kids are waving the gun in their faces.

STEVE ROGERS: Are we being "mugged" here?

MUGGER TWO: Damn right you bein' mugged. What's the matter wit' you, man? You HIGH or somethin'?

4/ Steve and Jan just aren't taking this seriously, smiling as they take off their sunglasses and baseball caps. The kids are becoming increasingly annoyed as we start to pull off-camera.

MUGGER ONE: What you SMILIN' about, bitch? You think this is FUNNY? What the hell's the MATTER with you people?

5/ The camera drifts off and we hear the voice from off from the scene, knowing full well what's coming next.

MUGGER (off): What the hell's so damn FUNNY?

Page Fifteen

1/ Cut to a full-page picture of The Triskelion. Remember, this is the sequel to The Ultimates and the first issue of the new trade and the new hardcover so we need to have a great establishing shot of the base here and a clear description of what it is and who it's for. This is as important as the other characters all being reintroduced this issue and next and the first time we saw the base in issue three.

CAPTION: THE TRISKELION:

SUB-CAPTION: The New York headquarters of The Ultimates, S.H.I.E.L.D.'s United States superhuman response unit.

Page Sixteen

1/ Cut to interior and we're in the security area near Banner's cell. We can see Hank Pym standing here getting checked over by the guards before he pays Banner a visit. They're trying to be friendly, but Pym's such an intellectual snob and his personality varies depending on what day of the week it is. He's got a bag here they're checking with a helmet (seen in issue two) and a box of ants.

GUARD #1: Hey, Doctor Pym. I see your wife's boyfriend hospitalized another couple of guys over in the Village this afternoon.

GUARD #1: You realize how much money you could make selling YOUR side of that story now?

HANK PYM: You really think I care? Newspapers are for idiots, boys. Anyone who pays MONEY to read that garbage needs to have their HEAD examined.

/ Pym takes his bag back and gives the guards a sarcastic reply. It might be kind of funny making this security bay look a little like the one in *X-Men 2*. We never saw the exterior and I like the idea of us making readers think The Ultimates might be upstairs next time they watch the movie.

GUARD #1 (small): Hey, just making conversation, man.

GUARD #2: You know the drill by now, right, Doc? No touching anything, no crossing that big, white line, no telling anybody you've even HEARD of Doctor Banner...

HANK PYM: Is that a fact? You think I should toss out that T-shirt that says The Hulk is really a top-secret S.H.I.E.L.D. employee?

/ Closer on the guards, clearly unimpressed.

GUARD #1: Jackass.

GUARD #1: I can't believe Fury even keeps that guy AROUND.

/ Cut to Pym wandering down this corridor towards Banner's new cell. We don't see Banner yet, but we can hear him from off.

BRUCE (off/P): I'm afraid you'll have to stop just DROPPING BY like this, Clarice...

/ Pull back for a biggish pic of Banner standing here in the pose of Hannibal Lecter, his hands by his side and that slightly spooky expression.

BRUCE BANNER: People will say we're IN LOVE.

age Seventeen

/ Switch angles and Pym breaks into a smile as he takes a little plastic seat outside the new cell you suggested, Bryan. Banner seems a lot more at ease with himself here too and has a bit of a laugh. He and Pym are both disgraced scientists and now Fury has them working together. They're both men who wanted to be bigger and really aren't all that different. This is where we see just how different the new quarters are from the old, he distance between the two scientists really just being thick plate of glass now that Banner is a little more in control of himself.

HANK PYM: And how long you been waiting to say THAT?

BRUCE BANNER: Twenty minutes.

/ Pym sits down, back at his feet, and looks genuinely nterested to see how Banner's doing. Banner seems

pleased.

HANK PYM: How's the new cell, Bruce? Those pills Doctor Brankin prescribed still keeping you nice and relaxed in there?

BRUCE BANNER: Only turned into the Hulk once in the last six weeks and you know what I did? I just sat on the bed and watched *Curb Your Enthusiasm* until I shrank back down to normal again.

3/ Closer on Banner, obviously excited about the idea of getting his end away soon.

BRUCE BANNER: These psychic sessions with Charlie Xavier have really helped suppress all the rage, Hank. Brankin's even talking about letting BETTY in here in a few weeks' time.

BRUCE BANNER: You know she's written him a letter a day for the last six months just asking for a little QUALITY TIME with me?

4/ Pym gives a little jokey laugh and Banner sits on the bed, excited to see what he's got for him. Pym's opening the little box of ants and Banner looks curious. They look like a couple of boys showing each other their comic-book collections.

HANK PYM: Well, SOMEBODY sounds like she's hitting her thirties...

BRUCE BANNER: Yeah, yeah, yeah. Listen, how did you get on with those new SUPER-HERO ideas last week?

BRUCE BANNER: Fury's sitting on another big chunk of federal cash and he's desperate for us to come up with something nice and bright to sell to the public. You think of anything good?

5/ Pull back and we see the open box of ants sitting on the floor before Pym as he plops the big Ant-Man helmet on again. Bruce sits back, excited to see what happens next.

HANK PYM: Actually, I came up with some AMAZING stuff. I'd nothing for days and then I just sat down and came up with five different super-soldiers all in a single night.

HANK PYM: Those notes you had for my ULTRON idea were absolutely brilliant, but I had this crazy notion for the ants I really wanted to run past you first.

BRUCE BANNER: Man, this is great. I can't believe you and me never worked together in the past. We've got such an amazing synergy going on here.

Page Eighteen

1/ Repeat perspective, except here we see that Pym's disappeared and his clothes are starting to lose their shape and fall against the floor and chair. Banner looks shocked.

BRUCE BANNER: Hank?

2/ Banner stands up and squints, approaching the glass with a hunch as though he's trying to read some incredibly small print. A voice booms through unseen loudspeakers.

BRUCE BANNER: I don't get it. What did you do? Turn INVISIBLE or something?

RADIO BALLOON: No, don't be crazy. The Fantastic Four's already GOT that light-sensitive girl. I just figured out a way to shrink myself down and still stay in contact with the INSECTS here.

3/ Shot from behind the tiny Hank Pym as he floats on the back of a termite (the only flying ant I've ever heard of) in his Ant-Man costume and wearing the helmet. This is

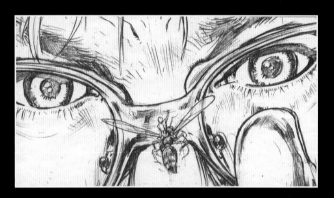

in the foreground and the huge, astonished face of Bruce Banner fills in the background.

RADIO BALLOON: Stand a little closer to the glass and you'll see me, Bruce. I'm speaking to you through the helmet's radio-system...

BRUCE BANNER: Oh my God.

BRUCE BANNER: I can't believe I'm even LOOKING at this...

4/ Closer on Pym riding the back of this flying ant, genuinely excited about the possibilities this has in store for him. Obviously, we've taken the naked thing as far as it can go and since we've seen Jan's costume shrink down we could give Hank something cool he's designed himself. The bright colors are important here because the team he joins in issue six are all in homemade, more traditional super-hero outfits.

RADIO BALLOON: What are you talking about? Thor's resigned, Tony's always too busy to do the Iron Man thing and there's no way people are going to let GIANT-MAN back on the team...

RADIO BALLOON: ...so I thought I'd ask Fury if he'd sneak me back with a brand-new name and a whole new background.

5/ Pull back and see what looks like Banner hunched and talking in disbelief to himself against the glass. The world is just getting madder and madder here.

RADIO BALLOON: Do you think ANT-MAN sounds RETARDED?

Page Nineteen

1/ Cut to a panoramic shot of New York City at nighttime, a tall posh restaurant in the middle of the view and a streak of lightning across the night sky. It's raining quite heavily here. Bryan, see the link for the restaurant up near Columbia I've sent separately.

CAPTION: Terrace In The Sky restaurant, Morningside Heights:

2/ Cut to the big, open balcony on the restaurant (all the diners are inside) and we see the lightning bolt striking the tiles from Thor. This is the arrival of Thor.

NO DIALOGUE

3/ Cut to the glass door between the glass balcony and the main restaurant opening and some big, wet, slightly sodden-looking boots coming in. We're looking at Thor from the knees down here as he slips inside this door.

THOR: Sorry I'm late, Volstagg.

THOR: I was creating a storm over a rice field in Ethiopia and none of the locals was wearing a watch.

4/ Pull back and a nice wide shot of Volstagg sitting here in the middle of this restaurant and eating the most preposterous amount of food you've ever seen. Thor is soaking wet and adjusting himself, everyone watching, the waiters all spinning around in disbelief. He's acting very casually, as though this bizarre dinner appointment was all quite normal. Dress Volstagg however you like here.

VOLSTAGG: Don't worry about it, Thor. I don't have any other plans.

VOLSTAGG: You'll have to forgive me for starting dinner without you, but it's been five hundred years since I set foot in this world and I'd honestly forgotten what chicken even TASTED like.

Page Twenty

1/ Closer as Thor sits down and Volstagg tucks into his enormous meal.

VOLSTAGG: I'm glad to hear you've finally left The Ultimates, by the way. The only thing that puzzles me is why you even associated with those idiots in the FIRST place.
THOR: Oh, I needed them as much as they needed me, old friend. Helping them out in a few little brawls is what gave me this global profile I'm enjoying at the moment.

2/ Thor seems quite charitable about The Ultimates and

Volstagg reprimands him, reminding him of his mission.

THOR: And they're not ALL idiots, you know. In fact, some of them are very fine men indeed.

VOLSTAGG: They're the agents of the New World Order, young man, and this agenda they're following puts them completely at odds with everything you've been sent here to do.

VOLSTAGG: It's essential that you remember that.

3/ Thor rolls his eyes, slightly irritated by all this. Volstagg suddenly becomes very serious.

THOR: Is this why you requested an AUDIENCE with me, Volstagg? To lecture me about the COMPANY I'm keeping?

VOLSTAGG: No, I'm here with a message from your father, Thor.

VOLSTAGG: Odin asked me to tell you that your brother has escaped from the ROOM WITHOUT DOORS and swears vengeance for your LAST encounter.

4/ Everyone is looking around, whispering to one another by this scene. Thor seems quite relaxed, but Volstagg explains the gravity of the situation.

THOR: That doesn't matter, does it? I beat him once, I'll beat him again. I beat Loki EVERY TIME we lock horns, right?

VOLSTAGG: But this time it's different. This time he's allied himself with something even you can't match and, if our wise men are correct, he'll assemble the super-people against you too.

5/ Close on Volstagg, very serious and very dark.

VOLSTAGG: Can't you feel him moving the scenery around us? Reality is being rewritten even as we speak and this warning should be taken with the UTMOST SERIOUSNESS.

VOLSTAGG: He's going to poison their minds AGAINST you, Thor. Be prepared: What comes next is like nothing you've ever SEEN before.

Page Twenty-One

1/ Reaction shot from Thor in close-up. He seems equally serious and convinced he can handle whatever's going to happen to him.

THOR: Don't worry, Volstagg.

THOR: I'll be ready.

2/ Pull back and we see the waiter looking a little embarrassed, standing here with a menu for Thor. Thor looks a little perplexed and motions over to his fat friend.

WAITER: Uh, excuse me, sir. Are you waiting for a FRIEND or just EATING ALONE here?

THOR: What are you talking about? I'm SITTING with a friend. This is VOLSTAGG THE VOLUMINOUS from ASGARD, for God's sake. He's hardly the type of man you don't NOTICE.

3/ The waiter looks awkward and other people are all watching, a little afraid. Thor looks confused.

WAITER: I'm sorry, sir. I don't mean to embarrass you, but you've actually just been talking to yourself for the last five minutes. The other diners are starting to get a little scared.

THOR: What?

4/ Close on Thor, a little scared. He thought he was talking to someone, but perhaps he's actually just as mad as everyone says.

THOR: Really?

5/ Pull back and Thor looks very uncomfortable as the waiter gestures around towards the empty chair opposite. Volstagg has never even been here. There's no food, no nothing. Is Thor just nuts?

WAITER: Take a look and see for YOURSELF, sir.

Page Twenty-Two

1/ Cut to the interior of one of the old New York Masonic lodges. All the old guys are in tuxedos after the roast and, since the wives are here, not wearing their aprons as they head through the main hallway. Everybody's having a laugh and they're treating Bucky and Cap like they're a couple of rock-stars. Jan and Gail are tagging along here too, both smiling and clearly enjoying the fun.

OLD FAT GUY: Aw, brother. That had to be the funniest roast I ever heard, Bucky. I can't believe you guys hid Cap's costume that time and he had to fight the Nazis in his underwear.

BUCKY BARNES: I swear to God, you shoulda seen their faces, Marty. Living legend he may be, but he looked like such a freakin' goofball in those long johns.

2/ Gail surprises Steve by taking his arm and holding him like she's on a date, everyone laughing as Bucky feigns anger and a little jealousy.

GAIL BARNES: Don't you listen to them, Steve, honey. I know for a fact you looked a PICTURE in those long johns.

BUCKY BARNES: Hey, hey, hey. You're not engaged to this clown no more, ya know. You moved onto bigger and better things, remember?

3/ Janet joins in the spirit of the whole thing as they head down the stairs, locking arms with Bucky and pretending she'll take him over Steve any day. Some of Bucky's laughing buddies join in the gag.

JANET PYM: Ah, Gail can have him, Bucky. Those two hooking up again just leaves things nice and open for you and me, huh?

BUCKY BARNES: Say, you got yourself a deal, doll. You see THIS, Carmine?

CARMINE: Careful how you squeeze him, Jan. Any tighter and you're gonna bust that colostomy bag o' his.

4/ Cut to downstairs in the lobby as they descend the main stairs and find reporters and TV cameras all waiting for them. Steve's being polite, but looks a little irked.

TV REPORTER: Captain America? Phil Nygun, NBC news. Have you any comment you'd like to make about the HULK situation, sir?

STEVE ROGERS: WHOA! WHOA! Hold your horses there, boys. This is a little PRIVATE TIME, huh? You can't just bust in here like this.

5/ Closer as the reporters all surge forward and stick mikes in Steve and Jan's faces, Bucky and Gail wondering what the hell is going on here too.

OTHER REPORTER: Cap, would you and The Wasp like to explain why you both repeatedly lied when you said you had no idea who the Hulk was or what his relationship was with Betty Ross?

JANET PYM: What?

BUCKY BARNES: What the hell are they talking about, Cap?

Page Twenty-Three

1/ Cut to inside a crowded bar at night and we see people gathering around to see a picture of the Hulk and a newscaster talking. We need this to emphasize that everyone is watching this out there.

NEWSCASTER: ...anonymous files sent to this and every major news network in the world explaining that The Hulk's name and origins have been known to the security services since the moment he appeared.

NEWSCASTER: General Nick Fury, commander-in-chief of S.H.I.E.L.D., refused to confirm that he participated in this cover-up to protect a man responsible for the deaths of more than eight hundred people...

2/ Cut to Tony's palatial bedroom and we see him lying unconscious here with a couple of bottles of champagne beside him, Natasha watching the TV and looking slightly horrified. The TV is facing away from us here and is the only light in a dark room.

NATASHA: Tony? I think you'd better wake up here, baby...

TV BALLOON: If these reports are accurate, and all signs indicate that they are, then the Hulk is in fact a federal employee whose identity was concealed to avoid a massive public outcry.

3/ Cut to a crowded TV studio where producers and researchers are torn between watching a report on one of the many screens and reading the new information coming in on their computers.

TV PRODUCER: Where the hell's this stuff coming from? I'm getting S.H.I.E.L.D. files ten levels over Presidential clearance here. Who the hell's SENDING this stuff?

NEWSCASTER: To repeat tonight's main headline: The identity of The Hulk has been confirmed as Doctor Robert Bruce Banner...

4/ The final panel in the sequence cuts to a wide shot in a busy, crowded outdoor environment. Times Square seems a good match because there has to be a sense of this just getting bigger and bigger. The newscast might be being played on someone's radio.

NEWSCASTER: ....former director of S.H.I.E.L.D.'s super-soldier program and, as you can see from these pictures, living comfortably in state-funded quarters one mile beneath The Triskelion.

NEWSCASTER: The Ultimates are expected to make an announcement shortly, but first we go live to the White House for an emergency statement from the President of the United States...

Page Twenty-Four

1/ Cut to a full-page splash of Bruce Banner sitting in his *Lord of the Rings* T-shirt and a pair of boxer-shorts as he slouches on the bed eating potato chips and watching his TV (also facing away from us). His eyes are wide and he looks stunned.

BRUCE (small): Oh $#&?...

To Be Continued

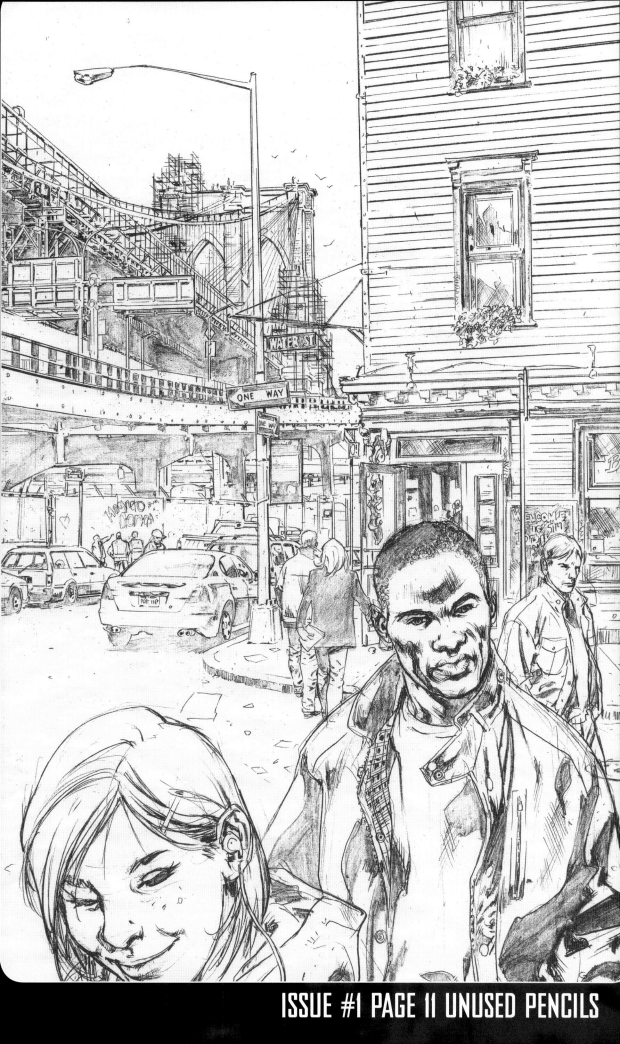

ISSUE #1 PAGE 11 UNUSED PENCILS

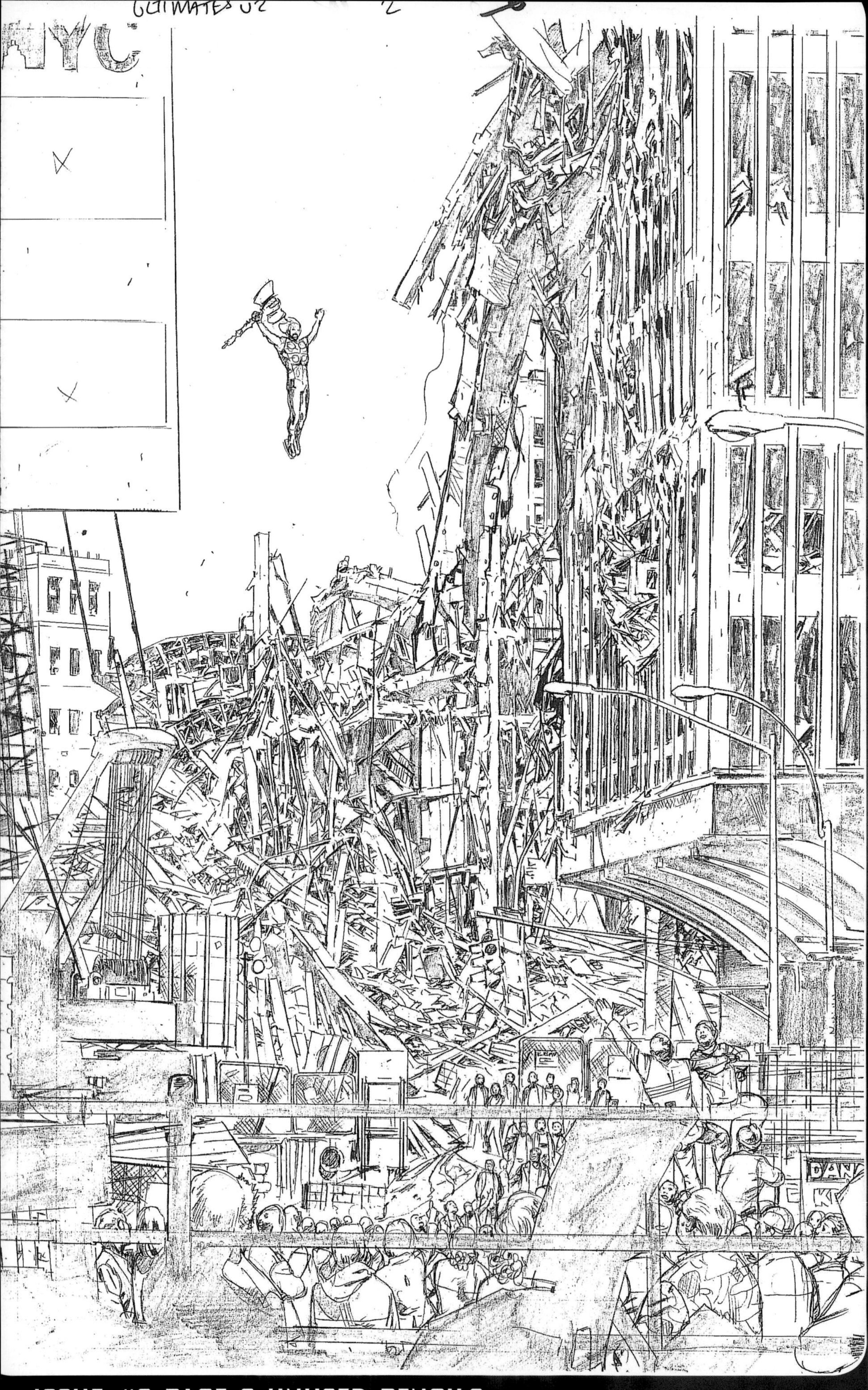
NYC

ISSUE #2 PAGE 8 UNUSED PENCILS

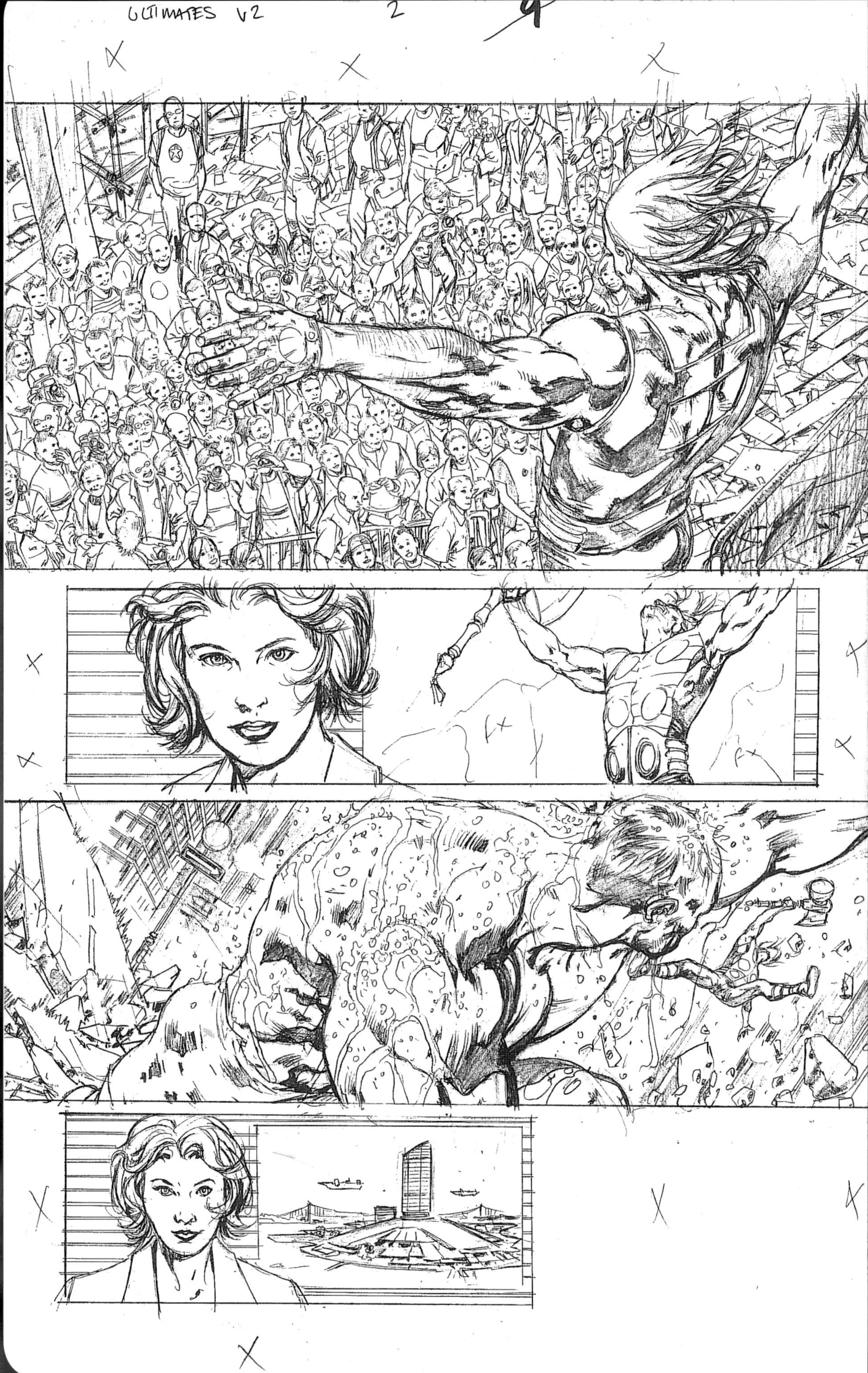
ULTIMATES V2 2 9

ISSUE #2 PAGE 9 UNUSED PENCILS

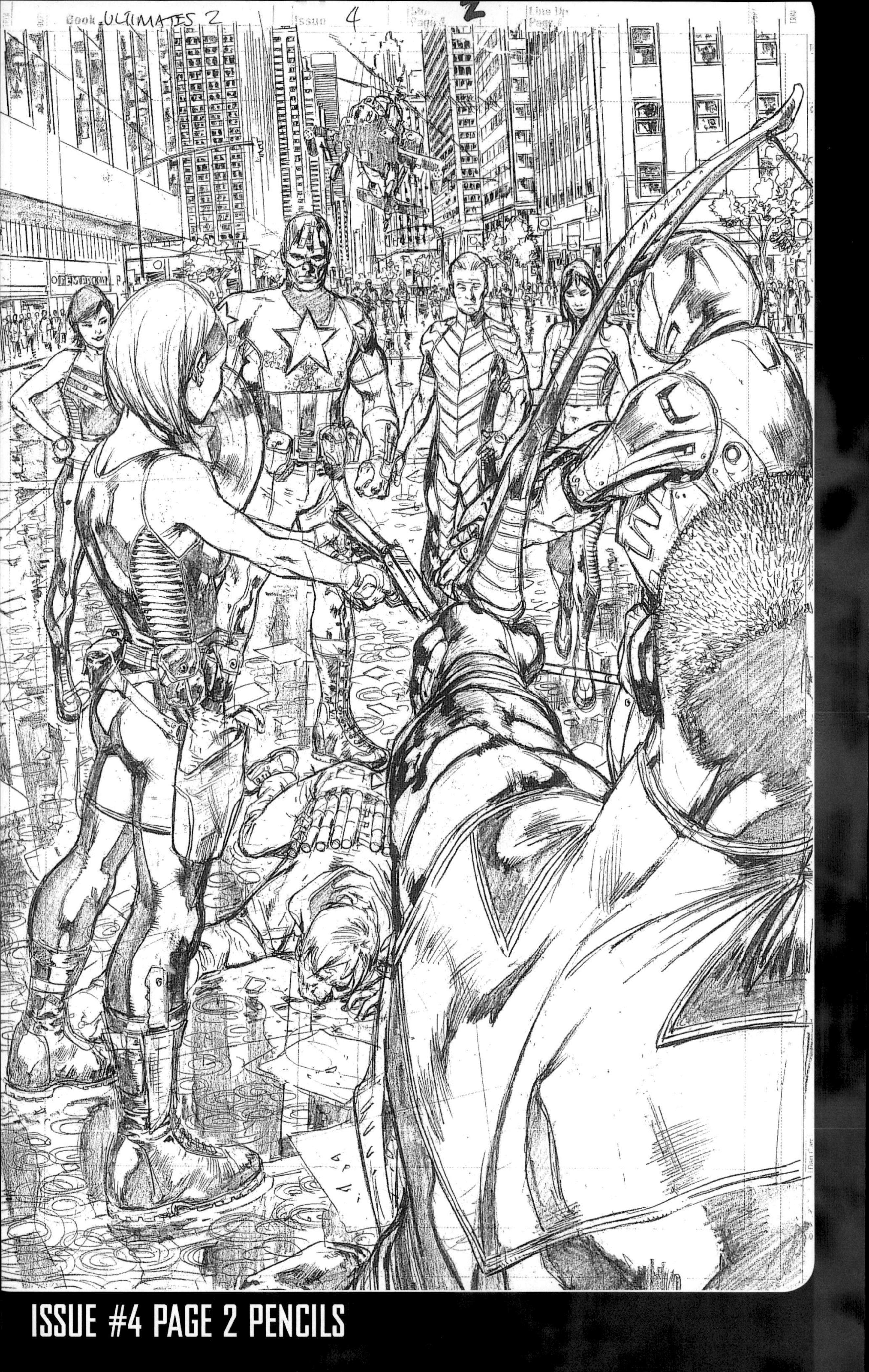
Book ULTIMATES 2
Issue 4

ISSUE #4 PAGE 2 PENCILS

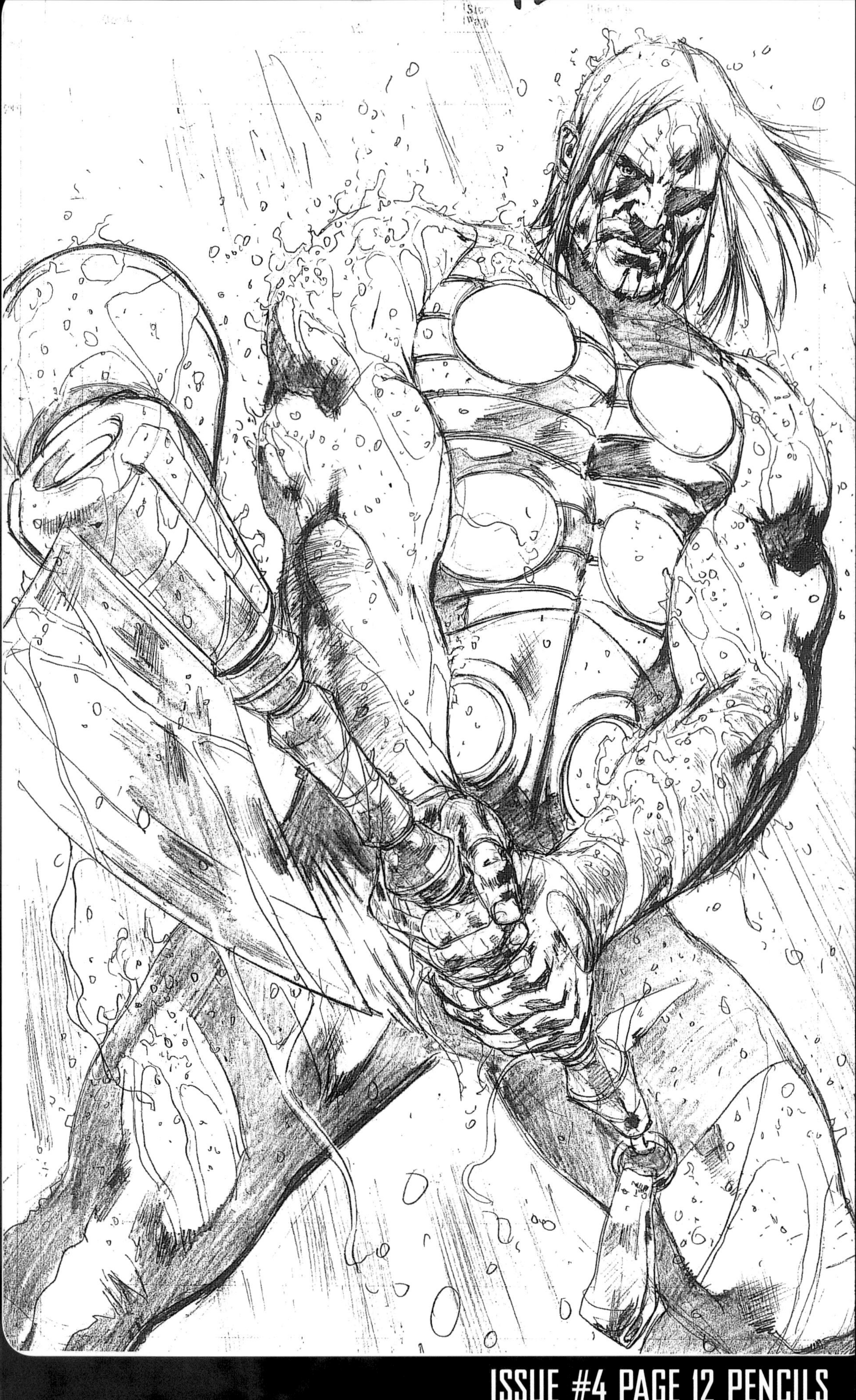

ISSUE #4 PAGE 12 PENCILS

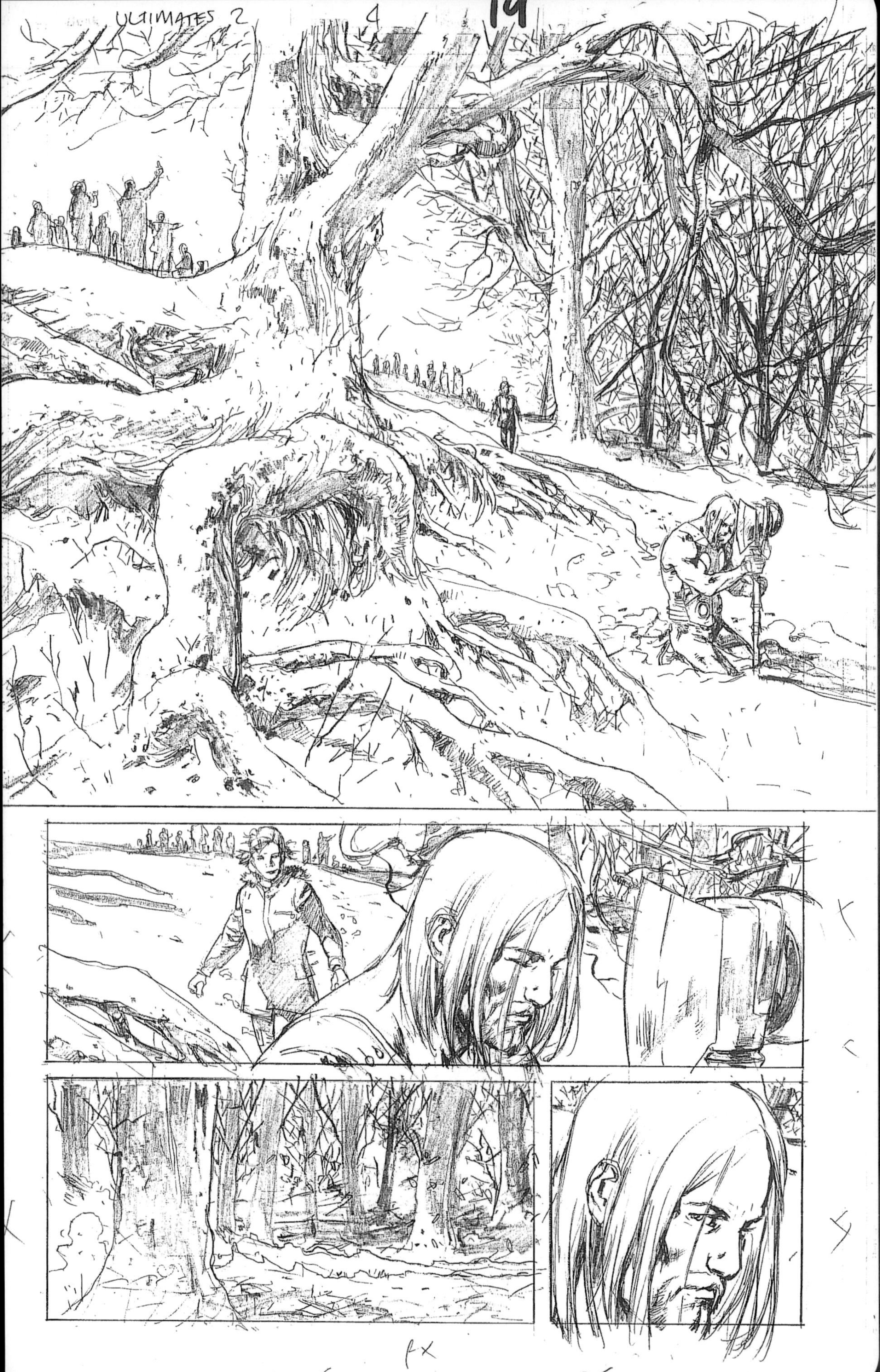
ULTIMATES 2
4
19
fx

ISSUE #4 PAGE 19 PENCILS

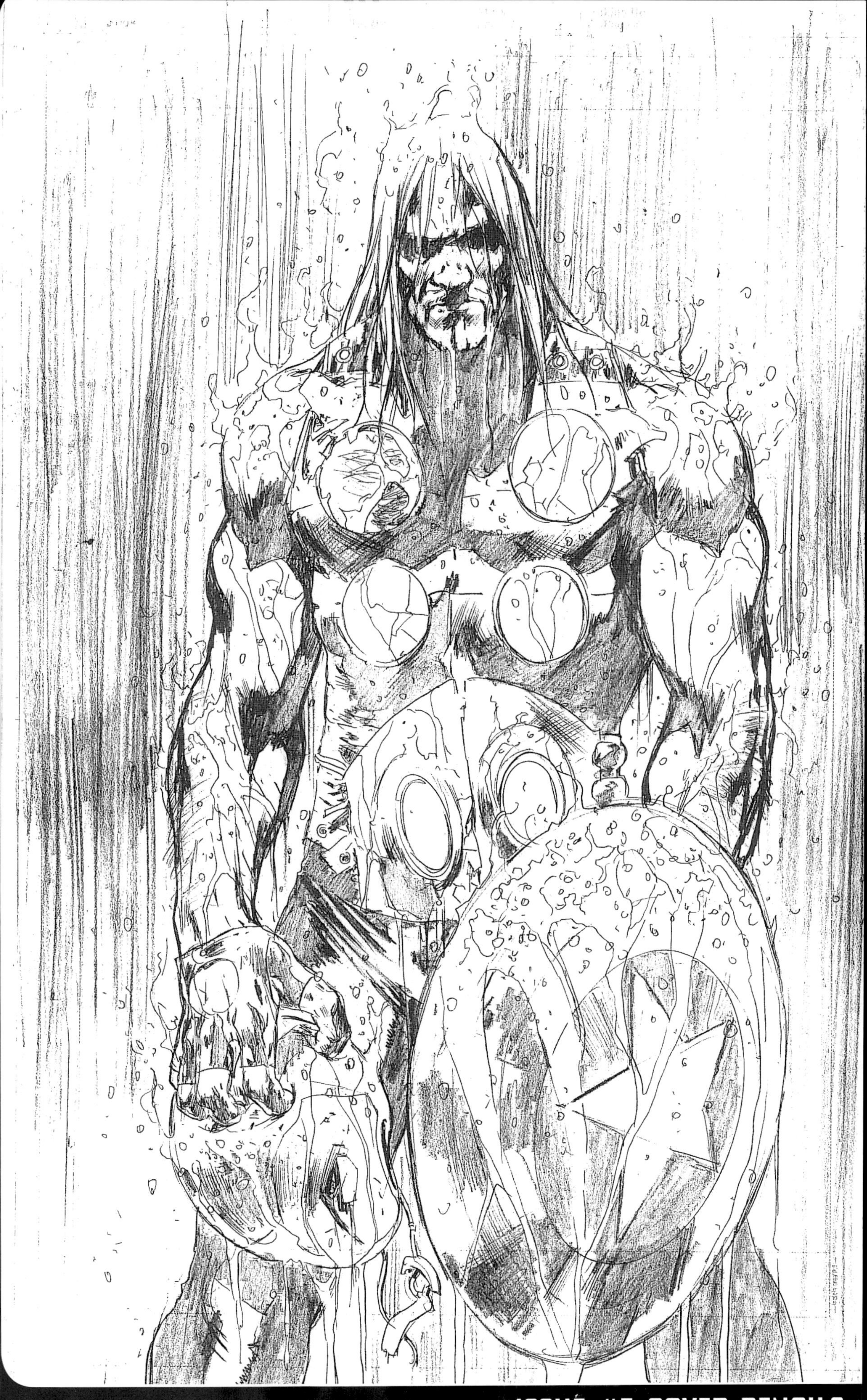

ISSUE #5 COVER PENCILS

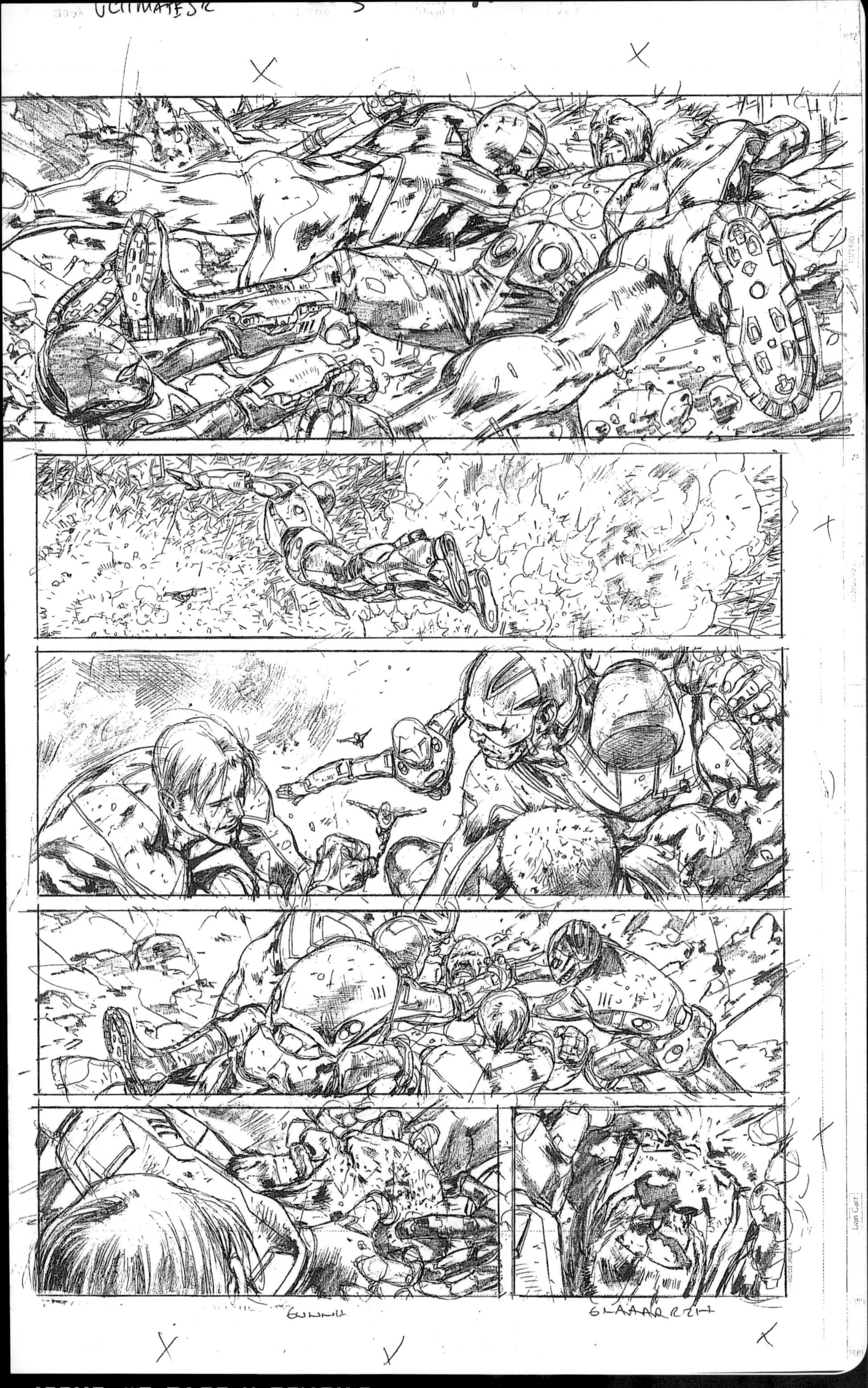
ULTIMATES 2
GUNNH
GLAAARRGH

ISSUE #5 PAGE 11 PENCILS

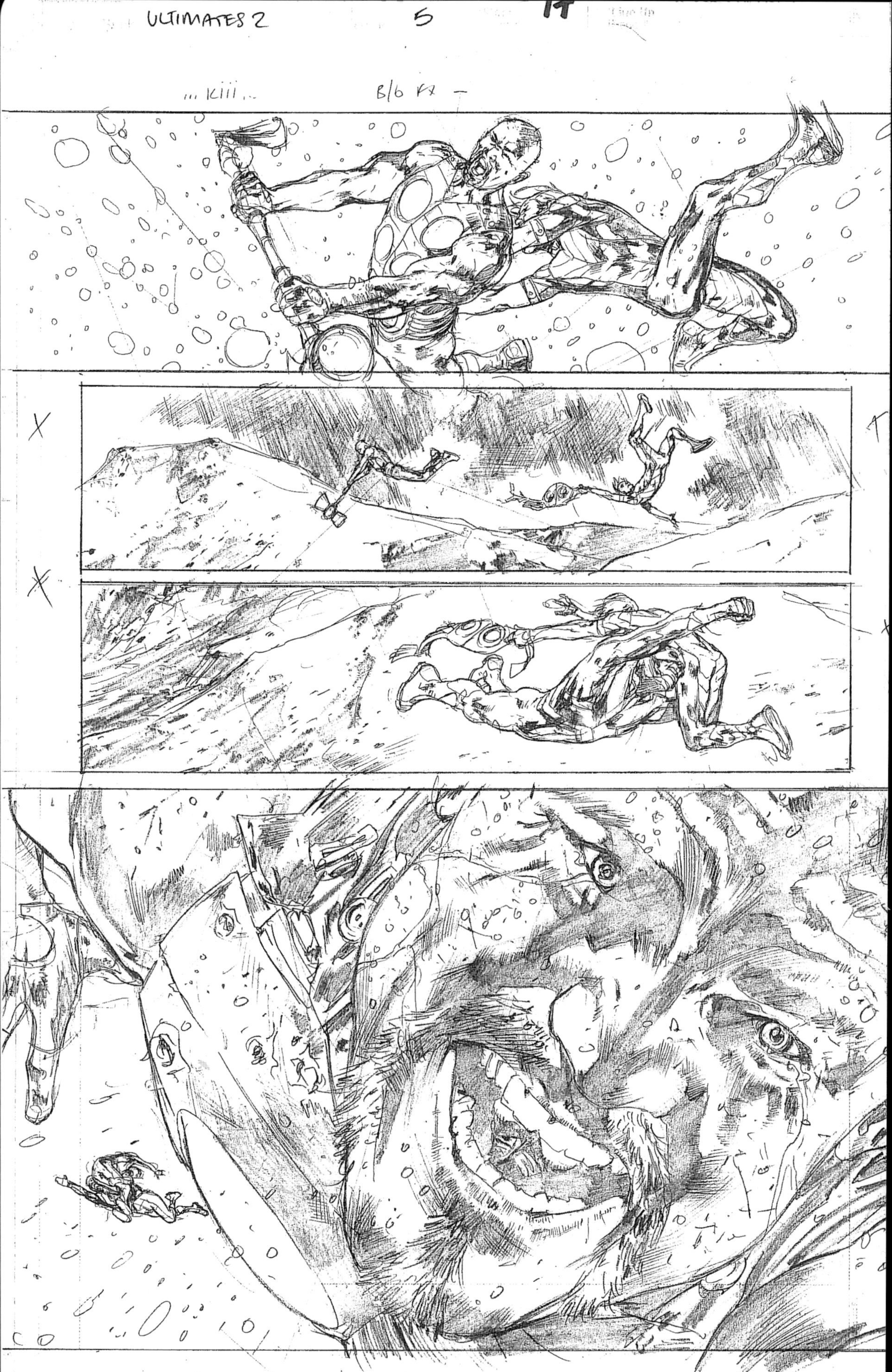
ULTIMATES 2
5
...Kiii...
B/G FX -

ISSUE #5 PAGE 17 PENCILS

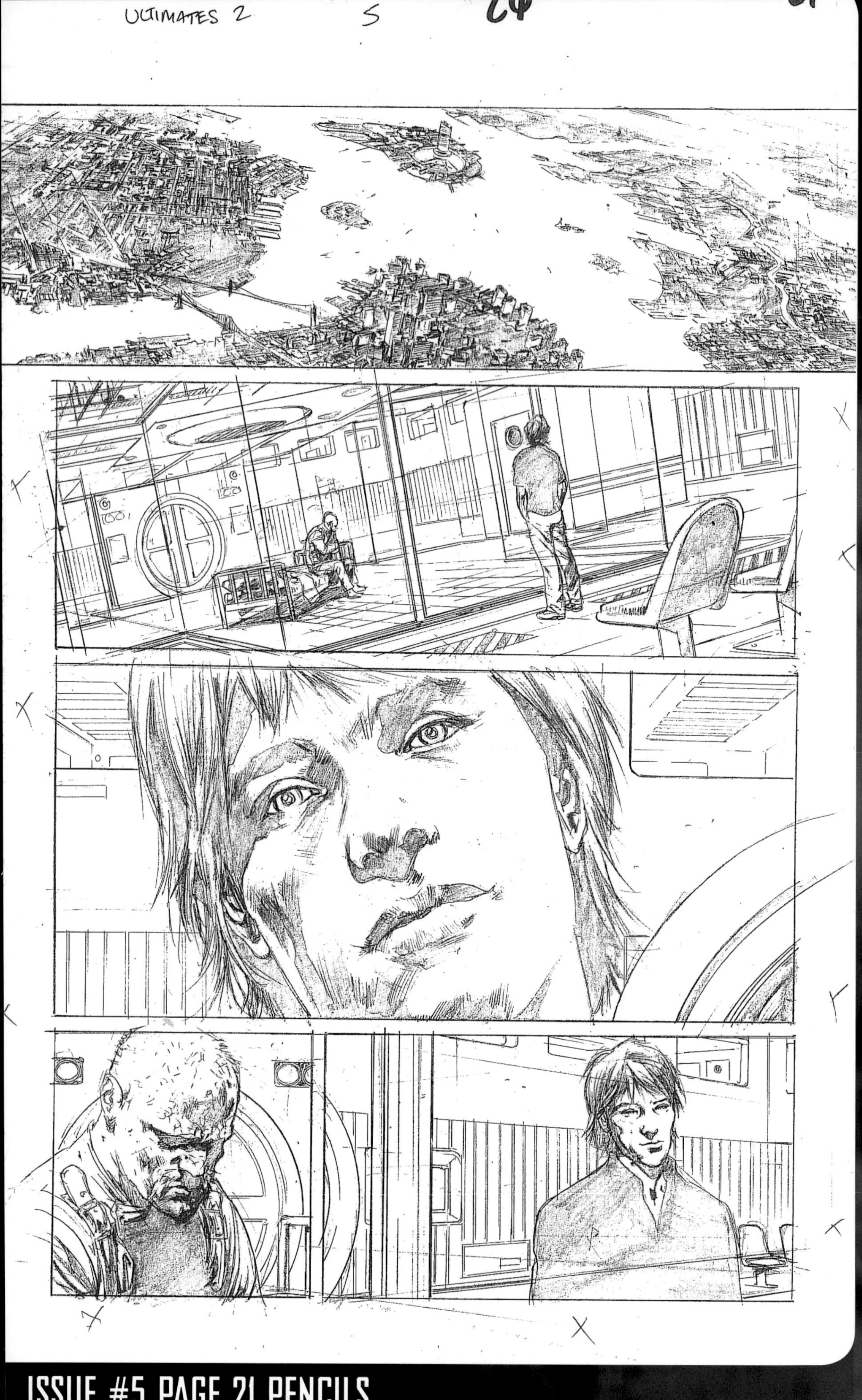
ULTIMATES 2
5

ISSUE #5 PAGE 21 PENCILS

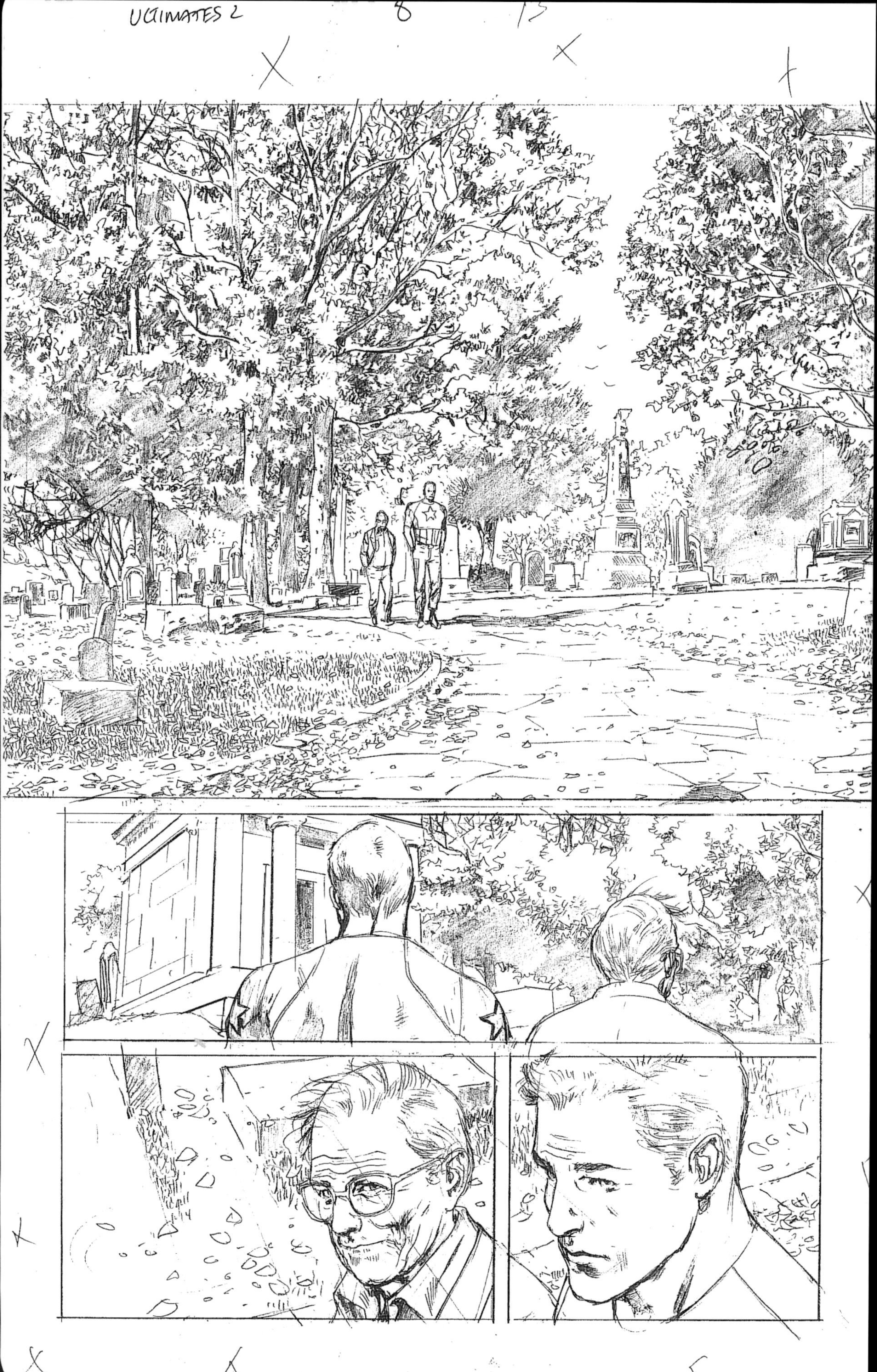
ULTIMATES 2
8
13

ISSUE #8 PAGE 13 PENCILS

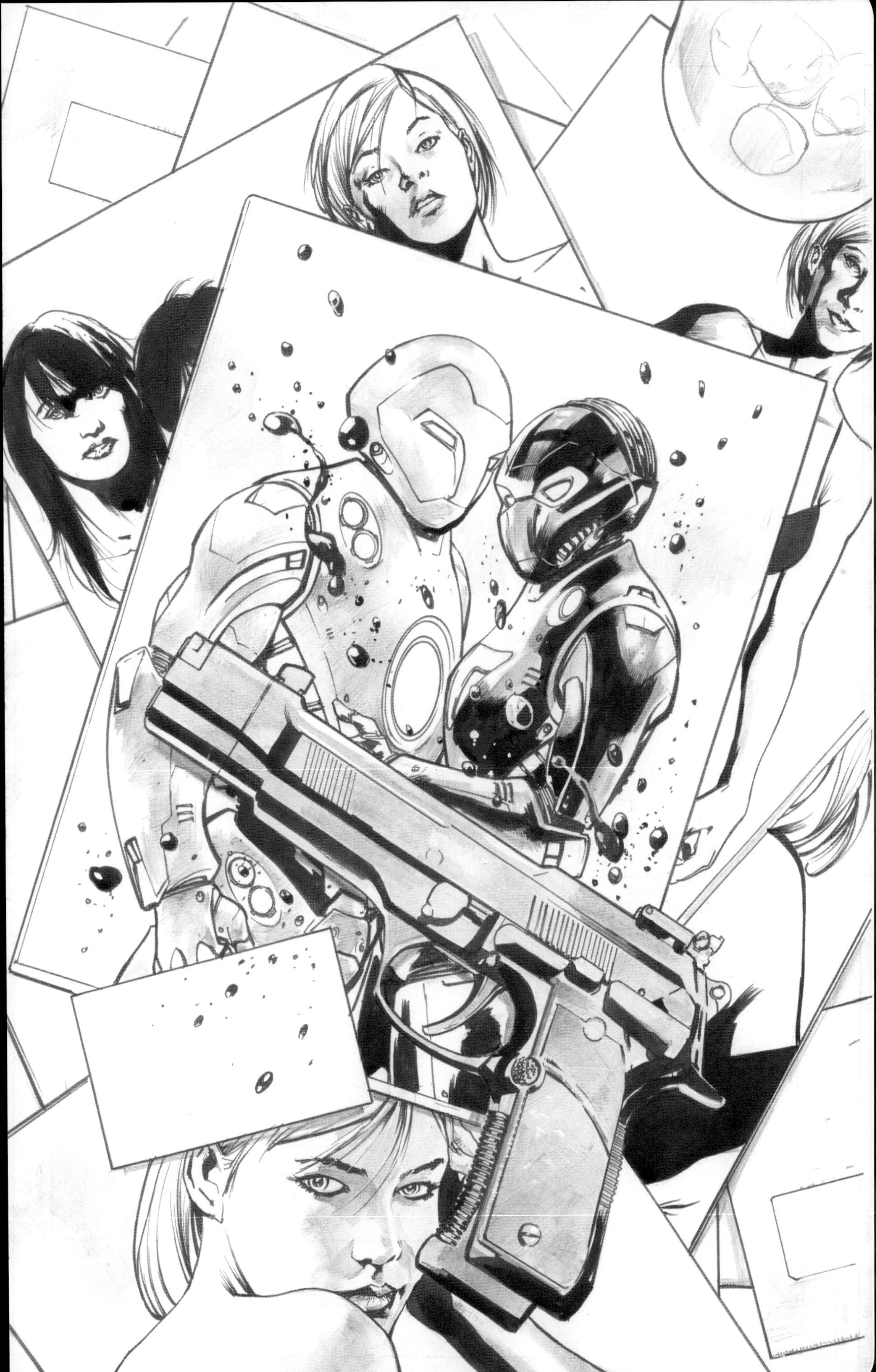

ISSUE #9 COVER INKS

ULTIMATES 2 10 21

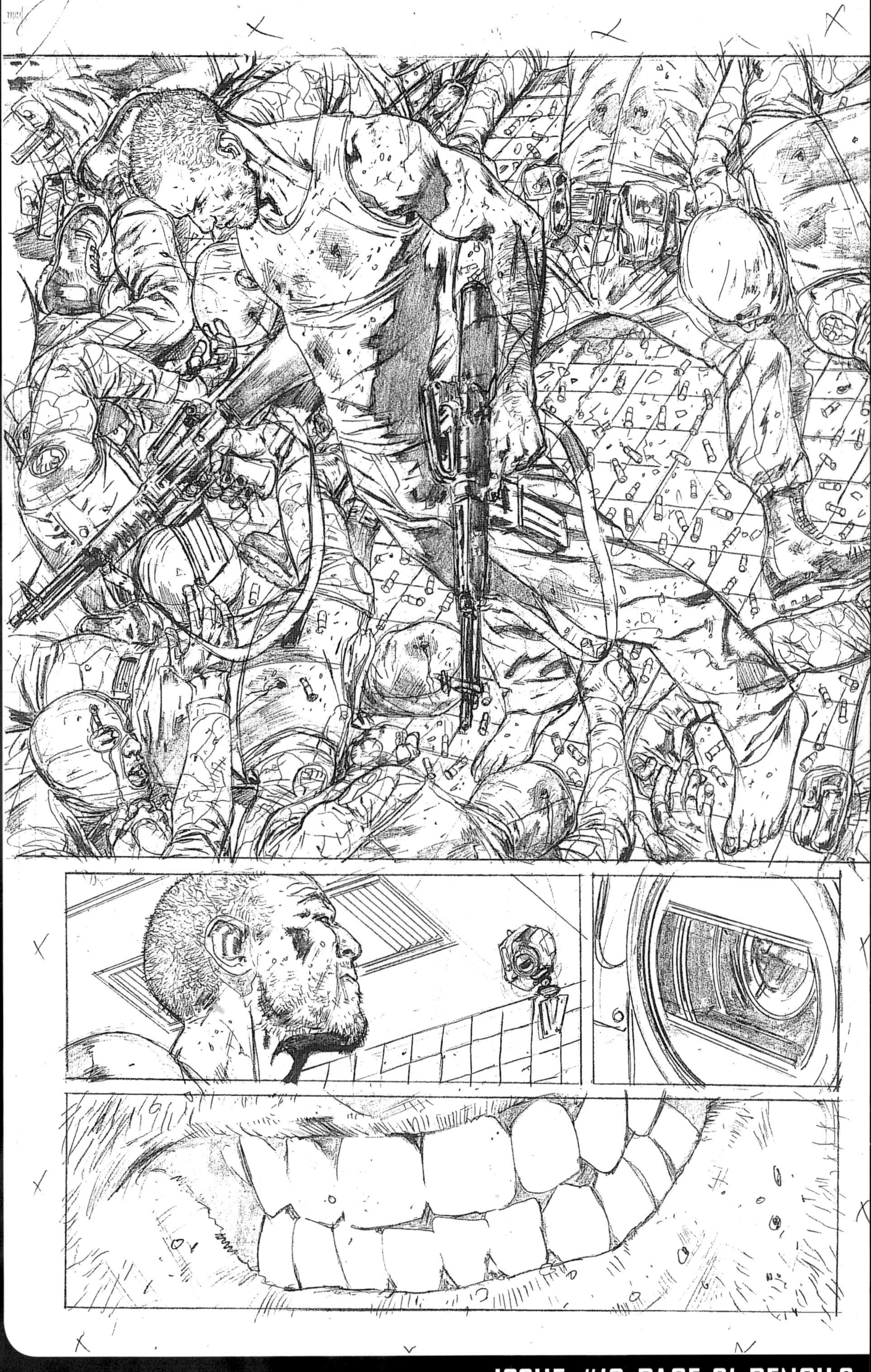

ISSUE #10 PAGE 21 PENCILS

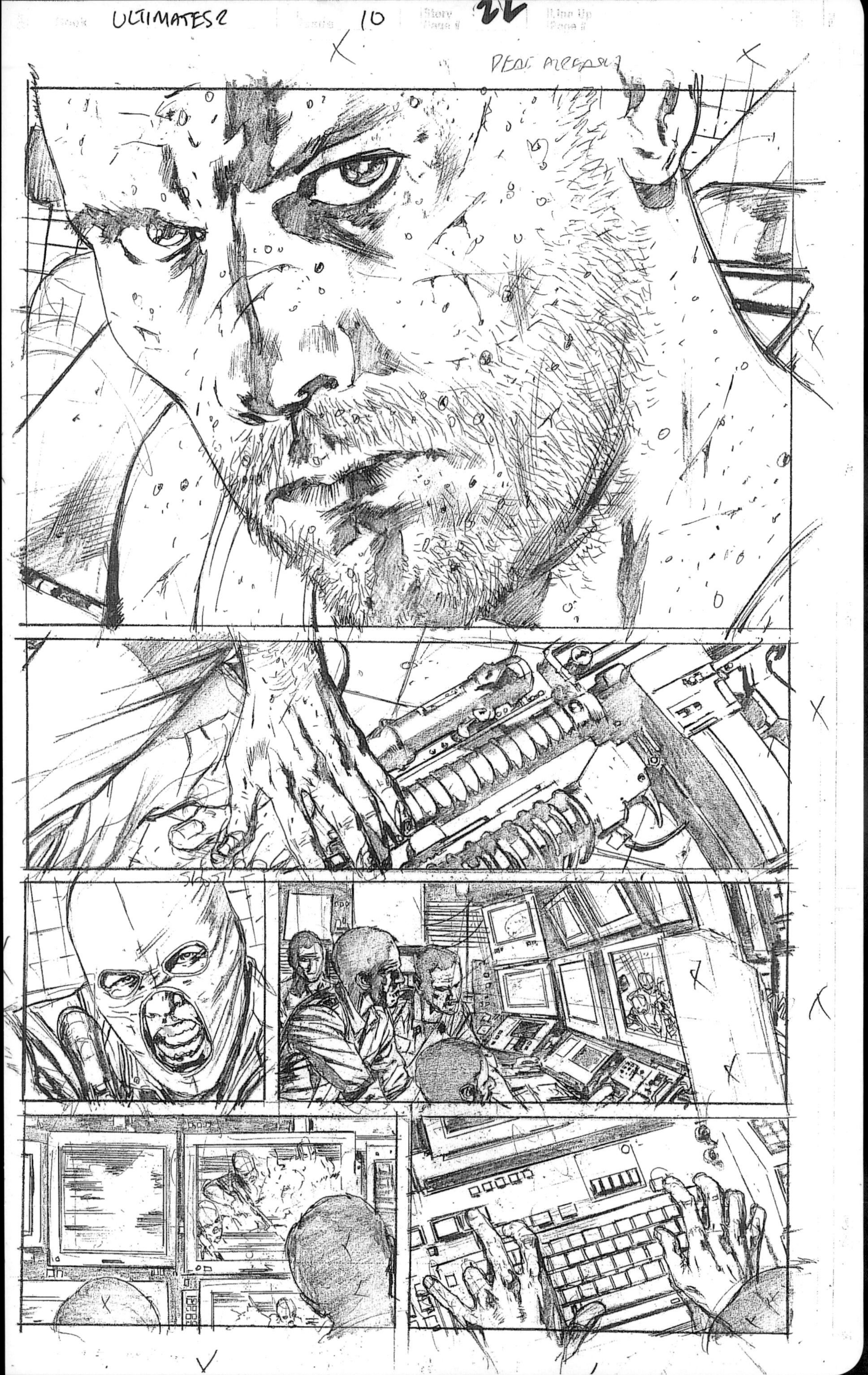
ULTIMATES 2
10
22

ISSUE #10 PAGE 22 PENCILS

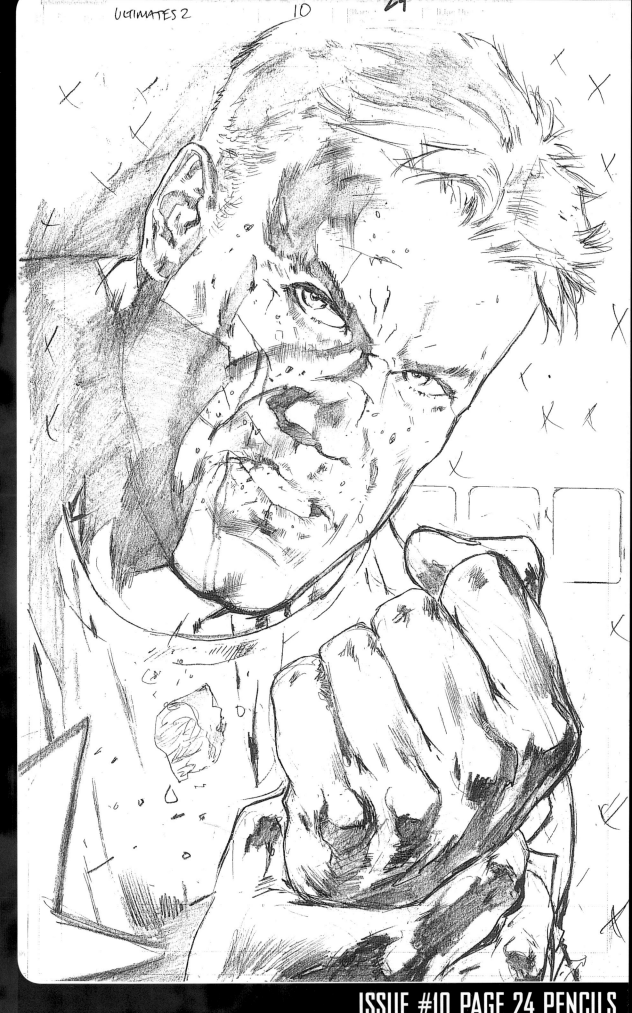

ULTIMATES 2   10   24

ISSUE #10 PAGE 24 PENCILS

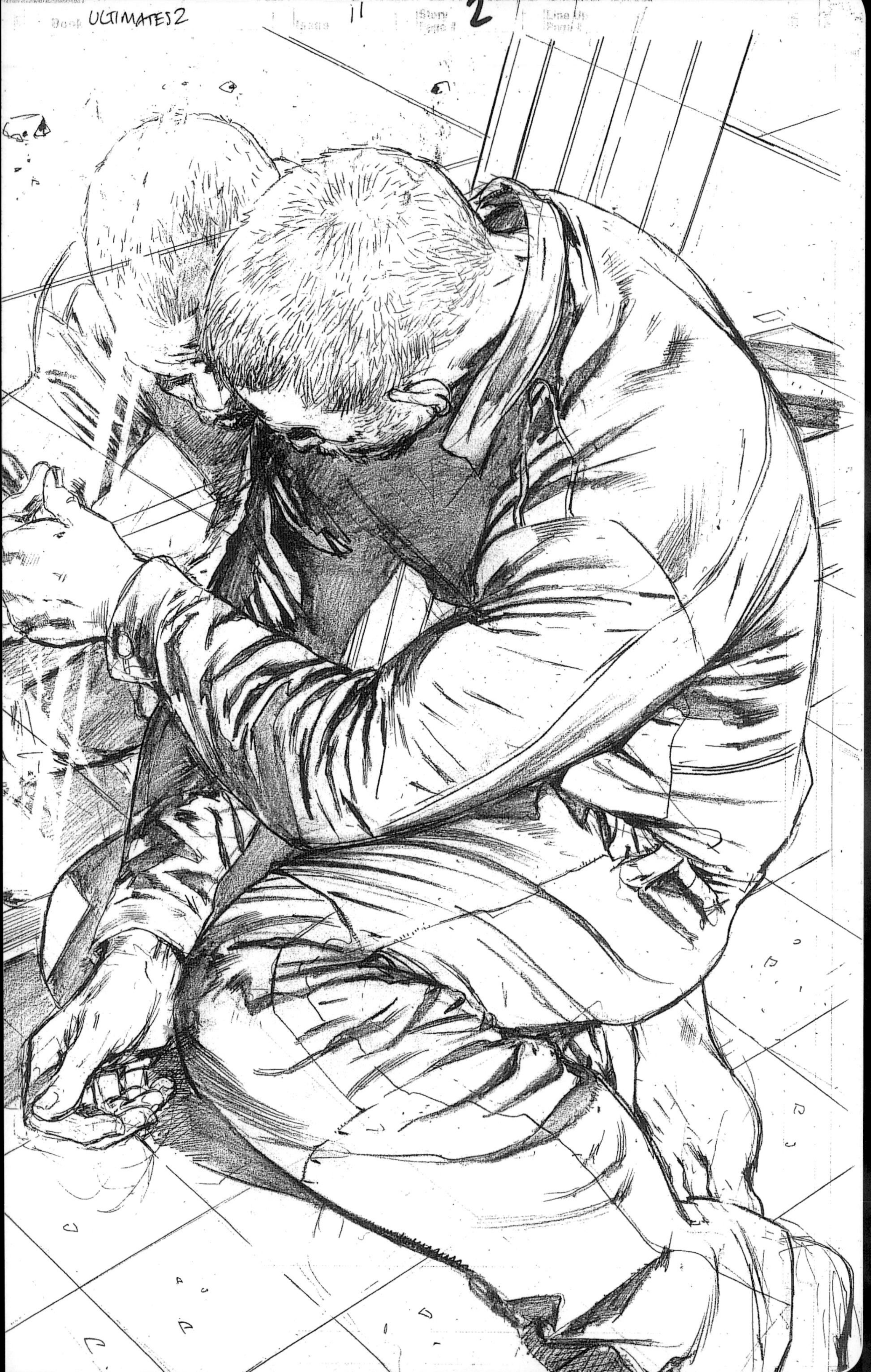
ULTIMATES 2
11
2

ISSUE #11 PAGE 2 PENCILS

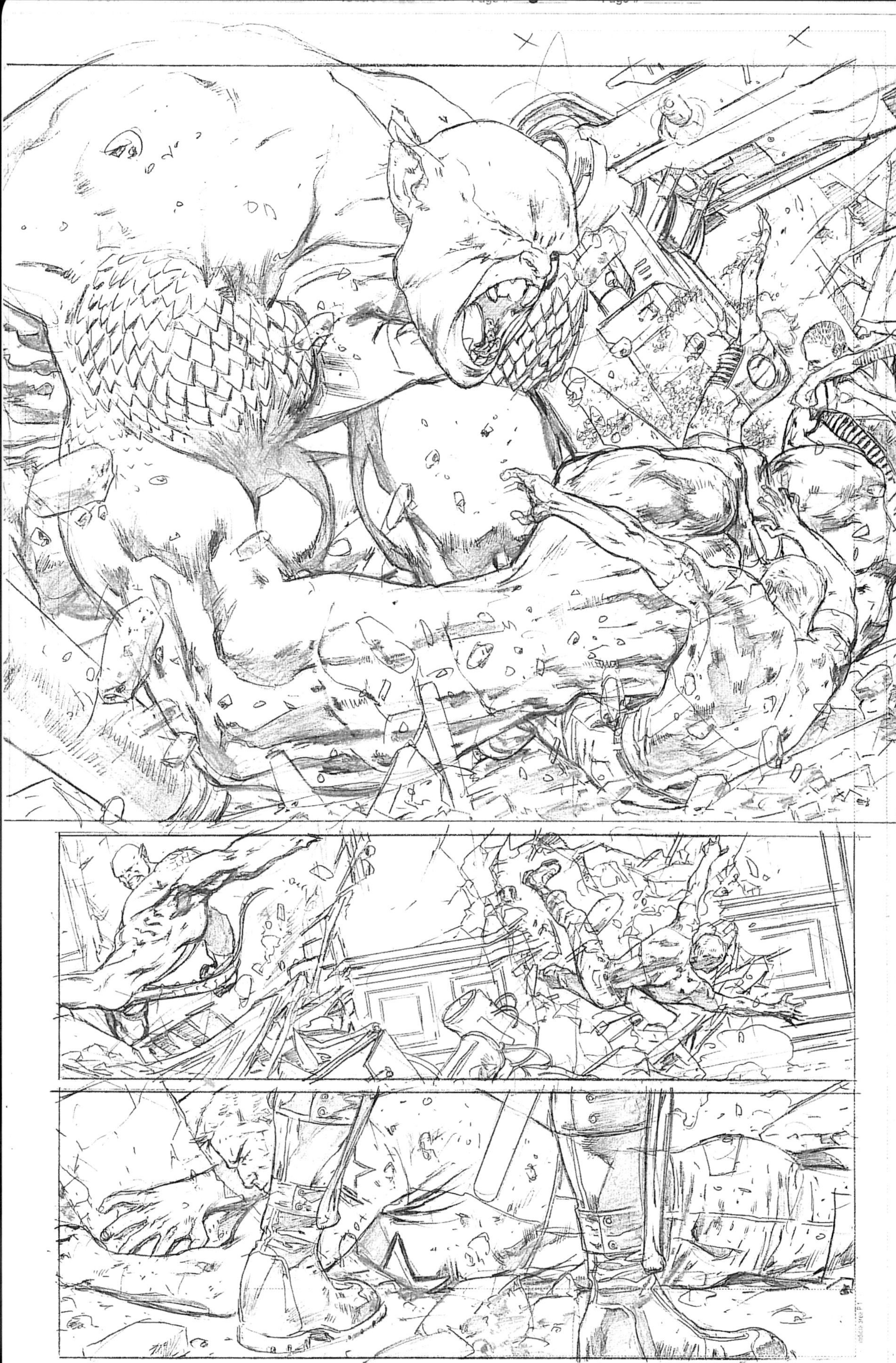
INSTRUCTIONS FOR DOUBLE PAGE SPREAD: CUT AS SHOWN. ABUT PAGE EDGES. TAPE ON BACK. DO NOT OVERLAP.

ISSUE #11 PAGE 20 PENCILS

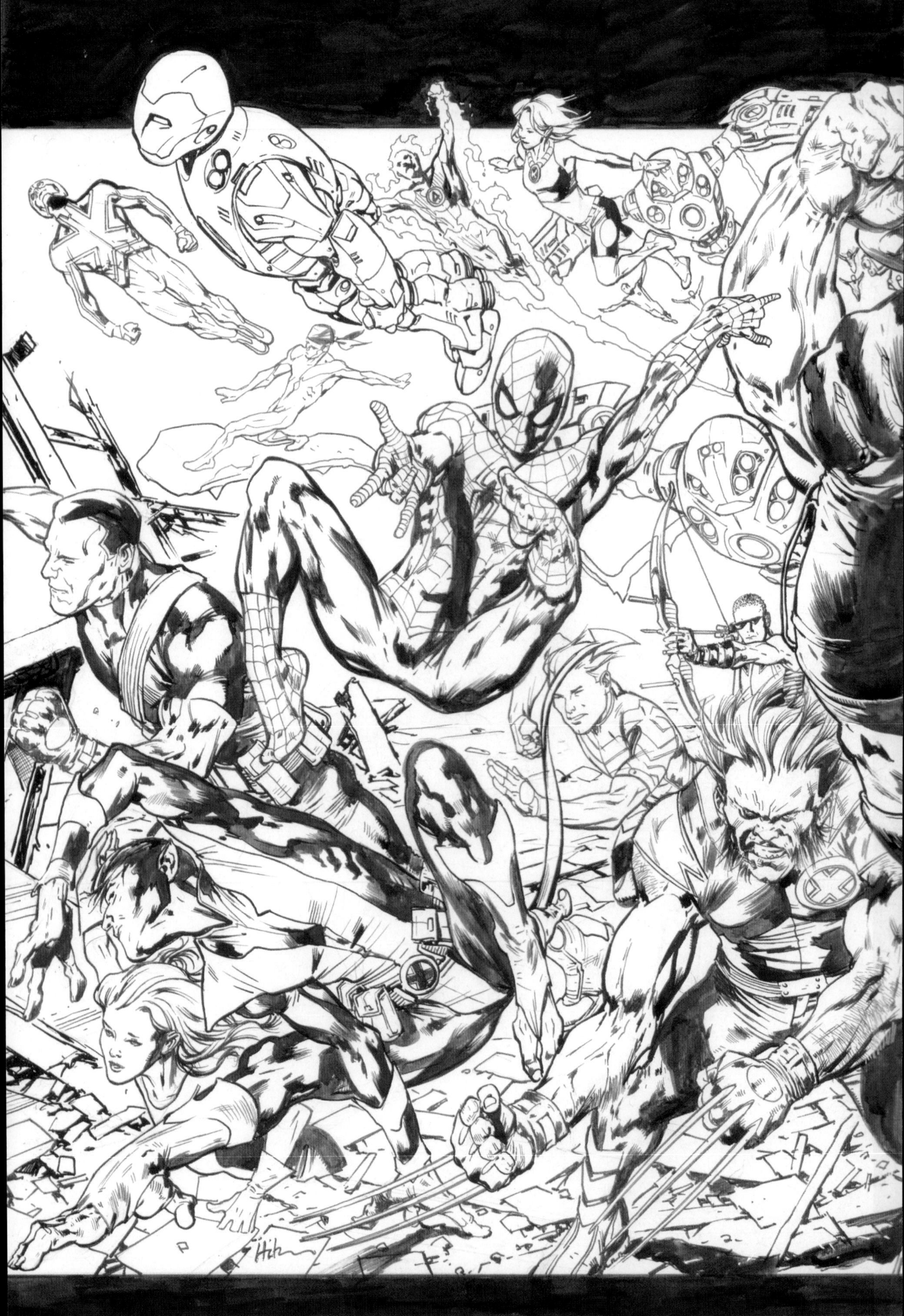

ISSUE #12 COVER INKS

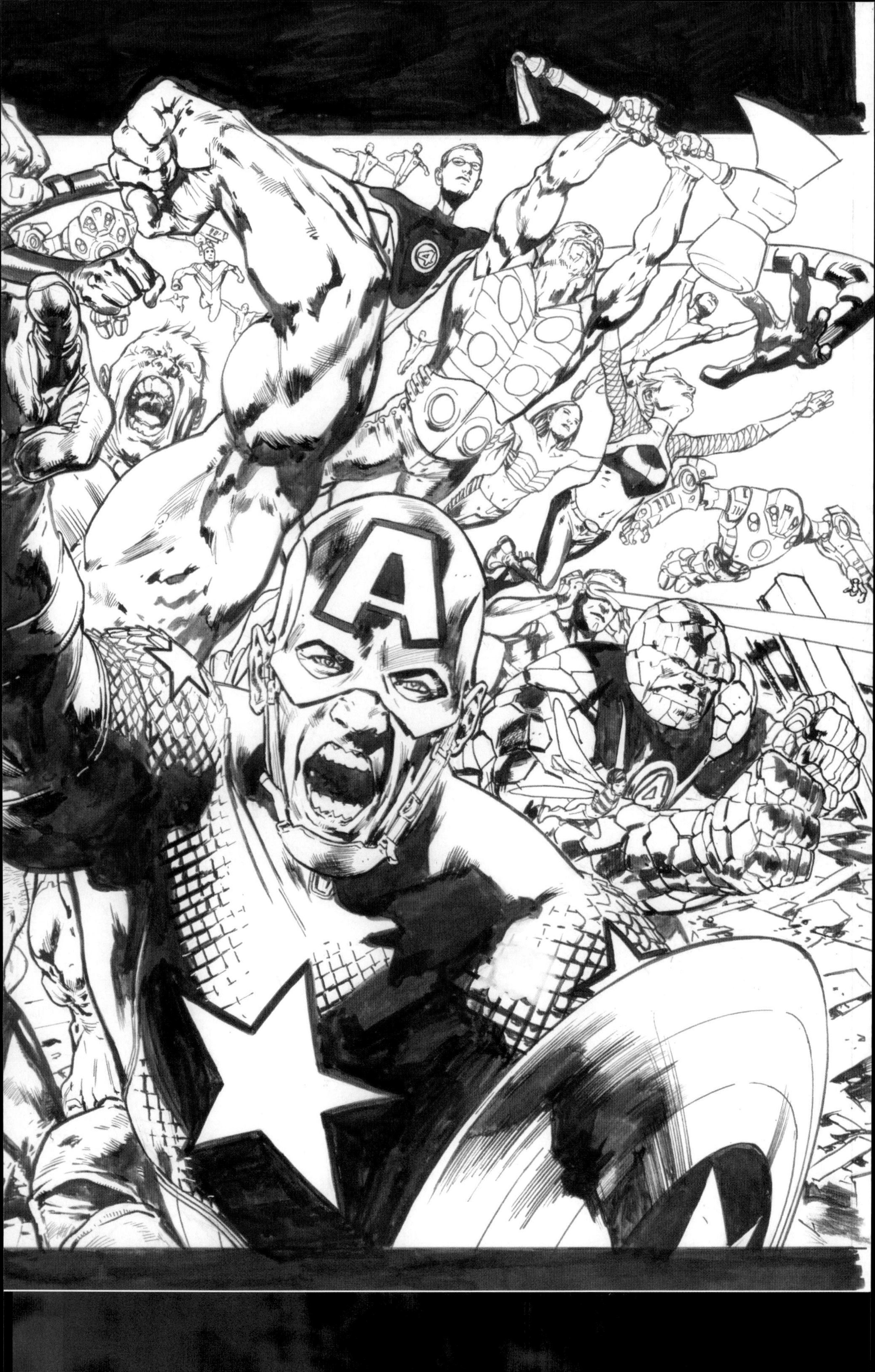

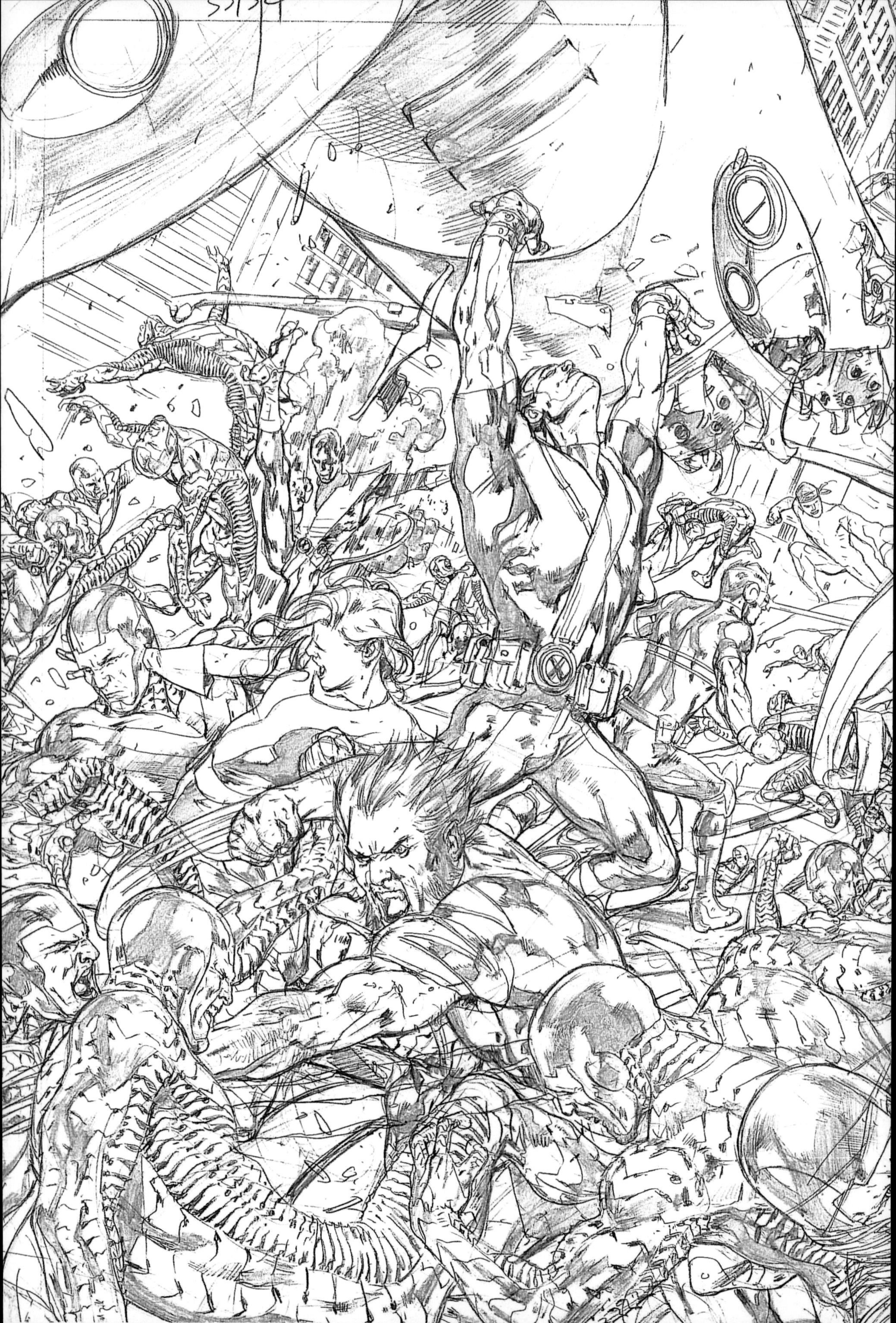

ISSUE #12 PAGE 33 PENCILS

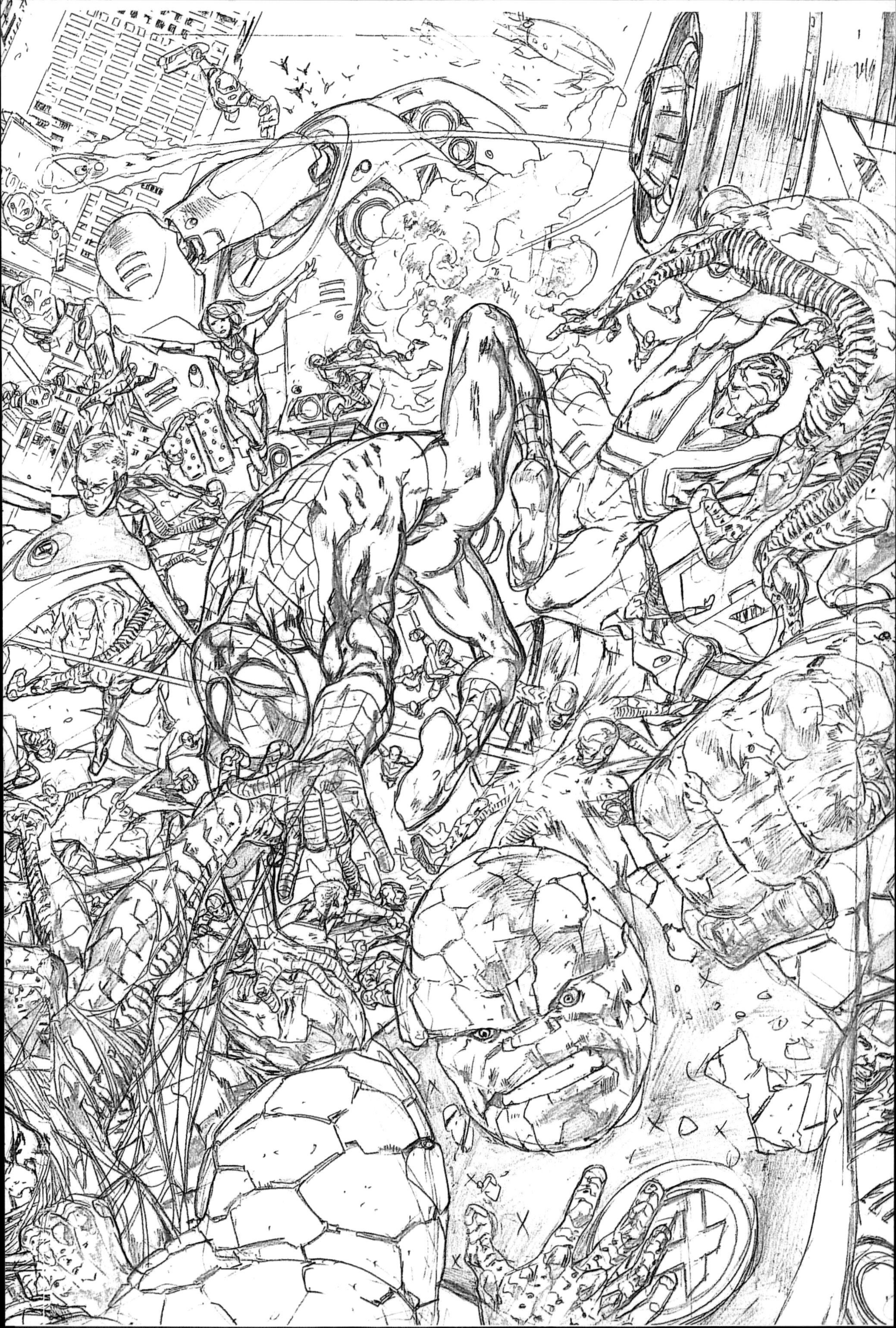

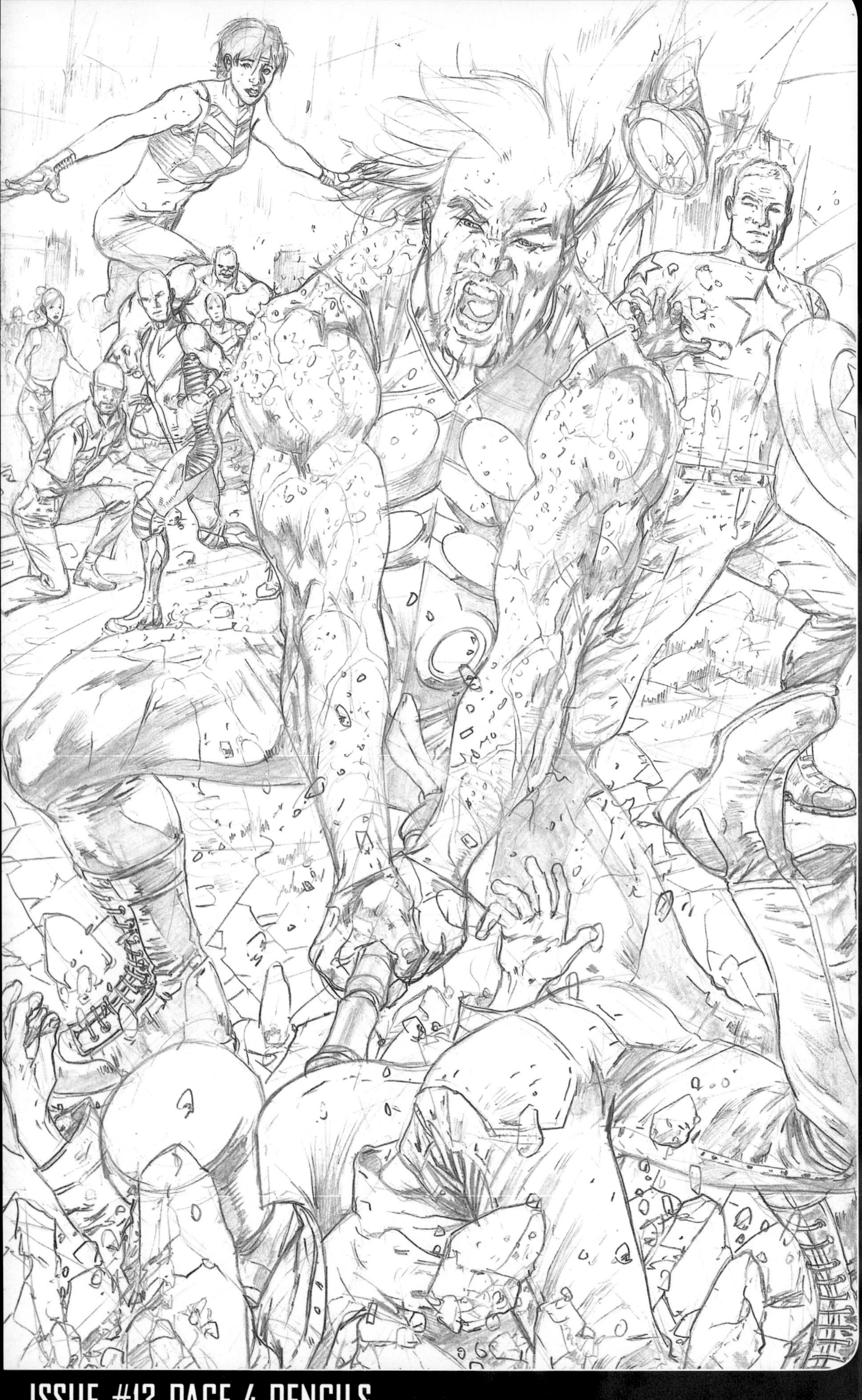

ISSUE #13 PAGE 4 PENCILS

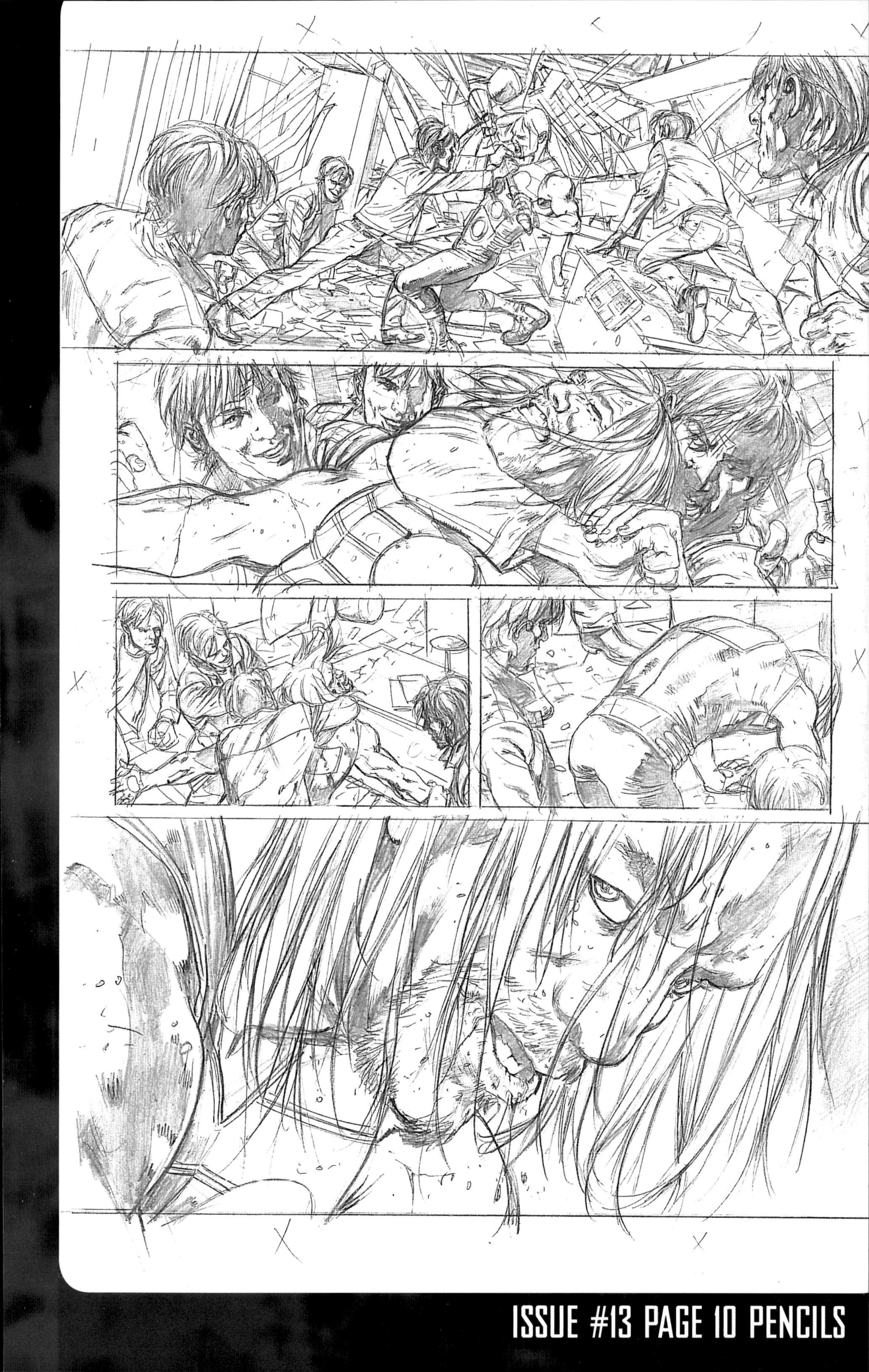

ISSUE #13 PAGE 10 PENCILS

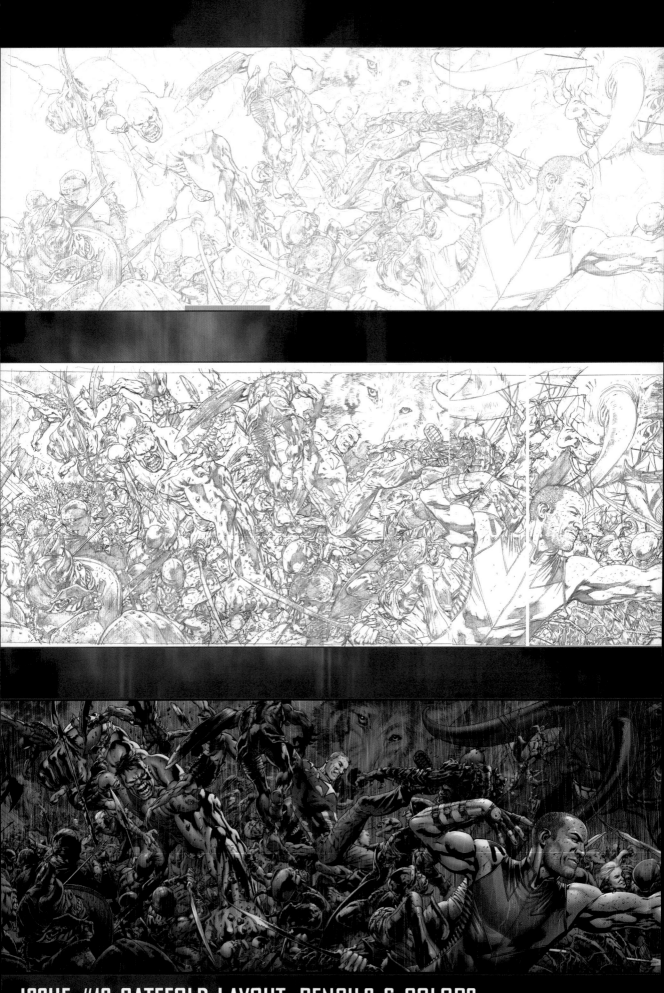

ISSUE #13 GATEFOLD LAYOUT, PENCILS & COLORS

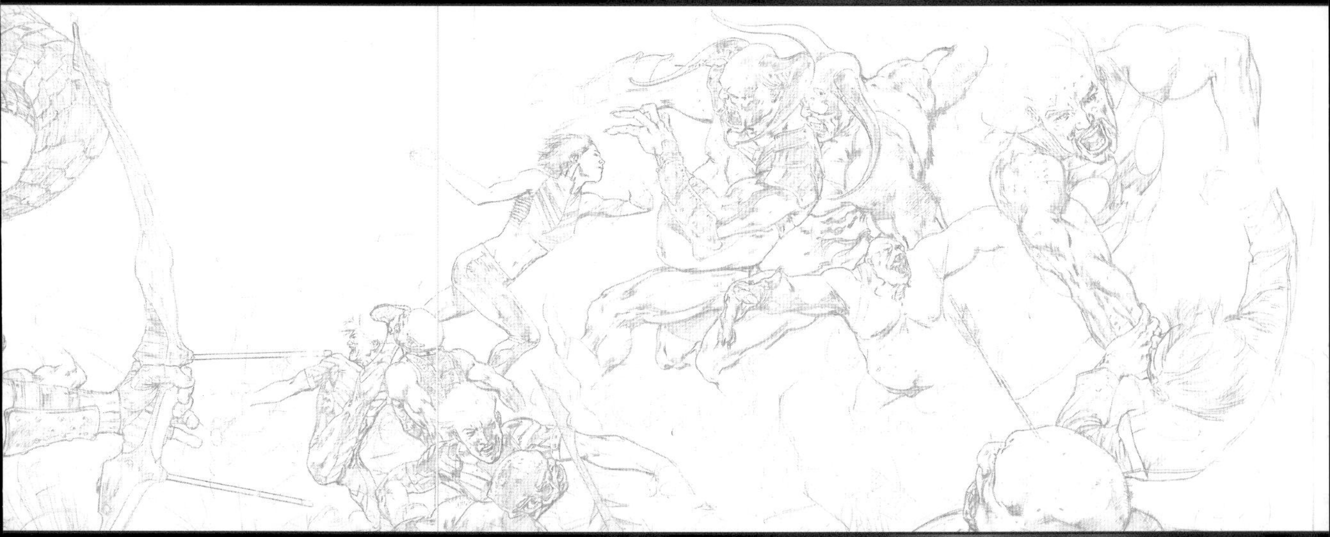

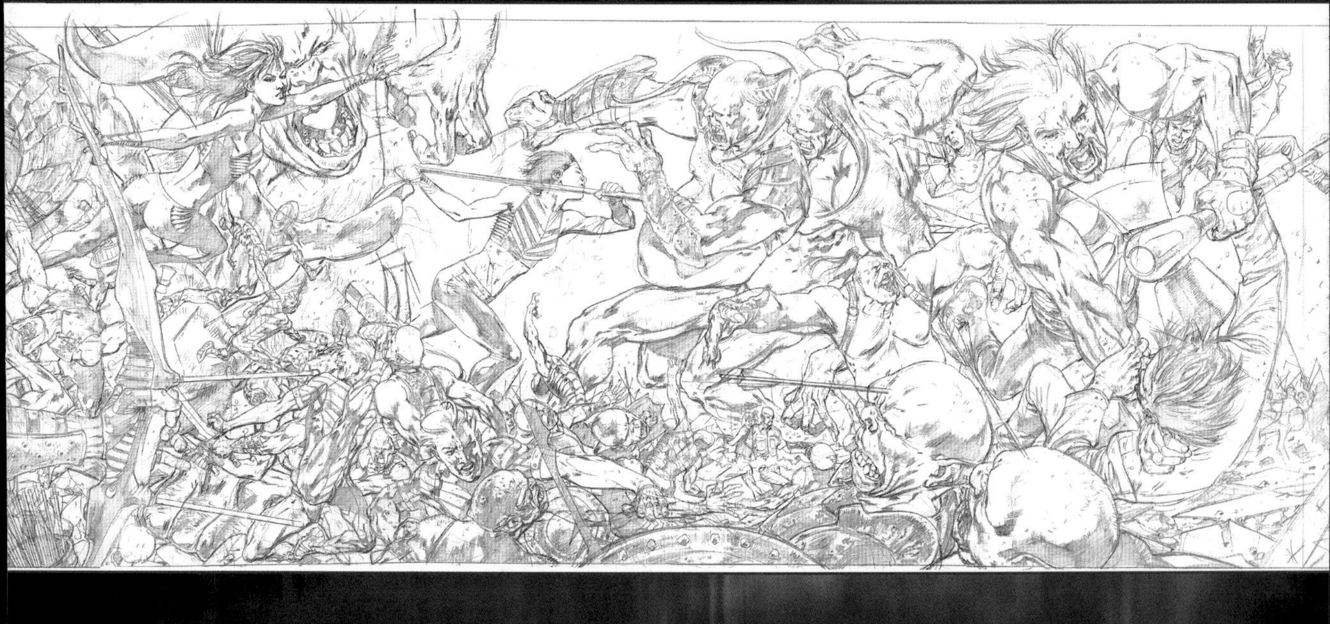

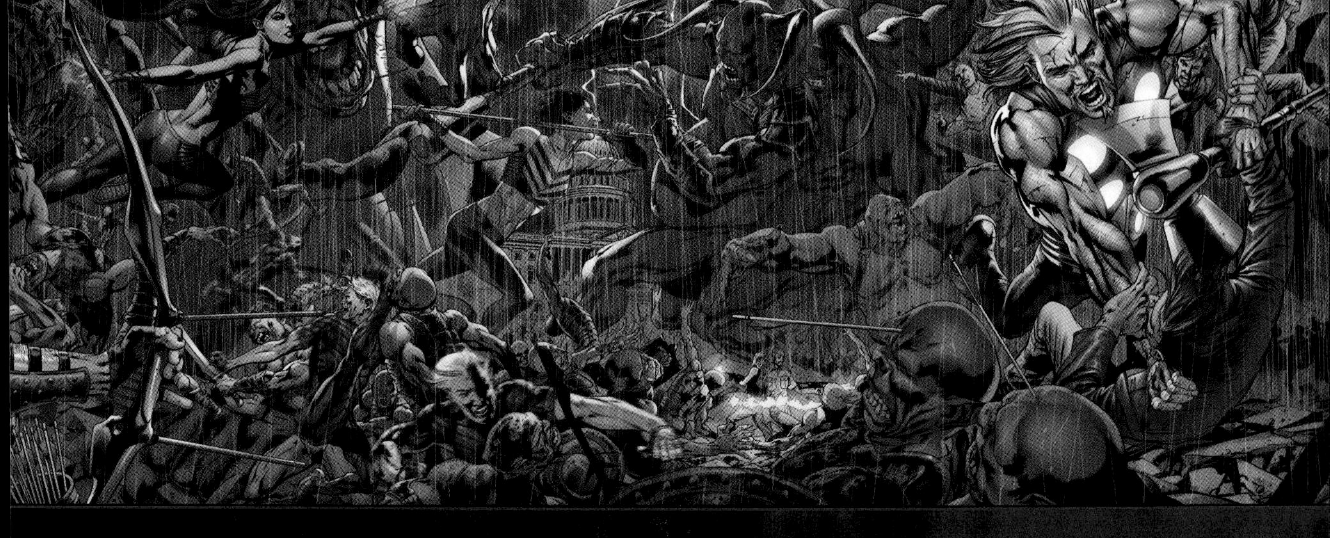

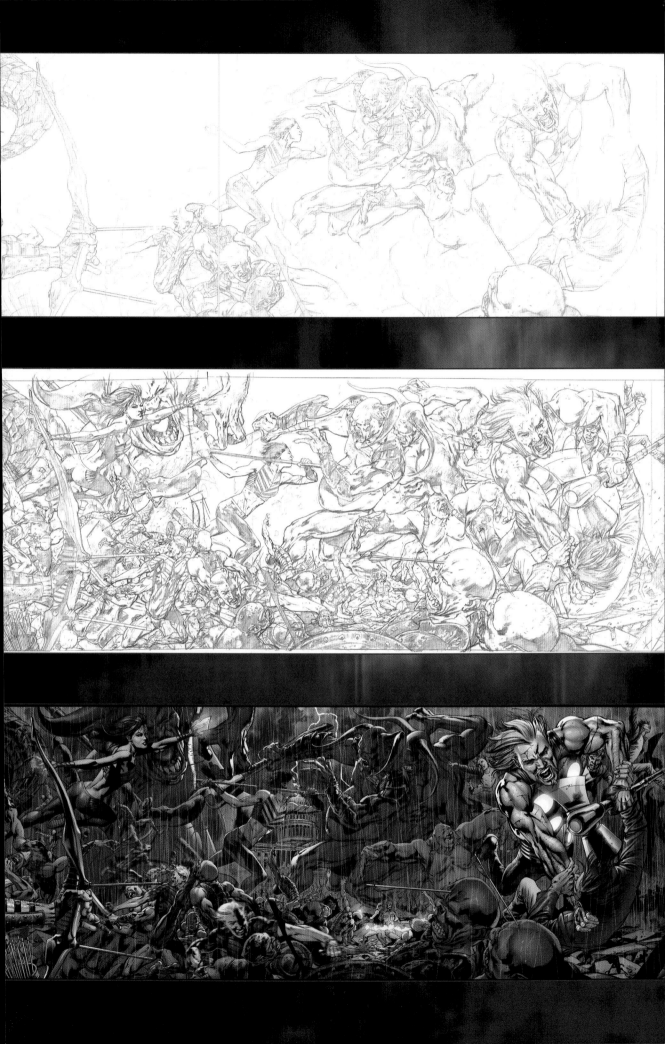

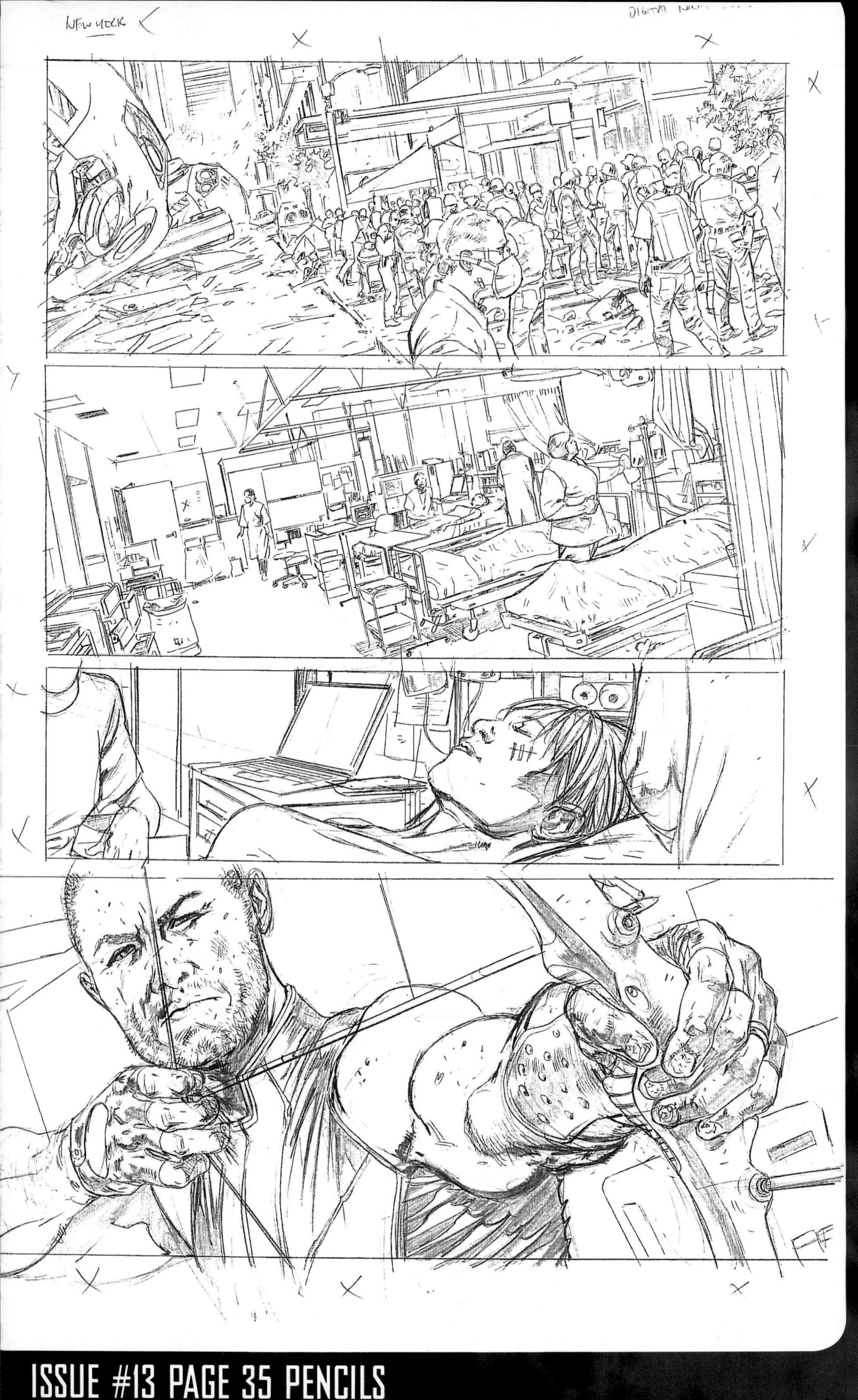
NEW YORK

ISSUE #13 PAGE 35 PENCILS

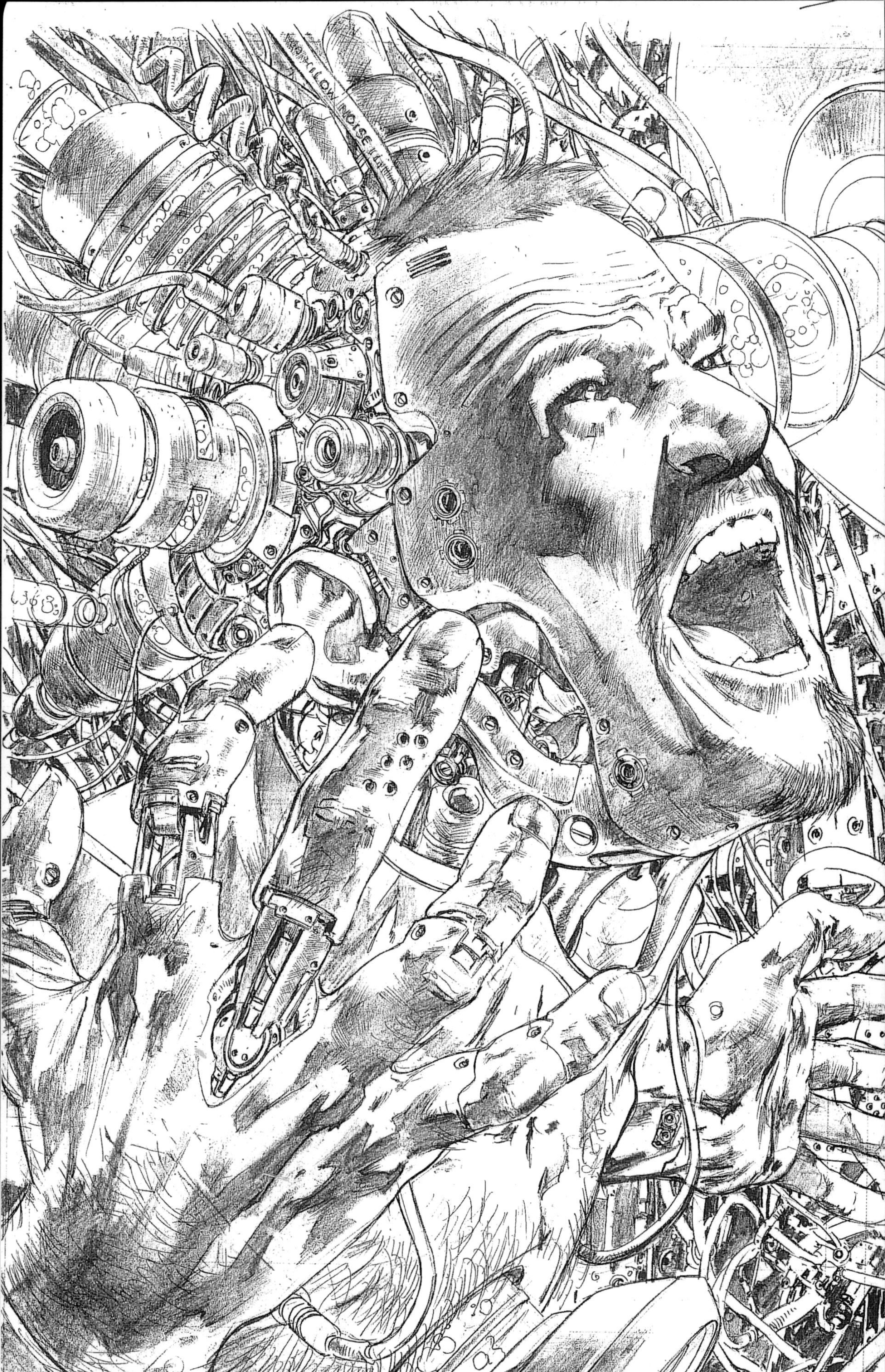

ULTIMATE IRON MAN #1 COVER PENCILS

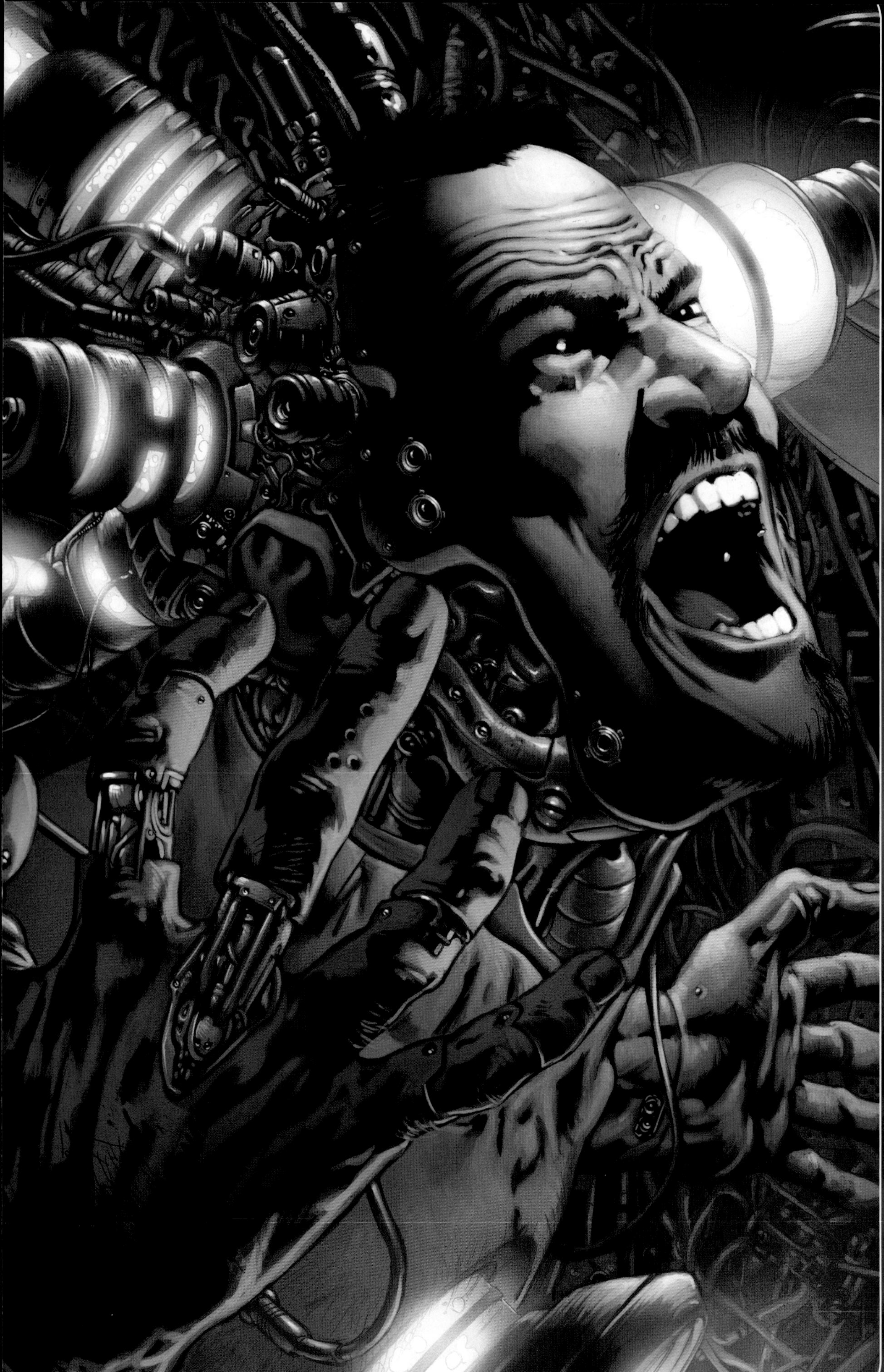

ULTIMATE IRON MAN #1 COVER

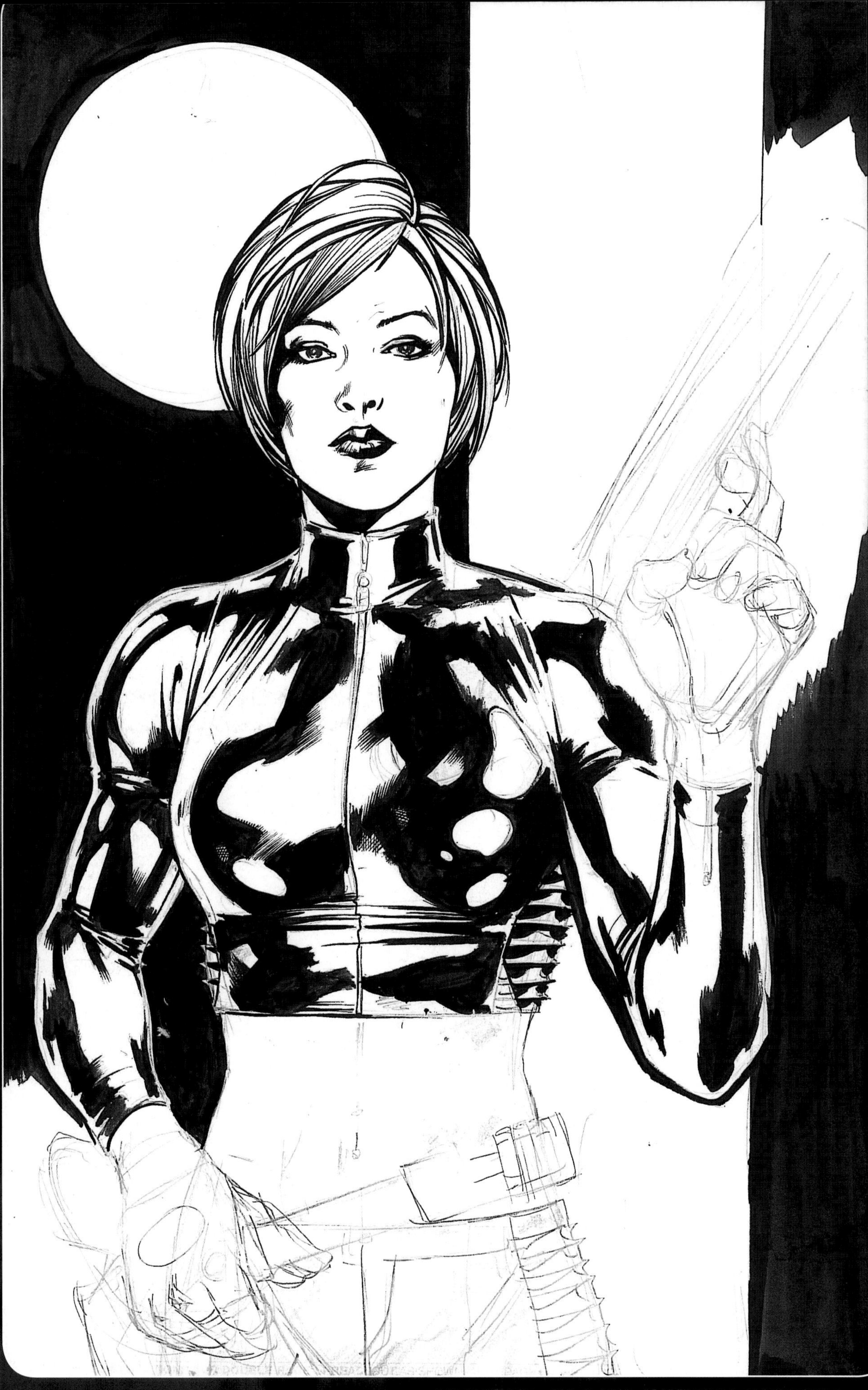

UNUSED BLACK WIDOW SKETCH

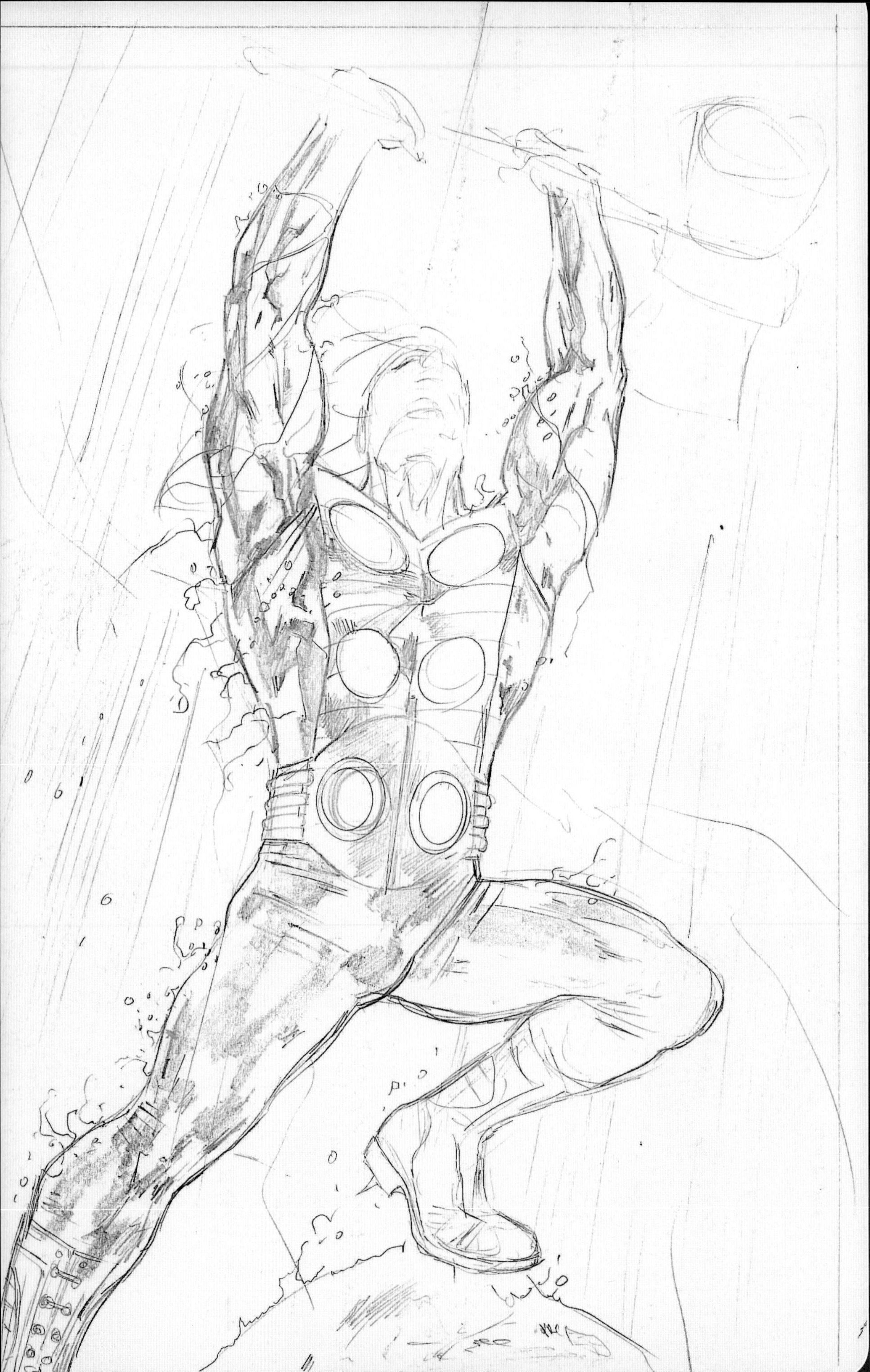

UNUSED THOR SKETCH